The Hornbook

Dr. Johnson described the hornbook as "the first book of children, covered with horn to keep it unsoiled." Pardon's New General English Dictionary (1758) defined it as "A leaf of written or printed paper pasted on a board, and covered with horn, for children to learn their letters by, and to prevent their being torn and daubed."

It was used throughout Europe and America between the late 1400s and the middle 1700s.

Shaped like an old-fashioned butter paddle, the first hornbooks were made of wood. The paper lesson the child was to learn was fastened to the wooden paddle and covered with a piece of horn. The transparent strip of horn was made by soaking a cow's horn in hot water and peeling it away at the thickness of a piece of celluloid. The horn was necessary to protect the lesson from the damp and perhaps grubby hands of the child. Hornbooks commonly contained the alphabet, the vowels, and the Lord's Prayer. Later hornbooks were made of various materials: brass, copper, silver, ivory, bronze, leather, and stone.

As the art of printing advanced, the hornbook was supplanted by the primer in the book form we know today. Subsequently West Group developed its "Hornbook Series", a series of scholarly and well-respected one volume treatises on particular areas of law. Today they are widely used by law students, lawyers and judges.

CIVIL PROCEDURE

Third Edition

By

Jack H. Friedenthal
Freda H. Alverson Professor of Law,
George Washington University
National Law Center

Mary Kay Kane
Dean, University of California
Hastings College of the Law

Arthur R. Miller
Bruce Bromley Professor of Law,
Harvard University

HORNBOOK SERIES®

WEST GROUP

ST. PAUL, MINN., 1999

 TEXT IS PRINTED ON 10% POST
CONSUMER RECYCLED PAPER

Preface

In some circumstances six years proves to be a long time in the life of the law. Since 1993 when the second edition of our Hornbook was published there have been a number of significant changes and developments in civil procedure. Our goal in this third edition is to update our volume to include these alterations. At the same time, however, we have preserved the basic format that we utilized in both of the prior editions. Comments we have received from a broad spectrum of those who have used these volumes indicate that the approach we have taken in the past has been a successful one.

As has been the case for some sixty years, many of the most significant procedural changes arise first, and sometimes exclusively, in the federal court system. The 1993 modifications to the Federal Rules of Civil Procedure have been tested and evaluated at some length. Especially in the areas of pretrial discovery and the enforcement of ethical requirements, there has been some dissatisfaction with the way in which those modifications have worked in practice and new proposed rules are currently on the table. Other important questions have arisen with respect to federal class actions and other forms of complex litigation and the Supreme Court has rendered several important decisions involving the right to jury trial and the judge/jury relationship. We have explored these matters in some detail. It is important to recognize, however, that our objective has been to identify and discuss the significant aspects of state as well as federal civil procedure. We have not been deterred from dealing with important questions merely because not all systems answer them alike.

We have tried to capture the complicated interrelationship between state and federal judicial systems in a coherent and systematic manner. Our approach is linear in time, beginning with the initial assertion of jurisdiction and challenges to it, progressing through the framing of matters to be litigated, the joinder of parties, and trial preparation, and continuing on to judgments—their binding effect, their enforcement, and their review on appeal.

The final Chapter is somewhat different in that it is not in chronological sequence. One of the fundamental challenges of our time is how the judicial system can cope with the increasing burden of complex, multiparty litigation that threatens to swamp our current procedural machinery, which, one must acknowledge, was devised for simpler disputes. That problem pervades from the beginning to the end of lawsuits. Thus, we have elected to gather all features of it in a single Chapter rather than distribute it throughout the text, which would create a risk of losing sight of it entirely, or, at the least, diminish its importance.

Our goal is to provide an important resource for law students, lawyers, judges, and researchers of all kinds who need information concerning the law of civil procedure. Thus, our book is far more comprehensive than any law school Civil Procedure course possibly could be. As a result we cover many significant topics which law school courses do not treat or which they handle only peripherally. Accordingly, we have addressed ourselves to Civil Procedure in the broad sense, embracing topics and issues whether or not they are typically covered in law school, and whether state or federal in origin. We also have been attentive to history and have tried to articulate the policies that have governed procedural practices and have led to their modification over time.

Certainly we do not claim that we have identified every procedural question that has arisen or might arise in the future. Nor have we provided answers to each of those we do discuss. But we have attempted to identify the important issues and to give readers sufficient information to allow them to understand what is at stake and why. In many situations our book is only a place to begin. Readers who need to go further are provided with references to another more detailed source in which additional inquiry can be pursued. Of the many instances of this throughout this volume, we call special mention to the numerous references to West Group's multi-volume treatise, Federal Practice and Procedure. That work has been authored by Charles A. Wright, in collaboration with two of the authors of this book, Arthur R. Miller and Mary Kay Kane, and Edward H. Cooper, Kenneth W. Graham, Michael H. Graham, and Victor Gold. For simplicity's sake, the citations to that work throughout this book omit its full title and refer to the specific volume number, the authors of the volume in question, the unit of the treatise involved—Criminal, Civil, Jurisdiction, or Evidence—and the particular section within the volume.

Finally, but certainly not of least importance, we gratefully acknowledge the help provided by our student research assistants, Joshua E. Gardner of the George Washington University Law School, and Rebecca Fewkes of Hastings College of the Law. Without their assistance, the task of reviewing and updating the wide range of sources and subjects covered in this text would have been virtually impossible. In addition we thank Jo Anne Friedenthal, whose encouragement and support were vital throughout the production of this volume.

JACK H. FRIEDENTHAL
MARY KAY KANE
ARTHUR R. MILLER

May, 1999

WESTLAW® Overview

Civil Procedure, Third Edition, by Jack H. Friedenthal, Mary Kay Kane and Arthur R. Miller, offers a detailed and comprehensive treatment of basic rules, principles and issues relating to civil procedure. To supplement the information contained in this book, you can access Westlaw, a computer-assisted legal research service of West Group. Westlaw contains a broad array of legal resources, including case law, statutes, rules, expert commentary, current developments and various other types of information.

Learning how to use these materials effectively will enhance your legal research abilities. To help you coordinate the information in the book with your Westlaw research, this volume contains an appendix listing Westlaw databases, search techniques and sample problems.

THE PUBLISHER

*

Summary of Contents

*

Table of Contents

*

CIVIL PROCEDURE

Third Edition

*

Chapter 1

INTRODUCTION

Analysis

§ 1.1 Civil Procedure Defined

The subject of this book is the field of civil procedure. Thus, its pages explore the principles surrounding the resolution of civil disputes[1] in the courts,[2] and in so doing examine the various tools available to the lawyer who must defend or bring a lawsuit. As distinguished from substantive matters, the civil procedure questions that will be studied in the Chapters that follow focus on how attorneys frame their cases in order to bring them properly before a particular court, and how the case proceeds from its institution until a judgment finally is reached and enforced. The availability of an appeal and the likely scope and effect of any judgment that is entered also are discussed.

In sum, then, this volume presents an exposition of how the procedural aspects of the civil justice system operate. In order to understand the rules of procedure, it is important to appreciate two things. First, the purpose underlying the establishment of most rules of civil procedure, in any judicial system, is to promote the just, efficient, and economical resolution of civil disputes.[3] This is not to say that these goals always

§ 1.1

1. Distinct bodies of procedural rules surround criminal, administrative, and other dispute resolution proceedings. Although many of the same devices and mechanisms are used in all of these contexts, important differences exist between the rules in civil court proceedings and those in other systems. Discussion of other dispute resolution systems is outside the scope of this volume.

2. For a classic description of the adjudicatory process, see Fuller, The Forms and Limits of Adjudication, 92 Harv.L.Rev. 353 (1978).

Although civil procedure traditionally focuses on court procedures and rules, serious problems of court congestion have resulted in increased attention by judges and commentators to alternative means by which parties may resolve private disputes. An excellent bibliography of articles and studies on alternative means of dispute resolution is A Selected Bibliography, Alternative Methods of Dispute Settlement, Compiled by the Special Comm. on Alternative Means of Dispute Resolution, American Bar Association (May, 1982).

3. Federal Civ.Proc.Rule 1, which governs civil litigation in the United States district courts, provides: "[These rules] shall be construed to secure the just, speedy, and inexpensive determination of every action." See American Bar Association, The Improvement of the Administra-

will be met or that they are entirely consistent, and many examples can be found throughout this volume of cases in which both judges and lawyers appear to have lost sight of them. Nonetheless, these objectives remain the foundation on which current procedural rules are based, and, as is explored in later Chapters, the desire to achieve them underlies many of the proposals for change in today's procedures.[4]

The second matter that must be remembered is that the Anglo–American judicial system is based on the adversary model. This differs from systems in civil law countries where the inquisitorial model prevails.[5] Under the inquisitorial system, the court conducts an active and independent inquiry into the merits of each case. This may include having the judge question and examine witnesses, as well as specifically ordering certain fact-finding.[6] The main feature of the adversary system that influences the development of particular procedures is that the parties (or their lawyers) control and shape the litigation. The traditional view is that the judge sits solely to decide disputed questions, most commonly questions of law and procedure. Issues not raised, objections not mentioned, and points not made are, with very few exceptions, waived. The case proceeds only in response to the demands of the litigants. Necessarily, then, the adversary model places enormous emphasis and responsibility on the lawyers; the court maintains a relatively passive role throughout the proceedings.

The ideal of the adversary system has come under increasing pressure in modern times.[7] Many judges have assumed more active roles in guiding the litigation before them.[8] This is seen in the participation of

tion of Justice 2–3 (5th ed.1971). See also Pound, The Causes of Popular Dissatisfaction with the Administration of Justice, 29 A.B.A.Rep. 395, 416–17 (1906).

4. For example, for more than twenty-five years many proposals have been made, and some adopted, to streamline the discovery process and to place controls on lawyers to discourage them from using it to delay or harass opponents. See, e.g., the 1983 amendment to Federal Rule 26, requiring the attorney to certify that a discovery request, response or objection is made in good faith, is not interposed for purposes of delay, and is not unduly burdensome or expensive, and the 1993 amendment to that rule, making the exchange of certain information mandatory. Discovery is discussed in Chapter 7, below.

5. Although the term "inquisitorial" brings to mind images of torture and trials with no true opportunity for defense, that is inappropriate in this context. As recognized by Judge Friendly of the United States Court of Appeals for the Second Circuit in testimony before Congress: "Whoever first characterized the continental European system as 'inquisitorial' did a profound disser-

vice to constructive legal thought. Substitute 'inquiring' and the bad becomes the good. The adversary system is not the only way to the truth; indeed, it has too often been a game in which both sides vie in their efforts to obscure the truth. Hopefully, by the year 2000, we will have learned where to preserve the adversary system and where to substitute something else." Hearings Before Commission on Revision of the Federal Court Appellate System, second phase, vol. I, at 205 (1974).

6. For a description of two different inquisitorial systems, see Kaplan, von Mehren & Schaefer, Phases of German Civil Procedure I, II, 71 Harv.L.Rev. 1193, 1443 (1958), and Osakwe, The Public Interest and the Role of the Procurator in Soviet Civil Litigation: A Critical Analysis, 18 Tex. Int'l L.J. 37, 37–49 (1983).

7. Frankel, The Search for Truth: An Umpireal View, 123 U.Pa.L.Rev. 1031 (1975); Miller, The Adversary System: Dinosaur or Phoenix, 69 Minn.L.Rev. 1 (1984).

8. To assist judges and lawyers in complex cases the Federal Judicial Center has

judges in the settlement process, during the pretrial conference stage,[9] and in the various management techniques by which courts are responding to complex modern litigation,[10] such as massive class actions charging discrimination, securities fraud, or environmental damage, or suits involving the reorganization of entire industries, schools, or prison systems.[11] These changes have been controversial and will continue to be so because they represent a reevaluation (and, to some degree, a weakening) of the adversary model itself. Nonetheless, it remains true that for the vast majority of civil actions, the ultimate responsibility for presenting the case remains with the attorneys and it is imperative that they be fully familiar with all the applicable procedural rules so as to ensure the most effective representation of their clients. Since this book examines the various rules that exist for each stage of litigation, it should aid the reader at least in avoiding the pitfall of overlooking some procedural matter or objection that it is his or her responsibility to raise.

The scope of civil procedure cannot be accurately defined more precisely than the broad description given above. The field necessarily overlaps with other matters that are related more directly to whether a claimant possesses a recognized legal right to recover, or, conversely, any defenses. This somewhat evanescent line between substance and procedure is discussed at various places throughout this volume.[12]

Note also that an attorney planning to institute litigation must consider what would be the best legal remedy available to meet the needs of the client. Although that inquiry frequently requires an examination of certain procedural rules, it nonetheless is not itself part of the typical study of court systems and thus is not emphasized in this book.

This was not always so. Historically, the type of remedy sought often dictated which court a litigant should enter to seek relief; special courts

---

produced several editions of a Manual on Complex Litigation, outlining procedures the federal courts may use to control "big" cases and administer the pretrial process to ensure that these cases are handled as expeditiously as possible.

9. Federal Rule 16, governing pretrial conferences, was amended in 1983 and 1993 to encourage active management and scheduling by the judges during all the pretrial phases of federal court litigation. See Chapter 8, below.

10. In major litigation in fields such as antitrust, securities fraud, and toxic torts, courts have begun to rely heavily on the services of magistrate judges and special masters to organize and move along the pretrial stages of the lawsuit. For an interesting description of their roles as special masters in the government antitrust suit against American Telephone & Telegraph Company, see Hazard & Price, Judicial Management of the Pretrial Process in Massive Litigation: Special Masters as Case Managers, 1982 ABF Res.J. 375.

11. In Chayes, The Role of the Judge in Public Law Litigation, 89 Harv.L.Rev. 1281 (1976), the author argues that the traditional model is not adequate to deal with modern public law litigation and that the courts must change to accommodate new forms of litigation that do not really arise between private parties. In Chayes, Public Law Litigation and the Burger Court, 96 Harv.L.Rev. 4 (1982), he demonstrates how the judiciary is responding to meet these new challenges. See also Aronow, The Special Master in School Desegregation Cases: The Evolution of Roles in the Reformation of Public Institutions Through Litigation, 7 Hast.Con.L.Q. 739 (1980); Brazil, Special Masters in the Pretrial Development of Big Cases: Potential and Problems, 1982 ABF Res.J. 287.

12. See Chapter 4, below, dealing with governing law questions; Chapter 5, below, discussing how to plead a claim for relief; and Chapter 14, below, concerning the scope of a claim for relief for res judicata purposes.

were established—law, equity, ecclesiastical—to dispense particular types of relief or to hear certain matters.[13] In the United States today, however, the courts are not so designated. With few exceptions,[14] modern civil court systems are authorized to dispense whatever remedy the evidence indicates is appropriate.[15] The problem of selecting a remedy, although essential in framing litigation, does not as a rule influence the selection of what court to use.

This volume speaks largely about civil procedure today, although some historical references will be made when relevant or helpful. Thus, insofar as the choice of a particular remedy is limited to certain facts or it influences the use of a particular procedure, that is outside the scope of this work.[16] But there remains a powerful need to remember the past in the utilization of juries; the impact of the remedy being sought and its historical antecedents on the right to jury trial is explored in depth in a later Chapter.[17]

§ 1.2   General Description of Court Systems

Each of the fifty states and the District of Columbia has its own judicial system. In addition, there is a separate federal court system, as well as courts for each of the United States territories and possessions. As is discussed in later Chapters, the potential availability of more than one court in which to litigate a given dispute poses some of the most important and often the most difficult questions facing a litigant.

For example, the tactical considerations that must be explored in choosing between a federal and state court are varied. An attorney might prefer a federal to a state forum in order to take advantage of certain features of the Federal Rules of Civil Procedure, most notably their liberal discovery procedures; the attorney may believe that federal judges and juries are of a higher caliber than their state counterparts; or she may desire to utilize a congested federal court calendar to wage a battle of attrition against her adversary. Conversely, a lawyer may prefer a state forum because he expects a state judge or jury to be more sympathetic to his client and his case, especially if the client is a local resident, or the lawyer may want to avoid one of the distinctive features of federal practice, such as liberal discovery or the power of a federal judge to comment to the jury on the evidence. Finally, many attorneys

---

13. For an excellent description of the historical divisions among the various courts, see R. Millar, Civil Procedure of the Trial Court in Historical Perspective (1952).

14. Some specialized courts deal only with certain matters and thus can provide only certain forms of relief. For example, a probate court can enter whatever order is necessary to distribute the assets of the estate of someone who has died. It cannot render a judgment giving money damages to the estate for acts done by some person or entity to the decedent. Those debts must

be collected through litigation in the general trial courts.

15. The notion that the prevailing party should receive the remedy or award that is supported by the evidence rather than what is demanded in the complaint often is embodied in the procedural rules of the judicial system. E.g., Fed.Civ.Proc.Rule 54(c).

16. See generally D. Dobbs, Remedies (2d ed.1993).

17. See Chapter 11, below.

simply are more experienced and comfortable litigating in one court system rather than the other. Similar considerations exist when choosing among different state court systems. In any event, each of these complex tactical questions must be evaluated in light of the various rules and statutes governing access to each court system.[1] This section merely describes some of the similarities and differences in existing courts.

Most judicial systems in the United States began as two-tiered structures, comprised of a trial tribunal and one court of review.[2] A few states remain so today.[3] As population and litigation increased, judicial systems became tri-partite, composed of a trial court, a court that engages in the initial appellate review, but is final for most cases, and a court of last resort that is empowered to select the cases that are lodged on its docket. The federal court system follows this organization, as do most state court systems today. Although the names of the specific courts may vary,[4] their functions remain basically comparable. A brief review of the federal court structure illustrates the interrelationship among the tiers of the system.[5]

The federal trial courts are denominated United States District Courts. There are today 91 judicial districts in the United States, each having its own court. Additionally, there are district courts for Puerto Rico, Guam, the Virgin Islands, and the Northern Mariana Islands. Every state, as well as the District of Columbia, has at least one judicial district, and many larger states are divided into two or three, or even (in the cases of Texas, New York, and California) four judicial districts. Congress' decision to divide a particular state into more than one judicial district depends on population, geography, and caseload.[6] Districts that cover an entire state or a large geographical area, as for example, Alaska, often have divisions that hear cases at different locations within the district.

The federal district courts exercise general trial competence (referred to as original jurisdiction). Thus, they act as the initial tribunal

---

§ 1.2

1. See Chapters 2 and 3, below.

2. In the federal court system the First Judiciary Act created district courts and circuit courts below the Supreme Court. However, the circuit courts had no judges of their own (borrowing them from the district courts and the Supreme Court) and had both original and appellate jurisdiction. Circuit courts of appeals, comparable to the present courts of appeals were not created until 1891 and it was not until 1911 that the circuit courts stopped operating as nisi prius courts. See 13 C. Wright, A. Miller & E. Cooper, Jurisdiction and Related Matters 2d §§ 3503–06.

3. E.g., Nebraska.

4. For example, in New York the trial court is denominated the Supreme Court, the intermediate court is the Appellate Division, and the highest appellate court is called the Court of Appeals. In California, the trial court is the Superior Court, the intermediate court is the Court of Appeal, and, like the federal system, the court of last resort is called the Supreme Court.

5. The structure and organization of the federal courts are controlled by provisions in Title 28 of the United States Code, commonly called the Judicial Code. For a more complete discussion of the organization of the federal court system, see 13 C. Wright, A. Miller & E. Cooper, Jurisdiction and Related Matters 2d §§ 3501–10.

6. Generally, federal judicial districts do not cross state lines. The one exception is the District of Wyoming, which includes Yellowstone National Park and thus covers small parts of Montana and Idaho. 28 U.S.C.A. § 131.

for almost all cases, civil and criminal, in the federal court system.[7] The federal district court's authority to hear a particular case commonly is concurrent or parallel to that of the state trial courts[8] so that litigants often can choose whether to sue in federal or state court.

A losing litigant in a federal district court generally may appeal a final decision to the United States Court of Appeals[9] for the circuit in which the district court is located. At present there are eleven numbered circuits, each embracing a largely geographically contiguous area, including anywhere from three to ten states and territories.[10] In addition, there is a Court of Appeals for the District of Columbia, which hears appeals from the federal district court there, and one for the Federal Circuit, which handles appeals on certain matters, such as patent disputes, and from various specialized federal tribunals, such as the Court of Federal Claims. Each court of appeals has four or more judges who sit in panels of three to review the cases brought before them. In addition to hearing appeals from the district courts, the courts of appeals often are the tribunals established by statute for initial judicial review of administrative agency action.[11]

At the apex of the federal court system is the Supreme Court of the United States, composed of nine justices. Unless disqualified or ill, all of the justices participate in each decision of the Court. Most cases reach the Court on discretionary writs of certiorari from the United States Courts of Appeals or the highest courts of the states.[12] The Supreme Court also has limited original (trial) jurisdiction extending to cases involving ambassadors, ministers, and consuls, and disputes between states.

Although, as already indicated, most states have a three-tiered model somewhat like the federal system, there are some differences in

---

7. There are certain specialized courts created by Congress to deal with particular subject matters, such as the United States Tax Court, just as in state court systems there typically are specialized tribunals to handle probate, estates, guardianships, and divorce or family law matters.

8. In some substantive areas Congress has made the federal courts the exclusive tribunal for handling certain matters. See § 2.2, below.

9. Prior to the enactment of the 1948 Judicial Code the federal appellate courts were denominated "Circuit Courts of Appeals" because those judges once literally rode circuit.

10. There were only ten numbered circuits until 1981, when the Fifth Circuit was split into two, and a new Eleventh Circuit was formed embracing Alabama, Florida, and Georgia. Act of Oct. 14, 1980, Pub.L. 96–452, 94 Stat.1994. Similar proposals have been made over the years to divide the overburdened Ninth Circuit, which presum-

ably would create a Twelfth Circuit. Commission on Revision of the Federal Court Appellate System, The Geographical Boundaries of the Several Judicial Circuits: Recommendations for Change, 62 F.R.D. 223 (1973). Disagreement continues over whether to make that change and, if it is to be done, how the circuit should be split.

11. Generally, a petitioner may secure judicial review of a federal administrative order either in the Court of Appeals for the District of Columbia or the court of appeals for the circuit within which the petitioner resides or has its principal place of business. See 16 C. Wright, A. Miller & E. Cooper, Jurisdiction and Related Matters 2d § 3940.

12. The statutory provisions governing petitions for certiorari to the Supreme Court are 28 U.S.C.A. §§ 1252–58. See 16B C. Wright, A. Miller & E. Cooper, Jurisdiction and Related Matters 2d §§ 4003–04. Prior to its abolition by Congress in 1988, the Supreme Court had mandatory appellate jurisdiction over certain cases.

the roles ascribed to various state courts of last resort.[13] In some states appeals as of right to the state supreme court are even more limited than those to the United States Supreme Court. In California, for example, only criminal cases in which capital punishment has been imposed may be appealed as of right; all other appeals to the state's highest tribunal are discretionary.[14] This restriction allows the supreme court of that state to manage its docket and to choose for review those cases that will provide some needed clarification in the law or that involve issues or facts of such public significance that the court deems its decision necessary. Litigants disappointed in the trial court have to be content with a full review by California's intermediate appellate court.

At the other end of the spectrum are states, such as New York, in which appeals as of right to the state's highest court are available in a large number of cases defined by statute.[15] The primary role of New York's Court of Appeals thus is to ensure that each case is correctly decided,[16] rather than to focus on resolving confusion in the law administered by the lower courts.

Regardless of the judicial system in which a lawsuit is filed, the basic progress through the courts remains the same: pleadings, discovery, and pretrial motions, followed by a trial at which the evidence is presented, witnesses are heard, and a decision is rendered and a judgment is entered. Although a right to at least one level of appeal normally exists, the losing party most often concludes that appeal is hopeless (or too expensive) and elects to abide by the trial court judgment. When an appeal is taken, the scope of the review is graduated. As is explored more fully in a later Chapter,[17] trial court rulings on law enjoy no deference; appellate courts exist to correct mistakes of law and sometimes even to declare new legal rules. At the opposite extreme are pure questions of fact. As to these matters, trial judges when they sit without a jury and juries when they act as the fact-finders are supreme and their findings subject to reversal only for egregious errors.

---

13. One of the roles filled by the United States Supreme Court is to resolve conflicts between the circuits and to oversee the lower federal courts to ensure uniformity in the application of federal law. With an ever increasing number of cases being filed in the Supreme Court, serious questions have been raised concerning whether the Court can act effectively in that capacity, and proposals have been made for a new National Court of Appeals to be formed to provide some of the necessary guidance to the lower federal courts. See Freund, Report of the Study Group on the Caseload of the Supreme Court, 57 F.R.D. 573 (1972). See also Haworth & Meador, A Proposed New Federal Intermediate Appellate Court, 12 Mich.J.L.Ref. 201 (1979). This proposal has been criticized by several commentators. See, e.g., Black, The National Court of Appeals: An Unwise Proposal, 83 Yale L.J. 883 (1974); Swygert, The Proposed National Court of Appeals: A Threat to Judicial Symmetry, 51 Ind.L.Rev. 327 (1976). In recent years the proposal has languished and in view of the reduced number of cases accepted by the Supreme Court for review, seems moribund.

14. West's Ann.Cal. Const. Art. 6, § 11.

15. N.Y.–McKinney's CPLR 5601.

16. For example, an appeal may be taken whenever there is a dissent in the intermediate appellate court on a question of law in favor of the appealing party. N.Y.–McKinney's CPLR 5601(a).

17. See § 13.4, below.

§§ 1.3–2.0 are reserved for supplementary material.

Chapter 2

SUBJECT-MATTER JURISDICTION AND VENUE

Analysis

---

§ 2.1 Overview

When deciding where to file suit one of the first questions that must be answered is whether the chosen court has the power or competence to decide the kind of controversy that is involved. This requirement most often is stated in terms of whether the court has subject-matter jurisdiction over the dispute and should be distinguished from questions of personal jurisdiction, which focus on the court's authority to enter a judgment that is binding on the particular defendants involved.[1]

§ 2.1

1. Personal jurisdiction is discussed in Chapter 3, below.

Questions of subject-matter jurisdiction typically are determined by reference to state or federal constitutional provisions or statutes that authorize particular courts to entertain certain categories of controversies.[2] These provisions distribute judicial power to hear disputes among a variety of courts within a system and in that sense regulate the flow of cases in those courts.[3] In some instances, certain types of litigation or problems are segregated and given to specialized tribunals; that is true in most states for probate and domestic relations matters.[4] Perhaps the most common method of limiting judicial power is by providing that certain courts can adjudicate only controversies involving more than a stated monetary amount or less than a maximum amount. For example, in California, most matters involving less than $25,000 are restricted to the Municipal Courts;[5] most matters involving more than $25,000 are assigned to the Superior Courts.[6] In either situation, the court in which suit is filed will be deemed to have "original" jurisdiction over the action. Other specifically designated courts will be given "appellate" jurisdiction and sit to review the decisions of these trial tribunals.

Thus, any decision about where to sue requires some investigation into the provisions governing the relevant court to determine whether it has been given authority to decide the particular matters involved. This inquiry becomes especially important when determining whether to file suit in federal or state court since, as is discussed in the next section, the federal courts' jurisdictional power is strictly limited by statute and by Article III of the Constitution. This Chapter focuses on the federal subject-matter jurisdiction scheme because it provides an excellent illustration of the kinds of problems that arise in the allocation of power between tribunals of equal trial competence and offers an opportunity to explore a number of important aspects of federalism.[7]

In addition to the rules delimiting a particular type of court's subject-matter competence, special rules exist that further allocate cases among the same type of courts within a given judicial system. This set of rules is referred to as venue. Every American court system, state and federal alike, has a number of venue statutes generally intended to channel litigation into those specific courts that are both convenient for litigants and witnesses, and efficient from a judicial administrative standpoint. The most common purpose of venue rules is to limit the plaintiff's forum choice in order to ensure that the locality of the lawsuit

2. One exception to the statutory bases for subject-matter jurisdiction is the development of the doctrine of supplemental jurisdiction by the federal courts, but even that has now been replaced by a statute. See §§ 2.12–2.14, below.

3. See generally Sunderland, Problems Connected with the Operation of a State Court System, 1950 Wis.L.Rev. 585.

4. The treatment of probate and domestic relations matters by specialized tribunals can be traced to England where those issues were tried in ecclesiastical courts. T. Plucknett, A Concise History of the Common Law 177 (2d ed.1936). This history is so strong that federal courts typically refuse to entertain these cases even though the action otherwise would meet federal statutory requirements. See § 2.5, below.

5. West's Ann.Cal.Code Civ.Proc. § 86.

6. West's Ann.Cal. Const. Art. 6, § 10.

7. See §§ 2.2–2.14, below.

has some logical relationship either to the litigants or to the subject matter of the dispute.[8]

Venue must be carefully distinguished from jurisdiction. Jurisdiction deals with the power of a court to hear and dispose of a given case; in the federal system, it involves questions of a constitutional dimension concerning the basic division of judicial power among the states and between state and federal courts. Venue is of a distinctly lower level of importance; it is simply a statutory device designed to facilitate and balance the objectives of optimum convenience for parties and witnesses and efficient allocation of judicial resources.[9]

Despite its lesser importance, venue must be considered in deciding where to file suit.[10] Further, general notions of convenience sometimes will be invoked to change the tribunal in which a particular suit is litigated, even though the chosen forum is one that meets the statutory venue requirements.[11] The conditions under which this will occur are discussed later in this Chapter.

A. FEDERAL SUBJECT–MATTER JURISDICTION

§ 2.2 The Nature of the Federal Courts

To understand the nature of the subject-matter limitations on the federal court system, it is necessary to know something of its history.[1] The present character of the federal courts derives largely from two seminal documents: Article III of the United States Constitution and the Judiciary Act of 1789. Subsequent jurisdictional enactments and judicial decisions have modified the contours of federal court jurisdiction, but its basic outlines retain the imprint of determinations made at the very outset of our nation's history.

Article III, Section 1 of the Constitution states: "The judicial Power of the United States, shall be vested in one supreme Court, and in such inferior Courts as the Congress may from time to time ordain and establish." Section 2 defines the permissible scope of federal judicial power, listing all those areas in which federal subject-matter jurisdiction may be asserted.[2] Congress has no power to extend the subject-matter

---

8. When venue is premised on some relationship between the forum and the subject matter of the dispute, the plaintiff's ability to file suit there also depends upon whether the forum state's long-arm statute will extend to bring the defendant within the personal jurisdiction of the court. See Comment, Federal Venue Amendment—Service of Process, Erie, and Other Limitations, 16 Cath.U.L.Rev. 297 (1967).

9. "Jurisdiction is a term of comprehensive import. * * * Venue in its modern and municipal sense * * * commonly has to do with geographical subdivisions, relates to practice or procedure, may be waived, and does not refer to jurisdiction at all." Paige v. Sinclair, 237 Mass. 482, 483–84, 130 N.E. 177, 178–79 (1921). See also Neirbo Co. v. Bethlehem Shipbuilding Corp., 308 U.S. 165, 167–68, 60 S.Ct. 153, 154, 84 L.Ed. 167 (1939).

10. See §§ 2.15–2.16, below.

11. See § 2.17, below.

§ 2.2

1. The classic history of the federal judiciary is F. Frankfurter & J. Landis, The Business of the Supreme Court (1928).

2. The Eleventh Amendment, constitutionally overriding Chisholm v. Georgia, 2 U.S. (2 Dall.) 419, 1 L.Ed. 440 (1793), with-

jurisdiction of the federal courts beyond the list in Article III.[3] To the extent that Congress purports to grant the federal courts power beyond those areas, the grant is unconstitutional.[4]

In fact, however, federal jurisdiction has been extended in some areas not specifically enumerated in the Constitution in order to effectuate the policies behind Article III. For example, statutes authorize the removal to federal courts of certain types of cases initially brought in state courts; even in this situation, however, the removed action must fall within the original jurisdiction of the federal courts as defined in the Constitution.[5] In addition, the judicially developed doctrines of ancillary and pendent jurisdiction, which have now been replaced by a statute and renamed supplemental jurisdiction, have permitted federal courts to assert jurisdiction over certain state-created claims that could not be entertained in a federal court if sued on separately in order to dispose more fully and effectively of related matters clearly within the federal courts' Article III power.[6] Finally, there is some authority suggesting that Congress is authorized by Article I as well as Article III to create federal jurisdiction to implement certain legislative goals.[7]

The 1789 Judiciary Act,[8] the second great historical cornerstone of the federal judicial system, is significant because it is the first and most authoritative expression of congressional understanding of Article III. In it, the first Congress created a system of federal courts inferior to the Supreme Court, as it was constitutionally authorized but not obligated to do. Congress also granted the lower courts some, but not all, of the jurisdictional power contained in Article III. It thus established the basic doctrine that although the outer limits of permissible federal judicial power are delineated by the Constitution, the actual scope of that jurisdiction at any given time is governed by the relevant jurisdictional statutes enacted by Congress. Despite an early challenge in a Supreme Court opinion by Justice Story,[9] it now is settled beyond any doubt that with respect to the federal courts, Congress constitutionally is free to grant or withhold subject-matter jurisdiction as it desires, within the

drew from the judicial power of the federal courts the ability to entertain actions against a state by citizens of another state or by aliens.

3. See 13 C. Wright, A. Miller & E. Cooper, Jurisdiction and Related Matters 2d § 3521.

4. Hodgson v. Bowerbank, 9 U.S. (5 Cranch) 303, 3 L.Ed. 108 (1809) (a statute could not confer federal jurisdiction over all suits involving aliens, since the Constitution extends the judicial power of the United States only to cases between aliens and American citizens).

5. See § 2.11, below.

6. See §§ 2.12–2.14, below.

7. National Mut. Ins. Co. of District of Columbia v. Tidewater Transfer Co., 337 U.S. 582, 69 S.Ct. 1173, 93 L.Ed. 1556 (1949) (Jackson, J.). The fact that Justice Jackson's opinion was joined by only two other justices, and that these two justices merely concurred in the result, makes his pronouncement on Article I courts somewhat doubtful authority. See 13 C. Wright, A. Miller & E. Cooper, Jurisdiction and Related Matters 2d § 3521.

8. Act of Sept. 24, 1789, 1 Stat. 73, c. 20. The best known work on the background of the First Judiciary Act is Warren, New Light on the Federal Judiciary Act of 1789, 37 Harv.L.Rev. 49 (1923).

9. Martin v. Hunter's Lessee, 14 U.S. (1 Wheat.) 304, 4 L.Ed. 97 (1816).

ultimate boundaries marked out by Article III.[10] As noted by one federal district judge, "when it comes to jurisdiction of the federal courts, truly, to paraphrase the scripture, the Congress giveth, and the Congress taketh away."[11]

From the twin principles discussed above—that Article III of the Constitution delineates the possible range of federal subject-matter jurisdiction and that congressional enactments define the actual scope of that jurisdiction at any given time—it follows that federal jurisdiction is limited in nature.[12] The practical effect of this proposition is that there is a presumption *against* federal jurisdiction: whereas the ability to hear a case is presumed in state courts of general jurisdiction, in the federal system the existence of subject-matter jurisdiction generally must be demonstrated at the outset by the party seeking to invoke it.[13] It cannot be conferred by consent of the parties,[14] nor can its absence be waived.[15] If a subject-matter jurisdiction defect exists, it may be raised at any time, even on appeal, and the court is under a duty to point it out if the parties do not.[16]

The early case of Capron v. Van Noorden[17] illustrates the way in which the foregoing principles are applied. In Capron, plaintiff brought a tort action against defendant in the North Carolina federal court. The plaintiff appealed from the jury's verdict for the defendant, alleging, among other things, that the trial court lacked subject-matter jurisdiction because the pleadings, although identifying the defendant as a citizen of North Carolina, were silent as to the citizenship of the plaintiff. Since federal jurisdiction would exist only if the plaintiff were of diverse citizenship from the defendant, and since diversity had not been demonstrated, the Supreme Court reversed the judgment. This case strikingly exemplifies the paramount importance attached to the limitations on federal court jurisdiction: the plaintiff, who had chosen the federal forum, was permitted to challenge, for the first time on appeal, the jurisdiction of the court of his own selection. The Supreme Court, in effect, declared that allowing unscrupulous or careless plaintiffs to escape adverse jury verdicts, thus wasting precious judicial resources,

---

10. Palmore v. U.S., 411 U.S. 389, 93 S.Ct. 1670, 36 L.Ed.2d 342 (1973); Kline v. Burke Constr. Co., 260 U.S. 226, 43 S.Ct. 79, 67 L.Ed. 226 (1922); Sheldon v. Sill, 49 U.S. (8 How.) 441, 12 L.Ed. 1147 (1850); Turner v. Bank of North America, 4 U.S. (4 Dall.) 8, 1 L.Ed. 718 (1799).

11. Senate Select Comm. on Presidential Campaign Activities v. Nixon, 366 F.Supp. 51, 55 (D.D.C.1973) (Sirica, J.).

12. See generally 13 C. Wright, A. Miller & E. Cooper, Jurisdiction and Related Matters 2d § 3522.

13. McNutt v. General Motors Acceptance Corp., 298 U.S. 178, 56 S.Ct. 780, 80 L.Ed. 1135 (1936); Turner v. Bank of North America, 4 U.S. (4 Dall.) 8, 11, 1 L.Ed. 718

(1799). Fed.Civ.Proc.Rule 8(a)(1) requires that the grounds for federal jurisdiction be pleaded in the plaintiff's complaint.

14. For example, People's Bank v. Calhoun, 102 U.S. (120 Otto) 256, 260–61, 26 L.Ed. 101 (1880), held that jurisdiction over a removed suit cannot be based upon a written stipulation of the parties.

15. Mitchell v. Maurer, 293 U.S. 237, 244, 55 S.Ct. 162, 164, 79 L.Ed. 338 (1934).

16. Louisville & Nashville Ry. Co. v. Mottley, 211 U.S. 149, 29 S.Ct. 42, 53 L.Ed. 126 (1908).

17. 6 U.S. (2 Cranch) 126, 2 L.Ed. 229 (1804).

was of less concern than the possibility of extending federal jurisdiction beyond its constitutional and statutory limits.

The major areas in which the federal courts presently exercise subject-matter jurisdiction are federal question cases[18] and diversity of citizenship cases.[19] In addition, federal jurisdiction is exercised in suits in which the United States is a party,[20] in admiralty and maritime cases,[21] in actions between two or more states,[22] and in a few other limited situations. By and large, federal court subject-matter jurisdiction is concurrent with that of the courts of the various states. This means that most cases over which the federal courts have jurisdiction also can be heard in the state courts. However, there are certain kinds of cases over which Congress has given the federal courts exclusive jurisdiction so that suit may be filed only in the federal courts on these matters.[23] In the absence of the specific designation of exclusive authority in an area, however, the presumption remains that federal subject-matter jurisdiction is concurrent.

As already emphasized, the jurisdiction of the federal courts is limited and should be construed narrowly to ensure that it is not extended beyond its proper bounds. However, once a final judgment has been rendered in a federal court action, the concern for stability and repose underlying the doctrine of preclusion, combined with the philosophy that courts of one system should give effect to the judgments of the courts of another system,[24] generally outweighs the principles of limited federal jurisdiction. Thus, although direct attacks on subject-matter jurisdiction are permitted even in the Supreme Court, as illustrated by Capron,[25] in the absence of extraordinary countervailing circumstances, collateral attacks on the judgment of a federal court in a later proceeding for an alleged defect in subject-matter jurisdiction are not permitted.[26] This is true even if jurisdiction is based upon a statute later found to be unconstitutional.[27]

§ 2.3 Federal Question Jurisdiction

Federal question jurisdiction stems from the Constitution's provision that the judicial power of the United States "shall extend to all

18. See §§ 2.3–2.4, below.

19. See §§ 2.5–2.7, below.

20. See § 2.10, below.

21. See § 2.10, below.

22. Actions between states fall within the original jurisdiction of the United States Supreme Court. See 13 C. Wright, A. Miller & E. Cooper, Jurisdiction and Related Matters 2d § 3524.

23. Some examples of exclusive jurisdiction are bankruptcy, 28 U.S.C.A. § 1334; patent and copyright cases, 28 U.S.C.A. § 1338(a); actions against consuls and vice-consuls, 28 U.S.C.A. § 1351; federal crimes, 18 U.S.C.A. § 3231; and actions under cer-

tain antitrust statutes 15 U.S.C.A. §§ 15, 26.

24. See Chapter 14, below.

25. See the discussion at note 17, above.

26. Des Moines Navigation & R. Co. v. Iowa Homestead Co., 123 U.S. 552, 8 S.Ct. 217, 31 L.Ed. 202 (1887). For an example of the extraordinary circumstances in which collateral attack predicated on a defect in subject-matter jurisdiction has been allowed, see Kalb v. Feuerstein, 308 U.S. 433, 60 S.Ct. 343, 84 L.Ed. 370 (1940).

27. Chicot County Drainage Dist. v. Baxter State Bank, 308 U.S. 371, 60 S.Ct. 317, 84 L.Ed. 329 (1940).

Cases, in Law and Equity, arising under this Constitution, the Laws of the United States, and Treaties made, or which shall be made, under their Authority * * *."[1] Congress did not confer jurisdiction over this category of cases in its original jurisdictional grant to the federal courts in the 1789 Judiciary Act. Federal question jurisdiction was briefly granted by the outgoing Federalist Congress in the so-called Midnight Judges Act of 1801,[2] but it was repealed only a year later, after the electoral triumph of the Jeffersonians who were ever distrustful of the power of the federal government.[3] Thus, cases arising under federal law were handled by the state courts. It was not until 1875 that general federal question jurisdiction was given to the federal courts on what has proved to be a permanent basis.[4]

Federal question jurisdiction is premised on the principle that the federal judiciary should have authority to interpret and apply federal law. The federal courts are considered to be in the best position to understand federal law, resolve disputes as to its meaning, and fill in the interstices of that law by judicial law-making. The federal judiciary also may be in the best position to enforce federal law, especially when it is unpopular in the forum state, as has been true, for example, of civil rights legislation in some parts of the nation. Therefore, both in terms of making certain that federal law is given a uniform application and in vindicating rights guaranteed by existing law, the federal courts have a unique role to play, the dimensions of which have expanded greatly with the increased involvement of the federal government in all areas of national life.[5]

The present general federal question statute is Section 1331 of the Judicial Code, a lineal descendant of the original 1875 act. In addition to Section 1331, there are a large number of other statutes, in the Judicial Code and elsewhere, that confer federal subject-matter jurisdiction over cases arising under a variety of federal laws.[6] These specific grants of federal question jurisdiction include the provisions for judicial review of administrative action found in numerous statutes creating or authorizing actions by administrative agencies, and statutes giving jurisdiction

---

§ 2.3

1. U.S. Const. Art. III, § 2.

2. Act of Feb. 13, 1801, § 11, 2 Stat. 89, 92.

3. Act of March 8, 1802, § 1, 2 Stat. 132.

4. Act of March 3, 1875, § 1, 18 Stat. 470.

5. For a discussion of the purposes of federal question jurisdiction and of the problems that arise in connection with it, see American Law Institute, Study of the Division of Jurisdiction Between State and Federal Courts, Official Draft, 162–82, 482–88 (1969); Chadbourn & Levin, Original Jurisdiction of Federal Questions, 90 U.Pa. L.Rev. 639 (1942); Cohen, The Broken Compass: The Requirement that a Case

Arise "Directly" Under Federal Law, 115 U.Pa.L.Rev. 890 (1967); Fraser, Some Problems in Federal Question Jurisdiction, 49 Mich.L.Rev. 73 (1950); London, "Federal Question" Jurisdiction—A Snare and a Delusion, 57 Mich.L.Rev. 835 (1959); Mishkin, The Federal "Question" in the District Courts, 53 Colum.L.Rev. 157 (1953); Shapiro, Jurisdiction and Discretion, 60 N.Y.U.L.Rev. 543 (1985).

6. The major difference between specific jurisdictional grants and the general federal question statute was that the latter contained a $10,000 amount in controversy requirement. However, Section 1331 was amended in 1980 to eliminate that requirement. See § 2.8, below.

over certain types of actions,[7] such as securities[8] and civil rights cases.[9] In most of these contexts, federal subject-matter jurisdiction is concurrent with that of the state courts; in a few areas, such as bankruptcy[10] and patent[11] law, federal jurisdiction is exclusive.

The most difficult single problem in determining whether federal question jurisdiction exists, either under the general federal question statute or under one of the specific jurisdictional grants, is deciding when the relation of federal law to a case is such that the action may be said to be one "arising under" that law. The inquiry ultimately is compelled by the Constitution. The general federal question statute uses the same language as Article III, Section 2, referring to "all civil actions" that arise under "the Constitution, laws or treaties of the United States." The "arising under" limitation applies by implication to the specific statutory grants of federal jurisdiction as well.[12]

The meaning of the words "arising under" thus assumes both a constitutional dimension, in that Congress has no *power* to grant the federal courts jurisdiction over cases that do not arise under federal law, and a statutory dimension, in that Congress did not *intend*, when it first enacted a federal question statute in 1875 and in subsequent enactments using the same words, to confer jurisdiction over cases not "arising under" federal law. Many of the problems of interpreting "arising under" have developed because of the failure to distinguish between the question of constitutional power and the question of legislative intent.

The first decision interpreting "arising under" addressed solely the constitutional aspect of the problem. Osborn v. Bank of United States[13] considered the constitutionality of a statute that gave the federal courts jurisdiction over actions involving the Bank of the United States, a federally chartered corporation. The Supreme Court upheld the statute. Chief Justice Marshall reasoned that because the Bank had been created by federal law, every act of the Bank necessarily grew out of the law that created it and endowed it with all the faculties and capacities that it possessed. Since the very right of the Bank to sue depended entirely upon those laws, every case involving the Bank automatically arose under the laws of the United States. This was true even if there were no actual dispute in the case, as there was unlikely to be, over the Bank's right to sue on the claim presented. The fact that a question of federal law might involve, at best, only a tangential connection to the actual dispute in the case did not disturb Chief Justice Marshall.

> [W]hen a question to which the judicial power of the Union is extended by the Constitution, forms an ingredient of the original

---

7. For an examination of the various specific grants of federal question jurisdiction, see 13B C. Wright, A. Miller, & E. Cooper, Jurisdiction and Related Matters 2d §§ 3568–85.

8. 15 U.S.C.A. §§ 77v, 77vvv(b), 78aa, 79y, 80a–43, 80b–14.

9. 28 U.S.C.A. § 1343.

10. 28 U.S.C.A. § 1334.

11. 28 U.S.C.A. § 1338.

12. See, e.g., Carlson v. Coca–Cola Co., 483 F.2d 279 (9th Cir.1973).

13. 22 U.S. (9 Wheat.) 738, 6 L.Ed. 204 (1824).

cause, it is in the power of Congress to give the Circuit Courts jurisdiction of that cause, although other questions of fact or of law may be involved in it.[14]

The Osborn holding is couched entirely in terms of what Congress constitutionally is empowered to do, and viewed in these terms, it is unobjectionable. With the passage of the general federal question statute in 1875, however, it became necessary for the federal courts to distinguish between the sweeping language of Osborn and the narrower scope of jurisdiction granted by statute. They did not always do so. For example, in the Pacific Railroad Removal Cases,[15] the Supreme Court mechanically applied Osborn's constitutional holding to the very different problem of construing the federal question statute, and held that any action by a federally incorporated corporation ipso facto arose under the laws of the United States within the meaning of the statute. But this decision has been characterized as a "sport" in the law,[16] and now it is well-settled that not every case in which a question of federal law forms an ingredient is covered by the "arising under" language of the jurisdictional statute.[17]

If the "ingredient" theory of Osborn now has been rejected definitively, what interpretation of "arising under" has replaced it? No clear, single line of authority emerges from the cases that have considered the question. One group of decisions focuses on whether federal law created the claim on which the plaintiff is suing. This approach was most clearly defined by Justice Holmes in American Well Works Company v. Layne & Bowler Company.[18] The action was for damages to the plaintiff's business caused by the defendant's slanderous accusations that the plaintiff had infringed a patent belonging to the defendant. Questions of patent law, an area of exclusive federal jurisdiction, were obviously an ingredient of the case. The plaintiff's cause of action for slander, however, was the creature of state common law; hence, the Court concluded that the case did not arise under federal law.

A federal statute also may permit an action to be brought without necessarily creating any federal substantive law or cause of action. Even though the authorization to sue was created by a federal statute, the suit itself does not necessarily arise under federal law. For example, when a federal law authorized miners to bring an "adverse suit" to assert claims to mining property, but the miners' rights to the disputed property were to be determined according to local mining rules and customs, it was held that an action brought under the statute was not one "arising

---

14. 22 U.S. (9 Wheat.) at 823. See also Cohens v. Virginia, 19 U.S. (6 Wheat.) 264, 5 L.Ed. 257 (1821) (Marshall, C.J.).

15. 115 U.S. 1, 5 S.Ct. 1113, 29 L.Ed. 319 (1885).

16. Mishkin, The Federal "Question" in the District Courts, 53 Colum.L.Rev. 157, 160 n. 24 (1953).

17. See, e.g., Romero v. International Terminal Operating Co., 358 U.S. 354, 379,

79 S.Ct. 468, 484, 3 L.Ed.2d 368 (1959) (Frankfurter, J.). See also People of Puerto Rico v. Russell & Co., 288 U.S. 476, 53 S.Ct. 447, 77 L.Ed. 903 (1933); Shoshone Mining Co. v. Rutter, 177 U.S. 505, 20 S.Ct. 726, 44 L.Ed. 864 (1900).

18. 241 U.S. 257, 260, 36 S.Ct. 585, 586, 60 L.Ed. 987 (1916).

under'' federal law.[19] Similarly, a substantive right may originate in federal law, and yet that source of the right may become so remote that the right loses its federal character for purposes of an action to vindicate it. For example, the mere fact that title to disputed land can be traced ultimately to the federal government and turn on federal law will not support federal question jurisdiction.[20] Were this otherwise, every suit to establish land title in the midwestern and western states would arise under federal law.

A case in apparent conflict with Justice Holmes' test is Smith v. Kansas City Title & Trust Company.[21] A majority of the Supreme Court, over a strong dissent by Justice Holmes, held that federal question jurisdiction existed in an action by a stockholder to enjoin a corporation from purchasing certain bonds on the ground that the bonds had been issued under an unconstitutional statute. The cause of action by the shareholder was created by state law, but the Supreme Court found federal jurisdiction to exist because the case turned on a dispute over the constitutionality of a federal statute. Although Smith has been cited approvingly in dictum,[22] it remains a fairly isolated authority.

These various strands of decisions are difficult to reconcile. Perhaps the best approach to deciding whether a given case arises under federal law is a common-sense, case-by-case method of analysis emphasizing the directness of the connection between federal law and the dispute in the case. This was the path taken by Justice Cardozo in Gully v. First National Bank in Meridian.[23] Gully involved a state action for back taxes brought by the Mississippi state tax collector against the bank. The bank attempted to remove the case to a federal court, claiming that the action arose under federal law because of a federal statute permitting suits against national banks under certain conditions. The Court rejected the bank's claim of federal jurisdiction. A federal statute may have authorized the action to be brought, but the plaintiff's claim was a state-created right to taxes, originating in an act by the Mississippi legislature. Federal consent might have been necessary to enable the enforcement of the state right, but the nature of the right was state, not federal.[24]

19. Shoshone Mining Co. v. Rutter, 177 U.S. 505, 20 S.Ct. 726, 44 L.Ed. 864 (1900). In the words of Justice Brewer: "A statute authorizing an action to establish a right is very different from one which creates a right to be established. An action brought under the one may involve no controversy as to the scope and effect of the statute, while in the other case it necessarily involves such a controversy, for the thing to be decided is the extent of the right given by the statute." 177 U.S. at 510, 20 S.Ct. at 728.

20. Shulthis v. McDougal, 225 U.S. 561, 32 S.Ct. 704, 56 L.Ed. 1205 (1912).

21. 255 U.S. 180, 41 S.Ct. 243, 65 L.Ed. 577 (1921).

22. T. B. Harms Co. v. Eliscu, 339 F.2d 823 (2d Cir.1964), (Friendly, J.), cert. denied 381 U.S. 915. The Supreme Court discussed Smith at length in Merrell Dow Pharmaceuticals Inc. v. Thompson, 478 U.S. 804, 106 S.Ct. 3229, 92 L.Ed.2d 650 (1986).

23. 299 U.S. 109, 57 S.Ct. 96, 81 L.Ed. 70 (1936).

24. See People of Puerto Rico v. Russell & Co., 288 U.S. 476, 483, 53 S.Ct. 447, 450, 77 L.Ed. 903 (1933); McGoon v. Northern Pacific Ry. Co., 204 Fed. 998 (D.C.N.D. 1913).

The Court in Gully recognized that a question of federal law might be lurking in the background. Nonetheless, it ruled that it is neither necessary nor desirable that every possible connection with federal law, no matter how remote or improbable be traced out in the federal courts. Rather, "the courts have formulated the distinction between controversies that are basic and those that are collateral, between disputes that are necessary and those that are merely possible."[25]

There are several sources of federal law that may provide the basis for finding that a particular case properly is brought under the general federal question statute. Most obviously, claims directly raising constitutional issues or depending for their resolution on constitutional construction clearly fall within the statute.[26] Although it may prove to be the case that the Constitution does not give a plaintiff the relief she seeks, as long as her claim that it does is substantial, federal court jurisdiction exists.[27]

Only one section of the Constitution will not independently support federal question jurisdiction because its connection with plaintiff's claim is not sufficiently direct to satisfy the "arising under" requirement. The Full Faith and Credit Clause[28] has been held to mandate only a rule of decision for state or federal courts when they encounter a question of the law or some aspect of the judicial proceedings of another state when hearing a case for which they otherwise have proper subject-matter jurisdiction;[29] if the Clause were permitted to serve as a basis for federal jurisdiction, the result would be to open the federal courts to every action to enforce a state statute or judgment in another state.[30]

Federal statutes,[31] and administrative regulations or executive orders made pursuant to an Act of Congress,[32] generally are considered to be "laws * * * of the United States" within the meaning of the Constitution and Section 1331 of Title 28.[33] In addition to statutory law, federal

---

25. 299 U.S. at 117–18, 57 S.Ct. at 100. For example, in Merrell Dow Pharmaceuticals Inc. v. Thompson, 478 U.S. 804, 106 S.Ct. 3229, 92 L.Ed.2d 650 (1986), the Supreme Court concluded that there was no federal question under the Food, Drug & Cosmetic Act simply because a violation of the federal statute would have to be shown by the plaintiff in order to recover under state tort law. The Court also concluded that Congress did not create a private federal cause of action when it enacted the statute.

26. See Powell v. McCormack, 395 U.S. 486, 516, 89 S.Ct. 1944, 1961, 23 L.Ed.2d 491 (1969); Hays v. Port of Seattle, 251 U.S. 233, 40 S.Ct. 125, 64 L.Ed. 243 (1920).

27. If the problem is that the Constitution does not provide for the relief the plaintiff is seeking, dismissal should be for failure to state a claim for relief, rather than for lack of subject-matter jurisdiction. Bell v. Hood, 327 U.S. 678, 66 S.Ct. 773, 90

L.Ed. 939 (1946); Keaukaha–Panaewa Community Ass'n v. Hawaiian Homes Comm'n, 588 F.2d 1216, 1227 (9th Cir.1978), cert. denied 444 U.S. 826.

28. U.S. Const. Art. IV, § 1.

29. Minnesota v. Northern Secs. Co., 194 U.S. 48, 72, 24 S.Ct. 598, 605, 48 L.Ed. 870 (1904).

30. California ex rel. McColgan v. Bruce, 129 F.2d 421, 424 (9th Cir.1942), cert. denied 317 U.S. 678.

31. Verlinden B.V. v. Central Bank of Nigeria, 461 U.S. 480, 103 S.Ct. 1962, 76 L.Ed.2d 81 (1983); Montana–Dakota Utilities Co. v. Northwestern Public Serv. Co., 341 U.S. 246, 249, 71 S.Ct. 692, 694, 95 L.Ed. 912 (1951).

32. Farmer v. Philadelphia Elec. Co., 329 F.2d 3, 7–8 (3d Cir.1964).

33. Jurisdiction cannot rest upon congressional acts passed exclusively as local law for the District of Columbia and lacking

question jurisdiction may be premised upon federal common law. Federal courts have developed several bodies of decisional law both to protect basic national interests and policies[34] and to interpret existing legislation, and this law is considered to be a part of the "laws * * * of the United States" referred to in the federal question statute.[35]

Federal decisional law does not provide a basis for federal question jurisdiction in the maritime and admiralty field, however. In Romero v. International Terminal Operating Company[36] the Supreme Court held that the framers of the original federal question statute did not intend to include cases within traditional admiralty jurisdiction in their grant of federal question jurisdiction to the federal courts, despite the unquestionably "federal" nature of admiralty law. Claims based on general maritime law (as opposed to claims based on specific maritime statutes such as the Jones Act)[37] thus cannot be instituted under Section 1331, but must be brought under Section 1333, the provision granting admiralty jurisdiction to the federal courts. This distinction is important mainly because of the unavailability of jury trial in admiralty cases.[38]

Finally, Section 1331 clearly grants the district courts jurisdiction over civil actions founded upon a claim or right arising under treaties of the United States.[39] This is not a very significant source of federal jurisdiction, however, since the relation of a treaty to a plaintiff's claim usually is not sufficiently direct to satisfy the "arising under" test.[40]

§ 2.4   Federal Question Jurisdiction—The Well–Pleaded Complaint Rule

For a litigant to invoke general federal question jurisdiction,[1] it is necessary both that the case "arise under" the Constitution or some

general application throughout the United States, however. American Sec. & Trust Co. v. Commissioners of District of Columbia, 224 U.S. 491, 32 S.Ct. 553, 56 L.Ed. 856 (1912).

34. See, e.g., Textile Workers Union of America v. Lincoln Mills, 353 U.S. 448, 77 S.Ct. 912, 1 L.Ed.2d 972 (1957) (federal common law of labor-management contracts developed to effectuate national labor policies). A more detailed discussion of federal common law is found in § 4.7, below.

35. Illinois v. City of Milwaukee, 406 U.S. 91, 92 S.Ct. 1385, 31 L.Ed.2d 712 (1972); Texas v. Pankey, 441 F.2d 236 (10th Cir.1971); Ivy Broadcasting Co. v. American Tel. & Tel. Co., 391 F.2d 486 (2d Cir.1968).

36. 358 U.S. 354, 79 S.Ct. 468, 3 L.Ed.2d 368 (1959). Romero has attracted a good deal of scholarly comment because Justice Frankfurter's opinion deals with a number of different facets of federal subject-matter jurisdiction. See, e.g., Currie, The Silver Oar and All That: A Study of the Romero Case, 27 U.Chi.L.Rev. 1 (1959); Kurland, The Romero Case and Some Problems of Federal Jurisdiction, 73 Harv.L.Rev. 817 (1960).

37. 46 U.S.C.A. § 688. The Jones Act permits recovery, by an action at law, for injury to or the death of a seaman sustained in the course of employment. Jones Act suits fall under general federal question jurisdiction, and also may be brought under 28 U.S.C.A. § 1337, since they arise under a law regulating interstate commerce.

38. See § 2.10, below, for a brief discussion of admiralty jurisdiction.

39. Continental Dredging Co. v. County of Los Angeles, 366 F.Supp. 1133, 1137 (C.D.Cal.1973).

40. Illustrative cases in which jurisdiction has been rejected because the relation between the plaintiff's claim and the treaty is too tenuous are Buechold v. Ortiz, 401 F.2d 371 (9th Cir.1968); Republic of Iraq v. First Nat. Bank, 350 F.2d 645 (7th Cir. 1965), cert. denied 382 U.S. 982.

§ 2.4

1. The well-pleaded complaint rule applies only to cases brought under 28

other aspect of federal law[2] and that this fact appear on the face of a well-pleaded complaint.[3] Issues that the defendant raises in the answer, or issues relating to a defense that the plaintiff anticipates in the complaint, are irrelevant for jurisdictional purposes. No matter how important, and even decisive, federal law may turn out to be in the later stages of the litigation, if a substantial federal issue is not raised as a legitimate part of the plaintiff's own claim for relief, there is no federal question jurisdiction under the statute.[4]

The classic case illustrating the application of these principles is Louisville & Nashville Railroad Company v. Mottley.[5] Mr. and Mrs. Mottley had been injured in a railway accident, and the railroad, as part of a settlement of their claims against it, had agreed to give them free passes for the rest of their lives. The railroad issued passes for twenty-nine years, but, after the enactment in 1907 of a federal statute making it unlawful for railroads to give free passes, it refused to renew the Mottleys' pass. The Mottleys brought suit in federal court against the railroad for specific performance, alleging that the statute did not apply to them, and that, if it did apply to them, it was an unconstitutional taking of their property. The trial court found for the plaintiffs, and an appeal followed.

The Supreme Court did not reach the merits of the case. Instead, it raised the issue of federal subject-matter jurisdiction on its own initiative and found that jurisdiction was lacking. In the words of Justice Moody: "It is not enough that the plaintiff alleges some anticipated defense to his cause of action, and asserts that the defense is invalidated by some provision of the Constitution of the United States."[6] The plaintiff's statement of his own cause of action must be based upon some federal law or the Constitution. Although the plaintiffs' complaint raised both a question of the construction of a federal law and a serious question as to its constitutionality, their own cause of action was a routine equitable action for specific performance of a contract governed entirely by state law; the federal questions merely anticipated the railroad's reliance on the federal statute as a defense.

On the basis of this reasoning, the Supreme Court reversed and remanded so that the action could be recommenced in a state court. As

---

U.S.C.A. § 1331 or actions removed from the state courts on the ground that they might have been brought in the federal courts under that statute. Verlinden B.V. v. Central Bank of Nigeria, 461 U.S. 480, 494–95, 103 S.Ct. 1962, 1972, 76 L.Ed.2d 81 (1983); Romero v. International Terminal Operating Co., 358 U.S. 354, 379, 79 S.Ct. 468, 484, 3 L.Ed.2d 368 (1959).

2. See § 2.3, above.

3. A more detailed discussion of the well-pleaded complaint rule can be found in 13B C. Wright, A. Miller, & E. Cooper, Jurisdiction and Related Matters 2d § 3566.

4. Franchise Tax Bd. v. Construction Laborers Vacation Trust for Southern California, 463 U.S. 1, 103 S.Ct. 2841, 77 L.Ed.2d 420 (1983); Phillips Petroleum Co. v. Texaco, Inc., 415 U.S. 125, 94 S.Ct. 1002, 39 L.Ed.2d 209 (1974); Skelly Oil Co. v. Phillips Petroleum Co., 339 U.S. 667, 70 S.Ct. 876, 94 L.Ed. 1194 (1950); Louisville & Nashville R.R. Co. v. Mottley, 211 U.S. 149, 29 S.Ct. 42, 53 L.Ed. 126 (1908); Metcalf v. City of Watertown, 128 U.S. 586, 9 S.Ct. 173, 32 L.Ed. 543 (1888).

5. 211 U.S. 149, 29 S.Ct. 42, 53 L.Ed. 126 (1908).

6. 211 U.S. at 152, 29 S.Ct. at 43.

might have been expected, the federal statutory and constitutional issues were raised in the state court, with the eventual result of another appeal to the United States Supreme Court, which finally disposed of the case on its merits.[7] The fact that the Supreme Court, which must have foreseen this result, was willing to permit the significant expenditure of judicial and party resources entailed by forcing the case to be litigated a second time strongly demonstrates the weight attached to the principle that federal court jurisdiction is limited and cannot be conferred by the parties.

Of course, overly strict adherence to any single legal principle is apt to cause difficulties. At times, application of the well-pleaded complaint rule has made the existence of federal jurisdiction in cases unquestionably involving issues of federal law turn on highly technical rules of pleading and on ancient principles regarding the forms of action that long since have lost their importance in other contexts of federal procedure.[8] For instance, when title to land is a matter of federal law, there is federal jurisdiction to hear an action to enjoin another from using the land,[9] but no jurisdiction over an action brought for ejectment because the latter is a possessory action that requires no allegation as to title in the complaint.[10]

By far the greatest difficulties in applying the well-pleaded complaint rule have occurred when the plaintiff seeks declaratory relief, because the plaintiff often is anticipating the defendant's action and is filing suit to avoid future litigation.[11] Although a broad view of the rule would uphold jurisdiction anytime the plaintiff sought a declaration as to the applicability or nonapplicability of some federal statute or the constitutionality of some state or federal law,[12] a more narrow interpretation prevails,[13] deriving in large measure from dictum in the Supreme

---

7. Louisville & Nashville R.R. Co. v. Mottley, 219 U.S. 467, 31 S.Ct. 265, 55 L.Ed. 297 (1911).

8. American Law Institute, Study of the Division of Jurisdiction Between State and Federal Courts, Official Draft, 169–70 (1969). See also Doernberg, There's No Reason for It; It's Just Our Policy: Why the Well–Pleaded Complaint Rule Sabotages the Purposes of Federal Question Jurisdiction, 38 Hast.L.J. 597 (1987).

9. Lancaster v. Kathleen Oil Co., 241 U.S. 551, 36 S.Ct. 711, 60 L.Ed. 1161 (1916).

10. Taylor v. Anderson, 234 U.S. 74, 34 S.Ct. 724, 58 L.Ed. 1218 (1914). But see Oneida Indian Nation v. County of Oneida, 414 U.S. 661, 94 S.Ct. 772, 39 L.Ed.2d 73 (1974) (when title to land is continuously a matter of federal law, as in the case of an Indian tribe claiming title under a treaty, there is federal jurisdiction over an ejectment action).

11. A fuller discussion of the well-pleaded complaint rule in the declaratory judgment context can be found in 10B C. Wright, A. Miller & M. Kane, Civil 3d § 2767.

12. A few courts seemingly have applied this broader interpretation. See, e.g., St. Louis Southwestern Ry. Co. v. City of Tyler, Texas, 375 F.2d 938 (5th Cir.1967); Regents of New Mexico v. Albuquerque Broadcasting Co., 158 F.2d 900 (10th Cir. 1947).

13. The Supreme Court reaffirmed its commitment to the narrow view in Franchise Tax Bd. v. Construction Laborers Vacation Trust for Southern California, 463 U.S. 1, 103 S.Ct. 2841, 77 L.Ed.2d 420 (1983). See Note, Federal Jurisdiction over Preemption Claims: A Post–Franchise Tax Board Analysis, 62 Texas L.Rev. 893 (1984).

Court's opinion in Skelly Oil Company v. Phillips Petroleum Company.[14] Thus, federal question jurisdiction will be found only if the coercive action that would have been brought were declaratory relief not available is within that jurisdiction. Utilizing this approach, then, the railroad in Mottley would not have been able to bring a federal court action seeking a declaration that the 1907 statute prevented it from issuing the Mottleys passes, for the railroad had no possible claim for injunctive relief; the only possible coercive action would be one by the Mottleys seeking specific performance of their contract—a claim involving purely state law questions.

The well-pleaded complaint rule fulfills a useful and necessary function. Given the limited nature of federal subject-matter jurisdiction, it is essential that the existence of jurisdiction be determined at the outset, rather than being contingent upon what *may* occur at later stages in the litigation. By demanding that a federal issue be raised in the complaint, the rule accomplishes this goal. But this achievement may be overshadowed by the fact that because general federal question jurisdiction exists only if a federal issue appears on the face of a well-pleaded complaint, in many cases federal courts are precluded from passing upon important issues of federal law, which leaves them for adjudication by state courts. Therefore, not surprisingly, the rule has been subjected to some rather trenchant criticism.[15]

Related to the well-pleaded complaint rule, and stemming also from a concern that the case be shown unequivocally to be one "arising under" federal law, is the doctrine that the federal issue raised by the complaint must be a substantial one. The substantiality doctrine requires a federal court to dismiss for lack of subject-matter jurisdiction whenever the federal claim that is asserted as the basis for jurisdiction is utterly frivolous or without merit.[16] The Supreme Court has held that a claim purportedly raising a federal question is "plainly unsubstantial" if it is "obviously without merit" or if " 'previous decisions of this court * * * foreclose the subject and leave no room for the inference that the questions sought to be raised can be subjects of controversy.' "[17] A claim that is of merely doubtful or questionable merit is not for that reason considered insubstantial for jurisdictional purposes; the claim may be dismissed for failure to state a claim on which relief can be granted,[18]

14.   339 U.S. 667, 673–74, 70 S.Ct. 876, 880, 94 L.Ed. 1194 (1950). See also Public Serv. Comm'n of Utah v. Wycoff Co., 344 U.S. 237, 248–49, 73 S.Ct. 236, 242–43, 97 L.Ed. 291 (1952).

15.   See, e.g., Cohen, The Broken Compass: The Requirement That a Case Arise "Directly" Under Federal Law, 115 U.Pa. L.Rev. 890 (1967); Fraser, Some Problems in Federal Question Jurisdiction, 49 Mich. L.Rev. 73 (1950).

16.   For a reaffirmation of the substantiality doctrine and a list of some of its formulations in prior decisions, see Hagans v. Lavine, 415 U.S. 528, 536–38, 94 S.Ct. 1372, 1378–79, 39 L.Ed.2d 577 (1974).

17.   Levering & Garrigues Co. v. Morrin, 289 U.S. 103, 105–06, 53 S.Ct. 549, 550, 77 L.Ed. 1062 (1933).

18.   Fed.Civ.Proc.Rule 12(b)(6). Compare Wheeldin v. Wheeler, 373 U.S. 647, 83 S.Ct. 1441, 10 L.Ed.2d 605 (1963) (no federal cause of action for violation of plaintiff's Fourth Amendment rights by an employee of House Unamerican Activities Committee), with Bivens v. Six Unknown Named Agents of Federal Bureau of Narcotics, 403 U.S. 388, 91 S.Ct. 1999, 29 L.Ed.2d 619

and yet be substantial enough to support federal jurisdiction.[19]

An "independent corollary" to the well-pleaded complaint rule is the principle that "a plaintiff may not defeat removal by omitting to plead necessary federal questions."[20] Thus, if a federal court concludes that a state court plaintiff has "artfully pleaded" claims in this fashion, the court may uphold removal from state court despite the fact that no federal question appears on the face of the state court complaint.[21]

§ 2.5 Diversity of Citizenship Jurisdiction—In General

Diversity of citizenship jurisdiction is among the oldest forms of federal judicial power; today, it is also the most controversial. The Constitution provides: "The judicial Power [of the United States] shall extend * * * to Controversies * * * between Citizens of different States, * * * and between a State, or the Citizens thereof and foreign States, Citizens, or Subjects."[1] In the 1789 Judiciary Act, the first Congress implemented a portion of this grant of judicial power by giving the United States circuit courts jurisdiction over cases in which "the suit is between a citizen of the State where the suit is brought, and a citizen of another State,"[2] as well as jurisdiction over suits involving aliens. In 1875, the requirement that one of the parties be a citizen of the forum state was eliminated,[3] and all subsequent legislation has conferred jurisdiction over all civil actions between citizens of different states, subject to many qualifications. The most obvious qualification is the explicit statutory requirement that a certain monetary minimum must be in controversy between the diverse citizens before a federal court can exercise jurisdiction over their dispute.[4]

There has been a long-standing scholarly dispute over the motivations that led the framers of the Constitution to include the provision for diversity jurisdiction. The classical rationale for diversity, enunciated by

---

(1971) (federal cause of action exists for Fourth Amendment violations by federal agents). In both cases, since the plaintiffs' constitutional claim was substantial, federal jurisdiction existed.

19. Rosado v. Wyman, 397 U.S. 397, 90 S.Ct. 1207, 25 L.Ed.2d 442 (1970); Bell v. Hood, 327 U.S. 678, 66 S.Ct. 773, 90 L.Ed. 939 (1946). This distinction may be important if additional supplemental claims are present since the court may have discretion to retain those claims if the dismissal was on the merits, rather than for lack of jurisdiction. See §§ 2.12–2.14, below.

20. Rivet v. Regions Bank of Louisiana, 522 U.S. 470, 118 S.Ct. 921, 925, 139 L.Ed.2d 912 (1998), quoting Franchise Tax Bd. of California v. Construction Laborers Vacation Trust for Southern California, 463 U.S. 1, 22, 103 S.Ct. 2841, 2853, 77 L.Ed.2d 420 (1983).

21. Rivet v. Regions Bank of Louisiana, 522 U.S. 470, 118 S.Ct. 921, 925, 139 L.Ed.2d 912 (1998). See generally Miller Artful Pleading: A Doctrine in Search of Definition, 76 Texas L.Rev. 1781 (1998); § 2.11, below.

§ 2.5

1. U.S. Const. Art. III, § 2.

2. Act of Sept. 24, 1789, § 11, 1 Stat. 73, 78. Congress is not required to grant, and never has granted, the full jurisdiction that the Constitution authorizes it to give the federal courts. See § 2.2, above.

3. Act of March 3, 1875, § 1, 18 Stat. 470.

4. See § 2.8, below. Other limitations on diversity jurisdiction are discussed at notes 20–25, below.

Chief Justice Marshall in Bank of United States v. Deveaux,[5] emphasized the avoidance of actual prejudice to out-of-state litigants in state courts, as well as the elimination of apprehensions and fears of prejudice by out-of-state litigants, whether justified or not. However, the real concern of the supporters of diversity at the Constitutional Convention and in the First Congress may have focused more on economic advantage than on the avoidance of abstract regional or state prejudice. The federal courts offered a means for protecting commercial groups from class bias on the part of democratically inclined state legislatures, which otherwise might pressure state courts into decisions hostile to commercial, manufacturing, and speculative land interests. According to this view, the problem that diversity addressed was not hostility among the states, but hostility among the classes.[6]

The controversy over the motives of the creators of diversity is equalled, if not surpassed in intensity, by the current disagreement over the desirability of perpetuating this basis of federal jurisdiction.[7] The opponents of diversity see it as an historical anachronism, destructive of judicial efficiency and prone to abuses that detract from the integrity of the legal system. For these critics, the alleged inefficiency stems from several by-products of diversity jurisdiction. First, and most simply, it adds to the case burden of the federal courts, which already are increasingly congested because of the dramatic expansion of federal question jurisdiction.[8] In addition, the doctrine of Erie Railroad Company v. Tompkins,[9] requiring federal courts to apply the substantive law of the forum state in diversity actions, tends to minimize the role of the federal judiciary in diversity cases and casts doubt on the wisdom of expending system time and energy on these cases.[10]

5. 9 U.S. (5 Cranch) 61, 3 L.Ed. 38 (1809).

6. Frank, Historical Bases of the Federal Judicial System, 13 Law & Contemp. Prob. 3, 22–28 (1948); Frankfurter, Distribution of Judicial Power Between United States and State Courts, 13 Cornell L.Q. 499, 521–22 (1928); Friendly, The Historic Basis of Diversity Jurisdiction, 41 Harv. L.Rev. 483 (1928).

7. The following list is a representative sample of the views of the participants in the debate over the merits and demerits of the continued existence of diversity jurisdiction: Justice Frankfurter's concurring opinion in Lumbermen's Mut. Cas. Co. v. Elbert, 348 U.S. 48, 53–60, 75 S.Ct. 151, 155–58, 99 L.Ed. 59 (1954); Doub, Time for Reevaluation: Shall We Curtail Diversity Jurisdiction?, 44 A.B.A.J. 243 (1958); Frank, For Maintaining Diversity Jurisdiction, 73 Yale L.J. 7 (1963); Moore & Weckstein, Diversity Jurisdiction: Past, Present, and Future, 43 Texas L.Rev. 1 (1964); Parker, Dual Sovereignty and the Federal Courts, 51 Nw.U.L.Rev. 407 (1956); Wechsler, Federal Jurisdiction and the Revision of the

Judicial Code, 13 Law & Contemp.Prob. 216, 234–40 (1948); Yntema, The Jurisdiction of the Federal Courts in Controversies Between Citizens of Different States, 19 A.B.A.J. 71, 149, 265 (1933).

8. Frankfurter, Distribution of Judicial Power Between United States and State Courts, 13 Cornell L.Q. 499, 523 (1928). The percentage of diversity cases on the federal docket steadily declined between 1960 and 1980, then remained relatively constant for a number of years, but has declined again since 1990. In fiscal year 1997, of the 272,027 civil cases commenced in the United States District Court, 55,278 (20.3%) were based on diversity. Annual Report of the Director of the Administrative Office of the United States Courts, Table C2 (1998).

9. 304 U.S. 64, 58 S.Ct. 817, 82 L.Ed. 1188 (1938). See Chapter 4 for full discussion of the Erie doctrine.

10. See Wright, The Federal Courts and the Nature and Quality of State Law, 13 Wayne L.Rev. 317, 321–26 (1967). It has

In addition to inefficiency and the misallocation of limited resources, diversity critics point to the opportunity it creates for abuse and injustice.[11] Further, diversity jurisdiction allows an alternative to the state forum that is open only to those litigants who fortuitously are of citizenship diverse from that of their adversaries.[12] One may question the propriety of according the privilege of having access to a federal forum to certain citizens, while others with cases no different on the merits are obliged to litigate only in the state courts.

The advocates of diversity jurisdiction claim that the spectre of prejudice against out-of-state litigants has not been laid entirely to rest.[13] Furthermore, they point to additional advantages of litigating in the federal courts, including the generally higher caliber of federal judges and the availability of the Federal Rules of Civil Procedure. Supporters of diversity also claim that the existence of two parallel court systems with concurrent jurisdiction over diversity cases creates a flow of ideas between the systems that improves the quality of practice in each.[14] Finally, the adoption by the states of uniform acts, most notably the Uniform Commercial Code, means that even under the doctrine of Erie Railroad Company v. Tompkins, a place remains for the federal courts to expound upon commercial law in a way that has nationwide applicability, one of the original historical functions of diversity jurisdiction.[15]

Between the extremes of wholesale abolition of diversity jurisdiction and total acceptance of the status quo, lies the realm of suggestions for change that, at least in the eyes of their proponents, would retain the valid features of diversity but eliminate its undesirable aspects. The most significant of these suggestions is the American Law Institute's proposal to prohibit a citizen of the forum state from invoking diversity jurisdiction in that state, regardless of the citizenship of the opposing party.[16] Since a resident of the forum state really cannot complain of prejudice in the courts of his or her home state, the classical justification for diversity jurisdiction is lacking. This proposal was considered most recently by Congress in 1978.[17] Further proposals to abolish diversity

been said that federal judges sitting in diversity are reduced to the status of "ventriloquist's dummies" for the courts of the forum state. Richardson v. Commissioner of Internal Revenue, 126 F.2d 562, 567 (2d Cir.1942) (Frank, J.), cited in Wechsler, Federal Jurisdiction and the Revision of the Judicial Code, 13 Law & Contemp.Prob. 216, 238–39 (1948).

11. See § 2.7, below, for a discussion of the devices used to manipulate diversity for tactical advantage.

12. Serious abuses may be perpetrated by a litigant trying to bring himself within this privileged group. See § 2.7, below.

13. See Brown, The Jurisdiction of the Federal Courts Based on Diversity of Citizenship, 78 U.Pa.L.Rev. 179 (1928); Moore

& Weckstein, Diversity Jurisdiction: Past, Present, and Future, 43 Texas L.Rev. 1, 16 (1964).

14. Frank, For Maintaining Diversity Jurisdiction, 73 Yale L.J. 7, 11–12 (1963).

15. Wright, The Federal Courts and the Nature and Quality of State Law, 13 Wayne L.Rev. 317 (1967).

16. American Law Institute, Study of the Division of Jurisdiction Between State and Federal Courts, Official Draft, 99–110 (1969). Other changes proposed by the Institute would make it more difficult for corporations to invoke diversity and would prevent improper manipulation of citizenship for diversity purposes by litigants.

17. S. 2094, 95th Cong., 2d Sess. (1978).

jurisdiction entirely were considered in 1979.[18] Although Congress did seem to be giving serious consideration to eliminating diversity jurisdiction in the late 1970s, interest in the subject appears to have subsided somewhat.[19]

Before turning to an examination of the application of the diversity statute's requirements, it is important to note that there are two areas of substantive law in which the federal courts traditionally have refused to exercise jurisdiction, despite the existence of all the necessary ingredients for diversity. These are domestic relations and probate cases. In the field of domestic relations, the established rule is that federal courts will not adjudicate cases involving marital status. A federal court will not grant a divorce, make an award of alimony, or settle a controversy over the custody of a child.[20] The rationale for this limitation is that family relations are uniquely a matter of state policy and state interest, with which the federal courts should not interfere. However, federal courts will take jurisdiction to enforce the obligations of a defaulting spouse under a final state court divorce decree.[21] The domestic relations exception to diversity jurisdiction has been criticized by a distinguished jurist,[22] but it continues to be widely honored by federal courts.

The probate exception to diversity stems from the doctrine that when "property is in the actual possession of one court, of competent jurisdiction, such possession cannot be disturbed by process out of another court."[23] Accordingly, a federal court cannot probate a will or appoint an administrator because the estate involves property already under the jurisdiction of the state probate court.[24] However, as part of its general equity jurisdiction, a federal court is free to hear diversity actions against administrators, executors, or other claimants by plaintiffs seeking to establish claims against an estate. As long as the federal court does not interfere with the state probate proceeding or attempt to assume control of property in the state court's custody, it has jurisdiction to render a binding in personam judgment concerning the shares of persons of diverse citizenship in the estate.[25]

---

18. H.R. 130 and 2202, 96th Cong., 1st Sess. (1979).

19. Five bills to curtail diversity were introduced by Congressman Kastenmeier in 1983, but none ever got out of committee. Occasional bills have appeared in the years since.

Thus, although some interest clearly remains, there does not appear to be an agreed-upon strategy for limiting diversity jurisdiction.

20. Ohio ex rel. Popovici v. Agler, 280 U.S. 379, 50 S.Ct. 154, 74 L.Ed. 489 (1930); Ex parte Burrus, 136 U.S. 586, 10 S.Ct. 850, 34 L.Ed. 500 (1890); Barber v. Barber, 62 U.S. (21 How.) 582, 16 L.Ed. 226 (1858).

21. Sutton v. Leib, 342 U.S. 402, 72 S.Ct. 398, 96 L.Ed. 448 (1952); Barber v. Barber, 62 U.S. (21 How.) 582, 16 L.Ed. 226 (1858). The scope of the exception is explored more fully in Note, The Domestic Relations Exception to Diversity Jurisdiction, 83 Colum.L.Rev. 1824 (1983).

22. See Spindel v. Spindel, 283 F.Supp. 797 (E.D.N.Y.1968) (Weinstein, J.).

23. Byers v. McAuley, 149 U.S. 608, 614, 13 S.Ct. 906, 908, 37 L.Ed. 867 (1893).

24. O'Callaghan v. O'Brien, 199 U.S. 89, 25 S.Ct. 727, 50 L.Ed. 101 (1905); Ellis v. Davis, 109 U.S. 485, 3 S.Ct. 327, 27 L.Ed. 1006 (1883); In re Broderick's Will, 88 U.S. (21 Wall.) 503, 22 L.Ed. 599 (1874).

25. Markham v. Allen, 326 U.S. 490, 66 S.Ct. 296, 90 L.Ed. 256 (1946); Waterman v. Canal–Louisiana Bank & Trust Co., 215 U.S. 33, 45, 30 S.Ct. 10, 13, 54 L.Ed. 80

Finally, as a corollary of the limited nature of federal subject-matter jurisdiction and the presumption against the existence of that jurisdiction,[26] the burden of pleading the citizenship of each party to an action is on the party seeking to invoke diversity jurisdiction.[27] The citizenship of each party must be alleged affirmatively in the complaint.[28] If and when diversity jurisdiction is challenged, the burden of proof remains on the party invoking federal court jurisdiction,[29] and citizenship must be established by a preponderance of the evidence.[30]

In determining whether diversity of citizenship exists, the critical moment is the time at which the suit is commenced; under the Federal Rules, this refers to when the complaint is filed in the district court.[31] Once diversity jurisdiction attaches, it is not impaired by a party's later change of domicile.[32] In the words of Chief Justice Marshall: " * * * after vesting, it [jurisdiction] cannot be ousted by subsequent events."[33] The rationale for this rule is the practical necessity of having a definite and easily ascertainable benchmark for determining whether jurisdiction has been established. The converse of the rule follows from the same need for definiteness and uniformity: if diversity does not exist at the time the action is commenced, it cannot be created by later events.[34]

§ 2.6　Diversity of Citizenship Jurisdiction—Application of Diversity Requirements

The diversity statute confers jurisdiction in general terms on the federal courts in all civil actions "between citizens of different states" in which the required jurisdictional amount is present.[1] There are, however, a number of crucial judicial interpretations of this language, the effect of which has been to reshape and limit the scope of diversity jurisdiction, placing certain actions involving citizens of different states beyond the ambit of the federal courts.

(1909); Lamberg v. Callahan, 455 F.2d 1213 (2d Cir.1972).

26. See § 2.2, above.

27. Cameron v. Hodges, 127 U.S. 322, 8 S.Ct. 1154, 32 L.Ed. 132 (1888).

28. The court will look to the entire record to determine whether it provides support for subject-matter jurisdiction if the pleadings are inadequate for that purpose, although the pleadings should clearly aver facts showing citizenship. Anderson v. Watt, 138 U.S. 694, 702, 11 S.Ct. 449, 451, 34 L.Ed. 1078 (1891).

29. Mas v. Perry, 489 F.2d 1396 (5th Cir.1974), cert. denied 419 U.S. 842; Janzen v. Goos, 302 F.2d 421 (8th Cir.1962). The plaintiff's burden may be relieved by one of several well-established presumptions, such as that a domicile once established continues until it is changed, that proof of residence in a state is prima facie evidence of citizenship thereof, and that the domicile of

a serviceman at the time of induction into military service persists.

30. Welsh v. American Sur. Co. of New York, 186 F.2d 16 (5th Cir.1951). As to the meaning of citizenship, see § 2.6, below.

31. Fed.Civ.Proc.Rule 3.

32. Smith v. Sperling, 354 U.S. 91, 77 S.Ct. 1112, 1 L.Ed.2d 1205 (1957); Smith v. Potomac Edison Co., 165 F.Supp. 681 (D.Md.1958).

33. Mollan v. Torrance, 22 U.S. (9 Wheat.) 537, 539, 6 L.Ed. 154 (1824).

34. Slaughter v. Toye Bros. Yellow Cab Co., 359 F.2d 954 (5th Cir.1966); Lyons v. Weltmer, 174 F.2d 473 (4th Cir.1949), cert. denied 338 U.S. 850.

§ 2.6

1. 28 U.S.C.A. § 1332(a)(1). Sections 2.8–2.9, below, discuss the jurisdictional amount requirement.

The most important of these interpretations is the rule of complete diversity, first enunciated by Chief Justice Marshall in the early case of Strawbridge v. Curtiss.[2] Strawbridge, which construed the language of the 1789 Judiciary Act, held that there is no diversity jurisdiction when any party on one side of the dispute is a citizen of the same state as any party on the other side. In multiparty suits, the presence of a single plaintiff who is a citizen of the same state as any defendant will defeat diversity.[3] Justice Marshall is reported to have regretted his Strawbridge decision in later life,[4] and it often has been criticized.[5] Nonetheless, the complete diversity requirement remains the unqualified rule in all types of diversity actions brought under Section 1332.[6]

The scope of diversity jurisdiction is affected further by a procedure known as realignment.[7] Since it would be unconstitutional for a federal court to assume jurisdiction based on diversity in a dispute involving nondiverse adversaries (assuming there is no other basis for federal jurisdiction), the court is obliged to scrutinize the nature of the controversy and if necessary, to realign the parties to reflect the actual clash of interests in the case. The citizenship of the parties as realigned will determine whether the requisite complete diversity exists.

In deciding whether the litigants should be realigned, an "ultimate interests" test is applied—the goal is to "look beyond the pleadings and arrange the parties according to their sides in the dispute."[8] Difficult problems of realignment arise when the interests of the parties are

2. 7 U.S. (3 Cranch) 267, 2 L.Ed. 435 (1806). Further discussion of the complete diversity requirement is found in 13B C. Wright, A. Miller & E. Cooper, Jurisdiction and Related Matters 2d § 3605.

3. Soderstrom v. Kungsholm Baking Co., 189 F.2d 1008, 1013–14 (7th Cir.1951).

4. Louisville, C. & C.R.R. Co. v. Letson, 43 U.S. (2 How.) 497, 555, 11 L.Ed. 353 (1844).

5. See, e.g., Currie, The Federal Courts and the American Law Institute, 36 U.Chi. L.Rev. 1, 18–21 (1968).

6. The requirement of complete diversity does not apply in actions brought under the interpleader statute, 28 U.S.C.A. § 1335. State Farm Fire & Cas. Co. v. Tashire, 386 U.S. 523, 87 S.Ct. 1199, 18 L.Ed.2d 270 (1967). See § 16.12, below, for a discussion of interpleader jurisdiction. Various other situations pose quasi-exceptions to the rule of complete diversity. Among them are the doctrine of supplemental claim jurisdiction, which permits the joinder of nondiverse parties in certain circumstances (see § 2.13, below); the doctrine of supplemental party jurisdiction, which similarly permits the joinder of nondiverse parties (see § 2.14, below); and the rule

that in many representative actions, only the citizenship of the named representative or representatives is relevant in determining whether diversity of citizenship exists (see § 16.4, below).

7. See 13B C. Wright, A. Miller & E. Cooper, Jurisdiction and Related Matters 2d § 3607.

8. City of Dawson v. Columbia Ave. Sav. Fund, Safe Deposit, Title & Trust Co., 197 U.S. 178, 180, 25 S.Ct. 420, 421, 49 L.Ed. 713 (1905) (Holmes, J.). In this case, a mortgagee sued to enforce a contract between its mortgagor, a water works, and the city. The plaintiff was a Pennsylvania corporation; the city and the water works were both citizens of Georgia. It was obvious to the Court that the mortgagor should have been aligned as a plaintiff, since there "was no difference or collision of interest or action" between it and its mortgagee. Realignment therefore was ordered, destroying diversity. See also Lee v. Lehigh Valley Coal Co., 267 U.S. 542, 45 S.Ct. 385, 69 L.Ed. 782 (1925) (lessor owning one-half interest in property must join other lessor as a plaintiff in suit against lessee and could not be named as a defendant in order to preserve complete diversity).

multiple, complex, and partially overlapping.[9] For example, in City of Indianapolis v. Chase National Bank,[10] the plaintiff (the Bank and trustee under a mortgage deed) sued the city and the gas company which was its mortgagor. The gas company owed the plaintiff a common interest on the mortgage but also shared with the plaintiff a common interest in obtaining a declaration that the city had succeeded to the obligations of the gas company's previous lessee. These obligations included payments to the company of the interest on its mortgage to the plaintiff. Faced with this complicated situation, the majority of the Court, in an opinion by Justice Frankfurter, held that the gas company should be realigned as a plaintiff because both it and the original plaintiff had the same interest in establishing the city's obligations. But four justices felt that the plaintiff and the gas company were fundamentally opposed, since the gas company would be liable for more than $1 million in back interest payments if the plaintiff prevailed.[11]

Since citizenship is the key to determining whether diversity jurisdiction may be asserted, it is critical to understand the meaning of that concept as applied to natural persons and corporations under the statute. With respect to litigants of United States citizenship, the courts have developed two basic requirements that must be satisfied before a person can sue or be sued in the federal courts under diversity jurisdiction. First, the party must be domiciled within a state.[12] The state citizenship of a natural person is treated as synonymous with an individual's domicile.[13] Second, the party must be a citizen of the United States.[14] Both requirements must be satisfied. A person who is domiciled in a state, but who is not a citizen of the United States, will be unable to invoke diversity jurisdiction;[15] a person who is a citizen of the United States, but who is not domiciled in any state, cannot satisfy the diversity

---

9. Special problems of realignment apply to shareholder derivative actions. See § 16.9, below.

10. 314 U.S. 63, 62 S.Ct. 15, 86 L.Ed. 47 (1941).

11. Since realignment had the effect of destroying diversity, perhaps Justice Frankfurter was motivated in part by his general opposition to diversity jurisdiction. For evidence of this opposition, see Frankfurter, Distribution of Judicial Power Between United States and State Courts, 13 Cornell L.Q. 499 (1928). See also Justice Frankfurter's concurring opinion in Lumbermen's Mut. Cas. Co. v. Elbert, 348 U.S. 48, 53–60, 75 S.Ct. 151, 155–58, 99 L.Ed. 59 (1954).

12. Gilbert v. David, 235 U.S. 561, 35 S.Ct. 164, 59 L.Ed. 360 (1915); Janzen v. Goos, 302 F.2d 421 (8th Cir.1962).

Early interpretations of the first Judiciary Act interpreted the word "state" narrowly to exclude citizens of the District of Columbia and the territories. See Corpora-tion of New Orleans v. Winter, 14 U.S. (1 Wheat.) 91, 4 L.Ed. 44 (1816); Hepburn & Dundas v. Ellzey, 6 U.S. (2 Cranch) 445, 2 L.Ed. 332 (1805). In 1940, Congress passed a statute clearly extending jurisdiction to those litigants. Act of April 20, 1940, 54 Stat. 143, presently codified in 28 U.S.C.A. § 1332(d). The validity of that statute was upheld in National Mut. Ins. Co. of District of Columbia v. Tidewater Transfer Co., 337 U.S. 582, 69 S.Ct. 1173, 93 L.Ed. 1556 (1949).

13. Ellis v. Southeast Constr. Co., 260 F.2d 280 (8th Cir.1958). See generally 13B C. Wright, A. Miller & E. Cooper, Jurisdiction and Related Matters 2d § 3611.

14. Scott v. Sanford, 60 U.S. (19 How.) 393, 15 L.Ed. 691 (1856).

15. One who is not a citizen of the United States may be able to invoke alienage jurisdiction under 28 U.S.C.A. § 1332(a)(2), however. See notes 34–40, below.

statute's requirements.[16]

Domicile is defined as residence in fact, combined with the intention of making the place of residence one's home for an indefinite period.[17] Both ingredients are necessary. The mere fact of residence in a given state does not establish domicile, although it generally provides prima facie evidence of domicile in that state; nor is the expression of an intention to move one's residence, without actually moving, sufficient to constitute a change in domicile.[18] Domicile, in other words, has both a physical and a mental dimension—it is the place where a person has a true, fixed home and principal establishment, and to which, whenever she is absent, she intends to return. Thus, a person may have only one domicile at any time,[19] despite the ownership of multiple residences (such as seasonal homes) or involvement in different businesses. Further, a domicile once established continues unless and until a new one is acquired.[20] Consequently, there is a presumption in favor of an established domicile that must be overcome by a party seeking to show a change in domicile.[21]

Because the test for domicile contains an element of intention to remain, resolution of a contested or doubtful citizenship question can be rather complex, involving a number of evidentiary factors, no one of which is necessarily controlling. These factors may include: current residence; voting or automobile registration; location of personal or real property or other economic interests, such as businesses; location of brokerage and bank accounts; place of employment; membership in unions, churches, clubs, and other associations; participation in civic affairs; and sometimes even a personal declaration of domicile.[22]

There are special rules for various categories of persons, each reflecting the accommodation of the basic domicile principles with other legal and factual considerations. A married woman, because of the historic legal identity of husband and wife, has been deemed to possess her husband's domicile, even if in fact they live apart.[23] This rule, however, has been relaxed considerably in cases in which there has been a breakdown in the marital relationship,[24] and there are signs of even

---

16. Twentieth Century–Fox Film Corp. v. Taylor, 239 F.Supp. 913 (S.D.N.Y.1965).

17. Gilbert v. David, 235 U.S. 561, 35 S.Ct. 164, 59 L.Ed. 360 (1915); Stine v. Moore, 213 F.2d 446 (5th Cir.1954).

18. Krasnov v. Dinan, 465 F.2d 1298 (3d Cir.1972). See also Steigleder v. McQuesten, 198 U.S. 141, 25 S.Ct. 616, 49 L.Ed. 986 (1905); Hendry v. Masonite Corp., 455 F.2d 955 (5th Cir.1972), cert. denied 409 U.S. 1023.

19. Williamson v. Osenton, 232 U.S. 619, 34 S.Ct. 442, 58 L.Ed. 758 (1914). Justice Holmes' opinion is a concise summary of many of the principles governing citizenship for diversity purposes.

20. Mitchell v. U.S., 88 U.S. (21 Wall.) 350, 22 L.Ed. 584 (1875).

21. Janzen v. Goos, 302 F.2d 421 (8th Cir.1962); Maple Island Farm, Inc. v. Bitterling, 196 F.2d 55 (8th Cir.1952), cert. denied 344 U.S. 832.

22. 13B C. Wright, A. Miller & E. Cooper, Jurisdiction and Related Matters 2d § 3612, at 530–33. See generally Note, Evidentiary Factors in the Determination of Domicile, 61 Harv.L.Rev. 1232 (1948).

23. Anderson v. Watt, 138 U.S. 694, 11 S.Ct. 449, 34 L.Ed. 1078 (1891).

24. Williamson v. Osenton, 232 U.S. 619, 34 S.Ct. 442, 58 L.Ed. 758 (1914); Gallagher v. Philadelphia Transp. Co., 185 F.2d 543 (3d Cir.1950).

further erosion as attitudes toward marriage and other social patterns change.[25] Minors, because the common law treated them as having a dependent status, are considered to share the domicile of the parent who is supporting them.[26] Thus, out-of-state students generally are deemed to retain their pre-school domicile, which typically is that of their families, although if emancipated or of age, they may acquire a domicile at the location of their school.[27]

Because a domicile must be chosen with the intention of settling there indefinitely, it follows that changes of residence that are coerced or otherwise involuntarily made will be disregarded. Consequently, military personnel[28] and prisoners[29] traditionally have been considered to possess the domicile they occupied before enlistment or incarceration, although this rule has been applied less mechanically. Also, someone who has been adjudged incompetent is presumed to have the domicile that he possessed when last competent, regardless of subsequent moves.[30]

Interesting problems arise when actions are brought by representatives for the benefit of others or for the estates of deceased persons. It always has been the rule that the citizenship of purely nominal or formal parties with no interest in the action is ignored for diversity purposes.[31] But the situation is different with regard to a representative who has actual power over the matter in litigation, such as a trustee litigating on behalf of beneficiaries, in which case the citizenship of the representative, not that of the represented individuals, controls.[32] The same does not apply to an executor or administratrix litigating on behalf of an estate, however. Congress provided in 1988 that "the legal representative of the estate of a decedent shall be deemed to be a citizen only of the same state as the decedent." Congress also stipulated that a legal representative of an infant or an incompetent should be deemed a citizen of the same state as the infant or incompetent.[33] These changes were an attempt to eliminate the fabrication or avoidance of diversity; however, they do not change the rule with regard to actions brought by other types of representatives.

---

25. See Napletana v. Hillsdale College, 385 F.2d 871 (6th Cir.1967) (wife who had a job in Ohio and whose husband had a job in Michigan was held to be a citizen of Ohio for purpose of diversity jurisdiction); Taylor v. Milam, 89 F.Supp. 880 (W.D.Ark.1950).

26. Delaware, L. & W. Ry. Co. v. Petrowsky, 250 Fed. 554 (2d Cir.1918), cert. denied 247 U.S. 508.

27. Mallon v. Lutz, 217 F.Supp. 454 (E.D.Mich.1963).

28. Ellis v. Southeast Constr. Co., 260 F.2d 280 (8th Cir.1958); Bowman v. Du-Bose, 267 F.Supp. 312 (D.S.C.1967).

29. White v. Fawcett Publications, 324 F.Supp. 403 (W.D.Mo.1970). But see Stifel v. Hopkins, 477 F.2d 1116 (6th Cir.1973), noted in 20 Wayne L.Rev. 1177 (1974). The Stifel opinion is an extremely rich summary and re-appraisal of most of the principles discussed in this section.

30. Foster v. Carlin, 200 F.2d 943 (4th Cir.1952). The presumption against an individual's change of domicile is rebuttable. Coppedge v. Clinton, 72 F.2d 531 (10th Cir.1934).

31. Salem Trust Co. v. Manufacturers' Finance Co., 264 U.S. 182, 44 S.Ct. 266, 68 L.Ed. 628 (1924); Walden v. Skinner, 101 U.S. (11 Otto) 577, 25 L.Ed. 963 (1880).

32. Mexican Cent. Ry. Co. v. Eckman, 187 U.S. 429, 23 S.Ct. 211, 47 L.Ed. 245 (1903); Janzen v. Goos, 302 F.2d 421 (8th Cir.1962). The appointment of a representative to create or destroy jurisdiction is discussed in § 2.7, below.

33. 28 U.S.C.A. § 1332(c)(2).

Persons who do not have American citizenship may invoke federal court jurisdiction by virtue of Section 1332(a)(2), providing for jurisdiction over actions between aliens and citizens of a state.[34] This jurisdiction commonly is called "alienage jurisdiction" to distinguish it from the diversity jurisdiction provided for in Section 1332(a)(1).[35] The rules of citizenship and domicile applicable to American citizens for purposes of alienage jurisdiction are the same as those just discussed: the person litigating against the alien must be a citizen of the United States and be domiciled within a state. A person is deemed an alien—and therefore able to sue or be sued in the federal courts under alienage jurisdiction—only if he or she is a citizen or subject of a foreign nation according to the laws of that country.[36] Thus, persons without a country cannot sue or be sued in the federal courts under either diversity or alienage jurisdiction.[37]

In 1988, Section 1332(a) was amended to limit alienage jurisdiction somewhat by providing that "an alien admitted to the United States for permanent residence shall be deemed a citizen of the State in which such alien is domiciled."[38] Prior to the enactment of this amendment, an alien, admitted for permanent residence to the United States and domiciled in Michigan, for example, could invoke alienage jurisdiction to bring suit in federal court against an American citizen who also was domiciled in Michigan. Under the amended language however, the permanent resident alien no longer can invoke federal jurisdiction in that situation. On the other hand, the plain meaning of the amendment also expands diversity jurisdiction, in theory at least, by permitting a permanent resident alien to invoke diversity jurisdiction against another permanent resident alien who is domiciled in a different state or against a nonresident alien. This application of the amendment would abrogate the longstanding rule that if aliens are on both sides of a dispute, diversity jurisdiction does not exist,[39] and also may represent an unconstitutional exercise of judicial power, since Article III, Section 2 of the Constitution does not authorize Congress to extend the power of the federal courts to controversies between aliens. Perhaps with this constitutional concern in mind, and despite the plain meaning of the statute, no court, to date, has upheld jurisdiction in such a situation.[40]

34. Since Mossman v. Higginson, 4 U.S. (4 Dall.) 12, 1 L.Ed. 720 (1800), the federal courts consistently have refused to hear suits between aliens, first on the ground that the Constitution does not authorize jurisdiction over those suits, and later on the additional ground that Congress has not granted such jurisdiction. But in the 1976 Foreign Sovereign Immunities Act, Congress did so provide, at least in actions involving foreign governments. 28 U.S.C.A. § 1330. Several years later, the Supreme Court upheld that statute as constitutional. Verlinden B.V. v. Central Bank of Nigeria, 461 U.S. 480, 103 S.Ct. 1962, 76 L.Ed.2d 81 (1983).

35. See generally 13B C. Wright, A. Miller & E. Cooper, Jurisdiction and Related Matters 2d § 3604.

36. 13B C. Wright, A. Miller & E. Cooper, Jurisdiction and Related Matters 2d § 3611. See Murarka v. Bachrack Bros., Inc., 215 F.2d 547 (2d Cir.1954).

37. Blair Holdings Corp. v. Rubinstein, 133 F.Supp. 496 (S.D.N.Y.1955).

38. 28 U.S.C.A. § 1332(a).

39. Hodgson v. Bowerbank, 9 U.S. (5 Cranch) 303, 3 L.Ed. 108 (1809).

40. But compare Singh v. Daimler-Benz AG, 9 F.3d 303 (3d Cir.1993), in which the administrator of the estate of an

The evolution of the law governing the treatment of the citizenship of corporations for purposes of diversity jurisdiction illustrates both the process of judicial adaptation to changing social and economic conditions, and evolving attitudes about the desirability and scope of diversity jurisdiction. Originally, a corporation was considered to be a "mere legal entity," which could not be a citizen of any state.[41] A suit by a corporation was treated as a suit by its members (stockholders) and it was necessary to look to the citizenship of all the individual stockholders to determine whether diversity existed.

This interpretation did not cause many problems in the early part of the Nineteenth Century because most corporations were small and local in nature. However, as the corporate form of business enterprise became more significant and the character of corporations changed, the notion that the corporation was not a citizen of any state became increasingly burdensome, often shutting the door to the federal courts to both corporations and their adversaries. The Supreme Court responded to this problem in 1844 by declaring that a corporation chartered by a state was a citizen of that state for purposes of suing and being sued.[42] Nine years later it retracted its direct bestowal of citizenship and instead established a conclusive presumption that all of the stockholders of a corporation are citizens of the state of its incorporation.[43] This was, of course, a complete fiction in many cases, but it did answer the need for a device by which a corporation could acquire citizenship. The presumption also reflected a favorable, sympathetic view of diversity jurisdiction—some-

alien, who was admitted for permanent residence to the United States and was domiciled in Virginia, brought a products liability suit in state court against a German car manufacturer and its American affiliate, which was domiciled in Delaware and New Jersey. The action was removed to federal court. The Third Circuit upheld jurisdiction on the basis of diversity, holding that the situation before it presented a case of at least minimal diversity, since someone deemed a citizen of Virginia opposed a citizen of New Jersey and Delaware, and that the 1988 amendment was a valid exercise of Congress's power to invest the federal courts with jurisdiction when minimal diversity exists. That is precisely what the Supreme Court in Strawbridge v. Curtis, which is discussed in note 2, above, said Congress had not done in the 1789 Judiciary Act. Of the situation in which two aliens might be the only parties in a lawsuit, in which not even minimal diversity would exist, Chief Judge Sloviter wrote, "[T]he resolution of the constitutional issue is not as clear as may appear at first glance. Even accepting the general view that the Supreme Court's decision in Hodgson v. Bowerbank (citation omitted) (diversity jurisdiction does not extend to actions between aliens) is a construction of the diversity clause of Article III, this would not necessarily preclude Congress from authorizing federal jurisdiction in suits between aliens grounded on other constitutional bases." 9 F.3d at 312. Several courts have disagreed with the Singh holding, finding that the 1988 amendment did not abrogate the complete diversity requirement but instead did no more than eliminate the federal courts' jurisdiction over suits between a citizen and a permanent resident alien when both are domiciled in the same state. See, e.g., Saadeh v. Farouki, 107 F.3d 52 (D.C.Cir.1997); Engstrom v. Hornseth, 959 F.Supp. 545 (D.Puerto Rico 1997), Buti v. Impressa Perosa, S.R.L., 935 F.Supp. 458 (S.D.N.Y. 1996), affirmed on other grounds 139 F.3d 98 (2d Cir.1998), cert. denied ___ U.S. ___, 119 S.Ct. 73.

41. Bank of U.S. v. Deveaux, 9 U.S. (5 Cranch) 61, 3 L.Ed. 38 (1809).

42. Louisville, Cincinnati, Charleston R.R. Co. v. Letson, 43 U.S. (2 How.) 497, 11 L.Ed. 353 (1844).

43. Marshall v. Baltimore & Ohio R.R. Co., 57 U.S. (16 How.) 314, 14 L.Ed. 953 (1853). For a criticism of the use of this conclusive presumption see McGovney, A Supreme Court Fiction, 56 Harv.L.Rev. 853 (1943).

thing that was seen as a valuable privilege, not to be curtailed by any metaphysical doubt as to whether corporations could be citizens.

Although it has been modified both judicially and statutorily as the perceived attractiveness of diversity jurisdiction has waned,[44] the presumption of corporate citizenship wherever a corporation is chartered continues today. The most significant modification has been Section 1332(c) of Title 28, which was added in 1958[45] and which provides that a corporation is to be deemed a citizen of any state in which it is incorporated and of the state in which it has its principal place of business. Hence, a corporation now has dual citizenship, unless its principal place of business is in its state of incorporation. By expanding the notion of corporate citizenship, Section 1332(c) restricted the scope of diversity jurisdiction[46] and thereby somewhat eased the workload of the federal courts. The statute also remedied two related abuses. No longer can an entirely local corporation invoke diversity merely because it has been incorporated in another state for tax purposes or other reasons.[47] Conversely, a corporation doing primarily local business under a foreign charter cannot escape local state jurisdiction by removing actions brought against it to a federal court.[48] As a result, cases arising from the activities of a corporation vis-à-vis the citizens of the state with which it has its closest connection are likely to be heard by the courts of that state.[49]

Because the activities of many corporate enterprises are widely and equally dispersed, and because Section 1332(c) clearly requires that every corporation must have one—and only one—principal place of business,[50] a major problem arises concerning how to identify that site.[51] Three tests have been developed by the federal courts. The "corporate nerve center" test looks to the place where corporate policy is made, the locus of the executive and administrative functions of the corporation.[52]

---

44. With respect to diversity jurisdiction and corporations specifically, see Doub, Time for Re-evaluation: Shall We Curtail Diversity Jurisdiction?, 44 A.B.A.J. 243, 279–84 (1958); Warren, Corporations and Diversity of Citizenship, 19 Va.L.Rev. 661 (1933).

45. 28 U.S.C.A. § 1332(c), as amended by Act of July 25, 1958, § 2, 72 Stat. 415.

46. If a corporation is incorporated in New Jersey and has its principal place of business in New York, for example, it cannot sue or be sued in a federal court under diversity jurisdiction if any adverse party is a citizen of either New Jersey or New York.

47. Riley v. Gulf, Mobile & Ohio R.R. Co., 173 F.Supp. 416 (S.D.Ill.1959).

48. Section 1332(c) provides that the dual citizenship of a corporation is applicable to 28 U.S.C.A. § 1441, governing the removal of actions from state to federal courts. See § 2.11, below.

49. For discussions of the impact of the 1958 amendment, see Friedenthal, New Limitations on Federal Jurisdiction, 11 Stan.L.Rev. 213 (1959); Moore & Weckstein, Corporations and Diversity of Citizenship Jurisdiction: A Supreme Court Fiction Re-visited, 77 Harv.L.Rev. 1426 (1964).

50. Egan v. American Airlines, Inc., 324 F.2d 565 (2d Cir.1963); Campbell v. Associated Press, 223 F.Supp. 151 (E.D.Pa. 1963).

51. See generally 13B C. Wright, A. Miller & E. Cooper, Jurisdiction and Related Matters 2d § 3625; Note, A Corporation's Principal Place of Business for Federal Diversity Jurisdiction, 38 N.Y.U.L.Rev. 148 (1963).

52. Scot Typewriter Co. v. Underwood Corp., 170 F.Supp. 862 (S.D.N.Y.1959) is a leading example of this approach, commonly known as the "nerve center" test. See also J.A. Olson Co. v. City of Winona, 818

The "corporate muscle" test identifies the corporation's principal place of business with the site of its major production or service activities, which generally is equivalent to the location of its major corporate assets.[53] A more recently developed test, and an increasingly popular one, is the "corporate activities" test. This test is a hybrid of the other two and considers all the circumstances surrounding a corporation's business to decide what is its principal place of business.[54] Insofar as there is a pattern among the cases, it seems that the central location of manufacturing or services controls, with the location of the corporate headquarters being determinative only when the corporation's operations are relatively evenly divided among several states.[55]

Another vexing problem arises when a corporation has been incorporated in more than one state: is it, for diversity purposes, a citizen of all the states in which it is incorporated? If not, of which state is it a citizen? Judicial solutions to this problem have been notoriously varied and at times even inconsistent,[56] but since the decision in Chicago & N.W. Railway Company v. Whitton's Administrator,[57] these solutions generally have entailed one application or another of the so-called "forum doctrine." This doctrine dictates that if a corporation is a litigant in a federal court in one of the states of its incorporation, it is to be considered a citizen of only that state in determining the existence of diversity. Thus, the corporation can sue or be sued in the federal courts of a state of its incorporation as long as no adverse party is a citizen of that state; it is irrelevant that an opposing party in fact may be a citizen of another state in which the corporation is incorporated.[58] The forum doctrine is inconsistent with the complete diversity requirement of Strawbridge v. Curtiss[59] and numerous qualifications of it[60] reflect general dissatisfaction with that resolution of the question.

F.2d 401 (5th Cir.1987) ("total activity" test).

53. Kelly v. U.S. Steel Corp., 284 F.2d 850 (3d Cir.1960).

54. White v. Halstead Indus., Inc., 750 F.Supp. 395 (E.D.Ark.1990). See 13B C. Wright, A. Miller & E. Cooper, Jurisdiction and Related Matters 2d § 3625.

55. See United Nuclear Corp. v. Moki Oil & Rare Metals Co., 364 F.2d 568 (10th Cir.1966), cert. denied 385 U.S. 960; Fellers v. Atchison, Topeka & Santa Fe Ry. Co., 330 F.Supp. 1334 (D.Kan.1971); Lurie Co. v. Loew's San Francisco Hotel Corp., 315 F.Supp. 405 (N.D.Cal.1970); Mahoney v. Northwestern Bell Tel. Co., 258 F.Supp. 500 (D.Neb.1966), affirmed per curiam 377 F.2d 549 (8th Cir.1967).

56. See 13B C. Wright, A. Miller & E. Cooper, Jurisdiction and Related Matters 2d § 3626; Friedenthal, New Limits on Federal Jurisdiction, 11 Stan.L.Rev. 213, 225–41 (1959); Weckstein, Multi-state Corporations and Diversity of Citizenship: A Field Day for Fictions, 31 Tenn.L.Rev. 195

(1964); Comment, Corporate Diversity of Citizenship Under 28 U.S.C. § 1332(c), 26 Baylor L.Rev. 211 (1974); Note, Citizenship of Multi–State Corporations for Diversity Jurisdiction Purposes, 48 Iowa L.Rev. 410 (1963).

57. 80 U.S. (13 Wall.) 270, 20 L.Ed. 571 (1871).

58. Jacobson v. New York, New Haven & Hartford R.R. Co., 347 U.S. 909, 74 S.Ct. 474, 98 L.Ed. 1067 (1954) (per curiam); Lake Shore & M.S. Ry. Co. v. Eder, 174 Fed. 944 (6th Cir.1909); Hudak v. Port Authority Trans–Hudson Corp., 238 F.Supp. 790 (S.D.N.Y.1965). But compare Lang v. Colonial Pipeline Co., 266 F.Supp. 552 (E.D.Pa.1967), affirmed per curiam 383 F.2d 986 (3d Cir.1967); Dodrill v. New York Cent. R.R. Co., 253 F.Supp. 564 (S.D.Ohio 1966); Evans–Hailey Co. v. Crane Co., 207 F.Supp. 193 (M.D.Tenn.1962), appeal dismissed 382 U.S. 801.

59. 7 U.S. (3 Cranch) 267, 2 L.Ed. 435 (1806). See note 2, above.

60. See, e.g., Patch v. Wabash R.R. Co., 207 U.S. 277, 28 S.Ct. 80, 52 L.Ed. 204

Another question involves the status of alien corporations. Traditionally, an alien corporation has been considered a citizen solely of the foreign nation in which it was incorporated.[61] Most federal courts have held that Section 1332(c) has no effect on that rule, just as the 1958 enactment generally has been held to leave the "forum doctrine" undisturbed. Thus, the "principal place of business" standard for citizenship does not apply to foreign corporations; for diversity purposes, only the country of a foreign corporation's incorporation is relevant.[62]

A 1964 amendment to the diversity statute[63] further restricts diversity jurisdiction in the context of "direct actions" against liability insurers.[64] The amendment provides that if the insured is not joined as a party defendant, the insurer-defendant "shall be deemed a citizen of the state of which the insured is a citizen, as well as of any state by which the insurer has been incorporated and of the state where it has its principal place of business." This provision was added in response to a particularly glaring abuse of diversity jurisdiction. A Louisiana statute allows tort plaintiffs to seek relief directly from the tortfeasor's insurer. Since corporate insurers frequently were not incorporated in Louisiana and did not have their principal place of business there, Louisiana tort plaintiffs were able to sue insurers in federal court on the basis of diversity. This allowed them to circumvent a Louisiana procedure giving its state appellate courts a much broader scope of review of jury verdicts than was available in the federal court system. The result was blatant forum-shopping with virtually all Louisiana personal injury actions being tried in federal courts. As amended, Section 1332(c) makes insurance companies citizens of at least three different states, at least when a direct action is brought by an injured party without joining the tortfeasor.[65] The court now must consider the residence of the particular insured, as well as the insurer's state of incorporation and its principal place of business.

The last context in which the determination of citizenship has caused some problems is cases in which unincorporated associations are parties. Unlike the treatment of corporations, there has been a rather steadfast refusal to utilize any presumption regarding the citizenship of

(1907) (corporation incorporated in several states was deemed to be a citizen of that state of incorporation in which the cause of action arose); Louisville, N. A. & C. Ry. Co. v. Louisville Trust Co., 174 U.S. 552, 19 S.Ct. 817, 43 L.Ed. 1081 (1899) (corporation incorporated in several states was deemed to be a citizen of the original state of its incorporation). See also the catalogue of variations on the forum doctrine in Gavin v. Hudson & Manhattan R.R. Co., 185 F.2d 104 (3d Cir.1950) and in the articles cited in note 56, above.

61. National S.S. Co. v. Tugman, 106 U.S. 118, 1 S.Ct. 58, 27 L.Ed. 87 (1882).

62. Eisenberg v. Commercial Union Assurance Co., 189 F.Supp. 500 (S.D.N.Y. 1960).

63. 28 U.S.C.A. § 1332(c), as amended by Act of August 14, 1964, Pub.L. 88–439, 78 Stat. 445.

64. A direct action is limited to cases in which an injured party brings a tort action directly against the insurer, sometimes joining the insured tortfeasor and sometimes omitting the alleged tortfeasor.

65. Some questions have arisen concerning the meaning and scope of the terms "direct action" and "liability insurer." See 13B C. Wright, A. Miller & E. Cooper, Jurisdiction and Related Matters 2d § 3629.

the members of unincorporated associations. The first explicit refusal to do so was in Chapman v. Barney,[66] in which the Supreme Court held that a joint stock company could not sue in a federal court as a citizen of New York when the record failed to disclose the citizenship of all of its members. This principle has been applied to labor unions,[67] partnerships,[68] and religious or charitable organizations.[69] In all these cases, if one member of the association is a citizen of the same state as an adverse party, the rule of complete diversity[70] dictates the failure of jurisdiction.

For a time, the Supreme Court seemed inclined to modify this approach, and adopt a more flexible standard involving ad hoc consideration of the essential characteristics of a particular unincorporated association and whether it possessed a discrete legal personality sufficient to treat it in the same fashion as a corporation for diversity purposes.[71] But in United Steelworkers of America AFL–CIO v. R. H. Bouligny, Inc.,[72] the Court re-affirmed the traditional sharp distinction between corporations and unincorporated associations for diversity purposes. In Bouligny, a labor union was sued for defamation in connection with an organizing drive in a small North Carolina town. The case for abolishing the distinction was particularly strong: not only was there the argument that labor unions and other associations often are "indistinguishable from corporations in terms of the reality of function and structure,"[73] but there also existed the distinct possibility that the union would encounter prejudice in the state court—the traditional rationale for federal diversity jurisdiction. Nevertheless, the Supreme Court held that any changes in the rule and expansions of diversity jurisdiction were matters for Congress.[74]

A few years ago the Supreme Court once again reaffirmed this position. In Carden v. Arkoma Associates,[75] a sharply divided Court held that limited partnerships are not juridical citizens as are corporations. Instead, the citizenship of all partners, limited as well as general, must be considered for diversity purposes. The Court's majority again deferred

---

66. 129 U.S. 677, 682, 9 S.Ct. 426, 428, 32 L.Ed. 800 (1889).

67. United Steelworkers of America, AFL–CIO v. R. H. Bouligny, Inc., 382 U.S. 145, 86 S.Ct. 272, 15 L.Ed.2d 217 (1965).

68. Great Southern Fire Proof Hotel Co. v. Jones, 177 U.S. 449, 20 S.Ct. 690, 44 L.Ed. 842 (1900).

69. Lawson v. United House of Prayer, 252 F.Supp. 52 (E.D.Pa.1966).

70. See note 2, above.

71. People of Puerto Rico v. Russell & Co., 288 U.S. 476, 53 S.Ct. 447, 77 L.Ed. 903 (1933). See also Mason v. American Express Co., 334 F.2d 392 (2d Cir.1964).

72. 382 U.S. 145, 86 S.Ct. 272, 15 L.Ed.2d 217 (1965).

73. 382 U.S. at 149, 86 S.Ct. at 274.

74. Although the effect of Bouligny is to limit the number of cases involving unincorporated associations that can be brought in the federal courts, most disputes involving labor unions raise federal questions, so that the inability to establish diversity jurisdiction usually is not significant. This restriction also has been circumvented by using representative actions authorized by Federal Rule 23.2, since in those suits only the citizenship of the named representative is considered for diversity purposes. Tunstall v. Brotherhood of Locomotive Firemen & Enginemen, 148 F.2d 403 (4th Cir.1945). See generally 7C C. Wright, A. Miller & M. Kane, Civil 2d § 1861, for a discussion of actions using Rule 23.2.

75. 494 U.S. 185, 110 S.Ct. 1015, 108 L.Ed.2d 157 (1990).

to Congress's ability to determine the citizenship status of unincorporated associations. The Carden decision well may indicate that the Court will treat all other business forms as unincorporated associations rather than corporations.

§ 2.7 Diversity of Citizenship Jurisdiction—Devices to Create and Destroy Diversity

There are many valid and proper tactical reasons for a litigant to prefer a federal forum over a state tribunal, or vice-versa. Attorneys may act on these preferences if concurrent jurisdiction exists in the state and federal courts in the particular case. However, when a litigant attempts to pursue a preference in circumstances in which there is no legitimate forum choice or seeks to prevent the opposing side from exercising its right of removal, problems of manipulation and abuse arise. In attempting to create or destroy diversity artificially, a litigant crosses the line between permissible tactical maneuvers and what has been characterized as a "fraud upon the law."[1] The manufacture of diversity is a serious affront to the fundamental principle that the federal courts have limited jurisdiction.[2] The artificial destruction of diversity is a deprivation of an opposing litigant's right of access to the federal courts.

Some of the devices used to create diversity are simple and obvious, and the responses to them by the federal judiciary accordingly have been straightforward. For example, probably the crudest way to manufacture diversity is simply to bring an action in the name of a diverse party. However, the federal courts long have followed the rule that an action must be brought by the real party in interest[3] and that the citizenship of that party is determinative in deciding whether diversity jurisdiction exists.[4] There is no jurisdiction if the party of record is merely formal or nominal and the real party in interest is a citizen of the same state as his adversary. A similar method of manufacturing diversity is for the plaintiff to align the parties in the pleadings contrary to their real interests, making it appear that diversity exists. As already indicated, however, a federal court is not bound by the plaintiff's formal alignment of the parties in the pleadings; if necessary, it will realign the parties so that those with the same ultimate interests in the outcome are on the same side.[5] Finally, a plaintiff cannot circumvent the statutory requirements simply by failing to join a nondiverse party if that person is "indispensable" to the litigation.[6] Other methods of manufacturing or defeating

§ 2.7

1. Morris v. Gilmer, 129 U.S. 315, 9 S.Ct. 289, 32 L.Ed. 690 (1889).

2. See § 2.2, above.

3. This requirement is embodied in Fed.Civ.Proc.Rule 17(a). For a discussion of Rule 17(a), see § 6.3, below, and 6A C. Wright, A. Miller & M. Kane, Civil 2d §§ 1541–58.

4. See 6A C. Wright, A. Miller & M. Kane, Civil 2d § 1556.

5. See § 2.6 at nn. 7–11, above.

6. This is mandated by Fed.Civ.Proc. Rule 19. For a discussion of Rule 19 and the concept of indispensable parties, see § 6.5, below.

diversity have presented greater problems for the courts and a more detailed discussion of their treatment follows.

The major restraint on the use of devices to create diversity is the anti-collusion statute, found in Section 1359 of Title 28.[7] It provides that a "district court shall not have jurisdiction of a civil action in which any party, by assignment or otherwise, has been improperly or collusively made or joined to invoke the jurisdiction of such court ." Although the courts originally were far from vigorous in their application of Section 1359 to combat the collusive creation of diversity,[8] in more modern times, there has been a trend toward more effective use of the statute to limit diversity jurisdiction to disputes to which it properly should attach.[9] This has involved decisions about which assignments, appointments of representatives, or changes in domicile should be strictly scrutinized to determine whether they fall within the scope of the anti-collusion statute.

The criteria for determining whether an assignment is collusive are relatively straightforward.[10] If the assignee is only a nominal party, with the assignor retaining an actual, substantial interest in the suit, a court likely will find that the assignment is collusive.[11] Another factor to be considered is whether the assignee possesses an independent interest or right of action that existed prior to the assignment; if so, a court probably will take jurisdiction over the assigned claim.[12] Also relevant, although not decisive, is whether the assignor solicited the assignee to bring suit, contributed to the expenses of the litigation, or controlled its conduct.[13] As indicated by the Supreme Court, a purported assignment probably will be held collusive, and therefore invalid for diversity purposes, when the assignee merely functions as a collection agent for the assignor.[14]

Another common device for manufacturing diversity has been the appointment of an out-of-state representative for the sole purpose of bringing a federal action on behalf of a resident of the same state as the

---

7. The first congressional attempt to check diversity abuses was directed solely at collusive assignments of choses in action. Act of Sept. 24, 1789, c. 20, § 11, 1 Stat. 73, 79. An 1875 statute allowed the courts to dismiss actions in which parties had been "improperly or collusively made or joined." Act of March 3, 1875, c. 137, § 5, 18 Stat. 470, 472, codified as 28 U.S.C.A. § 80. The two statutes were merged in 1948 into the present anti-collusion statute.

8. See, e.g., Corabi v. Auto Racing, Inc., 264 F.2d 784 (3d Cir.1959).

9. See, e.g., Bishop v. Hendricks, 495 F.2d 289 (4th Cir.1974), cert. denied 419 U.S. 1056; Rogers v. Bates, 431 F.2d 16 (8th Cir.1970). See also Comment, Manufactured Federal Diversity Jurisdiction and Section 1359, 69 Colum.L.Rev. 706 (1969).

10. See 14 C. Wright, A. Miller & E. Cooper, Jurisdiction and Related Matters

3d § 3639; Comment, Assignments and Transfers Affecting Federal Diversity Jurisdiction, 47 Wash.L.Rev. 681 (1972).

11. Little v. Giles, 118 U.S. 596, 7 S.Ct. 32, 30 L.Ed. 269 (1886); Farmington Village Corp. v. Pillsbury, 114 U.S. 138, 5 S.Ct. 807, 29 L.Ed. 114 (1885).

12. Wheeler v. City & County of Denver, 229 U.S. 342, 33 S.Ct. 842, 57 L.Ed. 1219 (1913).

13. Cashman v. Amador & Sacramento Canal Co., 118 U.S. 58, 6 S.Ct. 926, 30 L.Ed. 72 (1886). Cf. Wheeler v. City & County of Denver, 229 U.S. 342, 33 S.Ct. 842, 57 L.Ed. 1219 (1913).

14. Kramer v. Caribbean Mills, Inc., 394 U.S. 823, 89 S.Ct. 1487, 23 L.Ed.2d 9 (1969).

defendant.[15] The traditional doctrine was that the citizenship of the representative controlled for diversity purposes[16] and that the objective or motive underlying the appointment of a representative was irrelevant.[17] Although there are cogent reasons for avoiding a potentially difficult and time-consuming investigation into the motives underlying an appointment, the practice of accepting appointments at face value invited continued abuse.

Initially, courts were reluctant to use Section 1359 to combat this practice, in large measure because of a Third Circuit decision[18] that gave the term "collusive" in the statute a narrow dictionary meaning, disregarding the broad statutory goal of preventing unwarranted invocations of federal jurisdiction. But in McSparran v. Weist,[19] the Third Circuit overruled its earlier decision, and held that the appointment of a nonresident guardian of a minor for the express purpose of creating diversity was grounds for refusing federal jurisdiction under Section 1359. The McSparran court distinguished between the appointment of a genuine fiduciary, who undertook the litigation as a part of her larger duties under the law, and the appointment of a "straw fiduciary" solely for diversity purposes.

The McSparran approach was followed by a number of federal courts.[20] Judges using that approach employed factors such as the reason for the appointment, the nature of the suit, the identity of the representative and his relationship to the party represented, the scope of the representative's powers, and the existence of a nondiverse person who might be considered the more "natural" representative of the interests involved.[21] Moreover, as described in the preceding section, problems

---

15. See 14 C. Wright, A. Miller & E. Cooper, Jurisdiction and Related Matters 3d § 3640; Comment, Appointment of Nonresident Administrator to Create Diversity Jurisdiction, 73 Yale L.J. 873 (1964).

16. Guardians ad litem, whose citizenship is not considered in deciding whether diversity exists, are an exception to this rule.

17. Lang v. Elm City Constr. Co., 324 F.2d 235 (2d Cir.1963); Janzen v. Goos, 302 F.2d 421 (8th Cir.1962); Corabi v. Auto Racing, Inc., 264 F.2d 784 (3d Cir.1959).

18. Corabi v. Auto Racing, Inc., 264 F.2d 784 (3d Cir.1959). But see Caribbean Mills, Inc. v. Kramer, 392 F.2d 387 (5th Cir.1968), affirmed 394 U.S. 823, 89 S.Ct. 1487, 23 L.Ed.2d 9 (1969).

19. 402 F.2d 867 (3d Cir.1968), cert. denied 395 U.S. 903, noted in 69 Colum.L.Rev. 706 (1969), 44 N.Y.U.L.Rev. 212 (1969), 44 Notre Dame Law. 643 (1969), 47 Texas L.Rev. 1233 (1969).

20. Bishop v. Hendricks, 495 F.2d 289 (4th Cir.1974), cert. denied 419 U.S. 1056; Kenebrew v. Columbia Land & Timber Co.,

454 F.2d 1146 (5th Cir.1972); Groh v. Brooks, 421 F.2d 589 (3d Cir.1970); O'Brien v. AVCO Corporation, 425 F.2d 1030 (2d Cir.1969). See also Ferrara v. Philadelphia Labs., Inc., 272 F.Supp. 1000 (D.Vt.1967), affirmed per curiam 393 F.2d 934 (2d Cir. 1968), an excellent district court opinion that foreshadowed the reasoning of McSparran. Compare Miller v. Perry, 456 F.2d 63 (4th Cir.1972) (state law requiring the appointment of a resident as wrongful death representative for an out-of-state decedent did not bar the decedent's estate from bringing a diversity action against the tortfeasor).

21. Groh v. Brooks, 421 F.2d 589 (3d Cir.1970). This type of factor analysis is costly in terms of judicial time. Compare the proposal of the American Law Institute, Study of the Division of Jurisdiction Between State and Federal Courts § 1301(b)(4) and at 117–19 (1969), that in all cases the citizenship of the represented party should be imputed to the representative. See also Judge Haynsworth's support of the Institute's recommendation in Lester v. McFaddon, 415 F.2d 1101 (4th Cir.1969),

caused by the manufacturing of diversity jurisdiction through the appointment of the representative of an infant, as well as certain other representatives, ultimately were resolved by Congress in an amendment to the diversity statute requiring that diversity be tested by looking to the citizenship of the represented party rather than that of the representative.

Probably the most direct way to manufacture diversity jurisdiction is simply for a prospective litigant, before filing suit, to move to a state other than the one of the potential defendant's citizenship. For such a shift in residence to be effective as a change in domicile and, accordingly, a change in citizenship, a party must have the intention to remain in the new state of residence indefinitely.[22] When a natural person makes a bona fide change in domicile, courts generally do not question the motives behind the change even if they include the desire to establish diversity.[23] If the evidence does not support a finding that a party who has moved intends to remain indefinitely in the new state of residence, however, then the change of citizenship is ineffective and the suit may be dismissed for lack of jurisdiction.[24]

The corporate analogy to the feigned change of citizenship by a natural person is dissolution in one state and reincorporation in another.[25] Since dissolution and reincorporation may involve little more than some shuffling of papers, it once was particularly easy for corporations to manufacture diversity in this fashion. The 1958 enactment of Section 1332(c) of Title 28 has helped to curtail this practice, however, by making a corporation a citizen of its principal place of business as well as its state of incorporation.[26]

Much of what has been said concerning devices to create diversity applies as well to attempts to destroy diversity in order to force suit in a state forum. However, there are two important distinctions between the creation and destruction of diversity. First, the anti-collusion statute applies only to the creation of diversity when none legitimately exists.[27] There is no statutory prohibition of devices to destroy diversity. Second, the policy against extending diversity jurisdiction, stemming both from theoretical concerns of federalism, and the practical concern for lessening the caseload of the federal courts, does not apply to situations in

which contains an excellent and provocative discussion of the purposes and proper application of § 1359.

22. See § 2.6, above.

23. Williamson v. Osenton, 232 U.S. 619, 34 S.Ct. 442, 58 L.Ed. 758 (1914); Janzen v. Goos, 302 F.2d 421 (8th Cir. 1962).

24. Compare Janzen v. Goos, 302 F.2d 421 (8th Cir.1962) (jurisdiction sustained), with Korn v. Korn, 398 F.2d 689 (3d Cir. 1968) (jurisdiction lacking).

25. Black & White Taxicab & Transfer Co. v. Brown & Yellow Taxicab & Transfer Co., 276 U.S. 518, 48 S.Ct. 404, 72 L.Ed.

681 (1928). The authority of this case, which permitted a Kentucky corporation to reincorporate in Tennessee for the express purpose of bringing a diversity action against a Kentucky competitor, has been eroded considerably. See Greater Dev. Co. of Connecticut, Inc. v. Amelung, 471 F.2d 338 (1st Cir.1973).

26. See § 2.6, above.

27. Some courts have used Rule 11 to sanction the collusive creation of diversity jurisdiction. See, e.g., Wojan v. General Motors Corp., 851 F.2d 969 (7th Cir.1988).

which diversity jurisdiction is defeated. On the other hand, if the traditional rationale for diversity jurisdiction—the avoidance of local prejudice, both actual and imagined—remains at all sound, federal courts should protect their legitimate jurisdiction and a litigant's right to invoke it.[28]

One possible mode of destroying diversity is to join as a defendant a party of the same citizenship as the plaintiff. In response, the federal courts have been willing, upon a showing that a joined, nondiverse defendant has no real connection with the litigation, to pierce the guise of nondiversity and permit the exercise of diversity jurisdiction by way of removal.[29]

Appointment of a nondiverse representative, other than an executor of an estate or a representative of an infant or an incompetent, or the assignment of a claim to a nondiverse party also can be used to defeat diversity. In the past, the federal courts have not been very vigilant in dealing with this type of machination. The leading case of Mecom v. Fitzsimmons Drilling Company[30] long has stood for the proposition that courts will not investigate the motives behind the appointment of representatives, even if admittedly for the sole purpose of destroying diversity. However, this doctrine, based on deference to the authority of state courts in making or ratifying appointments, shows signs of breaking down even in cases in which collusive manipulation of diversity is not an issue.[31] It therefore may be expected that as time passes, more courts will be willing to follow the American Law Institute's recommendation that assignments and appointments made to prevent access to the federal courts be treated the same as are collusive attempts to create federal jurisdiction.[32]

§ 2.8   Amount-in-Controversy Requirements

Satisfaction of a minimum amount in controversy has been one of the prerequisites for federal subject-matter jurisdiction from the earliest days of the national judiciary. Although there is no constitutionally mandated monetary threshold for entry into the federal courts, Congress consistently has chosen to make jurisdiction, in at least some classes of cases, contingent upon a minimum amount in controversy. The Judiciary

---

28. Attempts to destroy diversity arise when a prospective plaintiff prefers to litigate in a particular state court, but none of the potential defendants is a citizen of that state. In that event, a nonresident defendant may remove the action to federal court thereby avoiding the plaintiff's forum choice. See § 2.11, below, on removal jurisdiction. The plaintiff can prevent removal only by utilizing some method to destroy diversity.

29. Wilson v. Republic Iron & Steel Co., 257 U.S. 92, 42 S.Ct. 35, 66 L.Ed. 144 (1921); Wecker v. National Enameling &

Stamping Co., 204 U.S. 176, 186, 27 S.Ct. 184, 188, 51 L.Ed. 430 (1907); Williams v. Atlantic Coast Line R.R. Co., 294 F.Supp. 815 (S.D.Ga.1968). See B., Inc. v. Miller Brewing Co., 663 F.2d 545 (5th Cir.1981).

30. 284 U.S. 183, 52 S.Ct. 84, 76 L.Ed. 233 (1931).

31. See Miller v. Perry, 456 F.2d 63 (4th Cir.1972).

32. American Law Institute, Study of the Division of Jurisdiction Between State and Federal Courts, Official Draft, § 1307(b) and at 160–61 (1969).

Act of 1789 imposed a $500 amount-in-controversy requirement,[1] and successive jurisdiction statutes revised the figure upward in response to inflation and increasing court congestion.[2] In 1958 it was raised to more than $10,000.[3] In 1988, Congress raised the jurisdictional amount to more than $50,000.[4] This change was in response to the tension between those who wished to eliminate diversity jurisdiction entirely and those who favored its retention. Most recently, in 1996, the amount-in-controversy requirement was increased again to its present level of more than $75,000.[5]

The amount-in-controversy requirement applied to both general federal question jurisdiction[6] and diversity jurisdiction[7] until 1980 when it was eliminated for almost all federal question cases.[8] Thus, other than diversity of citizenship cases, only a few specialized types of federal question actions, such as statutory interpleader[9] are governed by specific statutory jurisdictional amount requirements.[10]

Under the diversity statute, jurisdiction can be invoked only if "the matter in controversy exceeds the sum or value of $75,000, exclusive of interest and costs." The words are interpreted literally; if the matter in controversy is precisely $75,000 in value, or less, there is no jurisdiction.[11] Nor can "costs" or "interest" comprise part of the requisite amount.[12] However, attorney's fees, if they are provided for either by statute or by a contract upon which the suit is being brought, can make up part of the jurisdictional amount.[13] Interest that is a part of the principal claim itself at the time it arose (such as interest on a promissory note prior to maturity) also is outside the exclusion; but interest that accrues solely because of a delay in payment or that otherwise is

---

§ 2.8

1. Act of Sept. 24, 1789, § 11, 1 Stat. 73, 78.

2. In 1887 the amount was raised to $2,000. Act of March 3, 1887, 24 Stat. 552. It was increased to $3,000 in 1911. Act of March 3, 1911, 36 Stat. 1091.

3. Act of July 25, 1958, 72 Stat. 415.

4. Act of Nov. 19, 1988, § 201, 102 Stat. 4642, 28 U.S.C.A. § 1332(a).

5. Federal Courts Improvement Act of 1996, Act of Oct. 19, 1996, Pub.L. 104–317, § 205, 110 Stat. 3847, 3850.

6. See § 2.3, above.

7. See § 2.5, above.

8. In 1976, Congress limited the amount-in-controversy requirement in federal question cases under Section 1331 to actions not against federal officers or agencies. Act of Oct. 21, 1976, Pub.L. 94–574, 90 Stat. 2721. In 1980, the requirement was eliminated altogether. Act of Dec. 1, 1980, Pub.L. 96–486, 94 Stat. 2369.

9. 28 U.S.C.A. § 1335. Statutory interpleader requires a $500 jurisdictional amount. See § 16.12, below, for a discussion of interpleader jurisdiction.

10. For example, claims against the United States that do not arise under the internal revenue laws or out of a tort can be heard in the district courts only if the amount in controversy does not exceed $10,000; any claims greater than this amount must go to the Court of Federal Claims. 28 U.S.C.A. § 1346. Also, actions against carriers in state courts for delay, loss, or injury to goods may be removed to federal court only if the amount in controversy exceeds $10,000. 28 U.S.C.A. § 1445(b).

11. See, e.g., LeBlanc v. Spector, 378 F.Supp. 301, 307 (D.Conn.1973).

12. See 14B C. Wright, A. Miller & E. Cooper, Jurisdiction and Related Matters 3d § 3712; Note, The "Interest" and "Costs" Excluded in Determining Federal Jurisdiction, 45 Iowa L.Rev. 832 (1960).

13. Missouri State Life Ins. Co. v. Jones, 290 U.S. 199, 54 S.Ct. 133, 78 L.Ed. 267 (1933); Springstead v. Crawfordsville State Bank, 231 U.S. 541, 34 S.Ct. 195, 58 L.Ed. 354 (1913).

incidental to the principal claim cannot be used to satisfy the jurisdictional amount.[14]

The purpose of the successive enactments of a jurisdictional amount requirement has been to set a figure "not so high as to convert the Federal courts into courts of big business nor so low as to fritter away their time in the trial of petty controversies."[15] Although the goal of limiting the jurisdiction of the federal courts is sound in both theoretical and practical terms, commentators have questioned whether an arbitrary monetary requirement is the proper means to this end.[16]

Despite these considerations, Congress has retained the general jurisdictional amount requirement for diversity cases and it has enacted sanction provisions to discourage the bringing of claims that do not meet the jurisdictional minimum. Since 1958, the diversity statute has provided that a successful plaintiff who recovers less than the jurisdictional amount, computed without regard to any set-off or counterclaim awarded to the defendant, and exclusive of interest and costs, may be penalized either by refusing to award costs to or by imposing costs upon the plaintiff.[17] The impact of this legislation has been negligible, however, since the courts generally have refused to exercise the discretion given them as long as the plaintiff can show a shred of good faith in bringing the action.[18]

The judicial attitude toward the question whether the amount in controversy exceeds the jurisdictional minimum in a particular case involves two competing considerations.[19] On the one hand, mounting federal court case loads and the notion that federal jurisdiction cannot be extended beyond the limits of the congressional grant argue for strict enforcement of the requirement. On the other hand, a detailed inquiry into the preliminary jurisdictional question regarding recoverable damages could well become a trial of the merits of the case, thereby wasting judicial time and enlarging the costs of litigation.[20] A related consider-

---

14. Brown v. Webster, 156 U.S. 328, 15 S.Ct. 377, 39 L.Ed. 440 (1895); Regan v. Marshall, 309 F.2d 677 (1st Cir.1962).

15. Sen.Rep. No. 1830, 85 Cong., 2d Sess. 4 (1958), reprinted in 1958 U.S.Code Cong. & Admin.News 3099, 3101.

16. American Law Institute, Study of the Division of Jurisdiction Between State and Federal Courts, Official Draft, § 1311, at 172–76 (1969); Friedenthal, New Limitations on Federal Jurisdiction, 11 Stan. L.Rev. 213, 216–18 (1959); Wechsler, Federal Jurisdiction and the Revision of the Judicial Code, 13 Law & Contemp.Prob. 216, 225–26 (1948).

17. 28 U.S.C.A. § 1332(b). See, e.g., McCord v. Moore–McCormack Lines, Inc., 242 F.Supp. 493 (S.D.N.Y.1965). See also Zimmer v. Wells Management Corp., 366 F.Supp. 215 (S.D.N.Y.1973).

18. Sturmon v. Jetco, Inc., 510 F.Supp. 578 (E.D.Mo.1981), modified on other grounds 670 F.2d 101 (8th Cir.1982); Lutz v. McNair, 233 F.Supp. 871 (E.D.Va.1964), affirmed per curiam 340 F.2d 709 (4th Cir. 1965); Bochenek v. Germann, 191 F.Supp. 104 (E.D.Mich.1960). An additional factor detracting from the significance of this sanction is that costs in America, unlike in Britain, do not include attorney's fees, and thus are a rather minor part of the total expense of litigation.

19. See Note, Federal Jurisdictional Amount: Determination of the Matter in Controversy, 73 Harv.L.Rev. 1369 (1960). For more detailed discussion, see 14B C. Wright, A. Miller & E. Cooper, Jurisdiction and Related Matters 3d § 3702.

20. Deutsch v. Hewes St. Realty Corp., 359 F.2d 96 (2d Cir.1966). But cf. Nelson v. Keefer, 451 F.2d 289 (3d Cir.1971).

ation evolves from the principle that the existence of federal subject-matter jurisdiction is to be determined at the outset of the litigation. This early determination also argues against a protracted examination of whether the jurisdictional minimum has been satisfied and for a simple test of the jurisdictional amount.

The Supreme Court weighed these factors in the leading case of St. Paul Mercury Indemnity Corporation v. Red Cab Company[21] and enunciated the now well established test for amount in controversy. "[T]he sum claimed by the plaintiff controls if the claim is apparently made in good faith. It must appear to a legal certainty that the claim is really for less than the jurisdictional amount to justify dismissal."[22] Further, the Court held that "the inability of plaintiff to recover an amount adequate to give the court jurisdiction does not show his bad faith or oust the jurisdiction,"[23] and that "events occurring subsequent to the institution of suit which reduce the amount recoverable below the statutory limit do not oust jurisdiction."[24]

The "legal certainty" standard laid down in St. Paul Mercury effectively precludes dismissal unless it is patent on the face of the complaint that the plaintiff cannot possibly recover the sum demanded. Thus, it is only in a few rather well-defined situations that the jurisdictional minimum will not be found. For example, when the statute establishing the cause of action authorizes a maximum recovery of $75,000 or less, or the plaintiff claims $6,000 actual damages and $70,000 punitive damages, but the applicable substantive law, as described in court decisions too recent to be challenged, rules out the possibility of punitive damages in the particular type of action, there is a legal certainty that the plaintiff cannot recover the jurisdictional amount and the case will be dismissed.[25] On occasion, independent facts show that the claimed amount of damages was inflated merely to obtain federal jurisdiction, in which case the action also will be dismissed.[26] In general, however, the "legal certainty" standard is an exceedingly permissive test, presenting virtually no obstacle at all for the plaintiff in many types of cases, especially tort claims involving unliquidated damages.[27]

---

21. 303 U.S. 283, 58 S.Ct. 586, 82 L.Ed. 845 (1938).

22. 303 U.S. at 288–89, 58 S.Ct. at 590 (Roberts, J.). For an analysis of this "good faith"-"legal certainty" standard in the most troublesome area of its application, see Note, Determination of Federal Jurisdictional Amount in Suits on Unliquidated Claims, 64 Mich.L.Rev. 930 (1966).

23. 303 U.S. at 289, 58 S.Ct. at 590.

24. 303 U.S. at 289–90, 58 S.Ct. at 590–91.

25. See Ringsby Truck Lines, Inc. v. Beardsley, 331 F.2d 14 (8th Cir.1964).

26. See, e.g., Arnold v. Troccoli, 344 F.2d 842 (2d Cir.1965); Brown v. Bodak, 188 F.Supp. 532 (S.D.N.Y.1960).

27. See, e.g., Santiesteban v. Goodyear Tire & Rubber Co., 306 F.2d 9 (5th Cir. 1962) (jurisdiction upheld when plaintiff claimed damages in excess of $10,000 for humiliation and wounded feelings, resulting in two sleepless nights and the need for medication, caused by defendant's public repossession of the tires of plaintiff's car). But compare Turner v. Wilson Line of Massachusetts, Inc., 142 F.Supp. 264 (D.Mass. 1956), affirmed 242 F.2d 414 (1st Cir.1957) (pain for seven or eight hours was not severe enough to cause the sufferer to stop

The plaintiff has the burden of pleading an amount in controversy greater than the statutory minimum,[28] but she may discharge the burden by a simple formal allegation to that effect.[29] Legal certainty is equated with the plaintiff's good faith allegations of injury.[30] Only when the defendant, or the court on its own motion, challenges the amount in controversy is the plaintiff obligated to go beyond the formal allegation and adduce facts to support the invocation of federal jurisdiction.[31] Further, the fact that the plaintiff ultimately recovers less than the jurisdictional amount does not affect the validity of the judgment, once jurisdiction has been found to exist.[32]

Some problems do arise in determining the amount involved when the plaintiff seeks equitable relief. The general rule governing suits for injunctions is that jurisdiction is to be tested by the value of the right sought to be protected against the defendant's interference.[33] Illustratively, in a suit to enjoin infringement of a trade name in the state of Louisiana, the amount in controversy was held to be the value to the plaintiff of its claimed right to prevent the use of the name in that state.[34] Although this rule is easy to state, it often is difficult to apply.

In many injunction suits, the plaintiff is seeking to protect a right that is inherently incapable of being evaluated in monetary terms. In an early case,[35] the Supreme Court held that it had no jurisdiction over a custody dispute between estranged parents, on the ground that the matter in controversy was "evidently utterly incapable of being reduced to any pecuniary standard of value,"[36] and hence could not be said to exceed the jurisdictional minimum. Even though it may seem both incongruous and logically unnecessary that rights so precious as to defy reduction to a monetary equivalent should, for that reason alone, be considered as having a value less than the statutory monetary threshold, this approach generally has been followed by the federal courts.[37]

work or realize that anything serious was the matter with him, and could not warrant an award of $3,000, the requisite jurisdictional amount at that time).

28. McNutt v. General Motors Acceptance Corp., 298 U.S. 178, 56 S.Ct. 780, 80 L.Ed. 1135 (1936); Hedberg v. State Farm Mut. Automobile Ins. Co., 350 F.2d 924 (8th Cir.1965). A plaintiff who fails to meet this pleading requirement may avoid dismissal by proper amendment. 28 U.S.C.A. § 1653.

29. KVOS, Inc. v. Associated Press, 299 U.S. 269, 57 S.Ct. 197, 81 L.Ed. 183 (1936); Molokai Homesteaders Cooperative Ass'n v. Morton, 506 F.2d 572 (9th Cir. 1974); Hupp v. Port Brownsville Shipyard, Inc., 515 F.Supp. 546 (S.D.Tex.1981).

30. Jones v. Landry, 387 F.2d 102 (5th Cir.1967). See also Fehling v. Cantonwine, 522 F.2d 604 (10th Cir.1975).

31. Gibbs v. Buck, 307 U.S. 66, 59 S.Ct. 725, 83 L.Ed. 1111 (1939); Opelika

Nursing Home, Inc. v. Richardson, 448 F.2d 658 (5th Cir.1971).

32. See, e.g., Buffington v. Amchem Prods., Inc., 489 F.2d 1053 (8th Cir.1974). The plaintiff may be sanctioned by the denial or imposition of costs, however. See the text at notes 17–18, above.

33. McNutt v. General Motors Acceptance Corp., 298 U.S. 178, 56 S.Ct. 780, 80 L.Ed. 1135 (1936); Kimball v. Callahan, 493 F.2d 564 (9th Cir.1974), cert. denied 419 U.S. 1019.

34. Seaboard Finance Co. v. Martin, 244 F.2d 329 (5th Cir.1957).

35. Barry v. Mercein, 46 U.S. (5 How.) 103, 12 L.Ed. 70 (1847).

36. 46 U.S. (5 How.) at 120.

37. This approach to intangible rights produced the most difficulty in cases involving constitutional rights brought under general federal question jurisdiction, 28 U.S.C.A. § 1331. See Comment, A Federal

A second problem that arises in actions for injunctive relief concerns the viewpoint from which the amount in controversy is to be assessed. The value to the plaintiff of having a right enforced and the cost to the defendant of having to honor or comply with an injunction are not necessarily symmetrical. As a result, the amount in controversy in the case may vary according to whose viewpoint is adopted for measurement purposes.

The Supreme Court's early attempt to deal with this problem succeeded only in muddying already obscure waters. In Mississippi & Missouri Railroad Company v. Ward,[38] an action brought by a steamboat owner to abate the defendant's bridge across the Mississippi River as a public nuisance, the Court stated: "the removal of the obstruction is the matter in controversy, and the value of the object must govern."[39] This language, which Judge Learned Hand charitably characterized as "at best ambiguous,"[40] raises many questions and resolves none. What is the "value of the object"—the cost to the defendant of removing the obstruction, the benefit that the plaintiff will derive from its removal, or the value of the bridge itself? The opinion fails to answer this question.

Over time, a more coherent doctrine has emerged. Although there are cases holding that the viewpoint of either the plaintiff or the defendant may be used,[41] the majority rule is that the jurisdictional amount is to be tested by the value to the plaintiff of the object that is sought to be gained.[42] For example, in the leading case of Glenwood Light & Water Company v. Mutual Light, Heat & Power Company,[43] an action by one utility to compel another utility to remove equipment that interfered with the plaintiff's operations, the Supreme Court held that the district court had erred in testing jurisdiction by the amount that it would cost the defendant to remove its poles and wires that were conflicting or interfering with those of the complainant, and to replace them so as to avoid the interference. As explained Justice Pitney, the plaintiff sought the right to conduct its business free from wrongful interference by defendant. Thus, "the relief sought is the protection of

Question Question: Does Priceless Mean Worthless?, 14 St. Louis U.L.J. 268 (1969). See also Comment, A Dollars and Sense Approach to the Amount-in-Controversy Requirement, 57 Iowa L.Rev. 530 (1971). The 1980 amendment eliminating any jurisdictional amount requirement for federal question cases has largely resolved the problem.

38. 67 U.S. (2 Black) 485, 17 L.Ed. 311 (1862).

39. 67 U.S. (2 Black) at 492 (Catron, J.).

40. M & M Transportation Co. v. City of New York, 186 F.2d 157 (2d Cir.1950).

41. See, e.g., McCarty v. Amoco Pipeline Co., 595 F.2d 389 (7th Cir.1979); Ronzio v. Denver & R. G. W. Ry. Co., 116 F.2d 604 (10th Cir.1940).

42. Glenwood Light & Water Co. v. Mutual Light, Heat & Power Co., 239 U.S. 121, 36 S.Ct. 30, 60 L.Ed. 174 (1915); Massachusetts State Pharmaceutical Ass'n v. Federal Prescription Serv., Inc., 431 F.2d 130 (8th Cir.1970); Central Mexico Light & Power Co. v. Munch, 116 F.2d 85 (2d Cir. 1940); Hirsch v. Jewish War Veterans of U.S., 537 F.Supp. 242 (E.D.Pa.1982); Ehrenfeld v. Webber, 499 F.Supp. 1283 (D.Me. 1980); Zep Mfg. Corp. v. Haber, 202 F.Supp. 847 (S.D.Tex.1962). For the permutations of the plaintiff-viewpoint rule involved in removal cases, in which it is the defendant seeking federal jurisdiction, see Inman v. Milwhite Co., 261 F.Supp. 703 (E.D.Ark. 1966); Thomas v. General Elec. Co., 207 F.Supp. 792 (W.D.Ky.1962).

43. 239 U.S. 121, 36 S.Ct. 30, 60 L.Ed. 174 (1915).

that right, now and in the future, and the value of that protection is determinative of the jurisdiction."[44] The plaintiff's-viewpoint doctrine has the advantage of providing a uniform, rather than a variable, standard, and dovetails with the general approach of determining the existence of federal jurisdiction on the basis of the contents of the complaint.

Once it is established that the plaintiff's viewpoint controls, a court still must decide what type of injuries may be considered in determining whether the jurisdictional amount has been exceeded. A court will not consider injuries that are merely remote, speculative, or collateral in computing the amount in controversy; subject-matter jurisdiction cannot be extended on the basis of unsupported guesses. Thus, in an action to enjoin enforcement of a state tax alleged to be unconstitutional, the matter in controversy is the value of the tax, and not the possible loss to the plaintiff's business that might occur or the fine that might be imposed if the tax is not paid.[45]

On the other hand, some types of injuries, such as those giving rise to unliquidated tort claims, by their very nature are difficult or impossible to pin down to a precise amount. The courts' approach to these claims has been a liberal one; the plaintiff need only show a "present probability" of recovering damages in excess of the jurisdictional amount if she prevails, rather than an absolute certainty.[46] This liberality derives from the same concerns that are reflected in the "legal certainty" rule applied to the allegations of the plaintiff's good faith complaint—the feeling that it is better to ensure access for all cases that properly should be in a federal forum, even if that allows some inflated claims to be brought in, than to expend great energy in ferreting out inflated claims or to run the risk of closing the federal courts' doors to worthy claims.[47]

§ 2.9 Amount-in-Controversy Requirements—The Effect of Additional Claims and Additional Parties

In the preceding section, various applications of the jurisdictional amount requirement were discussed in the context of the traditional common law unitary action involving a single plaintiff, a single defendant, and a single claim. The modern civil action under the Federal

---

44. 239 U.S. at 126, 36 S.Ct. at 32.

45. Healy v. Ratta, 292 U.S. 263, 54 S.Ct. 700, 78 L.Ed. 1248 (1934); May v. Supreme Court of Colorado, 508 F.2d 136 (10th Cir.1974), cert. denied 422 U.S. 1008. Similarly, when a business regulation is challenged, "the question is not the value or net worth of the business, but the value of the right to be free from the regulation, and this may be measured by the loss, if any, that would follow the enforcement of the rule prescribed." Kroger Grocery & Baking Co. v. Lutz, 299 U.S. 300, 301, 57 S.Ct. 215, 215, 81 L.Ed. 251 (1936). Only if the effect of the regulation is to put the plaintiff totally out of business is the value of the business relevant.

46. Aetna Cas. & Sur. Co. v. Flowers, 330 U.S. 464, 67 S.Ct. 798, 91 L.Ed. 1024 (1947). Crowded federal court dockets have encouraged some courts to scrutinize the plaintiff's allegations more carefully, particularly in tort cases. See Burns v. Anderson, 502 F.2d 970 (5th Cir.1974); Nelson v. Keefer, 451 F.2d 289, 295 (3d Cir.1971), noted in 47 N.Y.U.L.Rev. 349 (1972), 26 Sw.L.J. 461 (1972), 45 Temple L.Q. 305 (1972).

47. Deutsch v. Hewes St. Realty Corp., 359 F.2d 96 (2d Cir.1966); Wade v. Rogala, 270 F.2d 280 (3d Cir.1959).

Rules, however, often is a multi-claim, multi-party controversy of a kind that would have been quite unrecognizable to a common law practitioner. The joinder of additional claims and additional parties inevitably raises questions concerning the computation of the matter in controversy, and a series of aggregation rules have been developed, although unfortunately not in a very coherent or logical fashion, to guide the courts in these determinations.[1]

The rules may be stated as follows. When a single plaintiff sues a single defendant, the plaintiff may aggregate several claims for the purpose of satisfying the jurisdictional amount requirement, whether or not the claims bear any relation to one another.[2] When two plaintiffs each have a jurisdictionally insufficient claim against a single defendant, on the other hand, aggregation is not permitted if the claims are "separate and distinct."[3] This is true even if the claims are similar and factually related, as in a case in which co-passenger plaintiffs sue a defendant for injuries arising out of a single automobile accident.[4] Only if the claims are based on a common undivided interest, as narrowly and technically defined by the applicable substantive law,[5] may multiple plaintiffs aggregate their claims to satisfy the amount-in-controversy requirement.[6] Similarly, when a single plaintiff sues multiple defendants on separate and distinct claims, the claim against each defendant must be jurisdictionally sufficient; aggregation is not permitted unless the defendants are jointly liable to the plaintiff.[7]

Thus, whenever multiple parties are involved,[8] the operative distinction is that between a common, undivided interest, and separate and

---

§ 2.9

1. For general discussions of the rules governing the aggregation of claims, see 14B C. Wright, A. Miller & E. Cooper, Jurisdiction and Related Matters 3d § 3704; Note, The Federal Jurisdictional Amount and Rule 20 Joinder of Parties: Aggregation of Claims, 53 Minn.L.Rev. 94 (1968).

2. Edwards v. Bates County, 163 U.S. 269, 16 S.Ct. 967, 41 L.Ed. 155 (1896); Lloyd v. Kull, 329 F.2d 168 (7th Cir.1964); Rake v. City Lumber Co. of Bridgeport, 283 F.Supp. 870, 872 (D.Or.1967).

3. Clark v. Paul Gray, Inc., 306 U.S. 583, 59 S.Ct. 744, 83 L.Ed. 1001 (1939); Pinel v. Pinel, 240 U.S. 594, 36 S.Ct. 416, 60 L.Ed. 817 (1916); Troy Bank v. G. A. Whitehead & Co., 222 U.S. 39, 32 S.Ct. 9, 56 L.Ed. 81 (1911).

4. Thomson v. Gaskill, 315 U.S. 442, 447, 62 S.Ct. 673, 675, 86 L.Ed. 951 (1942): "Aggregation of plaintiffs' claims cannot be made merely because the claims are derived from a single instrument * * * or because the plaintiffs have a community of interest * * *."

5. An example of a common, undivided interest is the case of a partnership suing for an $80,000 debt. Aggregation is allowed, even though the partnership is owned by two equal partners, each technically having only an interest of $40,000 in the claim.

6. Troy Bank v. G. A. Whitehead & Co., 222 U.S. 39, 32 S.Ct. 9, 56 L.Ed. 81 (1911); Berman v. Narragansett Racing Ass'n, 414 F.2d 311 (1st Cir.1969), cert. denied 396 U.S. 1037.

7. Jewell v. Grain Dealers Mut. Ins. Co., 290 F.2d 11 (5th Cir.1961); Cornell v. Mabe, 206 F.2d 514 (5th Cir.1953). A case in which aggregation against multiple defendants would be permitted is an action to recover a single tract of land claimed by the several defendants under a common title source. The matter in controversy would be the value of the entire tract of land.

8. The aggregation rules apply to class action suits. See § 16.4, below. They do not present difficulties in shareholder derivative suits because the test for amount in controversy in that context is "the damage asserted to have been sustained by the defendant corporation." Koster v. (American) Lumbermens Mut. Cas. Co., 330 U.S. 518, 523, 67 S.Ct. 828, 831, 91 L.Ed. 1067 (1947).

distinct claims.[9] Unfortunately, this formal and conceptual distinction is far from clear, and as long as the federal courts adhere to it, the difficulties in application and the metaphysical decisions that it has engendered can be expected to continue.[10]

Thus far, the problem of additional claims has been examined solely from the perspective of claims brought by one or more plaintiffs. Modern civil litigation also permits counterclaims by the defendant against the plaintiff, cross-claims by one party against a coparty, and claims against third parties.[11] Jurisdiction over these other types of claims also must be considered.[12] Generally, the resolution of jurisdiction questions involving claims presented by defending parties turns on whether the claims fall within the supplemental jurisdiction of the federal court hearing the original claim.[13] If they do, then they do not need to satisfy jurisdictional amount requirements.[14] Otherwise, the normal standards for satisfying the amount-in-controversy requirement apply.[15]

Another question that has arisen is whether a jurisdictionally insufficient claim by the plaintiff can be tied to a compulsory counterclaim to satisfy the requirements of federal jurisdiction.[16] In 1961, the Supreme Court, dividing five to four, handed down a somewhat surprising decision involving this problem in Horton v. Liberty Mutual Insurance Company.[17] Horton had been injured in an industrial accident, and filed a worker's compensation claim before the Texas Industrial Accident Board against Liberty Mutual, his employer's insurer. Horton sought $14,035, but the Board awarded him only $1,050. The day the Board's award was announced, Liberty Mutual brought a federal diversity action seeking to have the award set aside and alleging that Horton had claimed, was claiming, and would continue to claim $14,035; the insurer asserted he should receive nothing. A week later, Horton filed a state court action to set aside the award and recover the full $14,035. He moved to dismiss Liberty Mutual's federal court action for failure to meet the jurisdiction-

---

9. For examples of cases in which courts have found parties to have a common, undivided interest or have ruled their interests to be several and distinct, see 14B C. Wright, A. Miller & E. Cooper, Jurisdiction and Related Matters 3d § 3704.

10. The distinction has evoked a good deal of criticism. See, e.g., Note, Aggregation of Claims in Class Actions, 68 Colum.L.Rev. 1554, 1558–62 (1968).

11. See §§ 6.7–6.9, below.

12. See generally 14B C. Wright, A. Miller & E. Cooper, Jurisdiction and Related Matters 3d § 3706; Note, Federal Jurisdictional Amount: Determination of the Matter in Controversy, 73 Harv.L.Rev. 1369, 1376–81 (1960).

13. For a discussion of supplemental jurisdiction, see §§ 2.13–2.14, below.

14. E.g., Dery v. Wyer, 265 F.2d 804 (2d Cir.1959) (third-party claim); Coastal Air Lines, Inc. v. Dockery, 180 F.2d 874 (8th Cir.1950) (cross-claim); Arvey Corp. v. Peterson, 178 F.Supp. 132 (E.D.Pa.1959) (compulsory counterclaim).

15. For example, several permissive counterclaims of a single defendant may be aggregated, in the same manner as multiple claims by a single plaintiff. See McKnight v. Halliburton Oil Well Cementing Co., 20 F.R.D. 563 (N.D.W.Va.1957).

16. See generally 14B C. Wright, A. Miller & E. Cooper, Jurisdiction and Related Matters 3d § 3706.

17. 367 U.S. 348, 81 S.Ct. 1570, 6 L.Ed.2d 890 (1961).

al amount because the Board's award involved only $1,050; at the same time he filed a "conditional compulsory counterclaim" for $14,035.

The Court held that the then applicable $10,000 amount-in-controversy requirement had been met. Justice Black, writing for the majority, saw the dispute essentially as involving $14,035. Since the applicable Texas substantive law permitted a trial de novo on Horton's entire claim, Justice Black stated that in fact the entire claim was in controversy in the insurer's federal court action.[18]

Justice Clark dissented vehemently. To predicate federal subject-matter jurisdiction upon Liberty Mutual's allegations that Horton intended to counterclaim for $14,035, he argued, was to disregard the basic principle that the basis for federal jurisdiction must appear on the face of the plaintiff's complaint.[19] The practical result of the decision to allow the plaintiff to invoke federal jurisdiction on the basis of an anticipated counterclaim would be to permit insurers, in cases like Horton, to force impecunious workers into costly federal court litigation, thereby subverting the congressional prohibition against the removal of state worker's compensation cases.[20]

The peculiarities of its facts have limited the impact of the Horton decision. A number of lower courts have seen it as merely reflecting the special character of Texas worker's compensation law, with its trial de novo provision, and have confined its holding to cases of that type.[21] In addition, the Court majority undoubtedly was influenced by the fact that Horton actually had filed both a state court claim for $14,035 and a conditional compulsory counterclaim for the same amount in the federal court proceeding. Liberty Mutual's action also can be viewed as essentially a suit for a declaratory judgment, the object of which was a declaration of non-liability for the entire $14,035 originally claimed by Horton. In truth, the case really involved only one cause of action; the presentation of a claim and counterclaim typically involves two. The problem with the decision, however, is that it gives disproportionate attention to a rather unique legal and factual situation, at the expense of simplicity of analysis and to the possible derogation of fundamental principles of federal subject-matter jurisdiction.[22]

---

18. 367 U.S. at 354, 81 S.Ct. at 1574.

19. See § 2.4, above. A correlative problem on which the courts are split is whether a defendant can remove a case to federal court when the plaintiff's claim is less than the jurisdictional minimum but the defendant responds with a compulsory counterclaim in excess of the statutory minimum. Compare National Upholstery Corp. v. Corley, 144 F.Supp. 658 (M.D.N.C.1956) (removal permitted), with Burton Lines, Inc. v. Mansky, 265 F.Supp. 489 (N.D.N.C. 1967) (removal denied). See § 2.11, below, for a discussion of removal.

20. In 1958, Congress had prohibited the removal of worker's compensation ac-

tions in an attempt to aid claimants and ease federal court congestion. See 28 U.S.C.A. § 1445(c).

21. See, e.g., Insurance Co. of North America v. Keeling, 360 F.2d 88 (5th Cir. 1966), cert. denied 385 U.S. 840.

22. For a further discussion of Horton, see Note, The Effect of the Horton Case on the Determination of the Amount in Controversy under Statutes Limiting Federal Court Jurisdiction, 17 Rutgers L.Rev. 200 (1962). See also the case notes in 11 Amer. U.L.Rev. 102 (1961), 1962 Duke L.J. 123, 46 Minn.L.Rev. 960 (1962).

§ 2.10   Actions in Which the United States Is a Party and Admiralty and Maritime Cases

In addition to federal question and diversity jurisdiction, the two other major areas of federal judicial power are cases involving the United States and admiralty and maritime cases. Although these areas of federal subject-matter jurisdiction cannot be dealt with at length in a volume of this character, their existence and fundamental principles will be described.

Most civil actions instituted by the United States are brought under Section 1345 of Title 28, which states that the district courts shall have jurisdiction, except as otherwise provided, in "all civil actions, suits or proceedings commenced by the United States, or by an agency or officer thereof expressly authorized to sue by Act of Congress."[1] There is no statutory amount-in-controversy requirement.[2] The only important limitation on the ability of the United States to sue under Section 1345 is that it cannot lend its name to a lawsuit that is brought solely for the benefit of a private individual.[3] However, the mere fact that a suit by the United States operates to confer a benefit on a citizen does not, in and of itself, place the action outside the scope of the jurisdiction statute. In addition, the government's interest need not be pecuniary or proprietary; it legitimately may litigate to assure the proper implementation of its policies and programs,[4] to protect the "general welfare,"[5] to prevent the violation of constitutional rights,[6] or to protect its sovereign interest.[7] Most commonly, however, actions brought by the United States—for example, suits to collect notes, to quiet title, or to obtain a remedy for breach of contract or tort—are similar to those commenced by private litigants.

Although federal jurisdiction over suits brought by the United States generally poses no difficulties, jurisdiction over actions brought against the United States is complicated by the doctrine of sovereign immunity, which prevents the federal government from being sued without its consent.[8] Only Congress can waive the United States' sovereign immunity[9] and statutory consents to suit generally are strictly

---

§ 2.10

1. For a more detailed discussion, see 14 C. Wright, A. Miller & E. Cooper, Jurisdiction and Related Matters 3d §§ 3651–53.

2. See § 2.8, above, for a discussion of amount-in-controversy requirements.

3. U.S. v. San Jacinto Tin Co., 125 U.S. 273, 8 S.Ct. 850, 31 L.Ed. 747 (1888). This limitation is actually a question of standing—if a suit is not in the interest of the United States, then the United States has no standing to bring the action. See generally § 6.3, below.

4. Wyandotte Transportation Co. v. U.S., 389 U.S. 191, 88 S.Ct. 379, 19 L.Ed.2d 407 (1967).

5. In re Debs, 158 U.S. 564, 584, 15 S.Ct. 900, 906, 39 L.Ed. 1092 (1895).

6. U.S. v. City of Jackson, Mississippi, 318 F.2d 1 (5th Cir.1963).

7. U.S. v. Marchetti, 466 F.2d 1309 (4th Cir.1972), cert. denied 409 U.S. 1063.

8. U.S. v. Sherwood, 312 U.S. 584, 61 S.Ct. 767, 85 L.Ed. 1058 (1941); Turner v. U.S., 51 Ct.Cl. 125 (1916), affirmed 248 U.S. 354, 39 S.Ct. 109, 63 L.Ed. 291 (1919).

9. Minnesota v. U.S., 305 U.S. 382, 59 S.Ct. 292, 83 L.Ed. 235 (1939).

construed.[10] Congress has waived immunity in a number of statutes[11] and until the Supreme Court decided Lane v. Pena,[12] the defense of sovereign immunity had been viewed by many courts with increasing disfavor with respect to actions for damages. In Lane, however, the Supreme Court forcefully reaffirmed the doctrine of sovereign immunity by crafting a clear-statement rule to determine whether the United States has consented to be sued. According to the Court, unless a statute expressly and unequivocally waives sovereign immunity in its text, Congress has not granted consent to the bringing of an action against the federal government.

The doctrine of sovereign immunity continues to be strictly applied in actions for specific relief. The reasons supporting the different treatment of damage and injunction actions, as it existed pre-Lane, were aptly summarized by Chief Justice Vinson in Larson v. Domestic & Foreign Commerce Corporation.[13]

> For, it is one thing to provide a method by which a citizen may be compensated for a wrong done to him by the Government. It is a far different matter to permit a court to exercise its compulsive powers to restrain the Government from acting, or to compel it to act. * * * The Government as representative of the community as a whole, cannot be stopped in its tracks by any plaintiff who presents a disputed question of property or contract right.[14]

Sovereign immunity extends to actions against agencies and officers of the United States when the conduct in question was undertaken on behalf of the government. Consequently, a suit against a federal agency or officer usually must find its jurisdictional basis in one of the statutory waivers of sovereign immunity. The only major exceptions to this arise when a federal officer has acted either in his individual capacity or outside the scope of his authority, in which case suit can be brought against the officer in his individual capacity, or if it is claimed that the conduct itself or the statute or order on which it was based is unconstitutional.[15] If none of these exceptions applies and if there is no specific statute waiving immunity, jurisdiction is lacking and the suit must be dismissed.[16]

10. McMahon v. U.S., 342 U.S. 25, 72 S.Ct. 17, 96 L.Ed. 26 (1951); Nickerson v. U.S., 513 F.2d 31 (1st Cir.1975).

11. Various legislative exceptions to sovereign immunity are noted in 14 C. Wright, A. Miller & E. Cooper, Jurisdiction and Related Matters 3d §§ 3656–59. The two most important are the Tucker Act, authorizing claims based on the Constitution or other claims for damages not sounding in tort, 28 U.S.C.A. §§ 1346(a)(2), 1491, and the Federal Tort Claims Act, authorizing damage claims premised on the negligence of federal employees or agencies performing official functions, 28 U.S.C.A. §§ 2401–02, 2671–80.

12. 518 U.S. 187, 116 S.Ct. 2092, 135 L.Ed.2d 486 (1996).

13. 337 U.S. 682, 69 S.Ct. 1457, 93 L.Ed. 1628 (1949).

14. 337 U.S. at 703–04, 69 S.Ct. at 1468–69.

15. Larson v. Domestic & Foreign Commerce Corp., 337 U.S. 682, 69 S.Ct. 1457, 93 L.Ed. 1628 (1949).

16. Sovereign immunity in general, and its application to suits against federal agencies and officers, is discussed more fully in 14 C. Wright, A. Miller & E. Cooper, Jurisdiction and Related Matters 3d §§ 3654–55.

Federal jurisdiction over admiralty and maritime cases is a more complicated matter.[17] The subject also is somewhat unique because both substantive maritime law and admiralty jurisdiction are largely matters of common law development, rather than statutory definition.[18]

The current statute conferring admiralty jurisdiction on the federal courts is Section 1333 of the Judicial Code, which provides for original jurisdiction over any "civil case of admiralty or maritime jurisdiction, saving to suitors in all cases all other remedies to which they are otherwise entitled." Because of the last clause of the statute—known as the "saving to suitors" clause—federal jurisdiction over admiralty and maritime cases is not exclusive; rather, suitors also have the right to a common law remedy, whenever the common law is competent to give it. This means that a plaintiff with an in personam (but not an in rem or limitation of liability)[19] claim may bring either a libel in admiralty or an ordinary civil action.[20] If federal admiralty jurisdiction is invoked, there are no requirements of diversity of citizenship or a minimum amount in controversy. Alternatively, if there is complete diversity of citizenship and the jurisdictional amount requirement is satisfied, the plaintiff may sue at law in a federal district court under Section 1332.[21] The plaintiff also may file suit in a state court.[22]

The threshold problem under Section 1333 is determining whether a case is one of "admiralty or maritime jurisdiction." In the early leading case of DeLovio v. Boit,[23] Justice Story decided that federal admiralty jurisdiction was not confined to the narrowly circumscribed admiralty jurisdiction exercised by the English courts at the time the Constitution

17. See 14A C. Wright, A. Miller & E. Cooper, Jurisdiction and Related Matters 3d §§ 3671–79.

18. In The Lottawanna, 88 U.S. (21 Wall.) 558, 576, 22 L.Ed. 654 (1875), the Supreme Court stated that the limits of maritime law and admiralty jurisdiction were "exclusively a judicial question." Although this sweeping claim of exclusive judicial power no longer can be made, the Supreme Court more recently has observed that "Congress has largely left to this Court the responsibility for fashioning the controlling rules of admiralty law." Fitzgerald v. U.S. Lines Co., 374 U.S. 16, 20, 83 S.Ct. 1646, 1650, 10 L.Ed.2d 720 (1963).

19. The rationale for maintaining exclusive federal admiralty jurisdiction over suits in rem despite the "saving to suitors" clause has been that a proceeding in rem is not a "common law remedy" within the terms of the original "saving to suitors" clause in the Judiciary Act of 1789. See The Moses Taylor, 71 U.S. (4 Wall.) 411, 18 L.Ed. 397 (1866). Sections 183–189 of Title 46 provide for exclusive federal jurisdiction over limitation of liability proceedings.

20. See Panama R. Co. v. Vasquez, 271 U.S. 557, 46 S.Ct. 596, 70 L.Ed. 1085 (1926); Rounds v. Cloverport Foundry & Mach. Co., 237 U.S. 303, 35 S.Ct. 596, 59 L.Ed. 966 (1915).

21. Atlantic & Gulf Stevedores, Inc. v. Ellerman Lines, Ltd., 369 U.S. 355, 82 S.Ct. 780, 7 L.Ed.2d 798 (1962).

22. The choice between suing at law or in admiralty has important procedural consequences. Most particularly, a federal court sitting in admiralty under Section 1333 does so without a jury. Waring v. Clarke, 46 U.S. (5 How.) 441, 460, 12 L.Ed. 226 (1847). Trial by jury is available only for in personam actions brought under the "saving to suitors" clause. Atlantic & Gulf Stevedores, Inc. v. Ellerman Lines, Ltd., 369 U.S. 355, 82 S.Ct. 780, 7 L.Ed.2d 798 (1962). The classic work on admiralty litigation is G. Gilmore & C. Black, The Law of Admiralty (2d ed.1975).

23. 7 Fed.Cas. 418 (C.C.D.Mass.1815) (No. 3,776).

became effective.[24] He concluded that admiralty jurisdiction

> comprehends all maritime contracts, torts, and injuries. The latter branch is necessarily bounded by locality; the former extends over all contracts, (wheresoever they may be made or executed, or whatsoever may be the form of the stipulations,) which relate to the navigation, business or commerce of the sea.[25]

The federal courts have followed this liberal construction of their admiralty jurisdiction. And the two fundamental sources of admiralty jurisdiction remain clear: (1) events occurring on certain types of waters encompassed by the constitutional grant; and (2) particular classes of disputes historically governed by maritime law and adjudicated in admiralty courts. Nonetheless, the outer boundaries of admiralty jurisdiction remain uncertain. In addition to difficulties in defining exactly which bodies of water fall within its scope,[26] both the federal courts and the Congress have altered or supplemented the substantive maritime law of the United States, thereby affecting federal court jurisdiction.

For a case to fall within admiralty jurisdiction, there generally must be some nexus between the alleged wrong and maritime activity, however. Merely because a tort occurs on navigable waters does not necessarily mean that it is an admiralty or maritime case. This is illustrated by the case of Executive Jet Aviation, Inc. v. City of Cleveland,[27] the facts of which are quite interesting. A jet aircraft departing Cleveland struck a number of sea gulls while airborne over the runway, causing an almost total loss of power. The plane hit a fence and a truck before settling into Lake Erie just beyond the end of the runway. In a suit against the city, the federal air traffic controller, and others for negligent failure to keep the runway free of birds or to warn of their presence, the plane's owners attempted to invoke admiralty jurisdiction on the ground that the plane had crashed in navigable waters. The Supreme Court ruled that jurisdiction did not exist. Although it recognized that traditionally, if a tort "occurred on navigable waters, the action is within admiralty jurisdiction,"[28] the Court noted that this "strict locality" test created problems in "perverse and casuistic borderline situations" and was particularly inappropriate for deciding modern aeronautical torts. The Court concluded that it "is far more consistent with the history and purpose of

24. "The advantages resulting to the commerce and navigation of the United States, from a uniformity of rules and decisions in all maritime questions, authorize us to believe that national policy, as well as juridical logic, require the clause of the constitution to be so construed, as to embrace all maritime contracts, torts and injuries, or, in other words, to embrace all those causes, which originally and inherently belonged to the admiralty, before any statutory restriction." 7 Fed.Cas. at 443.

25. 7 Fed.Cas. at 444.

26. Admiralty jurisdiction includes "all navigable waters within the country." Southern S.S. Co. v. NLRB, 316 U.S. 31, 41, 62 S.Ct. 886, 892, 86 L.Ed. 1246 (1942). "Navigable waters" are defined further as bodies or streams of water "generally and commonly useful to some purpose of trade or agriculture." The Montello, 87 U.S. (20 Wall.) 430, 442, 22 L.Ed. 391 (1874).

27. 409 U.S. 249, 93 S.Ct. 493, 34 L.Ed.2d 454 (1972).

28. 409 U.S. at 253, 93 S.Ct. at 497.

admiralty to require * * * that the wrong bear a significant relationship to traditional maritime activity."[29]

On the other hand, if the conduct underlying the action is sufficiently related to navigable waters, admiralty jurisdiction will exist even though neither of the parties is engaged in commercial maritime activity. Thus, the Supreme Court upheld jurisdiction in a wrongful death action arising from the collision of two pleasure boats on a navigable river. In a five-to-four decision, Justice Marshall, writing for the majority, concluded that the federal interest in protecting maritime commerce could be vindicated fully "only if all operators of vessels on navigable waters are subject to uniform rules of conduct."[30]

§ 2.11 Removal Jurisdiction

Removal jurisdiction permits a defendant to force the plaintiff to litigate certain actions in federal court, rather than in the state forum originally selected.[1] In a case involving parties of diverse citizenship, removal protects a nonresident defendant against any local bias that might be encountered in the state court because of the defendant being a "foreigner." In a case involving a claim raising an issue of federal law, removal equalizes the ability of both parties to have a federal question litigated in its "natural" forum.

The Constitution contains no mention of removal jurisdiction. Nevertheless, since the original Judiciary Act of 1789,[2] there always have been statutory provisions for the removal of cases from state to federal courts.[3] Although it represents an intrusion upon the judicial power of the state courts, the constitutionality of federal removal jurisdiction consistently has been upheld.[4] Because the source of removal jurisdiction

29. 409 U.S. at 268, 93 S.Ct. at 505. See also Rubin v. Power Authority of New York, 356 F.Supp. 1169 (W.D.N.Y.1973).

30. Foremost Ins. Co. v. Richardson, 457 U.S. 668, 675, 102 S.Ct. 2654, 2659, 73 L.Ed.2d 300 (1982).

§ 2.11

1. For a comprehensive discussion of removal jurisdiction and removal procedure, see 14B & 14C C. Wright, A. Miller & E. Cooper, Jurisdiction and Related Matters 3d §§ 3721–40. For information concerning removal in the context of complex litigation, see American Law Institute, Complex Litigation: Statutory Recommendations and Analysis with Reporter's Study, 217–56 (1994).

2. Act of Sept. 24, 1789, c. 20, § 12, 1 Stat. 73.

3. This section discusses the general removal statute. Various other statutes specifically authorize removal of certain types of cases. For example, a right of removal is provided for suits involving federal officers

sued in state court, 28 U.S.C.A. § 1442; suits against members of the armed forces for acts done under color of military authority, 28 U.S.C.A. § 1442a; suits against federal employees for injuries caused by the employee's operation of a motor vehicle within the scope of his employment, 28 U.S.C.A. § 2679(d); suits involving property on which the United States has a lien, 28 U.S.C.A. § 1444; and suits in which the defendant cannot secure his or her civil rights in a state court, 28 U.S.C.A. § 1443. Other actions are made specifically nonremovable by statute, such as actions under the Federal Employers' Liability Act, 28 U.S.C.A. § 1445(a); the Jones Act, 46 U.S.C.A. § 688; and the state worker's compensation laws, 28 U.S.C.A. § 1445(c).

4. Tennessee v. Davis, 100 U.S. (10 Otto) 257, 25 L.Ed. 648 (1879); Gaines v. Fuentes, 92 U.S. (2 Otto) 10, 23 L.Ed. 524 (1876); Chicago & N.W. Ry. Co. v. Whitton's Adm'r, 80 U.S. (13 Wall.) 270, 20 L.Ed. 571 (1871). Constitutional support is found in the Judicial Power Clause, Art. III,

is purely statutory, the right to remove and the method by which the right may be exercised are entirely dependent upon the will of Congress.[5]

The current general removal statute is Section 1441 of Title 28 of the United States Code. The basic principles controlling removal are spelled out in Section 1441(a), which reiterates the principal characteristic of removal jurisdiction—subject to some statutory exceptions, an action is removable only if it originally could have been brought in a federal court. Three other general features also should be noted. First, cases may be removed only from a state to a federal court; there is no procedure for transferring a case instituted in a federal court to a state court or from a state court in one state to a state court in another. Second, the general removal statute is limited to civil actions; criminal, and perhaps penalty, cases are not removable except as otherwise provided by statute.[6] Finally, the right of removal is limited to defendants.[7]

The principle that only defendants may remove is rigorously adhered to, in keeping with the general policy of limiting federal jurisdiction by construing jurisdictional statutes narrowly. In the leading case of Shamrock Oil & Gas Corporation v. Sheets,[8] the Supreme Court reaffirmed an earlier holding[9] that "defendant" in the removal statute referred only to a party against whom a suit is brought by serving process upon him. The filing of a counterclaim in the state court action does not convert the plaintiff opposing the counterclaim into a "defendant" for purposes of removal.[10]

The Shamrock Oil decision has been criticized because its effect is to prevent removal in cases in which there would be no question of the opposing party's right to remove if the counterclaim were brought as a separate action.[11] On the other hand, the decision can be justified on the grounds that the plaintiff chose voluntarily to submit to the jurisdiction

and the Necessary and Proper Clause, Art. I, § 8, cl. 18.

5. Great Northern Ry. Co. v. Alexander, 246 U.S. 276, 280, 38 S.Ct. 237, 239, 62 L.Ed. 713 (1918).

6. Tasner v. U.S. Industries, Inc., 379 F.Supp. 803 (N.D.Ill.1974); Quinn v. A Book Named "Sixty Erotic Drawings from Juliette," 316 F.Supp. 289 (D.Mass.1970); Rand v. Arkansas, 191 F.Supp. 20 (W.D.Ark.1961). The term "civil action" has been construed to encompass proceedings for garnishment or condemnation and actions to compel arbitration or to confirm or vacate an arbitration award. Chicago, R.I. & P.R.R. Co. v. Stude, 346 U.S. 574, 74 S.Ct. 290, 98 L.Ed. 317 (1954); Johnson v. England, 356 F.2d 44 (9th Cir.1966), cert. denied 384 U.S. 961; Stoll v. Hawkeye Cas. Co., 185 F.2d 96 (8th Cir.1950). See generally Moore & VanDercreek, Federal Removal Jurisdiction—Civil Action Brought in a State Court, 14 Sw.L.J. 297 (1960).

7. In 1875, the right to remove was extended to plaintiffs as well as defendants, but the experiment was short-lived, and in 1887, the predecessor of 28 U.S.C.A. § 1441 once again restricted removal to defendants only.

8. 313 U.S. 100, 61 S.Ct. 868, 85 L.Ed. 1214 (1941).

9. West v. Aurora City, 73 U.S. (6 Wall.) 139, 18 L.Ed. 819 (1868).

10. Questions of whether a defendant can remove on the basis of a counterclaim, cross-claim or third-party claim are discussed in note 36, below.

11. See American Law Institute, Study of the Division of Jurisdiction Between State and Federal Courts, Official Draft, § 1304(c), at 147–48 (1969). The result seems particularly inappropriate when the defendant's counterclaim is permissive and is based on an unrelated transaction.

of the state court by filing suit there, and that the legislative history of the removal statute reflects a clear congressional desire to limit the scope of this branch of federal jurisdiction.

In determining whether a state action originally could have been brought in a federal court and therefore is removable, the basic rules governing federal question jurisdiction, diversity jurisdiction, and amount in controversy, discussed in earlier sections, apply. Thus, if the attempt to remove is predicated on diversity of citizenship or alienage, a lawsuit between two aliens, for example, cannot be removed because such an action does not fall within the original diversity or alienage jurisdiction of the federal courts.[12] Further, according to the well-pleaded complaint rule, the basis for removal must appear as part of the plaintiff's claim so that when removal is sought on the basis of a federal question, the allegations of the plaintiff's complaint must raise a substantial federal question.[13] Some difficult problems surround the amount-in-controversy requirement, although generally the amount claimed by the plaintiff is determinative.[14]

Despite the fact that removal is a defendant's option, the plaintiff retains considerable control over where the action is litigated. If the plaintiff fails to assert a federal claim, or fails to join a party who could remove the entire action, or joins a nondiverse party, or demands less than the requisite jurisdictional amount, the defendant cannot remove on the ground that an alternate course that would have permitted removal was available to the plaintiff.[15] Of course, a different result will be reached when the plaintiff conceals a legitimate ground of removal by fraud, mistake, or inadvertence.[16] Once a case is properly removed, the plaintiff may not defeat federal jurisdiction by reducing the claim to less than the jurisdictional amount or by joining a nondiverse party.[17]

12. Kavourgias v. Nicholaou Co., 148 F.2d 96 (9th Cir.1945).

13. Rivet v. Regions Bank of Louisiana, 522 U.S. 470, 118 S.Ct. 921, 139 L.Ed.2d 912 (1998); Great Northern Ry. Co. v. Alexander, 246 U.S. 276, 38 S.Ct. 237, 62 L.Ed. 713 (1918); Burgess v. Charlottesville Sav. & Loan Ass'n, 477 F.2d 40 (4th Cir. 1973); Old Reading Brewery, Inc. v. Lebanon Valley Brewing Co., 102 F.Supp. 434 (M.D.Pa.1952).

14. Davenport v. Proctor & Gamble Mfg. Co., 241 F.2d 511, 514 (2d Cir.1957). The most difficult problems arise in two general situations: (1) when the state in which the federal court is sitting does not require that the complaint contain a demand for a specific monetary amount, or expressly forbids the inclusion of such a demand, or requires only that more than a certain amount be alleged; and (2) when the local state practice permits recoveries in excess of the amount pleaded in the ad damnum clause and plaintiff has prayed for less than the jurisdictional amount neces-

sary for removal. For a discussion of these and other problems involving the amount-in-controversy requirement in the context of removal jurisdiction, see 14C C. Wright, A. Miller & E. Cooper, Jurisdiction and Related Matters 3d § 3725.

15. Greenshields v. Warren Petroleum Corp., 248 F.2d 61, 65 (10th Cir.1957), cert. denied 355 U.S. 907.

16. City of Galveston v. International Organization of Masters, Mates & Pilots, 338 F.Supp. 907, 909 (S.D.Tex.1972). See also Avco Corp. v. Aero Lodge No. 735, Int'l Ass'n of Machinists & Aerospace Workers, 376 F.2d 337 (6th Cir.1967), affirmed 390 U.S. 557, 88 S.Ct. 1235, 20 L.Ed.2d 126 (1968). For a discussion of the treatment of devices to defeat diversity, see § 2.7, above.

17. Albright v. R. J. Reynolds Tobacco Co., 531 F.2d 132 (3d Cir.1976), cert. denied 426 U.S. 907; Southern Pac. Co. v. Haight, 126 F.2d 900, 903 (9th Cir.1942), cert. denied 317 U.S. 676; Stanhope v. Ford Motor

Another limitation on the plaintiff's choice of forum is the artful-pleading doctrine, which bars a plaintiff from defeating "removal by omitting to plead necessary federal questions."[18] If a court concludes that a plaintiff has artfully pleaded her claims, it may permit removal despite the well-pleaded complaint rule.[19] Because of the threat that it presents to the rule that the plaintiff is master of her complaint, however, the artful-pleading doctrine is confined to two situations—(1) when Congress has made it clear that federal law in a certain area completely preempts corresponding state law and has replaced it with a federal claim, and (2) when a state cause of action actually turns on a substantial federal question.[20] The latter basis for invoking the artful-pleading doctrine is seldom used.[21]

In addition to the existence of original federal jurisdiction, until recently removal also required that the state court in which the action was commenced have had original jurisdiction over the action.[22] The theory was that removal jurisdiction is in some sense derivative. Therefore, if the state court lacked subject-matter jurisdiction, the federal court to which removal was sought could not acquire jurisdiction. This sometimes led to anomalous results.[23] For example, if a plaintiff brought a state court action that fell within the exclusive jurisdiction of the federal courts, such as a patent or antitrust action, removal technically would be improper, and the federal court would be forced to dismiss the action, leaving the plaintiff with the burden of filing again in federal court.[24] In response to this problem, Section 1441(e) was added in 1986, providing that the federal court "is not precluded from hearing and determining any claim in such civil action because the state court did not have jurisdiction over that claim." Further, once an action has been

Credit Co., 483 F.Supp. 275 (W.D.Ark. 1980).

18. Franchise Tax Bd. of California v. Construction Laborers Vacation Trust for Southern California, 463 U.S. 1, 22, 103 S.Ct. 2841, 2853, 77 L.Ed.2d 420 (1983).

19. Rivet v. Regions Bank of Louisiana, 522 U.S. 470, 118 S.Ct. 921, 925, 139 L.Ed.2d 912 (1998).

20. Merrell Dow Pharmaceuticals Inc. v. Thompson, 478 U.S. 804, 106 S.Ct. 3229, 92 L.Ed.2d 650 (1986); Avco Corp. v. Aero Lodge No. 735, Int'l Ass'n of Machinists & Aerospace Workers, 390 U.S. 557, 88 S.Ct. 1235, 20 L.Ed.2d 126 (1968). For a discussion of the artful pleading doctrine, see Miller, Artful Pleading: A Doctrine in Search of Definition, 76 Texas L. Rev. 1781 (1998).

21. City of Park City v. Rural Water District, 960 F.Supp. 255 (D.Kan.1997).

22. See, e.g., Garden Homes, Inc. v. Mason, 238 F.2d 651 (1st Cir.1956) (state court lacked personal jurisdiction because of insufficient service of process); Dunn v. Cedar Rapids Engineering Co., 152 F.2d 733 (9th Cir.1945) (state court lacked personal jurisdiction over foreign corporation); Keay v. Eastern Air Lines, Inc., 267 F.Supp. 77 (D.Mass.1967) (state court had no subject-matter jurisdiction over award of arbitration board).

23. The rule was given its most widely known articulation by Justice Brandeis in Lambert Run Coal Co. v. Baltimore & Ohio R.R. Co., 258 U.S. 377, 382, 42 S.Ct. 349, 351, 66 L.Ed. 671 (1922).

24. General Inv. Co. v. Lake Shore & M.S. Ry. Co., 260 U.S. 261, 43 S.Ct. 106, 67 L.Ed. 244 (1922) (Sherman and Clayton Acts); Koppers Co. v. Continental Cas. Co., 337 F.2d 499 (8th Cir.1964) (Miller Act); Leesona Corp. v. Concordia Mfg. Co., 312 F.Supp. 392 (D.R.I.1970) (Patent Act). The rule was criticized sharply as it prohibited removal in exactly those cases in which the federal courts were the only forum in which they could be brought. See, e.g., Washington v. American League of Professional Baseball Clubs, 460 F.2d 654, 658–59 (9th Cir.1972).

removed, the complaint may be amended to include additional claims that could not have been brought originally in the state court.[25]

As might be expected of a privilege that is wholly the creation of federal statute, a state may not restrict or limit a litigant's right of removal in any way.[26] For example, a state cannot constitutionally pass a statute exacting a waiver of the right to remove as a condition of any foreign corporation doing business in the state.[27] On the other hand, private contracts in which one of the parties agrees in advance to waive the right of removal in the event of a lawsuit have been upheld.[28]

In determining the general propriety of removal, an important distinction must be drawn between federal question and diversity cases. Section 1441(b) of the general removal statute provides that a case can be removed on the basis of diversity only if none of the defendants is a citizen of the forum state. Consequently, if a Missouri citizen sues a citizen of Iowa in a state court in Iowa, the defendant cannot remove if diversity of citizenship is the only basis for federal jurisdiction. This additional restriction is justified on the ground that the Iowa defendant hardly can expect to encounter prejudice against out-of-staters in the courts of his home state so there is no reason for extending federal jurisdiction over the action.[29] In federal question cases, the defendant can remove without regard to the citizenship of the parties.

A number of rules are brought to bear on the determination whether a diversity action is removable under Section 1441(b). As a general rule, removability is determined from the record as of the time the notice of removal is filed.[30] However, when diversity is the basis of removal jurisdiction, it must exist both at the time the original action is filed in the state court and at the time removal is sought; the defendant cannot change domicile after the initiation of the state action so as to establish diversity, and then seek removal.[31] On the other hand, an action that is initially nonremovable may become removable as a result of the plaintiff's subsequent action. If the plaintiff sues a foreign defendant and a resident defendant, for instance, removal will not be available at the outset of the action because all defendants must be both diverse from the

---

25. Freeman v. Bee Mach. Co., 319 U.S. 448, 63 S.Ct. 1146, 87 L.Ed. 1509 (1943). Removed actions are governed by the same procedures and rules as actions originally commenced in the federal courts. See 14C C. Wright, A. Miller & E. Cooper, Jurisdiction and Related Matters 3d § 3738.

26. Harrison v. St. Louis & S.F.R.R. Co., 232 U.S. 318, 34 S.Ct. 333, 58 L.Ed. 621 (1914); Fresquez v. Farnsworth & Chambers Co., 238 F.2d 709, 712 (10th Cir. 1956).

27. Terral v. Burke Constr. Co., 257 U.S. 529, 42 S.Ct. 188, 66 L.Ed. 352 (1922).

28. Monte v. Southern Delaware County Authority, 321 F.2d 870 (3d Cir.1963).

29. The availability of diversity jurisdiction for nonresident plaintiffs affords protection for the nonresident who is concerned about the possibility of local prejudice against an out-of-state litigant. The fear-of-prejudice rationale does not explain, however, why an in-state plaintiff suing an out-of-state defendant has the option of invoking diversity in the federal courts of his home state.

30. Salem Trust Co. v. Manufacturers' Finance Co., 264 U.S. 182, 189–90, 44 S.Ct. 266, 267, 68 L.Ed. 628 (1924).

31. Jackson v. Allen, 132 U.S. 27, 10 S.Ct. 9, 33 L.Ed. 249 (1889); Carlton Properties, Inc. v. Crescent City Leasing Corp., 212 F.Supp. 370 (E.D.Pa.1962).

plaintiff[32] and nonresidents of the forum state. But if the plaintiff later amends the complaint to drop the resident defendant from the action, the foreign defendant then gains the right to remove.[33] The elimination of the nondiverse defendant under these circumstances must be a voluntary act on the part of the plaintiff: if the resident defendant is eliminated involuntarily, for example, by a summary judgment in his favor, the diverse defendant is not permitted to remove.[34] The rationale for this voluntary-involuntary distinction never has been explicated very clearly, but it does serve the purpose of preventing removal when the resident defendant's dismissal has not been determined finally in the state courts, and may be reversed on appeal. A voluntary dismissal is final, and there then can be no doubt that original federal jurisdiction over the remaining parties exists.[35]

Special removal problems arise when claims that normally would be removable under the principles just outlined are joined with claims that are nonremovable.[36] In 1866, a statute was enacted providing that where "a separable controversy between citizens of different states" existed within a larger lawsuit, that controversy could be removed, leaving the rest of the case in the state court in which it originally had been brought.[37] The statute was amended in 1875 to allow the defendant in such a controversy to remove the entire lawsuit.[38] The "separable controversy" standard endured until 1948,[39] when it was replaced by Section 1441(c) of Title 28 of the United States Code. The current statute allows removal of the entire action "whenever a separate and independent [nondiversity] claim or cause of action * * *, is joined with one or more otherwise non-removable claims or causes of action * * *." The court is given discretion to take the entire case or to remand "all matters in which State law predominates."

There are two policy justifications for the discretion Section 1441(c) gives a district court to retain the otherwise nonremovable claims. First, when the otherwise nonremovable claims have a substantial factual or evidentiary overlap with the removable claims, retention and adjudica-

---

32. Strawbridge v. Curtiss, 7 U.S. (3 Cranch) 267, 2 L.Ed. 435 (1806). See also the discussion in § 2.6, above.

33. Powers v. Chesapeake & Ohio Ry. Co., 169 U.S. 92, 18 S.Ct. 264, 42 L.Ed. 673 (1898). This situation is now explicitly provided for in 28 U.S.C.A. § 1446(b).

34. Southern Ry. Co. v. Lloyd, 239 U.S. 496, 36 S.Ct. 210, 60 L.Ed. 402 (1916).

35. Weems v. Louis Dreyfus Corp., 380 F.2d 545 (5th Cir.1967).

36. One question that arises is whether a defendant can remove on the basis of a counterclaim, cross-claim, or third-party claim. The application of the well-pleaded complaint rule precludes removal in the first two situations because the suit is not one that could have been brought in federal court. However, when jurisdiction appears

on the basis of the defendant's well-pleaded third-party complaint, then removal may be proper if the standards of 28 U.S.C.A. § 1441(c) are satisfied. See, e.g., Carl Heck Engineers, Inc. v. Lafourche Parish Police Jury, 622 F.2d 133 (5th Cir.1980); Industrial Lithographic Co. v. Mendelsohn, 119 F.Supp. 284 (D.N.J.1954).

37. Act of July 27, 1866, 14 Stat. 306.

38. Act of March 3, 1875, 18 Stat. 470, as construed by the Supreme Court in Barney v. Latham, 103 U.S. (13 Otto) 205, 26 L.Ed. 514 (1881).

39. For a discussion of the "separable controversy" standard, see Holms, The Separable Controversy—A Federal Removal Concept, 12 Miss.L.J. 163 (1939); Keefe & Lacey, The Separable Controversy—A Federal Concept, 33 Cornell L.Q. 261 (1947).

tion of them by the district court promotes judicial economy by avoiding wasteful parallel state litigation. Second, and perhaps more important, is the consideration that defendants would be forced to defend two separate actions if the district court could not retain the entire lawsuit. Under those circumstances, defendants might be deterred from exercising their removal right and the federal interest in providing an opportunity to litigate in a federal forum would be thwarted.

The principal problem in applying Section 1441(c) has been determining whether a claim or cause of action is "separate and independent," and therefore removable. The leading case on this question is American Fire & Casualty Company v. Finn.[40] Finn, a Texan, sued two foreign insurance companies and their local agent, also a Texan, in a Texas state court. The complaint contained alternative claims for recovery for a fire loss suffered by the plaintiff, alleging that one or the other insurer had issued policies or that the local agent was liable for having failed to keep the plaintiff's property insured. The foreign insurers removed the case to federal court, relying on Section 1441(c). After a jury trial resulting in a judgment against one of the insurers, that company sought to vacate the judgment on the ground that the action had been removed improvidently and that the federal court lacked jurisdiction. The Supreme Court agreed with the contention. In the Court's view, the language of the statute was more restrictive than that of its predecessors. In particular "the addition of the word 'independent' gives emphasis to congressional intention to require more complete disassociation between the federally cognizable proceedings and those cognizable only in state courts before allowing removal."[41]

After an attempt to define the elusive concept of "cause of action," the Court held that "where there is a single wrong to plaintiff, for which relief is sought, arising from an interlocked series of transactions, there is no separate and independent claim or cause of action under § 1441(c)."[42] Applying this criterion to the facts of the case, the Court found that there was but a single wrong in the failure to pay the plaintiff, with only the question of liability uncertain as among the three defendants. Therefore, removal jurisdiction had been assumed improperly by the district court.

The major impact of the Finn construction of "separate and independent" was to limit removal in multi-party diversity cases,[43] which theoretically were removable under the language of the statute at that time. In 1990, Congress specifically amended Section 1441(c) to elimi-

40. 341 U.S. 6, 71 S.Ct. 534, 95 L.Ed. 702 (1951).

41. 341 U.S. at 12, 71 S.Ct. at 539.

42. 341 U.S. at 14, 71 S.Ct. at 540.

43. E.g., Clarence E. Morris, Inc. v. Vitek, 412 F.2d 1174, 1176 (9th Cir.1969) ("Claims are not separate and independent * * * if multiple claims grow out of a single actionable wrong."); Anderson v. Union Pac. Coal Co., 332 F.Supp. 605 (D.Wyo. 1971) (action by 54 ex-supervisory employees, four of whom were citizens of the same state as defendant, to enforce an oral pension agreement); South Carolina Elec. & Gas Co. v. Aetna Ins. Co., 114 F.Supp. 79 (E.D.S.C.1953) (action against 38 insurers for a single loss on 38 separate policies providing for pro rata liability).

nate diversity cases from its scope, thereby limiting removal based on a separate and independent claim to actions asserting federal question claims.[44] In those actions, removal may be appropriate under Section 1441(c) when a federal question claim is joined with a separate state claim. This situation may arise in cases between a single plaintiff and a single defendant, so that the multi-party problems seen in Finn are not present. Nonetheless, the application of Section 1441(c) in this context presents other questions. One is the relation between "separate and independent" claims that are removable and claims that are sufficiently connected to removable claims to satisfy the test for supplemental jurisdiction.[45]

Two possibilities suggest themselves. If the federal and state claims are separate and independent, the case is removable under Section 1441(c); and if they are not separate and independent, the case is removable under Section 1441(b) with the state claim being heard under federal supplemental jurisdiction. But this may be too facile an approach. Perhaps there are claims that are too closely related to be removed under Section 1441(c), yet not sufficiently related to qualify as supplemental claims. The cases are silent on this possibility. There is another, actively debated, constitutional question: if the federal cases defining supplemental jurisdiction reflect the constitutional limits of federal subject-matter jurisdiction, then Section 1441(c) may be unconstitutional if it permits the removal of claims that bear no relation to any federal question and that are between nondiverse defendants.[46]

The procedure followed by a defendant who wishes to remove a state action is dictated by Section 1446 of the removal statute.[47] The basic steps are as follows. The removing defendant files a notice of removal (usually within 30 days after receiving the complaint) with the federal district court for the district or division in which the action is pending, setting out the facts that justify removal. Until recently, the defendant posted a bond when filing the notice of removal to protect the plaintiff against a wrongful removal. The bond covered the plaintiff's costs and disbursements in contesting the wrongful removal. In 1988, Congress abolished the requirement after deciding that the combination of Section 1447(c), which grants the district court ordering remand the discretion to award costs and fees, and the sanction provisions in Rule 11 rendered the bond requirement superfluous. Defendants also must give written

44. Dec. 1, 1990, Pub.L. 101–650, § 312, 104 Stat. 5089.

45. For a discussion of supplemental jurisdiction and the concept of pendent claims, see § 2.13, below.

46. Compare Lewin, The Federal Courts' Hospitable Back Door—Removal of "Separate and Independent" Non–Federal Causes of Action, 66 Harv.L.Rev. 423 (1953) (Section 1441(c) is unconstitutional), with Moore & VanDercreek, Multi-party, Multi-claim Removal Problems: The Separate and Independent Claim under Section 1441(c), 46 Iowa L.Rev. 489 (1961) (Section 1441(c)

is constitutional). See also Cohen, Problems in the Removal of a "Separate and Independent Claim or Cause of Action," 46 Minn. L.Rev. 1 (1961) (the statute is constitutional but of only marginal utility); Steinman, Removal, Remand, and Review in Pendent Claim and Pendent Party Cases, 41 Vand. L.Rev. 923 (1988).

47. See 14C C. Wright, A. Miller & E. Cooper, Jurisdiction and Related Matters 3d §§ 3730–37, for a more detailed discussion of removal procedure.

notice of removal to the plaintiff and file a copy of the notice with the state court. Once the papers have been filed, specific language in Section 1446 prohibits the state court from proceeding further with the case, unless and until it is remanded. As long as the case has not been remanded, any subsequent state action is void, even if the case was removed improperly.

A plaintiff who wishes to challenge the defendant's removal of an action does so by filing a motion to remand in the federal court to which the action has been removed.[48] Despite the fact that it is the plaintiff who is the aggressor on the remand motion, the burden of showing the necessary facts supporting removal jurisdiction rests on the defendant, in line with the general presumption against the existence of federal subject-matter jurisdiction.[49] If jurisdiction is at all doubtful, the action must be remanded to the state court from which it was removed.[50] The federal court also will remand on its own initiative if, at any time prior to the final judgment, it appears that the case was removed improperly.[51] Appellate review of orders remanding removed actions to state courts, as well as those denying motions to remand, generally is not available.[52]

Finally, the defendant may waive the right to remove by taking some substantial defensive action in the state court before petitioning for removal,[53] such as by filing a counterclaim or engaging in discovery. Similarly, a plaintiff may waive the right to object to removal. For example, once the removed case proceeds to the merits, a plaintiff who fails to make a timely objection to defects in the removal procedure or the propriety of removal waives any objection to removal she might have asserted.[54] Of course, defects in the removal court's subject-matter jurisdiction are not waivable and may be raised at any time.

§ 2.12 Supplemental Jurisdiction—History

In contrast to state courts, which are forums of general jurisdiction, federal courts possess limited jurisdiction and are authorized to adjudi-

48. 28 U.S.C.A. § 1447(c). See Meredith v. Van Oosterhout, 286 F.2d 216 (8th Cir.1960), cert. denied 365 U.S. 835. For a further discussion of the remand procedure, see 14C C. Wright, A. Miller & E. Cooper, Jurisdiction and Related Matters 3d § 3739.

49. R. G. Barry Corp. v. Mushroom Makers, Inc., 612 F.2d 651 (2d Cir.1979); Jerro v. Home Lines, Inc., 377 F.Supp. 670 (S.D.N.Y.1974); Lassiter v. State Farm Mut. Auto. Ins. Co., 371 F.Supp. 1221 (E.D.Ark. 1974).

50. Williams v. Tri–County Community Center, 323 F.Supp. 286 (S.D.Miss.1971), affirmed 452 F.2d 221 (5th Cir.1971); Pabst v. Roxana Petroleum Co., 30 F.2d 953 (S.D.Tex.1929). If remand is ordered, the federal court may assess "just costs" against the removing parties; this award is enforceable against the bond filed with the removal petition. 28 U.S.C.A. § 1447(c).

51. In re MacNeil Bros. Co., 259 F.2d 386 (1st Cir.1958); Pettit v. Arkansas Louisiana Gas Co., 377 F.Supp. 108 (E.D.Okl. 1974).

52. Things Remembered, Inc. v. Petrarca, 516 U.S. 124, 116 S.Ct. 494, 133 L.Ed.2d 461 (1995).

53. Texas Wool & Mohair Marketing Ass'n v. Standard Acc. Ins. Co., 175 F.2d 835 (5th Cir.1949); Briggs v. Miami Window Corp., 158 F.Supp. 229 (M.D.Ga.1956). Waiver will not occur if the defendant's participation has not been substantial. See Hildreth v. General Instrument, Inc., 258 F.Supp. 29 (D.S.C.1966).

54. Grubbs v. General Elec. Credit Corp., 405 U.S. 699, 92 S.Ct. 1344, 31 L.Ed.2d 612 (1972); McLeod v. Cities Service Gas Co., 233 F.2d 242 (10th Cir.1956).

cate only those cases enumerated by Article III of the Constitution[1] and only to the extent authorized by Congress.[2] However, in many cases properly before a federal court, closely related claims or issues may exist that, by themselves, are jurisdictionally insufficient and could not be entertained by the federal court. Since the earliest days of the federal courts, judges have managed to accommodate this need to adjudicate matters technically not within their subject-matter jurisdiction. Eventually, two forms of federal jurisdiction, known as ancillary jurisdiction and pendent jurisdiction, were developed by the federal courts in order to address the need to decide certain nonfederal matters as part of the courts' obligation to discharge effectively their duties under constitutional and statutory grants of judicial power.[3] Over the years, these two doctrines have expanded the otherwise limited nature of federal court subject-matter jurisdiction and have provided a means to adjudicate an entire case or controversy in a manner that was both fair to the litigants and efficient in the use of judicial resources. Piecemeal litigation among federal and state courts thereby could be avoided.

An appreciation of the judicially created doctrines of ancillary and pendent jurisdiction is necessary to understand their successor—statutory supplemental jurisdiction. Although the resemblance between ancillary and pendent jurisdiction often has been noted,[4] the "separate and dissimilar development of the two doctrines * * * induced most federal courts to distinguish between them."[5] This section also treats them as two discrete concepts.

In its original form, the concept of ancillary jurisdiction was much narrower than it eventually came to be in that it was limited to situations in which its invocation was virtually a matter of necessity. This is illustrated by the early case of Freeman v. Howe.[6] Freeman, a United States marshal, had filed a federal diversity action and had seized

---

§ 2.12

1. U.S. Const. Art. III, § 2 provides that: "The judicial power shall extend to all Cases, in Law and Equity, arising under the Laws of the United States, and Treaties made, or which shall be made, under their Authority;—to all cases affecting ambassadors, other public Ministers and Consuls;—to all Cases of admiralty and maritime Jurisdiction;—to Controversies to which the United States shall be a Party;—to Controversies between two or more states;—between a State and Citizens of another State;—between citizens of different states;—between Citizens of the same State claiming Lands under the Grants of different States, and between a State, or the Citizens thereof, and foreign States, Citizens or Subjects."

2. U.S. Const. Art. I, § 8, cl. 9 ("The Congress shall have Power * * * To constitute Tribunals inferior to the supreme Court"), and Art. III, § 1 ("The judicial

Power of the United States, shall be vested in one supreme Court, and in such inferior Courts as the Congress may from time to time ordain and establish.").

3. For other discussions of ancillary jurisdiction, see 13 C. Wright, A. Miller & E. Cooper, Jurisdiction and Related Matters 2d § 3523; Note, Ancillary Jurisdiction of the Federal Courts, 48 Iowa L.Rev. 383 (1963).

4. For a provocative discussion of the interrelation between ancillary and pendent jurisdiction, see Comment, Pendent and Ancillary Jurisdiction: Towards a Synthesis of Two Doctrines, 22 U.C.L.A. L.Rev. 1263 (1975).

5. See Mouchawar, The Congressional Resurrection of Supplemental Jurisdiction in the Post–Finley Era, 42 Hast.L.J. 1611 (1991).

6. 65 U.S. (24 How.) 450, 16 L.Ed. 749 (1860).

certain railroad cars under writs of attachment issued by the federal court. Subsequently, the railroad's mortgagees, who were citizens of the same state as Freeman, successfully brought a replevin action against him in state court. On review of the state court decision, the Supreme Court held that the state court had no power to interfere with property under the control of a federal court. However, if the state court was powerless to grant the relief sought by the mortgagees, and if they were unable to invoke federal diversity jurisdiction, the mortgagees would be without a forum in which to press their claims to the railroad cars. Therefore, the Court held that the mortgagees could assert their claim in federal court. According to the Court, the claim of the mortgagees was "not an original suit, but ancillary and dependent, supplementary merely to the original suit out of which it had arisen * * *."[7] Under this conception, then, a controversy was not ancillary unless it had a "direct relation to property or assets actually or constructively drawn into the court's possession or control by the principal suit."[8]

In 1926, the scope of ancillary jurisdiction was broadened significantly by Moore v. New York Cotton Exchange[9] in which the Supreme Court held that although the defendant's compulsory counterclaim did not involve a federal question and there was no diversity of citizenship jurisdiction, it nevertheless fell under ancillary jurisdiction because of its intimate connection with the facts comprising the basis of the plaintiff's federal law claim.[10]

The most significant expansion of ancillary jurisdiction, however, occurred in the wake of the 1938 adoption of the Federal Rules of Civil Procedure. Although Federal Rule 82 clearly states that the rules "shall not be construed to extend or limit the jurisdiction of the United States district courts * * *," one of the effects of the rules was to increase the dimensions of the litigation unit through liberal provisions for the joinder of claims and parties. As a result, the dimension of individual federal actions was broadened through the availability of those flexible devices, creating a fertile field for the increased application of ancillary jurisdiction. Indeed, in many contexts the joinder rules would have lost much of their practical utility if ancillary jurisdiction could not have been used as a supplement to the federal subject-matter jurisdiction ground over the original suit, in order to permit the court to adjudicate related claims that often involved additional parties.[11] Thus, ancillary jurisdiction enabled federal courts to resolve claims for which no inde-

---

7. 65 U.S. (24 How.) at 460.

8. Fulton Nat. Bank of Atlanta v. Hozier, 267 U.S. 276, 280, 45 S.Ct. 261, 262, 69 L.Ed. 609 (1925).

9. 270 U.S. 593, 46 S.Ct. 367, 70 L.Ed. 750 (1926).

10. "So close is the connection between the case sought to be stated in the bill and that set up in the counterclaim that it only needs the failure of the former to establish a foundation for the latter * * *." 270 U.S. at 610, 46 S.Ct. at 371. The "mir-ror image" test that this quotation suggests also is used in Great Lakes Rubber Corp. v. Herbert Cooper Co., 286 F.2d 631 (3d Cir. 1961).

11. Judge Charles E. Clark, the chief architect of the Federal Rules, defended the position that the proper invocation of ancillary jurisdiction to effectuate the Rules does not illegitimately extend federal jurisdiction, in Lesnik v. Public Industrials Corp., 144 F.2d 968 (2d Cir.1944).

pendent basis of subject-matter jurisdiction existed; generally, this occurred in diversity of citizenship cases in which a claim was technically jurisdictionally deficient because it involved one or more nondiverse parties or less than the requisite jurisdictional amount.[12]

In deciding whether a federal court had ancillary jurisdiction over a particular claim, the first issue that the district court determined was whether that claim was "ancillary" to the claim that provided the basis for subject-matter jurisdiction. Under one formulation, a claim was ancillary when it possessed a "logical relationship to the aggregate core of operative facts which constitutes the main claim over which the court has an independent basis of federal jurisdiction."[13] Essentially, a logical relationship could be found if the claims arose from "the same aggregate of operative facts" or if "the aggregate core of facts upon which the original claim rests activates additional legal rights in a party defendant that would otherwise be dormant."[14]

An alternative verbal formulation of ancillary jurisdiction was one used in several of the Federal Rules: a claim that arises out of the same transaction or occurrence that is the subject matter of a claim already properly before the court.[15] Federal courts that adopted this transactional test held that ancillary jurisdiction was appropriate for compulsory counterclaims,[16] cross-claims,[17] additional parties to a compulsory counterclaim or cross-claim,[18] and impleader claims against third-party defendants.[19] In addition, ancillary jurisdiction was invoked in interpleader actions[20] and for intervention as of right;[21] however, it did not extend to

12. See §§ 2.5–2.6, above, on diversity jurisdiction and §§ 2.8–2.9, above, on the jurisdictional amount requirement.

13. Revere Copper & Brass Inc. v. Aetna Cas. & Sur. Co., 426 F.2d 709, 714 (5th Cir.1970).

Although most modern courts when examining whether additional claims or parties were within ancillary jurisdiction used the logical relationship terminology, the standard or objective was the same as when pendent jurisdiction was established and the courts looked to whether the claims arose out of a common nucleus of operative fact. Indeed, the Supreme Court noted this overlap in Owen Equipment & Erection Co. v. Kroger, 437 U.S. 365, 98 S.Ct. 2396, 57 L.Ed.2d 274 (1978). The Kroger case and pendent jurisdiction are discussed later in this section.

14. Revere Copper & Brass Inc. v. Aetna Cas. & Sur. Co., 426 F.2d 709, 715 (5th Cir.1970).

15. E.g., Fed.Civ.Proc.Rules 13(a), 13(g), 13(h), and 14(a).

16. Fed.Civ.Proc.Rule 13(a); U.S. for Use & Benefit of D'Agostino Excavators, Inc. v. Heyward–Robinson Co., 430 F.2d 1077 (2d Cir.1970), cert. denied 400 U.S.

1021; Berger v. Reynolds Metals Co., 39 F.R.D. 313 (E.D.Pa.1966).

17. Fed.Civ.Proc.Rule 13(g); Amco Constr. Co. v. Mississippi State Bldg. Comm'n, 602 F.2d 730 (5th Cir.1979); City of Boston v. Boston Edison Co., 260 F.2d 872, 874–75 (1st Cir.1958); Hoosier Cas. Co. v. Fox, 102 F.Supp. 214 (N.D.Iowa 1952).

18. Fed.Civ.Proc.Rule 13(h); United Artists Corp. v. Masterpiece Productions, Inc., 221 F.2d 213 (2d Cir.1955) (compulsory counterclaim); Watson v. Apex Ry. Products Co., 56 F.R.D. 1 (N.D.Ga.1972) (cross-claim).

19. Fed.Civ.Proc.Rule 14(a); Pennsylvania R.R. Co. v. Erie Ave. Warehouse Co., 302 F.2d 843, 845 (3d Cir.1962); Dery v. Wyer, 265 F.2d 804 (2d Cir.1959).

20. Fed.Civ.Proc.Rule 22; Walmac Co. v. Isaacs, 220 F.2d 108 (1st Cir.1955).

21. Fed.Civ.Proc.Rule 24(a); Lenz v. Wagner, 240 F.2d 666 (5th Cir.1957). Subsequent to the enactment of 28 U.S.C.A. § 1367, intervenors as of right require an independent basis of jurisdiction. See the discussion of Section 1367 in § 2.13, below.

permissive intervention under Federal Rule 24(b),[22] to indispensable parties under Federal Rule 19,[23] to parties joined under Rule 20,[24] or to permissive counterclaims[25] unless the counterclaim took the form of a purely defensive set-off, in which case a form of ancillary jurisdiction was available.[26]

Although a federal court typically did assert jurisdiction over any claim it found to be ancillary, this was not a mandatory obligation.[27] The exercise of ancillary jurisdiction was discretionary, and the court, when deciding whether to assert it, generally considered whether doing so would foster judicial economy or would unduly complicate or change the shape of the jurisdictionally sufficient litigation that originally was instituted. A good example of how policy concerns, as well as constitutional and statutory limitations, affected the decision whether to allow ancillary jurisdiction can be found in the treatment of claims between third-party defendants and the original plaintiff under Federal Rule 14.

In 1978, the Supreme Court ruled in Owen Equipment & Erection Company v. Kroger[28] that a claim asserted by the original plaintiff against a third-party defendant had to be supported by independent grounds of jurisdiction, even if that claim was transactionally related as required by Federal Rule 14. The Court noted that to allow ancillary jurisdiction would be inconsistent with the principle of complete diversity because the result would be to permit a plaintiff who could not have joined the third-party defendant as an original codefendant without destroying diversity, to achieve that same objective through indirect means. Ironically, a number of lower courts held that a third-party defendant's transactionally related claim against the original plaintiff (a situation roughly the converse of that in Kroger) was within the ancil-

---

22. Hougen v. Merkel, 47 F.R.D. 528 (D.Minn.1969).

23. Chance v. County Bd. of School Trustees of McHenry County, Illinois, 332 F.2d 971 (7th Cir.1964).

24. The extension of jurisdiction over parties joined under Rule 20 was more properly denominated "pendent party" jurisdiction and is discussed in § 2.14, below.

25. For more detailed discussions of ancillary jurisdiction and the Federal Rules, see Fraser, Ancillary Jurisdiction and the Joinder of Claims in the Federal Courts, 33 F.R.D. 27 (1964); Goldberg, Influence of Procedural Rules on Federal Jurisdiction, 28 Stan.L.Rev. 395 (1976); Note, The Ancillary Concept and the Federal Rules, 64 Harv.L.Rev. 968 (1951); Developments in the Law—Multiparty Litigation in the Federal Courts, 71 Harv.L.Rev. 874 (1958); Note, Ancillary Jurisdiction of the Federal Courts, 48 Iowa L.Rev. 383 (1963); Note, Rule 14 Claims and Ancillary Jurisdiction, 57 Va.L.Rev. 265 (1971).

26. Fraser v. Astra S.S. Corp., 18 F.R.D. 240 (S.D.N.Y.1955). The set-off exception existed largely for historical reasons and applied only to liquidated claims arising out of a contract or a judgment. Marks v. Spitz, 4 F.R.D. 348 (D.Mass.1945).

27. In some cases the courts simply would state that they would not exercise their discretion. In others, the definition of what constituted a "transaction" would be the means by which jurisdiction was limited. For example, compare the district court opinion in LASA Per L'Industria Del Marmo Societa Per Azioni of Lasa, Italy v. Southern Builders, Inc., of Tennessee, 45 F.R.D. 435 (W.D.Tenn.1967), which defined transaction narrowly as the specific contract between the plaintiff and defendants, with the Sixth Circuit opinion reversing it and defining the transaction as all disputes arising out of the construction project involved, 414 F.2d 143 (6th Cir.1969).

28. 437 U.S. 365, 98 S.Ct. 2396, 57 L.Ed.2d 274 (1978). See § 2.13, below.

lary jurisdiction of the court.[29] Although some cases reached the opposite conclusion and rejected jurisdiction,[30] those decisions were not premised on constitutional or statutory grounds. Instead, the courts in those cases typically concluded that the additional claim would have further complicated the litigation and distorted the plaintiff's original design. Thus, the decisions were based on the premise that the exercise of jurisdiction over the additional claim by the third-party defendant was discretionary so that the court could decide that it should not be tried together with the original claim.

Finally, it should be mentioned that when a federal court had ancillary jurisdiction over a claim or party, the normal venue requirements did not have to be satisfied. On the other hand, the fact that ancillary subject-matter jurisdiction had attached to a claim against an additional party, such as a third-party defendant, did not obviate the need for the court to acquire personal jurisdiction over him under the usual rules governing amenability and service of process.[31]

Turning to pendent jurisdiction, the original concept was developed by Chief Justice Marshall in Osborn v. Bank of United States:[32]

> [W]hen a question to which the judicial power of the Union is extended by the constitution, forms an ingredient of the original cause, it is in the power of Congress to give the Circuit Courts jurisdiction of that cause, although other questions of law or fact may be involved in it.[33]

This statement represented a judicial recognition of the fundamental principle that a federal court of original jurisdiction cannot function effectively unless it has the power to decide all the questions that a case presents to the court. Further development occurred in Siler v. Louisville & Nashville Railroad Company,[34] in which the Supreme Court held that a federal court need not reach a determination of the federal question claim, from which the court's jurisdiction originally derived, but instead could resolve the dispute based entirely on the pendent state law claim. This rule was unlike the Osborn principle in that it was not necessary for the effective functioning of the federal courts. Nevertheless, it was useful because it avoided the decision of constitutional questions when possible[35] and allowed for the resolution of the entire controversy in one lawsuit.

29. Evra Corp. v. Swiss Bank Corp., 673 F.2d 951 (7th Cir.1982), cert. denied 459 U.S. 1017; Revere Copper & Brass Inc. v. Aetna Cas. & Sur. Co., 426 F.2d 709 (5th Cir.1970); Finkel v. U.S., 385 F.Supp. 333 (S.D.N.Y.1974); Union Bank & Trust Co. v. St. Paul Fire & Marine Ins. Co., 38 F.R.D. 486 (D.Neb.1965); Heintz & Co. v. Provident Tradesmens Bank & Trust Co., 30 F.R.D. 171 (E.D.Pa.1962).

30. James King & Son, Inc. v. Indemnity Ins. Co. of North America, 178 F.Supp. 146, 148 (S.D.N.Y.1959).

31. See, e.g., James Talcott, Inc. v. Allahabad Bank, Ltd., 444 F.2d 451, 464 n. 11 (5th Cir.1971), cert. denied 404 U.S. 940; Doebler v. Stadium Productions Ltd., 91 F.R.D. 211 (W.D.Mich.1981); U.S. v. Rhoades, 14 F.R.D. 373 (D.Colo.1953).

32. 22 U.S. (9 Wheat.) 738, 6 L.Ed. 204 (1824).

33. 22 U.S. (9 Wheat.) at 823.

34. 213 U.S. 175, 29 S.Ct. 451, 53 L.Ed. 753 (1909).

35. This aspect of the Siler decision was given new emphasis in Hagans v. La-

As the doctrine matured, pendent jurisdiction most commonly was invoked when a plaintiff brought a federal question claim against a nondiverse defendant and sought to have a related state law claim against the same defendant adjudicated in the same action.[36] Like ancillary jurisdiction, pendent jurisdiction enabled a federal court to adjudicate a claim that was closely related to an action properly within the court's statutory jurisdiction, but that by itself would not satisfy subject-matter jurisdiction requirements. Consequently, pendent jurisdiction also advanced the objectives of judicial economy, convenience, and fairness to the litigants by the elimination of duplicative state court proceedings.

Pendent jurisdiction additionally effectuated the plaintiff's right to have her federal claim heard in a federal forum—a rationale for the doctrine usually not present in the ancillary jurisdiction context. Absent pendent jurisdiction, a plaintiff with a federal claim and a closely related state claim against the same defendant would have had three unsatisfactory options. First, plaintiff could have litigated the federal claim in federal court and the state claim in state court. In addition to the cost and inconvenience of conducting two lawsuits, this option was complicated by principles of former adjudication[37]—the issues resolved in the claim that first reached final judgment well might be treated as binding upon the parallel litigation of the other claim. Second, the plaintiff could have foregone one claim altogether and litigated the other solely in either federal or state court. If both claims were substantial, the price of this alternative would have been excessive. That especially would be true if different elements of damages were involved. However, in order to prosecute both claims without the difficulties of parallel litigation, the plaintiff probably would have pursued the third option—litigating both the state claim and the federal claim (assuming the latter is not one within exclusive federal jurisdiction)[38] in a state court, thereby depriving herself of the opportunity to have the federal claim adjudicated by a federal court—an opportunity Congress had bestowed on her.

The crucial question of what type of relationship between the jurisdictionally sufficient claim and the pendent claim was necessary to justify the assertion of jurisdiction over the latter was addressed in Hurn

vine, 415 U.S. 528, 546–47, 94 S.Ct. 1372, 1383–84, 39 L.Ed.2d 577 (1974).

36. See, e.g., Romero v. International Terminal Operating Co., 358 U.S. 354, 79 S.Ct. 468, 3 L.Ed.2d 368 (1959) (Jones Act claim under 28 U.S.C.A. § 1331 provides basis for pendent jurisdiction over maritime claim that, by itself, could be brought only on admiralty side of federal court). Romero is discussed in Kurland, The Romero case and Some Problems of Federal Jurisdiction, 73 Harv.L.Rev. 817, 833–50 (1960). Cf. Lefson v. Esperdy, 211 F.Supp. 769 (S.D.N.Y. 1962) (alien's action to review denial of application for adjustment of status, which

normally would be heard by district court, could be heard by court of appeals as pendent to the latter's review of a deportation order).

When the state law claim would be insufficient solely because it lacks the requisite amount in controversy, it can be heard by virtue of the rules of aggregation—pendent jurisdiction need not be invoked. See § 2.9, above.

37. See generally Chapter 14, below.

38. The major areas of exclusive federal jurisdiction are mentioned in § 2.3, above.

v. Oursler.[39] In that case, the Supreme Court held that if a plaintiff presented "two distinct grounds," one state and one federal, "in support of a single cause of action," the federal court had jurisdiction over the entire claim; but if the plaintiff's assertions comprised "two separate and distinct causes of action," there was jurisdiction only over the federal "cause of action."[40] This test for pendent jurisdiction was problematic due to its abstract and overly conceptualized nature. Specifically, "cause of action" is a concept notoriously difficult to define, and the distinction between parallel grounds of the same cause of action and separate causes of action is far easier to state than apply. Moreover, with the promulgation of the Federal Rules in 1938, which substituted the functional concept of "claim" for the notion of "cause of action," the Hurn test became anachronistic. The necessary reformulation occurred in the 1966 landmark case of United Mine Workers of America v. Gibbs.[41]

Gibbs sued the union in federal court, asserting both a federal claim that the union had violated the Taft–Hartley Act, and a Tennessee state law claim that the union had conspired unlawfully to interfere with his contract of employment. In holding that pendent jurisdiction over the state law claim existed, Justice Brennan, writing for the Court, discarded the Hurn analysis and substituted a two-step test. First, does the court have jurisdictional *power* to entertain the pendent claim? Second, if the court has the power, does the exercise of sound *discretion* indicate that the federal court ought to assert that jurisdiction?

As to the first question regarding the power to hear the pendent claim, the Court focused on the relationship between the federal and nonfederal claims, stating: "The state and federal claims must derive from a common nucleus of operative fact."[42] Further, the Court ruled that judicial power to hear the state claims existed if the federal issues were substantial and if "plaintiff's claims are such that he would ordinarily be expected to try them all in one judicial proceeding * * *."[43] If the federal claim was too insubstantial to be the basis for federal question jurisdiction, there could be no pendent jurisdiction over other claims.[44] But if jurisdiction existed for a substantial federal claim,[45] then claims that "derive from a common nucleus of operative fact," could be entertained if those claims typically would be tried in one judicial proceeding. The reference to how the claims ordinarily would be tried appears to require consideration of the principles of former adjudication. If adjudication of one of the claims normally would result in the application of res judicata or collateral estoppel with regard to any

---

39. 289 U.S. 238, 53 S.Ct. 586, 77 L.Ed. 1148 (1933). See generally Note, The Evolution and Scope of the Doctrine of Pendent Jurisdiction in the Federal Courts, 62 Colum.L.Rev. 1018 (1962).

40. 289 U.S. at 246, 53 S.Ct. at 589.

41. 383 U.S. 715, 86 S.Ct. 1130, 16 L.Ed.2d 218 (1966).

42. 383 U.S. at 725, 86 S.Ct. at 1138.

43. Ibid.

44. See Rivera v. Chapel, 493 F.2d 1302 (1st Cir.1974); Warrington Sewer Co. v. Tracy, 463 F.2d 771 (3d Cir.1972).

45. For a discussion of when a federal claim is considered "substantial" for jurisdictional purposes, see § 2.4 at note 16, above.

subsequent litigation of the other claim, then they are claims that ordinarily would be tried in one judicial proceeding.[46]

Once judicial power is found, the Gibbs opinion directed the trial court to a number of factors to be considered in making the discretionary decision whether to hear the pendent claim.[47] Would the interests of judicial economy, convenience, and fairness to the litigants be served by the court exercising pendent jurisdiction? Do the state issues predominate, or is the state claim so closely tied to questions of federal policy that it should be decided by a federal court? Which is stronger under the facts of the given case, the desire to avoid needless decisions of state law in the interest of federalism, or the need for a federal court to decide issues closely related to the application of federal law? Finally, would a jury be confused by combining the federal and state claims in a single trial?

Although the existence of power to hear a pendent claim ordinarily was determined on the pleadings, the question whether to exercise that power remained open throughout the litigation. If at any time it appeared unwise to resolve a pendent state claim, the court could dismiss it without prejudice and leave it to the proper state tribunal for resolution. Although language in Gibbs strongly suggested that jurisdiction over the state claim always should be refused if the federal claim was dismissed before trial,[48] many courts treated this circumstance as simply one element to be considered in making the ultimate discretionary decision.[49]

Overall, the effect of Gibbs probably was to enlarge pendent jurisdiction.[50] In part, this expansion was due to the tremendous growth in federal substantive law in the years following the decision creating new contexts in which pendency could be asserted. The flexibility of the Gibbs approach allowed the federal courts to accommodate these changes. Gibbs clearly defined the power to entertain pendent claims more broadly than did Hurn. Moreover, while Gibbs' extensive listing of discretionary reasons why the power should not be exercised in particular cases might have reduced the number of cases in which the federal courts actually would decide pendent claims, this was not the result. In general, a loose factual connection between the claims was found to satisfy the requirements that they arise from a common nucleus of

---

46. See Chapter 14, below.

47. The listing of discretionary factors is at 383 U.S. at 726–27, 86 S.Ct. at 1139–40.

48. 383 U.S. at 726, 86 S.Ct. at 1139.

49. See Brunswick v. Regent, 463 F.2d 1205 (5th Cir.1972); Springfield Television, Inc. v. Springfield, Missouri, 462 F.2d 21 (8th Cir.1972); Gray v. International Ass'n of Heat & Frost Insulators & Asbestos Workers, 447 F.2d 1118 (6th Cir.1971).

The practice of adjudicating the pendent claim even after dismissal of the federal claim was given support by the Supreme

Court's decision in Rosado v. Wyman, 397 U.S. 397, 402–05, 90 S.Ct. 1207, 1212–14, 25 L.Ed.2d 442 (1970), in which pendent jurisdiction was held to continue after the principal, constitutional claim was declared moot.

50. See Shakman, The New Pendent Jurisdiction of the Federal Courts, 20 Stan. L.Rev. 262 (1968); Note, UMW v. Gibbs and Pendent Jurisdiction, 81 Harv.L.Rev. 657 (1968). For a very expansive interpretation of Gibbs, see Baker, Toward a Relaxed View of Federal Ancillary and Pendent Jurisdiction, 33 U.Pitt.L.Rev. 759 (1972).

operative fact and that a plaintiff ordinarily would be expected to try them all in one judicial proceeding.[51] Only a few courts used their discretion to dismiss pendent claims.[52]

§ 2.13 Supplemental Jurisdiction—Joinder of Claims

Although both ancillary and pendent jurisdiction often were lauded as doctrines necessary to the objectives of judicial economy, convenience, and fairness to the litigants because they helped eliminate duplicative state court proceedings,[1] they also were criticized as representing an unwarranted expansion of federal subject-matter jurisdiction.[2] Consistent with this concern, and despite the long acceptance and judicial use of the doctrines,[3] the 1989 Supreme Court decision in Finley v. United States[4] dramatically diminished federal court access to pendent and ancillary jurisdiction.

In Finley, the plaintiff's husband and children were killed when a plane on which they were traveling struck electrical power lines during its approach to a San Diego airport. Mrs. Finley filed claims against the city and the utility company in state court, and later brought a federal court action under the Federal Tort Claims Act (FTCA) against the United States, on the basis that the Federal Aviation Administration had been negligent in failing to provide adequate runway lights. Finley subsequently attempted to append the state claims to the federal FTCA claim. As a result, the Supreme Court was compelled to determine whether a federal court possessed authority to assert jurisdiction over a nonfederal claim against a nondiverse party on the ground that the court had exclusive jurisdiction over the federal FTCA claim, which arose from the same set of facts as the state claim. The case was particularly appealing because the federal and state claims were closely related and the federal claim could not be heard in a state court.

---

51. See, e.g., Vanderboom v. Sexton, 422 F.2d 1233 (8th Cir.1970), cert. denied 400 U.S. 852 (violation of the Securities Exchange Act supplied pendent jurisdiction over a claim for common law fraud and deceit); Knuth v. Erie–Crawford Dairy Co-op. Ass'n, 395 F.2d 420 (3d Cir.1968) (claims for fraudulent conversion of money, tortious interference with business relations, and violations of state milk control statute pendent to federal claim based on Sherman Act violations); Bowman v. Hartig, 334 F.Supp. 1323 (S.D.N.Y.1971) (claims by customers against brokers for breach of contract, negligence, and breach of fiduciary duty pendent to claims under the federal securities laws).

52. See, e.g., Moor v. County of Alameda, 411 U.S. 693, 715–17, 93 S.Ct. 1785, 1799, 36 L.Ed.2d 596 (1973); Global Indus., Inc. v. Harris, 376 F.Supp. 1379, 1385–86 (N.D.Ga.1974); Hattell v. Public Serv. Co., 350 F.Supp. 240 (D.Colo.1972); Catalano v.

Department of Hosps. of City of New York, 299 F.Supp. 166, 175–76 (S.D.N.Y.1969).

§ 2.13

1. See the discussion in § 2.12, above.

2. See, e.g., Judge Lumbard's dissent in Dery v. Wyer, 265 F.2d 804, 810–11 (2d Cir.1959). As Judge Lumbard admits elsewhere in his dissent, 265 F.2d at 811 n. 2, there is a much stronger case for invoking ancillary jurisdiction over compulsory counterclaims because otherwise a party might be foreclosed from bringing those claims in another court by the doctrine of res judicata. See § 14.6, below, on res judicata.

3. See Mengler, Burbank & Rowe, Congress Accepts Supreme Court's Invitation to Codify Supplemental Jurisdiction, 74 Judicature 213 (1991).

4. 490 U.S. 545, 109 S.Ct. 2003, 104 L.Ed.2d 593 (1989).

Despite these circumstances, Justice Scalia, writing for a slender majority of the Court, determined that the concepts of ancillary and pendent jurisdiction represented an "unconstitutional usurpation of power"[5] because Congress had not explicitly authorized the assertion of subject-matter jurisdiction over the plaintiff's state law claim. The overall tone of the Finley opinion suggested that a majority of the justices were willing to diminish significantly the ability of federal courts to assert jurisdiction over pendent and ancillary claims and to reduce the availability of ancillary jurisdiction over a party;[6] the case also appeared to terminate the power of federal courts to utilize pendent party jurisdiction.[7] However, at the same time, the Supreme Court seemed to recognize the necessity for the existence of these forms of jurisdiction and appeared to invite congressional action; "Whatever we say regarding the scope of jurisdiction can of course be changed by Congress. What is of paramount importance is that Congress be able to legislate against a background of clear interpretive rules, so that it may know the effect of the language it adopts."[8]

On October 28, 1990, seventeen months after the Finley decision, Congress responded to the Court's invitation and enacted Section 1367 of Title 28 of the United States Code. The statute, which applies to all civil actions instituted after December 1, 1990,[9] primarily codified the doctrines of ancillary and pendent jurisdiction as they existed prior to Finley, and gave them the collective name "supplemental jurisdiction." Section 1367(a) provides federal courts with the power to exercise supplemental jurisdiction "over all claims that are so related to claims in the action within such original jurisdiction that they form part of the same case or controversy under Article III of the United States Constitution."[10] Consequently, Section 1367 not only embraces the prior doctrines of ancillary and pendent jurisdiction and the cases interpreting and applying them, it also eliminates the definitional and procedural

---

5. See Perdue, Finley v. United States: Unstringing Pendent Jurisdiction, 76 Va. L.Rev. 539, 567 (1990).

6. For a discussion of the effects of the Finley decision on the uses of ancillary and pendent jurisdiction, see Mouchawar, Congressional Resurrection of Supplemental Jurisdiction in the Post–Finley Era, 42 Hast.L.J. 1611 (1991).

7. See § 2.14, below.

8. 490 U.S. at 556, 109 S.Ct. at 2007.

9. The statute's application only to actions commenced after its effective date was made clear in Port Allen Marine Servs., Inc. v. Chotin, 765 F.Supp. 887, 891 (M.D.La. 1991), in which the court followed Finley's pronouncement that "pendent party jurisdiction does not exist" despite the reversal of this rule in Section 1367.

10. See, e.g., Hollman v. U.S., 783 F.Supp. 221 (M.D.Pa.1992) (federal court had supplemental jurisdiction, in a "slip and fall" victim's suit against a federal property owner, over the victim's claim against a private party who allegedly had contracted with the federal government to provide janitorial services for the building in question since the claims against the defendants formed part of the same case or controversy under 28 U.S.C.A. § 1367); Meritor Sav. Bank v. Camelback Canyon Investors, 783 F.Supp. 455 (D.Ariz.1991) (under Section 1367(a), the district court had jurisdiction to hear one defendant's cross-claim against another defendant in an action on a promissory note, even though there was no diversity jurisdiction over the cross-claim); Operative Plasterers & Cement Masons Int'l Ass'n of U.S. & Canada, AFL–CIO v. Benjamin, 776 F.Supp. 1360 (N.D.Ind.1991) (district court that had jurisdiction over the union's suit against its officers under federal labor law could exercise supplemental jurisdiction over the union's state law claims for damages).

distinctions between them[11] by providing a uniform standard by which a federal court may determine its authority to hear a nonfederal claim attached to a federal claim. Although the statute is silent as to what comprises the constitutional limits of the power of the federal courts, it commonly is understood that Section 1367(a) incorporates the constitutional analysis of United Mine Workers of America v. Gibbs.[12]

Despite the broad scope of supplemental jurisdiction provided by Section 1367(a),[13] subdivision (b) of the statute restricts its use in diversity of citizenship cases by codifying the result reached in Owen Equipment & Erection Company v. Kroger and the broader principle underlying it.[14] In particular, claims asserted by an original plaintiff against a third-party defendant must have independent grounds of jurisdiction, even if those claims are transactionally related, as required by the Federal Rule. Congress thus agreed with the Supreme Court that to permit supplemental jurisdiction under these circumstances would be inconsistent with the requirement of complete diversity because the result would be to permit a plaintiff, who could not have joined the third-party defendant as an original codefendant without destroying diversity of citizenship, simply to circumvent the requirement and achieve the same result through indirect means. Under the language of Section 1367(b), supplemental jurisdiction is not permitted over claims by plaintiffs against any individual made a party to the action through the use of any of the joinder devices of Federal Rule 14 (impleader), Federal Rule 19 (compulsory joinder), Federal Rule 20 (permissive joinder), or Federal Rule 24 (intervention) if doing so would be incompatible with the requirement of complete diversity of citizenship.

As discussed in the previous section, a federal court had discretion to accept or reject an assertion of ancillary or pendent jurisdiction. Section 1367(c) preserves that practice by listing a number of considerations federal courts should evaluate in deciding whether to exercise supplemental jurisdiction. This subsection effectively codifies the factors delineated in the Gibbs case, which provided guidance to federal courts in making the determination of whether to assert or to refuse jurisdiction over a pendent claim. Section 1367(c) specifies that the court may decline to exercise supplemental jurisdiction over a claim if it raises "a novel or complex issue of state law;" "the claim substantially predomi-

---

11. But see Stevedoring Servs. of America, Inc. v. Eggert, 953 F.2d 552 (9th Cir.1992), cert. denied 505 U.S. 1230 and Harris v. Blue Cross/Blue Shield of Alabama, Inc., 951 F.2d 325 (11th Cir.1992) (citing United Mine Workers of America v. Gibbs), in which both courts analyzed the appropriate usage of pendent claim jurisdiction, rather than supplemental jurisdiction.

12. See, e.g., Urban v. King, 783 F.Supp. 560 (D.Kan.1992), in which supplemental jurisdiction properly was exercised over state claims that were asserted against the defendants because the nature of the plaintiffs' injuries was such that the plaintiffs ordinarily would be expected to try all their claims together.

13. See, e.g., Jones v. Villa Park, 784 F.Supp. 533 (N.D.Ill.1992), which held that the district court could exercise jurisdiction over the state claims against the village even though the only federal claim against the village was dismissed, when the state claims were substantially related to the pending claim against the village police officers.

14. See § 2.12, above.

nates over the claim or claims over which the district court has original jurisdiction;" "the district court has dismissed all claims over which it has original jurisdiction;"[15] or if "in exceptional circumstances, there are other compelling reasons for declining jurisdiction."[16] In the event that a federal court refuses to assert supplemental jurisdiction and decides to dismiss the jurisdictionally insufficient state claim, Section 1367 also includes a tolling provision to preserve a litigant's right to seek relief in a state forum.

It should be noted that Section 1367 has been the subject of some criticism on the ground that it is poorly drafted, unduly confusing, and restrictive.[17] Whether these negative appraisals will prove valid remains to be seen since the statute has been in effect only a few years and time is needed to build up a body of judicial precedent. What is clear is that the legislation was necessary following the decision in Finley and it does permit the exercise of a type of subject-matter jurisdiction essential to the effective and efficient functioning of the federal courts.[18]

§ 2.14 Supplemental Jurisdiction—Joinder of Parties

Throughout most of its history, pendent jurisdiction was confined to the addition of jurisdictionally insufficient claims brought by one plaintiff against the same defendant.[1] In later years, however, a number of lower federal courts expanded its scope to permit the addition of parties with respect to whom federal subject-matter jurisdiction otherwise would not have existed.[2] This notion of pendent party jurisdiction was applied in at least three different contexts.[3]

In the first situation, some courts held that if diversity of citizenship existed and one claim exceeded the requisite amount in controversy, the

---

15. See, e.g., Manela v. Gottlieb, 784 F.Supp. 84 (S.D.N.Y.1992) (court declined to exercise jurisdiction over remaining state law claims after the dismissal of federal claims when there was no complete diversity of citizenship and the court's original jurisdiction was based solely on the federal law claims); Imperiale v. Hahnemann Univ., 776 F.Supp. 189 (E.D.Pa.1991), affirmed 966 F.2d 125 (3d Cir.1992) (court declined to retain supplemental jurisdiction over state law claims following denial of liability on sole federal claim presented since litigation of state claims was still in the relatively early stage and neither party would be prejudiced by returning to state court).

16. See also American Pfauter, Ltd. v. Freeman Decorating Co., 772 F.Supp. 1071, 1073 (N.D.Ill.1991).

17. See Freer, Compounding Confusion and Hampering Diversity: Life after Finley and the Supplemental Jurisdiction Statute, 40 Emory L.J. 445 (1991).

18. See, e.g., Mengler, Burbank & Rowe, Congress Accepts Supreme Court's Invitation to Codify Supplemental Jurisdiction, 74 Judicature 213 (1991).

§ 2.14

1. See § 2.12, above.

2. The impetus for this expansion was provided in dictum in United Mine Workers v. Gibbs, 383 U.S. 715, 724, 86 S.Ct. 1130, 1138, 16 L.Ed.2d 218 (1966): "Under the [Federal] Rules, the impulse is toward entertaining the broadest possible scope of action consistent with fairness to the parties; joinder of claims, parties and remedies is strongly encouraged."

3. See 13B C. Wright, A. Miller & E. Cooper, Jurisdiction and Related Matters 2d § 3567; Note, Federal Pendent Party Jurisdiction and United Mine Workers v. Gibbs—Federal Question and Diversity Cases, 62 Va.L.Rev. 194 (1976).

See also Steinman, Crosscurrents: Supplemental Jurisdiction, Removal, and the ALI Revision Project, 74 Ind.L.J. 75 (1998).

court also could hear another claim for or against another party that was for less than the required amount.[4] Although the only impediment to the joinder of the additional plaintiff or defendant under these circumstances was the purely statutory requirement of amount in controversy,[5] the Supreme Court's decision in Zahn v. International Paper Company[6] cast grave doubts on the propriety of this use of party pendency.

Pendent party jurisdiction also was invoked to allow a plaintiff with a federal question claim against one defendant to bring a closely related state claim against another defendant without regard to the citizenship of the added parties or the amount involved in the pendent claim. This situation arguably represented the most justifiable application of pendent party jurisdiction.[7] However, the Supreme Court's decision in Aldinger v. Howard[8] exposed the validity of this assertion of pendent jurisdiction to serious doubts.

The plaintiff in Aldinger had brought a federal civil rights action against county officials and then sought to append closely related state claims against the county itself, a nondiverse defendant over whom an independent basis of jurisdiction did not exist. In affirming the refusal of the lower court to assert pendent jurisdiction over the state claims, the Supreme Court distinguished United Mine Workers of America v. Gibbs[9] as a case in which the pendent claim was asserted against a party "already present in federal court by virtue of a case over which the court has jurisdiction."[10] According to the Court, the proposed extension of federal jurisdiction to pendent parties involved serious constitutional difficulties: "[T]he addition of a completely new party would run counter to the well-established principle that federal courts, as opposed to state trial courts of general jurisdiction, are courts of limited jurisdiction marked out by congress."[11]

The Aldinger decision did not renounce pendent party jurisdiction categorically. The opinion specifically recognized that: "Other statutory grants and other alignments of parties and claims might call for a

---

4. F.C. Stiles Contracting Co. v. Home Ins. Co., 431 F.2d 917 (6th Cir.1970); Hatridge v. Aetna Cas. & Sur. Co., 415 F.2d 809 (8th Cir.1969); Stone v. Stone, 405 F.2d 94 (4th Cir.1968); Jacobson v. Atlantic City Hosp., 392 F.2d 149 (3d Cir.1968).

5. See §§ 2.8–2.9, above.

6. 414 U.S. 291, 94 S.Ct. 505, 38 L.Ed.2d 511 (1973). The Zahn case is discussed in § 16.4, below. For the effect of Zahn upon pendent party jurisdiction, see United Pacific/Reliance Ins. Cos. v. City of Lewiston, 372 F.Supp. 700 (D.Idaho 1974); Bratton, Pendent Jurisdiction in Diversity Cases—Some Doubts, 11 San Diego L.Rev. 296, 322–23 (1974); Note, Federal Pendent Party Jurisdiction and United Mine Workers v. Gibbs—Federal Question and Diversity Cases, 62 Va.L.Rev. 194, 231–36. (1976).

7. See Fortune, Pendent Jurisdiction— The Problem of "Pendenting Parties," 34 U.Pitt.L.Rev. 1 (1972). See also Note, Federal Pendent Subject Matter Jurisdiction— The Doctrine of United Mine Workers v. Gibbs Extended to Persons Not Party to the Jurisdiction–Conferring Claim, 73 Colum.L.Rev. 153 (1973). But see Comment, The Extension of Pendent Jurisdiction to Parties Not in the Jurisdiction–Conferring Suit, 20 Loy.L.Rev. 176 (1974).

8. 427 U.S. 1, 96 S.Ct. 2413, 49 L.Ed.2d 276 (1976).

9. For a more complete discussion of the Gibbs case, see § 2.12, above.

10. 427 U.S. at 14, 96 S.Ct. at 2420.

11. 427 U.S. at 15, 96 S.Ct. at 2420.

different result."[12] As an example, the Court noted that if the federal claim were within the exclusive jurisdiction of the federal courts, then "the argument of judicial economy and convenience can be coupled with the additional argument that only in a federal court may all of the claims be tried together."[13] In Aldinger, however, the federal and state courts had concurrent jurisdiction over the federal claim; consequently, the Court determined that the objective of avoiding piecemeal litigation could be achieved by bringing both claims together in a state forum. But the validity of any use of party pendency seemingly was required to be tested against the Court's final caveat: jurisdiction must be permissible under Article III of the Constitution and must not be negated expressly or impliedly by the jurisdictional statutes.

The application of the Aldinger standard for pendent party jurisdiction soon was tested in the context of a diversity action in which a nondiverse third-party defendant was brought into the suit[14] and the original plaintiff then attempted to assert a claim directly against it. This was the third situation in which pendent party jurisdiction was applied. In Owen Equipment & Erection Company v. Kroger,[15] discussed previously, the Supreme Court ruled that jurisdiction[16] could not be asserted over a plaintiff's claim against a third-party defendant even though the claim arose out of the same transaction as the main action, which met diversity of citizenship requirements. Thus, the Court ended the debate among the lower courts, which previously had divided on the propriety of this form of jurisdiction,[17] by finding that it violated the requirement of complete diversity. Furthermore, it distinguished and left unimpaired those cases upholding ancillary jurisdiction over impleader claims, cross-claims, and counterclaims.[18]

Although both Aldinger and Kroger made clear that the availability of pendent party jurisdiction was extremely limited, exactly how great a restriction the Supreme Court meant to impose remained somewhat unclear. The issue was not definitively resolved until the case of Finley v. United States[19] in which the plaintiff asserted a federal claim, over which the federal courts had exclusive jurisdiction, and then later sought to append related state claims against nondiverse defendants. The Court effectively rejected the Aldinger conclusion that pendent party jurisdic-

---

12. 427 U.S. at 18, 96 S.Ct. at 2422.

13. Ibid.

14. Ancillary jurisdiction could be asserted over the third-party claim. See § 2.12, above.

15. 437 U.S. 365, 98 S.Ct. 2396, 57 L.Ed.2d 274 (1978).

16. Because Kroger was a diversity action, the jurisdiction being claimed over the additional claims may be viewed as ancillary, as well as a species of pendent party jurisdiction. As indicated earlier, the exact denomination was not critical as the standard remained similar for both. See § 2.12, above.

17. Compare Kenrose Mfg. Co. v. Fred Whitaker Co., 512 F.2d 890 (4th Cir.1972), and McPherson v. Hoffman, 275 F.2d 466 (6th Cir.1960) (jurisdiction asserted), with CCF Industrial Park, Inc. v. Hastings Indus., Inc., 392 F.Supp. 1259 (E.D.Pa.1975), and Buresch v. American LaFrance, 290 F.Supp. 265 (W.D.Pa.1968) (jurisdiction denied).

18. 437 U.S. at 376–77, 98 S.Ct. at 2403–04.

19. For a more thorough discussion of the Finley case and its consequences, see § 2.13, above.

tion was appropriate unless Congress had undertaken to negate it and, instead, held that a federal court must find explicit congressional authority to assert jurisdiction over claims involving parties over whom there was no subject-matter jurisdiction. Moreover, the Supreme Court rejected the Aldinger suggestion that exclusive jurisdiction over the federal claim was sufficient for the assertion of pendent party jurisdiction. Overall, then, one of the effects of the Finley decision was to limit the exercise of pendent party jurisdiction to those situations in which Congress specifically had authorized that form of jurisdiction. In fact, some courts interpreted the limitations imposed by Finley to be so restrictive as to have the effect of terminating the federal court's ability to assert pendent party jurisdiction altogether.[20]

As discussed in the preceding section, in 1990 Congress responded to the Finley decision by enacting Section 1367 of Title 28 of the United States Code, which gave the federal courts statutory authority to exercise supplemental jurisdiction. Section 1367(a) specifically states that supplemental jurisdiction "shall include claims that involve the joinder or intervention of additional parties." However, supplemental jurisdiction over pendent parties is available only in cases in which jurisdiction over the original action is premised, at least in part, on a federal question. In conformity with the decision in Kroger, when jurisdiction is based on diversity of citizenship, no supplemental jurisdiction exists for a nonfederal claim against a nondiverse third-party defendant. But supplemental jurisdiction does exist over otherwise jurisdictionally insufficient parties whether the federal question jurisdiction is concurrent or exclusive. Consequently, one of the principal purposes of the new statute is to make clear that pendent party jurisdiction is permissible in all federal question cases. The only exception would be if the court found that the federal statute conferring original jurisdiction specifically forbids the exercise of supplemental jurisdiction.

B. VENUE

§ 2.15 Venue Requirements

As noted earlier,[1] venue requirements are purely statutory and vary from jurisdiction to jurisdiction, although all are designed to identify a convenient forum for the resolution of particular types of disputes. Despite the variety of approaches taken, some generalizations can be offered.

Numerous factors have been utilized to prescribe where venue should be laid in a given type of action. In some jurisdictions a single

---

20. See, e.g., Sarmiento v. Texas Bd. of Veterinary Medical Examiners, 939 F.2d 1242, 1247 (5th Cir.1991) ("[T]his court, along with others, has read Finley as sounding the death knell for pendent-party jurisdiction.").

§ 2.15

1. See § 2.1, above.

factor is the exclusive basis of venue. In others, it is sufficient that any one of several factors is satisfied. Some of these factors serve functional goals; others have little more than antiquity to recommend them. In the first category are those venue statutes that provide for trial of the action (1) where the subject matter of the action is located, (2) where the cause of action arose, (3) where the defendant resides, does business, or retains an agent, (4) where the plaintiff resides, or (5) in suits involving governmental bodies, where the seat of government is located.

Most of these provisions either serve the convenience of one of the litigants or facilitate the process of proof at trial, thereby increasing the probability of the just disposition of a case. By contrast, nonfunctional criteria used in fixing venue are illustrated by those statutes that lay venue (1) where some fact connected with the case occurred, (2) where the defendant may be found, (3) where the defendant may be served with process, (4) in the county designated in the plaintiff's complaint, or (5) in any county at all.[2]

The present statute governing venue generally in the federal court system is Section 1391 of Title 28 of the United States Code.[3] Its major provisions may be summarized as follows.[4] In diversity actions, venue is proper in a district where one of the defendants resides, if all of the defendants reside in the same state, or in a district in which a substantial part of the events or omissions giving rise to the claim occurred or a substantial part of property that is the subject matter of the action is situated, or in a district in which the defendants are subject to personal jurisdiction.[5] In federal question cases, the action may be brought in a

---

2. See Stevens, Venue Statutes: Diagnosis and Proposed Cure, 49 Mich.L.Rev. 307 (1951), for a full discussion of these factors and some suggestions for reform.

3. There are a large number of specialized venue statutes that apply to particular kinds of actions. E.g., 28 U.S.C.A. § 1400 (copyright and patent litigation); 28 U.S.C.A. § 1397 (statutory interpleader actions); and 46 U.S.C.A. § 688 (Jones Act matters). Some of these statutes expand the plaintiff's forum choice. E.g., 15 U.S.C.A. § 15 (aggrieved competitor can bring treble damage antitrust suit wherever defendant "resides or is found or has an agent"). Others have been rendered largely superfluous by the general venue statute. E.g., 45 U.S.C.A. § 56 (FELA cases).

4. In addition to the provisions discussed in the text, the statute states that an alien may be sued in any district. 28 U.S.C.A. § 1391(d). When an alien is the plaintiff, however, suit must be in a district where any defendant resides, if all defendants reside in the same state; in the district where a substantial part of the events or omissions giving rise to the claim occurred or a substantial part of property that is the subject of the action is located; or in a

district in which the defendants are subject to personal jurisdiction. Further, actions against agencies, officers, or employees of the federal government must be brought under a special venue provision, 28 U.S.C.A. § 1391(e). For a discussion of venue in actions against federal officers, as well as the United States, see 15 C. Wright, A. Miller & E. Cooper, Jurisdiction and Related Matters 2d §§ 3814–15.

5. Prior to 1990, venue in diversity of citizenship cases also was proper at the plaintiff's residence. The reason for this distinction between venue in diversity and federal question cases was unclear. Moreover, it was anomalous that the venue provisions for bringing a federal question case were more restrictive than those for bringing a diversity case. Thirty years ago the American Law Institute proposed abolishing plaintiff's venue in diversity actions. American Law Institute, Study of the Division of Jurisdiction Between State and Federal Courts § 1303(a) (1969). In point of fact, the distinction was not of great practical importance, since a defendant often is not amenable to process in a plaintiff's home district unless that also was the dis-

district where one of the defendants resides, if all of the defendants reside in the same state, or a district in which a substantial part of the acts or omissions giving rise to the claim occurred or a substantial part of property that is the subject matter of the action is situated, or a district in which any defendant may be found. It is not at all clear why this slight distinction exists between venue in diversity and in federal question cases.[6]

The authorities are divided on whether the concept of residence in the venue statute is identical to the concept of citizenship in the diversity jurisdiction statute.[7] If the two words are given the same meaning, then the test of domicile used in determining citizenship for diversity purposes[8] is applicable to determining residence for venue purposes. The consequence of this construction is that a person who has a home in one district but has retained a legal domicile, and thus citizenship, in another state or district, cannot sue or be sued in the district in which the home is located.[9] This seems inconsistent with the idea of convenience that underlies venue, since presumably a party would find it convenient to litigate wherever she had a home. That reasoning obviously leads to residence having a wider scope of application than domicile. But the equation of the two concepts does avoid the confusion that otherwise would result from having one body of law on what is citizenship for diversity purposes and a different body of law on what is residence for venue purposes.

Prior to the amendment of the venue statute in 1990, courts and litigants were faced with the problem of determining "where the claim arose."[10] The lower courts struggled to find some method of determining where the claim arose, especially when the alleged injury was not a physical one, easily identified, or the conduct of the defendant that produced the alleged harm was not clearly isolated in one district.[11] Since

trict where the wrong giving rise to the plaintiff's claim occurred. See Korbel, The Law of Federal Venue and Choice of the Most Convenient Forum, 15 Rutgers L.Rev. 607, 609 (1961).

6. The third venue criterion in federal question cases, where a defendant may be "found," is a "fallback" provision that is available only when venue cannot be secured based either on the residence of all the defendants or on where a substantial part of the events or omissions giving rise to the claim occurred.

7. Townsend v. Bucyrus–Erie Co., 144 F.2d 106 (10th Cir.1944) (residence and citizenship are related, but not identical, terms); Lee v. Hunt, 410 F.Supp. 329, 332 (M.D.La.1976), on rehearing 415 F.Supp. 245 (M.D.La.1976) (residence refers to domicile); Schultz v. McAfee, 160 F.Supp. 210, 212 (D.Me.1958) (citizenship and residence both refer to domicile). See also Ex parte Shaw, 145 U.S. 444, 449, 12 S.Ct. 935, 937, 36 L.Ed. 768 (1892) (dictum).

8. The domicile test for determining citizenship for diversity purposes is discussed in § 2.6, above.

9. See MacNeil v. Whittemore, 254 F.2d 820 (2d Cir.1958).

10. The provision authorizing venue where the claim arose has been amended several times since 1963, when Congress went part of the way toward making the place where the claim arose a proper venue, but limited the amendment to motor vehicle tort cases. Act of Dec. 23, 1963, 77 Stat. 473. This provision was repealed in 1966, when the general provision authorizing venue where the claim arose was added. As of December 1, 1990, venue is proper where a substantial part of the events or omissions giving rise to the claim occurred or a substantial part of property that is the subject of the action is located.

11. See Comment, Federal Venue: Locating the Place Where the Claim Arose, 54 Texas L.Rev. 392 (1976). Compare Sheffield

the 1990 amendments, however, Section 1391(a)(2) for diversity cases, Section 1391(b)(2) for federal question cases, and Section 1391(e)(2) for suits against federal officers and agencies all permit venue to be laid in a district "in which a substantial part of the events or omissions giving rise to the claim occurred, or a substantial part of property that is the subject of the action is situated."[12] This adopts the language originally proposed by the American Law Institute and makes it much easier to apply the statute.[13] Even before the revision of Section 1391, a number of lower courts had interpreted the statute as if it contained the ALI language.[14]

The federal venue statute also includes special standards for establishing venue in actions against corporations.[15] Originally, for venue purposes a corporation was considered to be a resident only of the state in which it was incorporated.[16] This notion created unjustifiable restrictions on the ability of plaintiffs to sue corporations carrying on activities in many states. Therefore, in 1939, in the leading case of Neirbo Company v. Bethlehem Shipbuilding Corporation,[17] the Supreme Court expanded venue to permit suit against a corporation in any district in which it maintained an agent to receive service of process under state law. The venue statute was amended in 1948 to reflect this holding,[18] and corporate residence for venue purposes was defined as including not only the state of incorporation, but also any place in which the corporation was licensed to do business or was doing business.[19] In 1988, the

v. Texas, 411 F.Supp. 709 (N.D.Tex.1976) ("place of injury" test), with Lamont v. Haig, 590 F.2d 1124, 1134 (D.C.Cir.1978) ("substantial material events" test).

12. Act of Dec. 1, 1990, Pub.L. 101–650, § 311.

13. American Law Institute, Study of the Division of Jurisdiction between State and Federal Courts, Official Draft, §§ 1303(a)(1), 1314(a)(1), 1326(a)(1) (1969).

14. See, e.g., Lamont v. Haig, 590 F.2d 1124 (D.C.Cir.1978) (in a civil action in which jurisdiction is not based solely on diversity, venue may be laid in a district where a substantial portion of the acts or omissions giving rise to the action occurred, notwithstanding that venue also might lie in other districts, so long as the substantiality of the operative events is determined by assessment of their ramifications for efficient conduct of the suit). See also Missouri Housing Dev. Comm'n v. Brice, 919 F.2d 1306, 1310 (8th Cir.1990).

15. After the 1988 amendments to Section 1391(c), the statute clearly applies only to corporate defendants.

16. As revised in 1988, Section 1391(c) no longer makes any reference to the place where a corporation is "incorporated." That now will be only one factor in determining whether a corporation is subject to

personal jurisdiction in that district. If a corporation is incorporated in a state but does not have enough contacts with any particular district to be subject to personal jurisdiction there, it is deemed to reside in the district within which it has the most significant contacts. See 15 C. Wright, A. Miller & E. Cooper, Jurisdiction and Related Matters 2d § 3811.

17. 308 U.S. 165, 60 S.Ct. 153, 84 L.Ed. 167 (1939).

18. Act of June 25, 1948, 62 Stat. 935.

19. As a rule, the definition of corporate residence in Section 1391(c) is read into special venue provisions. See, e.g., Pure Oil Co. v. Suarez, 384 U.S. 202, 86 S.Ct. 1394, 16 L.Ed.2d 474 (1966) (Jones Act case). Historically, this did not hold for venue of patent infringement actions governed by 28 U.S.C.A. § 1400(b). See, e.g., Fourco Glass Co. v. Transmirra Prods. Corp., 353 U.S. 222, 77 S.Ct. 787, 1 L.Ed.2d 786 (1957). However, the 1988 amendment of 28 U.S.C.A. § 1391(c), under which suit against a corporation can be brought in any district in which it is subject to personal jurisdiction, applies to suits for patent infringement and modifies 28 U.S.C.A. § 1400(b). See, e.g., VE Holding Corp. v. Johnson Gas Appliance Co., 917 F.2d 1574 (Fed.Cir.1990), cert. denied 499 U.S. 922;

statute was amended again so that a corporation now is deemed to reside in any judicial district in which it is subject to personal jurisdiction at the time the action is commenced, thereby equating the tests for personal jurisdiction and venue.[20] In determining their residence for venue purposes, unincorporated associations such as labor unions are treated as if they were corporations and thus may be sued in any district in which they do business.[21]

Because venue requirements are premised on notions of convenience rather than on decisions reflecting the constitutional limitations on a given court's power, objections to the venue of a particular court are waived if not asserted promptly.[22] Thus, it generally is agreed that the federal venue requirements need not be met in actions that are removed to the federal courts.[23] Since the ability of a defendant to object to the venue of an action is a privilege that may be waived, it makes sense to say that waiver occurs when a defendant voluntarily removes an action to federal court.[24] The normal venue requirements also are dispensed with for claims that fall within the supplemental jurisdiction of the federal courts.[25] The same procedural considerations that permit them to be heard despite the fact that they are outside the statutory limitations on federal court jurisdiction argue even more strongly that the venue requirements should be disregarded for those claims.[26]

Regents of University of California v. Eli Lilly & Co., 734 F.Supp. 911 (N.D.Cal. 1990); Century Wrecker Corp. v. Vulcan Equipment Co., 733 F.Supp. 1170 (E.D.Tenn.1989), affirmed 923 F.2d 870 (Fed.Cir.1990). See also 15 C. Wright, A. Miller & E. Cooper, Jurisdiction and Related Matters 2d § 3823.

20. As revised in 1988, Section 1391(c) no longer makes reference to the place where a corporation is licensed to do business. Act of Nov. 19, 1988, Pub.L. 100–702, § 1013, 102 Stat. 4624, 4669. This will now be only one factor in determining whether a corporation is subject to personal jurisdiction in that district. If a corporation is licensed to do business throughout a state but actually is doing business only in a single district of the state, it appears that it will be deemed only to reside in that district. See Oakley, Recent Statutory Changes in the Law of Federal Jurisdiction and Venue: The Judicial Improvements Acts of 1988 and 1990, 24 U.C.Davis L.Rev. 735, 770–74 (1991); Siegel, Changes in Federal Jurisdiction and Practice Under the New Federal Judicial Improvements and Access to Justice Act, 123 F.R.D. 399, 405–08 (1989); Welkowitz, Some Thoughts on Corporate Venue and Other Foibles, 10 Whittier L.Rev. 721 (1989).

21. Denver & R. G. W. R.R. Co. v. Brotherhood of R.R. Trainmen, 387 U.S.

556, 87 S.Ct. 1746, 18 L.Ed.2d 954 (1967). This contrasts with the decision not to treat unincorporated associations like corporations for diversity jurisdiction purposes. See § 2.6, above.

22. In the federal courts, the defense of lack of venue must be asserted by pre-answer motion or in the answer itself or it will be waived. Fed.Civ.Proc.Rule 12(h)(1). See 15 C. Wright, A. Miller & E. Cooper, Jurisdiction and Related Matters 2d § 3829.

23. Lee v. Chesapeake & Ohio Ry. Co., 260 U.S. 653, 43 S.Ct. 230, 67 L.Ed. 443 (1923); General Inv. Co. v. Lake Shore & M.S. Ry. Co., 260 U.S. 261, 43 S.Ct. 106, 67 L.Ed. 244 (1922). Generally, the venue of a removed action is in the district and division embracing the state court where the action was initially brought. 28 U.S.C.A. § 1441(a). See § 2.11, above.

24. General Inv. Co. v. Lake Shore & M.S. Ry. Co., 260 U.S. 261, 275–76, 43 S.Ct. 106, 113, 67 L.Ed. 244 (1922).

25. See §§ 2.12–2.14, above, on supplemental jurisdiction.

26. See, e.g., Pelinski v. Goodyear Tire & Rubber Co., 499 F.Supp. 1092 (N.D.Ill. 1980) (Rule 14 claim); Payne v. AHFI Netherlands, B.V., 482 F.Supp. 1158 (N.D.Ill. 1980) (Rule 13(a) claim); R.E. Linder Steel Erection Co. v. Alumisteel Sys., Inc., 88 F.R.D. 629 (D.Md.1980) (Rule 13(g) claim).

§ 2.16 Local and Transitory Actions

One of the most troublesome venue problems arises from the distinction between "local" and "transitory" actions. The concept of a local action is a somewhat elusive one, but generally it includes actions concerning real property, particularly suits to gain possession of land, to foreclose a lien, or to quiet title. Other actions affecting realty—such as trespass or breach of contract to convey—often are subsumed under the concept as well. Because these types of actions involve a particular piece of land that necessarily is located within a given region, they have been deemed to be peculiarly "local." Standing in sharp contrast are those actions that theoretically might have arisen anywhere, such as a battery or the breach of a mercantile contract; these have been deemed to be "transitory."

The practical significance of the distinction is that in most jurisdictions a local action must be brought in the court where the res at issue is located; a transitory action can be brought wherever personal jurisdiction over the defendant can be obtained, subject to the general venue requirements.[1] In Reasor–Hill Corporation v. Harrison,[2] the Supreme Court of Arkansas identified three reasons traditionally given as justifying the local-transitory distinction. First, a court supposedly is not qualified to pass upon the title to land outside its geographical boundaries. Second, a plaintiff should be encouraged to pursue a remedy before the defendant leaves the jurisdiction in which the res at issue is located. Third, there is a strong tendency to refuse suits against one's own citizens by nonresidents, especially if the foreign courts would provide no redress should the situation be reversed. The Arkansas court found that although these reasons may have justified the local action principle historically, they are inadequate to warrant continued adherence to the rule, at least with regard to tort actions within the United States. But the weight of authority continues to rely on the distinction, either by judicial decision[3] or by codifying it in venue statutes.[4]

The federal venue statutes, except for a few oblique references,[5] never have been couched in terms of local or transitory actions. Nonethe-

---

§ 2.16

1. The restrictive venue of local actions probably traces primarily to the nature of the early English jury. In feudal England, the jury consisted of neighbors familiar with the litigants and the dispute so that it made sense to require that the trial be held in the place where the subject matter of the dispute was located. Initially, all actions were "local," since land was the primary form of wealth in medieval society, and hence the most common subject of contention in early lawsuits. By the Fourteenth Century, with the further development of the medieval economy, the transitory action had appeared. Because these actions could not be identified with any single geographic locality, the rationale for localizing them did not exist. For the historical develop-

ment of the local-transitory action distinction, see T. Plucknett, A Concise History of the Common Law 123–25 (4th ed.1948); Blume, Place of Trial in Civil Cases, 48 Mich.L.Rev. 1 (1949); Wicker, The Development of the Distinction Between Local and Transitory Actions, 4 Tenn.L.Rev. 55 (1925).

2. 220 Ark. 521, 249 S.W.2d 994 (1952).

3. See note 10, below.

4. E.g., West's Ann.Cal.Code Civ.Proc. § 392(1); Mich.Comp.Laws Ann. § 600.1605; N.Y.—McKinney's CPLR 507.

5. Section 1392(a) of Title 28 provides: "Any civil action, not of a local nature, against defendants residing in different dis-

less, the local action rule was engrafted upon federal jurisprudence at an early date in the famous case of Livingston v. Jefferson,[6] in which the plaintiff sued former President Thomas Jefferson, a Virginian, in a Virginia federal court for trespass against the plaintiff's property in the Louisiana Territory. The action was in personam and not in rem. However, an action for trespass to land traditionally was considered to be a local action, and the court consequently held that it could be brought only where the land was located—in Louisiana. Since the plaintiff could not obtain personal jurisdiction over Jefferson in Louisiana, this decision in effect deprived the plaintiff of any forum at all in which to bring the action. Chief Justice Marshall, sitting as a circuit justice, recognized that application of the local action rule under these circumstances "produces the inconvenience of a clear right without a remedy,"[7] but felt bound by English precedent to follow the rule and dismiss the plaintiff's action.[8]

The injustice of the local action principle is obvious: it often has allowed an unavoidable defect of venue to bar a plaintiff from seeking judicial redress in the only available forum. As a practical matter, its impact has been diminished considerably in the last thirty years as a result of expanded notions of personal jurisdiction under state long-arm statutes.[9] The rule itself, however, and its application to in personam actions such as trespass, continues to be followed in the vast majority of American jurisdictions.[10] Only a few states have mitigated its adverse effect by holding that trespass to property is a transitory, rather than a local, action.[11]

To this day it is unclear whether the local action rule is jurisdictional or merely a venue rule. If it is the latter, then it, or a misapplication of

tricts in the same State, may be brought in any of such districts." Section 1392(b) provides: "Any civil action, of a local nature, involving property located in different districts in the same State, may be brought in any of such districts." Section 1393(a) also pertains to civil actions "not of a local nature."

6. 15 Fed.Cas. 660 (C.C.Va.1811) (No. 8411). For a history of the Livingston case and an analysis of the parties' strategies, see Degnan, Livingston v. Jefferson—A Freestanding Footnote, 75 Calif.L.Rev. 115 (1987).

7. 15 Fed.Cas. at 665.

8. That the general federal venue statutes do not apply to local actions is reflected in the opinion by Chief Justice Waite in Casey v. Adams, 102 U.S. (12 Otto) 66, 67–68, 26 L.Ed. 52 (1880). The impact of the local action rule on federal practice is discussed in 15 C. Wright, A. Miller & E. Cooper, Jurisdiction and Related Matters 2d § 3822; Note, Local Actions in the Federal Courts, 70 Harv.L.Rev. 708 (1957).

9. For example, suppose that D cuts and sells timber on P's land without permission. In some states, this would be a local action, and, if P could not serve D with process issued out of the court where the land was located, he would be without a remedy. However, if the state has a long-arm statute that covers actions arising out of property within the state, P will be able to serve process on D and have his suit adjudicated in a court where the res is located, in accordance with the local action rule. See the discussion in §§ 3.1–3.13, below, on personal jurisdiction and long-arm statutes.

10. See Annot., 42 A.L.R. 196; Annot., 30 A.L.R.2d 1219.

11. Reasor–Hill Corp. v. Harrison, 220 Ark. 521, 249 S.W.2d 994 (1952); Little v. Chicago, St. P., M. & O. Ry. Co., 65 Minn. 48, 67 N.W. 846 (1896); Ingram v. Great Lakes Pipe Line Co., 153 S.W.2d 547 (Mo. App.1941); Jacobus v. Colgate, 217 N.Y. 235, 111 N.E. 837 (1916).

it, can be waived.[12] But if it expresses a limitation on subject-matter jurisdiction, and therefore is grounded in considerations of sovereignty, it cannot be waived, and suits that contravene it must be dismissed. Early cases, holding the defect of bringing a local action in a district where the property is not located nonwaivable, indicate that the rule is jurisdictional.[13] More recent cases, however, have tended to view it as a venue matter.[14]

§ 2.17 Forum Non Conveniens and Transfer

The venue scheme applicable to a particular judicial system normally is adequate to ensure that actions are litigated in convenient and sensible places. But a well-functioning venue system also must make provision for changes of venue when actions are brought in places that, for one reason or another, are inappropriate. The most obvious situation calling for a change in venue is when the plaintiff brings suit in a district that lacks proper venue, and the defendant interposes a timely objection to the venue of the action.[1] To dismiss the action in every case of this type often might work an injustice: when the statute of limitations has run on a plaintiff's claim after the action was instituted, the plaintiff would be barred permanently from obtaining redress simply because of the failure to comply with a procedural technicality largely intended for the convenience of litigants.

State judicial systems long have had provisions for transferring improperly located cases to a court within the jurisdiction where venue is proper. Under these provisions, transfer usually is attempted to the court most convenient to the parties and witnesses. In federal courts, the problem of transfer when venue is improper is somewhat more difficult, since transfer often will have to be to an entirely different state. However, since 1948 the federal courts have been authorized to make interstate venue transfers under Section 1406(a) of the 1948 Judicial Code, as amended in 1949.[2] Although the court has a choice between dismissing and transferring an action that has been commenced in an improper venue, the courts usually have concluded that the interests of justice are served better by transfer to a proper forum than by dismissal. Transfers can be made only between courts of the same judicial system,

12. In California, the codification of the local action rule explicitly provides that the failure to raise a local action objection at the outset results in its waiver. West's Ann.Cal.Code Civ.Proc. § 392(1).

13. See, e.g., Ellenwood v. Marietta Chair Co., 158 U.S. 105, 15 S.Ct. 771, 39 L.Ed. 913 (1895).

14. Wheatley v. Phillips, 228 F.Supp. 439 (W.D.N.C.1964); Eddington v. Texas & New Orleans R. Co., 83 F.Supp. 230 (S.D.Tex.1949); O'Shaughnessy v. Marchese, 60 A.D.2d 882, 401 N.Y.S.2d 285 (1978). But see Minichiello Realty Assocs., Inc. v. Britt, 460 F.Supp. 896 (D.N.J.1978),

affirmed without opinion 605 F.2d 1196 (3d Cir.1979) (court may raise local action objection sua sponte). In Note, Local Actions in the Federal Courts, 70 Harv.L.Rev. 708, 712–13 (1957), it is suggested that variances with the local action rule be treated as venue defects in actions in personam but as jurisdictional defects in actions in rem.

§ 2.17

1. See § 2.15 at n. 22, above.

2. Act of May 24, 1949, c. 139, § 81, 63 Stat. 101.

however; federal courts can transfer only to other federal courts, and state courts can transfer only to state courts in the same state.

As a result of the somewhat surprising decision by the Supreme Court in Goldlawr, Inc. v. Heiman,[3] it even is permissible for a federal court lacking personal jurisdiction over the defendant to transfer under Section 1406(a).[4] As long as service of process can be made in the transferee district and venue is proper there, transfer is appropriate.[5] This rule furthers the basic objective of facilitating the adjudication of cases on the merits, rather than on the basis of procedural niceties; however, it also may be viewed as an unwarranted derogation of the importance of personal jurisdiction in federal practice.[6]

Contractual forum-selection clauses also raise questions of proper venue. In general, the federal courts and most state systems will enforce these clauses, holding that forum selection is a valid and valuable commercial device, allowing parties to estimate more accurately the costs of any litigation that may arise. At least in theory, removing that element of uncertainty from commercial risk calculations allows a party to charge lower prices to the other party to the contract, and the savings eventually reach the consumer.[7]

Therefore, although forum-selection clauses remain subject to some statutory limitations,[8] in most jurisdictions the clauses arrive in court with a strong presumption of enforceability, particularly when the parties to the contract were both represented by competent counsel and possessed equal bargaining power.[9] A litigant wishing to avoid the forum-selection clause carries a heavy burden to show that the clause is unreasonable in the circumstances of the case, or that it was obtained unfairly, although the forum-selection clause is not automatically dispositive of its enforceability.[10] Courts generally refer to the test set out by the Supreme Court in The Bremen v. Zapata Off–Shore Company and consider whether (1) the incorporation of the forum-selection clause into the agreement was the product of fraud or overreaching; (2) the party

---

3. 369 U.S. 463, 466, 82 S.Ct. 913, 916, 8 L.Ed.2d 39 (1962). The ramifications of Goldlawr are discussed in Note, Change of Venue in Absence of Personal Jurisdiction Under 28 U.S.C.A. §§ 1404(a) and 1406(a), 30 U.Chi.L.Rev. 735 (1963); Comment, Personal Jurisdiction Requirements Under Federal Change of Venue Statutes, 1962 Wis.L.Rev. 342.

4. Further discussion of Section 1406(a) can be found in 15 C. Wright, A. Miller & E. Cooper, Jurisdiction and Related Matters 2d § 3827.

5. See Hydrotherm, Inc. v. Bastian–Morley Co., 207 F.Supp. 744, 745 (E.D.N.Y. 1962).

6. See generally Chapter 3, below.

7. See Carnival Cruise Lines, Inc. v. Shute, 499 U.S. 585, 593–594, 111 S.Ct.

1522, 1527, 113 L.Ed.2d 622 (1991); The Bremen v. Zapata Off–Shore Co., 407 U.S. 1, 10, 92 S.Ct. 1907, 1913, 32 L.Ed.2d 513 (1972).

8. See, e.g., Idaho Code § 29–110, Mont.Code.Ann. 28–2–708. For a general discussion of forum-selection clauses in modern jurisprudence, see Heiser, Forum Selection Clauses in Federal Courts: Limitations on Enforcement After Stewart and Carnival Cruise, 45 Fla. L. Rev. 553 (1993).

9. The Bremen v. Zapata Off–Shore Co., 407 U.S. 1, 15, 92 S.Ct. 1907, 1916, 32 L.Ed.2d 513 (1972).

10. Stewart Organization, Inc. v. Ricoh Corp., 487 U.S. 22, 22, 23, 108 S.Ct. 2239, 2249–2250, 101 L.Ed.2d 22 (1988). This case is summarized in Haynsworth v. Lloyd's of London, 121 F.3d 956 (5th Cir. 1997).

seeking to escape enforcement would for all practical purposes be deprived of her day in court because of the grave inconvenience or unfairness of the chosen forum; (3) the fundamental unfairness of the chosen law will deprive the plaintiff of a remedy; or (4) enforcement of the forum-selection clause would contravene a strong public policy of the forum state.[11]

One final factor to consider is whether the forum-selection clause is "permissive," meaning that it permits suit in a specific forum that may or may not otherwise have had personal jurisdiction or venue, but does not foreclose suits elsewhere, or whether the clause is "mandatory." A mandatory clause precludes any lawsuit that falls under the terms of the clause from being brought outside the designated forum.[12]

The fact that the plaintiff's forum choice is proper in the sense of conforming to the statutory venue requirements does not necessarily mean that the court chosen is the most appropriate, or even desirable, one from the standpoint of convenience and efficiency. For example, the plaintiff may sue in a district in which venue technically is proper because of minimal activities carried on there by a corporate defendant, but the forum may have little or no connection with the significant events forming the basis of the lawsuit.

The traditional response to these problems of a correct, but inconvenient, tribunal is the forum non conveniens doctrine,[13] which permits a court having jurisdiction over an action to refuse to exercise its jurisdiction when the litigation could be brought more appropriately in another forum. The leading federal case applying the doctrine is Gulf Oil Corporation v. Gilbert.[14] In that case, Gilbert, a resident of Virginia, sued Gulf in a New York federal court for damage from a fire allegedly caused by Gulf's negligence in the delivery of gasoline to the plaintiff's warehouse, located in Virginia. Gulf was a Pennsylvania corporation qualified to do business in both New York and Virginia, and the New York federal court was thus a proper venue for the action under the general venue statute.[15] But the Supreme Court looked beyond the technical propriety of venue and found virtually no connection between New York and the facts of the case. The injury complained of had occurred in Virginia, all potential trial witnesses lived in Virginia, with the possible exception of experts, and Virginia law would be applied to determine liability. In these circumstances, it was held to be a proper exercise of discretion for the New York federal court to dismiss the action, leaving the plaintiff free to bring it in the courts of his own community, rather than to permit it to be brought in an inconvenient forum.

11.   407 U.S. 1, 12–13, 15, 18, 92 S.Ct. 1907, 1914–1915, 1916, 1917, 32 L.Ed.2d 513 (1972).

12.   For a case drawing this distinction, see, e.g., Caldas & Sons, Inc. v. Willingham, 17 F.3d 123 (5th Cir.1994).

13.   See generally 15 C. Wright, A. Miller & E. Cooper, Jurisdiction and Related Matters 2d § 3828; Barrett, The Doctrine of Forum Non Conveniens, 35 Calif.L.Rev. 380 (1947); Braucher, The Inconvenient Federal Forum, 60 Harv.L.Rev. 908 (1947).

14.   330 U.S. 501, 67 S.Ct. 839, 91 L.Ed. 1055 (1947).

15.   See § 2.15, above, for a discussion of venue in actions against corporations.

It must be emphasized that forum non conveniens comes into play only when venue is proper in the first instance. As the Supreme Court stated in Gilbert:

> It is conceded that the venue statutes of the United States permitted the plaintiff to commence his action in the Southern District of New York and empower that court to entertain it. But that does not settle the question of whether it must do so. Indeed, the doctrine of *forum non conveniens* can never apply if there is absence of jurisdiction or mistake of venue.[16]

Forum non conveniens allows a court to exercise its discretion to avoid the oppression or vexation that might result from automatically honoring plaintiff's forum choice. However, dismissal on the basis of forum non conveniens also requires that there be an alternative forum in which the suit can be prosecuted.[17] It must appear that jurisdiction over all parties can be secured and that complete relief can be obtained in the supposedly more convenient court.[18] Further, in at least some states, it has been held that the doctrine cannot be successfully invoked when the plaintiff is a resident of the forum state since, effectively, one of the functions of the state courts is to provide a tribunal in which their residents can obtain an adjudication of their grievances.[19] But in most instances a balancing of the convenience to all the parties will be considered and no one factor will preclude a forum non dismissal, as long as another forum is available.

The need to balance all the factors suggesting the desirability or lack thereof of the forum in which suit is filed and the alternative tribunal was reinforced by the Supreme Court in Piper Aircraft Company v. Reyno.[20] In that case a wrongful death suit arising out of a plane crash in Scotland was brought in the California state courts by several Scottish persons against the manufacturer of the plane, a Pennsylvania corporation, and the manufacturer of the plane's propellers, an Ohio company. The action was removed to federal court and transferred to the Middle District of Pennsylvania, on motion of the defendants. The defendants then obtained a dismissal of the action on the ground of forum non conveniens. The Third Circuit held that dismissal was barred since the law of Scotland does not recognize strict liability and was less favorable to the plaintiff than the law of the forum. The Supreme Court reversed.

Justice Marshall, writing for the Court, noted "the possibility of a change in substantive law should ordinarily not be given conclusive or

---

16.   330 U.S. at 504, 67 S.Ct. at 840–41.

17.   See Note, Requirement of a Second Forum for Application of Forum Non Conveniens, 43 Minn.L.Rev. 1199 (1959). For an interesting example of the application of the doctrine, see Stangvik v. Shiley, Inc., 54 Cal.3d 744, 1 Cal.Rptr.2d 556, 819 P.2d 14 (1991) (action by foreign plaintiffs against domestic defendant dismissed).

18.   North Branch Prods., Inc. v. Fisher, 284 F.2d 611 (D.C.Cir.1960), cert. denied 365 U.S. 827.

19.   E.g., Ferreira v. Ferreira, 9 Cal.3d 824, 109 Cal.Rptr. 80, 512 P.2d 304 (1973); Goodwine v. Superior Court, 63 Cal.2d 481, 47 Cal.Rptr. 201, 407 P.2d 1 (1965).

20.   454 U.S. 235, 102 S.Ct. 252, 70 L.Ed.2d 419 (1981).

even substantial weight in the forum non conveniens inquiry."[21] He then went on to conclude: "Although the relatives of the decedents may not be able to rely on a strict liability theory, and although their potential damage award may be smaller, there is no danger that they will be deprived of any remedy or treated unfairly."[22] Thus, the trial court may consider the fact that the alternative tribunal is in a foreign country and that the law in that tribunal is not as favorable to the plaintiff as the law where the action is filed, but those facts are not determinative. They must be weighed against other factors suggesting why dismissal may be appropriate.[23]

Forum non conveniens often is too blunt an instrument to permit frequent use, especially when the dismissal of plaintiff's claim will bar relief completely because the statute of limitations has run while the action is pending in the inconvenient forum.[24] Accordingly, the 1948 Judicial Code not only codified the judicially announced doctrine of forum non conveniens for the federal courts, but also ameliorated its harshness by providing for changes of venue, rather than dismissal, when an action is brought initially in an inconvenient forum. The operative provision is Section 1404(a),[25] which authorizes transfer "for the convenience of parties and witnesses," and "in the interest of justice."[26] If that standard is met, the court may transfer the action "to any other district or division where it might have been brought."

21. 454 U.S. at 247, 102 S.Ct. at 261.

22. 454 U.S. at 255, 102 S.Ct. at 265.

23. Some of the factors relevant to dismissal for forum non conveniens are the location of the evidence, the cost of producing witnesses, the source of the governing law, the availability of procedures to compel the appearance of unwilling witnesses, and the desire not to overburden taxpayers or the judicial system with cases only tangentially related to the forum. Generally, state courts are reluctant to resort to forum non conveniens if there are any contacts between the parties and the initially chosen forum. This is especially true if the plaintiff is a citizen of that forum. See note 19, above. For some examples of how the courts balance these factors, see Silver v. Great Am. Ins. Co., 29 N.Y.2d 356, 328 N.Y.S.2d 398, 278 N.E.2d 619 (1972); Thomson v. Continental Ins. Co., 66 Cal.2d 738, 59 Cal. Rptr. 101, 427 P.2d 765 (1967); Lonergan v. Crucible Steel Co. of America, 37 Ill.2d 599, 229 N.E.2d 536 (1967); Goodwine v. Superior Court of Los Angeles, 63 Cal.2d 481, 47 Cal.Rptr. 201, 407 P.2d 1 (1965).

24. One method of alleviating this problem is for the court to enter a conditional dismissal tied to the defendant's agreement to litigate in the other tribunal. See, e.g., Wendel v. Hoffman, 259 App.Div.

732, 18 N.Y.S.2d 96 (1940), appeal dismissed 284 N.Y. 588, 29 N.E.2d 664 (1940). See also Vargas v. A. H. Bull S.S. Co., 44 N.J.Super. 536, 131 A.2d 39 (1957), affirmed 25 N.J. 293, 135 A.2d 857 (1957), cert. denied 355 U.S. 958. The imposition of conditions is consistent with the notion that a forum non dismissal is warranted "in the interests of justice" only if it is clear that an alternative forum is available.

25. The history and purpose of Section 1404(a) is summarized in 15 C. Wright, A. Miller & E. Cooper, Jurisdiction and Related Matters 2d § 3841. Detailed discussion of other aspects of the statute can be found in §§ 3842–55 of the same volume.

26. An excellent discussion of the factors that might influence a judge to grant a transfer and a sharp critique of the statute can be found in Kitch, Section 1404(a) of the Judicial Code: In the Interest of Justice or Injustice?, 40 Ind.L.J. 99 (1965). For other discussions of transfer practice, see Kaufman, Observation on Transfers Under Section 1404(a) of the New Judicial Code, 10 F.R.D. 595 (1951); Kaufman, Further Observations on Transfers Under Section 1404(a), 56 Colum.L.Rev. 1 (1956); Korbel, The Law of Federal Venue and Choice of the Most Convenient Forum, 15 Rutgers L.Rev. 607 (1961).

It now is well-settled that transfers under Section 1404(a) require a lesser showing of inconvenience than do outright dismissals under forum non conveniens.[27] Indeed, given the enactment of the federal transfer statute, the doctrine of forum non conveniens retains only a limited vitality in the federal courts. If the more convenient forum is another federal court, the case can be transferred and there is no need to dismiss.[28] It is only when the more convenient forum is in a foreign country[29]—or perhaps, under rare circumstances, is a state court[30]—that a suit brought in a proper federal venue will be dismissed on grounds of forum non conveniens. In contrast, the doctrine of forum non conveniens continues to play an important role in the state courts because a court in one state cannot transfer a case to a court in another state.

One of the numerous problems that has arisen in the application of Section 1404(a) is determining whether transfer to a given district is permissible. In particular, what does the statutory language "where it might have been brought" mean? The Supreme Court considered this question in Hoffman v. Blaski,[31] which involved a patent infringement action brought by Illinois plaintiffs against Texas defendants in the United States District Court for the Northern District of Texas. The defendants moved for a change of venue to the Northern District of Illinois under Section 1404(a). After the transfer was granted by the Texas district court and affirmed by the Fifth Circuit, the plaintiffs moved in the Illinois district court for a remand of the action to Texas.[32] The district court denied the motion, but the Seventh Circuit reversed and ordered the action remanded to the Texas federal court. The Supreme Court affirmed the Seventh Circuit. The Court announced the rule that a federal court in which an action properly had been brought was not empowered under Section 1404(a) to transfer a case to a district in which the plaintiff could not have instituted the action originally.

In Hoffman, the defendants were not amenable to process in the Northern District of Illinois, nor could the venue of an action against them be laid there under Section 1400(b), the special venue provision applicable to patent infringement actions. The Northern District of Illinois therefore was not a district in which the action "might have been brought" by the plaintiff. The fact that the defendants were willing, in effect, to waive their venue and personal jurisdiction objections to suit in

27. Norwood v. Kirkpatrick, 349 U.S. 29, 32, 75 S.Ct. 544, 546, 99 L.Ed. 789 (1955). See also All States Freight, Inc. v. Modarelli, 196 F.2d 1010 (3d Cir.1952).

28. Collins v. American Auto. Ins. Co., 230 F.2d 416, 418 (2d Cir.1956), cert. dismissed 352 U.S. 802.

29. See, e.g., Yerostathis v. A. Luisi, Ltd., 380 F.2d 377 (9th Cir.1967); In re Union Carbide Corp. Gas Plant Disaster at Bhopal, India in December, 1984, 634 F.Supp. 842 (S.D.N.Y.1986), modified and affirmed 809 F.2d 195 (2d Cir.1987), cert. denied 484 U.S. 871 (dismissed on ground of forum non conveniens with conditions of

defendant's consent to United States discovery regime in India, consent to personal jurisdiction, and waiver of statute of limitations defense).

30. See, e.g., Gross v. Owen, 221 F.2d 94 (D.C.Cir.1955).

31. 363 U.S. 335, 80 S.Ct. 1084, 4 L.Ed.2d 1254 (1960).

32. This skirmishing over venue probably was due more to the Fifth Circuit's more favorable attitude toward patent holders in infringement actions than to any considerations of convenience.

Illinois was held to be irrelevant: "We do not think the Section 1404(a) phrase 'where it might have been brought' can be interpreted to mean * * * 'where it may be rebrought, with defendant's consent.' "[33]

The Hoffman decision may be criticized for unnecessarily limiting the ability to use Section 1404(a) to facilitate changes of venue whenever those changes are demanded by the interests of justice and the convenience of the litigants or witnesses.[34] However, any other reading of the statute would discriminate against plaintiffs by giving defendants a unilateral opportunity to forum shop. That is, a plaintiff would be able to sue only in whatever tribunals were proper according to the requirements of subject-matter jurisdiction, personal jurisdiction, and venue, but that plaintiff's suit might be transferred to a more convenient forum with or without his consent. Moreover, a defendant could consent to transfer to a more convenient forum, but if the defendant refused to give consent, a court would lack the power to transfer the case to a place where it could not have been brought originally, no matter how convenient that place might be.[35]

Plaintiffs, as well as defendants, are entitled to seek a change of venue under Section 1404(a).[36] This permits a plaintiff to amend the complaint to include newly discovered defendants for whom venue would not be proper in the district in which the action was filed originally.[37] After initial uncertainty, it now is settled that a case cannot be transferred on the plaintiff's motion to a district in which the defendant is not subject to process and where, therefore, in personam jurisdiction could not be obtained.[38] This rule is necessary to prevent a plaintiff from acquiring personal jurisdiction by the back door in circumstances in which it has not been waived by the defendant.

Finally, another specialized transfer statute should be noted. Section 1407 of the Judicial Code, enacted in 1968,[39] authorizes the temporary transfer of two or more civil actions "involving one or more common questions of fact" that are pending in different districts, to a single

---

33. 363 U.S. at 342–43, 80 S.Ct. at 1089.

34. Most commentators have been highly critical of the Hoffman decision. See Korbel, The Law of Federal Venue and Choice of the Most Convenient Forum, 15 Rutgers L.Rev. 607, 613–15 (1961); Masington, Venue in the Federal Courts—The Problem of the Inconvenient Forum, 15 U.Miami L.Rev. 237 (1961); Note, Transfer of Actions Under 28 U.S.C. § 1404(a), 36 Ind.L.J. 344 (1961); Note, Change of Venue Under Section 1404(a) of the Judicial Code: The Meaning of "Might Have Been Brought," 45 Minn.L.Rev. 680 (1961); Case Comment, 46 Iowa L.Rev. 661 (1961). The ramifications of the Hoffman decision are discussed in 15 C. Wright, A. Miller & E. Cooper, Jurisdiction and Related Matters 2d § 3845.

35. This possibility of discrimination figured heavily in the majority decision in the Hoffman case. 363 U.S. at 344, 80 S.Ct. at 1090.

36. Philip Carey Mfg. Co. v. Taylor, 286 F.2d 782, 784 (6th Cir.1961), cert. denied 366 U.S. 948. See Korbel, Plaintiff's Right to Change of Venue in Federal Courts, 38 U.Det.L.J. 137 (1960).

37. E.g., Torres v. Walsh, 221 F.2d 319 (2d Cir.1955), cert. denied 350 U.S. 836.

38. Foster–Milburn Co. v. Knight, 181 F.2d 949 (2d Cir.1950). Approval of this rule is implicit in the Supreme Court decision in Hoffman v. Blaski, discussed in text at note 31, above.

39. Act of April 29, 1968, 82 Stat. 109.

district "for coordinated or consolidated pretrial proceedings." It also establishes a special Judicial Panel on Multidistrict Litigation to determine whether transfer is appropriate in a particular case, what district should be denominated the transferee forum, and who should serve as the transferee judge. The legislative history of the statute reveals the statute's purpose to be "to provide centralized management under court supervision of pretrial proceedings of multidistrict litigation to assure the 'just and efficient conduct' of such actions."[40] Transfer under these circumstances should avoid or minimize conflict and duplication in discovery and other pretrial procedures in related cases. The use of the statute to coordinate and consolidate pretrial proceedings in complex cases[41] thus promotes the just and efficient disposition of actions in a manner that is both fair to the litigants and conducive to the most efficient allocation of judicial resources.

Under the statute, the Judicial Panel on Multidistrict Litigation may order transfer sua sponte or on a motion seeking transfer made by any party involved in one of the actions sought to be consolidated. Transfer will be ordered only if the Panel determines that the three statutory prerequisites are satisfied: (1) there are common questions of fact; (2) transfer will serve the "convenience of parties and witnesses"; and (3) transfer will "promote the just and efficient conduct" of the actions to be consolidated.[42] Transfer is not automatic even when the requirements have been satisfied. For example, the Panel has demonstrated a tendency to refuse to order pretrial consolidation when it believes that the litigant seeking it has an ulterior motive, such as the circumvention of the personal jurisdiction requirements.[43]

Unlike transfers under the general transfer statute, actions may be transferred under Section 1407 without regard to the usual venue requirements.[44] However, the choice of a transferee court obviously is tied to the requirements and considerations underlying the initial deci-

---

40. House Rep. No. 1130, 90th Cong., 2d Sess. 2, reprinted in 1968 U.S.Code Cong. & Admin.News 1898, 1899–1900.

41. The statute itself does not specify any particular type of case to which it should be applied, although the House of Representatives Report accompanying the legislation identified civil antitrust actions, common disaster actions, patent and trademark suits, products liability and securities law violation actions as likely classes of litigation meriting coordinated pretrial treatment. House Rep. No. 1130, 90th Cong., 2d Sess. 3, reprinted in 1968 U.S.Code Cong. & Admin.News 1898, 1900.

The American Law Institute has proposed a major expansion of the multidistrict transfer statute that would allow for transfer for trial, as well as pretrial. See American Law Institute, Complex Litigation: Statutory Recommendations and Analysis with Reporters' Study (1994).

42. For examples of the Judicial Panel's determinations according to these requirements, see In re Air Disaster at Lockerbie, Scotland, 709 F.Supp. 231 (Jud.Pan. Mult.Lit.1989); In re Union Carbide Corp. Gas Plant Disaster at Bhopal, India in December, 1984, 634 F.Supp. 842 (S.D.N.Y. 1986), modified and affirmed 809 F.2d 195 (2d Cir.1987), cert. denied 484 U.S. 871; In re A.H. Robins Co., "Dalkon Shield" Litigation, 505 F.Supp. 221 (Jud.Pan.Mult.Lit. 1981). See generally 15 C. Wright, A. Miller & E. Cooper, Jurisdiction and Related Matters 2d §§ 3862–67.

43. In re Truck Acc. Near Alamagordo, New Mexico, 387 F.Supp. 732 (Jud.Pan. Mult.Lit.1975).

44. In re Revenue Properties Co., 309 F.Supp. 1002, 1004 (Jud.Pan. Mult.Lit.1970).

sion to transfer. And although Section 1407 clearly provides that any transferred action "shall be remanded" at the end of the pretrial proceedings, for many years transferee courts engaged in the efficient practice of retaining jurisdiction over the transferred actions, either by securing the consent of the parties involved, or by transferring the cases to themselves under Section 1404(a) so long as the usual Section 1404(a) requirements could be met. However, the Supreme Court explicitly invalidated this practice in Lexecon, Inc. v. Milberg Weiss Bershad Hynes & Lerach.[45] Relying on the plain language of the statute, the Court concluded that the use of the word "shall" placed an absolute obligation upon the Panel to remand cases under Section 1407.

Given this uncompromising assertion, it can be presumed that the Panel must order a remand to the courts in which the consolidated cases were initiated even if all the parties involved are willing to consent to the case proceeding to trial in the transferee forum. The Supreme Court did add, however, that "on any view of Section 1407(a), if an order may be made under Section 1404(a), it may be made after remand to the originating district court." Therefore, at least in those cases when all parties consent, the Court's decision may well simply have imposed an extra procedural step; the Panel will remand to the originating district courts, which then will transfer the cases back to the transferee forum, provided that venue there is proper under Section 1404(a). But the transferee court no longer may transfer the Section 1407 cases to itself, since to do so would preclude the Panel from fulfilling its statutory obligation to remand.[46]

---

45. 523 U.S. 26 , 118 S.Ct. 956, 140 L.Ed.2d 62 (1998).

46. Multidistrict litigation under Section 1407 is discussed in greater detail in 15 C. Wright, A. Miller & E. Cooper, Jurisdic-

tion and Related Matters 2d §§ 3861–68. See also Note, The Judicial Panel and the Conduct of Multidistrict Litigation, 87 Harv.L.Rev. 1001 (1974).

§§ 2.18–3.0 are reserved for supplementary material.

Chapter 3

PERSONAL JURISDICTION

Analysis

---

§ 3.1 Overview

Before a court can hear and decide a particular case, it not only must have jurisdiction over the subject matter of the dispute,[1] it also must have jurisdiction over the persons or property involved in the action. The latter type of jurisdiction is referred to as personal, or territorial, jurisdiction.[2] The scope of a particular court's personal jurisdiction is determined by the federal Constitution, which defines the outermost limits of a state's power over persons and things outside its borders, and by any additional limitations imposed by the state itself. A state cannot exercise its adjudicatory authority over a party or a piece of property unless it has both the statutory authority and the constitutionally recognized power to do so. Historically, personal jurisdiction was asserted on the basis of the presence of the person or thing involved in the litigation within the forum's territorial boundaries or the consent of the party.[3] More modern law allows the assertion of personal jurisdiction

§ 3.1

1. See Chapter 2, above.

2. The term "territorial jurisdiction" is suggested and used in Restatement Second of Judgments 55 (1982).

3. See §§ 3.2–3.9, below.

based upon a review of the relationship that exists among the place where the underlying transaction took place, the parties, and the territory of the state where suit is brought.[4]

In addition to a finding that the forum court has the statutory and constitutional power to assert personal jurisdiction over a particular defendant or piece of property, procedural due process notions require that a court not exercise its adjudicatory authority unless the persons whose rights will be affected have been given adequate notice and an opportunity to be heard.[5] A judgment that is entered without providing these protections is invalid. Thus, notions of procedural due process must be considered in conjunction with any assertion of personal or property jurisdiction for the method of asserting jurisdiction must be designed to meet these needs.

This Chapter explores in detail the statutory and constitutional requirements for asserting territorial jurisdiction, as well as the requirements and means of providing for adequate notice and an opportunity to be heard. It concludes with an examination of the way in which a party who wishes to challenge a court's authority because of a defect or failing of any one of these requirements may do so.[6]

A. HISTORICAL DEVELOPMENT OF JURISDICTIONAL DOCTRINE

1. Traditional Bases of Jurisdiction

§ 3.2 The Jurisdictional Categories

The historic premise for the assertion of personal jurisdiction rests on a court's power over a given defendant or her property, which enabled it to enforce legal obligations owed by that defendant. Each court's power in turn was limited by the territorial or geographical boundaries of the government of which it was a part.[1] Given these limitations, three categories of jurisdiction over a defendant evolved: in personam, in rem, and quasi in rem.

The earliest basis for a court's exercise of jurisdiction over a defendant was the defendant's actual presence within that tribunal's territory. Because many personal actions at common-law were quasi-criminal in nature,[2] a court could not enforce a judgment without first obtaining physical control over the defendant. Thus, the assertion of actual physical power over the defendant was a prerequisite to rendering a valid

---

4. See §§ 3.10–3.11, and 3.14–3.15, below.

5. See §§ 3.19–3.21, below.

6. See §§ 3.25–3.27, below.

§ 3.2

1. See generally Ehrenzweig, The Transient Rule of Personal Jurisdiction:

The "Power" Myth and Forum Conveniens, 65 Yale L.J. 289 (1965); Developments in the Law—State–Court Jurisdiction, 73 Harv.L.Rev. 909, 915 (1960).

2. 3 Holdsworth, A History of English Law 626 (5th ed. 1942).

judgment against him.[3] Usually the defendant was brought before the court by writ of arrest, and remained in custody until he posted a bond sufficient to cover the amount of the plaintiff's claims and costs against him.[4] Some historians have argued that from this notion of a court's physical power emerged the concept of the territorial basis of jurisdiction. Under this theory a court could subject a defendant to its decision-making power only if he were personally served with process within the court's territory[5] or consented to the court's jurisdiction.[6] When a judgment was entered on the basis of territorial control over the defendant himself, the court was said to be asserting in personam jurisdiction.

Some courts also recognized a right to levy execution against a defendant's land as well. Early American courts recognized this second type of jurisdiction by distinguishing between proceedings in which the court exercised jurisdiction over the person—jurisdiction in personam—and those in which it exercised jurisdiction over the property itself—jurisdiction in rem.[7] The traditional theory of territorial power, extended to property, gave a forum's courts the right to adjudicate the status or ownership of property located within its borders regardless of the whereabouts of those claiming an interest in it. Although a judgment with respect to property clearly affected the rights and duties of those who claimed an interest in it, in rem jurisdiction was said to operate directly on the property itself, and only indirectly on the claimants. Thus, a judgment rendered by a court proceeding in rem, unlike a judgment in personam, was said not to bind the defendant personally.[8]

Common law courts exercised a third type of jurisdiction, which has been characterized as "attachment jurisdiction."[9] A court would issue a writ of attachment directing the sheriff to seize and hold a defendant's goods in order to secure that defendant's presence at a trial in which personal claims against him were to be adjudicated.[10] At first, the attachment served merely to compel the defendant to appear, and the trial was not allowed to proceed in his absence.[11] Later on, the defendant's continued absence resulted in the attached property being turned over to the plaintiff in satisfaction of the latter's claim.[12] This third type

3. McDonald v. Mabee, 243 U.S. 90, 37 S.Ct. 343, 61 L.Ed. 608 (1917).

4. Mills v. Duryee, 11 U.S. (7 Cranch) 481, 484, 3 L.Ed. 411, 413 (1813); Barrell v. Benjamin, 15 Mass. 354 (1819).

5. Buchanan v. Rucker, 103 Eng.Rep. 546 (K.B.1808). See generally Hazard, A General Theory of State Court Jurisdiction, 1965 Sup.Ct.Rev. 241, 252.

6. See generally Ross, The Shifting Basis of Jurisdiction, 17 Minn.L.Rev. 146, 148 (1933).

7. Kibbe v. Kibbe, 1 Kirby 119, 126 (Conn.1786); Phelps v. Holker, 1 U.S. (1 Dall.) 261, 264, 1 L.Ed. 128 (1788); Fenton v. Garlick, 8 Johns 194, 197 (N.Y.1811).

8. Freeman v. Alderson, 119 U.S. 185, 7 S.Ct. 165, 30 L.Ed. 372 (1886); Boswell's Lessee v. Otis, 50 U.S. (9 How.) 336, 13 L.Ed. 164 (1850).

9. For a history of the development of attachment jurisdiction, see Levy, Mesne Process in Personal Actions at Common Law and the Power Doctrine, 78 Yale L.J. 52, 58–79 (1968).

10. See generally R. Millar, Civil Procedure of the Trial Court in Historical Perspective 74 (1952).

11. 2 F. Pollock & F. Maitland, The History of English Law 594–95 (2d ed.1959).

12. See C. Drake, A Treatise on the Law of Suits by Attachment in the United States 1–2 (6th ed.1885).

of jurisdiction evolved, in the American context, into quasi in rem jurisdiction.[13]

American tribunals asserted quasi in rem jurisdiction over property located within the forum in order to adjudicate a personal dispute that usually was unrelated to the property itself. Quasi in rem jurisdiction was a hybrid, combining elements of both jurisdiction in rem and jurisdiction in personam. Like in rem jurisdiction, quasi in rem jurisdiction was based on a court's power over a defendant's property rather than his person. Like in personam jurisdiction, quasi in rem jurisdiction gave the court authority to adjudicate personal claims against the defendant, with the judgment strictly limited by the value of the property.[14] The differences between these forms of jurisdiction are highlighted by reviewing the Supreme Court's decision in Pennoyer v. Neff, which is discussed in the next section.

2.   The Rule of Physical Presence

§ 3.3   Pennoyer v. Neff

A number of American judges adopted the territoriality principle of jurisdiction at an early date.[1] But it was not until the 1877 decision in the still-famous case of Pennoyer v. Neff[2] that the Supreme Court gave the territoriality concept constitutional approval.

Pennoyer was the second of two actions involving Neff, a resident of California. In 1866, Mitchell, an Oregon attorney, sued Neff in Oregon state court to recover unpaid legal fees. Mitchell published notice of the commencement of the action in an Oregon newspaper, pursuant to a state statute authorizing "service by publication" for actions against nonresident defendants. Neff was not personally served. When Neff failed to appear for trial, Mitchell obtained a default judgment against him. To satisfy that judgment, the court attached a tract of Oregon land that Neff had purchased under the Oregon Donation Laws. The land then was sold to Pennoyer at a sheriff's execution sale and the proceeds awarded to Mitchell.

Nine years later, Neff brought an action in ejectment against Pennoyer in the Oregon federal court, seeking to recover the land. Neff claimed ownership based on the Oregon Donation Laws; Pennoyer asserted his ownership rights on the basis of the deed issued as a result of the judicial sale. In reply, Neff argued that the Oregon state court had lacked jurisdiction over both him and his property and thus the judg-

13. See generally Silberman, Shaffer v. Heitner: The End of an Era, 53 N.Y.U.L.Rev. 33, 39–53 (1978).

14. Freeman v. Alderson, 119 U.S. 185, 7 S.Ct. 165, 30 L.Ed. 372 (1886); Cooper v. Reynolds, 77 U.S. (10 Wall.) 308, 19 L.Ed. 931 (1870).

§ 3.3

1. See, e.g., Mills v. Duryee, 11 U.S. (7 Cranch) 481, 486, 3 L.Ed. 411 (1813) (Johnson, J., dissenting).

2. 95 U.S. (5 Otto) 714, 24 L.Ed. 565 (1877).

ment in Mitchell v. Neff was invalid and Pennoyer's ownership claim must fail.

The Supreme Court upheld Neff's claim and nullified the Oregon court's sale of Neff's land to Pennoyer. In the majority opinion, Justice Field enunciated a "field theory" of state court jurisdiction that was to survive for almost a century. He based his theory on two interrelated "principles of public law": first, "that every State possesses exclusive jurisdiction and sovereignty over persons and property within its territory;"[3] and second, "that no state can exercise direct jurisdiction and authority over persons or property without its territory."[4] Thus, each state would be exclusively powerful over the persons and property inside its borders and absolutely powerless over all persons and property outside those borders. These principles, Justice Field argued, flowed from the fact that individual states resemble independent nations. But Justice Field recognized that a federalist system necessarily places limits on the exclusive sovereignty of individual states over their own persons and property. Although a state court was not allowed to exercise its powers so as to interfere with another state's exclusive dominion over its own people and property, it was obliged to protect its own citizens in their dealings with nonresidents.[5] Consequently, each state court had some authority to bind nonresident defendants to judgments within the state.

A state court could enter a binding personal judgment against an unwilling nonresident defendant if, and only if, he was personally served with process within the state or voluntarily appeared before the court. Personal service on the defendant sufficed both to assert the state's power over him and to give the defendant notice of the pending action. Without personal service within the state borders, however, a state could not assert in personam jurisdiction over a nonresident defendant. Mitchell had not served Neff within Oregon and thus the Oregon court had no in personam power to enter a judgment against Neff.

Justice Field also noted that a state court could exercise indirect jurisdiction over a nonresident defendant by finding and seizing at the outset of the action property belonging to the defendant that was located in the state. By attaching the nonresident's property at commencement, the state court asserted its power over the property and, at the same time, the attachment was deemed to notify the defendant that his property had been taken into custody. Since the seizure itself provided a form of notice, the Court decided that "substituted service by publication, or in any other authorized form, may be sufficient to inform parties of the object of proceedings * * *."[6]

The Pennoyer Court did not require that the property seized be in any way related to the plaintiff's claim. It did, however, limit a plaintiff's recovery against a defaulting nonresident defendant to the value of the

---

3. 95 U.S. at 722.

4. Ibid.

5. 95 U.S. at 723.

6. 95 U.S. at 727.

property that could be found and attached within state boundaries.[7] Since Mitchell had not seized Neff's property until after the judgment was entered in that action,[8] the Oregon court never had power even indirectly over Neff and the judgment was invalid.

The Pennoyer decision created two tiers of state court jurisdiction, one based on power over a person present in the state and the other based on power over a person's property present in the state. A state court asserted in personam jurisdiction by personal service on the defendant inside the state and in rem or quasi in rem jurisdiction by attachment of the defendant's in-state property. Each tier required a different degree of notice: although publication would suffice for in rem jurisdiction's limited personal liability, only personal service could provide the notice required when a state court subjected a nonconsenting nonresident to full in personam liability.[9]

Justice Field went on to assert that this two-tiered scheme of state court jurisdiction was rooted in the Due Process Clause of the Fourteenth Amendment.[10] Although this discussion was technically dictum because the Fourteenth Amendment did not take effect until after judgment had been rendered in Mitchell v. Neff, Justice Field's analysis effectively linked the Due Process Clause with the Full Faith and Credit Clause of Article IV as the constitutional measuring rod of state court assertions of personal jurisdiction. A state court's failure to assert power or provide notice in the appropriate manner would lead to invalidation of its judgment as a violation of due process. Any judgment so invalidated would not only be denied full faith and credit in any other state of the union, it would be unenforceable in the very state in which it was rendered.

By creating a strict rule of physical presence, Pennoyer v. Neff established a simple, formalistic framework for analyzing the constitutionality of all assertions of state court jurisdiction. A state had power to adjudicate a dispute involving a nonresident if and only if the defendant could be personally served or his property could be attached within the state. The Pennoyer Court recognized in its own opinion that some categories of cases might require less restrictive rules, such as jurisdiction over domestic relations cases and nonresident business entities.[11] Other shortcomings soon became readily apparent within each of the jurisdictional categories that the decision had approved.

3. Jurisdiction Over Persons: Exceptions to the Rule of Physical Presence

§ 3.4 The Presence Test: Some Problems and Limitations

The Pennoyer rule of presence allowed the physical presence of a defendant in the forum to be a sufficient basis for acquiring personal

---

7. 95 U.S. at 726.

8. In fact, Mitchell could not have attached Neff's property in order to assert jurisdiction because Neff obtained title to the property in March 1866, one month after judgment was reached in Mitchell v. Neff.

9. See §§ 3.19–3.20, below.

10. 95 U.S. at 733.

11. 95 U.S. at 735.

jurisdiction over that individual, no matter how brief his stay might be.[1] The metaphysics of this principle permitted a nonresident defendant to be served with process even while travelling through the state by car or flying over it in an airplane.[2] This principle led to fortuitous assertions of state court jurisdiction as society at large became more mobile.

Perhaps more troubling, the Pennoyer rule proved useless as more and more civil controversies came to involve multistate elements. As one commentator observed:

> [W]hen adjudication of civil controversies does involve multistate elements, it is fatuous to think of any court having *exclusive* jurisdiction of anything. The jurisdictional problem exists precisely because there is no single tribunal that has exclusive jurisdiction in the territorial sense.[3]

Even at its birth, the Pennoyer Court was forced to recognize exceptions to its rule of strict physical presence. These exceptions provided limited sources of flexibility for the rigid territoriality framework Pennoyer established and allowed the courts to bring jurisdiction more in line with changes in the means of transportation and communication and in the methods of carrying on economic activity. In particular, the courts relied on notions of consent, residence, or domicile as bases for a state court's assertion of full in personam jurisdiction.[4]

Application of the Pennoyer rule to corporations required additional refinements. In order to assert in personam jurisdiction over a corporation, the courts had to determine when a corporation was "physically present" in a particular forum. This was not a difficult task when dealing with domestic corporations. Because the chartering state was deemed to have power over the corporations it had created and subjected to its control,[5] domestic corporations could be sued in the states of their incorporation in connection with any cause of action.[6] Since corporations were deemed to be artificial persons existing within the territory of the sovereign that created them,[7] treating domestic corporations as present in their state of incorporation for purposes of service of process seemed a logical extension of the Pennoyer principle.

This reasoning created difficulties, however, when corporations began to engage actively in business in states in which they were not incorporated. These "foreign corporations" were legally present only in

---

§ 3.4

1. See, e.g., Barrell v. Benjamin, 15 Mass. 354 (1819).

2. Grace v. MacArthur, 170 F.Supp. 442 (E.D.Ark.1959).

3. Hazard, A General Theory of State–Court Jurisdiction, 1965 Sup.Ct.Rev. 241, 265.

4. For a full discussion of these exceptions in cases involving natural persons, see §§ 3.5–3.6, below.

5. See Pennoyer v. Neff, 95 U.S. (5 Otto) 714, 734, 24 L.Ed. 565, 573 (1877).

6. See E. Scoles & P. Hay, Conflict of Laws § 9.2 (2d ed.1992); A. Scott, Fundamentals of Procedure 47 (1922).

7. Bank of Augusta v. Earle, 38 U.S. (13 Pet.) 519, 588, 10 L.Ed. 274 (1839).

the states in which they were chartered,[8] no matter how actively they engaged in business in another state. The difficulty was compounded by the fact that personal service on the corporation's chief executive officer gave rise to in personam jurisdiction over the corporation only when the officer was served in the state of incorporation.[9] Because a corporate officer was deemed to shed his official character as soon as the officer left the corporation's charter state,[10] a state court could not obtain in personam jurisdiction over a foreign corporation even by personally serving the corporation's chief executive officer within its territory.

As state courts faced the economic reality that corporations were carrying on business activities on regional and national scales, they began to develop jurisdictional fictions to permit the assertion of in personam jurisdiction over foreign corporations operating within their territory. The concepts of "express and implied consent," "corporate presence," and "doing business," discussed below,[11] evolved as means to permit local private entities to sue and be sued by foreign corporations in state court.

§ 3.5 Jurisdiction Based on Consent

A party always may concede that a court has authority to render a binding enforceable judgment against him. Thus perhaps the biggest exception to the Pennoyer rule was the notion, still valid today, that a defendant not physically present in the state may consent to the jurisdiction of its courts. Consent may be given before or after a suit has been instituted, or by virtue of filing a court action. In some cases consent may be express, in others it will be implied. A look at the different forms that consent may take illustrates the importance of this method of asserting jurisdiction.

A defendant may stipulate to the jurisdiction of the court in advance of litigation; in this way express consent is given. For example, the defendant voluntarily submits to the jurisdiction of the courts of a particular forum whenever the defendant agrees to arbitration there.[1] Parties also may contract specifically that any dispute arising out of their contract will be adjudicated in the courts of a particular place.[2]

8. Ibid.

9. 1 Kyd, Corporations 272 (1793).

10. McQueen v. Middletown Mfg. Co., 16 Johns. 5, 7 (N.Y.Sup.Ct.1819). In Riverside & Dan River Cotton Mills v. Menefee, 237 U.S. 189, 195, 35 S.Ct. 579, 581, 59 L.Ed. 910 (1915), service on a resident president of a foreign corporation was held invalid.

11. See §§ 3.5 and 3.7, below.

§ 3.5

1. Farr & Co. v. Cia. Intercontinental de Navegacion de Cuba, S.A., 243 F.2d 342 (2d Cir.1957); Frey & Horgan Corp. v. Su-

perior Court, 5 Cal.2d 401, 55 P.2d 203 (1936), cert. denied 298 U.S. 684; Gilbert v. Burnstine, 255 N.Y. 348, 174 N.E. 706 (1931).

2. M/S Bremen & Unterweser Reederei v. Zapata Off–Shore Co., 407 U.S. 1, 92 S.Ct. 1907, 32 L.Ed.2d 513 (1972) (Houston based corporation and German corporation contract to resolve all disputes in "London Court of Justice"); Muller & Co. v. Swedish American Line Ltd., 224 F.2d 806 (2d Cir. 1955), cert. denied 350 U.S. 903 (although a court cannot be ousted of its jurisdiction by a contract, it can decline jurisdiction and relegate the litigant to the forum stipulated in the contract); Smith, Valentino & Smith,

Along these lines, parties to a contract may appoint an in-state agent to accept process in litigation arising out of the contract.[3]

A variation on the express contractual consent to personal jurisdiction is the cognovit clause in a loan agreement, which authorizes a creditor, upon the debtor's default in paying the loan, to use a confession-of-judgment provision to have judgment entered against the debtor without service of process or notice being given him. Cognovit notes have been upheld in some jurisdictions,[4] and judgments entered on the basis of cognovit notes have been accorded full faith and credit even when the enforcing state itself will not honor cognovit notes[5] themselves. Other states have enacted legislation to prohibit enforcement of cognovit notes.[6] The United States Supreme Court has indicated that cognovit clauses are not per se violative of due process, although such factors as the relative bargaining power of the creditor and debtor, as well as the knowledge, ability, and volition of the parties to the agreement are relevant to the legitimacy of any given clause.[7]

Besides express consent in a contract or a cognovit note, a second type of express consent was recognized in the era immediately following Pennoyer v. Neff. A state in effect could require a corporation to appoint an agent for service of process as a condition of conducting certain activities within the forum. In Lafayette Insurance Company v. French[8] and St. Clair v. Cox,[9] the Supreme Court held that a state could condition a corporation's right to do business within its borders on its consenting to service of process on an agent specifically designated by the corporation for that purpose, provided the agent was one likely to inform the corporation of service of process.[10] This rule rested on the premise that the corporation was not a citizen within the meaning of the Privileges and Immunities Clause of the United States Constitution;[11] therefore it had no inherent right to do business in any state in which it was not incorporated. That argument was of dubious validity, however. Other Supreme Court decisions make it clear that a state cannot constitutionally exclude a foreign corporation from transacting interstate

Inc. v. Superior Court, 17 Cal.3d 491, 131 Cal.Rptr. 374, 551 P.2d 1206 (1976).

3. National Equipment Rental, Ltd. v. Szukhent, 375 U.S. 311, 84 S.Ct. 411, 11 L.Ed.2d 354 (1964), noted 1964 U.Ill.L.F. 443. This subject is discussed more fully in § 3.20, below.

4. Swarb v. Lennox, 314 F.Supp. 1091 (E.D.Pa.1970), affirmed 405 U.S. 191, 92 S.Ct. 767, 31 L.Ed.2d 138 (1972).

5. McDade v. Moynihan, 330 Mass. 437, 115 N.E.2d 372 (1953). But see Atlas Credit Co. v. Ezrine, 25 N.Y.2d 219, 303 N.Y.S.2d 382, 250 N.E.2d 474 (1969).

6. Chapter 227 of the Indiana Acts of 1927 renders enforcement of cognovit notes a criminal misdemeanor. Comment, The Indiana Cognovit Note Statute, 5 Ind.L.J. 208 (1930).

7. D.H. Overmyer Co. v. Frick Co., 405 U.S. 174, 92 S.Ct. 775, 31 L.Ed.2d 124 (1972). See also Swarb v. Lennox, 314 F.Supp. 1091 (E.D.Pa.1970), affirmed 405 U.S. 191, 92 S.Ct. 767, 31 L.Ed.2d 138 (1972); Kosches & Son v. Nichols, 68 Misc.2d 795, 327 N.Y.S.2d 968 (1971).

8. 59 U.S. (18 How.) 404, 15 L.Ed. 451 (1856).

9. 106 U.S. (16 Otto) 350, 1 S.Ct. 354, 27 L.Ed. 222 (1882).

10. Commercial Mut. Acc. Co. v. Davis, 213 U.S. 245, 29 S.Ct. 445, 53 L.Ed. 782 (1909).

11. Blake v. McClung, 172 U.S. 239, 19 S.Ct. 165, 43 L.Ed. 432 (1898); Paul v. Virginia, 75 U.S. (8 Wall.) 168, 19 L.Ed. 357 (1869).

business within its territory.[12] And if the state cannot exclude the corporation, it then should not be able to exact its consent.[13]

Despite deficiencies in the very underpinnings of the corporate consent theory, the consent notion flourished and was expanded to include cases in which a foreign corporation was deemed to imply its consent to jurisdiction whenever it in fact was doing business in the forum.[14] By virtue of conducting business within the forum, the corporation was deemed to have impliedly appointed an agent designated by the state—such as the Secretary of State—to receive service of process on its behalf for any dispute arising out of its activities within the state.

The rationale behind the implied consent theory was sound. An uncooperative corporation that refused to furnish an express consent to the state's jurisdiction should not be in a more advantageous position than a compliant corporation.[15] Nevertheless, the implied consent doctrine was not without contradictions.[16] For example, a corporation that had filed an express consent was liable to suit on causes of action not arising out of its business activities in the forum.[17] On the other hand, suits against a corporation that only had impliedly consented to the court's jurisdiction by doing business within the state were limited to claims arising out of that business.[18] Justice Holmes explained the added breadth of jurisdictional power based on the defendant's express consent as follows:

> * * * when a power actually is conferred by a document, the party executing it takes the risk of interpretation that may be put upon it by the courts. The execution was the defendant's voluntary act.[19]

The distinction, said then Judge Cardozo, was "between a true consent and an imputed or implied consent * * * "; in other words, he went on, "between a fact and a fiction."[20] But even when the consent was implied, if service was made within the forum state upon an appropriate corpo-

12. Davis v. Farmers' Co-op. Equity Co., 262 U.S. 312, 43 S.Ct. 556, 67 L.Ed. 996 (1923); Sioux Remedy Co. v. Cope, 235 U.S. 197, 35 S.Ct. 57, 59 L.Ed. 193 (1914); International Text-Book Co. v. Pigg, 217 U.S. 91, 30 S.Ct. 481, 54 L.Ed. 678 (1910); Pensacola Telegraph Co. v. Western Union Telegraph Co., 96 U.S. (6 Otto) 1, 24 L.Ed. 708 (1878).

13. Kurland, The Supreme Court, the Due Process Clause and the In Personam Jurisdiction of State Courts—From Pennoyer to Denckla: A Review, 25 U.Chi.L.Rev. 569, 581 (1958).

14. St. Clair v. Cox, 106 U.S. (16 Otto) 350, 356, 1 S.Ct. 354, 360, 27 L.Ed. 222 (1882).

15. J. Beale, Conflict of Laws 377 n. 2 (1935).

16. Kurland, The Supreme Court, the Due Process Clause and the In Personam

Jurisdiction of State Courts—From Pennoyer to Denckla: A Review, 25 U.Chi.L.Rev. 569, 578 (1958).

17. Bagdon v. Philadelphia & Reading Coal & Iron Co., 217 N.Y. 432, 111 N.E. 1075 (1916).

18. Simon v. Southern R. Co., 236 U.S. 115, 35 S.Ct. 255, 59 L.Ed. 492 (1915); Old Wayne Mut. Life Ass'n v. McDonough, 204 U.S. 8, 27 S.Ct. 236, 51 L.Ed. 345 (1907).

19. Pennsylvania Fire Ins. Co. v. Gold Issue Mining & Milling Co., 243 U.S. 93, 96, 37 S.Ct. 344, 345, 61 L.Ed. 610 (1917). See also Smolik v. Philadelphia & Reading Coal & Iron Co., 222 Fed. 148 (S.D.N.Y.1915).

20. Bagdon v. Philadelphia & Reading Coal & Iron Co., 217 N.Y. 432, 437, 111 N.E. 1075, 1076 (1916).

rate officer or agent, jurisdiction might be upheld on an unrelated claim.[21]

Just as the idea of consent provided the theoretical justification for a court's assertion of jurisdiction over a foreign corporation, it also was twisted and stretched to allow jurisdiction over nonresident individual tortfeasors in certain instances. In 1916, in Kane v. New Jersey[22] the Supreme Court upheld the constitutionality of a New Jersey statute requiring that a nonresident motorist formally designate the Secretary of State as an agent on whom process could be served in any action arising out of the operation of a registered motor vehicle in the state. Use of automobiles, the Court noted, involved "constant and serious dangers to the public,"[23] and the ability to enforce penalties against defalcating motorists was vital to law enforcement. According to the Court, the "power of a state to regulate the use of motor vehicles on its highways"[24] conferred the power to condition the use of motor vehicles in the forum on the consent of the nonresident to the jurisdiction of the state and its courts.

But if the state could exercise its police powers to exact an express consent as a precondition to driving a motor vehicle in a given forum, then the state also could imply that the nonresident motorist had consented to its jurisdiction by appointing a local official his agent for process whenever the motorist drove within the state. Implied consent statutes expressing this proposition soon began to appear. The Supreme Court validated the procedure in Hess v. Pawloski in 1927.[25] A state could legislate that a nonresident motorist using its highways be deemed to have appointed a local official his agent to receive service of process in any action growing out of the use of the vehicle within the state, provided the statute required that the defendant be notified of the service on the official.[26] Again the Court stressed the inherent dangers of motor vehicles to persons and property and introduced the notion of the special interest in public safety as a basis for exercising jurisdiction.[27]

The Hess decision represented an attempt to strike a delicate balance between the state's police powers and the individual citizen's due process rights and privilege to travel freely throughout the country. Yet the Court was unwilling to extend the concept of implied consent to all activities of natural persons. In Flexner v. Farson,[28] decided in 1919, the Court declined to uphold jurisdiction over individual members of an out-of-state partnership that was doing business in Kentucky. Defendants had been sued under a Kentucky statute providing for service on the manager or agent of an out-of-state partnership, association, or joint stock company. Rejecting the Kentucky courts' construction of the

21. Tauza v. Susquehanna Coal Co., 220 N.Y. 259, 115 N.E. 915 (1917).

22. 242 U.S. 160, 37 S.Ct. 30, 61 L.Ed. 222 (1916).

23. 242 U.S. at 167, 37 S.Ct. at 32.

24. 242 U.S. at 167, 37 S.Ct. at 31.

25. 274 U.S. 352, 47 S.Ct. 632, 71 L.Ed. 1091 (1927).

26. See the discussion of notice in §§ 3.19–3.20, below.

27. 274 U.S. at 356, 47 S.Ct. at 633.

28. 248 U.S. 289, 39 S.Ct. 97, 63 L.Ed. 250 (1919).

statute to the effect that by doing business in Kentucky the defendants consented to be bound by service of process, the Court found implied consent to be a "mere fiction" that was inapplicable in the nonresident partnership context.[29] Although a state could exclude some foreign corporations from doing business within its borders, the state had no power to exclude the nonresident partners, as they were natural persons and protected by the Privileges and Immunities Clause of Article IV, Section 1.

Even though implied consent did not extend to the "mere transaction of business" according to the Court in Hess v. Pawloski,[30] it clearly provided a precedent for jurisdiction in a broader range of "dangerous activities" than simply driving automobiles within the state. Jurisdiction statutes applicable to aircraft[31] and watercraft operation,[32] as well as construction work[33] soon were enacted by state legislatures and sustained by the courts. Moreover, many courts were emboldened to construe existing jurisdiction statutes more broadly than they had in the past. Motorist statutes were applied when neither plaintiff nor defendant were residents of the state in which the accident occurred,[34] to actions against the representative of a deceased motorist,[35] and even to the nonresident automobile owner who never had been within the forum state but who had authorized use of the car within the state by another.[36]

Flexner v. Farson was further undercut, if not effectively overruled, by the decision in Doherty v. Goodman,[37] which upheld service on the district manager for a nonresident defendant who was engaged in selling corporate securities in the forum. Advancing the implied consent doctrine to support jurisdiction, the Supreme Court again highlighted the "exceptional" nature and dangers of corporate securities and the state interest in their regulation for the protection of citizens.

It should be noted that the recurrent reference by the Supreme Court to "state interest"[38] has persuaded some courts that the real basis of jurisdiction in the Hess–Doherty line of cases is the interest of the forum state rather than any notion of implied consent.[39] This view finds

---

29. 248 U.S. at 293, 39 S.Ct. at 98.

30. 274 U.S. 352, 355, 47 S.Ct. 632, 633, 71 L.Ed. 1091 (1927). But see Nelson v. Miller, 11 Ill.2d 378, 143 N.E.2d 673 (1957), for the proposition that Flexner v. Farson has been overruled by implication.

31. 2 P.S. § 1410 (Pa.). See also Peters v. Robin Airlines, 281 App.Div. 903, 120 N.Y.S.2d 1 (1953) (application of New York nonresident aircraft statute to accident occurring outside New York held unconstitutional).

32. La.Stat.Ann.–R.S. 13:3479 et seq., as amended Acts 1954, No. 137, § 1, upheld as constitutional in Goltzman v. Rougeot, 122 F.Supp. 700 (W.D.La.1954).

33. Sugg v. Hendrix, 142 F.2d 740 (5th Cir.1944), rehearing denied 153 F.2d 240 (5th Cir.1946).

34. Dart Transit Co. v. Wiggins, 1 Ill. App.2d 126, 117 N.E.2d 314 (1953).

35. Milam v. Sol Newman Co., 205 F.Supp. 649 (N.D.Ala.1962).

36. Davis v. St. Paul–Mercury Indem. Co., 294 F.2d 641 (4th Cir.1961).

37. 294 U.S. 623, 55 S.Ct. 553, 79 L.Ed. 1097 (1935).

38. E.g., International Shoe Co. v. Washington, 326 U.S. 310, 66 S.Ct. 154, 90 L.Ed. 95 (1945).

39. Olberding v. Illinois Cent. R. Co., 346 U.S. 338, 74 S.Ct. 83, 98 L.Ed. 39

continued support in decisions upholding "doing business" statutes that provide for jurisdiction over nonresident natural persons upon a finding that the business involved in the particular litigation is subject to special state regulation.[40]

In sum, then, implied consent prior to the filing of a lawsuit served as a major means of asserting in personam jurisdiction over a mobile, business citizenry when a strict application of territorial jurisdiction premised on physical presence would have precluded jurisdiction. Although implied consent theories necessarily rested on fictions, the courts were most careful to avoid undue prejudice to the defendant by simultaneously requiring strict notice obligations as a part of these devices[41] and by limiting their use to the corporate business context or to situations in which a strong state regulatory interest was paramount.

All of the discussion in this section has involved situations in which the defendant consented to jurisdiction prior to the time when the suit was filed. Consent also may be implied on the basis of the activities of the parties after commencement. For example, by commencing a lawsuit, a nonresident plaintiff will be deemed to have submitted to jurisdiction for purposes of any counterclaims that the defendant may want to assert.[42] More commonly, the failure of the defendant to comply with the applicable rules governing the methods for raising jurisdictional objections, whether done intentionally or unintentionally, will constitute a waiver of any objection. Stated alternatively, notions of waiver will act as implied consent.[43]

§ 3.6 Jurisdiction Based on Domicile and Residence

Although consent, either express or implied, afforded the courts their greatest leeway in broadening the base of in personam jurisdiction, it was not the first conceptual peg on which they seized. An individual defendant's domicile was the first exception to the Pennoyer rule of physical presence. Domicile was determined by two factors: the intent of an individual to make a particular location a permanent home, and facts indicating that the party had physically located there.[1]

The notion that a court could enter a personal judgment against a domiciliary who was absent from the jurisdiction and thus was not amenable to service of process there was not new. By the early Nine-

---

(1953); D. Currie, The Growth of the Long Arm: Eight Years of Extended Jurisdiction in Illinois, 1963 U.Ill.L.F. 533, 540.

40. Davis v. Nugent, 90 F.Supp. 522 (S.D.Miss.1950); Armi v. Huckabee, 266 Ala. 91, 94 So.2d 380 (1957); Ritholz v. Dodge, 210 Ark. 404, 196 S.W.2d 479 (1946). For a fuller discussion of the doing-business theory of jurisdiction, see § 3.7, below.

41. See §§ 3.19–3.20, below.

42. In Adam v. Saenger, 303 U.S. 59, 68, 58 S.Ct. 454, 458, 82 L.Ed. 649 (1938),

the Court ruled that the plaintiff corporation impliedly had consented to jurisdiction by initiating the original suit, saying: "It is the price which the state may exact as the condition of opening its courts to the plaintiff."

43. See §§ 3.25–3.26, below.

§ 3.6

1. See Restatement Second of Conflict of Laws §§ 11, 12 (1971). See also Bergner & Engel Brewing Co. v. Dreyfus, 172 Mass. 154, 157, 51 N.E. 531, 532 (1898).

teenth Century, English courts had adopted domicile as a basis of jurisdiction from the civil law, and the principle had been accepted by some American state courts.[2] In 1917, the United States Supreme Court hinted in dictum that a judgment based on domicile coupled with personal service outside the jurisdiction would be valid.[3] In the subsequent cases of Blackmer v. United States[4] and Milliken v. Meyer,[5] the Supreme Court made it clear that domicile and extraterritorial service would support an in personam judgment. The Court's focus in both cases was on whether the assertion of jurisdiction premised on domicile or citizenship was consistent with due process, rather than on means or methods of fitting these situations within Pennoyer's rule of territorial power.[6]

In Blackmer, the petitioner was an American citizen who had been cited for contempt for refusing to comply with a subpoena issued by a federal court and served upon him in France in connection with a proceeding that grew out of the Teapot Dome Scandal. Extraterritorial service was authorized by federal statute and the Supreme Court concluded that the scheme did not violate due process. In the Milliken case the Blackmer principle was applied to state court litigation. Milliken had sued Meyer, a Wyoming resident, in a Wyoming state court. Personal service was effected in Colorado under a Wyoming statute that permitted extraterritorial service in lieu of service by publication on absent residents. Meyer did not appear and an in personam judgment was entered against him by default. Four years later Meyer asked a Colorado court to restrain Milliken's enforcement of the Wyoming judgment. Eventually the United States Supreme Court held the Wyoming judgment valid and entitled to full faith and credit. According to the Court:

> Domicile in the state is alone sufficient to bring an absent defendant within the reach of the state's jurisdiction for purposes of a personal judgment by means of appropriate substituted service. * * * [T]he authority of a state over one of its citizens is not terminated by the mere fact of his absence from the state. The state which accords him privileges and affords protection to him and his property by virtue of his domicile may also exact reciprocal duties.[7]

Domicile continues to be a valid basis of jurisdiction.[8] The availability of defendant's domicile as a proper forum assures that there is one

---

2. Glover v. Glover, 18 Ala. 367 (1850); In re Denick's Estate, 71 N.Y.St.Rep. 549, 92 Hun 161, 36 N.Y.S. 518 (1895) (citizens and domiciliaries).

3. McDonald v. Mabee, 243 U.S. 90, 37 S.Ct. 343, 61 L.Ed. 608 (1917).

4. 284 U.S. 421, 52 S.Ct. 252, 76 L.Ed. 375 (1932).

5. 311 U.S. 457, 61 S.Ct. 339, 85 L.Ed. 278 (1940). See also Arakaki v. Arakaki, 54 Hawaii 60, 502 P.2d 380 (1972).

6. Given the focus of these decisions on due process rather than pure territoriality

concerns, they may be seen as direct precursors of the approach ultimately adopted in International Shoe Co. v. Washington, 326 U.S. 310, 66 S.Ct. 154, 90 L.Ed. 95 (1945). See § 3.10, below.

7. 311 U.S. at 264–63, 61 S.Ct. at 342–43.

8. For personal jurisdiction purposes, citizenship may be treated as coincident with domicile and thus, in actions under federal statutes, citizenship may support jurisdiction. E.g., Blackmer v. U.S., 284 U.S. 421, 52 S.Ct. 252, 76 L.Ed. 375 (1932).

place in which defendant always may be sued.[9] Indeed, domicile at the time the cause of action arose will support jurisdiction even though the defendant moved from the jurisdiction before the action was instituted.[10] Once established, domicile "continues until it is superceded by a new domicile"[11] so that a person is subject to the jurisdiction of the state even though absent from the state for an extended period on business or pleasure, or while in transit to a new domicile.[12]

It has been suggested that residence affords a more easily ascertainable basis for personal jurisdiction than does domicile[13] and some courts have upheld jurisdiction based on where the defendant is living,[14] particularly in divorce actions.[15] Certainly the Milliken rationale of reciprocal obligations between a domiciliary and the state applies as well to a resident. On the other hand, when the defendant has more than one residence, and residence is a valid basis of jurisdiction in each state, the plaintiff then can forum shop, which may have the effect of causing the defendant considerable inconvenience.[16] Whatever the merits of residency as a basis for jurisdiction, most courts cling to the domicile requirement, construing statutes drafted in terms of residency as requiring domicile.[17]

§ 3.7 Jurisdiction Based on Corporate Presence and "Doing Business"

Corporations proved difficult to fit into the Pennoyer regime of personal jurisdiction relating to natural persons because a corporation could not be said to be physically present anywhere. Initially, a corporation was held to be subject to a court's jurisdiction only in the state of its incorporation, beyond which it could have no legal existence.[1] As corporations began to carry on their activities beyond the state in which they were incorporated, however, courts were forced to evolve new jurisdictional theories while still abiding by the principles set out by the Pennoyer Court. The first was the consent theory, discussed earlier.[2] The second was the theory of corporate presence, which filled the gaps the consent theory did not cover. From those two theories emerged yet a

See Note, Citizenship as a Ground for Personal Jurisdiction, 27 Harv.L.Rev. 464 (1914).

9. See Restatement Second of Conflict of Laws § 29 (1971).

10. Owens v. Superior Court of Los Angeles County, 52 Cal.2d 822, 345 P.2d 921 (1959).

11. Stucky v. Stucky, 186 Neb. 636, 185 N.W.2d 656, 659 (1971).

12. Alvord & Alvord v. Patenotre, 196 Misc. 524, 92 N.Y.S.2d 514 (1949).

13. Myrick v. Superior Court, 256 P.2d 348 (Cal.App.1953), writ discharged 41 Cal.2d 519, 261 P.2d 255 (1953).

14. Stucky v. Stucky, 186 Neb. 636, 185 N.W.2d 656 (1971); Fishman v. Sand-

ers, 15 N.Y.2d 298, 258 N.Y.S.2d 380, 206 N.E.2d 326 (1965).

15. Sachs v. Sachs, 278 Ala. 464, 179 So.2d 46 (1965); Wheat v. Wheat, 229 Ark. 842, 318 S.W.2d 793 (1958).

16. Developments in the Law—State–Court Jurisdiction, 73 Harv.L.Rev. 909, 942 (1960).

17. See, e.g., Hartford v. Superior Court, 47 Cal.2d 447, 304 P.2d 1 (1956).

§ 3.7

1. Bank of Augusta v. Earle, 38 U.S. (13 Pet.) 519, 10 L.Ed. 274 (1839). See § 3.4, above.

2. See § 3.5, above.

third one—the "doing business" notion of jurisdiction—which was the foundation for both presence and consent.

The presence doctrine rested on the proposition that a foreign corporation should be amenable to process absent consent only if it was doing enough business within the state to justify the inference that it was present there.[3] Although the presence of a natural person in a state, which would permit "tagging" to support in personam jurisdiction, could be fleeting at best, corporate presence had to be evidenced by continuous dealings in the state.[4] For example, it was held that personal jurisdiction over a corporation was not necessarily supported by the temporary presence of corporate personnel conducting business in the state.[5] On the other hand, if the corporation was found to be present, jurisdiction would be sustained on claims unrelated to its local business dealings,[6] which was not true under the implied consent theory. But once a corporation ceased to do continuous business in a state, it no longer was present for purposes of acquiring jurisdiction over it. A corporation could escape a state's jurisdiction by ceasing to conduct business there even though the former corporate activities gave rise to the cause of action[7]— a loophole that did not exist under the consent doctrine.[8]

In addition to these anomalies, other problems with the corporate presence theory surfaced. Notably, jurisdiction based on corporate presence was inconsistent with the thesis that a corporation had no legal existence outside the state of its incorporation. Moreover, how much business constituted sufficient business for purposes of finding corporate presence was difficult to standardize and therefore was somewhat unpredictable. The sufficiency of the corporation's local business became a frequently litigated threshold question to be answered on the facts of each case.[9] The presence formulation did not offer any magical solution because, in reality, presence was a "conclusory term," which did "no more than put the question to be answered."[10]

"Presence" was but a conclusion based upon a finding of sufficient business activity in the forum to support the inference of presence.[11] Not

---

3. Philadelphia & Reading R. Co. v. McKibbin, 243 U.S. 264, 37 S.Ct. 280, 61 L.Ed. 710 (1917); International Harvester Co. of America v. Kentucky, 234 U.S. 579, 34 S.Ct. 944, 58 L.Ed. 1479 (1914); Bomze v. Nardis Sportswear, Inc., 165 F.2d 33 (2d Cir.1948); Hutchinson v. Chase & Gilbert, 45 F.2d 139 (2d Cir.1930). See also Frummer v. Hilton Hotels Int'l, Inc., 19 N.Y.2d 533, 281 N.Y.S.2d 41, 227 N.E.2d 851 (1967).

4. Hutchinson v. Chase & Gilbert, 45 F.2d 139 (2d Cir.1930).

5. James–Dickinson Farm Mortgage Co. v. Harry, 273 U.S. 119, 47 S.Ct. 308, 71 L.Ed. 569 (1927).

6. Kurland, The Supreme Court, the Due Process Clause and the In Personam Jurisdiction of State Courts—From Pennoy-

er to Denckla: A Review, 25 U.Chi.L.Rev. 569, 583 (1958).

7. Robert Mitchell Furniture Co. v. Selden Breck Constr. Co., 257 U.S. 213, 42 S.Ct. 84, 66 L.Ed. 201 (1921).

8. Simon v. Southern Ry. Co., 236 U.S. 115, 35 S.Ct. 255, 59 L.Ed. 492 (1915); Tauza v. Susquehanna Coal Co., 220 N.Y. 259, 115 N.E. 915 (1917).

9. Hutchinson v. Chase & Gilbert, 45 F.2d 139 (2d Cir.1930).

10. 45 F.2d at 141.

11. As Judge Hand wrote in a prescient opinion, "There must be some continuous dealings in the forum; enough to demand trial away from its home. * * * This last appears to us to be really the control-

surprisingly, therefore, courts soon began to inquire directly into the quantum of the foreign corporation's business activity and to use the "doing business" formulation itself as a basis for jurisdiction.[12] The standards for "doing business," however, remained elusive. Regular purchases within a state were held not to constitute doing business,[13] but solicitation of business combined with some other business activity did.[14] The maintenance of an office, the locus of negotiations, the execution of a contract, and the activities of subsidiary companies[15] were among a number of factors to be considered; these provided guidelines but hardly constituted hard and fast rules.

One final problem that plagued the courts was how to treat parent and subsidiary corporations for purposes of determining whether one or the other or both satisfied the presence or doing business standard. It is clear that jurisdiction over a parent corporation does not necessarily confer jurisdiction over any of its subsidiaries,[16] nor does jurisdiction over one of the subsidiaries give rise to jurisdiction over the parent.[17] There must be a jurisdictional peg that goes beyond mere ownership of stock in another company. If, for example, there is an agency relationship[18] or the parent exercises economic and operational control over the subsidiary, creating a dependent economic relationship between the two,[19] jurisdiction over the one will sustain jurisdiction over the other.

4. Jurisdiction Over Property

§ 3.8 In Rem and Quasi in Rem Jurisdiction: Traditional Doctrine

In Pennoyer v. Neff, the Supreme Court declared that the courts of each state had the power to determine the title of property within state borders; however, it declared states impotent to exercise jurisdiction in

---

ling consideration, expressed shortly by the word 'presence,' but involving an estimate of the inconvenience which would result from requiring it to defend, where it has been sued. We are to inquire whether the extent and continuity of what it has done in the state in question makes it reasonable to bring it before one of its courts." Hutchinson v. Chase & Gilbert, 45 F.2d 139, 141 (2d Cir.1930).

12. In response to judicial developments, a number of states enacted "doing business" statutes supporting jurisdiction in various situations. See § 3.13, below.

13. Rosenberg Bros. & Co. v. Curtis Brown Co., 260 U.S. 516, 43 S.Ct. 170, 67 L.Ed. 372 (1923).

14. St. Louis Sw. Ry. Co. v. Alexander, 227 U.S. 218, 33 S.Ct. 245, 57 L.Ed. 486 (1913).

15. Hutchinson v. Chase & Gilbert, 45 F.2d 139 (2d Cir.1930).

16. See, e.g., Blount v. Peerless Chemicals (P.R.) Inc., 316 F.2d 695 (2d Cir.1963), cert. denied 375 U.S. 831; Associated Metals & Minerals Corp. v. S.S. Rialto, 280 F.Supp. 207 (S.D.N.Y.1967).

17. Cannon Mfg. Co. v. Cudahy Packing Co., 267 U.S. 333, 45 S.Ct. 250, 69 L.Ed. 634 (1925); Velandra v. Regie Nationale Des Usines Renault, 336 F.2d 292 (6th Cir. 1964).

18. Luce & Co., S. en C. v. Alimentos Borinquenos, S.A., 283 F.Supp. 81 (D.Puerto Rico 1968).

19. Cannon Mfg. Co. v. Cudahy Packing Co., 267 U.S. 333, 45 S.Ct. 250, 69 L.Ed. 634 (1925); Mas v. Orange–Crush Co., 99 F.2d 675 (4th Cir.1938); Thys Co. v. Harvard Indus., Inc., 205 Pa.Super. 472, 210 A.2d 913 (1965).

rem over property located outside their borders.[1] In rem jurisdiction enables the court to determine the status of, interests in, or title to property itself. Because a court proceeding in rem adjudicates conflicting claims to local property, which already has been subjected to the forum's physical control by attachment, due process does not require the court to summon, or even to identify all those whose interests might be affected by the judgment. In rem judgments are effective "against all the world."[2] Proceedings in admiralty,[3] in probate,[4] in eminent domain,[5] to condemn[6] or to confiscate[7] property, to register title to property,[8] to partition or divide community property,[9] to declare bankruptcy,[10] to escheat,[11] or to establish ownership in corporate shares[12] are all properly characterized as proceedings in rem as each involves an adjudication as to property.

An important group of proceedings related to issues of personal status, such as family relationships,[13] also have been treated as in rem proceedings for jurisdictional purposes. The original rationale for this treatment was to allow the state most concerned with a particular relationship, such as a marriage between two of its residents or the custody of a child domiciled within its borders, to adjudicate the status of that relationship. However, courts have encountered major difficulties in determining the location of the disputed status or "res" for jurisdictional purposes. In part, this difficulty has resulted from recent alterations in the underlying substantive law.

In particular, state power to dissolve a marriage has undergone sweeping change in recent decades. The state of marital domicile—the state in which both parties last resided together—was once considered to be the "situs" of a marriage, since that state was thought to be the place where the marriage was practiced and thus the only state that could

---

§ 3.8

1. 95 U.S. (5 Otto) 714, 723, 24 L.Ed. 565, 569 (1877).

2. Arndt v. Griggs, 134 U.S. 316, 10 S.Ct. 557, 33 L.Ed. 918 (1890); Tyler v. Judges of the Court of Registration, 175 Mass. 71, 55 N.E. 812 (1900), writ of error dismissed 179 U.S. 405, 21 S.Ct. 206, 45 L.Ed. 252 (1900).

3. The Hine v. Trevor, 71 U.S. (4 Wall.) 555, 18 L.Ed. 451 (1866); The Moses Taylor, 71 U.S. (4 Wall.) 411, 18 L.Ed. 397 (1866); New v. Yacht Relaxin, 212 F.Supp. 703 (S.D.Cal.1962).

4. In re Estate of Nilson, 126 Neb. 541, 253 N.W. 675 (1934); In re Shew's Estate, 48 Wn.2d 732, 296 P.2d 667 (1956). See also Simes, The Administration of a Decedent's Estate as a Proceeding in Rem, 43 Mich. L.Rev. 675 (1945).

5. Housing Authority of City of Butte v. Bjork, 109 Mont. 552, 98 P.2d 324 (1940).

6. Huling v. Kaw Valley Ry. & Improvement Co., 130 U.S. 559, 9 S.Ct. 603, 32 L.Ed. 1045 (1889).

7. The Confiscation Cases, 87 U.S. (20 Wall.) 92, 22 L.Ed. 320 (1874).

8. Tyler v. Judges of the Court of Registration, 175 Mass. 71, 55 N.E. 812 (1900).

9. Freeman v. Alderson, 119 U.S. 185, 7 S.Ct. 165, 30 L.Ed. 372 (1886); Solomon v. Redona, 52 Cal.App. 300, 198 P. 643 (1921).

10. Bank of Marin v. England, 385 U.S. 99, 87 S.Ct. 274, 17 L.Ed.2d 197 (1966).

11. Texas v. New Jersey, 379 U.S. 674, 85 S.Ct. 626, 13 L.Ed.2d 596 (1965), opinion supplemented 380 U.S. 518, 85 S.Ct. 1136, 14 L.Ed.2d 49 (1965); Western Union Tel. Co. v. Pennsylvania, 368 U.S. 71, 82 S.Ct. 199, 7 L.Ed.2d 139 (1961).

12. Franz v. Buder, 11 F.2d 854 (8th Cir.1926), cert. denied 273 U.S. 756; First Trust Co. v. Matheson, 187 Minn. 468, 246 N.W. 1 (1932).

13. See generally A. Ehrenzweig, Conflict of Laws §§ 71–81 (1962); E. Scoles & P. Hay, Conflict of Laws § 15.4 (2d ed. 1992).

exercise divorce jurisdiction.[14] Today, however, a state can assert jurisdiction to dissolve a marriage if either spouse is domiciled there.[15] In some states, the mere residence of either spouse for a specified period of time will suffice to confer jurisdiction on state courts to adjudicate the status of the marriage ex parte[16]—the court can alter the marital status of one spouse even in the other's absence. In these cases, due process requires that the absent spouse be served with proper notice of the proceedings.[17]

It is misleading, however, to characterize an ex parte divorce proceeding as purely in rem, since a state has been held not to have jurisdiction to adjudicate an absent spouse's right to financial support simply because the spouse initiating the divorce action was domiciled in the forum. To adjudicate an absent defendant's property rights incident to a marriage, a state court either must have in personam jurisdiction over the missing spouse or quasi in rem jurisdiction over the property to be affected by the decree.[18] Similarly, a court must have in personam jurisdiction over the defendant to render a valid judgment in a proceeding to establish alimony[19] or child custody[20] because it is adjudicating personal as well as property rights. Thus, it may be best to consider the state's right to assert divorce jurisdiction as a specialized form of jurisdiction that sometimes has been referred to as in rem.[21]

Unlike in rem proceedings, quasi in rem actions are brought against known persons, rather than against property. By asserting quasi in rem jurisdiction, plaintiffs "seek to subject certain property of those persons to the discharge of the claims asserted."[22] Rather than affecting the interests of all persons, known or unknown, in designated property, a quasi in rem judgment affects only the interests in designated property[23] of known persons who are parties to the proceedings.[24]

A court may invoke quasi in rem jurisdiction in two distinct ways. It may assert quasi in rem jurisdiction over specific property when a plaintiff seeks both to secure a preexisting claim in the property and to extinguish or establish the nonexistence of other similar claims to the same property. Examples of this type of quasi in rem jurisdiction include a bill to remove a cloud on title[25] or to set aside a fraudulent convey-

---

14. Haddock v. Haddock, 201 U.S. 562, 26 S.Ct. 525, 50 L.Ed. 867 (1906).

15. Williams v. North Carolina, 317 U.S. 287, 63 S.Ct. 207, 87 L.Ed. 279 (1942). The Williams Court noted, however, that "such a suit is not a mere in personam action." 317 U.S. at 297, 63 S.Ct. at 213.

16. Sachs v. Sachs, 278 Ala. 464, 179 So.2d 46 (1965).

17. Mullane v. Central Hanover Bank & Trust Co., 339 U.S. 306, 70 S.Ct. 652, 94 L.Ed. 865 (1950). Notice is discussed in §§ 3.19–3.20, below.

18. Vanderbilt v. Vanderbilt, 354 U.S. 416, 77 S.Ct. 1360, 1 L.Ed.2d 1456 (1957).

19. Baldwin v. Baldwin, 28 Cal.2d 406, 170 P.2d 670 (1946).

20. May v. Anderson, 345 U.S. 528, 73 S.Ct. 840, 97 L.Ed. 1221 (1953).

21. Restatement Second of Judgments § 7 (1982).

22. Freeman v. Alderson, 119 U.S. 185, 187, 7 S.Ct. 165, 166–67, 30 L.Ed. 372, 373 (1886).

23. 119 U.S. at 188, 7 S.Ct. at 67.

24. Gassert v. Strong, 38 Mont. 18, 98 P. 497 (1908), appeal dismissed 215 U.S. 583, 30 S.Ct. 403, 54 L.Ed. 338 (1909).

25. Arndt v. Griggs, 134 U.S. 316, 10 S.Ct. 557, 33 L.Ed. 918 (1890).

ance,[26] a seller's action to foreclose any equity of a defaulting buyer in a piece of realty,[27] and a suit for specific performance of a contract to convey real estate.[28] These actions are very like in rem actions but have the additional element that the parties are litigating some underlying dispute; the property relates to the remedy only.

The second application of the quasi in rem concept is similar to an exercise of in personam jurisdiction. The plaintiff seeks to acquire jurisdiction over the defendant's property within the forum as a substitute for in personam jurisdiction over the defendant's person, typically because the nonresident defendant is not present in the forum. When utilized in this fashion, quasi in rem jurisdiction often is referred to as attachment jurisdiction.[29] The plaintiff does not seek to challenge the defendant's right to the property attached; rather the plaintiff seeks to use local property belonging to the defendant as a jurisdictional vehicle for litigating a personal claim unrelated to the property.

Even when the defendant is not subject to the in personam jurisdiction of the forum in which the plaintiff wishes to sue, the plaintiff may initiate proceedings by attaching any property the defendant may own in the forum and notifying the defendant of the attachment. Once the property comes under the court's control, whether by attachment, garnishment, or equitable sequestration, the court has power to adjudicate all phases of the action. The defendant must elect whether to appear and defend on the merits of the plaintiff's claim, or alternatively, to default and sacrifice the property.[30] If the plaintiff obtains judgment by default or full trial, the attached property can be sold and the proceeds awarded to the plaintiff in partial or full satisfaction of the judgment.

The plaintiff acquires two distinct advantages in actions based on attachment jurisdiction. By petitioning the court to seize the defendant's in-state property, the plaintiff forces the defendant to choose between appearing personally and defending on the merits of the claim or risking forfeiture of the property by default. Second, the seizure of the property assures the plaintiff of an asset from which the claim may be partially or fully satisfied.

On the other hand, the limited powers of a court exercising quasi in rem jurisdiction present plaintiffs with certain disadvantages. A quasi in rem judgment is strictly limited to the value of the property upon which the court's jurisdiction is based.[31] If the plaintiff's claim exceeds the value of the property, the court may not enter a deficiency judgment for

---

26. State ex rel. Hill v. District Court, 79 N.M. 33, 439 P.2d 551 (1968).

27. Prudential Ins. Co. v. Berry, 153 S.C. 496, 151 S.E. 63 (1930). See also Roller v. Holly, 176 U.S. 398, 20 S.Ct. 410, 44 L.Ed. 520 (1899).

28. Garfein v. McInnis, 248 N.Y. 261, 162 N.E. 73 (1928).

29. See Restatement Second of Judgments § 8 (1982).

30. See the discussion of the effect of a limited appearance in § 3.27, below. See also Simpson v. Loehmann, 21 N.Y.2d 990, 290 N.Y.S.2d 914, 238 N.E.2d 319 (1968) (appearance to defend on merits does not subject defendant to liability in excess of the attached debt).

31. Freeman v. Alderson, 119 U.S. 185, 7 S.Ct. 165, 30 L.Ed. 372 (1886); Cooper v. Reynolds, 77 U.S. (10 Wall.) 308, 19 L.Ed. 931 (1870).

the difference[32] unless the defendant has submitted to the court's in personam jurisdiction in the course of the quasi in rem proceeding.[33] Of course, if the property's value exceeds the amount of the judgment, the court returns to the defendant the balance of the proceeds remaining after the judgment has been deducted.

The court's power in quasi in rem actions also is limited by the fact that its judgment will not be given binding or res judicata effect in a subsequent action on the same personal claim.[34] In theory, the quasi in rem judgment concludes only the interests of the parties at bar in the particular property upon which jurisdiction is based. Res judicata operates to prevent a successful plaintiff from subsequently bringing the same personal claim against the same property. The plaintiff is not precluded from bringing a second quasi in rem action on the same personal claim by attaching additional property owned by the defendant, in the original forum or elsewhere, and suing for the difference between the full amount of the claim and the amount secured in the first action. If the plaintiff prevails again, the amount recovered in the first judgment will be deducted from the judgment awarded in the second action.[35] If the defendant wins the second action, the plaintiff is not required to restore any sum already received in the prior action.[36] Nor is the plaintiff precluded from bringing yet another action wherever the plaintiff can acquire in personam jurisdiction over the defendant.[37]

At the time of Pennoyer, the attachment form of quasi in rem jurisdiction provided a limited source of flexibility for ameliorating the effects of the rigid concept of exclusive territorial sovereignty. It afforded relatively immobile creditors some procedural protections against absconding debtors and allowed a state's courts to provide relief to resident plaintiffs against nonresident tortfeasors without violating another state's territorial sovereignty through direct assertions of in personam jurisdiction over its residents.[38] Because corporations could not be sued in personam outside of their states of incorporation,[39] quasi in rem jurisdiction provided the only means for resident creditors to sue foreign corporations in local courts for unpaid debts or personal injuries. When interstate travel was costly and difficult, quasi in rem jurisdiction provided some measure of fairness to plaintiffs who otherwise would have been forced to seek out and pursue nonresident defendants who had injured them in their own home state.

---

32. See, e.g., Cheshire Nat. Bank v. Jaynes, 224 Mass. 14, 112 N.E. 500 (1916).

33. The ways in which a defendant may waive a jurisdictional objection are explained in §§ 3.25–3.26, below.

34. Cheshire Nat. Bank v. Jaynes, 224 Mass. 14, 112 N.E. 500 (1916); Restatement Second of Judgments § 32 (1982). See the discussion in § 14.9, below, of the trend toward giving certain quasi in rem judgments limited former adjudication effect.

35. Restatement Second of Judgments § 32, comment c (1982).

36. Restatement First of Judgments § 34, comment h (1942).

37. Although multiple actions on the same claim theoretically are possible, they rarely happen.

38. Zammit, Quasi-in-Rem Jurisdiction: Outmoded and Unconstitutional?, 49 St. John's L.Rev. 668, 670 (1975).

39. See the discussion in § 3.7, above.

The Pennoyer Court did not tie the device of quasi in rem jurisdiction to notions of fairness. Its use depended solely on the presence or absence of the defendant's property in the forum, not on a broader evaluation of the defendant's continuing contacts with the forum. As standards of fairness rather than pure territoriality began to pervade the law surrounding in personam jurisdiction,[40] many argued that the distinctions between in personam, in rem, and quasi in rem jurisdiction promoted the evolution of artificially different standards for judging the validity of a state court's exercise of jurisdiction over a defendant's person and property. In particular, the constitutional legitimacy of attachment jurisdiction was questioned on both substantive and procedural due process grounds. These developments are discussed in the next section.

§ 3.9   Problems With Traditional Doctrine: Quasi in Rem Jurisdiction Under Stress

Pennoyer v. Neff[1] established a consistent albeit wooden conceptual framework for analyzing all assertions of a state court's jurisdiction over a defendant. If the defendant was physically present within the state and personally served, in personam jurisdiction could be asserted over him.[2] If the defendant's property was physically present in the state, it could be attached at the commencement of the proceedings and quasi in rem jurisdiction acquired over the defendant, making him liable for a judgment no greater than the value of the property once he received proper notice of the action.[3]

At its inception, the assertion of attachment jurisdiction under the guidelines of Pennoyer operated with relative certainty and predictability. Although it sometimes required a non-consenting nonresident defendant to appear in the courts of a distant state in order to defend his property, this was not considered to be unfair insofar as the defendant had availed himself of the benefit of the forum's laws by owning property in the state.

International Shoe Company v. State of Washington[4] shifted the focus of in personam jurisdiction from a state's physical power over the defendant to the defendant's minimum contacts with the state.[5] In Hanson v. Denckla,[6] the Supreme Court placed a limit on the expansion of in personam jurisdiction by requiring that the contacts take the form of a purposeful affiliation between the defendant and the forum.[7] Although both International Shoe and Hanson radically changed the in personam wing of jurisdiction, they left in rem and quasi in rem jurisdiction untouched. The continuing focus of those forms of jurisdic-

---

40. See § 3.10, below.

§ 3.9

1. 95 U.S. (5 Otto) 714, 24 L.Ed. 565 (1877).

2. See § 3.3, above.

3. See § 3.8, above.

4. 326 U.S. 310, 66 S.Ct. 154, 90 L.Ed. 95 (1945).

5. See § 3.10, below.

6. 357 U.S. 235, 78 S.Ct. 1228, 2 L.Ed.2d 1283 (1958).

7. See § 3.11, below.

tion on the state's physical power began to seem anachronistic, outmoded, and insensitive to a defendant's due process rights.[8] The attachment of intangible property made bizarre and fortuitous results possible in quasi in rem cases, depending on where a court found the situs of the property. The old concepts of quasi in rem jurisdiction were stretched to the breaking point. A brief exploration of some of the difficulties encountered illustrates the weaknesses of the traditional approach to attachment jurisdiction.

When the property attached in a quasi in rem proceeding is realty or tangible personalty, determining its situs poses little difficulty; tangibles have their legal situs in the state of their physical location. But the determination of the situs of intangible property, such as notes, bonds, and debts, has been a source of difficulty and confusion to the courts.[9] The situs of intangibles is a legal fiction and the "determination of situs for one purpose has no necessary bearing on its determination for another purpose."[10] For example, although the situs of an insurance policy is ordinarily the location of the policy itself, for purposes of taxing the cash surrender value of the policy, the situs is the taxpayer's residence, which may not be where the certificate is located.[11]

With documents and other written instruments that embody commercial obligations, situs often is identified exclusively with the paper itself as a matter of commercial convenience. Accordingly, jurisdiction ordinarily is permitted wherever the paper can be found and seized.[12] A more complicated problem arises when determining the situs of corporate securities.[13] At common law, the situs of stock was considered to be the domicile of the corporation.[14] The certificate (the writing) was viewed only as evidence of ownership of the stock, not as the embodiment of the property itself. Thus the presence of the certificate within the forum was considered insufficient to bring the actual property into the state where the certificate was held for jurisdictional purposes.

The common law approach to the situs of corporate securities generated some thorny problems. The state of incorporation alone had the power to determine whether a stock certificate embodied ownership

8. See Carrington, The Modern Utility of Quasi in Rem Jurisdiction, 76 Harv. L.Rev. 303 (1962); B. Currie, Attachment and Garnishment in the Federal Courts, 59 Mich.L.Rev. 337 (1961); Elliot & Green, Quasi in Rem Jurisdiction in Federal Courts: The Proposed Amendments to Rule 4, 48 Iowa L.Rev. 300 (1963).

9. Andrews, Situs of Intangibles in Suits Against Nonresident Claimants, 49 Yale L.J. 241 (1939); Carpenter, Jurisdiction over Debts for the Purpose of Administration, Garnishment & Taxation, 31 Harv. L.Rev. 905 (1918); Powell, Business Situs of Credits, 28 W.Va.L.Q. 89 (1922); Developments in the Law—State Court Jurisdiction, 73 Harv.L.Rev. 909, 950–53 (1960). See also U.S. v. First Nat. City Bank, 379

U.S. 378, 385, 404–09, 85 S.Ct. 528, 532, 542–45, 13 L.Ed.2d 365 (1965) (dissenting opinion) (situs of account payable).

10. Bankers Trust Co. v. Equitable Life Assurance Soc., 19 N.Y.2d 552, 281 N.Y.S.2d 57, 227 N.E.2d 863 (1967).

11. Ibid.

12. First Trust Co. v. Matheson, 187 Minn. 468, 246 N.W. 1 (1932) (bearer bonds). See also Restatement Second of Conflict of Laws § 61 (1969).

13. See generally Pomerance, The "Situs" of Stock, 17 Cornell L.Q. 43 (1931).

14. See, e.g., 15 Purdon's Statutes § 301.

of the stock or was merely evidence of that ownership. If the state of incorporation provided by statute that ownership of the stock was embodied in the certificate, then the attachment of the certificate could create a basis for quasi in rem jurisdiction in the state of its location. To avoid problems of doubtful jurisdiction and potential multiple liability, some, but not all, states adopted Section 13 of the Uniform Stock Transfer Act, which specified that the situs of the stock, for attachment purpose, is where the certificate is found. To have a valid attachment of the certificate, physical seizure of the written instrument or an injunction prohibiting the holder from transferring the stock was required.[15]

When an intangible property interest has not been embodied in a writing, additional problems occur. The quasi in rem regime of Pennoyer required that the interest be assigned a fictional presence for attachment purposes. Harris v. Balk[16] established the principle that for jurisdictional purposes, the situs of a debt is wherever the debtor is located.

Harris, a North Carolina resident, owed Balk, also of North Carolina, $180. Epstein, a resident of Baltimore, Maryland, claimed that Balk in turn owed him $340. While Harris was visiting Baltimore, Epstein served him personally with a writ of attachment garnishing his debt to Balk. Notice of the attachment was given to Balk by posting a declaration on the courthouse door in Baltimore, pursuant to Maryland procedure. Neither Harris, the garnishee, nor Balk, the principal debtor, entered an appearance despite the fact that both received actual notice of the attachment. The Maryland court entered a default judgment for $180 against Balk and enforced the judgment by ordering Harris to pay the money to Epstein.

When Balk later sued Harris in North Carolina to recover the $180, Harris interposed the Maryland judgment as a defense. Balk argued in reply that North Carolina was not obliged to give full faith and credit to the Maryland judgment, as Maryland had no jurisdiction to enter the judgment; since the obligation had been created in North Carolina between two North Carolinians, its situs was there and it could not be attached validly in Maryland. The North Carolina courts refused to recognize the Maryland judgment as a defense, but the United States Supreme Court reversed, holding that the Maryland judgment was valid and deserved full faith and credit from the North Carolina courts.

The Supreme Court reasoned that an intangible obligation to repay a debt "clings to and accompanies (the debtor) wherever he goes."[17] Thus the debt owed by Harris to Balk "traveled" with Harris to Maryland where it could be attached. The Maryland court had obtained

---

15. Mills v. Jacobs, 333 Pa. 231, 4 A.2d 152 (1939). See also Union Chemical & Materials Corp. v. Cannon, 38 Del.Ch. 203, 148 A.2d 348 (1959), noted 59 Colum.L.Rev. 803 (1959); Note, Attachment of Corporate Stock: The Conflicting Approaches of Delaware and the Uniform Stock Transfer Act, 73 Harv.L.Rev. 1579 (1960).

16. 198 U.S. 215, 25 S.Ct. 625, 49 L.Ed. 1023 (1905).

17. 198 U.S. at 222, 25 S.Ct. at 626.

valid quasi in rem jurisdiction over Balk's property—the debt owed by Harris—by personally serving Harris in Maryland.[18]

The doctrine of Harris v. Balk was widely criticized because it permitted jurisdiction over a defendant in a forum with which neither he nor his activities had any logical connection.[19] The logic of the case suggested that a creditor could seek to recover all or part of a debt by obtaining in personam jurisdiction over his debtor's debtor, thereby rendering a defendant subject to suit not only where he might be served personally, or where his realty or personalty might be located, but also in any state where his debtor might happen to wander. This problem was especially acute with regard to corporate debtors. If a plaintiff could garnish a defendant's corporate debtors wherever they happened to be doing business, the defendant could be subject to quasi in rem jurisdiction in any number of states.[20] The plaintiff could shop for a forum having procedural or substantive advantages, leading to endless opportunities for harassment of the defendant.

Despite these arguments, the Harris v. Balk principle was given broad application, and even taken to extremes with regard to the attachment of contractual obligations. In Seider v. Roth,[21] two New York residents injured in an automobile accident in Vermont obtained quasi in rem jurisdiction over the defendant, a Canadian, by attaching his auto liability insurance policy, issued in Canada by an insurer doing business in New York. The New York Court of Appeals found that the insurance company's obligation to defend the Canadian constituted a debt subject to attachment under New York law.[22]

The Seider case represented an expansion of attachment jurisdiction under Harris v. Balk because the debt attached was prospective and conjectural: the nature and the amount of the company's obligation to indemnify the defendant depended on the outcome of the suit. The majority opinion in Seider suggested that the insurer's obligation accrued when the accident occurred, subject to divestiture if the suit were unsuccessfully brought or not brought at all. The New York court did not consider the constitutionality of the procedure, however, nor the dilemma faced by a defendant whose insurance policy has been attached

---

18. The garnishee has a duty to notify its creditor of the attachment proceeding so that the creditor can appear at the proceeding to contest the claim of the person who has attached the debt. Failure of the garnishee to notify its creditor will not affect the validity of the judgment for the plaintiff against the creditor. It will, however, affect the right of the garnishee to plead that it already has paid the debt if the garnishee is later sued by the creditor to repay the loan. Thus, failure to give notice to the creditor can result in the debtor-garnishee paying its debt twice.

19. Beale, The Exercise of Jurisdiction in Rem to Compel Payment of a Debt, 27 Harv.L.Rev. 107 (1913). But see the defense of Harris in Carpenter, Jurisdiction over Debts for the Purpose of Administration, Garnishment and Taxation, 31 Harv.L.Rev. 905 (1918).

20. See, e.g., Steele v. G.D. Searle & Co., 483 F.2d 339 (5th Cir.1973), cert. denied 415 U.S. 958 (products liability action).

21. 17 N.Y.2d 111, 269 N.Y.S.2d 99, 216 N.E.2d 312 (1966), noted in 33 Brooklyn L.Rev. 368 (1967), 67 Colum.L.Rev. 550 (1967), 18 Syracuse L.Rev. 631 (1967), 35 U.Cinn.L.Rev. 691 (1966), 51 Minn.L.Rev. 158 (1966).

22. N.Y.—McKinney's CPLR 5201, 6202.

in a state that does not allow him to appear in court without submitting to the court's full in personam jurisdiction.[23] Most insurance policies require the insured party to appear in court or else forfeit any claims against the insurer. By attaching the policy as the predicate for quasi in rem jurisdiction, a plaintiff effectively could force the defendant to enter a personal appearance and submit to the full jurisdiction of the court. In this way a defendant ultimately was subjected to in personam jurisdiction by way of a procedure that applied the Harris fiction as to a debt's presence to a "debt" that might never be owed.

In the next few years, both the New York appellate courts and the Second Circuit attempted to quell constitutional doubts about the Seider procedure by restricting and modifying it. For example, the size of a Seider judgment was limited to the face amount of the liability insurance policy attached and a right of limited appearance in a Seider type case was recognized.[24] In addition, the plaintiff had to be a resident of New York or the cause of action had to arise there.[25] Even with these restrictions, the Seider procedure was highly controversial.[26] Although a few other states followed New York's lead,[27] most refused to extend quasi in rem jurisdiction so far.[28]

B. CONTEMPORARY JURISDICTION NOTIONS: IN PERSONAM JURISDICTION

1. Constitutional Requirements

§ 3.10 The Basic Rule of International Shoe: The Minimum Contacts and Fair Play and Substantial Justice Requirements

The judicially created exceptions to the physical presence rule[1] reflected judges' attempts to tailor nineteenth century jurisdictional doctrine to fit the realities of the twentieth century. Recognizing that the Pennoyer rule was anachronistic, the Supreme Court in a 1945 decision, International Shoe Company v. State of Washington,[2] adopted a new,

23. The device of a limited appearance is discussed in § 3.27, below.

24. Simpson v. Loehmann, 21 N.Y.2d 305, 287 N.Y.S.2d 633, 234 N.E.2d 669 (1967).

25. Minichiello v. Rosenberg, 410 F.2d 106 (2d Cir.1968), on rehearing en banc 410 F.2d 117 (2d Cir.1968), cert. denied 396 U.S. 844.

26. See generally Stein, Jurisdiction by Attachment of Liability Insurance, 43 N.Y.U.L.Rev. 1075 (1968); Comment, Garnishment of Intangibles: Contingent Obligations and the Interstate Corporation, 67 Colum.L.Rev. 550 (1967).

27. E.g., Rintala v. Shoemaker, 362 F.Supp. 1044 (D.Minn.1973); Forbes v.

Boynton, 113 N.H. 617, 313 A.2d 129 (1973).

28. E.g., Javorek v. Superior Court, 17 Cal.3d 629, 131 Cal.Rptr. 768, 552 P.2d 728 (1976); State ex rel. Government Employees Ins. Co. v. Lasky, 454 S.W.2d 942 (Mo.App. 1970); Howard v. Allen, 254 S.C. 455, 176 S.E.2d 127 (1970); De Rentiis v. Lewis, 106 R.I. 240, 258 A.2d 464 (1969); Housley v. Anaconda Co., 19 Utah 2d 124, 427 P.2d 390 (1967).

§ 3.10

1. See §§ 3.4–3.7, above.

2. 326 U.S. 310, 66 S.Ct. 154, 90 L.Ed. 95 (1945), analyzed in Kurland, The Supreme Court, the Due Process Clause and

more flexible standard for the assertion of personal jurisdiction, based upon a jurisdictional theory and standards better suited to a progressively more mobile society.

International Shoe Company was incorporated in Delaware and had its principal place of business in Missouri. The company employed salesmen who resided and solicited business in the state of Washington. The state assessed unemployment compensation taxes against the company based upon the annual commissions paid to its salesmen. When the company refused to pay the taxes, the State Tax Commissioner, acting pursuant to Washington statute, issued an order and notice of assessment, and effected service of process upon the company by personally serving one of the local sales agents and by mailing a copy of the notice to the company's Missouri offices.

Besides challenging its liability to taxation in the state, International Shoe Company challenged the propriety of the Commissioner's service of process upon it. It argued that the Washington salesmen were not agents of the company, and that the application of the statute authorizing service by mail violated the Due Process Clause of the Constitution. The state tax agency, trial court, and state supreme court held that service of process under the statute was constitutionally permissible, and that the company was subject to the jurisdiction of the state's courts.

The United States Supreme Court affirmed. In an opinion by Chief Justice Stone, the Court set out what continues to be the standard for determining whether a state may constitutionally subject a nonresident to the jurisdiction of its courts.

> [D]ue process requires only that in order to subject a defendant to a judgment in personam, if he be not present within the territory of the forum, he have certain minimum contacts with it such that the maintenance of the suit does not offend "traditional notions of fair play and substantial justice."[3]

In rejecting the company's argument that it was not present within the state, and that the state therefore was without jurisdiction, the Court noted that the concerns underlying the presence requirement may be met if the defendant has engaged in activities in the state "which courts will deem to be sufficient to satisfy the demands of due process."[4]

Dispensing with the legal fiction of "presence" as the test for asserting jurisdiction, the International Shoe decision focuses directly upon whether subjecting a particular defendant to jurisdiction in a particular case meets the demands of due process. "Those demands may be met," wrote Justice Stone, "by such contacts of the corporation with the * * * forum as make it reasonable * * * to require the corporation to defend the particular suit which is brought there."[5] The Court's

In Personam Jurisdiction of the State Courts—From Pennoyer to Denckla: A Review, 25 U.Chi.L.Rev. 569, 586 (1958).

3. 326 U.S. at 316, 66 S.Ct. at 158, quoting Milliken v. Meyer, 311 U.S. 457, 463, 61 S.Ct. 339, 343, 85 L.Ed. 278 (1940).

4. 326 U.S. at 319, 66 S.Ct. at 160.

5. 326 U.S. at 317, 66 S.Ct. at 158.

conclusion that the assertion of personal jurisdiction meets due process requirements when the defendant has minimum contacts with the state is based upon the premise that a nonresident's enjoyment of the privilege of conducting business in the forum carries with it an obligation to respond to suit there.[6] As is necessarily so of all due process questions, the criteria for determining whether a defendant has sufficient contact with the forum to permit its assertion of jurisdiction "cannot be simply mechanical or quantitative * * *." Rather, it must depend upon "the quality and nature of the activity in relation to the fair and orderly administration of the laws."[7]

The standard enunciated in the International Shoe decision repeatedly has been explained and refined, both by the Supreme Court and by lower federal and state courts.[8] One refinement was the conceptual separation of the notion of "minimum contacts" from that of "fair play and substantial justice," resulting in a two-step due process analysis: first, the court determines if the defendant has minimum contacts with the forum; if so, it remains to be determined whether the assertion of jurisdiction comports with "traditional notions of fair play and substantial justice."[9]

Cases applying the first prong of the International Shoe test—the requirement that the defendant have minimum contacts with the forum—may be categorized according to four principles suggested by Chief Justice Stone in the International Shoe decision itself. Although the Court eschewed a mechanistic determination of jurisdiction, it found in prior decisions certain standards that courts had applied in deciding whether a defendant was present in the forum state for jurisdictional purposes. From those decisions the Court derived four guideposts in applying the "minimum contacts" requirement:[10] (1) A defendant is subject to the jurisdiction of the courts in a forum in which its activities have been continuous and systematic, and have given rise to the cause of

6. 326 U.S. at 319, 66 S.Ct. at 160. See also Hanson v. Denckla, 357 U.S. 235, 78 S.Ct. 1228, 2 L.Ed.2d 1283 (1958), discussed in § 3.11, below, in which the Court explicitly makes the defendant's purposeful availment of the privilege of conducting activities in the forum a requirement for the forum court's assertion of jurisdiction.

7. 326 U.S. at 316, 66 S.Ct. at 158.

8. See Hazard, A General Theory of State Court Jurisdiction, 1965 Sup.Ct.Rev. 241; Kurland, The Supreme Court, the Due Process Clause and In Personam Jurisdiction of the State Courts—From Pennoyer to Denckla: A Review, 25 U.Chi.L.Rev. 569 (1958).

9. The language of the International Shoe opinion sets out the "fair play and substantial justice" formulation as the standard against which the sufficiency of minimum contacts is to be measured, thus tying the two standards together. Many later lower court decisions appeared to sever

the standard into a two-pronged test. These decisions neither explicitly admit that the test has been altered nor attempt to base the bifurcation upon the text of International Shoe itself. Other cases applying the International Shoe standard retained the unified approach more or less as it appears in Stone's opinion. The Supreme Court, in World–Wide Volkswagen Corp. v. Woodson, 444 U.S. 286, 100 S.Ct. 559, 62 L.Ed.2d 490 (1980), explicitly adopted the two-pronged approach, characterizing the minimum contacts inquiry as a threshold question. Only when minimum contacts are found to exist among the parties and the forum do fair play and substantial justice become relevant considerations. See § 3.11, below, for a more detailed discussion of the World–Wide Volkswagen decision.

10. 326 U.S. at 317, 318, 66 S.Ct. at 159.

action sued upon; (2) The sporadic or casual activities of a defendant in the forum, or his single isolated act there, are not enough to subject that defendant to suit in the forum on causes of action unrelated to his forum activities; (3) The continuous activity of a defendant within the forum may be of such nature as to subject the defendant to jurisdiction even upon causes of action unrelated to the forum activity; and (4) A defendant's sporadic forum activity, even a single act, may suffice under certain circumstances to render him subject to jurisdiction upon claims arising out of that activity. Thus, a minimum contacts analysis begins with two questions: first, were the defendant's activities in the forum continuous and systematic or only sporadic and casual; second, is the cause of action sued upon related or unrelated to the defendant's activities in the forum.[11]

The first principle—that jurisdiction is permissible when the defendant's activity in the forum is continuous and systematic and the cause of action is related to that activity—is amply illustrated by the International Shoe case itself. As the Court noted, the company's activities in the state of Washington were continuous and systematic and resulted in a large volume of business, and the obligation sued upon arose directly out of those activities. Therefore, the company had established "sufficient contacts * * * with the forum to make it reasonable and just according to our traditional conception of fair play and substantial justice to permit the state to enforce the obligations"[12] incurred by the company.

The second principle—that the sporadic or casual activity of the defendant in the forum does not justify assertion of jurisdiction on a cause of action unrelated to that forum activity—is illustrated by the Supreme Court's decision in Hanson v. Denckla.[13] That case held jurisdiction impermissible when the defendants' contact with the forum was negligible and, more importantly, not purposeful on their part.[14]

Cases covered by the third principle involve highly qualitative evaluations of the particular facts of the case at hand because the principle requires assessment of the nature, as well as the substantiality, of the defendant's contacts with the forum. The principle provides that a court may assert jurisdiction over a defendant whose continuous activities in the forum are unrelated to the cause of action sued upon when the defendant's contacts are sufficiently substantial and of such a nature as to make the state's assertion of jurisdiction reasonable. The Supreme

---

11. The need to consider these two questions at the outset is underscored by the Supreme Court's later decision in Helicopteros Nacionales de Colombia, S.A. v. Hall, 466 U.S. 408, 104 S.Ct. 1868, 80 L.Ed.2d 404 (1984).

12. 326 U.S. at 320, 66 S.Ct. at 160.

13. 357 U.S. 235, 78 S.Ct. 1228, 2 L.Ed.2d 1283 (1958), discussed in § 3.11, below.

14. But cf. Bryant v. Finnish Nat. Airline, 15 N.Y.2d 426, 260 N.Y.S.2d 625, 208 N.E.2d 439 (1965), discussed at note 30, below, in which the New York Court of Appeals sustained the assertion of jurisdiction over a defendant on a cause of action unrelated to the defendant's forum contacts, which were slight. The court's conclusion was based upon considerations of fairness and convenience.

Court generally has left to the states the discretion to assert or forego jurisdiction in cases in this category.[15]

The fourth principle provides that even a defendant whose activity in the forum is sporadic, or consists of only a single act, may be subject to the jurisdiction of the forum's courts when the cause of action arises out of that activity or act. Examples of this principle are plentiful in the field of tort claims against out-of-state motorists.[16] And, in McGee v. International Life Insurance Company,[17] the Supreme Court sustained a state's assertion of jurisdiction over a nonresident defendant whose only contacts with the state were its issuance of the insurance policy sued upon to a state resident and its receipt of policy premium payments from that resident.

In dealing with cases falling under these last two principles, a further refinement was made in a 1984 Supreme Court decision, Helicopteros Nacionales de Colombia, S.A. v. Hall.[18] In that case the Court recognized a distinction that had been made by some state courts between "general jurisdiction" and "specific jurisdiction."[19] When an action falls under the third principle and the cause of action does not arise out of defendant's forum related activities, general jurisdiction must be found; specific jurisdiction is asserted when the defendant's forum contacts are sporadic, but the cause of action arises out of those contacts.[20] This distinction is of great significance because in order to assert general jurisdiction there must be substantial forum-related activity on the part of the defendant. Thus, the threshold for satisfying minimum contacts, before considering convenience or more general fairness concerns, is higher in cases that are based on general jurisdiction than in those that are relying on specific jurisdiction. This is made clear by the Helicopteros Court's analysis of the standard as applied to the facts of that case.

15. See, e.g., Perkins v. Benguet Consolidated Mining Co., 342 U.S. 437, 72 S.Ct. 413, 96 L.Ed. 485 (1952). See also the discussion of example cases in § 3.13, below.

16. The principle of Hess v. Pawloski, 274 U.S. 352, 47 S.Ct. 632, 71 L.Ed. 1091 (1927), a pre-International Shoe case, discussed in § 3.5 at note 25, above, which enables a state to exact the implied consent to jurisdiction of a nonresident motorist, thus remains valid under modern jurisdictional standards. However, a state must provide nonresident motorists with notice and an opportunity to be heard. See §§ 3.19–3.20, below.

17. 355 U.S. 220, 78 S.Ct. 199, 2 L.Ed.2d 223 (1957). The case is discussed in § 3.11, below.

18. 466 U.S. 408, 104 S.Ct. 1868, 80 L.Ed.2d 404 (1984).

19. See, e.g., Cornelison v. Chaney, 16 Cal.3d 143, 127 Cal.Rptr. 352, 545 P.2d 264 (1976).

20. In a dissenting opinion, Justice Brennan argued that if the defendant's forum contacts were related to, even though not arising out of, the cause of action then the case might be treated as one asserting specific jurisdiction. 466 U.S. at 419, 104 S.Ct. at 1875. The majority refused to address that point stating that it was not properly before them since the parties and lower courts had treated the issue as one involving the "arising out of" standard. 466 U.S. at 416 n. 10, 104 S.Ct. at 1873 n. 10. Thus, a question remains whether yet a third level will be added to the minimum contacts threshold involving cases in which the defendant has forum contacts related to, but not arising out of, the cause of action. See the discussion at § 3.11 at note 59, below.

Helicopteros was a wrongful death action brought in Texas against a Colombian corporation and others for an accident that took place in Peru when one of the defendant's helicopters crashed. The evidence introduced showed that the defendant was engaged in the business of providing helicopter transportation for oil and construction companies in South America and that the decedents were United States citizens working for a Peruvian consortium that was the alter-ego of a joint venture that had its headquarters in Texas. The defendant had the contract to move personnel, materials, and equipment into and out of the construction area. Four Texas contacts were identified. (1) Defendant's chief executive officer flew, at the request of the consortium, to Houston to negotiate the transportation contract. (2) It had purchased most of its helicopters over a period of years from Bell Helicopter Company in Fort Worth. (3) It also had sent prospective pilots and management personnel for training to Bell in Texas. And (4) the checks paying for its transportation services were drawn on a Texas bank and paid into a New York account.

The Supreme Court ruled that jurisdiction could not be asserted. It treated the case as one requiring general jurisdiction because the parties had argued jurisdiction in the lower courts based on that characterization.[21] It concluded that defendant's contacts with Texas did not constitute continuous and systematic activity. The one trip by the corporation's chief executive officer was dismissed as sporadic. The fact that it had accepted checks for the consortium drawn on a Texas bank was "of negligible significance."[22] Finally, and perhaps most importantly, the Court ruled that the mere purchases of helicopters from Bell, even though they occurred at regular intervals, were not enough to warrant the state's assertion of in personam jurisdiction over the nonresident corporation when the cause of action was not related to those purchase transactions.[23] In this vein, the Court characterized the training of petitioner's pilots as "part of the package of goods and services purchased" and thus not a significant contact on which jurisdiction could be based. In sum, the Court's dismissal of each of Helicopteros contacts as not significant, as well as its failure to consider the effect of the aggregate of those contacts, suggests very strongly that the threshold contacts required for general jurisdiction are very substantial, indeed.

In addition, it must be remembered that the determination that a defendant has minimum contacts with the forum state is only the first step in the analysis of whether the assertion of jurisdiction comports with due process. The court then must consider if jurisdiction may be asserted consistent with "traditional notions of fair play and substantial

---

21.   466 U.S. at 415, 104 S.Ct. at 1872.

22.   466 U.S. at 416, 104 S.Ct. at 1873. The Court noted that the question of what bank a check is drawn upon is within the discretion of the drawer and unilateral activity on the part of the drawer does not constitute a contact on the part of the defendant. For a discussion of the need for purposeful conduct by defendant, see § 3.11, below.

23.   466 U.S. at 418, 104 S.Ct. at 1874.

justice."[24] The International Shoe decision gives little content to the ambiguous phrase "fair play and substantial justice." The opinion suggests that the fairness of maintaining a suit in a particular forum may depend in part upon the relative convenience of the forum to the respective parties. Compelling a nonresident defendant to submit to suit in an inconvenient forum may be unduly burdensome, and therefore inconsistent with the demands of due process, even though the defendant has some contacts with the forum state. No further guidance can be found in the decision itself.

Although detailed consideration of the kinds of factors used by the courts to assess this portion of the International Shoe standard is beyond the scope of this discussion,[25] a brief inquiry into some of the most important and common factors used is warranted. In Travelers Health Association v. Commonwealth of Virginia,[26] a divided Supreme Court upheld the assertion of jurisdiction over a nonresident insurance company that had used the mails to solicit business from state residents. The defendant's forum contacts were less substantial than those of the defendant in International Shoe, although the cause of action sued upon did arise out of the defendant's forum activities. The Court's conclusion that Virginia's assertion of jurisdiction over Travelers met due process requirements was based upon considerations of fairness and convenience. One compelling fairness factor noted by the Travelers Court was the interest of the forum state in adjudicating a dispute between a state resident and an insurance company doing business in the state. This state interest was evidenced by its regulation of the insurance business through statutory certification requirements.[27] The Court also stressed the inconvenience and unfairness to resident plaintiffs that would result if the local forum were not available for suits upon contracts solicited in the state.[28] The Travelers decision thus sets out three factors that have become recurrent considerations in later assessments of the fairness of jurisdiction under the International Shoe standard: the interest of the state in regulating the type of activity in which the defendant is engaged in the forum; the interest of the state in providing a convenient forum for its residents; and the relative convenience to the parties of suit in an alternative forum.[29]

The lack of an alternative forum may be an overriding factor in a court's conclusion that notions of fair play and substantial justice require a state's assertion of jurisdiction over a nonresident. Bryant v. Finnish National Airline,[30] involved a suit in a New York court by a state resident against a foreign corporation that maintained a small sales

---

24. International Shoe Co. v. Washington, 326 U.S. 310, 316, 66 S.Ct. 154, 158, 90 L.Ed. 95 (1945).

25. For a listing of cases applying the International Shoe criteria, see 4 C. Wright & A. Miller, Civil 2d § 1069.

26. 339 U.S. 643, 70 S.Ct. 927, 94 L.Ed. 1154 (1950).

27. 339 U.S. at 648, 70 S.Ct. at 930.

28. 339 U.S. at 649, 70 S.Ct. at 930.

29. Accord, McGee v. International Life Ins. Co., 355 U.S. 220, 78 S.Ct. 199, 2 L.Ed.2d 223 (1957).

30. 15 N.Y.2d 426, 260 N.Y.S.2d 625, 208 N.E.2d 439 (1965).

office in the state, its only office in the United States. Even though the plaintiff's claim was entirely unrelated to the defendant's forum activity, the New York Court of Appeals held that due process was accorded to the defendant in the state's assertion of jurisdiction since the alternative was effectively to bar the plaintiff altogether from relief in an American court.[31]

On the other hand, a court may find the assertion of jurisdiction unreasonable even when the defendant has systematic and continuous contacts with the forum. In Metropolitan Life Insurance Company v. Robertson–Ceco Corporation,[32] the Second Circuit found the exercise of general jurisdiction unreasonable given the absence of any interest on the part of either the forum state or the plaintiff in adjudicating the action in the forum. The dispute arose out of work done on the plaintiff's building in Florida. Metropolitan Life sued the two defendants in Vermont, where they had systematic and continuous contacts supporting general jurisdiction. The court held that neither Vermont nor Metropolitan Life had any interest in resolving the dispute in Vermont: the relevant acts had taken place in other states, no evidence or witnesses were located in Vermont, and all parties had their principal places of business elsewhere. The court did not consider the fact that Metropolitan Life apparently had chosen Vermont as the forum because its claim was barred by the statutes of limitations in other forums relevant to the question of reasonableness. Thus, the court held that it would be both inefficient and unreasonable for Vermont to exercise general jurisdiction over the defendants. The question of what constitutes reasonableness for purposes of general jurisdiction is not settled, however, since the Supreme Court has not directly addressed the issue.

Because of the inherent and necessary flexibility of the "fair play and substantial justice" standard, it is difficult to provide an exhaustive list of possible factors affecting a court's determination of fairness in a personal jurisdiction dispute. A fairly complete list of factors recurrently taken into account is set out in a well-known California opinion written by Justice Roger Traynor, Fisher Governor Company v. Superior Court:[33]

> The interest of the state in providing a forum for its residents * * *; or in regulating the business involved * * *; the relative availability of evidence and the burden of defense and prosecution in one place rather than another * * *; the ease of access to an alternative forum * * *; the avoidance of multiplicity of suits and conflicting adjudications * * *; and the extent to which the cause of action arose out of

---

31. Bryant may be seen as an exception to the second categorical principle of International Shoe that jurisdiction may not be asserted when the defendant's forum activities are only "casual" and the cause of action is unrelated to those activities. Alternatively, the case may be viewed as involving continuous, although slight, contacts, thus falling within the third principle. In either situation, the Bryant decision indicates how very slight forum contacts may sustain an assertion of jurisdiction when notions of fair play and substantial justice weigh heavily in favor of maintaining the suit in the forum.

32. 84 F.3d 560 (2d Cir.1996), cert. denied ___ U.S. ___, 117 S.Ct. 508.

33. 53 Cal.2d 222, 225–26, 1 Cal.Rptr. 1, 3–4, 347 P.2d 1, 3–4 (1959).

defendant's local activities * * * are all relevant to this inquiry. * * *

§ 3.11   Refinements of the Basic Standard: The Requirement of a Purposeful Act and Foreseeability

The application of the minimum-contacts-fair-play-and-substantial-justice standard allowed courts and state legislatures to effect a considerable expansion of state jurisdictional power. A good example of the broad reach of state judicial power under the standard is McGee v. International Life Insurance Company.[1] The case involved a Texas insurance company that had reinsured the life of a California resident. The earlier policy had been issued by an Arizona insurance company whose insurance obligations had been assumed by defendant. The certificate of insurance was mailed to the insured in California; he mailed the premium payments from his California home to the insurance company's Texas office. The company never maintained an office or agent in California, and the evidence did not show that it ever had solicited or done any insurance business in California apart from this one policy. When the company refused to pay the proceeds of the policy upon the death of the insured, the California beneficiary brought suit in that state making service by registered mail pursuant to a state statute that subjected foreign corporations to suit in California on insurance contracts entered into by residents of that state, even though those corporations could not be served with process in California. The beneficiary obtained a judgment against the insurer, and sued on that judgment in a Texas court. Texas refused to enforce the judgment, holding that the California court never obtained jurisdiction over the company and that its judgment was void.

A unanimous Supreme Court reversed and held that all of the due process elements had been satisfied. The Court said "it is sufficient for purposes of due process that the suit was based on a contract which had substantial connection with the state's courts."[2] Thus, jurisdiction was asserted based on a single act or a single contract entered into by the defendant.

If the McGee case suggested a newly unlimited jurisdictional reach for state courts, the Supreme Court was quick to remind them one year later that the territorial limits of Pennoyer still were relevant:

> But it is a mistake to assume that [the International Shoe] trend heralds the eventual demise of all restrictions on the personal jurisdiction of state courts. * * * Those restrictions are more than a guarantee of immunity from inconvenient or distant litigation. They are a consequence of territorial limitations on the power of the respective States. However minimal the burden of defending in a foreign tribunal, a defendant may not be called upon to do so unless

§ 3.11

1. 355 U.S. 220, 78 S.Ct. 199, 2 L.Ed.2d 223 (1957).

2. 355 U.S. at 223, 78 S.Ct. at 201.

he has had the "minimal contacts" with that State that are a prerequisite to its exercise of power over him.[3]

This passage is from the Court's opinion in Hanson v. Denckla.[4] In that case, a Pennsylvania domiciliary had executed a trust instrument in Delaware, naming a Delaware bank as trustee. The instrument gave the settlor certain powers over the trust during her lifetime, including a power of appointment as to the remainder in the trust. Subsequently, the settlor became a domiciliary of Florida. While there, she purported to exercise her power of appointment by appointing a substantial portion of the trust to two other trusts, previously established with another Delaware trustee for the benefit of two of her grandchildren.

After the settlor's death, the residuary legatees under her will brought an action in Florida, contending that the power of appointment had not been exercised effectively and that the amount in question passed to them with the residue of her estate. Personal service on the Delaware trustees or on certain other interested parties could not be effected in Florida; as a result, extraterritorial service was made by mail and by publication. Several defendants challenged the Florida court's jurisdiction. The Florida court concluded that it had jurisdiction over the Delaware trustee, that the trust was invalid, and that the settlor's exercise of the power of appointment was ineffective. Accordingly, the trust property passed under the will.

Before the Florida judgment was rendered, a parallel action was commenced in Delaware by one of the settlor's daughters to secure a declaratory judgment concerning the validity of the appointments under the trust. With minor exceptions, the parties were the same as in the Florida action. The Delaware court held the trust and the exercise of the power valid, refusing to be bound by the Florida judgment, which was entered and asserted prior to the Delaware court's ruling.

A divided Supreme Court held that the Delaware trustee did not have the minimum contacts with Florida that are prerequisite to a state's exercise of power over a party. Therefore, because jurisdiction over the trustee, an indispensable party to the action under Florida law, had not been obtained, the Florida judgment was not entitled to full faith and credit in the Delaware courts. The Court pointed out that the trust company had no office in Florida and transacted no business there, that none of the trust assets ever had been held or administered in Florida, and that there had been no solicitation of business in Florida by the trust company either in person or by mail. The Court further stated that the cause of action was not one arising out of an act done or a transaction consummated in Florida, but rather it involved the validity of an agreement that did not have any connection with Florida at the time it was signed.

---

3. Hanson v. Denckla, 357 U.S. 235, 251, 78 S.Ct. 1228, 1238, 2 L.Ed.2d 1283 (1958) (per Warren, C.J.).

4. Ibid.

The Court deemed it immaterial, so far as jurisdiction over the trustee was concerned, that the settlor and most of the appointees and beneficiaries were domiciled in Florida. Further, the unilateral act of the settlor, in exercising her power of appointment in Florida, was not enough to create jurisdiction over the trustee. Rather, Chief Justice Warren, writing for the majority, ruled that it was essential that "there be some act by which the defendant purposefully avails itself of the privilege of conducting activities within the forum State, thus invoking the benefits and protection of its laws."[5] The Court found no such purposeful activity by the defendant trust company in Hanson, distinguishing McGee in which the foreign insurance company consciously had solicited a contract with the California insured.

The Court's emphasis on a finding of some purposeful act on the part of the defendant in order to support jurisdiction is most important for this was not the only possible construction of the minimum contacts test. Indeed, dissenting Justice Black, joined by Justices Brennan and Burton, formulated the test in terms of the sufficiency of the relationship of the underlying transaction to the interest of the forum state.[6] In their view, principles of choice of law and forum non conveniens were thought relevant in applying the International Shoe standard. But the majority specifically rejected this formulation, stating that a court "does not acquire * * * jurisdiction by being the 'center of gravity' of the controversy, or the most convenient location for litigation."[7]

In the years following Hanson, the Supreme Court has continued to reaffirm the importance of a defendant's legitimate expectations in assessing the propriety of asserting jurisdiction and thus has continued to interpret the International Shoe standard in such a way as to place some limits on state court jurisdictional expansion.[8] Decisions limiting the courts' assertions of in rem and quasi in rem jurisdiction are discussed elsewhere.[9]

Two subsequent in personam jurisdiction decisions—Kulko v. Superior Court[10] and World–Wide Volkswagen Corporation v. Woodson[11]—illustrate what the Court sees as the outer boundaries of jurisdiction, beyond which a state may not constitutionally venture. In both decisions the Court deemphasized the interests of the forum state and the plaintiff in deciding whether the assertion of jurisdiction is consistent with due process and placed in the foreground the Hanson requirement that the defendant purposefully avail himself of the state's benefits. Other factors considered under the International Shoe standard such as forum convenience and the economic burden faced by the parties in litigating elsewhere are secondary considerations. They may affect the balance of

5. 357 U.S. at 253, 78 S.Ct. at 1240.

6. 357 U.S. at 258, 78 S.Ct. at 1242.

7. 357 U.S. at 254, 78 S.Ct. at 1240.

8. See generally Nordenberg, State Courts, Personal Jurisdiction and the Evolutionary Process, 54 N.D.Law. 587 (1969).

9. See §§ 3.14–3.15, below.

10. 436 U.S. 84, 98 S.Ct. 1690, 56 L.Ed.2d 132 (1978).

11. 444 U.S. 286, 100 S.Ct. 559, 62 L.Ed.2d 490 (1980).

factors indicating whether jurisdiction is proper, but, these considerations alone, without a finding of sufficient contacts with the state by the defendant cannot justify a court's assertion of jurisdiction.

In Kulko v. Superior Court,[12] a divorced wife residing in California brought an action in California against her former husband, a New York domiciliary, to gain custody of their children and to increase the husband's child support obligations. The couple had entered into a separation agreement in New York under which the children, a son and a daughter, were to live with the father in New York, but spend vacations with the mother in California. When the daughter expressed her desire to live permanently with her mother, the defendant consented and paid for her plane fare to California. The son later followed his sister to California without the father's consent or help. The California Supreme Court upheld personal jurisdiction over the nonresident father with respect to the claim for additional child support, finding that his act outside the state of sending his daughter to live with her mother had caused an "effect" in California by which he had purposefully availed himself of the benefits of the forum. Further, it ruled that because California had jurisdiction for the support action involving the daughter, it was fair to adjudicate the support of the son at the same time.

The Supreme Court reversed, declaring that the mere act of sending the daughter to California connoted neither intent to obtain nor expectation to receive a corresponding benefit in the state.[13] The Court's opinion suggested that the defendant's act had not been purposeful and volitional; it had constituted mere acquiescence in the event that had invoked the protection of the forum's law. Further, the cause of action arose not from the defendant's commercial transactions in interstate commerce but rather from his personal, domestic relations.[14] He did not purposefully derive any financial benefit from the children's move to California; any diminution in his household costs was due not to the children's presence in the forum state but rather their absence from New York. The Court concluded:

> This single act [of allowing the daughter to live with the mother] is surely not one that a reasonable parent would expect to result in the substantial financial burden and personal strain of litigating a child-support suit in a forum 3,000 miles away, and we therefore see no basis on which it can be said that appellant could reasonably have anticipated being "haled before [a California] court."[15]

The defendant's children, not the defendant, had invoked the protection of California's laws. And the unilateral activity of someone claiming a

12. 436 U.S. 84, 98 S.Ct. 1690, 56 L.Ed.2d 132 (1978).

13. See Note, The Long–Arm Reach of the Courts Under the Effects Test After Kulko v. Superior Court, 65 Va.L.Rev. 175 (1979).

14. 436 U.S. at 97, 98 S.Ct. at 1699.

15. 436 U.S. at 97, 98 S.Ct. at 1699–1700.

relationship to the defendant cannot be attributed to the defendant himself.[16]

Finally, the Court noted that any other approach to the problem would deter parents from cooperating in custody arrangements that were in the best interests of the children. Thus, the substantive policies underlying the action required that the courts find clearly purposeful conduct on the part of the defendant before asserting jurisdiction.[17]

The Kulko Court did consider California's interest in the litigation. It first noted that the state's interest in ensuring the support of children residing in California could be effectively vindicated by using alternative enforcement methods.[18] Even more important, however, the Court emphasized that the state's interest, though substantial and legitimate, did not make California a fair forum.[19] Although the forum state's interest may be considered along with the interest of the plaintiff in choosing the forum, the existence of contacts between the defendant and the forum state remains the essential criterion for jurisdiction.

In World–Wide Volkswagen Corporation v. Woodson,[20] two New York residents, Harry and Kay Robinson, brought a product-liability suit in Oklahoma state court against a group of defendants, including the New York auto retailer who sold them their car, and the Audi distributor for the New York–Connecticut–New Jersey region.[21] The Robinsons were on an Oklahoma freeway en route to their new home in Arizona when a car rear-ended their Audi, rupturing the gas tank and causing a fire. They asserted jurisdiction over the two New York defendants pursuant to the Oklahoma long-arm statute.[22] When the trial court denied a motion to dismiss for lack of personal jurisdiction over the New York retailer and the distributor, these two defendants sought a writ of prohibition from the state Supreme Court. In denying the writ, the Oklahoma court said that jurisdiction was proper under the Oklahoma statute because the defendants derived substantial revenues from automobiles they sell which are used "from time to time" in Oklahoma and because they allegedly had committed a tortious act outside the state having consequences within it.[23]

16. 436 U.S. at 94, 98 S.Ct. at 1698.

17. 436 U.S. at 93, 98 S.Ct. at 1698. See generally Bodenheimer & Neeley Kvarme, Jurisdiction Over Child Custody and Adoption after Shaffer and Kulko, 12 U.Cal.Davis L.Rev. 229 (1979).

18. The mother could have sued the husband more appropriately in New York. 436 U.S. at 98, 98 S.Ct. at 1700. Further, under state law the child support claim could be adjudicated using procedures in the Uniform Reciprocal Enforcement of Support Act and neither party then would be required to litigate away from his or her own domicile. 436 U.S. at 98 n. 13, 98 S.Ct. at 1700 n. 13.

19. 436 U.S. at 101, 98 S.Ct. at 1701.

20. 444 U.S. 286, 100 S.Ct. 559, 62 L.Ed.2d 490 (1980).

21. Also joined as defendants were the German auto manufacturer, Audi NSU Auto Union Aktiengesellschaft, and the American incorporated, but wholly German owned, importer, Volkswagen of America, neither of whom contested jurisdiction in the Supreme Court.

22. 12 Okl.Stat.Ann. §§ 1701.01 et seq. (repealed 1984).

23. World–Wide Volkswagen Corp. v. Woodson, 585 P.2d 351 (Okl.1978), reversed 444 U.S. 286, 100 S.Ct. 559, 62 L.Ed.2d 490 (1980). The state supreme court was concerned primarily with interpreting the Oklahoma statute, centering its discussion

In reversing, the Supreme Court said that the minimum contacts standard was designed to perform two functions: to protect the defendant and to ensure that states did not encroach on each other's sovereign interests.[24] Although the nationalization of the American economy had minimized the significance of state boundaries, loyalty to the intent of the Framers of the Constitution required that federalism itself not disappear. If the dual purpose of the minimum contacts test was to be met, the court should look first to a defendant's contacts with the forum. If no contacts are found, it is irrelevant that the defendant would suffer no actual burden by litigating away from home or that the forum chosen is a convenient one because witnesses and evidence are located there.[25] The Court gave little weight to the fact that the cause of action arose in Oklahoma, virtually ignoring the nexus between the litigation and the forum state.

Of particular importance in the Court's analysis is the fact that it found no connection between Oklahoma and the two New York defendants. The fact that the defendants arguably could foresee the entry of the Audi into Oklahoma was insufficient: foreseeability alone, without "affiliating circumstances" by which a defendant avails himself of the privileges and benefits of the forum state's law cannot support jurisdiction. If so, "every seller of chattels would in effect appoint the chattel his agent for service of process * * * [so that] his amenability to suit would travel with the chattel"[26]—a pointed reference to the discredited analysis in Harris v. Balk.[27] The Audi's presence in Oklahoma was a result of the plaintiff's unilateral activity, not the defendants' efforts. Due process requires that potential defendants be able "to structure their primary conduct with some minimum assurance as to where the conduct will and will not render them liable to suit."[28]

The Volkswagen majority refused jurisdiction only over the local auto retailer and the regional distributor. Through dictum, the Court approved the assertion of jurisdiction over the Audi's international manufacturer and national importer, the two other defendants in the case.[29] If the defendant purposefully caters to a national market, distributing its product across the country through its own efforts or the efforts of middlemen, jurisdiction over that defendant constitutionally may be asserted in virtually any state where the product malfunctions.[30] The assertion of jurisdiction is considered fair because the national or international manufacturer receives economic benefit from a countrywide market and reasonably should expect to be subject to suit in any state.

on whether the alleged tortious act was in or out of the state, making only passing mention of the fairness of the assertion of jurisdiction.

24. 444 U.S. at 291–92, 100 S.Ct. at 564.

25. 444 U.S. at 294, 100 S.Ct. at 565–66.

26. 444 U.S. at 296, 100 S.Ct. at 566.

27. See the discussion of Harris v. Balk in § 3.9, above.

28. 444 U.S. at 297, 100 S.Ct. at 567.

29. Several lower courts since Volkswagen have continued to uphold jurisdiction over manufacturers. See, e.g., Oswalt v. Scripto, Inc., 616 F.2d 191 (5th Cir.1980); Novinger v. E.I. DuPont deNemours & Co., 89 F.R.D. 588 (M.D.Pa.1981).

30. 444 U.S. at 297, 100 S.Ct. at 567.

Thus, the Volkswagen case indicates that the court must find purposeful conduct either by direct acts of the defendant in the forum state or by conduct outside the state that, because of its character, the defendant should have foreseen could result in suit being brought in the forum. A defendant serving a local area, albeit with a product that is inherently mobile,[31] has no way to foresee where that product ultimately may go and cannot, without more purposeful activity on its part, be held accountable in distant forums when the product malfunctions.

Although the approach of the Volkswagen Court may be viewed as a re-affirmation of the standard articulated in Hanson v. Denckla, some elements of the majority's opinion raise further questions. First, Justice White suggested in his opinion that the lower courts had forgotten that the minimum contacts standard serves two functions; it is designed not just to protect the defendant but also to preserve notions of federalism and recognize state sovereignty. These functions he felt would not be served were jurisdiction to be asserted over the New York retailer and regional distributor. After suggesting that some independent factor relating to state sovereignty ought to be considered, the remainder of the opinion discusses the lack of purposeful conduct and foreseeability to those defendants in being sued in Oklahoma. This left some question as to how federalism notions differed from concerns about the due process rights of the defendant and whether some new or additional element in the minimum contacts standard was being suggested by the Court.[32]

These questions were answered in a footnote in a later decision, Insurance Corporation of Ireland, Ltd. v. Compagnie des Bauxites de Guinee,[33] in which Justice White elaborated: "The restriction on state sovereign power described in World–Wide Volkswagen Corp., however, must be seen as ultimately a function of the individual liberty interest preserved by the Due Process Clause. That clause is the only source of the personal jurisdiction requirement and the clause itself makes no mention of federalism concerns."[34] Thus, it now is clear that the Court did not intend to inject a new factor into the analysis. Rather, defendant's conduct remains the central concern. By requiring clear evidence of some purposeful conduct on the part of the defendant, the defendant's individual liberty interests are protected and at the same time the state appropriately is recognizing the coequal sovereignty of its sister states.

The second question raised by Volkswagen stems from the majority's treatment of foreseeability as a critical factor in determining whether the minimum contacts standard is satisfied. In Volkswagen itself, the defendants' businesses were designed to serve local or regional areas and

---

31. Justice Blackmun in his dissenting opinion, argued that because of the nature of the product involved, jurisdiction was proper. He concluded that given the inherent mobility of the automobile, a dealer necessarily knows and should expect that it will be used beyond a limited area and thus subject him to suit outside of his home state.

32. See Comment, Federalism, Due Process, and Minimum Contacts: World–Wide Volkswagen Corp. v. Woodson, 80 Colum.L.Rev. 1341 (1980).

33. 456 U.S. 694, 102 S.Ct. 2099, 72 L.Ed.2d 492 (1982).

34. 456 U.S. at 702 n. 10, 102 S.Ct. at 2104–05 n. 10.

the plaintiffs purchased their car while they were residing in the defendant's business area. What if Oklahomans temporarily in New York purchased the auto, informing the defendant retailer that they were from Oklahoma and intended to return there with the car? Would the sale made with knowledge of where the product would be used mean that defendant should have foreseen being sued in Oklahoma and thus would be subject to suit, even though it did not solicit any business in that state and merely complied with the purchaser's request for the car?

The answer to this question is not absolutely clear. On the one hand, the retailer then has full knowledge and has benefitted from the sale. But this situation might be analogized to Kulko, where the father knew his children were moving to California and "benefitted" by the reduced costs of living in New York without his children. The Court in that case found that it was not sufficient that an act was done outside the state causing harm within the forum. However, the Kulko Court distinguished the products-liability situation, denying jurisdiction in large measure because substantive policies in the family law area suggested that jurisdictional barriers were important to encourage cooperation between parents on child custody arrangements. In the products-liability area, the trend has been to increase liability and the potential for suing in the state where the harm occurred.[35] Indeed, Volkswagen itself suggested that the manufacturer could not escape jurisdiction because it knowingly entered the United States market. Similarly, then, the retailer knowingly sold in the Oklahoma market. The regional distributor would remain outside the jurisdictional reach of Oklahoma, however, as it remains passive and would have no foreseeability about this sale.

The Volkswagen case does not mean that foreseeability may not be found in the absence of the defendant's purposeful direct contact with the forum state. Rather, the notion of foreseeability is restricted. It "is not the mere likelihood that a product will find its way into the forum State. Rather, it is that the defendant's conduct and connection with the forum State are such that he should reasonably anticipate being haled into court there."[36] Using this definition, our hypothetical New York retailer should have foreseen suit in Oklahoma and the minimum contacts threshold would be met so that consideration must be given to whether Oklahoma provides a fair forum for the dispute.

Although Justice Brennan, in his dissenting opinion in Volkswagen, criticized the majority's approach as ignoring the forum state's interest and giving the defendant "an unjustified veto power over certain appropriate fora,"[37] the clear trend since Hanson has been to raise the threshold for assertions of state jurisdiction and to inject some predictability and certainty into a test that is the source of so much litigation.[38]

---

35. See the discussion of long-arm jurisdiction in products liability actions in § 3.13, below.

36. 444 U.S. at 297, 100 S.Ct. at 567.

37. 444 U.S. at 286, 312, 100 S.Ct. at 580, 587.

38. Louis, The Grasp of Long–Arm Jurisdiction Finally Exceeds Its Reach: A Comment on World–Wide Volkswagen

In all its recent jurisdiction decisions, the Court has refused to credit the defendant with "contacts" that are the result of the activity of someone else. The definition of contacts is tied to the defendant's expectations: was defendant on clear notice that by acting in a certain way, he could be haled into a court outside of his home state?

The reference to the defendant's expectations will not always result in a complex subjective inquiry. In many instances, the answer to that question is clearly yes, as for example, when an intentional tort is involved.[39] Under those circumstances, the propriety of asserting jurisdiction over the defendant will be clear.

Further, the Court in even more recent decisions has made clear that if the defendant's contacts satisfy the minimum contacts threshold, then few other considerations are likely to tip the balance in favor of rejecting jurisdiction as unfair. In Keeton v. Hustler Magazine, Inc.,[40] it ruled that the fact that the plaintiff was not a resident of the forum state and had chosen the forum merely because of its uniquely long statute of limitations did not require the denial of jurisdiction as unfair.[41]

The Volkswagen test, by requiring that the court first examine a defendant's contacts rather than initially balancing several interests at one time, may be easier to apply and somewhat more predictable. Nonetheless, absolute predictability may prove elusive. As Justice Marshall acknowledged in the majority opinion in Kulko, the International Shoe test of "minimum contacts" is "one in which few answers will be written in black and white. The greys are dominant and even among them the shades are innumerable."[42]

Further refinements of the International Shoe "minimum contacts" standard were made in response to judicial developments in tort law that relaxed or dispensed with the requirements for privity between plaintiff and defendant in products-liability cases.[43] Early on, some courts applying the teachings of International Shoe were willing to find jurisdiction when a product caused damage in the forum state when the manufacturer merely had released it into the "stream of commerce" without knowing precisely where the product ultimately would be purchased or

Corp. v. Woodson and Rush v. Savchuk, 58 N.C.L.Rev. 409 (1980).

39. In Calder v. Jones, 465 U.S. 783, 104 S.Ct. 1482, 79 L.Ed.2d 804 (1984), the Supreme Court upheld jurisdiction over an out-of-state reporter and editor sued for libel. It rejected an argument that they should be treated as employees who had no authority to control the circulation of the publication and who derived no direct benefits from it, finding that they knew that any harm caused by the story likely would be felt at the home of the plaintiff and that it thus was foreseeable to them that they could be haled into court there.

40. 465 U.S. 770, 104 S.Ct. 1473, 79 L.Ed.2d 790 (1984).

41. In Metropolitan Life Ins. Co. v. Robertson–Ceco Corp., 84 F.3d 560 (2d Cir. 1996), cert. denied ___ U.S. ___, 117 S.Ct. 508, discussed in § 3.10, at note 32, above, the Second Circuit cited Keeton for a somewhat different proposition: if a plaintiff's claim is barred by the statute of limitations in all forums but one, fairness does not require the exercise of jurisdiction in the one remaining forum, even if the defendant is subject to general jurisdiction there.

42. 436 U.S. at 92, 98 S.Ct. at 1697.

43. For a discussion of the historical evolution of tort law in the area of products liability, see Prosser & Keeton on Torts §§ 95–104A (Dobbs, Keeton, Owen & Keeton ed.1984).

used. In Gray v. American Radiator & Standard Sanitary Corporation,[44] for example, the plaintiff, an Illinois resident, was injured in an explosion caused by a defective valve in a water heater she had purchased from an Illinois retailer. The valve had been produced by Titan Valve Manufacturing Company in Ohio, which shipped its product to Pennsylvania where American Radiator installed the valves into the water heaters. From Pennsylvania, the water heaters were shipped to retailers in states across the country, including Illinois, where they were purchased by the ultimate user. The plaintiff brought suit in Illinois state court, asserting jurisdiction over Titan Valve pursuant to the Illinois long-arm statute.

The Illinois Supreme Court held that Titan Valve had sufficient "minimum contacts" to justify the lower court's assertion of jurisdiction. Even though Titan Valve had made no sales in Illinois and had carried on no activity in that state, the court found that Titan's business was "directly affected by transactions occurring" in Illinois[45] and that Titan had "benefited * * * from the protection which [Illinois] law" provides to the marketing of water heaters containing their valves.[46] The court concluded that "[a]s a general proposition, if a corporation elects to sell its products for ultimate use in another State, it is not unjust to hold it answerable there for any damage caused by defects in those products."[47]

The United States Supreme Court considered the "stream of commerce" question in World–Wide Volkswagen Corporation v. Woodson,[48] which was discussed earlier.[49] In its opinion, the Court expressly endorsed the stream of commerce analysis as it was articulated in Gray: A forum state constitutionally may exercise personal jurisdiction over "a corporation that delivers its products into the stream of commerce with the expectation that they will be purchased by consumers in the forum State."[50] The Court held that the defendants in the Woodson case lacked this expectation and that therefore the Oklahoma court could not exercise in personam jurisdiction over them. The Court found that the automobile was present in Oklahoma only because it was taken there by the plaintiff. Even if it was "foreseeable" that an automobile sold in New York could be driven to Oklahoma, the Court held that "unilateral" actions on the part of a consumer "cannot satisfy the requirement of contact with the forum State" that is necessary for the assertion of personal jurisdiction.[51]

The Supreme Court's most recent statement on the "stream of commerce" theory appears in Asahi Metal Industry Company v. Superior

44. 22 Ill.2d 432, 176 N.E.2d 761 (1961). See the discussion in § 3.13, below.

45. 22 Ill.2d at 442, 176 N.E.2d at 766.

46. 22 Ill.2d at 442, 176 N.E.2d at 766.

47. 22 Ill.2d at 442, 176 N.E.2d at 766.

48. 444 U.S. 286, 100 S.Ct. 559, 62 L.Ed.2d 490 (1980).

49. See the discussion of the World–Wide Volkswagen decision at notes 20–32, above.

50. 444 U.S. at 297–98, 100 S.Ct. at 567 (citing Gray v. American Radiator & Standard Sanitary Corp.).

51. 444 U.S. at 297–98, 100 S.Ct. at 567.

Court of California.[52] In that case, the plaintiff and his passenger, both California residents, were injured when one of the tires of the motorcycle they were riding exploded. The plaintiff brought a products-liability action in California Superior Court against Cheng Shin Rubber Industrial Company, the Taiwanese manufacturer of the defective tire. Cheng Shin then filed a cross-complaint for indemnity against the Japanese manufacturer of the tire valve assembly, Asahi Metals. The plaintiff subsequently settled his claim against Cheng Shin, leaving the indemnity cross-claim between Cheng Shin and Asahi.

The United States Supreme Court unanimously held that the California state court could not constitutionally exercise jurisdiction over Asahi. The Court followed the two-step analysis it had developed in its previous decisions. First, inquiry was made into the sufficiency of the defendant's contacts with the forum state and then those contacts were examined in light of fairness considerations to determine if the exercise of jurisdiction would be reasonable.

Justice O'Connor, in her plurality opinion, understood the teaching of Volkswagen to be that a manufacturer's contacts must be "more purposefully directed at the forum State than the mere act of placing a product in the stream of commerce."[53] Asahi's mere awareness that the valve assemblies it sold to Cheng Shin eventually would end up in California was not sufficiently purposeful, in her opinion, to establish minimum contacts. Justice Brennan, in his concurrence, found no requirement in Volkswagen for any "additional conduct" beyond the placement of a product into "the regular and anticipated flow of products from manufacture to distribution to retail sale."[54] Since Asahi was aware that its products were being sold regularly in California, it had established "minimum contacts" with California. Justice Brennan also noted that the possibility of a lawsuit in California could neither "come as a surprise" to Asahi nor be considered a burden for which Asahi had received no corresponding benefit.[55]

On the facts of this case, a majority of the Court agreed with Justice Brennan that Asahi did have minimum contacts with California. However, the Court divided sharply on this point with three members endorsing the conclusion reached by Justice O'Connor. Given the division of the justices in Asahi and the changes in the Court's composition since, the question of what is the appropriate standard to be used to determine whether a manufacturer has established sufficient "minimum contacts" with a forum state has not been fully resolved.

The Court was in greater agreement on the question of whether, given minimum contacts, the assertion of jurisdiction was reasonable. Eight justices agreed that the California state court's exercise of jurisdiction over Asahi was unreasonable. The Court reached this conclusion by

52. 480 U.S. 102, 107 S.Ct. 1026, 94 L.Ed.2d 92 (1987).

53. 480 U.S. at 110, 107 S.Ct. at 1031.

54. 480 U.S. at 117, 107 S.Ct. at 1035 (Brennan, J., concurring).

55. 480 U.S. at 117, 107 S.Ct. at 1035.

balancing "several factors" including "the interests of the forum State, and the plaintiff's interest in obtaining relief" against "the burden on the defendant."[56] The Court found that the interests of California in litigating the lawsuit were minimal because, even though the original accident had occurred in California, the claim concerned the relationship between two corporations from foreign countries.[57] Likewise, the Court found the interest of Cheng Shin in litigating this matter in a California court not to be significant, especially when other forums were available. In contrast, the Court found the burden to Asahi would be great if it were forced to defend the claim in a California state court. The Court noted the international context of this case and indicated that great care should be exercised in deciding whether to hear a case that is truly foreign.[58]

Today, courts typically employ a three-step test to determine the constitutionality of asserting specific personal jurisdiction. First, did the defendant purposefully avail itself of the forum state? Second, did the cause of action arise from the defendant's contacts with the forum state? Finally, would the exercise of personal jurisdiction be reasonable?

Recently, some courts have expanded the scope of jurisdiction by relaxing the "relatedness" requirement of the three-part test. For example, the California Supreme Court in Vons Companies v. Seabest Foods, Inc.[59] exercised specific personal jurisdiction over two defendants for actions "substantially connected" to, but not arising directly out of, contacts with the forum state. Following a widely publicized outbreak of illness and death associated with bacteria in fast-food hamburgers, lawsuits were brought against, among others, the fast-food franchiser and Vons, a meat supplier, both of which had their principal place of business in California. Vons cross-complained against two out-of-state franchisees, Seabest Foods, Inc. ("Seabest") and Washington Restaurant Management, Inc. ("WRMI"), for failing to cook the offending hamburgers properly. Seabest and WRMI did not have enough contacts with California to warrant general jurisdiction, but they had purposefully availed themselves of an ongoing contractual relationship with the California franchiser. However, the alleged tortious activity did not arise directly out of contacts with the franchiser, and Seabest and WRMI had not directed their California contacts toward Vons. Nevertheless, the California Supreme Court held that Vons' claims were "substantially connected" to the contacts between the California franchiser and Seabest and WRMI; thus, California could exercise specific personal jurisdiction. The court noted that the appropriate question was not whether Seabest and WRMI had sufficient contacts with Vons, but whether they had sufficient contacts with California. As to fairness, the court pointed out that California had a strong interest in adjudicating the action and

---

56. 480 U.S. at 113, 107 S.Ct. at 1033–34.

57. 480 U.S. at 114–15, 107 S.Ct. at 1034.

58. 480 U.S. at 115–16, 107 S.Ct. at 1035.

59. 14 Cal.4th 434, 58 Cal.Rptr.2d 899, 926 P.2d 1085 (1996), cert. denied ___ U.S. ___, 118 S. Ct. 47.

any burden on Seabest and WRMI was mitigated by their agreement with the California franchiser that it would defend and indemnify them.

The California Supreme Court found support for its conclusions in decisions of the Sixth and Seventh Circuits, and the result in the Vons case may be indicative of a growing trend away from a strict interpretation of the requirement in specific jurisdiction cases that the cause of action "arises out of" the defendant's contacts with the forum. The California Supreme Court was careful to note that the United States Supreme Court never has addressed the particular degree of "relatedness" required by the minimum contacts doctrine; in line with the general reasoning of International Shoe, the California Supreme Court chose to focus on reasonableness and fairness rather than mechanical formulations.

Finally, it should be kept in mind that the Supreme Court decisions discussed in this section merely suggest how far the states can go in asserting jurisdiction over nonresident defendants. The states need not exhaust their powers under the Due Process Clause, although instances of such self-restraint are rare.[60] Similarly, a few courts have found constraints on the exercise of state court jurisdiction in constitutional clauses other than Due Process,[61] such as the Commerce Clause.[62] However, these additional limitations have not developed far. Perhaps the revival of federalism constraints in the Volkswagen and Hanson cases renders these additional limitations unnecessary.

2. Statutory Requirements

§ 3.12 The Growth and Use of Long–Arm Statutes

The Supreme Court decisions in Hess v. Pawloski,[1] upholding the validity of a nonresident motorist statute, and Doherty & Company v. Goodman,[2] upholding jurisdiction over a nonresident individual engaged in the sale of corporate securities, among other decisions, unquestionably encouraged states to enact jurisdictional statutes covering a wide range of supposedly hazardous activities. But it was the International Shoe decision with its validation of expanded state court jurisdiction under the Due Process Clause that inspired state legislatures to enact comprehen-

60. For example, in New York defamation is specifically excluded from the long-arm statute's tort provisions. N.Y.—McKinney's CPLR 302(a)(2), (3). For a further discussion of statutory restrictions in various long-arm provisions, see §§ 3.12–3.13, below.

61. At one time some lower courts found constraints on personal jurisdiction in the First Amendment. See, e.g., New York Times Co. v. Connor, 365 F.2d 567 (5th Cir.1966), noted 52 Iowa L.Rev. 1034 (1967), 20 Vand.L.Rev. 921 (1967). But the Supreme Court has now made clear that

First Amendment concerns are not to be injected into the jurisdictional inquiry. Calder v. Jones, 465 U.S. 783, 104 S.Ct. 1482, 79 L.Ed.2d 804 (1984).

62. See, e.g., Erlanger Mills, Inc. v. Cohoes Fibre Mills, Inc., 239 F.2d 502 (4th Cir.1956).

§ 3.12

1. 274 U.S. 352, 47 S.Ct. 632, 71 L.Ed. 1091 (1927).

2. 294 U.S. 623, 55 S.Ct. 553, 79 L.Ed. 1097 (1935).

sive jurisdictional statutes based on the defendant's conduct in the forum.[3] These long-arm or single-act statutes predicate jurisdiction over nonresidents upon a variety of contacts with the forum, including the transaction of business in the state, the commission of any one of a series of enumerated acts within the state, such as the commission of a tort, ownership of property, or entry into a contract, or, in some cases, the commission of a particular act outside the forum that has consequences within it.

In 1956, Illinois enacted the first single-act statute, which was thought to expand the in personam jurisdiction of the courts of that state "to the limits permitted under the due process clause."[4] The original Illinois statute is illustrative of the long-arm statutes that have been enacted in a majority of the states. It provided, in part:

(1) Any person, whether or not a citizen or resident of this State, who in person or through an agent does any of the acts hereinafter enumerated, thereby submits said person, and, if an individual, his personal representative, to the jurisdiction of the courts of this State as to any cause of action arising from the doing of any said acts:

(a) The transaction of any business within this State;

(b) The commission of a tortious act within this State;

(c) The ownership, use, or possession of any real estate situated in this State;

(d) Contracting to insure any person, property or risk located within this State at the time of contracting.[5]

In 1967, the statute was amended to include jurisdiction over claims against former residents that involve alimony, support, and property division.[6]

The Illinois statute just quoted is typical of, but by no means is identical to, the long-arm provisions in other states. For example, with respect to contract disputes, some long-arm provisions only apply to contracts with forum residents that are "to be performed in whole or in part" by either party in the forum;[7] many other long-arm provisions, like the Illinois statute, permit suit on causes of action arising out of the "transaction of any business" within the state.[8] The specific provisions in various long-arm statutes are explored in the next section.

---

3. D. Currie, The Growth of the Long–Arm: Eight Years of Extended Jurisdiction in Illinois, 1963 U.Ill.L.F. 533; Homburger, The Reach of New York's Long–Arm Statute: Today and Tomorrow, 15 Buffalo L.Rev. 61 (1965); Thode, In Personam Jurisdiction; Article 2031b, the Texas "Long–Arm" Statute; and the Appearance to Challenge Jurisdiction in Texas and Elsewhere, 42 Texas L.Rev. 279 (1964).

4. O'Hare Int'l Bank v. Hampton, 437 F.2d 1173, 1176 (7th Cir.1971); Nelson v. Miller, 11 Ill.2d 378, 143 N.E.2d 673 (1957).

5. Ill.—Smith–Hurd Ann. 735 ILCS 5/2–209 (original version at ch. 110, ¶ 17

(1956)). Some statutes explicitly preclude their use in defamation suits. See, e.g., Ga. Code § 9–10–91(2); N.Y.—McKinney's CPLR 302(a)(2), (3).

6. Ill.—Smith–Hurd Ann. 735 ILCS 5/2–209(a)(5) (original version at ch. 110, ¶ 17(1)(e) (1967)).

7. E.g., Miss.Code Ann. § 13–3–57; Tex.Civ.Prac. & Rem.Code Ann. § 17.042(1).

8. E.g., Ill—Smith–Hurd Ann. 735 ILCS 5/2–209(a)(1); N.Y.—McKinney's CPLR 302(a)(1).

A very different statutory approach has been taken in Rhode Island, however. That state's long-arm statute is drafted so that it can expand or contract with the construction given to due process by the Rhode Island and United States Supreme Courts.[9] It provides that:

> Every [defendant] that shall have the necessary minimum contacts with the state of Rhode Island, shall be subject to the jurisdiction of the state of Rhode Island, and the courts of this state shall hold * * * [defendant] amenable to suit in Rhode Island in every case not contrary to the provisions of the constitution or laws of the United States.

California has a statute modeled after Rhode Island's.[10] Because the California–Rhode Island type of statute is easy to draft and is completely nonspecific, it avoids many of the pitfalls of the detailed single-act provisions.[11] The price of this flexibility, however, is to reduce the predictability of the result, and, in a sense, to convert every jurisdictional issue into a constitutional question.[12]

The legislative rationale for the jurisdictional sweep of the modern long-arm statute is to ensure state citizens a local forum in which to litigate causes of action that arise from the activities of nonresidents; this convenience, of course, often is provided to the resident at the expense of the convenience of the nonresident defendant.

In a multiple claim action, the court must scrutinize each claim being asserted to make certain that the defendant is within its reach for purposes of adjudicating that claim. The defendant's appearance in the forum in response to process issued under the long-arm statute confers jurisdiction solely to adjudicate a claim covered by the provisions of the statute;[13] jurisdiction thus acquired does not extend to claims outside the scope of the statute.

In general, a plaintiff must negotiate three hurdles to obtain jurisdiction over a defendant under the applicable long-arm statute. First, the statutory language must apply to the cause of action alleged. For example, an action for invasion of privacy cannot be brought within a provision that is restricted to actions for physical injury. Second, even if the statutory language encompasses the particular cause of action at issue, the judicially developed standards that have emerged under the statute must be satisfied.[14] For example, judges in a particular forum

9. R.I.Gen.Laws 1956, § 9–5–33.

10. West's Ann.Cal.Code Civ.Proc. § 410.10 ("A court of this state may exercise jurisdiction on any basis not inconsistent with the Constitution of this state or of the United States.").

11. For a discussion of some of the interpretative problems in more specific long-arm statutes see § 3.13, below.

12. An effort to provide a model to guide state legislatures and provide for uniform treatment of the jurisdiction question is the Uniform Interstate and International Procedure Act § 1.03, 9B Uniform Laws Ann. 307. Patterned after the Illinois, Michigan, North Carolina, and Wisconsin statutes, the Act has been adopted in Oklahoma, Arkansas and the Virgin Islands and has been used as a model by a number of other state legislatures.

13. See N.Y.—McKinney's CPLR 302(c).

14. See § 3.13, below.

might require that sufficient state interest be shown before opening the forum courts to the plaintiff. Accordingly, the forum's case law always must be consulted to ascertain how its courts have interpreted the applicable long-arm statute. Third, and finally, jurisdiction must be exercised in a manner that is consistent with the federal, as well as any applicable state, constitutional standards. In practice, the constitutional inquiry is most important: almost twenty states have enacted statutes that explicitly allow the exercise of personal jurisdiction to the maximum extent permitted by the Constitution; another twenty-five or so have enacted long-arm statutes that have been interpreted, in whole or in part, to reach the limits of the Constitution.[15]

§ 3.13   Particular Applications of Long–Arm Statutes

Most states have long-arm statutes that are drafted to include very specific kinds of cases and defendants.[1] A full exploration of all of the different formulations that exist, as well as their varied interpretations, is beyond the scope of this discussion. However, a brief exploration of some of the common interpretative difficulties that have arisen will illustrate the varied extent of long-arm jurisdiction asserted by different states.

Many long-arm statutes speak in terms of "persons" and do not state whether the statute is intended to apply solely to natural persons or whether "persons" should be interpreted to include any natural person, partnership, corporation, and unincorporated association.[2] Although this language suggests that human and corporate defendants will be treated alike for purposes of long-arm jurisdiction, courts may apply a more demanding interpretation of the long-arm statute to cases involving natural persons. For example, the Iowa long-arm statute, which provided, as amended: "If a nonresident person * * * commits a tort in whole or in part in Iowa against a resident of Iowa, such acts shall be deemed to be doing business in Iowa by such person for the purpose of service of process"[3] was held not to permit the assertion of jurisdiction over an individual defendant once he had moved from the forum.[4] And in a Pennsylvania case the court refused to sustain jurisdiction over a physician who, although actively engaged in the practice of medicine at the time the cause of action accrued, had retired from his partnership by the time the plaintiff brought suit against all the partners.[5] The applica-

---

15. See, e.g., Glover v. Western Air Lines, Inc., 745 P.2d 1365 (Alaska 1987); Valspar Corp. v. Lukken Color Corp., 495 N.W.2d 408 (Minn.1992); CSR Limited v. Link, 925 S.W.2d 591 (Tex.1996).

§ 3.13

1. The exceptions to this pattern are statutes like those in force in certain states, such as Rhode Island and California, that basically adopt the constitutional standard as their sole limitation on the assertion of jurisdiction. See § 3.12 at nn. 9–10, above. Furthermore, note that many long-arm statutes have been interpreted to reach the limits of the Constitution. See § 3.12 at n. 15, above.

2. But see, e.g., Ark.Code Ann. § 16–4–101(A); Del.Code Ann. tit. 10, § 3104(a); N.C.Gen.Stat. § 1–75.2(1).

3. 42 Iowa Code Ann. § 617.3.

4. Fagan v. Fletcher, 257 Iowa 449, 451, 133 N.W.2d 116, 118 (1965).

5. Zalevsky v. Casillo, 421 Pa. 294, 218 A.2d 771 (1966).

ble statute provided for jurisdiction over "any person" who was not a resident of the forum who "shall engage in business" in the forum. Even though the physician's name remained on the partnership nameplate and he continued to collect fees still due him, the court found these activities fell short of the statutory standard of engaging in business in the forum.

Various statutory formulations exist permitting courts to exercise long-arm jurisdiction in tort actions and, depending on the exact language used, different questions have arisen. One common approach is to permit jurisdiction when the defendant commits a tortious act "within the state."[6] When the nonresident defendant allegedly acts tortiously within the forum, causing harm to the plaintiff in the forum—for example, by driving negligently or assaulting or defaming the plaintiff locally—the application of the statute is straightforward.

However, when the defendant acts outside the forum, allegedly causing injury within the forum, the courts have reached differing conclusions on whether the statutory standard is met. In Gray v. American Radiator & Standard Sanitary Corporation,[7] the Illinois Supreme Court set out the Illinois interpretation—a tortious act performed outside the forum that produces injury within the state falls within the language of the statute.[8] Other courts have distinguished between the place where the tortious act (typically negligence) was committed and the locus of the resultant injury, concluding that long-arm provisions do not extend to tortious conduct outside the forum.[9] Other distinctions have been drawn. One court has denied jurisdiction when a defectively manufactured item was purchased in the forum but the injury stemming from its use took place outside the forum,[10] even though the plaintiff was a resident of the forum; another court has upheld jurisdiction when a nonresident was injured outside the forum by a product purchased in the forum.[11]

In response to these problems, many legislatures, including that of New York, have amended their statutes to try to eliminate locus-of-the-tort ambiguities.[12] Other revised statutes use the language "commits a

---

6. E.g., Ill.—Smith-Hurd Ann. 735 ILCS 5/2–209(a)(2); N.Y.—McKinney's CPLR 302(a)(2).

7. 22 Ill.2d 432, 176 N.E.2d 761 (1961). This case is discussed more fully in § 3.11 at notes 44–47, above.

8. For additional courts following the same interpretation, see Scanlan v. Norma Projektil Fabrik, 345 F.Supp. 292 (D.Mont. 1972); Coe & Payne Co. v. Wood–Mosaic Corp., 230 Ga. 58, 195 S.E.2d 399 (1973); Myers v. Brickwedel, 259 Or. 457, 486 P.2d 1286 (1971); Nixon v. Cohn, 62 Wn.2d 987, 385 P.2d 305 (1963).

9. Lichina v. Futura, Inc., 260 F.Supp. 252 (D.Colo.1966); Feathers v. McLucas, 15 N.Y.2d 443, 261 N.Y.S.2d 8, 209 N.E.2d 68

(1965), cert. denied 382 U.S. 905 (N.Y.—McKinney's CPLR 302(a)(2), amended in 1966).

10. Black v. Oberle Rentals, Inc., 55 Misc.2d 398, 285 N.Y.S.2d 226 (1967).

11. Callahan v. Keystone Fireworks Mfg. Co., 72 Wn.2d 823, 435 P.2d 626 (1967).

12. The New York statute now provides, in part, for jurisdiction to be asserted over any defendant who "commits a tortious act without the state causing injury to person or property within the state * * * "if the defendant is engaged in business in the state or is in interstate or international commerce and should have foreseen that the act would have consequences

tort in whole or in part" in the state[13] to avoid arguments concerning what constitutes a tort or a tortious act.

Another problem that has faced the courts in construing tort long-arm provisions is whether the language "commission of a tortious act" includes an act of omission. It has been held, for example, that a corporate director's failure to perform duties in the forum state did not constitute a tortious act there.[14] An effort to resolve this particular problem has led to use of the formulation "causing tortious injury in this state by an act or omission outside this state."[15] Similarly, some questions have been raised concerning whether an economic loss in the forum represents an injury within the meaning of the statute.[16]

In contract actions, as in tort actions, the scope of jurisdiction under a long-arm statute will depend on the particular language used and the interpretation given by the forum's courts. Some statutes, for example, permit jurisdiction in actions based on contracts made with forum residents that are to be performed "in whole or in part" by either party in the forum.[17] Other statutes provide for jurisdiction over contracts "to supply services or things" in the forum.[18]

The major interpretative difficulties under these formulations center on the meaning of the terms "made" and "performed." It has been held that a contract is "made" in the forum state only when the final act necessary to make the contract a binding obligation takes place there, that is, acceptance must take place in the forum.[19] Even if negotiations have been conducted in the forum and draft contracts have been exchanged through the mail, if the contract is not accepted in the forum it will not have been "made" there for purposes of the long-arm statute, and jurisdiction cannot be asserted.[20] In a similar vein, courts have required a finding of substantial performance of the contract within the state in order to satisfy the long-arm requirement of performance in the state.[21]

A good case exemplifying these restrictions is Bowman v. Curt G. Joa, Inc.,[22] in which the buyer plaintiff, a North Carolina corporation,

---

in the state. N.Y.—McKinney's CPLR 302(a)(3). For a discussion of the interpretative difficulties with this provision, see 1 J. Weinstein, H. Korn & A. Miller, New York Civil Practice ¶¶ 302.10–10a.

13. E.g., Tex.Civ.Prac. & Rem.Code Ann. § 17.042(2).

14. Platt Corp. v. Platt, 17 N.Y.2d 234, 270 N.Y.S.2d 408, 217 N.E.2d 134 (1966). But see Nelson v. Miller, 11 Ill.2d 378, 393, 143 N.E.2d 673 (1957).

15. Uniform Interstate and International Procedure Act § 1.03(4), 9B Uniform Laws Ann. 307, 310.

16. Engine Specialties, Inc. v. Bombardier Ltd., 454 F.2d 527 (1st Cir.1972) (impairment of business). Cf. American Eutectic Welding Alloys Sales Co. v. Dy-

tron Alloys Corp., 439 F.2d 428 (2d Cir. 1971) (loss of profits is derivative commercial injury).

17. E.g., Miss.Code Ann. § 13–3–57; Tex.Civ.Prac. & Rem.Code Ann. § 17.042(1).

18. Uniform Interstate and International Procedure Act § 1.03(2), 9B Uniform Laws Ann. 307, 310.

19. Byham v. National Cibo House Corp., 265 N.C. 50, 143 S.E.2d 225, 233 (1965).

20. Bowman v. Curt G. Joa, Inc., 361 F.2d 706 (4th Cir.1966).

21. Ibid.

22. Ibid.

sought to assert jurisdiction over a Wisconsin defendant, a manufacturer of machinery, in a breach of contract action. The North Carolina long-arm statute at the time permitted jurisdiction for a cause of action arising "out of any contract made in this State or to be performed in this State."[23] Negotiations for the equipment had been conducted in North Carolina and the defendant seller had agreed to provide some supervision of the installation of its machinery in plaintiff's North Carolina plant, although the plaintiff was himself to install the equipment. The terms provided for shipment f.o.b. to the defendant's manufacturing plant in Wisconsin; plaintiff assumed all freight and shipping charges.

The Fourth Circuit affirmed the district court's finding that the final act of execution was the defendant's acceptance signature in Wisconsin so that the contract was not "made" in North Carolina. Distinguishing the North Carolina statute from others drafted in terms of a contract to be performed "in whole or in part" in the forum, the court construed the statute's language to require that the contract be performed to a "substantial degree" in the forum. Because the contract was to make or manufacture the requested machinery, it was substantially performed in Wisconsin, despite the seller's agreement to send a technician to North Carolina to advise the plaintiff on the machinery's installation and later to inspect the installation.

Another approach to jurisdiction over contractual claims is for the long-arm statute to provide for jurisdiction over a nondomiciliary who "transacts any business" in the forum.[24] This provision has been construed to reach both contract and tort claims,[25] although the claim for relief must arise out of the in-state activities of the defendant.[26] A range of factors are relevant to what constitutes the transaction of business, including the locus of contractual negotiations,[27] execution[28] and performance,[29] as well as who initiated the transaction.[30] Generally, the mere execution of a contract in the forum will not be deemed the transaction

23. N.C.Gen.Stat. § 55–145 (repealed 1989).

24. E.g., Ill—Smith–Hurd Ann. 735 ILCS 5/2–209(a)(1); N.Y.—McKinney's CPLR 302(a)(1).

25. Kramer v. Vogl, 17 N.Y.2d 27, 267 N.Y.S.2d 900, 215 N.E.2d 159 (1966); Singer v. Walker, 15 N.Y.2d 443, 464, 261 N.Y.S.2d 8, 24, 209 N.E.2d 68 (1965), cert. denied 382 U.S. 905.

26. Longines–Wittnauer Watch Co. v. Barnes & Reinecke, Inc., 15 N.Y.2d 443, 455, 261 N.Y.S.2d 8, 17, 209 N.E.2d 68 (1965), cert. denied 382 U.S. 905.

27. National Gas Appliance Corp. v. AB Electrolux, 270 F.2d 472 (7th Cir.1959), cert. denied 361 U.S. 959; Dahlberg Co. v. Western Hearing Aid Center, Ltd., 259 Minn. 330, 107 N.W.2d 381 (1961), cert. denied 366 U.S. 961.

28. Iroquois Gas Corp. v. Collins, 42 Misc.2d 632, 248 N.Y.S.2d 494 (1964), affirmed 23 A.D.2d 823, 258 N.Y.S.2d 376 (1965).

29. E.g., Longines–Wittnauer Watch Co. v. Barnes & Reinecke, Inc., 15 N.Y.2d 443, 445, 261 N.Y.S.2d 8, 17, 209 N.E.2d 68 (1965), cert. denied 382 U.S. 905.

30. Conn v. Whitmore, 9 Utah 2d 250, 342 P.2d 871 (1959) (jurisdiction improper when plaintiff initiated all contact with defendant). Cf. Agrashell, Inc. v. Bernard Sirotta Co., 344 F.2d 583, 587 (2d Cir.1965) (nonresident defendant's negotiation of goods contracts through the mails and by telephone with New York residents did not invoke the benefits and protections of New York).

of business,[31] but execution plus some additional contact has been held sufficient;[32] of course, execution is not indispensable[33] to the exercise of jurisdiction. A single "purposeful act," such as the participation in an auction by a special long distance telephone connection,[34] may sustain jurisdiction in some states; in others, the transaction of business requires "activities which are 'substantial,' 'continuous,' 'systematic,' and 'regular'" to create a jurisdictional base.[35]

In Burger King Corporation v. Rudzewicz[36] the Supreme Court addressed the issue of "whether and to what extent a contract can constitute a 'contact' for purposes of due process analysis."[37] The case involved a twenty-year franchise agreement between Rudzewicz, a resident of Michigan, and Burger King, a Florida corporation, for the operation of a fast-food restaurant in Michigan. The agreement was negotiated by Burger King representatives in Michigan and at no time did Rudzewicz have any physical contact with Florida. The agreement he signed, however, stipulated that the franchise relationship was to be "established" in Florida and governed by Florida law. It also committed Rudzewicz to send monthly rent and royalty payments to Burger King's headquarters in Florida. When Rudzewicz fell behind in his payments, Burger King terminated the franchise and brought a diversity action against him in a federal court in Florida for failure to meet his obligations under the franchise agreement. Jurisdiction over Rudzewicz was asserted under the Florida long-arm statute, which contained a provision authorizing jurisdiction based on breach of a contract in the state.[38]

Justice Brennan, writing for the majority, held that the exercise of long-arm jurisdiction over Rudzewicz did not violate due process. In reaching this conclusion, Justice Brennan utilized a two-step "minimum contacts" analysis. A preliminary inquiry was made into whether the defendant had "purposefully established 'minimum contacts' in the forum State."[39] According to the Court, the factors that must be evaluated in a contract case include the parties' "prior negotiations," the "contemplated future consequences" of the relationship, the "terms of the contract," and the "parties' actual course of dealing."[40] If sufficient

31. Aurea Jewelry Creations, Inc. v. Lissona, 344 F.Supp. 179 (S.D.N.Y.1972); Green & White Constr. Co. v. Columbus Asphalt Co., 293 F.Supp. 279 (S.D.N.Y. 1968). See also Keats v. Cates, 100 Ill. App.2d 177, 241 N.E.2d 645 (1968).

32. Atlantic Steamers Supply Co. v. International Maritime Supplies Co., 268 F.Supp. 1009 (S.D.N.Y.1967). See also Byham v. National Cibo House Corp., 265 N.C. 50, 143 S.E.2d 225 (1965).

33. Longines–Wittnauer Watch Co. v. Barnes & Reinecke, Inc., 15 N.Y.2d 443, 261 N.Y.S.2d 8, 209 N.E.2d 68 (1965), cert. denied 382 U.S. 905.

34. Parke–Bernet Galleries, Inc. v. Franklyn, 26 N.Y.2d 13, 308 N.Y.S.2d 337, 256 N.E.2d 506 (1970).

35. Bowman v. Curt G. Joa, Inc., 361 F.2d 706, 714 (4th Cir.1966).

36. 471 U.S. 462, 105 S.Ct. 2174, 85 L.Ed.2d 528 (1985).

37. 471 U.S. at 478, 105 S.Ct. at 2185.

38. West's Fla.Stat.Ann. § 48.193(1)(g) (Supp.1984).

39. 471 U.S. at 474, 105 S.Ct. at 2183 (citing International Shoe Co. v. Washington, 326 U.S. 310, 316, 66 S.Ct. 154, 158, 90 L.Ed. 95 (1945)). The International Shoe standard is explored in § 3.10, above.

40. 471 U.S. at 479, 105 S.Ct. at 2185.

contacts are present, Justice Brennan wrote, then the assertion of jurisdiction based on those contacts is presumptively reasonable. This presumption, however, may be overcome by a showing in the second inquiry that the assertion of personal jurisdiction would not comport with notions of "fair play and substantial justice."[41] Justice Brennan indicated that the considerations that must be addressed in this fairness determination include the burden on the defendant, the forum state's interest in adjudicating the dispute, the plaintiff's interest in obtaining convenient and effective relief, the interstate judicial system's interest in obtaining the most efficient resolution of controversies, and the shared interest of the several states in furthering fundamental substantive social policies.[42]

Applying this analysis to the facts of this case, the Court determined that Rudzewicz had established the "meaningful 'contacts, ties, or relations,'" required by the Constitution.[43] Rudzewicz, the Court held, deliberately had reached out and entered into a "carefully structured," "long term" agreement with Burger King in Florida.[44] By doing so, he established a "substantial and continuous relationship" with the Florida franchisor and had "purposely availed himself of the benefits and protections" of Florida's laws. The Court also noted that Rudzewicz was a "sophisticated and experienced" businessman, and that the stipulations in the contract regarding "choice of law" and situs of the agreement certainly had given him "fair warning" that he might be haled into court in Florida.

The Court found no support in the record for Rudzewicz's allegations that Florida's interests in adjudicating the dispute were minimal or that his burden in defending against the claim in Florida under Florida law would be great. The Court therefore concluded that Rudzewicz had "failed to demonstrate how jurisdiction in the forum would otherwise be fundamentally unfair,"[45] and consequently had not overcome the presumption that the assertion of jurisdiction over him in Florida was reasonable.

Another type of provision that is found in many long-arm statutes authorizes in personam jurisdiction in actions arising out of an interest in, use, or possession of property in the forum.[46] Although some of these provisions limit jurisdiction to the use or ownership of real property;[47] others permit jurisdiction for causes of action arising out of "ownership or possession of any interest in property."[48] The major interpretative

---

41.   471 U.S. at 476, 105 S.Ct. at 2184.

42.   471 U.S. at 477, 105 S.Ct. at 2184. This list of considerations essentially paraphrased those set forth in the Court's earlier decision in World–Wide Volkswagen Corp. v. Woodson, 444 U.S. 286, 292, 100 S.Ct. 559, 564, 62 L.Ed.2d 490 (1980). See § 3.11, above, for a more detailed discussion of the World–Wide Volkswagen decision.

43.   471 U.S. at 472, 105 S.Ct. at 2181.

44.   471 U.S. at 479–80, 105 S.Ct. at 2186.

45.   471 U.S. at 487, 105 S.Ct. at 2190.

46.   See Deleo v. Childs, 304 F.Supp. 593 (D.Mass.1969).

47.   E.g., Ill—Smith–Hurd Ann. 735 ILCS 5/2–209(a)(3);   N.Y.—McKinney's CPLR 302(a)(4).

48.   Tenn.Code Ann. § 20–2–214(a)(3).

difficulty in applying these statutes is determining what types of property interests fall within their scope. For example, it has been held that a guarantor of a lease does not "own, use, or possess" property for jurisdictional purposes in an action to recover damages because of the tenant's default.[49] Similarly, it has been ruled that an overnight guest in a motel does not "use" real property so as to support jurisdiction in an action to recover damages for destroyed property.[50] But a buyer who has signed a contract to purchase property has acquired an "interest" that will support jurisdiction in a breach of contract action.[51]

It should be noted that in response to judicial developments regarding the treatment of corporate defendants,[52] a number of states enacted "doing business" statutes that remain important bases of corporate jurisdiction today.[53] They also may be used to acquire jurisdiction over unincorporated associations.[54] Typically, if there is "continuity of dealing and activity,"[55] the corporation may be sued on a cause of action unrelated to the particular commercial acts carried on in the forum.[56] Consequently, it may be possible to obtain jurisdiction over a corporate defendant under this type of provision when jurisdiction would not be available under the more conduct-specific "long-arm" statutes, just discussed.

Finally, the Internet has begun to present new questions about the exercise of jurisdiction over distant defendants. Commentators have seized the initiative on this subject and written extensively about the new medium's significance;[57] several courts have tackled the issue,[58] but there are no definitive answers as yet. Because the Internet lowers price and regulatory barriers to communications, individuals have new opportunities to reach a global audience, raising the question of when these communications are sufficient to establish long-arm jurisdiction. The Internet conflates the characteristics of more traditional media into one,

---

49. Weinstein v. Talevi, 4 Conn.Cir. 330, 231 A.2d 660 (1966).

50. Messick v. Gordon, 434 Pa. 30, 252 A.2d 627 (1969).

51. Carmichael v. Snyder, 209 Va. 451, 164 S.E.2d 703 (1968).

52. See § 3.7, above.

53. E.g., Kan.Stat.Ann. § 17–7303; N.Y.—McKinney's Bus.Corp.Law 1301(b); 15 Pa.Consol.Stat.Ann. § 4122(a).

54. E.g., Schluter v. Trentonian Pub. Co., 4 N.J.Super. 294, 67 A.2d 189 (1949).

55. Dykes v. Reliable Furniture & Carpet, 3 Utah 2d 34, 37, 277 P.2d 969, 972 (1954).

56. E.g., Hoffman v. Air India, 393 F.2d 507 (5th Cir.1968), cert. denied 393 U.S. 924; Gelfand v. Tanner Motor Tours, Ltd., 385 F.2d 116 (2d Cir.1967), cert. denied 390 U.S. 996.

57. E.g., Johnson & Post, Law and Borders—The Rise of Law in Cyberspace, 48 Stan.L.Rev. 1367 (1996) (arguing that

"cyberspace" in general should not be confined to geographically defined territories); Sheehan, Predicting the Future: Personal Jurisdiction for the Twenty–First Century, 66 U.Cinc.L.Rev. 385 (1998) (arguing for continued, predictable notions of territoriality); Symposium, Jurisdiction in Cyberspace, 41 Vill.L.Rev. 1 (1996). Although these issues were posed by earlier communications media—mail, telegraphy, telephone, and facsimile transmission—they never received the attention now focused on the Internet.

58. E.g., Bensusan Restaurant Corp. v. King, 126 F.3d 25 (2d Cir.1997); CompuServe, Inc. v. Patterson, 89 F.3d 1257 (6th Cir.1996); Zippo Mfg. Co. v. Zippo Dot Com, Inc., 952 F.Supp. 1119 (W.D.Pa.1997); Maritz, Inc. v. Cybergold, 947 F.Supp. 1328 (E.D.Mo.1996); Inset Sys., Inc. v. Instruction Set, Inc., 937 F.Supp. 161 (D.Conn. 1996).

flexible medium: it permits communication that is broadcast or point-to-point, one-way or two-way, passive or interactive, synchronous or asynchronous, audio or visual, low-speed or high-speed, or any combination of the above. Thus the Internet is an electronic chameleon that does not fit squarely into a single analytical framework. Furthermore, the current "geography" of the Internet does not correspond to geopolitical boundaries, making it difficult for an Internet user to control, or even know about, contacts in distant fora. In addition, all the usual problems of defining the location of an activity are magnified in the metaphysical world of electrons.

The first cases to consider the application of long-arm statutes to activities on the Internet came to differing conclusions. One court held that a passive website accessible from anywhere in the country constituted "solicitation of business" in the forum state under the state long-arm statute and therefore met the minimum contacts requirement.[59] Another court held that a passive website did not commit a tortious act in the forum state within the meaning of the state long-arm statute.[60] A third court took a sliding-scale approach and looked at the interactivity and commercial nature of the website.[61] None of these cases provides an approach that is entirely satisfactory: a bright-line rule seems too wooden for such a flexible and dynamic medium and a balancing test seems too unpredictable to be of much use for planning purposes—"passive" and "interactive," "commercial" and "non-commercial" are poorly defined terms on the all-encompassing Internet. In the years to come, Internet activities promise to provide courts with many opportunities to refine the application of state long-arm statutes, as well as to give definition to the constitutional meaning of minimum contacts and fair play.

C. CONTEMPORARY JURISDICTION NOTIONS: IN REM AND QUASI IN REM JURISDICTION

§ 3.14 International Shoe Triumphant: A Uniform Standard for Jurisdiction

The Supreme Court hinted on a number of occasions after the decision in International Shoe Company v. State of Washington[1] that there was an inappropriate discrepancy between using a minimum contacts analysis to evaluate the propriety of asserting in personam

---

59. Inset Sys., Inc. v. Instruction Set, Inc., 937 F.Supp. 161 (D.Conn.1996). The Connecticut court noted that personal jurisdiction was "fair" because the Massachusetts defendant was geographically close to Connecticut and the action concerned Connecticut law.

60. Bensusan Restaurant Corp. v. King, 126 F.3d 25 (2d Cir.1997).

61. Zippo Mfg. Co. v. Zippo Dot Com, Inc., 952 F.Supp. 1119 (W.D.Pa.1997).

§ 3.14

1. 326 U.S. 310, 66 S.Ct. 154, 90 L.Ed. 95 (1945). This case is discussed in § 3.10, above.

jurisdiction while retaining the fictional "situs of the res" concept to determine the validity of quasi in rem jurisdiction. In Mullane v. Central Hanover Bank & Trust Company,[2] for example, the Court indicated that the traditional categories of jurisdiction were anachronistic and that the type of notice required by due process does not depend upon the classification of an action within one of the historical categories.

Moreover, on several occasions the Court acknowledged difficulties with the situs concept as a basis for jurisdiction. In Western Union Telegraph Company v. Commonwealth of Pennsylvania[3] and in State of Texas v. State of New Jersey,[4] the Court noted that at least in escheat proceedings, the application of a situs test could lead to the unfair imposition of multiple liability on the defendant because, using different theories of situs, several states could successfully escheat the same intangible property. An analogous problem was recognized with respect to different state theories about the proper situs of corporate stock.[5]

Recognizing these difficulties, commentators urged that the discrepancy between the due process standards for jurisdiction over people and over property be eliminated.[6] And in a California case, Atkinson v. Superior Court,[7] one of the severest critics of the jurisdictional categories, Chief Justice Roger Traynor, eschewed the situs approach in favor of an analysis based on what he deemed "general principles governing jurisdiction over persons and property."[8] In Hanson v. Denckla,[9] however, decided just one week before the Supreme Court denied certiorari in the Atkinson case, the Supreme Court appeared to reaffirm the traditional distinctions among the three types of jurisdiction since it structured its opinion along the lines of the historical jurisdictional categories.[10]

It was not until 1977 that the Supreme Court finally ruled in Shaffer v. Heitner[11] that the International Shoe standard should be

---

2. 339 U.S. 306, 70 S.Ct. 652, 94 L.Ed. 865 (1950). This case is discussed in § 3.19, below.

3. 368 U.S. 71, 82 S.Ct. 199, 7 L.Ed.2d 139 (1961).

4. 379 U.S. 674, 85 S.Ct. 626, 13 L.Ed.2d 596 (1965), opinion supplemented 380 U.S. 518, 85 S.Ct. 1136, 14 L.Ed.2d 49 (1965). See also Pennsylvania v. New York, 407 U.S. 206, 92 S.Ct. 2075, 32 L.Ed.2d 693 (1972).

5. Mills v. Jacobs, 333 Pa. 231, 4 A.2d 152 (1939).

6. Hazard, A General Theory of State-Court Jurisdiction, 1965 Sup.Ct.Rev. 241; von Mehren & Trautman, Jurisdiction to Adjudicate: A Suggested Analysis, 79 Harv. L.Rev. 1121 (1966).

7. 49 Cal.2d 338, 316 P.2d 960 (1957), cert. denied 357 U.S. 569 noted 46 Cal. L.Rev. 637 (1958).

8. 49 Cal.2d at 345, 216 P.2d at 964. See also Traynor, Is This Conflict Really Necessary?, 37 Texas L.Rev. 657 (1959).

9. 357 U.S. 235, 78 S.Ct. 1228, 2 L.Ed.2d 1283 (1958). See generally Kurland, The Supreme Court, the Due Process Clause and the In Personam Jurisdiction of State Courts—From Pennoyer to Denckla: A Review, 25 U.Chi.L.Rev. 569, 610 (1958).

10. The Hanson case is discussed in § 3.11, above.

11. 433 U.S. 186, 97 S.Ct. 2569, 53 L.Ed.2d 683 (1977). The case has been examined by various commentators. See generally Casad, Shaffer v. Heitner: An End to Ambivalence in Jurisdiction Theory?, 26 Kan.L.Rev. 61 (1977); Reisenfeld, Shaffer v. Heitner: Holding, Implications, Forebodings, 30 Hast.L.J. 1183 (1979); Silberman, Shaffer v. Heitner: The End of an Era, 53 N.Y.U.L.Rev. 33 (1978); Zammit, Reflections on Shaffer v. Heitner, 5 Hast.Con.L.Q. 15 (1978).

applied to the assertion of all forms of jurisdiction. As is explored below, the Shaffer decision does not eliminate the three jurisdictional categories; rather, it abolishes the discrepancy that existed in the constitutional test used for each category.

In the Shaffer case, Heitner brought a shareholder derivative suit[12] in the Delaware Court of Chancery against 28 individual defendants, consisting of the present and former officers and directors of the Greyhound Corporation and its subsidiary Greyhound Lines, Inc.[13] The plaintiff alleged that the individual defendants had violated their fiduciary duties by involving the corporation in activities in Oregon that had resulted in a sizable antitrust judgment and a criminal contempt fine against Greyhound. Although Greyhound had been incorporated in Delaware, its principal place of business was in Arizona. Neither the plaintiff Heitner nor any of the 28 individual defendants were residents of or domiciled in Delaware; indeed, nothing in the record indicated that any of the defendants had ever set foot in Delaware.[14] Nor was it alleged that any of the acts that gave rise to the antitrust liability occurred in Delaware.[15]

Under state law, Delaware courts could assert quasi in rem jurisdiction over an action by sequestering the defendant's property situated in the state.[16] Furthermore, another state statute provided that for the purpose of sequestration, securities issued by corporations incorporated in the state had their legal situs in Delaware, regardless of the location of the certificates of ownership.[17] Heitner sought to establish jurisdiction over 21 of the 28 defendants by obtaining an order to sequester approximately 82,000 shares of their Greyhound stock and options, valued at $1.2 million. The state sequestration statute did not provide for a hearing prior to the seizure, nor did it permit limited appearances;[18] nonresident defendants whose property had been sequestered had to choose between making a general appearance, subjecting themselves to the state's full in personam jurisdiction, or defaulting and sacrificing their property.

12. A shareholder's derivative suit allows a shareholder to sue on behalf of the corporation when the board of directors refuses to bring suit to vindicate the corporation's rights. The claimant is treated as the representative of the shareholders and must meet several procedural prerequisites. See § 16.9, below, on shareholder derivative actions.

13. Greyhound Corp. and Greyhound Lines, Inc. were corporate defendants in the suit.

14. 433 U.S. at 213, 97 S.Ct. at 2585.

15. Ibid.

16. 10 Del.Code § 366. For the subsequent history of the statute, see § 3.17 at note 6, below.

17. 8 Del.Code § 169. Like 49 other states, Delaware adopted the Uniform Commercial Code, but it did not adopt UCC § 8–317 or section 13 of the Uniform Stock Transfer Act, which provide that a "security" may be attached only by seizing the document embodying it. The Delaware approach, which was clearly anomalous, had been criticized by many commentators. See Folk & Moyer, Sequestration in Delaware: A Constitutional Analysis, 73 Colum.L.Rev. 749, 749–50 (1973); Note, Attachment of Corporate Stock: The Conflicting Approaches of Delaware and the Uniform Stock Transfer Act, 73 Harv.L.Rev. 1579 (1960).

18. For a discussion of limited appearances, see § 3.27, below.

The 21 defendants whose property had been sequestered challenged jurisdiction. They argued that the stock was not attachable in Delaware because it was present there only by virtue of the anomalous situs statute; that the ex parte sequestration procedure did not accord them procedural safeguards sufficient to satisfy due process;[19] and that under International Shoe they did not have sufficient minimum contacts with Delaware to sustain jurisdiction. After approving the sequestration procedure, the Delaware courts summarily rejected the defendants' last argument. Since quasi in rem, and not in personam, jurisdiction was being invoked, reference to minimum contacts was deemed irrelevant.[20]

The United States Supreme Court could have reversed the Delaware courts either by invalidating the statute locating the stock in Delaware or by declaring the sequestration statute unconstitutional due to inadequate procedural safeguards.[21] Instead, the Court, speaking through Justice Marshall, held that the assertion of jurisdiction violated due process because it was based solely on the seizure of the stock under the sequestration statutes and did not include consideration whether there were other contacts between the defendants and the forum. The Court unanimously agreed that the distinction between the three jurisdictional categories was artificial inasmuch as "all proceedings * * * are really against persons."[22] Given that jurisdiction over a thing is merely an "elliptical way of referring to jurisdiction over the interests of persons in a thing,"[23] the Court reasoned that it is "simple and straightforward" that an exercise of jurisdiction over a thing should be evaluated by the same standard that governs an exercise of jurisdiction over those persons with interests in the thing.[24] If a court could not exercise in personam jurisdiction directly over an owner of property without offending due process, it ought not circumvent his rights indirectly by exercising quasi in rem jurisdiction over his property.[25]

Having declared the use of a bifurcated jurisdictional standard to be both illogical and inconsistent with due process, the Court made a sweeping statement appearing to unite the divided world of state court personal and property jurisdiction under the uniform standard of minimum contacts: "We therefore conclude that all assertions of state-court jurisdiction must be evaluated according to the standards set forth in International Shoe and its progeny."[26] In this way, the Shaffer opinion

---

19. The Delaware courts had focused on appellants' contention that the sequestration statute violated the procedural due process requirements established by Sniadach v. Family Finance Corp., 395 U.S. 337, 89 S.Ct. 1820, 23 L.Ed.2d 349 (1969) and its progeny, because it did not provide the defendants with notice or an opportunity to be heard prior to the seizure of their corporate stock. See generally § 3.21, below, for a discussion of this problem.

20. Greyhound Corp. v. Heitner, 361 A.2d 225, 229 (Del.1976).

21. 433 U.S. at 194 n. 10, 97 S.Ct. at 2575 n. 10.

22. 433 U.S. at 207, 97 S.Ct. at 2581.

23. Ibid.

24. Ibid.

25. "The fiction that an assertion of jurisdiction over property is anything but an assertion of jurisdiction over the owner of the property * * * serve[s] only to allow state court jurisdiction that is fundamentally unfair to the defendant." 433 U.S. at 207, 97 S.Ct. at 2584.

26. 433 U.S. at 212, 97 S.Ct. at 2584–85. The Court's decision in Kulko v. Superior Court, 436 U.S. 84, 98 S.Ct. 1690, 56 L.Ed.2d 132 (1978), one year after Shaffer;

proclaims the triumph of a *general* theory of state court jurisdiction based on International Shoe, which displaces rather than supplements the barnacled conceptual structure of Pennoyer v. Neff regarding absent defendants.[27]

The Shaffer Court went on in the last part of its opinion to apply the minimum contacts standard to the specific facts of the case. A majority of the Court did not find the contacts among the defendants, the litigation, and the forum to be sufficient to support an assertion of Delaware jurisdiction over them, despite the situs of their property within the state. The Court's evaluation of the facts of Shaffer under the Shoe standard sheds new light on how that standard ought to be interpreted and applied. Thus, the Shaffer opinion is highly significant for two reasons. First, it extends the use of the Shoe standard to all jurisdictional areas. Second, it gives further insight into how that standard ought to be generally applied.

§ 3.15   International Shoe Applied to in Rem and Quasi in Rem Jurisdiction

The application of the minimum contacts standard to the facts of Shaffer v. Heitner resulted in a holding that jurisdiction was lacking. Justice Marshall, writing for the majority, noted that the property that was sequestered—the stock—was unrelated to the plaintiff's cause of action and the mere statutory presence of stock in Delaware could not provide sufficient contacts to support jurisdiction.[1] Further, under his analysis, the defendant directors had not committed any acts or caused any events within the forum justifying the exercise of jurisdiction. The mere fact that the defendants held directorships in Greyhound did not demonstrate purposeful availment of the benefits of the forum.[2] Because no state statutes specifically articulated Delaware's interest in asserting jurisdiction over its corporations' officers,[3] the Supreme Court decided that the state's interest in the outcome of suit would not permit jurisdiction nor make the state a fair forum for this particular litigation. Without such statutes, the Court concluded, the defendants had "no reason to expect to be haled before a Delaware court."[4] In sum, according to the majority's view, the case against jurisdiction was clear because there were no direct contacts by the defendants with Delaware and no foreseeability that suit would be brought there. The cause of action itself

closely followed the Shaffer interpretation of the Shoe standard by denying California jurisdiction over a New York domiciliary in a child custody suit, thus confirming that the Court intended the single standard of evaluation to apply across the spectrum of jurisdictional exercises. See § 3.11, above, for a discussion of Kulko.

27. The Court's later opinion in Burnham v. Superior Court, 495 U.S. 604, 110 S.Ct. 2105, 109 L.Ed.2d 631 (1990), clarifies that its broad statement in Shaffer was not intended to indicate that a person served within a state also must meet the minimum contacts standard to fall within the court's jurisdiction. Burnham is discussed in § 3.17, below.

§ 3.15

1. 433 U.S. 186, 213, 97 S.Ct. 2569, 2584, 53 L.Ed.2d 683 (1977).

2. 433 U.S. at 213–14, 97 S.Ct. at 2584–85.

3. 433 U.S. at 214, 97 S.Ct. at 2585.

4. 433 U.S. at 216, 97 S.Ct. at 2586.

arose out of activities in Oregon. Further, an alternative forum was available that would not be unfair.[5]

Although Justice Marshall noted in Shaffer that the presence of property in the forum state will not alone confer jurisdiction, he also went on to state that that fact is not irrelevant. In some cases, the presence of property may suggest contacts necessary and sufficient to permit an exercise of jurisdiction. These are controversies in which the defendant's property interest within the state, whether tangible or intangible, is directly related to the plaintiff's cause of action.

Two types of controversies clearly belong to this class of cases. The first occurs when the property within the state is itself the subject matter of the dispute, and encompasses both classic in rem proceedings and quasi in rem proceedings among specific claimants to a piece of property.[6] The Shaffer decision indicated that it would not be unfair for the state court to adjudicate this type of dispute in view of the close relationship that necessarily exists among the defendant, the forum, and the litigation. The fact that the defendants are asserting claims to property within the forum indicates that they expect to benefit from the protection of the forum's laws. Further, since the state normally would want to assure the marketability of property within its borders, its interests are served by providing a peaceful procedure to resolve these disputes.[7] From a systemic point of view, the local availability of witnesses and records makes adjudication of these disputes where the property is located in the forum both convenient and reasonable. Thus, the Shaffer Court suggested that it had no intention to disturb the assertion of jurisdiction in classic in rem or quasi in rem actions of this type. For similar reasons, the Court also declared that adjudications of status, by their very nature, are fairly made by the state that created the status.[8]

A second type of case in which the mere presence of property in the forum constitutes sufficient contact to confer quasi in rem jurisdiction occurs when the plaintiff's claim relates to rights and obligations arising out of the nonresident defendant's ownership of local property, as, for example, tortious injury suffered by the plaintiff on the defendant's property or because of the defendant's negligent use of his personalty.[9] Notably, in actions of this type the availability of quasi in rem jurisdiction usually is superfluous because most long-arm statutes allow full in personam jurisdiction to be exercised over a nonresident defendant in actions arising out of his ownership, use, or possession of local proper-

---

5. Plaintiff could have filed suit in Oregon, where the activities underlying his claim took place, or in Arizona, the principal place of business of Greyhound. The Court noted in a footnote that it was not faced with a situation in which suit was filed in the only available forum. 433 U.S. at 211 n. 37, 97 S.Ct. at 2583 n. 37.

6. See § 3.8, above.

7. 433 U.S. at 208, 97 S.Ct. at 2580.

8. 433 U.S. at 208 n. 30, 97 S.Ct. at 2582 n. 30.

9. 433 U.S. at 208, 97 S.Ct. at 2582, citing Dubin v. City of Philadelphia, 34 Pa.D. & C. 61 (Com.Pl.1939).

ty.[10] Since the cause of action arises locally, and the plaintiff is in many cases a local resident, a wealth of contacts typically exists between the dispute and the forum state to support in personam jurisdiction. In any case, exercises of jurisdiction in these types of actions necessarily satisfy the Shoe standard because the nonresident defendant's ownership of local property constitutes a purposeful, volitional, and continuous contact with the forum that directly gives rise to the plaintiff's cause of action.[11]

In the context of quasi in rem jurisdiction, the use of the International Shoe standard has its greatest practical impact when the plaintiff's cause of action is completely unrelated to the property that serves as the basis for jurisdiction. In those circumstances, quasi in rem jurisdiction operates as a type of judicially created long-arm, since

> the only role played by the property is to provide the basis for bringing the defendant into court. * * * In such cases, if a direct assertion of personal jurisdiction over the defendant would violate the Constitution, it would seem that an indirect assertion of that jurisdiction should be equally impermissible.[12]

It was this type of quasi in rem jurisdiction that the Shaffer Court concluded did not meet the Shoe standard of fairness.

Although the Court decided that jurisdiction could not be asserted on the facts before it, the Shaffer opinion was ambiguous as to whether the Court intended to eliminate all uses of quasi in rem jurisdiction when the property is unrelated to the claims involved.[13] It specifically recognized the possibility that the presence of defendant's property in the state, even when totally unrelated to the cause of action, might suggest the existence of other ties between the defendant, the forum, and the litigation permitting the assertion of jurisdiction.[14] Unfortunately, the opinion failed to give any examples of cases in which those ties might reasonably be implied.[15]

Lower federal courts have interpreted the Supreme Court's ambiguity on this point differently. There appears to be general agreement that Shaffer requires that the presence of the defendant's property within the forum must be viewed as only one contact with the state to be considered

10. See, e.g., N.Y.—McKinney's CPLR 302. See generally § 3.13 at nn. 46–51, above.

11. "[T]o the extent that a corporation exercises the privilege of conducting activities within a state, it enjoys the benefits and protection of the laws of that state. The exercise of that privilege may give rise to obligations, and, so far as those obligations arise out of or are connected with the activities within the state, a procedure which requires the corporation to respond to a suit brought to enforce them can, in most instances hardly be said to be undue." International Shoe Co. v. Washington, 326 U.S. 310, 319, 66 S.Ct. 154, 160, 90 L.Ed. 95 (1945). See generally § 3.10, above.

12. 433 U.S. at 209, 97 S.Ct. at 2583.

13. 433 U.S. at 212 n. 39, 97 S.Ct. at 2584 n. 39.

14. 433 U.S. at 209, 97 S.Ct. at 2582.

15. Note the analogy between the exercise of this type of jurisdiction, and the type allowed in Perkins v. Benguet Consolidated Mining Co., 342 U.S. 437, 72 S.Ct. 413, 96 L.Ed. 485 (1952) (corporation with systematic and continuous activities in state may be sued there on claims unrelated to in state activities).

along with other contacts of the defendant in deciding whether the assertion of jurisdiction is consistent with traditional notions of fair play and substantial justice.[16] However, at least in actions involving the attachment of real property, the very nature of the property may be recognized as creating contacts with the forum state sufficient to make it fair to subject the owner to suit there. Indeed, two of the concurring justices in Shaffer expressly reserved judgment on whether it still would be valid to use quasi in rem jurisdiction to adjudicate an unrelated claim when the property attached is of the type "whose situs is indisputably and permanently located within the forum."[17] Although the paradigm for this type of property would be realty, courts differ on where to draw the line as property becomes less tangible.

For example, a New York federal district court held in Feder v. Turkish Airlines (THY)[18] that quasi in rem jurisdiction could be obtained over a foreign airline by attaching its New York bank account even though the cause was totally unrelated to the property. The court reasoned that the defendant voluntarily had opened the bank account in New York in furtherance of its business and could reasonably expect to be amenable to suit there. The Second Circuit on the other hand has indicated in dictum[19] that a bank account may not provide a sound foundation for quasi in rem jurisdiction over claims unrelated to the account absent any other contacts by the defendant with the forum state.

For a few years, there was some debate over what effect Shaffer would have on quasi in rem jurisdiction based on the attachment of an insurer's contractual obligation to defend and indemnify the nonresident defendant, as approved by the New York Court of Appeals in Seider v. Roth.[20] Since Shaffer prohibited the assertion of jurisdiction based solely on the attachment of property in the forum state, it seemed to remove Seider's constitutional linchpin. But some saw Seider as possibly surviving Shaffer.[21] They argued that the real question in a Seider case is the plaintiff's right to the proceeds of the nonresident defendant's insurance policy, and the real defendant is the insurer who controls the defense of the suit—and who does have minimum contacts with the forum state. In Rush v. Savchuk,[22] the Supreme Court ended the speculation, overruling

---

16. See Intermeat, Inc. v. American Poultry, Inc., 575 F.2d 1017 (2d Cir.1978).

17. Justices Powell and Stevens both wrote concurring opinions. 433 U.S. at 217, 97 S.Ct. at 2586, 2587.

18. 441 F.Supp. 1273 (S.D.N.Y.1977).

19. O'Connor v. Lee–Hy Paving Corp., 579 F.2d 194, 198 (2d Cir.1978), cert. denied 439 U.S. 1034.

20. 17 N.Y.2d 111, 269 N.Y.S.2d 99, 216 N.E.2d 312 (1966). This form of attachment jurisdiction is discussed in § 3.9, above.

21. See generally Williams, The Validity of Assuming Jurisdiction by the Attachment of Automobile Liability Insurance Obligations: The Impact of Shaffer v. Heitner upon Seider v. Roth, 9 Rut.–Camden L.J. 241, 269 (1977). The Second Circuit sustained the constitutionality of Seider after Shaffer in O'Connor v. Lee–Hy Paving Corp., 579 F.2d 194 (2d Cir.1978), cert. denied 439 U.S. 1034.

22. 444 U.S. 320, 100 S.Ct. 571, 62 L.Ed.2d 516 (1980).

this controversial form of attachment jurisdiction and applying a straightforward minimum contacts analysis to strike down jurisdiction.

Finally, it should be noted that Shaffer does not affect the use of the remedies of attachment, garnishment, and sequestration for their original purpose of providing security for a judgment. The majority opinion in Shaffer specifically recognized that a state may assert jurisdiction over property consistent with the requirements of International Shoe despite the absence of minimum contacts with its owner if the attachment is accomplished for purposes of providing security for an in personam action being litigated against the owner elsewhere.[23] This ensures that defendants cannot remove their assets to states with which they do not have other contacts as a device for escaping valid personal judgments in states where they do have those contacts.[24]

Although the Shaffer opinion extends the International Shoe standard to all assertions of jurisdiction, there is a qualitative difference between attachment jurisdiction and in personam jurisdiction that may affect the balance that is struck between the minimum contacts and fair play and substantial justice factors. The primary argument in favor of a different standard is the differential effect between a quasi in rem judgment and an in personam judgment.[25] The existence of a uniform standard for determining jurisdiction does not necessarily suggest that the same "quantum" of contacts be required for all jurisdictional exercises. Arguably fair play and substantial justice requires fewer contacts between the defendant and the forum to enforce a judgment that is limited by the value of the attached property than it requires to enforce a full in personam judgment against the defendant. At least this would be true when the property involved is not worth as much or more than the claims being litigated. Fair play might be satisfied further if the defendant is permitted to make a limited appearance for purposes of defending the merits without consenting to full in personam liability.[26]

---

23. Shaffer v. Heitner, 433 U.S. 186, 210, 97 S.Ct. 2569, 2583, 53 L.Ed.2d 683 (1977).

24. In one case, for example, the Northern District of California permitted the ex parte attachment of a debt owed to the defendant, a French corporation, by a California corporation, although the defendant's contacts with California would not have supported an exercise of in personam jurisdiction by that state. The court relied on Shaffer to validate the attachment, since the North Carolina plaintiff sought the attachment solely as security for an award it was seeking in a valid in personam action being litigated against the French company in New York. The French defendant's California "property" was completely unrelated to the plaintiff's New York claim, but the court attached the property anyway not to adjudicate the claim on the merits, but to prevent the defendant from removing its property from the country. Carolina Power & Light Co. v. Uranex, 451 F.Supp. 1044 (N.D.Cal.1977). See generally Reisenfeld, Shaffer v. Heitner: Holding Implications, Forebodings, 30 Hast.L.J. 1183, 1196 (1979).

25. In personam judgments are entered for the full value of the claim, they are given res judicata and collateral estoppel effect, and they are entitled to full faith and credit for the full amount in all states of the Union. Quasi in rem judgments are limited to the amount of the property locally attached, have limited res judicata effect, no collateral estoppel effect, and are not entitled to full faith and credit. See generally § 3.2, above.

26. See § 3.27, below.

Whether the application of a differential minimum contacts threshold is appropriate is unclear. Certainly doing so is consistent with the fact noted by the Supreme Court in International Shoe that the propriety of assertions of jurisdiction must be decided on the facts of each case and requires a qualitative assessment of the facts therein.[27] From a systemic perspective, the injection of this distinction produces further uncertainty and raises concerns regarding whether the standards can be fairly and consistently administered. This point is likely to continue to be debated until the Supreme Court chooses to expand on the issue.

§ 3.16   The Seizure of Property: Requirements and Definition

A court's power to assert quasi in rem or in rem jurisdiction depends upon finding property that is within the forum court's jurisdiction at the time of suit.[1] In Pennoyer v. Neff[2] and again in Pennington v. Fourth National Bank,[3] the Supreme Court indicated that "seizure or some equivalent act" prior to judgment was necessary to endow the court with quasi in rem jurisdiction. In Pennoyer, Justice Field reasoned that the seizure of the property served three purposes. First, it formally announced that the court had taken custody of the property and thus, any condemnation and sale following adjudication would be backed by authority of law. Second, seizure reinforced the then customary notice by publication. This notion assumed that owners, either personally or through agent caretakers, would keep themselves informed "of what concerns or may concern their real estate"[4] and that a writ of attachment posted on the property would come to the owner's attention. Finally, it was asserted that seizure assured that the court could control the property and provide a resource against which the plaintiff could enforce the judgment. Without this control, the defendant might sell the property during the proceeding and render the action and any resulting judgment ineffectual.[5]

It may well be that pre-action seizure, although pragmatically expe-

---

27. International Shoe Co. v. Washington, 326 U.S. 310, 66 S.Ct. 154, 90 L.Ed. 95 (1945). The Court expressly endorsed a differential minimum contact threshold in the context of in personam jurisdiction in Burger King Corp. v. Rudzewicz, 471 U.S. 462, 477, 105 S.Ct. 2174, 2184, 85 L.Ed.2d 528 (1985) ("considerations [of fairness] sometimes serve to establish the reasonableness of jurisdiction upon a lesser showing of minimum contacts than would otherwise be required").

§ 3.16

1. Closson v. Chase, 158 Wis. 346, 149 N.W. 26 (1914).

2. 95 U.S. (5 Otto) 714, 24 L.Ed. 565 (1877).

3. 243 U.S. 269, 37 S.Ct. 282, 61 L.Ed. 713 (1917). See generally Note, The Requirement of Seizure in Quasi in Rem Jurisdiction: Pennoyer v. Neff Re-Examined, 63 Harv.L.Rev. 657 (1950); 1 J. Weinstein, H. Korn & A. Miller, New York Civil Practice ¶ 314.18.

4. Ballard v. Hunter, 204 U.S. 241, 27 S.Ct. 261, 51 L.Ed. 461 (1907).

5. See, e.g., Union Chemical & Materials Corp. v. Cannon, 38 Del.Ch. 203, 148 A.2d 348 (1959), noted in 59 Colum.L.Rev. 803 (1959) (jurisdiction of court defeated when attached shares of stock were converted by merger).

dient, is not a constitutional requirement in quasi in rem cases.[6] Indeed, Justice Hunt, dissenting in Pennoyer v. Neff,[7] so argued, positing that reasonable notice and an opportunity to defend per se met the constitutional mandates.[8] Thus, in suits to foreclose a mortgage or other lien created by statute or contract, it has been held that no seizure is required to give the court jurisdiction.[9] According to this view, the purpose of seizure is to create a lien not to create jurisdiction. When a lien already exists, the courts may proceed to enforce the lien as if the property had been seized upon attachment or execution.

Although pre-action seizure may not be constitutionally required, some, but not all,[10] states require seizure to establish quasi in rem jurisdiction.[11] Clearly, pre-action seizure is administratively advantageous. It eliminates the risk to the plaintiff[12]—and potential embarrassment to the court—that the property will be removed from the court's jurisdiction in the middle of the proceedings. Thus, it is not surprising that most often the plaintiff commences a quasi in rem proceeding by attaching the property, and the issue whether that seizure was necessary rarely arises.[13]

The preceding discussion has involved whether seizure of property is required for the assertion of quasi in rem jurisdiction. But what acts are equivalent to seizure is equally important.[14] The jurisdictional property need not be placed in the actual physical custody of the court. With land, for example, constructive seizure—that is, a levy under a writ of seizure—and the posting of notices on the land, suffices to bring it within the jurisdiction of the court.[15] Shares of stock may be brought under a court's jurisdiction by serving a writ of attachment and notice of the attachment on the proper corporate officer.[16]

6. Whether pre-judgment seizure for jurisdictional purposes satisfies the due process requirements of notice and an opportunity to be heard is discussed in § 3.21, below.

7. 95 U.S. (5 Otto) 714, 736, 24 L.Ed. 565 (1877).

8. Insofar as the seizure was designed to assure that the court had jurisdictional power, the change in the standard for asserting jurisdiction to one emphasizing defendant's contacts with the forum also may suggest that seizure is of less importance. See § 3.14, above.

9. Roller v. Holly, 176 U.S. 398, 20 S.Ct. 410, 44 L.Ed. 520 (1900).

10. See, e.g., Closson v. Chase, 158 Wis. 346, 149 N.W. 26 (1914); Gallun v. Weil, 116 Wis. 236, 92 N.W. 1091 (1903).

11. N.Y.—McKinney's CPLR 314.

12. See 4A C. Wright & A. Miller, Civil 2d § 1121. See also Deredito v. Winn, 23 A.D.2d 849, 259 N.Y.S.2d 200 (1965) (ser-

vice by publication not authorized when there had been no prior attachment of defendant's property).

13. In the federal courts, Federal Rule 4(n)(2) provides for the use of state procedures for service in actions commenced by seizure of the defendant's assets within the district when in personam jurisdiction cannot be obtained. As the Advisory Committee Note to the rule points out, however, given the liberal availability of long-arm jurisdiction, the exercise of quasi-in-rem jurisdiction has become almost an anachronism. See generally 4A C. Wright & A. Miller, Civil 2d §§ 1119–21.

14. For a discussion of the procedure surrounding attachments, see § 15.2, below.

15. Cooper v. Reynolds, 77 U.S. (10 Wall.) 308, 19 L.Ed. 931 (1870).

16. See, e.g., Woods v. Spoturno, 37 Del. (W.W.Harr.) 295, 183 A. 319 (1936), reversed on other grounds 38 Del. (W.W.Harr.) 378, 192 A. 689 (1937).

An indebtedness also is considered property for jurisdictional purposes, and therefore is subject to seizure.[17] To seize, or more properly, to garnish a debt, the plaintiff serves a writ of garnishment notifying the defendant's debtor that the obligation is to be appropriated to satisfy the plaintiff's claim.[18] The equitable device of sequestration, by which the court directs the debtor to pay the debt to the plaintiff, is yet another act equivalent to seizure. In Pennington v. Fourth National Bank,[19] for example, the plaintiff who had sued her husband for a divorce obtained a court decree ordering the bank in which her husband maintained assets to pay the amount of the debt to her. The choice of which of these devices is used depends largely on the state law in the forum.

D. THE IMPACT OF SHAFFER v. HEITNER ON PENNOYER'S SATELLITES

§ 3.17 The Current Viability of Consent, Domicile, and Transitory Presence Theories

The Pennoyer opinion recognized three corollaries to its general theory of territorial power: a state may exercise jurisdiction over defendants who have consented to its jurisdiction,[1] who are domiciled within the state,[2] or who have personally been served while transitorily present within the forum state's borders.[3] Each of these satellite rules continued to be followed after International Shoe, despite the fact that jurisdiction asserted under them required no reference to principles of minimum contacts or fundamental fairness. Their primary virtue rested in their simplicity and certainty of application. Plaintiffs could invoke these rules to choose fora for their suits in which there could be no possibility of a successful jurisdictional challenge; at the same time, defendants could refer to the rules to decide whether they could safely ignore a summons from a remote forum. Inasmuch as Shaffer v. Heitner purports to apply the International Shoe standard to all assertions of state-court jurisdiction, the continued vitality of each of these satellite rules must be re-examined.

The theory that the defendant always may consent to jurisdiction is not incompatible with the Court's decision in Shaffer to adopt the minimum contacts standard as the constitutional test for evaluating all assertions of jurisdiction. Shaffer, like International Shoe, merely speaks to the constitutional limitations imposed on the courts, suggesting when defendants legitimately may object to having to defend in a particular forum. If the defendant does not wish to object, jurisdiction may be asserted.

17. Pennington v. Fourth Nat. Bank, 243 U.S. 269, 37 S.Ct. 282, 61 L.Ed. 713 (1917).

18. Harris v. Balk, 198 U.S. 215, 25 S.Ct. 625, 49 L.Ed. 1023 (1905).

19. 243 U.S. 269, 37 S.Ct. 282, 61 L.Ed. 713 (1917).

§ 3.17

1. See § 3.5, above.

2. See § 3.6, above.

3. See § 3.3, above.

Notably, the Shaffer majority refused to imply the consent of the director-defendants to Delaware's jurisdiction simply because they held directorships in a Delaware corporation.[4] At the same time, the Court suggested that a state statute "that treats the acceptance of directorship as consent to jurisdiction in the State" would have been sufficient to confer jurisdiction over the individual defendants, even without other contacts with the forum.[5] The consequence of the Court's reasoning may be that states simply will replace their now invalid quasi in rem statutes with statutes equating an act (for example, the defendant's acceptance of a corporate directorship) with consent, thereby transforming the nonresident defendant's affiliation with the forum from an unwitting and reluctant one into a cognitive and voluntary relationship.[6] At first this seems to be yet another bit of jurisdictional sleight-of-hand. However, it can be justified on the ground that the Shaffer Court would allow states to protect certain important state interests by enacting statutes declaring certain acts by the defendant to constitute consent to state court jurisdiction. Labeling acceptance of a directorship as consent, for example, thus indicates the type of purposeful act by which the defendant necessarily avails himself of the benefit and protection of the state's laws. The use of implied consent statutes to protect key state interests has been historically upheld by the Court since Hess v. Pawloski.[7] Consequently, the fiction of implied consent likely will continue to be accepted as a basis for jurisdiction at least in those instances in which the forum state has expressed a legitimate desire to regulate certain activities by citizens and noncitizens.

Jurisdiction based on domicile also most likely will continue given that as a general rule, a "person's domicile in a state is a fair and reasonable basis upon which to ground his amenability to suit there."[8] Its preservation as a jurisdictional base serves a system interest by "assur[ing] the existence of a place in which a person is continuously amenable to suit."[9] Nonetheless, Shaffer may indicate that under unusual or unfair circumstances, the technical rule that domicile alone is sufficient to justify exercising jurisdiction over an absent domiciliary[10] should be discarded. For example, in personam jurisdiction may be deemed improper in the state of a person's domicile if the party has left his domicile and not yet established a new one. In those cases, the defendant traditionally is treated as a domiciliary of the state he left behind, despite the lack of any continuous and systematic contact with

---

4. Shaffer v. Heitner, 433 U.S. 186, 216, 97 S.Ct. 2569, 2586, 53 L.Ed.2d 683 (1977).

5. Ibid.

6. Indeed, in the aftermath of Shaffer, Delaware enacted a statute that treats acceptance of a directorship in a Delaware corporation as constituting consent to jurisdiction in that state over any cause of action arising from the director's corporate activities. 10 Del.Code § 3114.

7. 274 U.S. 352, 47 S.Ct. 632, 71 L.Ed. 1091 (1927). For a discussion of implied consent statutes, see § 3.5, above.

8. Restatement Second of Conflict of Laws § 29, comment a (1971).

9. Ibid.

10. Milliken v. Meyer, 311 U.S. 457, 61 S.Ct. 339, 85 L.Ed. 278 (1940).

the forum since his departure.[11] Applying the International Shoe standard to those facts, it might be found unfair to subject the defendant to suit in the state of his domicile of origin after a lengthy absence, especially if the defendant evinces no intent to return there and an alternate forum is available. The fact of the defendant's domicile in a state would become only one of many possible contacts with the forum that would aid in establishing jurisdiction.

A similar argument conceivably could be applied to the rule of "transitory presence." Strict application of the doctrine of territorial power would allow full in personam jurisdiction to be exercised by a state court over an individual personally served in the state even if the defendant was served while only passing through,[12] and even if there was no logical relationship among the defendant, the forum, and the litigation.[13] Although the Court in International Shoe was not directly concerned with transient jurisdiction, the Shaffer decision, with its assertion that "all assertions of state-court jurisdiction must be evaluated according to the standards set forth in International Shoe and its progeny,"[14] could be interpreted to mean that the "minimum contacts" standard must be applied to a state court's assertion of personal jurisdiction over a natural person physically present within a state's boundaries. Indeed, this was the understanding of many commentators and was consistent with the position taken by the 1989 revision of the Restatement Second of Conflicts of Laws.[15]

In Burnham v. Superior Court of California, County of Marin,[16] the Court was presented with the opportunity to address the continued viability of transient jurisdiction. Burnham, a resident of New Jersey, was served with process while temporarily in California to conduct business and visit his children. The subject of the suit did not arise out of or relate to his activities in California and Burnham challenged the court's exercise of jurisdiction over him, alleging that he did not have sufficient "minimum contacts" with California.

All of the justices concluded that personal jurisdiction could be constitutionally asserted over Burnham by the California court. The analytical approaches taken to reach this result, however, reveal a sharp

---

11. Mas v. Perry, 489 F.2d 1396, 1400 (5th Cir.1974), cert. denied 419 U.S. 842.

12. International Shoe Co. v. Washington, 326 U.S. 310, 316, 66 S.Ct. 154, 158, 90 L.Ed. 95 (1945).

13. See, e.g., Grace v. MacArthur, 170 F.Supp. 442 (E.D.Ark.1959) (defendant served in an airplane passing over Arkansas was subject to in personam jurisdiction of that state's courts because served while "present" in the state); Nielsen v. Braland, 264 Minn. 481, 119 N.W.2d 737 (1963) (nonresident defendant served on foreign cause of action while passing through Minnesota; his objection to service based on

transitory presence was characterized as frivolous).

14. Shaffer v. Heitner, 433 U.S. 186, 212, 97 S.Ct. 2569, 2584, 53 L.Ed.2d 683 (1977).

15. "A state has power to exercise judicial jurisdiction over an individual who is present within its territory unless the individual's relationship to the state is so attenuated as to make the exercise of such jurisdiction unreasonable." Restatement Second of Conflicts of Laws § 28 (1989).

16. 495 U.S. 604, 110 S.Ct. 2105, 109 L.Ed.2d 631 (1990).

division among members of the Court on this question. Justice Scalia,[17] who announced the judgment of the Court, wrote that the traditional theory of transient jurisdiction remains a viable basis for the assertion of in personam jurisdiction. His opinion examined the rule of territoriality from an historical perspective and noted that a state's jurisdiction over a natural person served within its boundaries "is one of the continuing traditions of our legal system" and therefore comports with "traditional notions of fair play and substantial justice" by definition. Thus, Justice Scalia concluded, jurisdiction based on "physical presence alone" does not violate due process,[18] and therefore need not be subjected to the International Shoe "minimum contacts" analysis. He added that the "minimum contacts" standard was developed to serve as a substitute for physical presence of the defendant in the forum, and that it would be perverse to turn this standard back on what is the "touchstone of jurisdiction."[19]

In his concurring opinion, Justice Brennan[20] acknowledged that personal service within the forum usually is sufficient to establish in personam jurisdiction, but emphasized that a categorical rule to that effect is not possible. In some cases transient jurisdiction may be unreasonable and violate due process and, like "all assertions of state-court jurisdiction," must undergo a "minimum contacts" analysis. Although not dispositive, tradition is relevant in this analysis, for example, in determining that an individual should have foreseen that he is amenable to suit in the forum.

The rule advocated by Justice Scalia has the advantages of certainty, predictability, and efficiency. It eliminates the need for a case-by-case inquiry into the multiple factors that have been identified as relevant to the "minimum contacts" standard because, if a defendant is "tagged" in the forum state, the state may exert in personam jurisdiction over him. However, like any categorical rule, it is vulnerable to criticism for being wooden and leading to unfair results in some cases.[21] Moreover, the service of a summons on a nonresident defendant during a temporary stay may be even more fortuitous than the presence there of the defendant's debtor or his intangible property, and it is unclear that the efficiencies of Justice Scalia's rule, in practice, would outweigh the costs of the injustices it may allow.

E. AMENABILITY TO SUIT

§ 3.18 Source of Governing Law

The sovereign power of the United States government is nationwide, just as that of each state is statewide. There is no question that Congress

17. Justice Scalia was joined by Chief Justice Rehnquist and Justices Kennedy and White.

18. 495 U.S. at 619, 110 S.Ct. at 2115 (1990).

19. Ibid.

20. Justice Brennan was joined by Justices Marshall, Blackmun, and O'Connor.

21. See, e.g., Ehrenzweig, The Transient Rule of Personal Jurisdiction: The "Power" Myth and Forum Conveniens, 65 Yale L.J. 289 (1956). Serious injustices, however, probably could be avoided by employing the doctrine of forum non conveniens. See § 2.17, above.

has the power to provide that the process of each of the United States district courts should extend into every state of the Union.[1] Congress has not so provided, however. Under existing law the process of each federal court is bounded by the territory of the state in which it sits,[2] absent a federal statute[3] or rule[4] extending or contracting the jurisdictional reach of the federal courts, or an applicable state statute that does so.[5]

The question whether a federal court is at liberty to apply federal standards allowing jurisdiction over defendants beyond the reach of state law was debated at length a number of years ago in the context of corporate defendants. Quite clearly, when suit is brought in a federal court on a federally created right, the terms of any applicable federal statute and general federal law control, as long as the assertion of jurisdiction is consistent with the demands of due process.[6]

Further, it has been suggested that in applying the minimum contacts standard to actions under some federal statutes, such as antitrust,[7] or in suits against alien defendants,[8] the court may consider the aggregate contacts of the defendants with the nation as a whole, rather than simply contacts with the forum state. This standard recognizes that the underlying nature of the claims (the subject that the federal statute addresses) involves nationwide activities and that the Fifth Amendment Due Process Clause limits the federal government's assertion of jurisdiction, rather than the Fourteenth Amendment.

In Omni Capital International v. Rudolf Wolff & Company,[9] however, the Supreme Court held that under certain circumstances, a federal

---

§ 3.18

1. Mississippi Pub. Corp. v. Murphree, 326 U.S. 438, 66 S.Ct. 242, 90 L.Ed. 185 (1946); Robertson v. Railroad Labor Bd., 268 U.S. 619, 45 S.Ct. 621, 69 L.Ed. 1119 (1925). See generally 4 C. Wright & A. Miller, Civil 2d § 1075.

2. Robertson v. Railroad Labor Bd., 268 U.S. 619, 45 S.Ct. 621, 69 L.Ed. 1119 (1925).

3. E.g., 28 U.S.C.A. § 2361 (nationwide service in federal interpleader actions); 15 U.S.C.A. §§ 5, 22, 25 (nationwide service in antitrust actions).

4. E.g., Fed.Civ.Proc.Rule 4(k). See generally 4A C. Wright & A. Miller, Civil 2d §§ 1124–29.

5. Federal Rule 4(e) and Rule 4(k)(1)(A) specifically authorize the federal courts to use state procedures in actions in the federal courts. See generally 4A C. Wright & A. Miller, Civil 2d §§ 1112–16.

6. Fraley v. Chesapeake & O. Ry. Co., 397 F.2d 1 (3d Cir.1968) (FELA suit); Lone Star Package Car Co. v. Baltimore & O.R.

Co., 212 F.2d 147 (5th Cir.1954) (action under Carmack Amendment, 49 U.S.C.A. § 20(11)); Goldberg v. Mutual Readers League, Inc., 195 F.Supp. 778 (E.D.Pa.1961) (Fair Labor Standards Act).

7. See Black v. Acme Markets, Inc., 564 F.2d 681 (5th Cir.1977); Leasco Data Processing Equip. Corp. v. Maxwell, 468 F.2d 1326 (2d Cir.1972); Hovenkamp, Personal Jurisdiction and Venue in Private Antitrust Actions in the Federal Courts: A Policy Analysis, 67 Iowa L.Rev. 485, 498 (1982).

8. See Texas Trading & Milling Corp. v. Federal Republic of Nigeria, 647 F.2d 300, 314 (2d Cir.1981), cert. denied 454 U.S. 1148; Kane, Suing Foreign Sovereigns: A Procedural Compass, 34 Stan.L.Rev. 385, 402 (1982); Comment, National Contacts as a Basis for In Personam Jurisdiction Over Aliens in Federal Question Suits, 70 Calif.L.Rev. 686 (1982); Note, Alien Corporations and Aggregate Contacts: A Genuinely Federal Jurisdictional Standard, 95 Harv. L.Rev. 470 (1981).

9. 484 U.S. 97, 108 S.Ct. 404, 98 L.Ed.2d 415 (1987).

court adjudicating federally created rights and exercising the sovereign power of the United States may be bound by limitations on the states developed under the Fourteenth Amendment. The plaintiff in Omni Capital sought to pursue a cause of action against a resident of a foreign country for violation of the Commodity Exchange Act. The federal service rule in force at the time authorized extraterritorial service on defendants either in accordance with an applicable federal statute or with the jurisdiction provisions of the forum state.[10] Because the Commodity Exchange Act did not contain a long-arm provision, the Court looked to the law of Louisiana, the state in which the federal court was located. Under Louisiana's long-arm statute, the alien defendant was not amenable to service of process and therefore the federal court could not exert jurisdiction.[11] Although this result is somewhat anomalous, the Court explicitly refused to create an ad hoc rule authorizing service of process under the Fifth Amendment, leaving that responsibility to "Congress" and "those who propose the Federal Rules of Civil Procedure."[12]

Rule 4(k), as amended in 1993, responds to the Supreme Court's suggestion and explicitly closes the "gap" exposed in Omni Capital. Paragraph (1) of the subdivision substantively reflects the old rule used in Omni Capital: it explicitly authorizes the exercise of personal jurisdiction when authorized by a federal statute or when consistent with the long-arm statute of the state in which the district court is located. Paragraph (2), which is new, corrects the gap in jurisdiction that existed when the defendant was a nonresident of the United States and had contact with the nation sufficient to justify the application of United States law and to satisfy federal jurisdiction standards, but did not have sufficient contact with any single state to support jurisdiction under the forum's long-arm statute or to meet the requirements of International Shoe. The new rule serves as a federal long-arm statute and authorizes personal jurisdiction over any defendant who has minimum contacts with the United States as a whole but is not subject to personal jurisdiction on the basis of contacts with any individual state. Thus, before invoking the doctrine of nationwide minimum contacts, a court may need to examine the long-arm statute of several states, which may entail performing the International Shoe analysis for the purpose of determining the propriety of jurisdiction in each of those states. Paragraph (2) rests on the Fifth, rather than the Fourteenth, Amendment; presumably the doctrine of nationwide minimum contacts includes a requirement of "fair play and substantial justice" similar to that applicable under the Fourteenth Amendment.

One source of current controversy is the propriety of exercising something in the nature of supplemental personal jurisdiction.[13] When a plaintiff brings federal and state law claims against a defendant who lacks minimal contacts with the state for purposes of the state claim but

10. See generally 4 C. Wright & A. Miller, Civil 2d §§ 1067–69.

11. 484 U.S. at 108, 108 S.Ct. at 411.

12. 484 U.S. at 111, 108 S.Ct. at 413.

13. See 4A C. Wright & A. Miller, Civil 2d § 1125.

is subject to nationwide service for the federal claim, there is some question whether a federal court may exercise personal jurisdiction over the defendant for the state claim.[14] Neither the plain meaning nor the legislative history of Section 1367, which codifies supplemental subject-matter jurisdiction, supports the conclusion that Congress intended the statute to expand personal jurisdiction in that fashion. Furthermore, the exercise of supplemental personal jurisdiction seems to violate the defendant's Fourteenth Amendment rights embodied in the minimum contacts test. Nevertheless, several courts[15] have upheld the doctrine; the Supreme Court has not yet considered the practice.

The question of what law governs the assertion of personal jurisdiction is more complex when the right sued on is state-created and subject-matter jurisdiction rests on diversity of citizenship. Whether state or federal law controls makes little difference when the state has chosen to extend its jurisdictional reach to the limits of the Constitution;[16] but when the state elects not to exercise its full jurisdictional power, may a federal court apply federal standards and assert jurisdiction further than the state in which it is sitting? The answer to this question may best be examined in the context of a well-known debate on the subject in the Second Circuit.

The Second Circuit initially upheld the use of a federal standard in Jaftex Corporation v. Randolph Mills, Inc.[17] only to reverse itself three years later in Arrowsmith v. United Press International.[18] In Jaftex, a diversity action for personal injuries instituted in the Southern District of New York, Randolph Mills, a North Carolina corporation that had been brought in as a third-party defendant, moved to vacate the service and to dismiss the third-party complaint on the ground that it was not "doing business" and thus was not amenable to suit in New York. The district court granted the motion, but the Second Circuit upheld the service under both New York and federal law. Judge Clark, writing for the majority, concluded that the question whether a foreign corporation is present in a district to permit service of process upon it is one of federal law.[19]

In Arrowsmith, the plaintiff, a resident of Maryland, had brought a libel action in the Vermont federal district court against United Press International. Subject-matter jurisdiction was based on diversity of citizenship and UPI was served under former Federal Rule 4(d)(3), which is similar to current Rule 4(i)(2), through its manager in Vermont. The complaint was dismissed by the district court for failure to state a claim

---

14. Of course, a federal court must have both personal and subject-matter jurisdiction before adjudicating a case. For a discussion of supplemental subject-matter jurisdiction, see §§ 2.12–2.14, above.

15. E.g., Rice v. Nova Biomedical Corp., 38 F.3d 909 (7th Cir.1994), cert. denied 514 U.S. 1111; IUE AFL–CIO v. Herrmann, 9 F.3d 1049 (2d Cir.1993), cert. denied 513 U.S. 822.

16. For a discussion of the scope of various long-arm statutes see §§ 3.12–3.13, above.

17. 282 F.2d 508 (2d Cir.1960).

18. 320 F.2d 219, 6 A.L.R.3d 1072 (2d Cir.1963).

19. 282 F.2d at 516.

for relief; plaintiff appealed to the court of appeals, which, sitting en banc, took the opportunity to review the Jaftex principle.

A majority of the court, in an opinion by Judge Friendly, found no basis for holding that a federal standard should be applied in determining amenability to suit in diversity litigation; it felt that Federal Rule 4 prescribed only the manner of service in federal court actions, rather than the amenability of corporations to federal process.

> No one reading the Rule would be likely to get the impression that Rule 4(d)(3) was a charter to the federal courts to make their own law as to when a foreign corporation is subject to suit and that the effect of Rule 4(d)(7) is to make state standards alternatively applicable.[20]

The result reached by the Second Circuit—that amenability of a foreign corporation to suit in a federal court in a diversity action is determined according to the law of the state in which the district court sits—has been adopted unanimously by the circuit courts.[21] State law also governs amenability questions in removed cases since removal jurisdiction is derivative and thus dependent on the personal jurisdiction of the state court in which the action was commenced.[22] This conclusion is clear when jurisdiction rests on Rule 4(k)(1)(A), which allows a federal court to adopt state law bases of jurisdiction.

Although the Arrowsmith principle is firmly established, one other amenability question remains: in a diversity action, which state's law should govern the assertion of personal jurisdiction when service is accomplished under Federal Rule 4(k)(1)(B), the special 100 mile provision that permits extraterritorial service on certain persons in multiparty actions?[23] The Second Circuit has adopted the view that either the law of the forum state or the state in which service actually is made may be used when serving persons outside the state pursuant to this 100–mile provision.[24] Inasmuch as the amendment to Federal Rule 4 adding this so-called "bulge" provision was intended to encourage complex controversies to be litigated in one action whenever the necessary third parties could be found within the 100 mile radius,[25] to restrict amenability by following the rules of the forum state would defeat the purpose of the provision. Regardless, with the recent creation of a federal long-arm provision, in addition to the ability to assert jurisdiction under any

20. 320 F.2d at 226. Former Rule 4(d)(7) is similar to current Rule 4(e)(1).

21. See, e.g., Donahue v. Far Eastern Air Transport Corp., 652 F.2d 1032 (D.C.Cir.1981); Wilkerson v. Fortuna Corp., 554 F.2d 745 (5th Cir.1977), cert. denied 434 U.S. 939; Amba Marketing Systems, Inc. v. Jobar Int'l, Inc., 551 F.2d 784 (9th Cir.1977); Davis H. Elliot Co. v. Caribbean Utilities Co., 513 F.2d 1176 (6th Cir.1975); Pujol v. U.S. Life Ins. Co., 396 F.2d 430 (1st Cir.1968).

22. Electric Regulator Corp. v. Sterling Extruder Corp., 280 F.Supp. 550 (D.Conn. 1968); Southern New England Distributing Corp. v. Berkeley Finance Corp., 30 F.R.D. 43 (D.Conn.1962).

23. See 4 C. Wright & A. Miller, Civil 2d § 1075.

24. Coleman v. American Export Isbrandtsen Lines, Inc., 405 F.2d 250 (2d Cir.1968).

25. 405 F.2d at 252.

applicable federal statute or the forum state's long-arm statute, personal jurisdiction is widely available to federal courts under Rule 4(k).

Finally, the question whether the exercise of jurisdiction is consistent with due process under the Fifth or Fourteenth Amendment always is a matter of federal law.[26] Accordingly, whether a nonresident can be held amenable to process in a federal court requires answers to two analytically distinct questions. First, do the state's procedural rules or statutes provide for jurisdiction over the defendant under the circumstances of the particular case? This is a question of state law.[27] Second, if the state's provisions are broad enough to assert jurisdiction under the facts of the case, or if no state can assert jurisdiction and thus the federal long-arm provision applies, is that exercise of jurisdiction consistent with due process? The latter question is a matter of federal law.[28]

F. NOTICE AND THE OPPORTUNITY TO BE HEARD

1. Due Process Requirements

§ 3.19 The Requirement of Reasonable Notice

Due process not only requires that the court must have power to adjudicate, it also demands that the defendant have notice of the institution of proceedings against him. The constitutional obligation to provide the defendant with proper notice and an opportunity to be heard is an additional aspect of the due process limitation on a court's ability to exercise jurisdiction.[1] If the defendant has not received proper notice, the court's power to adjudicate the dispute is imperfect; any judgment it renders is vulnerable to collateral attack.[2] As the constitutionally permissible bases for exercising jurisdiction over the defendant's person or property have expanded, notice requirements have received greater attention. Because the evolution of jurisdiction based on minimum contacts has obliged more people to defend lawsuits far from their domiciles, new standards for notice-giving have developed to ensure that the defendant is informed of the proceedings and has an opportunity to participate in them.

26. Arrowsmith v. United Press Int'l, 320 F.2d 219 (2d Cir.1963); Partin v. Michaels Art Bronze Co., 202 F.2d 541 (3d Cir.1953); Pulson v. American Rolling Mill Co., 170 F.2d 193 (1st Cir.1948).

27. Kansas City Structural Steel Co. v. Arkansas, 269 U.S. 148, 150, 46 S.Ct. 59, 60, 70 L.Ed. 204 (1925) ("We accept the decision of the Supreme Court of Arkansas as to what constitutes the doing of business in that state within the meaning of its own laws.") (Butler, J.).

28. Pulson v. American Rolling Mill Co., 170 F.2d 193 (1st Cir.1948); Bomze v. Nardis Sportswear, Inc., 165 F.2d 33 (2d Cir.1948).

§ 3.19

1. "[W]hen notice is a person's due, process which is a mere gesture is not due process." Mullane v. Central Hanover Bank & Trust Co., 339 U.S. 306, 314, 70 S.Ct. 652, 657, 94 L.Ed. 865 (1950) (Jackson, J.). See also 4 C. Wright & A. Miller, Civil 2d § 1074; Developments in the Law—State Court Jurisdiction, 73 Harv.L.Rev. 909, 987–91 (1960).

2. Smith v. U.S., 403 F.2d 448 (7th Cir.1968). See also Wuchter v. Pizzutti, 276 U.S. 13, 48 S.Ct. 259, 72 L.Ed. 446 (1928).

In general, the defendant has been provided notice when he has received the set of papers known as "process." Process consists of a summons, which directs the defendant to appear before the court under penalty of default, and, if the applicable procedural rules require, a copy of the complaint. For a court to have valid jurisdiction, process must have been properly served and the defendant must have been given sufficient notice of the pending action to satisfy due process. Although adhering to the applicable rules governing how process is served usually provides notice, this is not always the case.

Because the means of service should be designed to assure as much as possible that defendant receives notice of the action, it is not surprising that service by publication ordinarily is deemed constitutionally insufficient for actions in personam.[3] Publication has been upheld as proper service in actions in personam only when a state domiciliary could be served in no other way[4] or when a state resident deliberately concealed herself to avoid service.[5] The mere knowledge of a pending lawsuit does not satisfy the notice requirement, however, and this is true even when the defendant allegedly evaded service and the lawsuit was brought to his attention through personal correspondence and publicity in the media.[6]

Pennoyer v. Neff[7] made it clear that seizure of property owned by the defendant, coupled with publication of a notice of the action, provided constitutionally adequate notice in a proceeding based on in rem or quasi in rem jurisdiction. Courts required only minimal notice even when the defendant's name and address were known, either on the theory that the action was against the property itself, making the defendant's actual presence unnecessary, or on the theory that property owners always kept themselves aware of events concerning their property and thus would be aware of any seizure of their property and the litigation involving it.[8] The landmark decision of Mullane v. Central Hanover Bank & Trust Company[9] challenged many of these assumptions and, since Mullane, the possibility of utilizing publication as the method of service has been reduced drastically.

---

3. Greene v. Lindsey, 456 U.S. 444, 102 S.Ct. 1874, 72 L.Ed.2d 249 (1982); Polansky v. Richardson, 351 F.Supp. 1066 (E.D.N.Y. 1972) (actual receipt of process is not the test under due process and full faith and credit, rather it is whether "reasonable steps were taken to give notice to the adverse party").

4. Dobkin v. Chapman, 21 N.Y.2d 490, 289 N.Y.S.2d 161, 236 N.E.2d 451 (1968) (publication upheld after mailed notice returned).

5. Butler v. McKey, 138 F.2d 373 (9th Cir.1943), cert. denied 321 U.S. 780.

6. Chaplin v. Superior Court of Los Angeles County, 81 Cal.App. 367, 253 P. 954 (1927).

7. 95 U.S. (5 Otto) 714, 24 L.Ed. 565 (1877), discussed at § 3.3, above. See also Note, Requirements of Notice in In Rem Proceedings, 70 Harv.L.Rev. 1257 (1957).

8. Developments in the Law—State Court Jurisdiction, 73 Harv.L.Rev. 909, 989 (1960).

9. 339 U.S. 306, 70 S.Ct. 652, 94 L.Ed. 865 (1950), noted in 36 Cornell L.Q. 541 (1951), 50 Mich.L.Rev. 124 (1951), 100 U.Pa.L.Rev. 305 (1951), 36 Iowa L.Rev. 47 (1950), 25 N.Y.U.L.Rev. 896 (1950), 1950 Wis.L.Rev. 688.

In Mullane, the subject matter of the action was a $3 million common trust fund, administered by Central Hanover Bank as trustee. The fund had been established by the pooling of 113 smaller trust estates under a New York banking statute. The purpose of the statute was to enable small investors collectively to secure the services of professional money managers, which they could not have afforded on an individual basis. As required by state law, the bank petitioned the New York Surrogate Court to settle or audit the propriety of its first accounts as trustee of the common trust fund, giving notice of the Surrogate Court proceedings to the beneficiaries by publication in a local newspaper. Notice that this procedure would be followed for seeking judicial approval of the trustee's actions had been mailed to known beneficiaries at the time of each participating estate's first investment in the common fund, some twelve to fifteen months earlier.

The Surrogate Court appointed Mullane as special guardian and attorney under the statute to represent all persons with an interest in the income of the common trust fund; a separate guardian, appellee Vaughan, was appointed to represent persons interested in the fund's principal. Since the effect of the court's decree would be to "settle all questions respecting the management of the common trust fund" as well as the disposition of management fees for the prior period, it would foreclose any subsequent challenges by beneficiaries for mismanagement of their monies.

Mullane challenged the jurisdiction of the New York court on two grounds. First, Mullane argued that the proceeding was necessarily a proceeding in personam because it adjudicated personal rights of the nonresident beneficiaries by immunizing the trustee against their subsequent suits for negligence or breach of trust. Since process had not been served personally on these nonresident beneficiaries, then, according to Pennoyer, the court lacked in personam jurisdiction over them. Second, Mullane asserted that notice by publication did not constitute adequate notice comporting with due process.

The Supreme Court found that precise classification of the nature of the proceeding was unnecessary to a determination that the state court did have power to decide the case. Further, the Court held that the due process notice requirement did not depend on the classification of an action as in personam or in rem. Justice Jackson, writing for the Court, chose instead to declare a general standard for notice:

> An elementary and fundamental requirement of due process in any proceeding which is to be accorded finality is notice reasonably calculated, under all the circumstances, to apprise interested parties of the pendency of the action and afford them an opportunity to present their objections. * * * The notice must be of such nature as reasonably to convey the required information * * * and it must afford a reasonable time for those interested to make their appearance * * *. The means employed must be such as one desirous of

actually informing the absentee might reasonably adopt to accomplish it.[10]

Applying this standard to the facts of the case, the statutory notice by publication was deemed sufficient only for beneficiaries who were unknown and absent, or whose rights were conjectural when the proceedings were instituted. For present beneficiaries whose names and addresses were known to the trustee, or could be ascertained with reasonable diligence, the Court concluded that no less than notice by mail would be adequate.

The major impact of Mullane derives from its analytical approach. The Court chose first to separate the issue of judicial power from that of notice. It then analyzed the constituents of adequate notice in light of the peculiar circumstances of the case, balancing the need to assure that all who would be affected would be notified or represented against the practical difficulties associated with identifying and notifying every possible beneficiary.[11] Since the interests of all income beneficiaries and principal beneficiaries in overseeing the management efforts of the trustee were identical, it was not crucial that every beneficiary be personally served; notice "reasonably certain" to reach most of those interested was considered likely to safeguard the interests of all. Nor did the Court consider it essential to require "impracticable and extended searches" in the name of due process.[12] The Court compared the importance of direct notice to individual beneficiaries with the cost and administrative difficulty imposed on the trust if required to give individual notice and it required the maximum notice consistent with prudent financial management of the fund.

Although the common trust fund proceedings involved in Mullane were so specialized that the decision might have been limited to its facts, subsequent cases have shown that the Mullane standard applies equally to other types of actions.[13] In Walker v. City of Hutchinson,[14] a condemnation proceeding, the Court held notice by publication in an official city newspaper insufficient when direct notice could have been given to the property owners. Similarly, in an eminent domain proceeding, publication and posting notices on the land were held insufficient when the city could have located with relative ease the names and addresses of the affected riparian owners.[15] And notice of a forfeiture proceeding mailed

---

10. 339 U.S. at 314–15, 70 S.Ct. at 657–58.

11. "A construction of the Due Process Clause which would place impossible or impractical obstacles in the way could not be justified. Against this interest of the State we must balance the individual interest sought to be protected by the Fourteenth Amendment." 339 U.S. at 313–14, 70 S.Ct. at 657.

12. 339 U.S. at 317–18, 70 S.Ct. at 659.

13. For a discussion of the application of the Mullane standard in class actions, see § 16.6, below.

14. 352 U.S. 112, 77 S.Ct. 200, 1 L.Ed.2d 178 (1956). See also Hazard, A General Theory of State–Court Jurisdiction, 1965 Sup.Ct.Rev. 241, 248–52; Developments in the Law—State Court Jurisdiction, 73 Harv.L.Rev. 909, 987–91 (1960); Comment, in Rem Actions—Adequacy of Notice, 25 Tenn.L.Rev. 495 (1958).

15. Schroeder v. City of New York, 371 U.S. 208, 83 S.Ct. 279, 9 L.Ed.2d 255

to the defendant's house when the state knew the defendant was in prison was found not reasonably calculated to apprise the defendant of the proceedings.[16] Finally, posting a notice of a forcible entry and detainer action on an apartment door after only one effort to serve the tenant personally was found not to satisfy the minimum standards of due process when mailed notice could have been used and posted notices were not infrequently removed by children and other tenants before they had their intended effect.[17] Thus, constructive notice by publication is constitutionally suspect whenever plaintiff actually knows, or has reason to know, particularly as a matter of public record, the defendant's identity or address.

Since the test for notice is "reasonableness under the circumstances of the case," courts tend to take a permissive attitude toward the formalities of notice-giving when the defendant is, in fact, apprised,[18] however. Moreover, a party can knowingly and voluntarily waive notice.[19] In the absence of an adhesion contract or inequality of bargaining power between the parties to a contract,[20] waiver by contract, such as in a cognovit clause,[21] is not automatically deemed violative of due process.

§ 3.20 Service of Process as a Means of Notice

The traditional manner of providing notice is "personal service"—in hand delivery of the summons to the defendant by a sheriff, marshal, or someone similarly authorized by law. In Pennoyer v. Neff,[1] the Supreme Court validated personal service on the defendant within the forum state as a means of exercising jurisdiction; the act of service within the forum both provided evidence of the defendant's presence and notified the defendant of the proceedings. Personal service remains a sufficient, and in some ways, the preferred form of notice-giving.[2] Accordingly, personal service on defendants outside the forum constitutes adequate notice under "doing business" and long-arm statutes.[3] In the federal courts,

---

(1962). See also City of New York v. New York, N.H. & H.R. R. Co., 344 U.S. 293, 73 S.Ct. 299, 97 L.Ed. 333 (1953) (bankruptcy proceedings); Polansky v. Richardson, 351 F.Supp. 1066 (E.D.N.Y.1972) (divorce decree invalidated).

16. Robinson v. Hanrahan, 409 U.S. 38, 93 S.Ct. 30, 34 L.Ed.2d 47 (1972).

17. Greene v. Lindsey, 456 U.S. 444, 102 S.Ct. 1874, 72 L.Ed.2d 249 (1982); Sterling v. Environmental Bd. of the City of New York, 793 F.2d 52 (2d Cir.1986), cert. denied 479 U.S. 987.

18. Nowell v. Nowell, 384 F.2d 951 (5th Cir.1967), cert. denied 390 U.S. 956; Clemones v. Alabama Power Co., 250 F.Supp. 433 (N.D.Ga.1966).

19. National Equipment Rental, Ltd. v. Szukhent, 375 U.S. 311, 84 S.Ct. 411, 11 L.Ed.2d 354 (1964).

20. D.H. Overmyer Co. v. Frick Co., 405 U.S. 174, 92 S.Ct. 775, 31 L.Ed.2d 124

(1972); Kosches v. Nichols, 68 Misc.2d 795, 327 N.Y.S.2d 968 (1971) (absent showing of extraordinary circumstances, sellers may not obtain ex parte order to seize household goods).

21. See § 3.5, above, for a discussion of cognovit clauses.

§ 3.20

1. 95 U.S. (5 Otto) 714, 24 L.Ed. 565 (1877).

2. See generally Milliken v. Meyer, 311 U.S. 457, 61 S.Ct. 339, 85 L.Ed. 278 (1940); Hagen v. Payne, 222 F.Supp. 548 (W.D.Ark. 1963).

3. Milliken v. Meyer, 311 U.S. 457, 61 S.Ct. 339, 85 L.Ed. 278 (1940); Hagen v. Payne, 222 F.Supp. 548 (W.D.Ark.1963); Dobkin v. Chapman, 21 N.Y.S.2d 490, 289 N.Y.S.2d 161, 236 N.E.2d 451 (1968).

personal service both within the forum state and in other states is provided for expressly in Rule 4(e);[4] Rule 4(f) authorizes personal delivery of service outside of the United States.[5]

Due process does not *require* that the defendant be served personally. Many statutes now provide for forms of "substituted" or "constructive" service. These include: leaving the process at the defendant's home, mailing the process to the defendant, or, under very limited circumstances, publishing the contents of the summons in a newspaper for a prescribed number of times. In federal court, a plaintiff likely will have a choice among several methods of service: Rule 4(e)(2) authorizes leaving process at the defendant's usual place of abode and Rule 4(e)(1) authorizes service upon an individual pursuant to the law of either the state in which the district court is located or the state in which service is effected. These methods are scrutinized carefully by the courts, however, to ensure that they will give fair notice. In the early case of McDonald v. Mabee,[6] Justice Holmes suggested a standard by which to evaluate these alternative forms of service: "To dispense with personal service the substitute that is most likely to reach the defendant is the least that ought to be required if substantial justice is to be done."[7]

In actions against natural persons, the most common form of substituted service calls for a copy of the summons to be left at the defendant's "usual place of abode" with someone of "suitable age and discretion"[8] residing therein, typically a spouse or child of mature years. Under some statutes, this method of service is always an option; the plaintiff need not show an inability to obtain service by personal delivery before using substituted service.[9] When service is made by leaving process at the defendant's home, the return of service must show both that service was made at an appropriate place and upon a person of "suitable age and discretion."[10]

As a practical matter, it is the serving officer who determines who is of suitable age and discretion. However, the ultimate determination will be made by the court if the defendant chooses to place the matter in issue,[11] and service may be invalidated if process is left with a person later deemed unsuitable. For example, delivery to an illiterate maid has been held improper.[12] On the other hand, the person receiving process clearly need not be an adult—delivery to a defendant's sixteen year-old daughter has been upheld, for example.[13] In general, when substituted

---

4. See generally 4A C. Wright & A. Miller, Civil 2d §§ 1094–18.

5. See generally 4A C. Wright & A. Miller, Civil 2d §§ 1133–36.

6. 243 U.S. 90, 37 S.Ct. 343, 61 L.Ed. 608 (1917).

7. 243 U.S. at 92, 37 S.Ct. at 344.

8. N.Y.—McKinney's CPLR 308 (substituted service may be made at the defendant's actual place of business as well as usual place of abode); Fed.Civ.Proc.Rule 4(e)(2).

9. N.Y.—McKinney's CPLR 308(2–4).

10. Scheerger v. Wiencek, 34 F.Supp. 805 (W.D.N.Y.1940).

11. In re Carwell, 323 F.Supp. 590 (E.D.La.1971).

12. See, e.g., Joyce v. Bauman, 11 N.J.Misc. 237, 165 A. 425 (1933).

13. De George v. Mandata Poultry Co., 196 F.Supp. 192 (E.D.Pa.1961).

service is used, the person actually served must be someone so closely "related" to the defendant that there is a high probability that that person will give the defendant actual notice.

When substituted service is employed it is particularly important that the formalities in the applicable service of process statute be followed closely in order to assure that the notice-giving function of process has been effectuated.[14] Although substituted service may be deemed effective even if the defendant does not actually receive the papers—so long as he has had actual notice,[15] plaintiffs cannot rely on that result. The failure to meet the statutory requirements may render the service ineffective even if the defendant actually receives the papers.[16] Courts also have sought to prevent potential abuses by narrowly construing the terms "usual place of abode" and "suitable age and discretion residing therein."[17] Thus, service left at the defendant's place of employment has been ruled ineffective[18] unless the statute so provides. Similarly, if the statute requires that the person with whom the service is left be "residing" at the defendant's home, it will not be sufficient to leave the process with someone who performs part-time janitorial services in the defendant's apartment.[19]

In actions against corporate or other organizational defendants, detailed procedural rules typically specify how personal service is to be accomplished—that is, who is authorized to receive service of process on behalf of the organization.[20] In most cases, personal delivery to an officer or agent of the corporation who is likely to inform an appropriate corporate official of the receipt and content of the process suffices as service on the corporation, inasmuch as it affords reasonable assurance that the corporation has actual notice.[21] Similarly, a partnership or other

---

14. Varra v. Superior Court, 181 Cal. App.2d 12, 4 Cal.Rptr. 920 (1960); Southern Mills, Inc. v. Armstrong, 223 N.C. 495, 496, 27 S.E.2d 281 (1943).

15. Smith v. Kincaid, 249 F.2d 243 (6th Cir.1957); Adams v. School Bd. of Wyoming Valley West School District, 53 F.R.D. 267 (M.D.Pa.1971) (defendant had actual notice though record showed service made on a secretary who did not exist).

16. Maryland State Firemen's Ass'n v. Chaves, 166 F.R.D. 353 (D.Md.1996), discussed in § 3.22, below; Chilcote v. Shertzer, 372 F.Supp. 86 (E.D.Wis.1974) (substituted service on nonresident defendant's father at father's residence insufficient when no attempt made to comply with state long-arm statute's requirement).

17. Grammenos v. Lemos, 457 F.2d 1067 (2d Cir.1972) (service left at sister's apartment insufficient when there is no evidence that defendant regularly resided there); First Nat. Bank & Trust Co. of Tulsa v. Ingerton, 207 F.2d 793 (10th Cir. 1953) (service left with defendant's son at his Denver home during defendant's visit

quashed, since her usual place of abode was a New Mexico hotel). See generally 4A C. Wright & A. Miller, Civil 2d § 1096.

18. Bell v. Hosse, 31 F.R.D. 181 (M.D.Tenn.1962). See also Rabiolo v. Weinstein, 357 F.2d 167 (7th Cir.1966), cert. denied 391 U.S. 923.

19. Zuckerman v. McCulley, 7 F.R.D. 739 (E.D.Mo.1947), appeal dismissed 170 F.2d 1015 (8th Cir.1948).

20. E.g., Fed.Civ.Proc.Rule 4(h); Conn. Gen.Stat.Ann. §§ 52–57; N.Y.—McKinney's CPLR 308(3).

21. Commercial Mut. Acc. Co. v. Davis, 213 U.S. 245, 29 S.Ct. 445, 53 L.Ed. 782 (1909); Diapulse Corp. of America v. Birchter Corp., 362 F.2d 736 (2d Cir.1966), cert. dismissed 385 U.S. 801 (1966). But cf. Paramount Packaging Corp. v. H.B. Fuller Co., 190 F.Supp. 178 (E.D.Pa.1960) (service on switchboard operator, not the person in charge of the office, held invalid under the Pennsylvania rule). See generally 4A C. Wright & A. Miller, Civil 2d §§ 1100–05.

association sued in its firm name may be served by leaving a copy of the summons and complaint personally with any partner or officer of the firm, or with any agent of the partnership.[22]

In addition to the various means of substituted service, constructive service effected by registered or certified mail has been deemed constitutionally sufficient.[23] In order to ensure that the defendant has received the process, some statutes require a signed return receipt when constructive service is used.[24] Under the present text of Federal Rule 4(d), use of first-class mail[25] not only is authorized as a substitute for personal service, but is highly encouraged to save the cost of formal service. When Rule 4(d) is used to notify a defendant and to request a waiver of formal service, the defendant must be sent an extra copy of the notice and request as well as a prepaid means of providing the waiver in writing. The rule gives the defendant two incentives—a "carrot" and a "stick"— to encourage the waiver of formal service: (1) if waived, the defendant is given 60 days (or 90 days if the defendant is not within the United States) to answer the complaint instead of the usual 20 days allowed under Rule 12, and (2) if not waived, the defendant must bear the cost of formal service unless good cause for refusing to waive can be shown.[26] Under the rule, the defendant has at least 30 days from the date on which the request is sent (or 60 days if the defendant is not within the United States) to return the waiver;[27] waiving service does not also waive any objection to venue or personal jurisdiction.[28]

Nonresident motorist long-arm statutes once generally required delivery of process to a state official accompanied by a mailing of the papers to the out-of-state defendant. Today, service on the in-state official is recognized as being part of the fiction of implied consent and, having little notice value, often no longer is required.[29] When, however, such a statute still provides for service on a state official, the prescribed procedure must be followed.[30]

22. See, e.g., Ill.—Smith–Hurd Ann. 735 ILCS 5/2–205; Williams v. Egan, 308 P.2d 273 (Okl.1957).

23. Hess v. Pawloski, 274 U.S. 352, 47 S.Ct. 632, 71 L.Ed. 1091 (1927); Miller v. Steinbach, 43 F.R.D. 275 (S.D.N.Y.1967); Durfee v. Durfee, 293 Mass. 472, 200 N.E. 395 (1936).

24. Yox v. Durgan, 302 F.Supp. 1262 (E.D.Tenn.1969) (case dismissed for insufficiency of service because certified copy of process returned without being received by defendant when Tennessee statute required return receipt). But see Speir v. Robert C. Herd & Co., 189 F.Supp. 432 (D.Md.1960) (return receipt not constitutionally required for substituted service on foreign corporation).

25. Rule 4(d)(2)(B) recognizes the reality of facsimile machines and private express mail companies and thus also allows the use of "other reliable means." However, Rule 4(d)(2)(G) requires a prepaid means of providing written compliance, casting doubt on the utility of electronic correspondence.

26. Infants, incompetent persons, and the government do not have a duty to waive service, however. The Advisory Committee Note gives two somewhat questionable reasons for exempting the government: (1) government mail receiving facilities are inadequate, and (2) the government should not be confronted with the potential for bearing the cost of service.

27. Fed.Civ.Proc.Rule 4(d)(2).

28. Fed.Civ.Proc.Rule 4(d)(1).

29. See, e.g., Olberding v. Illinois Central R.R. Co., 346 U.S. 338, 340–41, 74 S.Ct. 83, 98 L.Ed. 39 (1953). See also Scott, Jurisdiction over Non-resident Motorists, 39 Harv.L.Rev. 563 (1926).

30. Bookout v. Beck, 354 F.2d 823 (9th Cir.1965); Peterson v. Dickison, 334 F.Supp. 551 (W.D.Pa.1971).

Finally, it should be noted that the parties may contract for a specific means of service that is not authorized by any of the otherwise applicable rules. When the defendant contractually consents in advance to the jurisdiction of a particular court, service of process may be made by any method consistent with due process.[31] Thus, the Supreme Court has held that in federal courts when service is made under what is now Rule 4(e)(2), the agent selected to receive service by the contracting parties need not be known personally by the defendant so long as that agent actually notifies the defendant of the pending lawsuit.[32]

§ 3.21 The Timing of Notice and the Opportunity to Be Heard

Due process requires that a defendant be afforded an opportunity to be heard.[1] In Mullane v. Central Hanover Bank & Trust Company,[2] the Supreme Court stated that the "right to be heard has little reality or worth unless one is informed that the matter is pending and can choose for himself whether to appear or default, acquiesce or contest."[3] The right to be heard is narrowed considerably if it cannot be exercised in a timely fashion. For example, the right to argue one's entitlement to welfare benefits clearly is circumscribed if a hearing does not precede the termination of benefits.[4]

The defendant's right to a hearing runs counter to the interest of creditors who wish to recover goods sold on credit or to collect debts after default in payments through garnishment or replevin. If recovery must await the outcome of proceedings of which the defendant has been informed and in which he has been given the opportunity to participate, the goods involved may be destroyed or concealed, or they simply may depreciate through the debtor's continued use. Similarly, assets may be withdrawn from banks so that they cannot be reached and jobs may be lost so that wages will not be available to satisfy an eventual judgment. An analogous problem arises in the context of quasi in rem jurisdiction[5] in which property, if not attached before the action is commenced, may be removed, destroying the court's jurisdiction. From a broader perspective, an excessive concern for the opportunity to be heard may have deleterious effects: courts may become paternalistic, at the expense of individual liberty, or creditors faced with higher costs due to increased litigation may exit the market, ultimately limiting credit opportunities

---

31. Lawn v. Franklin, 328 F.Supp. 791 (S.D.N.Y.1971). See also AAMCO Automatic Transmissions, Inc. v. Hagenbarth, 296 F.Supp. 1142 (E.D.Pa.1968) (service more than met minimum required by contract and so declared valid even though service imperfect by standards of Federal Rules).

32. National Equipment Rental, Ltd. v. Szukhent, 375 U.S. 311, 84 S.Ct. 411, 11 L.Ed.2d 354 (1964).

§ 3.21

1. Grannis v. Ordean, 234 U.S. 385, 394, 34 S.Ct. 779, 783, 58 L.Ed. 1363 (1914).

2. 339 U.S. 306, 70 S.Ct. 652, 94 L.Ed. 865 (1950).

3. 399 U.S. at 314, 70 S.Ct. at 657.

4. Goldberg v. Kelly, 397 U.S. 254, 90 S.Ct. 1011, 25 L.Ed.2d 287 (1970).

5. See § 3.16, above.

for the poor. The balance to be struck between these conflicting interests has posed some problems.

In 1932, the Supreme Court declared in American Surety Company v. Baldwin,[6] that "Due process requires that there be an opportunity to present every available defense; but it need not be before the entry of judgment."[7] The case involved a challenge by a surety company to a court order entering judgment against it without notice on a bond it had given. The state practice, which provided for a hearing on the construction of the bond by an appeal following the entry of judgment, was found constitutional.

Almost forty years later the Court reconsidered this issue in the context of a Wisconsin prejudgment garnishment procedure that permitted a creditor to freeze the debtor's wages prior to trial, and reached a different conclusion. In Sniadach v. Family Finance Corporation,[8] Justice Douglas, writing for the Court, noted that the practical consequence of statutory prejudgment garnishment was to "drive a wage-earning family to the wall."[9]

> Where the taking of one's property is so obvious, it needs no extended argument to conclude that absent notice and a prior hearing * * * this prejudgment garnishment procedure violates fundamental principles of due process.[10]

Two years after the Sniadach decision, the Court broadened the requirement of a prior hearing to include state replevin procedures. In Fuentes v. Shevin[11] the Court concluded that the Florida and Pennsylvania statutes permitting replevin without prior hearing were unconstitutional. The Court indicated that the replevin laws did not serve any general public interest sufficient to justify postponement of the defendant's right to a hearing, even though the owner was permitted to regain possession of the property by posting a bond. Read broadly, Fuentes seemed to suggest that any prejudgment sequestration that did not provide notice and an opportunity to be heard prior to the attachment was constitutionally suspect.

However, in the 1974 case of Mitchell v. W.T. Grant Company,[12] the Court appeared to retreat from Fuentes somewhat. In Mitchell, the Court, in a five-to-four decision upheld a Louisiana procedure for sequestration to avoid waste or alienation. The majority distinguished Fuentes on the grounds that the Louisiana writ required judicial approval, involved a vendor's lien, made available a procedure that enabled the

---

6. 287 U.S. 156, 53 S.Ct. 98, 77 L.Ed. 231 (1932).

7. 287 U.S. at 168, 53 S.Ct. at 102 (Brandeis, J.).

8. 395 U.S. 337, 89 S.Ct. 1820, 23 L.Ed.2d 349 (1969), noted 70 Colum.L.Rev. 942 (1970), 68 Mich.L.Rev. 986 (1970).

9. 395 U.S. at 341–42, 89 S.Ct. at 1823.

10. 395 U.S. at 342, 89 S.Ct. at 1823.

11. 407 U.S. 67, 92 S.Ct. 1983, 32 L.Ed.2d 556 (1972), noted 86 Harv.L.Rev. 85 (1972). See also Gardner, Fuentes v. Shevin: The New York Creditor and Replevin, 22 Buffalo L.Rev. 17 (1972).

12. 416 U.S. 600, 94 S.Ct. 1895, 40 L.Ed.2d 406 (1974), noted 88 Harv.L.Rev. 41, 71 (1974). Changes in the composition of the Court between Fuentes and Mitchell may explain more than fine nuances.

buyer to reclaim possession immediately, and forced the plaintiff to demonstrate the basis for sequestration rather than allowing sequestration based solely on conclusory allegations. The Court found that these added features adequately protected the debtor's interest.

Whether all of these features are necessary in order to satisfy due process concerns is unclear. One year after Mitchell, the Supreme Court again addressed the issue, striking down a Georgia garnishment statute that permitted the garnishment of the corporate defendant's bank accounts on the basis of the plaintiff's conclusory affidavits and the posting of a bond equal to double the amount due.[13] The court clerk issued the writ and no early hearing was provided, although the defendant could repossess its property upon posting a counter-bond. The Supreme Court's resolution of this case reenforces the significance of the procedural safeguards suggested in Mitchell.

More recently, in Connecticut v. Doehr,[14] the Supreme Court used a balancing test, as it often does in due process cases, to strike down the plaintiff's use of Connecticut's prejudgment attachment statute against the defendant's real estate to secure a potential judgment in an assault and battery case. The Connecticut statute only required a plaintiff to file an affidavit under oath that "there is probable cause to sustain the validity of the plaintiff's claims." The Supreme Court concluded that the statute posed "too great a risk of erroneous deprivation" of the defendant's property right since it permitted an attachment on little more than the plaintiff's belief that the defendant was liable and the ability to prepare a "facially valid complaint." Mitchell was distinguished because the plaintiff in that case had a vendor's lien on the attached property to protect, so that the risk of error was minimal since "the likelihood of recovery involved uncomplicated matters that lent themselves to documentary proof," and the plaintiff was required to post a bond.[15] Finally, the Court noted that the plaintiff had no interest in Doehr's real estate and was seeking only to ensure the availability of assets to satisfy the judgment if he prevailed in the action. The Court found that interest to be insubstantial since there was no allegation that the defendant was about to transfer or encumber the real estate during the action's pendency.[16]

An important question that remains somewhat in doubt due to this line of cases is whether prejudgment attachment for purposes of asserting quasi in rem jurisdiction can survive constitutional scrutiny.[17] As is discussed elsewhere, a necessary prerequisite to the assertion of quasi in rem jurisdiction is that the defendant's property must be attached at the outset of the litigation, before any hearing.[18] In Fuentes v. Shevin, itself, the Supreme Court noted that under some exigent circumstances notice

---

13. North Georgia Finishing, Inc. v. DiChem, Inc., 419 U.S. 601, 95 S.Ct. 719, 42 L.Ed.2d 751 (1975).

14. 501 U.S. 1, 111 S.Ct. 2105, 115 L.Ed.2d 1 (1991).

15. 501 U.S. at 15, 111 S.Ct. at 2115.

16. 501 U.S. at 16, 111 S.Ct. at 2115.

17. See Note, Quasi in Rem Jurisdiction and Due Process Requirements, 82 Yale L.J. 1023 (1973).

18. See § 3.16, above.

and a hearing prior to attachment were not required and, in this connection, it cited approvingly an earlier Supreme Court decision[19] that "involved attachment necessary to secure jurisdiction in state court— clearly a most basic and important public interest."[20] Whether attachment for jurisdiction purposes must meet the Mitchell criteria or should be considered an exception from that standard remains unclear. The issue was squarely before the Supreme Court in Shaffer v. Heitner,[21] but the Court failed to rule on the point, finding instead that the assertion of jurisdiction was unconstitutional because the defendant did not have the requisite minimum contacts with the forum state.

As is true with all due process rights, the defendant may waive the right to notice and a hearing prior to attachment. In D.H. Overmyer Co. v. Frick Company,[22] the Supreme Court held that a cognovit clause authorizing a creditor to use a confession of judgment provision upon default and enter a judgment against the debtor without notice was not per se violative of due process. The Court found significant the facts that the waiver was knowing and voluntary, that it was the result of negotiation between parties of equal bargaining power, that it was given for consideration from the creditor, and that the Ohio procedure authorized vacation of a confessed judgment upon the showing of a valid defense. In a companion case,[23] however, the Court indicated that it would look with disfavor on the enforcement of cognovit clauses, especially when the debtor is a person of limited income. Thus, although the circumstances under which courts will invalidate procedures that do not provide the defendant with prior notice and the opportunity to be heard must be evaluated on a case by case basis, the Mitchell and Overmyer cases lay to rest the notion that those procedures automatically violate due process.

2.   Service of Process Requirements and Limits

§ 3.22   The Etiquette and Sufficiency of Service of Process

The formalities of service of process may vary from state to state and must be closely followed.[1] The custom in most states is that process must include both a copy of the summons and the complaint,[2] although

---

19. Ownbey v. Morgan, 256 U.S. 94, 41 S.Ct. 433, 65 L.Ed. 837 (1921).

20. 407 U.S. at 91 n. 23, 92 S.Ct. at 1999 n. 23.

21. 433 U.S. 186, 97 S.Ct. 2569, 53 L.Ed.2d 683 (1977). This case is discussed in § 3.14, above.

22. 405 U.S. 174, 92 S.Ct. 775, 31 L.Ed.2d 124 (1972).

23. Swarb v. Lennox, 405 U.S. 191, 92 S.Ct. 767, 31 L.Ed.2d 138 (1972). See generally Countryman, The Bill of Rights and the Bill Collector, 15 Ariz.L.Rev. 521, 557 (1973).

§ 3.22

1. See, e.g., Chaney v. Reddin, 201 Okl. 264, 205 P.2d 310 (1949) (leaving a single copy of the summons and complaint for husband and wife, codefendants, held insufficient service when statute required copy to be left with each defendant). See also the discussion in § 3.20 at note 14, above.

2. In the case of quasi in rem jurisdiction, local law determines the methodology of service. In California, for example, the issuance of a writ of attachment cannot precede the issuance of the summons. See Rowe v. Stoddard, 15 Cal.App.2d 440, 59 P.2d 423 (1936).

personal service of a summons without a complaint has been found constitutionally adequate.[3] In the federal courts the Federal Rules dictate that the summons and complaint must be served together;[4] service of the summons without the complaint is not effective service.[5]

In many state courts, process is served by the sheriff or a deputy; some states permit the use of private process-servers as long as they have attained a certain age and are not a party to the action.[6] In the federal courts, except in certain special actions, any person not a party and not less than 18 years of age may serve process.[7]

A federal court may dismiss a plaintiff's action against each defendant that is not served within 120 days.[8] Completion of service typically is shown by the server's timely return of the completed and endorsed proof of service form. The sheriff's statement once was treated as conclusive proof of service and this practice was upheld against a Fourteenth Amendment challenge.[9] However, modern courts hold that the return of service is not conclusive; it is merely strong evidence of the facts stated therein and may be controverted upon a showing that it is inaccurate.[10]

The summons generally is a one page form, identifying the parties and plaintiff's attorney.[11] It also will contain a statement informing the defendant that he or she must file with the clerk of the court a written pleading in response to the complaint within a specified time after receipt of service, and that failure to so respond will result in a default judgment for damages or the other relief demanded in the complaint.[12] The form for proof of service, typically printed on the reverse side of the summons, calls for the name and address of the defendants, the date of service, the fees and charges for service, and the names of the process server and the court clerk. In federal court, if service is not waived, Rule 4(*l*) simply requires the person effecting service to make "proof thereof."

A challenge to the sufficiency of process refers to an attack based on a defect in the form of the process—that is, the content and completion of the summons. A summons that is defective on its face[13] because of a

---

3. Owens v. I.F.P. Corporation, 374 F.Supp. 1032 (W.D.Ky.1974), affirmed without opinion 419 U.S. 807, 95 S.Ct. 23, 42 L.Ed.2d 36 (1974).

4. Fed.Civ.Proc.Rule 4(c)(1).

5. Phillips v. Murchison, 194 F.Supp. 620 (S.D.N.Y.1961).

6. See, e.g., N.Y.—McKinney's CPLR 2103(a); West's Ann.Cal.Code Civ.Proc. § 414.10.

7. Fed.Civ.Proc.Rule 4(c)(2). A court has the discretion to refuse a plaintiff's request for service on the defendant by a United States marshal, but the court must appoint a marshal, deputy, or some other person to serve the defendant when the plaintiff may proceed in forma pauperis or as a seaman. See 28 U.S.C.A. §§ 1915–16.

8. Fed.Civ.Proc.Rule 4(m). This time limit does not apply to service in a foreign country or if the plaintiff shows good cause.

9. Miedreich v. Lauenstein, 232 U.S. 236, 34 S.Ct. 309, 58 L.Ed. 584 (1914).

10. See Gottlieb v. Sandia Am. Corp., 452 F.2d 510 (3d Cir.1971), cert. denied 404 U.S. 938; Taft v. Donellan Jerome, Inc., 407 F.2d 807 (7th Cir.1969).

11. See 4A C. Wright & A. Miller, Civil 2d § 1087.

12. See, e.g., Peterson v. W. Davis & Sons, 216 Minn. 60, 11 N.W.2d 800 (1943).

13. E.g., Harris v. Louisiana State Supreme Court, 334 F.Supp. 1289 (E.D.La. 1971); Tharp v. Tharp, 228 Minn. 23, 36 N.W.2d 1 (1949).

misnomer,[14] for example, or because it is not properly completed[15] will be invalidated by a court.

There are occasions, however, when the plaintiff does not know the defendant's name or whereabouts as, for example, in the context of a "hit and run" automobile accident. Many states have enacted "fictitious name" statutes enabling the plaintiff to file the complaint merely describing the defendant and to amend the complaint after he identifies and locates the defendant.[16] This procedure permits the defendant to be considered a party to the action from its commencement so that the statute of limitations is tolled as of the date of the filing of the original "John Doe" pleading.[17]

Provided the statute of limitations has not run, the court may permit the plaintiff to amend the process to correct a minor error such as a misnomer[18] or a non-prejudicial defect in the designation of the parties.[19] But the court well may not permit the plaintiff to amend a fundamental defect in the process, such as a failure to include the defendant's name when known.[20] If the court does not permit amendment, the plaintiff's action will be dismissed without prejudice for insufficient process. The plaintiff, of course, may institute another proceeding but there is always the risk that the statute of limitations has run in the interim.

The distinction between insufficient process and insufficient service of process is important to keep in mind. Insufficient process, which usually involves a summons with defective content or that is improperly completed, results in the invalidation of the process and dismissal without prejudice.[21] But if the process is insufficient because it is not served properly on the defendant, the court lacks jurisdiction over the

---

14. See Schiavone v. Fortune, 477 U.S. 21, 106 S.Ct. 2379, 91 L.Ed.2d 18 (1986) (notice found insufficient when caption read "Fortune" rather than "Time, Inc." even though Time's agent received the complaint and certainly knew that Time published Fortune magazine).

15. Pinkham v. Jennings, 123 Me. 343, 122 A. 873 (1923) (writ not signed by clerk of court); Rockefeller v. Hein, 176 Misc. 659, 28 N.Y.S.2d 266 (1941) (defendant's name omitted).

16. E.g., Mass.Gen.Laws Ann. c. 223, § 19.

17. Austin v. Massachusetts Bonding & Ins. Co., 56 Cal.2d 596, 15 Cal.Rptr. 817, 364 P.2d 681 (1961).

18. Tharp v. Tharp, 228 Minn. 23, 36 N.W.2d 1 (1949). Federal Rule 4(a) permits an amendment of proof of service and can be used to alleviate technical errors in the form of the summons, unless material prejudice would result to the rights of the per-

son served. See 4A C. Wright & A. Miller, Civil 2d §§ 1088, 1131–32.

19. Roe v. Borup, 500 F.Supp. 127 (E.D.Wis.1980); Vega Matta v. Alvarez, 440 F.Supp. 246 (D.Puerto Rico 1977), affirmed without opinion 577 F.2d 722 (1st Cir. 1978).

20. Rockefeller v. Hein, 176 Misc. 659, 28 N.Y.S.2d 266 (1941). See also Summerlott v. Goodyear Tire & Rubber Co., 253 Iowa 121, 111 N.W.2d 251 (1961) (service that notified defendant to appear at incorrect courthouse held fatally defective); Pinkham v. Jennings, 123 Me. 343, 122 A. 873 (1923) (failure to obtain clerk's signature); M. Fisher, Sons & Co. v. Crowley, 57 W.Va. 312, 50 S.E. 422 (1905) (writ returnable at time unauthorized by law is void and cannot be amended).

21. See Higgins v. Hampshire Prods., Inc., 319 Mich. 674, 30 N.W.2d 390 (1948) (trial court erred in dismissing suit but was correct in quashing service; summons may be reserved).

defendant.[22] The action will be dismissed for insufficiency of service of process and, if the statute of limitations has run, the action or any subsequent action, will be dismissed with prejudice.[23] Indeed, since improper service creates a jurisdictional defect, it can result in the setting aside of a judgment entered in the defendant's absence.[24]

That was the case in Maryland State Firemen's Association v. Chaves:[25] the court set aside a default judgment because of improper service even though the defendant had actual notice of the lawsuit. The plaintiff had sent the summons and complaint by first-class mail to the defendant, and counsel for both parties had spoken by telephone on three separate occasions. After that, however, nothing more was heard from the defendant. Because the plaintiff never had formally served the defendant, and the defendant never had formally waived service, the court lacked jurisdiction and refused to enter judgment against the defendant.

A defect in either the sufficiency of the process or its service may be challenged by a motion to quash or set aside service[26] or by a plea in abatement, as, for example, when the defendant alleges that he was tricked into the forum as a ground to abate the plaintiff's action.[27] In some states[28] and in the federal courts,[29] a motion to dismiss the proceeding is proper to challenge either the sufficiency of process or the sufficiency of service of process.

§ 3.23   Impermissible Uses of Service of Process

Jurisdiction cannot rest on service procured by force or fraud. When, for example, the plaintiff tricks the defendant into entering the forum state so that service may be made, any judgment entered for the plaintiff may be treated as null and void and attacked collaterally.[1] Similarly, an attachment or garnishment obtained by enticing the defendant to send

22. See, e.g., Bell v. Hosse, 31 F.R.D. 181 (M.D.Tenn.1962).

23. Bond v. Golden, 273 F.2d 265 (10th Cir.1959).

24. Chaney v. Reddin, 201 Okl. 264, 205 P.2d 310 (1949). Cf. State ex rel. Rakowsky v. Bates, 286 S.W. 420 (Mo.App. 1926) (writ of prohibition issued to bar entry of default judgment when process failed to state correct court at which defendant was to appear).

The defendant typically must raise the defective service within a specified period after judgment is entered or it will be waived. See Myers v. Mooney Aircraft, Inc., 429 Pa. 177, 240 A.2d 505 (1967). For a discussion of relief from judgment, see § 12.6, below.

25. 166 F.R.D. 353 (D.Md.1996).

26. E.g., Grabner v. Willys Motors, Inc., 282 F.2d 644 (9th Cir.1960); Higgins v. Hampshire Prods., Inc., 319 Mich. 674, 30 N.W.2d 390 (1948); M. Fisher, Sons & Co. v. Crowley, 57 W.Va. 312, 50 S.E. 422 (1905).

27. Goss v. Hall, 125 Ind.App. 25, 117 N.E.2d 649 (1954).

28. Lendsay v. Cotton, 123 So.2d 745 (Fla.App.1960).

29. Fed.Civ.Proc.Rule 12(b)(4), (b)(5). See generally 5A C. Wright & A. Miller, Civil 2d § 1353.

§ 3.23

1. Wyman v. Newhouse, 93 F.2d 313 (2d Cir.1937), cert. denied 303 U.S. 664. See generally A. Ehrenzweig, Conflict of Laws § 32 (1962); Note, Jurisdiction by Trickery: Enticement for Service of Process, 7 Duke L.J. 52 (1957); Comment, Jurisdiction over Persons Brought into a State by Force or Fraud, 39 Yale L.J. 889 (1930).

property into the state will be discharged.[2] By analogy, it also has been held that the plaintiff cannot serve the defendant with process when the latter is invited into the forum to negotiate a settlement to the dispute underlying the lawsuit.[3] Both during travel to and from the forum for negotiations and during the stay in the forum, the defendant is immune from service of process and process served under these circumstances generally will be void.

The use of trickery to accomplish service of process is not always prohibited, however. A defendant who is in hiding within the forum can be "flushed out" by trickery.[4] Moreover, a court will consider to what extent the defendant has voluntarily placed himself in a position so that he can be served in the forum. In Nowell v. Nowell,[5] for example, the defendant had been advised that process could not be served in Connecticut on Sundays. On this advice he returned on a Sunday afternoon to his former home to retrieve some personal effects. Having accepted his wife's invitation to tea, the defendant lingered and was served by the sheriff after sundown, as was permissible under local law. Service was upheld on the ground that the defendant had not been induced fraudulently to enter the forum. In a similar vein, when a stranger to the action has persuaded the defendant to enter the jurisdiction for purposes independent of the plaintiff's action, service of process on the defendant has been upheld.[6] And when the nonresident defendant had arranged for an agent bank to sell its traveler's checks in the forum, and a debt running from the bank to the defendant created by the purchase of the travelers' checks was attached, the court found nothing deceitful in the conduct of the plaintiff; it therefore concluded that the defendant had not been "enticed or induced" to bring its property within the jurisdiction.[7]

The theoretical underpinnings of the force or fraud rule have been the subject of some dispute. Some courts have stated that no jurisdiction is obtained by the court when service is procured by trickery.[8] Others have expressed the view that jurisdiction exists, but the court should decline to exercise it.[9] These discrepancies occasionally produce different results. Following the view that the court has but must decline jurisdiction, the defendant may have the action dismissed. However, if the

2. Forbess v. George Morgan Pontiac Co., 135 So.2d 594 (La.App.1961). Delaney Co. v. Freedman Co., 93 N.J.L. 456, 108 A. 435 (1919); Sessoms Grocery Co. v. International Sugar Feed Co., 188 Ala. 232, 66 So. 479 (1914); Pakas v. Steel Ball Co., 34 Misc. 811, 68 N.Y.S. 397 (1901).

3. Western States Refining Co. v. Berry, 6 Utah 2d 336, 313 P.2d 480 (1957).

4. Gumperz v. Hofmann, 245 App.Div. 622, 283 N.Y.S. 823 (1935), affirmed 271 N.Y. 544, 2 N.E.2d 687 (1936) (process server misrepresents himself as notebearer).

5. 24 Conn.Sup. 314, 190 A.2d 233 (1963).

6. Ex parte Taylor, 29 R.I. 129, 69 A. 553 (1908).

7. Siro v. American Express Co., 99 Conn. 95, 121 A. 280 (1923). See generally Annot., 98 A.L.R.2d 551 (1964).

8. Wyman v. Newhouse, 93 F.2d 313 (2d Cir.1937), cert. denied 303 U.S. 664; Blandin v. Ostrander, 239 Fed. 700 (2d Cir.1917).

9. See, e.g., Commercial Mut. Acc. Co. v. Davis, 213 U.S. 245, 29 S.Ct. 445, 53 L.Ed. 782 (1909).

defendant fails to challenge the court's jurisdiction, any judgment entered against him is valid and not subject to collateral attack elsewhere.[10] But the opposite result flows from the view that the court lacks jurisdiction. The defendant need not protest the court's jurisdiction in the original proceeding; rather she may attack the resulting judgment collaterally in the original or in any other forum in which its enforcement is sought.[11]

The need of a plaintiff to resort to trickery in order to serve process on the defendant has been obviated in large part by the widespread enactment of long-arm statutes.[12] These statutes enable the plaintiff to obtain jurisdiction over the defendant without serving process in the forum state and thus they avoid the need to find some means to bring a recalcitrant defendant into the state for that purpose.

§ 3.24 Immunity From Service of Process

The doctrine of immunity from process shields a nonresident from service while entering, staying in, or leaving a jurisdiction to attend judicial or quasi-judicial proceedings.[1] Immunity is a privilege accorded by the court and is rooted in the necessities of judicial administration; it is not an inherent right of the defendant. Proceedings could be "embarrassed, and sometimes interrupted, if the suitor might be vexed with process" while attending court proceedings in furtherance of justice.[2] In addition to protecting the court's dignity,[3] immunity also encourages the voluntary attendance of necessary parties and witnesses.[4] "Courts of justice ought everywhere to be open, accessible, free from interruption, and to cast a perfect protection around every man who necessarily approaches them."[5] Thus, immunity will be granted to parties, witnesses, and attorneys as long as their visit to the forum is not motivated by unrelated personal business.[6] Further, immunity applies to attendance at a trial[7] or at related proceedings such as depositions[8] and appellate proceedings.[9]

10. Restatement of Judgments, § 15, comment b (1942).

11. Wyman v. Newhouse, 93 F.2d 313 (2d Cir.1937), cert. denied 303 U.S. 664.

12. See the discussion of long-arm statutes in §§ 3.12–3.13, above.

§ 3.24

1. Stewart v. Ramsay, 242 U.S. 128, 37 S.Ct. 44, 61 L.Ed. 192 (1916). See also Mertens v. McMahon, 334 Mo. 175, 66 S.W.2d 127 (1933). See generally 4 C. Wright & A. Miller, Civil 2d §§ 1076–81; Keeffe & Roscia, Immunity and Sentimentality, 32 Cornell L.Q. 471 (1947); Nole, Immunity of Non–Resident Participants in a Judicial Proceeding from Service of Process—A Proposal for Renovation, 26 Ind.L.J. 459 (1951).

2. Stewart v. Ramsay, 242 U.S. 128, 130, 37 S.Ct. 44, 45, 61 L.Ed. 192 (1916) (Pitney, J.).

3. Parker v. Marco, 136 N.Y. 585, 32 N.E. 989 (1893).

4. Lamb v. Schmitt, 285 U.S. 222, 52 S.Ct. 317, 76 L.Ed. 720 (1932); Page Co. v. MacDonald, 261 U.S. 446, 43 S.Ct. 416, 67 L.Ed. 737 (1923); Stratton v. Hughes, 211 Fed. 557 (D.N.J.1914).

5. Stewart v. Ramsay, 242 U.S. 128, 129, 37 S.Ct. 44, 45, 61 L.Ed. 192 (1916).

6. Hammons v. Superior Court, 63 Cal. App. 700, 219 P. 1037 (1923).

7. Ibid.

8. Russell v. Landau, 127 Cal.App.2d 682, 274 P.2d 681 (1954).

9. Chase Nat. Bank v. Turner, 269 N.Y. 397, 199 N.E. 636 (1936).

In recent years the immunity doctrine has been applied more restrictively, particularly when service is made for a proceeding related to the one in which the nonresident is appearing. One rationale advanced for limiting immunity in these circumstances is to prevent the nonresident from selecting from the subject matter of the litigation only those portions in which he wishes to appear, thereby resulting in a hardship to the opposing party. For example, in the California case of Velkov v. Superior Court,[10] the plaintiff had instigated disciplinary proceedings before the State Bar Association against the defendants, her attorneys in a matrimonial action, because of a purportedly illegal assignment of royalties in oil properties that had been paid the attorneys as fees for their legal services. The attorneys had brought an action for a declaratory judgment to determine the rights of the parties under the assignment. Toward this end, they served process on the plaintiff while she was testifying at the State Bar proceedings. The court sustained the service on the grounds that the plaintiff was the initiating party in the disciplinary proceedings and the subject matter of the bar proceeding and the declaratory judgment action was the same. In a similar vein, immunity has been denied not only to the plaintiff,[11] but also to the defendant[12] and even to the plaintiff's attorney[13] whenever process is served in an action connected to the subject matter of the proceeding in which the party invokes the privilege.

To the extent that the early use of immunity served to prevent the obstruction of a trial that might ensue when a suitor or witness was physically wrested from the courtroom, it no longer may be necessary.[14] As early as 1888, one court, conceding the continued utility of extending immunity to witnesses, argued that nonresident suitors no longer need be exempt.[15]

> We think it would rarely happen that the attention of a non-resident plaintiff or defendant would be so distracted by the mere service of a summons from the immediate business at hand * * * that the interests of justice would suffer in consequence * * *.[16]

But it is in criminal proceedings that the need for immunity has been attacked most sharply. Protection of the defendant in a criminal action from being served in civil proceedings does not promote the administration of justice by encouraging the voluntary attendance of the

10.   40 Cal.2d 289, 253 P.2d 25 (1953).

11.   Eberlin v. Pennsylvania R.R. Co., 402 Pa. 520, 167 A.2d 155 (1961).

12.   St. John v. Superior Court, 178 Cal.App.2d 794, 3 Cal.Rptr. 535 (1960) (defendant appearing at an administrative license revocation hearing concerning particular shares of stock may be served at the hearing by plaintiff in an action to rescind the sale of the same shares). Cf. Grundy v. Refior, 312 Mich. 428, 20 N.W.2d 261 (1945) (plaintiff's suit against defendant for services rendered as accountant not sufficiently related with defendant's suit against

corporation to cancel stock of corporation so as to deny immunity to plaintiff from defendant's attempted service).

13.   Lamb v. Schmitt, 285 U.S. 222, 52 S.Ct. 317, 76 L.Ed. 720 (1932).

14.   Mertens v. McMahon, 334 Mo. 175, 66 S.W.2d 127 (1933).

15.   Baldwin v. Emerson, 16 R.I. 304, 15 A. 83 (1888).

16.   16 R.I. at 307, 308, 15 A. at 84, 85 (Matteson, J.).

defendant at trial since typically the defendant has been incarcerated in the state against his will to answer for the crime.[17] Thus, immunity may be denied when a nonresident criminal defendant has been arrested in the forum where the crime allegedly was committed and is served with civil process while in custody or after his discharge,[18] or when he has been extradited and is in custody.[19] On the other hand, courts have distinguished the situation in which the criminal defendant voluntarily returns to the forum to offer bail or to stand trial; the policy is to encourage this volitional conduct by granting immunity from civil process.[20]

G. CHALLENGES TO JURISDICTION

§ 3.25 Challenging Jurisdiction—An Introduction

Because issues of personal jurisdiction are tied to the due process rights of the defendant, the defendant can waive any objections to the court's power over him.[1] Thus, it is necessary to determine when the defendant has participated in the proceedings to such a degree that it would be appropriate to hold that the defendant impliedly has waived any objections and consents to jurisdiction. The method commonly used is to establish certain rules governing how the defendant can challenge jurisdiction and to find that the failure to comply with the specific procedures established constitutes consent. Although the precise methods for challenging jurisdiction vary from state to state, two basic approaches are taken: the utilization of the special appearance to challenge jurisdiction and the use of a pretrial motion to dismiss for lack of jurisdiction.

Before turning to an exploration of the methods of challenging jurisdiction, it is important to note that once the defendant raises a jurisdictional objection, the plaintiff has the burden to prove that jurisdiction is proper.[2] The defendant's challenge and the plaintiff's consequent burden of proof may be quite straightforward and raise a simple question of fact. For example, the defendant may assert that he never received a copy of the complaint and the plaintiff then must establish

17. Ryan v. Ebecke, 102 Conn. 12, 128 A. 14 (1925).

18. State ex rel. Sivnksty v. Duffield, 137 W.Va. 112, 71 S.E.2d 113 (1952); State ex rel. Alexander–Coplin & Co. v. Superior Court for King County, 186 Wash. 354, 57 P.2d 1262 (1936); Husby v. Emmons, 148 Wash. 333, 268 P. 886 (1928).

19. Rutledge v. Krauss, 73 N.J.Law 397, 63 A. 988 (1906); Williams v. Bacon, 10 Wend. 636 (N.Y.1834). But see Weale v. Clinton Circuit Judge, 158 Mich. 563, 123 N.W. 31 (1909) (after criminal proceedings are dismissed, defendant is immune from service in civil action).

20. Church v. Church, 270 Fed. 361 (D.C.Cir.1921); Benesch v. Foss, 31 F.2d 118 (D.Mass.1929); In re Hall, 296 Fed. 780 (S.D.N.Y.1924). But see Netograph Mfg. Co. v. Scrugham, 197 N.Y. 377, 90 N.E. 962 (1910) (service upheld in civil suit after acquittal in criminal proceeding when defendant voluntarily appeared).

§ 3.25

1. See § 3.5, above.

2. Tice v. Wilmington Chem. Corp., 259 Iowa 27, 141 N.W.2d 616 (1966), opinion supplemented 259 Iowa 27, 143 N.W.2d 86 (1966). See also Waukesha Bldg. Corp. v. Jameson, 246 F.Supp. 183 (W.D.Ark.1965).

that the complaint indeed was served upon the defendant. But the allocation of the burden of proof can be a much more complex matter, resulting in the shifting of the burden back and forth between the parties.[3]

§ 3.26   Methods of Challenging Jurisdiction

A common method in state courts of challenging the court's personal jurisdiction is by making a "special appearance."[1] A defendant who wishes to object to personal jurisdiction must enter a special appearance and typically is not permitted to introduce any other defenses prior to or simultaneously with raising the objection.[2] If he does so, he will be deemed to have made a "general appearance" and have waived all jurisdiction objections.[3]

Under this approach, when the defendant answers the plaintiff's complaint,[4] or requests a more definite statement of the plaintiff's claim,[5] or a continuance,[6] or challenges the plaintiff's standing to sue,[7] without challenging jurisdiction, the defendant will be held to have made a general appearance. The only exception to this obligation to limit defendant's response solely to personal jurisdiction objections is when defendant also wants to challenge the court's subject-matter jurisdiction.[8] The defendant may object to the court's subject-matter jurisdiction without submitting to the tribunal's in personam jurisdiction.[9] Further, it has been held that a special appearance to contest personal jurisdiction

3. See, e.g., Buckeye Boiler Co. v. Superior Court of Los Angeles County, 71 Cal.2d 893, 80 Cal.Rptr. 113, 458 P.2d 57 (1969); Gray v. American Radiator & Standard Sanitary Corp., 22 Ill.2d 432, 176 N.E.2d 761 (1961). The extent to which the shifting of the burden of proof to the defendant to show lack of foreseeability is permissible since World–Wide Volkswagen Corp. v. Woodson, 444 U.S. 286, 100 S.Ct. 559, 62 L.Ed.2d 490 (1980), is unclear.

§ 3.26

1. Harkness v. Hyde, 98 U.S. (8 Otto) 476, 25 L.Ed. 237 (1879). See generally Thode, In Personam Jurisdiction and Appearance to Challenge Jurisdiction, 42 Texas L.Rev. 279 (1964); Developments in the Law—State–Court Jurisdiction, 73 Harv. L.Rev. 909, 991 (1960).

2. See State ex rel. Dial Press, Inc. v. Sisemore, 263 Or. 460, 502 P.2d 1365 (1972).

3. A general appearance cannot be withdrawn without the permission of the court. Chapman v. Chapman, 284 App.Div. 504, 132 N.Y.S.2d 707 (1954), appeal denied 284 App.Div. 857, 134 N.Y.S.2d 173 (1954). This is true even though the plaintiff amends the complaint to add new causes of action. Everitt v. Everitt, 4 N.Y.2d 13, 171

N.Y.S.2d 836, 148 N.E.2d 891 (1958). But see Johnston v. Federal Land Bank of Omaha, 226 Iowa 496, 284 N.W. 393 (1939). However, the defendant's general appearance is limited to the original action; additional claimants, such as intervenors, cannot file new claims against the defendant simply because the defendant has waived personal jurisdiction objections to the original plaintiff's claims. Ex parte Indiana Transp. Co., 244 U.S. 456, 37 S.Ct. 717, 61 L.Ed. 1253 (1917).

4. Goodwine v. Superior Court of Los Angeles, 63 Cal.2d 481, 47 Cal.Rptr. 201, 407 P.2d 1 (1965).

5. Long v. Newhouse, 57 Ohio St. 348, 49 N.E. 79 (1897).

6. Pfeiffer v. Ash, 92 Cal.App.2d 102, 206 P.2d 438 (1949).

7. Davis v. Davis, 305 U.S. 32, 59 S.Ct. 3, 83 L.Ed. 26 (1938).

8. Subject-matter jurisdiction is discussed in Chapter 2, above.

9. Goodwine v. Superior Court of Los Angeles, 63 Cal.2d 481, 47 Cal.Rptr. 201, 407 P.2d 1 (1965). But see Smith v. Hoover, 39 Ohio St. 249 (1883); Handy v. Insurance Co., 37 Ohio St. 366 (1881).

combined with a petition to remove the case from state to federal court does not constitute a general appearance.[10]

A state need not permit a defendant to make a special appearance.[11] According to a very old Supreme Court decision, a state rule making any appearance a consent to jurisdiction does not violate due process.[12] The defendant is provided a choice—the defendant need not appear at all, and, if judgment is entered on the basis of invalid service or improper jurisdiction, jurisdiction may be attacked collaterally in any action brought to enforce the defective judgment.[13]

As a practical matter, since Texas[14] and Mississippi[15] now permit special appearances, the right to make some form of an appearance to contest the court's in personam jurisdiction exists in all states. The particular rules concerning what the defendant can or must do to preserve his objection if the trial court overrules it differ, however, from state to state. In some states, once the defendant's objection to the court's jurisdiction is rejected, he must choose between allowing a default judgment to be entered, which he then can appeal in the hope of obtaining a reversal on the jurisdictional ruling, or contesting the merits, which thereby waives the jurisdictional objection.[16] A number of states ease the defendant's dilemma by permitting an immediate review of the jurisdictional ruling by interlocutory appeal or by extraordinary writ.[17] If an opportunity for immediate appellate review is provided, and the defendant does not utilize that procedure, the opportunity to reassert the jurisdictional objection once a judgment on the merits has been rendered will be waived. The jurisdictional ruling also will be deemed final and binding for purposes of other proceedings.[18] Further, the jurisdictional objection may be waived whenever the defendant consents to a review of the judgment without reasserting the jurisdictional point.[19]

In most states, and in the federal courts, the defendant may defend on the merits following an unsuccessful challenge to the court's jurisdiction without waiving any jurisdiction objection. Following an adverse judgment on the merits, the defendant may challenge the jurisdiction

---

10. Lambert Run Coal Co. v. Baltimore & O.R. Co., 258 U.S. 377, 42 S.Ct. 349, 66 L.Ed. 671 (1922); Cain v. Commercial Pub. Co., 232 U.S. 124, 34 S.Ct. 284, 58 L.Ed. 534 (1914); Commercial Mut. Acc. Co. v. Davis, 213 U.S. 245, 29 S.Ct. 445, 53 L.Ed. 782 (1909).

11. Western Life Indem. Co. v. Rupp, 235 U.S. 261, 35 S.Ct. 37, 59 L.Ed. 220 (1914).

12. York v. Texas, 137 U.S. 15, 11 S.Ct. 9, 34 L.Ed. 604 (1890).

13. Thompson v. Whitman, 85 U.S. (18 Wall.) 457, 21 L.Ed. 897 (1874); Davis v. St. Paul Mercury Indem. Co., 294 F.2d 641 (4th Cir.1961).

14. Vernon's Ann.Tex.C.C.P. art. 120a.

15. Mladinich v. Kohn, 250 Miss. 138, 164 So.2d 785 (1964).

16. Corbett v. Physicians' Cas. Ass'n of America, 135 Wis. 505, 115 N.W. 365 (1908). The Wisconsin rule was changed in 1976 and now the federal approach is followed. Wis.Stat.Ann. 802.06.

17. See, e.g., West's Ann.Cal.Code Civ. Proc. § 418.10(c).

18. Baldwin v. Iowa State Traveling Men's Ass'n, 283 U.S. 522, 51 S.Ct. 517, 75 L.Ed. 1244 (1931); Wayside Transp. Co. v. Marcell's Motor Express, Inc., 284 F.2d 868 (1st Cir.1960).

19. E.g., Western Life Indem. Co. of Illinois v. Rupp, 235 U.S. 261, 35 S.Ct. 37, 59 L.Ed. 220 (1914).

ruling on appeal, which, if successful, will result in a reversal of the judgment and a dismissal of the action.[20]

The distinction between general and special appearances has been abolished in the federal courts and in those states that have adopted the federal rules.[21] Instead of requiring the defendant to make a special appearance to challenge jurisdiction, the defendant may raise the objection either in a pretrial motion to dismiss or in the answer.[22] The defendant's options are circumscribed primarily by timing constraints. Thus, the defendant may combine his objection with defenses on the merits in the responsive pleading rather than raise it by pre-answer motion.[23] If the jurisdictional objection is made in timely fashion, it will be preserved and may be advanced on appeal by the defendant following an adverse judgment.[24] Only the defendant's failure to include the jurisdiction objection in a pretrial motion when other defenses are raised by motions to dismiss[25] or to include it in the answer when no pretrial motions have been made[26] will result in the total waiver of the objection.

§ 3.27   Limited Appearances in Quasi in Rem Proceedings

Just as the defendant may seek to enter a special appearance to contest the in personam jurisdiction of a court without consenting to the tribunal's general jurisdiction,[1] so too the defendant may try to appear to contest the validity of an attachment or garnishment in a quasi in rem action without submitting to the full in personam jurisdiction of the court. A few state courts have held that any appearance converts the action to one in personam.[2] Others have held that once the defendant proceeds to defend the case on the merits, he opens himself up to an in personam judgment.[3] Those states that allow the defendant to try the case on the merits yet restrict liability to the value of the property recognize what is called the "limited appearance."[4] Even in those states

---

20. Toledo Rys. & Light Co. v. Hill, 244 U.S. 49, 37 S.Ct. 591, 61 L.Ed. 982 (1917); Harkness v. Hyde, 98 U.S. (8 Otto) 476, 25 L.Ed. 237 (1878).

21. See 5A C. Wright & A. Miller, Civil 2d § 1344.

22. See Fed.Civ.Proc.Rule 12(b).

23. "No defense or objection is waived by being joined with one or more other defenses or objections in a responsive pleading or motion." Fed.Civ.Proc.Rule 12(b); Mertens v. McMahon, 334 Mo. 175, 66 S.W.2d 127 (1933).

24. Harkness v. Hyde, 98 U.S. (8 Otto) 476, 25 L.Ed. 237 (1878).

25. Fed.Civ.Proc.Rule 12(g). See generally 5A C. Wright & A. Miller, Civil 2d §§ 1384–89.

26. Fed.Civ.Proc.Rule 12(h)(1). See generally 5A C. Wright & A. Miller, Civil 2d § 1391.

§ 3.27

1. See §§ 3.25–3.26, above.

2. See, e.g., Johnson v. Holt's Adm'r, 235 Ky. 518, 31 S.W.2d 895 (1930) (motion to contest attachment confers personal jurisdiction).

3. See, e.g., Sands v. Lefcourt Realty Corp., 35 Del.Ch. 340, 117 A.2d 365 (1955); State ex rel. Methodist Old People's Home v. Crawford, 159 Or. 377, 80 P.2d 873 (1938) (an answer to plaintiff's complaint confers personal jurisdiction).

4. Miller Bros. Co. v. State, 201 Md. 535, 95 A.2d 286 (1953), reversed on other grounds 347 U.S. 340, 74 S.Ct. 535, 98 L.Ed. 744 (1954); Cheshire Nat. Bank v. Jaynes, 224 Mass. 14, 112 N.E. 500 (1916).

that do recognize the limited appearance, however, the defendant may have to take affirmative steps to secure this right by moving to limit the scope of the hearing to the value of the property attached.[5]

The propriety of the limited appearance has been much debated and there is a sharp split of authority as to its desirability.[6] Proponents of the limited appearance argue that it is unfair to force the defendant to choose between forfeiting the attached property by default or appearing to protect his interest in the property, thereby risking the imposition of a judgment in excess of the property value. Since jurisdiction is based on the court's custody of the property, the forum may not be a convenient one nor bear any relationship to the events at issue. It even has been suggested that a state's refusal to recognize the limited appearance violates a defendant's due process rights by depriving the defendant of property without the opportunity to appear.[7]

Opponents argue that rejection of the limited appearance would mean that a case would be fully decided on the merits in one proceeding, thus avoiding a multiplicity of suits and relitigation of the same issues in violation of res judicata principles and the goal of judicial economy. It also avoids the risk of different adjudications by different courts of the underlying personal rights involved in a quasi in rem action; conflicting judgments could result when a defendant owns and the plaintiff seeks to attach property in more than one forum. Finally, a defendant who can appear in court to protect his property demonstrates a capacity to litigate the entire claim in the forum; no greater inconvenience would result by having the defendant submit to full in personam jurisdiction.

Federal Rule 4(n), which authorizes quasi in rem actions in federal court pursuant to the law of the state in which the district court is located, although only as a last resort, is silent as to whether limited appearances are available.[8] Federal judges have reached inconsistent

---

5. Salmon Falls Mfg. Co. v. Midland Tire & Rubber Co., 285 Fed. 214, 217 (6th Cir.1922) (if defendant had sought relief on the merits beyond the value of the property, he would have been deemed to have submitted to the court's personal jurisdiction).

6. Commentators favoring the limited appearance are: B. Currie, Attachment & Garnishment in the Federal Courts, 59 Mich.L.Rev. 337 (1961); Taintor, Foreign Judgment In–Rem; Full Faith and Credit v. Res Judicata In Personam, 8 U.Pitt.L.Rev. 232 (1942). Commentators opposing the limited appearance are: Blume, Actions Quasi-in-Rem Under Section 1655, Title 28 U.S.C., 50 Mich.L.Rev. 1 (1951); Note, Effect of a General Appearance to the In Rem Cause in a Quasi-in-Rem Action, 25 Iowa L.Rev. 329 (1940).

7. Developments in the Law—State Court Jurisdiction, 73 Harv.L.Rev. 909, 954 (1960).

8. Fed.Civ.Proc.Rule 13(a) provides, however, that the defendant need not assert a counterclaim that is otherwise compulsory if the action is brought by attachment. See generally 4A C. Wright & A. Miller, Civil 2d § 1123.

In the case of admiralty and maritime actions, Supplemental Rule E(8) states that an appearance "may be expressly restricted to the defense of such claim, and in that event shall not constitute an appearance for the purposes of any other claim with respect to which such process is not available or has not been served." The Advisory Committee Note to the rule says that in cases not covered by the rule, the question of limited appearances is to be left to a case-by-case development.

results, some permitting limited appearances,[9] but others denying them.[10] Courts[11] and commentators[12] also differ as to whether the federal courts should apply the forum state's rule in regard to limited appearances or feel free to fabricate a federal rule. The availability of a limited appearance may be a matter of procedure and therefore a proper subject for a single uniform federal practice. Yet, there is no federal policy on the point and the device could be said to be linked to a state's substantive policies regarding res judicata and amenability to suit, so that the federal courts should apply state rules.

The failure to allow a limited appearance in some jurisdictions has produced problems for those courts in determining whether the plaintiff should be allowed to amend the complaint seeking increased relief after the defendant has appeared.[13] This dilemma is caused by a recognition that the defendant may have appeared in order to free his property from attachment, weighing the objective against the potential liability stated in the complaint. Had the defendant understood the exact dimensions of the plaintiff's demands, however, he might have preferred to default and forfeit the property.

Because of these concerns, some courts have refused to allow the plaintiff to amend a complaint seeking in personam relief after the defendant appears in an action in rem on the ground that to permit an amendment that adds other causes of action will tend to deter general appearances.[14] Some courts allow the plaintiff to amend the original claim under these circumstances, but permit the defendant to challenge the court's jurisdiction to enter an in personam judgment.[15] Still other courts permit an amended pleading at least when quasi in rem attachment would be a permissible means to bring suit under the amended pleading. Thus, an amended pleading reiterating a cause of action for lost profits but adding an allegation for wrongful termination of an exclusive agency agreement and requesting additional damages was permitted after the defendant had filed an appearance and answer

---

9. See, e.g., McQuillen v. National Cash Register Co., 112 F.2d 877 (4th Cir. 1940), cert. denied 311 U.S. 695; Salmon Falls Mfg. Co. v. Midland Tire & Rubber Co., 285 Fed. 214 (6th Cir.1922); Grable v. Killits, 282 Fed. 185 (6th Cir.1922), cert. denied 260 U.S. 735.

10. See, e.g., Norris, Inc. v. M.H. Reed & Co., 278 Fed. 19 (5th Cir.1922); Anderson v. Benson, 117 F.Supp. 765 (D.Neb.1953), appeal dismissed 215 F.2d 752 (8th Cir. 1954); Campbell v. Murdock, 90 F.Supp. 297 (N.D.Ohio 1950); Bede Steam Shipping Co. v. New York Trust Co., 54 F.2d 658 (S.D.N.Y.1931).

11. Compare Dry Clime Lamp Corp. v. Edwards, 389 F.2d 590 (5th Cir.1968) (state law not relied on), with U.S. Industries, Inc. v. Gregg, 58 F.R.D. 469 (D.Del.1973) (state rule applied).

12. Compare B. Currie, Attachment & Garnishment in the Federal Courts, 59 Mich.L.Rev. 337 (1961) (argument for state law), with Carrington, The Modern Utility of Quasi–In–Rem Jurisdiction, 76 Harv. L.Rev. 303 (1962) (argument for federal law).

13. Frumer, Jurisdiction and Limited Appearance in New York: Dilemma of the Nonresident Defendant, 18 Ford.L.Rev. 73 (1949).

14. River Farms, Inc. v. Superior Court of San Bernadino County, 252 Cal. App.2d 604, 60 Cal.Rptr. 665 (1967); Alkalaj v. Alkalaj, 190 Misc. 326, 73 N.Y.S.2d 678 (1947).

15. Fidelity & Cas. Co. v. Bank of Plymouth, 213 Iowa 1058, 237 N.W. 234 (1931).

following attachment of his property.[16] The court failed to find, under the circumstances of the case, that the plaintiff had substituted a different cause of action.

Some commentators have proposed that when the plaintiff has chosen a reasonable forum, instead of permitting the defendant to enter a limited appearance, the court should protect the defendant against unforeseen risk by not permitting the plaintiff to amend the complaint to introduce a new cause of action.[17] The judgment in the action then would be given full binding effect.

It should be noted that many of these arguments as to the need for limited appearances and the problems of the relationship between the plaintiff's right to amend and the defendant's ability to decide whether to default or to enter a general appearance in a quasi in rem action are of decreasing importance today. The use of quasi in rem jurisdiction was significant when the courts' in personam jurisdictional power was limited by their territorial boundaries because it provided the only viable way to reach out-of-state and uncooperative defendants.[18] The expansion of long-arm jurisdiction has lessened the need to resort to quasi in rem jurisdiction, however. In the federal courts, the combination of Rule 4(k)'s expansion of federal jurisdiction[19] and Rule 4(n)'s requirement that quasi in rem proceedings be employed only as a last resort makes the question of limited appearances almost wholly academic. Also, as is discussed elsewhere,[20] the decision by the Supreme Court in Shaffer v. Heitner[21] requiring that all assertions of quasi in rem jurisdiction meet the same due process standards as in personam jurisdiction has reduced further the distinctions between these two forms of jurisdiction. Resort to quasi in rem jurisdiction has been restricted to many fewer cases and the satisfaction of the minimum contacts and fair play and substantial justice criteria in those cases means that the availability of limited appearances need not be considered the sole safeguard against unfairness to a defendant confronted by a lawsuit based on this form of jurisdiction.

§ 3.28 Protecting the Defendant Against Vexatious Litigation

The ease of instituting proceedings under the broad bases of jurisdiction that currently exist, in particular, under long-arm statutes, suggests that the defendant, from time to time, may need to be protected against unduly burdensome or vexatious litigation.[1] Accordingly, courts

---

16. Nicholas & Co. v. Societe Anonyme, 189 Misc. 863, 73 N.Y.S.2d 155 (1947), affirmed mem. 272 App.Div. 1002, 74 N.Y.S.2d 403 (1947), appeal denied 272 App.Div. 1047, 75 N.Y.S.2d 285 (1947).

17. E.g., Developments in the Law—State–Court Jurisdiction, 73 Harv.L.Rev. 909, 954 (1960).

18. See § 3.8, above.

19. See § 3.18, above.

20. See § 3.14, above.

21. 433 U.S. 186, 97 S.Ct. 2569, 53 L.Ed.2d 683 (1977).

§ 3.28

1. It should be kept in mind that venue requirements provide some shelter to defendants in both federal and state courts as they tend to ensure that the action is brought in a forum having some relation to

have made available to the defendant a variety of protective devices both in quasi in rem and in personam jurisdiction cases. For example, when the plaintiff has initiated proceedings in two forums, each court has discretion to stay the proceedings before it if it considers the other tribunal more appropriate to adjudicate the controversy.[2] In the event that quasi in rem proceedings are brought, the court's stay will preserve the attachment;[3] dismissal would have vacated the attachment.

The defendant also may seek to enjoin the plaintiff from instituting duplicative proceedings in another forum,[4] although this is not always an available or a satisfactory remedy. Even though a state court can enjoin its citizens from suing in the court of another state,[5] a state court may not enjoin an action under the Federal Employers' Liability Act brought in another state.[6] Federal courts also generally are prohibited from enjoining state proceedings.[7] More importantly, injunctions operate on parties, not the courts. Accordingly, the court in which an enjoined action is pending has the power to proceed despite the injunction.[8] Indeed, the original forum even may issue a counter-injunction to restrain the defendant from enforcing the injunction obtained in the second forum, thereby creating an unseemly squabble between the two courts.[9]

In instances in which the plaintiff only brings one suit but the plaintiff's choice of a forum is greatly inconvenient for the defendant, the court may protect the defendant by dismissing the action on the basis of forum non conveniens[10] or by transferring the action to a more convenient forum.[11] The rules circumscribing the court's power to use either of these two devices are discussed more fully elsewhere.[12]

the controversy or to the parties. Venue is discussed in §§ 2.15–2.16, above.

2. Fitch v. Whaples, 220 A.2d 170 (Me. 1966). Cf. Filtrol Corp. v. Kelleher, 467 F.2d 242 (9th Cir.1972), cert. denied 409 U.S. 1110 (motion to stay in order to try issue of patent infringement in California pending Connecticut trial determining validity of patent denied).

3. Fitch v. Whaples, 220 A.2d 170 (Me. 1966).

4. James v. Grand Trunk Western R.R. Co., 14 Ill.2d 356, 152 N.E.2d 858 (1958), cert. denied 358 U.S. 915, noted 43 Minn. L.Rev. 1249 (1959).

5. Pope v. Atlantic Coast Line R. Co., 345 U.S. 379, 73 S.Ct. 749, 97 L.Ed. 1094 (1953).

6. Ibid.

7. 28 U.S.C.A. § 2283.

8. Keck v. Keck, 8 Ill.App.3d 277, 290 N.E.2d 385 (1972), reversed on other grounds 56 Ill.2d 508, 309 N.E.2d 217 (1974).

9. E.g., James v. Grand Trunk Western R.R. Co., 14 Ill.2d 356, 152 N.E.2d 858 (1958), cert. denied 358 U.S. 915.

10. Plum v. Tampax, Inc., 402 Pa. 616, 168 A.2d 315 (1961), cert. denied 368 U.S. 826.

11. Jarvik v. Magic Mountain Corp., 290 F.Supp. 998 (S.D.N.Y.1968).

12. See § 2.17, above.

§§ 3.29–4.0 are reserved for supplementary material.

Chapter 4

ASCERTAINING THE APPLICABLE LAW

Analysis

A. FEDERAL COURTS

A. FEDERAL COURTS

§ 4.1 The Rules of Decision Act and Swift v. Tyson

Any analysis of the governing law in the federal courts must begin with Section 34 of the Judiciary Act of 1789,[1] also known as the Rules of Decision Act. That statute provides:

> [T]he laws of the several states, except where the constitution, treaties or statutes of the United States shall otherwise require or provide, shall be regarded as rules of decisions in trials at common law in the courts of the United States in cases where they apply.

Prior to 1842, the United States Supreme Court had failed to formulate a consistent interpretation of this provision.[2] Specifically,

---

§ 4.1

1. 1 Stat. 92 (1789). The Rules of Decision Act is now found in 28 U.S.C.A. § 1652. It has remained substantially unchanged since its adoption in 1789, except that the words "civil actions" have been substituted for "trials at common law."

2. Compare Brown v. Van Braam, 3 U.S. (3 Dall.) 344, 1 L.Ed. 629 (1797), with

Sim's Lessee v. Irvine, 3 U.S. (3 Dall.) 425, 1 L.Ed. 665 (1799), and Robinson v. Campbell, 16 U.S. (3 Wheat.) 212, 4 L.Ed. 372 (1818), with Wheaton v. Peters, 33 U.S. (8 Pet.) 591, 8 L.Ed. 1055 (1834). For a general discussion, see 2 W. Crosskey, Politics and the Constitution in the History of the United States 822–62 (1953).

when the subject matter of the suit did not involve the interpretation or application of the Constitution, a treaty, or federal statute, so that the reference to the "laws of the several states" was applicable, the federal courts differed as to whether that language included decisions of state courts, as well as state statutes and constitutions. Swift v. Tyson[3] represented the Court's attempt to resolve that question. In his opinion for the majority, Justice Story stated, "the laws of a state are more usually understood to mean the rules and enactments promulgated by the legislative authority thereof, or long-established local customs having the force of laws."[4] As a result, federal judges sitting in diversity jurisdiction were not necessarily bound by the previous decisions of the courts of the state whose law was otherwise being applied.[5]

The specific issue decided in Swift was whether a pre-existing debt constituted sufficient consideration for the endorsement of a bill of exchange so that the plaintiff-endorsee would be treated as a holder in due course. The debt had been accepted by the defendant as part of a fraudulent conveyance of property in Maine. Although it assumed that a New York state court would not have regarded the debt as sufficient consideration, the Supreme Court nevertheless held that federal interests relating to the development of a uniform body of commercial law justified an independent evaluation by the federal court, even if that meant reaching a contrary decision.[6] According to Justice Story: "The law respecting negotiable instruments may be truly declared * * * to be in great measure, not the law of a single country only, but of the commercial world."[7]

In addition to promoting the development of a uniform national law of commercial transactions, Justice Story believed that the federal judiciary should develop a comprehensive body of substantive law to serve as a model for state courts, thereby stimulating uniformity in the legal doctrines applied by state courts.[8] Some commentators also suggest that the Swift decision was motivated partially by the lack of adequate state court case reporting systems, which prevented the federal courts from ascertaining the content of state court decisions.[9]

As a result of Swift, the laws of the states that would be regarded as rules of decision in the federal courts under Section 34 of the Judiciary Act were limited to state constitutions, statutes, and state judicial opinions interpreting them. Federal courts were bound to follow these formulations, as well as state decisions on real estate, immovables, and other purely "local" questions. Conversely, so-called "general" matters, in the absence of a valid state statute, were to be determined by the

---

3. 41 U.S. (16 Pet.) 1, 10 L.Ed. 865 (1842).

4. 41 U.S. at 12–13.

5. 41 U.S. at 18.

6. "[T]he decisions of the local tribunals upon such subjects are entitled to, and will receive, the most deliberate attention and respect of this court; but they cannot furnish positive rules, or conclusive authori-

ty, by which our own judgments are to be bound up and governed." 41 U.S. at 13.

7. Ibid.

8. Ibid.

9. H. Hart & H. Wechsler, The Federal Courts and the Federal System 679 (Fallon, Meltzer & Shapiro, 4th ed.1996).

federal courts according to what they conceived to be widely held jurisprudential doctrines. Thus, ascertaining the applicable law often depended upon distinguishing matters of "local" concern, as to which federal courts were bound by the decision of the appropriate state's tribunals, from matters of "general" concern, as to which the federal courts were able to develop independently their own substantive body of law.

The problems inherent in drawing this distinction are exemplified by Gelpcke v. City of Dubuque,[10] which raised the question whether certain municipal bonds issued in connection with railroad construction were valid. The action was brought in a federal court in Iowa under diversity of citizenship jurisdiction. The Iowa Supreme Court, reversing a series of earlier decisions, had held in a similar case that the bonds were invalid under the state constitution. Even though the Iowa decision was based upon a construction of the state constitution, the United States Supreme Court refused to consider the decision binding and held the bonds to be valid, indicating that in certain exceptional cases, federal courts were free to apply their own conceptions of "truth, justice and the law" and disregard state court decisions.[11]

The Gelpcke decision aroused considerable adverse reaction. Critics noted that the increasing exclusion of state judicial decisions from the definition of "laws" in the Rules of Decision Act permitted federal courts to interfere arbitrarily in matters clearly within the purview of state law.[12] This criticism was reinforced by the publication of an article by Professor Charles Warren concerning a previously unexamined draft of Section 34 of the Judiciary Act.[13] According to Professor Warren, this draft indicated, contrary to Justice Story's belief at the time of Swift, that in 1789 Congress had intended the rules of decision in federal courts to include decisions of state courts as well as state constitutions and statutes.[14]

The implementation of the Swift doctrine did not bring about Justice Story's hoped for uniformity among the federal courts. Nor did it result in establishing federal decisions as models for state judges. The federal courts were hindered in developing a uniform body of law, notwithstanding the expansion of the category of "general" law questions, because many cases still involved "local" questions that were not subject to federal judicial discretion. In addition, state courts frequently

---

10. 68 U.S. (1 Wall.) 175, 17 L.Ed. 520 (1864).

11. 68 U.S. at 206. The exceptional circumstance in Gelpcke was a recent Iowa Supreme Court decision, which the majority viewed as aberrational. The holding can be narrowed further by noting that the Court emphasized the fact that the bonds in question were issued before the latest Iowa decision, and the Court was simply not giving it retroactive effect. See J. Gray, The Nature and Sources of the Law 248–59 (2d ed.1927).

12. Kuhn v. Fairmont Coal Co., 215 U.S. 349, 370–72, 30 S.Ct. 140, 147–48, 54 L.Ed. 228 (1910) (Holmes, J., dissenting).

13. Warren, New Light on the History of the Federal Judiciary Act of 1789, 37 Harv.L.Rev. 49 (1923).

14. For a commentary disagreeing with Professor Warren's interpretation, see 2 W. Crosskey, Politics and the Constitution in the History of the United States 867 (1953).

failed to follow federal common law decisions.[15] Finally, many federal courts rendered their decisions on "general" matters on the basis of the common law decisions of the jurisdiction in which they happened to sit, which meant that different federal courts handled the same question inconsistently.

The most dramatic demonstration of the problems raised by the implementation of the Swift doctrine came in 1928 with the decision in Black & White Taxicab & Transfer Company v. Brown & Yellow Taxicab & Transfer Company.[16] In that case, a former Kentucky corporation brought suit to enjoin another Kentucky corporation from operating taxis at a certain railroad station in violation of its exclusive contract with the railroad company. Kentucky state courts consistently had held exclusive dealing contracts to be unenforceable on the ground that they violated public policy.[17] The plaintiff attempted to circumvent this Kentucky policy by dissolving the corporation in Kentucky, reincorporating in Tennessee, and bringing a diversity action in a Kentucky federal court. Although the plaintiff apparently had created diversity of citizenship solely to escape the unfavorable application of Kentucky law,[18] the Supreme Court upheld the assertion of federal jurisdiction in the case. Further, it affirmed the lower court's determination that Kentucky state law need not be followed because the action involved questions of "general" commercial concern that were within the competence of the federal courts.[19]

Reaction to the majority opinion in the Black & White Taxicab case was more immediate and hostile than that following Gelpcke. Critics opined that the Supreme Court's decision would promote even more flagrant forum-shopping in federal courts by litigants seeking to avoid enforcement of specific state laws. In a strongly worded dissent, Justice Oliver Wendell Holmes denounced the majority's decision as an "unconstitutional assumption of powers by the Courts of the United States."[20] Although the Supreme Court responded to the adverse criticism by more closely limiting the discretion allowed federal courts in later diversity cases,[21] Justice Holmes' dissent, concurred in by Justices Brandeis and

15. Frankfurter, Distribution of Judicial Power Between United States and State Courts, 13 Cornell L.Q. 499, 529 n. 150 (1928).

16. 276 U.S. 518, 48 S.Ct. 404, 72 L.Ed. 681 (1928).

17. 276 U.S. at 526, 48 S.Ct. at 407.

18. See generally § 2.7, above, for a discussion of devices to create diversity jurisdiction.

19. 276 U.S. at 530, 48 S.Ct. at 407.

20. 276 U.S. at 533, 48 S.Ct. at 408. Justice Holmes expressed his personal disagreement with the general philosophy of the Swift doctrine, but most sharply criticized what he saw as a misapplication of that doctrine in the Taxicab case. He believed the dispute involved the regulation of activities upon state land, an area traditionally considered "local" in nature, and hence an area in which federal courts were bound by state decisions. 276 U.S. at 536, 48 S.Ct. at 410.

21. Burns Mortgage Co. v. Fried, 292 U.S. 487, 54 S.Ct. 813, 78 L.Ed. 1380 (1934) (state court ruling on Uniform Negotiable Instruments Law held binding on federal courts); Mutual Life Ins. Co. v. Johnson, 293 U.S. 335, 55 S.Ct. 154, 79 L.Ed. 398 (1934) (when there is no consensus upon a substantive issue of law, decisions of the appropriate state court should be applied).

Stone, proved prophetic of the final demise of the Swift doctrine ten years later.

§ 4.2 Erie Railroad Company v. Tompkins

Two profoundly important events occurred in 1938 that were to change fundamentally both the nature of civil procedure in the federal courts and the distribution of judicial power to make rules of decision between the federal government and the states. The first was the adoption of the Federal Rules of Civil Procedure, which established for the first time a unified set of rules to govern procedure in all the federal courts.[1] The second was the Supreme Court's decision in Erie Railroad Company v. Tompkins,[2] which has been called "one of the most important cases at law in American legal history."[3]

The decision in Erie was as unexpected as it was significant. The facts and issues involved were straightforward.[4] Harry Tompkins brought a tort action for injuries he received from a passing train while walking along the Erie Railroad's right-of-way in Hughestown, Pennsylvania. Under Pennsylvania common law, the railroad could be held liable only for gross or willful negligence because Tompkins was viewed as a trespasser. Under the "general" law of the federal courts, Tompkins would be considered a licensee and consequently the railroad could be held liable for ordinary negligence. Tompkins, a citizen of Pennsylvania, brought suit against the Erie, a citizen of New York, in a New York federal court on the basis of diversity of citizenship jurisdiction.[5] The district court concluded that the case involved issues of "general" as opposed to "local" law as defined by Swift v. Tyson,[6] so that the federal standard governed. Following trial, the jury awarded Tompkins $30,000 for the railroad's negligence and the Second Circuit affirmed.[7] The railroad successfully petitioned for certiorari.

Justice Brandeis' opinion for the majority in Erie caught both the litigants and the legal community by surprise.[8] Neither party had advo-

---

§ 4.2

1. The rules became effective September 16, 1938, and were promulgated under the authority of the Rules Enabling Act, c. 651, 48 Stat. 1064 (1934) (current version at 28 U.S.C.A. § 2072). For a discussion of the enactment of the statute and the promulgation of the rules and their importance for federal practice, see 4 C. Wright & A. Miller, Civil 2d §§ 1003–08.

2. 304 U.S. 64, 58 S.Ct. 817, 82 L.Ed. 1188 (1938).

3. Black, Address, 13 Mo.B.J. 173, 174 (1942).

4. For an entertaining and informative account of the lawsuit itself, see Younger, What Happened in Erie, 56 Texas L.Rev. 1011 (1978).

5. For a discussion of why the New York district court was considering Pennsylvania and not New York substantive law, see § 4.5, below.

6. 41 U.S. (16 Pet.) 1, 10 L.Ed. 865 (1842). See § 4.1, above.

7. 90 F.2d 603, 604 (2d Cir.1937).

8. Justice Butler's dissent noted that the Court had not notified the United States Attorney General and given him an opportunity to appear as was required by a federal statute when the constitutionality of a statute was in question. 304 U.S. at 80, 88–89, 58 S.Ct. at 823, 827. Since the Court's conclusion was that it was the Court's own course of conduct, not the statute itself, that was constitutionally suspect, arguably that objection has little merit.

cated overruling the Swift doctrine. Instead, each side recommended application of its particular interpretation of Swift. Nonetheless, the Supreme Court reversed the lower federal courts, stating that "there is no federal general common law,"[9] and remanded the case to the Second Circuit for a determination and application of Pennsylvania state law. On remand, the Court of Appeals held that the railroad was not liable, and Tompkins lost his $30,000 award.[10]

Three reasons were given by Justice Brandeis for overruling Swift and holding that under Section 34 of the Judiciary Act federal courts in diversity actions must apply judicially announced state-created substantive law, as well as state statutes and constitutions. First, the Justice noted that the "recent research of a competent scholar"[11] revealed that Justice Story's interpretation of that section of the Act was erroneous, and that a correct construction would require that, except on matters controlled by federal statutes, state law—written or unwritten—should be applied. Thus, the historical underpinnings of Swift were demolished.

Second, Justice Brandeis reviewed what had occurred under the regime of Swift, finding that "experience in applying the doctrine of Swift v. Tyson had revealed its defects, political and social; and the benefits expected to flow from the rule did not accrue."[12] The failure of the federal courts to develop a uniform national law, and the persistence of state courts in ignoring federal decisions and applying their own state doctrines had created two bodies of law, one applied in federal courts between litigants of diverse citizenship, and another applied in state courts between citizens of the same state. Discrimination resulted between the former and the latter group, with a plaintiff of diverse citizenship being able to choose whether state or federal law would apply by selecting the forum.[13] "In attempting to promote the uniformity of law throughout the United States, the doctrine had prevented uniformity in the administration of the law of the State."[14] Justice Brandeis concluded that these inadequacies, compounded by the great difficulty in distinguishing general issues from local ones, made it impossible to achieve the equal protection of the law, and required reevaluation of the Swift interpretation of Section 34.

However, the most surprising aspect of Erie was the language in the opinion indicating that the problems raised by Swift extended beyond a misinterpretation of the Rules of Decision Act. Indeed, Justice Brandeis suggested that the reasons discussed above would not have justified overruling ninety-six years of federal practice under Swift.[15] What made

---

9. 304 U.S. at 78, 58 S.Ct. at 822.

10. Tompkins v. Erie R.R. Co., 98 F.2d 49 (2d Cir.1938), cert. denied 305 U.S. 637.

11. 304 U.S. at 73, 58 S.Ct. at 819. The Court's reference was to Warren, New Light on the History of the Federal Judiciary Act of 1789, 37 Harv.L.Rev. 49 (1923).

12. 304 U.S. at 74, 58 S.Ct. at 820.

13. See the discussion of these effects in § 4.1, above.

14. 304 U.S. at 74–75, 58 S.Ct. at 820–21.

15. 304 U.S. at 77–78, 58 S.Ct. at 822.

termination of the Swift doctrine inescapable was that "the unconstitutionality of the course pursued has been made clear."[16]

This last section of the Erie opinion, holding that the Swift construction of Section 34 was itself unconstitutional, is at once the most important and most controversial reason given by Justice Brandeis for the decision.[17] Much time has been spent trying to determine precisely what constitutional provision was violated by Swift, and great disagreement exists among scholars as to the validity of Justice Brandeis' analysis.[18] Notably, Justice Brandeis failed to cite any particular section of the Constitution that the Swift doctrine violated. He did, however, incorporate language from earlier protests against Swift by Justices Field and Holmes.[19] Unfortunately, those references are not of much help in determining what the specific content of Justice Brandeis' argument is because both also fail to specify the exact constitutional violation.

Some guidance may be derived from the fact that Section 34 itself was not found to be unconstitutional. Rather, the Supreme Court's own failure to include state judicial decisions on substantive law as "rules of decision" under the statute was held unconstitutional since, "in applying the Swift doctrine this Court and the lower courts have invaded rights which in our opinion are reserved by the Constitution to the several states."[20] The most obvious conclusion to be drawn from these words is that Swift violated the Tenth Amendment, which preserves state power in areas not expressly delegated to the federal government by the Constitution. This interpretation of Erie's constitutional basis is supported by the Supreme Court's later decision in Hanna v. Plumer,[21] in which the Court said:

> we are reminded by the Erie opinion that neither Congress nor the federal courts can, under the guise of formulating rules of decision for federal courts, fashion rules which are not supported by a grant of federal authority contained in Article I or some other section of the Constitution; in such areas state law must govern because there can be no other law.[22]

---

16. Ibid. For a fuller discussion of the constitutional basis for Erie, see 19 C. Wright, A. Miller & E. Cooper, Jurisdiction and Related Matters 2d § 4505.

17. That Justice Brandeis should have sought to determine a constitutional question in Erie is surprising in itself, given his insistence in previous cases that the Supreme Court avoid deciding constitutional issues if any other means of resolving the matter is available. Ashwander v. TVA, 297 U.S. 288, 346–48, 56 S.Ct. 466, 482–84, 80 L.Ed. 688 (1936) (Brandeis, J., concurring).

18. Compare Friendly, In Praise of Erie—And of the New Federal Common Law, 39 N.Y.U.L.Rev. 383 (1964), supporting Justice Brandeis' position, with Keeffe, In Praise of Joseph Story, Swift v. Tyson

and "The" True National Common Law, 18 Am.U.L.Rev. 316 (1969), opposing the views of both Justice Brandeis and Judge Friendly.

19. See Baltimore & O. R.R. Co. v. Baugh, 149 U.S. 368, 391, 13 S.Ct. 914, 923, 37 L.Ed. 772 (1893) (Field, J., dissenting); Black & White Taxicab & Transfer Co. v. Brown & Yellow Taxicab & Transfer Co., 276 U.S. 518, 533, 48 S.Ct. 404, 408, 72 L.Ed. 681 (1928) (Holmes, J., dissenting).

20. 304 U.S. at 79–80, 58 S.Ct. at 823.

21. 380 U.S. 460, 85 S.Ct. 1136, 14 L.Ed.2d 8 (1965). The Hanna case is discussed more thoroughly in § 4.3, below.

22. 380 U.S. at 471–72, 85 S.Ct. at 1144.

But this reasoning does not totally answer the argument, first made by Justice Reed in his concurring opinion in Erie, that Article III, Section 2 of the Constitution, establishing the jurisdiction of the federal judiciary, coupled with the Necessary and Proper Clause found in Article I, Section 8, give to Congress the power to enact substantive rules for the federal courts.[23] This argument is especially convincing if one recalls Chief Justice Marshall's decision in McCulloch v. Maryland.[24] That case indicates that the Necessary and Proper Clause does not limit congressional action to areas that are absolutely necessary but permits Congress to employ all the means reasonably calculated to produce a constitutional objective. Applying this principle in admiralty cases, the Supreme Court has found that Congress does have the power to adopt substantive rules of law for the federal courts in that context.[25] Viewed from this perspective, the constitutional infirmity of Swift seems to be that the federal courts acted without congressional authority to create substantive law, raising serious separation of powers questions.

Although various explanations have been advanced as possible justifications for the Erie decision,[26] the constitutional questions raised by Justice Brandeis' opinion remain unsettled.[27] Regardless of this shortcoming, it is clear that the Supreme Court decision in Erie Railroad Company v. Tompkins must be regarded as one of the most significant opinions in the history of American jurisprudence.[28] The decision returns to the states a power that for nearly a century had been exercised by the federal judiciary and thus speaks to the heart of the relations between the federal government and the states.

§ 4.3   Evolution of the Erie Doctrine

The conceptual basis for the holding in Erie Railroad Company v. Tompkins[1] has been reformulated substantially by three landmark Su-

---

23. 304 U.S. at 91–92, 58 S.Ct. at 828.

24. 17 U.S. (4 Wheat.) 316, 324–25, 4 L.Ed. 579 (1819).

25. Southern Pac. Co. v. Jensen, 244 U.S. 205, 37 S.Ct. 524, 61 L.Ed. 1086 (1917).

26. One interesting argument suggests that the constitutional basis for Erie may lie in the Article I, Section 9 prohibition against ex post facto laws and bills of attainder. Under Swift and its progeny, this argument states, so much uncertainty existed in legal relationships because of the unpredictability of the application of state or federal law, that the constitutional safeguards of Article I, Section 9 were violated. See A. Von Mehren & D. Trautman, Law of Multistate Problems 1051 (1965). Language in Justice Harlan's concurring opinion in Hanna v. Plumer, 380 U.S. 460, 85 S.Ct. 1136, 14 L.Ed.2d 8 (1965), has been used in support of this position. "Erie recognized that there should not be two conflicting

systems of law controlling the primary activity of citizens, for such alternative governing authority must necessarily give rise to a debilitating uncertainty in the planning of everyday affairs." Id. at 474–75, 85 S.Ct. at 1145–46.

27. For an excellent overview of the constitutional status of Erie, see Ely, The Irrepressible Myth of Erie, 87 Harv.L.Rev. 693 (1974). For an unconventional and an historical view, see Westen & Lehman, Is There Life for Erie after the Death of Diversity?, 78 Mich.L.Rev. 311 (1980).

28. The case and its progeny have spawned countless articles. See 19 C. Wright, A. Miller & E. Cooper, Jurisdiction and Related Matters 2d §§ 4501–15, and all the articles cited therein.

§ 4.3

1. 304 U.S. 64, 58 S.Ct. 817, 82 L.Ed. 1188 (1938).

preme Court decisions.[2] The first of these was Guaranty Trust Company v. York,[3] decided in 1945. This diversity suit was instituted in a New York federal court as a class action on behalf of a group of noteholders who alleged that Guaranty, in sponsoring an exchange offer, had failed to protect their interests. Although a factually complicated case, for purposes of the present discussion the key issue was whether a federal court in a suit seeking equitable relief must apply the state statute of limitations, which effectively barred the action, rather than the more flexible federal equity defense of laches, which might have permitted the action to proceed. After acknowledging that the Erie case did not specifically address the rules of decision for federal courts sitting in equity, and noting that Congress provided for independent development of the "forms and modes of proceeding" for suits in equity,[4] the Court ruled that federal courts sitting in diversity of citizenship cases must rely upon state law in determining substantive rights even in equity matters.[5]

The Supreme Court rejected any conclusory labeling of statutes of limitations as substantive or procedural.[6] Instead, it found that the issue of the nature of the New York statute for Erie purposes turned on the following question: "[D]oes it significantly affect the result of a litigation for a federal court to disregard a law of a State that would be controlling in an action upon the same claim by the same parties in a State court?"[7] It was immaterial that, for purposes unrelated to the choice of applicable law, state court opinions had characterized statutes of limitation either as substantive or procedural. Rather, the Court focused on the purpose of the Erie decision, finding that it was to avoid the potential of state and federal courts reaching different outcomes. In Guaranty, if the federal court were to disregard the state statute, which appeared to bar recovery in the state court completely, and plaintiff prevailed, the

---

2. These decisions are discussed more fully in 19 C. Wright, A. Miller & E. Cooper, Jurisdiction and Related Matters 2d § 4504.

3. 326 U.S. 99, 65 S.Ct. 1464, 89 L.Ed. 2079 (1945).

4. The Act of May 8, 1792 (ch. 36, § 2, 1 Stat. 275, 276) provided that the procedure for suits in equity was to follow the existing principles and usages of the courts of equity, and empowered the Supreme Court to make any necessary changes by adopting rules. The Court first adopted equity rules in 1822. The second set of rules was adopted in 1842 and remained in effect until the Court promulgated the Equity Rules of 1912, which, in turn, remained in effect until the Federal Rules of Civil Procedure were adopted in 1938.

5. 326 U.S. at 108–09, 65 S.Ct. at 1469–70.

6. 326 U.S. at 109, 65 S.Ct. at 1470. The substance/procedure argument was precipitated by the fact that in Erie Justice

Brandeis had stated that Congress is powerless to declare "substantive rules of common law applicable in a State * * *," 304 U.S. at 78, 58 S.Ct. at 822, but Justice Reed had observed in his concurring opinion that "no one doubts federal power over procedure," 304 U.S. at 92, 58 S.Ct. at 828. Later cases seemed to rely on this distinction between the areas of substance and procedure. See Cities Serv. Oil Co. v. Dunlap, 308 U.S. 208, 60 S.Ct. 201, 84 L.Ed. 196 (1939) (burden of proof to be imposed in an action to quiet title involves a substantive right, necessitating the application of state law), and Palmer v. Hoffman, 318 U.S. 109, 63 S.Ct. 477, 87 L.Ed. 645 (1943) (the placement of the burden of establishing contributory negligence is a question of local law that federal courts must apply).

7. 326 U.S. at 109, 65 S.Ct. at 1470.

outcome of the case undoubtedly would be significantly affected. Consequently, the Court held that the New York statute governed.

York marks the emergence of the outcome determinative test, which was an attempt to prevent federal courts from reaching a decision at variance with the result that would obtain in a state court in a comparable case. Justice Frankfurter, who wrote the majority opinion, apparently felt that this policy was the essence of the Erie decision. He remarked:

> The nub of the policy that underlies Erie R. Co. v. Tompkins is that for the same transaction the accident of a suit by a non-resident litigant in a federal court instead of in a State court a block away should not lead to a substantially different result.[8]

Viewed this way, Erie reflects an attempt to achieve vertical uniformity, that is, the consistent application of local substantive law in both state and federal courts within the same state. The goal of horizontal uniformity of law throughout the federal court system that had been advocated in Swift v. Tyson[9] was abandoned. In addition, Justice Frankfurter wanted to eliminate a major incentive for litigants of diverse citizenship to forum shop—at least between state and federal courts.[10]

Problems soon developed with the application of York's outcome-determinative test. If the approach were applied literally, virtually every federal procedural rule would have to be displaced in diversity cases by any different state rule because all procedural rules could affect the outcome of a case to some degree.[11] Such an encompassing interpretation probably was not intended by the York Court. Nonetheless, the federal courts were faced with the task of divining the correct limits of the stated test, which remained obscure.[12] Prediction of whether the application or nonapplication of a particular federal practice might have a substantial effect on the outcome of a case is especially difficult at the outset of a lawsuit when the parties' factual and legal theories may be framed only in general terms.

Close examination of Justice Frankfurter's opinion in York reveals some limits on the application of the outcome-determinative test, however. For example, he indicated that in diversity cases the federal courts could continue to provide the traditional federal equitable remedies,[13] such as injunctions, whether or not the same remedy was available in

---

8. Ibid.

9. 41 U.S. (16 Pet.) 1, 10 L.Ed. 865 (1842). See § 4.1, above.

10. 326 U.S. at 109, 65 S.Ct. at 1470. Vertical uniformity may not completely discourage forum-shopping. Different procedural rules, docket congestion, the availability of interlocutory appeals, and the character and competence of judges may affect the choice of forum. See Hill, The Erie Doctrine and the Constitution, 53 Nw. U.L.Rev. 427, 451 (1958).

11. The fact that the application of the outcome-determinative test could result

in undercutting the Federal Rules was supported, at least in part, by three cases decided by the Supreme Court in 1949 involving clashes between that test and the Federal Rules. In all three, the Supreme Court ruled that state law should be applied. For a discussion of these three cases, see § 4.4 at notes 9–27, below.

12. Hart, The Relations Between State and Federal Law, 54 Colum.L.Rev. 489, 512 (1954).

13. 326 U.S. at 105–06, 65 S.Ct. at 1468–69.

the state courts.[14] He further noted that the federal practice in question must "significantly affect" the result of the lawsuit before it need be supplanted by a contrary state procedure.[15] However, these vaguely worded statements provided precious little guidance and comfort and some commentators concluded that every Federal Rule of Civil Procedure was endangered by York.[16]

In 1958, the Supreme Court reformulated the Erie doctrine again in Byrd v. Blue Ridge Rural Electric Cooperative, Inc.[17] In that case, the Supreme Court found that the mere possibility that a federal practice may alter the outcome of a diversity case is not conclusive in deciding whether to apply federal or state law. Instead, it devised an analysis calling for a comparison of the significance of the competing federal and state policies at issue in a particular case.

Byrd was a diversity action brought in a South Carolina federal court for personal injuries allegedly caused by the defendant's negligence. The defendant asserted that the action should be barred because the plaintiff was its employee for purposes of the South Carolina Workmen's Compensation Act, and the plaintiff's only remedy was to seek compensation from the appropriate administrative agency. The South Carolina Supreme Court had held that whether a plaintiff was a statutory employee was an issue to be determined by a judge, rather than a jury. Nonetheless, the United States Supreme Court ruled that in the federal courts a jury would decide the question.

Justice Brennan, writing for six members of the Court, divided his opinion on the judge-jury issue into three parts.[18] He first addressed the principle stated in Erie that federal courts in diversity litigation should respect the manner in which state created rights have been defined by the state courts. The Court observed that the South Carolina practice by which the judge, rather than the jury, decides the employee's status under the Act was not "bound up with the definition of the rights and obligations of the parties" created by the state statute.[19] Rather, it was simply a procedural or administrative practice established by the South Carolina Supreme Court with no strong policy to support it.

Second, Justice Brennan recognized the applicability of York's outcome-determinative test, but felt it should be reevaluated in light of the

14. For a discussion of this equitable remedial power and its modern vitality, see 19 C. Wright, A. Miller & E. Cooper, Jurisdiction and Related Matters 2d § 4513.

15. 326 U.S. at 109, 65 S.Ct. at 1470.

16. See generally Ely, The Irrepressible Myth of Erie, 87 Harv.L.Rev. 693 (1974); Hill, The Erie Doctrine and the Constitution, 53 Nw.U.L.Rev. 427 (1958); Merrigan, Erie to York to Ragan—A Triple Play on the Federal Rules, 3 Vand.L.Rev. 711 (1950).

17. 356 U.S. 525, 78 S.Ct. 893, 2 L.Ed.2d 953 (1958).

18. Justice Whittaker dissented on the governing law point. Justices Frankfurter and Harlan dissented on another issue and did not discuss the Erie questions in their opinion.

19. 356 U.S. at 536, 78 S.Ct. at 900. Compare the Court's language in this case with the discussion of the state statute involved in Ragan v. Merchants Transfer & Warehouse Co., 337 U.S. 530, 533–34, 69 S.Ct. 1233, 1235, 93 L.Ed. 1520 (1949). For a discussion of the Ragan case, see § 4.4, below.

"affirmative countervailing considerations at work here."[20] One such consideration was the potential for interference with the federal system of allocating functions between judge and jury. Although it refrained from holding that the seventh amendment right to jury trial extended to the disputed factual issue in Byrd, the Court recognized the amendment as evidence of a "strong federal policy against allowing state rules to disrupt the judge-jury relationship in the federal courts."[21]

In the third section of the opinion, Justice Brennan returned to the outcome-determinative principle and shed new light on its interpretation. He noted that in determining whether the outcome of the litigation may be substantially affected by applying federal rather than state law, it is necessary to look to the degree of certainty and predictability that a different result actually will occur when employing the federal rather than the state practice. In Byrd itself, there was no strong likelihood that the outcome of the suit would be affected were the jury to determine the issue rather than the judge.[22] Certainly, there was no ability to predict when a difference might occur. Thus, it was unnecessary to displace the federal practice with the state rule in the interest of uniformity of outcome.

What emerges from Byrd is a balancing test that requires weighing the policies underlying the respective federal and state rules. In Byrd, the state practice was found to reflect a weak state policy, not bound up with the underlying statute, of preferring a judge determination of the employment issue. When balanced against the strong federal policy embodied in the seventh amendment, and the fact that there was no substantial likelihood that a different result would be obtained because of the utilization of a jury, Justice Brennan concluded that federal practice was to be preferred.[23]

Commentators welcomed the Byrd decision and its balancing approach as an attempt to restore the proper equilibrium between federal and state interests that they thought had been unsettled by York.[24] But some courts had great difficulty in applying Byrd because of the lack of an objective standard by which to evaluate the competing practices.[25]

20. 356 U.S. at 537, 78 S.Ct. at 901.

21. 356 U.S. at 538, 78 S.Ct. at 901.

22. 356 U.S. at 540, 78 S.Ct. at 902.

23. 356 U.S. at 537–38, 78 S.Ct. at 901.

24. See generally Friendly, In Praise of Erie—And the New Federal Common Law, 39 N.Y.U.L.Rev. 383 (1964); Smith, Blue Ridge and Beyond: A Byrd's–Eye View of Federalism in Diversity Litigation, 36 Tul. L.Rev. 443 (1962); Note, Of Lawyers and Laymen: A Study of Federalism, the Judicial Process and Erie, 71 Yale L.J. 344 (1961).

25. One example of how the lower courts applied the Byrd test involves state door-closing statutes. In Szantay v. Beech Aircraft Corp., 349 F.2d 60 (4th Cir.1965), suit was brought in South Carolina by an Illinois citizen against a Delaware corporation on a cause of action arising in Tennessee. A state statute would have barred suit in a South Carolina state court. However, the Fourth Circuit identified three important federal interests that would be served by ignoring the state statute: (1) the prevention of discrimination against nonresidents in the Article III creation of diversity jurisdiction; (2) the federal policy of maximum enforcement in each state of rights created in sister states embodied in the Full Faith and Credit Clause of the Constitution; and (3) the federal interest in encouraging efficient joinder, since one of the defendants could not be served outside South Carolina. These interests were found to out-

One federal court might conclude that a particular state or federal policy was of some importance, but another court, or even the same court at a different time, would not accord the same policy any special consideration.

For example, in Jaftex Corporation v. Randolph Mills, Inc.,[26] a divided Second Circuit panel held that the issue whether a foreign corporation is "present" in New York and thus amenable to suit there would be determined by federal standards. In his opinion for the majority, Judge Clark found that the Article III establishment of diversity jurisdiction implied a policy of guaranteeing litigants "the essentials of a trial according to federal standards."[27] He also argued that the federal venue statutes and the provisions in Federal Rule 4 dealing with service of process evidenced a policy favoring uniform federal standards for amenability to suit.[28] Judge Clark found no significant state policies in opposition to these federal interests, noting that the service of process in the case probably would have been valid under both New York and federal standards.[29] Three years later, in Arrowsmith v. United Press International,[30] the same court, sitting en banc, overruled Jaftex, holding that state statutes limiting personal jurisdiction over foreign corporations reflected a deliberate state policy not to discourage corporate activity in the state. This policy was deemed sufficiently important to override the arguments for judicially creating a federal standard of amenability to suit.[31]

In 1965, the Supreme Court reviewed the Erie doctrine again in Hanna v. Plumer.[32] Chief Justice Warren wrote the opinion for the Court upholding the validity of substituted service of process under Federal Rule 4(d)(1) in a diversity case under circumstances in which the relevant state law required in-hand service. The Court rejected the defendant's argument that permitting the action to proceed in a federal court when a counterpart state action would have been dismissed because service had not been completed properly violated the Erie–York outcome determination policy.

> "Outcome-determination" analysis was never intended to serve as a talisman. * * * Indeed, the message of York itself is that choices between state and federal law are to be made not by application of any automatic, "litmus paper" criterion, but rather by reference to the policies underlying the Erie rule.[33]

weigh the state interest in having its door-closing statute applied because the court found no important state policy supporting that statute.

26. 282 F.2d 508 (2d Cir.1960).

27. 282 F.2d at 513.

28. 282 F.2d at 512.

29. 282 F.2d at 511.

30. 320 F.2d 219 (2d Cir.1963).

31. 320 F.2d at 229–30. The Second Circuit did intimate that, notwithstanding Erie, Congress could authorize a federal court to assume jurisdiction over a corporation even though a state court would not. 320 F.2d at 226.

32. 380 U.S. 460, 85 S.Ct. 1136, 14 L.Ed.2d 8 (1965).

33. 380 U.S. at 466–67, 85 S.Ct. at 1141.

The Court then went on to refine the outcome-determinative standard of Guaranty by tying it to the twin policies underlying the Erie rule—the discouragement of forum-shopping and the avoidance of the inequitable administration of the laws.[34] Further, a substantial alteration in the enforcement of state-created rights must exist before the equal protection problems alluded to in Erie arise.[35] The minor difference between using substituted service under Federal Rule 4(d)(1) and following the state rule of in-hand delivery could not result in such a significant benefit to a noncitizen plaintiff to induce forum-shopping between the state and federal courts.

As will be discussed further in the next section, Chief Justice Warren asserted the strong national interest in maintaining a uniform body of procedural rules for the United States district courts as an alternative ground supporting the applicability of Federal Rule 4. The Chief Justice stated that the Constitution's grant of power to Congress to create and regulate the federal courts,[36] exercised with regard to matters of procedure in the Rules Enabling Act,[37] allows the Federal Rules to be applied in diversity cases even though some of them may be different from comparable state procedures.[38]

Although concurring in the result, Justice Harlan rejected both of the arguments advanced by Chief Justice Warren. He expressed the view that "Erie was something more than an opinion which worried about 'forum-shopping and avoidance of inequitable administration of the laws.' "[39] He went on to point out that in rejecting the "outcome" test of York, and setting up a new "procedural, ergo constitutional" test, the Court was oversimplifying the basic principles of the Erie doctrine.[40] These, Justice Harlan believed, would be better served by a closer examination of the relevant federal and state practices, and an application of the state procedure, despite a contrary Federal Rule, whenever "primary decisions respecting human conduct which our constitutional system leaves to state regulation"[41] were involved.

Justice Harlan's approach requiring federal courts to determine what constitutes law governing the primary conduct and affairs of the forum state's citizens raises all of the problems of vagueness and nonobjectivity that plagued the balancing test of Byrd; in effect, it merely calls for a new definition of "substantive." In contrast, Chief Justice Warren's opinion has been praised as finally providing a simple and clear test for determining the validity of federal procedural practices under Erie,[42] and, as will be discussed in the next section, for safeguard-

---

34. 380 U.S. at 467–68, 85 S.Ct. at 1142.

35. 380 U.S. at 468–69, 85 S.Ct. at 1142–43.

36. U.S. Const. Art. III, § 2.

37. 28 U.S.C.A. § 2072.

38. 380 U.S. at 471–74, 85 S.Ct. at 1144–45.

39. 380 U.S. at 474, 85 S.Ct. at 1145.

40. 380 U.S. at 476, 85 S.Ct. at 1146–47.

41. 380 U.S. at 475, 85 S.Ct. at 1146.

42. See generally Ely, The Irrepressible Myth of Erie, 87 Harv.L.Rev. 693 (1974).

ing the Federal Rules from encroachment in diversity cases by conflicting state practices.

§ 4.4   The Erie Doctrine and the Federal Rules

Prior to the promulgation of the Federal Rules of Civil Procedure in 1938, practice in the federal courts was regulated by the Conformity Act of 1872,[1] which provided that each district court should follow the court procedure of the state in which it sat. Several problems developed as a result of this principle. The purpose of the Act was to provide a uniform procedure for all courts in the same state, but exceptions to its application caused adherence to state practice by the federal courts to be erratic.[2] In addition, the effect of the Act was to abdicate responsibility for formulating rules of procedure for the federal courts to state legislatures, instead of giving that responsibility to the federal courts, which are more qualified to undertake this task.[3]

In light of these shortcomings, Congress enacted the Rules Enabling Act in 1934, which authorized the Supreme Court to draft and promulgate an independent set of procedural rules for the federal courts.[4] Then, an advisory committee of prominent judges, attorneys, and scholars was appointed to assist the Court in preparing them. The rules were adopted by a majority of the Court on December 20, 1937, and became effective on September 1, 1938.

The adoption of a separate set of uniform federal rules completed the transformation of federal practice, which had begun earlier that year with the Supreme Court's decision in Erie Railroad Company v. Tompkins.[5] Taken together, the decision in Erie and the Court's promulgation of the Federal Rules indicate that a federal court sitting in diversity jurisdiction should apply the substantive law of the state in which it was located, and the procedural law prescribed in the Federal Rules.

This seemingly simple approach appeared to run aground when the Supreme Court decided Guaranty Trust Company v. York seven years later.[6] Rejecting the general utilization of a substance/procedure distinction, Justice Frankfurter instead indicated that state law would have to be applied to a number of matters that usually would be thought of as procedural in order that "the outcome of the litigation in the federal

---

§ 4.4

1. Act of June 1, 1872, ch. 255, § 5, 17 Stat. 197 (1872) (repealed 1934).

2. The Act did not require federal courts to conform to state procedure when the suit was in equity or admiralty; separate sets of Equity and Admiralty Rules controlled procedure in those cases. This not only frustrated the goal of procedural uniformity, but also tended to perpetuate the artificial division between law and equity actions, even in states that had unified their court systems.

3. For a detailed discussion of procedure in the federal courts prior to the Federal Rules of Civil Procedure, see 4 C. Wright & A. Miller, Civil 2d §§ 1001–04.

4. Act of June 19, 1934, ch. 651, 48 Stat. 1064 (codified at 28 U.S.C.A. § 2072). For a complete history of the Act, see Burbank, Rules Enabling Act, 130 U.Pa.L.Rev. 1015 (1982).

5. 304 U.S. 64, 58 S.Ct. 817, 82 L.Ed. 1188 (1938). See § 4.2, above.

6. 326 U.S. 99, 65 S.Ct. 1464, 89 L.Ed. 2079 (1945).

court should be substantially the same, so far as legal rules determine the outcome of a litigation, as it would be if tried in a State court."[7] Not surprisingly, many commentators expressed concern that many of the Federal Rules would have to be displaced in diversity actions by their corresponding state provisions because any procedural rule might affect the outcome of a case to some extent.[8]

This concern was greatly increased by three decisions handed down by the Court on the same day in 1949: Woods v. Interstate Realty Company,[9] Cohen v. Beneficial Industrial Loan Corporation,[10] and Ragan v. Merchants Transfer & Warehouse Company.[11] In each of these cases the federal courts were told to apply state law, despite arguments that adherence to state practice would represent a significant encroachment on federal interests in procedural uniformity.

In Woods v. Interstate Realty Company,[12] the plaintiff brought suit to recover a broker's commission alleged to be due for the sale of the defendant's real estate in Mississippi. Recovery was barred in state court under a Mississippi law establishing that a foreign corporation, such as the plaintiff, could not maintain an action in the courts of that state if it failed to appoint an agent upon whom process could be served. The Supreme Court held that a diversity action could not be brought in federal court if recovery was barred in the state courts.[13] It interpreted the premise of York to be "that a right which local law creates but which it does not supply with a remedy is no right at all for purposes of enforcement in * * * a diversity case."[14] A contrary result, the Court believed, would unfairly favor litigants fortuitously able to invoke diversity jurisdiction.[15]

Cohen v. Beneficial Industrial Loan Corporation,[16] was a shareholder derivative suit brought in New Jersey federal court against the managers of the Beneficial Industrial Loan Corporation, who allegedly had been involved in a conspiracy to enrich themselves at the expense of the corporation. The suit was initiated by a single shareholder who owned only a small portion of the total stock of the company. Before trial, the

7. 326 U.S. at 109, 65 S.Ct. at 1470.

8. Gavit, States' Rights and Federal Procedure, 25 Ind.L.J. 1 (1949); Merrigan, Erie to York to Ragan—A Triple Play on the Federal Rules, 3 Vand.L.Rev. 711 (1950); Note, Federal Procedure: The "Outcome" Test Applied in Actions Based on Diversity of Citizenship, 35 Cornell L.Q. 420, 423 (1950); Note, Substance, Procedure and Uniformity—Recent Extensions of Guaranty Trust Co. v. York, 38 Geo.L.J. 115, 128–30 (1949).

9. 337 U.S. 535, 69 S.Ct. 1235, 93 L.Ed. 1524 (1949).

10. 337 U.S. 541, 69 S.Ct. 1221, 93 L.Ed. 1528 (1949).

11. 337 U.S. 530, 69 S.Ct. 1233, 93 L.Ed. 1520 (1949).

12. 337 U.S. 535, 69 S.Ct. 1235, 93 L.Ed. 1524 (1949).

13. The Court relied on Justice Frankfurter's statements in Angel v. Bullington, 330 U.S. 183, 187, 67 S.Ct. 657, 659, 91 L.Ed. 832 (1947), quoting Guaranty Trust Co. v. York, 326 U.S. 99, 108, 65 S.Ct. 1464, 1469, 89 L.Ed. 2079 (1945), that "for purposes of diversity jurisdiction a federal court is in effect only another court of the State."

14. 337 U.S. at 538, 69 S.Ct. at 1237.

15. Ibid.

16. 337 U.S. 541, 69 S.Ct. 1221, 93 L.Ed. 1528 (1949).

defendants demanded that the plaintiff post an indemnity bond for expenses as required by state law.[17]

The district court held the state law inapplicable since the action was governed by the Federal Rule[18] covering shareholder derivative suits,[19] and the Court of Appeals for the Third Circuit reversed.[20] The Supreme Court affirmed the Third Circuit, observing that the New Jersey statute was not "merely a regulation of procedure."[21] Rather, it created a new liability that was imposed on the plaintiff in order to ensure that the corporate defendant would receive compensation for the expenses it incurred if the plaintiff failed to prove his claim. The Court commented: "We do not think a statute which so conditions the stockholder's action can be disregarded by the federal court as a mere procedural device."[22]

The third case, Ragan v. Merchants Transfer & Warehouse Company,[23] involved a diversity action brought in a Kansas federal court. The suit arose from a highway accident. Kansas had a two year statute of limitations, which was tolled by commencement of the action. State law provided that suits were not commenced until the defendant had been served with process. Federal Rule 3, on the other hand, provides that actions are commenced at the time the complaint is filed. In full compliance with the Federal Rules, the plaintiff filed the complaint within two years of the date of the accident; however, service of process was not effected until after that period had expired.

The Supreme Court eventually held that the case had to be dismissed because it had not been commenced in compliance with the time frame allowed by Kansas' statute of limitations. In his opinion for the Court, Justice Douglas wrote that since the

> cause of action is created by local law, the measure of it is to be found only in local law. * * * It accrues and comes to an end when local law so declares. * * * Where local law qualifies or abridges it, the federal court must follow suit. Otherwise there is a different measure of the cause of action in one court than in the other, and the principle of Erie R. Co. v. Tompkins is transgressed.[24]

Commentators who had been skeptical of the Court's decision in York were quick to point out that Ragan, Cohen, and Woods further

---

17. A New Jersey statute imposed liability for all the expenses of the corporate defendant on any plaintiff bringing a derivative suit who had only a small interest in the corporation if the action ultimately was determined to be unfounded. The statute also entitled the corporation to demand an indemnity bond from the plaintiff before a derivative suit would be heard. 337 U.S. at 544 n. 1, 69 S.Ct. at 1224 n. 1.

18. The rule was Fed.Civ.Proc.Rule 23(b), now renumbered as Rule 23.1.

19. 7 F.R.D. 352, 356 (D.N.J.1947). The district court also relied on Justice Frankfurter's reservation of the independence of federal equity practice from his outcome determinative analysis in York; historically, derivative suits were proceedings in equity. See Guaranty Trust Co. v. York, 326 U.S. at 105–06, 65 S.Ct. at 1468.

20. 170 F.2d 44, 54 (3d Cir.1948).

21. 337 U.S. at 555, 69 S.Ct. at 1230.

22. 337 U.S. at 556, 69 S.Ct. at 1230.

23. 337 U.S. 530, 69 S.Ct. 1233, 93 L.Ed. 1520 (1949).

24. 337 U.S. at 533, 69 S.Ct. at 1235.

threatened the continued applicability of the Federal Rules in state law based actions. The distinguished Reporter of the Federal Rules Advisory Committee that had drafted the Rules more than a decade earlier, Second Circuit Judge Charles E. Clark, observed that after these three decisions "hardly a one of the heralded Federal Rules can be considered safe from attack by shrewd lawyers and obedient lower tribunals."[25] Similarly, other scholars asserted that attorneys were unable to ascertain those Federal Rules that would remain "in effect" after Woods, Ragan, and Cohen.[26]

In retrospect, these statements were overreactions. Although Ragan and Cohen did superimpose state substantive law on the application of the Federal Rules, they did not, as was suggested, invalidate Federal Rule 3 or former Federal Rule 23(b). The Court did not actually displace federal law with state law; instead, it attempted to integrate state substantive policies with federal procedural ones. Ragan did not hold that Federal Rule 3 is inapplicable; rather, it concluded that in order to honor certain state-created rights it may be necessary to satisfy state procedural requirements in addition to the practice set out in the applicable Federal Rule. Similarly, Cohen suggested that a state can impose additional impediments on access to its own courts in shareholder derivative suits that go beyond the requirements of the Federal Rules. These requirements must be followed by the federal courts sitting in that state along with the conditions prescribed by the relevant Federal Rule. Thus, Ragan, Cohen, and Woods may be viewed as examples of a false conflict between federal and state law. The substantive policies embodied in the respective federal and state procedures could be advanced simultaneously; the state and federal procedures were not mutually exclusive.[27]

Fears that the Federal Rules of Civil Procedure would not survive further elaborations of the Erie doctrine were allayed somewhat by the decision in Byrd v. Blue Ridge Rural Electric Cooperative, Inc.[28] Although it did not involve a Federal Rule, the case seemed to suggest that the Rules and Erie could coexist—outcome-determination no longer was to be the only test applied by the federal courts. Recognizing the independent nature of the federal judiciary, the Court held that significant federal policies, such as the allocation of functions between the

25. Clark, Book Review, 36 Cornell L.Q. 181, 183 (1950).

26. Merrigan, Erie to York to Ragan—A Triple Play on the Federal Rules, 3 Vand. L.Rev. 711, 712 n. 5 (1950). See also Note, Substance, Procedure and Uniformity—Recent Extensions of Guaranty Trust Co. v. York, 38 Geo.L.J. 115, 118–24 (1949).

27. Two additional explanations of the decisions can be offered. The Court may have been indicating that under the Rules Enabling Act the "substantive" elements of a Federal Rule cannot be applied if they conflict with a significant state practice. On this point, see the discussion in Ely, The Irrepressible Myth of Erie, 87 Harv.L.Rev. 693, 729–32 (1974). Second, at least in Ragan, the Court may have been implying that Federal Rule 3 does not reflect any important federal policy that ought to be unswervingly applied in diversity cases. For a discussion of the Ragan decision, see 4 C. Wright & A. Miller, Civil 2d § 1057.

28. 356 U.S. 525, 78 S.Ct. 893, 2 L.Ed.2d 953 (1958). See § 4.3, above, for a more detailed discussion of the Byrd case.

judge and the jury, must be protected, despite conflicting state procedures.

However, as noted in the preceding section, although Byrd was welcomed as a retreat from the insensitivity of the York decision, the vagueness and nonspecificity of Byrd's balancing test resulted in confusion and contradictory results in the lower federal courts. For example, the Fifth Circuit[29] attached importance to the interest of the federal system in regulating procedure for the presentation of evidence in its courts, but the Seventh Circuit[30] held a general federal interest in controlling procedure to be of relatively minor importance. Lacking an absolute scale by which to assign weights to state and federal policies, the balancing process proved arbitrary.[31]

In Hanna v. Plumer,[32] the Supreme Court laid to rest the fears about the continued viability of the Federal Rules when it said:

> To hold that a Federal Rule of Civil Procedure must cease to function whenever it alters the mode of enforcing state-created rights would be to disembowel either the Constitution's grant of power over federal procedure or Congress' attempt to exercise that power in the Enabling Act.[33]

According to the Hanna Court, a Federal Rule is to be applied unless it can be demonstrated that the Advisory Committee on the Federal Rules, the Supreme Court, and Congress were mistaken in their judgment that the challenged rule falls within the ambit of the Enabling Act.[34]

Chief Justice Warren, writing for the Court, found support for the presumption favoring the validity of a Federal Rule in Sibbach v. Wilson & Company.[35] In Sibbach, the Court held that the authority to order physical examinations provided by Federal Rule 35 was a legitimate exercise of the power granted by Congress to the Supreme Court to promulgate rules of procedure. Federal Rule 35 was held not to abridge, modify, or enlarge the substantive rights of the litigants; it only operated to enforce rights and duties recognized and created by state substantive law. Chief Justice Warren also relied on Mississippi Publishing Corporation v. Murphree,[36] in which the Supreme Court decided that Federal

---

29. Monarch Ins. Co. v. Spach, 281 F.2d 401, 407 (5th Cir.1960). Accord Dallas County v. Commercial Union Assurance Co., 286 F.2d 388, 393 (5th Cir.1961) (admissibility of hearsay evidence determined under federal standard).

30. Allstate Ins. Co. v. Charneski, 286 F.2d 238 (7th Cir.1960) (specific state policy prohibiting declaratory judgment of insurance company nonliability outweighs federal practice of granting district courts discretion in awarding declaratory relief).

31. For further examples of the difficulties of applying the Byrd balancing standards, see § 4.3, above.

32. 380 U.S. 460, 85 S.Ct. 1136, 14 L.Ed.2d 8 (1965). See § 4.3 at notes 32–42,

above, for a summary of the facts and reasoning of the Court in Hanna.

33. 380 U.S. at 473–74, 85 S.Ct. at 1143.

34. 380 U.S. at 471, 85 S.Ct. at 1144.

35. 312 U.S. 1, 61 S.Ct. 422, 85 L.Ed. 479 (1941). The Sibbach case and Rule 35 are discussed in 8A C. Wright, A. Miller & R. Marcus, Civil 2d § 2231, and in Notes, 29 Calif.L.Rev. 543 (1941), 15 Tul.L.Rev. 612 (1941), and 27 Va.L.Rev. 706 (1941).

36. 326 U.S. 438, 445, 66 S.Ct. 242, 90 L.Ed. 185 (1946).

Rule 4(e), providing for service throughout the state in which the federal court is located did not enlarge the jurisdiction of the federal courts in violation of Federal Rule 82 and the Rules Enabling Act; rather, it only served to implement the jurisdiction conferred on the district courts by Congress.

The Court's opinion in Hanna suggests a tripartite analysis for determining the applicability of a particular federal practice. The first inquiry is whether a Federal Rule actually governs the practice under consideration in the particular case. If the answer is yes, then the federal court must determine whether a conflict between the Federal Rule and state law exists, or whether the Federal Rule is narrower in its coverage than the state statute, permitting the superimposition of the state requirements without interfering with the application of the Rule. The Chief Justice pointed to the Ragan and Cohen cases as examples of the latter situation. In both instances, the Federal Rules involved were narrower in their application than the relevant state procedures, and the additional requirements established by state law could be followed without doing violence to the Federal Rules.[37] If, however, there is a direct conflict between state practice and a Federal Rule, then the court must determine whether the latter is a valid exercise of the power granted to the Supreme Court under the Rules Enabling Act. This last step does not present any significant barrier to the application of federal law since, as already noted, Chief Justice Warren's analysis in Hanna suggests that the Federal Rules are presumed to be a valid exercise of the Supreme Court's authority to promulgate procedural rules for the federal courts.

In theory at least, matters governed by a Federal Rule no longer are subject to the Erie–York outcome-determination or forum-shopping analysis.[38] If the Federal Rule covers the specific matter in question, and if it is a valid exercise of the power delegated by Congress to the Supreme Court under Articles I and III, it will be controlling; state provisions to the contrary will not replace the procedures established by the Rule.

37. Following Hanna there was some debate about the validity of the Ragan decision, but the Supreme Court resolved the question in Walker v. Armco Steel Corp., 446 U.S. 740, 100 S.Ct. 1978, 64 L.Ed.2d 659 (1980), holding that Ragan is still good law. The Court found that Federal Rule 3 does not directly conflict with a state statute that prescribes that an action is "commenced" for limitations purposes only when service is made. Therefore, a federal court sitting in diversity must apply state law in such a situation and a Hanna analysis of the validity or supremacy of Rule 3 never is reached.

In Burlington Northern R.R. Co. v. Woods, 480 U.S. 1, 107 S.Ct. 967, 94 L.Ed.2d 1 (1987), the Court reaffirmed the Hanna test for determining the validity of a Federal Rule. The Court held that Federal Rule of Appellate Procedure 38 was "suffi-ciently broad" to conflict with a state rule specifying fixed penalties for judgments affirmed on appeal, and that the Federal Rule must be applied because it represents a "valid exercise of Congress' rule-making authority" under the Constitution and the Rules Enabling Act. The Court noted that Rule 38 is a procedural rule, and thus is "a priori constitutional" and does "satisfy the statutory constraints of the Rules Enabling Act." 480 U.S. at 9, 107 S.Ct. at 971.

38. See, e.g., Neifeld v. Steinberg, 438 F.2d 423, 426 (3d Cir.1971) (Rules 12(b) and 12(h) applicable in lieu of Pennsylvania procedural law on an issue raised by a permissive counterclaim); Har–Pen Truck Lines, Inc. v. Mills, 378 F.2d 705, 708 (5th Cir.1967) (Georgia statute prohibiting joinder of contract and tort claims inapplicable since the joinder issue was one governed by the Federal Rules).

Only when there is no Federal Rule directly governing the disputed matter or when both state and federal law may be applied concurrently is it necessary to test the competing state and federal practices against the twin aims of Erie—avoidance of forum-shopping and the inequitable administration of the laws.[39]

Despite the comparative clarity that Hanna has introduced into the process of determining governing law questions involving a Federal Rule, the Court's reasoning has not been accepted universally. As pointed out in the preceding section, Justice Harlan's concurring opinion in Hanna suggested that the majority's "arguably procedural ergo constitutional" test was overly broad and ignored the true foundations of the Erie doctrine.[40] Further, his opinion points out the difficulty under Hanna of determining when a Federal Rule is directly in conflict with a state practice and when the Rule exceeds the Supreme Court's rulemaking authority. Problems in determining the applicability of a Federal Rule also persist because there often are difficulties in defining the proper scope of a particular Rule.[41]

In Gasperini v. Center for Humanities,[42] for example, the Supreme Court recently faced the problem of determining the scope of a Federal Rule. The case presented the question whether a federal court had to apply the forum state's (New York) statutory standard for judicial review of jury-awarded damages in a diversity action.

Journalist William Gasperini had sued the Center for Humanities for losing his original photographic slides. The jury returned a verdict much larger than expected, and the Center for Humanities challenged the verdict for excessiveness, arguing that the federal district court should apply a New York statute that required state trial and appellate courts, on a motion for a new trial, to review a jury's damage award more critically than was required by the traditional federal standard of review.[43] The district judge refused to apply the state standard of review, but on appeal the Second Circuit reversed, holding that the New York statute should have been applied.

The Supreme Court granted certiorari and reviewed two issues: first, whether the district court should have applied the New York statute, and second, whether the Second Circuit had violated the Sev-

---

39. See Kuchenig v. California Co., 350 F.2d 551, 554–55 (5th Cir.1965), cert. denied 382 U.S. 985, in which Judge Wisdom concluded that a question of indispensability required a "run of the mine" Erie–Byrd balancing test. For a discussion of the balancing approach, see § 4.3, above.

40. 380 U.S. at 476, 85 S.Ct. at 1146–47.

41. For a detailed discussion of the problem of determining the proper scope of the rules, see 19 C. Wright, A. Miller & E. Cooper, Jurisdiction and Related Matters 2d § 4310.

42. 518 U.S. 415, 116 S.Ct. 2211, 135 L.Ed.2d 659 (1996). N.Y.-McKinney's CPLR 5501(c).

43. Under the New York statute, an award is excessive if it "deviates materially from what would be reasonable compensation." N.Y.-McKinney's CPLR 5501 (c); the more restrictive federal decisional rule allows the verdict to stand unless it "shocks the conscience of the court." 116 S.Ct. at 2211, 2236, 518 U.S. at 415, 459.

enth Amendment in reviewing the verdict de novo. As to the first question, Justice Ginsburg, writing for the Court, adopted Hanna's "twin aims" rationale of Erie, reasoning that the application of the federal standard would violate the first aim because substantial variations in recovery between a federal district court and a New York trial court would encourage forum-shopping. Applying a federal standard of review also would violate Hanna's second aim, which attempted to prevent the inequitable administration of the law as between federal and state courts. However, three dissenting justices argued the Hanna "twin aims" test was inapplicable because the trial court's standard of review fell within the broad scope of judicial discretion permitted by Federal Rule 59, and, in accordance with Hanna's interpretation of the Rules Enabling Act, the federal standard applied.[44]

Although the New York statute also authorized state appellate courts to reduce jury verdicts, the Court rejected the application of this appellate provision to a federal diversity action. The Court explicitly adopted the balancing test of Byrd v. Blue Ridge Rural Electric Cooperative, Inc., weighing the state policies underlying the statute's appellate provision against the federal interests embedded in the "Re-examination Clause" of the Seventh Amendment. The Court concluded that the latter prevailed.[45]

Commentators on Gasperini have noted the conspicuous absence of any reliance on Byrd in the Court's discussion of the first "Erie question"—whether to apply the state standard of review at all—as well as the conspicuous absence of a discussion of Hanna from the Court's consideration of the second Erie question—whether de novo appellate review of a New York trial court's jury-review standard endangers the Seventh Amendment.[46] Unfortunately, the Gasperini Court does not explain why the two questions required two different Erie analyses. On an even more general level, the Court does not provide any guidance in deciding whether one analysis is more relevant than the other on a given question. The Court only hints that the presence of "an essential characteristic of the [federal court] system" in the second question, which involved the Reexamination Clause and the New York statute's appellate provision, triggered the Byrd analysis because that mode of thinking is a better guide in cases that present "countervailing federal interests."[47] Even so, the Court does not explain how to discern the presence of a countervailing interest, or why there is none present in the

44. 116 S.Ct. 2211, 2229, 518 U.S. 415, 448 (Scalia, J., dissenting, joined by Thomas, J. and Rehnquist, C.J.). See also §§ 4.3–4.4, above, for elaboration on Hanna's "guided" Erie questions.

45. U.S.Const.Am. VII ("[N]o fact tried by jury, shall be otherwise re-examined in any Court of the United States, than according to the rules of the common law."). See also §§ 11.3–11.6, below, for an extended discussion of the Seventh Amendment.

46. See, e.g., Freer, The State of Erie after Gasperini, 76 Texas L.Rev. 1637 (1998); Rowe, Not Bad for Government Work: Does Anyone Else Think the Supreme Court Is Doing a Halfway Decent Job in its Erie–Hanna Jurisprudence?, 73 Notre Dame L.Rev. 963 (1998).

47. 116 S.Ct. at 2211, 2276, 518 U.S. 415, 459.

context of the Court's first question about the application of the New York standard rather than that of Federal Rule 59.

Nonetheless, the special status and standard for evaluating governing law questions when Federal Rules are involved can be justified as consistent with the constitutional concerns expressed by Justice Brandeis in Erie. For Erie not only expressed concern about the need to give due deference to the interests of the states in regulating certain substantive spheres, it also suggested that the conduct of the Court in developing federal common law under Swift v. Tyson was outside the authority delegated to the courts by the Rules of Decision Act. But in the situation in which a Federal Rule is present, a different statute is involved—the Rules Enabling Act—and that involves a context in which Congress specifically has delegated certain authority to the Court to promulgate rules regulating their own procedures.[48]

§ 4.5   Determining Which State's Law Controls

Throughout this Chapter we have been concerned with the question of how a federal court determines whether it is bound to follow state law or is free to apply federal law to the case before it. But an additional choice of law question is presented in any case having multistate elements—that question is, which state's law controls. Federal courts confronted with actions whose parties and events cross state lines must answer several choice of law questions: (1) What law, federal or state, provides the principles by which to determine which state's law should govern; (2) What do those choice of law principles direct with regard to the specific governing state law; and (3) Once a particular state law is chosen, is the federal court bound to apply that law in preference to federal law? The standards for answering the last question already have been fully explored in the preceding sections and the second question requires an analysis of the principles governing state-to-state choice of law decisions that is outside the scope of this volume.[1] However, the first question will be addressed in this Section since it involves the same federalism concerns that underlie the Erie doctrine, but, as will be seen, arguably does not necessitate the same resolution.[2]

In Erie Railroad Company v. Tompkins,[3] it will be remembered, the New York federal court was adjudicating a cause of action that had arisen out of an accident that occurred in Pennsylvania involving a Pennsylvania plaintiff. Although Justice Brandeis clearly stated that the federal court in New York was not free to disregard the Pennsylvania common law rule regarding a railroad's duty to trespassers on its right

48. For a discussion of Erie as reflecting a separation of powers determination, see Degnan, Law of Federal Evidence Reform, 76 Harv.L.Rev. 275 (1962).

§ 4.5

1. See generally E. Scoles & P. Hay, Conflict of Laws (1992).

2. For a more complete discussion of the standards governing which state's law controls in a federal diversity suit, see 19 C. Wright, A. Miller & E. Cooper, Jurisdiction and Related Matters 2d § 4506.

3. 304 U.S. 64, 58 S.Ct. 817, 82 L.Ed. 1188 (1938).

of way, he did not explain why Pennsylvania, rather than New York, law governed.

Justice Brandeis' conclusion that Pennsylvania law controlled could mean that the Court was applying a federal choice of law doctrine and accordingly had determined that a tort occurring in Pennsylvania and involving a local resident required the application of that state's law.[4] Alternatively, the Justice may have assumed that a New York state court, applying its own conflict of law rules, would have decided that Pennsylvania law controlled since it was the place of the accident. This analysis suggests that the forum state's conflicts rules should be binding in federal diversity cases.

Little insight can be gleaned from the language of the Erie opinion to determine the actual theory underlying Justice Brandeis' remarks.[5] Thus, federal courts in the immediate post-Erie period were unsure whether to use the forum state's conflict of laws rules, or to develop an independent federal choice of law doctrine. The most influential of the cases decided during these years was the 1940 First Circuit opinion in Sampson v. Channell,[6] authored by Judge Magruder, holding that Erie required the district court to follow the choice of law rules of the forum state.

It is worth noting that the decision the Sampson court reached on this point is not an inevitable one. Neither history nor the Constitution compels it. The Rules of Decision Act[7] refers only to "the laws of the several states * * * in cases where they apply," leaving open the question of which state's law applies in a particular case. Similarly, the Constitution does not direct that a federal court must follow state conflicts doctrines in diversity cases. In fact, it has been suggested that the Full Faith and Credit Clause of Article IV, Section 1, and the implications of the grant of judicial power in Article III provide a constitutional basis for the independent determination by the federal courts of conflicts questions.[8]

The 1941 Supreme Court decision in Sibbach v. Wilson & Company,[9] seemed to point the Court toward adopting a federal conflicts doctrine.

4. Hart, The Relations Between State and Federal Law, 54 Colum.L.Rev. 489, 514 n. 84 (1954).

5. In a case decided a week after Erie the Court by its own admission entirely avoided this choice of law issue. Ruhlin v. New York Life Ins. Co., 304 U.S. 202, 208 n. 2, 58 S.Ct. 860, 862 n. 2, 82 L.Ed. 1290 (1938).

6. "If the federal court in Massachusetts on points of conflicts of laws may disregard the law of Massachusetts as formulated by the Supreme Judicial Court and take its own view as a matter of 'general law,' then the ghost of Swift v. Tyson * * * still walks abroad, somewhat shrunken in size, yet capable of much mischief." 110

F.2d 754, 761 (1st Cir.1940), cert. denied 310 U.S. 650.

7. 28 U.S.C.A. § 1652.

8. Cheatham, Federal Control of Conflict of Laws, 6 Vand.L.Rev. 581 (1953). See also American Law Institute, Study of the Division of Jurisdiction Between State and Federal Courts 442–48 (1969); Friendly, In Praise of Erie—And of the New Federal Common Law, 39 N.Y.U.L.Rev. 383, 398–405 (1964); Hill, The Erie Doctrine and the Constitution: II, 53 Nw.U.L.Rev. 541 (1958); Jackson, Full Faith and Credit— The Lawyer's Clause of the Constitution, 45 Colum.L.Rev. 1 (1945).

9. 312 U.S. 1, 61 S.Ct. 422, 85 L.Ed. 479 (1941). The Court noted that if the

However, before the 1941 Term was over, the Supreme Court laid to rest any notion of federal conflicts principles for diversity cases. In two very important cases decided on the same day, it held that federal courts sitting in diversity must follow the choice of law rules that the forum state court would follow.

The first of these cases was Klaxon Company v. Stentor Electric Manufacturing Company.[10] The action had been brought in a Delaware federal court for breach of a contract that had been executed in New York, the state of incorporation of one of the parties to the contract. The Third Circuit held that a New York statute providing for interest in contract actions was to be applied. In so holding, it made no examination of Delaware law, presuming to follow what was known as the "better view" on the subject. The Supreme Court reversed, ordering that the conflicts principles of Delaware, the forum state, be applied. Speaking for the unanimous Court, Justice Reed observed:

> Any other ruling would do violence to the principle of uniformity within a state upon which the Tompkins decision is based. Whatever lack of uniformity this may produce between federal courts in different states is attributable to our federal system, which leaves to a state, within the limits permitted by the Constitution, the right to pursue local policies diverging from those of its neighbors. It is not for the federal courts to thwart such local policies by enforcing an independent "general law" of conflict of laws.[11]

This conclusion was reached without even considering the argument that the combined force of the Rules of Decision Act, the Full Faith and Credit Clause, and the Article III grant of judicial power permitted federal courts to formulate their own conflicts principles.

In the second case, Griffin v. McCoach,[12] the Court was even more explicit in requiring that the forum state's conflicts doctrine be applied. Administrators of an estate had brought the action in a Texas federal court to collect the proceeds of an insurance policy on the life of the deceased, a citizen and resident of Texas. The defendant insurance company filed a bill of interpleader, bringing into the suit all the other claimants to the policy benefits. The interpleader was allowed, and the insurance company was discharged from the litigation. Because the policy had been issued in New York, the district court found New York law controlling, and awarded the proceeds to members of a syndicate that had been formed to receive them. The Supreme Court reversed.

right to be exempt from discovery rules authorizing physical examinations was substantive, "the Rules of Decision Act required the District Court, though sitting in Illinois, to apply the law of Indiana, the state where the cause of action arose, and to order the examination." 312 U.S. at 10–11, 61 S.Ct. at 425. This language seemed to suggest that when the matter is not governed by a valid Federal Rule, the federal court should apply the practice of the place of the wrong rather than the practice, and the conflicts doctrine, of the forum state.

10. 313 U.S. 487, 61 S.Ct. 1020, 85 L.Ed. 1477 (1941).

11. 313 U.S. at 496, 61 S.Ct. at 1021–22.

12. 313 U.S. 498, 61 S.Ct. 1023, 85 L.Ed. 1481 (1941).

Texas had enacted a rather unusual law forbidding persons without an insurable interest in the insured's life, such as the syndicate members in Griffin, from collecting the proceeds of insurance policies. Since a Texas state court, using its conflicts principles, would apply this rule to a contract made in another jurisdiction, thereby denying recovery to the syndicate members, the case was remanded for a determination that would be consistent with Texas law.

The reasoning employed in both Klaxon and Griffin[13] has been criticized by many scholars and lawyers.[14] Although vertical forum-shopping arguably is reduced by the use of state conflicts principles in both state and federal courts in the same state,[15] horizontal forum-shopping—that is, among the federal courts in different states—is engendered. Litigants simply will gravitate toward federal courts in states whose conflicts principles best serve their purposes.[16]

It is especially unfortunate that federal courts should be so limited in their ability to formulate an independent approach to conflicts of law. They seem to be the logical fora for creating interstate conflicts of law doctrine because of their national character, their relatively neutral attitudes, and the generally high quality of the judges. By making the federal courts adhere to local conflicts practices, Klaxon and Griffin eliminate this potentially beneficial opportunity.

Despite these criticisms, the Supreme Court and the lower federal courts continue to follow the Klaxon principle. Klaxon was reaffirmed in

---

13. Special criticism has been directed at Griffin because the very nature of the statutory interpleader proceeding with its provisions for nationwide service of process suggested that no alternative state forum existed and thus there was no legitimate concern regarding forum-shopping. For a discussion of the implications of the Klaxon and Griffin principles on the question of the law governing interpleader actions, see 7 C. Wright, A. Miller & M. Kane, Civil 2d § 1713.

Several commentators have argued that whenever a litigant is made a party in a federal court by virtue of some special federal statute and personal jurisdiction would not have been possible in state court, federal conflicts rules should be utilized. See Friendly, In Praise of Erie—And of the New Federal Common Law, 39 N.Y.U.L.Rev. 383, 402 (1964); Horowitz, Toward a Federal Common Law of Choice of Law, 14 U.C.L.A.L.Rev. 1191 (1967); Weintraub, The Erie Doctrine and State Conflict of Laws Rules, 39 Ind.L.J. 228 (1964). The great growth of state long-arm statutes, see §§ 3.12–3.13, above, significantly weakens the relevance of this argument.

14. See Baxter, Choice of Law and the Federal System, 16 Stan.L.Rev. 1 (1963); Cheatham, Federal Control of Conflict of Laws, 6 Vand.L.Rev. 581 (1953); Cook, The

Federal Courts and the Conflict of Laws, 36 Ill.L.Rev. 493 (1942); Friendly, In Praise of Erie—And of the New Federal Common Law, 39 N.Y.U.L.Rev. 383, 402 (1964); Hart, The Relations Between State and Federal Law, 54 Colum.L.Rev. 489, 513–15 (1954); Horowitz, Toward a Federal Common Law of Choice of Law, 14 U.C.L.A.L.Rev. 1191 (1967). See also American Law Institute, Study of the Division of Jurisdiction Between State and Federal Courts, Official Draft, Commentary—Memorandum C 442 (1969).

15. Given the rapidity of change in conflicts law, Klaxon arguably may stimulate forum-shopping between federal and state courts in the same jurisdiction. Ideal Structures Corp. v. Levine Huntsville Dev. Corp., 396 F.2d 917 (5th Cir.1968). This may result when a litigant is encouraged to choose a federal court in which an outmoded state conflicts principle is likely to be mechanically applied because of Klaxon, or a state court in which the antiquated conflicts doctrine may be modified or abandoned.

16. Weintraub, The Erie Doctrine and State Conflict of Laws Rules, 39 Ind.L.J. 228, 241–46 (1964).

Bernhardt v. Polygraphic Company,[17] in which the Court held that Vermont law declaring arbitration agreements unenforceable must control in a case involving an employment contract entered into in New York but performable in Vermont. To eliminate any doubt on the subject, the Court reaffirmed the Klaxon principle even more recently in Day & Zimmermann, Inc. v. Challoner,[18] a 1975 decision. This was a diversity case brought in a Texas federal court to recover for death and personal injury resulting from an explosion of ammunition in Cambodia. The Supreme Court held that the governing substantive law was to be determined by the conflict of laws rules of the Texas state courts. As a result, the law of Cambodia, where the cause of action arose, applied.

It should be noted that the reach of the Klaxon decision is limited somewhat by two considerations. First, the state conflicts principle that is to be applied must be valid under the Full Faith and Credit and Due Process Clauses of the Constitution.[19] Second, when there is no precedent in the forum state describing the choice of law rule to be followed, a federal court may assume that the state would follow those conflicts doctrines accepted by the majority of jurisdictions.[20] This at least enables the federal court to select the law to be applied according to widely recognized conflicts rules.

Several Supreme Court decisions have refined the principles of the Klaxon and Griffin cases further. Nolan v. Transocean Air Lines[21] involved an action brought by a New York resident in a New York federal court for a wrongful death that occurred in California. New York choice of law principles provided that California substantive law controlled. The Court suggested that in such a situation, the federal court is to apply, not California law as the federal court understands it, but New York's conception, if there be any, of what California law is.[22]

Another wrinkle in the Klaxon principle was introduced by the Supreme Court in Van Dusen v. Barrack.[23] The issue in that case was whether the applicable state law changes when there is an interstate transfer of venue under Section 1404(a) of Title 28 of the United States

17. 350 U.S. 198, 76 S.Ct. 273, 100 L.Ed. 199 (1956).

18. 423 U.S. 3, 96 S.Ct. 167, 46 L.Ed.2d 3 (1975).

19. See generally Hughes v. Fetter, 341 U.S. 609, 71 S.Ct. 980, 95 L.Ed. 1212 (1951). But in most cases Full Faith and Credit is not a significant limitation on the states' abilities to develop whatever conflicts rules they deem appropriate. See Allstate Ins. Co. v. Hague, 449 U.S. 302, 101 S.Ct. 633, 66 L.Ed.2d 521 (1981).

20. Gates v. P. F. Collier, Inc., 378 F.2d 888 (9th Cir.1967), cert. denied 389 U.S. 1038. See also § 4.6, below.

21. 365 U.S. 293, 81 S.Ct. 555, 5 L.Ed.2d 571 (1961).

22. 365 U.S. at 295–96, 81 S.Ct. at 557. In a famous statement by Judge Friendly writing for the Second Circuit in Nolan, he points to the unreality of the process suggested by the Supreme Court, commenting that the federal court in New York would be called upon "to determine what the New York courts would think the California courts would think on an issue about which neither has thought." Nolan v. Transocean Air Lines, 276 F.2d 280, 281 (2d Cir.1960), vacated and remanded 365 U.S. 293, 81 S.Ct. 555, 5 L.Ed.2d 571 (1961).

23. 376 U.S. 612, 84 S.Ct. 805, 11 L.Ed.2d 945 (1964). For a discussion of Van Dusen, see Note, Choice of Law after Transfer of Venue, 75 Yale L.J. 90 (1965).

Code.[24] The Court held that when transfer is ordered pursuant to a motion by the defendant, the transferee court must apply the law that would have been applied in the transferor court. A change in forum only means a change in courtrooms, not a change of law. The Court strictly reaffirmed this view in Ferens v. John Deere Company.[25] A five-justice majority held that when transfer is on the plaintiff's motion under Section 1404(a), the same rule applies. The Court reasoned that to rule otherwise would "undermine the Erie rule in a serious way" in that it would result in a different law being applied in state courts and federal courts in diversity cases.[26] However, Justice Scalia, speaking for the four dissenters, said that the decision compromises Klaxon, and the " 'principle of uniformity within a state' which Klaxon says [the Rules of Decision Act] embodies" by allowing plaintiffs to choose a distant federal court instead of a state court "in order to obtain application of a different substantive law."[27] Thus, the plaintiff's initial forum choice, even if improper,[28] will govern which state's laws control when a case is transferred under Section 1404(a). It still is uncertain what law applies in the transferee court when a case is transferred for lack of venue under Section 1406(a), or when a court of the transferor state would have dismissed the original action on forum non conveniens grounds, although an extension of the Court's divided decision in Ferens probably leads to the application of the law of the transferor court.

Is Congress powerless to alter the Klaxon rule? A conclusion that the Constitution does not give Congress the power to authorize independent federal choice of law doctrines is incongruous with recognized congressional authority to administer the federal court system. Nor is it apparent why the judicial power of the United States should be inherently more limited than that of the individual states in the area of conflicts of laws.[29] Nonetheless, the prospect of congressional activity in this field seems slim and the Supreme Court has made clear that, at least in the absence of congressional direction, the federal courts are obliged to apply state choice of law principles.[30]

24. Transfer is discussed in § 2.17, above.

25. 494 U.S. 516, 110 S.Ct. 1274, 108 L.Ed.2d 443 (1990).

26. 494 U.S. at 526, 110 S.Ct. at 1276.

27. 494 U.S. at 539, 110 S.Ct. at 1286. In Ferens, the application of Mississippi's choice of law rules resulted in the use of Pennsylvania's substantive law and Mississippi's statute of limitations in a Pennsylvania tort action. However, other states' choice of law rules may implicate the "substantive" law to be applied in a transferred case.

28. The majority acknowledged that the plaintiffs filed their tort claim in Mississippi only in the hope of taking advantage of that state's longer statute of limitations, immediately transferring the claim to the Pennsylvania federal court, and consolidating it with their pending contract and warranty actions on the same facts.

29. See American Law Institute, Study of the Division of Jurisdiction Between State and Federal Courts, Official Draft, Commentary—Memorandum C, 442 (1969).

30. When Congress *has* spoken on a matter, federal courts must apply the congressional rule even in the face of a contrary state rule. In Stewart Organization, Inc. v. Ricoh Corp., 487 U.S. 22, 108 S.Ct. 2239, 101 L.Ed.2d 22 (1988), the Supreme Court held that the existence of a contractual forum-selection clause will be weighed as a factor in determining whether a transfer of forum is fair and convenient under Section 1404(a), despite the forum state's strong policy against those clauses. The

§ 4.6 Determining the Content of State Law

Once it has been decided what state's law will govern a dispute, the federal court then must ascertain the actual content of that law.[1] In Erie Railroad Company v. Tompkins,[2] Justice Brandeis stated that the law to be applied by the federal courts would be that "declared by its [the state's] Legislature in a statute or by its highest court * * *."[3] However, this formula for determining state law was modified substantially by several controversial Supreme Court decisions, culminating in the case of Fidelity Union Trust Company v. Field.[4]

In order to understand the facts in Fidelity Union Trust, some background information is necessary. Originally, New Jersey law had prohibited the establishment of a "Totten" or tentative trust. This type of trust is created when a bank deposit is made in the depositor's name as trustee for another. It is revocable at any time before the death of the depositor.[5] Statutes passed in 1932 reformed the state law and authorized use of the trust. In 1935, Edith Peck deposited a sum of money in Fidelity Union Trust for the benefit of Ethel Field. When Miss Peck died soon after, Miss Field brought suit against the bank in order to recover the balance of the account.

The federal district court, reviewing New Jersey law, found that two vice-chancellors, comparable to judges on an intermediate state law court, had decided in other cases that the legislation permitting the Totten trust was so "confused" and "difficult to comprehend" that this fiduciary arrangement would remain invalid in New Jersey.[6] Thus, the federal court applied these decisions and held that Ethel Field could not recover. The Third Circuit reversed, finding that the state statutes clearly permitted the trust. The court of appeals believed that because the highest court of the state had not ruled on the matter, the federal courts were free to interpret the statute as they saw fit.[7]

The Supreme Court reversed. The Court noted that an intermediate state court, such as the New Jersey Chancery Court, acts as an organ of the state when it declares and applies state law. Therefore, its decisions are binding on the federal courts, even though the state's highest court may not have ruled on the particular matter.[8]

Court held that because Section 1404(a) "represents a valid exercise of Congress's authority under the Constitution," and was sufficiently broad to cover the issues in the case, it must be applied. 487 U.S. at 31–32, 108 S.Ct. at 2245.

§ 4.6

1. For a more detailed discussion of the problem of ascertaining state law, see 19 C. Wright, A. Miller & E. Cooper, Jurisdiction and Related Matters 2d § 4507.

2. 304 U.S. 64, 58 S.Ct. 817, 82 L.Ed. 1188 (1938).

3. 304 U.S. at 78, 58 S.Ct. at 822.

4. 311 U.S. 169, 61 S.Ct. 176, 85 L.Ed. 109 (1940).

5. For a more detailed discussion of the characteristics of the "Totten Trust," see G. Bogert, The Law of Trusts and Trustees, § 47, at 333–36 (2d ed.1965).

6. 311 U.S. at 176, 61 S.Ct. at 177.

7. 108 F.2d 521 (3d Cir.1939).

8. 311 U.S. at 177–78, 61 S.Ct. at 178.

The Supreme Court's decision was subjected to immediate criticism. In a case decided by the Second Circuit shortly after the Field decision, Judge Frank observed that federal judges now would have "to play the role of ventriloquist's dummy to the courts of some particular state."[9] Judge Clark, referring to the Field holding, commented: "this, I say without hesitation, is the most troublesome, the most unsatisfying in its consequence, of all the rules based upon the Tompkins case."[10] Especially disturbing to many writers was that by forcing the federal courts to apply whatever state court opinion was available on a particular legal issue, the Supreme Court was binding the federal courts in diversity cases to state decisions that in many instances were of no precedential value within the same state court system. In the Field case, for example, the vice-chancellor's rulings were not binding on any other state court judge in New Jersey.[11]

Despite these objections, the federal courts continued to apply the Field doctrine in diversity cases. In fact, some lower courts seemed to carry the doctrine to extremes. For example, in Gustin v. Sun Life Assurance Company,[12] the Sixth Circuit held that even when the only available information regarding the particular state's law on a subject consists of an unreported state court decision, a federal court sitting in diversity is bound to follow that decision.[13]

The Supreme Court appeared to retreat somewhat from Field in King v. Order of United Commercial Travelers of America,[14] a 1948 decision. In that case, Chief Justice Vinson stated that Field had not formulated a general rule as to the respect that must be accorded state trial court decisions. Holding that the unpublished decision of a South Carolina Common Pleas court was not binding on a federal court, the Chief Justice noted, "it would be incongruous indeed to hold the federal court bound by a decision which would not be binding on any state court."[15] The Court was careful to caution federal courts not to assume that all state trial court decisions could be ignored, however, concluding "other situations may well call for a different result."[16]

The duty of the federal courts to ascertain state law does not end upon the entry of judgment. In a decision rendered the year after Field,

9. Richardson v. Commissioner of Internal Revenue, 126 F.2d 562, 567 (2d Cir. 1942).

10. Clark, State Law in the Federal Courts: The Brooding Omnipresence of Erie v. Tompkins, 55 Yale L.J. 267, 290 (1946).

11. When the highest court in New Jersey subsequently did address the issue raised in Field, it adopted the Third Circuit's view and permitted the Totten trust, as opposed to the view of the New Jersey vice-chancellors that had been forced upon the federal courts by the Supreme Court. See Hickey v. Kahl, 129 N.J.Eq. 233, 19 A.2d 33 (1941).

12. 154 F.2d 961 (6th Cir.1946), cert. denied 328 U.S. 866.

13. Judge Allen's opinion in Gustin suggests that the unreported decision of the Court of Appeals of Ohio was applied, in part, because there was no reason to suppose that the Court of Appeals would change the ruling or that the Supreme Court of Ohio would grant review of the intermediate court decision. 154 F.2d at 962.

14. 333 U.S. 153, 68 S.Ct. 488, 92 L.Ed. 608 (1948).

15. 333 U.S. at 161, 68 S.Ct. at 493.

16. 333 U.S. at 162, 68 S.Ct. at 493.

the Supreme Court ruled that a federal court of appeals must apply the latest state precedents, even though they may have been rendered after the trial court ruled on the matter that the appellate court is reviewing.[17] As Justice Reed noted: "Any other conclusion would but perpetuate the confusion and injustices arising from inconsistent federal and state interpretations of state law."[18]

This holding makes a good deal of sense insofar as it places the federal courts in the same position as the state appellate courts—able to correct erroneous rulings of the lower courts.[19] However, it raises a new problem. Is a federal court in matters being considered in a diversity case held to existing state decisions, no matter how antiquated and questionable they might be, or is it free to anticipate a revision of state law that, although imminent, has not yet been formally announced by the state courts? The issue is exemplified by a 1957 First Circuit case, Mason v. American Emery Wheel Works.[20] Suit had been brought in a Rhode Island federal court against a Rhode Island corporation by a Mississippi citizen for the negligent manufacture of an emery wheel. Since the injury occurred in Mississippi, the district court applied Mississippi local law to determine the tort liability of the corporation.[21] The district court reluctantly concluded that it was bound by a 1928 Mississippi state decision that required privity of contract between the user and manufacturer, contrary to the great weight of authority in the United States. Writing for the appellate court, Judge Magruder reversed, finding in a recent dictum by the Mississippi Supreme Court evidence to suggest that the 1928 decision soon would be revised. In a similar vein, Judge Frank, writing for the Second Circuit, noted that a federal judge in a diversity case should ask "what would be the decision of reasonable intelligent lawyers, sitting as judges of the highest New York court, and fully conversant with New York 'jurisprudence'?"[22]

Not all courts agree with this liberal approach to the federal judge's interpretative powers. For example, Judge Jones of the Fifth Circuit rejected any such approach as "attempting to psychoanalyze state court

---

17. Vandenbark v. Owens–Illinois Glass Co., 311 U.S. 538, 61 S.Ct. 347, 85 L.Ed. 327 (1941). See also Nolan v. Transocean Air Lines, 365 U.S. 293, 81 S.Ct. 555, 5 L.Ed.2d 571 (1961).

18. 311 U.S. at 543, 61 S.Ct. at 350.

19. This practice can produce unfair results, however. For example, in Atkins v. Schmutz Mfg. Co., 372 F.2d 762 (6th Cir. 1967), cert. denied 389 U.S. 829, the plaintiff had relied on three Kentucky cases that held foreign statutes of limitation applicable if the cause of action arose in the foreign jurisdiction. Before the case could be tried in the Kentucky federal court, the Kentucky Court of Appeals overruled this line of authority. Although the plaintiff had relied on the overruled cases, and although the cases were overruled only subsequent to the plaintiff's commencement of the action

in federal court, the federal court of appeals was compelled to dismiss the suit. An unfair result ultimately was avoided in Atkins when the plaintiff subsequently brought the same suit in a Virginia federal court. The Fourth Circuit en banc decided that given the peculiar facts involved, the previous Kentucky lawsuit had tolled the Virginia statute of limitations and therefore the Virginia suit was not time barred. 435 F.2d 527 (4th Cir.1970).

20. 241 F.2d 906 (1st Cir.1957), cert. denied 355 U.S. 815.

21. See § 4.5, above, for a discussion of the standard used to decide which state's law governs.

22. Cooper v. American Airlines, Inc., 149 F.2d 355, 359 (2d Cir.1945).

judges rather than to rationalize state court decisions."[23] The court concluded: "The Georgia courts can overrule their prior decisions. The Federal Courts cannot do so."[24]

Some light was shed on the problem by the Supreme Court's ruling in Bernhardt v. Polygraphic Company of America.[25] Bernhardt supports those federal judges advocating the right to anticipate changes on the part of a state's highest courts in appropriate situations. The Supreme Court held in Bernhardt that a 1910 decision by the Vermont Supreme Court was binding on the federal trial court in 1956. Justice Douglas found that it was still good law because, "there appears to be no confusion in the Vermont decisions, no developing line of authorities that casts a shadow over the established ones, no dicta, doubts or ambiguities in the opinions of Vermont judges on the question, no legislative development that promises to undermine the judicial rules."[26] These comments suggest that a federal court may consider these factors to determine if previous state precedents still should be followed by the federal courts.[27]

The Supreme Court's last general elaboration on the problem occurred in Commissioner of Internal Revenue v. Estate of Bosch.[28] That case held that whenever the highest court of the state has not spoken on a particular legal issue, decisions by intermediate courts will be highly persuasive data, but they are not binding, on the issue of what the law of the state is.[29] As a result of Bosch, federal courts sitting in diversity jurisdiction now are free to use all available information to ascertain how the highest court of the state in which they are sitting would determine the legal principle in issue.

In ascertaining the state law to be applied in diversity matters, federal courts must carefully achieve a balance between two extremes. On the one hand, they must avoid being rigid implementers of outmoded state doctrines that no longer would be embraced by the forum state's

---

23. Polk County, Georgia v. Lincoln Nat. Life Ins. Co., 262 F.2d 486, 489 (5th Cir.1959). Specifically, the court held that changes in the membership of the Georgia Supreme Court did not justify a conclusion by the district court that a change in the state law was imminent.

24. 262 F.2d at 490. See also the Eighth Circuit's decision in Yoder v. Nu–Enamel Corp., 117 F.2d 488, 489 (8th Cir. 1941), in which the court held that federal courts were not only to apply the "definitive decision" of the state courts, but were also to consider dicta and other "obvious implications and inferences."

25. 350 U.S. 198, 76 S.Ct. 273, 100 L.Ed. 199 (1956).

26. 350 U.S. at 205, 76 S.Ct. at 277.

27. Justice Frankfurter, concurring in Bernhardt, also implied that federal courts

are able to "estimate" whether a state court would consider itself bound by a precedent before blindly applying the rule of the case. 350 U.S. at 209, 76 S.Ct. at 279.

28. 387 U.S. 456, 87 S.Ct. 1776, 18 L.Ed.2d 886 (1967), noted 81 Harv.L.Rev. 69 (1967). Although not a diversity case, the Court nevertheless thought the issue to be one requiring an analysis similar to that undertaken in diversity litigation and therefore addressed the issues raised by Field and Bernhardt.

29. For articles written prior to Bosch that agree with the conclusions reached by the Court, see Corbin, The Laws of the Several States, 50 Yale L.J. 762 (1941); Corbin, The Common Law of the United States, 47 Yale L.J. 1351 (1938); Kurland, Mr. Justice Frankfurter, The Supreme Court and the Erie Doctrine in Diversity Cases, 67 Yale L.J. 187 (1957).

judiciary. On the other hand, district judges must shun the temptations of prematurely anticipating changes in state law, choosing principles they would prefer to apply rather than those actually used by state judges.[30] The authority of the federal courts to identify changes and follow developments in state doctrines is most important; otherwise, forum-shopping might be engendered if federal courts were obliged to apply rigidly outmoded state precedents that a state court could disregard. Further, as one scholar has pointed out, if federal courts are too tightly shackled in the exposition of state law, "federal justice in such matters is doomed to be second-rate justice, and the state systems will lose the benefit of valuable contributions to their growth."[31]

Later cases have refined the method suggested by Bernhardt and Bosch for determining the content of state law. Thus, it has been held that although obiter dicta need only be considered as illustrative of what state law actually is, considered dicta as well as actual state court holdings are binding on federal courts sitting in diversity jurisdiction.[32] Further, opinions of the state attorney general on particular questions of law are not binding, but are entitled to careful consideration.[33] Long-term practices by state agencies, whose responsibility it is to administer and interpret the particular state law concerned, also are good indicia in determining the content of the law to be applied.[34]

The most difficult situation arises when there is no existing state statute or judicial precedent controlling the legal problem before the federal court. The Supreme Court held, in Meredith v. City of Winter Haven,[35] that a federal court cannot refuse jurisdiction because there is no ascertainable state law on the topic. If the state has a procedure by which its highest court will answer questions certified to it by the federal court, the latter may be able to obtain an authoritative statement on important and unclear issues of state law.[36] But if certification to the

---

30. The comments of Judge Wyzanski in Pomerantz v. Clark, 101 F.Supp. 341 (D.Mass.1951), are illustrative. "A federal judge sitting in a diversity jurisdiction case has not a roving commission to do justice or to develop the law according to his, or what he believes to be the sounder, views. His problem is less philosophical and more psychological. His task is to divine the views of the state court judges." 101 F.Supp. at 345–46.

31. Hart, The Relations Between State and Federal Law, 54 Colum.L.Rev. 489, 510 (1954). See also Boner, Erie v. Tompkins: A Study in Judicial Precedent, II, 40 Texas L.Rev. 619 (1962).

32. Kirk v. Hanes Corp. of North Carolina, 16 F.3d 705 (6th Cir.1994); Rocky Mountain Fire & Cas. Co. v. Dairyland Ins. Co., 452 F.2d 603 (9th Cir.1971); Doucet v. Middleton, 328 F.2d 97 (5th Cir.1964); Hartford Acc. & Indem. Co. v. First Nat. Bank & Trust Co. of Tulsa, Oklahoma, 287

F.2d 69 (10th Cir.1961); U.S. Fidelity & Guar. Co. v. Anderson Constr. Co., 260 F.2d 172 (9th Cir.1958).

33. E.g., Bostick v. Smoot Sand & Gravel Corp., 260 F.2d 534, 541 (4th Cir. 1958).

34. Orme v. Lendahand Co., 128 F.2d 756 (D.C.Cir.1942). See also Rosenfeld, Administrative Determinations as State Law under Erie v. Tompkins, 24 N.Y.U.L.Rev. 319 (1949). But see the decision in Mogis v. Lyman–Richey Sand & Gravel Corp., 189 F.2d 130 (8th Cir.1951), cert. denied 342 U.S. 877 (administrative practice no longer was indicative of state law on the matter in question after amendment of the law by the state legislature).

35. 320 U.S. 228, 64 S.Ct. 7, 88 L.Ed. 9 (1943).

36. See generally Madden v. Creative Serv., Inc., 24 F.3d 394 (2d Cir.1994); Strange v. Krebs, 658 F.2d 268 (5th Cir.

state court is not possible or feasible, the federal court may consider all available legal sources. That includes scholarly works such as law review articles, textbooks, treatises, and the Restatements of the Law, as well as decisions of other states, federal decisions, or the general weight of authority. However, as pointed out earlier, the federal court must be careful to determine the law it believes the state court would choose were it to rule on the matter, not the law the district judge thinks is the best.

As a practical matter, once the district court has determined the state law, it probably will not be disturbed by the court of appeals. The district judge is usually a member of the bar of the state in which the federal court sits, and therefore is more conversant with the intricacies of state law than most federal appellate judges would be. Indeed, for a number of years some courts of appeal considered the ascertainment of state law by the district judge to be akin to a question of fact and hence reviewable only under very limited circumstances and reversible only when the trial judge was "clearly erroneous."[37] However, the majority considered the trial judge's finding to be subject to the same appellate review as any other legal question, although recognizing that the district judge's conclusion is worthy of great weight.[38]

Finally, in Salve Regina College v. Russell,[39] the Supreme Court held that a court of appeals should review de novo a district court's determination of state law. The Court stated that appellate deference to district court determinations of state law is inconsistent with the twin aims of the Erie doctrine—discouragement of forum-shopping and avoidance of inequitable administration of the laws—because it invites divergent development of state law among the federal trial courts within a single state and, by denying access to meaningful review of state-law claims, creates a dual system of enforcement of state-created rights, in which the substantive rule applied to a dispute may depend on the choice of forum.[40] The Court also reasoned that independent appellate review of legal issues best serves the dual goals of doctrinal coherence and economy of judicial administration since the courts of appeals are better suited to resolve complicated legal questions while district courts are better suited to resolve factual issues.[41]

1981); Flannery v. U.S., 649 F.2d 270 (4th Cir.1981).

37. See, e.g., Christensen v. Osakis Silo Co., 424 F.2d 1301 (8th Cir.1970); Rudd–Melikian, Inc. v. Merritt, 282 F.2d 924 (6th Cir.1960); Bower v. Bower, 255 F.2d 618 (9th Cir.1958).

38. Bernhardt v. Polygraphic Co. of America, 350 U.S. 198, 204, 76 S.Ct. 273, 277, 100 L.Ed. 199 (1956); Ward v. Hobart Mfg. Co., 450 F.2d 1176 (5th Cir.1971). See also Kurland, Mr. Justice Frankfurter, The Supreme Court and the Erie Doctrine in Diversity Cases, 67 Yale L.J. 187, 216–18

(1957), for a discussion of the role of the Supreme Court in reviewing cases in which lower federal courts have attempted to ascertain and apply state law.

39. 499 U.S. 225, 111 S.Ct. 1217, 113 L.Ed.2d 190 (1991).

40. 499 U.S. at 234, 111 S.Ct. at 1222.

41. 499 U.S. at 231, 111 S.Ct. at 1221. The rationale of Salve Regina was extended to the Supreme Court's review of lower court determinations of state law in Leavitt v. Jane L., 518 U.S. 137, 116 S.Ct. 2068, 135 L.Ed.2d 443 (1996).

§ 4.7 Federal Common Law

The decision in Erie Railroad Company v. Tompkins[1] clearly stated that "except in matters governed by the Federal Constitution or by acts of Congress, the law to be applied in any case is the law of the state," and that "there is no federal general common law."[2] But this language should not be read too broadly. Although Justice Brandeis stated that there is no "federal general common law," it nevertheless is apparent that he did recognize the existence of a "federal common law."[3]

The federal common law that has developed since Erie can be distinguished from the federal general common law applied by the federal courts under the rule of Swift v. Tyson[4] in three basic ways. First, federal common law displaces state statutory as well as state decisional law; federal general common law prior to Erie only displaced state court decisions.[5] Second, whenever federal common law governs a particular issue, it must be applied whether the case is in a state or in a federal court.[6] In addition, cases "arising under" federal common law fall within the federal courts' federal question jurisdiction[7] and diversity of citizenship is not required for them to be heard in federal court. Finally, federal courts are not free to develop federal common law on all matters of "general" as distinguished from "local" law as was true under Swift, but are restricted to matters of substantial national concern that fall within the powers given the federal government by the Constitution.[8]

§ 4.7

1. 304 U.S. 64, 58 S.Ct. 817, 82 L.Ed. 1188 (1938).

2. 304 U.S. at 78, 58 S.Ct. at 822.

3. In Hinderlider v. La Plata River & Cherry Creek Ditch Co., 304 U.S. 92, 110, 58 S.Ct. 803, 811, 82 L.Ed. 1202 (1938), decided the same day as Erie, Justice Brandeis wrote: "[W]hether the water of an interstate stream must be apportioned between the two states is a question of 'federal common law' upon which neither the statutes nor the decisions of either state can be conclusive." See Meltzer, State Court Forfeitures of Federal Rights, 99 Harv.L.Rev. 1128 (1986).

4. 41 U.S. (16 Pet.) 1, 10 L.Ed. 865 (1842). See § 4.1, above, for a discussion of the Swift decision.

5. See, e.g., Clearfield Trust Co. v. U.S., 318 U.S. 363, 63 S.Ct. 573, 87 L.Ed. 838 (1943); Hinderlider v. La Plata River & Cherry Creek Ditch Co., 304 U.S. 92, 58 S.Ct. 803, 82 L.Ed. 1202 (1938).

6. See, e.g., Yiatchos v. Yiatchos, 376 U.S. 306, 84 S.Ct. 742, 11 L.Ed.2d 724 (1964); Banco Nacional de Cuba v. Sabbatino, 376 U.S. 398, 84 S.Ct. 923, 11 L.Ed.2d 804 (1964); Local 174, Teamsters, Chauffeurs, Warehousemen & Helpers of America v. Lucas Flour Co., 369 U.S. 95, 82 S.Ct.

571, 7 L.Ed.2d 593 (1962). In Comment, Federal Common Law and Article III: A Jurisdictional Approach to Erie, 74 Yale L.J. 325, 329 (1964), it is observed that this line of decisions enforces the Erie policy of preventing forum-shopping by requiring that state and federal courts sitting in the same jurisdiction apply the same law.

7. 28 U.S.C.A. § 1331(a). This basis of subject-matter jurisdiction is discussed in § 2.3, above.

8. See generally Friendly, In Praise of Erie—And of the New Federal Common Law, 39 N.Y.U.L.Rev. 383 (1964); Hart, The Relations Between State and Federal Law, 54 Colum.L.Rev. 489 (1954); Hill, The Law-Making Power of the Federal Courts: Constitutional Preemption, 67 Colum.L.Rev. 1024 (1967); Mishkin, The Variousness of "Federal Law": Competence and Discretion in the Choice of National and State Rules for Decision, 105 U.Pa.L.Rev. 797 (1957); Note, The Federal Common Law, 82 Harv. L.Rev. 1512 (1969); Note, The Competence of Federal Courts to Formulate Rules of Decision, 77 Harv.L.Rev. 1084 (1964); Note, Federal Common Law and Article III: A Jurisdictional Approach to Erie, 74 Yale L.J. 325 (1964); Comment, Rules of Decision in Nondiversity Suits, 69 Yale L.J. 1428 (1960).

Beyond these few basic principles, however, very little is clear about the proper scope of federal common law.

The areas in which federal courts have applied federal common law most frequently include: (1) admiralty and maritime cases; (2) interstate disputes; (3) proceedings raising matters of international relations; (4) actions involving gaps in federal statutory provisions; and (5) cases concerning the legal relations and proprietary interests of the United States. These categories are neither exhaustive nor analytically precise.[9] Nonetheless, in each of them, there is good reason for permitting the federal courts to ignore the presumption in favor of state law and to develop an independent body of federal substantive law. The rationales behind requiring the application of state law—the logical utilization of local substantive law to solve local problems, the preservation of important state policies, and the orderliness and certainty of application of well-developed areas of state law—generally are not applicable in the situations listed.[10] In addition, there are various federal concerns present—the desire to have uniform law in areas in which definite federal interests should prevail, the need to foster and promote the federal policies, and a preference for decisionmaking by the federal judiciary, who are particularly suited to develop decisional law that advances federal policy. But as will be seen later, the fact that the district court is free to develop a federal substantive rule does not mean that state law will not be chosen as the most logical rule for a particular problem.

The first area in which federal common law was found to govern was admiralty. In Southern Pacific Company v. Jensen,[11] the Supreme Court ruled that the constitutional grant of admiralty jurisdiction in Article III gave the federal courts (and Congress) the power to develop a uniform body of substantive federal maritime law, which would constitute part of "national law." The dissent in Jensen argued that "the language of § 2 of art. III of the Constitution speaks only of establishing jurisdiction, and does not prescribe the mode in which or the substantive law by which the exercise of that jurisdiction is to be governed."[12] This construction of the Constitution was involved in Erie, decided after Jensen, in which Justice Brandeis made it clear that the constitutional grant of diversity jurisdiction was not in itself an adequate basis for judicial lawmaking power. Nevertheless, the majority view in Jensen has been reaffirmed since Erie and the principle that federal statutory and common law governs in admiralty cases is firmly established.[13]

9. For a fuller discussion of the development of federal common law, see 19 C. Wright, A. Miller & E. Cooper, Jurisdiction and Related Matters 2d §§ 4514–19.

10. See Note, The Federal Common Law, 82 Harv.L.Rev. 1512, 1517–31 (1969).

11. 244 U.S. 205, 214–15, 37 S.Ct. 524, 528, 61 L.Ed. 1086 (1917). See also Chelentis v. Luckenbach S.S. Co., 247 U.S. 372, 38 S.Ct. 501, 62 L.Ed. 1171 (1918) (federal common law of admiralty must be applied by state courts in admiralty cases).

12. 244 U.S. at 227, 37 S.Ct. at 533 (Pitney, J., dissenting).

13. See Kossick v. United Fruit Co., 365 U.S. 731, 81 S.Ct. 886, 6 L.Ed.2d 56 (1961); Romero v. International Terminal Operating Co., 358 U.S. 354, 360–61, 79 S.Ct. 468, 474, 3 L.Ed.2d 368 (1959). But see Wilburn Boat Co. v. Fireman's Fund Ins. Co., 348 U.S. 310, 75 S.Ct. 368, 99

Even though there may be disagreement over the source of power relied on by the Jensen Court, the use of federal common law in admiralty cases is consistent with the essential philosophy of the Erie doctrine. Parties to a lawsuit should not be exposed to potentially differing outcomes for the same conduct depending on whether the action is brought in an admiralty court rather than a federal court sitting in general jurisdiction or a state court. Additional support for the Jensen conclusion can be found in the national interest of having uniformity in the law that governs maritime commerce. It also is likely that in the field of admiralty, federal law should be the product of the greater special expertise regarding maritime matters possessed by federal judges.

Another substantive area in which federal common law has been applied involves disputes arising between two or more states. Although the Supreme Court never has identified the constitutional provision establishing the basis for this exercise of federal judicial lawmaking power, the general belief is that it can be found in the grant of jurisdiction in Article III, Section 2 over controversies between states. The authority for federal common lawmaking power also reflects the realization that application of a particular state's law to disputes between two states would be inconsistent with the equality and quasi-sovereignty of the states.[14] As the Supreme Court said in State of Kansas v. State of Colorado:[15]

> [W]henever * * * the action of one state reaches, through the agency of natural laws, into the territory of another state, the question of the extent and the limitations of the rights of the two states becomes a matter of justiciable dispute between them, and this court is called upon to settle that dispute in such a way as will recognize the equal rights of both and at the same time establish justice between them. In other words, through these successive disputes and decisions this court is practically building up what may not improperly be called interstate common law.[16]

Because the Supreme Court has both original and exclusive jurisdiction of suits between states,[17] the decision to allow the development of federal common law to decide these controversies also does not pose the danger of forum-shopping nor the threat of inconsistent bodies of law

L.Ed. 337 (1955), holding that in the absence of federal legislation or a conflicting rule established by the federal courts, the regulation of maritime insurance was left to the states. The case was severely criticized in G. Gilmore & C. Black, The Law of Admiralty Jurisdiction 44–55 (1957), and Currie, Federalism and the Admiralty: The Devil's Own Mess, 1960 Sup.Ct.Rev. 158, 215–18. For a history of the treatment of marine insurance in the era of Swift v. Tyson, see Fletcher, The General Common Law and Section 34 of the Judiciary Act of 1789: The Example of Marine Insurance, 97 Harv.L.Rev. 1513 (1984).

14. New Jersey v. New York, 283 U.S. 336, 51 S.Ct. 478, 75 L.Ed. 1104 (1931). See generally Note, The Federal Common Law, 82 Harv.L.Rev. 1512, 1520 (1960).

15. 206 U.S. 46, 27 S.Ct. 655, 51 L.Ed. 956 (1907).

16. 206 U.S. at 97–99, 27 S.Ct. at 667.

17. 28 U.S.C.A. § 1251(a)(1).

being potentially applicable to a case.[18] Thus, the Erie Court's concern over the use of federal common law in disputes over matters within state competence is not present.[19]

A third area in which federal common law is authorized involves the international relations of the United States. The leading case is Banco Nacional de Cuba v. Sabbatino.[20] Decided in 1964, the suit was brought by the bank, a financial agent of the Cuban government, to recover the proceeds of a shipment of sugar. The shipment, along with all the property of the defendant corporation, had been expropriated by the Cuban government. The district court granted summary judgment against Banco Nacional on the ground that the Cuban expropriation was a violation of international law. As a result, valid title to the sugar did not pass to the Cuban government. The Supreme Court reversed, holding that as a matter of federal common law, the act-of-state doctrine, which prohibits United States' courts from questioning the validity of public acts a foreign country commits within its territory, proscribed challenging the Cuban expropriation decree. Justice Harlan, writing for the Court's majority, recognized that an identical result would have been obtained had state law been applied because New York also recognized the act-of-state doctrine. However, he reasoned that the issue involved the basic competence of the federal executive and judicial branches to decide questions affecting the United States' foreign relations, and therefore must be treated as exclusively within the ambit of federal law.[21]

Sabbatino is important in defining the scope of federal common law. In contrast to matters of water apportionment or interstate boundary disputes, the Court admitted that neither the Constitution, nor any statute enacted by Congress, required the application of federal common

---

18. See Note, Federal Common Law and Interstate Pollution, 85 Harv.L.Rev. 1439, 1447–51 (1972); Note, The Original Jurisdiction of the United States Supreme Court, 11 Stan.L.Rev. 665, 683–85 (1959).

19. Another concern in Erie was the fact that the judiciary was acting without congressional authorization—a separation of powers argument. The importance of congressional silence in permitting the courts to create a body of federal interstate common law was reemphasized in City of Milwaukee v. Illinois, 451 U.S. 304, 101 S.Ct. 1784, 68 L.Ed.2d 114 (1981), a case involving interstate water pollution. The litigation began in 1972 when the parties invoked the original jurisdiction of the Supreme Court. 406 U.S. 91, 92 S.Ct. 1385, 31 L.Ed.2d 712 (1972). At that time the Court ruled that federal common law governed and thus the parties could invoke general federal question jurisdiction and were directed to file suit in the lower federal courts. Subsequently, Congress enacted a

new system of regulations for water pollution and when the case returned to the Court in 1981, it ruled that the congressional enactments displaced federal common law. Justice Rehnquist, writing for the Court, emphasized that federal common law is always subject to the "paramount authority of Congress." 451 U.S. at 313, 101 S.Ct. at 1791.

20. 376 U.S. 398, 84 S.Ct. 923, 11 L.Ed.2d 804 (1964). For a discussion of this case and the federal common law of foreign relations, see Edwards, The Erie Doctrine in Foreign Affairs Cases, 42 N.Y.U.L.Rev. 674 (1967); Henkin, The Foreign Affairs Power of the Federal Courts: Sabbatino, 64 Colum.L.Rev. 805 (1964); Hill, The Law-Making Power of the Federal Courts: Constitutional Preemption, 67 Colum.L.Rev. 1024 (1967).

21. 376 U.S. at 425–26, 84 S.Ct. at 939.

law in the area of international relations. Nonetheless, Justice Harlan found that:

> the act of state doctrine does * * * have "constitutional" underpinnings. It arises out of the basic relationships between branches of government in a system of separation of powers. It concerns the competency of dissimilar institutions to make and implement particular kinds of decisions in the area of international relations. Whatever considerations are thought to predominate, it is plain that the problems involved are uniquely federal in nature.[22]

Sabbatino elaborates the statement in United States v. Curtiss–Wright Export Corporation,[23] that the power to conduct international relations is not vested in the states individually but collectively in the government of the United States. Accordingly, power over international relations belongs to the federal government as a matter of sovereignty.[24]

The federal courts also have fashioned common law in situations in which Congress expressly or impliedly has delegated the authority to do so by statute or statutory scheme. There are two such types of judicial lawmaking. The first is a byproduct of the fact that statutes cannot be written with sufficient detail to cover every possible question of construction and application that might arise. As a result, federal courts often are obliged to interpret vague words,[25] supply omitted procedural rules,[26] or determine the viability of claims and defenses that may be asserted when the elements of a statutory cause of action have been established by Congress in very general terms.[27] This is the most prevalent form of federal common lawmaking power and it has arisen most frequently in the context of a federal statute that does not contain a statute of limitations.[28]

22. 376 U.S. at 423–24, 84 S.Ct. at 938.

23. 299 U.S. 304, 57 S.Ct. 216, 81 L.Ed. 255 (1936).

24. Some commentators have expressed concern over the potential Sabbatino creates for federal lawmaking. See, e.g., Henkin, The Foreign Affairs Power of the Federal Courts: Sabbatino, 64 Colum.L.Rev. 805, 831 (1964). Compare Horowitz, Toward a Federal Common Law of Choice of Law, 14 U.C.L.A.L.Rev. 1191, 1200–03 (1967), in which the author cites Sabbatino as support for "the development of a federal common law of choice of law."

25. E.g., Urie v. Thompson, 337 U.S. 163, 69 S.Ct. 1018, 93 L.Ed. 1282 (1949).

26. Note, Federal Statutes Without Limitations Provisions, 53 Colum.L.Rev. 68 (1953).

27. E.g., Lear, Inc. v. Adkins, 395 U.S. 653, 89 S.Ct. 1902, 23 L.Ed.2d 610 (1969).

28. Until 1985, the statute of limitations applied in civil rights actions brought under Section 1983 of Title 42 of the United States Code generally was the state statute of limitations for an analogous state claim, which was consistent with the general practice in other situations in which there was no limitations provision in a federal statute. This led to inconsistencies as state and district courts applied varying limitations rules to Section 1983 actions. To clarify the confusion, the Supreme Court created a uniform rule in Wilson v. Garcia, 471 U.S. 261, 105 S.Ct. 1938, 85 L.Ed.2d 254 (1985), holding that all Section 1983 actions should be characterized as actions involving claims for personal injuries for purposes of choosing the applicable limitations period. However, the Court failed to answer directly the question of which period to apply in states that have more than one personal injury statute of limitations.

In DelCostello v. International Bhd. of Teamsters, 462 U.S. 151, 103 S.Ct. 2281, 76 L.Ed.2d 476 (1983), the Court applied an analogous federal statute of limitations to suits over employer-union collective bargaining and arbitration agreements. The

The second type of statutory authorization occurs when Congress provides a skeletal legislative scheme and permits the federal courts to formulate a detailed body of substantive law under it. The leading Supreme Court case in which such an implied congressional delegation was found is Textile Workers Union v. Lincoln Mills of Alabama,[29] in which an employer sued a labor union for damages sustained as a result of an allegedly unauthorized strike. Congress had developed a statutory scheme indicating a federal interest in industrial peace and a policy in favor of the smooth functioning of the collective bargaining process. The Supreme Court, in an opinion by Justice Douglas, held that the federal courts must fashion a body of substantive principles of federal labor law from the legislative outline provided by Congress. In a later case, the Court also held that state courts are obliged to apply this judicially created federal law, regardless of the content of local law.[30]

The Lincoln Mills decision is of great significance in that it has opened the way for federal judicial lawmaking in many areas in which a general regulatory scheme has been enacted by Congress. For example, regulations established pursuant to statute and administered by the Securities and Exchange Commission have been used as a springboard for the development of an important body of federal common law in the area of securities regulation and corporate responsibility.[31] In an even more far-reaching decision, a lower court has held that private citizens have a federal common law cause of action against telephone companies even though the congressional regulatory statutes neither explicitly nor implicitly address the question of private remedies. The court based its decision on the significant national interest in the proper functioning of telephone companies.[32]

Court held that "when a rule from elsewhere in federal law [the National Labor Relations Act] clearly provides a closer analogy than available state statutes, and when the federal policies at stake and the practicalities of litigation make that rule a significantly more appropriate vehicle for interstitial lawmaking, we have not hesitated to turn away from state law." 462 U.S. at 172, 103 S.Ct. at 2294. See also Lampf, Pleva, Lipkind, Prupis & Petigrow v. Gilbertson, 501 U.S. 350, 111 S.Ct. 2773, 115 L.Ed.2d 321 (1991).

When a federal court borrows a state statute of limitations or one from another federal statute, it does not necessarily also borrow that statute's tolling provision. See West v. Conrail, 481 U.S. 35, 107 S.Ct. 1538, 95 L.Ed.2d 32 (1987).

In 1990, Congress enacted a general four-year statute of limitations for all federal statutory claims filed subsequent to its enactment. 28 U.S.C.A. § 1658. This should alleviate many of the problems described in this footnote.

29. 353 U.S. 448, 77 S.Ct. 912, 1 L.Ed.2d 972 (1957). For a favorable discussion of this decision, see Note, The Federal Common Law, 82 Harv.L.Rev. 1512, 1531–35 (1969). For a view opposing the decision, see Bickel & Wellington, Legislative Purpose and the Judicial Process: The Lincoln Mills Case, 71 Harv.L.Rev. 1 (1957).

30. Local 174, Teamsters, Chauffeurs, Warehousemen & Helpers of America v. Lucas Flour Co., 369 U.S. 95, 82 S.Ct. 571, 7 L.Ed.2d 593 (1962).

31. For a discussion of litigation in this context, see L. Loss & J. Seligman, Securities Regulation 2111–19, 3404–48 (3d ed. 1989, and Supp.1998).

32. Ivy Broadcasting Co. v. American Tel. & Tel. Co., 391 F.2d 486 (2d Cir.1968), noted 37 Geo.Wash.L.Rev. 425 (1968), 82 Harv.L.Rev. 479 (1968), 43 Tul.L.Rev. 168 (1968), 47 N.C.L.Rev. 447 (1969). The decision has been criticized by most writers.

On the other hand, the Supreme Court took an especially cautious attitude toward the creation of federal common law in Wheeldin v. Wheeler,[33] finding that Congress had not intended to create a private cause of action against a federal officer for abuse of the federal subpoena power. Thus, the imposition of any liability in a case of this character would have to be based on state law. Writing for the Court, Justice Douglas observed:

> As respects the creation by the Federal courts of common law rights, it is perhaps needless to state that we are not in the free-wheeling days antedating Erie R. Co. v. Tompkins * * * [I]t is difficult for us to see how the present statute, which only grants power to issue subpoenas, implies a cause of action for abuse of that power.[34]

And more recent Supreme Court decisions reveal an increasing reluctance to infer private remedies from congressional legislation.[35]

A related question is whether a federal court can imply the right to develop federal common law to enforce constitutional rights when there is congressional silence in the area. This issue was addressed in Bivens v. Six Unknown Named Agents,[36] in which the Court held that when a citizen's Fourth Amendment rights have been infringed, an action under federal common law will lie against the tortfeasor.[37] A significant jurisprudence has developed on the basis of Bivens.

Finally, the authority to apply federal common law has been recognized in matters involving the determination and definition of the

---

33. 373 U.S. 647, 83 S.Ct. 1441, 10 L.Ed.2d 605 (1963). See also Bell v. Hood, 327 U.S. 678, 684, 66 S.Ct. 773, 777, 90 L.Ed. 939 (1946).

34. 373 U.S. at 651, 83 S.Ct. at 1445.

35. E.g., Northwest Airlines, Inc. v. County of Kent, Michigan, 510 U.S. 355, 114 S.Ct. 855, 127 L.Ed.2d 183 (1994); Middlesex County Sewerage Authority v. National Sea Clammers Ass'n, 453 U.S. 1, 101 S.Ct. 2615, 69 L.Ed.2d 435 (1981); Northwest Airlines, Inc. v. Transport Workers Union of America, AFL–CIO, 451 U.S. 77, 101 S.Ct. 1571, 67 L.Ed.2d 750 (1981); Touche Ross & Co. v. Redington, 442 U.S. 560, 99 S.Ct. 2479, 61 L.Ed.2d 82 (1979). See also American Airlines, Inc. v. Wolens, 513 U.S. 219, 115 S.Ct. 817, 130 L.Ed.2d 715 (1995).

In Cort v. Ash, 422 U.S. 66, 95 S.Ct. 2080, 45 L.Ed.2d 26 (1975), the Court announced a four-part test for determining whether a private right of action should be implied from a federal statute that does not expressly provide for a private remedy. "First, is the plaintiff 'one of the class for whose especial benefit the statute was enacted,' * * *—that is, does the statute create a federal right in favor of the plaintiff? Second, is there any indication of legislative intent, explicit or implicit, either to create such a remedy or to deny one? * * * Third, is it consistent with the underlying purposes of the legislative scheme to imply such a remedy for the plaintiff? * * * And finally, is the cause of action one traditionally relegated to state law, in an area basically the concern of the States, so that it would be inappropriate to infer a cause of action based solely on federal law?" Id. at 78, 95 S.Ct. at 2088.

36. 403 U.S. 388, 91 S.Ct. 1999, 29 L.Ed.2d 619 (1971).

37. Insofar as Erie R.R. Co. v. Tompkins suggests that federal courts act unconstitutionally when they create common law based solely on the general judicial power given them under Article III, Section 2, Bivens recognizes that other provisions in the Constitution authorize judicial action without legislative authorization. The difference between the two cases then becomes the source of constitutional power being invoked by the Court, balanced against general Tenth Amendment deference to state interests. When a direct federal constitutional right is involved, as in Bivens, Tenth Amendment concerns are of lesser weight.

government's legal relations and proprietary interests.[38] The source of this lawmaking power has been characterized in various ways—for example, as emanating from the jurisdictional grant to the federal courts established in legislation that forms the basis of most of the legal relationships entered into by the United States; as implied when the federal government, or one of its instrumentalities, is a party to litigation; or as an outgrowth of federalism because the government in these cases is exercising constitutional or federal functions.[39] The final approach seems to have the most extensive support in court decisions.

In this category the most famous case is Clearfield Trust Company v. United States,[40] which involved a check printed by the United States that was stolen and cashed by means of a forged endorsement. The bank that accepted the check guaranteed prior endorsements and presented it for payment to the United States Treasury. After paying the bank the proceeds of the check, the United States learned of the forged endorsement and sued the bank on the latter's guarantee to recover the amount paid. Under the law of Pennsylvania, where the transactions had taken place, the United States would have been unable to prevail because of its delay in notifying the bank of the forgery. Nevertheless, the Supreme Court held that the United States could recover since the rights and duties of the Government on its commercial paper are controlled by federal common law. Writing for the Court, Justice Douglas observed:

> The authority to issue the check had its origin in the Constitution and the statutes of the United States and was in no way dependent on the laws of Pennsylvania or of any other state. * * * The duties imposed upon the United States and the rights acquired by it as a result of the issuance find their roots in the same federal sources.[41]

Thus, the federal courts could fashion the governing legal rule according to their own standards.

The Clearfield principle, which involved the government's contractual relations, has been extended to government tort litigation. In United States v. Standard Oil Company of California,[42] the Court held that the liability of a tortfeasor for injuring a United States soldier was to be determined under federal common law. Conversely, in Howard v.

---

38. See Hill, The Law–Making Power of the Federal Courts: Constitutional Preemption, 67 Colum.L.Rev. 1024, 1041–42 (1967). See also Mishkin, The Variousness of "Federal Law": Competence and Discretion in the Choice of National and State Rules for Decision, 105 U.Pa.L.Rev. 797 (1957).

39. In U.S. v. McCabe Co., 261 F.2d 539, 543 (8th Cir.1958), the court found that it was clear that the rule of Erie v. Tompkins was inapplicable when the United States "enters into large scale transactions requiring uniform administration," since under those circumstances "questions of rights and liabilities must be uniformly determined by federal law." Compare Jack-

son v. Johns–Manville Sales Corp., 750 F.2d 1314 (5th Cir.1985) (en banc), cert. denied 478 U.S. 1022 (asbestos litigation that presented questions as to the proper distribution of the resources of the asbestos industry was not a proper area for federal common law because it did not relate to congressional policy or directly implicate the authority and duties of the United States as sovereign).

40. 318 U.S. 363, 63 S.Ct. 573, 87 L.Ed. 838 (1943).

41. 318 U.S. at 366, 63 S.Ct. at 575.

42. 332 U.S. 301, 305, 67 S.Ct. 1604, 1607, 91 L.Ed. 2067 (1947).

Lyons,[43] the Court found that the validity of a defense by a federal officer being sued for tortious activity in the course of official duties also would have to be determined in accordance with federal common law. The Howard case is significant because it was solely a diversity action between private parties—neither the government nor any of its instrumentalities was a party to the lawsuit. Yet the Court concluded that federal common law applied because "the authority of a federal officer to act derives from federal sources, and the rule which recognizes a privilege under appropriate circumstances as to statements made in the course of duty is one designed to promote effective functioning of the Federal Government."[44]

The fact that an area of law has been recognized as requiring the application of federal common law does not necessarily mean that state law will be ignored. Federal courts in their discretion may decide that on a given matter state law is the most appropriate choice, and adopt it as the federal rule of decision. The decision to use state law may be based on numerous factors: (1) congressional intent as expressed in a statute or legislative history; (2) the existence of a substantial state interest that would be served by the incorporation of local law; (3) the fact that federal and state law are closely interwoven; (4) the furtherance of equity; or (5) as a matter of convenience when federal law is silent on a particular issue.[45]

The utilization of state law under any of these circumstances should not be confused with that required in situations governed by the Erie doctrine. When state law is adopted as the federal rule of decision in instances governed by federal common law, the district court is not just "another court of the state" and therefore is not bound by previous state court interpretations of the law involved.[46] The federal judge has much greater flexibility in ascertaining the substance of the state law.[47] As

---

43. 360 U.S. 593, 79 S.Ct. 1331, 3 L.Ed.2d 1454 (1959). See also Boyle v. United Technologies Corp., 487 U.S. 500, 108 S.Ct. 2510, 101 L.Ed.2d 442 (1988); Barr v. Matteo, 360 U.S. 564, 79 S.Ct. 1335, 3 L.Ed.2d 1434 (1959).

44. 360 U.S. at 597, 79 S.Ct. at 1334.

45. In U.S. v. Kimbell Foods, Inc., 440 U.S. 715, 99 S.Ct. 1448, 59 L.Ed.2d 711 (1979), the Court held that the priority of liens stemming from federal Small Business Administration and Farmers Home Administration loans were matters of federal law, but that federal courts were free to adopt state law as federal law. The Court reasoned that there was "little need for a nationally uniform body of law" in this context, and asked two questions, which have been adopted by lower federal courts, e.g., FDIC v. Jenkins, 888 F.2d 1537 (11th Cir.1989), to determine whether state law should be followed: (1) Would state law frustrate the specific objectives of federal programs? (2) Would a federal rule disrupt commercial relations predicated on state

law? See also Atherton v. Federal Deposit Ins. Corp., 519 U.S. 213, 117 S.Ct. 666, 136 L.Ed.2d 656 (1997); Kamen v. Kemper Financial Servs., Inc., 500 U.S. 90, 111 S.Ct. 1711, 114 L.Ed.2d 152 (1991); McCarthy v. Azure, 22 F.3d 351 (1st Cir.1994).

46. See De Sylva v. Ballentine, 351 U.S. 570, 581, 76 S.Ct. 974, 980, 100 L.Ed. 1415 (1956) (although state law would be used for certain definitional purposes under the Copyright Act, a state would not be permitted to define the word "children" in a way entirely strange to "ordinary usage"; only permissible variations in the ordinary concept of "children" would be used as part of the state's definition). See also Holmberg v. Armbrecht, 327 U.S. 392, 66 S.Ct. 582, 90 L.Ed. 743 (1946) (federal equitable tolling rule applied to state statute of limitations).

47. Commissioner of Internal Revenue v. Estate of Bosch, 387 U.S. 456, 465, 87 S.Ct. 1776, 1782, 18 L.Ed.2d 886 (1967).

Professor Mishkin has commented, "there remains a freedom, after decision to incorporate local law, to control the intent and methods of that adoption which is not present when a determination has been made that state law will apply because the court has no competence to do otherwise."[48] In addition, unlike cases in which Erie controls, state courts are bound by federal court decisions on matters of federal common law, even when these decisions deviate from state law or the interpretation thereof.[49]

The interwoven nature of federal and state interests, and the caution that must be exercised by a federal judge in formulating law that will protect the interests involved, is demonstrated by the decision in Bank of America National Trust & Savings Association v. Parnell.[50] As in Clearfield, United States commercial paper was involved. Unlike Clearfield, however, the suit was between private parties. The bank brought an action against Parnell to recover money he had acquired by cashing federal bonds that had been stolen from the bank. One issue raised was whether the bonds, which were not yet mature but had been called in by the United States for redemption, were "overdue." Two other issues were whether Parnell acted in good faith in redeeming the bonds and whether he or the bank had the burden of proving good faith or a lack thereof. In an opinion by Justice Frankfurter, the Supreme Court held that the issue whether the bonds were overdue was governed by federal law because it went to the nature of the rights and obligations created by United States' commercial instruments. But the burden of proof and good faith questions were considered to pertain to what was "essentially a private transaction"[51] and therefore were to be decided under the law of the state where the transaction took place.[52]

In United States v. Yazell,[53] the Court further elaborated this analysis. The United States brought suit against Mrs. Yazell to recover proceeds under a loan contract negotiated between the defendant, her husband, and the Small Business Administration. The Court barred recovery by the United States. The anachronistic law of coverture, which prevented married women from binding their property without a court order, still existed in the state where the transaction occurred; this law, the Court ruled, had to be applied. The Court emphasized in Yazell that

---

48. Mishkin, The Variousness of "Federal Law": Competence and Discretion in the Choice of National and State Rules for Decision, 105 U.Pa.L.Rev. 797, 804 (1957). See also Comment, Rules of Decision in Nondiversity Suits, 69 Yale L.J. 1428, 1449 (1960).

49. See note 6, above.

50. 352 U.S. 29, 77 S.Ct. 119, 1 L.Ed.2d 93 (1956). See also O'Melveny & Myers v. Federal Deposit Ins. Corp., 512 U.S. 79, 114 S.Ct. 2048, 129 L.Ed.2d 67 (1994)(federal interest too remote).

51. 352 U.S. at 34, 77 S.Ct. at 122.

52. 352 U.S. at 33–34, 77 S.Ct. at 121.

53. 382 U.S. 341, 352, 86 S.Ct. 500, 507, 15 L.Ed.2d 404 (1966). Justice Fortas wrote: "Each State has its complex of family and family-property arrangements. * * * We have no federal law relating to the protection of the separate property of married women. We should not * * * establish a principle which might cast doubt upon the effectiveness in relevant types of federal suits of the laws of 11 other States relating to the contractual positions of married women, which, as the Government's brief warns us, would be affected by our decision in the present case."

the contract was negotiated and entered into individually, and drafted with state law clearly in mind. This is different from Clearfield in which thousands of government checks had been issued, as well as the circumstances in Parnell in which thousands of United States bonds were involved. Justice Fortas, who wrote the Yazell opinion, did not decide whether the application of state law in this matter was required by the Rules of Decision Act, or by its adoption as a federal principle.

What can be seen from these cases is that neither the basis of subject-matter jurisdiction, the identity of the parties, nor the nature of the right in controversy necessarily justifies or prevents a federal court's development of federal common law. The decision to create and apply a federal rule of decision, or to adopt state law as the rule of decision in matters of federal common law, requires an in depth analysis of the specific facts and issues raised in a particular lawsuit and the relative significance of the federal and state interests intertwined in the resolution of the case.

B. STATE COURTS

§ 4.8 Federal Law in State Courts

Article III of the Constitution gives Congress the power to create exclusive jurisdiction in the federal courts over all matters within the judicial authority of the federal government.[1] However, the federal courts have exclusive jurisdiction only in those instances in which Congress explicitly has granted it and Congress has not done so in all contexts. Thus, in all disputes involving federal law matters as to which Congress has not made federal court jurisdiction exclusive, the state courts have concurrent jurisdiction with the federal courts.[2]

Because of concurrent jurisdiction, a state court often is required to construe and apply federal law.[3] This means that the state court must attempt to achieve a result consistent with federal jurisprudence. Due to certain similarities between this practice and the care with which federal courts must interpret and apply state law in diversity cases under the Erie doctrine, the enforcement of federal law by state courts has been called the "inverse-Erie" doctrine.[4]

---

§ 4.8

1. See generally § 2.2, above.

2. Claflin v. Houseman, 93 U.S. (3 Otto) 130, 23 L.Ed. 833 (1876). See generally Cullison, State Courts, State Law and Concurrent Jurisdiction of Federal Questions, 48 Iowa L.Rev. 230 (1963).

3. Federal law also may be introduced into state proceedings by way of defense. Thus, in Sola Elec. Co. v. Jefferson Elec. Co., 317 U.S. 173, 63 S.Ct. 172, 87 L.Ed. 165 (1942), the plaintiff brought a state court breach of contract action for the nonpayment of royalties due under a contract

licensing the use of a federal patent. The Supreme Court held that a state court defendant may assert the contract's invalidity under the federal Copyright or Patent Act, or defend on the ground that the plaintiff's copyright or patent has been used in violation of the federal antitrust laws. This result was permitted even though claims under the copyright and patent laws typically fall within the exclusive jurisdiction of the federal courts.

4. See Friendly, In Praise of Erie—And of the New Federal Common Law, 39 N.Y.U.L.Rev. 383 (1964); Hill, Substance

Although it has been apparent since 1789 that state courts have the power to adjudicate various federal claims, until 1912 doubt remained whether state courts were bound to hear these cases. However, in the Second Employers' Liability Cases,[5] the Supreme Court decided that whenever a state court is capable of adjudicating a right arising under the Federal Employers' Liability Act, it does not have any discretion to decide whether to hear the claim. The case had reached the Supreme Court when a Connecticut court had held that it would not enforce an FELA claim because doing so would be contrary to Connecticut state policy. The Court dismissed this reasoning, and stated that when Congress creates a national policy on a given subject, it overrides individual state policies to the contrary. The national policy is as powerful a directive to the state courts as if the statute had been enacted by the state legislature.[6]

Congress has enacted legislation creating numerous causes of action that can be litigated in the state courts. In some instances the plaintiff's choice of tribunal is final.[7] In those cases in which a state court adjudicates a claim under a federal statute, the Supremacy Clause of the Federal Constitution, Article VI, requires the application of federal law.[8] Furthermore, as established in Local 174, Teamsters, Chauffeurs, Warehousemen & Helpers of America v. Lucas Flour Company,[9] state courts are required to implement judicially created federal law—federal common law—as well as federal statutory law.

A particular problem for the state courts when they are adjudicating a federally created claim or defense is determining the extent to which they may follow their own procedural rules. Although the Supreme

and Procedure in State FELA Actions—The Converse of the Erie Problem?, 17 Ohio St.L.J. 384 (1956). See also Note, State Enforcement of Federally Created Rights, 73 Harv.L.Rev. 1551, 1561–64 (1960).

5. 223 U.S. 1, 32 S.Ct. 169, 56 L.Ed. 327 (1912).

6. 223 U.S. at 57–58, 32 S.Ct. at 178.

7. For example, an action under the Federal Employers' Liability Act can be brought in either a state or a federal court. 45 U.S.C.A. § 56. However, if the plaintiff has chosen the state forum, the defendant is not permitted to remove the litigation to federal court. 28 U.S.C.A. § 1445(a). For further discussion of the procedure involved in bringing an FELA action before a state court and the problems raised thereby, see generally Hill, Substance and Procedure in State FELA Actions—The Converse of the Erie Problem?, 17 Ohio St.L.J. 384 (1956); Note, State Enforcement of Federally Created Rights, 73 Harv.L.Rev. 1551, 1561–64 (1960).

8. Testa v. Katt, 330 U.S. 386, 67 S.Ct. 810, 91 L.Ed. 967 (1947). In Testa, the Rhode Island Supreme Court refused to enforce a provision for sanctions under the federal Emergency Price Control Act, stating that federal law was "foreign" to Rhode Island in the "private international" sense, and that it therefore had no duty to enforce the penal laws of a foreign government. The United States Supreme Court reversed in an opinion by Justice Black rejecting the contention that the United States was "foreign" in any manner. See Note, Utilization of State Courts to Enforce Federal Penal and Criminal Statutes: Development in Judicial Federalism, 60 Harv.L.Rev. 966 (1947). The Supreme Court's decision in Testa is criticized in Sandalow, Henry v. Mississippi and the Adequate State Ground: Proposals for a Revised Doctrine, 1965 Sup. Ct.Rev. 187, 203–07 (1965).

9. 369 U.S. 95, 82 S.Ct. 571, 7 L.Ed.2d 593 (1962). The Court held that the substantive principles of federal labor law being developed by the federal judiciary under § 301(a) of the Taft–Hartley Act, 29 U.S.C.A. § 185(a), are binding on state courts. For a discussion of federal common law in the labor field, see § 4.7 at notes 29–30, above.

Court has held that a state court may use its own procedural rules in adjudicating a federally created claim, it has limited this freedom to purely procedural issues in order to protect the implementation of federal rights in state courts, especially in cases involving the FELA. For example, in Brown v. Western Railway of Alabama,[10] the Supreme Court held that a state could not apply its usual rule of construing pleadings against the pleader. To prevent the debilitation of the federal rights created by the FELA, the state court was required to construe the pleadings in favor of the pleader, as would be the case in a federal court.

In Dice v. Akron, Canton & Youngstown Railroad Company,[11] the Supreme Court was even more explicit as to its readiness to override state procedural requirements in order to protect federally created rights.[12] In Dice, an Ohio court, following the equity tradition of that state, granted a judgment notwithstanding the verdict on the question whether a release signed by the plaintiff was invalid because of fraud in the procurement of the plaintiff's signature. Under Ohio law, the fraud issues properly were decided by the judge. The Supreme Court reversed, and ordered the issue submitted to the jury, holding that trial by jury was too important a part of the substantive rights provided through the FELA to be eliminated in a state action. After Dice, state courts, in effect, are required in FELA actions to adhere to federal notions of the judge-jury relationship.[13]

Some scholars have attempted to limit the significance of Dice by suggesting that the case reflects the Supreme Court's concern with protecting rights created under the FELA, and that its holding can be restricted to cases under that statute.[14] Although it is true that the Supreme Court traditionally has been vigorous in its protection of FELA rights, there is no indication that the holding in Dice was meant to be limited to this particular federal statute. In any event, the Dice case clearly supports the proposition that Congress has the constitutional power to enact legislation regulating the mechanics of trial in a state court whenever a federally created claim is involved.[15]

10. 338 U.S. 294, 70 S.Ct. 105, 94 L.Ed. 100 (1949).

11. 342 U.S. 359, 72 S.Ct. 312, 96 L.Ed. 398 (1952). See further the decision in Bowman v. Illinois Cent. R.R. Co., 11 Ill.2d 186, 142 N.E.2d 104 (1957), cert. denied 355 U.S. 837, in which the Illinois Supreme Court held that the scope of appellate review in FELA actions is governed by federal law.

12. For a discussion of the facts and the Court's opinion in Dice, see § 11.8, below.

13. Contrast the Dice result with the decision in Byrd v. Blue Ridge Rural Elec. Co-op., Inc., 356 U.S. 525, 78 S.Ct. 893, 2 L.Ed.2d 953 (1958), in which the Supreme Court decided that federal courts in diversity matters are not required to implement the judge-jury practices of the state in which they sit, but are free to apply federal notions on this subject, even though the source of the claim is state law. For a full discussion of the Byrd case, see §§ 4.3–4.4, above.

14. See Hill, Substance and Procedure in State FELA Actions—The Converse of the Erie Problems, 17 Ohio St.L.J. 384, 397–98 (1956).

15. See generally Note, Procedural Protection for Federal Rights in State Courts, 30 U.Cin.L.Rev. 184 (1961).

§§ 4.9–5.0 are reserved for supplementary material.

Chapter 5

MODERN PLEADING

Analysis

§ 5.1 Introduction

At common law the entire procedural system was inextricably interwoven with what was called the writ system.[1] An action was begun when
the court issued a writ ordering a defendant to appear and defend. A
coherent set of pleading rules did not exist for cases in the common law
courts. Each type of action had its own writ with its own rules for
pleading as well as other procedures. Thus, the requirements of pleading
were tied to the substantive law governing legal relationships. Pleading
in courts of equity operated differently. There, the pleadings consisted of
the detailed statements of the parties, which in large part constituted
both their contentions and the evidence upon which the case was
decided.[2]

Procedural reform in both the United States and England in the
second half of the nineteenth century freed the pleadings from their
entanglements with other procedural as well as substantive matters and
gave pleadings a clearcut function. Modern pleadings were to set forth
the parties' contentions of fact so as to guide the court as well as the
parties throughout the pendency of the case. Pleadings were to be used
as a means to a just determination.[3] By simplifying pleading it was hoped
that cases would turn on their substantive merits rather than on the
lawyers' technical and tactical skills,[4] as had been the case under the
common law system.

A vital aspect of pleading reform was the application of a uniform
set of rules to all cases, regardless of the nature of the substantive
cause.[5] Writs were abolished and pleading distinctions between cases at

---

§ 5.1

1. F. Maitland, The Forms of Action at Common Law (1948).

2. B. Shipman, Handbook of Common Law Pleading 11 (3d ed.1923).

3. C. Clark, Code Pleading 54 (2d ed.1947).

4. N.Y.Laws 1847, c. 59, § 8. See also New York, First Report of the Commissioners on Practice and Pleading 146, 147 (1848).

5. New York, First Report of the Commissioners on Practice and Pleading 146–47 (1848); J. Pomeroy, Remedies and Remedial

law and suits in equity were eliminated.[6]

These developments did not occur everywhere at the same pace or at the same time. In some jurisdictions, notably New York and California, the reforms came as early as 1848 and 1850 and were relatively complete.[7] By the late 1930s a majority of states had followed New York's lead by adopting what has come to be known as the code approach.[8] On the other hand, as late as 1947 at least seven states retained substantial vestiges of common-law practice.[9]

The federal courts were not early leaders in the reform movement. Although a simplified modern system of pleading was adopted for equity cases by the Equity Rules of 1912,[10] until 1938, procedure in actions at law was governed by the Conformity Act,[11] requiring each federal court to apply the rules of practice of the courts of the state in which it was located. Not until promulgation of the Federal Rules of Civil Procedure in 1938 was a uniform system of pleading established for all suits in the federal courts.[12] The federal reform, coming somewhat late, proved to be vitally important, for it represented a new approach to pleading, requiring only fair notice of a claim or defense, which thus stressed simplicity beyond that achieved by state court reform.

In the United States today, then, there are essentially two types of pleading, known generally as "fact" pleading and "notice" pleading. Fact pleading was developed as an integral part of the reform that began with the adoption in 1848 of the New York code of procedure.[13] Notice pleading was introduced by the Federal Rules of Civil Procedure. Although now a majority of states have, by statute or rule, adopted notice pleading provisions virtually identical to those used in the federal courts,[14] a number of states still adhere to the original code pleading formulations even though many other aspects of their procedural systems have been brought into line with the federal rules.[15] This Chapter will explore these two forms of pleading in some detail and note some of their differences from common-law pleading, when appropriate.

Rights § 13 (4th ed.1910); Clark, The Code Cause of Action, 33 Yale L.J. 817 (1924).

6. New York, First Report of the Commissioners on Practice and Pleading, 67–87 (1848); J. Pomeroy, Remedies and Remedial Rights §§ 4, 10 (4th ed.1910).

7. C. Hepburn, The Historical Development of Code Pleading 88, 89 (1897).

8. See C. Clark, Code Pleading § 8 (2d ed.1947).

9. The states were Delaware, Florida, Maine, Rhode Island, Tennessee, Vermont, and West Virginia.

10. 226 U.S. 627 (1912).

11. Act June 1, 1872, c. 255, 17 Stat. 197.

12. Sunderland, The New Federal Rules, 45 W.Va.L.Q. 5 (1938).

13. N.Y.Laws 1848, c. 379.

14. E.g., Alabama, Alaska, Arizona, Colorado, Delaware, Florida, Georgia, Hawaii, Idaho, Indiana, Kansas, Kentucky, Maine, Massachusetts, Minnesota, Missouri, Montana, Nevada, New Jersey, New Mexico, North Carolina, North Dakota, Ohio, Rhode Island, South Dakota, Tennessee, Utah, Vermont, Washington, West Virginia, Wisconsin, and Wyoming.

15. For example, statutes in California and Nebraska still require "fact" pleading, even though they have adopted federal type discovery provisions.

§ 5.2   The Function and Effectiveness of Modern Pleading

Generally speaking, pleadings have two functions. First, they permit the elimination from consideration of contentions that have no legal significance. Thus, if a plaintiff sets forth an alleged claim for which the law provides no redress, the matter should be disposed of immediately; there is no need for a trial to determine if the facts alleged to support the claim are true. The same logic applies whether the defective contention constitutes all or part of a plaintiff's claim or of a defendant's defense. To the extent that a contention cannot affect the result, it should be eliminated at once.

However, the use of the pleadings in this way can be much more than a means of eliminating ill-conceived claims and defenses that could result only in unnecessary costs and delays for the courts and the litigants. It is also a clean, effective method of focusing attention on difficult questions of law, helping them to develop in accord with the needs of society. For example, an injured plaintiff may seek redress on the basis of a novel legal theory or on one that previously had been rejected but that now, in light of technical or social developments, has substantial appeal. Given the precedents, the trial court, upon challenge from the opposing party, may eliminate the issue from the case. When that occurs the matter is squarely preserved in the record so that it can form the basis for appellate review, and, if the appellate court thinks it appropriate, a new legal doctrine will emerge.

The second purpose of modern pleading is to guide the parties and the court in the conduct of cases. A litigant cannot prepare for trial unless she has been informed adequately of the opponent's contentions. Equally vital is notice to the court. There is no way that the court can control an action unless it knows the nature of the parties' allegations. When questions as to the relevancy of certain evidence are raised, either on a motion involving pretrial discovery or on a request for a ruling on admissibility at trial, the court has to know what the case is about or it cannot decide. Similarly, a motion to dismiss all or part of a claim or defense would be meaningless unless the court has the framework provided by the pleadings as a guide.

For notice purposes, it is as important to settle what facts the parties agree occurred as it is to determine what matters are in controversy. If an alleged fact is conceded to be true by the opposing party, the court will consider that fact as established; the court will make legal rulings on that basis, and parties will not be permitted, let alone required, to introduce evidence with regard to the fact's existence.

Ever since modern pleading systems supplanted common-law pleading doctrine, there has been considerable debate as to how much reliance should be placed upon the pleadings to carry out these functions. Some believe that the pleadings should carry a substantial portion of the burden of shaping the case and eliminating irrelevant issues.[1] They argue that without a set of rules, rigidly applied, courts will be clogged with unjustified cases, some that never should have been brought and some that cannot legitimately be defended. Trials that do take place will be sloppy affairs, admitting as evidence testimony that bears remotely at best on the true issues at stake.

Opposing these views are people who argue that the need for reform of the common-law system resulted from the rigidity of its rules, making the results in cases turn on technical matters of procedure rather than the underlying facts or merits. Therefore, the pleadings should be general guides only. Other devices, such as pretrial discovery, summary judgment, and the pretrial conference, should be employed to assist in shaping the case for trial, but even these should be applied flexibly to avoid decisions based upon the technical errors of the lawyers.[2] Moreover these individuals contend that the advantage of eliminating improper issues alleged to be possible under a more rigid set of pleading rules will not materialize because any competent legal technician easily can set forth allegations that satisfy the requirements. Indeed, such a system places a premium on dishonesty; the more unscrupulous is the litigant, the easier it is to set forth the allegations necessary to avoid challenges at the pleading stage.

This debate has not been merely an academic exercise. The nature of the pleading reform in any particular state has depended in large part upon which view prevailed among its lawyers and judges at the time reform was undertaken. However, either through abrupt change or persistent tinkering over a long period of time, the vast majority of American courts now operate under a flexible pleading system that relies heavily on other devices to aid in the delineation and control of litigation.[3]

§ 5.3   Types of Pleadings

Modern rules limit the number and types of pleadings. The initial pleading is the complaint or petition in which plaintiff sets forth her allegations and prayer for relief. The complaint is followed by the answer in which defendant may deny allegations made in the complaint and, in

§ 5.2

1. See, e.g., Fee, The Lost Horizon in Pleading Under the Federal Rules of Civil Procedure, 48 Colum.L.Rev. 491 (1948); McCaskill, Actions and Causes of Action, 34 Yale L.J. 614, 641 (1935). See also Claim or Cause of Action, 13 F.R.D. 253 (1952).

2. C. Clark, Code Pleading 57 (2d ed.1947); Clark, Simplified Pleading, 2 F.R.D. 456 (1943). See also Pike & Willis, The New Federal Deposition–Discovery Procedure, 38 Colum.L.Rev. 1179 (1938). See generally James, The Revival of Bills of Particulars under the Federal Rules, 71 Harv.L.Rev. 1473 (1958); Comment, Federal Rule 12(e): Motion for More Definite Statement—History, Operation and Efficiency, 61 Mich.L.Rev. 1126 (1963).

3. Sutherland, Fact Pleading v. Notice Pleading: The Eternal Debate, 22 Loy. L.Rev. 47, 69–70 (1975–76). For a discussion of residual aspects of the pleading debate as they affect current practice in the federal courts, see Marcus, the Puzzling Persistence of Pleading Practice, 76 Texas L.Rev. 1749 (1998).

addition, may set forth affirmative allegations regarding defenses and counteractions.

It is as to pleadings subsequent to the answer that the rules of different jurisdictions vary, depending in large part on what the answer contains. If the answer merely denies plaintiff's allegations, delineating the issues for trial, further pleadings serve no purpose. If, however, the answer contains affirmative allegations setting forth defenses, it would be logical to require plaintiff to reply to them. Indeed, if a reply, in turn, contained affirmative allegations, logic would dictate that defendant rebut those allegations, and so on until the final pleading would be one that contained only denials. This generally was the practice at common law.[1] It proved so formalistic and impractical that those who drafted modern pleading provisions determined to limit the number of pleadings and to leave to other devices the elimination and delineation of the issues.

Modern courts are divided regarding where the line is to be drawn. Originally, most modern pleading rules required the plaintiff to file a reply to affirmative allegations of the defendant and eliminated all subsequent pleadings. Today many jurisdictions cut off the pleadings after the answer, subject only to the court's power to make a specific order, rarely done, requiring the plaintiff to file a reply.[2] If a party attempts to make an unauthorized response, favorable allegations will be treated as surplusage, subject to a motion to strike, and unfavorable statements will be used against the pleader to the extent that they constitute admissions.[3]

In addition to defending against a plaintiff's claims, the defendant may utilize the answer to file affirmative claims on his own behalf. These may be counterclaims against the plaintiff, cross-claims against a co-defendant, or third party claims against persons who previously have not been joined in the action. In virtually every jurisdiction, whether or not it ordinarily provides for a reply, a response to such an affirmative claim must be made by the party against whom it is asserted.[4] This response may be referred to as an "answer," or it may be called a "reply."

A number of different problems may arise if the response to a counterclaim, cross-claim, or third party claim itself attempts to set forth a claim for affirmative relief. First, by specifically cutting off the plead-

§ 5.3

1. J. Koffler & A. Reppy, Common Law Pleading §§ 292–94 (1969); B. Shipman, Common Law Pleading 31 (3d ed.1923); H. Stephen, Principles of Pleading 82 (1824).

2. Fed.Civ.Proc.Rule 7(a). See, e.g., Moviecolor Ltd. v. Eastman Kodak Co., 24 F.R.D. 325, 326 (S.D.N.Y.1959); Beckstrom v. Coastwise Line, 13 F.R.D. 480 (D.Alaska 1953); Keller–Dorian Colorfilm Corp. v. Eastman Kodak Co., 10 F.R.D. 39 (S.D.N.Y. 1950); Commentary, Effect of Unauthorized Reply, 4 Fed.R.Serv. 888 (1941). California does not even give the court the power to order a reply. West's Ann.Cal.Code Civ. Proc. § 422.10.

3. Berger v. State Farm Mut. Auto. Ins. Co., 291 F.2d 666, 668 (10th Cir.1961). See also C. Clark, Code Pleading 691 (2d ed.1947).

4. Fed.Civ.Proc.Rule 7(a); N.Y.— McKinney's CPLR 3011.

ings, the rules in some jurisdictions could be read to prohibit these claims entirely. Generally, however, courts in these jurisdictions have read their rules liberally to permit the claims.[5] If the claim is brought by a plaintiff against a defendant, the matter is less serious, because the plaintiff can seek leave to amend the original complaint to include the new claim. If the new claim belongs to a party other than the plaintiff, however, this alternative is not available. It seems clear that a person who is called upon to defend against a claim and wishes to make her own affirmative claim should not be prohibited from doing so just because the claim against her happens to be a cross-claim rather than an original complaint.[6] In these instances, then, an additional pleading may be appropriate.

A second problem is whether the party against whom such a claim for affirmative relief is filed, can or must reply to it. Again, the pleading provisions often are silent or ambiguous. For example, Federal Rule 7(a), which states that there shall be "a reply to a counterclaim denominated as such," makes no specific provision for a response to a counterclaim or cross-claim contained in the reply. And the rule goes on to state that no pleading other than those specifically enumerated "shall be allowed." Although there are sound reasons to cut off pleadings at some point to avoid proliferation, the general scheme of modern pleading systems is to require an answer to each affirmative claim; because any new claim for relief is, in reality, a complaint, an answer to it usually is held necessary.[7]

Finally, in a small number of jurisdictions, a demurrer, which is a challenge to the legal sufficiency of a complaint or answer, is denominated a "pleading."[8] Most courts, however, confine the term "pleading" to only those documents setting forth allegations or denials of facts. Whether a legal challenge to a pleading is or is not itself considered a pleading has little substantive effect; however, it may determine procedural matters such as when the challenge can be filed and heard.

A. PLEADING REQUIREMENTS

1. Code Pleading

§ 5.4 Pleading a Cause of Action: A Definition

A litigant under the codes typically is required to allege "a plain and concise statement of the facts constituting each cause of action (defense

---

5. Southeastern Industrial Tire Co. v. Duraprene Corp., 70 F.R.D. 585, 586 n. 2 (E.D.Pa.1976); Joseph Bancroft & Sons v. M. Lowenstein & Sons, Inc., 50 F.R.D. 415, 418 (D.Del.1970); Gretener, A. G. v. Dyson–Kissner Corp., 298 F.Supp. 350 (S.D.N.Y. 1969). But see Cornell v. Chase Brass & Copper Co., 48 F.Supp. 979, 980–81 (S.D.N.Y.1943), affirmed 142 F.2d 157 (2d Cir.1944). See also West's Ann.Cal.Code Civ.Proc. §§ 422.10, 431.30.

6. 5 C. Wright & A. Miller, Civil 2d § 1188.

7. Millar, Counterclaim Against Counterclaim, 48 Nw.U.L.Rev. 671, 690 (1954).

8. See, e.g., West's Ann.Cal.Code Civ. Proc. § 422.10.

or counterclaim) without unnecessary repetition."[1] This apparently simple formulation has proven to be deceptive, however, because the courts have had substantial problems defining the terms "cause of action" and "facts." So serious are these difficulties that they have cut deeply into the hoped-for effectiveness of code pleading reform.

At common law a pleader needed first to select a proper writ that would cover the general set of facts upon which relief was sought. The writ governed both substantive and procedural rights. If the facts, alleged and proved, fell within the proper scope of the writ, the relief available under the writ would be granted, provided that the pleader had followed the procedures that the writ required.

The codes abolished the writs and substituted a uniform procedural system, but nothing specific was provided for the matters of substance with which the procedural system had been intertwined. The codes had not been intended to alter substantive law and it was assumed that a party's right to relief would remain the same after procedural reform as before.[2] But this assumption merely avoided a number of problems, including that of what needed to be stated in a pleading to establish a right to relief.

The term "cause of action" is too ambiguous to provide a meaningful guide. At one extreme, the statement of a cause could require allegations identical to those required under a proper writ at common law. But this would provide little relief from the technicalities of common-law pleading. At the other extreme, a statement of a cause could require no more than a conclusion that a pleader had a right to prevail in the action. Under this view allegations would be sufficient to state a "cause" even though they gave no specific facts regarding the events at issue. For example, a complaint merely might say, "Plaintiff has been injured by acts of defendant, which acts entitle plaintiff to redress under the law." This view would rob the pleading of any meaningful role in the litigation process.

The problem of definition did not lend itself to a simple solution for several reasons. First, courts and scholars simply could not agree on a definition. Second, the term "cause of action" was used in several places in the codes and did not relate solely to the problems of pleading allegations. The concept of a "cause" governed such matters as joinder of parties and claims and the application of res judicata, the doctrine by which a judgment in one action precludes institution of another action based on the same or a related set of facts. The tendency of lawyers was to define "cause of action" the same way regardless of the context, in effect reverting to the system as it had been applied under the common law writs.

Despite these difficulties, there emerged two definitions of "cause of action" that gave the courts an opportunity to utilize pleadings in a

§ 5.4

1. N.Y.Laws 1851, c. 479, § 1.

2. New York, First Report of the Commissioners on Practice and Pleading 146, 147 (1848).

meaningful way without reverting to common-law technicalities. First was the so-called "primary right" theory advanced by Professor Pomeroy.[3] Under this view a cause of action is related to the nature of the injury alleged to have been suffered. Thus, a person has one primary right to be free from damage to her real estate, another to be free from breach of contract, another to be free from injury to her character, and so on. The advantage of this position is that it focuses on the harm rather than the acts that caused the harm or the specific remedy. A pleader may set forth the facts as they occurred and demand all the relief to which she might be entitled, even though those demands could not have been set forth and claimed within the scope of a single writ at common law.

The primary right theory has its own difficulties, however. Just what is a primary right? What does it include? Suppose an improperly maintained railroad engine sends out sparks setting fire to two adjacent pieces of plaintiff's real estate. How many causes of action arise? Would it make a difference if the properties are a mile apart? What if another fire is set by the same engine a week later? And if the same fire also destroys plaintiff's farming equipment, should a separate action ensue? These questions raise practical problems regarding convenience and cost.

Ultimately many of these problems have been solved by liberal rules that divorce the concept of cause of action from joinder of claims and parties and thus allow joinder despite the fact that the causes of action are different. Even today, however, the "primary right" view of a cause of action may have important consequences in deciding whether a plaintiff, having sued once and brought an action to a conclusion, can bring a separate action for a different type of harm.[4]

The second important view of a cause of action is the so-called "aggregate of operative facts" theory.[5] Under this position a cause of action is defined not by the substantive law to be applied, or the nature of relief sought, or the type of harm suffered, but solely by the events that give rise to a claim or claims for relief. For pleading purposes, one need only set forth the related set of facts. The pleader, upon proving those facts, may obtain every type of relief the law provides. It is as if the pleader had been allowed to join every applicable writ (and every

3. J. Pomeroy, Code Remedies § 347 (4th ed.1904), approved in Stone v. Case, 34 Okl. 5, 15, 21, 124 P. 960, 963, 964 (1912); Hurt v. Haering, 190 Cal. 198, 211 P. 228 (1923); State v. P. Lorillard Co., 181 Wis. 347, 193 N.W. 613 (1923); Comment, Code Pleading: Nature of a "Cause of Action," 12 Calif.L.Rev. 303 (1924).

4. See Blume, The Scope of a Civil Action, 42 Mich.L.Rev. 257 (1943); Shopflacher, What is a Single Cause of Action For the Purpose of the Doctrine of Res Judicata, 21 Or.L.Rev. 319 (1942); Comment, Res Judicata in California, 40 Calif.L.Rev. 412, 419 (1952). Compare Wulfjen

v. Dolton, 24 Cal.2d 891, 151 P.2d 846 (1944), with Holmes v. David H. Bricker, Inc., 71 Cal.Rptr. 562 (1968), affirmed 70 Cal.2d 786, 76 Cal.Rptr. 431, 452 P.2d 647 (1969). The scope of a cause of action for res judicata purposes is discussed in §§ 14.4–14.5, below.

5. See C. Clark, Code Pleading 137 (2d ed.1947); Phillips, Code Pleading § 187 (2d ed.1932); Harris, What Is a Cause of Action?, 16 Calif.L.Rev. 459 (1928). See also Elliott v. Mosgrove, 162 Or. 507, 93 P.2d 1070 (1939); Otto v. Village of Highland Park, 204 Mich. 74, 80, 169 N.W. 904, 906 (1918).

relevant equitable action) without the necessity of the technical pleading required at common law.

This view obviously provides a simple, straightforward formula. It has met with considerable resistance, however, for several reasons. First, it does not inform the opposing party or the court as to what law is claimed applicable. How is an opposing party to prepare to meet "all the law" that might apply? Second, how does one limit "operative facts" to define a single cause of action? The language often used to define a cause of action refers to all those matters "arising out of the same transaction or occurrence or set of transactions or occurrences." This begs the question, however, for it merely transfers the uncertainty to the definition of the word "same."

The uncertainty as to how much is contained in a single cause of action under the "aggregate of operative facts" approach is far more important for purposes of res judicata than it is for purposes of pleading. The chief danger in pleading is that a party, in an attempt to ensure that all possible legal rights are covered, will plead far more facts than necessary. This is a very real danger, as the reformers knew from the historic practice at equity, when parties tended to state and restate allegations until their pleadings evolved into voluminous reports. Because those equity "pleadings" also constituted the evidence in the case, there was potent incentive to make certain that one's facts were read and digested by the chancellor.

The problem of lengthy pleadings has been anticipated in the codes, in that they typically call for "plain and concise" pleading "without repetition." There are a number of ways to avoid the problem of prolix allegations. Some of them are: approval of concise pleadings as set out in reported cases, adoption of standard pleading forms for routine matters, motions to strike surplusage, and a humane amendment process covering the situation when a crucial allegation is omitted.

The concern that the court and opposing parties will not be able to ascertain what law applies—a problem that also is relevant to a lesser extent with respect to the "primary right" theory—led some courts to resort to the so-called "theory of the pleadings" doctrine that requires the pleader to tailor the pleadings to a specific legal theory.[6] Presumably the justification for this approach stemmed from a desire to ensure that neither the court nor the opposing parties would be misled as to the nature of the issues. In fact, the "theory of the pleadings" doctrine proved to be no more than a reversion to the common-law system.

Under the common law, a pleader, by selecting a writ, automatically selected the legal theory upon which the case would proceed. A party who selected the wrong writ would have no choice but to dismiss the

---

6. E.g., Vandalia R.R. Co. v. State, 166 Ind. 219, 76 N.E. 980 (1906), writ dismissed 207 U.S. 359 (1907) ; Mescall v. Tully, 91 Ind. 96, 99 (1883). See generally C. Clark, Code Pleading § 43 (2d ed.1947); Albertsworth, The Theory of Pleading in Code States, 10 Calif.L.Rev. 202 (1922); Page, Application of the Derogation Rule to the Code of Civil Procedure, 1955 Wis.L.Rev. 91; Whittier, The Theory of a Pleading, 8 Colum.L.Rev. 523 (1908).

action and begin again. The elimination of the writs and the substitution of fact pleading appeared to alter this situation drastically. If the properly pleaded facts would state a valid cause of action under any legal (or equitable) theory, the pleading would be legally sufficient. The case could proceed. If the facts might justify relief under more than one theory, the party could go forward on all of them. Many courts took this position without much question or significant difficulty. It is therefore somewhat surprising that a number of courts instead turned to the "theory of pleadings" doctrine.

The utilization of the "theory of the pleadings" doctrine penalized parties with valid claims who misconceived the proper legal basis for recovery. It also dealt unfairly with parties who sought relief when the law was confused or when no precedents existed. In some cases, when multiple theories might be available, it was held that the judge should determine on what theory plaintiff really had decided to proceed.[7] If the court picked a theory upon which the plaintiff ultimately could not recover, the plaintiff would lose despite a clear right to relief on a different basis.

There simply is no need for such rigidity. A defendant who wishes to explore the legal bases for the plaintiff's case may do so by challenging the legal sufficiency of the complaint. The plaintiff then must demonstrate that there is at least one theory upon which she might prevail. The only time that a serious problem might arise is if a party seeks to proceed on a new and different theory that theretofore had not been within the contemplation of the defendant or of the court, even though the facts to support that theory appear in the complaint. Under those circumstances the court, through continuance and other methods, may obviate any prejudice that otherwise might result.[8] Fortunately, the "theory of the pleadings" doctrine generally has been dying out. In those jurisdictions where it has been followed, however, the doctrine has limited the effectiveness of code reform.

Most courts following the code formulation for pleading a cause of action operate under flexible rules that require only a basic statement of facts without concern for technical pleadings or the extent to which the allegations may or may not go beyond the concept of "cause of action" as used in other contexts. However, there is one important aspect of the cause of action concept that affects the sufficiency of a pleader's allegations. In stating a claim or a defense, a party must provide an allegation to cover every element of that claim or defense. For example, in a defamation case, one vital element is the fact that the alleged libel or slander has been "published," that is, heard by a third person. Even if a plaintiff alleges that a false statement has been made about him by a defendant and that serious damages have ensued, the plaintiff's failure

---

7. Supervisors of Kewaunee County v. Decker, 30 Wis. 624, 633 (1872).

8. If new facts are to be added, Federal Rule 15, governing amendments, or its

state counterpart applies. See §§ 5.26–5.27, below.

to allege publication will render the complaint defective.[9] The court will not imply the missing allegation from the other allegations.

The defect is not often serious, however, since modern procedural rules normally will permit the plaintiff to amend the complaint to add the missing facts.[10] Nevertheless, in a few situations such a pleading mistake may have important consequences.[11] Moreover, when coupled with the problems of pleading resulting from the definition of "facts," the "cause of action" requirement does result in unnecessary technicality, leading to costly court battles that are a total waste, and that may provide an unjust tactical advantage for a wealthier litigant over a less affluent opponent.

§ 5.5 The Uncertain Meaning of "Facts" in the Code Pleading System

At common law a pleader was required to set forth facts according to the particular writ governing the case. However, these "facts" were less an explicit statement of what the pleader believed actually had occurred than they were a formal set of allegations long held necessary to satisfy the pleading technicalities required under the particular writ.[1] At times they were at a complete variance with the actual facts of the case.

One of the key aspects of reform, as seen by those who drafted the code, was a requirement that the pleader set forth the actual facts involved in the case.[2] This requirement was an adaptation of pleading in equity, with one substantial difference. In equity the pleadings were under oath and also constituted the evidence in the suit; the equity court heard no oral testimony.[3] As a result, pleadings in equity were extensive and repetitious. The code drafters had no intention of encouraging similarly prolix pleadings. They wanted a statement of a cause of action, but they wanted it to be short and simple. At the same time, they required more than a mere recitation that defendant was liable to plaintiff for a stated amount of damages.[4]

As is frequently stated by courts and commentators, the pleader is expected to set forth only the ultimate facts, free from evidentiary facts and conclusions of law.[5] There is some reason to believe that those who

---

9. See Collins v. Oklahoma State Hosp., 76 Okl. 229, 184 P. 946 (1916); Penry v. Dozier, 161 Ala. 292, 49 So. 909 (1909); Schoepflin v. Coffey, 162 N.Y. 12, 56 N.E. 502 (1900). See also West's Ann.Cal. Code Civ.Proc. § 460; 12 Okl.Stat.Ann. § 1441; Hall, Pleading Libel Actions in California, 12 So.Calif.L.Rev. 225 (1939).

10. See § 5.26, below.

11. For example, a default judgment may be set aside. Ness v. Greater Arizona Realty, Inc., 21 Ariz.App. 231, 517 P.2d 1278 (1974); Wayne Creamery v. Suyak, 10 Mich.App. 41, 158 N.W.2d 825 (1968); Thompson v. Hickman, 164 Ark. 469, 262 S.W. 20 (1924).

§ 5.5

1. J. Koffler & A. Reppy, Common Law Pleading § 21 (1969).

2. New York, First Report of the Commissioners on Practice and Pleading 137 (1848).

3. C. Langdell, Equity Pleading (2d ed.1883); F. Maitland, Equity (2d ed.1936).

4. New York, First Report of the Commissioners on Practice and Pleading 147 (1848).

5. Id. at 141–44.

drafted the code realized that these distinctions often would be difficult to draw and that all that should reasonably be required is a statement that could be understood by an ordinary person.[6] Nevertheless, goaded on by litigating attorneys, the courts turned the "fact" pleading requirement into a nightmare that in some jurisdictions all but destroyed the effectiveness of the reform.[7]

There simply is no clear cut line between an "ultimate" fact and an "evidentiary" fact or between an "ultimate" fact and a "conclusion of law." As many writers have noted,[8] the distinctions among the categories are matters of degree. Thus, the sufficiency of a particular allegation under the code system often was determined by the particular view of the judge before whom the matter was brought and uniformity among the lower courts could be obtained only by appealing the issue to the highest court in the jurisdiction.[9] The cost to the judicial system of resolving matters of pleading, on an item by item basis, by appeals to the state supreme court is immense and appears hardly worth the effort. Shifting the focus of procedure away from the just resolution of matters on their substantive merits to technical decisions as to the form of statements made in the complaint or answer is the very antithesis of the result desired from pleading reform.

Despite these criticisms, the utilization of the ultimate fact test continues to exist in a number of jurisdictions. Thus, a brief inquiry into some of the problems of ascertaining what is an ultimate fact is appropriate.

Courts often have not agreed on whether a particular allegation is or is not an ultimate fact.[10] For example, a general averment that defendant acted within the scope of his employment has been held by some courts to be a proper allegation of ultimate fact and by others to be an improper conclusion of law.[11] The same is true of a general allegation in a defamation suit that defendant acted "out of malice,"[12] or of a statement that pleader is an "heir,"[13] or that a promise was made in exchange for "a valuable consideration."[14] Given this uncertainty, unless there is a

---

6. Id. at 141, 150–51.

7. See C. Clark, Code Pleading § 38, at 226 (2d ed.1947); Cook, Statements of Fact in Pleading Under the Codes, 21 Colum.L.Rev. 416 (1921).

8. C. Clark, Code Pleading 233–36 (2d ed.1947); Cook, Statements of Fact in Pleading Under the Codes, 21 Colum.L.Rev. 416–19 (1921); Gavit, Legal Conclusions, 16 Minn.L.Rev. 378 (1932); Morris, Law and Fact, 55 Harv.L.Rev. 1303 (1942); Wheaton, Manner of Stating Cause of Action, 20 Cornell L.Q. 185 (1935).

9. See Cook, Statements of Fact in Pleading Under the Codes, 21 Colum.L.Rev. 416–19 (1921).

10. Ibid.

11. Compare Howell v. Simon, 225 Ark. 535, 283 S.W.2d 680 (1955) (conclusion of law), with Ledman v. Calvert Iron Works, Inc., 92 Ga.App. 733, 89 S.E.2d 832 (1955) (ultimate fact).

12. Compare Holden v. Pioneer Broadcasting Co., 228 Or. 405, 365 P.2d 845 (1961), cert. denied 370 U.S. 157 (conclusion of law), with Boston Nutrition Soc'y v. Stare, 342 Mass. 439, 173 N.E.2d 812 (1961) (general allegation of "malice" is proper).

13. Compare Dibble v. Winter, 247 Ill. 243, 93 N.E. 145 (1910) (statement of fact), with Combs v. Cardwell, 164 Ky. 542, 175 S.W. 1009 (1915) (statement of law).

14. Compare Andersen v. Charles, 52 Cal.App. 290, 198 P. 641 (1921) (insufficient), with Bank of River Falls v. German American Ins. Co., 72 Wis. 535, 40 N.W. 506 (1888) (good against general demurrer).

clear-cut decision regarding the matter in the relevant jurisdiction, the pleader will be wise to plead not only the "conclusion" but more detailed facts as well.

In some situations the difficulty of determining what is a properly pleaded "ultimate fact" appears to place an attorney in a "no win" situation; precedents are available to attack the pleadings no matter how the allegations are phrased. For example, in an action for trespass, if plaintiff alleges that she "was entitled to possession of the property," she could be attacked for having pleaded a conclusion of law.[15] If she amends the claim to state that she "had entered into an agreement to purchase the property, that a deed was delivered to her by the former owners, but that the former owners refused to turn over possession to her," the complaint could be held insufficient because she pleaded only evidence rather than the ultimate facts of ownership and right to possession.[16] Although it is unlikely that the holdings of an individual court would make it impossible for a party to state a meritorious case, finding the proper formula can be costly and time consuming;[17] a wrong choice by the trial judge can spell disaster for an innocent party on appeal.

In many cases the decision as to the sufficiency of the pleading is focused less on a specific allegation than it is on the whole document, raising the question of what amount of information generally must be conveyed to the opposing parties in order to satisfy the code requirements. This is a much more meaningful inquiry than one that attempts to pigeonhole a specific allegation; it relates to the underlying purpose of pleadings and the role they are to play in the litigation process. Consider, for example, one case in which plaintiff alleged that:

> On or about May 5, 1959 and May 6, 1959, the defendants, without cause or just excuse and maliciously came upon and trespassed upon the premises occupied by the plaintiff as a residence, and by the use of harsh and threatening language and physical force directed against the plaintiff assaulted the plaintiff and placed her in great fear, and humiliated and embarrassed her by subjecting her to public scorn and ridicule, and caused her to be seized and exhibited to the public as a prisoner, and to be confined in a public jail, all to her great humiliation, embarrassment and harm.[18]

The court held this pleading deficient for setting forth only conclusions of law and not specifying, "*What* occurred, *When* it occurred, *Where* it occurred, *Who* did *What* "and so on.

Should those details (and why would they not result in the pleading of evidence?) be set forth in the pleadings or should they be explored through formal discovery methods? Should a decision as to whether plaintiff's case is without factual foundation be made at the pleading

---

15. Sheridan v. Jackson, 72 N.Y. 170 (1878).

16. McCaughey v. Schuette, 117 Cal. 223, 48 P. 1088 (1897).

17. See Kirkpatric, Procedural Reform in Oregon, 56 Or.L.Rev. 539, 558–62 (1977).

18. Gillispie v. Goodyear Serv. Stores, 258 N.C. 487, 128 S.E.2d 762 (1963).

stage or at some later time, after plaintiff as well as defendant has had further opportunity to search for evidence?

Whether for philosophical reasons related to the ideal role of the pleadings or for practical reasons related to the inability of the courts to define the term "facts" so as to approach that ideal, many recent code pleading cases have loosened the requirement of fact pleading, in effect requiring little more than fair notice to the opposing party and the court of the general nature of the suit. Thus in one case the court upheld as sufficient a simple allegation, "that on or about July 1, 1956, on Amherst Street in the City of Buffalo, New York, the defendant assaulted, battered and beat plaintiff without any provocation or just cause."[19]

In a similar vein, the consequences for improperly pleading an evidentiary fact or a conclusion of law have changed. Initially courts operating under the codes tended to take a strict view toward improper pleading. Allegations of evidentiary facts or conclusions of law were ignored upon a challenge to a pleading.[20] If those improper allegations were essential to state a cause of action or defense, the pleading would be held insufficient.

This position has been altered substantially, especially with respect to the pleading of evidence. Most courts today will not uphold a challenge to the sufficiency of a pleading when the defect is the pleading of evidentiary facts from which the ultimate facts necessarily follow.[21] Thus, if the pleader states all of the facts establishing a right to possession, the failure to allege a right to possession in so many words will be overlooked.[22] That rule obviously makes sense in light of the uncertainty as to what is an ultimate fact. The only danger is that some pleaders may tend to include too much. But that is not a serious problem given the natural tendency of attorneys not to reveal more of their cases than necessary and the ability of courts to strike surplus allegations and to require a pleader to eliminate uncertainty and ambiguity.[23]

Although some courts have treated a conclusion of law as a nonexistent allegation,[24] many modern courts have taken the position that such an allegation can be considered in determining whether the complaint gives notice of the existence of a cause of action.[25] If it does, a challenge to the sufficiency of the complaint will be denied. The defect is treated

---

19. D'Auria v. Niemiec, 15 Misc.2d 449, 450, 182 N.Y.S.2d 378, 379 (1959). See also M. G. Chamberlain & Co. v. Simpson, 173 Cal.App.2d 263, 343 P.2d 438 (1959); Augustine v. Trucco, 124 Cal.App.2d 229, 268 P.2d 780 (1954).

20. Metropolis Trust & Savs. Bank v. Monnier, 169 Cal. 592, 147 P. 265 (1915); McCaughey v. Schuette, 117 Cal. 223, 48 P. 1088 (1897).

21. But see Curry v. Meier, 15 Misc.2d 418, 179 N.Y.S.2d 549 (1958); O'Regan v. Schermerhorn, 25 N.J.Misc. 1, 50 A.2d 10 (1946).

22. Robinson v. Meyer, 135 Conn. 691, 693–94, 68 A.2d 142, 143 (1949).

23. See Fed.Civ.Proc.Rule 12(f); N.Y.— McKinney's CPLR 3024(a); Utah Rules Civ. Proc., Rule 12(f). See also § 5.23, below.

24. Cousins v. Wilson, 94 Okl. 29, 220 P. 923 (1923); Smith v. Abel, 211 Or. 571, 577, 316 P.2d 793, 796 (1957); Callahan v. Broderick, 124 Cal. 80, 56 P. 782 (1899).

25. See, e.g., Rembold v. City & County of San Francisco, 113 Cal.App.2d 795, 249 P.2d 58 (1952). See also Krug v. Meehan, 109 Cal.App.2d 274, 240 P.2d 732 (1952).

solely as one of form that can be attacked only by a challenge that the pleading is indefinite or uncertain.[26]

§ 5.6　Challenges Based on Indefiniteness, Ambiguity, or Uncertainty

Almost all code states have some provision for attacking the form of a pleading on the ground that it is uncertain or ambiguous. This may be by means of a special type of demurrer[1] or by a motion to make more definite and certain.[2] There are some important differences between an attack on the form of a pleading and an attack on its substantive sufficiency. The latter, normally referred to as a "general demurrer," or motion to dismiss for failure to state a claim or defense, can be raised at any time up to and during trial, and perhaps even on appeal.[3] An attack on form is waived unless brought up at the earliest opportunity.[4] Moreover, a default judgment can be overturned if the complaint on which it is based fails to state a cause of action,[5] but not if the defect is considered one of form only.[6]

2.　Notice Pleading

§ 5.7　The Basic Requirements of Notice Pleading

When the Supreme Court promulgated a uniform set of procedural rules for all federal cases in 1938, a key feature of that reform was the adoption of Federal Rule of Civil Procedure 8, which closely followed the simple equity rules of pleading.[1] Federal Rule 8 not only revolutionized practice in law cases in the federal courts, it also proved to be an important catalyst for reform in many state courts, including a number of jurisdictions that long before had adopted the code pleading system.[2] The key provision is Federal Rule 8(a)(2), requiring a party to set forth "a short and plain statement of the claim showing that the pleader is entitled to relief." Although this appears close to the code requirement of "a statement of facts constituting a cause of action," the similarity is deceptive, for under the federal rule the last vestiges of pleading techni-

---

26. Fleischmann v. Lotito, 6 Cal.2d 365, 57 P.2d 922 (1936); Campbell v. Genshlea, 180 Cal. 213, 180 P. 336 (1919). Cf. Jerry v. Borden Co., 45 A.D.2d 344, 358 N.Y.S.2d 426 (1974) (under N.Y.—McKinney's CPLR 3013).

§ 5.6

1. West's Ann.Cal.Code Civ.Proc. § 430.10(g).

2. Neb.Rev.Stat. § 25–833.

3. West's Ann.Cal.Code Civ.Proc. § 430.80. See § 5.22, below; C. Clark, Code Pleading § 85a (2d ed.1947).

4. Mass.Rules Civ.Proc., Rule 12(h). See § 5.24, below; C. Clark, Code Pleading § 85 (2d ed.1947).

5. C & H Transp. Co. v. Wright, 396 S.W.2d 443 (Tex.Civ.App.1965). See Comment, Attacking a Default Judgment in California on the Grounds that the Complaint Failed to State a Cause of Action, 1 U.C.L.A.L.Rev. 195 (1954); Note, 49 Mich. L.Rev. 446 (1951); Note, 36 Texas L.Rev. 243 (1957).

6. See Ramey v. Myers, 111 Cal.App.2d 679, 245 P.2d 360 (1952).

§ 5.7

1. See Federal Equity Rule 25.

2. See § 5.1 n. 14, above.

calities are stripped away and the concept of "notice" pleading is firmly established.[3]

The advantages are clear. First, the rule eliminates the seemingly endless controversies concerning what constitutes a "cause of action" and what is a "fact" as opposed to mere evidence or a conclusion of law.[4] The issue becomes whether the opposing party has been sufficiently notified concerning the claim (or defense) so as to be able to prepare to meet it.[5] Second, the rule avoids the traumatic problems of the "theory of the pleadings" doctrine.[6] The doctrine clearly has no place in the federal scheme, which abolishes the requirement that a "cause of action" be stated. As the federal cases consistently hold, a party is permitted to recover whenever she has a valid claim, even though her attorney fails to perceive the proper basis of the claim at the pleading stage.[7]

It is true that notice pleading makes it less likely that the pleadings themselves will narrow issues for trial and provide for easy disposal of sham claims or defenses. But these supposed advantages of a strict pleading system have not materialized under the codes. A careful tactician almost always can plead a good "cause of action" using nothing but ultimate facts as declared by prior decisions. Courts in code states already have been forced to turn to other procedural devices to narrow issues and dispose of sham matters.[8] The federal rules by formally including broad rules of discovery[9] and an elaborate provision for summary judgment[10] adequately filled any gap left by less stringent pleading requirements.[11]

A number of commentators have objected to the use of the term "notice pleading" to describe pleading under Rule 8, preferring instead "modern pleading" or "simplified pleading."[12] The fear is that "notice" will be taken to mean that no more is required than a mere statement that a suit has been filed and damages are desired; whereas, in fact, the pleader must refer to the circumstances and events upon which the claim or defense is based. What the pleader need not do is worry about the particular form of the statement or that it fails to allege a specific fact to cover every element of the substantive law involved. As long as the opposing party and the court can obtain a basic understanding of the claim being made, the requirements are satisfied.[13] It is important to

3. For a discussion in a code state of the differences between pleading under the codes and pleading under the federal rules, see Christianson v. Educational Serv. Unit, 243 Neb. 553, 501 N.W.2d 281 (1993).

4. See § 5.5, above.

5. Leatherman v. Tarrant County Narcotics Intelligence & Coordination Unit, 507 U.S. 163, 113 S.Ct. 1160, 122 L.Ed.2d 517 (1993); Conley v. Gibson, 355 U.S. 41, 78 S.Ct. 99, 2 L.Ed.2d 80 (1957); Dioguardi v. Durning, 139 F.2d 774 (2d Cir.1944).

6. See § 5.4, above.

7. 5 C. Wright & A. Miller, Civil 2d § 1219.

8. See C. Clark, Code Pleading §§ 86, 88 (2d ed.1947).

9. Fed.Civ.Proc.Rules 26–37. See generally Chapter 7, below.

10. Fed.Civ.Proc.Rule 56. See generally §§ 9.1–9.3, below.

11. See C. Clark, Code Pleading § 88, at 566 (2d ed.1947).

12. Clark, Pleading Under the Federal Rules, 12 Wyo.L.J. 177, 181 (1958).

13. Leatherman v. Tarrant County Narcotics Intelligence & Coordination Unit, 507 U.S. 163, 113 S.Ct. 1160, 122 L.Ed.2d 517 (1993); Hospital Bldg. Co. v. Trustees

note, however, that cases do arise in which judges disagree as to whether the amount of detail is sufficient to state a claim and whether more facts are required to give "fair notice" to the opposing party.[14]

This elimination of technicalities is underscored by Federal Rule 8(f), which states simply that "all pleadings shall be so construed as to do substantial justice." Since no words are fully adequate to describe with precision the balance between simplicity and detail, the Federal Rules are followed by an Appendix of Forms, many of which are examples of various sufficient Complaints and Answers. These short and simple forms constitute important guidelines for parties to federal litigation.

§ 5.8   Adjustment of Federal and State Courts to Notice Pleading

The transition from more rigid pleading systems to notice pleading was not accomplished without resistance in some federal courts[1] as well as in state courts[2] that adopted the federal pleading rules. In a few isolated cases, federal trial judges even rejected pleadings that followed the forms contained in the Appendix to the Rules on the ground that the latter were not binding and that additional facts were required.[3] To clarify the matter, Federal Rule 84 was amended in 1946 to state that the forms were sufficient.[4] The forms themselves were not altered.

One of the most significant cases involving the interpretation to be given Federal Rule 8, Dioguardi v. Durning,[5] was decided in 1944. In that case, the plaintiff, who apparently distrusted all lawyers, formulated his own complaint in confused and broken English. The trial court dismissed the complaint for failure "to state facts sufficient to constitute a cause of action," using the language of the code formulation that had been

of Rex Hosp., 425 U.S. 738, 96 S.Ct. 1848, 48 L.Ed.2d 338 (1976); Conley v. Gibson, 355 U.S. 41, 78 S.Ct. 99, 2 L.Ed.2d 80 (1957). See McCardle, A Short Plain Statement: The Significance of *Leatherman v. Tarrant County*, 72 U.Det. Mercy L.Rev. 19 (1994).

14. See, e.g., the majority and dissenting opinions in Kyle v. Morton High School, 144 F.3d 448 (7th Cir.1998) (complaint dismissed). The majority in Kyle quoted Chaveriat v. Williams Pipe Line Co., 11 F.3d 1420, 1430 (7th Cir.1993), where the court stated, "It is true that the original theory of the Federal Rules of Civil Procedure was that the plaintiff ought to be permitted to fumble around searching for a meritorious claim within the elastic boundaries of a bare-bones complaint until the final pretrial conference. No judge or lawyer in this age of crowded dockets takes that completely seriously * * *." The dissenting judge in Kyle, in noting that Federal Rule 8 does not require a statement of facts, said, "A mo-

tion to dismiss is not properly granted unless it is beyond doubt that there could be no set of facts justifying relief. The majority's report of this principle's demise * * * is greatly exaggerated." 144 F.3d at 459.

§ 5.8

1. See, e.g., Employers' Mut. Liability Ins. Co. v. Blue Line Transfer Co., 2 F.R.D. 121 (W.D.Mo.1941); Washburn v. Moorman Mfg. Co., 25 F.Supp. 546 (S.D.Cal.1938).

2. See, e.g., Walden, The "New Rules" in New Mexico, 25 F.R.D. 107, 108–11 (1960).

3. Employers' Mut. Liability Ins. Co. v. Blue Line Transfer Co., 2 F.R.D. 121 (W.D.Mo.1941); Washburn v. Moorman Mfg. Co., 25 F.Supp. 546 (S.D.Cal.1938).

4. See Advisory Committee on Rules for Civil Procedure, Report of Proposed Amendments to Rules of Civil Procedure, 5 F.R.D. 433, 498 (1946).

5. 139 F.2d 774 (2d Cir.1944).

replaced by the new rules. The Second Circuit reversed. It held that the plaintiff's complaint, even though inarticulate and unclear, did reveal the basic nature of his dispute with the defendant and the specific incidents upon which the complaint was based.

The Dioguardi decision was sharply criticized[6] and became the focal point for opposition to the new rules. Critics noted that when the case later went to trial, the plaintiff was unable to prove his claims and lost on the merits.[7] The latter fact, of course, is irrelevant. Many a well-pleaded case has been lost at trial. It is the opposite problem that causes greater concern. How can the courts prevent meritorious claims and defenses from being lost through technical errors of procedure?

Although the critics persisted for some time in efforts to reestablish the code formulation for federal pleading,[8] they met with no success. However, their efforts were not all in vain, for the continuing controversy obviously had an impact on state reform. A number of jurisdictions that have adopted many of the other federal procedural rules have maintained the code pleading requirements.[9] Moreover, in some states that adopted Federal Rule 8 the controversy over its interpretation interfered with the transition; some state trial judges, at least in the early years, read the new rules as a mere restatement of the prior code provisions and applied all of the technicalities.[10] Modern decisions, however, tend to follow the rules as they have been interpreted in the federal courts.[11] A few states recognized the potential problems of making the transition to notice pleading at the outset and moved to avoid them. Colorado, for example, added a special clause not in Federal Rule 8, specifically stating that pleadings were not to be held insufficient merely because they failed to state ultimate facts as distinguished from conclusions of law.[12]

Finally, it should be kept in mind that not every jurisdiction that has liberalized its pleading rules has fully embraced notice pleading. For example, in 1962 New York eliminated its traditional code pleading rule and substituted Rule 3013 as follows:

> Statements in a pleading shall be sufficiently particular to give the court and parties notice of the transactions, occurrences, or series of

---

6. McCaskill, The Modern Philosophy of Pleading: A Dialogue Outside the Shades, 38 A.B.A.J. 123 (1952).

7. Ibid.

8. See Claim or Cause of Action, 13 F.R.D. 253 (1953).

9. See § 5.1 n. 15, above.

10. See, e.g., Walden, The "New Rules" in New Mexico, 25 F.R.D. 107, 108–11 (1960).

11. See Cole v. Cole Tomato Sales, Inc., 293 Ala. 731, 734, 310 So.2d 210, 212 (1975); Gardner v. Hollifield, 96 Idaho 609,

611, 533 P.2d 730, 732 (1975); Slife v. Kundtz Properties, Inc., 40 Ohio App.2d 179, 318 N.E.2d 557 (1974); Seattle Professional Photographers Ass'n v. Sears Roebuck Co., 9 Wn.App. 656, 662, 513 P.2d 840, 844 (1973); Davidson v. Dill, 180 Colo. 123, 131, 503 P.2d 157, 162 (1972); Hall v. Kim, 53 Hawaii 215, 219, 491 P.2d 541, 544 (1971); Brewer v. Harris, 279 N.C. 288, 292, 182 S.E.2d 345, 347 (1971).

12. Colo.Rules Civ.Proc., Rule 8(e)(1).

transactions or occurrences, intended to be proved and the material elements of each cause of action or defense.[13]

Precisely what this section requires is unclear and the New York courts have taken widely divergent positions although the trend is definitely toward federal-type notice pleading.[14] Another compromise provision reveals a similar attempt to borrow from both the federal and code approaches. In Florida, the plaintiff must set forth "a short and plain statement of the ultimate facts showing that the pleader is entitled to relief."[15]

§ 5.9   Special Rules for Specific Cases and Facts

From time to time judges operating under notice pleading rules have argued and, on rare occasions, have held that special pleading rules requiring greater specifics and detail should apply to certain cases, especially those involving a large number of issues, multiple parties, or complex legal problems.[1] Similar arguments have been made regarding categories of suits that usually prove to be without merit, such as civil rights cases brought by prisoners against government officials.[2] In gener-

---

13. N.Y.—McKinney's CPLR 3013.

14. Compare Gross v. Eannace, 44 Misc.2d 797, 255 N.Y.S.2d 625 (1964), with Card v. Budini, 29 A.D.2d 35, 285 N.Y.S.2d 734 (1967).

15. Fla.—West's F.S.A.Rules Civ.Proc., Rule 1.110(b)(2).

§ 5.9

1. See Baim & Blank, Inc. v. Warren–Connelly Co., 19 F.R.D. 108, 109–10 (S.D.N.Y.1956); 5 C. Wright & A. Miller, Civil 2d § 1221; Marcus, the Puzzling Persistence of Pleading Practice, 76 Texas L.Rev. 1749 (1998).

In at least one type of situation, that involving securities litigation, Congress has specified heightened pleading requirements inconsistent with Federal Rule 8(a)(2) and the last sentence of Federal Rule 9(b). See Private Securities Litigation Reform Act of 1995, Pub. L. 104–52, 109 Stat.737. One federal court has adopted a local rule, inconsistent with Rule 8(a)(2), requiring detailed pleading in actions under the Racketeer Influences and Corrupt Organizations Act (RICO). See Heiser, A Critical Review of the Local Rules of the United States Court for the Southern District of California, 33 San Diego L.Rev. 555, 566–70 (1996).

2. Civil Rights cases, especially those against government employees have posed special concerns since many are frivolous. Thus, a number of the federal courts began to require heightened, i.e., detailed, pleadings in these suits with the idea that many

could be dismissed on the pleadings. For an analysis of the development of these special standards, see Wingate, A Special Pleading Rule for Civil Rights Complaints: A Step Forward or a Step Back?, 49 Mo.L.Rev. 677 (1984). The Supreme Court appeared to put an end to this practice in Leatherman v. Tarrant County Narcotics & Intelligence Unit, 507 U.S. 163, 113 S.Ct. 1160, 122 L.Ed.2d 517 (1993), holding that only those matters listed in Federal Rule 9(b) required detailed pleading; everything else was covered by the notice pleading standards of Rule 8(a)(2). See McCardle, A Short Plain Statement: The Significance of *Leatherman v. Tarrant County*, 72 U.Det. Mercy L.Rev. 19 (1994). However, Leatherman was a suit against a municipality and several of the federal courts of appeals have refused to follow it in suits against individuals regarding the defense of limited immunity. See Comment, *Schultea* II—Fifth Circuit's Answer to *Leatherman*—Rule 7 Reply: More Questions Than Answers in Civil Rights Cases?, 37 So.Tex.L.Rev. 413, 439–41 (1996). Moreover, the Fifth Circuit in Schultea v. Wood, 47 F.3d 1427 (5th Cir. 1995), has added a wrinkle by holding that, Leatherman notwithstanding, federal trial judges, under Rule 7(a), can order a plaintiff to reply to a defendant's affirmative defense of limited immunity, and at least to the extent that the defendant has pleaded factual details in the defense, the plaintiff can be required to plead details in the reply. The court took the position that notice pleading under Rule 8(a)(2) applied only to complaints and that replies are subject only

al, however, the courts have resisted these calls for special pleading.[3] The rules do not authorize it, and it is doubtful that any benefits would accrue. The notion that pleadings can be used to limit the size and scope of an action seems unsound. A clever tactician will manage to include all that is desired whatever the pleading requirements. The client with inept counsel may suffer, regardless of the merits of the case. That is not to say that there should not be special treatment for complex litigation.[4] But alteration of pleading rules seems clearly not to be the answer.[5]

Given the obvious trend away from pleading technicalities, it is somewhat surprising that federal-type pleading rules do include a special provision, Rule 9, that requires detailed pleading of a small number of specific matters.[6] Federal Rule 9(b) states, "In all averments of fraud or mistake, the circumstances constituting fraud or mistake shall be stated with particularity," and Rule 9(g) requires that "when items of special damage are claimed, they shall be specifically stated." Some states go even further. For example, Wisconsin, in its version of 9(b) requires a plaintiff in an action for sale and delivery of goods or the performance of labor and services, on demand of the defendant, to set forth a statement of each item of the plaintiff's complaint and the reasonable value thereof.[7]

It is not easy to justify these deviations from the general philosophy of modern pleading, particularly since the sought-after details can be obtained through formal discovery. The requirements as to fraud are understandable from an historical point of view. Fraud was a so-called "disfavored action" at common law because it raised questions of defendant's morality. Specific pleading requirements were enforced in an

---

to Rule 8(e)(1), requiring pleadings to be "simple, concise, and direct."

The Supreme Court in Crawford–El v. Britton, 523 U.S. 574, 118 S.Ct. 1584, 1596–97, 140 L.Ed.2d 759 (1998), appears to have given some support to the Fifth Circuit approach and to heightened pleading requirements in civil rights cases in general by stating, "[T]he court may order a reply to the defendant's * * * answer under Federal Rule * * * 7(a), or grant the defendant's motion for a more definite statement under Rule 12(e). Thus the court may insist that the plaintiff 'put forward specific, nonconclusory factual' allegations * * * to survive a prediscovery motion for dismissal * * *. "The reference to Rule 12(e) is particularly questionable since that rule is to be used only when a pleading is so vague or uncertain that a party who is required to respond is unable to do so. See § 5.23 n. 9, below.

3. See Walker Distributing Co. v. Lucky Lager Brewing Co., 323 F.2d 1, 3 (9th Cir.1963); Nagler v. Admiral Corp., 248 F.2d 319 (2d Cir.1957); 5 C. Wright & A. Miller, Civil 2d § 1221.

4. For example, the Judicial Panel on Multidistrict Litigation has published a manual with a suggested set of general procedures to be used in the trial of complex actions. These focus on techniques of discovery, pretrial conferences, and other pretrial orders. See Manual for Complex Litigation, Third (1995).

5. See Report to the Judicial Conference of the United States, Procedure in Antitrust and Other Protracted Cases, 13 F.R.D. 62, 66–68 (1953); Clark, Special Pleading in the "Big Case," 21 F.R.D. 45 (1958); Freund, The Pleading and Pre–Trial of an Antitrust Claim, 46 Cornell L.Q. 555 (1961); Recent Developments, 58 Colum.L.Rev. 408 (1958).

6. In fact, Rule 9 simplifies pleading by allowing a number of averments to be made generally, such as the performance and occurrence of conditions precedent, a person's state of mind, and the existence of a relevant prior judgment. See 5 C. Wright & A. Miller, Civil 2d § 1291. For detailed analysis of these special matters, including a discussion of Rule 9(g), see § 5.16, below.

7. Wisconsin Stat.Ann. 802.03(7).

effort to suppress unjustified claims, and this strict attitude was carried forward by courts operating under the codes.[8] An additional argument for special pleading, applicable to mistake as well as to fraud, is the fact that these are the grounds for upsetting contracts, judicial orders, and similar matters, that should not be set aside lightly. Nonetheless, utilization of the pleadings to effectuate substantive policy makes little sense.

At least in the federal courts the special requirements generally have had limited impact. Although some cases have held complaints involving fraud insufficient for pleading too little detail, most have accepted generalized statements.[9] The courts have noted that Federal Rule 9(b) requires only that the "circumstances" of the fraud be set forth; it does not revive the requirement that "facts" be pleaded.[10] Perhaps more telling is Official Form 13, which contains a model allegation for an action to set aside a fraudulent conveyance. The operative language simply alleges that defendant "conveyed all his property" to a third person "for the purpose of defrauding plaintiff and hindering and delaying the collection of the indebtedness" which defendant owes to plaintiff. Decisions in state courts vary considerably, although it is clear that special pleading requirements do have some impact on the way in which courts view the sufficiency of particular allegations.[11]

§ 5.10 The Role of Motions to Clarify Pleadings

Most notice pleading jurisdictions provide a method for clarifying uncertain or ambiguous pleadings, even though, as a whole, the pleadings are sufficient to state a valid claim under modern pleading rules. The scope and interpretation of these provisions are extremely important for they can be used as a means of re-establishing traditional pleading requirements, forcing a pleader to state ultimate facts or even a legal theory.

Federal Rule 12(e) is the model for those jurisdictions that have adopted notice pleading. Prior to 1946 when it was radically amended, the rule provided for either a motion for more definite statement or a bill of particulars to enable the moving party to draft a responsive pleading or to prepare for trial. In this form the rule was utilized by some courts

8. See Chamberlain Mach. Works v. U.S., 270 U.S. 347, 46 S.Ct. 225, 70 L.Ed. 619 (1926); Stearns v. Page, 48 U.S. (7 How.) 819, 829, 12 L.Ed. 928 (1849); Duane v. Altenburg, 297 F.2d 515, 518 (7th Cir. 1962); Chicago Title & Trust Co. v. Fox Theatres Corp., 182 F.Supp. 18, 31 (S.D.N.Y.1960). See also C. Clark, Code Pleading 311–12, 617 (2d ed.1947).

9. See Massey–Ferguson, Inc. v. Bent Equip. Co., 283 F.2d 12, 15 (5th Cir.1960); Future Tech Int'l v. Tae Il Media, Ltd., 944 F.Supp. 1538, 1570–72 (S.D.Fla.1996); Textile Banking Co. v. S. Starensier, Inc., 38 F.R.D. 492 (D.Mass.1965); Gottlieb v. San-

dia Am. Corp., 35 F.R.D. 223 (E.D.Pa.1964); McMahon Bros. Realty Co. v. U.S. Fidelity & Guar. Co., 217 F.Supp. 567 (D.Del.1963); Lynn v. Valentine, 19 F.R.D. 250, 254 (S.D.N.Y.1956). See also Glus v. Brooklyn Eastern District Terminal, 359 U.S. 231, 79 S.Ct. 760, 3 L.Ed.2d 770 (1959); Commentary, Requirement of Particularity in Pleading Fraud, 6 F.R.Serv. 739 (1943).

10. Consumers Time Credit, Inc. v. Remark Corp., 227 F.Supp. 263 (E.D.Pa.1964).

11. E.g., Marcucilli v. Alicon Corp., 41 A.D.2d 932, 343 N.Y.S.2d 367 (1973).

to undercut the liberal pleading provisions of Rule 8. These courts emphasized that aspect of the rule regarding preparation for trial and required litigants to set forth detailed facts underlying their initial allegations, thus using the bill of particulars as a mode of discovery.[1] Although a majority of federal judges restricted the grant of the Federal Rule 12(e) motion to situations in which pleadings were so unclear or ambiguous that the moving party could not frame a proper response,[2] nevertheless, the rule was responsible for substantial uncertainty and was soundly and frequently criticized.[3]

In its revised form, Federal Rule 12(e) has limited scope. It provides only for clarification of a pleading that is so uncertain that a proper response cannot be made; it is not to be used as a substitute for discovery.[4] It is unavailable to a party who does not have to respond to an opponent's pleading, even though that pleading may be unclear.

Even with these limitations, some commentators and judges have argued that the rule should be abolished, because they view it as a device used primarily for delay.[5] Others note that there are several situations in which the motion serves a useful purpose.[6] First, it provides a means by which a court can enforce special pleading rules, such as those contained in Rule 9. The availability of a motion to clarify tends to reduce pressure to grant a motion to dismiss if a complaint states a claim under general pleading rules but fails to include details as required by the special pleading provisions. Second, a motion for a more definite statement can assist in establishing so-called "threshold defenses" that can allow certain cases to be disposed of immediately. For example, if defendant knows that the statute of limitations bars plaintiff's claim, but plaintiff has failed to allege the date on which the claim arose, a motion for more definite statement could force plaintiff to plead the date, with the result that the action then could be dismissed. Similar results could be obtained if the defense were based on the statute of frauds. Although the same results could be obtained by means of a motion for summary judgment, the latter involves a more elaborate procedure[7] that can be bypassed in simple cases. It appears that current practice under Rule 12(e) has

---

§ 5.10

1. See, e.g., Graham v. New York & Cuba Mail S.S. Co., 25 F.Supp. 224 (E.D.N.Y.1938).

2. Colonial Hardwood Flooring Co. v. International Union United Furniture Workers, 76 F.Supp. 493 (D.Md.1948); Creedon v. Hempel, 7 F.R.D. 601 (D.Neb. 1947); Miller & Hart, Inc. v. Morris Packing Co., 7 F.R.D. 592 (W.D.Mo.1947); Baret v. Koppers Co., 6 F.R.D. 465 (W.D.Pa.1947).

3. See generally 5A C. Wright & A. Miller, Civil 2d §§ 1374–79; Comment, Federal Civil Procedure—Federal Rule 12(E): Motion for More Definite Statement—History Operation and Efficacy, 61 Mich.L.Rev. 1126 (1963).

4. Amoco Chemical Co. v. Tex Tin Corp., 925 F.Supp. 1192, 1212 (S.D.Tex. 1996); Tagare v. NYNEX Network Sys. Co., 921 F.Supp. 1146, 1153 (S.D.N.Y.1996).

5. E.g., Blane v. Losh, 10 F.R.D. 273 (N.D.Ohio 1950); Walling v. American S.S. Co., 4 F.R.D. 355, 358 (W.D.N.Y.1945). See Comment, Federal Civil Procedure—Federal Rule 12(E): Motion for More Definite Statement—History, Operation and Efficacy, 61 Mich.L.Rev. 1126, 1138–39 (1963).

6. See 5A C. Wright & A. Miller, Civil 2d § 1376.

7. See Fed.Civ.Proc.Rule 56; 10A C. Wright, A. Miller, & M. Kane, Civil 3d § 2719.

achieved many of the results that the Advisory Committee had in mind when it proposed the revision.[8] Further, Rule 12(e) has not become a vehicle for dilatory tactics as courts have given it a restrictive application.[9]

3. Truthfulness in Pleading

§ 5.11 Devices to Assure Candor in Pleading

Lawyers commonly are faced with questions concerning how to plead a particular claim or defense with complete candor and yet preserve a particular issue for trial. This problem may arise, for example, when determining whether a defense attorney can justifiably deny certain allegations in the plaintiff's complaint based solely on information received from his client. Alternatively, can plaintiff's counsel file a complaint knowingly omitting certain adverse facts which are not necessary to state a sufficient claim on behalf of his client?

The answers to these questions are not always self-evident. An official comment to the American Bar Association Model Rules of Professional Conduct provides some guidance by prohibiting the filing of false pleadings for harassment or to inflict malicious injury.[1] Although a full exploration of the ethical problems presented in the pleading context is beyond the scope of this volume, various devices have been employed by judicial systems to ensure that the pleadings are truthful and made in good faith. This section will explore the two most common methods employed by jurisdictions to promote candor in pleading: the attorney signature requirement and verification.

In many jurisdictions pleading rules require that every pleading be signed, usually by the attorney, or, if a party is unrepresented, by the party who files it.[2] A pleading may be stricken if it is not properly signed;[3] however, the defect is a technical one and the courts permit it to be corrected at any time during the proceedings.[4]

The chief purpose of the signature requirement is to ensure truthful pleading and thus deter frivolous litigation.[5] The original version of

---

8. See 5A C. Wright & A. Miller, Civil 2d § 1377.

9. Scarbrough v. R–Way Furniture Co., 105 F.R.D. 90 (E.D.Wis.1985); Shore v. Cornell–Dubilier Elec. Corp., 33 F.R.D. 5 (D.Mass.1963).

§ 5.11

1. ABA Model Rules of Professional Conduct, Rule 3.1, Comment, adopted August 2, 1983.

2. E.g., Fed.Civ.Proc.Rule 11; West's Ann.Cal.Code Civ.Proc. § 446; Ind.Trial Proc.Rule 11(A); Vernon's Ann.Tex.Rules Civ.Proc., Rules 45, 57.

3. Fed.Civ.Proc.Rule 11; Or.Rules Civ. Proc., Rule 17B.

4. Holley Coal Co. v. Globe Indem. Co., 186 F.2d 291 (4th Cir.1950); Burak v. Pennsylvania, 339 F.Supp. 534 (E.D.Pa.1972).

5. "Greater attention by the district courts to pleading and motion abuses and the imposition of sanctions when appropriate, should discourage dilatory or abusive tactics and help streamline the litigation process by lessening frivolous claims or defenses." Advisory Committee's Note to the 1983 amendments to Rule 11, reprinted in 97 F.R.D. 165, 198.

Federal Rule 11, which has been adopted in many states,[6] provided that by signing a pleading an attorney certified that the attorney had read it, believed that there were good grounds to support it, and that it had not been interposed for delay. The rule further provided that if it were signed with the intent of defeating the purposes of the rule, the pleading could be stricken as sham and the case ordered to proceed as if the pleading had not been filed. The effect of this provision on an unrepresented party who had signed her own pleading was unclear because the original drafters of the rule rejected a proposal making the latter's signature a certification identical to that of an attorney.[7] At least one state that adopted original Rule 11, New Jersey, included a provision making the signature of an unrepresented party a certificate of good faith.[8]

The effect of the original version of Rule 11 was to place a virtually unenforceable obligation upon the attorney to satisfy herself that there were good grounds for the action or defense.[9] Because many signature rules did not include sanctions, it is not surprising that the rules had little impact on actual conduct.[10] Primarily the rules stood as a reminder to attorneys of their obligation to the legal system and to the interests of justice. Even then, the power of these rules was questionable. There was no clear determination as to the degree of investigation required by an attorney to ensure that a pleading was not false. It generally was believed that there should be no duty to go beyond the word of the client; occasional suggestions that some investigation was required were met with the objection that the results would not justify the cost burden to clients.[11]

Although sanctions were available prior to 1983, courts were reluctant to impose them. Of course, an attorney who was shown to have willfully filed a false pleading could be subjected to disciplinary measures. However, proof of willful misconduct is difficult indeed. Under the original version of Rule 11, there were only one or two cases in which disciplinary action had been sought. In one particularly egregious situation a federal trial judge did order an attorney disbarred.[12] The order was reversed, however, because the trial court had acted without notifying the attorney or giving the attorney an opportunity to be heard.[13]

Another possible sanction was to strike a pleading that contained allegations that were obviously false.[14] Judges would not do so, however,

---

6. E.g., Colo.Rules Civ.Proc., Rule 11; N.M.Civ.Proc.Rules, Rule 1–011.

7. Final Report of the Advisory Committee 10 (Nov.1937).

8. N.J.Civ.Prac.Rule 1:4–8.

9. See 5A C. Wright & A. Miller, Civil 2d § 1334.

10. See Risinger, Honesty in Pleading and Its Enforcement: Some "Striking" Problems with Federal Rule of Civil Procedure 11, 61 Minn.L.Rev. 1 (1976).

11. Recent Decision, 47 Va.L.Rev. 1434 (1961), criticizing Freeman v. Kirby, 27 F.R.D. 395 (S.D.N.Y.1961).

12. In re Lavine, 126 F.Supp. 39 (S.D.Cal.1954), reversed sub nom. In re Los Angeles County Pioneer Soc., 217 F.2d 190 (9th Cir.1954).

13. In re Los Angeles County Pioneer Soc., 217 F.2d 190 (9th Cir.1954).

14. E.g., Brown v. District Unemployment Compensation Bd., 411 F.Supp. 1001 (D.D.C.1975).

if the pleading contained any valid claim or defense because the loss of a meritorious action or the default of a case in which there is a legitimate defense was viewed as too severe a penalty, at least when the fault was that of the attorney rather than of the party who would suffer.[15] Further, although courts had imposed costs, and even attorney fees, for the willful violation of the certification or signature requirement,[16] these means of enforcement had not been utilized frequently.

In recognition of these enforcement problems, in 1983 a number of significant revisions of Rule 11 were promulgated. That amended Rule was also considered unsatisfactory, so a new version of Rule 11, with major alterations, took effect in 1993. However, the 1993 Rule has itself proved highly controversial and there have been proposals for additional alterations, many of which would restore provisions of the 1983 version.[17]

The 1983 Rule required signatures on all pleadings and motions, and was extended to cover discovery requests and responses. A person, by signing, attested that he (1) had read the document, (2) had concluded, after reasonable inquiry into both the facts and the law, that to the best of his knowledge, information, and belief the pleading or motion was well grounded, and (3) had acted in good faith, without any improper motivation. The 1993 Rule made a number of significant changes to the 1983 formulation.[18] First, the 1993 Rule extends the obligation to every "pleading, written motion, or other paper" presented to the court whether by signing, filing, submitting, or later advocating a position.[19] The 1983 provision considered a pleading or motion only at the time it was signed. The 1993 Rule requires a person, who may have signed a pleading or motion in good faith, to cease advocating a position that she has learned is untenable on the facts or the law. Second, it no longer applies to matters of discovery since they are governed by their own specific provisions.[20] Third, it specifically authorizes an individual to submit a document with factual allegations that "if specifically so identified, are likely to have evidentiary support after a reasonable opportunity for further investigation or discovery."[21] The 1983 formula-

15. See Charm Promotions, Ltd. v. Travelers Indem. Co., 489 F.2d 1092 (7th Cir.1973), cert. denied 416 U.S. 986; Lewis v. Wells, 325 F.Supp. 382 (S.D.N.Y.1971); Radtke Patents Corp. v. C. J. Tagliabue Mfg. Co., 31 F.Supp. 226 (E.D.N.Y.1939); Northridge Co-op. Section No. 1, Inc. v. 32nd Ave. Constr. Corp., 15 Misc.2d 927, 181 N.Y.S.2d 608 (1958), affirmed 10 A.D.2d 244, 197 N.Y.S.2d 991 (1960).

16. See, e.g., Hedison Mfg. Co. v. NLRB, 643 F.2d 32 (1st Cir.1981); Anderson v. Allstate Ins. Co., 630 F.2d 677 (9th Cir.1980).

17. Tobias, Reforming Common Sense Legal Reforms, 30 Conn.L.Rev. 537, 533–55 (1998).

18. For a comprehensive analysis of the differences between the 1983 and 1993 versions of Rule 11, see Comment, A Practitioner's Guide to the 1993 Amendment to Federal Rule of Civil Procedure 11, 67 Temple L.Rev. 265 (1994). See also Proposed Rules, Preliminary Draft of Proposed Amendments to the Federal Rules of Civil Procedure and the Federal Rules of Evidence, 137 F.R.D. 53, 74–82 (Advisory Committee notes on the proposed 1993 version of Rule 11).

19. Fed.Civ.Proc.Rule 11(b).

20. Fed.Civ.Proc.Rule 11(d).

21. Fed.Civ.Proc.Rule 11(b)(3).

tion required the person signing the document, at the time of signing, to have a basis for believing that the pleading or motion was well-grounded. It was argued that this penalized litigants who believed, in good faith, that they could develop facts supporting their allegations but only if they could obtain formal discovery.[22] The current provision, however, seems almost unworkable.[23] How is one to know when a factual allegation is "likely" to have evidentiary support? How is a court to decide if such a claim is or is not justifiable?

The 1983 Rule did not specify procedures for sanctioning those who were alleged to have violated its requirements. As a result, claims for sanctions, primarily for expenses and attorney fees, often were contained in a pleading or with other motions. This had the tendency to increase the number of challenges under Rule 11 and created a good deal of "satellite litigation,"[24] not to mention bitter feelings between counsel on opposing sides. The 1993 Rule addresses this problem by requiring a party who seeks sanctions to do so by separate motion that must be served on the alleged offender.[25] The latter then has a "safe-harbor" period of twenty-one days during which she can withdraw or amend the challenged allegation or denial. Only after a twenty-one day period during which ameliorative action is not taken may the motion be filed with the court.[26] This rule change has been controversial. A distinguished group of federal judges and practicing attorneys argued that it would result in additional challenges under Rule 11, making a bad situation much worse.[27] Moreover, it has been noted that the "safe harbor" provision actually can increase the number of frivolous actions because attorneys can file those suits with impunity, knowing that, if challenged, they can simply withdraw or amend their complaints within the twenty-one day period.[28] Under the 1993 Rule the court continues to have power sua sponte to enforce Rule 11, but only after issuing a show cause order[29] that will allow the challenged individual to respond and, if appropriate, to take action to eliminate the problem.

22. See Proposed Rules, Preliminary Draft of Proposed Amendments to the Federal Rules of Civil Procedure and the Federal Rules of Evidence, 137 F.R.D. 53, 78–79 (1991) (Advisory Committee note on the proposed 1993 Rule).

23. See Pandrom, Predicting the Unpredictable Under Rule 11(B)(3): When Are Allegations "Likely" To Have Evidentiary Support?, 43 UCLA L.Rev. 1393 (1996).

24. See Bench–Bar Proposal To Revise Civil Procedure Rule 11, 137 F.R.D. 159 (1991) (courts were "drowning in satellite litigation" under the 1983 Rule.) The concern over ancillary litigation—generated from determining the applicability of sanctions—is reflected in Cooter & Gell v. Hartmarx Corp., 496 U.S. 384, 110 S.Ct. 2447, 110 L.Ed.2d 359 (1990). In Cooter, the Supreme Court held that the Rule did not authorize recovery of fees incurred on ap-

peal, reasoning that allowing recovery would promote satellite litigation. Id. at 409, 110 S.Ct. at 2463.

25. Fed.Civ.Proc.Rule 11(c)(1)(A).

26. Ibid. See Corley v. Rosewood Care Center, Inc., 142 F.3d 1041, 1057–58 (7th Cir.1998) (imposition of sanctions when there has not been compliance with the "safe harbor" provisions is an abuse of discretion.)

27. Bench–Bar Proposal To Revise Civil Procedure Rule 11, 137 F.R.D. 159 (1991).

28. Ripps & Drowatsky, Federal Rule 11: Are the Federal District Courts Usurping the Disciplinary Functions of the Bar?, 32 Valparaiso L.Rev. 67, 89 (1997) (advocating elimination of the "safe-harbor" provision).

29. Fed.Civ.Proc. Rule 11(c)(1)(B).

Some of the most dramatic differences between the 1983 and 1993 versions of Rule 11 involve the provisions for sanctions. The 1993 Rule makes clear that the purpose of sanctions is to deter improper conduct and not to compensate the opposing party.[30] This, too, has been controversial. Indeed Justice Scalia, with whom Justice Thomas joined, dissented from the adoption of the 1993 Rule, in part because it de-emphasized the importance of compensation to an opposing party.[31] The 1983 Rule required sanctions to be applied if the court found that a violation had occurred. The 1993 Rule provides the court with discretion,[32] thus allowing it to overlook inconsequential violations. The 1983 Rule itself had been criticized for lack of uniformity since courts had different views as to what constituted a violation and what sanctions should be applied.[33] The 1993 Rule merely adds to the uncertainty. The concern is that an attorney will be afraid to engage in zealous advocacy or to take innovative positions on behalf of his clients,[34] fearing that by so doing he will come before a judge who will decide that he has acted improperly and is thus subject to sanctions, even though other judges would have found the attorney's actions to have been proper or the violations inconsequential.

The 1983 Rule was held to apply only to the specific individual who signed the challenged document[35]—the attorney or the client—whereas the 1993 Rule specifies that in the ordinary course a law firm may be held jointly responsible for violations committed by its partners, associates, and employees.[36] Finally, the 1993 Rule provides a number of limitations on what sanctions can be imposed. For example, monetary sanctions cannot be imposed on a represented party for frivolous legal arguments;[37] the latter are the responsibility of the attorney. In ordinary circumstances monetary sanctions cannot be imposed by a court acting on its own motion.[38] And when monetary sanctions are imposed, they can include only those attorney fees and expenses incurred as a direct result

---

30. Fed.Civ.Proc.Rule 11(c)(2). See Forbes v. Merrill, Lynch, Fenner & Smith, Inc., 179 F.R.D. 107, 111 (S.D.N.Y.1998).

31. Amendments to the Federal Rules of Civil Procedure, 146 F.R.D. 401, 507 (dissenting opinion of Justice Scalia).

32. Fed.Civ.Proc.Rule 11(c); The courts continue to retain substantial discretion as to the nature of the sanctions imposed. See Shepherdson v. Nigro, 179 F.R.D. 150 (E.D.Pa.1998) (an admonition was held sufficient to deter similar future conduct).

33. See, e.g., Schwarzer, Rule 11 Revisited, 101 Harv.L.Rev. 1013, 1015 (1988)("In interpreting and applying Rule 11, the courts have become a veritable Tower of Babel.").

34. See Ripps & Dowatsky, Federal Rule 11: Are the Federal District Courts Usurping the Disciplinary Function of the Bar?, 32 Valparaiso L.Rev. 67, 79–80 (1997); Nelken, Sanctions Under Amended Federal Rule 11—Some "Chilling" Problems in the Struggle Between Compensation and Punishment, 74 Geo.L.J. 1313, 1338–43(1986); Note, Plausible Pleadings: Developing Standards for Rule 11 Sanctions, 100 Harv.L.Rev. 630, 632 (1987).

35. Pavelic & LeFlore v. Marvel Entertainment Group, 493 U.S. 120, 110 S.Ct. 456, 107 L.Ed.2d 438 (1989) (under the 1983 Rule, sanctions may not be imposed vicariously on a law firm for the conduct of one of its members).

36. Fed.Civ.Proc.Rule 11(c).

37. Fed.Civ.Proc.Rule 11(c)(2)(A).

38. Fed.Civ.Proc.Rule 11(c)(2)(B).

of the violation.[39]

Supporters of the 1983 Rule resisted the changes, arguing that the rule was effective in deterring much frivolous litigation (thereby conserving judicial resources and hence, achieving its chief purpose), compensating the victims of vexatious litigation, and educating the bar about appropriate standards of conduct.[40] Even some who saw faults with the Rule argued that progress had been made toward the development of workable standards and that federal judges needed more time to refine its implementation.[41] Whether the somewhat relaxed 1993 Rule will be equally effective as its 1983 predecessor while substantially eliminating satellite litigation and the chilling effect on innovation in pursuing a client's case is yet to be decided.

The second device that various jurisdictions use to ensure candor in pleading is a verification requirement. In the code pleading system, as originally adopted in New York in 1848,[42] a party was required to verify all the pleadings, that is, swear under oath as to the truth of the allegations, except regarding matters as to which the party would be privileged from testifying at trial.

In 1849 this requirement was altered substantially to provide any party with an option to verify the pleadings.[43] Once a party exercised this option, however, both parties had to verify all subsequent pleadings. The latter provision thus gave a party an opportunity "to probe the conscience of his adversary."[44] Of course, it provided a substantial advantage to plaintiffs who could not be required by defendants to verify their complaints if they had opted not to do so.

Today American courts generally follow one of three patterns. Some have virtually abolished verification.[45] A few require nearly all pleadings to be verified.[46] A number of others that retain fact pleading follow the optional verification plan adopted in New York,[47] although they may require verification for special cases.[48] Primarily, these statutes allow the plaintiff, by exercising an option to verify the complaint, to require the

---

39. Fed.Civ.Proc.Rule 11(c)(2).

40. See Amendments to the Federal Rules of Civil Procedure, 146 F.R.D. 401, 509 (1991) (Justice Scalia dissenting); Parness, Groundless Pleading and Certifying Attorneys in the Federal Courts, 1985 Utah L.Rev. 325; Untereiner, A Uniform Approach to Rule 11 Sanctions, 97 Yale L.J. 901, 902 (1988); Note, Litigant Responsibility: Federal Rule of Civil Procedure 11 and Its Application, 27 B.C.L.Rev. 385, 406 (1986).

41. See, e.g., Miller, The New Certification Standard Under Rule 11, 130 F.R.D. 479, 505 (1990) (much practice pertaining to the 1983 certification requirement has "solidified into a reasonably harmonious and workable standard").

42. N.Y.Laws 1848, c. 379, § 133. New York retains such a provision today. See N.Y.—McKinney's CPLR 3020.

43. N.Y.Laws 1849, c. 438, § 157.

44. C. Clark, Code Pleading § 36, at 217 (2d ed.1947).

45. The Federal Rules and the rules in those states having similar provisions abolish verification except in a few special cases. E.g., Fed.Civ.Proc.Rules 11, 23.1, 65(b); Del.Super.Ct.Civ. Rule 11.

46. E.g., Pa.Rules Civ.Proc., Rule 1024.

47. West's Ann.Cal.Code Civ.Proc. § 446; Official Code Ga.Ann. § 9–10–111; Ill.—Smith–Hurd Ann. 735 ILCS 5/2–605.

48. West's Ann.Cal.Code Civ.Proc. § 446; Official Code Ga.Ann. §§ 19–5–5, 9–10–110.

defendant to verify the answer and thereby prohibit the defendant from utilizing a one-sentence general denial. Instead, the defendant must specifically admit or deny the plaintiff's allegations.[49]

The value of a scheme of optional verification is questionable. First, as has been noted, it gives a tactical advantage to the plaintiff. Second, the actual utility of a verified pleading is as an item of evidence at trial to be used against the party who verified, to point out inconsistencies between statements made in the pleadings and those made by that party's witnesses. This tends to put an undue amount of emphasis on pleadings, which are drafted at an early stage of the proceeding, before all the information has been gathered and digested. In effect, verification becomes a tactical weapon to force a defendant into specific positions. Third, a question arises as to the leeway a party has if he or she chooses not to verify. If verification is designed to elicit truthful pleading, an option not to verify could be considered a license to make unsupportable allegations.

Jurisdictions that have signature requirements still retain specific verification requirements in situations in which a special effort to obtain truthful allegations seems warranted. In the federal courts, for example, the complaint in a shareholder's derivative suit must be verified,[50] and a temporary restraining order will be granted only on the basis of an affidavit or verified complaint showing the likelihood of irreparable harm.[51] Special verification provisions in state courts vary widely but may include divorce complaints,[52] all pleadings in attachment proceedings,[53] pleas denying possession or claims of title or interest in ejectment actions,[54] and denials of the execution of a written instrument.[55]

Under standard code provisions,[56] verification has to be made by one of the parties (or an officer or managing agent of a party),[57] except in certain specified situations. A person who verifies a pleading must aver that he has personal information as to the facts alleged or that he has information concerning the facts and on that basis believes them to be true.[58] A pleader also may verify a denial of facts on information and belief, although this was not permitted at common law.[59]

---

49. West's Ann.Cal.Code Civ.Proc. § 431.30(d); Official Code Ga.Ann. § 9–10–111 (applies only to courts not of record); Ill.—Smith–Hurd Ann. 735 ILCS 5/2–605. See Huckaby v. Oklahoma Office Bldg. Co., 201 Okl. 141, 202 P.2d 996 (1949).

50. Fed.Civ.Proc.Rule 23.1.

51. Fed.Civ.Proc.Rule 65(b).

52. Official Code Ga.Ann. § 19–5–5.

53. Ill.—Smith–Hurd Ann. 735 ILCS 5/4–104, 5/4–131.

54. Ill.—Smith–Hurd Ann. 735 ILCS 5/6–118.

55. Ill.—Smith–Hurd Ann. 735 ILCS 5/2–605(b).

56. In courts requiring verification only in special cases, the rules frequently do not specify who is to verify. See, e.g., Fed. Civ.Proc. Rule 23.1. Presumably, verification can be made by anyone having knowledge of the facts. See Surowitz v. Hilton Hotels Corp., 383 U.S. 363, 86 S.Ct. 845, 15 L.Ed.2d 807 (1966) (Harlan, J., concurring).

57. Ill.—Smith–Hurd Ann. 735 ILCS 5/2–605.

58. West's Ann.Cal. Code Civ.Proc. § 446; Ill.—Smith–Hurd Ann. 735 ILCS 5/2–605.

59. C. Clark, Code Pleading § 36, at 220 (2d ed. 1947).

These rules naturally tend to weaken the value of verification but they are necessary in situations when verification is required and when the party will not have a full opportunity to obtain the facts unless her pleading is held sufficient so that she then may engage in discovery. Abuses are controlled to some extent by refusing to accept pleadings based on information and belief when the facts are either a matter of public record or necessarily are available to the pleader.[60]

Modern courts have refused to apply sanctions for technical violations of verification rules when the interests of justice would not be served thereby. Perhaps the leading case is Surowitz v. Hilton Hotels Corporation,[61] in which the Supreme Court reversed the dismissal of a shareholder's derivative action in which the plaintiff had verified the complaint under the federal rule even though it later appeared that her knowledge of the case was based solely on statements made to her by her son-in-law. The Court, noting that the son-in-law was an attorney who was merely looking out for the interests of the plaintiff and those of her fellow shareholders, held that verification rules should not be used as a "booby trap" to eliminate meritorious cases. The verification was upheld because it was reasonable for the plaintiff to rely on the advice she had received, and there was no indication that the suit was not brought in good faith.

4.   Alternative and Inconsistent Allegations

§ 5.12   Ability to Assert Alternative and Inconsistent Allegations

At common law, a party could not plead hypothetically or in the alternative.[1] Thus, an allegation that "defendant wrote and published or caused to be written and published, a libel" would be considered "uncertain" and subject to challenge by special demurrer.[2] The purpose of the rule was to require a pleader to state clearly and concisely her position in order that the opponent would know exactly what claims were being made. An equally precise response would focus the trial only on those few facts about which the parties disagreed. As direct and logical as the rule appeared, it could result in substantial injustice in practice, particularly in a situation in which the pleader was unable, at the outset of the case, to ascertain the precise facts. A plaintiff was, in effect, required to select among alternative sets of facts and legal theories, even when the information was known only to the adverse party. If the pleader made a wrong choice, the case would be lost, even if the proof showed that an

---

60.   Oliver v. Swiss Club Tell, 222 Cal. App.2d 528, 35 Cal.Rptr. 324 (1963).

61.   383 U.S. 363, 86 S.Ct. 845, 15 L.Ed.2d 807 (1966).

§ 5.12

1.   An hypothetical pleading is one that utilizes an "if * * * then * * * "allegation,

whereas alternative pleading involves an "either * * *, or * * * "approach. The distinction is mechanical. See 5 C. Wright & A. Miller, Civil 2d § 1282.

2.   J. Koffler & A. Reppy, Common Law Pleading § 71 (1969).

alternative route would have been successful. In situations when a pleader inadvertently or by design encompassed possible alternatives by use of ambiguous allegations, the common law was even more harsh; it construed the pleading in the manner most unfavorable to the pleader on the theory that every party states her case most favorably to herself.[3]

The codes, as originally drafted and construed, adopted these same common-law principles,[4] except that the courts adopted a rule of construction resolving ambiguities in favor of, rather than against, the pleader.[5] In addition, at least some courts provided a means of avoiding the prohibition against alternatives by permitting inconsistent claims if they were presented in entirely different counts. Thus, in a single action a pleader could plead one claim on the basis of a breach of a valid contract, and another claim for rescission based on the invalidity of the same contract, as long as the claims were completely separated.[6] To the extent this pleading was permissible under the codes, it was cumbersome and confusing[7] and it is questionable whether inconsistent separate statements would be proper if the pleading had to be verified.[8]

A logical and straightforward approach would permit a party honestly to plead in the alternative in a single count according to the facts at her disposal. Many code jurisdictions have recognized the legitimacy of alternative pleadings and have adopted specific provisions allowing them.[9] Such a specific rule might seem unnecessary in notice pleading jurisdictions. Nevertheless, Federal Rule 8(e)(2), as followed in many states,[10] specifically permits claims and defenses that are stated hypothetically or in the alternative or are inconsistent with one another, so long as they are filed in good faith.

Given the fact that litigation is becoming increasingly complex, and that some types of information are much more difficult to obtain in advance of suit, the elimination of any bar to good-faith alternative pleading is not only proper, but necessary. Once a party has filed an action and has access to information through methods of formal discovery,[11] she can begin to define the proper limits of her case. Thereafter, by use of stipulation, discovery, summary judgment, and pretrial conference, the opposing party can eliminate those matters included in the initial pleadings that no longer are in dispute.

---

3. Id. at § 70.

4. Pavalon v. Thomas Holmes Corp., 25 Wis.2d 540, 131 N.W.2d 331 (1964); Hartzell v. Bank of Murray, 211 Ky. 263, 277 S.W. 270 (1925); McCrossin v. Noyes Bros. & Cutler, 143 Minn. 181, 173 N.W. 566 (1919); Hankin, Alternative and Hypothetical Pleadings, 33 Yale L.J. 365 (1924).

5. Jones v. Monson, 137 Wis. 478, 119 N.W. 179 (1909); Emerson v. Nash, 124 Wis. 369, 102 N.W. 921 (1905). But see Smith v. Monroe, 82 Ga.App. 118, 60 S.E.2d 790 (1950); J. R. Watkins Co. v. Ellington, 70 Ga.App. 722, 29 S.E.2d 300 (1944).

6. See Bischoff v. Hustisford State Bank, 195 Wis. 312, 218 N.W. 353 (1928).

7. C. Clark, Code Pleading 257 (2d ed.1947).

8. See Bell v. Brown, 22 Cal. 671, 678 (1863). See also § 5.11, above.

9. Ill.—Smith–Hurd Ann. 735 ILCS 5/2–613; Vernon's Ann.Tex.Rules Civ.Proc., Rule 48.

10. See § 5.1 n. 14, above.

11. See generally Chapter 7, below.

Because most modern jurisdictions today permit alternative or inconsistent allegations and claims, a question arises as to when, if at all, a party must elect among them. The problem can arise in three separate situations. First, there are cases in which a party may wish to pursue alternative legal theories, when there is no reason that she should not prevail on each. This might occur, for example, when plaintiff seeks damages for injury to reputation based on both defamation and invasion of privacy.[12] Although it is important to ensure that there is no double recovery for the same harm, there is no reason to require a plaintiff to select one theory prior to a decision on the merits. The trier of fact should decide the facts under each theory, but should be instructed carefully as to damages so that, in the case of a plaintiff's verdict, there is no duplicate damage recovery.

The second situation in which a question arises regarding whether the plaintiff should elect among alternative theories occurs when the plaintiff presents antagonistic claims and thus can prevail only on one. In one case, Wallace v. Bounds,[13] plaintiff, an administrator, brought suit with respect to injuries to a decedent arising from an auto accident with defendant. If the decedent's death was the result of the accident, the plaintiff's exclusive remedy was under the state wrongful death act. If death was from some other cause, the plaintiff could collect only under a survival statute giving survivors the same rights that the decedent would have possessed had he lived. Since it was unclear whether death was due to the accident, the plaintiff sought to pursue both claims and to allow the trier of fact to decide the matter. However, the court required the plaintiff to select one theory prior to submission of the case to the jury. Verdict was for the defendant and on appeal the judgment was affirmed.

This result seems highly improper. There is absolutely no justification for requiring an election. The case should have been submitted on both theories, allowing the trier of fact to decide if the plaintiff should prevail on either.[14] The required election is little more than a reversion to the discredited "theory of pleadings" doctrine.[15] Thus, perhaps not surprisingly, courts in other cases of this type have recognized the need to permit the plaintiff to go forward on all legitimately stated counts, and, accordingly, have refused to require an election.[16]

A third situation involving alternative or inconsistent claims arises when a plaintiff has a choice among inconsistent remedies. This occurs, for example, when a party has fraudulently been induced to enter into a contract. The plaintiff either may affirm the contract and sue for rights under it or disaffirm the contract and sue for damages or rescission. It is in this area of conflict that the so-called "election of remedies" doctrine is applicable and that the plaintiff may have to make a selection. The

---

12. See Brink v. Griffith, 65 Wn.2d 253, 396 P.2d 793 (1964).

13. 369 S.W.2d 138 (Mo.1963).

14. See C. Clark, Code Pleading § 77 (2d ed.1947).

15. See § 5.4 at n. 6, above.

16. See, e.g., McCormick v. Kopmann, 23 Ill.App.2d 189, 161 N.E.2d 720 (1959).

problem involves a question of estoppel. At some point the opposing party is entitled to know whether he is expected to go through with the contract. What constitutes an election is therefore a matter of substantive law that should be related to the question of when the defendant would be prejudiced by a change in the plaintiff's position. Often this point is reached long before any suit is filed.[17] From the viewpoint of pleading, the only question is whether the final election, if not already made by the plaintiff's actions, must be taken in the plaintiff's first pleading. Although decisions have been divided,[18] the modern trend has not required the plaintiff to make a binding choice in the complaint,[19] and to require the defendant to raise the matter as an affirmative defense.[20] Even if the plaintiff initially demands one form of relief, unless and until some real prejudice to the defendant is shown, the plaintiff can amend the complaint to shift her position and demand an inconsistent remedy.[21]

§ 5.13 Method of Asserting Alternative and Inconsistent Allegations; Incorporation of Allegations by Reference

Since one of the major concerns regarding alternative and inconsistent allegations is notice and possible prejudice to the opposing party, under the code pleading system rules allowing alternative pleadings typically include provisions requiring each cause of action or defense to be "separately pleaded, designated and numbered."[1] The purpose of these provisions is to keep the pleadings simple and the issues clear.[2] Unfortunately, emphasis on the term "cause of action" as the basis for separate statements can obfuscate rather than clarify a complaint or counterclaim. To the extent that a different "cause of action" is held to exist for every different legal theory as applied to one set of facts[3] or to every alteration of a set of facts no matter how small, the separate-statement requirement can result in a lengthy complaint, containing innumerable counts that add nothing to a simple straightforward recitation of the facts in a single statement.

More modern rules, modeled after Federal Rule 10(b),[4] clearly divorce the substantive aspects of the case from the need for pleading clarity. Thus, Federal Rule 10(b) calls for a separate paragraph for each

---

17. See C. Clark, Code Pleading § 77, at 496 (2d ed.1947).

18. See Annot., 6 A.L.R.2d 10 (1949).

19. See, e.g., Walton v. Walton, 31 Cal. App.4th 277, 292–93, 36 Cal.Rptr.2d 901, 908 (1995). See Fines, The Doctrine of Election of Remedies in Missouri, 63 U.Mo. K.C.L.Rev. 599, 606 (1994).

20. Ibid.

21. Adelman & Grossman, Civil Practice Annual of New York § 3002 (1982); C. Clark, Code Pleading § 77, at 497–98 (2d ed.1947).

§ 5.13

1. See Ill.—Smith–Hurd Ann. 735 ILCS 5/2–603. See also id. at 5/2–613.

2. C. Clark, Code Pleading 458 (2d ed.1947).

3. For examples see note 5, below.

4. E.g., Fla.—West's F.S.A. Rules Civ. Proc., Rule 1.110(f); Mass.Rules Civ.Proc., Rule 10(b); N.M.Dist.Ct.Rules Civ.Proc., Rule 1–010(B); Ohio Rules Civ.Proc., Rule 10(b); Wn.Civ.Rule 10(b).

"single set of circumstances" insofar as that is practical. Separation into different counts of claims and defenses that are based on separate transactions is required only when "a separation facilitates the clear presentation of the matters set forth." Obviously, under these latter rules, parties need not spend their time alleging and re-alleging the same facts in a variety of counts and defenses. In a simple case, regardless of the fact that several legal theories may apply, a single statement should suffice.

Despite the limited requirements of modern rules, a number of cases, in applying those rules, have required the pleader to set forth separate claims when a single set of facts gives rise to relief under several different theories, at least when the court believes that segregation will be helpful to understanding the claims.[5] Some cases also have required separate statements when the action is brought by multiple plaintiffs or against multiple defendants in order to help clarify the rights and liabilities of each party even though the underlying claim involves but one set of facts.[6] This pragmatic approach, if administered wisely, makes much sense, even though the terms of Rule 10(b) and its state counterparts do not specifically call for separate statements in these situations.

The courts must rely on their inherent powers to require parties to amend their pleadings to set forth separate statements of claims and defenses. No specific provision exists to enforce the requirements. This generally is true both in jurisdictions following the traditional code view as well as in jurisdictions that have adopted Federal Rule 10(b), although specific requirements may vary from state to state.[7] Whatever the challenge is called, it requires an amended set of allegations curing the defect. If a party fails to provide the required alterations, then the case can be dismissed.[8]

The separate statement requirement need not result in prolix or repetitive pleadings. A party may be able to avoid needless repetition by incorporating facts, once alleged, into other portions of the same pleading. Federal Rule 10(c) and its state counterparts expressly permit incorporation as do the vast majority of cases under code pleading

---

5. Hare v. Family Publications Serv., Inc., 342 F.Supp. 678, 686 (D.Md.1972); Woody v. Sterling Aluminum Prods., Inc., 243 F.Supp. 755 (E.D.Mo.1965), affirmed on other grounds 365 F.2d 448 (8th Cir.1966), cert. denied 386 U.S. 957 (inconsistent claims must be separately stated); Harzfeld's, Inc. v. Otis Elevator Co., 116 F.Supp. 512 (W.D.Mo.1953) (claim for wanton and reckless conduct and claim for negligence); Ingenuities Corp. of America v. Trau, 1 F.R.D. 578 (S.D.N.Y.1941); Chambers v. National Battery Co., 34 F.Supp. 834 (W.D.Mo.1940).

6. See, e.g., Pamela Amusement Co. v. Scott Jewelry Co., 22 F.R.D. 255 (D.Mass.

1958); Townsend v. Fletcher, 9 F.R.D. 711 (N.D.Ohio 1949).

7. There are, for example: (1) Motions to separate. Trussell v. United Underwriters, Ltd., 228 F.Supp. 757, 777 (D.Colo. 1964); 1951 Conn.Prac.Book 309 (Form 252); (2) Motions to strike. Erspamer v. Oliver Iron Mining Co., 179 Minn. 475, 229 N.W. 583 (1930); and (3) Demurrers. Heath v. Kirkman, 240 N.C. 303, 82 S.E.2d 104 (1954).

8. Benoit v. Ocwen Financial Corp., 960 F.Supp. 287 (S.D.Fla.1997). See Sawyer v. Sawyer, 181 Okl. 567, 75 P.2d 423 (1937).

systems.[9] There is only one limitation. With rare exception,[10] courts hold that allegations from another section of a pleading will be incorporated only if there is a direct and explicit reference to the material to be included.[11]

A somewhat similar situation occurs when a pleader wishes to incorporate information contained in documents outside of the pleadings. Under the codes, most courts permit incorporation if the pleading contains an explicit reference to the information clearly making it part of the allegations, and if the documents are attached to the pleadings as exhibits.[12] Modern provisions such as Federal Rule 10(c), allow incorporation by reference; the rules are somewhat unclear, however, regarding the need for specific language of incorporation. For example, the last sentence of Federal Rule 10(c) simply says "A copy of any written instrument which is an exhibit to a pleading is a part thereof for all purposes." This would indicate that the mere attachment of a document is sufficient, although there is some indication that direct reference to the document is required.[13] The matter is of some importance because the exhibit may be used against a pleader as well as in the pleader's favor. If an attached exhibit shows that a complaint is fatally defective, some courts have held the complaint subject to dismissal.[14] Further, if the allegations of a pleading are inconsistent with an exhibit, the exhibit is controlling.[15]

A final question is whether a pleader may incorporate information in a document that is not attached as an exhibit if the reference is clear and the document is available to the court and the parties. In general the answer appears to be "no." The rules do not provide for such incorporation and the courts have been reluctant to allow it.[16] The only excep-

9. E.g., N.Y.—McKinney's CPLR 3014; Vernon's Ann.Tex.Rules Civ.Proc., Rule 58. See, e.g., Ogier v. Pacific Oil & Gas Dev. Corp., 132 Cal.App.2d 496, 282 P.2d 574 (1955).

10. See N.Y.—McKinney's CPLR 3014.

11. Heintz & Co. v. Provident Tradesmens Bank & Trust Co., 29 F.R.D. 144 (E.D.Pa.1961) (incorporation must be done with a degree of clarity that enables the responding party to ascertain the nature and the extent of the incorporation). Aktiebolaget Stille–Werner v. Stille–Scanlan, Inc., 1 F.R.D. 395 (S.D.N.Y.1940); Dry Milk Co. v. Dairy Prods. Co., 171 App.Div. 296, 156 N.Y.S. 869 (1916); Florida Cent. & Pacific R.R. Co. v. Foxworth, 41 Fla. 1, 25 So. 338 (1899); Treweek v. Howard, 105 Cal. 434, 39 P. 20 (1895); Rose v. Jackson, 40 Mich. 29 (1879); Crawford v. New Jersey R. & Transp. Co., 28 N.J.L. 479 (1860).

12. M. G. Chamberlain & Co. v. Simpson, 173 Cal.App.2d 263, 343 P.2d 438 (1959). Some codes even require that in any suit brought to collect an unpaid debt based upon a note or other written obligation, the instrument must be attached and incorporated. E.g., Neb.Rev.St. § 25–832.

13. See Heintz & Co. v. Provident Tradesmens Bank & Trust Co., 29 F.R.D. 144 (E.D.Pa.1961); Oppenheimer v. F.J. Young & Co., 3 F.R.D. 220 (S.D.N.Y.1943), modified on other grounds 144 F.2d 387 (2d Cir.1944); Michelson v. Shell Union Oil Corp., 1 F.R.D. 183 (D.Mass.1940).

14. E.g., Kolbeck v. LIT America, Inc., 923 F.Supp. 557, 565 (S.D.N.Y.1996); Simmons v. Peavy–Welsh Lumber Co., 113 F.2d 812 (5th Cir.1940), cert. denied 311 U.S. 685.

15. See, e.g., Olpin v. Ideal Nat. Ins. Co., 419 F.2d 1250 (10th Cir.1969), cert. denied 397 U.S. 1074; General Guar. Ins. Co. v. Parkerson, 369 F.2d 821 (5th Cir. 1966); Consolidated Jewelers, Inc. v. Standard Financial Corp., 325 F.2d 31 (6th Cir. 1963); Banco Del Estado v. Navistar Int'l Transp. Corp., 942 F.Supp. 1176, 1179 (N.D.Ill.1996).

16. Oppenheimer v. F. J. Young & Co., 3 F.R.D. 220 (S.D.N.Y.1943), modified on

tion is when the documents involved previously have been filed in the case.[17] In those circumstances some courts have permitted incorporation by reference.

B. THE COMPLAINT

§ 5.14 Format Requirements; The Basic Elements of the Complaint

The format of the complaint is tightly regulated by local rules that vary often from city to city. In some instances the state judicial council or other comparable body has drafted some official forms that may be used.[1] Use of those forms clearly will meet any of the local format requirements. Thus, it is imperative when drafting a complaint to consult the local rules of the court in which suit will be filed. Despite this lack of uniformity, there is general agreement about the essential elements that should be present and a brief look at those rules is in order.

First, all jurisdictions require that the complaint contain a caption giving the name of the court, the title of the action, and the names of the parties.[2] Errors in the caption are treated as matters of form, not of substance, and typically can be corrected by amendment. This is true in situations in which a party is misnamed or designated in the wrong capacity. A distinction must be drawn between situations when plaintiff has sued the proper defendant under the wrong name and when plaintiff has sued the wrong defendant, however. In the latter case the error is not merely formal, and plaintiff's ability to bring in the correct defendant will depend in large part upon whether the statute of limitations has run.[3]

The next element in the complaint is the jurisdiction allegation. Courts vary substantially as to whether the complaint must set forth facts showing that the chosen forum is an appropriate court for the action to be heard. In many states there is a general presumption that the chosen court is proper; thus plaintiff need not deal with the matter in the complaint and any defect must be raised by defendant.[4] On the other hand, especially in inferior courts, state provisions oftentimes

---

other grounds 144 F.2d 387 (2d Cir.1944); Michelson v. Shell Union Oil Corp., 1 F.R.D. 183 (D.Mass.1940).

17. Woody v. Sterling Aluminum Prods., Inc., 243 F.Supp. 755 (E.D.Mo. 1965), affirmed on other grounds 365 F.2d 448 (8th Cir.1966), cert. denied 386 U.S. 957; Ogier v. Pacific Oil & Gas Dev. Corp., 132 Cal.App.2d 496, 282 P.2d 574 (1955). But cf. Hill v. Hill Spinning Co., 244 N.C. 554, 94 S.E.2d 677 (1956) (documents filed in previous action cannot be incorporated).

§ 5.14

1. In California, the Judicial Council developed forms for the causes of action most commonly encountered: personal injury, property damage, wrongful death, unlawful detainer, breach of contract, and fraud. West's Ann.Cal.Code Civ.Proc. § 425.12.

2. E.g., Fed.Civ.Proc.Rule 10(a); Colo. Rules Civ.Proc., Rule 10(a). See also C. Clark, Code Pleading § 35 (2d ed.1947).

3. See, § 5.27, below.

4. See Civil Code Study Commission, State of Indiana, Indiana Rules of Civil Procedure at 34 (August 1968).

require that the court's jurisdiction be set forth in the complaint.[5] And some provisions even require a plaintiff to include statements regarding venue.[6]

In federal court, jurisdictional allegations are required.[7] Since federal courts have limited subject-matter jurisdiction, there is no general presumption that a federal forum is proper.[8] The pleading requirement helps to ensure that federal courts do not, through error or inadvertence, adjudicate cases that do not fall within their powers.

Although technical pleading of jurisdictional facts is not required, federal courts on occasion have seemed to take a restrictive view, requiring something more than mere notice of the jurisdiction alleged to exist. Thus, an allegation that "plaintiff and defendant are citizens of different states" has been held insufficient for purposes of diversity of citizenship jurisdiction, absent an allegation as to the particular states of which the parties are citizens,[9] and there are many cases holding that allegations of "residency" will not suffice to set forth "citizenship."[10] Similarly, when establishing the citizenship of a corporate party, it is not enough simply to aver that the corporation is a citizen of a particular state or states;[11] a specific statement must be made as to the state of incorporation and the principal place of business.[12] In cases based upon federal question jurisdiction, courts generally have taken a liberal view, upholding as sufficient any allegations that clearly show that the action is based on federal law, even when the provision relied upon is not specifically named or designated.[13]

5. E.g., West's Ann.Cal.Code Civ.Proc. § 396a.

6. Official Code Ga.Ann. § 9–11–8(a).

7. Fed.Civ.Proc.Rule 8(a)(1).

8. 5 C. Wright & A. Miller, Civil 2d § 1206.

9. Hammes v. AAMCO Transmissions, Inc., 33 F.3d 774, 778 (7th Cir.1994); Gerstman v. Poole, 88 F.Supp. 733 (E.D.Pa. 1950); Cooper v. Globe Indem. Co., 9 F.R.D. 430 (W.D.La.1949). For a discussion of the method of pleading the existence of federal-question jurisdiction, see Miller, Artful Pleading: A Doctrine in Search of Definition, 76 Texas L.Rev. 1781 (1998).

10. E.g., Prescription Plan Serv. Corp. v. Franco, 552 F.2d 493, 498 n. 6 (2d Cir. 1977); DeVries v. Starr, 393 F.2d 9 (10th Cir.1968); Congress of Racial Equality v. Clemmons, 323 F.2d 54 (5th Cir.1963), cert. denied 375 U.S. 992.

11. Thomas v. Board of Trustees of Ohio State Univ., 195 U.S. 207, 217–18, 25 S.Ct. 24, 49 L.Ed. 160 (1904); Fifty Assocs. v. Prudential Ins. Co. of America, 446 F.2d 1187 (9th Cir.1970).

12. E.g., Veeck v. Commodity Enterprises Inc., 487 F.2d 423 (9th Cir.1973);

Moore v. Sylvania Elec. Prods., Inc., 454 F.2d 81 (3d Cir.1972); Fawvor v. Texaco, Inc., 387 F.Supp. 626 (E.D.Tex.1975), remanded on other grounds 546 F.2d 636 (5th Cir.1977).

There is some uncertainty whether the location of the principal place of business must be set forth specifically. Compare Moore v. Sylvania Elec. Prods., Inc., 454 F.2d 81 (3d Cir.1972) (both state of incorporation and principal place of business must be positively alleged), with Guerrino v. Ohio Cas. Ins. Co., 423 F.2d 419, 421 (3d Cir. 1970) (allegation that defendant is incorporated in Ohio and has its principal place of business elsewhere would suffice only if all plaintiffs are citizens of Pennsylvania), and Cherry v. Alcoa S.S. Co., 202 F.Supp. 663, 664 (D.Md.1962) (leave given to amend complaint to negate the possibility that the defendant's principal place of business was in Maryland). Official Form 2 seems to suggest that rigid pleading of the precise location is unnecessary.

13. E.g., Hammes v. AAMCO Transmissions, Inc., 33 F.3d 774, 778–79 (7th Cir.1994); Blue v. Craig, 505 F.2d 830, 844 n. 31 (4th Cir.1974); Williams v. U.S., 405 F.2d 951 (9th Cir.1969); Maple v. Citizens

When jurisdiction requires an amount in controversy, a bare allegation in the terms of the jurisdictional statute, "that the matter in controversy exceeds, exclusive of costs and interest, the sum of $75,-000"[14] is sufficient unless the balance of the complaint somehow demonstrates that this averment is not credible. But the averment must refer clearly to the required statutory amount. Thus, an allegation that the suit involved "priceless rights" was held insufficient.[15] It should be recalled that in cases involving multiple parties, including class actions, the claim of every plaintiff must meet the jurisdictional amount[16] and the pleadings must be phrased to aver that.

Whenever it appears that a court lacks subject-matter jurisdiction, the traditional view is that the court, on its own motion, must dismiss the case,[17] or, when permitted or required by state law, transfer it to another court of the same state where subject-matter jurisdiction is appropriate.[18] The defect cannot be waived and can be raised at any time during the action, even on appeal.[19] When the defect is merely one of pleading and, in fact, jurisdiction is proper, an amendment is appropriate and will be freely allowed, either at trial or on appeal.[20]

The third and major element of the complaint is the body of allegations comprising the cause of action or claim for relief. As already discussed,[21] defining what should be contained in this portion of the complaint is not always easy and thus the most difficult pleading problems for plaintiffs involve stating this element sufficiently. The next two sections explore some of these problems and concerns.

The final portion of a complaint, the prayer, contains the demand for the relief to which the pleader believes he or she is entitled. The demand is not part of the substantive claim; thus, selection of an improper form of relief will not subject the complaint to dismissal for failure to state a claim or cause, provided that the substantive allegations show that some other form of relief would be appropriate.[22]

In most jurisdictions, the demand for relief has a major impact only in cases in which defendant defaults. In those situations, by statute or rule, the plaintiff cannot obtain relief in excess of, or different in kind

Nat. Bank & Trust Co., 437 F.Supp. 66 (W.D.Okl.1977).

14. See 28 U.S.C.A. § 1332(a).

15. Giancana v. Johnson, 335 F.2d 366, 371 (7th Cir.1964), cert. denied 379 U.S. 1001.

16. Zahn v. International Paper Co., 414 U.S. 291, 94 S.Ct. 505, 38 L.Ed.2d 511 (1973); Snyder v. Harris, 394 U.S. 332, 89 S.Ct. 1053, 22 L.Ed.2d 319 (1969).

17. Morgan v. Melchar, 442 F.2d 1082 (3d Cir.1971), judgment vacated 405 U.S. 1014, 92 S.Ct. 1280, 31 L.Ed.2d 477 (1972); Kamsler v. Zaslawsky, 355 F.2d 526 (7th Cir.1966); Thomas v. St. Luke's Health Systems, Inc., 869 F.Supp. 1413, 1424–25

(N.D.Iowa 1994), affirmed 61 F.3d 908 (8th Cir.1995). See Berry v. Consumer Credit of Valdosta, Inc., 131 Ga.App. 147, 205 S.E.2d 533 (1974); Roby v. South Park Comm'rs, 215 Ill. 200, 74 N.E. 125 (1905).

18. West's Ann.Cal.Code Civ.Proc. §§ 396, 396a; Ill.—Smith–Hurd Ann. 735 ILCS 5/2–106.

19. Fed.Civ.Proc.Rule 12(h)(3). See also Capron v. Van Noorden, 6 U.S. (2 Cranch) 126, 2 L.Ed. 229 (1804).

20. See 28 U.S.C.A. § 1653.

21. See §§ 5.4–5.5, and 5.7, above.

22. 5 C. Wright & A. Miller, Civil 2d § 1255.

from, that demanded in the prayer.[23] The purpose is to encourage defendants to default in cases in which the claim is justifiable, by ensuring that they will not suffer unforeseen judgments. Practically speaking these clauses have little effect on intentional defaults. When a defendant's position is so weak that he is willing to default, he normally will settle the action long before a complaint is filed.

If the case is litigated, the plaintiff will be awarded all the relief to which she is entitled, whether or not that relief was part of the demand.[24] This rule applies only to relief based on claims within the contemplation of the parties at the time the action is tried. It does not, and obviously should not, apply in situations in which the evidence admitted on pleaded claims also tends to establish an unpleaded claim that the defendant did not recognize and defend.[25]

It is important to note that some courts have rejected the general rule and prohibit recovery in excess of the demand even in litigated cases.[26] Even in these courts, however, a litigant whose demand is exceeded by a verdict may be allowed, in the discretion of the court, to amend the prayer to conform to the proof, thus allowing full recovery.[27] Since an amendment may be denied if prejudicial to the defendant, this rule has the unfortunate effect of encouraging plaintiffs to inflate their claims wildly, to ensure that they will not lose the benefit of any portion of a verdict in their favor.

In addition to the amount recoverable, the demand for relief also may have an effect on the jurisdiction of the court and the right to trial by jury. In those state courts in which a separate jurisdictional statement is not required, there are frequently two or more sets of trial courts whose jurisdiction depends on the nature or amount of relief sought by the plaintiff.[28] Moreover, in most jurisdictions, the right to trial by jury exists only in cases in which legal relief (in general, damages) is sought and not in cases in which only equitable remedies, such as injunctions, specific performance, or rescission, are demanded.[29]

In recent years a number of courts and commentators have expressed dissatisfaction with the requirement of a demand for relief,[30]

23. E.g., Fed.Civ.Proc.Rule 54(c); Official Code Ga.Ann. § 9–11–54(c)(1). However, at a hearing to establish damages a plaintiff may be awarded less than the demand. See 10 C. Wright, A. Miller & M. Kane, Civil 3d § 2663.

24. Fed.Civ.Proc.Rule 54(c); Colo.Rules Civ.Proc., Rule 54(c).

25. Old Republic Ins. Co. v. Employers Reinsurance Corp., 144 F.3d 1077 (7th Cir. 1998); Convertible Top Replacement Co. v. Aro Mfg. Co., 312 F.2d 52 (1st Cir.1962), modified on other grounds 377 U.S. 476, 84 S.Ct. 1526, 12 L.Ed.2d 457 (1964); Official Code Ga.Ann. § 9–11–54(c)(1). See also Fed.Civ.Proc.Rule 15(b) and § 5.26, below.

26. E.g., Stromberg v. Crowl, 257 Iowa 348, 353, 132 N.W.2d 462, 465 (1965).

27. Haney v. Burgin, 106 N.H. 213, 208 A.2d 448 (1965).

28. For example, in California the jurisdiction of municipal courts is limited to cases involving $25,000 or less and not involving equitable relief. West's Ann.Cal. Code Civ.Proc. § 86.

29. See C. Clark, Code Pleading § 16 (2d ed.1947). See generally Chapter 11, below, on the right to jury trial.

30. E.g., Bail v. Cunningham Bros., Inc., 452 F.2d 182, 190 (7th Cir.1971). See also 10 C. Wright, A. Miller & M. Kane, Civil 3d § 2663.

arguing that it does more harm than good. Courts have been concerned with the fact that demands for damages are inflated beyond reason, often in the hope that either through direct presentation in court or outside publicity the jury will be influenced in the plaintiff's favor. A few federal courts have ordered the demand stricken in such cases.[31] California has gone so far as to enact a statute that prohibits plaintiffs in personal injury cases from stating the amount demanded.[32] Although more stringent rules preventing the amount demanded from reaching the jurors in a case appears to be a sufficient cure, elimination of the demand would not cause substantial difficulty. Matters regarding court jurisdiction and the right to trial by jury can be handled through generalized allegations that avoid stating specified amounts.

§ 5.15   Pleading a Right to Relief

Although courts differ as to how detailed allegations must be and the form in which they must be phrased, under every pleading system the plaintiff (or a party filing a counterclaim, cross-claim, or third-party claim) must set forth sufficient information to allege a right to relief.[1] To do so the pleader first must know the essential elements upon which his claim or claims will be based. Even in the simplest of cases, the list of potential controlling factors is a long one. For example, in an action on a note, recovery can depend upon the existence and proper execution of the note, whether the note is due, whether it has been paid, whether the plaintiff has accepted some other consideration in lieu of payment, whether the plaintiff previously brought a separate action to enforce the identical claim, whether the statute of limitations has run, and, possibly several other matters.

The plaintiff is not required to allege the existence or nonexistence of each and every factor that might affect the outcome of the litigation; some matters are considered defenses to be raised by the defendant in the answer. The important question is how does one draw the line between factors that must be raised by the party seeking relief and those that constitute defenses?

The general rule is that a party bears the responsibility for pleading those matters upon which that party must produce proof at trial. The theory behind the rule is simple; if a party cannot produce the necessary proof, then that party will not be able, in good faith, to plead the issue and the issue, quite properly, will not be a part of the case. If the issue is crucial to recovery, the complaint can be dismissed and a wasteful trial avoided. If the issue is a matter the defendant must establish, it will be a factor only if the defendant raises it. This division of responsibility

---

31. Mitchell v. American Tobacco Co., 28 F.R.D. 315 (M.D.Pa.1961).

32. West's Ann.Cal.Code Civ.Proc. § 425.10(b). See also id. § 425.11. Michigan prohibits the statement of a specific amount in most cases, Mich.Ct.Rules 1985, 2.111 (B)(2), but other states have eliminated it

only in medical malpractice cases, N.Y.— McKinney's CPLR 3017(c).

§ 5.15

1. Fed.Civ.Proc.Rule 8(a)(2); West's Ann.Cal.Code Civ.Proc. § 425.10; N.C.Civ. Proc. Rules, Rule 8(a)(1).

between the plaintiff and the defendant is sound. If the plaintiff were required to raise and overcome every conceivable defense in the complaint, not only would the complaint be unnecessarily long and complex but one never could be certain just what defenses were seriously in contention.

The decision as to which party must produce evidence at trial is basically a question of substantive policy. Usually the party who seeks redress must establish those factors at the heart of the claim that are considered vital if recovery is to be allowed. The defending party has the duty to prove those special matters that would limit or avert recovery. Finally, the party seeking redress must assume the burden of establishing any additional matter that would avoid defenses established by the defending party. These latter matters of avoidance will be pleaded only if there is a reply to the answer.[2] When no reply is permitted, issues of avoidance can be placed in contention under the general provision that deems the answer to have been controverted and avoided on every material issue.[3]

Although courts usually agree as to which issues are so basic to the claim that the party seeking redress must prove and plead them, there are important disputes.[4] In some isolated instances, for historical or practical reasons, one party may have to plead certain factors, even though the opposing party has the burden of proof once the matter is raised. Perhaps the clearest case is one in which the plaintiff sues to collect on a note. The general rule is that payment of the note is a defense to be proved by the defendant who normally will have a receipt or other means of proof in his possession.[5] Nevertheless, nonpayment must be pleaded by the plaintiff for the simple reason that without such an allegation the complaint in effect says nothing.[6] Fortunately, incidents of this type are relatively few and are well known to lawyers in the particular jurisdictions where they apply.

A somewhat more serious problem sometimes has arisen when substantive rules place the burden of proof on the plaintiff, on whom the burden of pleading then logically would fall, but procedural rules list the matter as an affirmative defense to be raised by defendant. This can create considerable confusion.[7] For example, if lack of contributory negligence is a basic element of the plaintiff's right to relief, but the pleading rule lists contributory negligence as a defense, what happens if the defendant omits the issue? Must the plaintiff still prove lack of

---

2. With respect to the requirement of a reply, see § 5.3, above.

3. Fed.Civ.Proc.Rule 8(d).

4. For example, in personal injury actions based on negligence, most courts consider the plaintiff's contributory fault to be a defense to be proved and pleaded by the defendant. E.g., Hoffman v. Southern Pacific Co., 84 Cal.App. 337, 258 P. 397 (1927). But some jurisdictions have required the plaintiff to plead and prove lack of fault as part of the claim for relief. E.g., Hardware State Bank v. Cotner, 55 Ill.2d 240, 302 N.E.2d 257 (1973).

5. E.g., Pastene v. Pardini, 135 Cal. 431, 434, 67 P. 681, 682 (1902).

6. E.g., Fancher v. Brunger, 94 Cal. App.2d 727, 730, 211 P.2d 633, 636 (1949).

7. See Cleary, Presuming and Pleading: An Essay on Juristic Immaturity, 12 Stan.L.Rev. 5 (1959).

negligence in order to recover or is the issue waived? Since rules of pleading should serve to avoid confusion, the logical step would be to change the pleading rule. Courts have been reluctant to do so, however, and thus the uncertainty has had to be resolved by judicial intervention leading to customary practices known, it is hoped, by all attorneys involved in cases in which the particular problem arises.[8]

On occasion a pleading on its face will indicate a defect in the pleader's own claim or defense. The most common examples occur when a plaintiff's complaint reveals that the statute of limitations bars the action or that the defendant's alleged misconduct was privileged. In a few cases, the courts have insisted that allegations containing anticipated defenses, which normally must be pleaded and proved by the opposing party, are surplusage and should be ignored.[9] However, most courts have ruled that if a pleading contains a defect and fails to go on to show how the defect is avoided, the pleading is subject to challenge for failure to state a claim or defense.[10]

Under the majority view a problem arises as to the sufficiency of allegations necessary to avoid the defect. Courts utilizing a notice pleading system tend to be extremely lenient in finding that general allegations of liability are sufficient to overcome the anticipated matters. Thus, in one case in which allegations of slander included statements showing the remarks to be privileged unless they were uttered maliciously, the failure of the plaintiff to allege malice was held not to be an admission of the validity of the defense. As the court held,

> [W]hen allegations are sufficient to sustain the defense of conditional privilege they will be, generally, sufficient to permit the introduction of evidence tending to prove abuse of the privilege or actual malice. * * * [A]llegations which are adequate for the admission of evidence to prove the defense * * * are adequate for the admission of evidence to negative that defense.[11]

Of course, if the privilege shown is unqualified, and there is no way it can be avoided, then the complaint will be held defective.[12]

As one might expect, in states operating under the code pleading system, avoidance of anticipated defenses requires specific allegations of ultimate fact. The courts will not find that the allegations of the defense itself are sufficient to allow proof of the avoidance.[13]

8. Id. at 14–15.

9. See Ellis v. Black Diamond Coal Mining Co., 265 Ala. 264, 90 So.2d 770 (1956). See also C. Clark, Code Pleading § 82, at 522–23 (2d ed.1947).

10. See, e.g., Baggett v. Chavous, 107 Ga.App. 642, 131 S.E.2d 109 (1963); Marks v. McCune Constr. Co., 370 P.2d 560 (Okl. 1962).

11. Garcia v. Hilton Hotels Int'l, Inc., 97 F.Supp. 5, 9 (D.Puerto Rico 1951).

12. In Garcia, itself, one defense of absolute privilege could not be overcome and the corresponding count of the complaint was stricken. 97 F.Supp. at 10.

13. E.g., Wright v. Hix, 203 Ala. 425, 83 So. 341 (1919); Sternstein v. Heit, 186 App.Div. 45, 173 N.Y.S. 808 (1919).

§ 5.16 Special Problems of Pleading in Specific Cases

It would be impossible to set forth for each particular jurisdiction the specific allegations sufficient to state a claim or cause for every type of action. Nor would such an exercise be fruitful because many states follow the federal courts in supplying a set of official forms to guide attorneys.[1] There are, however, a certain number of specific matters that raise particular pleading problems and that merit special consideration.

The first is the pleading of conditions precedent. In order to establish a right to relief based upon a contract, or other duty, a plaintiff must show that all conditions precedent to the defendant's duty have occurred or been performed.[2] Under a fact pleading system, pleading of these conditions could prove onerous, since there may be a substantial number of conditions in a given contract. Moreover, detailed pleading usually would be wasteful because the defendant would have no intention of claiming that all or nearly all of the conditions had not been met. Even so, if the plaintiff inadvertently omitted to set forth facts showing satisfaction of any one condition, the complaint could be challenged successfully as insufficient.

Courts tended to eliminate these problems by stretching to find a condition to be either a condition subsequent, to be pleaded and proved as a defense, or an independent promise that did not affect the defendant's obligation under the contract.[3] To avoid technical arguments over the type of condition and the sufficiency of pleading, a number of code jurisdictions have enacted special statutes allowing a plaintiff to allege the simple "conclusion" that all conditions precedent have been duly performed.[4] The burden then shifts to the defendant to deny the allegations, in which event the plaintiff must bear the burden of proof.[5] As one would expect in notice-pleading systems, a general allegation of performance is specifically permitted.[6] On the other hand, when a plaintiff intends to rely on an excuse or waiver of a condition as opposed to performance, the general rule is that the plaintiff must plead the excuse or waiver; the plaintiff cannot rely solely on a general allegation of performance or occurrence.[7]

---

§ 5.16

1. E.g., Fed.Civ.Proc.Rules, Appendix of Forms; Colo.Civ.Proc.Rules, Appendix of Forms; Fla.—West's F.S.A. Rules Civ.Proc., Forms; Mo.Civ.Proc.Forms; N.Y.—McKinney's CPLR, Forms.

2. West's Ann.Cal.Code Civ.Proc. § 457.

3. C. Clark, Code Pleading § 45, at 280–82 (2d ed.1947). The distinction between a condition precedent and a condition subsequent depends largely on the way the obligation is worded and, from a substantive point of view, is of little material significance. See, e.g., 5 Williston, Contracts § 667A, at 148, 151–52 (3d ed.1961).

4. E.g., West's Ann.Cal.Code Civ.Proc. § 457; 12 Okl.Stat.Ann. § 2009.

5. See, e.g., 12 Okl.Stat.Ann. § 2009.

6. Fed.Civ.Proc.Rule 9(c).

7. See Redfield v. Continental Cas. Corp., 818 F.2d 596 (7th Cir.1987); Pearl Assur. Co. v. First Liberty Nat. Bank, 140 F.2d 200 (5th Cir.1944); Winter & Giordano Landscape Contracting Corp. v. Colaizzo, 17 Misc.2d 450, 191 N.Y.S.2d 565 (1959). But see Erskine v. Upham, 56 Cal.App.2d 235, 132 P.2d 219 (1942). See generally 5 C. Wright & A. Miller, Civil 2d § 1303.

The major benefits of the special pleading rules applicable to conditions precedent would be lost if the defendant, merely by denying the plaintiff's allegation of performance in general terms, could force the plaintiff to prove performance of every condition precedent, including those the defendant did not dispute. Thus, a concomitant of the rule allowing the plaintiff to plead performance or occurrence generally, is a rule, applied in most jurisdictions, requiring the defendant to deny performance or occurrence "specifically and with particularity."[8] The plaintiff need only give proof when performance or occurrence is actually in dispute.

Another situation in which there is a departure from the specificity usually required in fact pleading is with the use of so-called common counts. At common law under the writ system, very simple allegations were permitted to state an action for money due, whether the obligation was express or implied (indebitatus assumpsit), and whether for repayment of a loan, for goods sold and delivered (quantum valebant), for labor performed (quantum meruit), or because of an unjust enrichment (money had and received). The required allegations consisted basically of a one sentence claim that gave none of the details or facts of the particular situation.[9]

When the codes were adopted, these common counts posed a problem. Because the allegations consisted of simple conclusions, they did not conform to the general requirements of fact pleading and many commentators argued that they should be held insufficient.[10] But they were so well known, and so convenient, that their use has been generally[11] upheld. Although notice pleading provisions do not mention the common counts, the Official Forms attached to the Federal Rules clearly approve their use.[12] Thus, from a tactical point of view, whenever a plaintiff sues for money due, even if based on an express contract, she should, if allowed, add a common count to avoid dismissal. If the detailed account proves fatally defective, the common count will save the complaint.[13]

There also has been some difficulty in determining the level of pleading specificity required in negligence actions.[14] Regardless of the pleading system, courts typically have been lenient in permitting gener-

---

8. Fed.Civ.Proc.Rule 9(c); N.J.Civ. Prac.Rule 4:5–8(b); N.Y.—McKinney's CPLR 3015(a).

9. See J. Koffler & A. Reppy, Common Law Pleading § 175 (1969).

10. J. Pomeroy, Code Remedies §§ 436–38 (5th ed.1929). See also 1 J. Kerr, Pleading and Practice in the Western States § 26 (1919); Note, Pleading; Variance: Proof of an Express Contract in an Action upon an Implied Contract, 3 Cornell L.Q. 145 (1918).

11. E.g., Leoni v. Delany, 83 Cal. App.2d 303, 188 P.2d 765 (1948); See C. Clark, Code Pleading § 46, at 290 (2d ed.1947).

12. Fed.Civ.Proc.Rules Appendix of Forms, Forms 5, 6, 8.

13. A few courts have ruled that if an express count fails, a common count based on identical facts also must fail. E.g., Rose v. Ames, 53 Cal.App.2d 583, 128 P.2d 65 (1942); Hays v. Temple, 23 Cal.App.2d 690, 73 P.2d 1248 (1937). But this conclusion is not necessary since the common count rarely is designed to enforce an identical obligation to an express contract count. See, e.g., Leoni v. Delany, 83 Cal.App.2d 303, 188 P.2d 765 (1948).

14. Problems in pleading contributory negligence or the lack thereof are discussed in § 5.15, at n. 7, above.

alized allegations of negligence, so long as the complaint gives fair notice of the nature of the incident and its time and place. Some courts in fact pleading jurisdictions, however, have insisted that the specific negligent acts be set forth in detail.[15] This rigid application of the fact pleading requirements tends to be counter-productive; the plaintiff is likely to allege every detail in every possible manner, to avoid being barred at trial from establishing a case, no matter how the witnesses testify. Under modern pleading doctrine, it makes better sense to allow general pleadings; details can be developed through pretrial discovery.[16]

Another situation that has caused some problems in the past involves the utilization of res ipsa loquitur. In some courts, the allegation of specific acts of negligence has been held to prohibit the plaintiff's reliance on the doctrine, on the theory that, if the plaintiff knows what occurred, the doctrine is inapplicable.[17] Most courts have not imposed this limitation, however.[18] It makes little sense to force plaintiffs to plead only in general terms for fear that reliance on res ipsa loquitur otherwise will be precluded.

Thus far the discussion has involved situations in which general allegations are favored even in judicial systems adhering to fact pleading. There are instances in which the converse is true and a relatively high degree of specificity is required, even in those systems adhering to notice pleading. Jurisdictions vary regarding what types of actions require these detailed pleadings. New York, for example, requires a plaintiff, in an action for marital separation, to specify "the nature and circumstances of the defendant's misconduct and the time and place of each act complained of."[19] The most common areas in which a high degree of specificity is demanded are in actions for fraud and mistake, defamation, and in cases in which special damages are demanded.

At common law and under fact pleading systems, a plaintiff was required to set forth with specificity the details of fraud.[20] This requirement now generally is extended to include mistake as well. Even under liberal notice pleading rules, a special provision requires that the circumstances of the fraud and mistake be set forth with particularity.[21] Actions for fraud were disfavored because they involved allegations of immorality.[22] Moreover, fraud and mistake are means of avoiding deeds, contracts,

---

15. Mirto v. News–Journal Co., 50 Del. (11 Terry) 103, 123 A.2d 863 (1956); Sheing v. Remington Arms Co., 48 Del. (9 Terry) 591, 108 A.2d 364 (1954); See Gallion v. Woytassek, 244 Neb. 15, 504 N.W.2d 76 (1993).

16. See C. Clark, Code Pleading § 47, at 300–03 (2d ed.1947).

17. See generally Niles, Pleading Res Ipsa Loquitur; 7 N.Y.U.L.Rev. 415 (1929); Comment, The Effect of Specific Allegations on the Application of Res Ipsa Loquitur, 27 Fordham L.Rev. 411 (1958); Annot., 2 A.L.R.3d 1335 (1965); Annot., 160 A.L.R. 1450 (1946).

18. Comment, The Effect of Specific Allegations on the Application of Res Ipsa Loquitur, 27 Fordham L.Rev. 411 (1958). See Niles, Pleading Res Ipsa Loquitur, 7 N.Y.U.L.Rev. 415 (1929).

19. N.Y.—McKinney's CPLR 3016(c).

20. C. Clark, Code Pleading § 48, at 311–13 (2d ed.1947); J. Koffler & A. Reppy, Common Law Pleading § 93, at 194 (1969).

21. Fed.Civ.Proc.Rule 9(b). See § 5.9, at nn. 6–10, above.

22. C. Clark, Code Pleading § 48, at 311–13 (2d ed.1947).

and other similar documents that normally are the result of careful planning and should not be set aside lightly. For these reasons a higher pleading threshold seems warranted. Nonetheless, the special pleading requirements for fraud have not posed a significant barrier to those actions. Especially in notice pleading jurisdictions, general allegations giving fair notice as to the plaintiff's claim consistently have been upheld.[23] Only an allegation of the bare conclusion of "fraud" or "mistake" clearly is susceptible to a motion to dismiss.[24]

At common law, defamation suits also were disfavored and subjected to a number of pleading technicalities.[25] Code pleading states typically have eased these restrictions, particularly the common-law requirement of detailed averments showing that the words spoken were intended to refer to the plaintiff.[26] However, the attitude toward defamation suits has remained unfavorable as reflected by a generally imposed requirement that the defamatory words be set forth with precision.[27] Even in notice pleading jurisdictions, some judges have appeared to hold that the failure to set forth detailed averments will justify a dismissal or at least require a more definite statement.[28]

The need for greater specificity in pleading special damages arises from their very nature. The concept of special damages arises in two different contexts. First, in some types of actions, such as slander, trade libel, and malicious prosecution, special damages—defined as specific harm to one's personal or business reputation—must be pleaded and proved.[29] The trier of fact is not entitled to decide that the conduct of the defendant, assuming the defendant committed the alleged acts, necessarily would result in some harm to the plaintiff to be measured by a

---

23. See, e.g., Brady v. Games, 128 F.2d 754, 755 (D.C.Cir.1942); Cincinnati Gas & Elec. Co. v. General Elec. Co., 656 F.Supp. 49 (S.D.Ohio 1986); Gardner v. Surnamer, 599 F.Supp. 477 (E.D.Pa.1984); Consumers Time Credit, Inc. v. Remark Corp., 227 F.Supp. 263 (E.D.Pa.1964). See also Fed. Civ.Proc.Rules Appendix of Forms, Form 13.

24. Hayduk v. Lanna, 775 F.2d 441 (1st Cir.1985); C. I. T. Corp. v. Tyree, 268 N.C. 562, 151 S.E.2d 42 (1966); R.G. Wilmott Coal Co. v. State Purchasing Comm'n, 246 Ky. 115, 54 S.W.2d 634 (1932).

25. C. Clark, Code Pleading § 48, at 315 (2d ed.1947); J. Koffler & A. Reppy, Common Law Pleading § 93, at 195–96 (1969).

26. E.g., West's Ann.Cal.Code Civ. Proc. § 460; N.Y.—McKinney's CPLR 3016.

27. Holliday v. Great Atl. & Pac. Tea Co., 256 F.2d 297 (8th Cir.1958). See Nazeri v. Missouri Valley College, 860 S.W.2d 303, 313 (Mo.1993) (exact words of libelous, but not slanderous, statements must be pleaded).

28. Holliday v. Great Atl. & Pac. Tea Co., 256 F.2d 297 (8th Cir.1958); Garcia v. Hilton Hotels Int'l, Inc., 97 F.Supp. 5 (D.Puerto Rico 1951). In Holliday, the plaintiffs alleged only the import of the words of the defendant's employee rather than the actual words used. The court upholding a directed verdict for the defendant on the issue of slander ruled that the plaintiffs must not only allege and prove the actual words used, but also must allege and prove their falsity. Although more recent federal cases generally do not require allegations as to the specific words used, see, e.g., Levine v. McLeskey, 881 F.Supp. 1030, 1048 (E.D.Va.1995), affirmed in part, vacated in part on other grounds 164 F.3d 210 (4th Cir.1998); Thompson v. Campbell, 845 F.Supp. 665, 679–80 (D.Minn.1994), there are notable exceptions. See Ersek v. Township of Springfield, 822 F.Supp. 218, 223 (E.D.Pa.1993), aff'd, 102 F.3d 79 (3d Cir. 1996).

29. See C. Clark, Code Pleading § 51, at 330 (2d ed.1947); 5 C. Wright & A. Miller, Civil 2d § 1310.

general estimate of what the trier of fact, by its general experience, believes that harm would likely be. In this context, the failure to allege special damages will result in a dismissal of the complaint for failure to state a claim or cause of action.[30]

Second, in other cases a distinction is drawn between general damages that are a natural, expected result of the defendant's alleged conduct, and special damages that are a proximate result of the defendant's conduct but that occur only because of the specific situation of the plaintiff.[31] Since special damages are by their nature unique to the plaintiff's circumstances, it is important that the defendant be made aware of what is being claimed. Thus, although facts regarding general damages need not be pleaded,[32] special damages must be set out in detail.[33] This is true not only in code pleading jurisdictions, but under notice pleading rules as well.[34] A plaintiff who fails to plead special damages with the requisite specificity will be barred from introducing evidence on, and, as a result, recovering for those damages.[35]

The determination as to which damages are general and which are special is not as clear as one would hope. What appears to be a natural consequence of certain conduct from a practical standpoint may not be so, in a theoretical sense. For example, in a personal injury action, pain and suffering are considered general damages, but hospital and medical bills are not, at least in the vast majority of jurisdictions.[36] Similarly, loss of earning capacity is treated as general damage, whereas loss of profits is not.[37] In contract actions, the distinction is somewhat clearer because the substantive law itself addresses the matter. Thus, ordinary loss of the benefit of a bargain constitutes general damages, whereas additional losses, which are special damages, can be recovered only if the defendant had reason to foresee that they might result from the breach.[38]

Unfortunately, the area has been confused further by courts that themselves have not fully understood the distinction. This typically has occurred in personal injury actions in which the plaintiff has set forth in

---

30. See, e.g., Weiss v. Nippe, 5 A.D.2d 789, 170 N.Y.S.2d 642 (1958).

31. Roberts v. Graham, 73 U.S. (6 Wall.) 578, 579, 18 L.Ed. 791 (1867); Burlington Transp. Co. v. Josephson, 153 F.2d 372 (8th Cir.1946).

32. U.S. ex rel. Nourse v. Light, 3 F.R.D. 3 (M.D.Pa.1943).

33. Roberts v. Graham, 73 U.S. (6 Wall.) 578, 579, 18 L.Ed. 791 (1867); Radio Electronic Television Corp. v. Bartniew Distributing Corp., 32 F.Supp. 431 (S.D.N.Y. 1940). See generally C. Clark, Code Pleading § 51 (2d ed. 1947); Note, The Definition and Pleading of Special Damages Under the Federal Rules of Civil Procedure, 55 Va. L.Rev. 542 (1969).

34. Fed.Civ.Proc.Rule 9(g); C. Clark, Code Pleading § 51 (2d ed.1947).

The amount of detail required to plead special damages depends on the nature of the case, the type of damage involved, and the court's attitude toward pleading specificity. Courts following notice pleading tend to liberalize the requirements, although some specific mention of each item of special damages is necessary. See 5 C. Wright & A. Miller, Civil 2d § 1311.

35. Kendall v. Stokes, 44 U.S. (3 How.) 87, 102, 11 L.Ed. 506 (1845). The defect may be cured by an amendment, even at the trial, if no substantial prejudice is involved. See § 5.26, below.

36. See generally Annot., 98 A.L.R.2d 746 (1964).

37. Shaw v. Southern Pac. R.R. Co., 157 Cal. 240, 107 P. 108 (1910).

38. See 5 A. Corbin, Contracts §§ 1007, 1011 (1964).

some detail the nature and extent of his physical injuries and at trial seeks to prove some additional element not mentioned in the complaint. Since physical injuries, and the pain and suffering therefrom, constitute general damages, the details regarding the injuries in the pleadings are surplusage and should not bar recovery.[39] However, courts on occasion have lost sight of this fact and have termed the specified damages as "special," thus precluding proof of the additional element.[40] Had the plaintiff simply alleged "severe personal injuries, pain and suffering," the problem would not have arisen.

The difficulty in determining precisely what are special damages inevitably leads plaintiffs, who want to be on the safe side, to set forth in some detail all elements of the damages they might seek to collect. This casts substantial doubt on the justification for a special pleading requirement and raises the question why it should not be eliminated, particularly in jurisdictions that otherwise follow notice pleading rules and rely extensively on discovery to ascertain the matters at issue.

It should be noted that courts have sometimes been concerned over claims for punitive damages, concerned that allegations in the complaint may, if made public, unfairly destroy the reputations of some litigants, intimidate some into unjust settlements, or even influence jurors. Thus some states, by statute, prohibit allegations of punitive damages in an initial pleading. Only later, after a hearing to determine if claims for such damages are reasonably likely to be successful, is a party permitted to amend the complaint to include them in the demand.[41]

C.   THE ANSWER

§ 5.17   General Rules

Under modern pleading doctrine, the answer serves both to determine which allegations in the complaint a defendant intends to contest at trial and to permit the defendant to raise additional matters as defenses or claims.[1] Moreover, it allows the defendant to raise certain technical defenses, not going to the merits of the case, but challenging such matters as the jurisdiction or venue of the court, the misjoinder or lack of joinder of causes and parties, and the validity of service of process.[2] Problems involving the introduction of these defenses or of affirmative claims are discussed elsewhere.[3] The next three sections

---

39. Ephrem v. Phillips, 99 So.2d 257, 260–61 (Fla.App.1957).

40. E.g., Ziervogel v. Royal Packing Co., 225 S.W.2d 798 (Mo.App.1949).

41. Ill.—Smith–Hurd Ann. 735 ILCS 5/2–604.1; Kan.Stat.Ann 60–3703. See Fla.—West's F.S.A. § 768.72.

§ 5.17

1. Fed.Civ.Proc.Rules 8(b), 8(c); West's Ann.Cal.Code Civ.Proc. §§ 431.20, 431.30; Ill.—Smith–Hurd Ann. 735 ILCS 5/2–610,

5/2–613(d); Mo.Civ.Proc.Rules, Rules 55.07–55.09.

2. Fed.Civ.Proc.Rules 8(b), 12(b); Mo. Civ.Proc.Rules, Rule 55.27; 12 Okla.Stat. Ann. § 2012.

3. See §§ 5.23–5.24, below.

explore the rules surrounding the pleading of defenses going to the merits of the plaintiff's claim.

Before examining the various elements of the answer, it is important to note that the general pleading rules in force in a particular jurisdiction govern the level of detail required in affirmative allegations[4] and the extent to which separate statements of separate defenses are required.[5] Further, each jurisdiction provides the time limit by which an answer is to be filed.[6] The period is not jurisdictional, however, and thus can be, and very often is, extended upon consent of the opposing party or upon a motion.[7] A party who fails to file an answer on time will be subject to the entry of default and, ultimately, to a default judgment.[8]

§ 5.18　Admissions

A defendant will admit allegations in the complaint either by stating in the answer that they are true or by failing properly to deny them.[1] Unless the answer is amended, these admissions will bind the defendant at trial and obviate any need by the plaintiff to offer proof on the matters admitted.[2]

There are two reasons why a defendant might deliberately admit the plaintiff's allegations. First is the fact that a party has a duty to respond in good faith; if averments are true, they should be admitted. Second, for tactical reasons a party may admit allegations that legitimately could be contested. For example, if the defendant's conduct in a situation was reprehensible morally, but not necessarily sufficient to render him legally liable, the defendant nevertheless might admit liability to limit the trial to matters of damage; a jury is likely to award less to the plaintiff if it is not aware of the defendant's "bad" conduct.

Sometimes a defendant will admit an allegation by mistake, either because she has inadvertently failed to answer it at all, or because her purported denial is defective. This error is not fatal, however. In most cases, a defendant who acts with diligence, can cure the defect by amending the answer.[3]

---

4. See §§ 5.4, 5.7, above.

5. Fed.Civ.Proc.Rule 10(b); Ill.—Smith–Hurd Ann. 735 ILCS 5/2–613; Vernon's Ann.Mo.Civ.Proc.Rule 55.10.

6. E.g., Fed.Civ.Proc.Rule 12(a); Or. Rules Civ.Proc., Rule 15.

7. See Fed.Civ.Proc.Rule 6(b); Colo. Rules Civ.Proc., Rule 6(b).

8. Fed.Civ.Proc.Rule 55. See generally § 9.4, below.

§ 5.18

1. Fed.Civ.Proc.Rule 8(d); West's Ann. Cal.Code Civ.Proc. § 431.20; Ill.—Smith–Hurd Ann. 735 ILCS 5/2–610; Vernon's

Ann.Mo.Civ.Proc.Rule 55.09; N.Y.—McKinney's CPLR 3018.

2. C. Clark, Code Pleading § 91, at 579–80 (2d ed.1947). See Budget Rent–A–Car of Atlanta, Inc. v. Webb, 220 Ga.App. 278, 469 S.E.2d 712 (1996); Rembold v. City & County of San Francisco, 113 Cal.App.2d 795, 249 P.2d 58 (1952); Fed.Civ.Proc.Rule 8(d); West's Ann.Cal.Code Civ.Proc. § 431.20.

3. See § 5.26, below.

§ 5.19   Denials

The concept of a denial in the defendant's answer appears deceptively simple. Those matters that the defendant wishes to place into contention should be denied. In practice the exact form that the denial should take is much more complicated. To begin with, there are two basic forms of denials, general and specific.[1] A general denial consists of one sentence, simply stating that "defendant denies each and every allegation of plaintiff's complaint." A specific denial involves a sentence-by-sentence or paragraph-by-paragraph analysis of the complaint, denying only those allegations that the defendant intends to contest.[2]

From a tactical point of view the general denial has several advantages. First, it is simple and avoids technical errors associated with specific denials that can result in inadvertent admissions. Second, in some jurisdictions the general denial is used when the defendant contests the basic sum and substance of the complaint, even though a few of the allegations are true.[3] This tends to give the defendant an advantage by hiding from the plaintiff knowledge of precisely which issues the defendant will contest.

Because the general denial may tend to obscure rather than define the issues for trial, a substantial number of courts, including federal courts, specifically limit its use to those cases in which the defendant actually intends to controvert each and every one of the plaintiff's allegations.[4] This virtually eliminates use of the general denial because it will be an exceedingly rare complaint in which none of the facts alleged is true.[5] In some code-pleading systems, use of the general denial is prohibited in a verified answer.[6] Since in those jurisdictions if the plaintiff elects to verify the complaint, the answer also must be verified,[7] this gives the plaintiff the opportunity to require specificity by the defendant, but only if the plaintiff is willing to swear under oath to the truth of his own averments.[8]

When a general denial is impermissible or improper, the defendant must utilize a specific denial. This does not mean, however, that the defendant must respond to every sentence in the complaint, line by line. Very often the defendant can deny entire paragraphs and is permitted to do so by merely listing the paragraph number.[9] Thus, the specific denial

§ 5.19

1. See C. Clark, Code Pleading § 92, at 581 (2d ed.1947). See West's Ann.Cal.Code Civ.Proc. § 431.30; Colo.Rules Civ.Proc., Rule 8(b).

2. C. Clark, Code Pleading § 92, at 581, 587 (2d ed.1947). See West's Ann.Cal. Code Civ.Proc. § 431.30; Colo.Rules Civ. Proc., Rule 8(b).

3. J. Koffler & A. Reppy, Common Law Pleading § 224, at 457–58 (1969).

4. Fed.Civ.Proc.Rule 8(b); Ind.Trial Proc.Rule 8(B); N.C.Civ.Proc.Rules,, Rule

8(b). See 5 C. Wright & A. Miller, Civil 2d § 1265.

5. See Sunderland, The New Federal Rules, 45 W.Va.L.Q. 5, 13 (1938).

6. West's Ann.Cal.Code Civ.Proc. § 431.30(d).

7. West's Ann.Cal.Code Civ.Proc. § 446.

8. See the discussion of verification in § 5.11, above.

9. C. Clark, Code Pleading § 92, at 587 (2d ed.1947); 5 C. Wright & A. Miller, Civil 2d § 1266.

may not be much more detailed than a general denial except for the separate treatment accorded those matters that are conceded to be true and hence uncontested.

Even given this flexibility, difficulties arise in drafting an answer when some of the facts underlying the plaintiff's allegations are not within the defendant's immediate control or first hand knowledge. Thus most jurisdictions specifically provide that a party can deny an opposing party's allegations on information and belief or for lack of information and belief.[10] These provisions are particularly important when the answer must be verified; on occasion a defendant may need substantial investigation before learning the facts, as, for example, when suit is brought on the basis of acts allegedly committed by the defendant's agent acting within the scope of employment. A party cannot be required to default merely because he or she lacks sufficient knowledge to make a positive denial at the time the answer is required.[11]

Of course denials on information and belief or for lack thereof must be made in good faith and not as a means of harassment or delay. In general, courts will treat these denials as improper if they deal with matters of public record or facts about which the party may be presumed to have knowledge, such as things the party himself said or did.[12] Even then, if the party can show how and why a positive denial (or admission) cannot be made, the denial for lack of information will be accepted.[13]

Because a denial based on information or lack of information does present opportunity for abuse of the pleading process, some courts, especially in the past, have been extremely technical in requiring the use of specific words as set forth in the statutes. Thus, in one case a statement that "defendants do not have sufficient information to answer" was held an insufficient denial because it failed to use the statutory formula "defendant has no information or belief * * * sufficient to enable him to answer."[14] Most courts take a more lenient approach, however, since technical decisions merely penalize parties with careless attorneys and do not necessarily reach those acting in bad faith.[15]

---

10. Fed.Civ.Proc.Rule 8(b); West's Ann.Cal.Code Civ.Proc. § 431.30(d)–(e); N.Y.—McKinney's CPLR 3018; Iowa Rules Civ.Proc., Rule 72.

11. See Loew's Inc. v. Makinson, 10 F.R.D. 36 (N.D.Ohio 1950); Societe Norgan v. Schering Corp., 6 F.R.D. 367 (D.N.J. 1946); Ice Plant Equip. Co. v. Martocello, 43 F.Supp. 281 (E.D.Pa.1941); Nieman v. Long, 31 F.Supp. 30 (E.D.Pa.1939); Nordman v. Johnson City, 1 F.R.D. 51 (E.D.Ill. 1939).

12. See, e.g., American Photocopy Equip. Co. v. Rovico, Inc., 359 F.2d 745 (7th Cir.1966); Harvey Aluminum (Inc.) v. NLRB, 335 F.2d 749, 758 (9th Cir.1964); Mesirow v. Duggan, 240 F.2d 751 (8th Cir.

1957), modified on other grounds sub nom. Green v. Duggan, 243 F.2d 109 (8th Cir. 1957), cert. denied 355 U.S. 864; David v. Crompton & Knowles Corp., 58 F.R.D. 444 (E.D.Pa.1973).

13. See Oliver v. Swiss Club Tell, 222 Cal.App.2d 528, 35 Cal.Rptr. 324 (1963); C. Clark, Code Pleading § 93, at 595–97 (2d ed.1947); 5 C. Wright & A. Miller, Civil 2d § 1262.

14. Oliver v. Swiss Club Tell, 222 Cal. App.2d 528, 541, 35 Cal.Rptr. 324, 331 (1963).

15. C. Clark, Code Pleading § 93, at 595, 596 n. 66 (2d ed.1947).

Nonetheless, it is most important that the defendant utilize the proper form of denial. As previously noted, an allegation is admitted unless it is denied.[16] Because an improper denial is treated as no denial at all, it will result in an inadvertent admission of the facts sought to be denied. A denial on information and belief that is defective may be ignored and the opposing party's allegations treated as admitted.[17] Depending on the type of pleading system in force in the jurisdiction, there are a number of other different, well recognized types of improper denials that also should be avoided.

First, a defendant who files a general denial in bad faith (in a jurisdiction that permits such a denial only if no allegations are true), or who files a general denial when the verification laws prohibit it, may have the denial stricken and the allegations deemed admitted.[18] Courts are very reluctant, however, to make cases turn on pleading errors, even those that appear to be deliberate and in bad faith. Thus, judges may assume the denial to have been made in good faith,[19] or they may read the answer so as not to encompass facts that obviously are true.[20] But there is no assurance that the court will adopt this liberal attitude.[21]

Denials also may be deemed improper if the answer contains inconsistent responses or is evasive. For example, sometimes a defendant will deny generally all allegations in a complaint but then will admit specifically that some of the allegations are true. Courts in these cases follow the rule that specific allegations take precedence over general ones and the admissions are held to be effective.[22] This rule also has been followed in a case in which a defendant entered both general and specific denials. The court held that the general denial was to be ignored and all facts not specifically denied were admitted.[23] The latter result appears harsh and overly technical; nevertheless it is a means of preventing defendants from "tossing in" a general denial in every answer just to make certain that nothing is admitted.

Of greater concern are cases in which a defendant refuses to admit or deny the plaintiff's allegations, demanding that the plaintiff prove her case at trial. Such evasive denials are disapproved universally, often by statute, and result in the admission of the plaintiff's allegations.[24] It has

---

16. See the discussion in § 5.18, above.

17. See the cases cited in note 13, above.

18. E.g., Vrooman Floor Covering Inc. v. Dorsey, 267 Minn. 318, 126 N.W.2d 377 (1964).

19. See U.S. v. Long, 10 F.R.D. 443, 445 (D.Neb.1950).

20. See Biggs v. Public Serv. Coordinated Transp., 280 F.2d 311, 313–14 (3d Cir.1960).

21. A party interposing a general denial is also subject to the obligations of honesty set forth in Federal Rule 11. U.S. v. Minisee, 113 F.R.D. 121 (S.D.Ohio 1986) (Rule 11 sanctions were imposed on defense

counsel who signed a general denial to a complaint in which some of the averments were obviously true). Perhaps Rule 11, with its threat of sanctions for violation of the Rule, will curtail abuse of the general denial. For a discussion of the 1983 and 1993 amendments to Rule 11 and their effects, see § 5.11, above.

22. See Johnson v. School Dist. No. 3, 168 Neb. 547, 96 N.W.2d 623 (1959).

23. Fawcett v. Miller, 172 N.E.2d 328 (Ohio App.1961).

24. Mahanor v. U.S., 192 F.2d 873 (1st Cir.1951); Reed v. Hickey, 2 F.R.D. 92 (E.D.Pa.1941); Burnette v. McCarter, 211 Ga.App. 781, 440 S.E.2d 488 (1994); Rahal

been argued that it is grossly unfair to the defendant to require him to respond to a series of allegations, and even to admit some that are true but which the plaintiff could not prove.[25] These arguments invariably tend to confuse the rights of the criminally accused who have a clear cut privilege to remain silent, with a defendant in a civil action who can be called by the opposing party to testify at the trial.

A different situation exists when the defendant refuses to respond to an allegation in the complaint because the answer itself could be used against the defendant in a subsequent criminal prosecution. A legitimate exercise of the privilege against self-incrimination will be considered a denial, and accordingly, the refusal cannot result in an admission or other sanction.[26] Note, however, that the defendant cannot fail to respond altogether; the defendant must answer those parts of the complaint that do not fall within the claim of privilege.[27]

There are three types of denials that during the days of highly technical pleading presented traps for the unwary responding party: argumentative denials, negative pregnants, and conjunctive denials. Although modern courts typically resist deciding cases on technical rules and these types of defects no longer pose the same threat as before, the prudent lawyer should be aware of their forms and avoid them.

An argumentative denial is one that does not directly deny a fact alleged by an opposing party, but instead alleges the existence of inconsistent facts. For example, if the plaintiff alleged that the defendant was in San Francisco on a particular date and the defendant's answer averred that he was in Boston on that date the defendant's response would be considered argumentative. In some older cases decided under the codes, argumentative denials were held to be defective.[28] Today, however, it is unlikely that any court would treat such a denial other than as fully effective to dispute the opposing party's allegation.[29] Even so, there may be some danger that by pleading argumentatively, a responding party may be held to have assumed the burden of proof on the issue, when normally it would rest on the opponent.[30]

v. Titus, 107 Ga.App. 844, 131 S.E.2d 659 (1963); Sheldon, Hoyt & Co. v. Middleton, 10 Iowa 17 (1859). See also Ill.—Smith–Hurd Ann. 735 ILCS 5/2–610.

25. See Green, Restore the General Issue in Pleading, 42 Ill.B.J. 302, 303 (1954).

26. See de Antonio v. Solomon, 42 F.R.D. 320 (D.Mass.1967), modifying 41 F.R.D. 447 (D.Mass.1966); State v. Myers, 244 Miss. 778, 146 So.2d 334 (1962).

27. 5 C. Wright & A. Miller, Civil 2d § 1280.

28. Zwerling v. Annenberg, 38 Misc. 169, 77 N.Y.S. 275 (1902); Pullen v. Seaboard Trading Co., 165 App.Div. 117, 150 N.Y.S. 719 (1914); Altman v. Cochrane, 131 App.Div. 233, 115 N.Y.S. 870 (1909).

29. See C. Clark, Code Pleading § 92, at 591–92 (2d ed.1947); 5 C. Wright & A. Miller, Civil 2d § 1268.

30. A "defendant who voluntarily alleges a fact which could also have been proved under a simple denial presumably does so with the idea of making his defense appear to be stronger and more aggressive, and invites the court to charge that he has assumed the affirmative upon that particular issue." Page v. Brodoff, 22 Conn.Sup. 282, 169 A.2d 901 (1961). See also Comment, Effect of Unnecessary Affirmative Pleading upon the Burden of Proof, 39 Yale L.J. 117 (1929); Recent Cases: Evidence—Burden of Proof on Sub-issue Raised by Improper Pleadings, 4 U.Chi.L.Rev. 498 (1937).

A negative pregnant occurs when a responding party denies an allegation with such particularity that only immaterial allegations are at issue. The common situation (although place or time also could be involved) occurs when a plaintiff alleges that a certain sum is due, and defendant denies owing that specific sum.[31] In that situation, the defendant's denial is meaningless if the plaintiff's allegation proves to be a dollar more or a dollar less than that actually owed. Thus, if the plaintiff says he loaned the defendant $9000, and the defendant knows that the loan was for $8999, a denial "that plaintiff loaned $9000," although technically correct, is highly misleading. To be truthful, the defendant should deny that the plaintiff loaned him any sum in excess of $8999.

A conjunctive denial occurs when the plaintiff alleges a series of events and the defendant denies the entire series.[32] For example, the plaintiff may aver that the defendant "on April 16 of this year ordered $50,000 worth of goods from plaintiff, plaintiff delivered $50,000 worth of goods to defendant, defendant resold such goods at retail and that defendant never has paid plaintiff the value of the goods." If the defendant merely denies the existence of the acts alleged using the same terms as did the plaintiff, then, at least theoretically, all but one of the allegations could be true. Such a denial could be based solely on the fact that the alleged date was incorrect, or that no resale occurred. Since these are immaterial facts, the denial would be highly misleading. The defendant should delineate specifically which, if any, of the individual facts are true and which untrue.

Many older decisions held negative pregnants and conjunctive denials to be ineffective, admitting the truth of the allegations they were intended to deny.[33] This tended to penalize careless or ignorant pleaders as well as those few who were deliberately evasive. Neither the code nor the notice systems of pleading justify such a technical application of pleading rules,[34] and most courts either ignore the defect, treating the denial as adequate, or permit an amendment to cure it.[35]

§ 5.20   Affirmative Defenses

Even if all the plaintiff's allegations are true, the defendant may beable to present additional facts establishing a defense. In such a case, the defense is called an affirmative defense and the defendant must plead it in the answer so that the plaintiff is aware of the allegations and has an opportunity to prepare to meet them. Unless an affirmative defense is pleaded, it cannot be proved at trial,[1] although the court, in its

---

31. See, e.g., Janeway & Carpender v. Long Beach Paper & Paint Co., 190 Cal. 150, 211 P. 6 (1922).

32. E.g., Janeway & Carpender v. Long Beach Paper & Paint Co., 190 Cal. 150, 211 P. 6 (1922).

33. See C. Clark, Code Pleading § 92, at 588–91 (2d ed.1947).

34. C. Clark, Code Pleading § 92, at 590 (2d ed.1947); 5 C. Wright & A. Miller, Civil 2d § 1267.

35. E.g., Frank v. Solomon, 94 Ariz. 55, 381 P.2d 591 (1963).

§ 5.20

1. See C. Clark, Code Pleading § 96, at 607 (2d ed.1947).

discretion, may give the defendant leave to amend the answer to add the defense at any time.[2]

Because the failure to plead an affirmative defense may result in its waiver, it is most important to determine exactly what constitutes an affirmative defense. In particular, affirmative defenses should be distinguished from denials, pleas in abatement, and from possible counterclaims and cross-claims.

The best means to understand the difference between matter introduced for purposes of a denial and that introduced for purpose of an affirmative defense is to consider the burden of pleading and proof on the issue involved. As previously noted, in a vast majority of cases the burden of pleading is on the party who has the burden of proof on the issue.[3] If a fact does not form a portion of the plaintiff's case that is crucial to the plaintiff's recovery, in the ordinary course it will be part of an affirmative defense and will be at issue only if the defendant raises it.[4] From a logical point of view, therefore, one can distinguish a matter that must be raised by affirmative defense from one that can be raised by denial merely by determining whether the particular fact controverts one of the plaintiff's allegations or whether it deals with entirely new matter having nothing to do with whether the plaintiff's claims are or are not true.

Unfortunately, a few courts have complicated the situation unnecessarily by not recognizing the difference between new facts introduced by the defendant and positive evidence disproving facts alleged by the plaintiff.[5] The latter has nothing to do with affirmative defenses, since the means of disproving one of the plaintiff's allegations is not relevant as to who has the burden of pleading in the particular situation. For example, if the plaintiff alleges that he is the owner of a particular piece of property, the defendant upon denial of the plaintiff's ownership, should be able to attack the plaintiff's allegation at trial with any type of evidence that shows the allegation to be untrue. Thus, the defendant should be able to refute the existence of the plaintiff's title, or in the alternative, to establish that a superior title exists in a third party. Even though evidence of the latter would not directly refute the plaintiff's evidence as to his own purchase of the property, it still negates the plaintiff's allegations as to ownership.[6]

In some cases in which the defendant's evidence does not directly contradict evidence that the plaintiff has introduced, but instead is positive evidence overcoming the plaintiff's allegations, a few courts have erroneously taken the position that the defendant is presenting evidence involving an affirmative defense that, if not pleaded, cannot be proved.

2. Fed.Civ.Proc.Rule 15; Ariz.Rules Civ.Proc., Rule 15. See § 5.26, below.

3. See § 5.15, above.

4. C. Clark, Code Pleading § 96 (2d ed.1947); J. Pomeroy, Code Remedies §§ 548, 567 (5th ed., Carrington, 1929).

5. See, e.g., Young v. Marlas, 243 Iowa 367, 51 N.W.2d 443 (1952). See also C. Clark, Code Pleading § 96, at 606–10 (2d ed.1947).

6. Denham v. Cuddeback, 210 Or. 485, 311 P.2d 1014 (1957); Caldwell v. Bruggerman, 4 Minn. 270 (1860).

This has occurred, for example, in cases in which the plaintiff's allegation of the defendant's negligence has been met with evidence that the defendant's activities were "unavoidable," or resulted from "an act of God" or a "sudden emergency."[7]

It is arguable that the defendant should be required to plead affirmatively any evidentiary matters that might take the plaintiff by surprise, even though they refute essential allegations in the complaint that the defendant has denied. One state, New York,[8] has adopted a rule with such a requirement. This appears, however, to raise more problems than it solves. A careful pleader necessarily will set forth every conceivable fact that she might wish to prove as one never can be certain what a court will hold to be a "surprise." It seems far better to rely on the plaintiff's ability to utilize modern discovery techniques, rather than to encourage more detailed, all-encompassing pleadings.

There are, of course, many clear cut affirmative defenses that constitute new matter not refuting the plaintiff's allegations. Thus, matters of release or res judicata, or the applications of the statute of limitations, must be raised by a defendant who wishes to rely upon them to avoid liability.[9] It is important to note, as a matter of substantive law, that what is an affirmative defense in one jurisdiction may not be an affirmative defense in another. For example, in some states a plaintiff may have to allege and prove as part of his case his own lack of contributory negligence in order to recover,[10] whereas in other jurisdictions contributory fault may be a complete or partial defense that must be raised by the defendant.[11]

Frequently a defendant will have a challenge having nothing to do with the merits of the claim, but going solely to the jurisdiction or venue of the court or to some other procedural matter. Such a challenge is referred to as a plea in abatement. The means of raising pleas in abatement are governed by specific rules in each jurisdiction. In some jurisdictions they must be raised by motions at the outset of the case.[12] The Federal Rules of Civil Procedure, and the state rules that are similar, give the defendant the option of raising such pleas by motion or of including them as affirmative defenses in the answer.[13] When the

---

7. Young v. Marlas, 243 Iowa 367, 376, 51 N.W.2d 443, 448 (1952) (act of God); Fontana v. State Farm Mut. Auto. Ins. Co., 173 So.2d 284 (La.App.1965) (sudden emergency); Ashworth v. Morrison, 93 Ohio L.Abs. 503, 196 N.E.2d 465 (Ohio App.1963) (unavoidable).

8. N.Y.—McKinney's CPLR 3018(b).

9. These matters are set forth as examples of affirmative defenses in the governing rules and statutes. E.g., Fed.Civ.Proc. Rule 8(c); Colo.Rules Civ.Proc., Rule 8(c).

10. Hardware State Bank v. Cotner, 55 Ill.2d 240, 302 N.E.2d 257 (1973). See § 5.15, n. 7, above.

11. Martinelli v. Poley, 210 Cal. 450, 292 P. 451 (1930). See also Gyerman v. U.S. Lines Co., 7 Cal.3d 488, 102 Cal.Rptr. 795, 498 P.2d 1043 (1972).

12. West's Ann.Cal.Code Civ.Proc. §§ 396, 418.10; Ill.—Smith–Hurd Ann. 735 ILCS 5/2–104, 5/2–301.

13. Fed.Civ.Proc.Rule 12; Del.Super.Ct.Civ.Rule 12(b). If one such matter is raised by motion, all such matters not raised in that motion, except those specifically preserved by rule, i.e., subject-matter jurisdiction or failure to join an indispensable party, are waived; these matters may not be raised one by motion and another by

latter method is used, the defendant must set forth the facts upon which the plea is based in the same form and manner as she would an affirmative defense based on substantive grounds.

In most cases a plea in abatement should be heard prior to the substance of the action; only if the same evidence will be presented on the substantive issues as on the plea[14] does it make sense to defer procedural issues to the trial on the merits. It would be foolish to try a case on the merits only to have it dismissed for lack of venue. For that reason many jurisdictions, including the federal courts, specifically allow a special hearing on abatement matters to take place prior to trial.[15]

A counterclaim against the plaintiff or a cross-claim against a codefendant generally is included with the answer. Since those pleadings are not portions of an answer but constitute a new complaint against the parties to whom they are directed, counterclaims and cross-claims are treated quite differently than are affirmative defenses. For example, cross-claims and counterclaims must be answered by a reply pleading,[16] whereas in most jurisdictions an affirmative defense will be taken as denied without any further pleading on the part of the plaintiff.[17] Although the distinction between counterclaims and cross-claims and affirmative defenses is an important one, misdesignation is not fatal. If the defendant mistakenly has denominated a counterclaim or cross-claim as an affirmative defense, or vice-versa, the court will treat the allegations for what they are in fact and will ignore the erroneous label.[18]

Finally, it should be noted that a defendant who wishes to set forth affirmative defenses in the answer is required to do so with the same degree of specificity and detail as the plaintiff is required to use in the complaint. This, of course, will depend on the type of pleading system that exists in the particular jurisdiction.[19]

One potential problem arises in the situation in which the plaintiff has anticipated an affirmative defense in the complaint, and has sought to overcome it. In most jurisdictions that do not treat those allegations as surplusage,[20] a denial should be sufficient to raise the issue. If, however, the anticipated pleadings are treated as surplus and ignored, this could pose a trap for the defendant who may have denied the existence of any avoidance as alleged by the plaintiff. Some courts have held that a mere denial of surplus allegations is ineffective to raise the

---

answer or in two separate motions. Fed.Civ. Proc.Rule 12(g). See § 5.24, below.

14. This might occur, for example, when service is on an alleged agent and the agency is a substantive issue. See Fed.Civ. Proc.Rule 12(d); West's Ann.Cal.Code Civ. Proc. § 597.

15. Fed.Civ.Proc.Rule 12(d); Wyo.Rules Civ.Proc., Rule 12(d).

16. Fed.Civ.Proc.Rule 7(a); Fla.— West's F.S.A.Rules Civ.Proc., Rule 1.100(a).

17. Fed.Civ.Proc.Rule 8(d); Ariz.Rules Civ.Proc., Rule 8(e). See generally § 5.21, below.

18. Fed.Civ.Proc.Rule 8(c); Ariz.Rules Civ.Proc., Rule 8(d).

19. See generally §§ 5.4, and 5.7, above.

20. See § 5.16, above.

issue.[21] In those jurisdictions, the defendant would have to raise the affirmative defense herself, despite the plaintiff's anticipation and attempt at avoidance. From a logical point of view, and to avoid unnecessary technicalities, the defendant's denial of any allegation by the plaintiff should be sufficient to preserve the issue, even if it otherwise would have had to have been raised by affirmative defense.[22]

D.   THE REPLY AND SUBSEQUENT PLEADINGS

§ 5.21   The Propriety of Pleadings Beyond the Complaint and Answer

From a logical point of view if the defendant presents affirmative allegations either by way of affirmative defense, cross-claim or counterclaim, the plaintiff, and any other party to whom they are directed, should respond in order that the defendant may know what is admitted, what is denied, and what further matters will be raised at trial to overcome the new allegations. This process of responding to affirmative allegations should continue until the final pleading, in which only denials are presented. That was the process at common law.[1] Practically speaking, however, such a drawn out system of pleading bears little fruit,[2] providing opportunity for decisions based on technicalities, with little assistance in formulating issues for trial. Thus today, in almost all jurisdictions, the number of pleadings has been strictly limited.[3] To the extent that a plaintiff is permitted or required to respond to the defendant's allegations in the answer, the plaintiff's new pleading is designated a reply.[4]

Under the Federal Rules and similar provisions in most jurisdictions, the plaintiff normally is not permitted to reply to an affirmative defense set forth in the defendant's answer.[5] The allegations in the answer are taken both as denied and avoided.[6] At trial the plaintiff not only may present evidence refuting the defendant's allegations, but may introduce evidence of new matter to overcome those allegations even if they are true.[7] In a few jurisdictions, a reply to an affirmative defense is prohibited.[8] Under most procedural rules, however, a reply may be

---

21. Cf. Ellis v. Black Diamond Coal Mining Co., 265 Ala. 264, 90 So.2d 770 (1956) (even though complaint shows on its face that cause of action is barred by statute of limitations, the defense is not raised by pleading the general issue).

22. See C. Clark, Code Pleading § 40, at 250–52, § 98, at 621 (2d ed.1947).

§ 5.21

1. See the discussion in § 5.3, above.

2. See 5 C. Wright & A. Miller, Civil 2d § 1190.

3. See the discussion in § 5.3, above. See Fed.Civ.Proc.Rule 7(a); West's Ann.Cal. Code Civ.Proc. § 422.10.

4. Fed.Civ.Proc.Rule 7(a); Ariz.Rules Civ.Proc., Rule 7(a).

5. Fed.Civ.Proc.Rule 7(a); Me.Rules Civ.Proc., Rule 7(a).

6. Fed.Civ.Proc.Rule 8(d); Me.Rules Civ.Proc., Rule 8(d).

7. Vaughn v. Jonas, 31 Cal.2d 586, 191 P.2d 432 (1948); Walter v. Libby, 72 Cal. App.2d 138, 164 P.2d 21 (1945); Kenfield v. Weir, 16 Cal.App.2d 501, 60 P.2d 885 (1936).

8. General Credit Corp. v. Pichel, 44 Cal.App.3d 844, 118 Cal.Rptr. 913 (1975); West's Ann.Cal.Code Civ.Proc. §§ 422.10, 431.30.

permitted or required upon order of the court,[9] thereby giving the trial judge some flexibility to utilize the reply when it may prove useful in defining the issues. In fact, it is rare that a court will order a reply to be filed.[10]

In a few states, a contrary rule prevails. A plaintiff is required to respond to affirmative allegations in an affirmative defense.[11] Failure to do so will result in the admission of the truth of the defendant's allegations.[12] Even in these states, however, there is a limitation on the number of pleadings; if the plaintiff puts affirmative allegations in the reply, the defendant may not be permitted to respond thereto, at least without a specific court order.[13] Those affirmative allegations are taken as denied or avoided.

Litigants have experienced little difficulty because of these rules. The number of responses to affirmative defenses are limited as a matter of substantive law. A party who may be uncertain as to what an opponent intends to raise at trial in response to the last pleading may use modern techniques of discovery to ascertain what those claims will be.

Subsequent pleadings are necessary, however, when the defendant's answer contains a counterclaim or cross-claim. Under modern rules, a counterclaim or cross-claim is considered as if it were an original complaint.[14] Thus, the party against whom it is directed must respond or the allegations will be taken as true.[15] If such a claim is filed against a plaintiff, then the plaintiff's response normally is denominated a reply; if the claim is against a co-defendant or a new party, the response typically will be labeled an answer.[16]

The requirement that a party respond to a counterclaim or cross-claim directed against him is logical. There are a wide range of defenses available to a party who is in the position of a defendant and thus it is important that the latter notify the complaining party as to what will be denied, what will be admitted, and what affirmative defenses will be relied upon. The responding party is under the same obligation as if the counterclaim or cross-claim had been filed as an independent action.

E. CHALLENGES TO PLEADINGS

§ 5.22 Devices for Attacking the Substantive Sufficiency of the Pleadings

At common law and in the codes, a challenge to the substantive sufficiency of a complaint or an answer is termed a "general demurrer."[1]

---

9. Fed.Civ.Proc.Rule 7(a); Wis.Stat. Ann. 802.01(1).

10. See § 5.3, above.

11. Ill.—Smith–Hurd Ann. 735 ILCS 5/2–602.

12. See Hudson v. Mandabach, 22 Ill. App.2d 296, 160 N.E.2d 715 (1959).

13. Ill.—Smith–Hurd Ann. 735 ILCS 5/2–602; Neb.

14. See § 5.3, above.

15. Fed.Civ.Proc.Rule 8(d); West's Ann.Cal.Code Civ.Proc. § 431.20; Me.Rules Civ.Proc., Rule 8(d).

16. Fed.Civ.Proc.Rule 7(a); N.J.Civ. Prac.Rule 4:5–1.

Under the Federal Rules of Civil Procedure and the state provisions that follow them, demurrers have been abolished.[2] In their stead, the courts have adopted the motion to dismiss for failure to state a claim[3] and a motion to strike an insufficient answer.[4] From a functional point of view these latter motions operate exactly as do general demurrers to the complaint or to the answer. Each asks whether, if all the allegations are true, the pleader has stated a valid claim or defense under the law.[5]

In many jurisdictions, by rule or by practice, an alternative method of attacking the sufficiency of an opposing party's pleading is the "motion for judgment on the pleadings."[6] Unlike a general demurrer or a motion to dismiss for failure to state a claim or present a defense, the motion for judgment on the pleadings is reserved until all of the pleadings have been completed.[7] Otherwise, however, it raises issues identical to the other types of challenge and is dealt with by the courts in the same manner.[8]

It is important to note that the failure of a party sufficiently to plead a claim or defense is not necessarily fatal. Today all jurisdictions have extremely liberal rules permitting a party to amend a pleading that has been held defective as long as the pleader can in good faith alter the pleading to remedy the defect.[9]

A challenge also may be made to a portion of a pleading, such as to one claim or one defense.[10] In most jurisdictions a general challenge to the sufficiency of the pleading will be sufficient to eliminate any portion that is defective.[11] In a few jurisdictions, however, the courts will uphold a general challenge only if the entire pleading is defective.[12] In these, a litigant can eliminate defective portions of a complaint or answer only by specifying that portion of the pleading that is to be challenged.[13] For

---

§ 5.22

1. J. Koffler & A. Reppy, Common Law Pleading § 198 (1969); B. Shipman, Common Law Pleading 279 (3d ed., Ballantine, 1923).

2. Fed.Civ.Proc.Rule 7(c); Vt.Rules Civ. Proc., Rule 7(c).

3. Fed.Civ.Proc.Rule 12(b)(6).

4. N.C.Gen.Stat. § 1A–1, Rules Civ. Proc., Rule 12.

5. The term "demurrer" was eliminated to help ensure that the technicalities of common law and code pleading would not survive. Considering the functional similarity between a demurrer and a motion to dismiss for failure to state a claim upon which relief may be granted, the change in nomenclature seems to have been made mainly for psychological reasons. See 5A C. Wright & A. Miller, Civil 2d § 1355.

6. Fed.Civ.Proc.Rule 12(c); Official Code Ga.Ann. § 9–11–12(c).

7. Fed.Civ.Proc.Rule 12(c); Ind.Trial Proc.Rule 12(C).

8. See C. Clark, Code Pleading § 87 at 554–56 (2d ed.1947); 5A C. Wright & A. Miller, Civil 2d § 1367.

9. See § 5.26, below.

10. C. Clark, Code Pleading § 79, at 509 (2d ed.1947).

11. Alternatively, a motion to strike can be used to attack a portion of a pleading, such as one of several variants of a claim. E.g., Garcia v. Hilton Hotels Int'l, Inc., 97 F.Supp. 5 (D.Puerto Rico 1951).

12. See C. Clark, Code Pleading § 79, at 509, 511–12 (2d ed.1947). See also John Day Co. v. Alvine & Assocs., 1 Neb.App. 954, 510 N.W.2d 462 (1993); Cooper v. National R.R. Passenger Corp., 45 Cal.App.3d 389, 119 Cal.Rptr. 541 (1975); Brunson v. Babb, 145 Cal.App.2d 214, 302 P.2d 647 (1956).

13. Lord v. Garland, 27 Cal.2d 840, 168 P.2d 5 (1946); Donahue v. Stockton Gas & Elec. Co., 6 Cal.App. 276, 92 P. 196 (1907).

example, if the plaintiff brings suit against two defendants, alleging causes against each of them, a general demurrer brought by one of the defendants will be rejected if any one of the causes states a valid claim against any one of the defendants.[14]

When a party wishes to challenge the substantive sufficiency of the opponent's pleadings, the traditional rule permitted the challenge to be based solely upon the face of that pleading. No extrinsic material could be introduced to establish that claims or defenses, which appeared valid on their faces, could not, in fact, be supported by the evidence.[15] Technically this is still the rule even in most modern jurisdictions.[16] However, in most courts today a different procedure, called a motion for summary judgment,[17] is available to challenge the factual basis of a pleading that on its face is sufficient to state a claim or defense. Under the Federal Rules and comparable state rules, the distinction between a pleading challenge and a motion for summary judgment is blurred, since a pleading challenge simply is treated as a motion for summary judgment if outside matter is introduced.[18]

An exception to the rule limiting challenges to the face of the pleadings exists for matters of which the courts may take judicial notice. Traditionally, courts have accepted the existence of certain indisputable facts, treating them as having been established by the evidence, even though no proof of them has been introduced by the parties.[19] The purpose is to save the time and trouble that it would take to present evidence of matters, the truth of which no one can legitimately challenge. These may include the dates of notorious events, the location of public buildings, the existence of documents in the court's files, and a whole range of similar matters.[20] There are differences among jurisdictions as to what cannot be judicially noticed.[21] For pleading purposes it is important to note that in considering a challenge to the sufficiency of an allegation, the court will take into consideration not only what appears on the pleading itself, but also facts that it judicially notices.[22] For example, if plaintiff's complaint states a valid claim on its face, but the

---

14. C. Clark, Code Pleading § 79, at 511 (2d ed.1947).

15. See C. Clark, Code Pleading § 80, at 514 (2d ed.1947); J. Koffler & A. Reppy, Common Law Pleading § 195 (1969).

16. See Niece v. Sears, Roebuck & Co., 293 F.Supp. 792 (N.D.Okl.1968). See also 5A C. Wright & A. Miller, Civil 2d § 1357.

17. Fed.Civ.Proc.Rule 56; N.Y.— McKinney's CPLR 3212; Utah Rules Civ. Proc., Rule 56. For a full discussion of summary judgment, see §§ 9.1–9.3, below.

18. Fed.Civ.Proc.Rules 12(b), 12(c); R.I.Rules Civ.Proc., Rules 12(b), 12(c).

19. See C. Clark, Code Pleading § 80, at 513 (2d ed.1947); J. Koffler & A. Reppy, Common Law Pleading §§ 195, 199 (1969). See, e.g., Louisville & N.R. Co. v. Palmes, 109 U.S. 244, 3 S.Ct. 193, 27 L.Ed. 922 (1883); Masline v. New York, N. H. & H. R. Co., 95 Conn. 702, 112 A. 639 (1921).

20. See, e.g., West's Ann.Cal.Evid.Code §§ 451–53; Kan.Stat.Ann. 60–409; N.Y.— McKinney's CPLR 4511.

21. Compare Suren v. Oceanic S.S. Co., 85 F.2d 324, 325 (9th Cir.1936), cert. denied 300 U.S. 653 (court could take judicial notice of its own records in prior action based on the same facts), with James v. Unknown Trustees, 203 Okl. 312, 314, 220 P.2d 831, 833–34 (1950) (refusal to take judicial notice of another action previously brought in the same court by the same parties).

22. Colvig v. RKO General, Inc., 232 Cal.App.2d 56, 63–64, 42 Cal.Rptr. 473, 478 (1965).

court knows that plaintiff previously has brought suit on the same claim and has litigated it to a conclusion, the court may take into consideration the prior suit in holding that the principles of res judicata preclude the present action.[23] The case can be dismissed even though the pleading, on its face, shows no defect.

In a similar vein, when a party challenges an opponent's pleading, the court will go beyond the challenged pleading to consider any facts that have appeared in other pleadings in the case, including allegations by the party who is making the challenge.[24] Illustratively, if other pleadings present facts that cure the defect that is the basis for the attack, the court will consider the challenged pleading to contain those facts and will overrule the challenge.

Finally, a challenge to the substantive sufficiency of a pleading never is waived. At any time up to and even during a trial, a party may be permitted to challenge an opponent's pleading on the ground that it fails to state a claim or a defense under the law. It would make no sense whatsoever to allow evidence to come in on a claim or a defense that, if proved, would have no substantive effect in the case. Moreover, it would be improper to consider such a defect waived by failure to raise it, since the ultimate result would be recovery on nonexistent causes or the denial of recovery based on nonexistent defenses. As a result, in almost all jurisdictions, there are specific provisions against waiver of challenges based upon the substantive sufficiency of a pleading.[25] If a case actually goes to trial on such an issue, the matter can be raised by a motion for nonsuit[26] or directed verdict.[27] The matter even can be raised for the first time on appeal.[28]

On the other hand, if the case goes to trial, and the evidence presented in fact establishes the existence of a cause of action or a defense in spite of the failure to plead it, the pleading defect will be considered to have been cured.[29] It would make no sense to throw out a claim on the ground that it is insufficient in law if in fact the evidence establishes that a valid claim exists. The curing of defective pleadings

23. See Iacaponi v. New Amsterdam Cas. Co., 379 F.2d 311, 312 (3d Cir.1967), cert. denied 389 U.S. 1054.

24. C. Clark, Code Pleading § 119, at 735–36 (2d ed.1947); J. Koffler & A. Reppy, Common Law Pleading § 200 (1969); H. Stephen, Principles of Pleading in Civil Actions 160 (Tyler ed.1882). See Roberts v. Fuquay–Varina Tobacco Bd. of Trade, Inc., 223 F.Supp. 212 (E.D.N.C.1963), modified 332 F.2d 521 (4th Cir.1964) (summary judgment entered against moving party).

25. NLRB v. Weathercraft Co. of Topeka, Inc., 832 F.2d 1229 (10th Cir.1987); Gaynor v. Metals Reserve Co., 166 F.2d 1011 (8th Cir.1948), cert. denied 338 U.S. 909; Van Voorhis v. District of Columbia,

240 F.Supp. 822 (D.D.C.1965); Fed.Civ. Proc.Rule 12(h)(2); West's Ann.Cal.Code Civ.Proc. § 430.80; Mass.Rules Civ.Proc., Rule 12(h); N.Y.—McKinney's CPLR 3211(e).

26. West's Ann.Cal.Code Civ.Proc. § 581c; Conn.Gen.Stat.Ann. § 52–210. See § 9.5, below.

27. Fed.Civ.Proc.Rule 50(a); Colo.Rules Civ.Proc., Rule 50. See § 12.3, below.

28. Southard v. Southard, 305 F.2d 730 (2d Cir.1962).

29. See Fed.Civ.Proc.Rule 15(b); West's Ann.Cal.Code Civ.Proc. § 473; C. Clark, Code Pleading § 119, at 736–37 (2d ed.1947). See also § 5.26, below.

through the presentation of evidence is generally referred to as "aider by verdict."[30]

§ 5.23 Devices for Challenging Uncertainty or Ambiguity

In some circumstances a pleading will be sufficient to state a claim or a defense but will be so uncertain or ambiguous in some particulars that the opposing party cannot be certain exactly what is being alleged. Although this situation can arise in all courts, it is more likely to arise in notice pleading jurisdictions in which all the pleader must do is give a general idea as to the basic nature of the claims or defenses upon which she intends to rely at trial.

The traditional method of attacking uncertain or ambiguous pleadings was by use of a "special demurrer,"[1] to be distinguished from the "general demurrer" by which attacks on substance were made.[2] Modern courts, including those using the Federal Rules, which have abolished the use of demurrers[3] have substituted motions to make more definite and certain.[4] In some code pleading states a complaint may be attacked as being uncertain or ambiguous.[5] Under the Federal Rules and similar provisions in many states, such a challenge can be made only on the basis that the pleading is so vague or ambiguous that the challenging party cannot reasonably frame a responsive pleading.[6] Thus, the motion is unavailable to attack a pleading when no response is required; in most cases this means that the motion is available only to a defendant since, as previously noted,[7] most jurisdictions do not require the plaintiff to reply to an answer.

The differences among jurisdictions with respect to the scope of challenges for ambiguity and uncertainty exists in part because different purposes are involved. In those jurisdictions permitting a challenge to any pleading, the purpose is to ensure that each party is notified as to the claims of the opposing party not only so that a responsive pleading may be filed, but also to help the party with the investigation and preparation of the case.[8] Jurisdictions with the more restrictive rule take the position that litigants should ascertain facts necessary for trial not through pleading challenges, but by use of the extensive discovery

---

30. C. Clark, Code Pleading § 119, at 736–37 (2d ed.1947); J. Koffler & A. Reppy, Common Law Pleading § 299 (1969).

§ 5.23

1. Cameron v. Evans Securities Corp., 119 Cal.App. 164, 6 P.2d 272 (1931). See West's Ann.Cal.Code Civ.Proc. §§ 430.10(f), 430.60; C. Clark, Code Pleading § 79, at 507–09 (2d ed.1947); J. Koffler & A. Reppy, Common Law Pleading § 198 (1969).

2. See § 5.22, above.

3. Fed.Civ.Proc.Rule 7(c); Idaho Rules Civ.Proc., Rule 7(c).

4. Fed.Civ.Proc.Rule 12(e); Ala.Rules Civ.Proc., Rule 12(e).

5. E.g., West's Ann.Cal.Code Civ.Proc. § 430.10.

6. Fed.Civ.Proc.Rule 12(e); N.J.Civ. Prac.Rule 4:6–4. See also Elliott v. Perez, 751 F.2d 1472 (5th Cir.1985).

7. See § 5.21, above.

8. See generally Landau v. Salam, 4 Cal.3d 901, 95 Cal.Rptr. 46, 484 P.2d 1390 (1971); Fanning v. Lemay, 78 Ill.App.2d 166, 222 N.E.2d 815 (1966), reversed on other grounds 38 Ill.2d 209, 230 N.E.2d 182 (1967).

devices that are available.[9] Indeed one state, in adopting federal-type pleading rules, deliberately omitted a motion for a more definite statement as wasteful and unnecessary.[10]

Unlike a substantive challenge, a demurrer or motion based on uncertainty or ambiguity must be raised at the earliest opportunity—typically prior to the filing of a responsive pleading,[11] or, if no response is required, then within a specific number of days.[12] Otherwise such a defect is considered to have been waived.[13] Courts should not bother with technical challenges raised long after the case has been at issue.

If a challenge is timely and successful, then the pleader will be given a reasonable opportunity to amend the pleading to cure the defect.[14] Failure to do so ultimately will result in a judgment for the opposing party.

§ 5.24   Devices for Challenging Form and Other Procedural Irregularities

In addition to challenges directed toward the claims or defenses of the opposing party, various challenges directed to other procedural problems raised in the pleadings may be made. In every jurisdiction there are a number of technical details that govern the filing of pleadings. For example, there are time limits by which answers and other responsive pleadings must be filed.[1] Frequently, certain types of amended pleadings or replies can be filed only with leave of court.[2] If a pleading is filed in violation of a rule or regulation, the normal means of challenge is by a motion to strike the pleading.[3] In ruling upon such a motion, the court must determine whether the defect can be cured and, if so,

---

9. See Advisory Committee on the Rules for Civil Procedure, Report of Proposed Amendments to Rules of Civil Procedure 15–17 (June 1946). In its original form Federal Rule 12(e) provided for a bill of particulars so that defendant could prepare for trial. U.S.Sup.Ct.Rule 12(e), 308 U.S. 678 (1939). As a result the rule was used to force plaintiff to rely upon a specific set of facts, thereby converting the notice pleading system into a fact pleading procedure. Thus, the rule was amended in 1946 to state clearly that the only time a motion for a more definite statement could be used was when it was necessary to allow the opposing party to frame a responsive pleading. See also Scarbrough v. R–Way Furniture Co., 105 F.R.D. 90 (E.D.Wis.1985).

10. See Committee Comment following 12 Okla.Stat.Ann. § 2012.

11. Fed.Civ.Proc.Rule 12; N.Y.—McKinney's CPLR 3024(a).

12. West's Ann.Cal.Code Civ.Proc. §§ 430.20(b); 430.40.

13. See, e.g., West's Ann.Cal.Code Civ. Proc. §§ 430.10, 430.80.

14. See Lodge 743, Int'l Ass'n of Machinists v. United Aircraft Corp., 30 F.R.D. 142 (D.Conn.1962).

§ 5.24

1. Fed.Civ.Proc.Rule 12; Colo.Rules Civ.Proc., Rule 12(a); Idaho Rules Civ.Proc., Rule 12; N.Y.—McKinney's CPLR 3024(c), 3025(a).

2. Fed.Civ.Proc.Rules 7(a), 15(a), 15(b), 15(d); N.Y.—McKinney's CPLR 3025(b); Tenn.Rules Civ.Proc., Rules 7.01, 15.01, 15.02, 15.04.

3. Fed.Civ.Proc.Rule 12(f); N.Y.—McKinney's CPLR 3024(b). See Beverly Milk Yonkers Co. v. Conrad, 5 A.D.2d 682, 168 N.Y.S.2d 698 (1957); Buck v. Morrossis, 114 Cal.App.2d 461, 250 P.2d 270 (1952). Cf. Georgia Power Project v. Georgia Power Co., 409 F.Supp. 332 (N.D.Ga.1975) (when motion to dismiss was properly responsive to both original and amended complaint, motion to strike supplemental pleadings entered without leave of court was denied). See generally C. Clark, Code Pleading § 81 (2d ed.1947).

whether the court in its discretion should allow the pleader to cure the defect in the interest of justice.[4]

A motion to strike also may be utilized in many jurisdictions to eliminate allegations that are "sham," "frivolous," "irrelevant," "redundant," "unnecessary," "impertinent," or "scandalous."[5] The basic purpose of such a motion is to eliminate from the public record unfair attacks or charges designed solely to embarrass the party against whom the pleading is filed. However, as one might expect, from time to time attorneys have attempted to use a motion to strike to obtain a substantive advantage. Thus, they have sought to eliminate allegations necessary to the pleader's cause of action or defense.[6] The courts have held that the only allegations that can be stricken are those that are unnecessary to the substantive claims being set forth and that have no useful purpose in the pleading.[7]

The pleadings also may be challenged on the ground that they reveal some procedural defect such as improper jurisdiction or venue, the failure to join necessary parties or the improper joinder of claims, and other matters.[8] With the exception of a challenge to the subject-matter jurisdiction of the court or to the lack of an indispensable party, which normally can be raised at any time, even on appeal,[9] matters of abatement are waived if they are not raised in accordance with the rules of the jurisdiction.[10] As already noted,[11] these challenges often may be raised as affirmative defenses in the answer. However, each jurisdiction determines precisely how these claims may be raised.[12] In some cases, whether or not the defect appears on the face of the complaint, the defense must be raised by a special motion at the outset of the case.[13] It will be waived if one waits to assert it in a challenge to the pleadings or to the answer.[14] On the other hand, in a number of jurisdictions, if such a defense does appear on the face of the complaint, then the defendant may raise the matter by a motion or a special demurrer challenging the particular defect in question.[15] In the federal courts these issues can be

---

4. Fed.Civ.Proc.Rule 15(a); N.Y.—McKinney's CPLR 3025(b); Wyo.Rules Civ. Proc., Rule 15(a).

5. Fed.Civ.Proc.Rule 12(f); N.Y.—McKinney's CPLR 3024(b); Utah Rules Civ. Proc., Rule 12(f).

6. Gateway Bottling, Inc. v. Dad's Rootbeer Co., 53 F.R.D. 585 (W.D.Pa.1971).

7. See Atlantic City Elec. Co. v. General Elec. Co., 207 F.Supp. 620 (S.D.N.Y. 1962); McWhirter, Reeves, McGothlin, Davidson, Rief & Bakas v. Weiss, 704 So.2d 214 (Fla.App.1998). Cf. 3 J. Weinstein, H. Korn & A. Miller, New York Civil Practice ¶ 3024.01 (1977).

8. Fed.Civ.Proc.Rules 12(b)(1)–(5), 12(b)(7); Ill.—Smith–Hurd Ann. 735 ILCS 5/2–104, 2–301; Kan.Stat.Ann. 60–212(b)(1)–(5), (7).

9. Fed.Civ.Proc.Rule 12(h)(2), (3); Fla.—West's F.S.A. Rules Civ.Proc., Rule 1.140(h)(2).

10. Fed.Civ.Proc.Rule 12(h)(1); Colo. Rules Civ.Proc., Rule 12(h)(1).

11. See § 5.20, above.

12. See West's Ann.Cal.Code Civ.Proc. §§ 430.10, 430.30(b); Ill.—Smith–Hurd Ann. 735 ILCS 5/2–104, 5/2–301.

13. See, e.g., Ostrowski v. Miller, 226 Cal.App.2d 79, 37 Cal.Rptr. 790 (1964); Texas Secs. Corp. v. Peters, 463 S.W.2d 263 (Tex.Civ.App.1971).

14. West's Ann.Cal.Code Civ.Proc. § 430.80.

15. West's Ann.Cal.Code Civ.Proc. §§ 430.10, 430.30(a).

raised either by motion or in the answer.[16] However, a party who does file a motion based on one of these matters must raise all such defenses in the same motion; she will not be allowed to raise some of them by motion and later to raise others, either by a second motion or in the answer.[17]

§ 5.25   Consequences of a Ruling on a Challenge to the Pleadings

Whenever the court rules on a challenge to the pleadings, the losing party is faced with a choice of whether to go on with the case or to appeal. In those few jurisdictions where the losing party may appeal the ruling while the case continues,[1] there is no serious problem. But in the vast majority of jurisdictions an appeal can be taken only from a final judgment.[2] The decision to forgo all other means of defense and to allow the case to go to final judgment is an extremely important one and may pose a serious dilemma for the litigant who has lost a preliminary motion.

A party whose challenge to a pleading is rejected may continue with the case or allow a final judgment to be entered against her and appeal. If the party decides to continue, she may, by that act alone, give up the right to make the challenge at a later date on appeal.[3] For example, challenges to the form of pleadings, to venue, jurisdiction over the person, and the like, often are held to be waived if the party who has raised them and lost determines to go on with the case.[4] On the other hand, it is a very serious step indeed if the party who loses the challenge allows a judgment to be entered against her. Illustratively, if the defendant files an unsuccessful motion to dismiss for failure to state a claim and then allows a default judgment to be entered against her, she will give up her right to contest the merits in the event that the trial court's ruling on the motion is upheld on appeal.[5] Unless a party feels that the

---

16. Fed.Civ.Proc.Rule 12(b).

17. Fed.Civ.Proc.Rule 12(g); Official Code Ga.Ann. § 9–11–12(g).

§ 5.25

1. See e.g., N.Y.—McKinney's CPLR 5701(a).

2. See generally § 13.1, below.

3. See Blazer v. Black, 196 F.2d 139, 143–44 (10th Cir.1952); Leggett v. Montgomery Ward & Co., 178 F.2d 436, 438 (10th Cir.1949).

4. Ill.—Smith–Hurd Ann. 735 ILCS 5/2–301.

5. See Fish v. McGann, 205 Ill. 179, 68 N.E. 761 (1903); Cutler v. Wright, 22 N.Y. 472 (1860); C. Clark, Code Pleading § 84 (2d ed.1947); J. Koffler & A. Reppy, Common Law Pleading § 201, at 406 (1969). Cf. Elfman v. Glaser, 313 Mass. 370, 47 N.E.2d 925 (1943) (judgment for the defendant, after demurrer sustained with leave to amend and the plaintiff failed to amend, is res judicata to a subsequent action between the same parties on the same cause).

Note that this situation is a rare occurrence as a party has the option of preserving the objection raised in the overruled demurrer by scrupulously keeping the evidence at trial to that admissible under the challenged pleading and then moving for a directed verdict at the end of trial upon the same grounds as those underlying the demurrer. The plaintiff either will recognize his error during trial and amend to correct it, which he would be allowed to do after losing an appeal of the ruling on the demurrer, or defendant can appeal on the basis of the ruling on her motion for a directed verdict. The only loss suffered by defendant from taking this latter course is the expense of trial; thus, it is by far the more common choice.

best and only chance to win is on the pleading challenge, she is very unlikely to permit a judgment to be entered in favor of the opposing party.

When a challenge to a pleading is upheld, the losing party normally has a choice either to amend or to allow judgment to be entered and to appeal.[6] In most cases a party will amend if that is possible, and will proceed with the case on the basis of the amended pleading.[7] By doing so, however, the party may be held to have waived any error in the ruling on the original pleading.[8] Yet, if the party does not amend but allows a judgment to be entered against her, then she may appeal the ruling on the pleading, but if she loses on appeal, she will not be able to go back and contest the case on the merits. Given these risks, the latter is a drastic course that would be undertaken only if the challenged pleading cannot be amended or if the only successful amendment would require the interjection of new issues that the pleader would not likely be able to prove at trial.

F. AMENDED AND SUPPLEMENTAL PLEADINGS

§ 5.26 Amendments: In General

The rules of pleading, particularly in code pleading jurisdictions, sometimes appear highly technical, providing traps for the unwary or unsophisticated pleader. Almost every jurisdiction today, however, softens the impact of improper pleading through the adoption of liberal amendment rules, allowing a pleader to correct any defect that in good faith can be corrected, thus providing maximum opportunity for each claim to be decided on its merits rather than on procedural technicalities.

The Federal Rules, and the rules in most jurisdictions, permit a pleader to amend a pleading once as a matter of right, so long as no responsive pleading has been filed or, if the original pleading did not call for a response, within the normal time that responsive pleadings are required.[1] Thus, if an individual realizes that his pleading is insufficient, he immediately may file an amended pleading and the case may proceed. In many jurisdictions the filing by the opposing party of a challenge to the pleading does not cut off this right.[2] The pleader can avoid an unnecessary hearing on what is obviously a valid challenge by filing a corrected pleading.

---

6. See, e.g., Bertucelli v. Carreras, 467 F.2d 214 (9th Cir.1972); Breier v. Northern California Bowling Proprietors' Ass'n, 316 F.2d 787 (9th Cir.1963).

7. See Blazer v. Black, 196 F.2d 139, 143–44 (10th Cir.1952).

8. See State ex rel. Randolph v. Hancock Circuit Court, 243 Ind. 156, 182 N.E.2d 248 (1962).

§ 5.26

1. Fed.Civ.Proc.Rule 15(a); Ariz.Rules Civ.Proc., Rule 15(a).

2. E.g., Lipary v. Posner, 96 Misc.2d 578, 409 N.Y.S.2d 363 (1978).

A pleader also may amend a pleading by obtaining leave of court.[3] Although the court has discretion to reject leave, such rulings are rare, at least when the leave is sought at a reasonably early stage in the proceedings when the opposing party can adjust readily to the new allegations.[4] Indeed, it may be held an abuse of discretion for the court to deny leave to amend unless there is a demonstrable showing of prejudice to an opposing party.[5] This is the case whether the amendment is sought prior to a pleading challenge or after a successful challenge has been filed and upheld by the trial court. In California, if the trial court upholds a demurrer to a pleading, the judge's failure to grant leave to amend is, by statute, appealable, even though the pleader did not specifically ask for leave.[6]

Amendments, of course, may be denied in situations in which unfair advantage would be taken of the opposing side. This may occur, for example, when leave to amend is requested at or during trial, and would so alter the case that the opposing party would have to search for new witnesses and other evidence.[7] Similar prejudice might be found when the pleading is filed only after the death or disappearance of a key witness who would be necessary to disprove the new allegations. In addition to these rather obvious situations, leave may be denied to a party who has received leave to amend the identical pleading on numerous other occasions and who has been unable to set forth a claim or a defense.[8] At some point, when it appears that the pleader cannot in good faith file a satisfactory pleading, the court is entitled to cut off the availability of amendment.

A difficult situation arises when a pleader has included allegations that clearly would destroy her position, as, for example, when the face of the complaint reveals that the statute of limitations has elapsed. In this situation the court may withhold leave to amend when the pleader intends merely to eliminate from the pleading the allegations as to the time that the cause of action arose, unless the moving party convinces the court that it is not simply attempting to prolong a bad case to harass

---

3. Fed.Civ.Proc.Rule 15(a); Alaska Rules Civ.Proc., Rule 15(a); N.Y.—McKinney's CPLR 3025(b).

4. Compare Landis v. Superior Court, 232 Cal.App.2d 548, 42 Cal.Rptr. 893 (1965) (courts should show great liberality in granting amendments so that no litigant shall be deprived of his day in court by technicalities), and Posz v. Burchell, 209 Cal.App.2d 324, 25 Cal.Rptr. 896 (1962) (law allows great liberality in amendment prior to and even during trial), with Bedolla v. Logan, 52 Cal.App.3d 118, 125 Cal.Rptr. 59 (1975) (long deferred presentation of amendment without excuse is significant factor in upholding denial of leave to amend). See generally 6 C. Wright, A. Miller & M. Kane, Civil 2d §§ 1484, 1487–89.

5. See Foman v. Davis, 371 U.S. 178, 83 S.Ct. 227, 9 L.Ed.2d 222 (1962); Jackson v. Bank of Hawaii, 902 F.2d 1385 (9th Cir. 1990); Harkless v. Sweeny Independent School Dist., 554 F.2d 1353 (5th Cir.1977), cert. denied 434 U.S. 966; United Steelworkers of America v. Mesker Bros. Industries, Inc., 457 F.2d 91 (8th Cir.1972).

6. West's Ann.Cal.Code Civ.Proc. § 472.

7. Krumme v. WestPoint Stevens Inc., 143 F.3d 71, 87–88 (2d Cir.1998), cert. denied __ U.S. __, 119 S.Ct. 592.

8. Baker v. Murphy, 495 F.Supp. 462 (D.Puerto Rico 1980); Alvarez v. E & A Produce Corp., 708 So.2d 997 (Fla.App. 1998); Gautier v. General Tel. Co., 234 Cal. App.2d 302, 44 Cal.Rptr. 404 (1965); Martinez v. Cook, 57 N.M. 263, 258 P.2d 375 (1953).

the opponent, but in fact can establish that the statute has not run or is inapplicable.[9]

It should be noted that the trial judge has the power to allow an amendment at any time during the trial and even afterwards in the interests of justice.[10] Thus, the court can allow an amendment and reopen a case to take further testimony if that is an appropriate course. However, the later the timing of the amendment, the more likely it will be that the trial judge will find the amendment to be prejudicial to the opposing party.[11] Moreover, it is far less likely that an appellate court would overrule the exercise of discretion by a trial court in denying leave to amend at a late date.

Finally, a question arises whether the court, in ruling on a motion for leave to amend, should consider the legal sufficiency of the substance of the proposed amendment. A number of courts have said no.[12] But many courts have taken the position that leave to amend can and should be denied if the proposed amendment is frivolous or fails to advance the case in some way.[13]

Although amendments to conform the pleadings to the proof introduced at trial present the same policy considerations as any other amendment—namely whether allowing the amendment would prejudice the opposing party—historically, these amendments were treated differently. The traditional rule at common law was that the attempt to prove causes of action or defenses not pleaded would result in a "fatal variance" and these new issues could not be considered in the determination of the case.[14] This rule still prevails in some jurisdictions and the insertion of a new issue into the trial, at least if it advances a new cause of action or defense, will not be allowed, whether or not an amendment to conform to the proof is sought.[15]

In the federal courts and in states having similar rules, a party is given the right to amend the pleadings to conform to the proof at trial.[16]

---

9. Owens v. Traverso, 125 Cal.App.2d 803, 271 P.2d 164 (1954).

10. Fed.Civ.Proc.Rule 15(a); S.D.Codified Laws 15–6–15(a). See Browne v. R & R Engineering Co., 164 F.Supp. 315 (D.Del. 1958), reversed on other grounds 264 F.2d 219 (3d Cir.1959); Hemmer–Miller Dev. Co. v. Hudson Ins. Co., 63 S.D. 109, 256 N.W. 798 (1934).

11. See Nilsen v. City of Moss Point, Mississippi, 621 F.2d 117 (5th Cir.1980); Crawford v. City of Muncie, 655 N.E.2d 614, 622–23 (Ind.App.1995); Bedolla v. Logan, 52 Cal.App.3d 118, 125 Cal.Rptr. 59 (1975).

12. E.g., Fox v. City of West Palm Beach, 383 F.2d 189 (5th Cir.1967); Pearl Brewing Co. v. Jos. Schlitz Brewing Co., 415 F.Supp. 1122 (S.D.Tex.1976); Stanley Works v. Haeger Potteries, Inc., 35 F.R.D. 551, 554 (N.D.Ill.1964).

13. E.g., Pan–Islamic Trade Corp. v. Exxon Corp., 632 F.2d 539 (5th Cir.1980), cert. denied 454 U.S. 927; Norbeck v. Davenport Community School Dist., 545 F.2d 63 (8th Cir.1976), cert. denied 431 U.S. 917; Collyard v. Washington Capitals, 477 F.Supp. 1247 (D.Minn.1979).

14. See J. Koffler & A. Reppy, Common Law Pleading §§ 217, 302 (1969).

15. Neb.Rev.Stat. § 25–852; Farmers Union Co-op. Ins. Co. v. Reinwald, 194 Neb. 766, 235 N.W.2d 630 (1975). See Vines v. Branch, 244 Va. 185, 418 S.E.2d 890 (1992); Hall, Standards of Review in Texas, 29 St. Mary's L.Rev. 351, 438 (1998) (amendment that states a new cause or defense is " 'prejudicial on its face' ").

16. Fed.Civ.Proc.Rule 15(b); Ohio Rules Civ.Proc., Rule 15(b). See also West's Ann.Cal.Code Civ.Proc. §§ 469, 470; N.Y.—McKinney's CPLR 3025(c).

The amendment can be made at any time, even after judgment.[17] Indeed, under these rules even if a party does not seek to amend a pleading to conform to the proof, the pleading is treated in all respects as including all issues tried by express or implied consent of the parties.[18] The important factor here is the existence of knowing consent. If evidence is introduced on an issue that is pleaded, the fact that it also bears on an unpleaded issue will not justify a finding that the latter issue was tried by implied consent because the opposing party had no reason to object to the evidence in question.[19] On the other hand, if the opposing party responds to the evidence with testimony going only to the second issue, then that party no longer could oppose the amendment on the ground that the issue had not been tried.[20] Thus, consent generally is found when evidence is introduced without objection,[21] or when the party opposing the motion to amend actually produced evidence bearing on the new issue[22] or otherwise took action to oppose the unpleaded issue on the merits.[23]

§ 5.27   Amendments and the Statutes of Limitations

In the vast majority of jurisdictions today, for purposes of the statute of limitations, an amended pleading is treated as having been filed at the same time as the original pleading, provided that the claim or defense asserted in the amended pleading arose out of the same transaction or occurrence as that set forth in the original pleading.[1] The amended pleading is said to "relate back" to the original filing date. The relation back principle is consistent with the purpose of the statute of limitations, which is to prevent the assertion of stale claims, but not to

17. Fed.Civ.Proc.Rule 15(b); Ind.Trial Proc.Rule 15(B).

18. Fed.Civ.Proc.Rule 15(b); West's Ann.Cal.Code Civ.Proc. § 470.

19. Browning Debenture Holders' Comm. v. DASA Corp., 560 F.2d 1078 (2d Cir.1977); International Harvester Credit Corp. v. East Coast Truck, 547 F.2d 888, 890 (5th Cir.1977); Schultz v. Cally, 528 F.2d 470 (3d Cir.1975); Tomka v. Hoechst Celanese Corp., 528 N.W.2d 103 (Iowa 1995). Cf. Hayes v. Richfield Oil Corp., 38 Cal.2d 375, 240 P.2d 580 (1952) (party who objected to evidence at trial on grounds that the issue was not pleaded held to have been aware of the issue and thus not prejudiced. But see Nucor v. General Elec. Co., 812 S.W.2d 136, 145–46 (Ky.1991) (right to amend turns on "actual prejudice" rather than "actual consent").

20. See Hicks v. U.S., 486 F.2d 325 (10th Cir.1973), cert. denied 416 U.S. 938; Federal Savs. & Loan Ins. Corp. v. Hogan, 476 F.2d 1182 (7th Cir.1973).

21. Corsica Livestock Sales, Inc. v. Sumitomo Bank of California, 726 F.2d 374 (8th Cir.1983); Carlyle v. U.S. Department of the Army, 674 F.2d 554 (6th Cir.1982).

See generally 6A C. Wright, A. Miller & M. Kane, Civil 2d § 1493.

22. Fejta v. GAF Companies, Inc., 800 F.2d 1395 (5th Cir.1986); Davis & Cox v. Summa Corp., 751 F.2d 1507 (9th Cir. 1985); Weinstein Enterprises v. Cappelletti, 217 A.D.2d 616, 629 N.Y.S.2d 476 (1995). See generally 6A C. Wright, A. Miller & M. Kane, Civil 2d § 1493.

23. E.g., Whitaker v. T.J. Snow Co., 151 F.3d 661 (7th Cir.1998) (complaint treated as amended when, on defendant's motion for summary judgment, both parties briefed an issue not contained in the complaint). See also Suiter v. Mitchell Motor Coach Sales, Inc., 151 F.3d 1275 (10th Cir. 1998) (answer treated as amended when unpleaded affirmative defense was put forth and disputed on defendant's motion for judgment as a matter of law).

§ 5.27

1. LaBar v. Cooper, 376 Mich. 401, 137 N.W.2d 136 (1965); Fed.Civ.Proc.Rule 15(c); N.J.Civ.Prac.Rule 4:9–3; N.Y.—McKinney's CPLR 203(e). See generally 6A C. Wright, A. Miller & M. Kane, Civil 2d §§ 1496–97.

prohibit the augmentation or correction of claims that have been filed before the statute has run. On the other hand, a pleader is not allowed to utilize this rule to proceed on totally unrelated claims upon which the statute of limitations has run prior to the time that they appear in an amended pleading.[2]

A large majority,[3] although not all, courts have been liberal in finding that amendments do relate back to avoid statute of limitations problems. The most difficult cases are those amendments that add substantially different facts or otherwise alter the basic focus of the claim.[4] Thus, in one case a claim based on the manufacturer's failure to warn of an inherently dangerous condition in the product was held not to arise out of the same transaction or occurrence as a claim for negligent manufacture and breach of implied warranty of merchantability.[5] However, that decision is more restrictive than most. The courts normally would permit such an amendment to relate back because the underlying transaction and occurrence is considered to be the fact that the purchased product was dangerous and injured the buyer.[6]

It is clear that a mere change of the legal theory does not prevent an amendment from relating back.[7] An amendment may shift a case from a tort to a contract theory or vice versa[8] or alter a claim based on common law liability to one having a statutory basis.[9] Technical or mechanical tests will not be applied. Thus, a claim by a pedestrian that he was injured by the negligence of the vehicle that struck him was held to arise out of the same occurrence as a claim that the driver who struck him negligently failed to stop and render appropriate aid.[10] Although the facts

2. E.g., National Distillers & Chem. Corp. v. Brad's Mach. Prods., Inc., 666 F.2d 492 (11th Cir.1982); Barnes v. Callaghan & Co., 559 F.2d 1102 (7th Cir.1977); Illinois Tool Works, Inc. v. Foster Grant Co., 395 F.Supp. 234 (N.D.Ill.1974), affirmed 547 F.2d 1300 (7th Cir.1976), cert. denied 431 U.S. 929; Price v. J.C. Penney Co., 26 N.C.App. 249, 216 S.E.2d 154 (1975), cert. denied 288 N.C. 243, 217 S.E.2d 666.

3. Staren v. American Nat. Bank & Trust Co., 529 F.2d 1257 (7th Cir.1976); Williams v. U.S., 405 F.2d 234 (5th Cir. 1968). See also LaBar v. Cooper, 376 Mich. 401, 405–06, 137 N.W.2d 136, 138 (1965); Scott v. Newsom, 74 N.M. 399, 394 P.2d 253 (1964); Keel v. Brown, 162 So.2d 321 (Fla.App.1964), cert. denied 166 So.2d 753; Schlecht v. Schiel, 76 Ariz. 214, 262 P.2d 252 (1953).

4. See, e.g., Nason v. Jones, 278 Ala. 532, 179 So.2d 281 (1965); Johnson v. Bar-Mour, Inc., 27 Wis.2d 271, 133 N.W.2d 748 (1965).

5. Tarbert v. Ingraham Co., 190 F.Supp. 402 (D.Conn.1960).

6. See Tiller v. Atlantic Coast Line R.R. Co., 323 U.S. 574, 65 S.Ct. 421, 89

L.Ed. 465 (1945); LaBar v. Cooper, 376 Mich. 401, 137 N.W.2d 136 (1965); Scott v. Newsom, 74 N.M. 399, 394 P.2d 253 (1964). See generally Note, Federal Rule of Civil Procedure 15(c): Relation Back of Amendments, 57 Minn.L.Rev. 83 (1972).

7. Hageman v. Signal L.P. Gas, Inc., 486 F.2d 479 (6th Cir.1973); U.S. v. Johnson, 288 F.2d 40 (5th Cir.1961); Gridley v. Sayre & Fisher Co., 409 F.Supp. 1266 (D.S.D.1976).

8. Hood v. P. Ballantine & Sons, 38 F.R.D. 502 (S.D.N.Y.1965) (negligence to warranty); C. Corkin & Sons v. Tide Water Associated Oil Co., 20 F.R.D. 402 (D.Mass. 1957) (contract to tort).

9. Wall v. Chesapeake & Ohio Ry. Co., 339 F.2d 434 (4th Cir.1964); U.S. v. Johnson, 288 F.2d 40 (5th Cir.1961).

10. Brooks v. E.J. Willig Truck Transp. Co., 40 Cal.2d 669, 681, 255 P.2d 802, 810 (1953). See also O'Shaughnessy v. Bayonne News Co., 9 N.J.Misc. 345, 154 A. 13 (1931), affirmed per curiam 109 N.J.L. 271, 160 A. 696 (1932).

were different, the incident and the nature of the injury were clearly the same.

Whether amendments that change parties can relate back has been an ongoing source of controversy. The traditional rule stemmed from the notion that a claim against one party is an entirely separate matter from a claim against another, even though the claims arise out of the same transaction or occurrence. In addition, it was emphasized that one function of the statute of limitations is to protect potential defendants from stale claims; at some point the individual should be free from fear of lawsuits arising out of an incident that occurred many years before. Thus, it generally was accepted that new parties could not be added to an action by amendment after the applicable limitations period had expired unless their conduct misled plaintiff in filing against the wrong defendant. This rule often led to harsh, unjust results, allowing meritorious claims to be defeated on technical grounds.[11]

Federal Rule 15(c) was amended in 1966 to set forth specific conditions upon which new parties could be added by amendment. Rule 15(c), as then amended, provided that an amendment changing the party against whom a claim is asserted would be permitted to relate back if the new defendant, "within the period provided by law for commencing the action," (1) received notice of the institution of the action so that she would not be prejudiced in maintaining a defense, and (2) knew or should have known that but for a mistake concerning the identity of the proper party, the action would have been brought against her.[12] This standard was slightly more liberal than the traditional rule in that it was not necessary that the pleader's mistake resulted from confusion caused by the proposed new defendant. It was enough that confusion existed and that the proposed new defendant had reason to know about it.[13]

It seems obvious that a major distinction should be drawn between an amendment that merely corrects the name of the party against whom the action has been filed and an amendment that adds an entirely new party after the statute of limitations has run. Further, in keeping with the trend toward liberal pleading, in cases in which plaintiff has misspelled defendant's name or otherwise failed to denominate defendant correctly, an allowance should be made and the amendment should be readily granted. However, differing interpretations of Rule 15(c)'s language: "within the period provided by law for commencing the action," led to conflict and inconsistent rulings among courts. Some courts ruled that notice had to be received before the statute of limitations had run.[14]

---

11. See Jacobs v. McCloskey & Co., 40 F.R.D. 486 (E.D.Pa.1966); Martz v. Miller Bros. Co., 244 F.Supp. 246 (D.Del.1965); Robbins v. Esso Shipping Co., 190 F.Supp. 880 (S.D.N.Y.1960).

12. See the Advisory Committee Note on the 1966 amendment to Federal Rule 15(c); 6A C. Wright, A. Miller & M. Kane, Civil 2d § 1498.

13. See, e.g., Varlack v. SWC Caribbean, Inc., 550 F.2d 171 (3d Cir.1977); Mitchell v. Hendricks, 68 F.R.D. 564 (E.D.Pa. 1975); Ames v. Vavreck, 356 F.Supp. 931 (D.Minn.1973).

14. See Weisgal v. Smith, 774 F.2d 1277 (4th Cir.1985); Cooper v. U.S. Postal Serv., 740 F.2d 714 (9th Cir.1984), cert. denied 471 U.S. 1022; Hughes v. U.S., 701

Other courts adopted a more permissive posture, holding that the rule was satisfied as long as the action was filed within the statutory period and notice was accomplished within the time allowed for service of process.[15]

In 1986, the Supreme Court held that in the situation of a mis-named defendant, notice must be received within the statute of limitations and it was not sufficient to find that notice was given within the time for service.[16] Although the lower courts necessarily followed the decision,[17] the Court's rigid approach was severely criticized.[18] Indeed, the rules committee took notice of the repeated calls for reform and Rule 15(c) was amended again, as of December 1, 1991.[19] The effect of the 1991 amendment is to permit a name-correcting amendment if filed within the period provided by Rule 4(j) for service of process.[20] The purpose of the rule's revision is to prevent parties against whom claims are asserted from taking unjust advantage of otherwise inconsequential pleading errors, thus promoting litigation on the merits.[21] Whether the new amendment finally resolves the controversy over the relation back of amendments changing parties remains an open question.

Many states do not have specific statutes providing for joinder of

F.2d 56 (7th Cir.1982); Stewart v. U.S., 655 F.2d 741 (7th Cir.1981).

15. See Hendrix v. Memorial Hosp. of Galveston County, 776 F.2d 1255 (5th Cir. 1985); Kirk v. Cronvich, 629 F.2d 404 (5th Cir.1980); Ingram v. Kumar, 585 F.2d 566 (2d Cir.1978), cert. denied 440 U.S. 940.

16. Schiavone v. Fortune, 477 U.S. 21, 106 S.Ct. 2379, 91 L.Ed.2d 18 (1986).

17. See Slade v. U.S. Postal Serv., 875 F.2d 814 (10th Cir.1989); Giannini v. City of New York, 700 F.Supp. 202 (S.D.N.Y. 1988).

18. Schiavone was criticized for imposing too restrictive a reading of Rule 15(c). It has been argued that in adopting Rule 15(c), the Court recognized that on occasion a mistake will be made and plaintiff initially will sue a wrong party. If the intended party has not been prejudiced, the correction of the misnomer by amendment should be permitted. By ignoring this objective of Rule 15(c), the Schiavone Court foreclosed many cases from being litigated on their merits because of "procedural error." See Bauer, Schiavone: An Un–Fortunate Illustration of the Supreme Court's Role as Interpreter of the Federal Rules of Civil Procedure, 63 Notre Dame L.Rev. 101 (1988); Brussack, Outrageous Fortune: The Case for Amending Rule 15(c) Again, 61 S.Calif.L.Rev. 671 (1988); Epter, An Un–Fortune–Ate Decision: The Aftermath of the Supreme Court's Eradication of the Relation–Back Doctrine, 17 Fla.St.U.L.Rev. 713

(1990); Note, Looking Forward: A Fairer Application of the Relation Back Provisions of Federal Rule of Civil Procedure 15(c), 63 N.Y.U.L.Rev. 131 (1988).

19. Amendments to the Federal Rules of Civil Procedure, Revised Rule 15(c) (1991).

20. Amendments to the Federal Rules of Civil Procedure, Revised Rule 15(c)(3) (1991). The new rule actually read, "within the period provided by Rule 4(m) for service of the summons and complaint." This anticipated alteration of Rule 4 to redesignate Rule 4(j) as Rule 4(m). However, the alteration of Rule 4 was not adopted, but the reference in new Rule 15(c) to Rule 4(m), which does not exist, was not altered. Subsequently Congress passed legislation to correct the oversight by changing "Rule 4(m)" to read "Rule 4(j)". Public Law 102–198, § 11(a), Dec. 9, 1991, 105 Stat. 1623. Normally, Rule 4(j) requires service on a defendant within 120 days from the date the complaint is filed. A number of state courts have altered their versions of Federal Rule 15(c) to adopt the approach of the 1991 federal rule. See, e.g., Me.Rules Civ. Proc., Rule 15.

21. Indeed, one of the purposes of amended Rule 15(c) is specifically to prevent courts from reaching the result in Schiavone v. Fortune. See Advisory Committee Note to the 1991 amendments to Rule 15, reprinted in 134 F.R.D. 525, 637 (1991).

new defendants after the normal limitations period has elapsed.[22] Others follow the federal rule as it existed prior to the 1991 amendments,[23] while still others have provisions consistent with the current federal rule.[24]

Some states, such as California,[25] are more liberal. The California rule utilizes an entirely different technique for avoiding a statute of limitations problem. A plaintiff, by naming a number of "John Doe" defendants, whose names are not known, and by making certain that the causes of action in the complaint are stated against them as well as the named defendant, can substitute the true name of any defendant for a John Doe and avoid the limitations problem entirely. The naming of the specific defendant relates back to the time that the case was filed against the John Doe whom he replaces.[26] The existence of the California procedure may be explained in part at least by the fact that the state has a very short one-year statute of limitations for all personal injury actions,[27] and that full investigation of a case to determine who is responsible may take more time. In recent years litigants in federal courts have named John Doe defendants when they are unaware of the identity of the proper defendant. Often the identity of the correct defendant is unknown until after the statute of limitations has run. Plaintiffs then attempt to apply Rule 15(c) to amendments substituting the name of the correct defendant. Federal courts have had mixed reactions to this approach, some holding that Rule 15(c) does not apply because there was no "mistake" when the John Does were named, whereas others have permitted relation back if the requirements of Rule 15(c) have otherwise been met.[28]

The amendment rules usually do not purport to deal with cases in which a new plaintiff is added or substituted for the original plaintiff after the statute of limitations has run. The courts treat this problem as a less serious one because once the defendant has had a timely suit filed against him, it is not inconsistent with the statute of limitations to allow an appropriate plaintiff to be substituted for the person who originally brought the suit.[29] A person who is the real party in interest may be

---

22. E.g., N.C.Civ.Proc.Rules, Rule 15(c); Crossman v. Moore, 341 N.C. 185, 459 S.E.2d 715 (1995), noted in 74 N.C.L.Rev 2000 (1996) (no relation back in North Carolina for an amendment to correct a misnomer).

23. E.g., N.J.Civ.Proc.Rules, Rule 4:9-3.

24. E.g., 12 Okla.Stat.Ann. § 2015C.

25. West's Ann.Cal.Code Civ.Proc. § 474.

26. See Larson v. Barnett, 101 Cal. App.2d 282, 225 P.2d 297 (1950); Day v. Western Loan & Bldg. Co., 42 Cal.App.2d 226, 108 P.2d 702 (1940). See generally Hogan, California's Unique Doe Defendant Practice: A Fiction Stranger Than Truth, 30 Stan.L.Rev. 51 (1977).

27. West's Ann.Cal.Code Civ.Proc. § 340.

28. For analysis of the federal cases and their relation to state laws, see Rice, Meet John Doe: It Is Time for Federal Civil Procedure To Recognize John Doe Parties, 57 U.Pitt.L.Rev. 883 (1996); Note, Relation Back of "John Doe" Complaints in Federal Court: What You Don't Know Can Hurt You, 19 Cardozo L.Rev. 1235 (1997).

29. See Staren v. American Nat. Bank & Trust Co., 529 F.2d 1257 (7th Cir.1976); Brauer v. Republic Steel Corp., 460 F.2d 801 (10th Cir.1972); Garr v. Clayville, 71 F.R.D. 553 (D.Del.1976).

substituted for the individual who originally filed the suit, provided that the claim is the same and that the original action was timely.[30] This of course does not mean that a new plaintiff can join in an action in order to raise a stale claim unrelated to the on-going case.[31] Whatever claims the new plaintiff has must be identical with those originally filed or arise out of the same transaction or occurrence, so that any new claims clearly would relate back to the time of the original filing.

Finally, one must distinguish carefully the situation in which a new party is sought to be joined from one in which a successor in interest is sought to be substituted for the initial plaintiff or defendant. An executor or personal representative of a deceased or incompetent party may be substituted readily without fear that the limitations period will have continued to run against the new party.[32] No new claims or parties actually are presented in this instance; the substitution merely reflects the party who now is legally responsible for maintaining or defending the action.

§ 5.28 Supplemental Pleadings

In a number of jurisdictions special statutes or rules specifically provide for supplemental pleadings.[1] A supplemental pleading is distinguished from an amended pleading in that the latter covers only those matters that had occurred at the time the original pleading was filed, whereas the supplemental pleading covers matters that occur subsequently.[2] For example, a supplemental pleading can be used to alter or augment the amount of relief demanded in the original complaint,[3] or add related claims that have newly arisen,[4] or provide for new defenses,[5] as might occur if there has been a new release signed or if a prior case has been resolved so as to have preclusive effect[6] on the present one.

Sometimes a party who seeks to alter a pleading mislabels the new pleading as an amended rather than a supplemental pleading. Courts invariably ignore the erroneous label, treating the pleading for what it is in substance.[7] However, there may be adverse consequences if a party

30. Wadsworth v. U.S. Postal Serv., 511 F.2d 64 (7th Cir.1975); Metropolitan Paving Co. v. International Union of Operating Engineers, 439 F.2d 300 (10th Cir. 1971), cert. denied 404 U.S. 829. See § 6.3, below, for a discussion of the real party in interest requirement.

31. E.g., Higgins, Inc. v. Kiekhaefer Corp., 246 F.Supp. 610 (E.D.Wis.1965).

32. Fed.Civ.Proc.Rule 25; Colo.Rules Civ.Proc., Rule 25. See Staggers v. Otto Gerdau Co., 359 F.2d 292 (2d Cir.1966).

§ 5.28

1. Fed.Civ.Proc.Rule 15(d); N.Y.— McKinney's CPLR 3025(b).

2. Slavenburg Corp. v. Boston Ins. Co., 30 F.R.D. 123 (S.D.N.Y.1962); U.S. v. L. D. Caulk Co., 114 F.Supp. 939 (D.Del.1953);

Magee v. McNany, 10 F.R.D. 5 (W.D.Pa. 1950); Williams v. Rutherford Freight Lines, Inc., 10 N.C.App. 384, 179 S.E.2d 319 (1971).

3. City of Texarkana v. Arkansas, Louisiana Gas Co., 306 U.S. 188, 59 S.Ct. 448, 83 L.Ed. 598 (1939).

4. Smith, Kline & French Labs. v. A. H. Robins Co., 61 F.R.D. 24 (E.D.Pa.1973).

5. Slavenburg Corp. v. Boston Ins. Co., 30 F.R.D. 123 (S.D.N.Y.1962).

6. Kimmel v. Yankee Lines, Inc., 125 F.Supp. 702 (W.D.Pa.1954), affirmed 224 F.2d 644 (3d Cir.1955).

7. U.S. v. Vorachek, 563 F.2d 884 (8th Cir.1977); U.S. ex rel. Atkins v. Reiten, 313 F.2d 673 (9th Cir.1963); U.S. v. Russell, 241

makes the wrong choice. For example, because a party who wishes to file a supplemental pleading normally must request leave from the court,[8] a supplemental pleading may be stricken if leave to file is not obtained, even though, had it qualified as an amendment, leave would not have been required.[9] Courts are liberal in granting leave,[10] denying it only when it would cause prejudice to the opposing party.[11] When the moving party has been guilty of inexcusable delay in seeking to supplement a pleading, leave also may be denied.[12]

In the past some courts have taken the position that, unlike an amendment, a supplemental pleading cannot cure a defect in the original pleading.[13] Normally the problem arises when the pleader has failed to take some step that is a prerequisite to the bringing of the type of action in question—for example, when a party has not exhausted the administrative remedies before filing suit.[14] In 1963, Federal Rule 15(d) was amended to permit use of a supplemental pleading to cure an original pleading that was defective.[15] It seemed wasteful and unnecessary to require the pleader to file anew once he in fact had taken the appropriate steps necessary to perfect a claim or defense.

A somewhat similar problem exists when a pleader attempts to set up an entirely new claim for relief by way of a supplemental pleading. A minority of courts have taken the position that newly arising claims can be brought only in an entirely new action.[16] Although one might be able to consolidate the actions for trial,[17] consolidation may not be available if the actions must be brought in different jurisdictions.[18] In any event, the cost and expense of filing two separate suits hardly seems justifiable so long as the original claims and the new claims could have been joined together in a single action, had they all occurred at the same time.[19]

F.2d 879 (1st Cir.1957); Dells, Inc. v. Mundt, 400 F.Supp. 1293 (S.D.N.Y.1975); Macaluso v. Easley, 81 Colo. 50, 253 P. 397 (1927).

8. Fed.Civ.Proc.Rule 15(d); N.C.Gen. Stat. § 1A–1, Rules Civ.Proc., Rule 15(d). See Deutsch v. Fisher, 32 N.C.App. 688, 233 S.E.2d 646 (1977).

9. See 6A C. Wright, A. Miller & M. Kane, Civil 2d § 1504.

10. Bell v. U.S. Department of Defense, 71 F.R.D. 349 (D.N.H.1976), affirmed 563 F.2d 484 (1st Cir.1977).

11. See Rowe v. U.S. Fidelity & Guar. Co., 421 F.2d 937 (4th Cir.1970).

12. Garrison v. Baltimore & O.R.R. Co., 20 F.R.D. 190 (W.D.Pa.1957).

13. La Salle Nat. Bank v. 222 East Chestnut Street Corp., 267 F.2d 247 (7th Cir.1959), cert. denied 361 U.S. 836; Bonner v. Elizabeth Arden, Inc., 177 F.2d 703 (2d Cir.1949); Walton v. Kern County, 39 Cal. App.2d 32, 102 P.2d 531 (1940).

14. See, e.g., Security Ins. Co. v. U.S. ex rel. Haydis, 338 F.2d 444 (9th Cir.1964).

15. See Advisory Committee on the Rules for Civil Procedure, Proposed Amendments to Rules of Civil Procedure, 31 F.R.D. 621, 637 (1962).

16. General Bronze Corp. v. Cupples Prods. Corp., 9 F.R.D. 269 (E.D.Mo.1949), affirmed 189 F.2d 154 (8th Cir.1951); Popovitch v. Kasperlik, 76 F.Supp. 233 (W.D.Pa. 1947); Ebel v. Drum, 55 F.Supp. 186 (D.Mass.1944). But see Rowe v. U.S. Fidelity & Guar. Co., 421 F.2d 937 (4th Cir.1970); Montgomery Environmental Coalition v. Fri, 366 F.Supp. 261 (D.D.C.1973).

17. Fed.Civ.Proc.Rule 42(a); Mont. Rules Civ.Proc., Rule 42(a). See § 6.2, below.

18. Swindell–Dressler Corp. v. Dumbauld, 308 F.2d 267 (3d Cir.1962); Silver v. Goodman, 234 F.Supp. 415 (D.Conn.1964).

19. The rules governing joinder of claims are discussed in Chapter 6, below.

To the extent that new claims are permitted in a supplemental pleading, the question arises as to whether those claims relate back for statute of limitations purposes to the time that the original complaint was filed. Even though there is no specific provision dealing with the relation back of supplemental pleadings,[20] many courts have taken the position that a supplemental pleading may relate back to the time of the filing of the original complaint provided that it arises from the same transaction or occurrence as the claims in the original complaint.[21] This is a logical extension of the rule with respect to the relation back of amendments. Once the defendant has had proper notification that a suit has been brought against him with respect to a particular transaction or occurrence, it is legitimate to permit augmentation of the claim to include every aspect of that transaction or occurrence.[22] If the proposed supplemental pleading would introduce a new and unrelated cause, the new claim should not relate back to the time that the original claim was filed.[23]

The question of relation back of supplemental pleadings will arise infrequently since, by definition, the new claim must have arisen after the original pleading was filed. Therefore it is only in rare cases, involving very short statutes of limitations, when the supplemental pleading will not be filed before the statute of limitations on the new claim has run.

20. Security Ins. Co. v. U.S. ex rel. Haydis, 338 F.2d 444 (9th Cir.1964).

21. Missouri, Kansas & Texas R.R. Co. v. Wulf, 226 U.S. 570, 33 S.Ct. 135, 57 L.Ed. 355 (1913); Security Ins. Co. v. U.S. ex rel. Haydis, 338 F.2d 444 (9th Cir.1964); Bates v. Western Elec., 420 F.Supp. 521 (E.D.Pa. 1976).

22. See William Inglis & Sons Baking Co. v. ITT Continental Baking Co., 668 F.2d 1014 (9th Cir.1981), cert. denied 459 U.S. 825.

23. See Blau v. Lamb, 191 F.Supp. 906 (S.D.N.Y.1961).

§§ 5.29–6.0 are reserved for supplementary material.

Chapter 6

JOINDER OF PARTIES
AND CLAIMS

Analysis

A. IN GENERAL

A. IN GENERAL

§ 6.1 History and Policy Behind Party and Claim Joinder

A number of contemporary procedural devices used in multiparty-
multiclaim actions have their genesis in equity. The common law tied
many procedural rules to the objective of reducing the scope of litigation
to the fewest possible issues, a limitation not imposed by the equity
courts. Procedural reform and the consolidation of law and equity both
in England[1] and the United States[2] extended the application of the
equity joinder procedures, especially those permitting complex cases to

---

§ 6.1

1. See the Common Law Procedure
Acts of 1852, 1854, and 1860, which expanded joinder and the Judicature Acts of
1873 and 1875, which fused law and equity.
See 15 W. Holdsworth, A History of English

Law 104–38 (Goodhart & Hanbury ed.
1965).

2. The most significant illustration of
this reform movement in the United States
is the Field Code of Civil Practice in New
York. N.Y.Laws 1848, c. 379.

be resolved in a single action. New York's Field Code, for example, eliminated many barriers to multiple party actions and the stated objectives of the Code acknowledge the influence of equity practice.[3]

Modern party joinder practice seeks to maximize the ability of the court to meet the distinctive needs of particular controversies. A great deal of authority is given to the court to grant, withhold, or modify permission to expand the number of the parties to the action before it. But there are limits to this discretion. The court operates within the following constraints regarding the joinder of parties: (1) the action must be brought by the "real party in interest"; (2) the parties must have the "capacity" to sue or be sued; (3) persons joined must be "proper" parties if their joinder is to be permitted; (4) persons so related to the dispute that their joinder is "necessary if feasible" must be joined if that can be reasonably accomplished; and (5) actions may not proceed if persons "indispensable" to the litigation cannot be joined.[4]

The tests for whether claims may be joined in a single lawsuit vary widely. As is true of party joinder, the trend clearly is toward giving broad discretion to the court to combine claims in a single action. Although the limits of this discretion have been defined somewhat imprecisely in some instances, all but the most traditional claim joinder rules hinge on considerations of judicial efficiency, procedural rationality, and (especially when the fact-finder is a jury) the potential for confusion and prejudice that might be engendered by the joint treatment of claims.[5]

Two generalizations concerning claim joinder rules can be offered. First, claims from divergent areas of substantive law—for example, tort, contracts, and property—generally may be processed in the same action if they are sufficiently related so that their joint adjudication would promote judicial efficiency without sacrificing standards of justice. This practice reflects an evolution from prior systems under which joinder was a function of certain groupings of right-duty relationships. Early joinder rules provided that claims and parties could be brought into a single action only if they fell within the same writs or causes of action, or if they were classified together by the code of the particular jurisdiction.[6] Modern procedure groups claims into factual clusters that are easily handled by the courts.

Second, as will become more apparent in discussing the various joinder devices,[7] simple notions about the adversary system developed in the age of two-party civil litigation no longer are sufficient to meet the needs of many contemporary cases. Courts today are called upon to manage large-scale actions. Yet, the emerging role of the judge as

---

3. First Report of New York Commissioners on Practice and Pleadings 137–38 (1948).

4. These requirements are discussed in §§ 6.3–6.5, below.

5. See, e.g., Sporn v. Hudson Transit Lines, 265 App.Div. 360, 38 N.Y.S.2d 512 (1942).

6. See Harris v. Avery, 5 Kan. 146 (1869).

7. See §§ 6.6–6.10, below.

"justice manager" by no means is accepted universally; resistance to it creates one of the counterforces limiting the receptivity of the courts to complex actions, and correspondingly, to the joinder of parties and claims.

§ 6.2   Consolidation, Separation, and Severance

Three devices—consolidation of actions, separation of claims, and severance of claims—are the means by which courts sort out the undesirable side-effects of liberal party and claim joinder under contemporary procedural regimes.[1] These devices are necessary for the adequate management of the very complex multiparty and multiclaim actions that are possible today.[2]

Consolidation permits the amalgamation of actions or issues involving at least one common question of law or fact.[3] A court may consolidate two or more entire actions, require a joint hearing or trial of the issues common to several actions, or combine actions or issues only for the pretrial phase of litigation. The obvious virtue of consolidation is that it increases the productivity of the judicial system by arranging for simultaneous resolution of issues or entire actions.

Procedurally, the term consolidation has been used to describe three different situations: (1) when the court stays all but one of several actions and the judgment in the trial of that one action proves conclusive as to the others; (2) when the court combines several actions into one and renders a single judgment for what has become a single action (illustrated by the situation in which several actions are pending between identical parties involving claims that might have been brought as separate counts in one complaint); and (3) when the court orders several actions to be tried together but each action retains a distinct character and requires a separate judgment.[4] Although Federal Rule 42(a) makes separate reference to ordering a joint trial and to ordering actions consolidated and thus appears to encompass at least the last two of these general categories, the Rule clearly has been limited by the case law to

---

§ 6.2

1. For a more detailed discussion, see 7 C. Wright, A. Miller & M. Kane, Civil 2d §§ 1681–89; 9 C. Wright & A. Miller, Civil 2d §§ 2381–92.

As a means of dealing with the modern phenomenon of multiparty, multidistrict litigation arising out of mass torts and other nationwide business activities, the American Law Institute proposed an expansion of the current rules to allow cases filed in different districts to be transferred and consolidated in a single transferee court, which would be given the authority to structure and even sever and retransfer claims in the litigation so as to produce the fair, just, and efficient adjudication of the controversy.

See ALI, Complex Litigation: Statutory Recommendations and Analysis (1994).

2. See Marcus, Confronting the Consolidation Conundrum, 1995 B.Y.U.L.Rev. 879. For an example of modern mass tort consolidation, see In re New York Asbestos Litigation, 149 F.R.D. 490 (S.D.N.Y.1993) (considering and denying motions for separate trials and to reconsider the prior consolidation of six mass tort cases based on asbestos exposure).

3. See 9 C. Wright & A. Miller, Civil § 2382.

4. Ibid. See also Minnesota v. U.S. Steel Corp., 44 F.R.D. 559 (D.Minn.1968); Lumiansky v. Tessier, 213 Mass. 182, 99 N.E. 1051 (1912).

the third category.[5] Actions do not lose their separate identity because of consolidation.[6]

Except for this relatively unimportant constraint, the federal courts have virtually unfettered discretion regarding consolidation.[7] The court can exercise the power to consolidate actions without the consent of the parties,[8] for purposes of trial or merely for pretrial activity,[9] and without the parties being identical in all the actions.[10] In deciding whether to consolidate, the judge will weigh the saving of time and effort that consolidation would produce against any inconvenience, delay or expense that it would cause. Illustratively, in a series of actions that arose entirely out of a private placement of convertible debentures, the court consolidated for trial two actions in which the chief defendant was the same. The court, however, refused to consolidate two other cases involving both issues and parties not raised or named in the consolidated actions.[11]

As might be expected, the three management devices discussed in this section are interrelated and may be employed in conjunction. Separation of claims or issues and severance of claims are particularly interdependent. In fact, the terms frequently are used interchangeably to refer to a court's order dividing a single lawsuit into smaller parts for more efficient processing.[12] Yet there is a clear theoretical distinction

5. See Johnson v. Manhattan Ry. Co., 289 U.S. 479, 496–97, 53 S.Ct. 721, 727–29, 77 L.Ed. 1331 (1933).

6. But compare Roden v. Empire Printing Co., 135 F.Supp. 665, 16 Alaska 28 (1955), affirmed 247 F.2d 8, 17 Alaska 209 (9th Cir.1957).

The possible effects of consolidation on various traditional procedural rights are explored in two articles by Professor Steinman. Steinman, The Effects of Case Consolidation on the Procedural Rights of Litigants: What They Are, What They Might Be Part 1: Justiciability and Jurisdiction (Original and Appellate), 42 UCLA L.Rev. 717 (1995), and Steinman, The Effects of Case Consolidation on the Procedural Rights of Litigants: What They Are, What They Might Be Part II: Non–Jurisdictional Matters, 42 UCLA L.Rev. 967 (1995).

7. See 9 C. Wright & A. Miller, Civil 2d § 2383. At the federal level, the discretion to consolidate exists principally within judicial districts; consolidation is not allowed when suits are filed in different districts. However, the possibility of consolidation may be one factor in the determination of whether an action may be transferred to another district under 28 U.S.C.A. § 1404. Moreover, the consolidation of actions pending in different districts may be ordered for pretrial purposes by the Judicial Panel on Multidistrict Litigation, pursuant to 28

U.S.C.A. § 1407. See § 2.17, above. See also the American Law Institute's proposal, discussed in note 1, above. Some states have similar restrictions, not allowing consolidation if the actions are in different courts. See Horn v. Rincker, 84 Ill.2d 139, 49 Ill. Dec. 315, 417 N.E.2d 1329 (1981). Other states allow consolidation even under those circumstances. West's Ann.Cal.Code Civ. Proc. § 404 et seq. and Rule 1501 et seq.; Mich.Comp.Laws Ann. § 600.6421.

8. See American Photocopy Equipment Co. v. Fair (Inc.), 35 F.R.D. 236 (N.D.Ill. 1963).

9. See MacAlister v. Guterma, 263 F.2d 65 (2d Cir.1958). The court also may join only a few issues out of the entire case. See Mays v. Liberty Mut. Ins. Co., 35 F.R.D. 234 (E.D.Pa.1964).

10. Attala Hydratane Gas, Inc. v. Lowry Tims Co., 41 F.R.D. 164 (N.D.Miss.1966).

11. See also Connell v. Bernstein–Macauley, Inc., 67 F.R.D. 111 (S.D.N.Y.1975).

12. See Fischer & Porter Co. v. Haskett, 51 F.R.D. 305, 306 (E.D.Pa.1970), in which the terms "separate trials" and "severance" are used interchangeably within the same sentence. See also Note, Separate Trial of a Claim or Issue in Modern Pleading: Rule 42(b) of the Federal Rules of Civil Procedure, 39 Minn.L.Rev. 743, 744–45 (1955).

between these two devices.[13] The typical application of separation (oftentimes also referred to as bifurcation) is the division of an action into two or more claims or groups of claims. These groups are tried separately, but a single judgment encompassing the entire original action is rendered. Severance consists of dividing the claims in a single action into separate actions, with independent judgments entered on each of the severed claims.[14]

The question whether separate trials should be ordered is addressed to the trial court's discretion. The test is broad and looks to whether one trial or separate trials will be most convenient, will avoid prejudice, and will minimize expense and delay.[15] Underlying this balancing test is a desire to use the procedure most likely to result in a just final disposition of the litigation.[16] Along these lines, separation cannot be used to deny a party's right to a jury trial on any of the issues. If separation is ordered in a case involving both legal and equitable claims, the issues common to both claims must be tried to a jury first.[17] Only thereafter may the court decide any remaining equitable issues in light of the jury's resolution of the common issues.

A typical use of separation is to divide the issue of liability from that of damages.[18] Especially when one or both of these issues are to be determined by a jury, separation helps to ensure that the emotional impact of evidence regarding the extent of injury suffered by the plaintiff will not affect the decision on the defendant's fault.[19] According to one study, the separation of liability from damage issues resulted in a significantly greater percentage of defendant victories than occurred in cases that were not bifurcated.[20] This finding strongly suggests that juries in fact are moved by sympathy when they have heard evidence of

---

13. See 9 C. Wright & A. Miller, Civil 2d § 2387.

14. See the discussion in In re Plumbing Fixture Cases, 298 F.Supp. 484, 490 (Jud.Pan.Mult.Lit.1968).

15. See 9 C. Wright & A. Miller, Civil 2d § 2388. See also Ammesmaki v. Interlake S.S. Co., 342 F.2d 627 (7th Cir.1965).

16. See the extensive discussion in Eichinger v. Fireman's Fund Ins. Co., 20 F.R.D. 204 (D.Neb.1957). See also Montana ex rel. Stenberg v. Nelson, 157 Mont. 310, 486 P.2d 870 (1971).

17. See § 11.5, below, on the right to jury trial.

18. E.g., Beeck v. Aquaslide 'N' Dive Corp., 562 F.2d 537 (8th Cir.1977); Kushner v. Hendon Constr., Inc., 81 F.R.D. 93 (M.D.Pa.1979), affirmed without opinion 609 F.2d 501 (3d Cir.1979); Morley v. Superior Ct. of Arizona In and For Maricopa County, 131 Ariz. 85, 638 P.2d 1331 (1981); Kaiser Steel Corp. v. Westinghouse Elec.

Corp., 55 Cal.App.3d 737, 127 Cal.Rptr. 838 (1976).

19. See Granholm & Richards, Bifurcated Justice: How Trial–Splitting Devices Defeat the Jury's Role, 26 U.Tol.L.Rev. 505 (1995); Henderson, Bertram & Toke, Optimal Issue Separation in Modern Products Liability Litigation, 73 Texas L.Rev. 1653 (1995); Comment, Implications of Bifurcation in the Ordinary Negligence Case, 26 U.Pitt.L.Rev. 99, 107–10 (1964). See, e.g., In re Bendectin Litigation, 857 F.2d 290 (6th Cir.1988), cert. denied 488 U.S. 1006. Compare In re Beverly Hills Fire Litigation, 695 F.2d 207, 217 (6th Cir.1982), cert. denied 461 U.S. 929 (bifurcation may create a sterile, laboratory environment), and Comment, Polyfurcation and the Right to a Civil Jury Trial: Little Grace in the Woburn Case, 25 B.C.Envtl.Aff.L.Rev. 649 (1998).

20. Rosenberg, Court Congestion: Status, Causes, and Proposed Remedies, in The Courts, The Public and the Law Explosion 29, 49 (Jones ed.1965).

the extent of plaintiff's injuries and that this influences their decisions on the liability issue.

The use of separation to eliminate influences of this type illustrates one of its underlying policies—the desire to avoid what is thought to be prejudice to one of the parties.[21] In other cases, bifurcation acknowledges a second policy—the desire to improve judicial economy by adjudicating first issues that may dispose of the entire action. For example, if the fact-finder first determines that the defendant is not liable, there will be no need to resolve the issue of damages.[22]

Any party may move for separation, or the court may order separation on its own motion.[23] Ideally, the decision should be made at the pretrial conference stage,[24] although it may be made later; it would be inconsistent to impose strict time requirements on what is in other respects a discretionary matter. In most jurisdictions, an appeal from a decision on a motion for separate trials is not likely to succeed inasmuch as the order is not a final judgment and therefore cannot be appealed immediately.[25] Therefore, the only way in which to challenge such an order is by an appeal following final judgment on the ground that the separation was prejudicial to a party.[26] Even in jurisdictions that do allow an immediate appeal, the appeal is not likely to succeed because of the discretionary nature of the trial court's finding.[27]

The third procedural device mentioned, severance of claims, is permitted whenever it appears that the continued joint litigation of actions would be inefficient or prejudicial.[28] Severance is most useful when party joinder, although appropriate, produces a lawsuit that would be cumbersome to prosecute and adjudicate if left in that form. For example, in one case the court permitted the severance of claims of two properly joined plaintiffs in order to permit a defendant to implead one

---

21. See 9 C. Wright & A. Miller, Civil 2d § 2390. In light of this purpose, separation should not be ordered if the issues are so interwoven that their independent submission to a single jury would cause prejudice. See Williams v. Adams, 46 A.D.2d 952, 362 N.Y.S.2d 68 (1974).

22. See, e.g., McKinney's 1983 New York Rules of Court § 699.14.

One early study concluded that cases handled in this fashion take twenty percent less time than cases in which the liability and damage issues are submitted to the jury simultaneously. See Zeisel & Callahan, Split Trials and Time Savings: A Statistical Analysis, 76 Harv.L.Rev. 1606, 1619 (1963).

23. Moss v. Associated Transport, Inc., 33 F.R.D. 335 (D.Tenn.1963), affirmed 344 F.2d 23 (6th Cir.1965); Rosen v. Rosen, 78 A.D.2d 911, 432 N.Y.S.2d 921 (1980).

24. American Mach. & Metals, Inc. v. De Bothezat Impeller Co., 8 F.R.D. 459 (S.D.N.Y.1948).

25. Courts have rebuffed attempts to obtain review of a separation order under the collateral order doctrine, see Travelers Indem. Co. v. Miller Mfg. Co., 276 F.2d 955 (6th Cir.1960), or by extraordinary writ, see Regec v. Thornton, 275 F.2d 801 (6th Cir. 1960). See generally Chapter 13, below.

26. See, e.g., United Air Lines, Inc. v. Wiener, 286 F.2d 302 (9th Cir.1961), cert. denied 366 U.S. 924.

27. See generally Korn, Civil Jurisdiction of the New York Court of Appeals and Appellate Divisions, 16 Buffalo L.Rev. 307 (1967).

28. See 7 C. Wright, A. Miller & M. Kane, Civil 2d § 1689. Severance also can embrace the procedure for dropping or adding parties as a remedy for misjoinder or nonjoinder.

of them under Federal Rule 14.[29] The defendant could not have impleaded the plaintiff in the original action because the federal rule bars impleading someone who is a "party to the action." But, after the court had severed the plaintiffs' claims for independent adjudication, the defendant was able to implead the original plaintiff as a new defendant in the separate action. In this way, the court protected the defendant's right of contribution and promoted a more efficient processing of the case. As this illustration suggests, severance shares many of the characteristics and underlying policies of separation of claims.[30]

Another typical application of severance occurs when a defendant who has been joined properly objects to the venue of the court. If persuaded that venue is not proper, the court can sever the claims against the objecting party.[31] Even when venue is proper as to all defendants, the court may sever a claim against a party and transfer it to a more convenient forum or it may sever an unrelated claim and give it separate treatment when doing so would be in the interest of some or all of the parties.[32]

Because of the interrelationship between severance and claim joinder, the former procedure must be interpreted in conjunction with the claim joinder provisions found in modern procedural rules. For example, if the claims in the preceding illustration were severed, a court could order the severed action consolidated for trial in a location where venue would be proper or could permit additional claims to be joined.[33] Similarly, particularly in the federal context, the court could transfer the severed action to another court where venue would be proper.[34]

B. PARTIES TO THE ACTION

§ 6.3 Who Is a Proper Party—Real Parties in Interest, Capacity to Sue, and Standing

A threshold issue in all civil litigation is whether the parties to the action meet the necessary criteria to warrant them invoking the judicial process. This question involves several different considerations. In particular, it is necessary to determine (1) whether the party is a "real party in interest"; (2) whether the parties have the legal "capacity" to sue or be sued; and (3) whether the plaintiff has "standing." An examination of each of these requirements follows.

---

29. Sporia v. Pennsylvania Greyhound Lines, Inc., 143 F.2d 105 (3d Cir.1944).

30. See the discussion accompanying notes 15–22, above.

31. See Wyndham Assocs. v. Bintliff, 398 F.2d 614 (2d Cir.1968), cert. denied 393 U.S. 977 (district court severed claims against one or more defendants for the purpose of permitting transfer of the action against the other defendants).

32. E.g., International Patent Dev. Corp. v. Wyomont Partners, 489 F.Supp. 226 (D.Nev.1980).

33. See the discussion of claim joinder in § 6.6, below. For a discussion of when the claim against the objecting party should be dismissed and when it should be transferred to another district, see Goldberg v. Wharf Constructers, 209 F.Supp. 499, 508 (N.D.Ala.1962).

34. See, e.g., O'Shatz v. Bailey, 220 F.Supp. 444 (D.Md.1963).

Although the real party in interest requirement most commonly is applied to original plaintiffs, any party asserting a claim—for instance, intervenors, cross-claimants, or counterclaimants—must be shown to be the real party in interest with regard to that particular claim.[1] In general, the rule insists that the named plaintiff possess, under the governing substantive law, the right sought to be enforced.[2] It does not speak to what parties must be joined to the action; it merely ensures that those present are proper parties.[3]

Historically, the real party in interest concept was applied more restrictively in law than in equity. Only someone with legal title to the right affected by the defendant's conduct could sue at law; in equity anyone whose equitable or beneficial rights were at issue could sue.[4] Under modern procedure, the real party in interest need not be the person who ultimately will benefit from the successful prosecution of the action,[5] a factor that often complicates the identification of the real party in interest. The court first must ascertain the nature of the substantive right being asserted and then must determine whether the party asserting that right is recognized as the real party in interest under the forum's procedural code. That a party stands to gain from the litigation is not necessarily controlling.

A good illustration is an action under a state wrongful death statute. In Pennsylvania, for example, the real party in interest is restricted by statute to only certain persons, namely spouses, children or parents of the deceased.[6] No other relatives qualify under the statute as real parties in interest. The personal representative of the estate can sue only if none of the other specified parties exist and then is limited in the type of recovery that can be obtained to special damages.[7]

The assignment of choses in action provides another common context for real party in interest questions. In order to determine who is a real party in interest, the court first must ascertain what has been assigned to decide whether the assignee has a legally cognizable claim.[8]

---

§ 6.3

1. 6A C. Wright, A. Miller & M. Kane, Civil 2d § 1543.

2. Ellis Canning Co. v. International Harvester Co., 174 Kan. 357, 255 P.2d 658 (1953).

3. If a partial assignment is involved, for example, it is necessary to consider whether the plaintiff—a partial assignee—is a real party in interest and then to consider whether joinder rules require the assignor also to be present. See Boris v. Moore, 152 F.Supp. 595 (E.D.Wis.1957), affirmed on other grounds 253 F.2d 523 (7th Cir.1958). The rules governing compulsory joinder of parties are discussed in § 6.5, below.

4. 6A C. Wright, A. Miller & M. Kane, Civil 2d § 1541.

5. Race v. Hay, 28 F.R.D. 354 (N.D.Ind.1961). At common law, if the action was for the benefit of another, the plaintiff would sue "for the use of" the beneficiary. See C. Clark, Code Pleading § 21 (2d ed.1947).

6. 42 Penn.Stat. § 8301(b).

7. 42 Penn.Stat. § 8301(d).

8. If what was assigned is not sufficiently connected with the claim for relief, the assignee cannot use the assignment as the basis for the action. See Farm Bureau Co-op. Mill & Supply, Inc. v. Blue Star Foods, Inc., 238 F.2d 326 (8th Cir.1956) (assignment of chattel mortgage did not transfer tort claim arising out of alleged conversion of mortgaged property).

Then, the court must determine if the purported assignment is valid.[9] In this sense, whether a party claiming to possess an assigned claim is a real party in interest ultimately rests on the substantive law governing the assignability of the chose in action. For example, if a retail firm assigns to a bank its right to collect the contract price for a particular sale and the contract is not performed, the bank may sue for breach, but the merchant may not. The merchant no longer has a substantive right to demand performance of the contract and therefore no longer is the real party in interest.

In the federal courts, the real party in interest requirement is found in Federal Rule 17(a), which provides that "every action shall be prosecuted in the name of the real party in interest."[10] Most other procedural systems contain the same general directive.[11] Almost all provisions also offer more specific guidelines regarding certain legal relations. Federal Rule 17(a), for example, states that executors, administrators, guardians, bailees, trustees, and parties to contracts made for the benefit of others may sue in their own names without joining the party for whose benefit the action is maintained.

The value of the real party in interest rule is a matter of some dispute. Those who support the rule maintain that a defendant must be allowed to insist upon being opposed by the real party in interest in order to be protected from further suits regarding the same claim.[12] Under this rationale, the requirement benefits defendants because "the defendant can insist upon a plaintiff who will afford him a setup providing good res judicata protection if the struggle is carried through on the merits to the end."[13] This argument is undercut, however, by the fact that the defendant always may move to dismiss should the plaintiff not have a right to relief under the applicable substantive law. It is difficult to see what a formal real party in interest rule adds to this procedure.

Not surprisingly, therefore, some commentators argue that the rule is superfluous and misleading.[14] They contend that substantive law,

---

9. For example, some states do not allow the assignment of tort claims. Young v. Garrett, 149 F.2d 223 (8th Cir.1945). Under the Anti–Assignment Act, 31 U.S.C.A. § 3727, claims against the United States cannot be assigned.

10. For a detailed examination of the application of the real party in interest rule in various contexts, see 6A C. Wright, A. Miller & M. Kane, Civil 2d §§ 1541–58.

One exception to the need to name the real party in interest occurs when courts allow a plaintiff to prosecute an action under a fictitious name to protect confidentiality. E.g., Coe v. U.S. District Ct. for District of Colorado, 676 F.2d 411 (10th Cir.1982); Doe v. State Bar of California, 415 F.Supp. 308, 309 n. 1 (N.D.Cal.1976), affirmed on other grounds 582 F.2d 25 (9th Cir.1978).

See generally Steinman, Public Trial, Pseudonymous Parties: When Should Litigants Be Permitted to Keep Their Identities Confidential?, 37 Hast.L.J. 1 (1985).

11. E.g., Kan.Stat.Ann. 60–217(a); Mich.Comp.Laws Ann. § 600.2041.

12. See the Advisory Committee Note to the 1966 Amendment to Rule 17(a), reprinted in 39 F.R.D. 84–85 (1966).

13. Kaplan, Continuing Work of the Civil Committee: 1966 Amendments of the Federal Rules of Civil Procedure, 81 Harv. L.Rev. 356, 412 (1967).

14. See, e.g., Atkinson, Real Party in Interest: A Plea for Its Abolition, 32 N.Y.U.L.Rev. 926 (1957); Entman, More Reasons for Abolishing Federal Rule of Civil

rather than parallel procedural directives, should be the basis for analyzing whether the proper party has brought the action. In some jurisdictions, this view has prevailed.[15]

The real party in interest requirement is tactically important to some litigants because of the effect that the identity of the claimant may have upon the jury. An insurance company in a personal injury case may prefer that its insured be the plaintiff on the theory that the jury will be more sympathetic to an individual. To achieve this objective, the insurance company may indemnify the insured for all but a relatively small amount of the policyholder's claim or provide indemnification in the form of a "loan." The insured thereby would retain a substantive right to sue, continuing to be a real party in interest, and the insurance company would not be required to appear in the action at all.

In the federal courts, real party in interest questions often present complicated choice of law problems.[16] This is well illustrated by the common situation, just mentioned, when an insurance company seeks to maintain the insured's status as the real party in interest in a personal injury case by indemnifying through the means of a "loan receipt."[17] In order for a federal diversity court to determine whether the insured is the real party in interest, it must look to the law of the forum state to decide whether the insured still retains a substantive right to relief. When the loan arrangement is sanctioned by state law, the federal courts have accepted the parties' characterization of the loan receipt and have held the insured to be the real party in interest.[18] By way of contrast, under federal question jurisdiction, federal substantive law would be applied to determine who possessed the right to sue and, under United States v. Aetna Casualty & Surety Company,[19] the federal court probably would hold that the loan receipt arrangement did not avoid total indemnification and that the insurer was the real party in interest.

On occasion, even when the federal court is exercising federal question jurisdiction, state substantive law is applied to determine who is the real party in interest. For example, state law controls when the federal law or regulation that forms the jurisdictional basis for the action merely has created a federal remedy for a traditional state-created right of action.[20] In contrast, when the claim is based on a law that creates a

---

Procedure 17(a): The Problem of the Proper Plaintiff and Insurance Subrogation, 68 N.C.L.Rev. 893, 920 (1990).

15. E.g., New York. See 2 J. Weinstein, H. Korn & A. Miller, New York Civil Practice ¶ 1004.01.

16. For a discussion of choice of law problems in the federal courts, see Chapter 4, above. Not only may the court face questions whether federal or state law governs various aspects of the real party in interest issue, but also a choice between different state standards may be presented. See, e.g., Koepp v. Northwest Freight Lines, 10 F.R.D. 524 (D.Minn.1950).

17. See Boynton, The Myth of the 'Loan Receipt' Revisited under Rule 17(a), 18 S.C.L.Rev. 624 (1966).

18. See Watsontown Brick Co. v. Hercules Powder Co., 201 F.Supp. 343 (M.D.Pa. 1962).

19. 338 U.S. 366, 70 S.Ct. 207, 94 L.Ed. 171 (1949). See also the Anti–Assignment Act, 31 U.S.C.A. § 3729.

20. See Hoeppner Constr. Co. v. U.S. for Use of Mangum, 287 F.2d 108 (10th Cir.1960) (action under Miller Act); U.S. for Use & Benefit of Allen Constr. Corp. v. Verrier, 179 F.Supp. 336 (D.Me.1959) (ac-

new federal cause of action, federal substantive law normally will be invoked in deciding the real party in interest question.[21]

In either case, state procedural rules are irrelevant to the real party in interest determination. If a state provision concerning in whose name an action may be brought to enforce the right of a subrogee conflicts with the federal rules, Rule 17(a) is controlling. Consequently, a party who could not bring the action in his own name in state court may be able to do so in federal court.[22]

Since a challenge that the action has not been brought by the real party in interest presents a threshold defense, it should be raised in the answer or by a preliminary motion.[23] In any event, the objection should be raised as soon as possible. If the objection is not interposed early, it may be considered waived.[24] The general trend seems to be to allow the courts as much discretion as possible in handling a real party in interest objection, as well as any delays in raising it. In one case, for example, an objection was deemed untimely when it was made four days before trial in a case that had been filed two years earlier.[25] But this need not always be the result. The test, as in other cases in which unreasonable delay is claimed, should be whether the opposing party has been prejudiced.[26]

Even if an objection to the plaintiff's real party in interest status is sustained, the defect may not be fatal. The court usually will allow a reasonable time for the substitution or joinder of the real party in interest.[27] Further, an amendment substituting the real party in interest typically will be allowed to relate back to the date of the original filing of

---

tion under Miller Act). The same rationale would apply to suits under the Federal Tort Claims Act, since that statute contains no standard for determining the liability of the United States; it merely incorporates state tort law and applies it to federal employees.

21. See Etherington v. Hardee, 290 F.2d 28 (5th Cir.1961) (Patent Act). For a further discussion of the decisions under the Patent Act, see 6A C. Wright, A. Miller & M. Kane, Civil 2d § 1547.

22. See 6A C. Wright, A. Miller & M. Kane, Civil 2d § 1544.

23. See, e.g., Blau v. Lamb, 314 F.2d 618 (2d Cir.1963), cert. denied 375 U.S. 813; Powers v. Ashton, 45 Cal.App.3d 783, 119 Cal.Rptr. 729 (1975); Ellis Canning Co. v. International Harvester Co., 174 Kan. 357, 255 P.2d 658 (1953); Or.Rules Civ. Proc., Rule 21A.

The court's power to raise the objection sua sponte is unclear. Compare U.S. Fidelity & Guar. Co. v. Slifkin, 200 F.Supp. 563 (N.D.Ala.1961) (a court should not raise the objection itself), with General Inv. & Serv. Corp. v. Wichita Water Co., 236 F.2d 464 (10th Cir.1956) (dictum) (objection should be raised sua sponte).

24. The court's characterization of the real party in interest objection may influence the decision on waiver. See, e.g., E. Brooke Matlack, Inc. v. Walrath, 24 F.R.D. 263 (D.Md.1959) (objection equivalent to challenge for failure to plead capacity); Kincaid v. City of Anchorage, 99 F.Supp. 1017, 13 Alaska 285 (1951) (motion analogous to one to dismiss for failure to join an indispensable party).

25. McLouth Steel Corp. v. Mesta Mach. Co., 116 F.Supp. 689 (E.D.Pa.1953), affirmed on other grounds 214 F.2d 608 (3d Cir.1954), cert. denied 348 U.S. 873. See also Hefley v. Jones, 687 F.2d 1383 (10th Cir.1982).

26. See Pace v. General Elec. Co., 55 F.R.D. 215 (W.D.Pa.1972); U.S. Fidelity & Guar. Co. v. Slifkin, 200 F.Supp. 563 (N.D.Ala.1961).

27. See Fed.Civ.Proc.Rule 17(a). See also the Advisory Committee's Note to the 1966 Amendment to Rule 17(a), reprinted in 39 F.R.D. 84, 85. The failure to cure the defect in a reasonable time may be fatal, however. E.g., Weissman v. Weener, 12 F.3d 84 (7th Cir.1993).

the action in order to escape the statute of limitations.[28] Only if the real party in interest is not substituted, will the action be dismissed. But this dismissal is not on the merits; a later action on the same claim may be brought by the real party in interest.[29]

Capacity to sue or be sued refers to an individual's ability to represent her interests in a lawsuit without the assistance of another. In a sense, the requirement reflects a series of "bright line" rules concerning certain categories of persons or entities[30] who are deemed to lack the personal qualifications necessary to litigate. Capacity is determined without regard to the nature of the action—a characteristic that distinguishes it from the real party in interest requirement, which can change depending on the substantive rights at issue. Accordingly, a plaintiff may possess a legal right under the substantive law but be barred from suing because her age indicates a lack of capacity; another plaintiff may have a direct stake in the outcome of the dispute and not be entitled to bring the action under the law of his domicile because he is represented by a guardian.

In general, incapacity can be organized along two functional lines: (1) incapacity based on physio-psychological condition, and (2) incapacity due to organizational status or legal relationship. Court treatment of those incapacitated differs according to the categories they fall into. Typically, those who lack capacity because of their physical or psychological condition—for example, infants or the mentally incompetent—are regarded as wards of the court and the court will appoint a party to represent them.[31] Those deprived of capacity because of their status as organizations[32] or representatives—for example, labor unions or receivers in some jurisdictions—do not receive this special treatment. No surrogate will be appointed; they must sue or be sued in different forums or qualify to litigate on some other basis.[33]

---

28. The key factors in deciding whether to allow an amendment substituting the real party in interest will be whether the delay will prejudice the defendant, see Crowder v. Gordons Transports, Inc., 387 F.2d 413, 418–19 (8th Cir.1967), and whether the plaintiff has some reasonable excuse for the error as to the real party in interest, see Hobbs v. Police Jury of Morehouse Parish, 49 F.R.D. 176 (W.D.La.1970). For a general discussion of the relation back of amendments, see § 5.27, above.

29. Ronsick v. Phariss, 286 F.2d 316, 318 (10th Cir.1960).

30. The most common categories of parties who may lack capacity are: infants; the mentally incompetent; married women, although this was true only under the common law; convicts and alien enemies (who are sometimes only denied capacity to sue but can *be* sued); individuals acting in representative capacities in jurisdictions other than that of their appointment; foreign and dissolved corporations; and partnerships and unincorporated associations. For a more detailed discussion of these categories, see 6A C. Wright, A. Miller & M. Kane, Civil 2d §§ 1559–70.

31. See the discussion of measures that federal courts will take to protect such parties in 6A C. Wright, A. Miller & M. Kane, Civil 2d § 1570.

32. This is the common law rule for all unincorporated associations. See Kaplan, Suits Against Unincorporated Associations under the Federal Rules, 43 Mich.L.Rev. 945 (1955). Examples of statutes changing the common law rule are N.Y.—McKinney's General Association Law § 13; N.C.Gen. Stat. § 1–69.1.

33. See 6A C. Wright, A. Miller & M. Kane, Civil 2d § 1564, discussing the efficacy of using class actions against partnerships and unincorporated associations.

The different treatment accorded the two classes of parties reflects the disparate policies giving rise to their incapacities. There is a desire to protect individuals in the first group who cannot be expected to act for themselves. With regard to those in the latter class, the forum simply is carrying out policies designed to control the litigation activities of certain types of organizations.[34]

The possibility always exists that a party will gain or lose the capacity to sue or be sued during the course of litigation. When a litigant who formerly lacked capacity sheds the disability, most jurisdictions hold that the authority of the guardian, whether appointed by the court or not, terminates.[35] Conversely, when a party loses capacity during litigation, the suit should be dismissed. For example, in Mather Construction Company v. United States,[36] approximately twenty days after filing its claim, the plaintiff corporation was suspended under state law for failing to pay its taxes. The court dismissed the action because the suspension rendered the corporation "incompetent" to bring suit. Capacity, the court held, "is not only the power to bring an action, but is also the power to maintain it."[37]

In the federal courts, the issue of capacity is governed primarily by state law.[38] Federal Rule 17(b) provides that the capacity of an individual, other than one acting in a representative capacity, is determined by the law of the individual's domicile; the capacity of a corporation is determined by the law under which it was organized, and in all other cases, with only a few minor exceptions, capacity is determined by the law of the state in which the district court is sitting. There are only two exceptions to the applicability of state law: (1) partnerships and unincorporated associations that lack capacity under state law can sue under a common name in federal question cases,[39] and (2) federal receivers have special capacity under the United States Code, even if they lack capacity under state laws.[40] Thus, the Federal Rule serves as an accommodation between those desiring local rules to govern capacity matters and those advocating uniform national standards to determine access to the federal courts.[41]

34. For an interesting case study of policies and implementing rules in Florida, see Note, Hazards of Enforcing Claims Against Unincorporated Associations in Florida, 17 U.Fla.L.Rev. 211 (1964).

35. As a matter of practice, the court should be asked to remove the representative by a timely motion. Ju Shu Cheung v. Dulles, 16 F.R.D. 550 (D.Mass.1954).

36. 201 Ct.Cl. 219, 475 F.2d 1152 (1973).

37. 475 F.2d at 1155.

38. For a complete discussion of capacity in the federal courts, see 6A C. Wright, A. Miller & M. Kane, Civil 2d §§ 1559–73.

39. This policy is derived from the landmark case of United Mine Workers of America v. Coronado Coal Co., 259 U.S. 344, 42 S.Ct. 570, 66 L.Ed. 975 (1922). See 6A C. Wright, A. Miller & M. Kane, Civil 2d § 1564.

40. See 2 U.S.C.A. §§ 754, 959(a). A state receiver's capacity is determined by the law of the forum state. See 6A C. Wright, A. Miller & M. Kane, Civil 2d § 1567.

41. See Van Dusen v. Barrack, 376 U.S. 612, 642, 84 S.Ct. 805, 822, 11 L.Ed.2d 945 (1964); Clark & Moore, A New Federal Civil Procedure II. Pleadings and Parties, 44 Yale L.J. 1291, 1312–17 (1935).

Unfortunately, the governing law question on capacity matters can become more complicated when the forum state's law varies from the law referred to in the Federal Rule.[42] The leading decision on this issue is Woods v. Interstate Realty Company[43] decided in 1949. In Woods, the Supreme Court held that a corporation organized in Tennessee could not sue a Mississippian in a Mississippi federal court when the action would have been barred in a Mississippi state court, despite the fact that the corporation had capacity under the law of the state in which it was organized. The corporation did not qualify under Mississippi's corporate capacity rules because it had failed to register to do business there.

The subsequent Supreme Court decision in Hanna v. Plumer,[44] which held that, unless it clearly violates the Rules Enabling Act,[45] a federal procedural rule should be applied in diversity cases,[46] may affect the precedential value of the Woods decision, however.[47] The second sentence of Federal Rule 17(b) clearly refers corporate capacity questions to the law under which the corporation is organized, not the forum state. Nonetheless, when the forum has expressed important policies in the context of its capacity rules, the proper resolution seems to be to require the action to meet both the law referred to in Rule 17(b) and the law of the forum. In this way a conflict between the laws is avoided and the regulatory interests of the forum state are fostered.

Because capacity rarely is challenged, most contemporary procedural systems do not require the plaintiff to establish the parties' capacity to sue or be sued at the outset of the action.[48] If a party's capacity is in doubt, a challenge must be raised by the opposing party by means of a specific negative averment; the issue will be waived if not raised in the answer or by a preliminary motion before trial.[49]

42. See 6A C. Wright, A. Miller & M. Kane, Civil 2d § 1569. Questions of governing law in the federal courts are discussed in more detail in Chapter 4, above.

43. 337 U.S. 535, 69 S.Ct. 1235, 93 L.Ed. 1524 (1949).

44. 380 U.S. 460, 85 S.Ct. 1136, 14 L.Ed.2d 8 (1965). The Hanna Court distinguished Woods as involving "a situation where application of the state rule would wholly bar recovery." Id. at 469, 85 S.Ct. at 1143. In Hanna, application of the state rule "would have resulted only in altering the way in which process was served." Ibid.

45. 28 U.S.C.A. § 2072.

46. For a discussion of the Hanna case, see § 4.4, above.

47. See, e.g., Stock West, Inc. v. Confederated Tribes of the Colville Reservation, 873 F.2d 1221 (9th Cir.1989).

48. Parties typically need not plead capacity, unless it is necessary to show the court's jurisdiction. Fed.Civ.Proc.Rule 9(a); West's Fla.Stat.Ann.Rules Civ.Proc.Rule 1.120(a); Official Code Ga.Ann. § 9-11-18(a); Minn.Rules Civ.Proc., Rule 9.01. But compare Vernon's Ann.Mo.Civ.Proc.Rule 55.13 ("sufficient to aver ultimate fact of capacity").

49. 5 C. Wright & A. Miller, Civil 2d §§ 1294-95. This practice is typical in most common law and code pleading jurisdictions. Society for Propagation of the Gospel v. Town of Pawlet, 29 U.S. (4 Pet.) 480, 7 L.Ed. 927 (1830); C. Clark, Code Pleading § 50 (2d ed.1947).

A minority of courts have treated capacity as a subject-matter jurisdiction requirement. E.g., Pasos v. Eastern S.S. Co., 9 F.R.D. 279 (D.Del.1949); Clemente Engineering Co. v. DeLiso Constr. Co., 53 F.Supp. 434 (D.Conn.1944). Under this approach capacity objections never are waived. That result is clearly inconsistent with the intentions of the drafters of Federal Rule 9(a) and its many state counterparts and thus is wrong. See 6A C. Wright, A. Miller & M. Kane, Civil 2d § 1559.

In addition to the threshold requirements of real party in interest and capacity, a party must have "standing" to sue—a doctrine typically in issue when the plaintiff seeks to challenge a statute or an executive or administrative decision by a governmental agency.[50] Like the principle of judicial noninvolvement in political questions, the judge-made standing rule is a control mechanism used to limit the types of issues that may be brought before the courts.[51] The policy considerations that underlie this notion of judicial restraint cannot be given full treatment in this work.[52] Nonetheless, these issues must be kept in mind when dealing with the procedural aspects of the standing requirement.

Although considered primarily a federal doctrine, the standing concept also is employed by state courts, with its most common application being taxpayer suits. Nearly all states permit taxpayers to bring suits to challenge expenditures by municipalities.[53] A smaller number of states also permit taxpayers to contest state spending decisions in their courts.[54] Although this discrepancy may appear peculiar, it reflects the states' perception of the proper role of the courts in reviewing legislative and executive decisions.[55]

In the federal courts, standing has gained importance and considerable publicity because of the increasing number of challenges to federal regulatory and executive decisions regarding consumer and environmental matters and the expenditure of public funds. Unfortunately, federal standing doctrine is in a nebulous state. As Justice Douglas commented: "Generalizations about standing to sue are largely worthless as such."[56]

One principle with regard to the federal courts that can be stated with some confidence, however, is that all standing issues are rooted in the constitutional restriction that courts may adjudicate only "cases or controversies."[57] If a federal court decides that the party bringing the

---

50. Standing has received extensive attention from the commentators. For an interesting historical and theoretical overview, see Jaffe, Standing to Secure Judicial Review: Public Actions, 74 Harv.L.Rev. 1265 (1961), and Comment, Taxpayers' Suits: A Survey and Summary, 69 Yale L.J. 895 (1959). See also L. Tribe, American Constitutional Law §§ 3–14—3–21 (1988).

51. Warth v. Seldin, 422 U.S. 490, 519, 95 S.Ct. 2197, 2215, 45 L.Ed.2d 343 (1975) (Douglas, J., dissenting).

52. A fuller discussion can be found in 13 and 13A C. Wright, A. Miller & E. Cooper, Jurisdiction and Related Matters 2d §§ 3529–35.

53. An interesting application of this power is Wirin v. Parker, 48 Cal.2d 890, 313 P.2d 844 (1957) (Los Angeles taxpayer granted standing to sue police commissioner to prevent expenditure of public funds for electronic eavesdropping equipment). For a contrasting opinion in a surveillance case in the federal system, see Laird v.

Tatum, 408 U.S. 1, 92 S.Ct. 2318, 33 L.Ed.2d 154 (1972).

54. See Jaffe, Standing to Secure Judicial Review: Public Actions, 74 Harv.L.Rev. 1265, 1278 (1961).

55. See the discussion in Comment, Taxpayers' Suits: A Survey and Summary, 69 Yale L.J. 895, 902 (1959). No jurisdiction has gone so far as to allow "citizen standing"; some connection with the subject of the action, at least through payment of taxes that are used in part in the contested program, must be alleged. See 13 C. Wright, A. Miller & E. Cooper, Jurisdiction and Related Matters 2d § 3531.10.

56. Association of Data Processing Serv. Organizations, Inc. v. Camp, 397 U.S. 150, 151, 90 S.Ct. 827, 829, 25 L.Ed.2d 184 (1970).

57. "Article III's requirement remains: the plaintiff still must allege a distinct and palpable injury to himself, even if it is an injury shared by a larger class of other

action is not associated sufficiently with the controversy, the court is prohibited by Article III from hearing the action. Courts therefore are obliged to approach the problem on a case-by-case basis. In some instances, separate standing determinations may be required for several parts of a single case; a party may have standing to challenge some aspects of a public act or activity, but not others.[58] The constitutional foundation of standing converts what otherwise would appear to be a routine threshold issue into one of fundamental importance in certain types of litigation.

In addition to constitutional restrictions, several policy considerations are involved in standing.[59] The importance of the prudential aspects of standing, as well as the standards for determining whether those objectives are satisfied has varied over time.[60] The current standard is the two-part test announced by the Supreme Court in the companion cases of Association of Data Processing Service Organizations, Inc. v. Camp,[61] and Barlow v. Collins.[62] To have standing, a plaintiff must show: (1) that the challenged conduct has caused injury in fact, and (2) that the interest sought to be protected is within the zone of interests to be protected or regulated by the statutory or constitutional guarantee in question.

The second part of this test, known as the "zone of protection standard," is still ill-defined, but indications exist that it will be satisfied whenever there is no special reason to deny standing.[63] Consequently, the first part of the standing test remains the most important. Several Supreme Court cases, including Sierra Club v. Morton,[64] United States v. Students Challenging Regulatory Agency Procedures (SCRAP),[65] and

possible litigants." Warth v. Seldin, 422 U.S. 490, 501, 95 S.Ct. 2197, 2206, 45 L.Ed.2d 343 (1975) (Powell, J.).

58. See, e.g., Ray Baillie Trash Hauling, Inc. v. Kleppe, 477 F.2d 696 (5th Cir. 1973), cert. denied 415 U.S. 914 (refuse haulers have standing to challenge the institution, but not the actual administration, of a Small Business Administration program to help minority businesses).

59. See Warth v. Seldin, 422 U.S. 490, 498–99, 95 S.Ct. 2197, 2205, 45 L.Ed.2d 343 (1975); Massachusetts v. Mellon, 262 U.S. 447, 448–89, 43 S.Ct. 597, 601, 67 L.Ed. 1078 (1923).

60. In Massachusetts v. Mellon, 262 U.S. 447, 43 S.Ct. 597, 67 L.Ed. 1078 (1923), the Supreme Court established the "direct injury" standard: a plaintiff did not have standing unless she could show that defendant's conduct produced a direct injury to her. The next step in the evolution of standing doctrine was the adoption of the "legal rights" test. See Tennessee Elec. Power Co. v. TVA, 306 U.S. 118, 59 S.Ct. 366, 83 L.Ed. 543 (1939). Plaintiff had to

have a claim that was cognizable under an existing statute or the case law; plaintiff challenging a government decision had to show that his injury would support recovery if he had brought a similar action against a private party. Additional gloss was added to this standard in Baker v. Carr, 369 U.S. 186, 82 S.Ct. 691, 7 L.Ed.2d 663 (1962), and Flast v. Cohen, 392 U.S. 83, 88 S.Ct. 1942, 20 L.Ed.2d 947 (1968). These standards are all now subsumed under the two-part test discussed in text at notes 61–70, below.

61. 397 U.S. 150, 90 S.Ct. 827, 25 L.Ed.2d 184 (1970).

62. 397 U.S. 159, 90 S.Ct. 832, 25 L.Ed.2d 192 (1970).

63. This is the conclusion reached in Sedler, Standing, Justiciability, and All That: A Behavioral Analysis, 25 Vand. L.Rev. 479 (1972).

64. 405 U.S. 727, 92 S.Ct. 1361, 31 L.Ed.2d 636 (1972).

65. 412 U.S. 669, 93 S.Ct. 2405, 37 L.Ed.2d 254 (1973).

Warth v. Seldin,[66] have turned on the "injury" aspect of the standing issue. In the Sierra Club case, plaintiff challenged a licensing agreement between the Department of the Interior and Walt Disney Enterprises, Inc., to develop a part of the Sequoia National Forest into a major ski resort. The Court concluded that the environmentalist group did not have standing because they were not personally injured and the injury alleged was not to a legally protected right.[67] In the SCRAP case, on the other hand, plaintiffs—law students—challenged an ICC decision raising railroad freight rates on the ground that it indirectly would discourage the use of recycled goods. This discouragement allegedly would lead to greater exploitation of forests and other natural resources and would deprive plaintiffs of protectable interests such as the enjoyment of hiking and other outdoor activities.[68] The Court accepted this argument as a basis for standing. In contrast, in Warth the Court decided that taxpayer-plaintiffs did not have standing to contest restrictive zoning in a suburb near Rochester, New York. The zoning regulations allegedly increased the need for subsidized housing in Rochester and therefore increased local taxes.[69] A sharp dissent was filed by four justices.[70]

The evolution of standing doctrine seems to point to greater freedom of action for plaintiffs. However, the courts still have not articulated how the balance is to be struck between the relevant and often competing interests: the plaintiff's right to relief and the legislature's right to carry out its policies without judicial interference. Nor has the judiciary's competence to rule on these interests been analyzed systematically or its limits defined. Courts essentially continue to be free to reconcile these competing values on an ad hoc basis.

It is important to note, however, that standing, because of its constitutional and public policy underpinnings, is very different from questions relating to whether a particular plaintiff is the real party in interest or has capacity to sue. Although all three requirements are directed toward ensuring that only certain parties can maintain an action, standing restrictions also require a partial consideration of the merits, as well as of broader policy concerns relating to the proper role of the judiciary in certain areas.

§ 6.4 Permissive Party Joinder

The traditional legal model is two-party litigation. However, modern transactions frequently embrace more than two individuals and when

66. 422 U.S. 490, 95 S.Ct. 2197, 45 L.Ed.2d 343 (1975).

67. 405 U.S. at 732–33, 92 S.Ct. at 1364–65.

68. 412 U.S. at 678, 93 S.Ct. at 2411. One reaction to the reasoning in the SCRAP case should be noted: "If these be thought gossamer distinctions, we can only rejoin that SCRAP's ingenious law students have caused us to be translated into ethere-al realms, where we must function as best we are able." Florida v. Weinberger, 492 F.2d 488, 495 (5th Cir.1974) (per Gee, J.).

69. Warth v. Seldin, 422 U.S. 490, 95 S.Ct. 2197, 45 L.Ed.2d 343 (1975).

70. Justices Brennan, Douglas, Marshall, and White dissented. 422 U.S. at 518, 95 S.Ct. at 2216.

those transactions go awry or some injury occurs, it becomes necessary to decide what persons properly may be joined in a single lawsuit.

Common-law procedure severely limited the permissive joinder of parties by tying it to the substantive rights of the parties to the action. The interests of plaintiffs were classified as either joint or several: if joint, they could sue in the same action; if several, they could not. Indeed, in most cases in which the rights contested were joint, joinder was compelled, so that there really was no permissive joinder of plaintiffs at all. The common-law rules governing joinder of defendants were somewhat more flexible. Under the rules relating to multiparty liability for torts, a plaintiff could join joint tortfeasors or sue them separately. A plaintiff had the same option with regard to defendants whose contractual obligations were both joint and several. If the defendant obligors were jointly liable, however, they had to be sued jointly.[1]

The equity courts permitted joinder of parties more readily than did the law courts. Rather than resting their determinations on an abstract joint-several classification, equity resolved joinder questions on the basis of the objectives of rendering complete justice among all those whose interests were involved and avoiding multiplicity of actions. Thus, the chancellors permitted all persons having an interest in the subject matter of the action or in the relief sought to join as plaintiffs or defendants in a single action. Moreover, even this liberal formulation was regarded as merely a guide, not an absolute requirement governing party joinder in all cases.[2]

Procedural codes imposed new tests for joinder of parties. Under the early codes some courts held that parties were "proper" and could be joined if their interests in the subject matter and in the relief sought were co-extensive. Thus, two owners of separate but adjacent property could not join to sue a tortfeasor who had injured their respective parcels because both the owners were uninterested in part of the relief sought.[3] This general rule left virtually no room for permissive joinder because nonparties who had an identity of interest with parties already litigating probably would be compelled to join the action under the existing compulsory joinder rules.[4]

Modern party joinder doctrine rejects the absolutism of the early codes. Overlapping interests still are required before a party may be joined under permissive joinder rules, but the extent of the overlap required can be less than total. A brief look at how the permissive joinder requirements are applied illustrates their flexibility.

§ 6.4

1. See C. Clark, Code Pleading §§ 56, 59 (2d ed.1947). See also B. Shipman, Common Law Pleading §§ 226–28 (3d ed.1923).

2. J. Story, Equity Pleadings § 76 (9th ed.1879).

3. Burghen v. Erie R. Co., 123 App.Div. 204, 108 N.Y.S. 311 (1908).

4. C. Clark, Code Pleading § 60 (2d ed.1947). See the historical analysis of the development of permissive joinder in New York in Clark & Wright, The Judicial Council and the Rule–Making Power: A Dissent and a Protest, 1 Syracuse L.Rev. 346 (1950). See also Blume, Joinder of Actions, 26 Mich.L.Rev. 1 (1927).

The first requirement for permissive party joinder under most modern procedural rules is that the persons to be joined must assert or have asserted against them some right to relief arising out of the transaction or occurrence or series of transactions or occurrences that comprise the subject matter of the action. The second requirement is that there must be a question of law or fact common to the parties who are to be joined and those already in the action.[5] In the federal courts,[6] both standards must be met in order to sustain joinder of parties.[7] The two requirements seem straightforward; however, they have been subject to varying interpretations and applications.

Although the first requirement has the advantage of being amenable to flexible application, the case law offers little guidance as to what is a transaction or occurrence. Most courts have used a case-by-case approach determining whether joinder should be permitted depending on the facts of each case,[8] rather than adopting generalized formulas as to when factual similarities are so extensive that the same transaction or occurrence is presented.

Usually, a court applies the transaction or occurrence requirement in a particular case by asking whether there is a logical relationship between the claim involving the party to be joined and the rest of the case.[9] This standard was developed initially as a judicial gloss on the transaction or occurrence standard used under the federal equity rules to determine whether a counterclaim was compulsory.[10] Under the logical relationship test, party joinder may be permitted when there is enough factual overlap so that it would be efficient to have the parties litigate together. "Logical relation" therefore is defined in terms of judicial economy and convenience.

---

5. See Fed.Civ.Proc.Rule 20(a); West's Ann.Cal.Code Civ.Proc. §§ 378(a), 379(a); N.Y.—McKinney's CPLR 1002(a), (b); Vernon's Ann.Texas Rules Civ.Proc., Rule 40. For an illustrative case, see Stone v. Stone, 405 F.2d 94 (4th Cir.1968).

6. State restrictions on joinder generally are inapplicable in the federal courts. For example, the joinder of several tortfeasors as defendants is permissible even though state law permits only joint tortfeasors to be joined. See Siebrand v. Gossnell, 234 F.2d 81 (9th Cir.1956). See also Doyle v. Stanolind Oil & Gas Co., 123 F.2d 900 (5th Cir.1941). In some instances, however, the federal court may honor important state policies restricting joinder. Thus, even though an insured subrogated his rights to the insurance company, the federal court sustained a motion challenging the joinder of the insurer when state substantive law prohibited joinder. American Fidelity Fire Ins. Co. v. Hood, 37 F.R.D. 17 (E.D.S.C. 1965).

7. The same transaction requirement may be avoided through a different procedural approach. Separate actions can be instituted, then, at the court's discretion, they may be consolidated for trial under provisions such as Federal Rule 42(a), as long as there exists a question of law or fact common to all the parties. See § 6.2, above, for a discussion of consolidation.

8. See the discussion in 7 C. Wright, A. Miller & M. Kane, Civil 2d § 1653. See also Eastern Fireproofing Co. v. U.S. Gypsum Co., 160 F.Supp. 580 (D.Mass.1958).

9. The test was articulated in Moore v. New York Cotton Exchange, 270 U.S. 593, 610, 46 S.Ct. 367, 371, 70 L.Ed. 750 (1926), as follows: "Transaction is a word of flexible meaning. It may comprehend a series of many occurrences, depending not so much upon the immediateness of their connection as upon their logical relationship." See, e.g., Duke v. Uniroyal Inc., 928 F.2d 1413 (4th Cir.1991) (age discrimination suit arising out of a single reduction in work force).

10. See § 6.7, below, for a discussion of compulsory counterclaims.

On occasion, relationships found to meet the standard may seem less than logical. For example, permissive joinder commonly is sought in cases in which a plaintiff is injured by one defendant's negligence, and those injuries later are aggravated by the negligence of a second defendant. In one case, the second defendant's activity did not occur until 18 days after the original injury, but the court permitted the two defendants to be joined in a single action.[11] In a similar case, a plaintiff who was a passenger in a car that was struck in the rear twice in one day—once on the way to work and once on the way home—was permitted to join both other drivers in one action.[12] The apparent separateness of the torts in these two actions was outweighed by the fact that under the applicable substantive law the initial tortfeasor could be held liable for the total injury in both cases.

On the other hand, one court refused to join as defendants persons who allegedly had injured plaintiff's property along with the insurers who had issued the policy for that property. Even though the claims against the two defendants involved significant factual overlap, the disparity in the underlying substantive law proved determinative.[13] Thus, the logical relationship test represents only the most general guide for deciding permissive joinder questions. As described by one federal district court, "the approach must be the general one of whether there are enough ultimate factual concurrences that it would be fair to the parties to require them to defend jointly [the several claims] against them."[14]

The second modern requisite for permissive party joinder is that a question of law or fact common to all the parties must be present. This test is not nearly so restrictive as the rule of the early codes that required complete commonality of interest,[15] but it does limit permissive joinder to cases in which all the parties share at least one common litigation interest in the form of an issue of law or fact. Note that the rules require only a single common question and that it does not have to be contested; thus admission by the defendant of a fact that is the only common question would not preclude joinder.

Ascertaining whether there is a common question of fact is relatively simple. For example, parties injured in a mass air disaster will be able to join together to sue on the basis of their relationship to a single event.[16]

---

11. Lucas v. City of Juneau, 127 F.Supp. 730, 15 Alaska 413 (1955).

12. Watts v. Smith, 375 Mich. 120, 134 N.W.2d 194 (1965). The Michigan court, under its permissive joinder rule, decided that in the absence of joinder each defendant could argue that it was uncertain which of the plaintiff's injuries were attributable to which accident and thus both might escape liability altogether.

13. State ex rel. Campbell v. James, 263 S.W.2d 402 (Mo.1953). Contract law would determine the insurer's liability, but tort principles would govern the claim against the other defendant.

14. Eastern Fireproofing Co. v. U.S. Gypsum Co., 160 F.Supp. 580, 581 (D.Mass. 1958).

15. See Music Merchants, Inc. v. Capitol Records, Inc., 20 F.R.D. 462 (E.D.N.Y. 1957).

16. For a discussion of multiparty litigation in mass disaster cases, see Note, The Challenge of the Mass Trial, 38 Harv.L.Rev. 1046 (1955). The tactical considerations are noted in Friedenthal, Whom to Sue—Multiple Defendants, 5 Am.Jur., Trials 1 (1966).

A somewhat more complex instance is posed by a suit based on the violation of the federal antitrust laws in which the plaintiff alleges that four defendants have conspired to fix the price of phonograph records. In additional counts, the plaintiff alleges that the first defendant conspired with the second to set prices on one record label and that the third conspired with the fourth to set prices on a different label. Although it is true that there will be many questions of fact not common to all the defendants, their joinder should be permitted because there is at least one common factual question—the existence of a conspiracy among all four defendants.

Whether a common question of law is involved, however, depends upon how broadly a court defines "question of law." In Federal Housing Administrator v. Christianson,[17] a United States district court held that the reference in the federal rules to common questions of law meant only those questions of law arising out of the claims in the particular case before the court—not those arising out of general principles of law. The court said that the alternative view would permit, for example, a creditor to join in a single action all debtors obligated to it, no matter how disparate the sources of their obligations might be.

But this analysis is faulty. Two factors make it unlikely that the common question test could be contorted to permit joinder in the hypothetical multiple debt case. First, the underlying policy of Federal Rule 20 and similar joinder rules is to enhance judicial economy; the supposed mass debt action almost certainly would not advance that goal. Second, the permissive joinder test, in addition to legal or factual commonality, requires that the parties to be joined satisfy the transaction and occurrence standard, which clearly would not be met in the hypothetical situation.[18]

Adherence to the Christianson view might cause a return to the restrictive joinder practice common under the early codes. If a common question of law must arise out of a common claim, only joint liability would provide the necessary conditions for joinder.[19] Recent cases have rejected this narrow interpretation of the question-of-law requirement.[20] For instance, in one case a plaintiff was allowed to join six voting registrars in a discrimination suit in which the only common question of law was whether a number of acts that were separate both chronologically and geographically constituted discrimination.[21]

17. 26 F.Supp. 419 (D.Conn.1939). The holding in Christianson is criticized in Wright, Joinder of Claims and Parties Under Modern Pleading Rules, 26 Minn.L.Rev. 580, 601–11 (1952). The actual holding was repudiated by the 1966 amendment to Federal Rule 18(a). However, the discussion in text of the matter of "common questions of law" was unaffected by the 1966 amendment.

18. See the discussion in 7 C. Wright, A. Miller & M. Kane, Civil 2d § 1653.

19. See Wright, Joinder of Claims and Parties Under Modern Pleading Rules, 36 Minn.L.Rev. 580, 605–06 (1952).

20. For a thoughtful discussion of the common question requirement under a state rule similar to Federal Rule 20, see Akely v. Kinnicutt, 238 N.Y. 466, 144 N.E. 682 (1924).

21. See U.S. v. Mississippi, 380 U.S. 128, 85 S.Ct. 808, 13 L.Ed.2d 717 (1965).

It should be stressed again that both parts of the test for permissive party joinder are flexible. The policy goals underlying contemporary permissive joinder provisions are much the same as those that quickened the equity rules: to render complete justice in one action, and, as a corollary, to avoid multiplicity of actions.[22] Balanced against these objectives is the policy that joinder should not be permitted when it would prejudice the parties to be joined or those already involved in the litigation. Thus, the trial court, in ruling on a motion challenging joinder, must weigh the convenience to itself and the parties of having a single adjudication against the prejudice that might result from joinder.[23]

In general, the standards for permissive party joinder are applied expansively to promote judicial economy. Consistent with this flexibility, modern practice permits the joinder of plaintiffs or defendants when the claims asserted by or against them are joint, several, or in the alternative as long as the two requisites for joinder described in this section are met.[24] Alternative joinder is illustrated by a suit by the spouse of a deceased railroad worker under the Federal Employers' Liability Act.[25] If the spouse is unsure which of several companies employed the worker at the time of his death, she may sue them in the alternative in one action, recovering only from the company determined at trial to have been the worker's employer. Allowing alternative joinder avoids multiple suits with the ever-present danger of inconsistent jury verdicts.

This liberal approach to party joinder seems sound since little difficulty or inconvenience is likely to result from the joinder at the pleading stage of even minimally related parties.[26] The court has discretion to sever at any time those parties who could try their claims more conveniently in separate actions or who would be prejudiced by their joinder in the initial action.[27]

In a similar vein, the general view is that no action will be dismissed merely for the misjoinder of a party. If a party is improperly joined, the appropriate remedy is to move to drop him as a party or for severance of the claim by or against him.[28] These possibilities obviously are qualified in that the party to be dropped or severed cannot be an indispensable party.[29] Most commonly, misjoinder in the federal courts involves a party who would be proper but whose presence destroys diversity. The pre-

---

22. See the discussion in Rumbaugh v. Winifrede R.R. Co., 331 F.2d 530 (4th Cir. 1964), cert. denied 379 U.S. 929.

23. See Desert Empire Bank v. Insurance Co. of North America, 623 F.2d 1371 (9th Cir.1980); U.S. v. American Sur. Co., 25 F.Supp. 700, 701 (E.D.N.Y.1939).

24. See Wyant v. National R.R. Passenger Corp., 881 F.Supp. 919 (S.D.N.Y. 1995) (alternative joinder of defendants); Amalgamated Packaging Indus., Ltd. v. National Container Corp., 14 F.R.D. 194 (S.D.N.Y.1953) (alternative joinder of plaintiffs).

25. Texas Employers Ins. Ass'n v. Felt, 150 F.2d 227 (5th Cir.1945).

26. Poindexter v. Louisiana Financial Assistance Comm'n, 258 F.Supp. 158 (E.D.La.1966); Kaplan, Continuing Work of the Civil Committee: 1966 Amendments of the Federal Rules of Civil Procedure (II), 81 Harv.L.Rev. 591, 595 (1968).

27. See § 6.2, above. See also the discussion in 7 C. Wright, A. Miller & M. Kane, Civil 2d § 1660.

28. See Fed.Civ.Proc.Rule 21.

29. See § 6.5, below, for a discussion of who constitutes an indispensable party.

ferred course in this situation is for the court to drop the party rather than dismissing the action for lack of subject-matter jurisdiction.[30]

Finally, it must be cautioned that joinder of claims is treated quite independently of joinder of parties. Typically, joinder of claims is much more inclusive than joinder of parties.[31] Therefore, even if the claim joinder requirements have been met, the party joinder requirements also must be satisfied before parties can be added with regard to the new claims. Accordingly, a plaintiff may join multiple defendants in a single action only if at least one claim arising out of the same transaction or occurrence is applicable to all the defendants *and* if a question of law or fact also is common to them all.[32]

§ 6.5 Compulsory Party Joinder

The joinder of persons to an action can be classified in either of two ways, permissive or compulsory. The latter classification can be divided further into two subcategories—"necessary" parties who must be joined if feasible but whose nonjoinder will not result in dismissal and "indispensable" parties whose joinder is compelled even at the cost of dismissing the action.[1] Compulsory party joinder may be viewed as the joinder of persons who are necessary for a just adjudication.[2] Under modern procedure, a court will order these persons joined "if feasible."[3] If joinder is not feasible, the action may have to be abated, but only if "in equity and good conscience" it cannot proceed without the absentees.[4]

These categories represent portions of a continuum onto which parties are placed in terms of the significance of their interests in the litigation. In order to qualify for joinder as a proper party, the person must have some interest in common with those already parties to the

30. See Safeco Ins. Co. v. City of White House, Tennessee, 36 F.3d 540 (6th Cir. 1994); Farahmand v. Local Properties, Inc., 88 F.R.D. 80 (N.D.Ga.1980); Padbury v. Dairymen's League Co-op. Ass'n, 15 F.R.D. 484 (M.D.Pa.1954). See also Newman–Green, Inc. v. Alfonzo–Larrain, 490 U.S. 826, 109 S.Ct. 2218, 104 L.Ed.2d 893 (1989) (court of appeals may drop a nondiverse party when that defect is recognized at the appellate stage, rather than dismissing the action or remanding it to the district court).

31. See § 6.6, below.

32. See Shaw v. Munford, 526 F.Supp. 1209 (S.D.N.Y.1981); Pennsylvania R. Co. v. Lattavo Bros., Inc., 9 F.R.D. 205 (N.D.Ohio 1949).

§ 6.5

1. See 7 C. Wright, A. Miller & M. Kane, Civil 2d §§ 1601–26, for a detailed discussion of compulsory party joinder in the federal courts. See generally Bone, Mapping the Boundaries of a Dispute: Conceptions of Ideal Lawsuit Structure from the Field Code to the Federal Rules, 89 Colum.L.Rev. 1 (1989).

2. The title of Federal Rule 19, governing compulsory party joinder was amended in 1966 to read: "Joinder of Persons Needed for Just Adjudication." The title prior to that year was "Necessary Joinder of Parties." See Kaplan, Continuing Work of the Civil Committee: 1966 Amendments of the Federal Rules of Civil Procedure (I), 81 Harv.L.Rev. 356, 365 (1967).

3. See the discussion at notes 43–45, below.

4. The phrase "equity and good conscience" is taken from Federal Rule 19(b). The use of this concept signifies the important role of substantive justice in deciding whether a party should be joined, even at the cost of dismissing the entire action. See Reed, Compulsory Joinder of Parties in Civil Actions, 55 Mich.L.Rev. 327, 356 (1957); Tobias, Rule 19 and the Public Rights Exception to Party Joinder, 65 N.C.L.Rev. 745 (1987).

action.[5] Compulsory joinder requires a closer relation between the persons to be joined and the action so that their absence would imperil some aspect of the litigation or their own rights. "Persons who must be joined if feasible," therefore, are those whose absence threatens undesirable consequences beyond merely impairing judicial efficiency.[6]

The distinction between necessary and indispensable parties is not always easy to ascertain. Perhaps the best approach to the problem is to define an indispensable party as one who must be joined because nonjoinder is so prejudicial to the absentee's rights or to those already parties to the action, that the action cannot proceed without joinder.[7] Viewed in terms of this continuum of interests, the categories demand a flexible case-by-case analysis to determine the proper classification of persons not already parties to the action.

The evolution of the compulsory party joinder rules reveals a history of rigid application. The nineteenth century decision of Shields v. Barrow[8] played an important role in this unhappy history. In that case, the Supreme Court distinguished necessary from indispensable parties. Necessary parties were those "having an interest in the controversy, and who ought to be made parties, in order that the court may act on that rule which requires it to decide on, and finally determine the entire controversy, and do complete justice, by adjusting all the rights involved in it." However, necessary parties were not deemed indispensable "if their interests are separable from those of the parties before the court, so that the court can proceed to a decree, and do complete and final justice, without affecting other persons not before the court * * *." A person was deemed indispensable only if she had "an interest of such a nature that a final decree cannot be made without either affecting that interest or leaving the controversy in such a condition that its final determination may be wholly inconsistent with equity and good conscience."[9]

Although these definitions appear reasonably flexible, courts tended to use the labels in a conclusory fashion.[10] Much of the confusion and

---

5. See § 6.4, above.

6. Compulsory joinder is governed by more restrictive criteria than the encompassing transaction and occurrence test prescribed by permissive joinder rules. The different standards reflect the fact that the question of whether someone should be joined typically raises a much more significant problem than does the question of whether the absentee is a proper party who may be joined. See Bevan v. Columbia Broadcasting Sys., Inc., 293 F.Supp. 1366, 1369(S.D.N.Y.1968). See also 7 C. Wright, A. Miller & M. Kane, Civil 2d § 1604.

7. It should be noted that the philosophy of the compulsory joinder rule in the federal courts is to avoid dismissal whenever possible. See Travelers Indem. Co. v. Household Int'l, Inc., 775 F.Supp. 518

(D.Conn.1991); Heath v. Aspen Skiing Corp., 325 F.Supp. 223, 229 (D.Colo.1971).

8. 58 U.S. (17 How.) 130, 15 L.Ed. 158 (1855).

9. 58 U.S. (17 How.) at 139 (per Curtis, J.).

10. See the discussions in Kaplan, Continuing Work of the Civil Committee: 1966 Amendments of the Federal Rules of Civil Procedure (I), 81 Harv.L.Rev. 346, 362 (1967); Reed, Compulsory Joinder of Parties in Civil Actions, 55 Mich.L.Rev. 327 (1957); Wright, Recent Changes in the Federal Rules of Procedure, 42 F.R.D. 552, 561 (1966).

misapplication of the rules stemmed from a failure to examine the basic principles underlying compulsory party joinder. Modern rulemakers and courts have attempted to return to these principles in devising guidelines to aid in determining whether to compel the joinder of a person in a particular situation.

The basic objective underlying all claim and party joinder rules is rendering complete justice with as little litigation as possible.[11] When compulsory party joinder is sought, however, this goal may conflict with other important concerns. One of these is the possibility that joinder might prejudice the interests of the individuals whose joinder is requested or of those who already are parties to the action.[12] Another important concern is whether the court will have jurisdiction over all the parties it seeks to add.[13] Courts also must consider the potential effect of a judgment on a person who is absent but might be joined. A court cannot predetermine the binding effects of its own judgment, nor can a court bind a person to a decision against a party with whom the nonparty is not in privity.[14] Yet, in a practical sense, an absentee's claim or defense may be impaired by a judgment in a variety of situations.[15]

A potential constitutional concern also exists in the right of a party to insist upon the joinder of others in a single lawsuit. In Western Union Telegraph Company v. Commonwealth of Pennsylvania,[16] an escheat case involving potentially conflicting claims by several states, the Supreme Court held that an action had to be dismissed if other persons claiming an interest in the subject matter of the dispute were not joined and a real possibility existed that the defendant would be exposed to multiple liability in their absence. The Court stated that if the effect of fragmented adjudications was to subject a defendant to the risk of paying the same debt more than once, there would be a taking without due process.[17] Although the Western Union holding has not been applied to private claims by multiple parties interested in a single res, there is no logical way to restrict its applicability so as not to reach this latter situation.[18]

---

11. See generally § 6.1, above. See also Freer, Avoiding Duplicative Litigation: Rethinking Plaintiff Autonomy and the Court's Role in Defining the Litigative Unit, 50 U.Pitt.L.Rev. 809 (1989); Note, Mandatory Joinder of Parties: The Wave of the Future?, 49 Rutgers L.Rev. 53 (1990).

12. See the discussion at notes 27–40, below.

13. The federal court may be able to obtain personal jurisdiction over the absentees, but the attempt to exercise this jurisdiction might destroy diversity of citizenship leaving the plaintiff without a remedy in a federal forum. See Haas v. Jefferson Nat. Bank of Miami Beach, 442 F.2d 394 (5th Cir.1971).

14. Compare Independent Wireless Tel. Co. v. Radio Corp. of America, 269 U.S. 459, 46 S.Ct. 166, 70 L.Ed. 357 (1926) (nonparty bound by res judicata).

15. See Haas v. Jefferson Nat. Bank of Miami Beach, 442 F.2d 394 (5th Cir.1971).

16. 368 U.S. 71, 82 S.Ct. 199, 7 L.Ed.2d 139 (1961).

17. 368 U.S. at 76, 77, 82 S.Ct. at 202.

18. See the discussion, without a decision, of this issue in Hunt v. Nevada State Bank, 285 Minn. 77, 90, 172 N.W.2d 292, 300 (1969), cert. denied 397 U.S. 1010. And see Kaplan, Continuing Work of the Civil Committee: 1966 Amendments of the Federal Rules of Civil Procedure (I), 81 Harv. L.Rev. 356, 368 (1967).

Despite the above, the practice of dismissing actions when indispensable parties cannot be joined is at odds with the natural desire of judges to resolve disputes brought before them—especially if dismissal leaves a party without a remedy.[19] This conflict, of course, is present in all party joinder determinations. For some years before the revision of the federal compulsory joinder rules, judges often strained to categorize absent parties as necessary rather than indispensable in order to allow cases to be heard.[20] There even were instances in which the courts expressly categorized absent parties as indispensable but refused to order their joinder because they believed the consequent termination of the action would be contrary to the dominant purpose underlying the compulsory joinder rules[21]—to provide a final adjudication for legitimate claims.

Federal Rule 19, as amended in 1966, explicitly recognizes the inherent conflicts among the policies involved in compulsory party joinder.[22] By forcing the courts to abandon the mechanical use of legal categories—the "jurisprudence of labels"[23]—and to adopt a pragmatic approach to these policy dilemmas, the current rule requires a judicial evaluation of the party's right to a remedy despite the inability to join an absentee.

The Supreme Court clarified the significance of the changes in the Federal Rule in Provident Tradesmens Bank & Trust Company v. Patterson,[24] when it overturned a Third Circuit ruling to the effect that an absentee who may be affected by the litigation must be made a party.[25] The Court noted that "the inflexible approach adopted by the Court of Appeals in this case exemplifies the kind of reasoning that the Rule [for compulsory joinder] was designed to avoid * * *."[26] A look at the approach taken by modern courts to questions of compulsory joinder best illustrates the flexibility and careful balancing of competing interests that is required.

To determine whether an absentee's joinder should be compelled—whether the party is "necessary"—courts must evaluate the strength of the nonparty's interest in the pending litigation.[27] This inquiry can be

19. See Bourdieu v. Pacific Western Oil Co., 299 U.S. 65, 57 S.Ct. 51, 81 L.Ed. 42 (1936). See also Rush & Halloran, Inc. v. Delaware Valley Financial Corp., 180 F.Supp. 63, 65–66 (E.D.Pa.1960).

20. See Bourdieu v. Pacific Western Oil Co., 299 U.S. 65, 57 S.Ct. 51, 81 L.Ed. 42 (1936). See also Mackintosh v. Marks' Estate, 225 F.2d 211 (5th Cir.1955), cert. denied 350 U.S. 934.

21. See Parker Rust–Proof Co. v. Western Union Telegraph Co., 105 F.2d 976 (2d Cir.1939), cert. denied 308 U.S. 597. See also Benger Labs., Ltd. v. R. K. Laros Co., 24 F.R.D. 450, 452 (E.D.Pa.1959).

22. The factor analysis called for by Federal Rule 19 requires the trial court to balance conflicting considerations pertinent to particular absentees. See the discussion in Provident Tradesmens Bank & Trust Co. v. Patterson, 390 U.S. 102, 88 S.Ct. 733, 19 L.Ed.2d 936 (1968). See also Freer, Rethinking Compulsory Joinder: A Proposal to Restructure Federal Rule 19, 60 N.Y.U.L.Rev. 1061 (1985).

23. C. Wright, Federal Courts § 70 at 496 (5th ed.1994).

24. 390 U.S. 102, 88 S.Ct. 733, 19 L.Ed.2d 936 (1968).

25. 365 F.2d 802, 805 (3d Cir.1966). The Court of Appeals cited as authority Russell v. Clark's Executors, 11 U.S. (7 Cranch) 69, 3 L.Ed. 271 (1812).

26. 390 U.S. at 107, 88 S.Ct. at 736.

27. See 7 C. Wright, A. Miller & M. Kane, Civil 2d §§ 1601–04.

broken down into three questions: (1) In the absence of joinder, can complete relief be accorded those already parties to the action? (2) Will a judgment in the absence of the nonparty as a practical matter impair that individual's interest in the subject matter of the action? and (3) Will those already parties be subject to a substantial risk of incurring inconsistent obligations in separate suits?[28] If the answer to any of these questions is affirmative, the nonparty must be joined "if feasible."[29] Thus, the standard is phrased in terms of what harm may accrue if party joinder is not ordered, rather than what policies should be satisfied through joinder.

The implications of each of these questions are apparent. The first requires the joinder of a nonparty if, in her absence, complete relief cannot be accorded among those already parties. This standard serves to aid those seeking relief to adjudicate their grievances in a single action, furthering the overall efficiency of the judicial system.[30] For example, when an injured party sues a nonparty's insurer, if the insurance policy covers only losses in excess of a certain sum, a verdict for less than that sum would be worthless—requiring a second lawsuit against the insured on virtually identical facts. To avoid this possibility, the joinder of the insured with the insurance company should be ordered.[31]

The second principle—that joinder is necessary if the interest of nonparties would be impaired by nonjoinder—protects the nonparty from the adverse effects of a judgment rendered in her absence.[32] The problem is to determine which interests of the nonparties will be affected by nonjoinder and to what extent they might be prejudiced. This requires an analysis of the possible consequences of the action at the time the joinder question is raised.

Provident Tradesmens Bank & Trust v. Patterson[33] indicates the importance—and difficulty—of this analysis. In Provident Tradesmens, the Third Circuit reversed a verdict for plaintiffs and dismissed their suit on the ground that an interested absentee had not been joined at trial. The losing defendant had objected to the nonjoinder neither at trial nor on appeal. On certiorari, the Supreme Court held that the absentee was

---

28. The second and third questions are combined in the Federal Rules, but are treated separately in this discussion. See Fed.Civ.Proc.Rule 19(a)(1)–(2).

29. See text at notes 43–45, below, for a discussion of when joinder is not feasible.

30. See Evergreen Park Nursing & Convalescent Home, Inc. v. American Equitable Assurance Co., 417 F.2d 1113 (7th Cir.1969). However, efficiency concerns alone do not merit a finding that an individual is a necessary party who should be joined if feasible. This point is underscored by the Supreme Court's opinion in Temple v. Synthes Corp., 498 U.S. 5, 111 S.Ct. 315, 112 L.Ed.2d 263 (1990), holding that joint tortfeasors are merely permissive parties and do not meet the Rule 19(a) standard.

31. Prestenback v. Employers' Ins. Companies, 47 F.R.D. 163 (E.D.La.1969). A similar concern for judicial efficiency compelled the joinder of a contract vendee in an action by the contract vendor against the vendor's insurer after a fire destroyed the property. Sullivan v. Merchants Property Ins. Co. of Indiana, 68 Ill.App.3d 260, 24 Ill.Dec. 756, 385 N.E.2d 897 (1979). Compare Truckweld Equip. Co. v. Swenson Trucking & Excavating, Inc., 649 P.2d 234 (Alaska 1982) (when recovery sought for claim of partially subrogated insurer, insurer must be joined).

32. Zwack v. Kraus Bros. & Co., 93 F.Supp. 963, 965 (S.D.N.Y.1950).

33. 390 U.S. 102, 88 S.Ct. 733, 19 L.Ed.2d 936 (1968).

not an indispensable party, in part because by the time the case had reached the appellate level, it had become clear that the absentee had not been prejudiced by his nonjoinder in the action. Therefore, it was unreasonable for the Court of Appeals to dismiss the action on the ground that the nonparty should have been joined because his interests were in potential peril.[34]

The Supreme Court's opinion in Provident Tradesmens repeatedly stressed the importance of pragmatic considerations, including the actual effect of past litigation, in applying compulsory joinder tests,[35] especially in evaluating the extent of the prejudice to the nonparty that failure to join might cause. The Federal Rule states that the trial court must prevent practical—not merely legal—impairment of a nonparty's interests. Thus, joinder will be compelled when the outsider has an interest in a lump sum insurance policy, because, even though the nonparty's claims will not be affected by preclusion rules, there is the practical risk that the first judgment will exhaust the fund. All that is required is that the adjudication threaten the absentee's ability to prosecute or defend a subsequent action.[36]

The third element under Rule 19(a) also has its roots in the policy of avoiding prejudice. This consideration, a complement to the preceding one, aims at avoiding prejudice to those already parties. It is unclear how likely the threat of prejudice must be before the nonparty's joinder will be compelled.[37] Examples may best illustrate how it is applied.

In one case, a labor union brought an action against an employer to impose a grievance procedure and binding arbitration under a collective bargaining agreement.[38] The court recognized that what appeared to be a two-party disagreement was "an incipient jurisdictional dispute between two unions."[39] Failure to join the rival union would expose the employer to a second suit in which the rival would press a similar claim under the collective bargaining agreement. Consequently, the court ordered the competing union joined.

In another case, Haas v. Jefferson National Bank of Miami Beach,[40] Haas brought suit against the bank for conversion of shares of stock. Haas alleged that he and another party, Alveck, had jointly purchased the stock and that Haas had asked Alveck to direct the bank to issue shares that reflected Haas' half ownership. In fact, all the shares were

34. 390 U.S. at 113–16, 88 S.Ct. at 739–41.

35. 390 U.S. at 119–20, 88 S.Ct. at 743.

36. See Smith v. American Federation of Musicians of U.S. & Canada, 46 F.R.D. 24 (S.D.N.Y.1968). See also Imperial Appliance Corp. v. Hamilton Mfg. Co., 263 F.Supp. 1015 (E.D.Wis.1967).

37. Fed.Civ.Proc.Rule 19(a) states that the parties must be subject to "a substantial risk of incurring double, multiple, or otherwise inconsistent obligations," but "a

possibility" of hazard to a party's interest has been deemed sufficient. See Window Glass Cutters League of America AFL–CIO v. American St. Gobain Corp., 47 F.R.D. 255, 258 (W.D.Pa.1969), affirmed 428 F.2d 353 (3d Cir.1970).

38. Window Glass Cutters League of America AFL–CIO v. American St. Gobain Corp., 47 F.R.D. 255 (W.D.Pa.1969), affirmed 428 F.2d 353 (3d Cir.1970).

39. 47 F.R.D. at 256.

40. 442 F.2d 394 (5th Cir.1971).

issued in Alveck's name. The court held that Alveck had to be joined if feasible because an adjudication of the plaintiff's half-ownership of the stock without Alveck would subject the bank to the threat of double liability. Since Alveck would not be bound by the judgment in the action, he could bring a subsequent action against the bank claiming ownership of all the stock.

After it has been determined that a nonparty's joinder should be compelled and that joinder is feasible, the party seeking joinder usually is given a reasonable opportunity to serve the nonparty and bring him into the action. Dismissal of the action for nonjoinder should be the last resort, used only when there has been willful disobedience of the court's orders.

If the nonparty's interest in the subject matter of the litigation is such that he should be included as a plaintiff but he refuses to do so, the court, if it has jurisdiction over the nonparty, may order the nonparty joined as a defendant.[41] That person later may be realigned as a plaintiff. Realignment can preserve a federal court's jurisdiction when the action is based on diversity of citizenship. Of course, if the interests of the party joined involuntarily render him hostile to the original plaintiff, he must remain as a defendant. For instance, if a stockholder brings a derivative suit against the president of a corporation seeking compensation from the latter because the president's wrongful conduct damages the corporation, the corporation is an indispensable party because its rights are being litigated and it stands to benefit from the suit.[42] However, since the corporation is under the control of the president—a person obviously antagonistic to the plaintiff's action—the corporation should not be realigned as a plaintiff if it is joined involuntarily as a defendant.

In some instances, the court will not be able to order the joinder of a nonparty. This may occur when joinder will defeat the subject-matter jurisdiction of the court,[43] when the court cannot obtain personal jurisdiction over the person sought to be joined,[44] or when the person sought to be joined has a valid objection to the venue of the court.[45] In these situations, the court must decide whether "in equity and good conscience"[46] it should proceed with the action in the nonparty's absence. If the court concludes that proceeding would be so prejudicial to the rights

---

41. In a few special circumstances, particularly involving patent and copyright infringement actions, a nonparty may be joined as an involuntary plaintiff. See 7 C. Wright, A. Miller & M. Kane, Civil 2d § 1606. Joinder is required because patent and, until recently copyright, law specified that an exclusive licensee cannot sue for infringement without joining the patent or copyright owner. See Waterman v. Mackenzie, 138 U.S. 252, 11 S.Ct. 334, 34 L.Ed. 923 (1891). An owner who is outside the court's jurisdiction will be joined as an involuntary plaintiff; an owner who is within the court's jurisdiction may be joined as an involuntary defendant. See Independent

Wireless Telegraph Co. v. Radio Corp. of America, 269 U.S. 459, 46 S.Ct. 166, 70 L.Ed. 357 (1926).

42. See Ross v. Bernhard, 396 U.S. 531, 538, 90 S.Ct. 733, 738, 24 L.Ed.2d 729 (1970).

43. See §§ 2.1–2.14, above.

44. See §§ 3.1–3.17, above.

45. See §§ 2.15–2.17, above.

46. This test was first cited in Shields v. Barrow, 58 U.S. (17 How.) 130, 15 L.Ed. 158 (1855), and is now incorporated into Federal Rule 19(b).

of both the nonparty and those persons already in the action that the case should not go forward, the absentee will be labelled indispensable.[47]

Determining whether a party is indispensable requires the careful exercise of judicial discretion on a case-by-case basis.[48] Federal Rule 19(b) and its state counterparts recommend a four-part test.[49] It should be emphasized that the elements are meant to be a guide to the judge confronted with a joinder problem, not a complete list of relevant concerns.[50] Moreover, the four parts are interdependent and therefore must be considered in relation to each other as well as to the facts of the case. Rule 19(b) does not indicate the relative weight to be given to each factor; the decision ultimately must be made on the basis of "equity and good conscience."[51]

The first part of the current indispensable party test requires the court to determine whether "a judgment rendered in the person's absence might be prejudicial to him or those already parties."[52] As seen earlier, the goal of avoiding prejudice is a recurrent theme in deciding joinder motions. In the context of indispensable party joinder, the courts must consider the practical likelihood of prejudice, which includes whether there is a real possibility of subsequent litigation. As the Fifth Circuit pointed out: "In applying Rule 19 the courts must refrain from taking a view either too broad or too narrow in determining 'prejudicial' effect of a judgment. The watchwords of Rule 19 in this regard are 'pragmatism' and 'practicality'."[53]

The second part of the test—whether the court can reduce or eliminate prejudice or other ill-effects of nonjoinder by "the shaping of relief, or other measures"[54]—shows the need for judicial initiative in dealing with problems posed by compulsory joinder. The measures available to avoid a dismissal because of nonjoinder are limited mainly by the constraints of the particular case. Experience suggests several ways of

---

47. Compare Pulitzer–Polster v. Pulitzer, 784 F.2d 1305 (5th Cir.1986) (an action seeking damages against an uncle for improprieties when acting as the sole voting trustee of the family company), with Bank of California Nat. Ass'n v. Superior Court, 16 Cal.2d 516, 106 P.2d 879 (1940) (absent legatees were not indispensable to an action to declare valid a contract to make a will).

48. See Hunt v. DelCollo, 317 A.2d 545, 551 (Del.Ch.1974); Revoir v. Kansas Super Motels of North Dakota, Inc., 224 N.W.2d 549 (N.D.1974); Oxley v. Mine & Smelter Supply Co., 439 P.2d 661 (Wyo. 1968).

49. See the general discussion in 7 C. Wright, A. Miller & M. Kane, Civil 2d § 1608.

50. See the discussion of the other relevant factors in Provident Tradesmens Bank & Trust Co. v. Patterson, 390 U.S. 102, 88 S.Ct. 733, 19 L.Ed.2d 936 (1968). See also the 1966 Advisory Committee Note to Rule 19, reprinted in 39 F.R.D. 89, 92 (1966).

51. The lack of hierarchical weighting is noted in Fisk, Indispensable Parties and the Proposed Amendment to Federal Rule 19, 74 Yale L.J. 403, 424 (1965). See also the analysis in Jones Knitting Corp. v. A. M. Pullen & Co., 50 F.R.D. 311 (S.D.N.Y. 1970).

52. This is in part a reiteration of the standard of Federal Rule 19(a)(2). See Haas v. Jefferson Nat. Bank of Miami Beach, 442 F.2d 394 (5th Cir.1971).

53. Schutten v. Shell Oil Co., 421 F.2d 869, 874 (5th Cir.1970) (per Carswell, J.). See Freer, Avoiding Duplicative Litigation: Rethinking Plaintiff Autonomy and the Court's Role in Defining the Litigative Unit, 50 U.Pitt.L.Rev. 809 (1989).

54. See the early examination of this problem in Roos v. Texas Co., 23 F.2d 171 (2d Cir.1927), cert. denied 277 U.S. 587.

modifying a judgment to protect the interests of those who cannot be joined.[55] For example, when an absentee's insurance fund might be vulnerable to exhaustion by a few of many claimants, the court could order the payment of judgments against the fund delayed until all litigation concerning the fund—including a later action by the absentee if she chose to bring it—had been concluded.[56] The absent person also may be protected if relief is awarded in a form different from that initially sought by the plaintiff. Giving a money judgment when the requested rescission of a transaction would damage the interests of an absentee is a good example.[57]

Prejudice to absent parties also may be avoided through informal arrangements between the actual parties to encourage them to take procedural steps to avoid the possibility of prejudice,[58] such as bringing in an absentee by defensive interpleader and joining the nonparty to a counterclaim.[59] Conversely, absent persons who cannot be compelled by the court to appear and whose absence may prejudice their own or others' interests can be given the chance to join the action voluntarily, waiving personal jurisdiction or venue objections.[60] A failure to take these steps may be relevant to the court's determination of the possible prejudice to the recalcitrant absentee.[61]

The third factor to consider is whether a judgment rendered without the outsider will be "adequate." This determination requires the court to assess the impact of its decision on those actually before it and to decide whether there is some way it can tailor a judgment to minimize the necessity for additional litigation.[62] In one interesting case, the court decided that although it could not directly grant the request for an order declaring corporate dividends (because it could not join all the defen-

---

55. For example, in one case plaintiff brought suit to enforce an alleged will contract in her favor, naming as defendants all the will beneficiaries, but serving only the residuary legatee. Because the trial court could protect the absent parties' interests by shaping plaintiff's relief to impose a constructive trust in her favor upon only the interest of the present defendant, the California Supreme Court classified the absent parties as "necessary" rather than "indispensable" and allowed the suit to go forward. Bank of California, Nat. Ass'n v. Superior Court, 16 Cal.2d 516, 106 P.2d 879 (1940).

56. This suggestion was made by the Supreme Court in the Provident Tradesmen's case, 390 U.S. at 115–16, 88 S.Ct. at 741.

57. See Tardan v. California Oil Co., 323 F.2d 717 (5th Cir.1963).

58. See the 1966 Advisory Committee Note to Rule 19, reprinted in 39 F.R.D. 89, 92 (1966). See also Kaplan, Continuing Work of the Civil Committee: 1966 Amend-

ments of the Federal Rules of Civil Procedure (I), 81 Harv.L.Rev. 356, 365–66 (1967).

59. See Associated Dry Goods Corp. v. Towers Financial Corp., 920 F.2d 1121 (2d Cir.1990) (counterclaim); Gauss v. Kirk, 198 F.2d 83 (D.C.Cir.1952) (interpleader); B. L. Schrader, Inc. v. Anderson Lumber Co., 257 F.Supp. 794, 797–98 (D.Md.1966) (impleader).

60. See Sandobal v. Armour & Co., 429 F.2d 249 (8th Cir.1970).

61. In the Provident Tradesmens case, Justice Harlan suggested that a person who has "purposely bypassed an adequate opportunity to intervene" as a party in an earlier action may be bound by the decree by his own inaction. He then qualified this suggestion by leaving open the question of whether such an argument would be correct under the circumstances of that case. 390 U.S. at 114, 88 S.Ct. at 740.

62. See the 1966 Advisory Committee Note to Rule 19, reprinted in 39 F.R.D. 89, 93 (1966).

dants necessary under state law to achieve that objective), it could secure the result indirectly by sequestering the corporation's assets.[63]

Finally, under the fourth factor, the court must take into account the costs to the plaintiff of a dismissal for nonjoinder.[64] The most common alternative for a plaintiff whose federal case is dismissed for lack of an indispensable party is to bring the same action in state court. Therefore, the federal judge must decide if a state court action is a practical possibility. It may be, for example, that such an action would be barred by the applicable statute of limitations. Other impediments also might render a state action inadequate. Illustratively, one federal district judge decided that because the state in which he was sitting would require that all beneficiaries be joined in a trust action, the case, in practicality, could not be brought in a state court. Consequently, the action was retained by the federal court.[65]

Objections to the nonjoinder of necessary and indispensable parties should be made in a pre-answer motion, a demurrer, or in the answer itself in the form of a "defense of non-joinder."[66] The importance of a failure to join someone necessary to the litigation may be seen in the fact that objections to nonjoinder are not waived automatically by delay, but may be raised at any time.[67]

Yet, this conclusion must be qualified. The untimeliness of the motion may have some bearing on the court's determination of the prejudice that will result if joinder is not required. If, for example, the moving party is seeking to protect herself from a suit by an absentee (not to protect the absentee from a prejudicial judgment), the court may reason that the delay in making the motion is grounds for denial.[68] That nonjoinder will prejudice the moving party's case is counterbalanced by considerations of judicial efficiency and of the moving party's own responsibility for the possibility of prejudice.[69]

In the absence of a motion by one party to compel joinder of an absentee, the court may order joinder sua sponte. This may occur at the trial or appellate level.[70] However, raising the issue of nonjoinder at the

63. Kroese v. General Steel Castings Corp., 179 F.2d 760 (3d Cir.1950), cert. denied 339 U.S. 983.

64. See Broussard v. Columbia Gulf Transmission Co., 398 F.2d 885, 888 (5th Cir.1968) (per Goldberg, J.).

65. Rippey v. Denver U.S. Nat. Bank, 260 F.Supp. 704, 711–12 (D.Colo.1966).

66. See Fed.Civ.Proc.Rule 12(b)(7); West's Ann.Cal.Code Civ.Proc. §§ 430.10(d), 430.60. See generally 5A C. Wright & A. Miller, Civil 2d §§ 1347–49, 1359.

67. Fed.Civ.Proc.Rule 12(h)(2). See, for example, Haas v. Jefferson Nat. Bank of Miami Beach, 442 F.2d 394, 396 n. 2 (5th Cir.1971). See also Rippey v. Denver U.S.

Nat. Bank, 42 F.R.D. 316 (D.Colo.1967) (changed circumstances provided reason for reconsideration of indispensability, because it is an "equitable" issue).

68. See, e.g., Provident Tradesmens Bank & Trust Co. v. Patterson, 390 U.S. 102, 110, 88 S.Ct. 733, 738, 19 L.Ed.2d 936 (1968).

69. See the Advisory Committee Note to the 1966 Amendment to Rule 19, 39 F.R.D. 89, 93 (1966).

70. Provident Tradesmens Bank & Trust Co. v. Patterson, 390 U.S. 102, 110–11, 88 S.Ct. 733, 739, 19 L.Ed.2d 936 (1968). See also Dredge Corp. v. Penny, 338 F.2d 456, 464 (9th Cir.1964); Haby v. Stanolind Oil & Gas Co., 225 F.2d 723 (5th Cir.1955).

appellate level creates special problems. Considerations of judicial economy and fairness dictate that the court closely examine the merits of any such challenge to be certain that nonjoinder really will have prejudicial effects. When the judgment does not prejudice the absent party or when the objection has been raised for the first time on appeal, strong reasons exist for refusing to overturn the trial decision on the merits for nonjoinder.[71]

A dismissal for nonjoinder usually is not on the merits and is without prejudice to the institution of a later action.[72] The defect of nonjoinder generally is regarded as an equitable flaw, rather than a jurisdictional one.[73] Having jurisdiction over the parties before it, the court concludes that it cannot proceed "in equity and good conscience" without the absent party.

C. CLAIMS

§ 6.6 The Standard for Claim Joinder—In General

Under modern procedural rules, it is easier to join claims than it is to join parties.[1] This fact may be explained by two considerations. First, a stronger policy prevails against bringing into an action persons who have little or nothing to do with those already involved than prevails against bringing in minimally related claims between litigants already before the court. Second, the desire to use the resources of the judicial system efficiently and to spare the parties multiple lawsuits supports settling as much judicial business at one time as possible. As a result, modern procedural rules allow a party to join as many claims, counterclaims, cross-claims, and third-party claims as he has against another party.[2]

This has not always been the general practice. Under common-law pleading, only claims brought under the same writ, or "form of action," could be joined in one suit.[3] This restriction on claim joinder was a

71. See Judge Hutcheson's dissent in Calcote v. Texas Pacific Coal & Oil Co., 157 F.2d 216, 224 (5th Cir.1946), cert. denied 329 U.S. 782.

72. See 5A C. Wright & A. Miller, Civil 2d § 1359.

73. Swift v. Boonslick Sav. & Loan Ass'n, 78 F.R.D. 342 (W.D.Mo.1978); Sierra Club, Inc. v. California Coastal Comm'n, 95 Cal.App.3d 495, 157 Cal.Rptr. 190 (1979); Hoppmann v. Reid, 86 Wis.2d 531, 273 N.W.2d 298 (1979). But see Coughlin v. Ryder, 260 F.Supp. 256 (E.D.Pa.1966); Frost v. Gazaway, 122 Ga.App. 244, 176 S.E.2d 476 (1970).

§ 6.6

1. For a discussion of party joinder rules, see §§ 6.3–6.5, above. Although claim and party joinder function independently and typically pursuant to different standards, the two sometimes are intertwined incorrectly. See, e.g., U.S. v. Anchor Line, Ltd., 232 F.Supp. 379 (S.D.N.Y.1964); Man–Sew Pinking Attachment Corp. v. Chandler Mach. Co., 29 F.Supp. 480 (D.Mass.1939).

2. The remainder of this section discusses the joinder of claims generally. The rules surrounding counterclaims, cross-claims, and third-party claims are discussed in §§ 6.7–6.9, below.

3. Common-law joinder rules are discussed in 1 J. Chitty, Pleadings 222–23 (16th Am. ed.1885); B. Shipman, Common-Law Pleading § 80 (3d ed.1923). One exception to the form of action restriction existed: debt could be joined with detinue even though debt was ex contractu and detinue was ex delicto. 1 J. Chitty, Pleadings 223 (16th Am. ed.1885).

natural corollary of the common-law policy that cases should be reduced to the fewest possible issues for a single trial; courts refused to entertain more than one form of action at one trial. This policy stemmed from a fear that juries would be confused by the multiplicity of issues possible when separate claims are asserted, especially in cases involving multiple parties as well.[4] However justified this concern, the common-law rule hampered efficient disposition of transactionally related injuries. A theoretical result of the rule was that a plaintiff could combine in a single action for trespass to chattel, for example, multiple claims relating to entirely different items of property and concerning events occurring at different times. Yet, a plaintiff who had been beaten and insulted in public while being arrested without reasonable cause would have to bring three completely separate actions for redress against the culpable defendant—one for assault, one for defamation, and one for false imprisonment.[5]

In sharp contrast, equity allowed claim joinder at the chancellor's discretion in an effort to resolve as many issues with as little inconvenience to the court and the parties as possible. In general, equity permitted unlimited joinder of claims in cases between a single plaintiff and a single defendant. In multiparty suits, the chancellor allowed joinder when efficiency would be promoted.[6] On the other hand, because law and equity were themselves separate judicial systems, legal and equitable claims could not be joined in the same action.[7]

Some early state codes borrowed heavily from the common-law tradition.[8] Under these codes, claims could be joined only if they fell within the same statutory cause of action. Although the categories of causes of action generally were defined more broadly than those under the common-law writ system,[9] joinder across categorical divisions was not permitted. However, an early modification in many codes permitted the joinder of claims arising out of the same transaction or occurrence. In this way, the codes amalgamated the common law and equity tests.[10]

---

4. See Hinton, An American Experiment with the English Rules of Court, 20 Ill.L.Rev. 533, 535 (1926).

5. This example is taken from a discussion in Harris v. Avery, 5 Kan. 146 (1869).

6. The tests for efficiency and convenience developed by the chancellors sometimes involved considerations of transactional relationships and factual and legal commonality. See Blume, Joinder of Causes of Action, 26 Mich.L.Rev. 1, 16 (1927).

7. See J. Story, Equity Pleadings §§ 271–84 (9th ed.1879).

8. See C. Clark, Code Pleading § 67 (2d ed.1947), which contains a good general discussion of some historical and contemporary facets of claim joinder.

9. The usual classes included some combination of the following: (1) contracts, express or implied; (2) injuries to person;

(3) injuries to character; (4) injuries to property; (5) actions to recover real property with or without damages; (6) actions to recover chattels with or without damages; (7) claims against a trustee by virtue of a contract or operation of law; and (8) actions arising out of the same transaction or transactions connected with the same subject of action. Often certain of the tort classes were combined, and in some codes the last class was omitted. See C. Clark, Code Pleading §§ 68–70 (2d ed.1947).

10. These provisions sometimes were narrowly construed by the courts, however, limiting the extent to which the rigor of the common-law policy was mitigated by the influence of equity.

Under the Federal Rules, the categories known as causes of action are done away with altogether.[11] Court involvement in claim joinder is minimal at the pleading stage; the parties may add as many claims as they wish. Later, of course, the court may separate issues for trial,[12] but even that decision will rest on the facts of the particular case and the relationships among the claims, rather than on the categories of legal rights into which those facts fit. The policy behind this fundamental change in approach has been stated clearly by the Supreme Court: "Under the Rules, the impulse is toward entertaining the broadest possible scope of action consistent with fairness to the parties; joinder of claims, parties and remedies is strongly encouraged."[13] This philosophy now has been adopted by a majority of states.[14]

Consistent with this impulse toward broad joinder, contemporary procedural rules commonly permit joinder of claims in the alternative so that the plaintiff need not make an election of legal theories or remedies at the pleading stage.[15] Modern rules also authorize the joinder of prospective claims, even when, had the claims been prosecuted separately, rendition of a favorable judgment on one of them would have been required before litigation could proceed on the other. For example, when a creditor sued a debtor to recover on a loan and joined another person to set aside as fraudulent a transfer to that third party of the property that was the security for the loan, courts formerly required that the creditor obtain a money judgment before asking for nullification of the transfer. Under present rules, both claims may be joined in one suit.[16]

Typically claim joinder rules are permissive;[17] there is no compulsory claim joinder corresponding to compulsory party joinder.[18] However, there are indirect sanctions against "claim splitting."[19] These stem from the requirements of res judicata, which in a number of states demand that all the grounds or theories of a cause of action be asserted in one action or be barred in subsequent litigation.[20] The requisite overlap of

11. See Fed.Civ.Proc.Rule 18.

12. See § 6.2, above.

13. United Mine Workers of America v. Gibbs, 383 U.S. 715, 724, 86 S.Ct. 1130, 1138, 16 L.Ed.2d 218 (1966). .

14. See Del.Code Ann.R.Civ.P. 18; Official Code Ga.Ann. § 9–11–18(a); Ill.— Smith–Hurd Ann. 735 ILCS 5/2–614; Vernon's Ann.Mo.Civ.Proc. Rule 55.06. But see La.Stat.Ann.–Code Civ.Proc. art. 462.

15. Parties also may add inconsistent claims under the usual provision for alternative pleadings. See §§ 5.12–5.13, above. The only limit is that these pleadings must be made in good faith. See § 5.11, above.

16. See Fed.Civ.Proc.Rule 18(b); 6A C. Wright, A. Miller & M. Kane, Civil 2d §§ 1590–94.

17. See West's Ann.Cal.Code Civ.Proc. §§ 427.10, 428.30; Iowa Rules Civ.Proc.,

Rules 22, 31; Or.Rules Civ.Proc., Rules 22A, 24A.

18. An exception is Mich.Gen.Ct.Rule 1963, 203.1, which compels parties to join claims arising out of the transaction or occurrence that is the subject matter of the action but that do not require for their adjudication the presence of third parties over whom the court cannot acquire jurisdiction. This interesting rule is examined in Meisenholder, The New Michigan Pre–Trial Procedural Rules—Models for Other States?, 61 Mich.L.Rev. 1389, 1417–18 (1963).

19. See C. Clark, Code Pleading § 73 (2d ed.1947); 6A C. Wright, A. Miller & M. Kane, Civil 2d § 1582; Blume, Required Joinder of Claims, 45 Mich.L.Rev. 797 (1947).

20. See §§ 14.4–14.6, below.

claims necessary for the doctrine to apply is both unclear and often unascertainable in the first action.[21] Consequently, the indirect effect of res judicata is to encourage cautious claimants to join claims that might be related in any way to their principal cause of action.

Because there are no threshold requirements to claim joinder in most jurisdictions, there can be no penalty for misjoinder.[22] Pleaders having multiple claims, however, must present them clearly.[23] The failure to present a clearly drafted complaint will result in an order to redraft it to conform to reasonable standards of good pleading.[24]

The major restraint on the joinder of claims results from jurisdiction and venue rules. Thus, in the federal courts, each claim generally must have an independent basis for subject-matter jurisdiction.[25] Personal jurisdiction[26] and venue[27] also must be proper as to each claim. Special personal jurisdiction questions are presented when a party has been served properly with process under a statute—typically a long-arm provision—with regard to one claim but is not subject to process under the same statute for purposes of a joined claim.[28] Venue concerns are resolved most easily; if venue is proper for one of the claims brought by the plaintiff, the desire for judicial economy dictates that a venue defect of the joined claim should be disregarded.[29]

§ 6.7 Counterclaims

A counterclaim is any affirmative claim for relief asserted by a pleader—typically the defendant—in the defensive pleadings against an opposing party—typically the plaintiff.[1] Although a minority of jurisdictions have limited the scope of counterclaims, modern procedure encourages the use of the counterclaim as part of a policy of promoting the settlement of all disputes between two parties as expeditiously and economically as possible.[2]

---

21. "The search for an automatic rule of thumb is illusory as in law generally, particularly in procedural law." C. Clark, Code Pleading § 73 (2d ed.1947).

22. See Atlantic Lumber Corp. v. Southern Pacific Co., 2 F.R.D. 313 (D.Or. 1941); Hundley v. Gossett, 278 S.W.2d 65 (Ky.1955). See also Gadd v. Pearson, 351 F.Supp. 895, 904 (M.D.Fla.1972).

23. See C. Clark, Code Pleading § 71 (2d ed.1947). See generally §§ 5.14–5.16, above, for a discussion of pleading requirements.

24. See 5 C. Wright & A. Miller, Civil 2d § 1324; 6 C. Wright, A. Miller & M. Kane, Civil 2d § 1584.

25. In diversity cases, the problem becomes whether a party may aggregate all the claims against the opposing party to satisfy the amount in controversy requirement. See § 2.9, above. When federal ques-

tion jurisdiction exists, the issue is whether additional claims may be brought under the court's supplemental jurisdiction. See § 2.13, above.

26. See generally §§ 3.10–3.17, above.

27. See generally § 2.15, above.

28. See Robinson v. Penn Cent. Co., 484 F.2d 553 (3d Cir.1973); Puma v. Marriott, 294 F.Supp. 1116, 1120 (D.Del.1969).

29. See Carolyn Chenilles, Inc. v. Ostow & Jacobs, Inc., 168 F.Supp. 894 (S.D.N.Y.1958).

§ 6.7

1. In some jurisdictions, counterclaims are denominated cross-complaints. See, e.g., West's Ann.Cal.Code Civ.Proc. § 428.10(a).

2. See Millar, Counterclaims Against Counterclaims, 48 Nw.U.L.Rev. 671, 691 (1954).

Counterclaim procedure has its roots in the common-law practices of set-off and recoupment.[3] At common law, recoupment allowed a defendant to assert against a plaintiff a claim that arose out of the same transaction as the plaintiff's complaint, but this assertion could be made only defensively. Thus, recoupment was available only to defeat or diminish the plaintiff's recovery—affirmative relief was prohibited.[4] A set-off was a claim by defendant that was unrelated to the plaintiff's claims. Although this device permitted the defendant to make an affirmative demand for relief, the utility of set-offs was limited because the claims either had to be for a liquidated amount or they had to arise out of a contract or judgment.[5]

Early state codes reflected this same narrow approach. Often, they required, expressly or through judicial interpretation, that the counterclaim directly defeat or diminish the plaintiff's claim in some way.[6] Moreover, most state codes limited counterclaims to certain types of actions—such as claims arising out of the same transaction, or involving liquidated sums, or representing prescribed causes, such as contract or tort claims. In short, early code practice continued to reward the party who first initiated a legal proceeding and put the onus on the defendant to bring an entirely separate action to pursue most claims against the opposing party.

There were restrictions on counterclaims even in equity. Under Federal Equity Rule 30 of 1912, counterclaims were allowed only if they arose "out of the transaction which is the subject matter of the suit."[7] Furthermore, equitable counterclaims were permitted only against equitable, not legal, claims.[8]

Under modern procedural rules, the ability to interpose a counterclaim is not limited in any way as to nature,[9] subject matter,[10] or relationship to the original claim.[11] Indeed, the Federal Rules permit the later addition of a counterclaim that matures or is acquired after the defendant has filed the original answer.[12] This liberal counterclaim

---

3. See 6 C. Wright, A. Miller & M. Kane, Civil 2d § 1401.

4. See 3 A. Sedgwick, Damages §§ 1042, 1049 (9th ed.1912); 3 J. Story, Equity Jurisprudence § 1878 (14th ed.1918).

5. See O.L. Barbour, Law of Set–Off 24–26 (1841); Waterman, Law of Set–Off, Recoupment and Counterclaim §§ 302–03 (2d ed.1872).

6. See C. Clark, Code Pleading § 101, at 650 (2d ed.1947).

7. J. Hopkins, Federal Equity Rules 209 (8th ed.1933).

8. See, e.g., American Mills Co. v. American Sur. Co., 260 U.S. 360, 43 S.Ct. 149, 67 L.Ed. 306 (1922).

9. With the merger of law and equity, prohibitions against pleading equitable counterclaims in legal actions, and vice-versa, were eliminated. See 6 C. Wright, A. Miller & M. Kane, Civil 2d § 1403.

10. See Fed.Civ.Proc.Rule 13(c).

11. The relationship between the counterclaim and original claim may determine whether the counterclaim is compulsory or permissive. See the discussion at notes 14–17, below.

12. Fed.Civ.Proc.Rule 13(e). See 6 C. Wright, A. Miller & M. Kane, Civil 2d §§ 1428–29.

policy, now followed in most states as well, seeks to eliminate circuity of action and multiple litigation.[13]

As counterclaim procedure now operates, any claim that a defendant has against a plaintiff, or that a third-party defendant has against a third-party plaintiff, may be asserted as a counterclaim.[14] However, many contemporary procedural rules distinguish between those counterclaims that arise out of the same transaction and occurrence as the opposing party's claim, and those that do not. The former type of counterclaim is designated "compulsory," the latter is "permissive."[15] Parties are required to assert any compulsory counterclaims they may have against opposing parties; if they fail to do so, they may not bring those claims subsequently as a separate action.[16] Permissive counterclaims may be postponed at the pleader's option without diminishing their future viability.[17]

This bifurcated categorization of counterclaims represents a compromise between two competing policies: (1) the desire to adjudicate all legal disputes between two parties in one action—which would compel all counterclaims to be asserted, regardless of how tenuously they were related to the original action, and (2) the importance of preventing lawsuits from becoming unduly complicated.[18] A rule that would make all counterclaims compulsory is not desirable because it would force a defendant or third-party defendant to litigate all claims in a forum dictated by the opponent. On the other hand, the court may determine that a counterclaim should be handled separately to promote economy or convenience, and, in that event, the court is empowered to order a separate trial of the claim.[19]

Despite the apparent simplicity of the transaction or occurrence standard for compulsory counterclaims, the concept continues to be elusive and ambiguous.[20] The most widely followed definition was formulated by the United States Supreme Court in Moore v. New York Cotton Exchange:[21]

---

13. See Price v. U.S., 42 F.3d 1068 (7th Cir.1994); LASA Per L'Industria Del Marmo Societa Per Azioni v. Alexander, 414 F.2d 143 (6th Cir.1969); Ortega, Snead, Dixon & Hanna v. Gennitti, 93 N.M. 135, 139, 597 P.2d 745 (1979); Gardner v. Gardner, 294 N.C. 172, 240 S.E.2d 399 (1978).

14. See generally 6 C. Wright, A. Miller & M. Kane, Civil 2d § 1403.

15. See, e.g., Fed.Civ.Proc.Rule 13(a), (b); West's Ann.Cal.Code Civ.Proc. §§ 426.10, 426.30–40; West's Fla.Stat.Ann. R.Civ.Proc.Rule 1.170(a), (b); Vernon's Ann.Mo.Civ.Proc.Rule 55.32(a), (b). Some states have expressly rejected the idea of compulsory counterclaims, relying instead upon court-created extensions of res judicata to encourage defendants to assert transactionally related claims. See, e.g., R.I.Rules Civ.Proc.Rule 13(a). See also 3 J. Weinstein,

H. Korn & A. Miller, New York Civil Practice ¶ 3019.12.

16. See the discussion at notes 46–54, below.

17. See American Triticale, Inc. v. Nytco Servs., Inc., 664 F.2d 1136, 1148 (9th Cir.1981); Jones v. Sonny Gerber Auto Sales, Inc., 71 F.R.D. 695 (D.Neb.1976).

18. See 6 C. Wright, A. Miller & M. Kane, Civil 2d § 1409.

19. See § 6.2, above.

20. See the detailed discussion in 6 C. Wright, A. Miller & M. Kane, Civil 2d § 1410. See generally Kane, Original Sin and the Transaction in Federal Civil Procedure, 76 Texas L.Rev. 1723 (1998).

21. 270 U.S. 593, 46 S.Ct. 367, 70 L.Ed. 750 (1926).

[The transaction or occurrence] is the one circumstance without which neither party would have found it necessary to seek relief. Essential facts alleged by appellant enter into and constitute in part the cause of action set forth in the counterclaim. That they are not precisely identical, or that the counterclaim embraces additional allegations * * * does not matter.[22]

The value of this definition is uncertain. Obviously, the Moore standard gives the courts rather wide latitude in making case-by-case determinations of whether counterclaims are compulsory.[23]

A number of courts have sought more concrete standards and four additional tests have emerged for deciding whether a counterclaim is compulsory.[24] First, would res judicata bar a subsequent suit on defendant's claim absent the compulsory counterclaim rule?[25] Second, are the issues of fact and law raised by the claim and counterclaim largely the same?[26] Third, will substantially the same evidence support or refute plaintiff's claim as well as defendant's counterclaim?[27] And fourth, is there any logical relationship between the claim and counterclaim?[28] In all of these tests, an affirmative answer means that the counterclaim is compulsory.

Each of these standards is subject to criticism. The first test merely imparts the ambiguity of another uncertain field of civil procedure— namely, former adjudication.[29] Moreover, the premise of the test is logically faulty; in jurisdictions that do not have a compulsory counterclaim rule, a pleader typically will not be barred by res judicata from suing independently on a claim that could have been brought as a counterclaim in a previous action.[30]

The second and third tests reflect roughly similar outlooks and suffer analogous shortcomings. The second test, insofar as it demands identity of issues, narrows the scope of the compulsory counterclaim rule unduly. And if complete issue identity is not really demanded, then there

22. 270 U.S. at 610, 46 S.Ct. at 371.

23. Many courts have been willing to interpret the terms "transaction or occurrence" liberally to encourage the parties to settle as much of their business as possible at one time. See, e.g., Albright v. Gates, 362 F.2d 928 (9th Cir.1966); Magna Pictures Corp. v. Paramount Pictures Corp., 265 F.Supp. 144 (C.D.Cal.1967).

24. For additional cases applying these tests, see 6 C. Wright, A. Miller & M. Kane, Civil 2d § 1410.

25. See Libbey–Owens–Ford Glass Co. v. Sylvania Indus. Corp., 154 F.2d 814, 816 (2d Cir.1946) (Frank, J. dissenting), cert. denied 328 U.S. 859.

26. See, e.g., Whigham v. Beneficial Finance Co. of Fayetteville, Inc., 599 F.2d 1322 (4th Cir.1979); Connecticut Indem. Co. v. Lee, 168 F.2d 420, 423 (1st Cir.1948).

27. See, e.g., Columbia Plaza Corp. v. Security Nat. Bank, 525 F.2d 620 (D.C.Cir. 1975); Non–Ferrous Metals, Inc. v. Saramar Aluminum Co., 25 F.R.D. 102, 105 (N.D.Ohio 1960).

28. See, e.g., Revere Copper & Brass Inc. v. Aetna Cas. & Sur. Co., 426 F.2d 709 (5th Cir.1970).

29. See generally Chapter 14, below.

30. See Restatement Second of Judgments § 22 (1982). The exception to this rule is that res judicata will bar a counterclaim when the relationship between that claim and the original plaintiff's claim is such that the successful prosecution of the counterclaim would nullify the initial judgment or impair rights established in the first action. Id., comment f.

is no convenient measuring rod to determine how much issue overlap must exist to bring the compulsory counterclaim rule into play. Although the third test suggests the necessity of overlapping claims and counterclaims, this time at the level of evidence rather than of issues, it excludes an entire group of cases in which the counterclaim arises out of the same events as does the main claim but involves substantially different evidence.

Unlike the other three, under the fourth test—frequently referred to as the "logical relationship" standard[31]—the principal consideration in determining whether a counterclaim is compulsory rests on the efficiency or economy of trying the counterclaim in the same litigation as the main claim. As a result, the convenience of the court, rather than solely the counterclaim's relationship to the facts or issues of the opposing claim, is controlling. The hallmark of this approach is flexibility. Although the fourth test has been criticized for being overly broad in scope and uncertain in application,[32] it has by far the widest acceptance among the courts.[33]

Examples of cases in which courts have ruled on the question whether given counterclaims were compulsory may provide further illumination. In one action in which the plaintiff claimed that the defendants had slandered him with respect to his sale of oil securities, the defendants' counterclaim for the price they had paid to the plaintiff for the allegedly worthless oil securities was found to arise out of the same transaction and was compulsory.[34] In another case, the defendant patients' medical malpractice claim was held to be compulsory in an action by the medical center for unpaid medical bills arising from the same treatment.[35] Also, when an insurer sues for a declaratory judgment of nonliability, the insured's claim under the policy is treated as a compulsory counterclaim.[36] However, if the persons injured by the event forming the basis of the dispute about the policy are brought in as codefendants in the insurer's suit for a declaratory judgment of nonliability, their counterclaims for injuries are not compulsory because their claims grow out of the insured's tort liability, not the contractual rights existing between the insured and the insurer.[37]

---

31. See the parallel discussion of the transaction and occurrence problem in the context of party joinder in § 6.4, above.

32. Bose Corp. v. Consumers Union of the U.S., Inc., 384 F.Supp. 600 (D.Mass. 1974); Comment, Narrowing the Scope of Rule 13(a), 60 U.Chi.L.Rev. 141 (1993).

33. E.g., Xerox Corp. v. SCM Corp., 576 F.2d 1057 (3d Cir.1978); Newburger, Loeb & Co. v. Gross, 563 F.2d 1057, 1071 (2d Cir.1977), cert. denied 434 U.S. 1035; Jack LaLanne Fitness Centers, Inc. v. Jimlar, Inc., 884 F.Supp. 162 (D.N.J.1995); Rettig Enterprises, Inc. v. Koehler, 68 Ohio

St.3d 274, 626 N.E.2d 99 (1994). For additional cases, see 6 C. Wright, A. Miller & M. Kane, Civil 2d § 1410.

34. Albright v. Gates, 362 F.2d 928 (9th Cir.1966).

35. Geisinger Medical Center v. Gough, 160 F.R.D. 467 (M.D.Pa.1994).

36. Plains Ins. Co. v. Sandoval, 35 F.R.D. 293 (D.Colo.1964).

37. E.g., Aetna Ins. Co. v. Pennsylvania Mfrs. Ass'n Ins. Co., 456 F.Supp. 627 (E.D.Pa.1978); Globe Indem. Co. v. Teixeira, 230 F.Supp. 444 (D.Hawai'i 1963).

The typical compulsory counterclaim rule contains several explicit exceptions[38] and a party who fails to assert a counterclaim that qualifies under one of these exceptions may present that claim in a subsequent action.[39] Exceptions to the compulsory counterclaim rule are based on equitable policies that override the goal of encouraging resolution of as many disputes as possible in a single action. For example, a party need not assert a claim that has not fully matured at the time the responsive pleading is served.[40] Without this exception, a plaintiff, who fears a claim will be brought after it has been more thoroughly developed, would have the unfair tactical advantage of being able to force the defendant's hand. A party also need not assert a counterclaim for a cause of action that is the subject of another pending action.[41] It would be inappropriate to allow the mere fact that the plaintiff has chosen a different forum to litigate her claim to override the prior forum choice for the counterclaim. In addition, a party need not raise a counterclaim if its adjudication would require a third party over whom personal jurisdiction cannot be obtained.[42] This exception simply recognizes that it would be self-defeating to oblige a pleader to assert a counterclaim if that counterclaim will be dismissed for lack of a required third party.[43] In a similar vein, an exception exists if the original claim was brought on the basis of attachment jurisdiction, rather than in personam jurisdiction.[44] If a court cannot obtain full in personam jurisdiction over the defendant, it would be inequitable to penalize the defendant for not asserting his counterclaims.[45] Yet, if the defendant chooses to assert any counterclaim, it seems appropriate to compel him to assert all other counterclaims that normally would be compulsory.

The threat that a court will refuse to entertain in a later suit a claim not previously raised as a compulsory counterclaim lies at the heart of the procedure. It has been argued that the preclusion of an unpleaded compulsory counterclaim is based on an extension of the doctrine of former adjudication[46] and most of the courts that have dealt with the question have spoken of "res judicata" as preventing the later assertion

---

38. In addition to express rule exceptions, some case law exceptions to the compulsory counterclaim requirement have developed. See 6 C. Wright, A. Miller & M. Kane, Civil 2d § 1412.

39. See generally 6 C. Wright, A. Miller & M. Kane, Civil 2d § 1411. Since the exceptions are designed to protect the defending party, that party may waive the right of nonassertion. An excepted counterclaim that is asserted will be treated like a compulsory counterclaim. See Union Paving Co. v. Downer Corp., 276 F.2d 468 (9th Cir. 1960).

40. See, e.g., Dillard v. Security Pac. Brokers, Inc., 835 F.2d 607 (5th Cir.1988); Stahl v. Ohio River Co., 424 F.2d 52 (3d Cir.1970).

41. See, e.g., U.S. v. Sarman, 699 F.2d 469 (9th Cir.1983).

42. See Dragor Shipping Corp. v. Union Tank Car Co., 378 F.2d 241 (9th Cir. 1967).

43. See 6 C. Wright, A. Miller & M. Kane, Civil 2d §§ 1434–36, for a discussion of the ability to add parties to a counterclaim under Federal Rule 13(h).

44. See 6 C. Wright, A. Miller & M. Kane, Civil 2d § 1411.

45. See the Advisory Committee Note to the 1963 Amendment to Rule 13(a), reprinted in 31 F.R.D. at 635. The change in standards for asserting attachment jurisdiction may make this exception less useful or meaningful. See §§ 3.14–3.15, above.

46. See Wright, Estoppel by Rule: The Compulsory Counterclaim Under Modern Pleading, 38 Minn.L.Rev. 423 (1954).

of the claim.[47] Some courts have relied upon theories of waiver or estoppel.[48] As one state court expressed it, preclusion of the counterclaim is "a bar created by rule * * * which logically is in the nature of an estoppel arising from the culpable conduct of a litigant in failing to assert a proper claim."[49] This second analysis provides a more flexible approach and affords a means of extricating a defendant who has not knowingly refrained from asserting his claim from the severe consequences of the counterclaim rule.[50] This safety valve might be useful, for example, when an insurance company controlled the defense of the first action and the actual defendant in that action lacked a realistic opportunity to assert a claim.[51]

A question remains as to the effect of the failure to assert a compulsory counterclaim in the courts of another jurisdiction. Does the failure preclude the defendant from bringing a subsequent action on the claim in another judicial system? Analytically, if the compulsory counterclaim rule is viewed as purely procedural, then a court in a different jurisdiction should be free to hear the claim because the rule has no effect outside the judicial system in which it was rendered.[52] But if the compulsory counterclaim rule is conceptualized as defining the scope of a cause of action for res judicata purposes or creating a conclusive presumption of waiver, then the defendant should be barred in all courts. Most state courts that have considered this issue have barred a claim that should have been brought as a compulsory counterclaim in a previous federal court action.[53] The same problem can arise when the action in which the counterclaim is not asserted is brought in a state court having a compulsory counterclaim rule. Again, the result when the claim is advanced may depend on how the original forum's rule is analyzed and whether the second forum, which can be either state or federal, has a compulsory counterclaim rule.[54]

The difference between compulsory and permissive counterclaims also becomes important for statute of limitations purposes. The institution of an action by the plaintiff is held by most courts to suspend the

---

47. See Baker v. Southern Pacific Transp., 542 F.2d 1123 (9th Cir.1976); U.S. v. Hampton Tree Farms, Inc., 860 F.Supp. 741 (D.Or.1994); Rich v. Tudor, 123 Ariz. 393, 599 P.2d 846 (App.1979).

48. See, e.g., Kane v. Magna Mixer Co., 71 F.3d 555 (6th Cir.1995), cert. denied 517 U.S. 1220; Twin Disc, Inc. v. Lowell, 69 F.R.D. 64 (E.D.Wis.1975); Reynolds v. Hartford Acc. & Indem. Co., 278 F.Supp. 331 (S.D.N.Y.1967); Suchta v. Robinett, 596 P.2d 1380 (Wyo.1979).

49. House v. Hanson, 245 Minn. 466, 470, 72 N.W.2d 874, 877 (1955).

50. In Douglas v. Wisconsin Alumni Research Foundation, 81 F.Supp. 167 (N.D.Ill.1948), for example, the action in which defendant failed to interpose the compulsory counterclaim terminated without a decision on the merits. The court concluded that the first action ended before the defendant waived the counterclaim.

51. See Reynolds v. Hartford Acc. & Indem. Co., 278 F.Supp. 331 (S.D.N.Y. 1967).

52. See 6 C. Wright, A. Miller & M. Kane, Civil 2d § 1417.

53. London v. City of Philadelphia, 412 Pa. 496, 194 A.2d 901 (1963). See also Adams v. KVWO, Inc., 570 P.2d 458, 461 (Wyo.1977).

54. E.g., Springs v. First Nat. Bank of Cut Bank, 835 F.2d 1293 (9th Cir.1988); Cleckner v. Republic Van & Storage Co., 556 F.2d 766 (5th Cir.1977).

running of the statute of limitations on any compulsory counterclaim.[55] Permissive counterclaims are barred in this situation.[56] The problem becomes more complicated when the statute of limitations already has run on the counterclaim before the plaintiff commences the action, although compulsory counterclaims have been allowed by some courts in that situation.[57] Fairness, however, requires that the statute of limitations not be tolled by the commencement of an action with regard to additional parties to a counterclaim brought in under provisions like Federal Rule 13(h). If those parties could not have been sued in an independent action because the statute had run, they should not be subject to that claim when it is asserted in the guise of a counterclaim.

The broad scope of the modern counterclaim poses several secondary procedural questions. One is the effect on the right of jury trial of the assertion of a legal counterclaim against an equitable claim, or an equitable counterclaim against a legal claim.[58] Until the merger of law and equity, courts frequently held that a defendant asserting a legal counterclaim in an equity suit waived the jury trial right.[59] Yet, in many jurisdictions, a party who does not assert a counterclaim arising out of the same transaction as the original action loses the right to bring that claim at a later time, thus forcing a counterclaimant to choose between losing the right of action and losing the right to a jury trial. This limitation on jury trial rights arguably was unconstitutional.[60] It now is clear that the right to a jury trial does not depend on the characterization of the main claim as legal; if the counterclaim would be jury-triable if sued upon alone, it will be so even if presented in an equitable action.[61]

A second problem area under modern counterclaim rules stems from the requirement that counterclaims be filed only against opposing parties—that is, persons in an adversarial relationship. Whether such a relationship exists becomes complicated when the original plaintiff or third-party plaintiff acts in more than one capacity. The rule appears to be that a counterclaim can be asserted only against a party in the capacity in which she appears in the action.[62] Illustratively, when a plaintiff sues in her capacity as a representative of the government, the defendant cannot counterclaim against the plaintiff in her individual

55. See Trindade v. Superior Ct. In & For Contra Costa County, 29 Cal.App.3d 857, 106 Cal.Rptr. 48 (1973); Armstrong v. Logsdon, 469 S.W.2d 342 (Ky.1971).

56. Spartan Grain & Mill Co. v. Ayers, 581 F.2d 419, 430 (5th Cir.1978), cert. denied 444 U.S. 831.

57. Notions of recoupment and set-off typically are invoked to support allowing a counterclaim to be asserted when the limitations statute has run before the plaintiff filed suit. See U.S. v. Southern Cal. Edison Co., 229 F.Supp. 268 (S.D.Cal.1964).

58. See the discussion in 6 C. Wright, A. Miller & M. Kane, Civil 2d § 1405.

59. See American Mills Co. v. American Sur. Co., 260 U.S. 360, 43 S.Ct. 149, 67 L.Ed. 306 (1922).

60. See Lisle Mills, Inc. v. Arkay Infants Wear, Inc., 90 F.Supp. 676, 678–79 (E.D.N.Y.1950); Harada v. Burns, 50 Hawaii 528, 445 P.2d 376, 382 (1968); James, Right to a Jury Trial in Civil Actions, 72 Yale L.J. 655, 684 (1963).

61. Beacon Theatres, Inc. v. Westover, 359 U.S. 500, 79 S.Ct. 948, 3 L.Ed.2d 988 (1959). This case is discussed more fully in § 11.5, below.

62. See Banco Nacional de Cuba v. Chase Manhattan Bank, 658 F.2d 875, 886 (2d Cir.1981); Rhodes, Inc. v. Morrow, 937 F.Supp. 1202 (M.D.N.C.1996).

capacity. Conversely, in an action against a municipal tax official for allegedly causing the unlawful arrest and detention of a taxpayer, the court held that the official could not assert a counterclaim on behalf of the city for the recovery of the taxes.[63] Because this limitation restricts the possibility of settling all disputes between the litigants in one action, some cases have looked behind the stated capacities of the parties to see if they are in fact "opposing,"[64] and have eliminated the restriction altogether when the relationship between the two distinct capacities appears exceptionally close.[65]

A third area in counterclaim procedure that should be considered is the pleading rules pertinent thereto. Mislabeling frequently occurs in the pleading of counterclaims in that they are referred to erroneously as cross-claims or affirmative defenses, and vice-versa. Most modern pleading rules do not place much emphasis on proper labeling, however.[66] The courts generally ignore the nomenclature used and look to the substance of the claim to determine its correct classification.[67] There is also the question of the proper response to a defendant's counterclaim. Some early decisions under the new liberal counterclaim rules instructed a plaintiff confronted with a counterclaim to amend the original complaint in order to assert any new affirmative claims that arose out of the same transaction or occurrence as the defendant's counterclaim.[68] The question, of course, has greater significance in a jurisdiction in which those counterclaims are compulsory and thus must be asserted or lost. Yet, in some cases, this course of pleading may be awkward.[69] The weight of authority now appears to be that the right and obligation to interpose a counterclaim applies to plaintiffs as well as to defendants; thus, a counterclaim against a counterclaim is an appropriate manner of proceeding.[70]

§ 6.8 Cross–Claims

A cross-claim is any claim asserted by one party against a coparty. Under Federal Rule 13(g), a cross-claim must arise out of the transaction or occurrence that is the subject matter either of the original action or of

63. Durham v. Bunn, 85 F.Supp. 530 (E.D.Pa.1949).

64. See, e.g., Scott v. U.S., 173 Ct.Cl. 650, 354 F.2d 292 (1965) (defendant allowed to assert counterclaim against member of partnership in an individual capacity, although the plaintiff was suing as a representative of the partnership).

65. See Moore–McCormack Lines, Inc. v. McMahon, 235 F.2d 142 (2d Cir.1956) (widow, who had been sued as an administratrix, permitted to assert counterclaim in capacity as a special statutory trustee under Jones Act for the benefit of the named defendant).

66. See the discussion of the liberal pleading requirements in most jurisdictions in §§ 5.1–5.21, above.

67. See Reiter v. Cooper, 507 U.S. 258, 113 S.Ct. 1213, 122 L.Ed.2d 604 (1993); Brown v. Johns, 312 So.2d 526 (Fla.App. 1975).

68. See Millar, Counterclaim Against Counterclaim, 48 Nw.U.L.Rev. 671, 671–72 (1954).

69. See the discussion in Bethlehem Fabricators, Inc. v. John Bowen Co., 1 F.R.D. 274 (D.Mass.1940).

70. See Electroglas, Inc. v. Dynatex Corp., 473 F.Supp. 1167 (N.D.Cal.1979); Millar, Counterclaim Against Counterclaim, 48 Nw.U.L.Rev. 671, 671 (1954).

a counterclaim therein, or it must relate to property that is the subject matter of the original action.[1] The same test is used in numerous states.[2]

Before the merger of law and equity, the cross-claim device was available in equity and under some procedural codes, but was not termed a cross-claim. In equity the device was known as the cross-bill. It permitted a claim against any other party or coparty to the action. In the federal courts, Federal Equity Rule 30 introduced counterclaims, and cross-claims became devices available only against coparties.[3]

In code jurisdictions, cross-bills frequently were renamed cross-complaints. Generally, these devices required that the cause of action set forth in the cross-complaint arise out of the facts supporting the original complaint.[4] Today's rules, although generally similar to the cross-complaint devices,[5] are more liberal in scope in that they also direct the court to bring in parties necessary for granting complete relief.[6] In addition, in most jurisdictions, a cross-claimant can seek either affirmative relief or indemnification for any liability to another party in an action.[7]

The same policy underlies the modern cross-claim that animates the modern transactional or compulsory[8] counterclaim—the desire to avoid multiple suits and to encourage resolution of the entire controversy among the parties with a minimum of procedural steps.[9] In pursuing this objective, most courts have construed cross-claim provisions liberally.[10] Moreover, the assertion of a legal cross-claim in an equitable action does not waive the right to a jury trial on the legal claim.[11] Any ill effects from the expansive application of the device—for example, the chance that the

---

§ 6.8

1. See generally 6 C. Wright, A. Miller & M. Kane, Civil 2d § 1431.

2. E.g., Ala.Rules Civ.Proc., Rule 13(g); West's Ann.Cal.Code Civ.Proc. § 428.10(b); Iowa Rules Civ.Proc., Rule 33; Md.Dist.Rule 3–331(b). But see N.Y.—McKinney's CPLR 3019(b) (any claim may be asserted between defendants).

3. See J. Hopkins, Federal Equity Rules Annotated, Rule 30, Note 1 (8th ed.1933).

4. See C. Clark, Code Pleading § 105 (2d ed.1947).

5. Some code states still retain the term "cross-complaint." E.g., West's Ann. Cal.Code Civ.Proc. § 428.10.

6. C. Clark, Code Pleading § 105 (2d ed.1947). See also Fed.Civ.Proc.Rule 13(h).

7. Chappell v. Scarborough, 224 So.2d 791 (Fla.App.1969); Board of Educ., School District 16 v. Standhardt, 80 N.M. 543, 458 P.2d 795 (1969).

8. See § 6.7 at n. 18, above.

9. See Lenske v. Knutsen, 410 F.2d 583 (9th Cir.1969); Werneth v. Cook, 487 F.Supp. 144 (N.D.Miss.1979); Selective Ins.

Co. v. NCNB Nat. Bank, 324 N.C. 560, 380 S.E.2d 521 (1989).

In federal court if the original claim or counterclaim is dismissed for lack of subject-matter jurisdiction, then the cross-claim also must be dismissed unless it is supported by an independent base of jurisdiction. See 6 C. Wright, A. Miller & M. Kane, Civil 2d § 1433. If the main claim is dismissed on nonjurisdictional grounds, however, then depending on how far the action has progressed, the court may retain the cross-claim even if it fails to satisfy jurisdiction requirements. See Fairview Park Excavating Co. v. Al Monzo Constr. Co., 560 F.2d 1122 (3d Cir.1977); Parris v. St. Johnsbury Trucking Co., 395 F.2d 543 (2d Cir.1968). See also the discussion in §§ 2.12–2.14, above.

10. See LASA Per L'Industria Del Marmo Societa Per Azioni v. Alexander, 414 F.2d 143 (6th Cir.1969); First Tennessee Nat. Bank, Chattanooga v. Federal Deposit Ins. Corp., 421 F.Supp. 35 (E.D.Tenn.1976).

11. Black v. Boyd, 248 F.2d 156 (6th Cir.1957), modified per curiam 249 F.2d 441 (6th Cir.1957). See also § 11.5, below, on the right to jury trial in multiple claim settings.

action may become unduly complicated and the rights of parties may be prejudiced—can be eliminated by invoking the provision for separate trials now found in all procedural systems.[12]

As already intimated, two limitations exist on the court's ability to allow claims to be brought in by way of cross-claim: (1) the cross-claim may be asserted only against a coparty and (2) it must present a claim transactionally related to the original claim or to a counterclaim, or related to property that is the subject matter of the original action.[13] Unlike transactionally related counterclaims in some jurisdictions, cross-claims are totally permissive and may be asserted in the action at the party's option or brought in a subsequent independent action.[14]

The requirement that a cross-claim be against a coparty typically is satisfied when the claim is asserted between original defendants. Technically, co-plaintiffs also fall within the language of modern cross-claim rules. However, case law generally has prohibited the assertion of cross-claims between co-plaintiffs unless a counterclaim has been interposed against them by a defendant.[15]

The coparty requirement distinguishes cross-claims from counterclaims, which may be asserted only against opposing parties.[16] Unfortunately, counterclaims still occasionally are confused with cross-claims, possibly because the terms "cross-complaint" and "cross-bill" continue to be used in some states for what now are called counterclaims under the Federal Rules and their state counterparts.[17] In most cases, opposing parties are distinguished easily from coparties; furthermore, a mislabeling of a properly asserted cross-claim or counterclaim will not prejudice the pleader.[18]

Those difficulties that do arise in deciding who is a coparty often stem from the question whether a coparty necessarily must be a party at the same level of a multiparty action. This question arises, for example, when a plaintiff sues two defendants, one of whom asserts a third-party claim for indemnification against another new party. If the third-party defendant is considered a codefendant, then the original defendant can assert, by way of cross-claim, any claim he has against the impleaded

---

12. See § 6.2, above.

13. Once one transactionally related claim is asserted, Rule 18 controls and parties may join any additional claims they have against their coparties. See generally § 6.6, above.

14. See U.S. v. Confederate Acres Sanitary Sewage & Drainage Sys., Inc., 935 F.2d 796 (6th Cir.1991); Hall v. General Motors Corp., 647 F.2d 175, 207 (D.C.Cir.1980); Farm Credit Servs. of Mandan, FLCA v. Crow, 501 N.W.2d 756 (N.D.1993); Thomas v. Hawaii, 57 Hawaii 639, 562 P.2d 425 (1977).

15. See Danner v. Anskis, 256 F.2d 123 (3d Cir.1958). This conclusion is reached by interpreting the transaction requirement narrowly as the group of facts relating to the claims already asserted directly against the cross-claimant, rather than to those facts on which the entire lawsuit is based.

16. See § 6.7 nn. 62–65, above. For a discussion of when co-parties may become opposing parties, see Rainbow Management Group, Ltd. v. Atlantis Submarines Hawaii, L.P., 158 F.R.D. 656 (D.Hawai'i 1994).

17. See the general discussion in 6 C. Wright, A. Miller & M. Kane, Civil 2d § 1431; Greenbaum, Jacks or Better to Open: Procedural Limitations on Co–Party and Third Party Claims, 74 Minn.L.Rev. 507 (1990).

18. See 6 C. Wright, A. Miller & M. Kane, Civil 2d § 1407.

party that arises out of the subject matter of the original action. If the third-party defendant is not considered a coparty, then any claim that is asserted must satisfy the requirements of the impleader rules, which generally limit claims against third-party defendants to those alleging the liability of the impleaded party to the original defendant for all or part of the plaintiff's claim against that defendant.[19] The courts have not agreed on the treatment of this problem.[20] However, the interpretation that best reflects the original intent of the cross-claim provision limits coparties to those on the same level of litigation.[21]

The other major cross-claim requirement is that the right of action asserted in the cross-claim must arise out of the transaction or occurrence underlying the original claim or counterclaim or it must involve property that is the subject matter of the original action. The test for transactional relatedness is very similar to that used to decide whether a counterclaim is compulsory.[22] Accordingly, most courts have made the determination on the basis of the logical relationship standard, which examines whether the cross-claim involves many of the same factual and legal issues present in the main action.[23]

The application of this standard is illustrated by an insurer's action for a declaratory judgment of nonliability with regard to a car accident in which the insured and the injured person are named as codefendants. In this situation, the injured individual may assert a cross-claim for his injuries against the insured if that claim bears a logical relationship to the principal claim raised in the insurance company's action. This relationship would exist if the insurer seeks the declaration of nonliability on the ground that the car in question was not under the insured's control at the time of the accident and the insured raises the same defense against the injured person.[24] On the other hand, if the declaratory action is to determine whether the terms of the policy extend to the accident at issue, the investigations required for the original claim and the cross-claim might involve totally different factual and legal issues. Consequently, the logical relationship test would not be satisfied.[25]

Notably, unlike counterclaim practice, cross-claim provisions do not extend to a transactionally unrelated claim. The requirement of a transactional nexus is to help ensure that plaintiff's case will not be complicated by a totally unrelated series of claims among codefendants. Once a defendant files a valid cross-claim against a codefendant, howev-

---

19. See the lengthy discussion of what types of claims may be brought against a third-party defendant in 6 C. Wright, A. Miller & M. Kane, Civil 2d §§ 1446–52. See also § 6.9, below.

20. Compare Fogel v. United Gas Improvement Co., 32 F.R.D. 202 (E.D.Pa.1963) (cross-claim allowed), with Murray v. Haverford Hosp. Corp., 278 F.Supp. 5, 6 (E.D.Pa.1968) (cross-claims disallowed).

21. See 6 C. Wright, A. Miller & M. Kane, Civil 2d § 1431.

22. See the discussion in § 6.7 at nn. 20–37, above.

23. See LASA Per L'Industria Del Marmo Societa Per Azioni v. Alexander, 414 F.2d 143, 147 (6th Cir.1969).

24. See Collier v. Harvey, 179 F.2d 664 (10th Cir.1949).

25. See Allstate Ins. Co. v. Daniels, 87 F.R.D. 1 (W.D.Okl.1978); Globe Indem. Co. v. Teixeira, 230 F.Supp. 444 (D.Hawai'i 1963).

er, the former can join all other claims he has against that codefendant under the general claim joinder rules, even though the additional claims are totally unrelated to the plaintiff's original claim.[26] Moreover, the compulsory and permissive counterclaim provisions apply with respect to the codefendant's answer.[27]

The right to assert a cross-claim that is related to property that is the subject matter of the original action[28] also may authorize a cross-claim beyond the transactional nexus because the basis of the cross-claim's relation to the property may have no factual or legal connection with the transaction or occurrence underlying the original action.[29] For example, in an action by the United States to foreclose a mortgage, defendant's mortgagor was allowed to file a cross-claim for fraud against a coparty, relying on the property connection.[30]

§ 6.9   Third–Party Practice (Impleader)

Impleader, or third-party practice, is the procedural device enabling the defendant in a lawsuit to bring into the action an additional party who may be liable for all or part of the original plaintiff's claim against the defendant.[1] This additional party is known as a third-party defendant, and the original defendant who brings an impleader claim is called the third-party plaintiff. Unlike counterclaim procedure, impleader is entirely optional; the defendant may assert the claim against the third party in a completely separate action.[2]

The historical antecedents of impleader are found in the practice of "vouching to warranty" at common law. That procedure permitted a defendant sued for the recovery of property to vouch in a third party who had given a warranty to title to the defendant. Later developments broadened the scope of impleader to other situations as well.[3]

As is true of the theory underlying counterclaim provisions,[4] impleader is intended "to avoid circuity of action and to dispose of the entire subject matter arising from one set of facts in one action, thus

26. Fed.Civ.Proc.Rule 18. See the discussion in § 6.6, above.

27. See § 6.7, above.

28. See the discussion in 6 C. Wright, A. Miller & M. Kane, Civil 2d § 1432.

29. See, e.g., Claude A. Hinton, Jr., Inc. v. Institutional Investors Trust, 133 Ga.App. 364, 211 S.E.2d 169 (1974).

30. Lenske v. Knutsen, 410 F.2d 583, 585–86 (9th Cir.1969).

§ 6.9

1. Impleader also may be used by a plaintiff who is facing a counterclaim. Fed. Civ.Proc.Rule 14(b); Va.Sup.Ct.Rules, Rule 3:10(b); Wis.Stat.Ann. 803.05(2). See Kaiser Aluminum & Chem. Sales, Inc. v. Ralston

Steel Corp., 25 F.R.D. 23 (N.D.Ill.1959); New York, New Haven & Hartford R. Co. v. U.S., 21 F.R.D. 328 (S.D.N.Y.1958); Welch v. Crown–Zellerbach Corp., 365 So.2d 586 (La.App.1978).

2. See DeVore Brokerage Co. v. Goodyear Tire & Rubber Co., 308 F.Supp. 279 (M.D.Tenn.1969); Union Paving Co. v. Thomas, 9 F.R.D. 612 (E.D.Pa.1949).

3. See 2 W. Holdsworth, History of English Law, 112–14 (4th ed.1936); Degnan & Barton, Vouching to Quality Warranty: Case Law and Commercial Code, 51 Calif.L.Rev. 471 (1963); Developments in the Law—Multiparty Litigation in the Federal Courts, 71 Harv.L.Rev. 874, 906–13 (1958).

4. See § 6.7, above.

administering * * * justice expeditiously and economically."[5] The availability of impleader saves the time and cost of duplicating evidence in two proceedings, avoids inconsistent results on related claims based on identical or similar evidence, and eliminates the serious prejudice to the original defendant that might result from a time lag between the plaintiff's judgment against him and a judgment in the defendant's favor against the third-party defendant.[6]

An illustration of how impleader fulfills these purposes is provided by the case of a plaintiff suing a railroad for injuries sustained when the plaintiff was hit by a mail pouch thrown from the defendant's moving train. A mail clerk employed by the United States government was responsible for any judgment that might be entered against the railroad on the plaintiff's claim. It would be senseless to require a separate action by the defendant clerk against the third-party defendant under these circumstances—the facts concerning the plaintiff's injury that would have to be litigated in each action would be identical.[7]

Federal Rule 14 governs impleader in the federal courts; similar provisions are found in a number of states.[8] Rule 14 permits a defendant to serve a third-party complaint "upon a person not a party to the action who is or may be liable to the third-party plaintiff for all or part of the plaintiff's claim against the third-party plaintiff." Using this provision, defendant may implead someone whom the plaintiff could not sue directly[9] as, for example, when the statute of limitations would have barred an action against that person by the original plaintiff.[10] This is because a third-party plaintiff's right of indemnity or subrogation does not arise until he has been held liable on the original claim.

The basis of the third-party claim may be indemnity,[11] subrogation,[12] contribution,[13] breach of warranty,[14] or any other legal theory supporting derivative liability. It is not enough that the impleader claim arise out of the same transaction or occurrence as the plaintiff's claim against the original defendant; it must involve a transfer of liability based on

---

5. LASA Per L'Industria Del Marmo Societa Per Azioni v. Alexander, 414 F.2d 143, 146 (6th Cir.1969). See additionally Hood v. Security Bank of Huntington, 562 F.Supp. 749 (S.D.Ohio 1983).

6. Dery v. Wyer, 265 F.2d 804 (2d Cir. 1959).

7. This example is suggested by the facts in U.S. v. Acord, 209 F.2d 709 (10th Cir.1954), cert. denied 347 U.S. 975.

8. E.g., Vernon's Ann.Mo.Civ.Proc. Rule 52.11; N.Y.—McKinney's CPLR 1007; Pa.Rules Civ.Proc., Rule 2252.

9. See 6 C. Wright, A. Miller & M. Kane, Civil 2d § 1447.

10. TSZ Ki Yim v. Home Indem. Co., 95 F.R.D. 349 (D.D.C.1982). But see Rambone v. Critzer, 548 F.Supp. 660 (W.D.Va. 1982).

11. E.g., John Mohr & Sons v. GMR Associates, Inc., 388 F.2d 907 (7th Cir. 1968); Yelin v. Carvel Corp., 119 N.M. 554, 893 P.2d 450 (1995); Funt v. Ruiz, 58 A.D.2d 801, 396 N.Y.S.2d 418 (1977), affirmed 51 N.Y.2d 358, 434 N.Y.S.2d 189, 414 N.E.2d 689 (1980).

12. E.g., Glens Falls Indem. Co. v. Atlantic Bldg. Corp., 199 F.2d 60 (4th Cir. 1952); Attorneys' Title v. Punta Gorda Isles, Inc., 547 So.2d 1250 (Fla.App.1989).

13. E.g., Craigie v. General Motors Corp., 740 F.Supp. 353 (E.D.Pa.1990); New Hampshire Ins. Co. v. Petrik, 343 So.2d 48 (Fla.App.1977).

14. E.g., Altec, Inc. v. FWD Corp., 399 F.2d 860 (5th Cir.1968); Adalman v. Baker, Watts & Co., 599 F.Supp. 752 (D.Md.1984).

plaintiff's original claim.[15] Further, the legal theory underlying the claim must be one that is recognized by the relevant substantive law.[16] Impleader cannot be used to create a cause of action that previously has not been recognized.[17] The device is a procedural mechanism acting merely to accelerate the prosecution of otherwise recognized claims.[18] Impleader permits the bringing in of a third party against whom the original defendant's claim has not yet accrued; defendant's claim will not exist until and unless the plaintiff succeeds in the original action. Thus, allowing impleader under these circumstances has the effect of accelerating the determination of the contingent claim.

In federal practice,[19] and in many states,[20] impleader of a third party because she is directly liable to the plaintiff in the original action is forbidden. Accordingly, impleader is not suitable when the defendant believes that someone other than himself is responsible for the breach of legal duty giving rise to plaintiff's claim. A defendant sued for negligence, for example, cannot implead a third party on the theory that that person's negligence was totally responsible for plaintiff's injury.[21] When a third party's conduct furnishes a complete defense against the defendant's liability, the defendant may raise that conduct defensively in the answer but may not use it as a foundation for impleader. If the plaintiff has brought separate actions against two defendants, one of them who claims that the other is solely responsible for plaintiff's harm may be able to effectuate joinder by means of a consolidation of the actions.[22]

15. U.S. v. Joe Grasso & Son, Inc., 380 F.2d 749 (5th Cir.1967); Lopez v. U.S., 162 F.R.D. 256 (D.P.R.1995); National Bank of Canada v. Artex Indus., Inc., 627 F.Supp. 610, 613 (S.D.N.Y.1986). The facts supporting derivative liability almost always will stem from the same transaction or occurrence as plaintiff's original claim. But compare U.S. Fidelity & Guar. Co. v. Perkins, 388 F.2d 771 (10th Cir.1968).

16. Kim v. Fujikawa, 871 F.2d 1427 (9th Cir.1989) (when ERISA did not provide a right of contribution between fund trustees, impleader by a fund representative against the other trustees was denied); Howard v. Wilson Concrete Co., 57 F.R.D. 8 (W.D.Mo.1972) (when no indemnitor-indemnitee relationship existed under Missouri law, defendant could not use Rule 14(a) to implead plaintiff's employer).

17. Fraley v. Worthington, 64 F.R.D. 726 (D.Wyo.1974); Fontenot v. Roach, 120 F.Supp. 788 (E.D.Tenn.1954). Federal Rule 14 cannot be read as creating any form of derivative liability for to do so would violate the Rules Enabling Act's prohibition against abridging, enlarging, or modifying substantive rights. See 28 U.S.C.A. § 2072.

18. Holzhauser v. Container Corp. of America, 93 F.R.D. 837 (W.D.Ark.1982); Savings Bank of Manchester v. Kane, 35 Conn.Sup. 82, 396 A.2d 952 (1978).

19. This has been true since 1948, when the wording of the Federal Rule was changed to achieve this result. See 6 C. Wright, A. Miller & M. Kane, Civil 2d § 1441.

20. Ariz.Rules Civ.Proc., Rule 14(a); Official Code Ga.Ann. § 9–11–14(a); Minn. Rules Civ.Proc., Rule 14.01. See Chrysler Corp. v. McCarthy, 14 Ariz.App. 536, 484 P.2d 1065 (1971).

21. Murray v. Reliance Ins. Co., 60 F.R.D. 390 (D.Minn.1973) (when insured and judgment creditor brought action against insurer for refusal to defend earlier tort action, insurer could not implead counsel for insured on a theory of negligence in allowing a default judgment in the earlier action, since counsel, if liable to anyone, was liable to insured rather than to insurer); Donaldson v. U.S. Steel Corp., 53 F.R.D. 228 (W.D.Pa.1971) (when plaintiff sued under Jones Act for injuries aboard defendant's ship, defendant could not implead three motorists whom it claimed actually were responsible for injuring plaintiff in an entirely unrelated automobile accident, since those motorists could not be liable in any way to defendant).

22. See generally § 6.2, above, for a discussion of consolidation.

Even when it has been determined that the impleader requirements have been met, it does not follow that the third-party defendant may be brought in as a matter of right.[23] The court must decide whether the procedural efficiency to be gained from allowing joinder will be outweighed by the possibility of prejudice to any of the parties. The basic rule is that impleader should be permitted unless it clearly will prejudice the plaintiff or third-party defendant either by complicating unduly the original suit or by delaying its resolution.[24] The possibility of significant prejudice is handled best by permitting the third party to be joined and, if it appears later that the fear of prejudice was justified, the court then can order the third-party claim to be severed or tried separately.[25]

It is important to distinguish impleader from the other claim joinder devices that are available.[26] Unlike counterclaims and cross-claims, impleader seeks to assert a claim against someone who is not already a party to the action. Impleader technically is inappropriate when the prospective third party already is involved in the action.[27] Should the defendant wish to assert a claim against someone already a party to the action, the appropriate devices are counterclaims for claims against opposing parties, or cross-claims for those against coparties.

The third-party plaintiff may join with a proper third-party claim as many other claims as he may have against the third-party defendant.[28] Thus, in one case,[29] a subcontractor being sued by a general contractor was permitted to implead its supplier, asserting that the supplier's negligence had caused the subcontractor both to breach its contract with the plaintiff and to lose the profit it would have received if the price of

23. Under the Federal Rules, if the defendant files a third-party complaint within ten days of filing the original answer, leave of court need not be obtained. Fed.Civ.Proc. Rule 14(a). However, objections still can be raised by making a motion to strike the third-party complaint. Defendants seeking to implead after the ten-day period must seek leave of court to do so and thus impleader is subjected to judicial scrutiny at that time. See 6 C. Wright, A. Miller & M. Kane, Civil 2d §§ 1453–54.

24. See Hicks v. Long Island R.R., 165 F.R.D. 377 (E.D.N.Y.1996); Eastman Chem. Int'l, Ltd. v. Virginia Nat. Bank, 94 F.R.D. 21 (E.D.Tenn.1981); Powell v. Kull, 53 F.R.D. 380 (M.D.Pa.1971).

25. See Thompson v. United Artists Theatre Circuit, Inc., 43 F.R.D. 197 (S.D.N.Y.1967); Miskell v. W.T. Cown, Inc., 10 F.R.D. 617 (E.D.Pa.1950).

26. In some states, such as California, the term "cross-complaint" is used for all claim joinder devices after the initial claim has been filed. West's Ann.Cal.Code Civ. Proc. §§ 428.10–428.70.

27. See Henz v. Superior Trucking Co., 96 F.R.D. 219 (M.D.Pa.1982); Horton v. Continental Can Co., 19 F.R.D. 429 (D.Neb.

1956); Kuris v. Pepper Poultry Co., 2 F.R.D. 361 (S.D.N.Y.1941).

A special situation arises when the defendant has a contingent claim against one of several plaintiffs, as in an automobile accident case in which a driver and a passenger sue defendant and defendant contends that the driver-plaintiff was negligent, making her liable for any amount that defendant is found to owe to the passenger-plaintiff. Defendant cannot counterclaim against the driver under these circumstances, since a counterclaim cannot be contingent. Thus courts have permitted an impleader claim to be used against the driver, simultaneously severing the driver's claim from the passenger's claim. Sporia v. Pennsylvania Greyhound Lines, 143 F.2d 105 (3d Cir.1944).

28. Fed.Civ.Proc.Rule 18(a). See Schwab v. Erie Lackawanna R.R. Co., 438 F.2d 62 (3d Cir.1971); Middlesex Mut. Assur. Co. v. Black, 40 Conn.Sup. 63, 480 A.2d 614 (1984).

29. Noland Co. v. Graver Tank & Mfg. Co., 301 F.2d 43 (4th Cir.1962).

the article supplied had been as represented originally by the supplier. This holding permitted the third-party plaintiff to claim a greater sum from the third-party defendant than the original plaintiff had claimed from the third-party plaintiff.[30]

Finally, it should be kept in mind that a court must obtain personal jurisdiction over a third-party defendant before it can proceed to adjudicate a third-party claim.[31] Although the federal courts gradually have extended the concept of supplemental subject-matter jurisdiction to embrace most claims under Federal Rule 14,[32] they have declined to employ the mechanism to eliminate the need for establishing personal jurisdiction over third-party defendants.[33] On the other hand, third-party claims typically are considered ancillary for purposes of statutory venue requirements.[34]

Once impleader has been allowed, the third-party defendant proceeds much like a defendant in a normal action. The third-party defendant may counterclaim against the third-party plaintiff, cross-claim against other third-party defendants, and bring in a fourth party who may be liable to him derivatively for any part of his liability to the third-party plaintiff.[35] The third-party defendant also may assert against the original plaintiff any claim arising out of the same transaction or occurrence as the original action,[36] and the plaintiff similarly may assert transactionally related claims against the third-party defendant.[37] The assertion of these claims is optional; they may be withheld and made the subject of separate actions if the parties so desire. Further, although the required transactional nexus assures that all claims will be somewhat related and thus fosters the policy of judicial economy that underlies impleader,[38] the court may determine that the addition of certain claims

30. For an additional example, see George Cohen Agency, Inc. v. Donald S. Perlman Agency, Inc., 69 A.D.2d 725, 419 N.Y.S.2d 584 (1979), affirmed 51 N.Y.2d 358, 434 N.Y.S.2d 189, 414 N.E.2d 689 (1980).

31. Coleman v. American Export Isbrandtsen Lines, Inc., 405 F.2d 250 (2d Cir.1968); National Gypsum Co. v. Dalemark Indus., Inc., 779 F.Supp. 147 (D.Kan. 1991); Doebler v. Stadium Productions Ltd., 91 F.R.D. 211 (W.D.Mich.1981).

32. See § 2.14, above.

33. James Talcott, Inc. v. Allahabad Bank, Ltd., 444 F.2d 451, 464–65 n. 11 (5th Cir.1971), cert. denied 404 U.S. 940.

34. U.S. v. Acord, 209 F.2d 709 (10th Cir.1954), cert. denied 347 U.S. 975; ABCKO Music, Inc. v. Beverly Glen Music, Inc., 554 F.Supp. 410 (S.D.N.Y.1983).

35. See 6 C. Wright, A. Miller & M. Kane, Civil 2d § 1461. E.g., Weber v. Weber, 44 F.R.D. 227 (E.D.Pa.1968) (counter-

claim against third-party plaintiff); Caplen v. Sturge, 35 F.R.D. 176 (E.D.Pa.1964) (fourth party complaint).

36. E.g., Finkel v. U.S., 385 F.Supp. 333 (S.D.N.Y.1974). See 6 C. Wright, A. Miller & M. Kane, Civil 2d § 1458.

37. E.g., Northbrook Nat. Ins. Co. v. J & R Vending Corp., 167 F.R.D. 643 (E.D.N.Y.1996) (claim against fifth party defendant allowed); Kenrose Mfg. Co. v. Fred Whitaker Co., 53 F.R.D. 491 (W.D.Va. 1971), affirmed 512 F.2d 890 (4th Cir.1972). See 6 C. Wright, A. Miller & M. Kane, Civil 2d § 1459.

38. In the federal courts, although claims between the original plaintiff and third-party defendant are transactionally related to the main action, this does not mean that jurisdiction may be asserted over them; independent subject-matter jurisdiction may be required. 28 U.S.C.A. § 1367(b). See §§ 2.12–2.14, above, for a discussion of supplemental jurisdiction in multiclaim, multiparty settings.

unduly complicates the litigation and may order those claims severed or dismissed.[39]

The third-party defendant also may assert any defenses that the third-party plaintiff may have against the original plaintiff's claim.[40] Because the third-party defendant cannot relitigate the question of the defendant's liability to the plaintiff, this provision prevents any prejudice that might result from the third-party plaintiff's failure to assert a particular defense against the original plaintiff.[41] It also reduces the possibility of collusion between the original plaintiff and defendant.

§ 6.10   Intervention

Intervention is the procedure that permits someone who is not a party to an action to join the litigation to protect her interests.[1] Its origins can be traced to Roman law in which it was used extensively for the purpose of giving a nonparty a means of protecting a claim against the possibility that the losing party in an action might choose not to appeal a decision that was adverse to the outsider's interests.[2]

The evolution of intervention in English practice was gradual, assuming different forms in the ecclesiastical, admiralty, common law, and chancery courts.[3] The English courts viewed the primary justification for intervention as the need for a device that would enable litigation to continue without prejudice to the rights of nonparties. Thus, the development was most advanced in those types of proceedings in which injury to outsiders was likely to occur.[4] For example, since a judgment in an admiralty in rem proceeding was binding against the world, a nonparty with an interest in property held by the court would be precluded from presenting a claim after the conclusion of the action unless he were allowed to participate. Similarly, both at law and in equity, the disposition of certain claims to property in the court's custody, although not binding on nonparties, could be seriously prejudicial to their interests as a practical matter. The evolution of this procedure in the English system was affected, however, by the historical belief that the plaintiff should be allowed to control the shape and

---

39. See Kosters v. Seven–Up Co., 595 F.2d 347 (6th Cir.1979); Beights v. W. R. Grace & Co., 62 F.R.D. 546 (W.D.Okl.1974).

40. Fed.Civ.Proc.Rule 14(a); N.Y.—McKinney's CPLR 1008. See U.S. v. Lumbermens Mut. Cas. Co., 917 F.2d 654 (1st Cir.1990); Administrative Management Servs., Inc. v. Fidelity & Deposit Co. of Maryland, 129 Cal.App.3d 484, 181 Cal. Rptr. 141 (1982).

41. See Carey v. Schuldt, 42 F.R.D. 390 (E.D.La.1967).

§ 6.10

1. The proper procedure is for the person seeking to enter the action to file a motion accompanied by a statement of the claim or defense that is the basis for intervention. Fed.Civ.Proc.Rule 24(c); Ill.—Smith–Hurd Ann. 735 ILCS 5/2–408; Pa. Rules Civ.Proc., Rules 2327, 2328.

2. Moore & Levi, Federal Intervention: I. The Right to Intervene and Reorganization, 45 Yale L.J. 565, 568 (1936).

3. Moore & Levi, Federal Intervention: II. The Procedure, Status, and Federal Jurisdictional Requirements, 47 Yale L.J. 898 (1938).

4. Moore & Levi, Federal Intervention: I. The Right to Intervene and Reorganization, 45 Yale L.J. 565, 573 (1936).

direction of the action.[5] The wider the permissible range of intervention, the greater the possibility that the interests of the original parties would be prejudiced by delay, expense, and complexity.

Today, the liberality of joinder of parties and claims coupled with the increased incidence of complex substantive regulations have provided a fertile soil for multiparty, multi-issue litigation. This has diminished the power of the original parties to control the lawsuit, and correspondingly increased the discretionary power of the trial judge to determine who are the appropriate participants in the litigation.[6] The increasing availability of intervention is a concomitant of the attempt to satisfy the growing demands for economy and sensitivity to due process concerns in the administration of the judicial system.[7] Rules governing intervention seek to balance two competing policies: (1) the interest of the legal system in ensuring adequate representation to those who are not parties to an action but who have interests that may be affected by its outcome, and (2) the interests of the initial parties, who bear the primary expense of the litigation, in the prompt disposition of their claims and defenses. These interests must be evaluated and balanced in light of the circumstances of each case. As described by one commentator, "the primary task of the rules is to serve as guidelines for the trial judge to use in fashioning an equitable result in a particular case."[8]

Federal Rule 24[9] and many comparable state provisions,[10] which establish intervention requirements, distinguish between intervention as of right and permissive intervention.[11] This dichotomy represents an attempt to accommodate the competing interests of the original parties and those seeking to participate. When intervention is of right, there is an implicit judgment that the nonparty's right to participate should predominate; when intervention is declared to be permissive only, the court first must ascertain whether the interests of the original parties

5. Id. at 569.

6. Kennedy, Let's All Join In: Intervention Under Federal Rule 24, 57 Ky.L.J. 329, 381 (1969); Note, When a Permissive Intervenor Impairs the Plaintiff's Control, 35 Hast.L.J. 707 (1984).

7. An example of the courts' sensitivity to the need to encourage intervention in appropriate cases is the Supreme Court's decision in Independent Federation of Flight Attendants v. Zipes, 491 U.S. 754, 109 S.Ct. 2732, 105 L.Ed.2d 639 (1989), holding that, despite an attorney fee-shifting statute, parties who intervene as defendants in Title VII cases for employment discrimination in order to protect their own rights should not be assessed their opponents' attorneys fees if the plaintiff prevails unless it is found that their intervention was frivolous, unreasonable, or without foundation. The Court determined that assessing the fees was not central to the statute's purpose and could have the effect of encouraging parties to remain outside the litigation, waiting to collaterally attack any unfavorable decree that was entered.

8. Comment, The Litigant and the Absentee in Federal Multiparty Practice, 116 U.Pa.L.Rev. 531, 532 (1968).

9. Rule 24 is examined at length in 7C C. Wright, A. Miller & M. Kane, Civil 2d §§ 1901–23.

10. E.g., West's Ann.Cal.Code Civ. Proc. § 387; Ind.Code Ann.Ct.R.Trial 24; Md.Dist.Rule 3–214(a), (b); N.Y.—McKinney's CPLR 1012, 1013. But see Iowa Rules Civ.Proc., Rules 75, 76.

11. This division of intervention into permissive and "as of right" has been criticized as generating needless confusion and difficulties. Shreve, Questioning Intervention of Right: Toward a New Methodology of Decisionmaking, 74 Nw.U.L.Rev. 894 (1980).

will be prejudiced by allowing the outsider access to the litigation.[12] A review of the criteria for both types of intervention underscores this difference.

Modern intervention provisions typically contain a tripartite standard for intervention of right.[13] First, the potential intervenor must have an interest relating to the property or transaction that is the subject of the action. Second, disposition of the action in the intervenor's absence, as a practical matter, must be likely to impair the intervenor's ability to protect that interest. Finally, it must be shown that the existing parties to the action do not adequately represent the intervenor's interests.[14] In addition to these criteria, intervention of right is allowed when a statute provides an unconditional right to intervene.[15]

A substantial judicial gloss has been developed for the concepts of "interest," "impairment of interest as a practical matter," and "adequacy of representation." Several federal courts have broadened the scope of intervention under Federal Rule 24 significantly, prompting some observers to question whether the balance has not shifted too heavily in favor of the applicant.[16] However, these decisions are consistent with the thrust of the 1966 amendments to the other federal joinder rules, which were designed to accommodate multiparty and multi-issue litigation more easily than had been possible under the original rules.[17] In addition, the trial judge has discretion to impose conditions and restrictions on intervention of right so as to redress whatever imbalances occur between the interests of the intervenor and those of the original parties.[18]

---

12. Cohn, The New Federal Rules of Civil Procedure, 54 Geo.L.J. 1204, 1232 (1966).

13. E.g., West's Ann.Cal.Code Civ. Proc. § 387(b); Vernon's Ann.Mo.Rule Civ. Proc.Rule 52.12(a); Wis.Stat.Ann. 803.09.

14. Prior to the amendment of Federal Rule 24(a) in 1966, the standards for federal intervention were highly rigid and conceptualistic. Intervention as of right was allowed only when the absentee might be bound in a strict res judicata sense by the pending action, Sam Fox Pub. Co. v. U.S., 366 U.S. 683, 81 S.Ct. 1309, 6 L.Ed.2d 604 (1961), or when the court had control over property whose distribution might adversely affect the absentee. Cohn, The New Federal Rules of Civil Procedure, 54 Geo.L.J. 1204, 1230 (1966). The amended rule discards this approach, shifting the focus to the policies underlying intervention. See Comment, The Litigant and the Absentee in Federal Multiparty Practice, 116 U.Pa. L.Rev. 531, 542 (1968).

15. In order to ensure adequate consideration of constitutional issues in actions between private parties, Federal Rule 24(a) also provides that the court must notify the Attorney General whenever the constitutionality of a federal law affecting the public interest is questioned in an action in which the government is not a party so that the government may intervene pursuant to 28 U.S.C.A. § 2403. See Developments in the Law—Multiparty Litigation in the Federal Courts, 71 Harv.L.Rev. 874, 899 (1958). Section 2403 is invoked properly only when the constitutionality of a statute has been questioned; issues of statutory construction are insufficient. See Note, Federal Intervention in Private Actions Involving the Public Interest, 65 Harv.L.Rev. 319, 323 (1951).

16. See Shapiro, Some Thoughts on Intervention Before Courts, Agencies, and Arbitrators, 81 Harv.L.Rev. 721, 722 (1968).

17. See Kennedy, Let's All Join In: Intervention Under Federal Rule 24, 57 Ky. L.J. 329, 374 (1969), in which the author discusses the interrelationship of the 1966 amendments to Federal Rules 19, 23 and 24. See also § 6.5, above, for a discussion of Federal Rule 19, and § 16.2, below, for a discussion of Federal Rule 23.

18. See, e.g., Stringfellow v. Concerned Neighbors in Action, 480 U.S. 370, 107 S.Ct. 1177, 94 L.Ed.2d 389 (1987).

A closer examination of the three separate elements of the intervention of right standard, using the federal provision as a model, provides a useful picture of the availability of this procedure. The first requirement is that the potential intervenor show "an interest relating to the property or transaction which is the subject of the action." The boundaries imposed by this language are uncertain. Perhaps for this reason, cases decided on the basis of this criterion are few in number.

Attempts to read this passage restrictively seem foreclosed by the Supreme Court's decision in Cascade Natural Gas Corporation v. El Paso Natural Gas Company.[19] In El Paso, three appellants sought to intervene in a divestiture proceeding in which the defendant, El Paso, a major supplier of natural gas, was forced to give up its control over another company that sold natural gas, Pacific Northwest, in order to restore competition in the California market. The State of California sought intervention to guarantee that Pacific Northwest or its successor would be restored so as to provide effective competition. Southern California Edison, a large industrial user of natural gas, which purchased from El Paso sources, also sought intervention in the interest of restoring competition in California. Cascade Natural Gas, a distributor in Oregon and Washington whose sole supplier of natural gas was Pacific Northwest, applied to intervene in order to guarantee that Pacific Northwest would be able to perform effectively as a supplier. All three applicants were denied intervention by the district court.

The Supreme Court first decided that both the State of California and Southern California Edison were " 'so situated' geographically as to be 'adversely affected' within the meaning of [original] Rule 24(a)(3) by a merger that reduces the competitive factor in natural gas," and therefore, denial of intervention had been error.[20] Further, because the merits of the case had to be reopened to allow intervention by those entities, the Supreme Court held that the requirement of amended Rule 24(a)(2) that the intervenor "claim an interest in the transaction which is the subject of the action" was sufficiently broad to include Cascade.

Arguably the El Paso case should be limited to its facts since the outcome reflects, in large measure, the dissatisfaction of the Supreme Court with the substance of the divestiture plan adopted by the district court.[21] Nonetheless, a review of subsequent lower court decisions shows that the case has not been so limited and that a wide spectrum of interests exists for which intervention as of right will be permitted under current Rule 24(a).[22]

19. 386 U.S. 129, 87 S.Ct. 932, 17 L.Ed.2d 814 (1967).

20. 386 U.S. at 135–36, 87 S.Ct. at 936–37.

21. See Kaplan, Continuing Work of the Civil Committee: 1966 Amendment of the Federal Rules of Civil Procedure (I), 81 Harv.L.Rev. 356, 406 (1967), in which the author suggests that the Court's expansive reading of the "interest" requirement should be restricted to antitrust cases involving attacks on decrees inconsistent with Supreme Court mandates.

22. This is not to suggest that an applicant may qualify for intervention by asserting any claim that arguably is related to the subject matter of the action; indeed the Supreme Court has denied one such motion to intervene under amended Rule

For example, in Smuck v. Hobson,[23] the United States Court of Appeals for the District of Columbia found that a group of parents had a sufficient interest in the education of their children to intervene to appeal a district court finding that the Board of Education had violated the Constitution in administering the District of Columbia schools. The court noted that "there is no apparent reason why an 'economic interest' should always be necessary to justify intervention."[24] It then went on to conclude that allowing intervention would foster "the goal of 'disposing of lawsuits by involving as many apparently concerned persons as is compatible with efficiency and due process'."[25] The conceptual framework utilized by the court is instructive. The focus clearly is directed at achieving judicial economy and satisfying due process, and that approach is sufficiently flexible to accommodate a wide variety of asserted interests under Rule 24(a).[26]

The second requirement for establishing a right to intervene under Federal Rule 24(a) is that the applicant must be "so situated that the disposition of the action may as a practical matter impair or impede the applicant's ability to protect that interest." This language makes clear that the issue that must be considered is not one of res judicata but simply the degree to which the applicant may be "practically harmed" by a judgment in a pending action.

In what is certainly among the most liberal readings of this requirement, the Fifth Circuit has held that the adverse impact of stare decisis is sufficient to support the right of intervention. In Atlantis Development Corporation v. United States,[27] Atlantis sought leave to intervene in a suit brought by the United States against three defendants to enjoin the erection of caissons on certain coral reefs. In its proposed answer and cross-claim against the defendants in the main action, Atlantis asserted that the United States had no territorial jurisdiction, dominion, or ownership in or over the reefs and therefore could not maintain the action for an injunction, and, conversely, that Atlantis had title to the property by discovery and occupation. In the cross-claim, Atlantis charged the defendants with being trespassers on its land.

24. In Donaldson v. U.S., 400 U.S. 517, 91 S.Ct. 534, 27 L.Ed.2d 580 (1971), a taxpayer filed a motion to intervene in proceedings to enforce Internal Revenue Service summonses directed to a former employer of the taxpayer and to the employer's accountant for the production of the employer's records of the taxpayer's employment and compensation during years as to which the taxpayer-applicant's returns were under investigation. The Supreme Court held that the taxpayer's interest in his employer's routine business records was insufficient to entitle him to intervene. The Donaldson decision may be restricted to its special facts, however, suggesting that intervention may be denied in those instances in which the interest in maintaining a mechanism for speedy adjudication outweighs the applicant's interest in intervention.

23. 408 F.2d 175 (D.C.Cir.1969).

24. 408 F.2d at 179.

25. Ibid. In an earlier case, Nuesse v. Camp, 385 F.2d 694, 700 (D.C.Cir.1967), the same court had characterized the interest requirement as "primarily a practical guide" to disposing of lawsuits economically, but consistent with due process concerns.

26. For an exploration of the kinds of interests that have been deemed sufficient, see 7C C. Wright, A. Miller & M. Kane, Civil 2d § 1908.

27. 379 F.2d 818 (5th Cir.1967).

The Fifth Circuit ruled that the controlling inquiry was the question of the extent to which the intervenor would be practically harmed by the action's disposition in its absence. The court pointed out that a judgment resolving the dispute between the United States and the defendants could not have any direct effect on Atlantis Corporation; the intervenor would not be bound by any principle of res judicata. However, two basic questions of law inescapably present in Atlantis' claim against the Government would have to be resolved by the court in adjudicating the main action. If these issues were decided adversely to the position favoring Atlantis, the court felt that the impact of stare decisis would make it extremely difficult for Atlantis to prevail in any subsequent action and render its claim "for all practical purposes * * * worthless."[28]

The court qualified its holding somewhat by noting that intervention is not appropriate in every circumstance in which stare decisis might afford a substantial obstacle to the intervenor in a subsequent action.[29] Rather, it is only when this factor is combined with a claim to the very property or transaction that is the subject of the main action that intervention should be granted.[30] Nevertheless, the Fifth Circuit's decision marks an important extension of the right to intervene for it applies the requirements in light of the policies that underlie intervention, rather than relying on a narrow categorization and inventory of formal requirements.[31]

The final test for intervention as of right under Federal Rule 24(a) provides that if the other prerequisites are satisfied intervention should be granted "unless the applicant's interest is adequately represented by existing parties."[32] Adequacy of representation is a highly complex variable. At one extreme, the applicant may seek to interpose a separate claim

28. 379 F.2d at 828. The court noted that the Fifth Circuit followed the practice in which a decision by one panel is adhered to by all others until it is reversed by the Supreme Court or by the Circuit in en banc proceedings, and characterized the prospect for a rehearing en banc or certiorari as "formidable."

29. In Ionian Shipping Co. v. British Law Ins. Co., 426 F.2d 186 (2d Cir.1970), a mortgagor brought an action against an insurer on a marine hull policy and the assignee of the mortgagee, Allied Chemical Corporation, sought and was denied intervention as of right in the main suit. The Second Circuit found no practical considerations that would indicate any impairment of Allied's opportunity to present its claim in a subsequent suit. Unlike the Atlantis case, the court noted that "there is little likelihood that novel issues of law will be determined that will have the effect of stare decisis." 426 F.2d at 191.

30. 379 F.2d at 828–29. See, e.g., Chiles v. Thornburgh, 865 F.2d 1197 (11th Cir.1989); Oneida Indian Nation of Wisconsin v. New York, 732 F.2d 261 (2d Cir. 1984).

31. For additional cases applying a policy analysis, see Natural Resources Defense Council, Inc. v. U.S. Nuclear Regulatory Comm'n, 578 F.2d 1341 (10th Cir.1978); O'Hara Group Denver, Ltd. v. Marcor Housing Sys., Inc., 197 Colo. 530, 595 P.2d 679 (1979).

32. Prior to the 1966 amendments, Rule 24(a) allowed intervention "when the representation of the applicant's interest by existing parties is or may be inadequate." The current language appears to shift the burden of establishing inadequate representation from the intervenor to the parties opposing intervention. See Caterino v. Barry, 922 F.2d 37 (1st Cir.1990); Smuck v. Hobson, 408 F.2d 175, 179 (D.C.Cir.1969). There is some judicial indication to the contrary, however. See Trbovich v. United Mine Workers of America, 404 U.S. 528, 538 n. 10, 92 S.Ct. 630, 636 n. 10, 30 L.Ed.2d 686 (1972).

for relief against one of the parties; when this occurs, her interests clearly are not represented at all, and intervention should be granted.[33] At the other extreme, petitioner may seek to assert exactly the same claim as one of the litigants, making the case for intervention rather weak.[34] In situations that fall between these poles, courts must weigh certain factors and be on the lookout for extenuating circumstances.[35] Evidence of fraud or collusion clearly is indicative of inadequate representation;[36] similarly, a showing that a case was mishandled, or that the representative and petitioner have adverse interests may provide sufficient grounds for intervention.[37]

A good illustration of the kind of inadequacy of representation that warrants intervention is presented in Trbovich v. United Mine Workers of America,[38] in which a union member who had filed an initial complaint with the Secretary of Labor, sought to intervene in a subsequent suit brought by the Secretary under the Labor–Management Reporting and Disclosure Act to set aside the election of certain union officers. The Secretary opposed intervention arguing that petitioner's interests were adequately represented by him in the pending action, and that the only way the Court could find otherwise would be to find that the Secretary had failed to perform his statutory duty.[39]

The Supreme Court ultimately disagreed. In reviewing the history and purposes of the labor statute, the Court found that it imposes two distinct duties on the Secretary of Labor—to represent individual union members against their union, and to protect the larger public interest in free and democratic union elections.[40] Both functions, although clearly important, did not dictate the same approach to the conduct of litigation under the statute. Consequently, the representation of petitioner's narrower interest was inadequate in the litigation even if the Secretary was performing his duties as well as could be expected. When a party to an action is obliged to represent two separate interests that, although not adverse, may require different judgments regarding tactical considerations, intervention as of right is appropriate in order to guarantee that the interests of the absentee are given full and vigorous attention.[41]

---

33. E.g., Duff v. Draper, 96 Idaho 299, 527 P.2d 1257 (1974).

34. E.g., Maryland Radiological Soc., Inc. v. Health Servs. Cost Review Comm'n, 285 Md. 383, 402 A.2d 907 (1979).

35. See the discussion and the cases cited in Note, Intervention of Private Parties under Federal Rule 24, 52 Colum.L.Rev. 922, 925 (1952).

36. See Shump v. Balka, 574 F.2d 1341 (10th Cir.1978); Cuthill v. Ortman–Miller Mach. Co., 216 F.2d 336 (7th Cir.1954).

37. See Smith v. Clark Sherwood Oil Field Contractors, 457 F.2d 1339 (5th Cir. 1972), cert. denied 409 U.S. 980.

38. 404 U.S. 528, 92 S.Ct. 630, 30 L.Ed.2d 686 (1972).

39. Generally, adequacy of representation is found when the government is the named party representing the interests of the person seeking intervention. See 7C C. Wright, A. Miller & M. Kane, Civil 2d § 1909, nn. 25–28, and accompanying text.

40. 404 U.S. at 538–39, 92 S.Ct. at 636–37.

41. See Nuesse v. Camp, 385 F.2d 694 (D.C.Cir.1967) (party pursuing its own narrow interests might not adequately represent the broader interest of the intervenor).

When taken together, the three criteria set out in Rule 24(a) establish a pragmatic and flexible test for determining the scope of the right to intervene. It is clear that the concepts of interest, practical harm, and adequacy of representation are not to be viewed in isolation from each other, but rather as related factors to be considered in balancing the competing interests of those who already are litigants and those who would like to be.

When an absentee does not qualify for intervention as of right, the court may grant permissive intervention under certain conditions. Federal Rule 24(b) and its many state counterparts provide that "anyone may be permitted to intervene in an action: 1) when a statute of the United States confers a conditional right to intervene; or 2) when an applicant's claim or defense and the main action have a question of law or fact in common."[42]

A motion seeking permissive intervention is addressed to the trial court's discretion. The court will consider whether the benefits of intervention outweigh the possibility of proliferating the controversy so as to cause delay and expense.[43] Intervention should not be permitted at all when the applicant's presence would serve no useful purpose, as, for example, when the common question is being presented effectively by the parties to the action.[44] Further, if intervention is allowed, any attempt by the intervenor to raise issues that are remote from the mainstream of the original action will be resisted, even though the intervenor might have been able to raise them had he been a party to the action initially.

As an illustration, consider the case in which P sues for damages and an injunction, claiming that D is infringing P's patent. X seeks to intervene as a defendant in the infringement suit, and to interpose a counterclaim against P for unfair competition. Since D is wholly disinterested in the unfair competition claim, the court in its discretion may deny intervention or it may permit intervention on condition that the issue of unfair competition not be raised. On the other hand, X's counterclaim may be permitted if it has a close transactional relationship with the original infringement action.

Some difficult analytical problems are posed by the requirement that the applicant raise a question of fact or law common to an issue involved in the claim or defenses raised by the original parties. This relatively minimal requirement allows the court to permit someone to intervene even though that person would not be a proper party for joinder purposes because there is no requirement that the intervenor's claim be transactionally related to claims in the main action, as is true of

---

42. See 7C C. Wright, A. Miller & M. Kane, Civil 2d §§ 1910–12.

43. See Developments in the Law— Multiparty Litigation in the Federal Courts, 71 Harv.L.Rev. 874, 903 (1958).

44. See Note, Intervention of Private Parties Under Federal Rule 24, 52 Colum.L.Rev. 922, 927–28 (1952).

permissive joinder.[45] But intervention is far from automatic. As previously noted, the matter is directed to the trial court's discretion and the judge will deny intervention when the absentee seeks to interpose a claim that is not related to the main action and would delay the trial and prejudice the rights of the original parties.

An interesting discussion of the circumstances under which permissive intervention may be warranted is found in Ionian Shipping Company v. British Law Insurance Company,[46] in which the assignee of the mortgages on a marine hull insurance policy sought and was refused intervention of right in an action brought by the mortgagor against the insurer. However, the court stated that permissive intervention clearly was appropriate. The court noted that the putative intervenor shared a strong interest in common questions of law and fact with the mortgagor, and that intervention would comport with the policy underlying the revision of the federal joinder rules to dispose of as many issues in a single action as is consistent with due process.[47] Moreover, the court felt that the burden intervention would impose on the original parties was slight compared with the burden that would be imposed on the judicial system if the applicant were forced to bring a second action. Any confusion or prejudice to the existing parties could be alleviated by the imposition of conditions on the discretionary intervenor.[48]

One important problem that has arisen under the common question requirement of Federal Rule 24(b)(2) is the scope of the government's right to intervene in an action in which a party relies on a statute, order, or regulation that is administered by a government officer or agency. This is not the same situation as when a party challenges the constitutionality of an act of Congress; in that context the government has an unconditional right to intervene under Section 2403 of the Judicial Code. When a litigant argues that a certain construction or application should be given a federal statute, the issue is one of permissive intervention.

As is true generally, a request for permissive intervention even by the government, is addressed to the discretion of the trial judge. However, a 1946 amendment to the Rule[49] makes it clear that the interest of the government agency charged with the administration of a statute or executive order is sufficient to satisfy the prerequisites to the exercise of that discretion; in many instances, the public interest in assuring that all the implications of an issue under a federal statute are brought to the

---

45. See § 6.4, above.

46. 426 F.2d 186 (2d Cir.1970).

47. 426 F.2d at 191.

48. 426 F.2d at 191–92. For an example of a case in which permissive intervention was denied, see Commonwealth Edison Co. v. Allis–Chalmers Mfg. Co., 207 F.Supp. 252 (N.D.Ill.1962), affirmed 315 F.2d 564 (7th Cir.1963), cert. denied 375 U.S. 834.

49. Prior to the amendment, there had been some confusion about the propriety of intervention under these circumstances because the government was not raising "a claim or a defense" having a question in common with the issue in the main proceeding, but was merely seeking to interject its interest in the application of a particular statute. See Note, Federal Intervention in Private Actions Involving the Public Interest, 65 Harv.L.Rev. 319, 324–25 (1951).

attention of the court outweighs any resulting delay.[50]

Whether the intervention sought is permissive or as of right, an application for leave to intervene must be timely. Timeliness varies depending on the circumstances of each case. The stage of the action reached when intervention is sought necessarily is an important factor in determining whether an applicant's motion is timely. It is not the actual length of the delay in requesting intervention that is significant, but rather the degree to which adding a party at a certain point would be disruptive of the proceedings and prejudicial to those already parties.[51] As a general rule, therefore, a petition interposed before the beginning of trial will be held timely,[52] but a petition submitted after judgment will be rejected as untimely absent very unusual circumstances.[53] In deciding a motion to intervene made at some point between these extremes, the court must balance various considerations.[54]

For example, the decision often will be affected by the type of intervention that is sought. When the absentee seeks intervention as of right because his rights will be affected by the decision in a pending suit and he may be unable to vindicate them in subsequent litigation, the equities clearly favor the putative intervenor who may be left without a remedy.[55] On the other hand, when the nonparty's rights will not be prejudiced in a future action, and she applies for permissive intervention, the court should give careful consideration to the degree to which this will hinder or impair the rights of the original litigants. Under this approach, the timeliness requirement in Rule 24 is not really designed to punish an intervenor for failing to be more diligent, but is intended to ensure that the original parties will not be prejudiced by the absentee's failure to apply sooner.[56]

The preceding discussion has focussed solely on the rule or code requirements surrounding intervention. However, it is important to note that intervention must be denied even if those requirements are met if the intervenor's presence in a federal court action would destroy the court's subject-matter jurisdiction. An intervenor whose presence would have created jurisdictional problems if he was made a party initially—for

---

50. See Developments in the Law—Multiparty Litigation in the Federal Courts, 71 Harv.L.Rev. 874, 904 (1958). For an example of the kind of policy analysis that is involved, see Nuesse v. Camp, 385 F.2d 694 (D.C.Cir.1967).

51. Note, Intervention of Private Parties Under Federal Rule 24, 52 Colum.L.Rev. 922, 929 (1952).

52. E.g., Reeves v. International Tel. & Tel. Corp., 616 F.2d 1342 (5th Cir.1980), cert. denied 449 U.S. 1077; State ex rel. Keeler v. Port of Peninsula, 89 Wn.2d 764, 575 P.2d 713 (1978).

53. Special circumstances were found, for example, in Brink v. DaLesio, 667 F.2d 420 (4th Cir.1981); Nesbit v. City of Albu-

querque, 91 N.M. 455, 575 P.2d 1340 (1977).

54. See Kozak v. Wells, 278 F.2d 104 (8th Cir.1960), in which the motion to intervene, although made five months after the filing of the complaint, was held to be timely when the issues had not yet been clearly drawn and prejudice resulting from the passage of time was not apparent.

55. Comment, The Litigant and the Absentee in Federal Multiparty Practice, 116 U.Pa.L.Rev. 531, 544–45 (1968).

56. Note, The Requirement of Timeliness Under Rule 24 of the Federal Rules of Civil Procedure, 37 Va.L.Rev. 863, 867 (1951).

example, a nondiverse party—cannot avoid those problems by entering the lawsuit through a different means.[57] Conversely, when a federal court lacks subject-matter jurisdiction over a pending action, it must be dismissed; intervention may not be allowed for the purpose of curing the defect.[58]

Finally, in jurisdictions adhering to the final judgment rule,[59] there has been some confusion over the appealability of an order either granting or denying intervention. Clearly an order granting intervention is not final and is not appealable as such; the party opposing intervention must await the entry of judgment before contesting the intervention decision.[60] When the district court denies intervention, arguably an immediate appeal by the disappointed applicant should be available; a refusal to allow intervention is not a final decision on the merits of the action, but it is a final decision on the intervenor's request. The intervenor's rights may be impaired substantially if he is forced to await the outcome of the litigation.[61]

Judicial opinions, although generally supporting this conclusion, have generated some ambiguity. A practice has developed under which an order denying intervention is appealable only if it was sought as of right; an order denying permissive intervention is appealable only if the court has abused its discretion.[62] This rule is really a somewhat evanescent barrier in terms of its restriction on appellate review.[63] Whether the appellate court determines that intervention did or did not exist as of right, or it determines that the trial court did or did not abuse its discretion in denying intervention, it first must examine the merits of the case.[64] Thus, there really is a form of appellate review of an order

---

57. See 28 U.S.C.A. § 1367(b). This statute, which was enacted in 1990, explicitly prohibits supplemental jurisdiction over intervenors in diversity cases. It effectively overrules prior lower court cases, which distinguished between intervenors as of right and permissive intervenors and authorized ancillary jurisdiction to be applied to claims by intervenors as of right as long as those parties would not be classified as indispensable parties under Rule 19(b). E.g., Drillers Engine & Supply, Inc. v. Burckhalter, 327 F.Supp. 648 (W.D.Okl.1971). For a more extended discussion, see 7C C. Wright, A. Miller & M. Kane, Civil 2d § 1917.

58. See Fuller v. Volk, 351 F.2d 323, 328 (3d Cir.1965).

59. See § 13.1, below for a discussion of the final judgment rule.

60. It also generally is true that once the litigation has been completed an appeal from an order granting intervention has little hope for success. See Note, Intervention of Private Parties under Federal Rule 23, 52 Colum.L.Rev. 922, 930–31 (1952).

An order denying intervention as of right, but granting permissive intervention

with significant conditions also is nonappealable under the final judgment rule. Stringfellow v. Concerned Neighbors in Action, 480 U.S. 370, 107 S.Ct. 1177, 94 L.Ed.2d 389 (1987).

61. See Shapiro, Some Thoughts on Intervention Before Courts, Agencies, and Arbitrators, 81 Harv.L.Rev. 721, 748–49 (1968).

62. For a collection of the cases following this approach, see 7C C. Wright, A. Miller & M. Kane, Civil 2d § 1923.

63. See Kennedy, Let's All Join In: Intervention Under Federal Rule 24, 57 Ky. L.J. 329, 368–69 (1969).

64. One court held that all orders denying intervention are final for purposes of appeal, stating that because the aim of the 1966 amendments was to substitute a practical emphasis on questions of intervention, the sensible course is to go directly to the merits without inquiring whether intervention was sought permissively or as of right. Ionian Shipping Co. v. British Law Ins. Co., 426 F.2d 186, 188–89 (2d Cir.1970).

denying permissive intervention as well as from an order denying intervention as of right. In the former situation, however, there will be a reversal only if it is determined that the denial constituted an abuse of discretion.[65]

65. See Shapiro, Some Thoughts on Intervention Before Courts, Agencies, and Arbitrators, 81 Harv.L.Rev. 721, 751 (1968); Comment, Federal Practice: Appealability of an Order Denying Intervention, 11 Okla. L.Rev. 80 (1958).

§§ 6.11–7.0 are reserved for supplementary material.

Chapter 7

DISCOVERY

Analysis

A. INTRODUCTION

A. INTRODUCTION

§ 7.1 History, Purposes, and Techniques of Modern Discovery

The term "discovery" encompasses the methods by which a party or a potential party to a lawsuit obtains and preserves information regarding the action.[1] Historically, discovery was not an integral part of the litigation process.[2] The parties learned the outlines of their opponent's case from the pleadings and thereafter did the best they could to support their own position and refute that of the opponent by employing whatever private means of investigation they could afford.[3] At common law, discovery was limited to a motion for a bill of particulars, which could be used only to require a plaintiff to set forth in detail any items of account upon which the plaintiff was suing.[4] To reach other types of information, a party could file a separate action in equity, asking for a bill of discovery; that allowed a person to uncover facts to support his own case, but could not be used to ascertain evidence that the opposing parties had available for trial.[5] The net effect was to leave many litigants in the dark about what their adversary's position or evidence would be at trial.

Although various techniques for obtaining information were developed over the years,[6] it was not until the adoption of Federal Rules of Civil Procedure 26–37, in 1938, that discovery became a vital part of the litigation process. These discovery rules virtually revolutionized the practice of law in the United States.[7] Of all the Federal Rules, they have been the most widely copied; nearly every state has adopted a similar set of provisions permitting broad, intensive discovery.[8]

Modern discovery has three major purposes. First is the preservation of relevant information that might not be available at trial.[9] The earliest discovery procedures in the federal courts were designed basical-

---

§ 7.1

1. Developments in the Law—Discovery, 74 Harv.L.Rev. 940, 942 (1961).

2. E. Sunderland, Cases & Materials on Trial and Appellate Practice 1–4 (3d ed.1941).

3. Developments in the Law—Discovery, 74 Harv.L.Rev. 940, 946 (1961).

4. Id. at 947.

5. Sinclair Refining Co. v. Jenkins Petroleum Process Co., 289 U.S. 689, 53 S.Ct. 736, 77 L.Ed. 1449 (1933); Kelly v. Nationwide Mut. Ins. Co., 23 O.Op.2d 29, 188 N.E.2d 445 (1963).

6. See G. Ragland, Discovery Before Trial 1–5 (1932); James, Discovery, 38 Yale L.J. 746 (1929); Sunderland, The New Federal Rules, 45 W.Va.L.Q. 5, 19, 22 (1938); Developments in the Law—Discovery, 74 Harv.L.Rev. 940, 949 (1961). See also Rev.

Stat. §§ 863–75, formerly at 28 U.S.C.A. §§ 639–53 (1940).

7. See Developments in the Law—Discovery, 74 Harv.L.Rev. 940, 950 (1961).

8. Among such states are Alabama, Alaska, Arizona, Arkansas, California, Colorado, Delaware, Florida, Georgia, Hawaii, Idaho, Indiana, Iowa, Kansas, Maine, Maryland, Massachusetts, Michigan, Minnesota, Missouri, Montana, Nevada, New Jersey, New Mexico, New York, North Carolina, North Dakota, Ohio, Oklahoma, Oregon, Pennsylvania, Rhode Island, South Dakota, Tennessee, Texas, Utah, Vermont, Virginia, Washington, West Virginia. Wisconsin, and Wyoming. See 8 C. Wright, A. Miller & R. Marcus, Civil 2d § 2001.

9. Fed.Civ.Proc.Rule 27; Ala.Rules Civ. Proc., Rule 27; Alaska Rules Civ.Proc., Rule 27.

ly for this purpose.[10] If a witness is ill or infirm, or will be out of the country at the time of trial, the testimony of that witness can be taken and preserved, and ultimately used at trial.[11] A second purpose of discovery is to ascertain the issues that actually are in controversy between the parties.[12] Frequently, if one looks only to the pleadings, one will find a substantial number of factual disputes that actually do not exist.[13] Discovery can be utilized to determine what really is at issue so that the parties can concentrate on obtaining evidence on those matters that actually are disputed.[14] Finally, modern discovery allows a party to obtain information that will lead to admissible evidence on the issues that are in dispute.[15] Thus, if an eyewitness to an event is reluctant to talk to a party,[16] that party can require the witness to submit to a deposition,[17] during which the witness, under oath, must reveal her knowledge about the facts.[18] In addition, one party can obtain from the opposing party, relevant facts regarding the case and documents and other items that pertain to it.[19]

An increasingly important consideration regarding modern discovery involves the procedures used for discovery when evidence is located abroad.[20] The United States has been a party to the Hague Convention on the Taking of Evidence Abroad since 1972. That Convention provides procedures on requesting evidence located in foreign countries.[21] The interrelation between international discovery procedures and the Federal Rules of Civil Procedure was not clear until 1987, however, when the Supreme Court held that the Hague Convention procedures are a supplemental consideration rather than a mandatory replacement of the federal discovery rules.[22]

10. See Developments in the Law— Discovery, 74 Harv.L.Rev. 940, 949 (1961).

11. Fed.Civ.Proc.Rule 32(a)(3); Brown v. Pryor, 954 P.2d 1349 (Wyo.1998).

12. See Fed.Civ.Proc.Rule 36; Ariz. Rules Civ.Proc., Rule 36; Ark.Rules Civ. Proc., Rule 36.

13. Nutt v. Black Hills Stage Lines, Inc., 452 F.2d 480 (8th Cir.1971); Perry v. Creech Coal Co., 55 F.Supp. 998 (E.D.Ky. 1944); Eichenberger v. Wilhelm, 244 N.W.2d 691, 695 (N.D.1976).

14. Nutt v. Black Hills Stage Lines, Inc., 452 F.2d 480 (8th Cir.1971); Perry v. Creech Coal Co., 55 F.Supp. 998 (E.D.Ky. 1944).

15. E.I. du Pont De Nemours & Co. v. Phillips Petroleum Co., 24 F.R.D.416 (D.Del.1959); Stanzler v. Loew's Theatre & Realty Corp., 19 F.R.D. 286 (D.R.I.1955).

16. Pennsylvania R.R. Co. v. The Marie Leonhardt, 179 F.Supp. 437 (E.D.Pa. 1959); Czuprynski v. Shenango Furnace Co., 2 F.R.D. 412 (W.D.N.Y.1942).

17. Fed.Civ.Proc.Rule 30(c); Colo.Rules Civ.Proc., Rule 30(c); Fla.—West's F.S.A. Rules Civ.Proc., Rule 1.310(c).

18. Marshall v. Electric Hose & Rubber Co., 68 F.R.D. 287 (D.Del.1975); Falk v. U.S., 53 F.R.D. 113 (D.Conn.1971).

19. Fed.Civ.Proc.Rules 26(b), 33, 34; Official Code Ga.Ann. §§ 9–11–26; 9–11–33, 34; Idaho Rules Civ.Proc., Rules 26(b), 33, 34.

20. See generally 8 C. Wright, A. Miller & R. Marcus, Civil 2d § 2005; Alley & Prescott, Recent Developments in the United States Under the Hague Evidence Convention, 2 Leiden J. Int'l Law 19 (1989); Weis, The Federal Rules and the Hague Conventions: Concerns of Conformity and Comity, 50 U.Pitt.L.Rev. 903 (1989).

21. Hague Convention on the Taking of Evidence Abroad in Civil or Commercial Matters, opened for signature Mar. 18, 1970, 23 U.S.T. 2555, T.I.A.S. No. 7444, 847 U.N.T.S. 231, text of Convention located in note to 28 U.S.C.A. § 1781.

22. Société Nationale Industrielle Aérospatiale v. U.S. District Court, 482 U.S. 522, 529–32, 107 S.Ct. 2542, 2548–50, 96 L.Ed.2d 461, 474–77 (1987). See also In re Aircrash Disaster Near Roselawn, Indiana, 172 F.R.D. 295, 307–11 (N.D.Ill.1997).

In the early 1990s, some jurisdictions,[23] including the federal courts,[24] introduced a new dimension to pretrial discovery by requiring mandatory initial disclosure by which attorneys automatically exchange basic information about the identity of witnesses and relevant documents or other tangible evidence.[25] At least one state also requires a statement of the factual basis of each pleaded claim and defense and of the legal theory upon which each is based.[26] These changes were in response to criticism within and outside the legal community that attorneys were abusing discovery by harassing opposing parties and that the existing system was costly and inefficient.[27] This move toward mandatory initial disclosure has been highly controversial.[28] The federal rules permit any judicial district to opt out and to follow local rules that either exclude or modify the initial disclosure requirements.[29] Many districts have exercised the opt-out provision resulting in a striking array of local discovery rules.[30] This has, in turn, spawned substantial support for a return to national uniformity by elimination of the opt-out provision.[31]

B. SCOPE OF DISCOVERY

§ 7.2 Scope—In General

The scope of discovery is extremely broad under the Federal Rules and comparable state practice. Information can be obtained regarding

In an effort to give more weight to international discovery treaties, the Advisory Committee in 1990 proposed an amendment to Rule 26(a), which would have incorporated the trend toward balanced accommodation to international agreements bearing on discovery methods. The proposed amendment would have added language creating a preference for internationally agreed methods of discovery when those methods are available, unless the court were to deem those methods inadequate or inequitable. However, this proposed amendment was neither adopted in 1991 nor included in the 1991 proposed amendments. Report of the Judicial Conference Committee on Rules of Practice and Procedure, Committee Notes, September 1990 and August 1991.

23. Arizona appears to have been the first jurisdiction to adopt mandatory disclosure. See Ariz.Rules Civ.Proc., Rule 26.1. See also Colo.Rules Civ.Proc., Rule 26(a).

24. Fed.Civ.Proc.Rule 26(a).

25. See § 7.7, below.

26. Ariz.Rules Civ.Proc., Rule 26.1(a)(1),(2).

27. For a discussion of pre-amendment criticism of the discovery rules, see Barnes, The Litigation Crisis: Competitiveness and Other Measures of Quality of Life, 71 Den. U.L.Rev. 71 (1993); Niemeyer, Here We Go Again: Are the Federal Discovery Rules Really in Need of Amendment?, 39 B.C.L.Rev. 517 (1998).

28. For criticism concerning the 1993 amendments to the federal rules, see Justice Scalia's dissenting statement to the adoption of the amendments, Amendments to the Federal Rules of Civil Procedure, reprinted in 146 F.R.D. 401, 507. In Justice Scalia's view, the reforms are "potentially disastrous and certainly premature–particularly the imposition on litigants of a continuing duty to disclose to opposing counsel, without awaiting any request, various information 'relevant to the disputed facts with alleged particularity.'" For a defense of mandatory initial discovery, see Note, Mandatory Disclosure Can Improve the Discovery System, 70 Ind.L.J. 657 (1995).

29. Fed.Civ.Proc.Rule 26(a)(1).

30. Preliminary Draft of Proposed Amendments to the Federal Rules of Civil Procedure 48, reprinted in 181 F.R.D. 18, at 71 (1998).

31. Id. at 49.

any matter, not privileged,[1] that is relevant to the subject matter involved in the action,[2] whether or not the information sought will be admissible at trial, just so long as it is reasonably calculated to lead to the discovery of admissible evidence.[3]

One of the key passages in contemporary provisions governing the scope of discovery is that it extends to any matter that is "relevant to the subject matter involved in the pending action." This clause has become the focus of a serious attempt to reform the discovery provisions by narrowing their scope.[4]

At present, relevance is interpreted very broadly.[5] As already noted, it is proper to discover facts not necessarily admissible themselves, so long as they may lead to admissible evidence.[6] For example, a party not only may obtain information with respect to the names of eyewitnesses to an incident, but also information with respect to persons who have talked to or seen those witnesses.[7] Thus, a party can request information regarding hearsay statements and the like as long as it may assist the inquiring party in obtaining additional information with respect to the case.[8] It is proper to discover facts concerning what the opponent intends

§ 7.2

1. The exception for privileged matters is discussed in § 7.4, below.

2. See Fed.Civ.Proc.Rule 26(b); Ind.Trial Proc.Rule 26(B); Kan.Stat.Ann. 60–226(b); Me.Rules Civ.Proc., Rule 26(b).

3. Fed.Civ.Proc.Rule 26(b); West's Ann.Cal.Code Civ.Proc. § 2017(a); Ind.Trial Proc.Rule 26(B); Kan.Stat.Ann. 60–226(b); Me.Rules Civ.Proc., Rule 26(b). See generally 8 C. Wright, A. Miller & R. Marcus, Civil 2d §§ 2007–15.

4. See Liman, The Quantum of Discovery vs. The Quality of Justice: More is Less, 4 Litigation 8 (1977); Lundquist & Schechter, The New Relevancy: An End to Trial by Ordeal, 64 A.B.A.J. 59 (1978); Rifkind, Addresses Delivered to the National Conference on the Causes of Popular Dissatisfaction with the Administration of Justice, 70 F.R.D. 79, 107 (1976); Spann, Abuse of Discovery: Some Proposed Reforms, 25 N.C.St. B.Q. 1 (1978). For a discussion on the future of discovery, see § 7.18, below.

In 1998, the Advisory Committee on the Federal Rules proposed an alteration of Federal Rule 26(b) that would, in the absence of a court order, limit discovery to matters "relevant to the claim or defense of any party." For good cause, the court could expand the scope of discovery to its current state by ordering discovery of any information "relevant to the subject matter involved in the action." The purpose of the change would be to eliminate abuses by some litigants who engage in wide-ranging discovery seemingly unrelated to the issues in the case. The extent to which the altera-

tion would affect the practice in the large majority of cases is unclear. It very well could, however, result in a flood of motions claiming that the new limits had been exceeded. This proposed change is currently being considered by members of the bench and bar.

5. See, e.g., National Organization for Women, Inc. (NOW), St. Paul Chapter v. Minnesota Mining & Mfg. Co., 73 F.R.D. 467 (D.Minn.1977); Bowman v. General Motors Corp., 64 F.R.D. 62, 69 (E.D.Pa. 1974). See generally 8 C. Wright, A. Miller & R. Marcus, Civil 2d § 2008.

6. In Mellon v. Cooper–Jarrett, Inc., 424 F.2d 499 (6th Cir.1970), an automobile accident case, the court reversed a judgment for plaintiff because the trial court had denied defendant the right to discover plaintiff's prior misdemeanor driving conviction even though it could not have been introduced into evidence to impeach the plaintiff. The court held that the information could have led to admissible evidence. See also Edgar v. Finley, 312 F.2d 533 (8th Cir.1963); Bell v. Swift & Co., 283 F.2d 407 (5th Cir.1960); Balas v. Ruzzo, 703 So.2d 1076 (Fla.App.1997).

7. Federal Deposit Ins. Corp. v. St. Paul Fire & Marine Ins. Co., 53 F.R.D. 260, 263 (W.D.Okl.1971); Cogdill v. TVA, 7 F.R.D. 411 (E.D.Tenn.1947); Baltimore Transit Co. v. Mezzanotti, 227 Md. 8, 174 A.2d 768 (1961).

8. Technograph, Inc. v. Texas Instruments Inc., 43 F.R.D. 416 (S.D.N.Y.1967); Lowe's of Roanoke, Inc. v. Jefferson Stan-

to prove as well as to obtain information supporting one's own case.[9] Along those lines, it generally is held that information may be sought for the purpose of impeaching a witness likely to be called by the opposing side.[10] However, in a few situations, courts have limited the obligation of a party to come forward with impeachment evidence.[11] Difficulties have arisen over the question of what constitutes impeachment. It should be clear that evidence on the issues to be proved in the case, even though it contradicts evidence presented by the opposing party, is not impeachment. The latter refers only to evidence that does not go to the merits of the case, but tends only to show that the testimony of a witness is unreliable.[12] Evidence may both impeach a witness and help determine an issue in the case; in that situation the evidence should fall within the ambit of open discovery.[13]

The traditional view of discovery has been that a party cannot delve into the trial tactics of opposing counsel.[14] For example, it generally has been thought inappropriate to ask what witnesses will be called in what particular order.[15] Those questions have nothing to do with the disclosure of information that would lead to admissible evidence.[16] At least in the federal courts, however, that viewpoint has given way to a requirement of automatic disclosure, at least 30 days before trial, of the identity

dard Life Ins. Co., 219 F.Supp. 181 (S.D.N.Y.1963); Taylor v. Sound S.S. Lines, Inc., 100 F.Supp. 388 (D.Conn.1951).

9. See Timken Roller Bearing Co. v. U.S., 38 F.R.D. 57 (N.D.Ohio 1964); U.S. v. General Motors Corp., 2 F.R.D. 528 (N.D.Ill.1942); Nichols v. Sanborn Co., 24 F.Supp. 908 (D.Mass.1938).

There currently is no distinction in the federal courts as to the scope of discovery between matters that must automatically be disclosed and as to those that need be disclosed only at the request of another party. However, a 1998 proposal would limit the former to the names of witnesses and the existence of other evidence that support the claims and defenses of the party making disclosure; automatically required disclosures would not include the names of witnesses or the existence of evidence that would harm the disclosing party's case. See Preliminary Draft of Proposed Amendments to the Federal Rules of Civil Procedure and Evidence 34–35, 50, reprinted in 181 F.R.D. 18, at 57–58, 73 (1998).

10. Adventures in Good Eating v. Best Places to Eat, 131 F.2d 809 (7th Cir.1942); Davidson Pipe Co. v. Laventhol & Horwath, 120 F.R.D. 455, 461 (S.D.N.Y.1988); U.S. v. International Business Mach. Corp., 66 F.R.D. 215 (S.D.N.Y.1974); RCA Mfg. Co. v. Decca Records, 1 F.R.D. 433 (S.D.N.Y. 1940).

11. For example, under Fed.Civ.Proc. Rule 26(c) one party, even though not formally requested to do so by another party,

must automatically provide information regarding the evidence it may present at trial, "other than solely for impeachment purposes."

12. See Klonoski v. Mahlab, 156 F.3d 255, 269–70 (1st Cir.1998).

13. Klonoski v. Mahlab, 156 F.3d 255, 269–70 (1st Cir.1998); Chiasson v. Zapata Gulf Marine Corp., 988 F.2d 513 (5th Cir. 1993).

14. Hickman v. Taylor, 329 U.S. 495, 511, 67 S.Ct. 385, 91 L.Ed. 451 (1947); Communist Party of U.S. v. Subversive Activities Control Bd., 254 F.2d 314 (D.C.Cir. 1958); U.S. v. International Business Mach. Corp., 66 F.R.D. 215 (S.D.N.Y.1974). See § 7.5, below, for a discussion of the work-product doctrine.

15. Brennan v. Engineered Prods., Inc., 506 F.2d 299, 303 (8th Cir.1974); Wirtz v. Continental Finance & Loan Co., 326 F.2d 561 (5th Cir.1964); Wirtz v. B. A. C. Steel Prods., Inc., 312 F.2d 14, 16 (4th Cir.1962); City of Long Beach v. Superior Court, 64 Cal.App.3d 65, 74–79, 134 Cal. Rptr. 468, 474–77 (1976); Employers Mut. Liability Ins. Co. v. Butler, 511 S.W.2d 323, 325 (Tex.Civ.App.1974).

16. Cf. Aktiebolaget Vargos v. Clark, 8 F.R.D. 635 (D.D.C.1949) (enumeration of items of evidence to be introduced by opponent disallowed).

of witnesses, documents, and other evidence that are expected to be presented at trial or the identity of any witness whose deposition is expected to be used at trial.[17]

A special aspect of the broad scope of discovery is the treatment of the discovery of insurance policy limits. In the federal courts and in a large majority of the states today, a party may discover not only the fact that the potential liability of the defendant is covered by insurance, but the monetary limits of the policy as well.[18] Normally, this information does not lead to admissible evidence, and thus, some courts originally ruled that discovery of this information was improper.[19] Because the existence and extent of insurance is deemed important for the settlement of cases, however, disclosure was strongly encouraged and, in jurisdictions where restrictions had been applied, special rules were promulgated explicitly authorizing discovery of this information.[20] This approach was justified further by the fact that disclosure of the policy limits does not involve a serious invasion of the privacy of the individual litigant. Thus, when balanced against the strong desire to settle cases on a realistic basis, it generally was felt that discovery should be permitted.[21]

If the monetary limits of a defendant's insurance policy can be discovered in order to obtain reasonable settlements, then it can be argued forcefully that a defendant's general financial ability should be discoverable for the same purpose, particularly if the defendant is self-insured. Unlike the insurance situation, however, general discovery of a defendant's assets involves an invasion of privacy of such a magnitude

---

17. Fed.Civ.Proc.Rule 26(a)(3). The names of expert witnesses who will be expected to testify must be revealed at least 90 days before trial. Fed.Civ.Proc.Rule 26(a)(2)(A). See also Fed.Civ.Proc.Rule 16(c)(7), making the "identification of witness[es] and documents" an appropriate subject for action by the court at a pretrial conference.

For a state provision requiring a party to disclose not only the factual basis of her case but also the legal theories upon which it rests, including legal citations if necessary, see Ariz.Rules.Civ.Proc., Rule 26.1(a)(1),(2).

18. Mass.Rules Civ.Proc. Rule 26(b)(2); Minn.Rules Civ.Proc., Rule 26.02(b); Vernon's Ann.Mo.Civ.Proc.Rule 56.01(b)(2); Mont.Rules Civ.Proc., Rule 26(b)(2). See generally 8 C. Wright, A. Miller & R. Marcus, Civil 2d § 2010.

Federal Rule 26(a)(1)(D) requires parties automatically, and without any request therefor, to turn over for inspection and copying any insurance agreement under which the insurer "may be liable to satisfy part or all of a judgment which may be entered in the action."

19. E.g., Childers v. Nicolopoulos, 296 F.Supp. 547 (D.Okl.1969); Beal v. Zambelli Fireworks Mfg. Co., 46 F.R.D. 449, 451 (W.D.Pa.1969); Great Am. Ins. Co. v. Murray, 437 S.W.2d 264 (Tex.1969); Muck v. Claflin, 197 Kan. 594, 419 P.2d 1017 (1966); Sanders v. Ayrhart, 89 Idaho 302, 404 P.2d 589 (1965).

20. E.g., Or.Rules Civ.Proc., Rule 36(b)(2); R.I.Rules Civ.Proc., Rule 26(b)(2). See Advisory Committee Notes to the 1970 amendments to Rule 26(b)(2), reprinted in 48 F.R.D. 487, 498.

21. Davis, Pretrial Discovery of Insurance Coverage, 16 Wayne L.Rev. 1047 (1970); Jenkins, Discovery of Automobile Insurance Limits: Quillets of the Law, 14 Kan.L.Rev. 59 (1965); Thode, Some Reflections on the 1957 Amendments to the Texas Rules of Civil Procedure Pertaining to Witnesses, Depositions, and Discovery, 37 Texas L.Rev. 33, 40–42 (1958); Williams, Discovery of Dollar Limits in Liability Policies in Automobile Tort Cases, 10 Ala.L.Rev. 355 (1958); Note, The Scope of Discovery in New York: Liability Insurance Policies, 25 Syracuse L.Rev. 646 (1974).

that courts typically have not allowed it.[22] The information is not deemed relevant and no special rules have been promulgated to overcome this. Of course, in some situations a party's finances are at issue in the case and then evidence of financial standing and ability are directly relevant and the information is discoverable.[23] This may occur, for example, whenever punitive damages are sought,[24] as the trier of fact must relate any such award to the defendant's ability to pay in order that a suitable "punishment" be imposed.[25]

§ 7.3 Discovery Prior to the Commencement of the Case

As previously noted,[1] one of the basic purposes of discovery is to preserve evidence when a potential witness is ill or infirm, or will be unavailable at trial.[2] This may have to be done even prior to the bringing of an action. Situations may arise when a potential plaintiff cannot bring a suit because it would be premature to do so and yet a key witness to any suit that would be brought is about to die.[3] Modern discovery rules provide a means by which this testimony can be preserved.

A difficult question, however, is the extent to which presuit discovery can be utilized purely to ascertain facts, as opposed to preserving testimony.[4] Further, if prelitigation discovery is allowed, should it be confined to ascertaining facts that will be admissible in evidence in the event that a trial subsequently does take place? Courts have not given a clear answer to this question, in part because there are few cases and because it is difficult to know before suit is filed exactly what will and what will not be relevant; some leeway must be afforded even if only the basic objective of preserving testimony is to be accomplished.

Many jurisdictions have enacted provisions allowing a party to uncover information, prior to the filing of suit, in order to assist that party in preparing the complaint.[5] Nonetheless, nearly all courts[6] agree

22. See generally Payne v. Howard, 75 F.R.D. 465 (D.D.C.1977); Ranney–Brown Distributors, Inc. v. E. T. Barwick Indus., 75 F.R.D. 3 (S.D.Ohio 1977); Bogosian v. Gulf Oil Corp., 337 F.Supp. 1228 (E.D.Pa. 1971); Hillman v. Penny, 29 F.R.D. 159, 161 (D.Tenn.1962); Sawyer v. Boufford, 113 N.H. 627, 312 A.2d 693 (1973); Doak v. Superior Court, 257 Cal.App.2d 825, 65 Cal. Rptr. 193 (1968).

23. Vollert v. Summa Corp., 389 F.Supp. 1348 (D.Hawai'i 1975); Holliman v. Redman Dev. Corp., 61 F.R.D. 488 (D.S.C. 1973).

24. Brackett v. Woodall Food Prods., Inc., 12 F.R.D. 4 (E.D.Tenn.1951).

25. Renshaw v. Ravert, 82 F.R.D. 361 (E.D.Pa.1979); Miller v. Doctor's General Hosp., 76 F.R.D. 136 (W.D.Okl.1977); Lewis v. Moody, 195 So.2d 260 (Fla.App.1967); Coy v. Superior Court, 58 Cal.2d 210, 23 Cal.Rptr. 393, 373 P.2d 457 (1962); Gierman v. Toman, 77 N.J.Super. 18, 185 A.2d

241 (Law Div.1962). See Hughes v. Groves, 47 F.R.D. 52, 55 (W.D.Mo.1969).

§ 7.3

1. See § 7.1 at n.9, above.

2. Fed.Civ.Proc.Rule 27.

3. See De Wagenknecht v. Stinnes, 250 F.2d 414 (D.C.Cir.1957).

4. Compare Martin v. Reynolds Metals Corp., 297 F.2d 49, 55 (9th Cir.1961) (allowed), with C.F. Simonin's Sons, Inc. v. American Can Co., 26 F.Supp. 420 (E.D.Pa. 1939) (not allowed). See generally Note, The Preservation and Discovery of Evidence Under Federal Rule of Civil Procedure 27, 78 Geo.L.J. 593 (1990) (advocating discovery before filing of suit both to preserve evidence and to help frame complaint).

5. E.g., Mass.Rules Civ.Proc., Rule 27; N.Y.—McKinney's CPLR 3102(c).

6. In Benner v. Walker Ambulance Co., 118 Ohio App.3d 341, 692 N.E.2d 1053

that discovery is not to be used as a means of determining whether a case exists at all; discovery is prohibited unless and until it is clear that a viable suit exists.[7] Given this conclusion, these special statutes for presuit discovery are of limited value. The same result can be obtained if a court permits a plaintiff to file a complaint which, if insufficient to withstand a demurrer or motion to dismiss, can be amended on the basis of information obtained as a result of discovery taken after suit has been initiated.[8] To the extent that the filing of even a defective complaint will permit a plaintiff to engage in discovery regarding the general subject of the suit, there is little harm in providing for discovery only after an action has been commenced.

§ 7.4   Privileged Matters

All jurisdictions provide that a party cannot obtain privileged matter through discovery.[1] Privileged matter refers to information that falls under the formal privileges as recognized under the rules of evidence.[2] The person asserting a claim of privilege has the burden of establishing its existence.[3] This matter is excluded from discovery in order to protect the privacy and secrecy of individuals in certain relationships. These include the lawyer-client,[4] doctor-patient,[5] priest-penitent,[6] husband-wife,[7] and other similar privileges that exist in particular jurisdictions.

(1997), the court stated that it was appropriate to utilize presuit discovery to determine if a valid cause of action existed against a known party. However the court seems to have misread the governing Ohio Rule of Civil Procedure 34(D)(3), which appears to apply only if a party needs discovery to identify a potential adverse party.

7. In re Boland, 79 F.R.D. 665 (D.D.C. 1978); Matter of Vermilion Parish School Bd., 357 So.2d 1295, 1297 (La.App.1978); Simpson v. Traum, 63 A.D.2d 583, 404 N.Y.S.2d 619 (1978); L–Tron Corp. v. Davco Systems, Inc., 60 A.D.2d 25, 400 N.Y.S.2d 243 (1977); In re Lewis, 11 N.C.App. 541, 181 S.E.2d 806 (1971), cert. denied 279 N.C. 394, 183 S.E.2d 242.

8. Keely v. Price, 27 Cal.App.3d 209, 103 Cal.Rptr. 531 (1972) (discovery permitted).

§ 7.4

1. Fed.Civ.Proc.Rule 26(b)(1); Ill.S.Ct. Rule 201(b)(2); N.Y.—McKinney's CPLR 3101(b). See generally 8 C. Wright, A. Miller & R. Marcus, Civil 2d §§ 2016–20.

2. U.S. v. Reynolds, 345 U.S. 1, 6, 73 S.Ct. 528, 531, 97 L.Ed. 727 (1953); Southern Ry. Co. v. Lanham, 403 F.2d 119, 134 (5th Cir.1968); Oliver v. Committee for Re–Election of the President, 66 F.R.D. 553, 556 (D.D.C.1975). See also Fed.Evid.Rule

501; McCormick on Evidence §§ 72–143 (4th ed.1992); § 10.2 at nn. 19–28, below.

3. Heathman v. U.S. District Ct., 503 F.2d 1032, 1033 (9th Cir.1974); Brock v. Gerace, 110 F.R.D. 58, 63 (D.N.J.1986); International Paper Co. v. Fibreboard Corp., 63 F.R.D. 88 (D.Del.1974).

In 1993, the Supreme Court added Federal Rule 26(b)(5), which imposes on a party asserting a privilege a duty to disclose information sufficient to enable an adversary party to assess the validity of the claim of privilege. This addition to Rule 26(b) applies to claims of work product as well as claims of privilege. See § 7.5, below.

Also in 1993. Rule 45, that covers discovery from nonparties by use of subpoenas, was completely rewritten and now includes a provision similar to the proposed amendment to Rule 26(b), enabling a discovering party to contest claims of privilege or work-product protection. Fed.Civ.Proc. Rule 45(d)(2).

4. West's Ann.Cal.Evid.Code §§ 950–62. See also Upjohn Co. v. U.S., 449 U.S. 383, 101 S.Ct. 677, 66 L.Ed.2d 584 (1981).

5. West's Ann.Cal.Evid.Code §§ 990–1007.

6. West's Ann.Cal.Evid.Code §§ 1030–34.

7. West's Ann.Cal.Evid.Code §§ 970–73, 980–87.

Persons in a privileged relationship need not reveal any communication that occurred between them. Encouraging confidence in these relationships is deemed more important than allowing full access to this information for litigation purposes.

In addition, there are certain testimonial limitations such as the privilege against self-incrimination,[8] the privilege of one spouse not to testify against another,[9] and the privilege not to reveal the identity of confidential police informants,[10] which also are applicable. This information is not to be revealed at any time under the compulsion of the courts, or of any branch of government. As a matter of policy, the protection to the individuals involved is deemed to outweigh any harm that might occur because the information is not disclosed. The law simply has considered it too coercive to compel a person to testify against himself, and this notion has been extended to spouses.[11] The need to protect the identity of police informants stems from the belief that only if such privacy is guaranteed will the police be able to obtain critical information.[12]

Finally, there has been increasing attention given to the need to protect the privacy of third persons from discovery.[13] In this field a "semi-privilege" appears to be evolving to prevent the disclosure of certain information that would invade the privacy of persons not parties to the action.[14] Thus, for example, in a wrongful death action brought by decedent's husband, defense counsel sought the disclosure of plaintiff's extramarital affairs; and the court ordered plaintiff to respond, but the names, addresses, and phone numbers of the nonlitigant paramours did not have to be revealed.[15]

§ 7.5 Material Prepared for Litigation—The "Work–Product" Doctrine

In the initial federal discovery rules and the state rules that copied them, there was no provision limiting discovery of information prepared

8. U.S.C.A. Const.Amend. 5; West's Ann.Cal.Evid.Code §§ 930, 940.

9. West's Ann.Cal.Evid.Code §§ 970–73.

10. West's Ann.Cal.Evid.Code § 1041.

11. See 18 U.S.C.A. § 3500; McCormick on Evidence § 66 (4th ed.1992).

12. The privilege to protect police informants is a qualified one in the sense that the court must balance the need to protect the government's source against the requesting party's right to prepare the defense of his criminal case. Roviaro v. U.S., 353 U.S. 53, 62, 77 S.Ct. 623, 628, 1 L.Ed.2d 639 (1957). The same balance must be made in a civil suit, as, for example, one for false arrest, although the need of the litigant may not seem as compelling.

13. The problem has been particularly acute in employment discrimination cases in the academic setting. See EEOC v. University of New Mexico, 504 F.2d 1296 (10th Cir.1974) (university required to produce personnel files of entire faculty at School of Engineering); Zaustinsky v. University of California, 96 F.R.D. 622 (N.D.Cal.1983), affirmed 782 F.2d 1055 (9th Cir.1985) (peer evaluations of tenured faculty member protected). See generally Note, Preventing Unnecessary Intrusion on University Autonomy: A Proposed Academic Privilege, 67 Calif.L.Rev. 1538 (1981).

14. See Valley Bank of Nevada v. Superior Court, 15 Cal.3d 652, 125 Cal.Rptr. 553, 542 P.2d 977 (1975) (information disclosed to bank in confidence by customer).

15. Morales v. Superior Court, 99 Cal. App.3d 283, 160 Cal.Rptr. 194 (1979).

for litigation. Not long after the rules went into operation, however, it became evident that a problem existed with respect to that type of information.[1] A lawyer, to make certain that he had left no stone unturned, simply would send a set of inquiries to an opposing party seeking whatever information the latter or opposing counsel might have regarding the case. In 1947 the Supreme Court, in the now famous case of Hickman v. Taylor,[2] engrafted a judicial exception on the generally broad federal discovery rules, holding that, in the absence of a showing of need, an opposing party could not discover information obtained by an attorney while preparing for litigation. This so-called "work-product" rule was based on the idea that every attorney should be free to investigate all aspects of a case, whether favorable or unfavorable to the attorney's client, without fear that the opposing party simply could obtain unfavorable matters and put them to use. Conversely, every attorney should be encouraged to investigate his own case, and not to remain passive, waiting for the opposing counsel to do all the investigative work.[3]

The notion of a work-product exception to discovery[4] did not meet with immediate success and several states did not follow Hickman in applying their own discovery rules.[5] In 1970, a new rule, Federal Rule 26(b)(3), was promulgated to cover the matter in federal courts, and many states have followed that lead in revising their own provisions.[6] Thus, today the work-product exception to discovery is vitally important and an exploration of its scope is necessary.

At the outset, the difference between the work-product exception to discovery and the exception for privileged matter should be kept in mind. Privileged information is immune totally from discovery, no matter how compelling the need for the information seems to be.[7] Information that is

§ 7.5

1. See generally 8 C. Wright, A. Miller & R. Marcus, Civil 2d §§ 2021–28.

2. 329 U.S. 495, 67 S.Ct. 385, 91 L.Ed. 451 (1947).

3. As Justice Jackson observed, "Discovery was hardly intended to enable a learned profession to perform its functions either without wits or on wits borrowed from the adversary." 329 U.S. at 516, 67 S.Ct. at 396.

This philosophy has been eroded somewhat by the adoption in 1993 of alterations to Federal Rule 26(a) that impose on each party an automatic duty, early in the case, to disclose substantial information, including the names of persons with information regarding the case, the description and location of documentary evidence, expert opinions that may be offered at trial, and the persons and exhibits to be offered at trial.

4. Although the work-product notion originally was devised in civil discovery, it has evolved into an independent restriction on compulsory disclosure in other settings. See, e.g., Upjohn Co. v. U.S., 449 U.S. 383, 101 S.Ct. 677, 66 L.Ed.2d 584 (1981); People v. Collie, 30 Cal.3d 43, 177 Cal.Rptr. 458, 634 P.2d 534 (1981).

5. See, e.g., Monier v. Chamberlain, 35 Ill.2d 351, 221 N.E.2d 410 (1966); Alseike v. Miller, 196 Kan. 547, 412 P.2d 1007 (1966).

6. See, e.g., Vernon's Ann.Mo.Civ.Proc. Rule 56.01(b)(4). Amendments to the Federal Rules to provide a specific work-product exception were proposed, but not adopted in 1946, 1955, and 1967. Nonetheless, several states base their rule provisions on these proposals. Thus, although most states now have codified the work-product doctrine in some form, there are many variations in the statutes and rules on this subject. For a listing of many of the variations, see 8 C. Wright, A. Miller & R. Marcus, Civil 2d § 2022 n. 24.

7. See § 7.4, above.

collected in anticipation of litigation or trial is protected from discovery, but that protection may yield to a showing of need on the part of the requesting party.[8] Mental impressions of the attorney enjoy the highest level of protection under the work-product doctrine, but, as will be seen, even they may be revealed, at least in part, upon a sufficient showing.[9] Thus, the application of the work-product rule often requires a balancing of the competing needs of the parties, as well as an inquiry into whether the material involved properly falls within the concerns that originally produced this discovery exception.

The most basic principle is that any notes, working papers, memoranda, or similar materials, prepared by an attorney in anticipation of litigation, are protected from discovery.[10] There has been some uncertainty when, if at all, protection exists for papers and materials prepared prior to the institution of litigation.[11] It is clear that protection does not exist when the information is formulated without reference to a potential lawsuit.[12] But a question arises if such a suit is contemplated but no claim of any kind has yet been made. Protection seems likely in such a case if the lawyer "had a subjective belief that litigation was a real possibility, and that belief * * * [was] objectively reasonable."[13]

It is somewhat strange that the written federal work-product rule refers only to documents and tangible things, and does not refer to information gathered by the attorney that is not reflected in a writing.[14] In the Hickman case itself, the Supreme Court noted that it would be a serious matter indeed to require an attorney to testify as to his mental impressions or ideas and theories regarding a case.[15] It could be extremely demoralizing if an attorney were required to summarize oral statements of eyewitnesses to an incident and the opposing party then could utilize the attorney's account at trial to impeach witnesses whom the

---

8. See text at notes 30–35, below. See generally 8 C. Wright, A. Miller & R. Marcus, Civil 2d § 2025.

The party claiming work-product protection must lay a proper foundation for the claim before the requesting party must show good cause. See, e.g., Delco Wire & Cable, Inc. v. Weinberger, 109 F.R.D. 680, 690–92 (E.D.Pa.1986). And see Federal Rule 26(b)(5), added in 1993, that requires the party asserting work-product protection to provide detailed information as to the justification for the protection sufficient to enable other parties to make any legitimate arguments that protection is improper. This addition to Rule 26(b) applies to claims of privilege, as well as to claims of work product. See § 7.4 above.

9. See notes 36–39, below. See generally 8 C. Wright, A. Miller & R. Marcus, Civil 2d § 2026.

10. Natta v. Zletz, 418 F.2d 633 (7th Cir.1969); Natta v. Hogan, 392 F.2d 686

(10th Cir.1968); U.S. v. Aluminum Co. of America, 34 F.R.D. 241 (E.D.Mo.1963).

11. See In re Sealed Case, 146 F.3d 881 (D.C.Cir.1998).

12. Only documents prepared in anticipation of litigation, and not in the ordinary course of business, are eligible for work-product status. See Simon v. G.D. Searle & Co., 816 F.2d 397, 401 (8th Cir.1987), cert. denied 484 U.S. 917; Grossman v. Schwarz, 125 F.R.D. 376, 388 (S.D.N.Y.1989); E.E.O.C. v. Commonwealth Edison, 119 F.R.D. 394 (N.D.Ill.1988).

13. In re Sealed Case, 146 F.3d 881, 884 (D.C.Cir.1998). See Broadnax v. ABF Freight Sys., Inc., 180 F.R.D. 343 (N.D.Ill. 1998); Dimeglio v. Briggs–Mugrauer, 708 So.2d 637 (Fla.App.1998).

14. Fed.Civ.Proc.Rule 26(b)(3). See also various state rules, e.g., Ohio Rules Civ.Proc., Rule 26(B)(3); Utah Rules Civ. Proc., Rule 26(b)(3).

15. 329 U.S. at 513, 67 S.Ct. at 395.

attorney called to the stand.[16] Even the existence of minor discrepancies could be used to indicate either that the witness or the attorney who called the witness was lying. It was so obvious that unwritten matters would need to have protection under the work-product doctrine that one of the major arguments for extending the doctrine to written matters was the fact that unless that were done, attorneys would have strong incentives not to write anything down and to avoid keeping written accounts by witnesses.[17] Thus, there is little doubt today that the work-product doctrine extends to unwritten as well as to written information.[18]

Further, the current federal rule gives the most complete protection to information regarding "the mental impressions, conclusions, opinions, or legal theories of an attorney or other representatives of a party concerning the litigation,"[19] whether that information is written or unwritten. This formulation reflects the approach taken by the Hickman Court to the need to allow attorneys to prepare their cases fully without concern that their opponents will be allowed to wait and take advantage at the last minute. The strategy of counsel is immune from discovery; only equal access to the facts is assured by the discovery system.

Another question regarding the scope of the work-product doctrine is whether it protects information obtained in anticipation of litigation by the party or insurance agent, or accountant, or similar consultants other than the attorney. The Hickman case did not address this question,[20] and although some courts provided protection from discovery of this information,[21] others did not.[22] Those jurisdictions that have adopted specific work-product rules as part of their discovery provisions generally have resolved the question in favor of protection by including parties and nonattorney agents within the scope of the specific provisions setting forth the doctrine.[23] The policy behind this extended protection is that without it an attorney would be under an obligation to do all of the investigative work without help from others, in order to immunize the reports from discovery. This result is highly undesirable because it would be inefficient or uneconomical to have the lawyers doing nonlegal work. Since the ultimate purpose of the doctrine is to promote full investigation by each party of his own case, extension of it to all those who are working for the client in anticipation of litigation seems most reasonable.

---

16. 329 U.S. at 517, 67 S.Ct. at 396 (Jackson, J., concurring).

17. 329 U.S. at 510, 67 S.Ct. at 393.

18. Transmirra Prods. Corp. v. Monsanto Chem. Co., 26 F.R.D. 572, 579 (S.D.N.Y.1960).

19. Fed.Civ.Proc.Rule 26(b)(3). Compare Duplan Corp. v. Moulinage et Retorderie de Chavanoz, 509 F.2d 730, 734 (4th Cir.1974), cert. denied 420 U.S. 997 (holding protection absolute), with In re Grand Jury Investigation, 599 F.2d 1224 (3d Cir. 1979) and Charlotte Motor Speedway, Inc. v. International Ins. Co., 125 F.R.D. 127

(M.D.N.C.1989) (both holding protection qualified).

20. Hickman v. Taylor, 329 U.S. 495, 67 S.Ct. 385, 91 L.Ed. 451 (1947).

21. Alltmont v. U.S., 177 F.2d 971 (3d Cir.1949), cert. denied 339 U.S. 967; Ownby v. U.S., 293 F.Supp. 989 (W.D.Okl.1968).

22. Southern Ry. Co. v. Lanham, 403 F.2d 119 (5th Cir.1968); Whitaker v. Davis, 45 F.R.D. 270, 273 (W.D.Mo.1968).

23. Fed.Civ.Proc.Rule 26(b)(3); Va.Sup. Ct.Rules, Rule 4:1(b)(3); Wn.Civ.Rule 26(b)(3).

An exception to the work-product doctrine permits any party to obtain a copy of her own statement, even though that statement otherwise would be protected from disclosure.[24] This exception is justified by the fact that a party's statement always may be used as direct evidence at trial by an opposing party, whether or not the party who made the statement is called to the witness stand.[25] Because the statement is likely to have a substantial impact on the trier of fact, it would be unfair to preclude the party who made the statement from examining it prior to trial.

It should be noted that under Federal Rule 26(b)(3) and its state counterparts, any nonparty witness also may obtain a copy of a prior statement given to a party or attorney, even though that statement is otherwise within the work-product doctrine. The reason for this exception is to allow the witness to avoid embarrassment at trial by being confronted with statements inconsistent with the testimony given.[26] This special exception seems unwarranted to many and not every state has endorsed it.[27]

Unlike the statement of a party, the statement of a witness can be used in court to impeach only when it is inconsistent with testimony given by the witness on the stand.[28] The very purpose of the rule allowing a witness to be impeached by a prior inconsistent statement is to assist the trier of fact in determining whether a witness has told the truth at trial.[29] Embarrassment of a witness who tells different stories at different times is not too high a price to pay for that information. Thus, the need to provide access to the statement is not clear.

More important, however, is the fact that this exception is subject to abuse and unfairness. Suppose the witness has given a statement to one of the parties. The opposing attorney has asked for a copy of the statement but it has been refused on work-product grounds. Under the federal rule, the requesting attorney may obtain the statement by asking the witness to obtain a copy of his statement from the opposing party and then turn it over to the attorney seeking discovery, thereby undercutting the work-product protection. What is worse is the fact that this approach can be used only when the witness is friendly to the attorney seeking discovery, and thus is willing to cooperate in making the request. It seems unfortunate to allow disclosure to turn on the question of which party or attorney is more friendly to the witness.

---

24. This exception is written into the federal rule as well as into the rules of many states. See Fed.Civ.Proc.Rule 26(b)(3); Fla.—West's F.S.A.Rules Civ. Proc., Rule 1.280(b)(3); Official Code Ga. Ann. § 9–11–26(b)(3).

25. Straughan v. Barge MVL No. 802, 291 F.Supp. 282, 285 (S.D.Tex.1968); Reed v. McCord, 160 N.Y. 330, 54 N.E. 737 (1899). See Fed.Evid.Rule 801(d)(2); West's Ann.Cal.Evid.Code § 1220.

26. See Advisory Committee Notes to the 1970 amendments to Rule 26(b)(3), reprinted in 48 F.R.D. 457, 503.

27. See N.Y.—McKinney's CPLR 3101(e). The vast majority of states have followed the federal rule, see, e.g., Iowa Rules Civ.Proc., Rule 122(c); Idaho Rules Civ.Proc., Rule 26(b)(3).

28. See McCormick on Evidence §§ 34–38 (4th ed.1992). But see id. § 251.

29. McCormick on Evidence § 34 (4th ed.1992).

Even though the policies supporting nondisclosure are very strong, the protection provided by the work-product doctrine is not absolute.[30] In addition to the few rule exceptions just mentioned,[31] all other information that falls within the doctrine's scope will be subject to discovery if the requesting party makes a showing of good cause based on a necessity for disclosure of the information.[32] But what constitutes necessity or good cause?

Good cause will rarely exist in situations like that in the Hickman v. Taylor case, involving the attempt by one party to obtain the statements of witnesses that had been taken by opposing counsel.[33] If a party wants to learn what a witness knows about a particular incident, and if the witness refuses to talk informally, the party always may subpoena the witness to a deposition and force the witness under oath to reveal that knowledge.[34] Thus, in the absence of a showing by the requesting party that the witness no longer is available, perhaps because of death, age, or infirmity, there is no need to overcome the protection accorded that information.[35] Other situations depend on the facts of each case.

In some states a good cause exception to the work-product rule is not applicable to any material revealing an attorney's impressions, conclusions, or legal theories.[36] That material is not discoverable under any circumstances. The federal work-product rule and those of the states that follow it do not appear specifically to prohibit such discovery; rather the rule states that the courts should "guard against" disclosure of that matter.[37] It is unclear whether this was intended to be an absolute prohibition or whether it merely requires extreme necessity before this information should be held discoverable.[38]

In the ordinary course of events an attorney's impressions and theories can be eliminated from a response to a discovery request without seriously curtailing the disclosure of relevant information. But

30. Chaney By & Through Guilliam v. Slack, 99 F.R.D. 531, 534 (S.D.Ga.1983). See also Cohn, The Work Product Doctrine: Protection, Not Privilege, 71 Geo.L.J. 917 (1983).

31. Information regarding expert witnesses also receives special treatment under the rules. See § 7.6, below.

32. American Standard, Inc. v. Bendix Corp., 71 F.R.D. 443, 447 (W.D.Mo.1976); Truck Ins. Exchange v. St. Paul Fire & Marine Ins. Co., 66 F.R.D. 129 (E.D.Pa. 1975); Burlington Indus. v. Exxon Corp., 65 F.R.D. 26 (D.Md.1974). See generally 8 C. Wright, A. Miller & R. Marcus, Civil 2d § 2025.

33. 329 U.S. 495, 67 S.Ct. 385, 91 L.Ed. 451 (1947).

34. Fed.Civ.Proc.Rules 26(a), 30, 31, 45(a); Ariz.Rules Civ.Proc., Rules 26(a), 30, 31, 45(a); Colo.Rules Civ.Proc., Rules 26(a), 30, 31, 45(a). See also § 7.8,.

35. See In re Grand Jury Investigation, 599 F.2d 1224, 1231–32 (3d Cir.1979); McNulty v. Bally's Park Place, Inc., 120 F.R.D. 27 (E.D.Pa.1988); Rackers v. Siegfried, 54 F.R.D. 24 (W.D.Mo.1971); McDonald v. Prowdley, 38 F.R.D. 1 (W.D.Mich. 1965); Hanson v. Gartland S. S. Co., 34 F.R.D. 493 (N.D.Ohio 1964).

36. In re PCB File No. 92.27, ___ Vt. ___, 708 A.2d 568 (1998); Kenford Co. v. Erie County, 55 A.D.2d 466, 390 N.Y.S.2d 715 (1977). See N.Y.—McKinney's CPLR 3101(c).

37. Fed.Civ.Proc.Rule 26(b)(3); Kan. Stat.Ann. 60–226(b)(3); Me.Rules Civ.Proc., Rule 26(b)(3).

38. See Peterson v. U.S., 52 F.R.D. 317 (S.D.Ill.1971); Willis v. Duke Power Co., 291 N.C. 19, 229 S.E.2d 191 (1976); Coleman v. Imbruglia, 166 So.2d 780 (Fla.App. 1964); Baltimore Transit Co. v. Mezzanotti, 227 Md. 8, 174 A.2d 768 (1961).

situations can arise in which it would be highly unfair and unfortunate if an absolute prohibition existed. For example, if an attorney had reason to believe that an opposing party ultimately might be able to show necessity for discovering an important statement of a witness, the attorney taking the statement might do so in question and answer fashion, forming the questions in such a way that they call only for yes and no answers. It then could be argued that the statement could not be revealed under any circumstances because the attorney's questions necessarily revealed the impressions and theories of the case; the answers alone would be worthless. It seems improper to apply the "attorney's theories" limitation to prevent necessary disclosure under those circumstances.[39]

As the foregoing analysis indicates, the work-product doctrine cannot be used to hide evidence or avoid revelation of the facts of a case.[40] Only the thoughts, ideas, and theories of the people who gather information in preparation for trial are subject to protection. Thus, if a party tells her attorney all that she knows about a case, the attorney need not reveal the information but the party, on direct questioning, must do so.[41] Similarly, the fact that an attorney has found the contract upon which the suit is brought, does not make the contract itself part of the attorney's work-product; the attorney cannot refuse to turn it over to the opposing party for examination,[42] and one side cannot refuse to disclose the names of eyewitnesses that it has uncovered, even though considerable time and expense were involved in obtaining that information.[43]

§ 7.6 Expert Information

In a great many cases, experts are employed to assist in preparing a case for trial. Taking a superficial view, the work-product doctrine seems to encompass experts just as it covers the party or insurance agent who is assisting the attorney. Indeed, the need for protection appears somewhat greater with regard to an expert, for if the expert renders an unfavorable report, which could be presented by the opposing party at trial, it would have a devastating effect on the party who had employed the expert. No one would hire an expert unless assured that any report

---

39. See In re Murphy, 560 F.2d 326, 336 (8th Cir.1977); Duplan Corp. v. Deering Milliken, Inc., 540 F.2d 1215 (4th Cir.1976); Duplan Corp. v. Moulinage et Retorderie de Chavanoz, 509 F.2d 730, 734, 737 (4th Cir. 1974), cert. denied 420 U.S. 997.

40. See, e.g., Nutmeg Ins. Co. v. Atwell, Vogel & Sterling, 120 F.R.D. 504, 509 (W.D.La.1988); Hoffman v. United Telecommunications, Inc., 117 F.R.D. 436, 439 (D.Kan.1987); Wonneman v. Stratford Secs. Co., 23 F.R.D. 281, 285 (S.D.N.Y.1959). See also McCormick on Evidence § 96 (4th ed.1992).

41. Gaynor v. Atlantic Greyhound Corp., 8 F.R.D. 302 (E.D.Pa.1948).

42. See Natta v. Hogan, 392 F.2d 686 (10th Cir.1968); In re Penn Cent. Commercial Paper Litigation, 61 F.R.D. 453 (S.D.N.Y.1973).

43. Cedolia v. C. S. Hill Saw Mills, Inc., 41 F.R.D. 524 (M.D.N.C.1967); Taylor v. Atchison, T. & S. F. Ry. Co., 33 F.R.D. 283 (W.D.Mo.1962). Cf. In re San Juan Dupont Plaza Hotel Fire Litigation, 859 F.2d 1007 (1st Cir.1988) (requiring parties, before deposition, to provide list of exhibits to be used during deposition).

would not be detrimental, thereby preventing a party or an attorney from obtaining an honest appraisal of the case.

The situation is altered dramatically, however, if the party who hires the expert determines to call the latter to testify at trial. In that event, the opposing party must have some way of ascertaining what the expert is likely to say. Indeed, it is more important that the opposition have access to this material than information regarding the possible testimony of ordinary eyewitnesses. The expert's theories and opinions may be based on the nature of his training and certain assumptions that are part of his expertise. The opposing party must be able to ascertain what those assumptions are in order to be able to counter them at trial. Thus, different specialized rules have developed with regard to access to expert information gathered in anticipation of trial.[1]

First, when an expert is an eyewitness to material events in a case,[2] or a party to an action,[3] as opposed to being hired in anticipation of litigation, no work-product protection exists. Thus, a doctor who provides emergency treatment to an accident victim may be questioned as to the condition of the patient, the nature of the victim's treatment, and similar matters.[4] Discovery will be curtailed only to the extent that the information sought is privileged.[5]

Special rules also have been developed for information gathered in the course of a medical examination. Under modern discovery rules a party whose mental or physical condition is in controversy may be required to submit to an examination by a doctor or doctors employed by an opposing party.[6] The examined party may demand and obtain a copy of the examiner's report but, in exchange, must supply copies of medical reports from her own doctors regarding the conditions involved.[7] In this situation the general rules regarding discovery from experts employed in anticipation of litigation do not apply.[8]

§ 7.6

1. Compare Fed.Civ.Proc.Rules 26(a)(2) and 26(b)(4)(A) with Fed.Civ.Proc. Rule 26(b)(4)(B). See generally Note, Proposed 1967 Amendments to the Federal Discovery Rules, 68 Colum.L.Rev. 271, 282 (1968).

2. Keith v. Van Dorn Plastic Machinery Co., 86 F.R.D. 458 (E.D.Pa.1980); Franks v. National Dairy Prods. Corp., 41 F.R.D. 234, 237 (W.D.Tex.1966).

3. Williams v. Thomas Jefferson Univ., 54 F.R.D. 615 (E.D.Pa.1972); Anderson v. Florence, 288 Minn. 351, 181 N.W.2d 873 (1970). But see Meltzer v. Coralluzzo, 499 So.2d 69 (Fla.App.1986)

Note that if a party, who is an expert, wants to testify as an expert as to matters to which the party was not an eyewitness, the party is subject to disclosure provisions regarding expert witnesses and failure to obey those rules can result in the exclusion of the party's expert testimony. Pedigo v. UNUM Life Ins. Co., 145 F.3d 804 (6th Cir.1998).

4. Franks v. National Dairy Prods. Corp., 41 F.R.D. 234 (W.D.Tex.1966).

5. See § 7.4, above. For a discussion of discovery by means of mental and physical examinations, see § 7.12, below.

6. Fed.Civ.Proc.Rule 35. See Sarka v. Rush Presbyterian—St. Luke's Medical Center, 207 Ill.App.3d 587, 152 Ill.Dec. 614, 566 N.E.2d 301 (1990). Federal Rule 35 was amended in 1991 to allow licensed and qualified professionals, other than just medical doctors, to conduct examinations.

7. See 8A C. Wright, A. Miller & R. Marcus, Civil 2d § 2237.

8. Dimeglio v. Briggs–Mugrauer, 708 So.2d 637 (Fla.App.1998).

Outside of the latter area, however, experts hired to assist in preparation for trial, are treated differently depending on whether the expert will be called to testify at trial. The discovery rules typically require discovery of the facts and opinions of those experts who have been retained for trial; non-testifying experts are accorded protection from discovery in keeping with general work-product notions.[9]

The typical provision for discovery of expert information in state courts is based on an earlier version of Federal Rule 26(b)(4), which has since been altered substantially,[10] and the cases which interpreted it. Under the typical state rule, if the party who hired the expert intends to call that expert to testify at trial, the party must answer an interrogatory, stating the subject matter on which the expert is expected to testify, and giving the substance of the facts and opinions that will be expressed, as well as a summary of the grounds for each opinion.[11] In light of the need for a party to understand fully the nature of the testimony of the opponent's expert, this access often may be too restrictive. Therefore, a number of states authorize a party to take the expert's deposition without seeking a court order.[12] In other states the court has the power to order additional discovery, such as the taking of depositions and the revelation of written opinions.[13] The problem is that no standards are set forth as to when additional discovery is appropriate,[14] and in a few older cases courts restricted discovery to cursory answers to interrogatories that gave only a very general outline of the expert testimony without sufficient detail to apprise the opposing party of the underlying basis for the expert's opinion.[15] Any restriction on the ability of a party to learn

---

9. See the discussion at notes 23–26, below. Experts who are not retained but are informally consulted fall directly within work-product notions and neither their names nor their opinions are discoverable. See Advisory Committee Note to 1970 amendments to Rule 26(b)(4), reprinted in 48 F.R.D. 487, 504. See also Healy v. Counts, 100 F.R.D. 493 (D.Colo.1984).

10. See text at notes 16–20, below. See also § 7.7, below.

11. E.g., Mich.Ct.Rules 1985, 2.302(B)(4)(a)(i); Vernon's Ann.Mo.Civ. Proc.Rule 56.01(b)(4)(a); N.Y—McKinney's CPLR 3101(d)(i).

12. E.g., Mich.Ct.Rules 1985, 2.302(B)(4)(a)(ii); Vernon's Ann.Mo.Civ. Proc.Rule 56.01(b)(4)(b); NY—McKinney's CPLR 3101(d)(iii).

Some states provide for wide ranging discovery regarding information about an expert who will testify and her opinions. E.g., Fla Rules 1.280(b)(4); Iowa Rules Civ. Proc., Rule 125(a)(2)(B).

13. E.g., Kan.Stat.Ann. 60– 226(b)(4)(A)(ii); Utah Rules Civ.Proc., Rule 26(b)(4)(A)(ii); W.Va.Rules Civ.Proc., Rule 26(B)(4)(a)(ii). Discovery of reports of trial

experts is routinely granted in New Hampshire. See Workman v. Public Serv. Co., 113 N.H. 422, 308 A.2d 540 (1973).

14. Graham, Discovery of Experts Under Rule 26(b)(4) of the Federal Rules of Civil Procedure: Part One, An Analytical Study, 1976 U.Ill.L.F. 895, 939; Comment, Rule 26(b)(4) of the Federal Rules of Civil Procedure: Discovery of Expert Information, 42 U.Miami L.Rev. 1101, 1129 (1988); Comment, Discovery of Expert Information Under the Federal Rules, 10 U.Rich.L.Rev. 706, 714 (1976).

New York permits such additional discovery "only by court order upon a showing of special circumstances." N.Y.—McKinney's CPLR 3101(d)(iii).

15. E.g., Wilson v. Resnick, 51 F.R.D. 510 (E.D.Pa.1970). It has been suggested that additional discovery by deposition should be restricted to the opinions the expert will give on direct examination. In re IBM Peripheral EDP Devices Antitrust Litigation, 77 F.R.D. 39 (N.D.Cal.1977); Bailey v. Meister Brau, Inc., 57 F.R.D. 11 (N.D.Ill. 1972). See also Connors, A New Look at an Old Concern—Protecting Expert Information from Discovery Under the Federal

the nature and basis of the opinions of another party's expert who will testify at trial seems unwarranted.

In 1993, the federal discovery rules were substantially altered with regard to experts who are expected to testify at trial. Within specific time limits, normally not less than 90 days prior to trial, a party must automatically reveal to the other parties in the case the identity of any such experts and must provide a written report prepared and signed by the expert.[16] The report must include the expert's opinion and the basis and reasons therefor, and must contain any data or information upon which the opinion was based and any exhibits to be used in support of the opinion.[17] Moreover, the statement must list the qualifications of the expert, the expert's publications over a ten-year period, other cases in which the expert has testified, during the past four years and the compensation paid or to be paid for the expert's opinion in the current case.[18] After such a report has been provided, any party may depose the expert,[19] and may obtain other expert information through other discovery methods.[20]

When an expert, who will testify, was not hired in anticipation of litigation, federal courts have split on how the regulations are to be applied. It is agreed that the party who will call the expert must reveal the latter's identity, but the issue is whether the expert must file a report even when she will provide some opinion testimony. The large majority of decisions do not require a report so long as the testimony does not go beyond the expert's observations as a witness and the opinions based on those observations. Thus, a treating physician is not considered an expert hired for litigation if the doctor describes the patient's injuries and treatment and, on that basis, gives an opinion as to

---

Rules, 18 Duquesne L.Rev. 271, 277–80 (1980).

16. Fed.Civ.Proc.Rule 26(a)(2). Under the rule a party must disclose his own intentions to testify as an expert. Failure to do so can result in the exclusion of his expert testimony. Pedigo v. UNUM Life Ins. Co., 145 F.3d 804 (6th Cir.1998).

Similar rules are found in Arizona and Colorado. See Ariz.Rules Civ.Proc., Rule 26.1(a)(6); Colo.Rules Civ. Proc., Rule 26(a)(2).

17. Federal courts are divided on whether a party can object to disclosure of information supplied to the expert to assist him in forming his opinion on the ground that the information constituted work product of the attorney. See Cohen, Expert Witness Discovery Versus the Work Product Doctrine: Choosing a Winner in Government Contracts Litigation, 27 Pub.Contract L.J. 719, 729–35 (1998); Note, Discoverability of Attorney Work Product Reviewed by Expert Witnesses: Have the 1993 Revisions to the Federal Rules of Civil Procedure

Changed Anything?, 69 Temple L.Rev. 451 (1996). Compare Lamonds v. General Motors Corp., 180 F.R.D. 302 (W.D.Va.1998)(disclosure required) with Haworth, Inc. v. Herman Miller, Inc., 162 F.R.D. 289 (W.D.Mich.1995)(materials held not discoverable).

18. Fed.Civ.Proc.Rule 26(a)(2).

19. Fed.Civ.Proc.Rule 26(b)(4)(A).

20. Fed.Civ.Proc.Rule 26(a)(5) contemplates the use of other forms of discovery. See Joseph, Emerging Issues Under the 1993 Amendment to the Federal Civil Rules, 583 PLI/lit 325, 344 (1998), citing Corrigan v. Methodist Hosp., 158 F.R.D. 54, 58 (E.D.Pa.1994)(documents attorney gives to expert in formulating opinion are subject to discovery); Caruso v. Coleman Co., No. 93–CV–6733, 1994 WL 719759 (E.D.Pa. 1994)(drafts of experts "reports and notes" used to formulate opinion are subject to discovery); All West Pet Supply Co. v. Hill's Pet Prods., 152 F.R.D. 634, 639–40 (D.Kan.1993)(other testimony given by expert is subject to discovery).

the causation of the injury and the prognosis for recovery.[21] If the physician goes beyond observations as a witness, and provides an opinion based on facts other than those ascertained during care and treatment, then the physician becomes a "retained" expert subject to the rules governing those hired in anticipation of litigation.[22]

In the ordinary course, a party will not be permitted to discover the opinions or findings of an expert hired by the opposing party to aid in the preparation of litigation when the latter party does not intend to call the expert to testify.[23] There is, however, an exception to this rule when special circumstances make it impossible or highly impracticable for the party seeking the information to obtain his own expert's opinions.[24] This could occur, for example, in a situation in which one party hires the only available expert, or when one party's expert had an opportunity to study a particular item of evidence that is lost or destroyed before experts from the opposing side have had an opportunity to examine it.[25] It has been held that such discovery is appropriate when the cost of obtaining duplicate opinions would be "judicially prohibitive."[26]

When a party is permitted to discover information from an expert hired by an opposing party, the Federal Rules and those of some states specifically provide that the court may order the discovering party to pay a portion of the expert's fee.[27] The court is required, however, to provide for fee sharing when the discovery involves an expert who will not be called to the stand by the party who hired him.[28] The court has broad discretion to determine what is a fair portion of the fee that should be so paid.[29]

---

21. Sprague v. Liberty Mut. Ins. Co., 177 F.R.D. 78 (D.N.H.1998). Contra Thomas v. Consolidated Rail Corp., 169 F.R.D. 1 (D.Mass.1996)(physician who gives opinions as to cause of patient's injuries and prognosis is to be considered retained in anticipation of litigation).

22. Brown v. Best Foods, 169 F.R.D. 385 (N.D.Ala.1996).

23. Fed.Civ.Proc.Rule 26(b)(4)(B); Mass.Rules Civ.Proc., Rule 26(b)(4)(B); Minn.Rules Civ.Proc., Rule 26.02(d)(2).

24. Fed.Civ.Proc.Rule 26(b)(4)(B); Mont.Rules Civ.Proc., Rule 26(b)(4)(B); N.J.Civ.Prac.Rule 4:10–2(d)(3). In addition, a party may subpoena an expert witness not retained by any party to the action. Fed.Civ.Proc.Rule 45(c)(3)(B)(ii) (see §§ 7.8, 7.11) provides appropriate protection for unretained experts. See Report of the Judicial Conference Committee on Rules of Practice and Procedure, Proposed Amendments to the Federal Rules of Civil Procedure, September 1990. See generally Maurer, Compelling the Expert Witness: Fairness and Utility Under the Federal Rules of Civil Procedure, 19 Ga.L.Rev. 71 (1984); Note, Discovery and Testimony of Unretained Experts: Creating a Clear and Equitable Standard to Govern Compliance With Subpoenas, 1987 Duke L.J. 140 (1987).

25. Sanford Constr. Co. v. Kaiser Aluminum & Chem. Sales, Inc., 45 F.R.D. 465 (E.D.Ky.1968); Walsh v. Reynolds Metals Co., 15 F.R.D. 376 (D.N.J.1954); Town of North Kingstown v. Ashley, 118 R.I. 505, 374 A.2d 1033, 1036 (1977); Wasmuth v. Hinds–Toomey Auto Corp., 39 A.D.2d 723, 331 N.Y.S.2d 804 (1972).

26. Bank Brussels Lambert v. Chase Manhattan Bank, 175 F.R.D. 34, 44–45 (S.D.N.Y.1997).

27. Fed.Civ.Proc.Rule 26(b)(4)(c); Ohio Rules Civ.Proc., Rule 26(B)(4)(c); Utah Rules Civ.Proc., Rule 26(b)(4)(C)(ii).

28. Fed.Civ.Proc.Rule 26(b)(4)(c); U.S. v. 50.34 Acres of Land in Village of East Hills, 13 F.R.D. 19 (E.D.N.Y.1952).

29. See, e.g., Worley v. Massey–Ferguson, Inc., 79 F.R.D. 534 (N.D.Miss.1978).

Additionally, when an expert is required to spend time responding to discovery requests by a party who did not employ him, modern rules provide that the court should require the discovering party to pay reasonable compensation to the expert "unless manifest injustice would result."[30] Presumably, if the party desperately needed the information but was not financially able to pay, the court could refuse to order compensation.[31] It should be noted, however, that compensation is not required when the only discovery sought is by a set of interrogatories to an expert who will testify for the opposing party. Normally this information does not require further efforts by the expert.[32]

C. THE MECHANICS OF MODERN DISCOVERY DEVICES

§ 7.7 Mandatory Planning Conference and Required Initial Disclosures

The federal courts in 1993 adopted a new set of rules requiring parties to meet early in the case to develop a proposed discovery plan[1] and, unless they otherwise stipulate, requiring each of them, within ten days thereafter[2] and without waiting for a discovery request, to disclose to all other parties basic types of information.[3] Several states have adopted similar provisions.[4]

The information that must initially be disclosed under the federal rule[5] includes (1) the names and addresses of those individuals "likely to have discoverable information relevant to the disputed facts alleged with particularity in the pleadings," (2) a copy or description of all documents or tangible items in the party's custody or control that are relevant to such disputed facts, (3) a computation of any damages claimed, including documents, not privileged or otherwise protected from discovery, upon which those computations are based, and (4) copies of any insurance agreements that may be liable to satisfy all or part of a judgment against the party. Until a party makes these automatic disclosures, she cannot

30. Fed.Civ.Proc.Rule 26(b)(4)(C); Va. Sup.Ct.Rules, Rule 4:1(b)(4)(C); Wn. Civ.Rule 26(b)(4)(C). See, e.g., Benjamin v. Gloz, 130 F.R.D. 455 (D.Colo.1990); Herbst v. International Tel. & Tel. Corp., 65 F.R.D. 528 (D.Conn.1975).

31. See Advisory Committee Note to 1970 amendments to Rule 26(b)(4), reprinted in 48 F.R.D. 487, 505.

32. Cf. Russo v. Merck & Co., 21 F.R.D. 237, 239 (D.R.I.1957).

§ 7.7

1. Fed.Civ.Proc.Rule 26(f). The meeting is to take place as soon as is practicable and no later than 14 days prior to a pretrial conference under Federal Rule 16. See

§ 8.2, below. A 1998 proposed amendment to Rule 26(f) would raise the number of days from 14 to 21. Preliminary Draft of Proposed Amendments to the Federal Rules of Civil Procedure and Evidence 45, reprinted in 181 F.R.D. 18, at 68 (1998).

2. A 1998 proposed amendment to Rule 26(a)(1) would raise the number of days from 10 to 14. Preliminary Draft of Proposed Amendments to the Federal Rules of Civil Procedure and Evidence 37, reprinted in 181 F.R.D. 18, at 60 (1998).

3. Fed.Civ.Proc.Rule 26(a).

4. Ariz.Rules Civ.Proc., Rule 26.1; Colo.Rules Civ.Proc., Rule 26(a).

5. Fed.Civ.Proc.Rule 26(a)(1).

engage in any formal discovery using traditional methods for obtaining information.

In addition to these initial disclosures, other automatic disclosures are required at various times before trial. Thus, at least 90 days before trial, parties must identify any expert witnesses who will testify at trial on their behalf, and must include a written report, signed by the witness, giving a "complete statement of the opinions to be expressed and the basis and reasons therefor."[6] Additional information regarding the basis for the opinion and the qualifications of the expert also must be included.[7] Moreover, at least 30 days before trial, a party must automatically disclose the names of witnesses she expects to call at trial and the names of others who may be called if the need arises; the names of witnesses whose testimony will be presented by deposition; and an identification of each document the party intends to introduce at trial and each document which she will introduce if the need arises.[8] It should be noted that the court is given the power to modify these automatic disclosure provisions if the situation so warrants.[9]

Automatic disclosure provisions are by no means given universal acclaim.[10] The federal rule has included a provision permitting each district court by local rule to opt out of the mandatory disclosure system and a substantial number have done so.[11] The loss of uniformity of practice under the federal rules has proved particularly troublesome. As a result, in 1998 a proposal was circulated that would amend Rule 26 substantially to limit the scope of mandatory disclosure[12] and to do away

---

6. Fed.Civ.Proc.Rule 26(a)(2)

7. This includes "the data or other information considered by the witness in forming the opinions; any exhibits to be used as a summary of or support for the opinions; the qualifications of the witness, including a list of all publications authored by the witness within the preceding ten years; the compensation to be paid for the study and testimony; and a listing of any other cases in which the witness has testified as an expert at trial or by deposition within the preceding four years." Fed.Civ. Proc.Rule 26(a)(2)(B).

8. Fed.Civ.Proc.Rule 26(a)(2)(C). Another party who wishes to object to the use of a witness' deposition or to the admissibility of a listed document, other than on relevancy grounds, must do so within 14 days or the court may declare the objection waived.

9. Fed.Civ.Proc.Rule 8(a)(1).

10. See § 7.1 nn. 27 & 28, above, for views pro and con. See also Hench, Mandatory Disclosure and Equal Access to Justice: The 1993 Federal Discovery Rules Amendments and the Just, Speedy and Inexpensive Determination of Every Action, 67 Temple L.Rev. 179, 198–228 (1994); Sorenson, Disclosure Under Federal Rule of Civil

Procedure 26(A)-"Much Ado About Nothing?", 46 Hastings L.J. 679 (1995); Willging, Stienstra, Shapard, & Miletich, An Empirical Study of Discovery and Disclosure Practice Under the 1993 Federal Rule Amendments, 39 B.C.L.Rev. 525 (1998).

11. Preliminary Draft of Proposed Amendments to the Federal Rules of Civil Procedure and Evidence 48–49 (August 1998), reprinted in 181 F.R.D. 18, at 71–72.

For views of the members of the bench and bar, see Willging, Stienstra, Shapard & Miletich, An Empirical Study of Discovery and Disclosure Practice Under the 1993 Federal Rule Amendments, 39 B.C.L.Rev. 525 (1998).

12. The proposal would exempt eight categories of cases from mandatory initial disclosure and also from the requirement of a discovery conference under Rule 26(f). These include: actions for review of an administrative record, petitions for habeas corpus to challenge convictions or sentences, cases brought by pro se litigants who are in custody, motions to quash administrative summonses or subpoenas, actions by the United States to recover benefit payments, actions by the United States to collect on student loan guarantees, pro-

with the opt-out provision by local rule or standing orders.[13] Courts would remain free to eliminate mandatory disclosure requirements on a case-by-case basis. The exemptions would have a major impact since it is estimated that they would affect about one-third of all civil filings in federal courts and would cover types of actions where there is not likely to be a need for discovery or where early discovery will not effectively contribute to the development of the case.[14]

§ 7.8   Oral Depositions and Depositions on Written Questions

An oral deposition allows the attorneys for the various parties in the case to confront and question any person, including a party, regarding the subject matter of the case.[1] That person (the "deponent") is placed under oath by an officer who is in charge of the deposition. This can be anyone who is authorized to administer oaths[2] or anyone upon whom the parties agree.[3] Although the deponent will normally be present, the parties, by written agreement or through a court order, can take a deposition over the telephone or by other remote electronic means.[4] Invariably the parties designate as officer the reporter who records the questions, the answers, and any objections made by the parties or by the witness.[5] In most jurisdictions, when the deposition has been concluded, the reporter prepares a transcript, which the deponent then is called upon to sign.[6] This requirement has proven difficult for reporters who frequently have trouble contacting non-party witnesses. Therefore, Federal Rule 30(e), as amended in 1993, provides only that a deponent will be offered a chance to review the transcript or the recording of the deposition if the deponent or a party so requests prior to the completion

---

ceedings ancillary to proceedings in other courts, and actions to enforce arbitration awards. Proposed Rule 26(a)(1)(E), Preliminary Draft of Proposed Rules of Civil Procedure and Evidence 36–37 (August 1998).

13. Preliminary Draft of Proposed Amendments to the Federal Rules of Civil Procedure 49–50 (August 1998), reprinted in 181 F.R.D. 18, at 72–73 . .

14. Id. at 51–52.

§ 7.8

1. Fed.Civ.Proc.Rule 30(c); Ala.Rules Civ.Proc., Rule 30(c); Iowa Rules Civ.Proc., Rule 153.

2. Fed.Civ.Proc.Rule 28; Ariz.Rules Civ.Proc.Rule 28; Ark.Rules Civ.Proc., Rule 28. See Ott v. Stipe Law Firm, 169 F.R.D. 380 (E.D.Okla.1996)(deposition inadmissible because plaintiff administered the oath to the deponent).

3. Fed.Civ.Proc.Rule 29; Fla.—West's F.S.A.Rules Civ.Proc., Rule 1.300(c); Ill. S.Ct.Rule 201(i); Texas Rules Civ.Proc., Rule 166(c).

4. Fed.Civ.Proc.Rule 30(b)(7).

5. There must be a reporter recording the deposition. Fed.Civ.Proc.Rule 30(c); Colo.Rules Civ.Proc., Rule 30(c); Fla.—West's F.S.A.Rules Civ.Proc., Rule 1.310(c).

Some courts have provided for audio or audiovisual transcriptions of depositions. See, e.g., Fed.Civ.Proc.Rule 30(b)(2)(approval of court or consent of other parties not required); N.J.Civ.Prac.Rule 4:14–9; N.Y.—McKinney's CPLR 3113. However, any party can insist that a stenographer also be present as a backup to the mechanical methods. See, e.g., Fed.Civ.Proc.Rule 30(b)(3). For cases in which video depositions were utilized, see Morrison v. Reichhold Chemicals, Inc., 97 F.3d 460 (11th Cir.1996); Hudson v. Spellman High Voltage, 178 F.R.D. 29 (E.D.N.Y.1998); Ott v. Stipe Law Firm, 169 F.R.D. 380 (E.D.Okla. 1996).

6. Official Code Ga.Ann. § 9–11–30(e); Idaho Rules Civ.Proc., Rule 30(e); Iowa Rules Civ.Proc., Rule 149(b).

of the deposition. In such a case, the deponent may, within 30 days after notice that the transcript or recording is available, sign a statement reciting any changes in form or substance and the reasons for making them. These latter provisions may become important if the deposition, or a portion of it, is offered into evidence at trial.[7]

Oral depositions have several advantages and disadvantages. An oral deposition permits the attorney to observe a potential witness while undergoing examination, thus giving a strong indication of how the witness will appear at trial if called to testify. It also permits the attorney to pin down the witness with regard to the details of his observations, which can be an advantage both to the attorney who will call the witness at trial and to an opposing attorney who may cross-examine the witness as to any inconsistencies. The fact that the witness is present and answering the questions directly is extremely important because the answer to one question often dictates what the next one will be. Thus, this form of discovery has distinct advantages over a procedure in which a witness responds in writing to questions while at home or in his office, with the benefit of counsel, and with no direct confrontation by the questioning attorney.[8]

The chief drawback to oral depositions is their expense. Typically, each party must pay for the time that his attorney spends in connection with the deposition.[9] In addition, a party will have to pay for any transcriptions of the deposition received and, perhaps, some witness fees and expenses.[10] Although some of the latter ultimately may be recovered by the successful party as part of the judgment,[11] that usually will not be a major consideration in deciding to what extent depositions should be taken. In the first place reimbursement is usually a long time off. Second, the very purpose of the discovery will be to help determine how likely a party is to prevail if a trial takes place, and thus at the time the

---

7. Modern discovery rules specify when a deposition may be admitted into evidence at trial. See § 7.17, below. Even if a deposition meets the requirements of these rules, however, the court, as it can with any item of evidence, may find the deposition to be so unreliable that admissibility is not justified. See Fenstermacher v. Philadelphia Nat. Bank, 493 F.2d 333 (3d Cir.1974); Zimmerman v. Safeway Stores, Inc., 410 F.2d 1041 (D.C.Cir.1969); U.S. v. Schwartz, 213 F.Supp. 306, 313 (E.D.Pa.1963), reversed on other grounds 325 F.2d 355 (3d Cir.1963); Shives v. Furst, 70 Md.App. 328, 521 A.2d 332 (Ct.Spec.App.1987), cert. denied 309 Md. 521, 525 A.2d 636.

8. See § 7.9, below. Of course some of the benefits of the oral deposition may be lost if it is taken by telephone or other remote electronic means. See Fed.Civ.Proc. Rule 30(b)(7).

9. E.g., West's Ann.Cal.Code Civ.Proc. § 1032.7. See id. §§ 1021–34.

10. Corona Foothill Lemon Co. v. Lillibridge, 12 Cal.App.2d 549, 55 P.2d 1210 (1936).

Expert witness fees typically are paid by the party who employed the expert and are not recoverable in the judgment. Crawford Fitting Co. v. J.T. Gibbons, Inc., 482 U.S. 437, 107 S.Ct. 2494, 96 L.Ed.2d 385 (1987), on remand 826 F.2d 309 (5th Cir.1987); Henkel v. Chicago, St. Paul, Minneapolis & Omaha Ry. Co., 284 U.S. 444, 52 S.Ct. 223, 76 L.Ed. 386 (1932). See 10 C. Wright, A. Miller & M. Kane, Civil 3d § 2678, at 480. However, if a party obtains information from his opponent's expert during discovery, the court may require the party to share a portion of the fee. See § 7.6 at nn. 27–29, above.

11. See 10 C. Wright, A. Miller & M. Kane, Civil 3d § 2676.

party must decide to use a deposition, it may not be very clear who will prevail. Third, most cases are settled without trial, frequently at a figure dictated by what the parties have learned through the discovery process.

Due to the costs in time and money to the deponent as well as the parties and their attorneys, some jurisdictions have placed certain limitations on the taking of depositions without a court order.[12] In the federal courts, for example, a party must receive permission to take more than ten depositions, whether orally or by written questions,[13] Court approval also must be sought if the proposed deponent already has been deposed in the case.[14]

A party may take the deposition of any person, whether or not a party, who has information relevant to the subject matter of a case.[15] In addition, many rules provide that a party may notice the deposition of a corporation or association, requiring the latter to produce the person or persons having knowledge of the subject matter upon which the deposition is to be taken.[16] Of course, the party seeking the information must detail the issues that are to be explored in order that the organization can ascertain which of its personnel has the relevant knowledge.[17] This form of corporate depositions is particularly useful when the party taking the deposition is unaware of which individual or individuals within a large organization has the information that is needed.

Under modern discovery rules, an attorney may schedule a deposition merely by notifying the opposing attorney of the time and the place where the deposition is to be taken;[18] no court order is required except when plaintiff seeks to take a deposition prior to the time when the defendant must file an answer to the plaintiff's complaint.[19] This exception is made in order to ensure that the defendant will have sufficient

---

12. A 1998 proposal to amend the Federal Rule 30(d)(2) would limit oral depositions to "one day of seven hours," unless otherwise authorized by court order or by a stipulation of the parties and the deponent. Preliminary Draft of Proposed Amendments to the Federal Rules of Civil Procedure and Evidence 60, 62–63, reprinted in 181 F.R.D. 18, at 83, 85–86 (1998). At present Federal Rule 30(d)(2) gives power to the federal courts to limit the length of depositions, either by local rule, or on a case by case basis.

13. Fed.Civ.Proc.Rule 30(a)(2)(A). Depositions on written questions are discussed at notes 37-42, below.

14. Fed.Civ.Proc.Rule 30(a)(2)(B).

15. Fed.Civ.Proc.Rule 30(a)(1); Me. Rules Civ.Proc., Rule 30(a); Mass.Rules Civ. Proc., Rule 30(a).

16. Fed.Civ.Proc.Rule 30(b)(6); Minn. Rules Civ.Proc., Rule 30.02(f); Vernon's Ann.Mo.Civ.Proc.Rule 57.03(b)(4). The identity of those individuals within the corporation who have the requisite information can be obtained by other discovery

devices, such as interrogatories, but those methods may be cumbersome and certainly are not as direct as the one used by the federal courts and comparable state provisions. See also Marker v. Union Fidelity Life Ins. Co., 125 F.R.D. 121, 126 (M.D.N.C. 1989); Volz, Depositions of Organizations: The Designation Procedure Under the Federal Rules, 33 S.D.L.Rev. 236 (1988).

17. Fed.Civ.Proc.Rule 30(b)(6); Ohio Rules Civ.Proc., Rule 30(B)(5); Utah Rules Civ.Proc., Rule 30(b)(6).

18. Fed.Civ.Proc.Rule 30(b); Kan.Stat. Ann. 60–230(b); Me.Rules Civ.Proc., Rule 30(b).

19. Fed.Civ.Proc.Rule 30(a)(2)(C); Ark. Rules Civ.Proc., Rule 30(a); Mass.Rules Civ. Proc., Rule 30(a); Minn.Rules Civ.Proc., Rule 30.01; Vernon's Ann.Mo.Civ.Proc.Rule 57.03(a). Cf. Md.Rule 401a (no court order required once jurisdiction obtained over defendant). The requirement of a court order is eliminated if the defendant takes an active role in the case by seeking her own discovery.

time to obtain a lawyer before a deposition takes place.[20] In federal courts, a deposition normally cannot be noticed, except by a stipulation of the parties or by leave of court, until the parties have met and developed a proposed discovery plan.[21]

Most commonly, the details as to a deposition are worked out among all of the attorneys in order to accommodate their schedules and that of the person to be deposed.[22] If the parties cannot agree on the time, place, or details of the examination, then one may obtain a court order with respect to the disputed matters.[23] When private arrangements fail, recourse to the guidelines set out in the rules is necessary.[24] In addition, there are specific rules that come into play when objections are made as to the conduct of the attorneys or the deponent during the course of the deposition or to the questions asked.[25]

Whenever, as is often the case, the person whose testimony is sought is one of the parties, there is no need for a subpoena. A party can be

20. A party may notice a deposition before the opponent has responded if the party attaches a certificate setting forth facts indicating that the deponent is about to leave the country or go more than one hundred miles from the place of trial, making the deponent unavailable for a deposition there at a later date. Me.Rules Civ. Proc., Rule 30(b)(2); Utah Rules Civ.Proc., Rule 30(b)(2); Va.Sup.Ct.Rules, Rule 4:5(b)(2); Wn.Civ.Rule 30(b)(2). If the defendant later shows that he was unable to obtain counsel to represent him at the deposition, the deposition cannot be used against him at trial. Ala.Rules Civ.Proc., Rule 30(b)(2); Idaho Rules Civ.Proc., Rule 30(b)(2).

21. Fed.Civ.Proc.Rule 30(a)(2)(C), which refers to Fed.Civ.Proc.Rule 26(f). An exception exists if the moving party in a notice of deposition includes a certificate showing that the person to be examined is about to leave the United States and will otherwise be available for examination. Such a deposition shall not be used against a party who later shows that, despite due diligence, she was unable to obtain counsel to represent her at the deposition. Fed.Civ. Proc.Rule 32(a)(3).

22. See Fed.Civ.Proc.Rule 29; Ala. Rules Civ.Proc., Rule 29; Idaho Rules Civ. Proc., Rule 29.

23. See Hudson v. Spellman High Voltage, 178 F.R.D. 29 (E.D.N.Y.1998).

24. Many timing disputes involve questions of priority. See, e.g., Stover v. Universal Moulded Prods. Corp., 11 F.R.D. 90 (E.D.Pa.1950). The traditional rule requires depositions to be taken in the order that

they were noticed. See, e.g., Story v. Quarterback Sports Federation, Inc., 46 F.R.D. 432, 433 (D.Minn.1969); Suplee, Yeatman, Mosley Co. v. Shapiro, 42 F.R.D. 34 (E.D.Pa.1966); Md.Rule 405c. Allowing depositions to be taken in order of their respective notices results in some advantage to defendants who may notice a deposition at anytime whereas plaintiffs, in the absence of a court order, must wait until defendant has had an opportunity to respond. See the discussion at notes 18–21, above. Thus, the court always has discretion to alter the order in light of the particular circumstances of the case. See Fed.Civ. Proc.Rule 26(d); Ind.Trial Proc.Rule 26(D); Iowa Rules Civ.Proc., Rule 147(b).

25. E.g., Fed.Civ.Proc.Rule 30(d). Under current Federal Rule 30(d)(1) a "party" is prohibited from instructing a deponent not to answer except when necessary to preserve a privilege, comply with a court order, or to permit a motion to limit the inquiry. See Bristol–Myers Squibb Co. v. Rhone–Poulenc Rorer, Inc., 1998 WL 2829 (S.D.N.Y.1998); Boyd v. University of Maryland Medical Sys., 173 F.R.D. 143 (D.Md. 1997); Damaj v. Farmers Ins. Co., 164 F.R.D. 559 (N.D.Okla.1995). See generally 8A C. Wright, A. Miller & R. Marcus, Civil 2d § 2113 (Supp.1998). A proposed 1998 amendment would, if adopted, change the word "party" to "person". Preliminary Draft of Proposed Amendments to the Federal Rules of Civil Procedure and Evidence 59 (August 1998), reprinted in 181 F.R.D. 18, 82. See the discussion at § 7.15, below.

For a discussion of how attorneys can best react to abusive or disruptive tactics during the course of a deposition, see Dick-

required to attend and to bring to the deposition documents and other items of evidence in his possession merely by including a demand therefore in the notice of a deposition.[26] A party who fails to appear at a properly set deposition may face serious sanctions that can result in the loss of the case.[27]

There is no requirement that a nonparty be subpoenaed to a deposition.[28] However, a nonparty who is not subpoenaed and does not appear, or who appears but fails to bring requested documents or other items faces no sanctions.[29] A person who fails to respond to a subpoena will be subject to a citation for contempt of court.[30] If a party notices a deposition, but does not subpoena the witness thereto, and if the witness fails to appear, that party may be ordered to pay the reasonable expenses, including attorney's fees, of any other party for wasting time appearing at the place where the deposition was to be taken.[31] Thus, unless full cooperation of a nonparty witness is certain, the use of a subpoena is advisable. If a party or attorney for the party who called a deposition does not appear, then an opposing party who did appear can collect expenses, including attorney's fees.[32]

If an action is filed in one state but the deponent lives in another, the court where the action is filed normally will not have the power to subpoena the witness to a deposition in the forum state.[33] Instead, the deposing party will be required to go to the state or country in which the deponent can be found, file documents in accordance with the latter's laws, and take the deposition pursuant to the rules and regulations as set down by that state or country.[34] It is important to recognize that resort to the courts in other jurisdictions is required only if a subpoena is necessary. If the deponent is a party, the court where the action is pending can order the deposition to be taken anywhere in the world,

erson, The Law and Ethics of Civil Depositions, 57 Md.L.Rev.273 (1998).

26. Fed.Civ.Proc.Rule 30(b)(5); Fla.— West's F.S.A.Rules Civ.Proc., Rule 1.310(b)(5); Official Code Ga.Ann. § 9–11–30(b)(5).

27. Fed.Civ.Proc.Rule 37(b)(2), (d); Ariz.Rules Civ.Proc., Rule 37(b)(2), (d); Colo.Rules Civ.Proc., Rule 37(b)(2), (d).

28. See El Salto, S.A. v. PSG Company, 444 F.2d 477 (9th Cir.1971), cert. denied 404 U.S. 940.

29. See Srybnik v. Epstein, 13 F.R.D. 248 (S.D.N.Y.1952); Chemical Specialties Co. v. Ciba Pharmaceutical Prods., Inc., 10 F.R.D. 500 (D.N.J.1950).

Since 1991, Fed.Civ.Proc.Rule 45(a)(1) has provided for the issuance of a subpoena compelling a nonparty to produce evidentiary material independent of a deposition. Many states have followed suit. See, e.g., Ky.Rules Civ.Proc., Rule 45.01(court order required); Mich.Ct.Rules 1985, 2.310(c);

N.Car.Rules Civ.Proc., Rule 45(c). See also § 7.11, below.

30. Fed.Civ.Proc.Rule 45(e); Idaho Rules Civ.Proc., Rule 45(f); Ind.Trial Proc. Rule 45(F).

31. Fed.Civ.Proc.Rule 30(g); Iowa Rules Civ.Proc., Rule 140(c)(2); Kan.Stat. Ann. 60–230(g)(2).

32. Fed.Civ.Proc.Rule 30(g)(1); Me. Rules Civ.Proc., Rule 30(g)(1); Md.Rule 414a.

33. E.g. West's Ann.Cal.Code Civ.Proc. § 1989.

34. Mass.Gen.Laws Ann. c. 233, § 45. The procedure is less complicated if the action is in federal court because the party seeking the deposition only need file for a subpoena in the federal district court where the deposition will be located and the same federal discovery rules will apply as if the deposition was taken where suit was brought. Fed.Civ.Proc.Rule 45(a)(2).

pursuant to its own discovery rules.[35] Similarly, if a nonparty deponent is amenable, his deposition may be taken anywhere.[36]

A deposition on written questions, sometimes referred to as a written deposition, operates much as does an oral deposition with one major exception—the attorneys usually are not present. Instead, they send their questions in advance to the officer who then proceeds to read them aloud to the witness who answers orally and whose responses are duly recorded.[37]

The time and place of a written deposition, as well as the need for a subpoena, the times when leave of court must be obtained,[38] any signature requirements, and similar matters are virtually the same as for an oral deposition.[39] However, in the early stage of a case it typically is not necessary that plaintiff either obtain a court order or wait until a certain number of days have passed so that other parties will have had time to obtain counsel.[40] The opposing party is provided ample time to prepare because each party has a certain number of days in which to send their written questions to the officer designated to take the deposition;[41] this delay permits the defendant to obtain counsel who will make preparations to take the deposition, or in the alternative, seek a delay from the court.[42]

Written depositions are used infrequently. Although they have the advantage of being less expensive than oral depositions because the attorneys need not be present, they have few of the advantages. It is difficult to draw a set of questions that can penetrate into the heart of a case and expose its strengths and its weaknesses without having some sense of what the individual responses are likely to be. Written depositions do not offer the opportunity to shape the questions in light of the

---

35. See, e.g., Gitto v. "Italia" Societá Anonima Di Navigazione, Genova, 28 F.Supp. 309 (E.D.N.Y.1939). The place selected for deposing a party is subject to the power of the court to grant a protective order under Rule 26(c)(2) designating a different place. See, e.g., Turner v. Prudential Ins. Co., 119 F.R.D. 381, 383 (M.D.N.C. 1988); Pinkham v. Paul, 91 F.R.D. 613, 614 (D.Me.1981).

36. Moore v. George A. Hormel & Co., 4 F.R.D. 15 (S.D.N.Y.1942).

37. Fed.Civ.Proc.Rule 31; Minn.Rules Civ.Proc., Rule 31; Vernon's Ann.Mo.Civ. Proc.Rule 57.04.

38. In federal courts a total of ten depositions, whether taken orally or by written questions, are permitted without a prior court order. Fed.Civ.Proc.Rule 31(a)(2)(A). Moreover, a court order is required before a deponent can be called to testify at more than one deposition. Fed.Civ.Proc.Rule 31(a)(2)(B).

39. Fed.Civ.Proc.Rule 31; Mont.Rules Civ.Proc., Rule 31; N.J.Civ.Prac.Rule 4:15–1.

40. N.M.Rules Civ.Proc., Rule 1–031(a); Ohio Rules Civ.Proc., Rule 31(A). Under Fed.Civ.Proc.Rule 31(a)(2)(C) a party needs a court order, or the stipulation of the other parties, to take a deposition on written questions prior to a meeting of the parties under Fed.Civ.Proc.Rule 26(f) to establish a proposed discovery plan.

41. Fed.Civ.Proc.Rule 31(a)(4).

42. The general procedure is that the deposing party submits written questions to all opposing parties who then have a certain number of days in which to serve their cross-questions. Fed.Civ.Proc.Rule 31(a)(4)(14 days). The party who noticed the deposition then has a period in which to send a set of redirect questions to which the other parties may serve recross questions. Fed.Civ.Proc.Rule 31(a)(4)(7 days). The court may allow additional sets of questions, if necessary. See Baron v. Leo Feist, Inc., 7 F.R.D. 71 (S.D.N.Y.1946).

type of answers that are received and they are of no help at all in producing answers from shy or reluctant witnesses. As a result, written depositions are used primarily to obtain routine information that is not in substantial dispute. They also may be used in suits in which the amounts involved are small and the investment in terms of investigation and discovery necessarily must be kept at a minimum.

§ 7.9   Written Interrogatories

Written interrogatories allow one party to send to another a series of questions, to be answered under oath within a specific time.[1] The procedure is extremely simple. No court order is required[2] and no officers need be appointed; the entire exchange is accomplished by mail. If a question, or any portion of it, is thought to be improper, the responding party may say so, and state the grounds for the objection, rather than answering.[3] The interrogating party then has the option of seeking a court order requiring an answer.[4]

Unlike a deposition, a set of interrogatories may not be sent to any person who has information regarding the subject matter of the case, but only to parties.[5] The rationale for this limitation is a sound one. A party who is called upon to answer a set of interrogatories will consult with counsel before doing so, and will be careful to answer with precision, knowing that the answers may be used in court against him. However, a nonparty, who has no stake in the case, and who would not in the ordinary course be protected by counsel, could be led very easily into inadvertent misleading statements in response to one-sided questions.[6] It also seems unfair to burden a nonparty with a lengthy set of interrogatories.

A minority of states allow interrogatories to be sent only to adverse parties.[7] This limitation is deemed justifiable because only an adverse party can introduce the answers into evidence;[8] therefore, a mere coparty would not be as careful in answering questions as would an adverse party. This reasoning is unsound for several reasons. First, even though the answers may be in response to questions from a nonadverse party,

§ 7.9

1. Fed.Civ.Proc.Rule 33; Utah Rules Civ.Proc., Rule 33; Va.Sup.Ct.Rules, Rule 4:8.

2. Because the usual time for a response is reasonably long, most courts have eliminated any requirements that leave be obtained. For example, in the federal courts, absent a specific court order, interrogatories cannot be sent before the parties convene to discuss a discovery plan. Fed. Civ.Proc.Rules 33(a), 26(d), 26(f). Defendant thus has ample time to obtain counsel before being required to answer.

3. Fed.Civ.Proc.Rule 33(b); Ala.Rules Civ.Proc., Rule 33(a); Wn.Civ.Rule 33(a).

4. Fed.Civ.Proc.Rules 33(b)(5), 37(a); Alaska Rules Civ.Proc., Rules 33(a), 37(a); Ariz.Rules Civ.Proc., Rules 33(a), 37(a).

5. McNamara v. Erschen, 8 F.R.D. 427, 429 (D.Del.1948); Fed.Civ.Proc.Rule 33(a).

6. Information may be obtained from nonparties at a deposition with counsel present to ensure that the questions asked are not ambiguous or misleading and that the responses reflect the witness's actual knowledge about the incidents about which she is testifying.

7. Kan.Stat.Ann. 60–236; N.H.Sup.Ct. Rules, Rule 36.

8. See Developments in the Law—Discovery, 74 Harv.L.Rev. 940, 1020 (1961).

those answers can be introduced into evidence by another party who is adverse.[9] Second, courts have had difficulty in deciding just who should be considered an adverse party for purposes of allowing interrogatories,[10] leading to conflicting decisions and distorting the purpose behind the requirement.[11] Finally, interrogatories are an inexpensive and useful way to get basic information from people who are knowledgeable. Even when parties are not technically adverse, their interests may not coincide and they may not cooperate fully with one another with respect to divulging information.

A party has the duty to respond to interrogatories not only on the basis of personal knowledge but also with regard to the knowledge of other individuals that reasonably can be obtained through investigation.[12] Thus, a party must consult with her attorney, employees, and other agents who have or might have knowledge that would be important in making a response.

In addition to the duty to investigate, some jurisdictions, including the federal courts, require the responding party to state any opinions or contentions as to the facts that are relevant to the subject matter of the action.[13] Under this approach, it would be appropriate to ask a defendant whether she was negligently driving the vehicle at the time of the accident. The defendant would be free to answer the question "No," but she could not refuse to answer on the ground that it was somehow inappropriate.

Special rules have been adopted regarding a party's duty to respond to interrogatories requiring an investigation of its business records. When the answer may be derived from the answering party's business records, and when it would be just as easy for the requesting party to search those records as it would be for the responding party, then the responding party, instead of answering, may specify the records from which the answers may be obtained and give the inquiring party a

---

9. Fed.Evid.Rule 801(d)(2); West's Ann.Cal.Evid.Code §§ 1220, 1222.

10. See Jones v. Rederai A/B Soya, 31 F.R.D. 524, 525 (D.Md.1962); M.V.M., Inc. v. St. Paul Fire & Marine Ins. Co., 20 F.R.D. 296 (S.D.N.Y.1957).

11. Originally the Federal Rules allowed interrogatories to be sent only to adverse parties, but courts did not agree regarding what determined adversity. See Anuszewski v. Toepfer, 48 F.R.D. 433 (D.Md.1970); Carey v. Schuldt, 42 F.R.D. 390 (E.D.La.1967). Thus, in an action for breach of warranty for the sale of machinery in which the manufacturer was joined as a third-party defendant, some courts ruled that the plaintiff could not send interrogatories to the manufacturer as the pleadings controlled adversity. Since the plaintiff only had sued the seller, the plaintiff was not adverse from the third-party defendant. See Rogers v. Tri–State Materi-

als Corp., 51 F.R.D. 234, 245 (N.D.W.Va. 1970). Other courts permitted the interrogatories since the very nature of the case made the plaintiff adverse from the manufacturer. See General Dynamics Corp. v. Selb Mfg. Co., 481 F.2d 1204 (8th Cir.1973), cert. denied 414 U.S. 1162; Holt v. Southern Ry. Co., 51 F.R.D. 296 (E.D.Tenn.1969). The adverse party limitation was removed in the 1970 amendments to Rule 33(a).

12. Fed.Civ.Proc.Rule 33(a); Fla.— West's F.S.A.Rules Civ.Proc., Rule 1.340(b); Idaho Rules Civ.Proc., Rule 33(b). See, e.g., Brunswick Corp. v. Suzuki Motor Co., Ltd., 96 F.R.D. 684 (E.D.Wis.1983).

13. Ex parte Dorsey Trailers, Inc., 397 So.2d 98, 105 (Ala.1981); Rogers v. Tri–State Materials Corp., 51 F.R.D. 234, 245 (N.D.W.Va.1970). But see Needles v. F. W. Woolworth Co., 13 F.R.D. 460 (E.D.Pa. 1952).

reasonable opportunity to look at them.[14] This does not mean that the responding party can simply say, "The answer is in our records," and then turn all records over to the inquiring party, knowing full well that the latter never will be able to locate the appropriate documents. The responding party must designate with some specificity just what documents contain the information so that the inquiring party can find it.[15] Further, if there would be a far greater burden on the inquiring party to ascertain the information than there would be on the responding party, then the latter must ascertain the answer itself.[16]

There are several advantages to interrogatories. They are a relatively inexpensive way of obtaining important information. In addition, they enable the inquiring party to obtain all the information known to the responding party, not just that which is known by a series of individual deponents. Access to a greater range of information is likely since prior to answering the responding party must investigate and ascertain the knowledge of all of its agents and employees.

The disadvantage of using interrogatories lies primarily in the fact that the answers are not spontaneous. The responding party, in consultation with counsel, may answer as cryptically as possible; any ambiguity may be utilized so as to give the least informative response.[17] Perhaps because of this and because it is extremely easy to ask questions and impose heavy burdens on their adversaries in the process, some litigants have abused the process by asking hundreds of questions detailing every aspect of the case from the most trivial to the most complex. In doing so, they cross the line from legitimate inquiry into the area of unnecessary and unjust harassment.[18]

Indeed, because of these abuses, federal courts and many states have adopted provisions limiting the number of interrogatories that can be served without leave of court.[19] It is easier to justify such limitations in

---

14. Fed.Civ.Proc.Rule 33(d); Ind.Trial Proc.Rule 33(E); Iowa Rules Civ.Proc., Rule 126(c).

15. Rainbow Pioneer No. 44–18–04A v. Hawaii–Nevada Inv. Corp., 711 F.2d 902 (9th Cir.1983); Avramidis v. Atlantic Richfield Co., 120 F.R.D. 450 (D.Mass.1988); Budget Rent–A–Car of Missouri, Inc. v. Hertz Corp., 55 F.R.D. 354, 357 (W.D.Mo. 1972). See Advisory Committee Note to the 1970 Amendment of Rule 33(c), reprinted in 48 F.R.D. 487, 524–25.

16. See American Rockwool, Inc. v. Owens–Corning Fiberglas Corp., 109 F.R.D. 263 (E.D.N.C.1985); Thomason v. Leiter, 52 F.R.D. 290, 291 (M.D.Ala.1971).

17. In re Convergent Technologies Secs. Litigation, 108 F.R.D. 328, 338 (N.D.Cal.1985). See also Brazil, View From the Front Line: Observations by Chicago Lawyers About the System of Civil Discovery, 1980 A.B.F.Res.J. 217, 233.

18. Courts may attempt to curb these abuses by providing for sanctions against an offending party, his lawyer, or both. See, e.g., Fed.Civ.Proc.Rule 26(g).

19. In 1993, Federal Rule 33 was amended to limit the number of interrogatories to 25; leave of court is required to serve more. Previously, many federal trial courts had adopted local rules limiting the number of interrogatories permitted. See Sherman & Kinnard, Federal Court Discovery in the 80's: Making the Rules Work, 95 F.R.D. 245, 263 (1983). See also Official Code Ga.Ann. § 9–11–33(a); Minn.Rules Civ.Proc., Rule 33.01(a).

To avoid an end run around a limitation on the number of interrogatories permitted, the rules typically provide that each discrete subpart of a question is to be counted separately. Courts have split on how such provisions should be interpreted. Some hold that all subparts must be counted separate-

those jurisdictions that follow Federal Rule 26(a), requiring mandatory disclosure of much of the information that was previously elicited through interrogatories.

§ 7.10 Requests for Admission

One party may serve upon any other party a written request to admit the truth of certain matters of fact that are in dispute or to admit the genuineness of any relevant document, thereby avoiding the necessity of formally authenticating the document at trial.[1] A request for admission may be served without the necessity of a court order.[2] The time given to respond is sufficient to ensure that there will be no unfairness to a defendant who is served with requests at the same time he is served with a summons and complaint.

The party who receives a request to admit must respond under oath, either denying the matter sought to be admitted or setting forth in detail the reasons why the party cannot truthfully admit or deny the matter. The responding party also may object to a request as improper or claim a privilege that excuses a response.[3] If the responding party fails to respond within the prescribed time, then the party may be held to have admitted the matters set out in the request for admission.[4] The court may grant relief to a party who failed to respond and now is faced with an admission, however, provided that the failure was not a willful attempt to evade discovery.[5] This may create problems for the requesting

---

ly. See Aetna Cas. & Sur. Co. v. W.W. Grainger, Inc., 170 F.R.D. 454 (E.D.Wis. 1997); Valdez v. Ford Motor Co., 134 F.R.D. 296, 298 (D.Nev.1991). The majority hold, however, that if the subparts are "subsumed within" or "necessarily related" to the "primary question," then the subparts are to be counted as a single interrogatory. See Safeco v. Rawstron, 181 F.R.D. 441 (C.D.Cal.1998); Ginn v. Gemini Inc., 137 F.R.D. 320 (D.Nev.1991); Clark v. Burlington Northern R.R., 112 F.R.D. 117 (N.D.Miss.1986).

The test for whether a subpart of an interrogatory is "subsumed" is whether it is "secondary" to a "primary" question. See Kendall v. GES Exposition Servs., Inc., 174 F.R.D. 684 (D.Nev.1997) For varying state views of the test, see Holme, Colorado's New Rules of Civil Procedure, Part II: Rediscovering Discovery, 23 Colo.Law. 2711, 2716 (1994); Morris & Pickering, Recent Developments in Deposition Practice and Document Discovery, C380 ALI–ABA 127, at 166 (Feb. 1, 1989); Selig, The 1994 Amendments to the Wyoming Rules of Civil Procedure, 30 LWLR 151, 170 (1995).

§ 7.10

1. Fed.Civ.Proc.Rule 36; Iowa Rules Civ.Proc., Rule 127; Kan.Stat.Ann. 60–236; Me.Rules Civ.Proc., Rule 36; Mass.Rules Civ.Proc., Rule 36(a); Mich.Ct.Rules 1985, 2.312.

2. Fed.Civ.Proc.Rule 36(a); Minn.Rules Civ.Proc., Rule 36.01; Mont.Rules Civ.Proc., Rule 36(a).

Subject to a court order, Federal Rule 36(a) prevents a party from seeking requests for admissions until the parties have met and conferred on a discovery plan as required under Federal Rule 12(f). See § 7.7, above.

3. Fed.Civ.Proc.Rule 36(a); Ohio Rules Civ.Proc., Rule 36(A); Tenn.Rules Civ.Proc., Rule 36.01. See also § 7.4, above.

4. Fed.Civ.Proc.Rule 36(a); Utah Rules Civ.Proc., Rule 36(a); Va.Sup.Ct.Rules, Rule 4:11(a).

5. See, e.g., Marshall v. Sunshine & Leisure, Inc., 496 F.Supp. 354 (M.D.Fla. 1980); Westmoreland v. Triumph Motorcycle Corp., 71 F.R.D. 192 (D.Conn.1976); U.S. v. Cannon, 363 F.Supp. 1045 (D.Del. 1973); Williams v. Krieger, 61 F.R.D. 142 (S.D.N.Y.1973); Pleasant Hill Bank v. U.S., 60 F.R.D. 1 (W.D.Mo.1973).

party who cannot be certain that a failure to respond will be binding so that it is not necessary to prepare evidence for trial on the issue involved. This difficulty may have been obviated by an amendment to the Federal Rules which permits the party who made the request to seek an order deeming an issue to be admitted.[6]

There are three areas in which there has been some confusion about the duty of the responding party. The first issue is whether the request for an admission requires a response only if the party can do so based on immediate, personal knowledge. The answer to this question is no. A party cannot deny a request for admission on the basis of insufficient information, if the necessary information is readily available.[7] If a reasonable investigation does not provide sufficient facts to allow the party to admit or deny, however, then the answering party may refuse to admit on that ground.[8]

The second area of concern is whether a party must admit or deny a request requiring the application of law to fact. The federal rule and some of its state counterparts specifically permit requests involving the application of law to fact.[9] For example, it is proper to ask an opposing party to admit facts that, taken together, constitute evidence that its employee was "negligent."[10] In other jurisdictions in which no specific provision is made for this type of request, courts on occasion have held them improper on the ground that they call for an attorney's work-product.[11]

Requests for admissions on vital or key issues present the third problem. In most jurisdictions a request to admit may encompass any issue in the case, no matter how important and no matter whether an admission would result in the termination of the action.[12] Although some courts have ruled improper any requests directed to crucial issues disputed in the pleadings upon which the case or any major portion of it rests,[13] the reason for this limitation is not clear. Perhaps it is based on

---

6. Fed.Civ.Proc.Rule 36(a). See Advisory Committee Note to the 1970 Amendment of Rule 36(a), reprinted in 48 F.R.D. 487, 532. The court in ruling on the motion may grant the relief sought or permit a response denying the allegations. It should be noted that the rule refers to an "answer [that] does not comply with the requirements" of the rule and not to the failure to submit an answer, leaving some doubt as to whether a court can order that the matter be admitted in the latter case.

7. O'Meara–Sterling v. Mitchell, 299 F.2d 401 (5th Cir.1962); Lumpkin v. Meskill, 64 F.R.D. 673 (D.Conn.1974); Adley Express Co. v. Highway Truck Drivers & Helpers, Local No. 107, 349 F.Supp. 436, 451 (E.D.Pa.1972); Fickett v. Superior Court, 27 Ariz.App. 793, 558 P.2d 988 (1976); Rosales v. Thermex–Thermatron, Inc., 67 Cal.App.4th 187, 78 Cal.Rptr.2d 861, 867–68 (1998).

8. See Alexander v. Rizzo, 52 F.R.D. 235 (E.D.Pa.1971).

9. Fed.Civ.Proc.Rule 36(a); Ala.Rules Civ.Proc., Rule 36(a); Alaska Rules Civ. Proc., Rule 36(a). See Advisory Committee Note to the 1970 Amendment of Rule 36(a), reprinted in 48 F.R.D. 487, 532.

10. Jones v. Boyd Truck Lines, Inc., 11 F.R.D. 67, 70 (W.D.Mo.1951).

11. General Acc. Fire & Life Assur. Corp. v. Cohen, 203 Va. 810, 127 S.E.2d 399 (1962). See also § 7.5, above, for a discussion of the work-product doctrine.

12. See City of Rome v. U.S., 450 F.Supp. 378, 383 (D.D.C.1978), affirmed 446 U.S. 156, 100 S.Ct. 1548, 64 L.Ed.2d 119 (1980).

13. Prior to the 1970 amendment to Federal Rule 36, a majority of federal courts ruled those requests improper. E.g., Pickens

the notion that it is unrealistic to expect a litigant to admit away her case; thus, a rule is unjustified if it presents an overwhelming incentive for improper denials. Such reasoning is faulty. Otherwise a party could not be required to respond to other forms of discovery or to take the stand at trial. If a responding party is not certain that a fact is true, he may deny it or state why he cannot admit or deny.[14]

Unlike other forms of discovery, requests to admit involve primarily the elimination of undisputed matters, rather than the ascertainment of facts or the preservation of testimony for trial. An admission generally is binding on the party who made it, and supersedes the pleadings pro tanto.[15] No evidence is necessary to establish an admitted fact, and no evidence is permitted to refute it.[16] In the event that a party admitted a fact in good faith that it later finds to be untrue, the party may move to amend the admission in the same way and under the same circumstances as amending its pleadings.[17]

In a few cases, admissions have not been treated as binding, but only as evidence of the existence of the fact admitted,[18] and the party who made the admission may introduce evidence to contradict it at trial.[19] Obviously this cuts the heart out of the value of a request to admit, since an opposing party cannot rely upon the admission to avoid the time and expense of preparing his own evidence. On the other hand, even the federal discovery rules specifically provide that admissions are binding only in the present case and cannot be used in any way in other litigation.[20] One cannot always foresee precisely when an issue might arise again in a different context, perhaps with much more at stake. A responding party would be extremely reluctant to admit anything, if it possibly could be avoided, if the respondent thought that an admission might have unforeseen consequences.

v. Equitable Life Assur. Soc., 413 F.2d 1390 (5th Cir.1969); Syracuse Broadcasting Corp. v. Newhouse, 271 F.2d 910 (2d Cir.1959).

14. See Advisory Committee Note to the 1970 Amendment of Rule 36(a), reprinted in 48 F.R.D. 487, 532.

15. Fed.Civ.Proc.Rule 36(b); Ariz.Rules Civ.Proc., Rule 36(b); Colo.Rules Civ.Proc., Rule 36(b).

16. See Fleitz v. Van Westrienen, 114 Ariz. 246, 560 P.2d 430 (App.1977); Advisory Committee Note to the 1970 Amendment of Rule 36(b), reprinted in 48 F.R.D. 487, 534.

17. Gardner v. Southern Ry. Sys., 675 F.2d 949 (7th Cir.1982); St. Regis Paper Co. v. Upgrade Corp., 86 F.R.D. 355 (W.D.Mich. 1980); Nicholson v. Bailey, 182 F.Supp. 509 (S.D.Fla.1960); U.S. v. Wimbley, 125 F.Supp. 691, 693–94 (W.D.Ark.1954); Jackson v. Hearn Bros., Inc., 59 Del. 7, 212 A.2d

726 (1965). But compare American Auto. Ass'n v. AAA Legal Clinic of Jefferson Crooke, 930 F.2d 1117 (5th Cir.1991), and Brook Village North Assocs. v. General Elec. Co., 686 F.2d 66 (1st Cir.1982) (both concluding that amendment to withdraw admission is governed by Federal Rule 16 "manifest injustice" standard, rather than by more liberal Federal Rule 15 amendment standard for pleadings).

18. Williams v. Howard Johnson's Inc., 323 F.2d 102, 105 n. 9 (4th Cir.1963); Dorsey v. RFC, 197 F.2d 468, 472 (7th Cir. 1952).

19. See, e.g., Hartley & Parker, Inc. v. Florida Beverage Corp., 348 F.2d 161, 162–64 (5th Cir.1965); Ark.–Tenn. Distributing Corp. v. Breidt, 209 F.2d 359, 360 (3d Cir. 1954).

20. Fed.Civ.Proc.Rule 36(b). See Seay v. International Ass'n of Machinists, 360 F.Supp. 123 (C.D.Cal.1973).

On their face, requests to admit provide great advantages in that they are inexpensive to use, and are quite direct. Unlike interrogatories, a party cannot answer them cryptically or with explanations and qualifications. If an admission is forthcoming, it can save substantial time and money, since the matter at issue need not be litigated.[21] This benefits the court and those who would have to be called as witnesses, as well as the parties to the case.

Requests to admit the genuineness of documents have proven quite useful. Unfortunately, however, requests to admit facts upon which a claim or defense is based have not proved to be very effective in practice. First, responding parties normally will deny all but the clearest, most unmistakable matters. There is an inherent problem of philosophy in determining when one "knows" something, to the extent that it must be admitted. Thus, a lawyer can advise his client, in good conscience, to deny nearly every major controversial request for admission. More unfortunate is the fact that the sanctions for a false denial usually are so weak that even when issues are extremely clear and the evidence totally one-sided, requests still will be denied.[22] The reluctance of courts and legislators to provide severe sanctions for willful perjury has seriously undermined the usefulness of requests to admit so that they are one of the least effective of the discovery devices.

Another troublesome aspect of requests to admit involves the situation when a party who has been served with a set of requests does not respond to them. In such a case, under typical rules, the matter is deemed admitted.[23] However, the responding party is always free to seek relief from the court on the ground of mistake or excusable neglect. As a result, the party who served the requests cannot be certain whether or not to prepare to prove the "admitted" facts at trial. The rules typically provide that the party who has served requests may move to determine the sufficiency of the answers. The court is then free to enter an order that the subject matter of a request be admitted or an amended answer be served. The rules do not specifically provide that a party can move for a decision that a failure to answer has resulted in a binding admission although that would be a logical result.[24] However, such a motion would undoubtedly be met with a countermotion to permit a late response.

§ 7.11   Discovery and Production of Property

Modern federal discovery rules provide means by which a party may inspect documents and other personal or real property in possession or

---

21. See, e.g., O'Campo v. Hardisty, 262 F.2d 621 (9th Cir.1958); Berry v. Federated Mut. Ins. Co., 110 F.R.D. 441, 443 (N.D.Ind. 1986); Irons v. Le Sueur, 487 So.2d 1352, 1355 (Ala.1986); Morast v. Auble, 164 Mont. 100, 519 P.2d 157 (1974); Kissinger v. School Dist. No. 49, 163 Neb. 33, 77 N.W.2d 767 (1956).

22. See § 7.16, text at notes 31–33, below.

23. See, e.g., Fed.Civ.Proc.Rule 36(a); Ill.S.Ct.Rule 216(c).

24. See Deloge v. Cortez, 131 Idaho 201, 953 P.2d 641 (App.1998)(failure of a party to respond after several extensions were granted resulted in admissions leading to summary judgment for the opposing party).

control of parties and nonparties.[1] However, many states have yet to adopt a similar approach with respect to nonparties;[2] consequently, the procedure and scope of discovery varies depending on whether discovery is sought of a party or a nonparty and each must be considered separately.

Whenever disclosure could lead to admissible evidence, a party is entitled to inspect and copy any document or inspect any real or personal property under the custody or control of another party.[3] Under the Federal Rule and many of its state counterparts, inspection of property in the control of a party is permitted on notice without a court order,[4] although there are limits as to how early in the case such a notice can be served.[5] The party seeking discovery must designate the particular items sought to be inspected, copied, or otherwise tested.[6] It is the responding party who must go to court in the event that he believes that the evidence is not relevant, or that the time and place set forth in the notice are inconvenient, or otherwise inappropriate.[7]

The major problem involving requests for production of property controlled by a party has been in determining when the respondent legitimately can refuse a request on the ground that the property involved is not within its possession or control. Parties cannot evade

§ 7.11

1. Fed.Civ.Proc.Rule 34. As amended in 1991, Federal Rule of Civil Procedure 34(c) now provides that nonparties may be subpoenaed directly to produce documents and things or to submit their property to an inspection. Previously, the rule permitted a subpoena for documents and other items only in connection with a deposition and there was no provision for inspection of real property.

2. Fla.—West's F.S.A. Rules Civ.Proc., Rule 1.350; Ohio Rules Civ.Proc., Rule 34.

3. Fed.Civ.Proc.Rule 34(a); Idaho Rules Civ.Proc., Rule 34(a); Ind.Trial Proc. Rule 34(A); Iowa Rules Civ.Proc., Rule 129; Kan.Stat.Ann. 60–234(a). The discovering party may photograph, measure, survey, test, or sample the property, if necessary.

4. Fed.Civ.Proc.Rule 34(b); Me.Rules Civ.Proc., Rule 34(b); Mass.Rules Civ.Proc., Rule 34(b). The notice must set forth the time, place, and manner of inspection.

Initially, Federal Rule 34 required that the party seeking discovery obtain a court order based upon a showing of good cause. Many state courts adopted that provision. However, recognizing that this was leading to unnecessary court appearances, the requirement was dropped from the Federal Rules in 1970, leaving it to the person from whom discovery was sought to make any objection. The various state courts that over the years adopted the good cause requirement are now eliminating it. See Advisory

Committee Note to the 1970 Amendment of Rule 34(b), reprinted in 48 F.R.D. 487, 527. See also Guilford Nat. Bank v. Southern Ry. Co., 297 F.2d 921 (4th Cir.1962).

5. Of course, a defendant must be given sufficient time to obtain legal counsel. In federal courts the notice cannot be served until after the parties have met to discuss a discovery plan. Fed.Civ.Proc.Rules 34(b), 26(d), 26(f). In most states, the rules provide that a request for discovery of documents and other relevant items can be served along with the summons and complaint and specify the amount of time after that service that the defendant has to respond. E.g., Ind.Trial Proc.Rule 34(B)(30 days); Minn.Rules Civ.Proc., Rule 34.02 (45 days); Wn.Civ.Rule 34(b)(45 days).

6. Fed.Civ.Proc.Rule 34(b); Mich.Ct. Rules 1985, 2.310; Minn.Rules Civ.Proc., Rule 34.01; Vernon's Ann.Mo.Civ.Proc.Rule 58.01(b); Mont.Rules Civ.Proc., Rule 34(b).

The party may designate the property by category if specific items are not known. However, the designation must leave no doubt as to the type of items involved. See Scuderi v. Boston Ins. Co., 34 F.R.D. 463, 466 (D.Del.1964); Bowers v. City of Kansas City, 202 Kan. 268, 270, 448 P.2d 6, 8 (1968); Dean v. Superior Court, 84 Ariz. 104, 324 P.2d 764 (1958).

7. Fed.Civ.Proc.Rules 26(c), 34(b), 37(a); Alaska Rules Civ.Proc., Rules 26(c), 34(b), 37(a); Wn.Civ.Rule 26(c), 34(b), 37(a).

discovery requests by placing material evidence in the hands of others. A refusal is clearly inappropriate if the party can obtain the property by requesting it from the person or entity that has physical possession of it.[8] Further, control need not mean legal control. In the one case to reach the United States Supreme Court on this issue, Societe Internationale v. Rogers,[9] the Court ruled that defendant would have to deliver documents even though the revelation of those documents could result in a criminal penalty under Swiss law. The Rogers case should not be read too broadly, however, since there were some intimations there that defendants deliberately had placed the requested documents outside the country to avoid disclosure. Thus, the Court felt justified in ruling that the party had the ability to influence the Swiss government to change the law or to create an exception to it and thus it had "control" over the documents. Nonetheless, the case does clearly indicate that parties cannot easily plead lack of possession or control to avoid discovery.[10]

An additional problem occurs when, as is often the case, the party seeking disclosure is not certain just what documents or items exist. A request for categories of items is proper if they are reasonably designated.[11] Thus, in a suit for the price of goods allegedly delivered to defendant, the latter may obtain discovery of all documents pertaining to those deliveries. In responding to demands for documents, some parties have attempted to thwart the value of discovery by delivering them in a jumbled mass, hoping that any unfavorable information they contain will not be recognized. In 1980, the Federal Rules were altered to require the responding party to turn over documents "as they are kept in the usual course of business or [to] * * * organize and label them to correspond with the categories in the request."[12]

A party's response to a request for documents and other items, especially when designated by category, can prove expensive and often disproportionate to the needs of the party seeking disclosure.[13] As a result, amendments have been proposed that would enable the court to shift the cost burden to the requesting party in appropriate situations.[14]

Since the 1991 amendments of Federal Rules 34(c) and 45, nonparties may be subpoenaed to produce documents and things and to submit to inspections of premises.[15] Now attorneys, as officers of the court, may

---

8. See, e.g., In re Uranium Antitrust Litigation, 480 F.Supp. 1138 (N.D.Ill.1979); Kozlowski v. Sears Roebuck & Co., 73 F.R.D. 73 (D.Mass.1976).

9. 357 U.S. 197, 78 S.Ct. 1087, 2 L.Ed.2d 1255 (1958).

10. See generally 8A C. Wright, A. Miller & R. Marcus, Civil 2d § 2210.

11. Fed.Civ.Proc.Rule 34(b); Fla.— West's F.S.A.Rules Civ.Proc., Rule 1.350(b); Idaho Rules Civ.Proc., Rule 34(b)(1); Vernon's Ann.Mo.Civ.Proc.Rule 58.01(b); N.Car.Rules Civ.Proc., Rule 34(b).

12. Fed.Civ.Proc.Rule 34(b). Many state courts have adopted a similar provi-

sion, but some have declined to do so. See, e.g., Idaho Rules Civ.Proc., Rule 34(b) and note following entitled "Federal Rules Comparison."

13. See Preliminary Draft of Proposed Amendments to the Federal Rule of Civil Procedure and Evidence 66–68, reprinted in 181 F.R.D. 18 (1998).

14. Id. at 64–66.

15. A party no longer needs to initiate independent actions against nonparties to produce documents or things or for permission to enter upon land. Advisory Committee Note to the 1991 Amendment of Rule

themselves issue subpoenas in limited circumstances.[16] However, the attorney has a duty to avoid imposing any undue burden or expense on a person subject to the subpoena and may be sanctioned for a breach of that duty.[17] The protection of persons subject to subpoenas is expressly defined.[18] Nonparties must submit a specific written objection to the party or attorney designated in the subpoena when withholding information on a claim of privilege.[19] When objecting on other grounds, a timely motion must be made to the court by which the subpoena was issued.[20] Nonparties are entitled to the same protections as parties with regard to demands for discovery where the costs outweigh the relevance or where the required disclosure would otherwise be abusive.[21]

A few states have adopted detailed provisions similar to those of the federal rules[22] but most have not. Nevertheless, those states do provide for the issuance of subpoenas to nonparties to produce documents and other items in their possession and they provide protection against undue burden and unfairness to the deponent by authorizing the court to quash the subpoena or condition its enforcement on payment by the discovering party of the reasonable cost of compliance.[23] A nonparty also ought to have the right to object to a subpoena when discovery would not lead to admissible evidence and certainly when the property is not within the nonparty's control.[24]

Initially the federal courts permitted a subpoena for documents and other items issued to a nonparty only in connection with the taking of the nonparty's deposition. This requirement made little sense when there was no reason to obtain the nonparty's testimony. Thus, in 1991,

34, Excerpt from the Report of the Judicial Conference on Rules of Practice and Procedure, September 1990.

In New York, nonparties and parties have for some time been treated identically with respect to discovery of property. N.Y.—McKinney's CPLR 3120(b).

16. Fed.Civ.Proc.Rule 45(a)(2), (a)(3). See Advisory Committee Note to the 1991 Amendment of Rule 45, Excerpt from the Report of the Judicial Conference on Rules of Practice and Procedure, September 1990 (noting two courts of appeals have described lawyer-issued subpoenas as mandates of the court).

17. Fed.Civ.Proc.Rule 45(c)(1).

18. Fed.Civ.Proc.Rule 45(c).

19. Fed.Civ.Proc.Rule 45(c)(2)(b), (d)(2).

20. Fed.Civ.Proc.Rule 45(c)(3)(A). Rule 45 does not require an objecting party to accompany a motion with a certificate that the movant has made a good faith effort to confer with other affected parties to resolve a dispute over discovery without court action. Rule 26(c), however, does require such

action by "a party or by the person from whom discovery is sought," which would seem to encompass nonparties. Cf. Echostar Communications Corp. v. The News Corp., 180 F.R.D. 391 (D.Colo.1998)(application of local rule to discovering party).

21. See Fed.Civ.Proc.Rule 26(c). If a nonparty establishes that a request for information, even though marginally relevant, would be unduly oppressive or unreasonable, the court may quash the subpoena, or may limit the discovery, or may require that the discovering party pay all or a portion of the costs associated with obtaining the information. See Linder v. Calero–Portocarrero, 180 F.R.D. 168 (D.D.C.1998)(modification of subpoena preferred to outright quashing). See also Echostar Communications Corp. v. The News Corp., 180 F.R.D. 391 (D.Colo.1998). See generally § 7.15, below.

22. E.g., Ala.Rules Civ.Proc., Rule 45.

23. See, e.g., Colo.Rules Civ.Proc., Rule 45(d)(1); Ind.Trial Proc. Rule 45(B); Minn. Rules Civ.Proc., Rules 45.01,45.02.

24. See text at notes 8–10, above.

the requirement was eliminated and state courts have followed suit, allowing a subpoena for the items alone.[25]

As one means of avoiding problems obtaining disclosure under the rules, most discovery provisions specifically preserve the traditional equity suit for discovery.[26] Thus, in cases in which it is necessary to inspect real property in the hands of a nonparty that may not fall within the terms of the discovery rules, a separate action seeking discovery can be brought against the nonparty. Although independent actions generally have fallen into disuse because they are subject to equitable defenses and restrictions, they can be useful in appropriate situations.

§ 7.12 Physical and Mental Examinations

In many cases the physical or mental state of a person will be in issue. That person, and those with whom the person is on friendly terms, will have access to current medical records and past medical history, but, because such information generally is privileged,[1] an opposing party will not. The latter, therefore, needs to have a method by which his own medical professionals have an opportunity to observe the person whose condition is in controversy to help prepare for trial and, if necessary, to testify.

Traditionally, only parties were subject to physical or mental examinations requested by opposing parties.[2] However, a number of jurisdictions have extended the rule to encompass persons under the legal custody or control of a party.[3] Thus, if a parent, whose child has been injured in an accident, sues to collect medical expenses without joining the child as a named party, the opposing party may obtain an order requiring the parent to produce the child for an examination.[4] A few states have gone even further, permitting physical examination of a party's agent—such as a driver or employee—when the condition of the agent is in controversy.[5]

It is important to note that the rules and statutes permitting examination of persons other than parties do not provide for an order directing them to submit to physical or mental examinations. Rather, the rules operate only upon those who are parties, requiring them to produce

25. Fed.Civ.Proc.Rule 45(c)(2)(A); Mich.Ct.Rules 1985, 2.310(c); N.Car.Rules Civ.Proc., Rule 45(c). But see Ky.Rules Civ. Proc., Rule 45.01, requiring a court order to issue a subpoena for items without taking the custodian's deposition.

26. Alaska Rules Civ.Proc., Rule 34(c); Ariz.Rules Civ.Proc., Rule 34(c).

§ 7.12

1. See § 7.4, above.

2. Advisory Committee Note to the 1970 Amendment of Rule 35(a), reprinted in 48 F.R.D. 487, 529. See Clark v. Geiger, 31 F.R.D. 268 (E.D.Pa.1962).

3. Fed.Civ.Proc.Rule 35(a); West's Ann.Cal.Code Civ.Proc. § 2032; Colo.Rules Civ.Proc., Rule 35(a); Fla.—West's F.S.A. Rules Civ.Proc., Rule 1.360(a); Idaho Rules Civ.Proc., Rule 35; Ill.S.Ct.Rule 215(a); Md. Rule 2–423; Mich.Ct.Rules 1985, 2.311; Minn.Rules Civ.Proc., Rule 35; Vernon's Ann.Mo.Civ.Proc.Rule 60.01; N.Dak.Rules Civ.Proc., Rule 35; Wyo.Rules Civ.Proc., Rule 35.

4. Beckwith v. Beckwith, 355 A.2d 537 (D.C.App.1976), cert. denied 436 U.S. 907.

5. West's Ann.Cal.Code Civ.Proc. § 2032(a); Minn.Rules Civ.Proc., Rule 35.01; Vernon's Ann.Mo.Civ.Proc.Rule 60.01(a).

for examination persons under their control whose physical condition is at issue in the case.[6] Because a party can be required only to make a good-faith effort to produce another person for examination, if the proposed examinee absolutely refuses to cooperate, the request for an examination will be thwarted and no sanctions can be imposed.[7] That result can be avoided only by joining as a formal party the person whose examination is sought.

Because of its intrusiveness, an examination will be permitted only when a person's physical or mental condition is a key issue in the case.[8] The most common situation in which a medical condition is in controversy is when the plaintiff sues for personal injuries received in an accident. But it also may be appropriate to obtain an examination of a defendant in a situation in which it is alleged that defendant's motor skills were insufficient to operate a vehicle or other machinery causing injuries to the plaintiff.[9] Physical or mental condition also may arise in contract cases, such as those providing for disability payments to employees or excusing breaches of performance due to illness or injury.[10]

On the other hand, physical or mental condition is not "in controversy" simply because evidence of the condition might be used at trial. For example, one might question a witness to an accident concerning his eyesight; nevertheless every eyewitness cannot be required to submit to an eye examination. The witness' vision is not "in controversy" as required by the statutes and rules governing examinations.

No party has a right to an examination without first obtaining a court order on the basis of a showing of good cause.[11] A physical or mental examination involves an invasion of a person's privacy that ought not to be required without serious consideration of the circumstances.[12] In the ordinary case in which the plaintiff seeks damages for personal injuries, good cause is established by showing that the defendant has not

6. Fed.Civ.Proc.Rule 35(a); Mont.Rules Civ.Proc., Rule 35(a); Ohio Rules Civ.Proc., Rule 35(A); Utah Rules Civ.Proc., Rule 35(a); Va.Sup.Ct.Rules, Rule 4:10(a).

7. See Fed.Civ.Proc.Rule 37(b)(2)(E); Ala.Rules Civ.Proc., Rule 37(b)(2)(E); Advisory Committee Note to the 1970 Amendment of Rule 35(a), reprinted in 48 F.R.D. 487, 540.

8. The Rule 35 requirements "are not met by mere conclusory allegations of the pleadings—nor by mere relevance to the case—but require an affirmative showing by the movant that each condition as to which the examination is sought is really and genuinely in controversy and that good cause exists for ordering each particular examination." Schlagenhauf v. Holder, 379 U.S. 104, 118, 85 S.Ct. 234, 242–43, 13 L.Ed.2d 152 (1964).

9. E.g., Schlagenhauf v. Holder, 379 U.S. 104, 85 S.Ct. 234, 13 L.Ed.2d 152 (1964).

10. Balfour v. Balfour, 413 So.2d 1167 (Ala.Civ.App.1982); Raymond v. Raymond, 105 R.I. 380, 252 A.2d 345 (1969); Landau v. Laughren, 357 S.W.2d 74 (Mo.1962).

11. Fed.Civ.Proc.Rule 35(a); Alaska Rules Civ.Proc., Rule 35(a); Ariz.Rules Civ. Proc., Rule 35(a). An untimely motion, such as one filed just prior to the scheduled trial date, may be denied. See Romero v. Boyd Bros. Transp. Co., Civ.A.No. 93–0085–H, 1994 WL 507475 (W.D.Va.1994).

12. After the Federal Rule was adopted, the Supreme Court held it constitutional despite claims that it violated the Rules Enabling Act because it abridged the examined party's right to privacy. Sibbach v. Wilson & Co., 312 U.S. 1, 61 S.Ct. 422, 85 L.Ed. 479 (1941). It now also is clear that the application of the rule to both plaintiffs and defendants is constitutional. Schlagenhauf v. Holder, 379 U.S. 104, 118, 85 S.Ct. 234, 242, 13 L.Ed.2d 152 (1964).

had an opportunity for independent analysis of the plaintiff's condition; obviously the defendant is not required to accept the statements of the plaintiff's own medical experts. However, if the requesting party can obtain the necessary information from other sources, good cause will not be found.[13]

The court has broad control over the time and place of the examination, the examiner or examiners[14] who will conduct it, the scope that the examination will take, and other details such as who will be present when the examination takes place.[15] For example, it can refuse to require a party to submit to a painful or dangerous examination, particularly when the examination previously had been performed by a competent professional and there is no reason to suspect that the results are inaccurate.[16] If the person to be examined is fearful or embarrassed, the court may order a companion to be allowed into the examining room.[17]

Because of the importance and character of the information in a report of a physical or mental examination, special rules exist requiring exchange of examiners' reports. A party who is examined pursuant to the discovery rules, even when the examination is agreed to by stipulation without court order, is entitled, upon request, to receive a copy of the examiner's report, including all findings, results of tests, diagnoses, and other conclusions.[18] The normal limits imposed on discovery of another party's expert do not apply to physical or mental examinations.[19]

13. See In re Certain Asbestos Cases, 113 F.R.D. 612 (N.D.Tex.1986); Marroni v. Matey, 82 F.R.D. 371 (E.D.Pa.1979); Martin v. Tindell, 98 So.2d 473 (Fla.1957), cert. denied 355 U.S. 959.

14. Initially Rule 35 only permitted examinations by medical doctors. As revised in 1991, however, Rule 35 authorizes the court to require physical or mental examinations by anyone who is suitably licensed or certified. The rule extends the 1988 revision, which authorized mental examinations by licensed clinical psychologists, to include other professionals, such as dentists or occupational therapists. See Advisory Committee Note to the 1991 Amendment of Rule 35(a), reprinted in 134 F.R.D. 525, 651. See also Fla.—West's F.S.A.Rules Civ. Proc., Rule 1.360 (amended in 1988 to allow experts other than physicians to conduct physical and mental exams.) See generally 8A C. Wright, A. Miller & R. Marcus, Civil 2d § 2234.

15. Fed.Civ.Proc.Rule 35(a). Most examinations take place without any court order, however, pursuant to agreement of opposing counsel. It is only the unusual case in which the courts are asked to intercede.

16. Vopelak v. Williams, 42 F.R.D. 387 (N.D.Ohio 1967); Hildyard v. Western Fasteners, Inc., 33 Colo.App. 396, 522 P.2d 596 (1974); Roskovics v. Ashtabula Water

Works Co., 174 N.E.2d 295 (Ohio Com.Pl. 1961).

17. Langfeldt–Haaland v. Saupe Enterprises, Inc., 768 P.2d 1144 (Alaska 1989) (allowing attorney to be present during examination); Cline v. Firestone Tire & Rubber Co., 118 F.R.D. 588 (S.D.W.Va.1988) (not permitting attorney to be present during examination); McDaniel v. Toledo, Peoria & Western R. Co., 97 F.R.D. 525 (C.D.Ill.1983); Brandenberg v. El Al Israel Airlines, 79 F.R.D. 543 (S.D.N.Y.1978); Warrick v. Brode, 46 F.R.D. 427 (D.Del. 1969); Simon v. Castille, 174 So.2d 660, 665 (La.App.1965), application denied 247 La. 1088, 176 So.2d 145 (1965), cert. denied 382 U.S. 932.

18. Fed.Civ.Proc.Rule 35(b); Colo. Rules Civ.Proc., Rule 35(b); Fla.—West's F.S.A.Rules Civ.Proc., Rule 1.360(b); Official Code Ga.Ann. § 9–11–35(b); Idaho Rules Civ.Proc., Rule 35(b)(2). See Dimeglio v. Briggs–Mugrauer, 708 So.2d 637 (Fla. App.1998)(rule applies to presuit examination pursuant to clause in insurance contract requiring insured to submit to examination).

19. Fed.Civ.Proc.Rule 35(b)(2); Ind.Trial Proc.Rule 35(B)(2); Iowa Rules Civ.Proc., Rule 133(b).

In order that the examined party not have an unfair advantage, the rules also provide that once he requests a copy of the examiner's report, he in turn must turn over to the opposing party all prior reports of his own examiners regarding the same condition.[20] By making the request for the report, the examined party waives any doctor-patient privilege upon which he otherwise might rely to avoid disclosure.

D. SPECIAL RULES AND PROBLEMS REGARDING THE DETAILS AND SCOPE OF DISCOVERY

§ 7.13   The Duty to Supplement Responses

In nearly all jurisdictions, including the federal courts, specific provisions require a party, to a limited extent, to update and supplement responses to previous discovery requests and orders,[1] and, in jurisdictions where automatic disclosures are required, to update and correct those disclosures.[2] In almost all courts a party has an affirmative obligation to amend a prior disclosure of witnesses to reveal the names of any new witnesses who have been uncovered.[3] There is also an obligation to amend other prior responses, but only to correct any answer or disclosure that the party learns was incorrect when made or which was correct when made but is no longer true and when the failure to amend would amount to a knowing concealment.[4] In addition, the rules provide that the court may order further corrections and amendments.[5]

At least one state does not require supplementation.[6] Other jurisdictions have limited which types of discovery methods require supplementation.[7] In those jurisdictions, an inquiring party may need to send a new interrogatory, just prior to trial, asking what additional information may

---

20. A plaintiff who puts his own physical condition into controversy normally is held to have waived any privilege regarding that condition. However, when the condition of a defendant is put in controversy by the plaintiff, no waiver takes place. It is here that the rule regarding the request for a copy of the examiner's report becomes significant, since the defendant otherwise would retain a privilege against disclosure by his own examiner.

§ 7.13

1. Fed.Civ.Proc.Rule 26(e); Kan.Stat. Ann. 60–226(e); Me.Rules Civ.Proc., Rule 26(e). See generally 8 C. Wright, A. Miller & R. Marcus, Civil 2d §§ 2048–50.

2. Fed.Civ.Proc.Rule 26(e); Colo.Rules Civ.Proc. 26(e).

3. Fed.Civ.Proc.Rule 26(e)(1); Ind.Trial Proc.Rule 26(E)(1); Me.Rules Civ.Proc., Rule 26(e)(1); Wis.Stat.Ann. 804.01(5)(1).

4. Ind.Trial Proc.Rule 26(E)(2); Ky. Rules Civ.Proc., Rule 26.05(b); Me.Rules Civ.Proc, Rule 26(e)(2); Wis.Stat.Ann. 804.01(5)(2). Fed.Civ.Proc.Rule 26(e)(2) appears to be more extensive by requiring amendment of a prior response if the party learns that the response is "in some material respect incomplete or incorrect" and the other parties are unaware of the supplemental information.

5. See, e.g., Ky.Rules Civ.Proc. 26.05(c); Me.Rules Civ.Proc., Rule 26(e)(3); Minn.Rules Civ.Proc., Rule 26.05(c).

6. Fla.—West's F.S.A.Rules Civ.Proc., Rule 1.280(e).

7. In general, there is no duty to supplement answers given in depositions. See, e.g., Fed.Civ.Proc.Rule 26(e); Md.Rule 2–401(c). See also Vernon's Ann.Mo.Civ.Proc. Rule 56.01(e) and N.J.Civ.Prac.Rule 4:17–7, providing only for the supplementation of answers to interrogatories.

have been uncovered. A duty to update responses also has been imposed when that request is set forth in the original inquiries themselves.[8]

The reluctance of courts to require wholesale, automatic updating of discovery responses is due to a recognition that a rigid supplementation requirement could prove to be a substantial burden on a litigant to whom information flows in bits and pieces on a daily basis.[9] The significance of certain information may not even be recognized until the trial is underway.

Although there are specific sanctions provided for derelictions in a party's obligation to cooperate with discovery under the rules, often there is no specific provision dealing with sanctions for a failure to update responses.[10] The absence of rule authority does not mean that noncompliance will be ignored, however. Rather, courts must rely upon their inherent powers to control the litigation before them and to determine whether some sanction is necessary.[11] For example, in those situations in which a party wishes to call to the stand a witness whose identity should have been included in an update of prior discovery responses, the court may prohibit the introduction of that witness' testimony if a willful violation is shown.[12] A specific provision in the federal rules provides sanctions for a party who fails to update its automatic disclosures, including the exclusion of the undisclosed matters,[13] but the rule does not include sanctions if the party does not update responses to interrogatories, requests for production of documents or other items, or requests for admission. A rule amendment to cover those devices has been proposed.[14]

§ 7.14   Discovery Directed to Nominal Parties

Many of the techniques of formal discovery are designed to elicit

---

8. McNally v. Yellow Cab Co., 16 F.R.D. 460 (E.D.Pa.1954); Furmanek v. Southern Trading Co., 15 F.R.D. 405 (E.D.Pa.1953).

9. See, e.g., Gebhard v. Niedzwiecki, 265 Minn. 471, 478, 122 N.W.2d 110, 115 (1963).

10. Mass.Rules Civ.Proc., Rule 37; Mich.Ct.Rules 1985, 2.313. See generally 8 C. Wright, A. Miller & R. Marcus, Civil 2d § 2050. But see Lucas v. Titus County Hosp. Dist., 964 S.W.2d 144 (Tex.App.1998)(relying on Rule 215(5) of the Texas Rules of Civil Procedure, which requires exclusion in the absence of a showing of good cause to require admission).

11. Royalty Petroleum Co. v. Arkla, Inc., 129 F.R.D. 674 (D.Okl.1990); Kilpatrick v. Mississippi Baptist Medical Center, 461 So.2d 765 (Miss.1984): Prager v. Meckling, 172 W.Va. 785, 310 S.E.2d 852 (1983).

12. Alimenta (U.S.A.), Inc. v. Anheuser–Busch Cos., 803 F.2d 1160 (11th Cir. 1986); Davis v. Marathon Oil Co., 528 F.2d

395 (6th Cir.1975), cert. denied 429 U.S. 823; Schearbrook Land & Livestock Co. v. U.S., 124 F.R.D. 221 (M.D.Fla.1988); Barnes v. St. Francis Hosp. & School of Nursing, Inc., 211 Kan. 315, 507 P.2d 288 (1973); Carver v. Salt River Valley Water Users' Ass'n, 104 Ariz. 513, 456 P.2d 371 (1969); Nissley v. Pennsylvania R.R. Co., 435 Pa. 503, 259 A.2d 451 (1969), cert. denied 397 U.S. 1078; Gebhard v. Niedzwiecki, 265 Minn. 471, 122 N.W.2d 110 (1963); D'Agostino v. Schaffer, 45 N.J.Super. 395, 133 A.2d 45 (App.Div.1957).

13. Fed.Civ.Proc.Rule 37(c)(1).

14. Preliminary Draft of Proposed Amendments to the Federal Rules of Civil Procedure and Evidence 69–70 (August 1998), reprinted in 181 F.R.D. 18, at 92–93. Without such an amendment a court must rely on its inherent powers, "an uncertain and unregulated ground for imposing sanctions." Id. at 70.

information from parties.[1] Nonparties generally are immune from discovery except upon deposition, requests for production of documents and things, or inspection of premises.[2] Even then, unlike parties, nonparties do not have to comply with those requests unless they are formally subpoenaed.[3] An interesting question arises therefore when persons have been made parties to an action without formal consent and perhaps without even their knowledge such as occurs in class actions. Should these nominal parties be subject to discovery as parties or should they be treated as ordinary witnesses?

The decisions have gone both ways.[4] Those courts holding nominal parties to be "parties" within the meaning of the discovery rules generally have been very careful to recognize the unique role that the affected nominal parties occupy and have made special rulings to protect their interests.[5] These protections seem warranted. Unlike an ordinary party to a lawsuit, a nominal party does not have a personal relationship with the attorney and may not have direct access to the attorney. Yet, if this individual fails to respond to an appropriate discovery request and is treated like an ordinary party, severe sanctions may be imposed causing the nominal party to lose valuable rights or even to be held liable to an opposing party in the action.[6] Thus, although discovery clearly is authorized, the courts must take care to ensure that the interests of any nominal party are not limited unreasonably or forfeited unknowingly.

§ 7.15 Controlling Harassment or Oppression: Protective Orders

The manner and scope of discovery must be tailored to some extent depending upon the nature of the case. Flexibility is required to eliminate situations in which discovery may be used for harassment or to oppress an opposing party. At the same time courts must not issue orders prohibiting a litigant from obtaining vital, up-to-date information necessary to allow proper presentation of the case.

Modern discovery provisions follow Federal Rule 26(c), which provides the courts with broad discretion to protect a party or other person from "annoyance, embarrassment, oppression, or undue burden or ex-

---

§ 7.14

1. See §§ 7.9, 7.10, 7.12, above.

2. As amended in 1991, Federal Rule 34(c) authorizes use of a subpoena, as provided in amended Rule 45, to compel a nonparty to produce documents and things or to submit to an inspection of premises.

3. Fed.Civ.Proc.Rule 45. See the discussion in § 7.8 at nn. 28–32, above.

4. Compare Brennan v. Midwestern United Life Ins. Co., 450 F.2d 999 (7th Cir.1971), cert. denied 405 U.S. 921 (unnamed parties are parties with respect to discovery), with Wainwright v. Kraftco

Corp., 54 F.R.D. 532 (N.D.Ga.1972) (unnamed parties not subject to discovery). See Cox v. American Cast Iron Pipe Co., 784 F.2d 1546 (11th Cir.1986), cert. denied 479 U.S. 883; Spoon v. Superior Court, 130 Cal. App.3d 735, 182 Cal.Rptr. 44 (1982); Danzig v. Superior Court of Alameda County, 87 Cal.App.3d 604, 151 Cal.Rptr. 185 (1978).

5. See Southern California Edison Co. v. Superior Court, 7 Cal.3d 832, 103 Cal. Rptr. 709, 500 P.2d 621 (1972).

6. Fed.Civ.Proc.Rule 37; Minn.Rules Civ.Proc., Rule 37; Vernon's Ann.Mo.Civ. Proc.Rule 61.01. See generally § 7.16, below.

pense."[1] A decision to curtail discovery may result from a balance between the value of the information sought to be obtained and the undue hardship that discovery would impose although the party seeking to limit disclosure, even of information of marginal relevance, carries a heavy burden of establishing reasons for the limitation.[2] When the purpose of the discovery is harassment or to obtain information for reasons other than the prosecution or defense of the lawsuit, such as a case in which a party seeks a competitive advantage by obtaining information of a competitor, the court may eliminate discovery entirely.[3] But a court should not take that drastic step lightly, especially when vital information is at stake. In that event, it should use other methods of control. If, for example, a party's motives are uncertain when it seeks a competitor's trade secrets, the court may structure the discovery so that the results are initially available only to the court or a neutral party to determine whether the information is sufficiently relevant to justify disclosure.[4] Indeed in such a case it may be an abuse of discretion for the court to permit discovery without conducting an in camera inspection of sensitive material or holding a special hearing to determine how and to what extent discovery is proper.[5]

In many instances, anticipating what a court probably would do, the parties enter into stipulations regarding what information will be exchanged. Thus, protective orders limiting discovery and private agreements to do so act to speed up the discovery process and avoid discovery disputes.[6] To encourage parties to resolve discovery disputes without

---

§ 7.15

1. See generally 8 C. Wright, A. Miller & R. Marcus, Civil 2d §§ 2037–44; Dickerson, The Law and Ethics of Civil Depositions, 57 Md.L.Rev. 273 (1998). Federal Rule 26(b)(1) was amended in 1983 to encourage judges to be more aggressive in identifying and discouraging discovery overuse. The Federal Rule now specifically provides that the court, on its own initiative, should limit discovery whenever it appears unreasonably cumulative, or the information is obtainable in some other less burdensome way; the party seeking discovery already has had ample opportunity to obtain the information sought; or discovery is unduly burdensome or expensive. See also N.Y.—McKinney's CPLR 3130(1)(without leave of court one party in a negligence case for injury to person or property cannot both depose an opposing party and send that party a set of interrogatories).

2. See Jones v. Clinton, 993 F.Supp. 1217, 1222 (E.D.Ark.1998).

3. See Echostar Communications Corp. v. News Corp., 180 F.R.D. 391, 395–96 (D.Colo.1998).

4. In most cases discovery is not totally denied. Rather, it is structured to protect the responding party as much as possible while giving the requesting party needed information. See Guerra v. Board of Trustees of California State Universities & Colleges, 567 F.2d 352 (9th Cir.1977); Covey Oil Co. v. Continental Oil Co., 340 F.2d 993 (10th Cir.1965), cert. denied 380 U.S. 964. See also Note, Trade Secrets in Discovery: From First Amendment Disclosure to Fifth Amendment Protection, 104 Harv.L.Rev. 1330 (1991); Note, The White Knight Privilege in Litigated Takeovers: Leveling the Playing Field in Discovery, 43 Stan.L.Rev. 445 (1991) (denying competitors access to confidential business information).

5. See Beck v. Dumas, 709 So.2d 601 (Fla.App.1998).

6. See Marcus, Myth and Reality in Protective Order Litigation, 69 Corn.L.Rev. 1 (1983). In some cases a "public right to know" has been raised to overcome these protections. Professor Marcus explores the dangers of this trend and effectively demonstrates why the notion of public trial does not automatically prevail at the civil discovery stage. In addition, the Supreme Court ruled in 1984 that there is no First Amendment right to disseminate information gained through civil discovery so that a protective order preventing dissemination of discovery information was constitutional.

court interference, Federal Rule 26(c) requires a party who seeks court interference to provide a certificate stating that the movant has made a good faith attempt to confer with the other affected parties in an effort to resolve the matter.

As a further means of discouraging discovery abuse, the Federal Rules were amended in 1983 and 1993 to include a signature requirement. Each federal discovery request, response, and objection made by a party now must be signed by the attorney, or by a party who is unrepresented. The signature constitutes certification that, after a reasonable inquiry, the request is thought to be "consistent with the rules," "not interposed for any improper purpose," and "not unreasonable or unduly burdensome or expensive."[7] Although these provisions cannot ensure that discovery abuse will be curbed, they are designed to remind attorneys that there is an affirmative duty to engage in pretrial discovery in a responsible manner consistent with the spirit and purposes of the discovery rules. Thus, the rule obliges each attorney to stop and think about the legitimacy of a discovery request or response.[8] A person who signs a discovery request, response, or objection in bad faith is subject to sanctions under the rule.[9]

The court also may control potential harassment by limiting discovery only to certain types of issues, until those issues are firmly established and it is clear that it will be necessary to go forward on other matters.[10] For example, if a preliminary issue is whether the court has proper jurisdiction over the defendant, discovery may be restricted to that issue so that if jurisdiction ultimately is not established, the defendant will not have been required to go through costly discovery with respect to substantive issues that never will be reached.[11]

The court also has power to control the time, place, and atmosphere of the discovery situation.[12] It may make orders with respect to the way in which the discovery is to be recorded,[13] and it may be creative in its

Seattle Times Co. v. Rhinehart, 467 U.S. 20, 104 S.Ct. 2199, 81 L.Ed.2d 17 (1984).

7. Fed.Civ.Proc.Rule 26(g).

8. See the Advisory Committee Notes to the 1983 Amendment to Rule 26, reprinted in 97 F.R.D. at 165, 218.

The 1993 amendment removed the signature request with regard to discovery from Rule 11, which governs ethical obligations regarding pleadings, see § 5.11, above, and placed it under Rule 26(g), which governs discovery.

9. Fed.Civ.Proc.Rule 26(g)(3). Courts still will look to cases decided under Federal Rule 11 in deciding when and to what extent sanctions are appropriate in discovery matters. Banco de Ponce v. Buxbaum, 99 F.3d 402 (2d Cir.1995).

10. See, e.g., Sogmose Realties, Inc. v. Twentieth Century–Fox Film Corp., 15 F.R.D. 496 (S.D.N.Y.1954); Newton v.

Yates, 170 Ind.App. 486, 353 N.E.2d 485 (1976).

11. Investment Properties Int'l, Ltd. v. IOS, Ltd., 459 F.2d 705 (2d Cir.1972); Cannon v. United Ins. Co., 352 F.Supp. 1212 (D.S.C.1973); Inter–State Milk Producers' Co-op. v. Metropolitan Co-op. Milk Producers Bargaining Agency, Inc., 236 F.Supp. 558 (M.D.Pa.1964); State ex rel. Deere & Co. v. Pinnell, 454 S.W.2d 889 (Mo.1970).

12. The court has the power to ensure that the deposition is conducted in a reasonable manner. Fed.Civ.Proc.Rule 30(d)(3). See the discussion of the timing and place of depositions in § 7.8, above. The courts also may order the sequence of discovery. See § 7.8 n. 23, above.

13. See § 7.8 n. 5, above (video depositions).

attempts to ascertain the extent to which discovery is appropriate in a given situation.[14] In all these ways the court may structure or limit discovery to provide for the open exchange of information desired by the rules,[15] at the same time assuring that the discovery process is used only for legitimate and non-abusive purposes.

§ 7.16   Sanctions and Motions to Compel Response

Modern discovery rules contain specific provisions setting forth sanctions available for abuse of the discovery process.[1] When a party violates the discovery rules by failing to comply with mandatory disclosure provisions or to appear at a requested deposition or to answer interrogatories, the opposing party may request sanctions despite the fact that no court order has been issued.[2] Because no specific court ruling was violated, the erring party cannot be held in contempt.[3] Under the federal rules, in the event that a party fails to make the automatic mandatory disclosures, a standard penalty would appear to be the exclusion of the undisclosed information during any phase of the trial process,[4] unless the error is harmless.[5] Courts will not enforce this sanction, however, if the party had "substantial justification" for failing to make the disclosure,[6] or if the court otherwise believes such a sanction is unwarranted.[7]

---

14. See notes 1–2, above.

15. See generally § 7.1, above.

§ 7.16

1. Fed.Civ.Proc.Rule 37; Alaska Rules Civ.Proc., Rule 37; Ariz.Rules Civ.Proc., Rule 37. See generally 8A C. Wright, A. Miller & R. Marcus, Civil 2d §§ 2281–93. For a comprehensive analysis of the imposition of sanctions in federal courts, see Note, The Second Circuit's Imposition of Litigation Ending Sanctions for Failure To Comply with Discovery Orders: Should Rule 37(b)(2) Defaults and Dismissals Be Determined by a Roll of the Dice?, 62 Brook. L.Rev. 585 (1996).

2. Fed.Civ.Proc.Rule 37(d); Colo.Rules Civ.Proc., Rule 37(d); Fla.—West's F.S.A.Rules Civ.Proc., Rule 1.380(d). Sanctions also are available against corporate parties whose officers, directors, or managing agents willfully refuse to cooperate in discovery. Fed.Civ.Proc.Rule 37(d); Kan. Stat.Ann. 60–237(d); Me.Rules Civ.Proc., Rule 37(d).

3. Sanctions under Federal Rule 11, see § 5.12, above, would not be available because violations of the discovery rules are governed exclusively by Federal Rule 26(g). See Banco de Ponce v. Buxbaum, 99 F.3d 402 (2d Cir.1995)(court, in interpreting Rule 26(g), should look to Rule 11 caselaw).

4. Fed.Civ.Proc.Rule 37(c)(1). See Asia Strategic Investment Alliances, Ltd. v. General Elec. Capital Serv. 173 F.R.D. 305 (D.Kan.1997); Chrysler Credit Corp. v. Bert Cote.s L/A Auto Sales, 707 A.2d 1311 (Me. 1998) The federal rule provides for additional sanctions in the discretion of the court including notification of the jury of the party's failure to make disclosure. The court can order the derelict party to pay the costs associated with additional discovery that became necessary due to the failure to make disclosure automatically. In the Complaint of Kreta Shipping, S.A., 181 F.R.D. 273 (S.D.N.Y.1998).

5. Newman v. GHS Osteopathic, Inc., 60 F.3d 153 (3d Cir.1995)(omission harmless when other party had reason to know the information).

6. See Fitz, Inc. v. Ralph Wilson Plastics Co., 174 F.R.D. 587 (D.N.J.1997)(substantial justification requires "justification to degree it could satisfy a reasonable person that parties could differ as whether nonmovant was required to comply with disclosure request"). See also Ames v. Van Dyne, 100 F.3d 956 (6th Cir.1996).

7. For a discussion of factors to be considered by the court; see In the Complaint of Kreta Shipping, S.A., 181 F.R.D. 273 (S.D.N.Y.1998)(citing In Re Paoli R.R. Yard PCB Litig., 35 F.3d 717, 791 (3d Cir. 1994)).

In all cases of impropriety regarding discovery, the court may strike all or any portion of a party's claim or defense, thus limiting what evidence may be introduced at trial. In truly egregious situations the court may go so far as to dismiss a plaintiff's complaint or enter a default judgment against a defendant.[8] Courts are reluctant to do so, however, unless it is clear that a party's actions are "flagrant and wanton,"[9] or a "deliberate, contumacious or unwarranted disregard of the court's authority."[10] Courts have broad discretion regarding the imposition of sanctions. As a result their standards vary when deciding what conduct will justify a finding of abuse sufficiently serious to result in litigation-ending penalties.[11] In addition to or in lieu of direct sanctions, the court can order a party to pay an opponent the reasonable expenses of obtaining sanctions, including attorneys' fees.[12]

In the absence of a court order to respond, courts have been particularly reluctant to hold that a party's default was flagrant and deliberate rather than merely negligent.[13] Therefore, the most that an aggrieved party typically can do is to seek a court order requiring the opposing party to attend the deposition, to produce requested documents, or to respond to the interrogatories under the rules.[14] Only if that order is disregarded will the most serious sanctions be imposed,[15]

As just indicated, when the discovery process breaks down, an aggrieved party most often will seek a court order.[16] Under the federal

---

8. Fed.Civ.Proc.Rule 37(b)(2), (d); Official Code Ga.Ann. § 9–11–37(b)(2), (d); Idaho Rules Civ.Proc., Rule 37(b)(2), (d). See Guex v. Allmerica Financial Life Ins., 146 F.3d 40 (1st Cir.1998)(unexcused failures of plaintiff to appear for deposition justified dismissal); Kami & Sons, Inc. v. Pipe, 248 A.D.2d 312, 670 N.Y.S.2d 484 (1998)(willful failure to provide discovery pursuant to court order justified dismissal).

9. Traxler v. Ford Motor Co., 227 Mich.App. 276, 576 N.W.2d 398 (1998)(default judgment against defendant set aside until trial court conducted hearing to determine reasons for defendant's failure to meet discovery requirements). See Communispond, Inc. v. Kelley & T.C.E. Assocs., No. 96 Civ. 1487, 1998 WL 473951 (S.D.N.Y.1998)(defendant's willful failure to comply with discovery orders resulted in default judgment for plaintiff). See also Cody v. Mello, 59 F.3d 13 (2d Cir.1995).

10. Shimanovsky v. General Motors Corp., 181 Ill.2d 112, 229 Ill.Dec. 513, 692 N.E.2d 286 (1998)(dismissal of plaintiff's complaint set aside when plaintiff's actions were not in bad faith).

11. See Note, The Second Circuit's Imposition of Litigation–Ending Sanctions For Failures To Comply with Discovery Orders: Should Rule 37(b)(2) Defaults and Dismiss-

als Be Determined by a Roll of the Dice?, 62 Brook.L.Rev 585 (1996).

12. Fed.Civ.Proc.Rule 37(d); Mass. Rules Civ.Proc., Rule 37(d); Minn.Rules Civ.Proc., Rule 37.04.

13. Flaks v. Koegel, 504 F.2d 702 (2d Cir.1974); Dorsey v. Academy Moving & Storage, Inc., 423 F.2d 858 (5th Cir.1970); Bon Air Hotel, Inc. v. Time, Inc., 376 F.2d 118 (5th Cir.1967), cert. denied 393 U.S. 859.

14. See W. Glaser, Pretrial Discovery and the Adversary System 154–56 (1968); Rosenberg, Sanctions to Effectuate Pretrial Discovery, 58 Colum.L.Rev. 480, 494–96 (1958).

15. Any sanction that is imposed must be tailored to the conduct of the non-responding party. Overly broad or too harsh sanctions may be subject to attack on due process grounds. E.g., Harrigan v. Mason & Winograd, Inc., 121 R.I. 209, 397 A.2d 514 (1979); Schulze v. Coykendall, 218 Kan. 653, 545 P.2d 392 (1976). For a discussion of the constitutional limits imposed on the court's sanctioning power, see 8A C. Wright, A. Miller & R. Marcus, Civil 2d § 2283.

16. See Fed.Civ.Proc.Rule 37(a)(2), (3); Ohio Rules Civ.Proc., Rule 37(A)(2), (3); Utah Rules Civ.Proc., Rule 37(a)(2), (3);

rules a party who moves for an order requiring discovery or for sanctions must include a certification that he or she in good faith conferred or attempted to confer with the person or party who had failed to respond in an effort to obtain compliance without court intervention.[17] Thus, if a party fails to cooperate with a discovery request, the discovering party may move for an order or orders to ensure that discovery is carried out properly. The same is true with respect to a witness who appears pursuant to a subpoena, but who fails to answer the questions asked or refuses to go beyond cryptic, uncertain, or incomplete responses. However, although the court where the action is pending has control over all discovery orders with respect to the parties to the case,[18] only a court having personal jurisdiction over a witness can issue orders directing that witness to make further responses to discovery.[19]

In addition to the order itself, the court may assess a party who has been unreasonable in refusing discovery to pay the opposing party's expenses of the motion, including reasonable attorneys' fees.[20] Conversely, if the party seeking sanctions was demanding improper discovery, such as irrelevant or privileged information, the court has the power to order that the responding party be paid the cost of contesting the motion, including reasonable attorneys' fees.[21]

Once an order has been issued, if it is not obeyed, the disobedient party or witness can be held in contempt of court.[22] A person who is in contempt can be fined or even jailed until such time as she complies with the court's discovery order,[23] except that the rules of discovery provide that no person shall be jailed for failure to submit to a physical or mental examination.[24] This latter exception is based on the general notion that a person has a right to privacy regarding his physical or mental state and should not be forced to relinquish it; other, less direct, sanctions are available for failure to comply with a court-ordered examination.[25]

Va.Sup.Ct.Rules, Rule 4:12(a)(2), (3); Wn. Civ.Rule 37(a)(2), (3).

17. Fed.Civ.Proc.Rule 37(a)(2)(A), (a)(2)(B), (d). The provisions do not require such a certificate in situations in which a party fails to appear for a properly scheduled deposition.

18. Fed.Civ.Proc.Rule 37(a)(1); Fla.— West's F.S.A.Rules Civ.Proc., Rule 1.380(a)(1); Official Code Ga.Ann. § 9–11–37(a)(1).

19. Fed.Civ.Proc.Rule 37(a)(1); Ind.Trial Proc.Rule 37(A)(1); Kan.Stat.Ann. 60–237(a)(1).

20. Fed.Civ.Proc.Rule 37(a)(4); Ala. Rules Civ.Proc., Rule 37(a)(4); Alaska Rules Civ.Proc., Rule 37(a)(4).

21. Fed.Civ.Proc.Rule 37(a)(4); Ariz. Rules Civ.Proc., Rule 37(a)(4); Colo.Rules Civ.Proc., Rule 37(a)(3).

22. Sheila's Shine Prods., Inc. v. Sheila Shine, Inc., 486 F.2d 114 (5th Cir.1973); Hodgson v. Mahoney, 460 F.2d 326 (1st Cir.1972), cert. denied 409 U.S. 1039; Southern Ry. Co. v. Lanham, 403 F.2d 119 (5th Cir.1968).

23. Southern Ry. Co. v. Lanham, 403 F.2d 119 (5th Cir.1968); Fenton v. Walling, 139 F.2d 608 (9th Cir.1943), cert. denied 321 U.S. 798.

24. Sibbach v. Wilson & Co., 312 U.S. 1, 61 S.Ct. 422, 85 L.Ed. 479 (1941); Fed. Civ.Proc.Rule 37(b)(2)(D); Mass.Rules Civ. Proc.; Rule 37(b)(2)(D). See § 7.12, above.

25. Fed.Civ.Proc.Rule 37(b)(2)(E); Mont.Rules Civ.Proc., Rule 37(b)(2)(E).

A court need not jail someone for contempt for failure to comply with its order. The rules specify a number of lesser penalties that may be utilized. These include striking a portion of the party's case, granting a default judgment, dismissing the action, limiting the testimony available at trial, or assessing the expenses of the opposing party in obtaining the sanctions.[26] The trial judge has wide discretion to determine what is appropriate and reasonable, given the nature of the discovery sought and the reason for the refusal.[27] As noted above, the harshest sanctions generally are reserved for the most flagrant cases,[28] and the courts, as a matter of policy, attempt to issue sanctions that will encourage compliance, rather than simply be punitive.[29]

A difficult problem exists when a party cannot comply with an order to produce documents or other items because they were lost or altered prior to the time suit was filed or their discovery was requested. It has been held that a party or potential party has a duty not to destroy evidence, but if the individual acted in good faith at all times, and the prejudice to another party is not severe, then the extreme sanction of dismissal of a plaintiff's case or a default judgment against the defendant is unwarranted.[30]

Failure to comply with the rules regarding requests for admission has received special treatment. Under the rules, a party who fails to respond to any request admits the facts contained therein.[31] Theoretically, this means that the requesting party would not have to prepare any evidence with respect to such an issue. Courts have been extremely reluctant, however, at least in the absence of a showing of bad faith, to hold a party to this type of an admission. Thus, to clarify these situations

---

26. Fed.Civ.Proc.Rule 37(b)(2); Ohio Rules Civ.Proc., Rule 37(B)(2); Utah Rules Civ.Proc., Rule 37(b)(2); Va.Sup.Ct.Rules, Rule 4:12(b)(2); Wn.Civ.Rule 37(b)(2).

27. See, e.g., National Hockey League v. Metropolitan Hockey Club, Inc., 427 U.S. 639, 96 S.Ct. 2778, 49 L.Ed.2d 747 (1976); Fox v. Studebaker–Worthington, Inc., 516 F.2d 989 (8th Cir.1975); Flaks v. Koegel, 504 F.2d 702, 707 (2d Cir.1974); Industrial Aircraft Lodge 707 v. United Technologies Corp., 104 F.R.D. 471 (D.Conn.1985); Martin v. Solon Automated Servs., Inc., 84 N.C.App. 197, 352 S.E.2d 278 (1987); Bell v. Inland Mut. Ins. Co., 175 W.Va. 165, 332 S.E.2d 127 (1985), appeal dismissed, cert. denied 474 U.S. 936; Mercer v. Raine, 443 So.2d 944 (Fla.1983); Lorson v. Falcon Coach, Inc., 214 Kan. 670, 678, 522 P.2d 449, 456 (1974).

28. See text at nn. 8–10, above. See also Insurance Corp. of Ireland, Ltd. v. Compagnie des Bauxites de Guinee, 456 U.S. 694, 102 S.Ct. 2099, 72 L.Ed.2d 492 (1982) (permissible sanction is to take as established the matters regarding which the discovery order was made, including a find-

ing of personal jurisdiction over the defendants).

29. Robison v. Transamerica Ins. Co., 368 F.2d 37 (10th Cir.1966); Jones v. Smith, 99 F.R.D. 4 (M.D.Pa.1983), affirmed 734 F.2d 6 (3d Cir.1984) (plaintiff had to comply with court order within 20 days or the action would be dismissed).

30. Webb v. District of Columbia, 146 F.3d 964 (D.C.Cir.1998)(routine destruction of some of plaintiff's personnel files in employment discrimination case did not justify trial court's entry of default judgment against defendant); Shimanovsky v. General Motors Corp., 181 Ill.2d 112, 229 Ill.Dec. 513, 692 N.E.2d 286 (1998)(dismissal of plaintiff's case reversed despite fact that plaintiff's expert had done "destructive testing" on important evidence in order that plaintiff could ascertain whether he could file suit in good faith). In both of the above cases the appellate courts left to the trial judges the nature of any lesser sanctions that would be appropriate.

31. Fed.Civ.Proc.Rule 36(a); Ala.Rules Civ.Proc., Rule 36(a); Alaska Rules Civ. Proc., Rule 36(a).

so that the requesting party knows whether a failure to respond will be deemed deliberate and treated as an admission rather than an inadvertent error, a number of jurisdictions, including the federal courts, have amended their rules to provide that the requesting party can move for an order to have the facts involved deemed admitted.[32] At the hearing the responding party will have to explain the failure to respond and both sides will know whether the issues in question are to be tried or whether they in fact are admitted.

On the other hand, if a party knowingly makes a false denial in response to a request to admit, and the matter subsequently is proved at trial, the discovery rules provide that the party who sought the admission is entitled to be paid the reasonable costs incurred in proving the matter.[33] These costs can be substantial.[34] Unfortunately, this sanction is far too weak to make requests to admit as effective as they otherwise might be. For one thing, it may be difficult if not impossible to establish that the matter in fact was "proved at trial." For example, if the aggrieved party is a defendant who put forth three defenses at trial and the request to admit involved only one of them, a general verdict in defendant's favor will give no clue as to what was or was not proved. Second, it may be extremely difficult for an aggrieved party to establish the reasonable costs of proving a matter. In most cases it will be impossible to ascertain how much time an attorney spent on a specific issue, particularly in the usual situation in which the same witnesses who testified on that issue also testified on other issues. It certainly seems that a deliberately false denial, signed under oath, would justify more severe sanctions, including the possibility of a substantial fine or even a stay in jail. Reported cases do not reveal that the courts have been willing to go that far, however.

E.　USE OF DISCOVERY AT TRIAL

§ 7.17　Use of Discovery at Trial

Modern discovery rules specifically set out when responses to discovery may be admitted in evidence at trial.[1] In many situations discovery responses would be admissible under the normal evidence rules.[2] But in some cases, those responses would be inadmissible; it is in these latter situations that the discovery provisions have a substantial impact.

---

32. Fed.Civ.Proc.Rule 36(a); Ariz.Rules Civ.Proc., Rule 36(a); Colo.Rules Civ.Proc., Rule 36(a).

33. Fed.Civ.Proc.Rule 37(c); Fla.— West's F.S.A.Rules Civ.Proc., Rule 1.380(c); Official Code Ga.Ann. § 9–11–37(c). See Bradshaw v. Thompson, 454 F.2d 75 (6th Cir.1972), cert. denied 409 U.S. 878.

34. See Rosales v. Thermex–Thermatron, Inc., 67 Cal.App.4th 187, 78 Cal. Rptr.2d 861 (1998)(upholding an award of $123,002).

§ 7.17

1. Fed.Civ.Proc.Rule 32.

An admission in response to a request to admit establishes the facts involved and thus no evidence is necessary to prove the admitted facts and no evidence may be introduced to refute them. Fed.Civ.Proc.Rule 36(b); Alaska Rules Civ.Proc., Rule 36(b); Colo.Rules Civ.Proc., Rule 36(b). See § 7.10 at nn. 15–19, above.

2. See generally McCormick on Evidence §§ 244–327 (4th ed.1992).

Typically, evidence rules provide that one party is entitled to introduce at trial any relevant statement of an opposing party, whether or not the latter takes the witness stand.[3] Any answer to an interrogatory or statement on deposition qualifies under these provisions. Indeed, because they are under oath, statements made during discovery may be more acceptable for use as evidence than the ordinary out-of-court casual remark.

Similarly, under the normal evidence rules, certain statements made by agents or employees of a party may be used as evidence by an opposing party.[4] Typically, these are restricted to statements of (1) managing agents, (2) persons specifically authorized to speak for a party on a matter, or (3) an employee regarding his or her particular duties.[5] Thus, a discovery answer made by an agent or an employee will be admissible against the principal or employer if the statement otherwise would be admissible under the rules of evidence.

Arguably, the employer has the opportunity to consult with an employee prior to discovery, so that the employee's statements, made under oath, will not be inadvertent or misleading and thus can be utilized fairly against the party.[6] Most jurisdictions do not have special rules authorizing this use because of a concern that an ordinary employee is not subject to much control by the employer. Thus, the employee's statements are treated as those of an ordinary witness for purposes of deciding whether they may be used as evidence at trial.

Discovery rules in a few jurisdictions also expand a party's ability to use answers on a deposition to contradict a witness' testimony at trial. A basic rule of evidence permits any witness to be impeached by establishing that the witness made a prior statement inconsistent with the current testimony.[7] This rule extends to prior statements made under oath in response to discovery orders. In a few jurisdictions, some prior inconsistent statements not only may be used to impeach the witness, but also may be admitted into evidence as proof of the fact stated.[8]

Except as just discussed, evidence rules typically provide that out-of-court statements are hearsay and cannot be introduced at trial.[9] The discovery rules offer a substantial exception to this general preclusion by allowing into evidence answers given on deposition, if the person who gave the responses is dead, ill, incompetent, or beyond the subpoena powers of the trial court.[10] The justification for this exception is that the evidence is given under oath, subject to examination and cross-examina-

---

3. E.g., Fed.Evid.Rule 801(d)(2); West's Ann.Cal.Evid.Code §§ 1220–25.

4. Fed.Evid.Rule 801(d)(2); West's Ann.Cal.Evid.Code §§ 1222, 1224.

5. Ibid.

6. See Fed.Civ.Proc.Rule 32 (admissibility of statements made at a deposition).

7. Fed.Evid.Rule 613; West's Ann.Cal. Evid.Code §§ 769, 770.

8. See, e.g., West's Ann.Cal.Evid.Code § 1235.

9. See generally McCormick on Evidence §§ 244–327 (4th ed.1992).

10. Fed.Civ.Proc.Rule 32(a)(3); Mont. Rules Civ.Proc., Rule 32(a)(3); N.J.Civ.Prac. Rule 4:16–1(c). See Brown v. Pryor, 954 P.2d 1349 (Wyo.1998)(video deposition of party's sole expert witness admitted when expert was out of state at time of trial).

tion; hence it is better than no evidence at all. Several states permit the introduction into evidence of the deposition of a physician or surgeon regardless of the deponent's availability.[11] This can save a party the high cost of calling the doctor to give live testimony at trial.

In the vast majority of cases, which condition admissibility of a deposition on the unavailability of the witness, the discovery rules specifically provide that a party who has procured a deponent's absence cannot use his deposition at trial.[12] A party whose witness has given a favorable deposition will not be allowed to avoid in-court scrutiny of the witness by inducing the witness to be out of the state or out of the country at the time that the trial takes place.

The special rule regarding the procuring of a witness' absence also applies when a party seeks to utilize her own deposition in lieu of appearing at trial. If the party normally lives outside the scope of the court's subpoena power, the party's attorney may introduce the client's deposition into evidence.[13] If the party lives within the reach of the court's subpoena power and elects not to attend trial for reasons of tactics or convenience, then the party is considered to have procured her own absence and the deposition cannot be used.[14]

It is important to note that the rules permitting parties to utilize their own discovery answers at trial apply only to depositions in which there has been a chance for the opposing side to cross-examine. A party is not permitted to introduce her answers to interrogatories;[15] this limitation is imposed to avoid encouraging responses to interrogatories that would be long, drawn-out, self-serving analyses of every aspect of the case.

F. THE FUTURE OF DISCOVERY

§ 7.18 Discovery Reform

The liberal discovery rules used in nearly all state and federal courts have accomplished much in terms of reducing, if not eliminating, trial

---

11. Ill—Smith–Hurd S.Ct.Rules 212(b), 202: Wis.Stat.Ann. 804.07(i)(c)(2). Under the Illinois provisions only a deposition taken for evidentiary purposes is admissible. A party who takes a deposition must state in advance whether it is taken for discovery or evidentiary purposes. Unless the parties otherwise agree, a party who wants to depose an individual both for discovery and evidentiary purposes must do so in separate depositions.

A 1991 proposed amendment to Federal Rule 32, that was not promulgated, would have allowed the use of the depositions of experts without having to establish their unavailability to testify in person.

12. Fed.Civ.Proc.Rule   32(a)(3)(B); Ohio Rules Civ.Proc., Rule 32(A)(3)(b); Utah Rules Civ.Proc., Rule 32(a)(3)(B).

13. Eferakeya v. Twin City State Bank, 13 Kan.App.2d 197, 766 P.2d 837 (1988), affirmed as modified 245 Kan. 154, 777 P.2d 759 (1989); Stewart v. Meyers, 353 F.2d 691 (7th Cir.1965).

14. Knox v. Anderson, 21 F.R.D. 97 (D.Hawai'i 1957); King v. International Harvester Co., 212 Va. 78, 181 S.E.2d 656 (1971). If a party is too ill to attend the trial, then the deposition may be used regardless of where the party resides. Van Sciver v. Rothensies, 122 F.2d 697 (3d Cir. 1941).

15. Haskell Plumbing & Heating Co. v. Weeks, 237 F.2d 263 (9th Cir.1956); Great Plains Supply Co. v. Mobil Oil Co., 172 N.W.2d 241, 253 (N.D.1969).

victories based on surprise tactics. At the same time, there is no question that they have been seriously abused and that, although the rules provide the courts with various tools to curb harassing or otherwise abusive discovery practices,[1] abuses continue to occur. Demands for massive numbers of documents and service of huge numbers of needless and burdensome interrogatories have raised litigation costs substantially. Both large corporations and individual litigants suffer from the overuse of discovery. Large corporate parties may coerce settlements when they are sued by individuals or small businesses by threatening them with long and involved discovery. Conversely, a corporation faced with enormous document demands or ceaseless interrogatories may feel that settlement is the only alternative, even though it believes it has a strong case on the merits. Whatever the cause, when discovery is being used not to search out facts but to force settlement, justice is being subverted. The ethics of these practices can be seriously questioned and concern has been shown by judges,[2] bar associations[3] and commentators.[4]

In response to these problems, there have been numerous reforms, led largely by a comprehensive set of amendments to the federal rules in 1993. These alterations are discussed or noted throughout this chapter.

Previous reforms in federal discovery tended to increase court control, encouraging judges to protect against abuse.[5] A 1980 amendment provided for discovery conferences, if an attorney cannot work out a reasonable program of discovery with opposing counsel.[6] Amendments in 1983 gave the courts specific authority to limit discovery if it appears unreasonably duplicative or oppressive or disproportionate to the matters involved in the case.[7] A certification requirement also was added so that federal discovery requests must be signed by the attorneys, attest-

---

§ 7.18

1. See §§ 7.15–7.16, above.

2. See Blue Chip Stamps v. Manor Drug Stores, 421 U.S. 723, 741, 95 S.Ct. 1917, 1928, 44 L.Ed.2d 539 (1975) (per Rehnquist, J.). See also Justice Powell's dissent from the adoption of the 1980 discovery rule amendments, reprinted in 85 F.R.D. 521.

3. See the two reports of the Section of Litigation, American Bar Association Special Committee for the Study of Discovery Abuse. The October 1977 report is reprinted at 92 F.R.D. 149 (1982); the November 1980 report is reprinted at 92 F.R.D. 137 (1982).

4. Dickerson, The Law and Ethics of Civil Depositions, 57 Md.L.Rev. 273 (1998); Hazard, Discovery Vices and Trans–Substantive Virtues in the Federal Rules of Civil Procedure, 137 U.Pa.L.Rev. 2237 (1989); Rosenberg, Federal Rules of Civil Procedure in Action: Assessing Their Impact, 137 U.Pa.L.Rev. 2197, 2203 (1989); Schwarzer, The Federal Rules, The Adver-

sary Process, and Discovery Reform, 50 U.Pitt.L.Rev. 703 (1989); Wendel, Rediscovering Discovery Ethics, 79 Marquette L.Rev. 895 (1996). See, e.g., McElroy, Federal Pre–Trial Procedure in an Antitrust Suit, 31 Sw.L.J. 649, 681 (1977); Symposium, Discovery in Civil Antitrust, 44 Antitrust L.J. 1, 3, 24 (1975). See generally Segal, Survey of Literature on Discovery From 1970 to Present: Expressed Dissatisfactions and Proposed Reforms (Fed.Jud.Center 1978).

5. Lambros, The Federal Rules of Civil Procedure: A New Adversarial Model for a New Era, 50 U.Pitt.L.Rev. 789, 804 (1989).

6. The attorney requesting the conference must include in the motion, among other things, a statement showing a reasonable effort to reach an agreement with opposing counsel on the matters set forth in the motion. Fed.Civ.Proc.Rule 26(f)(5). See also Advisory Committee Note to the 1980 Amendment of Rule 26(f), reprinted in 85 F.R.D. 521, 526.

7. Fed.Civ.Proc.Rule 26(b)(1).

ing to their propriety.[8] However, some states have been slow to adopt similar measures.[9]

Over the years there has been considerable disagreement over what reforms are needed and how drastic the measures should be.[10] Some studies have been undertaken to better understand what problems are occurring.[11] A brief look at some of the various proposals that have surfaced is useful.

One problem that has been raised is that the scope of permissible discovery is too broad, allowing investigation of any matter related to the "subject matter of the action." Litigants sometimes require opposing parties to answer innumerable questions under oath, and to produce literally thousands of documents, many of which, although related to the "subject matter of the action" are unlikely to be of any assistance in preparation for trial.[12] As a result, in some cases at least, discovery has become costly, time-consuming, and wasteful. In response to a call for reform, a Task Force created by the American Bar Association studied the problem and in the first of two reports, proposed to change the words "relevant to the subject matter" to "relevant to the issues raised by the claims or defenses of any party."[13] This change, by itself, does not seem to be sufficiently precise to alter prior practices with regard to the scope of allowable discovery. It was argued, however, that the reason why the alteration was made would be well known and would appear in the history of a new rule, with the result that courts would tend to restrict discovery. Such a proposed change to Federal Rule 26 has been circulated for comment in 1998; it would allow the court, for good cause shown, to expand the scope of discovery to its current scope, i.e, to discover information relevant to the subject matter.[14]

Just where the line would be drawn in any particular case would depend on the facts in the action. The proposed change would not likely

8. Fed.Civ.Proc.Rule 26(g). See also § 7.15, above.

9. Subrin, Federal Rules, Local Rules, and State Rules: Uniformity, Divergence, and Emerging Procedural Patterns, 137 U.Pa.L.Rev. 1999, 2037 (1989) (noting eight states have adopted all three amendments).

10. Compare Amendments to the Federal Rules of Civil Procedure, 146 F.R.D. 401, 507 (1993)(dissenting opinion of Justice Scalia) with Note, Mandatory Disclosure Can Improve the Discovery System, 70 Ind.L.J. 657 (1995). See also Easterbrook, Comment: Discovery As Abuse, 69 B.U.L.Rev. 635 (1989); Setear, The Barrister and the Bomb: The Dynamics of Cooperation, Nuclear Deterrence, and Discovery Abuse, 69 B.U.L.Rev. 569 (1989); Weinstein, Comment: What Discovery Abuse?, 69 B.U.L.Rev. 649 (1989).

11. See Brazil, Civil Discovery: Lawyers' Views of Its Effectiveness, Its Principal Problems and Abuses, 1980 A.B.F.Res.J. 787; Brazil, Views from the Front Lines:

Observations by Chicago Lawyers About the System of Civil Discovery, 1980 A.B.F.Res.J. 217; Willging, Stienstra, Shapard & Miletich, An Empirical Study of Discovery and Disclosure Practice Under the 1993 Federal Rule Amendments, 39 B.C.L.Rev. 525 (1998).

12. Report of the Arizona State University Discovery Conference on the Advisory Committee's Proposed Revision of the Rules of Civil Procedure (Discovery) 1978 Ariz.St.L.J. 494.

13. Section of Litigation, American Bar Association Special Committee for the Study of Discovery Abuse, 92 F.R.D. 149, 157 (1982). See also § 7.2, above.

14. See Proposed Rule 26(b)(1) in Preliminary Draft of Proposed Amendments to the Federal Rules of Civil Procedure and Evidence 41–42, 54–56 (August 1998), reprinted in 181 F.R.D. 18, at 64–65, 77–79.

affect smaller, more direct cases such as those involving automobile collisions, and the like, in which discovery is confined primarily to information obtained from eyewitnesses, plus the medical examinations of the injured parties. The altered language would have a much greater impact in business litigation, such as antitrust actions, in which, in addition to obtaining direct evidence regarding the alleged improper activities of defendants, plaintiffs often seek numerous background matters regarding the past practices of the industry, the economic history of a particular defendant, and other materials that may go back a generation or more. Whatever the merits of the proposal, the suggested change was not adopted in either the 1980,[15] 1983 or 1991 amendments to the Federal Rules. It remains to be seen whether it will have better success in 1999.

Another proposed change in Federal Rule 26(a), circulated for comment in 1998, would restrict mandatory, automatic disclosure to information supporting the disclosing party's claims or defenses.[16] The current rule requires disclosure of information regardless of whose claims or defenses the information would support. It is not at all clear what justification there is for such a limitation. If a party is aware of a witness whose testimony might support the opponent's case, there seems precious little justification for not including the witness on a list of those persons who may have relevant information. It would simply mean that each party will need routinely to send an interrogatory to all other parties asking for the names of any such witnesses. This practical requirement would be reinforced by the fact that a party would not need to update the mandatory disclosures if the party learns about such a witness later during the pretrial phase of the case but would need to update an interrogatory. The process that would ensue seems in conflict with the purpose of mandatory disclosure to limit the need for interrogatories, which now are restricted in the number that can be served without a court order.[17]

Perhaps the most significant proposed change in the federal rules is the elimination of the current opt-out provisions that allow federal courts, by local rule, to operate under a set of discovery rules entirely different from those set out in the formal Federal Rules of Civil Procedure.[18] So many districts have exercised this option in one way or another that it has eliminated uniform discovery practice in federal courts throughout the nation. The idea that local courts could tailor their discovery rules to their specific needs was reasonable, but a significant feature of the federal rules always has been the fact that one

15. See Friedenthal, A Divided Supreme Court Adopts Discovery Amendments to the Federal Rules of Civil Procedure, 69 Calif.L.Rev. 806 (1981).

16. Proposed Rule 26(a)(1)(A),(B) in Preliminary Draft of Proposed Amendments to the Federal Rules of Civil Procedure and Evidence 34–35, 50 (August 1998), reprinted in 181 F.R.D. 18, at 57–58, 73.

17. See Fed.Civ.Proc.Rule 33(a).

18. Proposed Rule 26(a)(1),(4) in Preliminary Draft of Proposed Amendments to the Federal Rules of Civil Procedure and Evidence 34, 41, 48–50 (August 1998), reprinted in 181 F.R.D. 18, at 57, 64, 71–73.

could count on uniformity regardless of which federal court one entered[19] —a fact still true, of course, of the rules not related to discovery. It also should be noted that even before the opt-out provisions were promulgated, local rules did govern certain aspects of discovery, such as limitations on the number of interrogatories permitted. There has been significant adverse criticism of the opt-out provisions and their elimination is certainly a valid topic for discussion. One feature of uniform federal discovery has been the extent to which state courts have used the federal provisions as a model. Today, nearly all states have adopted the rules as they existed prior to the 1993 amendments. The subsequent lack of uniformity in federal courts may explain why the new federal mandatory, automatic disclosure rules adopted in 1993 have not caught on.

It should be noted that if the opt-out provisions in the federal rules are eliminated, there is likely to be pressure from those courts that have determined not to follow the mandatory automatic discovery provisions, and perhaps from others, to eliminate the latter provisions. It is not at all certain what the result would be.

19. See Preliminary Draft of Proposed Amendments to the Federal Rules of Civil Procedure and Evidence 49 (August 1998), reprinted in 181 F.R.D. 18, at 72.

§§ 7.19–8.0 are reserved for supplementary material.

Chapter 8

THE PRETRIAL CONFERENCE

Analysis

§ 8.1 Nature and Purposes of a Pretrial Conference

Aspects of modern litigation—especially expanded joinder of parties and claims,[1] virtually unlimited discovery,[2] less informative pleadings,[3] and increasingly complex and protracted cases—have created a need for greater judicial intervention to focus controversies before trial. In many jurisdictions, including the federal courts, this has been accomplished by use of the pretrial conference,[4] which is a meeting of the attorneys (and sometimes the parties) with a trial judge or with a magistrate possessing certain judicial powers.[5]

The pretrial conference was unknown at common law.[6] It was introduced in 1929, in Wayne County, Michigan, as a device for relieving an extremely congested court calendar.[7] In 1938 the pretrial conference

---

§ 8.1

1. See generally Chapters 6 and 16.

2. See generally §§ 7.1–7.6, above.

3. See generally § 5.2, above.

4. Fed.Civ.Proc.Rule 16; Ala.Rules Civ. Proc., Rule 16; Ariz.Rules Civ.Proc., Rule 16(a); Cal.Rules of Ct., Rule 212; Fla.— West's F.S.A. Rules Civ.Proc., Rule 1.200; Vernon's Ann.Mo.Civ.Proc.Rule 62.01. See generally 6A C. Wright, A. Miller & M. Kane, Civil 2d §§ 1521–31.

5. In recent years the increase in the number of very large and complicated lawsuits has placed considerable pressure on the judicial system to develop special procedures to keep these cases from unduly clogging the calendar. Among the recommendations to combat this problem is an expanded use of multiple pretrial conferences, commencing prior to discovery, to formulate issues, to channel discovery, to avoid the excessive use of motions, and to set timetables to keep the case moving. See generally Manual for Complex Litigation, Third (1995). This carefully structured and expanded use of the pretrial conference may help significantly in easing the progress of these difficult cases.

Federal Rule 16 was amended in 1983 to promote better pretrial management. The amended rule encourages scheduling through a series of conferences and expands the list of matters that may be considered by the court at the pretrial conference in order to allow for better management of the case.

6. See 6A C. Wright, A. Miller & M. Kane, Civil 2d § 1521, at 214.

7. Id. at 215–16.

was embodied in Federal Rule 16, which now has many state counterparts.[8]

Today Federal Rule 26(f), regarding plans for pretrial discovery, works in conjunction with Rule 16 to cover virtually all aspects of the pretrial process. Thus pretrial conferences and plans may be used as a management tool, controlling motion and discovery practice, preparing for and guiding the trial,[9] informing the parties what issues and facts are in controversy,[10] and facilitating the decision of the case on its merits.[11] They also may be utilized to encourage settlement of cases,[12] directly or through alternative dispute resolution procedures,[13] thereby relieving the pressure on court calendars.[14] There is a continuing debate over which role should be primary, although there is a definite trend toward settlement, at least in the federal courts. Those emphasizing settlement tend to stress its utility to judges in urban areas with extremely crowded trial calendars.[15] Those emphasizing preparation for trial argue that too active judicial intervention causes coerced settlements,[16] which leads to dissatisfaction with the judicial system and raises the possibility of prejudice in the settlement process. Properly used to prepare for trial,

8. Fed.Civ.Proc.Rule 16; Mass.Rules Civ.Proc., Rule 16; Ohio Rules Civ.Proc., Rule 16. Some states have adopted modified versions of the federal rule. See, e.g., Ind.Trial Proc.Rule 16; N.J.Civ.Prac.Rule 4:25.

9. Ely v. Reading Co., 424 F.2d 758 (3d Cir.1970); Padovani v. Bruchhausen, 293 F.2d 546, 548 (2d Cir.1961); Lockwood v. Hercules Powder Co., 7 F.R.D. 24, 28 (W.D.Mo.1947).

10. Japanese War Notes Claimants Ass'n of the Phillipines, Inc. v. U.S., 178 Ct.Cl. 630, 373 F.2d 356 (1967), cert. denied 389 U.S. 971; Meadow Gold Prods. Co. v. Wright, 278 F.2d 867, 868–69 (D.C.Cir. 1960); Lockwood v. Hercules Powder Co., 7 F.R.D. 24, 28 (W.D.Mo.1947).

11. See Clark v. Pennsylvania R.R. Co., 328 F.2d 591, 594 (2d Cir.1964), cert. denied 377 U.S. 1006; Mays v. Disneyland, Inc., 213 Cal.App.2d 297, 28 Cal.Rptr. 689 (1963); 6A C. Wright, A. Miller & M. Kane, Civil 2d § 1522, at 221; Laws, Pre–Trial Procedure, 1 F.R.D. 397, 399 (1940).

12. Federal Rules, as amended in 1983 and 1993, place significant emphasis on settlement as a goal. See Fed.Civ.Proc.Rules 16(a)(5), 16(c)(9) and 26(f). See also Mott v. City of Flora, 3 F.R.D. 232 (E.D.Ill.1943). For a criticism of the trend to encourage facilitating settlement, see, Fiss, Against Settlement, 93 Yale L.J. 1073, 1075 (1984) ("Like plea bargaining, settlement is a capitulation to the conditions of mass society and should be neither encouraged nor praised.").

13. Federal Rule 16(c)(9) provides for "the use of special procedures to assist in resolving the dispute when authorized by statute or local rule." These may include such procedures as mediation, non-binding arbitration and non-binding summary jury trials. Federal courts disagree on the extent to which, if at all, federal judges can mandate use of these techniques whereas some states have enacted statutes specifically permitting their courts to require participation in various types of alternative dispute resolution. Federal and state courts have been concerned with the nature of appropriate penalties when a party fails to participate in good faith. For a comprehensive discussion of these matters, see Note, "Case Dismissed"—or is it? Sanctions for Failure to Participate in Court–Mandated ADR, 13 Ohio St.J. on ADR 975 (1998). See also Fed.Civ.Proc.Rule 16(c)(12) permitting the court to consider "adopting special procedures for managing potentially difficult or protracted actions."

14. Identiseal Corp. v. Positive Identification Sys., Inc., 560 F.2d 298 (7th Cir. 1977); Elder–Beerman Stores Corp. v. Federated Dep't Stores, Inc., 459 F.2d 138 (6th Cir.1972); Thermo King Corp. v. White's Trucking Serv., Inc., 292 F.2d 668, 671 (5th Cir.1961).

15. See Note, Pretrial Conference Procedures, 26 S.C.L.Rev. 481, 485–86 (1974).

16. See Clark, Objectives of Pre–Trial Procedure, 17 Ohio St.L.J. 163 (1956); Moscowitz, Glimpses of Federal Trials and Procedure, 4 F.R.D. 216, 218 (1944).

the pretrial conference undoubtedly also encourages settlements because it makes parties aware of the strengths and weaknesses of their cases.[17]

Studies of the pretrial conference have attempted to evaluate its performance in terms of two criteria. First, does it encourage settlement and reduce congestion?[18] Second, does it increase the quality of those trials that do take place and of the settlement process?[19] The studies focusing on settlement do not resolve the first question; they indicate that congestion has been reduced in some parts of the country[20] and not in others.[21] The results of studies agree, however, that the issues and evidence in pretried cases are better presented, there is less likely to be surprise, trials are fairer, and settlements are more informed.[22]

§ 8.2   Procedural Aspects of the Pretrial Conference

Normally, the court is given discretion to order a pretrial conference either on its own motion or at the request of a party.[1] In some areas local rules actually require its use in all cases.[2] Mandatory use generally has been rejected, however, because a conference is a waste of time in simple cases and the procedure will not work unless the judge believes it will be useful.[3] Thus, some jurisdictions that in the past have used mandatory pretrial conferences have eliminated them;[4] in too many cases they took more time and cost more than they were worth. In some situations, jurisdictions have employed mandatory provisions forcing parties to confer outside of a formal pretrial conference setting. For example, in 1993, Federal Rule of Civil Procedure 26(f) was amended to require parties, subject to a local rule of exemption, to meet early on in the case to develop a written discovery plan to be presented to the trial court.

17. Clark, To an Understanding Use of Pre–Trial, 29 F.R.D. 454, 456 (1961). But see Walker & Thibaut, An Experimental Examination of Pretrial Conference Techniques, 55 Minn.L.Rev. 1113, 1134 (1971).

18. M. Rosenberg, The Pretrial Conference and Effective Justice 25 (1964); Gourley, Effective Pretrial Must Be the Beginning of Trial, 28 F.R.D. 165 (1962); Martz, Pretrial Preparation, 28 F.R.D. 137 (1962); Comment, California Pretrial in Action, 49 Calif.L.Rev. 909 (1961); Note, Pretrial Conferences in the District Court for Salt Lake County, 6 Utah L.Rev. 259 (1959).

19. M. Rosenberg, The Pretrial Conference and Effective Justice 25 (1964); Lynch, Pretrial Procedure, 39 N.D.L.Rev. 176 (1963).

20. Gourley, Effective Pretrial Must Be the Beginning of Trial, 28 F.R.D. 165, 168 (1962); Martz, Pretrial Preparation, 28 F.R.D. 137, 137–38 (1962); Note, Pretrial Conferences in the District Court for Salt Lake County, 6 Utah L.Rev. 259 (1959).

21. M. Rosenberg, The Pretrial Conference and Effective Justice 45 (1964); Com-

ment, California Pretrial in Action, 49 Calif.L.Rev. 909, 917 (1961).

22. M. Rosenberg, The Pretrial Conference and Effective Justice 29 (1964); Lynch, Pretrial Procedure, 39 N.D.L.Rev. 176 (1963).

§ 8.2

1. McCargo v. Hedrick, 545 F.2d 393 (4th Cir.1976); Sleek v. J. C. Penney Co., 324 F.2d 467 (3d Cir.1963); Hayden v. Chalfant Press, Inc., 281 F.2d 543 (9th Cir. 1960); Fed.Civ.Proc.Rule 16; Ala.Rules Civ. Proc., Rule 16; N.J.Civ.Prac.Rule 4:25–1(a).

2. E.g., Local Rule 235–5, U.S.Dist. Court, Hawaii; Local Rule 16, U.S.Dist. Court, Kan.; Local Rule 5, U.S.Dist.Court, W.D.Mich.

3. Proceedings, Cleveland Institute on the Federal Rules 299 (1938); Comment, California Pretrial in Action, 49 Calif.L.Rev. 909, 924, 926 (1961); Note, Pretrial Conference Procedures, 26 S.C.L.Rev. 481, 496 (1974).

4. E.g., Cal.Rules of Ct., Rule 212.

The procedure governing a particular pretrial conference is largely within the discretion of the judge. In many instances local court rules provide guidance.[5] Despite the variety of practices, some general observations can be made.

Once the court has called a pretrial conference, the attendance of the attorneys is compulsory;[6] and pre-pretrial preparation, usually including the submission of a special pretrial conference memorandum, may be required.[7] Many courts require the presence at pretrial of the same attorneys who will present the case at trial[8] or at least one who knows the case and has full power to make admissions of fact and enter into stipulations.[9] Some courts also require the presence of someone at pretrial who has settlement authority.[10] Sanctions may be imposed for failure to meet the court's requirements; these may range from the assessment of costs[11] against an offending party who is late filing a memorandum, to the entry of a default or a dismissal for failure to prosecute in the event of complete nonattendance,[12] failure to file a memorandum[13] or failure to obey the pretrial order.[14]

The court is not limited to one pretrial conference, but may call several as the nature of the case indicates.[15] In highly complex litigation several pretrial conferences may be appropriate.[16] When a series of

---

5. An examination of some of the local rules that have been adopted may be found in Note, Pretrial Conference: A Critical Examination of Local Rules Adopted by Federal District Courts, 64 Va.L.Rev. 467 (1978).

6. Identiseal Corp. v. Positive Identification Sys., Inc., 560 F.2d 298 (7th Cir. 1977); Padovani v. Bruchhausen, 293 F.2d 546 (2d Cir.1961).

7. Local Rule 5.4(D), U.S.Dist.Court, Del.; Local Civ.Rule 25.02, U.S.Dist.Court, E.Dist.N.C.; Local Rule 300.6, U.S.Dist. Court, W.Dist.Tex.; 6A C. Wright, A. Miller & M. Kane, Civil 2d § 1524, at 235–36, 238.

8. Fed.Civ.Proc.Rule 16(d) requires the presence of an attorney who will conduct the trial at the final pretrial conference when a trial plan is formulated. See also Ariz.Civ.Proc.Rule 16(d).

9. Fed.Civ.Proc.Rule 16(c) (last paragraph). See Ha–Lo Indus., Inc. v. Your Favorite Producers, Inc., 164 F.R.D. 233 (N.D.Ill.1995).

10. G. Heileman Brewing Co. v. Joseph Oat Corp., 871 F.2d 648 (7th Cir.1989) (en banc); Dvorak v. Shibata, 123 F.R.D. 608 (D.Neb.1988); Abney v. Patten, 696 F.Supp. 567 (W.D.Okl.1987).

11. Bradley v. U.S., 866 F.2d 120 (5th Cir.1989); Ikerd v. Lacy, 852 F.2d 1256 (10th Cir.1988).

Federal Rule 16, as amended in 1983, mandates that the judge require the party or attorney representing him, or both, to pay the reasonable expenses, including attorney fees, incurred by the opposing party because of any noncompliance with a scheduling of a pretrial order. This sanction can be avoided only if the judge finds the noncompliance substantially justified or if such an award would be unjust. Fed.Civ.Proc. Rule 16(f). Courts are reluctant to impose sanctions against a party because of the improper conduct of the party's attorney, at least when the party did not engage directly in the improper conduct. See, e.g., Gundacker v. Unisys Corp., 151 F.3d 842, 849 (8th Cir.1998).

12. Link v. Wabash R.R. Co., 370 U.S. 626, 82 S.Ct. 1386, 8 L.Ed.2d 734 (1962); Suarez v. Yellow Cab Co., 112 Ill.App.2d 390, 251 N.E.2d 340 (1969).

13. American Electronic Labs., Inc. v. Dopp, 369 F.Supp. 1245 (D.Del.1974); Sleek v. J. C. Penney Co., 26 F.R.D. 209 (W.D.Pa. 1960), vacated on other grounds 292 F.2d 256 (3d Cir.1961).

14. See § 8.3, below.

15. Napolitano v. Compania Sud Americana De Vapores, 421 F.2d 382 (2d Cir. 1970); Life Music, Inc. v. Edelstein, 309 F.2d 242 (2d Cir.1962) (23 pretrial conferences held).

16. Manual for Complex Litigation, Third § 21.22 (1995).

conferences is scheduled, the first may take place prior to discovery, to take care of preliminary matters and to schedule the discovery and pretrial phase of the action.[17] This prediscovery conference helps to frame the issues, as well as to keep the cost of discovery in check.[18] However, in many cases, the pretrial conference is held after discovery is essentially completed and shortly before trial.[19] This is logical because at that time each side should be thoroughly familiar with the strengths and weaknesses of its case and know which issues and facts it wishes to contest and which it is willing to concede. Thus, the parties are at an excellent point either to make an informed settlement or to narrow the case for trial to those matters that genuinely are disputed.

In most jurisdictions a wide range of matters may be dealt with at a pretrial conference. It may be used to define the issues and facts still in contention,[20] to weed out extraneous issues,[21] and to make rulings relating to the remedies that might be awarded.[22] Amendments to the pleadings may be ordered if necessary.[23] To facilitate the presentation of evidence at trial, unnecessary items of proof may be eliminated,[24] the authenticity of documents may be determined,[25] rulings on the admissibility of evidence may be made,[26] and lists of documents and witnesses to be presented at trial may be required.[27] Matters also may be referred to a master whose findings may be introduced as evidence in a jury trial.[28]

---

17. Under Fed.Civ.Proc.Rule 16(b), subject to exemption by local rule, a scheduling order now is required within 120 days after filing the complaint. The court normally will have discussed the schedule with the parties and will have received from the parties, pursuant to Fed.Civ.Proc.Rule 26(f), a discovery plan prior to issuing a scheduling order. This order may be issued with or without a formal scheduling conference. Once issued, the order can only be modified upon a showing of good cause. Fed.Civ.Proc.Rule 16(b) (last paragraph).

18. Manual for Complex Litigation, Third § 21.21 (1995).

19. Commercial Ins. Co. v. Smith, 417 F.2d 1330 (10th Cir.1969); Century Refining Co. v. Hall, 316 F.2d 15 (10th Cir.1963); Clark, Objectives of Pre–Trial Procedure, 17 Ohio St.L.J. 163, 165 (1956).

20. FDIC v. Glickman, 450 F.2d 416, 419 (9th Cir.1971); Manbeck v. Ostrowski, 384 F.2d 970 (D.C.Cir.1967), cert. denied 390 U.S. 966.

21. Manbeck v. Ostrowski, 384 F.2d 970 (D.C.Cir.1967), cert. denied 390 U.S. 966; Mull v. Ford Motor Co., 368 F.2d 713 (2d Cir.1966).

22. Lundberg v. Welles, 93 F.Supp. 359, 361 (S.D.N.Y.1950).

23. FDIC v. Glickman, 450 F.2d 416 (9th Cir.1971); Hatridge v. Seaboard Sur.,

74 F.R.D. 6 (E.D.Okl.1976); Taylor v. S & M Lamp Co., 190 Cal.App.2d 700, 12 Cal. Rptr. 323 (1961).

24. FDIC v. Glickman, 450 F.2d 416 (9th Cir.1971); Manbeck v. Ostrowski, 384 F.2d 970 (D.C.Cir.1967), cert. denied 390 U.S. 966. The 1993 amendments to the federal rule permit the court to make rulings restricting or limiting expert testimony. Fed.Civ.Proc.Rule 16(c)(4).

25. Pritchett v. Etheridge, 172 F.2d 822 (5th Cir.1949).

26. Pritchett v. Etheridge, 172 F.2d 822 (5th Cir.1949); In re Panoceanic Tankers Corp., 54 F.R.D. 283 (S.D.N.Y.1971); Edenfield v. Crisp, 186 So.2d 545 (Fla.App. 1966).

27. Brock v. R.J. Auto Parts & Serv., Inc., 864 F.2d 677 (10th Cir.1988); Clark v. Pennsylvania R.R. Co., 328 F.2d 591 (2d Cir.1964), cert. denied 377 U.S. 1006; Syracuse Broadcasting Corp. v. Newhouse, 295 F.2d 269 (2d Cir.1961); Uinta Oil Refining Co. v. Continental Oil Co., 226 F.Supp. 495, 505 n. 39 (D.Utah 1964); Bodnar v. Jackson, 205 Kan. 469, 470 P.2d 726 (1970); Fairbanks Publishing Co. v. Francisco, 390 P.2d 784 (Alaska 1964); Glisan v. Kurth, 153 Colo. 102, 384 P.2d 946 (1963).

28. Fed.Civ.Proc.Rule 53(e). See Wilson v. Kennedy, 75 F.Supp. 592 (W.D.Pa. 1948); Fed.Civ.Proc.Rule 16.

Under broad catchall provisions in the federal type of pretrial conference rule, courts also have used the conference to rule on preliminary matters such as jurisdiction,[29] rather than taking those issues up by motion at the beginning of trial. Thus, courts have decided questions relating to stays,[30] consolidation or separation of issues for trial,[31] the right to a jury trial,[32] and the details of ongoing discovery[33] at pretrial conferences. In view of the wide range of matters that may be determined at pretrial and that will control the trial, counsel need to be fully prepared on all aspects of their cases at the final pretrial conference.

Certain matters have been definitely excluded from the purview of the pretrial conference, however. One party may not use it to steal his opponent's trial preparation; counsel are not to use the conference as a separate discovery device or for a fishing expedition.[34] Further, the conference may not serve as a substitute for trial.[35] Although the pretrial judge may grant summary judgment if there are no triable issues remaining,[36] the judge has no power to determine issues of fact.[37] The purpose of the conference is to achieve voluntary agreements; it is improper for the court to force concessions or settlement upon unwilling parties.[38] Nevertheless, some courts have required parties to engage in

29. A. H. Emery Co. v. Marcan Prods. Corp., 389 F.2d 11 (2d Cir.1968), cert. denied 393 U.S. 835.

30. Royster v. Ruggerio, 2 F.R.D. 429 (E.D.Mich.1941), modified on other grounds 128 F.2d 197 (6th Cir.1942); Niazi v. St. Paul Mercury Ins. Co., 265 Minn. 222, 121 N.W.2d 349 (1963).

31. Joseph v. Donover Co., 261 F.2d 812 (9th Cir.1958).

In 1993, Federal Rule 16(c)(13) was introduced to make clear that consideration of an order for a separate trial with respect to a claim, counterclaim, cross-claim or any particular issue of fact is a proper subject of discussion at a pretrial conference.

32. In re 1208, Inc., 188 F.Supp. 664 (E.D.Pa.1960); Schram v. Kolowich, 2 F.R.D. 343 (E.D.Mich.1942).

33. E.g., Buffington v. Wood, 351 F.2d 292 (3d Cir.1965); Di Donna v. Zigarelli, 61 N.J.Super. 302, 160 A.2d 655 (1960). See Judicial Conference of the United States, Proposed Amendments to the Federal Rules of Civil Procedure Relating to Discovery, 48 F.R.D. 485, 524, 532 (1969). Pretrial matters regarding discovery are now governed by a combination of Fed.Civ.Proc.Rules 16 and 26(f).

34. Berger v. Brannan, 172 F.2d 241 (10th Cir.1949), cert. denied 337 U.S. 941; Package Machinery Co. v. Hayssen Mfg. Co., 164 F.Supp. 904 (E.D.Wis.1958), affirmed on other grounds 266 F.2d 56 (7th Cir.1959). But see Brister, Lonesome Docket: Using the Texas Rules to Shorten Trials

and Delay, 46 Baylor L.Rev. 525, 532 (1994).

35. Lynn v. Smith, 281 F.2d 501 (3d Cir.1960); Syracuse Broadcasting Corp. v. Newhouse, 271 F.2d 910 (2d Cir.1959). See Gullett v. McCormick, 421 S.W.2d 352 (Ky. 1967).

36. Newman v. Granger, 141 F.Supp. 37 (W.D.Pa.1956), affirmed per curiam 239 F.2d 384 (3d Cir.1957); McComb v. Trimmer, 85 F.Supp. 565 (D.N.J.1949); Green v. Kaesler–Allen Lumber Co., 197 Kan. 788, 420 P.2d 1019 (1966); Ellis v. Woods, 453 S.W.2d 509 (Tex.Civ.App.1970).

The 1993 amendments to the federal rules added Federal Rule !6(c)(14) whereby the court may direct that a party or parties present evidence early in the trial on an issue that could be the basis for a judgment as a matter of law.

37. Fidelity & Deposit Co. v. Southern Utilities, Inc., 726 F.2d 692 (11th Cir.1984); Lynn v. Smith, 281 F.2d 501 (3d Cir.1960).

38. J. F. Edwards Constr. Co. v. Anderson Safeway Guard Rail Corp., 542 F.2d 1318 (7th Cir.1976) (cannot force parties to stipulate facts); Gullett v. McCormick, 421 S.W.2d 352 (Ky.1967); People ex rel. Horwitz v. Canel, 34 Ill.2d 306, 215 N.E.2d 255 (1966). Cf. Krattenstein v. G. Fox & Co., 155 Conn. 609, 236 A.2d 466 (1967). See also the first paragraph of the Advisory Committee Note to the 1993 Amendment to Fed.Civ.Proc.Rule 16(c).

various alternate dispute resolution procedures and to do so in good faith.[39]

Given the broad scope of the pretrial conference, and the powers of the presiding judge, there has been some discussion whether the pretrial judge should be the judge who will try the case. When the conference is used primarily as a tool to induce settlement, a separate judge for pretrial is to be preferred because this reduces coercion and lessens attorneys' fears that positions taken in pretrial discussions will prejudice them with the judge at trial if a settlement is not reached.[40] Generally, if the conference is designed primarily for trial preparation, most lawyers would favor having the same judge for pretrial and trial; they view the conference as focusing the case not only for the parties but also for the court, allowing the judge to spend time prior to trial becoming familiar with the issues and preparing background on the rulings that will have to be made at trial.[41] Some states deal with this problem by using a separate settlement calendar;[42] in these jurisdictions, the pretrial judge will try the case without having participated in the settlement conference.

The broad discretionary powers of trial judges to conduct pretrial conferences, especially as those powers have been increased over the years, have not been without adverse criticism. This is particularly true when the result is to obviate a trial on the merits on some matters.[43] There is concern over the fact that judges, without controls, have been arbitrary and have even acted out of bias, with a heavy impact on the outcome of their cases.[44]

§ 8.3 The Pretrial Order

Although some state pretrial regulations do not mandate it,[1] the federal rule and most of its state counterparts require the court to issue a pretrial order embodying the rulings made and matters agreed upon at the pretrial conference.[2] The pretrial order should incorporate all admis-

---

39. See § 8.1 n.13, above.

40. Thomas, The Story of Pretrial in the Common Pleas Courts of Cuyahoga County, 7 W.Res.L.Rev. 368, 391 (1953); Note, Pretrial Conference Procedures, 26 S.C.L.Rev. 481, 497 (1974); Note, Pretrial Conferences in the District Court for Salt Lake County, 6 Utah L.Rev. 259, 261 (1959).

41. See Clark, Objectives of Pre–Trial Procedure, 17 Ohio St.L.J. 163, 165 (1956); Kincaid, A Judge's Handbook of Pre–Trial Procedure, 17 F.R.D. 437, 445 (1955); Lynch, Pretrial Procedure, 39 N.D.L.Rev. 176, 185–86 (1963); Wright, The Pretrial Conference, 28 F.R.D. 141, 148 (1962); Note, Pretrial Conference Procedures, 26 S.C.L.Rev. 481, 496 (1974).

42. E.g., Cal.Rules of Ct., Rule 222.

43. Hench, Mandatory Disclosure and Equal Access to Justice: The 1993 Federal Discovery Rules Amendments and the Just, Speedy and Inexpensive Determination of Every Action, 67 Temple. L.Rev. 179, 233 (1994) ("'[T]he procrustean 1993 amendments [to the federal pretrial rules] are ill-conceived, at best, and will have to be repealed before serious progress [regarding case management] can be made.'").

44. Peterson, Restoring Structural Checks on Judicial Power in the Era of Managerial Judging, 29 UC Davis L.Rev. 41, 67–83 (1995).

§ 8.3

1. E.g., N.C.Gen.Stat. § 1A–1, Rules Civ.Proc., Rule 16.

2. Fed.Civ.Proc.Rule 16(e); N.M.Dist. Ct.Rules Civ.Proc., Rule 1–016.

sions and stipulations of the parties, list the issues remaining for trial, and note any requirements for filing statements or lists of evidence and witnesses.[3] In order to preserve the work done at pretrial for use at trial and to avoid its duplication there, the pretrial order is particularly necessary in those cases in which the pretrial judge will not try the case.[4]

The method of formulating the pretrial order is within the court's discretion; it frequently is done by requiring all counsel to draft an order and to present it for the court's approval.[5] If counsel cannot agree upon an order, the court will formulate its own.[6]

The order controls the subsequent course of the action.[7] Although it can be modified to prevent manifest injustice,[8] some courts may require a substantial showing of cause and may require any possibility of prejudice to the opposing party to be overcome.[9] The burden placed on a party seeking to amend a pretrial order is greater than that imposed when an amendment to the pleadings is sought.[10] This simply reflects the different functions of the pleadings[11] and the pretrial conference[12] and recognizes that the best way to make the conference an effective means of controlling or shaping the trial is to enforce the pretrial orders.[13] Thus, instructions given or evidence introduced outside the scope of the pretrial order may result in a mistrial or in the reopening of the case following appeal.[14] Failure to comply with the order may result in striking a defense,[15] the exclusion of evidence,[16] or, in an extreme case, dismissal of the action.[17] Thus great care must be taken in drafting the

3. U.S. v. An Article of Drug, etc., Acnotabs, 207 F.Supp. 758 (D.N.J.1962); Clark v. U.S., 13 F.R.D. 342, 344 (D.Or. 1952).

4. See Clark, Objectives of Pre–Trial Procedure, 17 Ohio St.L.J. 163, 169 (1956).

5. Bradford Novelty Co. v. Samuel Eppy & Co., 164 F.Supp. 798 (E.D.N.Y. 1958); Curto v. International Longshoremen's & Warehousemen's Union, 107 F.Supp. 805 (D.Or.1952), affirmed on other grounds 226 F.2d 875 (9th Cir.1955), cert. denied 351 U.S. 963.

6. See Life Music Inc. v. Edelstein, 309 F.2d 242, 243 (2d Cir.1962); Brinn v. Bull Insular Lines, Inc., 28 F.R.D. 578 (E.D.Pa. 1961).

7. Smith v. Washington Sheraton Corp., 135 F.3d 779 (D.C.Cir.1998); American Home Assurance Co. v. Cessna Aircraft Co., 551 F.2d 804 (10th Cir.1977); Colvin v. U.S. ex rel. Magini Leasing & Contracting, 549 F.2d 1338 (9th Cir.1977).

8. Summers v. Missouri Pac. R.R., 132 F.3d 599, 604–06 (10th Cir.1997) (failure to admit amendment was an abuse of discretion); Stahlin v. Hilton Hotels Corp., 484 F.2d 580 (7th Cir.1973); Wallin v. Fuller, 476 F.2d 1204 (5th Cir.1973); Herrell v. Maddux, 217 Kan. 192, 535 P.2d 935

(1975). See also HBE Leasing Corp. v. Frank, 22 F.3d 41, 44–45 (2d Cir.1994).

9. McKey v. Fairbairn, 345 F.2d 739 (D.C.Cir.1965); City of Lakeland v. Union Oil Co., 352 F.Supp. 758 (M.D.Fla.1973); Cornish v. U.S., 221 F.Supp. 658 (D.Or. 1963), reversed on other grounds 348 F.2d 175 (9th Cir.1965).

10. See § 5.26, above.

11. See § 5.2, above.

12. See § 8.1, above.

13. Note, Variance From the Pre–Trial Order, 60 Yale L.J. 175 (1951).

14. Clark v. Pennsylvania R. Co., 328 F.2d 591 (2d Cir.1964), cert. denied 377 U.S. 1006; Seaboldt v. Pennsylvania R. Co., 290 F.2d 296 (3d Cir.1961).

15. G & R Corp. v. American Sec. & Trust Co., 523 F.2d 1164 (D.C.Cir.1975); Associated Press v. Cook, 513 F.2d 1300 (10th Cir.1975).

16. Matheny v. Porter, 158 F.2d 478 (10th Cir.1946); Mellone v. Lewis, 233 Cal. App.2d 4, 43 Cal.Rptr. 412 (1965).

17. Delta Theatres, Inc. v. Paramount Pictures, Inc., 398 F.2d 323 (5th Cir.1968), cert. denied 393 U.S. 1050; Wirtz v. Hooper–Holmes Bureau, Inc., 327 F.2d 939 (5th

pretrial order. Objections to it are waived if not raised at the outset of the trial,[18] and they will lead to reversal upon appeal only if the order was an abuse of the trial court's discretion.[19]

Cir.1964); Kromat v. Vestevich, 14 Mich. App. 291, 165 N.W.2d 428 (1968). Cf. Uxmal Corp. Ltd. v. Wall Indus., Inc., 55 F.R.D. 219 (S.D.Fla.1972) (defendant's failure to comply with order or respond to plaintiff's motion for summary judgment resulted in judgment for plaintiff).

18. Hodgson v. Humphries, 454 F.2d 1279 (10th Cir.1972); Community Nat. Life

Ins. Co. v. Parker Square Sav. & Loan Ass'n, 406 F.2d 603 (10th Cir.1969).

19. Summers v. Missouri Pac. R.R., 132 F.3d 599, 604–06 (10th Cir.1997); Spellacy v. Southern Pacific Co., 428 F.2d 619 (9th Cir.1970); Ely v. Reading Co., 424 F.2d 758 (3d Cir.1970); Cruz v. U.S. Lines Co., 386 F.2d 803, 804 (2d Cir.1967).

§§ 8.4–9.0 are reserved for supplementary material.

Chapter 9

ADJUDICATION WITHOUT TRIAL

Analysis

A. SUMMARY JUDGMENT

A. SUMMARY JUDGMENT

§ 9.1 History and Purpose

Under traditional common law and code pleading rules a party's demurrer or equivalent motion was determined solely upon the face of the pleadings. The attacking party could not "go behind the pleading" to show that it had no basis in fact; so-called "speaking demurrers" were not allowed. It was assumed that pleadings were all made in good faith, based on evidence that could be presented at trial. Therefore, any challenge to the truth of a pleading that was sufficient in law to state a claim or a defense would necessitate a trial.[1]

Modern courts have recognized, however, that there are occasions in which it appears from the pleadings that a legitimate legal dispute exists when in fact one does not.[2] When the existence or nonexistence of the particular facts underlying a dispute can be established conclusively without trial, it would be wasteful to proceed as if they were actually in dispute.[3] The need for some kind of adjudicatory procedure to deal with

---

§ 9.1

1. See C. Clark, Code Pleading § 80 (2d ed.1947).

2. See R. Millar, Civil Procedure of the Trial Court in Historical Perspective 237–50 (1952).

3. Comment, Summary Judgment, 25 Wash.L.Rev. 71, 74 (1950). See 10A C.

this situation is particularly evident when the undisputed issues are crucial ones that can determine the entire case without trial.

Initially some jurisdictions avoided the normal rule prohibiting "speaking demurrers," by recognizing an inherent power in the court to strike "sham" pleadings.[4] The difficulty was that there was no standard for determining what was sham and what was not.[5] It was unclear, for example, whether a pleading was sham only if it was filed in bad faith or because there was overwhelming evidence to refute it. It also was unclear just what evidence was available to establish that a pleading was sham and how much evidence was necessary before a pleading or a portion of it would be stricken.

As a result, most jurisdictions today have adopted a formal procedure, called a motion for summary judgment,[6] to determine whether an issue set forth in the pleadings is in fact in dispute and, if not, to eliminate any portion of the case for which trial is not required. Summary judgment can be sought and granted not only on an entire claim or defense, but as to any portion thereof.[7] The court can make a determination on any single claim, counterclaim, defense, or a portion of a claim, such as the existence of liability or the amount of damages to be awarded if liability is established at trial.[8]

In many instances the lines between traditional challenges to the pleadings and motions for summary judgment have been blurred.[9] Thus, under modern rules a motion to dismiss for failure to state a claim or a motion for judgment on the pleadings can be treated as a motion for

Wright, A. Miller & M. Kane, Civil 3d § 2712.

4. See C. Clark, Code Pleading § 41, at 254 (2d ed.1947). The power to disregard, strike, or nullify sham pleadings generally was invoked only against sham defenses, the object being to "prevent delay and expense to the plaintiff." Pogson, Truth in Pleading, 8 N.Y.U.L.Q.Rev. 41, 57–58 (1930), quoting Brewster v. Hall, 6 Cow. 34 (N.Y.1826).

5. See C. Clark, Code Pleading § 87, at 550–54 (2d ed.1947); Pogson, Truth in Pleading, 8 N.Y.U.L.Q.Rev. 41 (1930).

6. See, e.g., Fed.Civ.Proc.Rule 56. For the history and nature of summary judgment procedure, see generally Bauman, The Evolution of the Summary Judgment Procedure, 31 Ind.L.J. 329 (1956); Clark & Somenow, The Summary Judgment, 38 Yale L.J. 423 (1929); Korn & Paley, Survey of Summary Judgment, Judgment on the Pleadings and Related Pre–Trial Procedures, 42 Cornell L.Q. 483 (1957).

7. E.g., Fed.Civ.Proc.Rule 56(c), (d); West's Ann.Cal.Code Civ.Proc. § 437c; Mich.Ct.Rules 1985, 2.116; Pa.Rules Civ. Proc., Rule 1035.5, See 10B C. Wright, A. Miller & M. Kane, Civil 3d §§ 2736–37.

8. Many courts hold that summary judgment on less than an entire claim or defense—partial summary judgment—is not a final judgment. Rather, it is an interlocutory order that certain issues shall be deemed established at trial and, as such, the order is not immediately appealable. Clark v. Kraftco Corp., 447 F.2d 933, 936 (2d Cir.1971); Hibbard Office World, Inc. v. F. Jay, 580 S.W.2d 55, 57 (Tex.Civ.App. 1979). But see N.Y.—McKinney's CPLR 3212(e), authorizing courts to enter final summary judgment as to any part of one or more causes of action, or alternatively to hold the entry of summary judgment in abeyance pending the determination of any remaining cause of action.

The nature and effect of partial summary judgment may vary greatly depending upon the law of the jurisdiction and the facts of the particular action. See generally Comment, Partial Summary Judgment Under Rule 56(a), 32 U.Chi.L.Rev. 816 (1965); Annot., 75 A.L.R.2d 1201 (1961); Annot., 67 A.L.R.2d 1456 (1959).

9. See 10A C. Wright, A. Miller & M. Kane, Civil 3d § 2713.

summary judgment when the moving party introduces outside matter and clearly intends to test not only whether the allegations are sufficient on their face to state a claim, but also whether there is any factual basis for those allegations.[10] Thus, when a party includes affidavits or other appropriate materials with a pleading challenge in order to refute the existence of a genuine factual dispute, the trial judge has discretion to treat the challenge as a motion for summary judgment.[11] This discretion typically will be exercised in favor of converting the motion, unless the responding party was so taken by surprise that he would be prejudiced thereby.[12] Of course, the court always can delay a hearing on the summary judgment motion until the respondent has had time to prepare,[13] thereby mitigating any possible prejudice.

Although the main purpose of summary judgment is to avoid useless trials[14] and at the same time achieve a final determination on the merits, the device also may be used to simplify trial or better prepare for trial.[15] This will occur if summary judgment is entered only on certain issues or claims, eliminating them from the trial process. Further, even if sum-

---

10. E.g., Fed.Civ.Proc.Rule 12(b), (c); Official Code Ga.Ann. § 9–11–12(b), (c); N.Y.—McKinney's CPLR 3211(c).

No other pretrial motion under Federal Rule 12 may be transformed into a summary judgment. For example, Rule 12(f) does not permit a court to treat a motion to strike an insufficient defense as a motion for summary judgment. See Uniroyal, Inc. v. Heller, 65 F.R.D. 83 (S.D.N.Y.1974). Compare N.Y.—McKinney's CPLR 3211(c), which gives New York courts the option of converting other pretrial motions into summary judgment motions.

11. See, e.g., Carter v. Stanton, 405 U.S. 669, 671, 92 S.Ct. 1232, 31 L.Ed.2d 569 (1972); Barrett v. United Hosp., 376 F.Supp. 791 (S.D.N.Y.1974), affirmed without opinion 506 F.2d 1395 (2d Cir.1974); Parks v. Macro–Dynamics, Inc., 121 Ariz. 517, 591 P.2d 1005 (App.1979); SaBell's, Inc. v. Flens, 42 Colo.App. 421, 599 P.2d 950 (1979), affirmed on the merits 627 P.2d 750 (Colo.1981); Kocsor v. Eastland, 44 A.D.2d 869, 355 N.Y.S.2d 503 (1974); Lineberger v. Welsh, 290 A.2d 847 (Del.Ch. 1972).

12. See, e.g., Burick v. Edward Rose & Sons, 18 F.3d 514 (7th Cir.1994)(trial court erred in converting a Rule 12(b)(6) motion to dismiss to a motion for summary judgment without giving plaintiff notice of the conversion and an opportunity to respond). But see C.B. Trucking, Inc. v. Waste Management, Inc., 137 F.3d 41 (1st Cir.1998) (express notice of conversion of motion to dismiss into a summary judgment motion is unnecessary if surrounding circumstances give reasonable notice and the parties have

an opportunity to present all pertinent materials).

The problem of surprising an unsuspecting litigant by converting a pleading challenge to a judgment on the merits also is presented by the issue of whether the court can grant summary judgment for the nonmoving party or sua sponte. See § 9.2, below.

13. Federal Rules 12(b) and 12(c), and their state counterparts, provide that before a motion to dismiss or for judgment on the pleadings may be treated as one for summary judgment, all parties shall be given a "reasonable opportunity" to present all pertinent material. See Plante v. Shivar, 540 F.2d 1233 (4th Cir.1976); Adams v. Campbell County School Dist., 483 F.2d 1351 (10th Cir.1973); Parks v. Macro–Dynamics, Inc., 121 Ariz. 517, 591 P.2d 1005 (App. 1979); Gronim v. Dessau, 58 A.D.2d 566, 396 N.Y.S.2d 326 (1977).

14. Even though summary judgment obviates the need for trial, it does not impinge on any jury trial rights. The court's role on summary judgment is not to weigh the evidence. Rather, it is to determine whether there are any factual questions for the jury to decide. Soria v. Oxnard School Dist. Bd. of Trustees, 488 F.2d 579 (9th Cir.1973), cert. denied 416 U.S. 951; Church v. Arko, 75 Cal.App.3d 291, 142 Cal.Rptr. 92 (1977); Harrell v. Wilson, 233 Ga. 899, 213 S.E.2d 871 (1975); Earl M. Jorgensen Co. v. Mark Constr., Inc., 56 Hawaii 466, 540 P.2d 978 (1975).

15. See 10A C. Wright, A. Miller & M. Kane, Civil 3d § 2712.

mary judgment ultimately is denied,[16] the exchange of information that occurs in order for the court to rule on the motion may help both parties in shaping their cases for trial.[17]

§ 9.2 Procedure for Obtaining a Summary Judgment

Summary judgment typically is granted upon a motion by one of the parties.[1] The exact timing of summary judgment motions varies in each judicial system, although some general observations can be made. If the moving party also is the one seeking relief in the case, some jurisdictions require the movant to wait a period of time, usually the time given the defending party to file an answer, before permitting the motion to be made.[2] This is to ensure that the opposing party will have an opportunity to obtain legal counsel and prepare a response to the motion. Other jurisdictions allow the motion to be filed at any time, relying upon the discretion of the trial judge to ensure that the responding party has time to prepare.[3] Typically, summary judgment motions are not made until each side has had a chance to engage in formal discovery to gather what evidence there is in support of his or her position.[4]

---

16. There is some evidence that at least in federal practice, the number of cases dismissed on a motion for summary judgment actually is relatively small. McLaughlan, An Empirical Study of The Federal Summary Judgment Role, 6 J.Legal Studies 427 (1977).

17. It should be noted that summary judgment may be used tactically as a discovery device, particularly to ascertain details of an opposing party's legal contentions that cannot be obtained through normal discovery. See § 7.5, above.

§ 9.2

1. In some cases both parties file summary judgment motions. In that event, the court must rule on each motion separately; the filing of cross-motions is not treated as a concession by the parties that no genuine factual issues remain for trial. See 10A C. Wright, A. Miller & M. Kane, Civil 3d § 2720.

Also, in some cases summary judgment will be granted by the court sua sponte, absent any motion by either party. See notes 11 and 12, below.

2. In the federal courts, a party seeking relief may move for summary judgment 20 days after the commencement of the action or after service of a motion by the adverse party; the adverse party may move for summary judgment at any time. Fed. Civ.Proc.Rule 56(a), (b). See N.Y.—McKinney's CPLR 3212(a) (motion allowed after defendant files answer); West's Ann.Cal. Code Civ.Proc. § 437c(a) (motion allowed after 60 days from adverse party's appear-

ance in the action or at such earlier time as the court may direct). See generally Annot., 85 A.L.R.2d 825 (1962).

In 1990 the Advisory Committee proposed an amendment to Rule 56 to eliminate the time requirement for filing a summary judgment motion. The amendment was not adopted.

3. Even when a court is allowed to entertain a summary judgment motion before the defendant has answered, e.g., Fla.—West's F.S.A.Rules Civ.Proc., Rule 1.510, courts generally will not grant the motion unless it appears that an answer could not raise a material fact issue. Coast Cities Coaches, Inc. v. Whyte, 130 So.2d 121 (Fla.App.1961); Goldstein v. Florida Fishermen's Supply Co., 116 So.2d 453 (Fla.App. 1959).

4. Under Federal Rule 56(f) and similar state rules, the trial court has broad discretion to delay hearing summary judgment motions. See Littlejohn v. Shell Oil Co., 483 F.2d 1140 (5th Cir.1973), cert. denied 414 U.S. 1116, vacating summary judgment to permit additional discovery. See also § 9.3, below.

There appears to be a current trend by which a nonmovant's failure formally to request a Rule 56(f) extension may result in the trial court's grant of summary judgment before completion of discovery. See, e.g., Springfield Terminal Ry. v. Canadian Pacific Ltd., 133 F.3d 103 (1st Cir.1997); Rivera–Flores v. Bristol–Myers Squibb Caribbean, 112 F.3d 9 (1st Cir.1997). See also Duffy v. Wolle, 123 F.3d 1026 (8th Cir.

Since the object of summary judgment is to pierce the pleadings and allow a judgment on the merits without the necessity of a trial, the moving party most often will support the motion with outside evidence. Thus, it is very important that the opposing side have an opportunity to present whatever countervailing evidence might exist to establish the need for a trial. Recognizing this, most summary judgment provisions require the movant to serve the motion on the opponent a number of days before the court hearing on the matter.[5]

On occasion, the affidavits and other information submitted with a summary judgment motion make it clear that not only should summary judgment for the moving party be denied, but it should be granted for the opposing side. Some state rules specifically authorize summary judgment under these circumstances.[6] In most jurisdictions the generally applicable summary judgment provision does not address this issue,[7] and some jurisdictions have refused to grant summary judgment absent a motion;[8] the trend, however, is clearly to allow judgment for the non-moving party.[9] This conclusion seems particularly justified as long as the

1997), cert. denied ＿ U.S. ＿, 118 S.Ct. 1839 (trial judge granted summary judgment despite plaintiff's motion under Rule 56(f) because plaintiff failed to make supportable showing of discrimination. The court in the Duffy case stated that plaintiff had an obligation to make a good faith showing of how additional time for discovery would establish the existence of material issues of fact.) There are cases appearing to go the other way. See, e.g. Kachmar v. SunGard Data Sys., Inc., 109 F.3d 173 (3d Cir.1997)(grant of summary judgment reversed; trial court failed to explain why plaintiff's Rule 56(f) motion had not been granted); Burick v. Edward Rose & Sons, 18 F.3d 514 (7th Cir.1994).

Under an amendment proposed in 1991, Rule 56(g) would have been revised to give explicit recognition of the court's broad discretion in conducting Rule 56 proceedings. Proposed Amendments to the Federal Rules of Civil Procedure, Revised Rule 56(g) (1991).

5. In the federal courts, the summary judgment motion must be served "at least 10 days before the time fixed for the hearing." Fed.Civ.Proc.Rule 56(c). See West's Ann.Cal.Code Civ.Proc. § 437c(a) ("at least 28 days before * * * "); Mass.Rules Civ. Proc., Rule 56(c) ("at least 10 days before * * * "); Ohio Rules Civ.Proc., Rule 56(C) ("at least 14 days before * * * ").

In 1991 a proposed amendment to Rule 56(c) would have replaced the 10 day limit with a standard of "reasonable opportunity" and "sufficient time" to marshal and present evidentiary materials to the court. Proposed Amendments to the Federal Rules

of Civil Procedure, Revised Rule 56(c) (1991).

6. E.g., Md.Rule 2–501(e); Me.Rules Civ.Proc., Rule 56(c); Mich.Ct.Rules 1985, 2.116(I)(2); N.Y.—McKinney's CPLR 3212(b); N.D.Rules Civ.Proc., Rule 56(c); Wis.Stat.Ann. 802.08(6).

7. E.g., Fed.Civ.Proc.Rule 56; Ariz. Rules Civ.Proc., Rule 56. For a discussion of the federal courts' power to grant summary judgment for a nonmoving party, see 10A C. Wright, A. Miller & M. Kane, Civil 3d § 2720.

Federal Rule 56(a) has not been changed specifically to permit summary judgment for the nonmoving party despite a proposed revision that would have read, "The court * * * may enter summary judgment *for or against* a claimant * * * "(Emphasis added). Proposed Amendments to the Federal Rules of Civil Procedure, Revised Rule 56(a) (1991).

8. See, e.g., Denton v. Mr. Swiss of Missouri, Inc., 564 F.2d 236, 241 n. 9 (8th Cir.1977); Bell v. Taca, Inc., 493 S.W.2d 281 (Tex.Civ.App.1973). The impact of these decisions often is negligible because of the willingness to give the party deserving summary judgment sufficient time to file a cross-motion. E.g., Pinkus v. Reilly, 71 F.Supp. 993 (D.N.J.1947), affirmed on other grounds 170 F.2d 786 (3d Cir.1948), affirmed on other grounds 338 U.S. 269.

9. See Lowenschuss v. Kane, 520 F.2d 255 (2d Cir.1975); Giovanelli v. First Fed. Sav. & Loan Ass'n, 120 Ariz. 577, 587 P.2d 763 (App.1978); Green v. Higgins, 217 Kan. 217, 535 P.2d 446 (1975); Port Authority of

party against whom the motion is to be granted is provided an opportunity to show that she needs time to obtain and present additional information that could establish the existence of a factual dispute.[10]

A similar issue arises concerning whether the court can enter summary judgment in the absence of any motion by the parties.[11] Although this situation does raise concerns about whether the party against whom summary judgment is being entered has had an opportunity to obtain and present evidence showing that a genuine fact issue does exist, allowing summary judgment seems consistent with the purpose of avoiding unnecessary trials. As long as the opposing party is not taken by surprise, and has a chance to show why summary judgment should not be entered, the absence of a formal motion should not preclude the entry of summary judgment.[12]

Because summary judgment is, in effect, a preview of the evidence the parties intend to introduce at trial, any admissible evidence is appropriate,[13] even the oral testimony of potential witnesses.[14] However, since the purpose of summary judgment is only to determine if a dispute exists, oral testimony rarely will be offered and, if it is, the court, in its discretion, may refuse to hear it,[15] preferring to save time by requiring the evidence to be presented in affidavit form. Summary judgment hearings thus typically involve only the argument of counsel and the court may dispense with a hearing if it determines that the papers contain sufficient information to allow a ruling on the motion.[16]

Allegheny County v. Flaherty, 6 Pa. Cmwlth. 135, 293 A.2d 152 (1972).

10. See Memphis Trust Co. v. Board of Governors of Federal Reserve Sys., 584 F.2d 921 (6th Cir.1978); Dabney v. Cunningham, 317 F.Supp. 57 (E.D.Va.1970).

11. Compare Matter of Hailey, 621 F.2d 169 (5th Cir.1980); Choudhry v. Jenkins, 559 F.2d 1085 (7th Cir.1977), cert. denied 434 U.S. 997 (summary judgment sua sponte not allowed), with Kistner v. Califano, 579 F.2d 1004 (6th Cir.1978), and FLLI Moretti Cereali v. Continental Grain Co., 563 F.2d 563 (2d Cir.1977) (summary judgment sua sponte allowed if notice and opportunity to be heard given).

12. See U.S. v. Grayson, 879 F.2d 620 (9th Cir.1989); Kennedy v. Whitehurst, 509 F.Supp. 226 (D.D.C.1981), affirmed 690 F.2d 951 (D.C.Cir.1982); Southern Erectors, Inc. v. Olga Coal Co., 159 W.Va. 385, 223 S.E.2d 46, 51 (1976). See also Wood v. Santa Barbara Chamber of Commerce, Inc., 507 F.Supp. 1128 (D.Nev.1980).

13. Miller v. City of Fairbanks, 509 P.2d 826 (Alaska 1973) (parties may utilize pleadings, affidavits and any other materials otherwise admissible in evidence). See 10A C. Wright, A. Miller & M. Kane, Civil

3d §§ 2721–24, for a discussion of the various materials that may be used.

14. Federal Rule 43(e), which authorizes the use of oral testimony on motions, has been held applicable to motions for summary judgment, even though Federal Rule 56 is silent on the point. See, e.g., Schultz v. Young Men's Christian Ass'n, 139 F.3d 286 (1st Cir.1998); Arrington v. City of Fairfield, 414 F.2d 687 (5th Cir. 1969); Hazelgrove v. Ford Motor Co., 428 F.Supp. 1096 (E.D.Va.1977). Accord, Tasco, Inc. v. Winkel, 281 N.W.2d 280 (Iowa 1979); Daniels v. Paddock, 145 Mont. 207, 399 P.2d 740 (1965). But see Mallory v. Dorothy Prinzhorn Real Estate, Inc., 535 S.W.2d 371 (Tex.Civ.App.1976) (Texas courts prohibited from hearing oral testimony on summary judgment motion).

15. E.g., McGuire v. Columbia Broadcasting System, Inc., 399 F.2d 902 (9th Cir. 1968); James Burrough Ltd. v. Lesher, 309 F.Supp. 1154 (S.D.Ind.1969).

16. There is no right to a hearing on summary judgment motions. Pagan v. Horton, 464 A.2d 146 (D.C.App.1983); People In Interest of F. L. G., 39 Colo.App. 194, 563 P.2d 379 (1977). See generally 10A C. Wright, A. Miller & M. Kane, Civil 3d § 2720.1.

The most common means of supporting or challenging summary judgment is by affidavits—written statements of potential witnesses signed under oath. Equally acceptable are formal responses to discovery such as depositions, answers to interrogatories and admissions. In addition, some courts have accepted verified pleadings,[17] that is, those signed under oath, but only to the extent they state specific facts and otherwise meet all the requirements of proper affidavits.[18] In any event, only material that would be admissible under the rules of evidence at trial will be considered.[19]

Modern summary judgment provisions typically provide that any affidavits that are offered must state that the matters contained therein are based on the affiant's personal knowledge and that affiant is competent to testify as to those matters at trial.[20] Some courts have tended to relax these requirements with regard to the party opposing summary judgment, especially in circumstances in which the opponent is at a disadvantage in obtaining access to relevant evidence.[21] Thus, some judges have overruled objections to affidavits offered in opposition to summary judgment when the affiants have firsthand knowledge but their testimony at trial would be excluded under a "dead man's" statute[22] or a rule of privilege.[23] In addition, some courts have suggested that although the affidavits of the moving party are strictly construed, those of the opposing party are treated more leniently.[24] However, a

17. Verified pleadings are discussed in § 5.11, above.

18. E.g., Runnels v. Rosendale, 499 F.2d 733, 734 n. 1 (9th Cir.1974); Forts v. Malcolm, 426 F.Supp. 464 (S.D.N.Y.1977); Talbert v. Choplin, 40 N.C.App. 360, 253 S.E.2d 37 (1979).

19. Inadmissible evidence may not be used to support or challenge a summary judgment motion. See, e.g., Adickes v. S. H. Kress & Co., 398 U.S. 144, 159 n. 19, 90 S.Ct. 1598, 1609 n. 19, 26 L.Ed.2d 142 (1970) (hearsay statement in deposition not proper support for summary judgment motion). Accord, Hunter v. Farmers Ins. Group, 554 P.2d 1239 (Wyo.1976); Gallo Painting, Inc. v. Aetna Ins. Co., 49 A.D.2d 746, 372 N.Y.S.2d 699 (1975). See generally 10B C. Wright, A. Miller & M. Kane, Civil 3d § 2738.

For the view that information in affidavits submitted in summary judgment proceedings should not be considered hearsay because it is used only as an indicator of potential testimony at trial, see Duane, The Four Greatest Myths About Summary Judgment, 52 Wash. & Lee L.Rev. 1523, 1534 (1995).

20. E.g., Fed.Civ.Proc.Rule 56(e); West's Ann.Cal.Code Civ.Proc. § 437c(d); Fla.—West's F.S.A. Rules Civ.Proc., Rule 1.510(e); Ohio Rules Civ.Proc., Rule 56(E).

21. See e.g., Costlow v. U.S., 552 F.2d 560 (3d Cir.1977); Argus Inc. v. Eastman Kodak Co., 552 F.Supp. 589 (S.D.N.Y.1982).

22. E.g., Moyer v. Briggs, 47 A.D.2d 64, 364 N.Y.S.2d 532 (1975); Phillips v. Joseph Kantor & Co., 31 N.Y.2d 307, 338 N.Y.S.2d 882, 291 N.E.2d 129 (1972); Raybin v. Raybin, 15 A.D.2d 679, 224 N.Y.S.2d 165 (1962). See Annot., 67 A.L.R.3d 970 (1975).

23. In Banco de Espana v. Federal Reserve Bank, 114 F.2d 438, 445 (2d Cir. 1940), the court accepted the affidavit of the Spanish ambassador without requiring him to make an express surrender of his immunity to process to "show affirmatively" that he was "competent to testify" within the meaning of Federal Rule 56(e).

24. Lodge Hall Music, Inc. v. Waco Wrangler Club, Inc., 831 F.2d 77, 80 (5th Cir.1987); R. D. Reeder Lathing Co. v. Allen, 66 Cal.2d 373, 57 Cal.Rptr. 841, 425 P.2d 785 (1967); Meadows v. Grant's Auto Brokers, Inc., 71 Wn.2d 874, 431 P.2d 216 (1967). See also Whaley v. Fowler, 152 Cal. App.2d 379, 313 P.2d 97 (1957) (counteraffidavits may state ultimate facts and conclusions of law). And see Zack, California Summary Judgment: The Need for Legislative Reform, 59 Calif.L.Rev. 439, 466 (1971).

number of courts have strictly adhered to the requirements for affidavits as set out in the summary judgment provisions,[25] regardless of whose affidavits are being scrutinized.

Any defect in the material submitted must be raised or it will be waived. If either party to a motion for summary judgment submits an improper affidavit that is not objected to by the opposing side, the court may consider that affidavit in making its decision,[26] in the same way that a court will permit introduction of unchallenged evidence at trial.[27] Further, when an affidavit contains both competent and incompetent evidence, and an objection is raised, the court will disregard the portions of the affidavit containing the incompetent evidence, but will consider fully that which is competent.[28] The entire affidavit need not be stricken.

§ 9.3 The Standard for Determining Whether to Grant a Summary Judgment

Summary judgment may be rendered when the court finds that there is no genuine issue of material fact and that the moving party is entitled to judgment as a matter of law.[1] Immaterial or minor facts[2] and feigned issues[3] will not prevent summary judgment. Only those facts that are central to a claim or defense[4] and over which there is a real dispute prevent summary judgment from being granted.[5]

When the issue is whether a specific act or event has occurred and the information submitted relates directly thereto, courts have little difficulty in deciding whether a dispute exists and, hence, whether summary judgment should be granted.[6] A problem arises, however, when

---

25. E.g., Joseph F. Trionfo & Sons v. Board of Educ., 41 Md.App. 103, 395 A.2d 1207 (1979) (fact conclusions must be ignored); Whitney's at the Beach v. Superior Court, 3 Cal.App.3d 258, 83 Cal.Rptr. 237 (1970) (conclusions of law raise no triable issue); Kellner v. Blaschke, 334 S.W.2d 315 (Tex.Civ.App.1960) (evidence inadmissible under "dead man's" statute must be disregarded).

26. Lamon v. McDonnell Douglas Corp., 91 Wn.2d 345, 588 P.2d 1346 (1979). See U.S. ex rel. Harrison v. Pace, 380 F.Supp. 107 (E.D.Pa.1974); 10B C. Wright, A. Miller & M. Kane, Civil 3d § 2738.

27. See McCormick on Evidence § 54 (4th ed.1992).

28. U.S. v. Alessi, 599 F.2d 513 (2d Cir.1979); Hopper v. City of Madison, 79 Wis.2d 120, 256 N.W.2d 139 (1977).

§ 9.3

1. Fed.Civ.Proc.Rule 56(c). State rules provide similar standards. E.g., West's Ann. Cal.Code Civ.Proc. § 437c(c); Mich.Ct.Rules 1985, 2.116; N.Y.—McKinney's CPLR 3212(b); Vernon's Ann.Tex.Civ.Proc., Rule 166–A.

2. See, e.g., Church of Scientology of California v. Cazares, 638 F.2d 1272 (5th Cir.1981).

3. E.g., Nabhani v. Coglianese, 552 F.Supp. 657 (N.D.Ill.1982).

4. E.g., Ruhs v. Pacific Power & Light, 671 F.2d 1268 (10th Cir.1982); Commodity Futures Trading Comm'n v. Savage, 611 F.2d 270 (9th Cir.1979).

5. Although courts have no discretion to grant summary judgment if the standard is not met, they can deny summary judgment even though it appears that there is no genuine dispute over any material fact. See 10A C. Wright, A. Miller & M. Kane, Civil 3d § 2728.

6. Courts often analogize summary judgment to a directed verdict. In both situations the moving party must present such proof of the existence of the facts that no fact finder reasonably could find against him. See Mihalchak v. American Dredging Co., 266 F.2d 875, 877 (3d Cir.1959), cert. denied 361 U.S. 901; Fail v. Lee, 535 S.W.2d 203 (Tex.Civ.App.1976); Gerard v. Inglese, 11 A.D.2d 381, 206 N.Y.S.2d 879 (1960).

the existence of a central act or event must be inferred. For example, should a court be permitted to conclude that a party had actual knowledge of a dangerous condition on her land on the basis of unrefuted affidavits establishing that the condition existed openly and visibly for more than a year? Although the failure of the property owner to come forward and testify as to her lack of knowledge might be considered crucial at a trial on the merits, the general rule is that those inferences or conclusions should not be taken into account on summary judgment motions.[7] Questions of this type are generally resolved in favor of the party opposing the summary judgment motion and the issue left to the trier of fact.[8] This reflects the deference of judges to jury trial and the recognition that the court's role is limited to deciding whether any genuine factual issues exist, rather than in determining the issues themselves.[9]

Another problem arises when the responding party's evidentiary material to defeat summary judgment appears to involve competing inferences—one that would support respondent's case and one that would defeat it.[10] Consistent with the recent trend toward a more liberal, expansive use of summary judgment,[11] the decision between competing

For a discussion of how and why the directed verdict standard applies to summary judgment motions, see Sonenshein, State of Mind and Credibility In the Summary Judgment Context: A Better Approach, 78 Nw. U.L.Rev. 774 (1983). For the argument that a rise in the number of motions for summary judgment should lead to a corresponding decrease in directed verdicts, see Gregory, One Too Many Rivers To Cross: Rule 50 Practice in the Modern Era of Summary Judgment, 23 Fla.St.U.L.Rev. 689, 691 (1996).

7. Cross v. U.S., 336 F.2d 431 (2d Cir. 1964); Bragen v. Hudson County News Co., 278 F.2d 615 (3d Cir.1960). For an interesting discussion as to whether matters of inference and credibility are questions of fact thus making summary judgment inappropriate, see Note, Summary Judgment Under Federal Rule of Civil Procedure 56— A Need for a Clarifying Amendment, 48 Iowa L.Rev. 453, 461–63, 468–69 (1963).

8. E.g., U.S. v. Diebold, Inc., 369 U.S. 654, 82 S.Ct. 993, 8 L.Ed.2d 176 (1962); Schmidt v. McKay, 555 F.2d 30 (2d Cir. 1977); Dicker v. Lomas & Nettleton Financial Corp., 576 S.W.2d 672 (Tex.Civ.App. 1978); Summers v. Milcon Corp., 134 Ga. App. 182, 213 S.E.2d 515 (1975); Green v. Southern Bell Tel. & Tel. Co., 204 So.2d 648 (La.App.1967).

9. Hoover v. Switlik Parachute Co., 663 F.2d 964 (9th Cir.1981).

10. For a discussion of the problem of equal inferences, see Friedenthal, Cases on Summary Judgment: Has There Been a Ma-

terial Change in Standards?, 63 Notre Dame L.Rev. 770, 784–87 (1988).

11. Three 1986 Supreme Court decisions regarding summary judgment appear to signal a more widespread use of this procedural device. The three cases are: Matsushita Elec. Industrial Co. v. Zenith Radio Corp., 475 U.S. 574, 106 S.Ct. 1348, 89 L.Ed.2d 538 (1986); Anderson v. Liberty Lobby, Inc., 477 U.S. 242, 106 S.Ct. 2505, 91 L.Ed.2d 202 (1986); Celotex Corp. v. Catrett, 477 U.S. 317, 106 S.Ct. 2548, 91 L.Ed.2d 265 (1986).

For discussion of the implications of these three decisions, see Friedenthal, Cases on Summary Judgment: Has There Been a Material Change in Standards?, 63 Notre Dame L.Rev. 770 (1988); Risinger, Another Step in the Counter–Revolution: A Summary Judgment on the Supreme Court's New Approach to Summary Judgment, 54 Brooklyn L.Rev. 35 (1988); Sinclair & Hanes, Summary judgment: A Proposal for Procedural Reform in the Core Motion Context, 36 Wm. & Mary L.Rev. 1633 (1995); Comment, Summary Judgment: The Majority View Undergoes a Complete Reversal in the 1986 Supreme Court, 37 Emory L.J. 171 (1988); Note, Summary Judgment in Federal Court: New Maxims for a Familiar Rule, 34 N.Y.L.Sch.L.Rev. 201 (1989); Note, Federal Summary Judgment: The "New" Workhorse for an Overburdened Federal Court System, 20 UC Davis L.Rev. 955 (1987).

For the argument that summary judgment is applied too broadly, see Wald, Sum-

inferences is not always for the jury; it is permissible for such a determination to be made by the court in granting summary judgment if one of the inferences is more plausible than the other.[12]

Although federal judges may evaluate evidence in determining whether it is sufficient to create a genuine issue of material fact, in no case can the proffered evidence be weighed by comparing it to opposing evidence. Thus, the trial judge need only determine that the nonmovant's evidence on an issue is "facially plausible and capable of being accepted by a rational factfinder"[13] in order to deny a summary judgment motion even though the moving party's affidavits, taken by themselves, would justify granting the motion on that issue.

Courts are aided in evaluating summary judgment motions by certain widely recognized rules concerning the burden of proof. The moving party has the initial burden of presenting information that clearly establishes that there is no factual dispute regarding the matter upon which summary judgment is sought.[14] This is so even if the adverse party would bear the burden of persuasion on that issue at trial.[15] The movant is held to a strict standard. Any doubts as to the existence of a genuine issue of material fact will be resolved against the movant[16] and the evidence will be construed in the light most favorable to the party opposing the motion.[17]

To meet this burden, the moving party normally submits outside evidence such as affidavits of witnesses setting forth facts[18] to which they

mary Judgment at Sixty, 76 Texas L.Rev. 1897, 1944 (1998). Judge Wald asserts that summary judgment has grown from a device to weed out frivolous and sham cases to "something more of a gestalt verdict based on an early snapshot of the case," transforming summary judgment into "a potential juggernaut." See id. at 1917.

12. In Matsushita Elec. Industrial Co. v. Zenith Radio Corp., 475 U.S. 574, 106 S.Ct. 1348, 89 L.Ed.2d 538 (1986), a complex antitrust suit, the Court maintained that because there was a lack of motive to conspire, a reasonable inference that there was no conspiracy could thus be drawn. The Court stated that only when a trier of fact is confronted with two equally plausible, competing inferences should summary judgment be denied. The effect of employing such a case-by-case analysis of the facts is that many cases may be properly disposed of at the summary judgment stage. Comment, Summary Judgment: The Majority View Undergoes a Complete Reversal in the 1986 Supreme Court, 37 Emory L.J. 171, 196 (1988).

It should be noted that this does not mean that a court is permitted to make credibility choices as to conflicting evidence about which reasonable persons might disagree. See Advisory Committee Notes, Pro-

posed Amendments to the Federal Rules of Civil Procedure, Revised Rule 56(b) (1991).

13. See Duane, The Four Greatest Myths About Summary Judgment, 52 Wash. & Lee L.Rev. 1523, 1560 (1995).

14. See Franklin Nat. Bank v. L. B. Meadows & Co., 318 F.Supp. 1339, 1343 (E.D.N.Y.1970); Tasco, Inc. v. Winkel, 281 N.W.2d 280, 282 (Iowa 1979).

15. See Gual Morales v. Hernandez Vega, 579 F.2d 677 (1st Cir.1978); Mack v. Cape Elizabeth School Bd., 553 F.2d 720 (1st Cir.1977).

16. Ely v. Hall's Motor Transit Co., 590 F.2d 62 (3d Cir.1978); Moyer v. Briggs, 47 A.D.2d 64, 364 N.Y.S.2d 532 (1975).

17. Harold Friedman, Inc. v. Thorofare Markets Inc., 587 F.2d 127 (3d Cir.1978); Partridge v. Younghein, 202 Neb. 756, 277 N.W.2d 100 (1979).

18. Affidavits in summary judgment proceedings—both in support and opposition to the motion—should set forth evidentiary facts. Ultimate facts and conclusions of law are not sufficient. E.g., Hatch v. Bush, 215 Cal.App.2d 692, 30 Cal.Rptr. 397 (1963); City of Quincy v. Sturhahn, 18 Ill.2d 604, 165 N.E.2d 271 (1960). For further discussion of the requirements for affidavits, see § 9.2, above.

could testify at trial.[19] If the information presented, taken as true, fails to establish that no factual dispute exists, summary judgment will be denied, even if the opposing party has presented no counter-evidence.[20] If, but only if, the moving party produces information that appears to establish that no factual dispute exists,[21] then the responding party normally[22] must come forward with materials to show that there indeed is a genuine issue of fact.[23] If the responding party fails to meet this burden, summary judgment should be granted.[24] The responding party cannot rely on the allegations in the pleadings since the essence of summary judgment is to go beyond the pleadings to determine if what appears to be a factual dispute is or is not genuine.[25] If, however, the

One proposed amendment to Rule 56(c) would have required particular specificity with regard to each fact claimed not to be in genuine dispute. Thus, to support a contention that a fact is or is not in genuine dispute, cross-references to the specific portions of evidentiary materials relied upon would have had to have been provided. Proposed Amendments to the Federal Rules of Civil Procedure, Revised Rule 56(c) (1991).

19. Although supporting affidavits are the most common evidence, summary judgment may be granted without affidavits, so long as the standard for summary judgment is satisfied. Celotex Corp. v. Catrett, 477 U.S. 317, 106 S.Ct. 2548, 91 L.Ed.2d 265 (1986).

20. E.g., Adickes v. S. H. Kress & Co., 398 U.S. 144, 160, 90 S.Ct. 1598, 26 L.Ed.2d 142 (1970); Becker v. Kodel, 355 So.2d 852 (Fla.App.1978); Jacobsen v. State, 89 Wn.2d 104, 569 P.2d 1152 (1977). See Currie, Thoughts on Directed Verdicts and Summary Judgments, 45 U.Chi.L.Rev. 72, 76–79 (1977).

21. When the moving party will not have the burden of proof at trial, she need not establish that the facts alleged are not true, but only that the opposing party has no evidence by which the latter can carry the burden of proof. In such a situation it is not sufficient for the moving party merely to state a belief that no such evidence exists. The moving party, to be successful, must establish a record by means of affidavits, depositions, interrogatories, requests to admit, and other relevant material showing such a lack of evidentiary support. See Maley, 1994 Federal Civil Practice and Procedure Update for the Seventh Circuit Practitioner: A Year of Adjustment, 28 Ind. L.Rev. 891, 906 (1995); Price, Reconsidering Celotex: What is the Burden of Production When a Defendant Moves for Summary Judgment on the Ground that the Plaintiff Lacks Evidence?, 11 Utah B.J. 14 (May 1998).

22. In certain unusual situations, the responding party may not have access to evidence showing a factual dispute, for example, when the nature of the issue gives control of the facts to the moving party. In those cases, summary judgment should not be granted. See notes 35–39, below, and accompanying text.

23. The context of the case may affect the amount of evidence a party must proffer to defeat a motion for summary judgment. For instance, the federal appellate courts are split as to the amount of evidence a plaintiff needs to defeat a motion for summary judgment in an employment harassment suit. See Acosta & Von Vorys, Bursting Bubbles and Burdens of Proof: The Deepening Disagreement on the Summary Judgment Standard in Disparate Treatment Employment Discrimination Cases, 2 Texas Rev.L. & Pol. 207 (1998). The First, Second (en banc), Fifth (en banc), and Eighth (en banc) Circuits have held that an employee has the duty to raise genuine issues of fact as to whether the employer intentionally discriminated. The Third (en banc), Seventh, Tenth (en banc) and Eleventh Circuits hold the employee to a somewhat lesser burden. Id. at 208.

24. See, e.g., Boulware v. Parker, 457 F.2d 450 (3d Cir.1972); Scott v. Dollahite, 54 F.R.D. 430 (N.D.Miss.1972); Phillips–Van Heusen Corp. v. Shark Bros., Inc., 289 N.W.2d 216 (N.D.1980); Gelb v. Bucknell Press, Inc., 69 A.D.2d 829, 415 N.Y.S.2d 89 (1979); Mayo v. Knapton, 118 N.H. 926, 395 A.2d 1254 (1978); Northern Contracting Co. v. Allis–Chalmers Corp., 117 Ariz. 374, 573 P.2d 65 (1977).

25. Federal Rule 56(e) was amended in 1963 to overcome a line of cases, chiefly in the Third Circuit, holding that the responding party could defeat a summary judgment motion without filing affidavits if "well pleaded" averments in her pleadings contradicted the moving party's affidavit on a material issue. See the Advisory Committee

responding party does produce information contradicting that of the moving party or otherwise showing that a factual dispute exists, summary judgment must be denied; the matter is then for the trier of fact after a trial on the merits.

Although the party moving for summary judgment always bears the burden of establishing the nonexistence of an issue of material fact,[26] the nature of the showing depends on who would bear the burden of persuasion at trial,[27] and what standard of proof is required.[28] In most cases, it is the nonmoving party who has the burden of persuasion at trial. If that party cannot come forward with information to establish the existence of questions of fact crucial to his case, summary judgment obviously is appropriate.[29] But suppose it is the movant who has the burden of persuasion. At trial the nonmoving party would be free to sit back, offer no evidence whatsoever and argue that he should prevail because the movant's witnesses were not credible. Logically, then, the nonmoving party should be able to avoid summary judgment merely by claiming that the case must go to trial when the moving party's wit-

Notes to the 1963 amendment of Rule 56, reprinted in 31 F.R.D. 648 (1963); 10B C. Wright, A. Miller & M. Kane, Civil 3d § 2739.

State rules of procedure are generally in accord with amended Federal Rule 56(e). See, e.g., Eakman v. Brutger, 285 N.W.2d 95 (Minn.1979); Cullincini v. Deming, 53 Cal.App.3d 908, 126 Cal.Rptr. 427 (1975); S.J. Capelin Assocs., Inc. v. Globe Mfg. Corp., 34 N.Y.2d 338, 357 N.Y.S.2d 478, 313 N.E.2d 776 (1974). But see Atkins v. Atkins, 376 A.2d 856, 859 n. 4 (Me.1977) ("[T]he pleadings raise sufficient issues of fact to warrant jury consideration and hence summary judgment is not 'appropriate'."); Glosser v. City of New Haven, 256 Ind. 33, 267 N.E.2d 67 (1971) (failure to file counteraffidavits does not entitle movant to summary judgment as a matter of law; verified complaint raised factual issues).

26. In Celotex Corp. v. Catrett, 477 U.S. 317, 106 S.Ct. 2548, 91 L.Ed.2d 265 (1986), the Court reduced the moving party's initial burden. A movant satisfies the initial burden by either affirmatively negating the nonmoving party's claim, or by demonstrating to the court that the nonmoving party is unable to prove an essential element of that claim. The Court's lessening of the moving party's burden will facilitate more frequent entries of summary judgment. See Note, Federal Summary Judgment: The "New" Workhorse for an Overburdened Federal Court System, 20 UC Davis L.Rev. 955, 967 (1987). See also Lujan v. National Wildlife Federation, 497 U.S. 871, 110 S.Ct. 3177, 111 L.Ed.2d 695 (1990) (following the Celotex case).

27. If the movants would have the burden of persuasion—either because they are the plaintiffs or because they are asserting an affirmative defense—then they must establish all essential elements of the claim or defense. A moving party who would not bear the burden of persuasion can obtain summary judgment simply by showing the nonexistence of any essential element of the opposing party's claim. See Louis, Federal Summary Judgment Doctrine: A Critical Analysis, 83 Yale L.J. 745, 747–48 (1974).

28. In Anderson v. Liberty Lobby, Inc., 477 U.S. 242, 106 S.Ct. 2505, 91 L.Ed.2d 202 (1986), the nonmovant's heightened evidentiary standard was taken into consideration. In this defamation suit, existence of malice had to be established by clear and convincing evidence, rather than by a preponderance of the evidence. By requiring the nonmoving party to produce evidence sufficient to withstand a directed verdict motion, the Court effectively increased the nonmoving party's burden, thus, facilitating the entry of summary judgment.

29. For example, in Dyer v. MacDougall, 201 F.2d 265 (2d Cir.1952), defendant countered a slander allegation with affidavits signed by all witnesses to the supposed defamation, each denying that the wrong had occurred. The court granted summary judgment for defendant. Even if plaintiff succeeded in impeaching the credibility of defendant's witnesses at trial, he nevertheless would be unable to discharge his burden of persuasion; there would be no competent evidence that could support a verdict for plaintiff.

nesses might be disbelieved.[30] But this is not the case.

The resolution of the question involves both burden of proof and credibility problems.[31] Courts typically have granted summary judgment when the opposing party's sole arguments for allowing the case to go to trial rest on a desire to test the credibility of the movant's witnesses. They have relied on the absence of specific language in summary judgment provisions placing limitations on which parties can move for relief or on the availability of summary judgment when credibility or motive issues are raised.[32] And they have pointed to the language in the rules requiring the party opposing summary judgment to controvert the movant's allegations.[33] Although courts should be cautious in granting summary judgment for a party with the burden of proof,[34] a mere allegation that the opponent desires to rest his case on the credibility of the witnesses is not enough, standing alone, to preclude summary judgment.[35] Summary judgment should be denied only if the nonmoving party provides affidavits supporting her case on the merits or casting doubt on the veracity of those persons who made affidavits for the movant.[36] If the opponent can show some reason why the movant's witness might be disbelieved at trial, as, for example, if the witness would profit personally from an outcome in favor of the movant,[37]

30. Professor David Currie has argued that when a "jury would be free to disbelieve an uncontradicted witness at trial, as is sometimes the case, to grant summary judgment for a party having the burden of proof on the basis of an affidavit embodying such a witness's testimony would infringe the right to jury trial." Currie, Thoughts on Directed Verdicts and Summary Judgment, 45 U.Chi.L.Rev. 72, 76–77 (1977).

31. See Sonenshein, State of Mind and Credibility in the Summary Judgment Context: A Better Approach, 78 Nw.U.L.Rev. 774 (1983).

32. Compare West's Ann.Cal.Code Civ. Proc. § 437c(e): "If a party is otherwise entitled to a summary judgment pursuant to the provisions of this section, summary judgment shall not be denied on grounds of credibility or for want of cross-examination of witnesses furnishing affidavits or declarations in support of the summary judgment * * *."

33. E.g., Lundeen v. Cordner, 354 F.2d 401 (8th Cir.1966); Spalding, Div. of Questor Corp. v. Antonious, 68 F.R.D. 222 (D.Md.1975); Rinieri v. Scanlon, 254 F.Supp. 469 (S.D.N.Y.1966). Cf. Swecker v. Dorn, 181 Mont. 436, 593 P.2d 1055 (1979) (since defendant did not controvert plaintiff's assertions, they were taken as true); Hurwitz v. Kohm, 516 S.W.2d 33 (Mo.App. 1974) (uncontroverted affidavits are admitted on plaintiff's motion for summary judgment).

34. See generally Louis, Federal Summary Judgment Doctrine: A Critical Analysis, 83 Yale L.J. 745 (1974) (criticizing summary judgment statutes because they do not expressly distinguish between those who have the burden of proof at trial and those who do not).

35. Vantage Point, Inc. v. Parker Bros., Inc., 529 F.Supp. 1204 (E.D.N.Y. 1981), affirmed without opinion 697 F.2d 301 (2d Cir.1982); Spalding, Div. of Questor Corp. v. Antonious, 68 F.R.D. 222 (D.Md. 1975).

36. It generally is said that the opposing party must produce specific facts that put the affiants' credibility in issue. See, e.g., Lundeen v. Cordner, 354 F.2d 401 (8th Cir.1966) (summary judgment granted for party with burden of persuasion when there was no positive showing that witness' testimony could be impeached or that affiant might have additional testimony valuable to opposing party). In Lundeen, Judge Gibson noted that cross-examination would be necessary, and thus summary judgment inappropriate, whenever there is an "indication that the affiant was biased, dishonest, mistaken, unaware or unsure of the facts." Id. at 408.

37. In Texas, uncontradicted evidence favoring the movant's position cannot be considered if it is from an interested witness, except when it is clear, direct, and positive and there are no circumstances in evidence tending to discredit or impeach it.

summary judgment is inappropriate as the credibility of the witness clearly is in issue.

As already indicated, in some instances the responding party may be unable to obtain information necessary to show that a material factual dispute exists. Summary judgment provisions typically provide that a motion may be denied, or the hearing on it delayed, if the responding party shows that more time is needed to obtain facts.[38] Courts generally are lenient in providing reasonable extra time for locating witnesses, taking depositions, and finding documents.[39]

The problem takes on an added dimension in the unusual case in which no amount of added time will suffice to provide the responding party with a fair opportunity to obtain necessary information. This occurs when the nature of the issue gives control of the facts to the moving party—for example, when the issue is the latter's state of mind at a particular time. In many circumstances, the only way to counter a person's affidavit as to his own intent is to have that person appear at trial and be subjected to formal examination before the trier of fact.[40] In these cases, summary judgment is denied.[41]

It is important to recognize a difference between situations in which it is unfair to expect the responding party to obtain countering information and those in which due search reveals that no countering evidence exists. In the latter cases, summary judgment is clearly appropriate. Even so, some courts may deny relief when the motion is based on the affidavit or deposition of the only witness to the relevant facts,[42] on the

Evans v. Fort Worth Star Telegram, 548 S.W.2d 819 (Tex.Civ.App.1977); Fagin v. North Dallas Moving & Storage Co., 503 S.W.2d 308 (Tex.Civ.App.1973).

38. E.g., Fed.Civ.Proc.Rule 56(f). Under Rule 56(f) a party must state by affidavit the reasons why he is unable to present the necessary opposing material and the court then may refuse to grant the summary judgment motion, order a continuance to permit additional discovery, or "make such order as is just." See Annot., 47 A.L.R.Fed. 206 (1980). Most states have similar provisions. E.g., West's Ann.Cal. Code Civ.Proc. § 437c(h); Official Code Ga. Ann. § 9-11-56; Neb.Rev.Stat. § 25-1335; N.Y.—McKinney's CPLR 3212(f).

39. See, e.g., Littlejohn v. Shell Oil Co., 483 F.2d 1140 (5th Cir.1973), cert. denied 414 U.S. 1116; Catanzaro v. Masco Corp., 408 F.Supp. 862 (D.Del.1976); Carter v. Jernigan, 227 N.W.2d 131 (Iowa 1975); Monmouth Lumber Co. v. Indemnity Ins. Co., 21 N.J. 439, 122 A.2d 604 (1956).

40. In Cross v. U.S., 336 F.2d 431 (2d Cir.1964), for example, plaintiff taxpayer, a professor of languages, attempted to prove that his overseas trip was intended primarily to maintain or improve his language

skills so that the trip expenses would qualify as a business deduction. Government attorneys had no extrinsic evidence to refute the taxpayer's own affidavit attesting to his state of mind when embarking on his travels. Yet the Second Circuit overturned summary judgment for plaintiff, preserving the government's "right to call and examine the adverse party * * * before the jury." Id. at 434.

41. See West's Ann.Cal.Code Civ.Proc. § 437c(e) ("[S]ummary judgment may be denied in the discretion of the court * * * where a material fact is an individual's state of mind, or lack thereof, and such fact is sought to be established solely by the individual's affirmation thereof."); Petro v. McCullough, 179 Ind.App. 438, 385 N.E.2d 1195 (1979); Louis, Summary Judgment and the Actual Malice Controversy in Constitutional Defamation Cases, 57 S.Calif.L.Rev. 707 (1984). But see Vern Walton Motors v. Taylor, 121 Ariz. 463, 591 P.2d 555 (App.1978). See generally 10B C. Wright, A. Miller & M. Kane, Civil 3d § 2730, for an examination of summary judgment when state of mind is in issue.

42. See West's Ann.Cal.Code Civ.Proc. § 437c(e). ("[S]ummary judgment may be

ground that it is unfair to decide the case without requiring that witness to testify to the facts in open court.

B.   DEFAULT JUDGMENT

§ 9.4   The Entry of Default and Default Judgment

It is important to keep in mind the difference between the entry of a default and a default judgment.[1] An entry of default does not constitute a judgment; it is merely a notation by the court clerk precluding the defaulting party from making any new defenses regarding liability.[2] The notation of default records the fact that the defending party has failed to plead or otherwise defend against a claim.

Default judgments may be entered in three types of situations. In the first, the defendant never appears or answers in response to the plaintiff's complaint. In the second, defendant makes an appearance, but fails to file a formal answer or appear at trial.[3] In the third, the defendant fails to comply with some procedural requirement, time frame or court order during the pretrial proceedings and the court enters a default judgment as a penalty. As is discussed elsewhere, authority for penalty defaults may be found in most discovery rules[4] and they have been recognized as within the inherent power of the court in order to force compliance or cooperation at the pretrial conference stage.[5] The other two default situations are dealt with in specially designed rules present in each court system and are discussed below.[6]

Default judgments are a drastic action because they confront the judicial preference for disposition of litigation on the merits, especially

---

denied in the discretion of the court, where the only proof of a material fact offered in support of the summary judgment is an affidavit or declaration made by an individual who was the sole witness to such fact * * *.").

§ 9.4

1. The distinction between defaults and default judgments becomes important when relief is sought. As might be expected, relief from the entry of default is more readily granted than from a default judgment. Jackson v. Beech, 636 F.2d 831 (D.C.Cir.1980); Peebles v. Moore, 48 N.C.App. 497, 269 S.E.2d 694 (1980), modified and affirmed 302 N.C. 351, 275 S.E.2d 833 (1981). See Rappleyea v. Campbell, 8 Cal.4th 975, 35 Cal.Rptr.2d 669, 884 P.2d 126 (1994), noted in California Supreme Court Survey: X Judgments, 23 Pepp.L.Rev. 354 (1995).

2. Arango v. Guzman Travel Advisors, 761 F.2d 1527 (11th Cir.1985), cert. denied 474 U.S. 995; Citizens Nat. Bank of Grant

County v. First Nat. Bank in Marion, Indiana, 165 Ind.App. 116, 331 N.E.2d 471 (1975).

3. A failure to answer or defend should be distinguished from a failure to appear at trial after answering the complaint. In the former situation, the case never has been placed formally at issue and a default judgment may be entered. In the latter, issue has been joined, and the trial proceeds, but without the absent party. See Coulas v. Smith, 96 Ariz. 325, 395 P.2d 527 (1964).

4. See § 7.16, above.

5. See § 8.2, above.

6. A penalty default may not be governed by all the protections set out in the rules governing default judgments. For example, the damages may not be limited to the amount claimed in the complaint. See text at note 18, below; Aljassim v. S.S. South Star, 323 F.Supp. 918 (S.D.N.Y. 1971); Sarlie v. E. L. Bruce Co., 265 F.Supp. 371 (S.D.N.Y.1967). However, the defending party will be entitled to notice and a right

when the defendant has been otherwise diligent. The actual judgment is based on a prior entry of default by the court clerk as provided by rule or statute.[7] The judgment may be entered either by the clerk or by the court, depending on the governing rule or statute and the nature of the underlying claim.

If default has been entered and it is clear from the complaint that a certain sum and only that sum is due to the complainant, most rules provide that the clerk then may enter a default judgment for that amount.[8] This requirement typically is satisfied when the damages claimed are for a liquidated amount and the amount requested is reasonable under the circumstances, conditions commonly fulfilled only in some contract actions.[9]

Aside from these few instances, most rules give the court discretion to decide whether or not to enter a default judgment. In exercising its discretion the court will consider various factors,[10] including whether the default is largely technical and the defendant now is ready to defend,[11] whether the plaintiff has been prejudiced by defendant's delay in responding,[12] and the amounts involved or the significance of the issues at stake.[13] These factors will be evaluated in light of the general preference for decisions rendered after a full adjudication on the merits.[14]

When deciding whether to enter a judgment, the court may hold a hearing.[15] Indeed, Federal Rule 55(b)(2) empowers the district judge to hold hearings or "order such references as it deems necessary and proper." A hearing often is particularly appropriate because defendant's default serves only to concede the factual allegations in the complaint

to appear at the default hearing. See Eisler v. Stritzler, 535 F.2d 148 (1st Cir.1976).

7. See, e.g., Fed.Civ.Proc.Rule 55(a); West's Ann.Cal.Code Civ.Proc. §§ 585(a) and (b), 586; Md.Rule 613; Ohio Rules Civ. Proc., Rule 55(A).

8. Fed.Civ.Proc.Rule 55(b)(1); West's Ann.Cal.Code Civ.Proc. § 585(a); Idaho Rules Civ.Proc., Rule 55(b)(1). See generally 10A C. Wright, A. Miller & M. Kane, Civil 3d § 2683.

9. Compare Galanti v. Emerald City Records, Inc., 144 Ga.App. 773, 242 S.E.2d 368 (1978) (damages for breach of rental agreement by tenant were liquidated because easily calculable), with Ford v. Superior Ct. for Orange County, 34 Cal.App.3d 338, 109 Cal.Rptr. 844 (1973) (clerk could not enter default judgment on a promissory note secured by a trust deed on real property because complaint alleged that the security had become "worthless" and court must hear that evidence). See also Byrd v. Keene Corp., 104 F.R.D. 10 (E.D.Pa.1984) (plaintiff cannot satisfy the certainty requirement simply by requesting a specific amount).

10. For a more detailed listing of the factors considered, see 10A C. Wright, A. Miller & M. Kane, Civil 3d § 2685.

11. See McKnight v. Webster, 499 F.Supp. 420 (E.D.Pa.1980); Franzen v. Carmichael, 398 N.E.2d 1379 (Ind.App.1980).

12. See Davis v. Mercier–Freres, 368 F.Supp. 498 (E.D.Wis.1973) (no prejudice); Seanor v. Bair Transport Co. of Delaware, Inc., 54 F.R.D. 35 (E.D.Pa.1971) (prejudice).

13. See Hutton v. Fisher, 359 F.2d 913 (3d Cir.1966); General Motors Corp. v. Blevins, 144 F.Supp. 381 (D.Colo.1956).

14. The preference for a full adversary presentation also influences a trial court's decision to allow relief from a default judgment. See § 12.6, below. On appeal, however, a trial court's discretionary determination to grant a default judgment will only be reversed for an abuse of discretion. See Rappleyea v. Campbell, 8 Cal.4th 975, 35 Cal.Rptr.2d 669, 884 P.2d 126 (1994), noted in California Supreme Court Survey: X Judgments, 23 Pepp.L.Rev. 354 (1995).

15. Ariz.Rules Civ.Proc., Rule 55(b)(2); Fla.—West's F.S.A.Rules Civ.Proc., Rule

regarding liability.[16] The default does not preclude a defendant from claiming that those factual allegations fail to state a claim for relief.[17] Pursuant to most default rules, once there has been a default the claimant cannot recover more than the amount demanded or the type of relief requested in the complaint.[18] But the default does not concede plaintiff's right to the relief requested;[19] the amount of damages to be awarded must be determined by the court.[20] A default hearing to determine damages may proceed like any other trial.[21] However, witnesses usually do not appear in person at a default judgment hearing. Rather, evidence is submitted by affidavit.[22]

An important issue is whether the defaulting party is entitled to notice of an impending judgment and hearing.[23] The resolution of this question varies depending on what type of default is involved. The entry of default usually is without notice, as is a default judgment entered by the clerk.[24] However, if the default judgment is to be entered by the court, then most jurisdictions follow the approach of Federal Rule 55(b)(2), which provides for three days' notice of a motion for default judgment if, but only if, the defendant has "appeared" in the case.[25] This distinction between "appearing" and "nonappearing" defendants recognizes that the former have taken some action in the case—shown some

---

1.500(e). See generally 10A C. Wright, A. Miller & M. Kane, Civil 3d § 2688.

16. See Thomson v. Wooster, 114 U.S. 104, 5 S.Ct. 788, 29 L.Ed. 105 (1885); Southern Arizona School for Boys, Inc. v. Chery, 119 Ariz. 277, 580 P.2d 738 (App. 1978).

17. Bonilla v. Trebol Motors Corp., 150 F.3d 77, 80 (1st Cir.1998).

18. E.g., Fed.Civ.Proc.Rule 54(c); Ariz. Rules Civ.Proc., Rule 54(d); Official Code Ga.Ann. § 9–11–54(c)(1).

19. The defendant may claim at the default hearing that the facts, even taken as true, will not support a judgment for plaintiff. Ohio Cent. R. Co. v. Central Trust Co., 133 U.S. 83, 91, 10 S.Ct. 235, 237, 33 L.Ed. 561 (1890); Clague v. Bednarski, 105 F.R.D. 552 (E.D.N.Y.1985); Productora E Importadora De Papel, S.A. v. Fleming, 376 Mass. 826, 383 N.E.2d 1129 (1978). But see Trans World Airlines, Inc. v. Hughes, 449 F.2d 51 (2d Cir.1971), reversed on other grounds 409 U.S. 363, 93 S.Ct. 647, 34 L.Ed.2d 577 (1973).

20. Pope v. U.S., 323 U.S. 1, 65 S.Ct. 16, 89 L.Ed. 3 (1944); Insurance Co. of N. America v. S/S "Hellenic Challenger," 88 F.R.D. 545 (S.D.N.Y.1980); Kelly Broadcasting Co. v. Sovereign Broadcast, Inc., 96 Nev. 188, 606 P.2d 1089 (1980).

21. Defendant may obtain a jury trial on the question of damages if the court decides it would be appropriate. See Bonilla v. Trebol Motors Corp., 150 F.3d 77, 82 (1st

Cir.1998); Barber v. Turberville, 218 F.2d 34 (D.C.Cir.1954). But neither side has a right to demand a jury trial on the issue of damages. Eisler v. Stritzler, 535 F.2d 148 (1st Cir.1976). But compare Devlin v. Kearny Mesa AMC/Jeep/Renault, Inc., 155 Cal. App.3d 381, 202 Cal.Rptr. 204 (1984) (defendant may not participate in default judgment hearing determining punitive damages).

22. See West's Ann.Cal.Code Civ.Proc. § 585(d).

23. The failure to provide the required notice justifies the reversal or setting aside of a default judgment. See Marshall v. Boyd, 658 F.2d 552 (8th Cir.1981); Wilver v. Fisher, 387 F.2d 66 (10th Cir.1967). The failure does not always mean that the judgment is void and subject to collateral attack, however. See Radioear Corp. v. Crouse, 97 Idaho 501, 547 P.2d 546 (1975). See also Winfield Assocs., Inc. v. Stonecipher, 429 F.2d 1087 (10th Cir.1970). But see Bass v. Hoagland, 172 F.2d 205 (5th Cir.1949), cert. denied 338 U.S. 816. For a more detailed discussion of notice, see 10A C. Wright, A. Miller & M. Kane, Civil 3d § 2687.

24. Harp v. Loux, 54 Or.App. 840, 636 P.2d 976 (1981); Zettler v. Ehrlich, 384 So.2d 928 (Fla.App.1980).

25. Ala.Rules Civ.Proc., Rule 55(b)(2); Ariz.Rules Civ.Proc., Rule 55(a), (b)(1); Idaho Rules Civ.Proc., Rule 55(a)(1), (b)(1). See also S.C.Rules Civ.Proc., Rule 55(b)(1); Wis.

interest—so that it is thought appropriate to provide them the opportunity to contest the amount, extent, or type of relief granted at the hearing or, if the pleadings are insufficient, to argue that plaintiff's claims should be dismissed because the pleadings fail to assert a claim upon which relief may be granted.[26]

Serious questions arise as to what constitutes an appearance sufficient to trigger these notice requirements.[27] One example is when a party has defended solely on a procedural ground such as lack of jurisdiction and, after losing that challenge, fails to defend the merits of the case.[28] But even less formal activity on the part of a defendant may constitute an appearance,[29] such as the exchange of letters between the parties concerning settlement.[30] The liberal approach of many courts in determining what constitutes an appearance reflects, once again, the general distaste for judgments entered without an adversary presentation and the desire to provide notice before a judgment is entered so as to encourage defaulting parties to appear and defend.

C. DISMISSALS

§ 9.5 Voluntary and Involuntary Dismissals

At common law plaintiff was viewed as the master of his case until a judgment was rendered, and therefore was permitted to dismiss the case voluntarily and without prejudice anytime prior to judgment.[1] Today, plaintiff's right to dismiss is governed by rule or statute, and most jurisdictions reject the common-law approach. Plaintiff's unilateral right to dismiss a case voluntarily generally exists as long as defendant has not been unduly burdened by plaintiff's suit. This has been codified as anytime before "trial"[2] or before "commencement of trial."[3] Exactly what defines "commencement of trial" or "trial" is a matter of judicial construction[4] and varies from the empaneling of jurors, to the entering of evidence, to the submission of the case to the jury. The Federal Rules[5] limit plaintiff's absolute right to dismiss to the point in the proceedings before defendant has answered[6] or moved for summary judgment.[7] A

Stat.Ann. 806.02(1) (notice required to any appearing party).

26. See Lutomski v. Panther Valley Coin Exchange, 653 F.2d 270 (6th Cir. 1981); H. F. Livermore Corp. v. Aktiengesellschaft Gebruder Loepfe, 432 F.2d 689 (D.C.Cir.1970).

27. See generally 10A C. Wright, A. Miller & M. Kane, Civil 3d § 2686.

28. See Cockrell v. World's Finest Chocolate Co., 349 So.2d 1117 (Ala.1977).

29. See, e.g., U.S. v. One 1966 Chevrolet Pickup Truck, 56 F.R.D. 459 (E.D.Tex. 1972).

30. H. F. Livermore Corp. v. Aktiengesellschaft Gebruder Loepfe, 432 F.2d 689 (D.C.Cir.1970).

§ 9.5

1. Bulkley v. Treadway, 1 Root 552 (Conn.1793).

2. Ill.—Smith Hurd Ann. 735 ILCS 5/2–1009(a).

3. West's Ann.Cal.Code Civ.Proc. § 581(1).

4. See generally 1 A.L.R.3d 711 (1965); 89 A.L.R. 53 (1934).

5. Fed.Civ.Proc.Rule 41(a)(1).

6. "Answer" generally is construed to be independent of appearance; an appearance by the defendant will not extinguish the right of voluntary dismissal if defendant has neither answered nor moved for dismissal or summary judgment. Compania Plomari De Vapores, S.A. v. American Hellenic Corp., 8 F.R.D. 426 (S.D.N.Y.1948).

7. Under Federal Rule 12(b)(6) a motion to dismiss for failure to state a claim is

motion to dismiss for failure to state a claim does not cut off plaintiff's right.[8] However, after the filing of an answer or motion for summary judgment, dismissal is only by leave of court or upon a stipulation of the parties.

Although the first voluntary dismissal as of right is almost always without prejudice, a second dismissal may act as an adjudication upon the merits of any of the claims included in both dismissals. Plaintiff will be precluded from successfully prosecuting a third suit based upon those claims.[9] The purpose of this "two dismissal rule" is to minimize both the harassment to the defendant and the undue expense to the court that would result from plaintiff's repeated filings and dismissals. On the other hand, a prior voluntary dismissal entered into by stipulation of the parties[10] or a second dismissal by leave of court usually will not be treated as on the merits as both of those procedures presume the imposition of terms and conditions that themselves may alleviate any undue prejudice to the defendant.

As just suggested, most jurisdictions[11] also provide for dismissal without prejudice by leave of court after plaintiff's power to dismiss as of right has terminated.[12] Whether to grant the dismissal and whether any terms or conditions will be attached to the dismissal are discretionary,[13] and the judge may, or often must,[14] hold a hearing to ensure substantial justice to both parties. In deciding whether to grant the dismissal, the benefits to the plaintiff as well as any prejudice or other detriments to the defendant are to be considered.[15] The court should not be swayed by its own inconvenience; nor should the motion be denied merely because

treated as a motion for summary judgment under Federal Rule 56 if "matters outside the pleading are presented to and not excluded by the court." However, federal courts are not in accord as to whether or when a 12(b)(6) motion to which outside materials are attached is to be treated as a motion for summary judgment so as to defeat a plaintiff's right to a voluntary dismissal. Aamot v. Kassel, 1 F.3d 441 (6th Cir.1993). See also § 9.1, above, regarding the conversion of a motion to dismiss into a motion for summary judgment.

8. Aamot v. Kassel, 1 F.3d 441 (6th Cir.1993); Horton v. Trans World Airlines Corp., 169 F.R.D. 11 (E.D.N.Y.1996).

9. As to what constitutes the "same claim," see 9 C. Wright & A. Miller, Civil 2d § 2368.

10. Poloron Prods., Inc. v. Lybrand Ross Bros., 534 F.2d 1012 (2d Cir.1976).

11. Iowa Rules Civ.Proc., Rule 215; Vernon's Ann.Mo.Stat. § 510.130(1), (2).

12. Leave of court always is required under Federal Rule 41(a)(1) in certain types of cases, as, for example, class action suits, or an action brought on behalf of incompetents. There is no dismissal by right in these cases in recognition of the fact that the effect of dismissal goes beyond those present in the court to represent their own interests. See, e.g., Evans v. Jeff D., 475 U.S. 717, 106 S.Ct. 1531, 89 L.Ed.2d 747 (1986).

13. Witzman v. Gross, 148 F.3d 988, 991–92 (8th Cir.1998). For comprehensive discussions of judicial discretion under Federal Rule 41(a)(2), see Note, Exercise of Discretion in Permitting Dismissals Without Prejudice Under Federal Rule 41(a), 54 Colum.L.Rev. 616 (1954); Note, Voluntary Dismissal by Order of Court—Federal Rule of Civil Procedure 41(a)(2) and Judicial Discretion, 48 Notre Dame Law. 446 (1972).

14. See, e.g., Cass v. Pacific Fire Ins. Co., 7 F.R.D. 348 (W.D.Mo.1947).

15. Ohlander v. Larson, 114 F.3d 1531 (10th Cir.1997), cert. denied __ U.S. __, 118 S.Ct. 702.

plaintiff may gain some tactical, as opposed to a legal, advantage.[16] The court may impose conditions on its dismissal in order to alleviate any prejudice that otherwise might occur. For example, courts have conditioned dismissal upon payment of money to the defendant for expenses,[17] or they have required plaintiff to produce certain discovery documents before dismissal would be allowed.[18]

In addition to the power to grant a motion for a voluntary dismissal, judges long have been regarded as possessing inherent discretion to dismiss an action with prejudice if the plaintiff does not proceed to trial with "due diligence." This authority derives from the courts' power to manage and administer their own affairs to ensure the orderly and expeditious disposition of cases.[19] A few jurisdictions set specific time limits before which dismissal is not allowed,[20] or after which dismissal is mandatory.[21] However, most jurisdictions[22] leave the issue completely to the court's discretion.[23]

In deciding whether to grant a motion to dismiss for failure to prosecute, the court must look to the factual circumstances surrounding each case.[24] Most jurisdictions do not require defendant to show prejudice; this is presumed from the delay. However, because the law favors deciding cases on the merits, courts are hesitant to dismiss for want of prosecution and will weigh this reluctance against the presumed prejudice to the defendant.[25] Generally, dismissal will not be ordered when the delay has not otherwise prejudiced the defendant, when the defendant is

16. Hoffmann v. Alside, Inc., 596 F.2d 822 (8th Cir.1979); Grynberg Production Corp. v. British Gas, P.L.C., 149 F.R.D. 135, 139 (E.D.Tex.1993); Kennedy v. State Farm Mut. Auto. Ins. Co., 46 F.R.D. 12 (E.D.Ark. 1969). But see Doyle v. Stanley Works, 60 F.R.D. 132 (E.D.Pa.1973), affirmed without opinion 492 F.2d 1238 (3d Cir.1974). Plaintiff will not be permitted to dismiss when the tactical advantage gained is unjust, however. Piedmont Interstate Fair Ass'n v. Bean, 209 F.2d 942 (4th Cir.1954); International Shoe Co. v. Cool, 154 F.2d 778 (8th Cir.1946), cert. denied 329 U.S. 726.

17. LeBlang v. Subaru, 148 F.3d 680 (7th Cir.1998); Davis v. McLaughlin, 326 F.2d 881 (9th Cir.1964), cert. denied 379 U.S. 833.

18. Eaddy v. Little, 234 F.Supp. 377 (E.D.S.C.1964).

19. Link v. Wabash R.R. Co., 370 U.S. 626, 82 S.Ct. 1386, 8 L.Ed.2d 734 (1962).

20. For example, West's Ann.Cal.Code Civ.Proc., § 583.420 allows dismissal only after the passage of two years from the filing of the complaint; within 2 to 5 years from filing, it is within the court's discretion as to whether to dismiss. See West's Fla.Stat.Ann. § 1.420(e) (defendant may bring motion one year after no activity in the case). Compare Ind.Trial Proc.Rule

41(E) (dismissal only when no action taken in civil case for 60 days).

21. West's Ann.Cal.Code Civ.Proc. § 583.310 (dismissal is mandatory after five years have elapsed); Official Code Ga.Ann. § 9–11–41(e) (automatic dismissal after five years of inactivity).

22. See Fed.Civ.Proc.Rule 41(b); Kan. Stat.Ann. 60–241(b); Vernon's Ann.Mo. Stat. § 510.140.

23. This discretion goes not only to the terms and conditions but also to whether to dismiss. It also frequently has been recognized that the trial judge on his own motion may dismiss for failure to prosecute. Koury v. International Bhd. of Teamsters, Chauffeurs, Warehousemen & Helpers of America, 69 F.R.D. 474 (E.D.Pa.1975), affirmed without opinion 547 F.2d 1161 (3d Cir. 1976).

24. Link v. Wabash R.R. Co., 370 U.S. 626, 82 S.Ct. 1386, 8 L.Ed.2d 734 (1962); Moore v. St. Louis Music Supply Co., 539 F.2d 1191 (8th Cir.1976); Asociacion de Empleados v. Rodriguez Morales, 538 F.2d 915 (1st Cir.1976).

25. Citizens Utilities Co. v. American Tel. & Tel. Co., 595 F.2d 1171 (9th Cir. 1979), cert. denied 444 U.S. 931.

at least partially responsible for the delay, or when the delay is due to the derelictions of counsel rather than of the client, who ought not to lose an otherwise meritorious case.[26] Dismissals for failure to prosecute are granted only when the plaintiff has been particularly dilatory.[27]

The inherent power of courts to control their own administrative matters also allows them to dismiss a case if plaintiff fails to comply with a court order.[28] However, dismissal is such a drastic sanction that it is seldom imposed,[29] except for an extreme case of a wilful violation of a discovery or pretrial conference order.[30] When dismissal occurs under these circumstances it is usually with prejudice and thus acts as an adjudication on the merits. This impact is especially important for it means that plaintiff cannot avoid the penalty merely by filing suit again; the dismissal will be given full preclusive effect.[31] This harsh effect can be avoided only if the court enters the dismissal without prejudice, which it may do if the conduct precipitating the dismissal is not viewed as too heinous.

26. Adams v. Trustees of the New Jersey Brewery Employees' Pension Trust Fund, 29 F.3d 863 (3d Cir.1994); Donnelly v. Johns–Manville Sales Corp., 677 F.2d 339 (3d Cir.1982); Hildebrand v. Honeywell, Inc., 622 F.2d 179 (5th Cir.1980); Ahmad v. Independent Order of Foresters, 81 F.R.D. 722 (E.D.Pa.1979), affirmed without opinion 707 F.2d 1399 (3d Cir.1983).

27. See, e.g., Edwards v. Harris County Sheriff's Dep't, 864 F.Supp. 633 (S.D.Tex. 1994).

28. See generally 9 C. Wright & A. Miller, Civil 2d §§ 2369–73. The judge also may dismiss upon a motion by defendant at the end of plaintiff's case due to insufficiency of evidence. When dismissal occurs at this stage, however, it is essentially a motion for a directed verdict. See § 12.3, below, on directed verdicts.

It should be noted that 1991 amendments to Federal Rule 41 deleted language authorizing use of Rule 41 as a device for evaluating the sufficiency of the evidence presented at trial by a plaintiff. That language was replaced by a new provision found in Rule 52(c) that would be more broadly useful. See Committee on Rules of Practice and Procedure, Judicial Conference of the United States (1990).

29. C. Wright, Federal Courts 696 (5th ed.1994).

30. See Calvert Fire Ins. Co. v. Cropper, 141 Cal.App.3d 901, 190 Cal.Rptr. 593 (1983) (dismissal for wilful failure to admit as requested in discovery). See generally § 7.16, above, on discovery sanctions.

31. See Phillips v. Arizona Bd. of Regents, 123 Ariz. 596, 601 P.2d 596 (1979); Scudder v. Haug, 197 Neb. 638, 250 N.W.2d 611 (1977); Anguiano v. Transcontinental Bus System, Inc., 76 Ariz. 246, 263 P.2d 305 (1953).

§§ 9.6–10.0 are reserved for supplementary material.

Chapter 10

THE TRIAL PROCESS

Analysis

Sec.
10.1 A General Description.
10.2 The Law of Evidence.

---

§ 10.1 A General Description

An attorney must be familiar with the specific rules of a forum in order to know just how a case is placed upon its trial calendar.[1] In some courts, in which each suit is assigned to a specific judge who handles every aspect of it, the procedural details for bringing a case to trial are left entirely in the judge's discretion.[2] In most jurisdictions, however, there are special rules and regulations to be followed. Most commonly, the party who desires assignment of a trial date must file a memorandum with the court stating that the case is "at issue," which means that the pleadings have been completed and filed.[3] Other information may be required such as whether the case is entitled to a preference on the calendar, the extent to which discovery has been completed, and whether a jury trial is demanded.[4] Upon submission of a properly completed memorandum, the case then is placed on the calendar list, normally according to when the memorandum was received.

The fact that a case is placed upon the trial calendar does not guarantee an early disposition. To the contrary, many courts have serious backlogs, sometimes as long as four or five years. Generally speaking these delays relate primarily to cases awaiting trial by jury.[5]

---

§ 10.1

1. See, e.g., Fed.Civ.Proc.Rule 40, which authorizes the federal district courts to adopt local rules governing the placing of actions upon the trial calendar.

2. See, e.g., Local Rules 12 and 16, U.S. Dist. Court, N.Dist.N.Y. (July 1975).

3. See, e.g., Cal.Rules of Ct., Rule 209(a); Fla.—West's F.S.A.Rules Civ.Proc., Rule 1.440; N.Y.—McKinney's CPLR 3402. Some jurisdictions do not require a trial-setting memorandum; they automatically place the case on the trial calendar when the pleadings are filed. See, e.g., N.J.Civ. Prac. Rule 4:36–2. In Iowa, no later than 120 days after a case has been commenced, the clerk of the court automatically sends a notice of a trial setting conference to all parties who are not in default. Iowa Rules Civ.Proc., Rule 181.

4. See Cal.Rules of Ct., Rule 209(a); Fla.—West's F.S.A.Rules Civ.Proc., Rule 1.440; N.Y.—McKinney's CPLR 3402.

5. H. Zeisel, H. Kalven & B. Buchholz, Delay in the Court 71–81 (1959); Peck, Do Juries Delay Justice?, 18 F.R.D. 455 (1955).

Courts maintain separate calendars for nonjury cases, and sometimes provide for early hearings for so-called "short causes," when the parties agree that the matter can be disposed of in less than one day.[6]

Because of long delays, a number of jurisdictions have adopted special statutes and rules giving preference to certain types of cases, thus advancing them to the top of the calendar list.[7] These include actions involving local government agencies, eminent domain, requests for temporary injunctions, unlawful detainer, and demands for wages.[8] Several states have provided for priority on the application of any litigant who has reached the age of seventy[9] or whose doctor certifies is not likely to live for more than six months.[10] Finally, some courts are given discretion to advance any case when the interests of justice will be served by an early trial.[11]

The placing of a case upon the trial calendar does not end the search for a precise trial date. Depending upon the rules of the particular forum, the attorneys for the litigants will be called to court sometime before their case reaches the top of the calendar to try to identify a specific date. This will then depend upon the estimated length of the trial, the attorneys' own schedules with respect to other cases, and similar factors. Inevitably, there will be a certain amount of jockeying among the judge and lawyers. Last minute adjustments frequently are required, since some prior scheduled cases may be settled on the eve of trial whereas others, already in trial, may take longer than was estimated. An experienced trial judge or administrator can do a great deal to eliminate unnecessary delay, particularly in conjunction with cooperative counsel. Nevertheless, there will be times when schedule changes, illness, and conflicting demands will result in unused courtrooms. In areas with large populations served by courts having many judges, the search for a particular trial date may be impossible; a tentative date will be set and then the parties and their attorneys simply may have to wait until a courtroom becomes available, all the while trying to avoid the scheduling of other, conflicting obligations. One of the major challenges to modern day courts is to find ways to minimize the backlog of cases by maximizing the utilization of existing resources, without compromising the quality of the trial process.[12]

In cases in which there is a right to jury trial, one of the major decisions that must be made is whether to invoke the right or to proceed

---

6. See, e.g., Cal.Rules of Ct., Rule 216.

7. See, e.g., West's Ann.Cal.Code Civ. Proc. § 36(a); N.Y.—McKinney's CPLR 3403; Pa.Rules Civ.Proc., Rule 214.

8. See authorities cited in note 7, above.

9. West's Ann.Cal.Code Civ.Proc. § 36(a); N.Y.—McKinney's CPLR 3403(a)(4).

10. West's Ann.Cal.Code Civ.Proc. § 36(d).

11. West's Ann.Cal.Code Civ.Proc. § 36(e); N.Y.—McKinney's CPLR 3403(a)(3); Pa.Rules Civ.Proc., Rule 214.

12. Burger, Isn't There a Better Way?, 68 A.B.A.J. 274–77 (1982); McCree, Bureaucratic Justice: An Early Warning, 129 U.Pa. L.Rev. 777–97 (1981); Posner, Will the Federal Courts of Appeal Survive Until 1984?, 56 S.Calif.L.Rev. 761–91 (1983).

to trial before a judge. As is discussed in the next Chapter, the right to a trial by jury in civil litigation depends upon the constitutional and statutory provisions in each jurisdiction.[13] The right must be properly invoked or it will be waived and the case tried by the judge as if no right existed.[14] In federal courts, as well as in many states, a judge has power to empanel an advisory jury when a right does not exist or has been waived.[15]

A variety of factors determine whether a particular litigant would prefer a judge or a jury trial. In many courts the nonjury calendar is fairly short whereas there are substantial delays before one can obtain a jury trial. If a litigant has a strong case and needs money to pay bills, the less delay, the better. Statistical studies indicate that judges and juries tend to agree on liability in the large majority of cases, although juries seem to have a greater disposition to find against government and corporate defendants and to provide larger awards in those cases.[16] Much depends upon the specific case, the nature of the community in which it is to be tried, the lawyer's personal success in past jury cases, and the effect that a jury demand will have on the settlement process. Much of pretrial decisionmaking is designed to raise the stakes for the opposing party in order to improve the level of the settlement that each side believes will occur. The cost—and risks—of going to trial, especially before a jury, are so high that settlement is often the only rational course.[17] Jury trials take considerably longer than do court trials; there is an elaborate jury selection process, arguments are longer, recesses are more frequent, and, in general, more witnesses will be called.[18] During a jury trial an attorney will have less sense of how she is doing than during a trial before a judge, who through comments and rulings on specific points often will make known what is and what is not considered to be significant. The following brief description of a trial illuminates further some of the differences between judge and jury cases.

The first order of business in a jury trial is selecting the jurors, the mechanics of which are discussed later.[19] Counsel for each of the parties will attempt to assess which of the potential jurors will identify with her client or the client's interests. In general, the lawyer can make only an educated guess as to which individuals will be favorably disposed.[20] Even after fairly extensive questioning on voir dire, a person's true feelings

---

13. See §§ 11.3–11.8, below.

14. See Fed.Civ.Proc.Rule 38(b), (d).

15. See Fed.Civ.Proc.Rule 38(c).

16. Broeder, The University of Chicago Jury Project, 38 Neb.L.Rev. 744, 750–51 (1959). But see Bledsoe, Jury or Nonjury Trial—A Defense Viewpoint, in 5 Am.Jur.Trials 123, 129, 139 (1966) (on the average juries do not give larger awards than do judges).

17. Tarangelo, Early Settlement: The Key to Cutting Legal Costs, 23 For the Defense 26–27 (Dec.1981).

18. See H. Zeisel, H. Kalven & B. Buchholz, Delay in the Court 71–81 (1959).

19. See § 11.10, below.

20. The existence and discovery of jurors' biases are complex matters that have not as yet been fully explored scientifically. See Hans & Vidmar, Jury Selection, in R. Kerr & N. Bray, The Psychology of the Courtroom 39–82 (1982).

may remain hidden.[21] Nevertheless, it is important that in courts in which such questioning is permitted, an attorney make an effort to establish a dialogue with each potential juror and to listen carefully for possible biases and hostilities.[22]

In addition to seeking favorable jurors on an individual basis, a careful lawyer also will pay attention to how various potential jurors will work together and affect each other's views. The presence of one dominant personality on the panel may be of far greater importance than a number of others who are favorably disposed toward one's client. People who exude confidence or who exhibit relevant expertise may control the course of the deliberations and, ultimately, the verdict itself.[23]

Generally speaking, in jury cases the order of trial will be as follows:

1. Plaintiff's opening statement

2. Defendant's opening statement

3. Plaintiff's presentation of direct evidence

4. Defendant's presentation of direct evidence

5. Plaintiff's presentation of rebuttal evidence

6. Defendant's presentation of rebuttal evidence

7. Opening final argument by plaintiff

8. Defendant's final argument

9. Plaintiff's closing final argument

10. Instructions to the jury

In some jurisdictions there are no special rules and the sequence is left to the discretion of the court.[24] In others the order is specified, subject to alteration by the judge in the interest of justice.[25] When the issues in the action are such that the burden of proof falls mainly upon defendant, the order of the parties often will be switched.[26]

---

21. See Kaplan, Cognitive Processes in the Individual Juror, in R. Kerr & N. Bray, The Psychology of the Courtroom 211–14 (1982).

22. See Keiner, Jury Selection: The Prejudice Syndrome, 19 Trial 48 (July 1983); Suggs & Sales, Using Communication Clues To Evaluate Prospective Jurors During the Voir Dire, 20 Ariz.L.Rev. 629 (1978); Turley, Voir Dire: Preparation and Execution, 8 Litigation 19, 21–22, 60 (Spring 1982). See also Broeder, Plaintiff's Family Status as Affecting Jury Behavior: Some Tentative Insights, 14 J.Pub.L. 131 (1965); Ziegler, Young Adults as a Cognizable Group in Jury Selection, 76 Mich.L.Rev. 1045 (1978).

23. See Bevan, Albert, Loiseaux, Mayfield & Wright, Jury Behavior as a Function of the Prestige of the Foreman and the Nature of His Leadership, 7 J.Pub.L. 419 (1958); Broeder, Occupational Expertise and Bias as Affecting Jury Behavior: A Preliminary Look, 40 N.Y.U.L.Rev. 1079 (1965); Vinson, Shadow Juries: Monitoring Jurors' Reactions, 19 Trial 75, 77–78 (Sept. 1983); Vinson, The Shadow Jury: An Experiment in Litigation Science, 68 A.B.A.J. 1242, 1245 (1982).

24. See N.Y.—McKinney's CPLR 4011.

25. See, e.g., Ky.Rules Civ.Proc., Rule 43.02; Neb.Rev.Stat. § 25–1107; Vernon's Ann.Tex.Rules Civ.Proc., Rule 265. But see Iowa Rules Civ.Proc., Rule 191, which appears to require the courts to follow a specified order.

26. See authorities cited in note 25, above.

In nonjury cases, the order is strictly up to the trial judge and the proceedings generally will be far less formal. Often the court will dispense with opening statements because the judge will have become familiar with the issues through conferences with counsel. Frequently, the court will request that the attorneys forego closing arguments,[27] and there never will be a need for formal instructions.

In jury tried cases, the opening statements are considered by most litigating attorneys as crucial. According to one author, they determine the outcome in more than fifty percent of the cases, perhaps in as many as eighty-five percent.[28]

As previously noted,[29] the presentation of the case typically begins with plaintiff's opening statement. However, in a case in which defendant has the burden of proof on all of the issues in the action, such as when the defendant admits all of plaintiff's allegations and the trial goes forward solely on the affirmative defenses, the roles will be reversed, and defendant will give the first statement. In general, lawyers regard the right to speak first as vital; plaintiff's attorneys, therefore, will attempt to structure their pleadings so as to include some issues that defendant must deny. At the outset of the trial the jurors are fresh and attentive. They know little about the action and are somewhat eager to learn what is at stake. An attorney who presents a coherent, plausible story may be able to make an indelible impression that will carry through to a favorable verdict. At the very least, it will put substantial pressure on the opposing attorney to overcome this initial advantage.[30]

In most jurisdictions, defendant (or plaintiff when defendant delivers the initial opening statement) has the option of presenting an opening statement immediately after plaintiff opens or after plaintiff has put on the direct evidence. Most expert trial attorneys recommend that defendant open at the earliest opportunity. That way the facts as stated by plaintiff do not become more deeply embedded in the minds of the jurors by hearing evidence that seems to support plaintiff's point of view. In a well-constructed opening statement, defendant can show that there is another view of the facts to be considered and the jurors will tend to be more cautious about making up their minds. Moreover, points made on cross-examination of plaintiff's initial witnesses will be more meaningful if the jurors have some idea of what defendant is attempting to show. Some trial lawyers, however, think defendant's opening statement has its maximum effect when it refutes the evidence plaintiff already has presented.[31]

27. There is no right to give a closing argument in a nonjury civil action. See J. Tanford, The Trial Process; Law, Tactics and Ethics 139 (1983); Gordon, Nonjury Summations, in 6 Am.Jur.Trials § 5, at 778–80 (1967).

28. Lindquist, Advocacy in Opening Statements, 8 Litigation 23 (Spring 1982).

29. See authorities cited in note 25, above.

30. For a discussion of experimental studies on the significance of the order of the arguments and proof, see Walker, Thibault & Andreoli, Order of Presentation at Trial, 82 Yale L.J. 216 (1972). See also Lawson, Order of Presentation as a Factor in Jury Presentation, 56 Ky.L.J. 523 (1968).

31. See, e.g., Stramondo & Goodspeed, Defendant's Presentation, 57 Mass.L.Q. 179 (1972).

Evidence is presented through witnesses, by the introduction of documents and, occasionally, other items that bear on the issues. There are elaborate, intricate sets of rules with regard to what is and what is not admissible evidence. These are summarized in the next section.

When a witness is called to testify, she is first sworn to tell the truth.[32] Then the attorney who called the witness proceeds to ask questions on direct examination. The questions may be pointed and sharp or they may call for a narrative of events, depending upon the nature of the issues and the personality of the particular witness. Normally, on direct examination the attorney is not permitted to ask leading questions,[33] that is, questions that suggest the answer desired. For example, a witness may be asked, "What color was the traffic light when defendant entered the intersection?," but not, "Defendant drove right through the red light, didn't he?" This general rule is not applied when the witness is an opposing party or otherwise is shown to be hostile to the party who called her.[34] Moreover, the trial judge has discretion to permit the use of leading questions to expedite the introduction of background information.[35]

When the direct examination has been completed, the opposing party is entitled to cross-examine the witness. The proscription against leading questions does not apply to cross-examination.[36] Normally cross-examination is confined to those matters that were explored on direct.[37] An attorney who wants to go beyond, into new areas, must obtain court permission or wait to call the witness himself. In either case the questioning at that point will be treated as direct examination.[38] When cross-examination has been completed, the attorney who called the witness may conduct redirect examination to clarify the testimony. If the attorney does that, the opposing party will be permitted to recross-examine.

A party who wishes to introduce a document or other item into evidence first presents it for identification, so that all references to it in the record will be clear. Usually this is done by assigning an identification number to each item. Then, unless the parties previously have stipulated to the item's admissibility, the proponent must present testimony to establish the item's admissibility.[39] Once that is accomplished the item will be accepted formally into evidence and the trier of fact may consider it.[40]

---

32. See Fed.Evid.Rule 603.

33. See Fed.Evid.Rule 611(c).

34. Ibid.

35. Ibid.

36. Ibid.

37. See Fed.Evid.Rule 611(b); Annot., 45 A.L.R.Fed. 639 (1979).

38. See Fed.Evid.Rule 611(b).

39. See McCormick on Evidence § 212 (4th ed.1992); Fed.Evid.Rule 901(a).

40. On occasion, evidence will be admissible for a limited purpose in a situation in which it might be used more generally. For example, under some circumstances if a witness has made a prior statement inconsistent with her testimony at trial, the prior statement is admissible to show that the witness is unreliable, but is not admissible for its truth. In a jury case, the judge will issue a so-called limiting instruction, telling the jury to consider the evidence only for

Under the adversary system, strictly applied, the trial judge acts merely as an impartial umpire, deciding only upon the admissibility of evidence as offered by the parties. Thus, in the past, it has been held improper for a judge to intervene in the presentation of evidence by asking extensive questions.[41] Generally speaking, however, modern courts permit the judge to call witnesses,[42] particularly experts,[43] and to interrogate any witness, regardless of who called her, if justice so demands.[44] Nevertheless, courts are reluctant to interfere in counsel's planned presentation, even if one of the attorneys seems overmatched. It is never quite clear whether what appears as an inadequate examination is in fact a carefully calculated trial tactic designed to disarm the opposing side, or whether the failure to call someone who seems to be a key witness for a party is a wise move in light of some highly detrimental testimony that might emerge on cross-examination.

An important change in the role of the trial judge has occurred in recent years in connection with the growth of so-called "public interest litigation." Today, a case brought by one individual or organization against another may have a dramatic effect on others who are not parties. This may occur with respect to charges of racial or sexual discrimination against a large employer, improper administrative actions by government officials, or violations of environmental protection laws, for example. An individual plaintiff may not have the resources or the vision to see the full implications of the case he has brought. The remedy sought may be sufficient for the plaintiff, but not sufficient to protect others who will be affected. The trial judge must be an activist, involved in the development of evidence and the establishment of an appropriate remedy, if any. In this type of litigation, "we have left the passive arbiter of the traditional model a long way behind."[45]

During the course of trial, no matter how well planned, the presentation of evidence necessarily is done in piecemeal fashion. Each witness may cover certain aspects of an issue, but not all. In addition there are inevitable interruptions and diversions that make it difficult, if not impossible, for the trier of fact, particularly a jury, to obtain a coherent picture of a party's case. Final argument provides the opportunity for each side to bring it all together, without interruption, and to set forth the logical implications of the evidence that has been presented. Knowledgeable practitioners urge attorneys to outline their final arguments as soon as they begin work on the case. "Your objective from the beginning of legal research and factual investigation is to develop the theory for

---

the appropriate purpose. See Fed.Evid.Rule 105.

41. See Laub, Trial and Submission of a Case From a Judge's Standpoint, 34 Temple L.Q. 1, 5–6 (1960).

42. Fed.Evid.Rule 614(a); Annot., 53 A.L.R.Fed. 498 (1981).

43. Fed.Evid.Rule 706; Annot., 95 A.L.R.2d 390 (1964).

44. Fed.Evid.Rule 614(b). See generally Gitelson & Gitelson, A Trial Judge's Credo Must Include His Affirmative Duty To Be an Instrumentality of Justice, 7 Santa Clara Law. 7 (1966).

45. Chayes, The Role of the Judge in Public Law Litigation, 89 Harv.L.Rev. 1281, 1298 (1976).

final argument. The theory becomes the framework on which the rest of trial preparation takes place.''[46]

Final argument usually is in three parts. The plaintiff is given the right to speak both first and last unless defendant had the burden of proof on the major issues tried, in which case the roles will be reversed.[47] Often the court will impose time limits on each of the parties.[48] Whether or not formal limits are imposed, however, an attorney should make her argument concise and to the point, emphasizing in direct and simple language the vital aspects of the case.[49] Trial judges tend to be lenient with lawyers, allowing them to argue emotionally and to "puff" their clients' cases, so long as the evidence or the law is not distorted.[50] It is not proper to argue on the basis of facts that are not in evidence or to couch statements in a way that assumes or implies that facts are in evidence when they are not.[51] Furthermore, it is improper to discuss a proposition of law that the trier of fact would be required to apply, at least until the court has formally accepted that proposition as correct.[52]

Whenever a case is tried before a jury, it must be instructed with respect to the law to be applied and the technical aspects of its deliberations. Courts differ on when the instructions should be given. The majority require them to be given after the final arguments on the ground that the judge, rather than one of the parties, should have the last word.[53] Others, however, believe that they are appropriate just prior to the final arguments so that the attorneys can refer to the instructions during the course of their summations.[54] Many writers believe that the court should instruct the jurors throughout the course of the trial, not to replace the final charge, but to make certain that the jury has some knowledge of the case and the significance of the evidence at the time it is presented. They advocate that a preliminary set of instructions be given at the very outset, before the opening statements, and that mid-trial instructions be presented whenever they would be useful, such as in complex or protracted cases.[55]

---

46. Cicero, Nondefensive Final Argument for the Defense, 8 Litigation 45 (Spring 1982).

47. See Annot., 53 A.L.R.Fed. 900 (1981).

48. Annot., 71 A.L.R.4th 130 (1989).

49. See Cleary, The Final Argument in a Criminal Case, 27 Practical Law. 39, 51 (Sept.1981); Sisson, The Closing Argument, 57 Mass.L.Q. 319 (1972).

50. See Argument to Jury—Permissible Limits, 22 Defense L.J. 277, 282–87 (1973).

51. See Levin & Levy, Persuading the Jury with Facts Not in Evidence: The Fiction–Science Spectrum, 105 U.Pa.L.Rev. 139 (1956); Annot., 37 A.L.R.2d 662 (1954).

52. See Gair, Summations for the Plaintiff, in 6 Am.Jur.Trials 641, 660–61 (1967).

53. See Schwarzer, Communication with Juries: Problems and Remedies, 69 Calif.L.Rev. 731, 755 (1981). The 1987 Amendment to Federal Rule of Civil Procedure 51 allows the judge to instruct the jury before or after final arguments, or both. Fed.Civ.Proc.Rule 51.

54. See, e.g., Ky.Rules Civ.Proc., Rule 51(2). Nebraska provides that on motion of a party, instructions will be given in advance of closing arguments. However, the court may charge the jury again after the arguments have been concluded. Neb.Rev. Stat. § 25–1107.

55. Schwarzer, Communication with Juries: Problems and Remedies, 69 Calif.L.Rev. 731, 755–56 (1981); Note, Jury Instructions v. Jury Charges, 82 W.Va.L.Rev. 555, 562–67 (1980).

Under modern rules in nearly all jurisdictions, the trial judge controls the time when the parties must submit proposed instructions.[56] The court, after consultation with and sometimes argument by the parties, determines which of these to give and which of its own to add or substitute. The lawyers are informed and given an opportunity to object. In most jurisdictions the failure to object to an instruction or to request that an instruction be given precludes appeal on the ground that the instructions were improper,[57] unless the error is grievous and resulted in a miscarriage of justice.[58]

In recent years, a good deal of attention has been given to the specific language and form of instructions to make them understandable and capable of application.[59] Studies show a definite need to simplify the language and to avoid legal jargon; the problems that jurors have are linguistic not conceptual.[60] Unfortunately, recent changes in jury instructions appear to have eased the burden of the court and the lawyers, but have not necessarily aided the jurors. Perhaps the most dramatic development has been the utilization of so-called "pattern instructions," those that have been formally approved as "correct" in a particular jurisdiction.[61] In some places their use is mandatory as to certain issues.[62] Pattern instructions are used even when not mandatory because they will not result in a reversal. However, they are not drafted for the benefit of the jurors and tend to be as difficult to understand as instructions proposed by counsel on a case-by-case basis.[63] Courts must recognize the need for sets of instructions that are as short as possible, comprehensible by ordinary citizens, and set forth in a logical fashion so as to let the jury know just what it is that it is deciding.

After all arguments are completed and the instructions given, the jury retires to deliberate. Technically, at least, the jurors are in the custody of the bailiff who keeps them together and protects them from interference from outsiders. Sometimes in criminal cases jurors will be kept together even at night when their deliberations are recessed.[64] Rarely, if ever, will a civil jury be so restrained;[65] the jurors will be

---

56. See Fed.Civ.Proc.Rule 51.

57. Fed.Civ.Proc.Rule 51.

58. Appellate courts have not always agreed as to when the trial judge has committed "plain error" in failing properly to instruct so as to permit reversal even though no requests or objections were made. Compare Alexander v. Kramer Bros. Freight Lines, Inc., 273 F.2d 373 (2d Cir. 1959), with Beardshall v. Minuteman Press Int'l, Inc., 664 F.2d 23, 26–27 (3d Cir.1981). As to the required specificity of objections to instructions, see Annot., 35 A.L.R.Fed. 727 (1977).

59. See Farrell, Communication in the Courtroom: Jury Instructions, 85 W.Va. L.Rev. 5 (1982); Schwarzer, Communication with Juries: Problems and Remedies, 69 Calif.L.Rev. 731, 740 (1981).

60. Ibid.

61. See Farrell, Communication in the Courtroom: Jury Instructions, 85 W.Va. L.Rev. 5, 12–13 (1982); Schwarzer, Communication with Juries: Problems and Remedies, 69 Calif.L.Rev. 731, 736 (1981).

62. Schwarzer, Communication with Juries: Problems and Remedies, 69 Calif.L.Rev. 731, 737 (1981).

63. Id. at 739.

64. Rizzi, The Period After Closing Arguments—An Important But Overlooked Part of a Trial, Part II, 69 Ill.B.J. 631, 637–38 (1981).

65. See generally Annot., 77 A.L.R.2d 1086 (1961).

allowed to go home after being admonished by the judge not to discuss the case with anyone outside the jury room and not to read or listen to anything in the media concerning the case.

During the course of the deliberations it is not unusual for the jury to ask for clarification of the instructions or for the reading of certain portions of the testimony. In general, the court will inform all counsel of the request, hear any arguments for or against granting it, and then exercise its discretion in deciding what steps, if any, should be taken.[66] The jury request may be denied if it could be misleading—for example, if it would emphasize one portion of the testimony that should not be considered out of context. A failure to notify the attorneys and give them an opportunity to be heard before ruling on the jury's request may lead to reversal of the judgment.[67]

In some instances, the jury may report that it is deadlocked and cannot reach a verdict. Trial judges understandably are reluctant to dismiss a jury that cannot reach a verdict because of the waste of time and expense. Thus they may send the jurors back for further deliberations, sometimes with a special instruction asking them to consider each other's views. The fact that a jury says that it is deadlocked is not in itself sufficient to declare a mistrial. Jurors often give up whenever a serious disagreement appears without deliberating for a sufficient time to be able to reconcile or alter their views, particularly in a case with complex issues or multiple parties. When asked to try again, they frequently do manage to reach a verdict.[68] However, the court must be careful not to appear to order them to agree. It is improper to tell them that a deadlock will result in a costly new trial or anything else that will exert pressure on any juror to come to a decision contrary to his convictions as to what the evidence shows.[69] It also is improper to keep them in session long after a true deadlock has been reached so that they believe that the only way the trial will ever end is to arrive at a verdict regardless of its content.[70]

In most jurisdictions the jury is handed a set of forms upon which to set out its verdict. In a simple tort case, for example, one form may state, "We find for the defendant," while another will read, "We find for the plaintiff in the amount of $_____." In cases with complex issues or multiple parties, there may be a stack of forms, each dealing with a separate issue, claim, or party.

After the jury has rendered its verdict, the court or one of the parties may wish to have the jury "polled," in order to make certain that in fact the verdict was agreed upon by the requisite number of jurors

66. See Rizzi, The Period After Closing Arguments—An Important But Overlooked Part of a Trial, Part I, 69 Ill.B.J. 548, 552–56 (1981).

67. See Annot., 32 A.L.R.Fed. 392 (1977); Annot., 84 A.L.R. 220 (1933).

68. See Rizzi, The Period After Closing Arguments—An Important But Overlooked

Part of a Trial, Part II, 69 Ill.B.J. 631, 635 (1981).

69. See id. at 634–37 (1981); Annot., 38 A.L.R.3d 1281 (1971); Annot., 41 A.L.R.3d 845, 1154 (1972).

70. See Annot., 164 A.L.R. 1265 (1946).

required in the particular jurisdiction to constitute a verdict. In many jurisdictions a party has a right to a poll; in others it is a matter of discretion.[71] The trial judge conducts the poll by asking each juror whether he or she agrees with the verdict, making certain that any expressed doubts are fully explored.[72] If it turns out that the requisite number of jurors do not support the verdict as initially rendered, the court may send the jury back for further deliberations or declare a mistrial, depending on whether continued jury discussions might lead to a valid verdict without fear that any of the jurors will feel undue pressure to decide one way or another.

One of the more difficult questions involving the validity of a verdict is whether the jurors must all agree on each of the issues. Consider, for example, a personal injury action in which plaintiff alleges three separate factual bases for finding that defendant was negligent. Suppose that the jurors split eight to four against a finding of negligence on each of these bases, but as to every determination, a different four jurors thought that negligence had been established. Thus, despite their disagreements on the specific factual issues, all twelve jurors find defendant at fault and return a verdict for plaintiff.[73] The existence of this situation will not often come to light because it usually is not known just how individual jurors voted,[74] except when the situation is exposed by a post-verdict poll. But when the court does learn how the votes were divided, should the verdict be allowed to stand? Courts have split on the matter, although the trend seems to be in favor of upholding the verdict.[75] The result turns on whether the particular jurisdiction views the proper role of the jury merely to decide specific factual issues or to determine the overall outcome of the case.

§ 10.2 The Law of Evidence

The law of evidence is a special branch of the law of procedure. Today, a large majority of state,[1] as well as federal,[2] courts are governed

---

71. See generally Annot., 71 A.L.R.2d 640 (1960).

72. See Rizzi, The Period After Closing Arguments—An Important But Overlooked Part of a Trial, Part II, 69 Ill.B.J. 631, 638–41 (1981).

73. A similar difficulty sometimes arises in jurisdictions where unanimity of the jury is not required. See § 11.11 at n. 23, below. For example, in a jurisdiction in which a two-thirds vote is required, eight out of twelve jurors may vote in favor of plaintiff on the issue of liability and eight may agree on the amount of damages to be awarded. The problem arises if the eight who voted for liability are not the same eight who voted on damages.

74. See Trubitt, Patchwork Verdicts, Different–Jurors Verdicts, and American Jury Theory: Whether Verdicts Are Invalidated By Juror Disagreement On Issues, 36 Okla.L.Rev. 473, 516–17 (1983).

75. Id. at 523, 526–28.

§ 10.2

1. A few states, such as California, Kansas and New Jersey, adopted comprehensive evidence regulations long before the federal courts did so. These states followed the 1953 version of the Uniform Rules of Evidence. See 13 Uniform Laws Ann., Uniform Rules of Evidence, Historical Note 209. In 1974, a new set of Uniform Rules of Evidence were adopted. They are nearly identical to the Federal Rules of Evidence except for rules of privilege, which the federal provisions leave to common-law development and application. See Fed.Evid.Rule 501. The similarities between the 1953 Uniform Rules and the 1974 version strongly outweigh their differences.

---

2. See note 2 on page 483.

by comprehensive sets of statutes or rules of evidence, just as they are governed by comprehensive rules of procedure. The evidence provisions are detailed and complex. What follows is of necessity an incomplete sketch designed to give only an overall outline of the most significant areas of those provisions. However, it is worth noting that well over half of the states now have adopted evidence provisions modeled after the Federal Rules of Evidence, which became effective in 1975.

At the outset it is important to understand the necessity for any rules of evidence. Why should litigants not have an absolute right to present to the court and the trier of fact whatever information they feel might be helpful to them in establishing their cases? There are three basic reasons for limiting the scope of information that parties otherwise might present, and all of the evidentiary rules controlling admissibility follow directly from those reasons.

First, courts should not waste time receiving worthless information. If litigants, or their attorneys, were permitted to introduce into evidence anything they desired, the courts would have even greater problems than they now have in controlling their workloads. Lawyers who were not subject to controls of any kind might feel compelled to include information that they believed to be useless, on the off chance that a judge or jury might find it helpful. Attorneys, caught in suits that appear hopelessly lost, could drag out the proceedings for weeks or even years in the hope that something of real value might turn up to turn the tide.

It is for this reason that courts have developed the rule of relevancy, requiring that evidence, to be admissible, must be of possible aid to the trier of fact in making its decision.[3] Although the rule may seem simple on its face, it often is difficult to administer for several reasons.

To be relevant, evidence need only have the capacity to help in the decision. It in fact may not play a role at all, such as when testimony is disregarded because the jury believes the witness to be a liar. Furthermore, evidence may be relevant even though it is not conclusive of the matter to be decided.[4] If, for example, the issue was whether defendant had been warned of a dangerous condition on his premises, testimony that someone waiting immediately outside the open door to defendant's office had complained loudly about the condition would be considered relevant even though that evidence, standing alone, would not be sufficient to justify a finding of defendant's knowledge. Indeed, one might argue that the evidence is irrelevant—that is, totally worthless—unless some evidence is produced that defendant was in the office at the time the statement was made or that defendant heard it or was in a position to do so. When the relevance of different items thus are interdependent, the court will admit one on the attorney's promise that the other will be

2. See Federal Evidence Rules, effective July 1, 1975. See generally C. Wright & K. Graham, Evidence, vols. 21–26; C. Wright & V. Gold, Evidence, vols. 27–29.

3. See Fed.Evid.Rule 402.

4. See Fed.Evid.Rule 401; West's Ann. Cal.Evid.Code § 210.

produced.[5] If the promise is not kept, the court may strike the item that was admitted,[6] warning the jury to ignore it, or, if the opposing party is seriously prejudiced, the court may order a new trial.

Reasonable people also may differ as to whether an item is relevant. Suppose, for example, that Z wants to "break" his deceased father's will by establishing that the latter was mentally incompetent at the time the will was written. As evidence, Z offers the fact that at the time of making the will, the father, although quite wealthy, was living in a county-operated "old folks home" that has long since been abandoned. In the past, at least in some places, such homes may have been reserved only for those who could not afford to live elsewhere and those whose mental state made it impossible for them to care for themselves. Whether the evidence is considered "helpful" well may depend on the trial judge's general experience and beliefs as to the admissions policies of these institutions in the jurisdiction. Of course, decisions as to relevancy are subject to appellate review, so that a panel of three or more judges will be able to control decisions based on a single judge's idiosyncratic views; in any event, however, the determination will be made by members of the judiciary and may not coincide with generally held views of the public at large.

A second reason for excluding information from trial exists when that information, though relevant, may engender such harm that it should not be admitted into evidence. Even if everyone agrees that an item of evidence would be of some assistance to the trier of fact, the amount of help may be insignificant in light of the prejudice it is likely to cause. Suppose, for example, that plaintiff alleges that defendant entered into a contract in New York on a particular day, but defendant claims that he was in another city. Although plaintiff knows a number of businessmen willing to testify that they saw defendant in New York on the day in question, plaintiff elects to call instead a New York police officer to testify that on that day he arrested defendant on a drunk driving charge. On defendant's objection, the officer's testimony normally would be held inadmissible; there is no need to introduce the irrelevant and highly prejudicial fact of defendant's arrest when other evidence is available to prove his location. It is important to recognize that evidence is not prejudicial merely because it tends strongly to refute a litigant's position. Evidence is prejudicial when it will induce the trier of fact to rely on irrelevant aspects of an otherwise relevant item.[7]

There are two different methods by which the value of a specific item of evidence is determined to be outweighed by its likely prejudicial effects. First, the trial judge, in her discretion may so decide on a case-by-case basis, taking into consideration all the factors that pertain to the particular suit involved.[8] That decision is subject to appellate review, but only on the ground that the trial judge has abused her discretion.

---

5. See Fed.Evid.Rule 104(b); 1 S. Saltzburg & M. Martin, Federal Rules of Evidence Manual 40 & n. 1 (5th ed.1990).

6. See McCormick on Evidence § 58 (4th ed.1992.)

7. See id. § 185.

8. See Fed.Evid.Rule 403.

Second, the law, through elaborate sets of evidence rules, established by common law, rule or legislation, in effect declares certain types of evidence to be so prejudicial that they are inadmissible per se, taking the matter out of the hands of the trial judge. Some of the major types of evidence subject to these regulations, such as hearsay, are discussed below.

Hearsay is defined as a statement made out of court that is offered to prove the truth of the matter stated.[9] Hearsay is considered inherently prejudicial because the party against whom it would be used would not have an opportunity to cross-examine the person who made the statement at the time it was made.[10] The speaker may have been joking, or guessing, or even deliberately lying.

It cannot be said that hearsay is never of value, only that the dangers are thought to be so grave that the excess of harm over good dictates exclusion of the information. The trouble with this view is that the law recognizes many circumstances when the balance favors admissibility. To deal with these situations, the evidence rules define a large number of specific exceptions to the general prohibition against hearsay evidence.[11] These exceptions fall into two basic categories, one in which circumstances help to assure that the evidence is reliable, and another in which the nature of the issue is such that it is not likely that other evidence exists to prove the matter in question. Examples of the first category include spontaneous utterances when the person making the statement had no time to reflect or fabricate; business records that are important to the day-to-day operations of the business involved; and statements of physical symptoms made by a patient to a doctor for purposes of diagnosis and treatment. Examples of the second category include statements by a person as to his state of mind, such as his intent, plan or motive, and statements of a person, now deceased, as to the existence, identification, or revocation of her will.

It is important to realize that even though an item of hearsay information falls within one of the exceptions to the hearsay rule, the evidence will not necessarily be admitted. The trial judge retains discretion to exclude the item if the judge finds that in the particular action the value of the item is outweighed by its likely prejudicial effect.

Character information also receives special treatment because of its potentially prejudicial effect. With but few exceptions, evidence of a person's character is not admitted to show that he acted in conformity with his character on any particular occasion.[12] "Character" is broadly defined for this purpose to include any general propensity to act in a certain way. For example, the fact that a person has had a number of convictions for reckless driving is inadmissible in a suit against that person for negligently causing a traffic accident. The danger that the trier will assume that a poor driver was acting improperly on the

---

9. See Fed.Evid.Rule 801(c).

10. See McCormick on Evidence § 245 (4th ed.1992).

11. See Fed.Evid.Rules 803, 804.

12. See Fed.Evid.Rule 404(a).

occasion in question, or that the driver might be held liable as punishment for past acts, is considered to outweigh any slight value the evidence might have in establishing what occurred in the particular case.

This does not mean, of course, that evidence of past activity never is admissible. It can be introduced if it is offered for some purpose, other than to establish character,[13] that is directly relevant to the case before the court. For instance, evidence regarding a prior accident will be allowed if it would show that the driver knew that at the time of the current accident, he was operating a vehicle with defective brakes. Moreover, as an exception to the general rule, certain evidence of a witness' past propensity to tell the truth is permissible to cast doubt upon or revitalize that witness' credibility.[14]

Another type of evidence that receives special treatment are compromise offers. It is not unusual during the course of pretrial jockeying among the parties, that an offer is made to compromise. If the offer is rejected, under modern rules neither it nor statements made in connection with it are admissible.[15] There are two reasons. First, the value of the evidence is limited; offers may be made not because a person is liable or guilty, but because the person does not want to gamble on an unfavorable result, or because the cost of going forward is far out of proportion with the value of an ultimate victory. Nevertheless, upon hearing that an offer has been extended, a trier of fact may jump to the conclusion that the offering party has conceded responsibility. Second, it is desirable to encourage out-of-court settlements. Litigants would be extremely reluctant to make offers if they could be used against them at trial. A number of jurisdictions have extended the rule prohibiting the admission of offers to compromise to include humanitarian gestures, such as a guarantee by one party to an accident to pay the hospital bills of another.[16]

For similar reasons, evidence of subsequent repairs or insurance also generally is inadmissible because of its potential for prejudice. Thus, in a tort action, the fact that subsequent to the accident or injury, defendant made repairs to the instrumentality that caused the harm is not admissible to establish that defendant was at fault for not making the repairs prior to the time of the injury.[17] Moreover, the fact that defendant was insured for the harm that resulted is not admissible to show that defendant had less reason to take steps to avoid the harm in the first place.[18] Here, as in the case with offers to compromise, there are two basic reasons for excluding the information. First, the fact that an individual insures against the possibility of injury or that, after an injury, she takes steps to keep it from happening again, does not provide strong evidence that the individual was negligent or otherwise liable for wrongdoing. Yet that is precisely what a trier of fact may conclude.

13. See Fed.Evid.Rule 404(b).

14. See Fed.Evid.Rules 404(a)(3), 608, 609.

15. See Fed.Evid.Rules 408, 410.

16. See Fed.Evid.Rule 409.

17. See Fed.Evid.Rule 407.

18. See Fed.Evid.Rule 411.

Moreover, with respect to insurance, the trier of fact simply may find liability on an "ability to pay" theory. Second, society wants to encourage people to eliminate dangerous situations and to insure against potential harm. Therefore, they should not be "penalized" for doing so.

A third major justification for excluding information from trial is based on important social policy reasons. Thus, some evidence, although valuable and nonprejudicial, will be inadmissible even though its exclusion might result in an incorrect factual determination at trial. In general, these exclusions fall within the laws of "evidentiary privilege."

There are several different kinds of privilege. The most common are the so-called "communication" privileges that protect conversations between individuals who are in a special relationship. The most notable are those involving attorneys and clients,[19] doctors and patients,[20] mental health practitioners and patients,[21] religious leaders and parishioners,[22] and husbands and wives.[23] Individual jurisdictions sometimes include other relationships, such as accountants and clients.[24] To be privileged, a conversation must be in confidence and, except for conversations between spouses, must be in the course of seeking professional advice. These privileges are based on the idea that society wants to encourage its members to seek appropriate advice when they need it, and, further, that it must protect professionals if they are to feel free to ascertain the true nature of the problems presented.

A second type of privilege, the so-called "testimonial privilege," goes much further. It does not merely protect against disclosure of statements made by one person to another, rather, it actually allows eyewitnesses to refuse to testify at all. This category includes the privilege against self-incrimination[25] and the privilege of one spouse not to testify against another in a criminal trial.[26] These protections are based on the notion that it is too much to ask a person who is sworn to tell the truth to incriminate himself or a spouse; society ought not place individuals in such delicate situations.

Other privileges exist to protect specific types of information in special circumstances. For example, in many situations neither the government[27] nor members of the news media[28] are required to reveal the names of their informants. Without that protection, sources of important information needed by society would not be willing to come forward.

In addition to these basic rules and regulations regarding admissibility, the laws of evidence provide a number of other safeguards to ensure that information sought to be introduced is reliable. The first of these

---

19. See Uniform Evid.Rule 502.

20. See Uniform Evid.Rule 503.

21. See Uniform Evid.Rule 503.

22. See Uniform Evid.Rule 505.

23. See Uniform Evid.Rule 504.

24. About one third of the states have established this privilege. McCormick on Evidence § 76.2 (4th ed.1992).

25. See McCormick on Evidence § 116 (4th ed.1992).

26. See Trammel v. U.S., 445 U.S. 40, 100 S.Ct. 906, 63 L.Ed.2d 186 (1980).

27. See Uniform Evid.Rule 509. The leading case is Roviaro v. U.S., 353 U.S. 53, 77 S.Ct. 623, 1 L.Ed.2d 639 (1957).

28. See Annot., 99 A.L.R.3d 37 (1980).

are found in provisions governing documents and other real evidence. An attorney often will attempt to introduce into evidence a tangible item that bears favorably on her client's case. In order to do so, the attorney must lay a proper foundation for admissibility by showing, through testimony, exactly how the item relates to the suit. Thus, if the prosecution wants to introduce a pistol into a robbery case, it must establish facts to show how that particular pistol is relevant. Not only must witnesses testify that the robber displayed a gun at the time the crime was committed, but the prosecution must go on to show some evidence by which it can be inferred that the gun being offered is the same one that was used. This is no more than an application of the ordinary rule of relevancy. Courts tend to apply the rule stringently, however, when real evidence is involved because, unlike testimony, tangible items may have a more indelible impact on the jurors.

Most of the real evidence introduced at trial is in the form of documents. There are two special rules that govern the admissibility of documents. First is the rule of authentication, that requires a showing that a document is what its proponent claims it to be before it will be admitted into evidence.[29] In the ordinary situation, this means only that the person offering the document must produce evidence that it was signed or prepared by the person who is claimed to have signed or prepared it. The fact that a signature, "James Q. Johnson," appears on the face of the paper is not by itself sufficient to show that James Q. Johnson signed it. Other testimony must be elicited before the document will be admitted. Of course, Johnson may testify that the signature is his, or someone familiar with Johnson's handwriting may so testify, or an expert can be called to compare known samples of Johnson's handwriting with the signature. Once this testimony has been produced, the document can be admitted; obviously, however, that does not mean that the jury must believe the document is genuine. The opposing party still is free to introduce testimony that it is a forgery.[30]

A second rule relating to documents is the so-called "best evidence" rule. The name "best evidence" is highly misleading. No rule of evidence requires a party to introduce the "best" or strongest evidence that might be available to prove a matter. Rather, the best evidence rule requires a party to introduce the original of a document or to establish that the original has been lost or destroyed before other evidence of the document's contents will be admitted.[31] The basis of the rule seems to be the fact that the precise wording of documents can be extremely important in the law. Therefore, whenever an original is available it should be used.

Other types of safeguards exist to ensure the reliability of testimonial evidence. One fundamental requirement is that every witness must

---

29. See Fed.Evid.Rule 901(a).

30. 1 S. Saltzburg & M. Martin, Federal Rules of Evidence Manual 43 (5th ed.1990). See Fed.Evid.Rule 104(e).

31. See Fed.Evid.Rules 1002, 1004.

have first-hand knowledge of the matters about which he testifies.[32] This is, of course, a necessary corollary to the hearsay rule. Ordinarily, a witness is not allowed to speculate or give an opinion about matters involved in the case, but this restriction is relaxed when the use of opinion appears to be the best means of informing the trier of fact what actually occurred.[33] Thus, a witness may be permitted to state that an individual was "drunk" rather than simply try to describe in detail the person's actions leading to that conclusion. The witness can be asked about the details in order to test the validity of the opinion. An important exception to the general rule prohibiting opinion evidence allows an expert witness to give an opinion regarding matters within his expertise.[34] Of course, the witness first must be qualified as an expert by testimony as to his credentials. Since 1993, as the result of a ruling of the United States Supreme Court,[35] there has been considerable debate about the extent to which evidence of a scientific and technical nature can and should be admitted. Based on the wording of Federal Evidence Rule 702, the Court decided that such evidence could be admitted if the trial court found it to be relevant and to rest upon a reliable foundation. Previously many courts had held that such evidence was admissible only if the scientific foundation upon which it rested was generally accepted by those in the field to which it belonged.[36] That position, of course, required exclusion of information newly developed in our modern, fast-moving scientific world. At the same time, however, it lessened the danger that cases could be determined by important-sounding, innovative theories that would prove to be incorrect.[37] Under the Supreme Court's new approach, it is important that the trial court exercise a "gatekeeper" function to exclude expert testimony when it is unreliable.[38]

This brief sketch of the law of evidence is far from complete. It is important to recognize that although, on the whole, evidentiary rules are much the same throughout the United States, there are significant variations in detail from jurisdiction to jurisdiction.[39] Before litigating in any court, an attorney must become thoroughly familiar with the specific provisions that will be applied there.

32. See, e.g., Fed.Evid.Rule 602.

33. See Fed.Evid.Rule 701.

34. See Fed.Evid.Rule 702, 703.

35. Daubert v. Merrell Dow Pharmaceuticals, Inc., 509 U.S. 579, 113 S.Ct. 2786, 125 L.Ed.2d 469 (1993).

36. The leading case was Frye v. United States, 293 Fed. 1013 (D.C.Cir.1923).

37. For a comprehensive view of the history and current debate of the admissibility of scientific evidence, see R. Park, D.

Leonard & S. Goldberg, Evidence Law § 10.04 (1998).

38. See General Elec. Co. v. Joiner, 522 U.S. 136, 118 S.Ct. 512, 139 L.Ed.2d 508 (1997) (upholding a trial court's discretionary decision to exclude expert testimony).

39. See Fed.Evid.Rule 501, providing that state evidentiary rules of privilege will be applied in diversity of citizenship cases in federal courts, whereas federal "common law" will govern the existence and scope of privileges in cases arising under federal law.

§§ 10.3–11.0 are reserved for supplementary material.

Chapter 11

JURY TRIAL

Analysis

A. INTRODUCTION

A. INTRODUCTION

§ 11.1 The Origins and Role of Jury Trial in Modern Society

The Seventh Amendment to the United States Constitution, which became effective in 1791, provides that: "In suits at common law, where the value in controversy shall exceed twenty dollars, the right of trial by jury shall be preserved, and no fact tried by a jury, shall be otherwise re-examined in any court of the United States, than according to the rules of the common law."[1] A similar guarantee can be found in nearly every state constitution.[2]

---

§ 11.1

1. U.S. Const.Amend. 7.

2. Colorado, Louisiana, and Wyoming have no constitutional guarantee to jury trial in civil cases. See West's Colo.R.S.A. Const.Art. 2, § 23; La.Stat.Ann.–Const. Art. 1, § 17; Wyo. Const. Art. 1, § 9. See generally O'Connell, Jury Trial in Civil Cases?,

Yet despite this long-standing commitment to the institution, jury trial and the manner of its operation continue to excite an extraordinary amount of debate. The focal point of discussion is whether the civil jury has sufficient utility to justify its retention in light of the need to streamline our complex and increasingly burdened judicial system. The principal lines of attack on jury trial divide along two axes. The first challenges the basic unfairness and inefficiency of trial by a group of citizens unskilled in the application of frequently particularized and difficult legal concepts; the second is concerned with the cost to the judicial system caused by the delays inherent in the jury process.

The ambivalence over what role—if any—the jury should play in the modern legal system is reflected in certain judicial attitudes toward the right to jury trial and the development of a number of procedural rules governing its utilization. For example, even though the right guaranteed by the Seventh Amendment has deep historical roots and is part of the foundation of the federal court system, as evidenced by its inclusion in the Bill of Rights, it has not been made binding on the states through the due process clause of the Fourteenth Amendment as have many other provisions in the first ten amendments to the Constitution.[3] In addition, Federal Rule 38(b) requires a litigant to make a timely demand for a jury trial, and Rule 38(d) provides that this right is waived if there is a failure to do so.[4] Even more significantly, there has been a clear recognition of the court's prerogative to regulate various procedural aspects of jury trials, by granting motions for summary judgment, new trial, directed verdict, and judgment notwithstanding the verdict[5] and by altering the traditional size of the jury.[6] Yet, there has been significant movement in the opposite direction. As will be discussed in later sections,[7] the Supreme Court has construed the availability of the right to jury trial under the Seventh Amendment expansively so as to give it a highly dynamic quality.

The contemporary uncertainty over the efficacy of the jury system should be seen against its historical background. The development of the power of juries was an important element in the emergence of democratic-egalitarian values in Anglo–American society.[8] Imported into England

---

58 Ill.Bar J. 796 (1970), urging the Illinois constitutional convention to abolish the constitutional right to jury trial for civil cases.

3. Justice Holmes' comments in Chicago, Rock Island & Pacific Ry. Co. v. Cole, 251 U.S. 54, 56, 40 S.Ct. 68, 69, 64 L.Ed. 133 (1919), although only dictum, are representative of the Supreme Court's beliefs in this area.

4. See the discussion in § 11.9, below.

5. See, e.g., Galloway v. U.S., 319 U.S. 372, 63 S.Ct. 1077, 87 L.Ed. 1458 (1943). According to the so-called "purist" school, represented principally in modern dialogue by Justices Black and Douglas (the former's

dissent in Galloway is illustrative), these inroads on what is assumed to be the historical functions of juries cannot be reconciled with the mandate of the Seventh Amendment. For an interesting view to the contrary, see Henderson, The Background of the Seventh Amendment, 80 Harv.L.Rev. 289 (1966). For a discussion of the four motions, and their constitutional status, see §§ 9.1–9.3, above, and §§ 12.3–12.5, below.

6. See § 11.11, below.

7. See §§ 11.5–11.6, below.

8. See Story, Commentaries on the Constitution § 1779 (1833). A somewhat romantic, but nonetheless fairly typical nineteenth century view of the jury is this pas-

in the eleventh century by William the Conqueror, by the end of the fifteenth century the jury had replaced trial by ordeal as the principal method of fact-finding; by the seventeenth century it had become popular as a political check on the judges of the Stuart monarchy. In colonial America, juries emerged as a potent instrument for resisting encroachment on colonial liberties by the British government and its appointed judges, and they continued to play an important political role in the early nineteenth century struggle between the Jeffersonian Republicans and the Federalist judiciary.[9] Historically then, the jury, because of its relative independence, was an extremely valuable bulwark against government oppression. In addition, its populist, lay quality was attractive and was thought to justify its utilization in cases having no political overtones to them at all.

Today, it is that very lay independence that has come under attack by those who see the jury as an oppressive force, functioning in an essentially unpredictable, unknowledgeable, and unregulated manner.[10] In an increasingly globalized economy, those same concerns underscore the reluctance of many foreign litigants to entrust the resolution of their disputes to the American court system. Judge Frank, who probably was the nation's most outspoken critic of jury trial during his lifetime, criticized the present jury structure on the ground that there is no effective judicial supervision over the process by which juries render verdicts.[11] His criticism is based upon an even more fundamental skepticism about the ability of the jurors to absorb and evaluate the testimony that they hear and to apply the explanations of the law tendered to them by the court.[12]

Moreover, given the litigious character of American society, trial by jury is seen by many as an enormous and disproportionate drain on the limited resources of the judicial system, a luxury that cannot be afforded. It is contended that jury trials take more time than cases tried directly to the judge, and that the costs of the procedure far outweigh whatever benefits once might have been thought to flow from it.[13]

sage in Sioux City & Pacific R.R. Co. v. Stout, 84 U.S. (17 Wall.) 657, 664, 21 L.Ed. 745, 749 (1873): "Twelve men of the average of the community, comprising men of education and men of little education, men of learning and men whose learning consists only in what they have themselves seen and heard, the merchant, the mechanic, the farmer, the laborer; these sit together, consult, apply their separate experience of the affairs of life to the facts proven, and draw a unanimous conclusion. This average judgment thus given it is the great effort of the law to obtain. It is assumed that twelve men know more of the common affairs of life than does one man, that they can draw wiser and safer conclusions from admitted facts thus occurring than can a single judge."

9. For discussion of the role of the jury in history, see 1 W. Holdsworth, A History of English Law 298–350 (7th ed.1956); 1 F. Pollock & F. Maitland, The History of English Law 138–50 (2d ed.1898); Thayer, The Jury and Its Development, 5 Harv.L.Rev. 249, 295, 357 (1892).

10. See Judge Frank's opinion in Skidmore v. Baltimore & Ohio R. Co., 167 F.2d 54 (2d Cir.1948), cert. denied 335 U.S. 816.

11. J. Frank, Courts on Trial 120 (1949).

12. Id. at 116.

13. See Peck, Do Juries Delay Justice?, 18 F.R.D. 455 (1956); O'Connell, Jury Trials in Civil Cases?, 58 Ill.Bar J. 796 (1970). In this connection it is interesting to note that jury trial has been substantially elimi-

There are various responses to these charges. Most proceed from a basic assumption that trial by jury preserves certain fundamental American perceptions about the nature of justice and its interaction with various social processes. As one study points out, it is inadequate to measure the jury's cost to the system merely in terms of added expense and time; rather, it must be measured in terms of the benefit that the system derives from the "quality" of the jury verdict.[14] Other commentators have viewed the jury's independence and discretion as its most valuable characteristics. The claim is that juries allow for the interplay of social judgments as to what is fair and equitable, which the law, in its orientation toward general principles and rules, often fails to take into consideration.[15]

Despite the controversy that currently exists in the literature and an occasional restrictive judicial decision, the Supreme Court in the case of Beacon Theatres, Inc. v. Westover[16] and its progeny has reaffirmed the historical commitment to, and continuing importance of, the right to civil jury trial in the American system, at least for the federal courts. Thus, the Seventh Amendment has been interpreted as meaning that trial by jury is

> the normal and preferable mode of disposing of issues of fact in civil cases at law as well as in criminal cases. Maintenance of the jury as a fact-finding body is of such importance and occupies so firm a place in our history and jurisprudence that any seeming curtailment of the right to a jury trial should be scrutinized with the utmost care.[17]

In attempting to understand the position of jury trial in the existing American process of civil dispute resolution, it is important to bear in mind the relationship between the substantive policy embodied by the Seventh Amendment and the changing historical context in which we view that constitutional guarantee. Much of the current law regarding the right to a jury trial and the character of the jury trial has developed from the conflict between, and the integration of, competing perceptions about jury behavior. It is in the trade-off between the constitutional mandate and a growing awareness of the operational costs to the overall legal system that we find much of the explanation for the uneven treatment accorded jury trial.

nated in civil cases in England. See Devitt, Should Jury Trial Be Required in Civil Cases? A Challenge to the Seventh Amendment, 47 J.Air L. & Comm. 495 (1982).

14. Kalven, The Dignity of the Civil Jury, 60 Va.L.Rev. 1055 (1964). On the sociological implications of jury trial, see Wolf, Trial by Jury: A Sociological Analysis, 1966 Wis.L.Rev. 820.

15. See Pound, Law in Books and Law in Action, 44 Am.L.Rev. 12 (1910); Wigmore, A Program for the Trial of Jury Trial, 12 Am.Jud.Soc. 166, 170 (1929). See also Dooley, Our Juries, Our Selves: The Power,

Perception, and Politics of the Civil Jury, 80 Cornell L.Rev. 325 (1995).

16. 359 U.S. 500, 79 S.Ct. 948, 3 L.Ed.2d 988 (1959). This case is discussed in § 11.5, below.

17. Dimick v. Schiedt, 293 U.S. 474, 486, 55 S.Ct. 296, 301, 79 L.Ed. 603 (1935) (per Sutherland, J.). The last sentence of this passage is quoted approvingly in Beacon Theatres, note 16, above, 359 U.S. at 501, 55 S.Ct. at 952. In reality, jury trial is waived by the parties in a very significant number of cases.

§ 11.2 The Judge–Jury Relationship

An understanding of the division of responsibility between the judge and jury in the adjudicatory process is of great significance to understanding the trial of civil actions. The allocation of various functions often is very subtle and proves to be basic to the effective operation of the litigation system. It involves a balancing of the frequently competing values of the commitment to the jury as "finders of fact" and the legal system's goal of achieving both consistency and efficiency.

Most civil trials in the United States are conducted before a judge sitting without a jury and acting both as a fact finder and a law applier. This will be true when there is no constitutional or statutory right to jury trial, when the right to jury trial has been waived by the parties' failure to demand a jury as required by the applicable procedural rules, or when the parties agree to a nonjury trial. But assuming that a right to a jury exists and has been properly exercised, the key inquiry is: What is the jury's function? Further, what is the role of the judge in attempting to help structure, without impinging upon, the work of the jury, and what are the implications of this division of labor?

To understand the jury's role better, it is useful to examine briefly the evolution of the jury since its inception in England in the eleventh century. Originally, jurors were chosen on the basis of their fitness as witnesses. They typically were selected from the neighborhood in which the facts in issue occurred. The assumption was that they would have the best possible background for evaluating the evidence in light of their own experiences in the locale.[1] The jurors were expected to inform each other on the issues, relying on their personal knowledge of the events, and to consult any other reliable sources, including direct communication with the parties. They were entitled to decide a case on the basis of their knowledge, even when this contradicted the testimony.[2]

Over time, the inquisitorial nature of the jury's role changed, and the emphasis shifted from the jury as witness-adjudicator to the jury as impartial finder of fact. This transformation came about as a result of two principal developments: (1) the evolution of the manner in which the jury became informed of the circumstances of the case, and (2) the growth of the law regarding the parties' ability to object to certain persons serving as jurors.[3] As this process advanced, jurors became increasingly dependent on the materials presented to them at trial and the responsibility for providing this information shifted to the parties themselves. This foreshadowed the establishment of the now familiar adversarial system, which is based on the philosophy that the fairest and most efficient process for arriving at justice is the evaluation by the jury of testimony presented by both parties in open court.

---

§ 11.2

1. See generally W. Holdsworth, A History of English Common Law 332–50 (7th ed.1956); Thayer, The Jury and Its Development, 5 Harv.L.Rev. 249 (1892).

2. M. Hale, The History and Analysis of the Common Law of England 260–61 (1713).

3. W. Holdsworth, A History of English Common Law 332 (7th ed.1956).

Today the jury performs three main functions: (1) determining what the facts are; (2) evaluating the facts in terms of the legal consequences as formulated by the trial judge in the jury instructions; and (3) presenting the result of its deliberations in the form of a verdict.

Typically, the jury's province does not extend to determining factual issues raised by questions of the admissibility and exclusion of evidence, claims of privilege, and threshold defenses, such as jurisdiction, pleading, and joinder questions. The heartland of the jury's domain is determining, often from competing and conflicting evidence, the facts germane to a given dispute, and deciding how the relevant law should apply to those facts. On occasion, the evidence is incomplete and the jury must infer the existence or nonexistence of certain facts from other facts on which evidence has been given. In other circumstances the evidence on a particular point will support inconsistent inferences. Although there is some dispute on the matter, in most jurisdictions the jury is allowed to choose from among competing inference chains, as long as there is some reasonable basis for each of them.

For example, consider the facts of one well-known case on this subject. A railroad switchman was found unconscious in a dark railway yard near a switching point on the track. He later died, apparently from a blow to the back of his head, without regaining consciousness. There were no known eye-witnesses to the fatal event. The railroad advanced the theory that the decedent was murdered; the decedent's estate offered the theory that a mail hook negligently left dangling from the side of a mail car on a passing train struck and killed the decedent. Although the facts seemed to support the inference chains that formed the basis of both theories equally, the jury was allowed to render a verdict in terms of what it felt was the more reasonable set of inferences and to discard or disbelieve facts inconsistent with its conclusion.[4] In discussing the role of the jury in this situation, the Supreme Court said:

> It is no answer to say that the jury's verdict involved speculation and conjecture. When ever facts are in dispute or the evidence is such that fair-minded men may draw different inferences, a measure of speculation and conjecture is required on the part of those whose duty it is to settle the dispute by choosing what seems to them to be the most reasonable inference.[5]

The functions and prerogatives of the jury are not discrete and easily categorized and they have shifted continuously over time. These shifts reflect changes in attitudes toward what tasks should be assigned to the jury, as well as changes in the availability of methods for structuring and directing the jury's performance to ensure that it operates in a legitimate manner.

---

4. Lavender v. Kurn, 327 U.S. 645, 66 S.Ct. 740, 90 L.Ed. 916 (1946).

5. 327 U.S. at 653, 66 S.Ct. at 744. Not all state courts allow the jury this latitude in choosing between competing inference chains. Compare Smith v. First Nat. Bank in Westfield, 99 Mass. 605, 612 (1868). See also Blid v. Chicago & N.W. Ry. Co., 89 Neb. 689, 691–92, 131 N.W. 1027, 1028 (1911); White v. Lehigh Valley R.R. Co., 220 N.Y. 131, 135, 115 N.E. 439, 441 (1917).

It is commonplace to say that it is the jury's responsibility to determine what the facts are. The law/fact dichotomy has come to represent the division between the functions of the court and those of the jury.[6] This relationship has not always existed, however. During the seventeenth century, when English juries were at the height of their powers in resisting the Stuart judges, expansive claims were made for the role of the jury as arbiters of both fact and law. By the turn of the eighteenth century, the judges had escaped domination by the Crown by having been awarded life appointments. The confidence of the people in the judiciary was restored, and by the time of the American Revolution, the law/fact division of responsibility had become established in England.[7]

In America, the refinement of the judge-jury relationship also occurred over a lengthy time period. The right of juries to decide questions of law was widely accepted in the colonies, especially in criminal cases.[8] Prior to 1850, the judge and jury were viewed as partners in many jurisdictions. The jury could decide questions of both law and fact, and the judge helped guide that decisionmaking process by comments on the witnesses and the evidence.[9] Legal theory and political philosophy emphasized the importance of the jury in divining natural law, which was thought to be a better source for decision than the "authority of a black-letter maxim."[10] Since natural law was accessible to laypeople, it was held to be the duty of each juror to determine for himself whether a particular rule of law embodied the principles of the higher, natural law.[11] Indeed, it was argued that the United States Constitution embodied a codification of natural rights so that "the reliance by the jury on a higher law was usually viewed as a constitutional judgment * * *."[12]

In the middle of the nineteenth century, this philosophy began to lose its acceptance, and the law/fact dichotomy became more sharply delineated. This resulted, on the one hand, in the introduction of several of today's jury "control mechanisms," and, on the other hand, in a

6. Slocum v. New York Life Ins. Co., 228 U.S. 364, 387–88, 33 S.Ct. 523, 532, 57 L.Ed. 879, 890 (1913). See also Hodges v. Easton, 106 U.S. 408, 1 S.Ct. 307, 27 L.Ed. 169 (1882); Dobson v. Masonite Corp., 359 F.2d 921 (5th Cir.1966). Compare Jerke v. Delmont State Bank, 54 S.D. 446, 456, 223 N.W. 585, 589 (1929): "The power and right and duty of the jury is not 'to say what the facts are,' but to adjudge and determine what the facts are by the usual and ordinary intellectual processes * * *."

7. Scott, Trial by Jury and the Reform of Civil Procedure, 31 Harv.L.Rev. 669, 675–78 (1918).

8. Howe, Juries as Judges of Criminal Law, 52 Harv.L.Rev. 582, 583–84, 589 (1939).

9. Note, The Changing Role of the Jury in the Nineteenth Century, 74 Yale L.J. 170, 173 (1964). But see Henderson, The Background of the Seventh Amendment, 80 Harv.L.Rev. 289 (1966), for the thesis that early American civil juries did not possess the right to decide questions of law, as evidenced by the availability and acknowledged legitimacy of early jury control devices.

10. Note, The Changing Role of the Jury in the Nineteenth Century, 74 Yale L.J. 170, 172 (1964).

11. See Georgia v. Brailsford, 3 U.S. (3 Dall.) 1, 4, 1 L.Ed. 483, 484 (1794).

12. Note, The Changing Role of the Jury in the Nineteenth Century, 74 Yale L.J. 170, 178 (1964). See 3 Debates and Proceedings in the State Convention to Revise and Amend the Constitution (Mass.) 455 (1853).

tendency to restrain the judge from commenting on the evidence presented to the jury. By the end of the nineteenth century, mistrust of juries was on the rise. With the movement away from the natural law philosophy, the system began to search for a mode of decisionmaking that would be stable and predictable. Increasingly, it appeared that juries did not function in this manner, but rather treated similar cases unevenly, often according to their own standard of "popular justice."[13]

Today, the law/fact distinction is well established, but the administration of the line between the two remains extremely difficult. The division necessarily is imprecise and varies with the nature of the litigation and from jurisdiction to jurisdiction. This is well illustrated by an examination of the functions performed by the jury in contract and negligence actions.

The typical distribution of responsibility between judge and jury in an action on a written instrument is as follows: The jury decides whether a contract exists. The judge determines whether that contract is ambiguous. When the contract is ambiguous, its meaning is determined by the jury from evidence introduced by the parties; if the contract is unambiguous, the court interprets and applies its language. In an action on an oral contract, the terms will be ascertained by the jury.

In an action in tort for injuries allegedly sustained as the result of the defendant's negligent driving, factual questions, such as whether the driver slowed down approaching an intersection or maintained a proper lookout at the time of the accident, ordinarily are determined by the jury. But if the trial judge considers the evidence to be so clear that no reasonable person could conclude that the driver did slow down or that a proper lookout was maintained, the issue may be withdrawn from the jury and a finding directed by the judge. Whether the driver had the duty to slow down is a question of law to be determined by the judge, as is the task of defining the general standard of conduct of the hypothetical reasonably prudent person. Application of that standard of conduct to the circumstances of the case—namely, was the defendant driving with sufficient caution in approaching the intersection to meet the reasonable person test—is ordinarily a jury question.[14]

Even when it theoretically is possible to draw a distinction between issues of fact and law, it often is difficult in practice to limit the jury to a decision concerning the former. Indeed, the very capacity of a jury to understand the difference between matters of law and fact and to apply the latter within their province has been questioned.[15] It is precisely because of the difficulty of separating law from fact that the role of the judge is so critical in the modern jury trial. Consequently, it is important to understand both the manner in which the judge interacts with the

13. See O.W. Holmes, Collected Legal Papers 237–38 (1920).

14. See Weiner, The Civil Jury Trial and the Law–Fact Distinction, 54 Cal-

if.L.Rev. 1867 (1966), for an interesting discussion of questions of "law application."

15. J. Frank, Courts on Trial iii (1949).

jury, and the tools the legal system provides the bench for limiting the jury to its legitimate sphere of responsibility.

The judge performs several major duties in a jury case. In addition to ruling on all the pretrial motions and preliminary issues, the trial judge screens the evidence and determines what is relevant and how much is sufficient to permit the jury to make a finding on a given proposition. The judge also decides when judicial notice is taken of certain issues so that they need not be proven at trial, as well as what rules of substantive law should be applied, how best to instruct the jury regarding those rules, and what type of verdict should be rendered. The judge also has wide latitude in structuring the trial.

Although the jury has considerable capacity to enlarge upon its role, the judge is not without resources in shaping and limiting the jury decisionmaking process. Through control over the admission of evidence, the court may so narrow the scope of triable factual issues that the jury's range of inquiry is very limited or it becomes appropriate to withdraw the case from the jury and direct a verdict.[16] Moreover, through the instructions given the jury, the judge may circumscribe the capacity of the jury to ignore the line between questions of law and fact.[17] The more precise the instructions, the less opportunity there is for the jury to invoke its own standard of conduct. For example, in the case of the motorist who allegedly failed to slow down at an intersection, the court simply might tell the jury that a reasonable driver would reduce speed at an intersection. This formulation gives the jury wide latitude to determine whether the defendant acted reasonably under the circumstances. On the other hand, the trial judge might formulate the standard of care for the jury with greater specificity by stating that a reasonable person would approach the intersection at five or ten miles per hour. Should the court do so, the jury theoretically retains only the prerogative to decide whether defendant did slow down to that particular speed.

In addition to the power to control the evidence and jury instructions, the judge has the power to choose the type of verdict to be rendered by the jury.[18] As the form of a verdict becomes more specific, the freedom of the jury to go its own way necessarily is reduced. A general verdict may mask very real inconsistencies in the views of the jurors and in their findings on particular issues, enabling them to ignore the judge's instructions by conforming the facts to notions of popular justice. But this clearly is more difficult to do when the jury is required to answer certain specific questions submitted by the judge. Finally, there are various other procedural mechanisms, such as additur/remittitur,[19] summary judgment,[20] directed verdict,[21] new trial,[22] and judgment

16. Coleman v. CIR, 791 F.2d 68 (7th Cir.1986) (in ordinary litigation the Seventh Amendment does not require a jury trial when no facts are in dispute).

17. See Thornburg, The Power and the Process: Instructions and the Civil Jury, 66 Fordham L.Rev. 1837 (1998). Instructions are discussed in § 10.1 at notes 53–63, above.

18. Verdicts are discussed in § 12.1, below.

19. See § 12.4, below.

20. See §§ 9.1–9.3, above.

21. See § 12.3, below.

22. See § 12.4, below.

notwithstanding the verdict,[23] that enable the judge to maintain a considerable degree of control over jury behavior.[24]

In sum, the judge has an important and active role in conducting a jury trial, representing the legal system's commitment to a fair, efficient, and consistent adjudicatory procedure. This must be achieved, however, within the context and strong influence of the jury trial guarantee. The judge's ability to shape and contour the jury's conduct exists only insofar as that management proceeds within constitutional bounds.

As the discussion in this section suggests, the relationship between judge and jury essentially is dynamic, changing as perceptions of the legal system develop according to contemporary needs and problems. As is discussed in the following sections, although the American judicial system increasingly has utilized procedural mechanisms to circumscribe the unfettered exercise of jury power, it also has significantly reaffirmed the commitment to jury trial in civil cases.

B.   THE RIGHT TO JURY TRIAL

§ 11.3   The Right to Jury Trial—In General

There are three general sources for the right to jury trial: (1) state and federal constitutional provisions that preserve the common law right in various forms;[1] (2) statutorily created causes of action that expressly or impliedly provide for jury trial;[2] and (3) the historic discretion of a court to empanel an advisory jury in equity proceedings. This section outlines these three sources of the jury trial right in general terms and examines some of the important principles that govern the right.

The Seventh Amendment to the United States Constitution[3] does not "create" a right to jury trial; rather, it preserves that right in the federal courts as it existed at common law in 1791, the date of the amendment's ratification by the original states.[4] Although the purpose and language of the jury trial guarantee appear to be straightforward, over the years it has proven to be one of the most difficult constitutional provisions to apply. This is due largely to the ambiguities surrounding the availability of jury trial in English and American practice in 1791. For example, historically there was no right to a jury in suits that sought only equitable relief, such as an injunction or specific performance. However, at the time of the Seventh Amendment's ratification, the

---

23. See § 12.3, below.

24. Although the judge maintains considerable control, the Seventh Amendment does provide some restrictions on that control. See, e.g., Henson v. Falls, 912 F.2d 977 (8th Cir.1990) (judge cannot make credibility determination on directed verdict motion).

§ 11.3

1. See § 11.4, below.

2. See § 11.6, below.

3. U.S. Const.Amend. 7.

4. Baltimore & Carolina Line, Inc. v. Redman, 295 U.S. 654, 55 S.Ct. 890, 79 L.Ed. 1636 (1935); Dimick v. Schiedt, 293 U.S. 474, 55 S.Ct. 296, 79 L.Ed. 603 (1935).

law/equity dichotomy was by no means well-defined. The respective jurisdiction of both courts was blurred and shifting, so that application of the historical test created by the Seventh Amendment necessarily has been confusing and imprecise.[5]

In the federal courts, Federal Rule 38(a) preserves "the right of trial by jury as declared by the Seventh Amendment * * * to the parties inviolate."[6] Although this standard, like the Seventh Amendment itself, appears to be neutral—that is, merely preserving a right that already exists—the merger of law and equity in the federal courts has had profound implications for the modern scope of the jury trial right in those courts.[7] As will be discussed later, the effect of the Federal Rules has been to consolidate what formerly were two separate jurisdictions into a single form of action, with the result that remedies once available only in equitable proceedings now are available in "civil" actions having the attributes of both equity and law. Since the Supreme Court has held that the constitutional right to jury trial is applicable to these proceedings, the clear effect of the Rules has been to enlarge the availability of the jury right.[8]

The Seventh Amendment jury trial right is not restricted to those relatively few common law actions that actually existed in 1791. The right also applies to all statutory causes of action that have been created since and are analogous to actions that were triable to a jury in 1791, whether the statute expressly says so or not.[9] Because there is no constitutional right to nonjury trial in the federal court system,[10] nothing in the Seventh Amendment or in Article III precludes Congress from extending jury trial to non-common law actions. Hence, when a statute expressly provides for trial by jury, there is no doubt that the right obtains.[11] For example, because the Seventh Amendment applies only to

5. See § 11.5, below.

6. Fed.Civ.Proc.Rule 38(a). See 9 C. Wright & A. Miller, Civil 2d §§ 2301–17. The preservation of the right to jury trial in the rule is mandated by the Rules Enabling Act pursuant to which the rules were promulgated. 28 U.S.C.A. § 2072.

Note, however, that the interposition of a mediation requirement has been held not to violate the Seventh Amendment. See Rhea v. Massey–Ferguson, Inc., 767 F.2d 266 (6th Cir.1985).

7. See § 11.5, below.

The merger of admiralty with law and equity in 1966 complicated the straightforward rule that there is no right to jury trial in suits in admiralty, as well. See Note, The Jury on the Quarterdeck: The Effect of Pleading Admiralty Jurisdiction Where the Proceeding Turns Hybrid, 63 Texas L.Rev. 533 (1984).

8. This point is recognized in Beacon Theatres, Inc. v. Westover, 359 U.S. 500, 79

S.Ct. 948, 3 L.Ed.2d 988 (1959), which is discussed in § 11.5, below.

9. See § 11.6, below.

10. See Beacon Theatres, Inc. v. Westover, 359 U.S. 500, 510, 79 S.Ct. 948, 956, 3 L.Ed.2d 988 (1959). See also Fitzgerald v. U.S. Lines Co., 374 U.S. 16, 83 S.Ct. 1646, 10 L.Ed.2d 720 (1963); Hurwitz v. Hurwitz, 136 F.2d 796 (D.C.Cir.1943). For a criticism of the Beacon Theatres position regarding the lack of constitutional protection for nonjury trial, see Note, The Right to A Nonjury Trial, 74 Harv.L.Rev. 1176, 1177–78 (1961). Some state courts have held that the state legislature cannot extend the jury trial to an equitable proceeding. See Brown v. Kalamazoo Circuit Judge, 75 Mich. 274, 42 N.W. 827 (1889); Callanan v. Judd, 23 Wis. 343 (1868). See generally Van Hecke, Trial by Jury in Equity Cases, 31 N.C.L.Rev. 157 (1953).

11. An example is an action under the Federal Employers' Liability Act, 35 Stat.

suits at common law, and because there was no right to sue the sovereign at common law, there is no constitutional right to a jury trial in an action brought against the United States.[12] A jury trial right in a suit against the United States may exist, however, when a statute expressly or impliedly so provides.[13]

Although the Seventh Amendment guarantee is not binding upon the states,[14] most state constitutions contain a comparable provision.[15] One difference between the jury right in the state and federal systems is that the scope of the right existing at the state level usually is determined by reference to the date of ratification of the state constitution, rather than 1791. Thus, for purposes of applying the historical test for determining the availability of jury trial in a particular state, the division between law and equity may have been quite different from that which existed on the reference date for the federal system.[16] These differences also raise important questions concerning whether federal or state rules are to be applied for determining the right to jury trial[17] when an action involving a federally created right is heard in a state court.[18]

The advisory jury has deep roots in the historic division between law and equity.[19] Although the emergence of equity as a separate system of courts with a defined jurisdiction meant that something in the nature of a right to a nonjury trial on certain issues developed,[20] the chancellor always retained the discretion to empanel and submit issues to a jury for an advisory verdict, which he was free to follow or to disregard.[21] Typically, an equity court would utilize an advisory jury whenever it needed assistance in determining an issue thought to be within the special competence of a jury. This often included questions concerning the credibility of witnesses. Since the jury's verdict was not binding, the principle that equity adjudications were judicial in character was pre-

65, 45 U.S.C.A. § 51 et seq. The jury right obtains even when the suit is filed in a state court that would not allow jury trial as to certain issues. See Dice v. Akron, Canton & Youngstown R.R. Co., 342 U.S. 359, 72 S.Ct. 312, 96 L.Ed. 398 (1952), discussed in § 11.8, below. See also Van Hecke, Trial by Jury in Equity Cases, 31 N.C.L.Rev. 157, 172–73 (1953).

12. See McElrath v. U.S., 102 U.S. (12 Otto) 426, 44026 L.Ed. 189, 192 (1880).

When the United States brings an action, the right to a jury trial will depend on the same analysis as applied to purely private litigation. See, e.g., Austin v. Shalala, 994 F.2d 1170 (5th Cir.1993).

13. For example, 28 U.S.C.A. § 2402, provides that any action brought against the United States shall be tried without a jury. There is an exception, however, for actions brought under 28 U.S.C.A. § 1346(a)(1) for the recovery of taxes erroneously or illegally assessed or collected under the internal revenue laws. For two di-

vergent solutions to the opposite question, namely, whether the right to trial by jury exists in an action by the United States against allegedly delinquent taxpayers, see Damsky v. Zavatt, 289 F.2d 46 (2d Cir. 1961).

14. See Walker v. Sauvinet, 92 U.S. (2 Otto) 90, 23 L.Ed. 678 (1875). See generally § 11.7, below.

15. See § 11.1, n. 2, above.

16. See § 11.4, below.

17. See § 11.8, below.

18. The New York jury trial provisions are outlined and discussed in § 11.7, below, as an illustration of the kinds of problems raised when interpreting state jury trial provisions.

19. See generally Note, The Right to a Nonjury Trial, 74 Harv.L.Rev. 1176 (1961).

20. Id. at 1179. See § 11.5, below.

21. See 9 C. Wright & A. Miller, Civil 2d § 2335.

served; in practice, however, the chancellor gave considerable weight to the advisory jury's determination.[22]

The trial judge's prerogative to empanel an advisory jury is preserved in Federal Rule 39(c)[23] and comparable state provisions.[24] As with its historical antecedent, the role of the contemporary advisory jury is to assist the court in determining any issue that the trial judge must decide. The court may utilize an advisory jury in deciding equitable issues to which no jury right attaches,[25] or in trying a case in which the right to a jury has been waived by the parties.[26]

Jurisdictions vary on the degree to which an advisory verdict is binding on the court. In the federal courts, the traditional practice continues and the judge has discretion about whether to abide by the decision of the advisory jury.[27] This also is true in most state courts, although some states provide that, unless the verdict is set aside on post-trial motion, it is binding on the court,[28] and other jurisdictions allow the trial judge to disregard the verdict only upon a showing of good cause.[29]

§ 11.4 Jury Trial in the Federal Courts—The Seventh Amendment and the Historical Test

The Seventh Amendment to the Constitution preserves the right to jury trial in the federal courts as it existed at common law.[1] It thus frequently is said to create an "historical test" for determining when the jury right attaches.[2] It was decided at an early period in the development of American jurisprudence that the "common law" referred to in the Seventh Amendment was that existing in England in 1791, the date of the Amendment's ratification,[3] not the common law of the several states.[4] It therefore is necessary to examine the contours of the jury trial

---

22. See Note, The Right to a Nonjury Trial, 74 Harv.L.Rev. 1176, 1183 (1961).

23. Fed.Civ.Proc.Rule 39(c).

24. See, e.g., N.Y.—McKinney's CPLR 4212. See generally 4 J. Weinstein, H. Korn & A. Miller, New York Civil Practice ¶¶ 4212.01–4212.08.

25. At least one jurisdiction recognizes a right to an advisory jury for disputed issues of fact in equitable proceedings. See Greer v. Goesling, 54 Ariz. 488, 97 P.2d 218 (1939); Stukey v. Stephens, 37 Ariz. 514, 295 P. 973 (1931).

26. For a discussion of advisory juries in the federal courts, see Aetna Ins. Co. v. Paddock, 301 F.2d 807 (5th Cir.1962); (American) Lumbermens Mut. Cas. Co. v. Timms & Howard, Inc., 108 F.2d 497 (2d Cir.1939).

27. See Kohn v. McNulta, 147 U.S. 238, 13 S.Ct. 298, 37 L.Ed. 150 (1893).

28. See Dose v. Insurance Co. of Pennsylvania, 206 Minn. 114, 287 N.W. 866

(1939); First Nat. Bank v. Quevli, 182 Minn. 238, 234 N.W. 318 (1931).

29. See Crocker v. Crocker, 188 Mass. 16, 73 N.E. 1068 (1905).

§ 11.4

1. See § 11.1, above. See also 9 C. Wright & A. Miller, Civil 2d § 2301.

2. Judicial notions concerning the historical test have undergone extensive revision in the past two decades. See §§ 11.5–11.6, below.

3. See Dimick v. Schiedt, 293 U.S. 474, 476, 55 S.Ct. 296, 297, 79 L.Ed. 603 (1935). State courts with state constitutional provisions comparable to the Seventh Amendment generally look to the date of ratification of the state constitution to determine the status of the right to a state jury trial. See § 11.3, above.

4. U.S. v. Wonson, 28 Fed.Cas. 745, 750 (C.C.Mass.1812) (No. 16,750) (per Story, J.).

right at English common law to understand the scope of the present-day right.

As discussed earlier,[5] in 1791 the English legal system was divided into separate equity and common-law courts.[6] Equity developed as a distinct system of justice largely in order to compensate for the deficiencies of the common-law courts. Because pleading and practice in the law courts had become inflexible and highly technical, injustice frequently resulted, for which equity provided a partial safety valve.[7] There was a right to jury trial only in the common-law courts; suits in equity were tried to one of the King's chancellors. For several important historical reasons, the chancellor did not utilize a jury.[8] Thus, one of the major distinctions between law and equity always has been the availability of the right to a jury trial at law.

Determining which actions belonged to law and which to equity for the purpose of delimiting the jury trial right continues to be one of the most perplexing questions of trial administration. The major problem is that a great deal of overlap existed between the two English systems in 1791. Further, the fusion of law and equity into a single civil action with the adoption of the Federal Rules of Civil Procedure in 1938[9] destroyed whatever jurisdictional and procedural distinctions might have existed for the purpose of applying the Seventh Amendment.

Originally, a suit in equity was brought as an appeal to the "King's conscience." It was a plea for relief that could not be secured at law because of the harsh and uncompromising rules that governed actions in those courts. As a result, a fierce competition developed between the chancery and the law courts in the fifteenth century and continued during the sixteenth and first part of the seventeenth centuries. Both systems attempted to enlarge their power and influence while jealously guarding their own distinct jurisdiction. For example, equity sought to expand the range of its own remedies through the chancellor's exercise of discretion, a reform measure not possible at law due to that system's comparative rigidity. Nonetheless, equity remained a supplemental system and would not assume jurisdiction when an adequate remedy at law existed.[10]

5. See §§ 11.1–11.3, above.

6. Valuable historical background on the development of the English bifurcated court system can be found in 3 W. Blackstone, Commentaries (1st ed. 1766–69); 1 W. Holdsworth, A History of English Law, (7th ed.1956); F. Maitland, Equity (2d ed.1936); W. Walsh, Equity, c. 2 (1930).

7. Note, The Right to a Nonjury Trial, 74 Harv.L.Rev. 1176, 1179 (1961).

8. The following statement offers some of the historical reasons for limiting the role of the jury in equity: "The idea of the jury as a protector of individual liberties and its psychological role as a group of the parties' peers passing upon their claims were more significant in criminal cases than in the civil jurisdiction of equity. Since equity courts were so long intimately associated with the royal power it is not strange that they should have been cool to a supposed bulwark of individual liberty. * * * Finally, it may have been that the chancellor was sufficiently dubious of the abilities of a jury to fulfill the function assigned to it to bar the wholesale adoption of the jury system." Id. at 1180–81.

9. See Fed.Civ.Proc.Rules 1, 2.

10. See Note, The Right to a Nonjury Trial, 74 Harv.L.Rev. 1176, 1181–82 (1961). See also 3 W. Blackstone, Commentaries 434 (1st ed.1766–69).

By the latter half of the seventeenth century, however, the differences between the two courts started to narrow. As cases decided in chancery began to be reported, those decisions were cited as authorities and followed.[11] The chancellors themselves began to exercise their discretion in accordance with precedent, and general practices began to emerge in equity for the trial of cases, giving that tribunal a procedure similar in many respects to that of the law courts.[12] In contrast, the rigidity of the common-law courts began to break down, and new principles of law that originated in equity were introduced in King's or Queen's Bench.[13] The rivalry between the two systems actually ameliorated the harshness of the common law, and the jurisdictional line separating them became much less precise.[14] This "borrowing" upon the resources of the other judicial branch was well advanced by 1791.[15]

The effect of this jurisdiction overlap upon modern procedure has been to confuse the application of the historical test embodied in the Seventh Amendment. Because the dividing line between law and equity was vague in 1791, no clear standards exist for interpreting the constitutional jury trial mandate. As already intimated, the task has been complicated even further by the adoption of the Federal Rules.[16] Although the Rules purport neither to abridge nor to modify the scope of the Seventh Amendment,[17] the merger of law and equity and the increased opportunity for the joinder of claims achieved by the Federal Rules necessarily has impinged upon the domain of equity by expanding the range of claims and remedies that historically were available at law.[18] With this increased competence of law, the circumstances under which the right to jury trial can obtain have been broadened significantly.[19]

The historical test in the federal courts after law and equity merged required that claims formerly triable "at law" were entitled to a jury and those formerly maintainable "in equity" did not merit a jury as of

---

11. 1 W. Holdsworth, A History of English Law 468 (7th ed.1956).

12. 1 W. Holdsworth, A History of English Law 453 (7th ed.1956); D. Kerly, An Historical Sketch of the Equitable Jurisdiction of the Court of Chancery 167 (1890). See also 1 J. Story, Equity Jurisprudence c. 2 (14th ed.1918).

13. D. Kerly, An Historical Sketch of the Equitable Jurisdiction of the Court of Chancery 288–89 (1890); Note, The Right to Nonjury Trial, 74 Harv.L.Rev. 1176, 1182 (1961).

14. See 1 W. Holdsworth, A History of English Law 467 (7th ed.1956); D. Kerly, An Historical Sketch of the Equitable Jurisdiction of the Court of Chancery 166, 180 (1890).

15. 3 W. Blackstone, Commentaries 436–37 (1st ed.1766–69).

16. See generally § 11.1, above.

17. City of Morgantown, West Virginia v. Royal Ins. Co., 337 U.S. 254, 258, 69 S.Ct. 1067, 1069, 93 L.Ed. 1347 (1949); Ettelson v. Metropolitan Life Ins. Co., 137 F.2d 62, 65 (3d Cir.1943), cert. denied 320 U.S. 777. See also Morris, Jury Trial under the Federal Fusion of Law and Equity, 20 Texas L.Rev. 427, 430–33, 443–44 (1942); Comment, The Right to Trial by Jury in Declaratory Judgment Actions, 3 Conn. L.Rev. 564 (1971).

18. See Note, The Right to Jury Trial under Merged Procedures, 65 Harv.L.Rev. 453 (1952); Comment, From Beacon Theatres to Dairy Queen to Ross: The Seventh Amendment, the Federal Rules and a Receding Law–Equity Dichotomy, 48 J. Urban Law 459, 470–71 (1971).

19. Beacon Theatres, Inc. v. Westover, 359 U.S. 500, 509, 79 S.Ct. 948, 956, 3 L.Ed.2d 988 (1959).

right.[20] But the assertion of both legal and equitable claims in a single action produced confusion as to how the historical test should be applied. Courts utilized tests attempting to determine whether the action was "basically" legal or equitable.[21] If the action was basically legal, all issues as to which the jury right applied were sent to the jury; after its verdict, the judge determined any undecided issues and ruled on the equitable claims. If the action was basically equitable, the court not only decided the equitable issues, but it also could invoke the "clean-up doctrine," and rule on any "incidental" legal issues in the case, thereby obviating the need for a jury.[22]

Another relevant factor in the reformulation of the jury trial guarantee's application was the enactment of the Declaratory Judgments Act.[23] This legislation was intended to adopt a neutral position with regard to the jury trial right.[24] Indeed, Federal Rule 57, which governs the procedure for obtaining a declaratory judgment in the federal courts, expressly preserves the right as set out in Federal Rules 38 and 39.[25] This means that the normal inquiry required by the Seventh Amendment for determining the availability of jury trial is applicable in the declaratory judgment context. The major difficulty with applying the historical test to this type of action is that the declaratory judgment was unknown in 1791. It cannot simply be classified as either legal or equitable because, depending on the circumstances, a declaratory judgment action might cover ground that formerly belonged to either judicial branch, or it might raise both legal and equitable issues in the same suit. Hence, due to the vague character of the historical analogy, any examination using the historical test is necessarily confusing.[26]

Prior to 1959, the right to jury trial in a declaratory judgment action turned on an inquiry into the nature of the "basic question" raised by the case.[27] When the declaratory judgment action did not fit into one of the basic patterns for equitable relief, but was merely an "inverted lawsuit," jury trial would be available.[28] When the declaratory judgment

---

20. See 8 J. Moore's Federal Practice ¶ 38.10[2][c] for a list of actions formerly at law and ¶ 38.10[3][b][iii] for a list of actions formerly in equity.

21. See Rosanna Knitted Sportswear, Inc. v. Lass O'Scotland, Ltd., 13 F.R.D. 325 (S.D.N.Y.1952). See also Thermo–Stitch, Inc. v. Chemi–Cord Processing Corp., 294 F.2d 486 (5th Cir.1961) (dictum).

22. See James, Right to a Jury Trial in Civil Actions, 72 Yale L.J. 655, 658–59, 670 (1963).

23. 28 U.S.C.A. §§ 2201, 2202.

24. See James v. Pennsylvania Gen. Ins. Co., 349 F.2d 228, 230 (D.C.Cir.1965); E. Borchard, Declaratory Judgments 1041 (2d ed. 1941).

25. See 9 C. Wright & A. Miller, Civil 2d § 2313; 10B C. Wright, A. Miller & M. Kane, Civil 3d § 2769.

26. Comment, Right to Trial by Jury in Declaratory Judgment Actions, 3 Conn. L.Rev. 564, 566 (1971).

27. Id. at 573–79. See (American) Lumbermens Mut. Cas. Co. v. Timms & Howard, Inc., 108 F.2d 497, 499 (2d Cir.1939).

28. Johnson v. Fidelity & Cas. Co., 238 F.2d 322 (8th Cir.1956); Hargrove v. American Cent. Ins. Co., 125 F.2d 225 (10th Cir. 1942). See James, Right to a Jury Trial in Civil Actions, 72 Yale L.J. 655, 686 (1963). "Inverted lawsuit" means a declaratory action in which one party seeks equitable relief in anticipation of a suit at law, typically for damages, by the opposing party. This was essentially the circumstance of Beacon Theatres, Inc. v. Westover, 359 U.S. 500, 79 S.Ct. 948, 3 L.Ed.2d 988 (1959).

was the counterpart of a suit in equity, however, no right would exist.[29] The holdings in Beacon Theatres, Inc. v. Westover[30] and its progeny have altered radically the application of the historical test to declaratory judgment actions. These cases make clear that it is the issue to be adjudicated, not the underlying nature of the case, that is determinative of the right to jury trial.[31] As is discussed in the next section, Supreme Court decisions since 1959 have recognized that the Declaratory Judgment Act has expanded the situations in which a legal remedy may be sought and this necessarily has contracted the scope of equity.[32] Thus, the Declaratory Judgments Act, like the Federal Rules, has enlarged significantly the range of issues for which there is a right to jury trial, with the result that the utility of the law/equity dichotomy, embodied in the historical test, has been diminished further.

Given all these developments, it is now clear that proper Seventh Amendment analysis requires application of a dynamic concept, one establishing a standard for jury trial rights that is not tied to the actual division between law and equity as it existed in 1791, but that evaluates the matters being litigated in terms of the way in which law and equity historically have interacted in defining the scope of jury trial. Inasmuch as equity would intervene only when the remedy at law was inadequate, there is a built-in capacity for adjustment in the scope of the Seventh Amendment as procedural alterations expand or contract the category of actions at law. As the range of remedies available at law has been expanded by modern procedural advances, the historical balance between law and equity has shifted. The next section examines the manner in which this contemporary, more refined view of the historical test has been applied, and what the implications of this development have been for the right to jury trial in the federal judicial system.

§ 11.5 Problems of Law and Equity in the Federal Courts—Modern Developments

Because the English practice with respect to the division between law and equity was rather flexible in 1791,[1] the historical interpretation and application of the Seventh Amendment, until recently, proceeded with much confusion and little consistency.[2] Indeed, one of the draw-

---

29. See Beaunit Mills, Inc. v. Eday Fabric Sales Corp., 124 F.2d 563 (2d Cir. 1942).

30. 359 U.S. 500, 79 S.Ct. 948, 3 L.Ed.2d 988 (1959). This case is discussed in detail in § 11.5, below.

31. See Dairy Queen, Inc. v. Wood, 369 U.S. 469, 82 S.Ct. 894, 8 L.Ed.2d 44 (1962); Ross v. Bernhard, 396 U.S. 531, 90 S.Ct. 733, 24 L.Ed.2d 729 (1970). These cases are discussed in § 11.5, below.

32. This development is criticized in James, Right to a Jury Trial in Civil Actions, 72 Yale L.J. 655, 689–90 (1963), and Rothstein, Beacon Theatres and the Consti-

tutional Right to Jury Trial, 51 A.B.A.J. 1145, 1146 (1965).

§ 11.5

1. See § 11.4, above. For an excellent study of the jury trial practices of the various colonies before ratification of the Constitution, see Henderson, The Background of the Seventh Amendment, 80 Harv.L.Rev. 289 (1966).

2. Compare Enelow v. New York Life Ins. Co., 293 U.S. 379, 55 S.Ct. 310, 79 L.Ed. 440 (1935), with American Life Ins. Co. v. Stewart, 300 U.S. 203, 57 S.Ct. 377, 81 L.Ed. 605 (1937). Enelow ultimately was

backs of defining the right to jury trial according to 1791 practices is that it allows a constitutional right to be defined in terms of an historical accident. Any test that is entirely directed to an historical inquiry inevitably fails to take account of the underlying policies of economy and efficiency with which any intelligent allocation of jury trial rights must be concerned.[3] Of course, there are limits to the extent to which the federal courts are free to employ these policy-related factors since the Constitution seems to provide for an historically based test.[4] Yet, when the historical test gives no clear direction, it has been argued that it is constitutionally acceptable to take into account such matters as the relative competence of the judge and jury.[5]

Criticism of the historical test, and the dysfunctional results that its rigid application often produces, have been widespread both in the courts[6] and the academic literature.[7] Yet, its continued utilization seems required to honor the constitutional mandate. The struggle has been to develop an interpretation of the Seventh Amendment that is both consistent with its historical basis, and capable of integrating modern procedural developments that promote the efficient functioning of the judicial system.

The current interpretation is reflected in the Supreme Court decisions in Beacon Theatres, Inc. v. Westover, Dairy Queen, Inc. v. Wood, Ross v. Bernhard, and Chauffers, Teamsters & Helpers, Local 391 v. Terry.[8] In these cases the Court adopted what might be termed a "dynamic concept" of the jury trial right. Under this approach, the inquiry is directed not to the actual arrangement of legal and equitable issues in 1791, but, as one author has stated, "to the distinctive common law process of adjudication and lawmaking that then and now, in England and in the United States, was recognized as flexible and changing."[9] The Beacon Theatres holding, for example, requires that the right to jury trial be measured in light of modern procedural developments, especially reforms that make available a remedy at law that

---

overruled by Gulfstream Aerospace Corp. v. Mayacamas, 485 U.S. 271, 108 S.Ct. 1133, 99 L.Ed.2d 296 (1988).

3. See the material discussed in § 11.1, above, concerning the contemporary debate over the utility of jury trial.

4. See James, The Right to a Jury Trial in Civil Actions, 72 Yale L.J. 655, 691 (1963).

5. Note, The Right to Nonjury Trial, 74 Harv.L.Rev. 1176, 1189–90 (1961).

6. See particularly, the dissent of Judge Clark in Damsky v. Zavatt, 289 F.2d 46, 57 (2d Cir.1961). See also Gefen v. U.S., 400 F.2d 476, 479 (5th Cir.1968), cert. denied 393 U.S. 1119, in which the court stated: " * * * although the classification of pre–1791 standards does not capture our unqualified enthusiasm, we follow Damsky

until the Supreme Court frees us from its validated historical bondage."

7. Kane, Civil Jury Trial: The Case for Reasoned Iconoclasm, 28 Hast.L.J. 1 (1976); Note, The Right to Jury Trial Under Title VII, 37 U.Chi.L.Rev. 167, 172–73 (1969).

8. Beacon Theatres, Inc. v. Westover, 359 U.S. 500, 79 S.Ct. 948, 3 L.Ed.2d 988 (1959); Dairy Queen, Inc. v. Wood, 369 U.S. 469, 82 S.Ct. 894, 8 L.Ed.2d 44 (1962); Ross v. Bernhard, 396 U.S. 531, 90 S.Ct. 733, 24 L.Ed.2d 729 (1970); Chauffeurs, Teamsters & Helpers, Local 391 v. Terry, 494 U.S. 558, 110 S.Ct. 1339, 108 L.Ed.2d 519 (1990). See the detailed discussion of these cases below. See also 9 C. Wright & A. Miller, Civil 2d §§ 2301–07.

9. Wolfram, The Constitutional History of the Seventh Amendment, 57 Minn. L.Rev. 639, 745 (1973).

previously did not exist.[10] This clearly changes the historic balance between law and equity. As the circumstances and setting of Beacon and its progeny are examined more closely, it will be apparent that these cases reflect the Court's judgment about the utility and value of jury trial in a modern civil litigation system, as well as the Court's attempt to formulate a constitutionally principled approach to determining jury trial rights.

In Beacon Theatres, Inc. v. Westover, plaintiff—Fox West Coast Theatres, Inc.—sought declaratory relief against Beacon Theatres, alleging a controversy under the antitrust laws. Fox operated a movie theatre in San Bernardino, California, exhibiting films under contracts with movie distributors. These agreements granted Fox an exclusive right to show first-run motion pictures in the San Bernardino area, and provided for a "clearance"—a period of time during which no other theatre in the area could exhibit the same pictures. Defendant Beacon constructed a drive-in theatre about 11 miles from San Bernardino, and, according to the complaint, notified Fox that it considered the exclusive distribution contracts to be violative of the antitrust laws. Fox instituted an action in a California federal district court seeking a declaration that the agreements were reasonable and did not violate the antitrust laws. Plaintiff also asked for a preliminary injunction to prevent defendant from instituting the threatened antitrust actions until the ongoing action was completed.

Beacon filed an answer, a counterclaim against Fox, and a cross-claim against an exhibitor who had intervened. Those pleadings denied the threats and asserted that no substantial competition existed between the two theatres, that the clearances therefore were not reasonable, and that Fox and its distributors had conspired to manipulate contracts and clearances so as to restrain trade and monopolize first-run pictures in violation of the antitrust laws. Treble damages were sought.

Defendant Beacon demanded a jury trial. The district court viewed the issues raised by Fox's complaint as essentially equitable and, purporting to act under the authority of Federal Rules 42(b) and 57, directed they be tried to the court before a jury determined the validity of the antitrust charges advanced in the counterclaim and cross-claim. Beacon sought a writ of mandamus to vacate the district court's orders.

The Ninth Circuit held that the jury trial question was to be determined solely from Fox's complaint, which the court construed as stating a claim traditionally cognizable in equity. The court rejected the argument that Beacon's interposition of the counterclaim afforded Fox an adequate remedy at law, rendering equitable relief unnecessary. The Ninth Circuit invoked the principle, discussed later, that equity jurisdiction properly acquired is unaffected by the subsequent availability of a

---

10. See McCoid, Procedural Reform and the Right to Jury Trial: A Study of Beacon Theatres, Inc. v. Westover, 116 U.Pa.L.Rev. 1, 6 (1967); Comment, The Right to Jury Trial in Declaratory Judgment Actions, 3 Conn.L.Rev. 564, 583 (1971).

legal remedy. In those instances, the pre-merger equity court had the discretion to enjoin the later lawsuit in order to allow the entire dispute to be determined in a single court as a single case. The court of appeals viewed the district court's order as analogous to such an injunction, because a determination by the district judge of the issue of the reasonableness of the clearances would operate by way of collateral estoppel to deprive Beacon of a jury determination of the same issue in the subsequent trial of the treble damage claim. The court concluded that the district judge had acted within the discretion granted by Federal Rule 42(b) and refused the writ of mandamus.

Beacon then appealed to the Supreme Court, which reversed and ordered that prior to the trial of any equitable issues by the court, all factual issues raised by the legal aspects of the case must be tried to a jury. The decision represents a dramatic re-evaluation of the right to jury trial in the federal courts.

Historically, when a case had both legal and equitable aspects, the chancery courts employed the so-called "clean-up doctrine." This meant that once it was determined that equitable jurisdiction over an action existed, the chancellor would decide all aspects of the controversy, both legal and equitable, thereby obviating the need for two proceedings. But the doctrine would be applied only when the legal aspects of the case were subordinate to the equitable issues. Thus, prior to Beacon Theatres, the Seventh Amendment inquiry had focused largely on ascertaining the "basic nature of the case" to determine whether a sufficiently important legal claim had been presented giving rise to a right to jury trial.

Judge Kalodner in Fraser v. Geist[11] succinctly stated the problem: "Where the complaint states one cause of action giving rise to alternative remedies in law or in equity, and where the complainant similarly prays for relief in the alternative, what is the rule as respects the right of trial by jury?"[12] His answer illustrates the typical pre-Beacon analysis. "The decision as to whether or not the plaintiff is entitled to jury trial 'as of right' must rest upon a prior determination as to whether the action, in its essence, is one at law or in equity."[13] Under this approach, when an action was classified as "essentially equitable," the federal court could dispose of any incidental legal claims without a jury.[14] Beacon Theatres expressly overruled this interpretation of the Seventh Amendment and held that no test utilizing traditional equity procedure could interfere with the right to have a jury determine all the factual issues associated with a legal claim.[15]

11. 1 F.R.D. 267 (E.D.Pa.1940).

12. 1 F.R.D. at 268.

13. 1 F.R.D. at 267.

14. This practice is criticized in Morris, Jury Trial Under the Federal Fusion of Law and Equity, 20 Texas L.Rev. 427 (1942).

15. See Comment, The Right to Jury Trial in Declaratory Judgment Actions, 3 Conn.L.Rev. 564, 584 (1971).

The analysis employed by the majority in Beacon focused on the extent to which procedural reforms, embodied in the Federal Rules and in the Declaratory Judgment Act, had shifted the traditional balance between the availability of equitable and legal relief.[16] The Court held that when a remedy at law has been made available, there is a constitutional right to a jury trial regardless of whether historically the action would have been tried in equity. The proper inquiry is not to be directed at the relationship between law and equity as of 1791, but rather at the process of accommodation between the two jurisdictions that has been developing over the past two centuries.[17]

Applying this principle to the facts of the case, the Court found that the Declaratory Judgment Act and the liberal joinder provisions of the Federal Rules offered an adequate remedy at law. Consequently, the assertion of equitable jurisdiction over Fox's complaint and Beacon's counterclaim and cross-claim on the ground that the remedy at law was inadequate, was not justified.[18] The Court reasoned that "if Beacon would have been entitled to a jury trial in a treble damage suit against Fox, it cannot be deprived of the right merely because Fox took advantage of the availability of declaratory relief to sue Beacon first."[19] Looking at the underlying basis of the treble damage claim, the Court concluded that the issue of the "reasonableness" of the clearance scheme under the federal antitrust laws was clearly appropriate for jury determination.[20]

The Court also noted that even assuming that Fox had stated a claim cognizable in equity, it would have been error to try that claim prior to the counterclaim.[21] Because ordering the trial of equitable issues first may operate, under the principles of former adjudication,[22] to bar the subsequent trial of the legal issues,[23] the rule of Beacon Theatres is that " * * * all order-of-trial problems be resolved in favor of jury trial unless there are special and compelling reasons for granting a nonjury trial."[24] Further, the right to jury trial attaches to issues, not causes of

---

16. Comment, From Beacon Theatres to Dairy Queen to Ross: The Seventh Amendment, the Federal Rules and a Receding Law—Equity Dichotomy, 48 J. Urban Law 459, 483–84 (1971).

17. McCoid, Procedural Reform and the Right to Jury Trial: A Study of Beacon Theatres, Inc. v. Westover, 116 U.Pa.L.Rev. 1, 23–24 (1967).

18. 359 U.S. at 507–08, 79 S.Ct. at 955.

19. 359 U.S. at 504, 79 S.Ct. at 953.

20. Ibid.

21. Comment, The Right to Jury Trial in Declaratory Judgment Actions, 3 Conn. L.Rev. 564, 581 (1971).

22. See generally §§ 14.9–14.12, below.

23. See Note, Ross v. Bernhard: The Uncertain Future of the Seventh Amendment, 81 Yale L.J. 112, 114 (1971).

24. Note, The Right to a Nonjury Trial, 74 Harv.L.Rev. 1176, 1187 (1961). See the Beacon opinion, 359 U.S. at 510–11, 79 S.Ct. at 956–57. The Court cited Leimer v. Woods, 196 F.2d 828, 833–36 (8th Cir. 1952), as stating a policy preference for jury, rather than court, trials whenever possible.

This policy preference has been strengthened in subsequent cases. See Lytle v. Household Mfg., Inc., 494 U.S. 545, 110 S.Ct. 1331, 108 L.Ed.2d 504 (1990) (collateral estoppel does not preclude the relitigation of issues resolved in the trial of an equitable claim when the issues in the legal claim are remanded to be tried to a jury); Lindsey v. American Cast Iron Pipe Co., 810 F.2d 1094 (11th Cir.1987) (court may not make new findings of fact inconsistent with facts established by the jury verdict); Kitchen v. Chippewa Valley Schools, 825

action, so that the fact that a traditionally equitable claim is filed first does not determine whether a jury trial first must occur on designated legal issues.

These two principles—(1)that the scope of equitable jurisdiction must be measured in light of the legal remedies and procedures currently available, and (2)that when an issue is common to both legal and equitable claims in the same proceeding, it must be tried first to a jury— are the backbone of the Beacon Theatres decision. These principles are not unbounded however; they apply only when legal issues are present in an action. Beacon Theatres does not require a jury trial in a proceeding seeking purely equitable relief. What it does direct is that the court's analysis of whether a jury triable issue is present must consider the effect of procedural innovation upon the historic balance between law and equity.[25]

In a real sense, Beacon Theatres was an "easy" case. Standing alone, it reveals little about the extent to which the Court intended to pursue the full implications of some of the language in its opinion. The claim by Fox and the counterclaim by Beacon presented a substantial common legal issue—the "reasonableness" of the movie distribution scheme under the contract. Given the basic thrust of the lawsuit once the counterclaim was interposed, this issue should have been tried to a jury even under the pre-Beacon "center-of-gravity" test. Accordingly, if the case is construed narrowly, the Beacon Court might have been saying that when the important issues in a lawsuit, as raised by all the pleadings, are clearly legal in nature, and the equitable issues are merely incidental, it is an abuse of the trial judge's discretion to utilize the equity clean-up doctrine for the purpose of avoiding a jury trial on the predominantly legal claims. Stated differently, the Supreme Court might have been saying that the trial court had used the right test, but had applied it incorrectly reaching the wrong result. It became apparent that Beacon Theatres was dramatically more significant than this, and that its philosophy regarding the dynamism of the Seventh Amendment was much more embracive, three years later in Dairy Queen, Inc. v. Wood.[26]

The dispute in Dairy Queen involved a failure to make payments under a trademark licensing agreement. Plaintiffs brought an action for breach of contract praying for: (1) temporary and permanent injunctions to restrain petitioner from any future use of or dealing in the franchise and the trademark; (2) an accounting to determine the exact amount of money owed by petitioner and a judgment for that amount; and (3) an injunction pending the accounting to prevent petitioner from collecting any money from Dairy Queen outlets in the territory.

F.2d 1004 (6th Cir.1987) (judge deciding retaliation claim is bound by jury findings on retaliation issue).

25. See McCoid, Procedural Reform and the Right to Jury Trial: A Study of Beacon Theatres, Inc. v. Westover, 116 U.Pa.L.Rev. 1, 12–13 (1967); Rothstein,

Beacon Theatres and the Constitutional Right to Jury Trial, 51 A.B.A.J. 1145, 1148 (1965).

26. 369 U.S. 469, 82 S.Ct. 894, 8 L.Ed.2d 44 (1962).

The federal court in the Eastern District of Pennsylvania granted a motion to strike petitioner's demand for a jury trial on the alternative grounds that the action was "purely equitable" or, if not purely equitable, the legal issues were "incidental" to the equitable issues. The Third Circuit refused to issue a writ of mandamus. The Supreme Court took jurisdiction and reversed.

At the outset, it should be noted that the claims in Dairy Queen were essentially equitable in nature, in contrast to the declaratory judgment and counterclaim in Beacon Theatres. The relief sought was entirely equitable and the issues concerning the liabilities under the contract raised questions that historically would have been tried to the court. Even though an accounting is quite similar to a damage remedy, its origins were in equity. This was because an accounting required skills that generally were thought to be beyond the competence of jurors, who, in an earlier era, were largely illiterate. Thus, Dairy Queen involved a situation in which application of the equitable clean-up doctrine would have been clearly appropriate and it presented a good case for testing the limits of the rule announced in Beacon Theatres.

The Court in Dairy Queen made it clear that virtually no application of the clean-up doctrine was constitutionally acceptable.[27] Writing for the majority, Justice Black stated:

> The holding in Beacon Theatres was that where both legal and equitable issues are presented in a single case, "only under the most imperative circumstances, circumstances which in view of the flexible procedures of the Federal Rules we cannot now anticipate, can the right to a jury trial of legal issues be lost through prior determination of equitable claims." That holding, of course, applies whether the trial judge chooses to characterize the legal issues presented as "incidental" to equitable issues or not. Consequently, in a case such as this where there cannot even be a contention of such "imperative circumstances," Beacon Theatres requires that any legal issues for which a trial by jury is timely and properly demanded be submitted to a jury.[28]

The Court then concluded: "insofar as the complaint requests a money judgment it presents a claim which is unquestionably legal."[29]

It is most important to understand the Court's analysis regarding the legal character of the action. In rejecting respondent's contention that the money claim was purely equitable because it was cast in terms of an accounting rather than in the language of an action for "debt" or "damages," Justice Black stated:

> But the constitutional right to trial by jury cannot be made to depend upon the choice of words used in the pleadings. The neces-

---

27. See Note, Congressional Provision for Nonjury Trial Under the Seventh Amendment, 83 Yale L.J. 401, 406–07 (1973). See also Comment, The Right to Jury Trial in Declaratory Judgment Actions, 3 Conn.L.Rev. 564, 585 (1971).

28. 369 U.S. at 472–73, 82 S.Ct. at 897.

29. 369 U.S. at 476, 82 S.Ct. at 899.

sary prerequisite to the right to maintain a suit for an equitable accounting, like all other equitable remedies, is, as we pointed out in Beacon Theatres, the absence of an adequate remedy at law.[30]

Starting from the basic premise of the Beacon Theatres decision that the right to jury trial exists as to any claim for which a legal remedy is available, the Court found that the power of the court to appoint masters under Federal Rule 53(b)[31] in order to assist the jury in computing money awards had obviated the historical necessity of a court trial. Accordingly, the Dairy Queen Court made clear that the right to jury trial exists as to any issue that is an element of a claim cognizable at law, even if the claim appears to be less significant than the equitable elements of the case. In addition, a determination of the "legal" nature of an issue must turn on an examination of the range of remedies that have been made available by procedural reforms since the ratification of the Seventh Amendment.[32]

Illustratively, suppose plaintiff alleges that defendant is a constant trespasser on her land. Although no serious tangible damage is done, defendant's trespass interferes with plaintiff's peaceful enjoyment of her property. Plaintiff sues to enjoin this continuing trespass—an equitable remedy—and for token money damages—a legal remedy. Despite the centrality of the equitable claim and the relative triviality of the legal claim, a right to jury trial exists for ascertainment of the facts regarding the trespasses.

Taken together, Beacon Theatres and Dairy Queen represent a significant affirmation of the right to jury trial on all issues common to legal and equitable claims.[33] However, because both cases involved actions with elements that might have been tried historically at law, the question remained whether the right to jury trial extended to an action that could not have been brought historically at law, because it required the use of a procedure not recognized by the law courts. The Supreme Court answered this question affirmatively in Ross v. Bernhard.[34]

In Ross, petitioners, stockholders of the Lehman Corporation, brought a derivative suit in federal court against the directors of the corporation and against Lehman Brothers, the corporation's brokers. Petitioners alleged gross negligence, abuse of trust, waste and conversion of corporate assets by the directors, breach of fiduciary duty by all defendants, and breach of the brokerage contract. Petitioners prayed for an accounting and for repayment to the corporation of the excessive commissions, and they demanded a jury trial.

30. 369 U.S. at 477–78, 82 S.Ct. at 899–900.

31. Fed.Civ.Proc.Rule 53(b).

32. See McCoid, Procedural Reform and the Right to Jury Trial: A Study of Beacon Theatres, Inc. v. Westover, 116 U.Pa.L.Rev. 1, 8–9 (1967).

33. Not all commentators view the cases with approval. See James, The Right to a Jury Trial in Civil Actions, 72 Yale L.J. 655, 687–88 n. 189 (1963).

34. 396 U.S. 531, 90 S.Ct. 733, 24 L.Ed.2d 729 (1970).

The main issue presented by Ross was whether the jury right attached to legal issues presented in a proceeding that historically was entirely equitable.[35] Recall that in Dairy Queen, the declaratory judgment procedure was neither purely equitable nor legal—it was a twentieth century statutory procedural innovation that was expressly neutral regarding jury trial. But this was not true of the stockholder derivative suit. Although derivative actions did not exist in England in 1791, either at common law or in equity, equitable analogies were present at that time. In addition, from its inception in the nineteenth century both in England and in the United States, the derivative suit had been treated as a purely equitable procedure.[36] Despite this history, the Supreme Court ruled that "the right to jury trial attaches to those issues in derivative actions as to which the corporation, if it had been suing in its own right, would have been entitled to a jury."[37]

The opinion of the Ross Court followed the rationale of Beacon Theatres and Dairy Queen. It stressed the "dual nature" of the derivative suit and noted that two things were to be determined: first, the plaintiffs' right to assert the claims of the corporation, and second, the merits of the claims asserted.[38] Although conceding that the question of the plaintiff's standing to sue on behalf of the corporation was historically an equitable matter, the Court concluded that the underlying corporate claim might be either legal or equitable, and, if legal, the right to jury trial had to be preserved.[39] Moreover, in determining that the underlying corporate claim was legal, the Court adopted the principle established in Beacon Theatres—equitable jurisdiction no longer exists when procedural reform has developed an adequate remedy at law.[40] It noted: "The historical rule preventing a court of law from entertaining a shareholder's suit on behalf of the corporation is obsolete * * *."[41]

The Ross Court also reaffirmed the principle that it is the individual issue, rather than either the basic nature of the case or the form of the action, that is determinative of the right to jury trial.[42] In developing a

35. Ross involved the resolution of this question in the context of a shareholder derivative suit. The same issue arises in two other actions that are historically equitable—interpleader, see Pan American Fire & Cas. Co. v. Revere, 188 F.Supp. 474, 483 (E.D.La.1960); Savannah Bank & Trust Co. v. Block, 175 F.Supp. 798, 801 (S.D.Ga. 1959); 7 C. Wright, A. Miller & M. Kane, Civil 2d § 1718, and class actions, see Canuel v. Oskoian, 23 F.R.D. 307, 314–15 (D.R.I.1959), affirmed on other grounds 269 F.2d 311 (1st Cir.1959); 7B C. Wright, A Miller & M. Kane, Civil 2d § 1801. Compare Richland v. Crandall, 259 F.Supp. 274 (S.D.N.Y.1966), with Ross.

36. See Cohen v. Beneficial Indus. Loan Corp., 337 U.S. 541, 548, 69 S.Ct. 1221, 1226, 93 L.Ed. 1528 (1949); Dodge v. Woolsey, 59 U.S. (18 How.) 331, 341–44, 15 L.Ed. 401 (1855). See also Note, Ross v.

Bernhard: The Uncertain Future of the Seventh Amendment, 81 Yale L.J. 112, 115–16 (1971).

37. 396 U.S. at 532–33, 90 S.Ct. at 735.

38. 396 U.S. at 534–35, 90 S.Ct. at 736.

39. 396 U.S. at 538–39, 90 S.Ct. at 738.

40. See Forward, The Supreme Court, 1969 Term, 84 Harv.L.Rev. 172, 175 (1970); Note, Ross v. Bernhard: The Uncertain Future of the Seventh Amendment, 81 Yale L.J. 112, 119 (1971).

41. 396 U.S. at 540, 90 S.Ct. at 739.

42. See Simler v. Conner, 372 U.S. 221, 83 S.Ct. 609, 9 L.Ed.2d 691 (1963), cited in Ross at 396 U.S. at 538, 90 S.Ct. at 738. See also the discussion of this point in Comment, The Right to Jury Trial in Declaratory Judgment Actions, 3 Conn.L.Rev. 564, 594–97 (1971).

test for defining the character of an issue, the Court, in an important footnote, stated:

> As our cases indicate, the "legal" nature of an issue is determined by considering, first, the pre-merger custom with reference to such questions; second, the remedy sought; and third, the practical abilities and limitations of juries * * *.[43]

Although it did make clear that the nature of the overall action, which in Ross was the derivative suit, no longer determined the mode of trial of all the issues, the test outlined by the Court led some observers to believe that another re-examination of the scope of the Seventh Amendment might be forthcoming.[44] This is because the Court left vague the content of its third criterion for determining the legal nature of an issue—"the practical abilities and limitations of juries"—and it was clear that a broad and critical examination under that standard could lead to a contraction of the jury trial right announced in Beacon Theatres.

An excellent example of this is the debate concerning whether a federal court can deny a jury trial on the ground that the litigation is so complex that it is beyond the competence of the jury.[45] This argument has been raised in a number of district courts[46] in the context of highly complex business litigation.[47] Its advocates point to the fact that historically equity took jurisdiction over certain cases and procedures such as accountings because they were deemed too complicated for the ordinary jury.[48] They rely on this historical ground for finding the remedy at law inadequate, as well as on the Ross recognition that the determination of the legal nature of an issue properly involves consideration of the abilities of the jury.[49] The Ninth Circuit and the Federal Circuit have rejected these arguments finding that there is no complexity exception to the Seventh Amendment.[50] The Third Circuit has concurred, but has

---

43. 396 U.S. at 538 n. 10, 90 S.Ct. at 738 n. 10.

44. See Wolfram, The Constitutional History of the Seventh Amendment, 57 Minn.L.Rev. 639 (1973).

45. For a discussion of the problems of complex litigation in the context of the right to jury trial, see Devitt, Should Jury Trial Be Required in Civil Cases? A Challenge to the Seventh Amendment, 47 J.Air L. & Comm. 495 (1982); Kirst, The Jury's Historic Domain in Complex Cases, 58 Wash.L.Rev. 1 (1982); Note, Complex Litigation and the Seventh Amendment Right to a Jury Trial, 51 U.Chi.L.Rev. 581 (1984).

46. See Kian v. Mirro Aluminum Co., 88 F.R.D. 351 (E.D.Mich.1980); Bernstein v. Universal Pictures, Inc., 79 F.R.D. 59 (S.D.N.Y.1978); In re Boise Cascade Secs. Litigation, 420 F.Supp. 99 (W.D.Wash. 1976). See also Hyde Properties v. McCoy, 507 F.2d 301, 306 (6th Cir.1974).

47. Another alternative to eliminating juries in highly complex litigation is to al-

low special "blue ribbon" juries chosen for their ability to understand the matters presented. See Note, The Case for Special Juries in Complex Civil Litigation, 89 Yale L.J. 1155 (1980).

48. See Campbell & LePoidevin, Complex Cases and Jury Trials: A Reply to Professor Arnold, 128 U.Pa.L.Rev. 965 (1980); Devlin, Jury Trial of Complex Cases: English Practice at the Time of the Seventh Amendment, 80 Colum.L.Rev. 43 (1980). But see Arnold, A Historical Inquiry into the Right to Trial by Jury in Complex Civil Litigation, 128 U.Pa.L.Rev. 829 (1980).

49. See Note, The Right to a Jury Trial in Complex Civil Litigation, 92 Harv.L.Rev. 898 (1979). But see Note, Taking the "Complexity" Out of Complex Litigation: Preserving the Constitutional Right to Civil Jury Trial, 28 Val.U.L.Rev. 337 (1993).

50. In re U.S. Financial Secs. Litigation, 609 F.2d 411 (9th Cir.1979), cert. denied 446 U.S. 929; SRI International v.

stated that there may be some instances in which a case is so complex that the use of a jury would violate Fifth Amendment Due Process rights.[51] The Fifth Circuit has declined to rule on whether a complexity exception exists, holding only that even if complexity properly may be considered, it will not support the denial of a jury trial based on a trial court finding that "it would be most difficult, if not impossible, for a jury to reach a rational decision."[52] Whether the Supreme Court will be willing to utilize the Ross test, particularly the third criterion, in setting a limit on the Beacon Theatres principle is highly debatable. In the more than twenty-five years since Ross, there has been little indication that the Court is likely to retreat from its expansive interpretation of the Seventh Amendment to adopt a broad complexity exception.[53]

Indeed, in 1990, the Court reaffirmed the expansive approach to finding a right to jury trial exhibited in Ross in the case of Chauffeurs, Teamsters & Helpers, Local 391 v. Terry.[54] The Court confronted the question whether employees seeking back pay from their union for an alleged breach of its duty of fair representation were entitled under the Seventh Amendment to a jury trial. Justice Marshall, writing for a divided Court, concluded that a jury trial right attached to the claim. In doing so, he reaffirmed that the nature of the issues to be tried, not the action as a whole, and, more importantly, the remedy being sought determine the right to a jury trial. In the case at hand, both elements were found to be legal in character. Although Justice Marshall found that the action was analogous to a suit by a beneficiary against a trustee—an historically equitable proceeding—he went on to look at the underlying issues in the claim and found them to be comparable to a breach of contract claim, and thus legal in character.[55] Further, the remedy involved a monetary award, damages, which typically also are legal. Notably, three members of the Court dissented, stating: "Although we have divided self-standing legal claims from equitable declaratory, accounting, and derivative procedures, we have never parsed legal elements out of equitable claims absent specific procedural justifications."[56] Thus, the dissenters criticized the expansive view exhibited by the Court, concluding: "If we abandon the plain language of the Constitution to

Matsushita Elec. Corp. of America, 775 F.2d 1107 (Fed.Cir.1985).

51. In re Japanese Electronic Prods. Antitrust Litigation, 631 F.2d 1069 (3d Cir. 1980).

52. Cotten v. Witco Chemical Corp., 651 F.2d 274, 276 (5th Cir.1981), cert. denied 455 U.S. 909. See also, Soderbeck v. Burnett County, Wisconsin, 752 F.2d 285 (7th Cir.1985), cert. denied 471 U.S. 1117.

53. See the measured approach taken by the Court in Markman v. Westview Instruments, Inc., 517 U.S. 370, 116 S.Ct. 1384, 134 L.Ed.2d 577 (1996), discussed at notes 58–59, below.

There have been suggestions that Congress may depart from this expansive view of the right to a jury trial. See Kane, Civil Jury Trial: The Case for Reasoned Iconoclasm, 28 Hast.L.J. 1, 11 (1976). The issue of the extent to which Congress may be able to provide for a nonjury trial by statute is discussed in § 11.6, below.

54. 494 U.S. 558, 110 S.Ct. 1339, 108 L.Ed.2d 519 (1990).

55. 494 U.S. at 569, 110 S.Ct. at 1347.

56. 494 U.S. at 590, 110 S.Ct. at 1358.

expand the jury right, we may expect Courts with opposing views to curtail it in the future."[57]

Interestingly, a 1996 Supreme Court decision may illustrate the dissenters' concerns. In Markman v. Westview Instruments, Inc.,[58] the Supreme Court had before it a patent infringement case in which its Seventh Amendment analysis focussed on issues, rather than claims, as well as on functional considerations as to whether the judge was in a better position than the jury to determine the construction of a patent claim document. When a review of history provided no clear answers as to whether the issue was one for the jury or for the judge to decide, the Court ruled that the issue could be determined by the judge since "judges, not juries, are the better suited to find the acquired meaning of patent terms."[59]

It would be wrong, however, to assume that this one decision marks a retreat by the Court from its general preference for jury trials because the outcome may be very tied to the peculiar facts before the Court. Taken as a whole, the Supreme Court's decisions in this area stand as a reaffirmation of the historic American commitment to the jury, a reaffirmation that, somewhat ironically, has taken place during a period in which this system of trial has been increasingly subject to criticism. Markman does indicate, however, the continued vitality of an inquiry into the practical ability of the jury to act as the decisionmaker as the basis for making a Seventh Amendment analysis, at least when history provides no clear guidance.

§ 11.6 Jury Trial in the Federal Courts—Statutory Causes of Action

In addition to constitutional jury trial rights, when Congress creates a statutory cause of action it may state that jury trial must be provided, thereby conferring a statutory jury trial right.[1] Further, when Congress has failed to provide expressly for trial by jury of a statutory cause of action, the federal courts often have found that Congress implicitly provided for the right or relied on the presence of the constitutional guarantee to supply it.[2] In either of these cases the right to jury trial is unassailable as Congress clearly has the power to confer broader jury trial rights than those guaranteed by the Seventh Amendment.

Serious and complicated Seventh Amendment problems occur, however, when Congress appears to have expressed a preference for nonjury trial because that preference must be reconciled with the jury trial

---

57. 494 U.S. at 593, 110 S.Ct. at 1359.

58. 517 U.S. 370, 116 S.Ct. 1384, 134 L.Ed.2d 577 (1996).

59. 517 U.S. at 388, 116 S.Ct. at 1395.

§ 11.6

1. E.g., 46 U.S.C.A. § 688 (1970) (Jones Act). The extent of this jury trial right is explored in Fitzgerald v. U.S. Lines Co., 374 U.S. 16, 20–21, 83 S.Ct. 1646, 1650, 10 L.Ed.2d 720 (1963).

2. E.g., Beacon Theatres, Inc. v. Westover, 359 U.S. 500, 504, 79 S.Ct. 948, 953, 3 L.Ed.2d 988 (1959) (antitrust laws); Dice v. Akron, Canton & Youngstown R. Co., 342 U.S. 359, 72 S.Ct. 312, 96 L.Ed. 398 (1952) (Federal Employers' Liability Act).

guarantee. The right to trial by jury guaranteed by the Seventh Amendment is not restricted to those common-law actions that actually existed in 1791.[3] Congress may create new causes of action by statute, or legislatively replace or modify actions that existed in 1791, without changing the applicability of the Seventh Amendment guarantee. This point was made clear at an early date by Justice Story, when he wrote in Parsons v. Bedford[4] that the Seventh Amendment "may well be construed to embrace all suits which are not of equity and admiralty jurisdiction, whatever may be the peculiar form which they may assume to settle legal rights."[5] Since the vast majority of liability statutes merely codify existing common law rights, most also fall within the scope of the Seventh Amendment.[6]

The Supreme Court has addressed the question of congressional power to provide for nonjury trial in a series of cases that fall into two broad categories. In the first, Congress has established a statutory cause of action and has provided that enforcement of those rights must proceed in a specialized statutory proceeding. In the second, the statutory right is to be enforced in the federal district courts. An examination of each of these situations follows.

The Supreme Court has spoken on four separate occasions regarding the power of Congress to take some causes of action outside the scope of the Seventh Amendment by providing for their enforcement through a statutory proceeding or in a specialized court. In three of these circumstances the statutory enactment was upheld against a Seventh Amendment challenge.

In NLRB v. Jones & Laughlin Steel Corporation,[7] the Supreme Court upheld a provision of the National Labor Relations Act empowering the Board to make findings of fact that were conclusive on review and to issue orders concerning challenged labor practices. The Court overruled defendant's Seventh Amendment objections, stating: "the instant case is not a suit at common law or in the nature of such a suit. The proceeding is one unknown to the common law. It is a statutory proceeding."[8] Thus, it appears that when Congress determines that administrative, rather than judicial, remedies are appropriate, it may so provide and the Seventh Amendment will not compel a jury trial in those proceedings. This conclusion may reflect the fact that Congress' decision

---

3. Curtis v. Loether, 415 U.S. 189, 194, 94 S.Ct. 1005, 1008, 39 L.Ed.2d 260 (1974). See, e.g., Chauffeurs, Teamsters & Helpers, Local 391 v. Terry, 494 U.S. 558, 110 S.Ct. 1339, 108 L.Ed.2d 519 (1990).

4. 28 U.S. (3 Pet.) 433, 7 L.Ed. 732 (1830).

5. 28 U.S. at 445–46, 7 L.Ed. at 736–37.

6. See, e.g., Feltner v. Columbia Pictures Television, Inc., 523 U.S. 340, 118 S.Ct. 1279, 140 L.Ed.2d 438 (1998) (Seventh Amendment provides a right to jury trial on all issues pertinent to the award of statutory damages for infringement under the Copyright Act); Tull v. U.S., 481 U.S. 412, 107 S.Ct. 1831, 95 L.Ed.2d 365 (1987) (Seventh Amendment guarantee applies to liability determination in actions by the government for civil penalties under the Clean Water Act; there is no jury trial right for the assessment of the penalty, however).

7. 301 U.S. 1, 57 S.Ct. 615, 81 L.Ed. 893 (1937).

8. 301 U.S. at 48, 57 S.Ct. at 629.

to remit certain causes of action to the administrative process involves the consideration that in some instances complex problems not easily comprehended by laypeople should be decided by a specialized group of experts; to inject a jury into that process would seriously impair its utility and effectiveness.[9]

In addition to its power to create administrative agencies for the enforcement of statutory rights, Congress may act under its Article I, Section 8 authority to establish specialized courts for the trial of certain actions historically cognizable in equity. Thus, in Katchen v. Landy[10] the Supreme Court upheld the summary jurisdiction of the bankruptcy court, which was established by Congress under the Bankruptcy Act, against a challenge that a summary proceeding before that court deprived the petitioner of its Seventh Amendment right to a jury trial. Although the Court noted that historically bankruptcy matters were not suits at common law and hence not under the scope of the Seventh Amendment, it also rested its decision on the power of Congress to establish a legislative court under Article I, Section 8 in order to provide for a prompt trial of a disputed claim without the intervention of a jury.[11]

The third case regarding congressional authority in this area is Atlas Roofing Company v. Occupational Safety & Health Review Commission,[12] decided in 1977. In that case the petitioners challenged the constitutionality of the Occupational Safety and Health Act under the Seventh Amendment insofar as it provides for civil penalties to be levied by a review commission against employers found to be violating the Act. The Supreme Court upheld the statute. Justice White, writing for a unanimous Court, stated that the Seventh Amendment does not prohibit Congress from committing the factfinding function and initial adjudication to an administrative tribunal that is incompatible with a jury. Further, the right to a jury trial "turns not solely on the nature of the issue to be resolved, but also on the forum in which it is to be resolved."[13] Congressional power is not unlimited, however.

A preference for administrative factfinding is justifiable only in situations involving " 'public rights,' e.g., where the Government is involved in its sovereign capacity under an otherwise valid statute creating enforceable public rights."[14] Cases involving wholly private

---

9. See Brown, Administrative Commissions and the Judicial Power, 19 Minn. L.Rev. 261 (1935); Note, Application of Constitutional Guarantees of Jury Trial to the Administrative Process, 56 Harv.L.Rev. 282 (1942).

10. 382 U.S. 323, 86 S.Ct. 467, 15 L.Ed.2d 391 (1966).

11. 382 U.S. at 336–37, 86 S.Ct. at 476.

12. 430 U.S. 442, 97 S.Ct. 1261, 51 L.Ed.2d 464 (1977). This case is discussed extensively in Kirst, Administrative Penalties and the Civil Jury: The Supreme Court's Assault on the Seventh Amendment, 126 U.Pa.L.Rev. 1281 (1978).

13. 430 U.S. at 461, 97 S.Ct. at 1272.

14. 430 U.S. at 458, 97 S.Ct. at 1270.

Public rights are not limited to those actions arising between the government and others, but are found when "Congress, acting for a valid legislative purpose * * * [has created] a seemingly 'private' right that is so closely integrated into a public regulatory scheme as to be a matter appropriate for agency resolution with limited involvement by the Article III judiciary." Thomas v. Union Carbide Agricultural Prods. Co., 473 U.S. 568, 593–94, 105 S.Ct. 3325, 3339–40, 87 L.Ed.2d 409 (1985).

matters between private individuals are not implicated. As summarized by the Court,

> We cannot conclude that the Amendment rendered Congress power-less—when it concluded that remedies available in courts of law were inadequate to cope with a problem within Congress' power to regulate—to create new public rights and remedies by statute and commit their enforcement, if it chose, to a tribunal other than a court of law—such as an administrative agency—in which facts are not found by juries.[15]

The importance of the distinction between private and public rights as elaborated in Atlas Roofing is underscored in the Supreme Court's most recent pronouncement on this question, Granfinanciera, S.A. v. Nordberg.[16] In Granfinanciera, a bankruptcy trustee filed suit in bankruptcy court against petitioners, who had not filed a claim against the estate, seeking to avoid allegedly fraudulent transfers made to the petitioners. The Court initially determined that the cause of action was legal, rather than equitable.[17] Thus, petitioners were entitled to a jury trial unless Congress had created a novel cause of action involving public rights. Although fraudulent transfers have been designated core proceedings which bankruptcy judges may adjudicate, the Court held that the trustee's right to recover a fraudulent conveyance from a party who had not filed a claim against the estate was a private, rather than a public, right. Thus, Congress simply had reclassified a pre-existing common-law cause of action, and a jury trial was required.[18] Congress could not eliminate a party's Seventh Amendment jury trial right merely by relabeling a cause of action and giving exclusive jurisdiction to a non-Article III tribunal.[19]

A problem of another dimension is presented when Congress expresses a preference for nonjury trial but provides for the remedies to be enforced under the normal Article III jurisdiction of the federal district courts. The Supreme Court addressed this question in Curtis v. Loether,[20] in which a black woman brought suit under Title VIII of the 1968 Civil Rights Act claiming that defendants racially discriminated against her in violation of the statute by refusing to rent her an apartment. Although originally she sought injunctive relief, compensatory and punitive damages, and attorney's fees, the injunction claim was dropped and the trial involved only the monetary claims. The question was whether

---

15. 430 U.S. at 460, 97 S.Ct. at 1271.

16. 492 U.S. 33, 109 S.Ct. 2782, 106 L.Ed.2d 26 (1989).

17. 492 U.S. at 49, 109 S.Ct. at 2794. The Court based its determination on the test set out in Tull v. U.S., 481 U.S. 412, 107 S.Ct. 1831, 95 L.Ed.2d 365 (1987).

18. Granfinanciera left unresolved whether bankruptcy courts can actually conduct jury trials or whether, once a Seventh Amendment right is found, the parties are remitted to an Article III court to deter-mine that issue before a jury. The lower courts are divided on the question. Compare In re Ben Cooper, 896 F.2d 1394 (2d Cir.1990) (bankruptcy court may conduct jury trials), with In re Stansbury Poplar Place, Inc., 13 F.3d 122 (4th Cir.1993) (bankruptcy court cannot conduct jury trial).

19. 492 U.S. at 61, 109 S.Ct. at 2800.

20. 415 U.S. 189, 94 S.Ct. 1005, 39 L.Ed.2d 260 (1974).

the defendants could claim a Seventh Amendment right to jury trial when the statute was silent and there were arguments that Congress did not want cases under the Act to be tried to a jury because of fears of delay and jury prejudice. The Supreme Court ruled that a jury trial was required constitutionally, finding that Congress in Title VIII had created a statutory right "in the nature of a suit at common law" and thus within the jury trial guarantee.[21] The Court avoided, however, the question of statutory intent, merely commenting on the sparsity and ambiguity of the legislative history.[22] Further, it noted that the policy arguments of avoiding delay and jury prejudice were "insufficient to overcome the clear command of the Seventh Amendment."[23]

The importance of the tribunal in which the statutory cause of action is enforced is made even clearer by the Supreme Court's decision in Pernell v. Southall Realty,[24] a jury trial decision rendered shortly after Curtis. Pernell involved a landlord's action for the summary recovery of possession of real property under the District of Columbia Code. An earlier statute governing those suits had contained an explicit jury trial provision,[25] but the Court Reform and Criminal Procedure Act of 1970[26] repealed that provision. It was argued that this change evidenced a congressional desire to dispense with jury trials because juries would delay and clog the courts in those cases, contrary to the express purpose of the 1970 Act. The Court ruled that the Seventh Amendment required a jury trial regardless of Congress' desires because an action for the recovery of real property is clearly analogous to a suit at common law. It noted that although the Constitution "would not be a bar to a congressional effort to entrust landlord-tenant disputes, including those over the right to possession, to an administrative agency,"[27] since Congress had committed those suits to ordinary courts of general jurisdiction, and the action involved rights and remedies recognized at common law, the jury trial right must be preserved.

Read most broadly, Curtis and Pernell seem to indicate that a congressional indication that nonjury trial is preferable, unaccompanied by the creation of a specific statutory, nonjudicial proceeding, cannot insulate a particular action from the Seventh Amendment. However, that reading appears too broad. In both cases Congress was silent as to jury trial. Thus, the Supreme Court has not yet been faced with the situation in which Congress has expressed a strong preference for nonjury trial and has provided reasons supporting that preference. Read more narrowly, then, the cases do not foreclose the possibility that Congress can provide for a statutory cause of action that is not purely equitable to be enforced in the district courts without a jury trial.

---

21. 415 U.S. at 195–96, 94 S.Ct. at 1009.

22. 415 U.S. at 191, 94 S.Ct. at 1007.

23. 415 U.S. at 198, 94 S.Ct. at 1010.

24. 416 U.S. 363, 94 S.Ct. 1723, 40 L.Ed.2d 198 (1974).

25. Act of Dec. 23, 1963, Pub.L. No. 88–241, § 1, 77 Stat. 517.

26. Act of July 29, 1970, Pub.L. No. 91–358, § 142(5)(A), 85 Stat. 552.

27. 416 U.S. at 383, 94 S.Ct. at 1733.

However, there is a constitutional presumption for jury trial and a very heavy burden of proof is placed on those desiring to overcome it.[28]

Two contemporary situations that have arisen in the lower courts allow for further exploration of the exact scope of congressional power in this area. The first involves claims brought under the 1976 Foreign Sovereign Immunities Act.[29] Among other things, that statute provides for subject-matter jurisdiction in the federal courts for actions against foreign governments or their instrumentalities and contains explicit language that jurisdiction is limited to nonjury proceedings.[30] Not only is the congressional preference for nonjury trials explicit, but the legislative history reveals that the Congress determined to provide only for nonjury trials because of a desire to promote uniformity in decisions and to avoid the international friction that might occur because of a perceived aberrant verdict rendered by a jury.[31] These provisions have been upheld by the circuit courts against challenges that the Seventh Amendment requires a jury trial if the underlying nature of the claim for relief was one that would have been brought at common law.[32] Essentially, they have found that actions against foreign sovereigns are by nature not actions at common law and that Congress thus effectuated a valid policy choice in deciding to provide for nonjury trials in these proceedings. In effect, the courts have recognized that, unlike Curtis, there was a functional justification for denying jury trial and that Congress had expressed itself clearly and satisfactorily on the question.[33]

The second, more controversial, area concerning the power of Congress to create statutory rights to be enforced in the federal courts without a jury trial involves suits under various civil rights statutes. Although Curtis has settled the question of the right to jury trial for actions under Title VIII of the 1968 Civil Rights Act, the right to a jury trial for actions under the other civil rights statutes still is in doubt.

The problem presented in these cases is similar to Curtis: that is, Congress is silent in the statute regarding the right to jury trial, but strong arguments are advanced that only a judge trial adequately can assure that the statutes are enforced as intended by Congress.[34] Argu-

---

28. See Kane, Civil Jury Trial: The Case for Reasoned Iconoclasm, 28 Hast.L.J. 1, 20–27 (1976).

29. Pub.L. No. 94–583, 90 Stat. 2891 (codified at 28 U.S.C.A. §§ 1330, 1332(a)(2), (4), 1391(f), 1441(d), 1602–11) (1976).

30. 28 U.S.C.A. §§ 1330(a), 1441(d).

31. See H.R.Rep. No. 1487, 94th Cong., 2d Sess. 14, reprinted in [1976] U.S.Code Cong. & Ad.News 6604, 6611–12.

32. In re Air Crash Disaster Near Roselawn, Indiana on October 31, 1994, 96 F.3d 932 (7th Cir.1996); Universal Consolidated Cos. v. Bank of China, 35 F.3d 243 (6th Cir.1994); Arango v. Guzman Travel Advisors, 761 F.2d 1527 (11th Cir.1985), cert. denied 474 U.S. 995; Goar v. Compa-

nia Peruana de Vapores, 688 F.2d 417 (5th Cir.1982); Rex v. Cia. Pervana De Vapores, S.A., 660 F.2d 61 (3d Cir.1981), cert. denied 456 U.S. 926; Williams v. Shipping Corp. of India, 653 F.2d 875 (4th Cir.1981), cert. denied 455 U.S. 982; Ruggiero v. Compania Peruana de Vapores, "Inca Capac Yupanqui", 639 F.2d 872 (2d Cir.1981).

33. See Kane, Suing Foreign Sovereigns: A Procedural Compass, 34 Stan. L.Rev. 385, 421–24 (1982).

34. See generally, Note, Jones v. Mayer: The Thirteenth Amendment and the Federal Anti–Discrimination Laws, 69 Colum.L.Rev. 1019 (1969); Comment, Jury Trial in Employment Discrimination Cases—Constitutionally Mandated?, 53

ably, the courts may take into account the possibility of jury prejudice as a factor indicating a practical limitation on the jury system and, applying the criteria in Ross v. Bernhard,[35] may determine that the Seventh Amendment does not compel a jury trial. Curtis itself does not answer this question because in that case the Court explicitly refused to rule on the extent to which Congress could impinge upon the Seventh Amendment under its power to enforce the Thirteenth and Fourteenth Amendments.[36] Further the Court compared the statutory language of Title VII (employment discrimination) and Title VIII (housing discrimination) and found, without deciding the issue, that congressional intent under the former statute was to provide for nonjury trial, but that no similar intent was expressed for Title VIII actions.[37]

The litigant suing under the civil rights laws and arguing for a nonjury trial must show that Congress impliedly expressed a preference for judge trials (that Congress intended to create an equitable remedy), that that preference is supported by a legitimate concern regarding the ability of the jury to decide these cases, and, finally, that jury ability is a proper factor by which to discriminate between cases falling within and without the Seventh Amendment. In employment discrimination suits, most lower courts have continued after Curtis to rule that the Seventh Amendment does not compel a jury trial on the issue of back pay, finding evidence in the type of remedies provided and the statutory language that Congress intended to establish an equitable scheme for redressing race discrimination in employment.[38] However, the propriety of jury inadequacy as a ground to support denying jury trial remains in doubt. It is possible that the Supreme Court might find sufficient congressional indication of jury inadequacy under Title VII so as to rule against jury trial under the criteria of Ross v. Bernhard. The Court's discussion in Curtis of Title VII does not preclude this result. Nonetheless, the fact that, to date, the Supreme Court never has found a preference for nonjury trial based on jury inadequacy to be sufficiently stated or supported[39] may indicate the Court's reluctance to accept these arguments in any context.

§ 11.7   Jury Trial in State Courts—The New York Approach

Although under current constitutional construction the Seventh

Texas L.Rev. 483 (1975); Comment, The Right to Jury Trial Under Title VII of the Civil Rights Act of 1964, 37 U.Chi.L.Rev. 167 (1969).

35. See the discussion of this case in § 11.5 at notes 34–53, above.

36. 415 U.S. 189, 198 n. 15, 94 S.Ct. 1005, 1010 n. 15, 39 L.Ed.2d 260 (1974).

37. 415 U.S. at 196–97, 94 S.Ct. at 1009–10.

38. E.g., Slack v. Havens, 522 F.2d 1091 (9th Cir.1975); EEOC v. Detroit Edison Co., 515 F.2d 301 (6th Cir.1975), vacated on other grounds 431 U.S. 951, 97 S.Ct. 2668, 53 L.Ed.2d 267 (1977).

39. The Supreme Court has ruled that cases under the Age Discrimination in Employment Act of 1967 are within the constitutional guarantee, finding that the remedies provided under that statute indicate congressional intent that jury trial be available. Lorillard v. Pons, 434 U.S. 575, 98 S.Ct. 866, 55 L.Ed.2d 40 (1978).

Amendment is not applicable to the states,[1] almost all states have comparable constitutional guarantees.[2] The interpretation generally given these provisions has been that the right to jury trial is to be applied as it existed at the time the state's constitution was adopted.[3] Since most state constitutional provisions describe the jury trial right in terms of the same law/equity distinction embodied in the Seventh Amendment, many of the same problems of applying the historical test under a merged procedural system arise in the state courts. Some states have avoided the confusion surrounding the law/equity dichotomy by providing for trial by jury in all cases, making the jury verdict binding in equity cases as well as those at law.[4] Most states, however, have maintained the law/equity dichotomy for purposes of applying their state constitutional standard.

An examination of the New York jury trial provisions reveals the way in which the content of this right can vary between the state and federal systems. The New York approach also presents some additional interpretative problems not pertinent to the federal jury trial guarantee. The original New York constitution, adopted in 1777, provided that: "Trial by jury, in all cases, in which it hath heretofore been used in the colony of New York, shall be established and remain inviolate, forever."[5] The Constitution of 1821 modernized this language to provide that "trial by jury, in all cases in which it has been heretofore used, shall remain inviolate forever."[6] This provision was reenacted in the Constitutions of 1846 and 1894.[7] The New York courts generally held that the 1821, 1846, and 1894 reenactments of the jury trial provision expanded the constitutional guarantee to embrace all cases in which there was a right prior to the promulgation of the 1894 Constitution.[8] The effect of the reenactment of the jury trial guarantee was

§ 11.7

1. See Minneapolis & St. Louis R.R. Co. v. Bombolis, 241 U.S. 211, 36 S.Ct. 595, 60 L.Ed. 961 (1916); Walker v. Sauvinet, 92 U.S. (2 Otto) 90, 23 L.Ed. 678 (1875); Melancon v. McKeithen, 345 F.Supp. 1025 (E.D.La.1972), affirmed sub nom. Davis v. Edwards, 409 U.S. 1098, 93 S.Ct. 908, 34 L.Ed.2d 679 (1973).

2. See § 11.1 n. 2, above.

3. See Barrett, The Constitutional Right to Jury Trial: An Historical Exception for Small Monetary Claims, 39 Hast.L.J. 125 (1987); Note, The Right to Jury Trial Under Merged Procedures, 65 Harv.L.Rev. 453 (1952).

4. See Van Hecke, Trial by Jury in Equity Cases, 31 N.C.L.Rev. 157 (1953).

5. N.Y.—McKinney's Const. Art. (1777), XLI.

6. N.Y.—McKinney's Const. Art. (1821), VII, § 2.

7. N.Y.—McKinney's Const. Art. (1846) I, § 2; N.Y.—McKinney's Const. Art. (1894), I, § 2.

8. See In re Littman's Will, 15 Misc.2d 430, 182 N.Y.S.2d 90 (1958); Matter of Britton's Will, 187 Misc. 70, 60 N.Y.S.2d 466 (1946). However, some cases determined the right to jury trial by returning to the custom as of 1846, rather than 1894. See Moot v. Moot, 214 N.Y. 204, 108 N.E. 424 (1915); Wynehamer v. People, 13 N.Y. (3 Kern) 378, 427 (1856); Conderman v. Conderman, 51 N.Y.S. (44 Hun) 181 (1887). Moreover, one case held that the words "heretofore used" meant only the common law prior to the adoption of the 1846 Constitution, not the right to jury trial accorded by statutory law. See Matter of Gurland, 286 App.Div. 704, 146 N.Y.S.2d 830 (1955), appeal dismissed 309 N.Y. 969, 132 N.E.2d 331 (1956). The holdings in these cases appear to be unsound. See 4 J. Weinstein, H. Korn & A. Miller, New York Civil Practice ¶ 4101.07.

to extend the constitutional guarantee to new classes of cases—those new cases in which jury trial was, at the time of the adoption of the new constitution, in use by virtue of legislation enacted since the adoption of the previous constitution.[9]

The 1938 New York Constitution, however, changed the nature of the jury trial guarantee by altering the language to read, "Trial by jury in all cases in which it has heretofore been guaranteed by constitutional provision shall remain inviolate forever."[10] The effect of this provision has been to "freeze" the constitutional right to jury trial to that which had been guaranteed by the 1894 Constitution.[11] Thus, the New York constitutional jury trial right is derived from two sources: 1) actions of the type in which a jury had been "heretofore used" at the time of adoption of the Constitution of 1777, and 2) actions in which the right to jury trial had been statutorily created between 1777 and 1894.[12] The clear effect of the 1938 Constitution was that statutory provisions for jury trial in the post–1894 period have not been accorded constitutional status.[13]

As to the first source, the right to jury trial in New York had been accorded only in proceedings at law prior to 1777. The Constitution of that year therefore incorporated the law/equity dichotomy and this test has been retained in the 1894 and 1938 Constitutions. But determining the incidence of the civil jury right was complicated by the merger of law and equity in New York in 1846.[14] In theory, only the right to jury trial remains to distinguish law and equity in New York. Thus, as in the federal courts, many New York courts have had serious difficulties in harmonizing the constitutional mandate and the unification of the procedural system.[15]

The various states' procedural rules or statutes that implement their respective constitutional jury trial guarantees adopt three different approaches: first, a simple declaration that the right as declared by constitution or by statute shall be preserved;[16] second, a general provi-

9. Mayers, The Constitutional Guarantee of Jury Trial in New York, 7 Brooklyn L.Rev. 180, 182–83 (1937).

10. N.Y.—McKinney's Const. Art. (1938), I, § 2.

11. See 2 Rev.Record, N.Y. State Const. Convention 1278 (1938). See also Matter of Leary's Estate, 175 Misc. 254, 23 N.Y.S.2d 13 (1940), affirmed mem. sub nom. Werner v. Reid, 260 App.Div. 1000, 24 N.Y.S.2d 1000 (1940), affirmed mem. 285 N.Y. 693, 34 N.E.2d 383 (1941).

12. There is no constitutional right to trial by court or referee in New York. See Susquehanna S.S. Co. v. A. O. Andersen & Co., 239 N.Y. 285, 295, 146 N.E. 381, 385 (1925); Phillips v. Gorham, 17 N.Y. 270, 273 (1858).

13. Kharas, A Century of Law Equity Merger in New York, 1 Syracuse L.Rev. 186, 200 (1949).

14. The Constitution of 1846 and the Code of Procedure of 1848 authorized by that Constitution accomplished three reforms: first, substitution of one "civil action" for all the different forms of action at law and equity; second, simplification of the technical common law rules concerning parties, pleadings, and final judgment; and third, fusion of law and equity. See note 18, below.

15. See 4 J. Weinstein, H. Korn & A. Miller, New York Civil Practice ¶ 4101.04.

16. This is the approach of the Federal Rules, which simply provide for jury trial as of right without attempting to define the cases in which that right exists. See Fed. Civ.Proc.Rule 38(a).

sion that all cases not triable in equity are accorded the right to jury trial; or, third, an enumeration of the specific types of cases in which the right exists.[17] New York's Civil Practice Law and Rules (CPLR)[18] is of the third type, purporting to list the classes of actions in which the jury trial right exists. This categorization generally has reflected the historical distinction between law and equity.[19]

Section 4101(1) of the CPLR guarantees the right to a jury trial in "an action in which a party demands and sets forth facts which would permit a judgment for a sum of money only."[20] Section 4101(2) of the CPLR lists "an action of ejectment; for dower; for waste; for abatement of and damages for a nuisance; to recover a chattel; or for determination of a claim to real property under article fifteen of the real property actions and proceedings law" as actions in which a right to jury trial exists. All of these, except the last category, are actions in which the jury right existed before 1777.[21] Section 4101(3) of the CPLR is a general reminder that the enumerations in paragraphs (1) and (2) are not exhaustive, and that in some cases historical research is necessary to determine whether a constitutional jury trial right exists.[22] The paragraph also protects statutory jury rights that were created since 1894 and therefore are not covered by a constitutional guarantee.[23]

Although application of the historical test in the federal courts requires a determination on an issue by issue basis whether the jury right would have existed historically,[24] this is not necessarily true in the states. New York has adopted what may be termed an "action orientation." Under this approach, the court will characterize an action as either "legal" or "equitable" in its entirety, and decide on this basis whether the action is jury triable. This method has been criticized as

---

17. See Note, The Right to Jury Trial Under Merged Procedures, 65 Harv.L.Rev. 453 (1952).

18. New York led the reform movement during the nineteenth century in adopting a merged procedural system. The Code of Procedure of 1848, popularly known as the Field Code in honor of its principal architect, implemented the revolutionary concepts of the 1846 Constitution. See 4 J. Weinstein, H. Korn & A. Miller, New York Civil Practice ¶ 4101.03.

19. Note, The Right to Jury Trial Under Merged Procedures, 65 Harv.L.Rev. 453, 454 (1952).

20. This passage has been interpreted to mean an action at law for a sum of money, rather than an action of an equitable nature in which a money judgment might afford adequate relief. See Bell v. Merrifield, 109 N.Y. 202, 16 N.E. 55 (1888); Clearview Gardens First Corp. v. Weisman, 206 Misc. 526, 134 N.Y.S.2d 288 (1954), affirmed without opinion 285 App.Div. 927,

139 N.Y.S.2d 881 (1955) (action deemed one for an equitable accounting, to which no jury right attaches).

21. See 4 J. Weinstein, H. Korn & A. Miller, New York Civil Practice ¶ 4101.10. Although there was no jury trial statute in 1777, the use of the civil jury was regulated by custom. See Malone v. Sts. Peter & Paul's Church, 172 N.Y. 269, 64 N.E. 961 (1902).

22. Ibid. See also Sporza v. German Savs. Bank, 192 N.Y. 8, 84 N.E. 406 (1908).

23. The CPLR does not explicitly deal with the right to jury trial in a declaratory judgment action. Like the federal courts, the New York courts have preserved the jury right when it would have existed had the action been brought for coercive relief. See Teperman v. Amron, 7 A.D.2d 857, 182 N.Y.S.2d 763 (1959); Allstate Ins. Co. v. Coe, 36 Misc.2d 323, 232 N.Y.S.2d 655 (1962).

24. See § 11.4, above.

being both rigid and out of harmony with the philosophy of merger.[25] It also has been viewed as creating artificial and unsound theoretical distinctions between "legal" and "equitable" actions that further have complicated the process of determining the scope of the right to jury trial.[26] In particular, the treatment of two situations provide good examples of the differences between many state constitutional guarantees and the Seventh Amendment—when defendant seeks affirmative equitable relief and when plaintiff joins legal and equitable claims.

At the time New York's first Constitution was adopted a defendant in an equitable action was not permitted to interpose a legal counterclaim. Thus, when it became procedurally possible to assert such a counterclaim, it is not surprising that it was held that no constitutional right to a jury trial existed.[27] In the 1876 revision of the New York Code, however, a new provision[28] created a statutory right to a jury in those cases and this provision has been continued in New York law.[29]

Although the language of the 1894 Constitution clothed pre–1894 statutory rights to trial by jury with constitutional protection, and therefore should have embraced the 1876 revision of the New York Code, the New York courts consistently have held that there is no constitutional right to trial by jury of a legal counterclaim in an equitable action.[30] In addition, the New York courts read into the successors of the 1876 provision the rule that equitable defenses, as distinguished from equitable counterclaims, are triable in the same way as legal defenses—to a jury.[31] The distinction between an equitable counterclaim and an equitable defense apparently depended upon "whether the facts stated in the so-called counterclaim show a need for affirmative relief for the complete protection of the defendants or if proven would merely defeat the plaintiff's cause of action."[32] Application of this distinction created inconsistency and confusion in determining the right to jury trial, and the distinction was abolished by CPLR 4101, which provides that "equitable defenses and equitable counterclaims shall be tried by the court."

Additional difficulties are presented under the New York categorization approach when plaintiff joins legal and equitable claims in one action. In the federal courts, the right to jury trial would apply to the legal claim.[33] In the New York system, the analysis is somewhat more complicated. No jury would have existed at common law when the two claims arose out of the same transaction because the chancellor could

25. Note, the Right to Jury Trial Under Merged Procedures, 65 Harv.L.Rev. 453, 456–57 (1952).

26. Id. at 455.

27. See MacKellar v. Rogers, 109 N.Y. 468, 17 N.E. 350 (1888).

28. Section 974, Code of Civil Procedure of 1876.

29. Section 424 of the Civil Practice Act of 1920 continued the 1876 provision unchanged. For the current text, see N.Y.—McKinney's CPLR 4102(c).

30. See Petition of Bryan, 242 App.Div. 689, 272 N.Y.S. 864 (1934); Manhattan Life Ins. Co. v. Hammerstein Opera Co., 184 App.Div. 440, 171 N.Y.S. 678 (1918).

31. See Susquehanna S.S. Co. v. A. O. Andersen & Co., 239 N.Y. 285, 146 N.E. 381 (1925); McGurty v. Delaware, L. & W. R.R. Co., 172 App.Div. 46, 158 N.Y.S. 285 (1916).

32. U.S. Fidelity & Guar. Co. v. Goetz, 285 N.Y. 74, 78, 32 N.E.2d 798, 800 (1941).

33. See § 11.5, above.

grant damages incidental to equitable relief under the equity clean-up doctrine.[34] Consequently, post-merger cases in New York have held that there is no jury trial right in this situation.[35] However, if at common law the two claims were based on two separate transactions, then two different actions would have been brought and the right to jury trial would have existed as to the legal claim. The New York post-merger decisions were divided as to what happened in this situation. Some cases held that plaintiff waived the right to jury trial on the legal claim by asserting the equitable claim in the same action;[36] other cases held that there was no waiver.[37] This conflict has now been resolved by CPLR 4102(c), which provides that plaintiff does not waive the jury right by joinder.

Even before adoption of the Civil Practice Law and Rules, it was clear that the defendant could not be deprived of a jury trial when plaintiff joined legal and equitable claims arising out of two separate transactions.[38] Furthermore, when plaintiff joins demands for both legal and equitable relief regarding one cause of action, and the main issue to be determined is legal, defendant maintains a right to jury trial.[39] Plaintiff cannot circumvent defendant's jury right merely by asserting an equitable claim in an action that is clearly legal in character. When plaintiff joins diverse claims arising out of a single transaction, however, neither plaintiff nor defendant has a right to jury trial on the legal action because equity would have assumed jurisdiction over both during the pre-merger period.[40]

§ 11.8 Problems of Federalism

Because state and federal constitutional provisions may differ regarding the scope and availability of the right to jury trial, it is necessary to determine which governs should a conflict arise. An issue concerning the appropriate source of the jury trial right presents itself in two situations: first, when an action asserting a federally-created right is brought in a state court, and second, when a state-created right is adjudicated in a federal court.

---

34. The equity clean-up doctrine is discussed in § 11.5 at notes 11–15, above.

35. See Di Menna v. Cooper & Evans Co., 220 N.Y. 391, 115 N.E. 993 (1917); Cogswell v. New York N. H. & H. R. Co., 105 N.Y. 319, 11 N.E. 518 (1887); Noto v. Headley, 21 A.D.2d 686, 250 N.Y.S.2d 503 (1964).

36. See Lavisch v. Schwartz, 235 App. Div. 18, 256 N.Y.S. 416 (1932); Eisenberg v. 230 Kent Corp., 229 N.Y.S.2d 109 (1962).

37. See City of Syracuse v. Hogan, 234 N.Y. 457, 138 N.E. 406 (1923); Duane Jones Co. v. Burke, 280 App.Div. 889, 115 N.Y.S.2d 529 (1952).

38. See Carroll v. Bullock, 207 N.Y. 567, 576, 101 N.E. 438, 439 (1913); Ehrle v. Sutton Place Apartments, Inc., 137 Misc. 122, 241 N.Y.S. 386 (1930), affirmed mem. 231 App.Div. 712, 246 N.Y.S. 866 (1930).

39. See City of Syracuse v. Hogan, 234 N.Y. 457, 461, 138 N.E. 406, 408 (1923).

40. See Jamaica Savs. Bank v. M. S. Investing Co., 274 N.Y. 215, 219, 8 N.E.2d 493, 494 (1937); Lynch v. Metropolitan Elevated Ry. Co., 129 N.Y. 274, 29 N.E. 315 (1891).

An example of the first arose in Dice v. Akron, Canton & Youngstown Railroad Company.[1] In that case petitioner was injured seriously when an engine in which he was riding jumped the track. He brought an action for damages under the Federal Employers' Liability Act in an Ohio court of common pleas. Respondent answered by denying any negligence, and by submitting a written document signed by petitioner purporting to release it in full for $924.63. Petitioner alleged that the release was void because he had signed it relying on the railroad's deliberately false statement that it was nothing more than a receipt for back wages. The jury awarded the petitioner $25,000. The trial judge later entered a judgment notwithstanding the verdict. In doing so, he reappraised the evidence as to fraud, found that petitioner had been "guilty of supine negligence" in failing to read the release, and accordingly held that the facts did not "sustain either in law or equity the allegations of fraud by clear, unequivocal and convincing evidence."

The judgment notwithstanding the verdict was reversed by the Ohio court of appeals on the ground that under the controlling federal law the jury's verdict must stand because there was ample evidence to support its finding of fraud. The Ohio Supreme Court reversed and sustained the trial court's action, holding: first, Ohio law, not federal law, governed; second, under Ohio law a man of ordinary intelligence who could read was bound by the release, even though he had been induced to sign it by a deliberately false statement; third, under Ohio law factual issues as to fraud in the execution of the release properly were decided by the judge, rather than by the jury.

The United States Supreme Court reversed, and held that federal law governs the mode of adjudicating cases arising under the Federal Employers' Liability Act. The Court reasoned that only if federal law controlled could the statute be given uniform application throughout the country.[2] The Court examined the right of action created by Congress, and concluded that jury trial was an integral element of the relief afforded. Therefore, it felt that federal rather than state rules concerning the jury function had to be followed. Since the issue of fraudulent release was jury triable in the federal courts, Ohio was obliged to provide a jury trial on that issue in a FELA action in one of its courts. As the Court stated, " * * * the right to trial by jury is too substantial a part of the rights accorded by the Act to permit it to be classified as a mere 'local rule of procedure' for denial in the manner that Ohio has here used."[3] Thus, the Dice decision makes clear that the state courts must grant a jury trial in proceedings involving federally-created causes of action whenever there is a strong federal policy in favor of jury trial in the particular case.[4]

§ 11.8

1. 342 U.S. 359, 72 S.Ct. 312, 96 L.Ed. 398 (1952).

2. 342 U.S. at 361, 72 S.Ct. at 314.

3. 342 U.S. at 363, 72 S.Ct. at 315.

4. For a discussion of the constitutional status of federally created rights in state courts, and the limitations on the use of state procedure in such cases, see Note, State Enforcement of Federally Created Rights, 73 Harv.L.Rev. 1551 (1960).

When state-created rights are adjudicated in a federal diversity action, jury trial problems arise whenever state law denies a jury trial but the Seventh Amendment requires it; state law denies a jury trial but federal law customarily grants one; or state law grants a jury trial but federal law denies that right. In each of these situations, federal jury trial criteria control. Even though the underlying substantive claim derives from state law, its characterization as legal or equitable—and therefore the question whether it is jury triable or not—is determined by federal law.

In a very early decision, the Supreme Court held that a federal court sitting in a diversity action does not have to apply state law in determining the scope of the jury trial right. In Parsons v. Bedford,[5] suit was instituted in a Louisiana parish court, and the action was removed on the basis of diversity of citizenship to the Eastern District of Louisiana. By an act of Congress of May 26, 1824, the procedure of civil cases in the federal courts in Louisiana was to conform to the practice in the district courts of the state, subject to such alterations as the federal judges should establish by rule. According to the practice in the Louisiana state courts, upon motion by either party in a case tried to a jury, verbal evidence would be recorded by the clerk to serve as a statement of facts in case of an appeal. Defendant argued that under the statute it had been error for the federal trial judge to refuse to allow the verbal evidence to be recorded in accordance with Louisiana procedure. Justice Story, writing for the Court, rejected this argument. He reasoned that since the Seventh Amendment prohibited the re-examination of any fact tried to a jury in a federal court, other than by the rules of the common law, the trial judge could not have followed state practice in this instance. He went on to state that the 1824 statute could not be interpreted, consistent with the Constitution, as having granted this power to the federal courts, and that therefore, federal notions regarding jury trial had to be preserved.

> No general words, purporting only to regulate the practice of a particular court, to confirm its modes of proceeding to those prescribed by the State to its own courts ought, in our judgment, to receive an interpretation which would create so important an alteration in the laws of the United States, securing the trial by jury.[6]

This conclusion was reaffirmed in the post-Erie Railroad Company v. Tompkins[7] era in Simler v. Conner.[8] In Simler, the Supreme Court held that the Seventh Amendment requires a federal court sitting in a diversity action to apply federal law in determining whether an action is "legal" or "equitable" for purposes of the right to jury trial. The Court noted that "the federal policy favoring jury trials is of historic and

---

5. 28 U.S. (3 Pet.) 433, 7 L.Ed. 732 (1830).

6. 28 U.S. at 448, 7 L.Ed. at 746.

7. 304 U.S. 64, 58 S.Ct. 817, 82 L.Ed. 1188 (1938). Erie is discussed at length in Chapter 4, above.

8. 372 U.S. 221, 83 S.Ct. 609, 9 L.Ed.2d 691 (1963).

continuing strength."⁹ Thus, it concluded that "only through a holding that the jury-trial right is to be determined according to federal law can the uniformity in its exercise which is demanded by the Seventh Amendment be achieved."¹⁰ Simler makes clear that the command of the Seventh Amendment controls the incidence of the jury right in a federal diversity action.

The second situation in which a conflict exists between state and federal practice is when the Seventh Amendment does not expressly mandate a jury trial, but federal law customarily grants one and state law does not. The Court apparently treated Byrd v. Blue Ridge Rural Electric Cooperative, Inc.,¹¹ which is discussed in an earlier Chapter, as such a case. Byrd involved a diversity action brought in the Western District of South Carolina by petitioner for damages for injuries allegedly caused by respondent's negligence. A judgment was entered in his favor on a jury verdict. The Fourth Circuit reversed and directed the entry of judgment for the respondent. It held that the petitioner had the status of a statutory employee under the South Carolina Workmen's Compensation Act and was obliged to accept statutory compensation as the exclusive remedy for his injuries. Petitioner appealed, arguing that he should have been given an opportunity to introduce further evidence on the issue, and that he was entitled to a jury trial on the factual questions raised by respondent's defense, despite contrary state practice.

After remanding to the trial court to allow petitioner an opportunity to present further evidence, the Supreme Court addressed the important question whether state or federal practice controlled the identity of the trier. The Court concluded that the state practice allowing the judge to decide the question of who was a statutory employee was not "a rule intended to be bound up with the definition of the rights and obligations of the parties."¹² Therefore, a federal court sitting in a diversity action was not bound by this state procedure.¹³ Although noting that federal courts should conform as nearly as possible to state procedures when the state rule may have a substantial bearing on the outcome of the case,¹⁴ the Court found "affirmative countervailing considerations at work" in the Byrd situation.

> The federal system is an independent system for administering justice to litigants who properly invoke its jurisdiction. An essential characteristic of that system is the manner in which, in civil common-law actions, it distributes trial functions between judge and jury and, under the influence—if not the command—of the Seventh Amendment, assigns the decisions of disputed questions of fact to the jury.¹⁵

9. 372 U.S. at 222, 83 S.Ct. at 610.

10. 372 U.S. at 222, 83 S.Ct. at 611.

11. 356 U.S. 525, 78 S.Ct. 893, 2 L.Ed.2d 953 (1958). See §§ 4.3–4.4, above.

12. 356 U.S. at 536, 78 S.Ct. at 900.

13. See the discussion in § 4.3, above.

14. 356 U.S. at 536–37, 78 S.Ct. at 900.

15. 356 U.S. at 536, 78 S.Ct. at 901.

Thus, the Court concluded: "It cannot be gainsaid that there is a strong federal policy against allowing state rules to disrupt the judge-jury relationship in the federal courts."[16]

As this passage suggests, Byrd was not decided under the command of the Seventh Amendment. The Court specifically reserved the constitutional question whether the right to jury trial in the federal courts embraces the issue of statutory immunity when asserted as an affirmative defense in a common-law negligence action.[17] Thus, Byrd establishes the proposition that federal practice controls the scope and incidence of jury trial, even when federal practice is not constitutionally required.[18]

The third set of circumstances under which a conflict between state and federal practice may arise in a federal diversity action is when state law would grant a jury trial that would be unavailable in a federal court. In Herron v. Southern Pacific Company,[19] the trial judge in a personal-injury diversity action brought in the Arizona federal court directed a verdict for the defendant when it appeared to him as a matter of law that the plaintiff was guilty of contributory negligence. This was contrary to the mandate of the Arizona Constitution, which provided: "The defense of contributory negligence or of assumption of risk shall, in all cases whatsoever, be a question of fact and shall, at all times, be left to the jury."[20] The Supreme Court upheld the trial judge's decision, stating: "The controlling principle governing the decision of the present question is that state laws cannot alter the essential character or function of federal court."[21] Because of this principle, "a federal court is not subject to state regulations, whether found in constitutional provisions or in statutes."[22] The Herron case was decided before the Erie decision, but as the Court in Byrd v. Blue Ridge Rural Electric Cooperative, Inc. makes clear, its principle has survived.[23]

Thus, whether a federally-created right is being adjudicated in a state court, or a state right is being tried in a federal diversity action, it appears that federal law controls the scope of the jury trial right. This is true whether the federal practice is constitutionally required or has been established by statute or custom.

A 1996 Supreme Court decision, Gasperini v. Center for Humanities, Inc.,[24] indicates, however, that the Court will attempt to accommodate

---

16. 356 U.S. at 537, 78 S.Ct. at 901.

17. 356 U.S. at 537 n. 10, 78 S.Ct. at 901 n. 10.

18. This view was advanced by Professor Green in an article written one year before the decision in Byrd v. Blue Ridge. Green, Protection of Jury Trial in Diversity Cases Against State Invasions, 35 Texas L.Rev. 768 (1957).

19. 283 U.S. 91, 51 S.Ct. 383, 75 L.Ed. 857 (1931).

20. Ariz.R.S. Const. Art. 18, § 5.

21. 283 U.S. at 94, 51 S.Ct. at 384.

22. Ibid.

23. 356 U.S. 525, 539, 78 S.Ct. 893, 902, 2 L.Ed.2d 953 (1958).

24. 518 U.S. 415, 116 S.Ct. 2211, 135 L.Ed.2d 659 (1996). Gasperini has been analyzed by several commentators, focussing on various aspects of the Court's opinion. For two articles discussing its implications on jury trials, see Note, The Supreme Court Sets New Standards of Review for Excessive Verdicts in Federal Court in Gasperini v. Center for Humanities, Inc., 50 Ark.L.Rev. 591 (1997); Note, Gasperini v. Center For Humanities, Inc: State Jury Award Con-

important state substantive policies that may implicate the federal jury right. In Gasperini, the Court ruled that a New York law, which attempted to control jury awards for excessiveness or inadequacy by allowing new trials to be ordered whenever the trial judge concluded that the award "deviates materially from what would be reasonable compensation,"[25] should be applied by the federal trial judge sitting in diversity. The New York new trial standard was in contrast to the narrower "shocks the consciousness" review standard typically applied by federal courts. The Court concluded that the state's objective in adopting the "deviates materially" standard was manifestly substantive and could be applied by the trial judge without disrupting the federal system because historically the discretion lodged in trial judges to grant new trials always had been large and thus could embrace New York's approach. However, federal appellate courts would be confined to the abuse of discretion standard generally applied when reviewing new trial decisions based on the inadequacy or excessiveness of the verdict because that standard was compatible with the re-examination clause in the jury trial guarantee. In that way, Seventh Amendment rights would be preserved.

§ 11.9   Procedure for Obtaining Jury Trial

The type of procedure that a party must follow in order to secure a jury trial has implications for the litigant, for the other parties to the action, and for the legal system. The ideal of guaranteeing the constitutional right to a jury trial to each litigant who wishes to exercise it cannot completely ignore the system's need for efficiency. A relatively simple and certain determination early in the proceedings as to whether any party wishes to assert a right to a jury not only promotes efficiency in the scheduling of trials, but also provides notice to the other litigants. The procedure for obtaining jury trial also must take into consideration the various situations in which jury-triable issues can arise in a lawsuit given today's merged procedures.

Under state code procedure, an express waiver by the litigants has been required to forestall jury trial on the issues as to which the right exists.[1] As a result, absent waiver, it is uncertain whether the litigants have elected jury trial.

Federal Rule 38 attempts to alleviate this ambiguous situation in the federal courts by requiring a party who wishes to have the case tried to a jury to make an affirmative demand for one.[2] A number of states also require a litigant to make a demand for a jury trial.[3] This type of

trols Supplant Seventh Amendment Protections, 18 Pace L.Rev. 199 (1997).

25. New York—McKinney's Civ.Prac. Law & Rules (CPLR) § 5501(c).

§ 11.9

1. See 4 J. Weinstein, H. Korn & A. Miller, New York Civil Practice ¶ 4102.01; C. Clark, Code Pleading § 17, at 113–14 (2d ed.1947).

2. See in 9 C. Wright & A. Miller, Civil 2d § 2318.

3. New York, for example, requires that a demand be made. See 4 J. Weinstein, H. Korn & A. Miller, New York Civil Practice ¶ ¶ 4102.01–4102.08.

provision has the virtue of eliminating unnecessary procedural skirmishing by determining the mode of proceeding before the trial begins.[4]

Failure to make the required demand will result in a waiver of the jury trial right. The notes of the Advisory Committee that drafted Rule 38 make it clear that the provision for demand and waiver was considered an integral element of the jury trial scheme,[5] and was regarded as consistent with preserving the constitutional right to jury trial as directed by Congress in the Rules Enabling Act.[6] The cases suggest that the demand requirement does not violate the Seventh Amendment guarantee.[7]

Similar statutory provisions have been consistently upheld in state courts, and the general trend appears to be toward requiring affirmative action by a party who wishes to invoke the right to jury trial.[8] This movement typically has been approved by the courts and commentators because it reduces the incidence of jury trial, which should relieve court congestion, and because it establishes what the mode of trial will be early in the case.[9]

These demand provisions illustrate the ambivalence of many American courts towards the civil jury trial. Although it is true that other constitutional rights may be waived only by stipulation, the demand requirements mean that an affirmative act is required in order for a litigant to secure a jury trial; the right will be waived by inaction.[10] This treatment may be appropriate insofar as it contributes to the systemic goal of reducing the average time it takes to adjudicate an action because there is no question that civil jury trial is a significant source of delay.[11] But the demand requirement seems to stand in sharp contrast to the spirit of a number of Supreme Court decisions during the past forty years[12] that have drastically expanded the jury trial right.

The right to a jury trial, once demanded, is determined by examining all the pleadings—claims, defenses, counterclaims, and third-party pleadings.[13] Even if the complaint does not present a jury-triable issue,

4. "With this system * * * there is less opportunity for a party to await events and use his claim as a strategic lever to secure delay or at times a reversal and another trial. It is a method fair to litigants in protecting the rights of those who have a real desire for jury trial, and yet reasonably expeditious of litigation * * *." C. Clark, Code Pleading § 17, at 113–14 (2d ed.1947).

5. See The Advisory Committee Notes for Rule 38 in 12 C. Wright & A. Miller, Civil Appendix C.

6. 28 U.S.C.A. § 2072.

7. See Moore v. U.S., 196 F.2d 906 (5th Cir.1952); Wilson v. Corning Glass Works, 195 F.2d 825 (9th Cir.1952).

8. See Annot., Withdrawal or Disregard of Waiver of Jury Trial in Civil Action, 64 A.L.R.2d 506, 511–14 (1959).

9. James, Trial by Jury and the New Federal Rules of Procedure, 45 Yale L.J. 1022, 1047 (1936).

10. Participation in a bench trial or a trial after the jury has been dismissed also will waive the right to a jury trial. See Matter of Muller, 851 F.2d 916 (7th Cir. 1988), cert. denied 490 U.S. 1007; Pope v. Savings Bank of Puget Sound, 850 F.2d 1345 (9th Cir.1988).

11. See § 11.1, above.

12. See § 11.5, above.

13. See Beacon Theatres, Inc. v. Westover, 359 U.S. 500, 79 S.Ct. 948, 3 L.Ed.2d 988 (1959).

the subsequent pleadings must be examined to see if they raise issues that should be tried by a jury. Neither the nature of the action, nor the label given it, is determinative.[14] Rather, as was discussed more fully earlier, in the federal courts the individual issue is the appropriate unit to be considered, and the existence of the right with regard to each issue must be judged in light of modern procedural developments.[15]

As to details, Federal Rule 38(b) requires that the demand be in writing and filed in timely fashion; an untimely or oral demand is insufficient to secure a jury trial.[16] No particular form of writing is required, and the demand "may be indorsed upon a pleading of the party."[17] It is desirable that the demand be set off from the main body of the pleading, however, so as to make it readily recognizable.[18] The demand must be served on all parties.

A litigant may limit the extent of the demand by requesting jury trial only on certain specified issues. If the other parties desire jury trial of any or all of the remaining issues, they must file a timely demand as to those issues or waive their rights. A general demand for a jury trial that does not specify issues for submission to the jury will result in a jury trial of all issues as to which the right applies.[19]

Once a proper demand has been made, Federal Rule 38(d) establishes that it may not be withdrawn without the consent of all the parties.[20] This is necessary to protect the other parties who may have relied on the demand. Once a general demand has been filed by one party, the rights of the other parties to a jury trial of all issues thus triable are secured without further action by them.[21] The sole exception to this rule is that plaintiff's jury trial demand does not extend to issues raised between the defendant and any third-party defendants.[22]

In the federal courts, the timeliness of a jury trial demand is judged by its relationship to the pleadings and the issues raised in them. Federal Rule 38(b) requires that a demand be made within ten days after the last pleading directed to the issue on which jury trial is sought.[23] Accordingly, when the answer and complaint are the only pleadings in

---

14. See Laskaris v. Thornburgh, 733 F.2d 260 (3d Cir.1984), cert. denied 469 U.S. 886; Kerr–McGee Corp. v. Bokum Corp., 453 F.2d 1067 (10th Cir.1972); Beaunit Mills v. Eday Fabric Sales Corp., 124 F.2d 563 (2d Cir.1942).

15. See § 11.5, above.

16. See Tri–State Tire Serv., Inc. v. Gates Rubber Co. Sales Div., Inc., 339 F.2d 573 (5th Cir.1964).

17. See Fed.Civ.Proc.Rule 38(b).

18. See Allstate Ins. Co. v. Cross, 2 F.R.D. 120 (E.D.Pa.1941).

19. See U.S. v. Anderson, 584 F.2d 369 (10th Cir.1978).

20. See Yates v. Dann, 223 F.2d 64 (3d Cir.1955); Thiel v. Southern Pacific Co., 149

F.2d 783 (9th Cir.1945), reversed on other grounds 328 U.S. 217, 66 S.Ct. 984, 90 L.Ed. 1181 (1946).

21. See Dell'Orfano v. Romano, 962 F.2d 199 (2d Cir.1992); Cram v. Sun Ins. Office, Ltd., 375 F.2d 670 (4th Cir.1967).

22. See Aligheri v. Long Island R.R., 156 F.R.D. 55 (S.D.N.Y.1994); Banks v. Hanover S.S. Corp., 43 F.R.D. 374 (D.Md. 1967). However, when the original defendant makes a general demand for jury trial at the time she serves both an answer to the plaintiff and a third-party complaint, the demand is said to secure a jury trial as to issues in both the original action and the third-party action.

23. Different jurisdictions vary as to the time limit imposed for demand.

the case, the demand must be filed within ten days of the service of the answer.[24] Of course, it may be made before the answer is served.[25] But when a counterclaim is asserted, which necessitates a reply, determining the timeliness of a demand becomes more complicated. If the counterclaim raises the same issues as the answer, then a demand made within ten days after the reply is effective as to those issues.[26] However, if the counterclaim and the reply raise new issues that were not contained in the complaint and answer, a demand served more than ten days after the answer, but within ten days after the reply, preserves the right to jury trial only for those issues raised by the counterclaim and reply and not those in the complaint and answer.[27]

For example, suppose that a seller brings an action against a buyer for breach of a contract to pay for goods on a certain shipment. Defendant responds that there was a prior breach by plaintiff because of a failure to ship the goods on a predetermined date; in addition, the buyer asserts a permissive counterclaim for damages resulting from the tardy delivery of several past shipments. Plaintiff replies that the tardy deliveries were excusable. Defendant serves a demand for jury trial later than ten days after the answer, but within ten days after the reply. This demand is ineffective as to issues concerning the shipment in the original complaint and answer, but will preserve a jury trial on the issues involving the other shipments that are the subject of the counterclaim.

The same approach applies to amended and supplemental pleadings; a timely demand may be made within ten days after the service of any such pleading raising a new issue. If a general demand already has been made, however, a new demand after the amendment is not required. On the other hand, if the amended or supplemental pleading does not raise a new issue, but merely changes the theory of the case or the relief requested, then a jury trial right waived by a failure to demand it in connection with the original pleading is not revived.[28]

Analysis of what constitutes a "new issue" has been somewhat complicated by the merger of law and equity and the adoption of simplified pleading. It is now certain that merely recasting an action in either "legal" or "equitable" terms does not constitute a "new issue" for purposes of Federal Rule 38(b), since Federal Rule 54(c) makes any amendment seeking to change the relief requested unnecessary.[29] Fur-

---

24. See McCorstin v. U.S. Department of Labor, 630 F.2d 242 (5th Cir.1980); May v. Melvin, 141 F.2d 22 (D.C.Cir.1944).

25. Christiansen v. Interstate Motor Lines, Inc., 20 F.R.D. 105 (D.Neb.1956).

26. See Tights, Inc. v. Stanley, 441 F.2d 336 (4th Cir.1971), cert. denied 404 U.S. 852; Monolith Portland Midwest Co. v. RFC, 240 F.2d 444 (9th Cir.1957), cert. denied 354 U.S. 921.

27. See Western Geophysical Co. of America v. Bolt Associates, Inc., 440 F.2d 765 (2d Cir.1971); Goldblatt v. Inch, 203 F.2d 79 (2d Cir.1953).

28. See Daniel Int'l Corp. v. Fischbach & Moore, Inc., 916 F.2d 1061 (5th Cir. 1990); In re Kaiser Steel Corp., 911 F.2d 380 (10th Cir.1990).

29. Fed.Civ.Proc.Rule 54(c) provides in part: "Except as to a party against whom a judgment is entered by default, every final judgment shall grant the relief to which the party in whose favor it is rendered is enti-

ther, a party may not reserve an election of the form of trial beyond the time "when it becomes reasonably apparent that under some aspects or legal theories of the case there may be a jury issue."[30] When the amended pleading refers to the same transaction as did the original complaint, the parties were on notice from the beginning that the facts alleged would support the grant of legal relief, and their opportunity to preserve a jury trial by demand, once waived, ought not to be revived.[31]

Originally there was some confusion whether a demand for jury trial in a state proceeding survived removal of the action to federal court, or whether a new demand had to be timely made.[32] This issue was resolved by a 1963 amendment to Federal Rule 81(c), which makes it clear that a timely express demand in state court is sufficient to secure the jury right upon removal. Further, a demand need not be made if the procedure of the state court from which the case is removed does not require an express demand to claim trial by jury.[33] The federal court may order that a request be made specifying the jury triable issues, however, in order to set and appraise its calendar.[34]

The opportunity to demand a jury trial, once waived, is not automatically revived by a reversal on appeal or the grant of a new trial. In this situation, it is within the discretion of the trial court whether to grant a jury trial to a party who has waived that right.[35] The trial court may consider such factors as the circumstances surrounding the waiver,[36] the suitability of the case for jury determination,[37] and the mode of trial most likely to expedite the suit.[38] No single circumstance is likely to be determinative and the trial court's action will be reversed only if an abuse of discretion can be demonstrated.[39]

tled, even if the party has not demanded such relief in the party's pleadings."

30. C. Clark, Code Pleading § 17, at 120 (2d ed.1947).

31. Clark, "Clarifying" Amendments to the Federal Rules?, 14 Ohio St.L.J. 241, 248 (1953). See, e.g., American Fidelity & Cas. Co. v. All American Bus Lines, Inc., 190 F.2d 234 (10th Cir.1951), cert. denied 342 U.S. 851 (amended complaint substituting the real party in interest as the party plaintiff did not change in any substantial respect any other issue of fact in the case). See also Gulbenkian v. Gulbenkian, 147 F.2d 173 (2d Cir.1945).

32. Compare Zakoscielny v. Waterman S.S. Corp., 16 F.R.D. 314 (D.Md.1954); Talley v. American Bakeries Co., 15 F.R.D. 391 (E.D.Tenn.1954); Rehrer v. Service Trucking Co., 15 F.R.D. 113 (D.Del.1953), holding a renewed demand unnecessary, with Petsel v. Chicago, B. & Q. R.R. Co., 101 F.Supp. 1006 (S.D.Iowa 1951); Nelson v. American Nat. Bank & Trust Co., 9 F.R.D. 680 (E.D.Tenn.1950), holding new demand required.

33. See Segal v. American Cas. Co., 250 F.Supp. 936 (D.Md.1966).

34. Kaplan, Amendments of the Federal Rules of Civil Procedure, 1961–1963 (II), 77 Harv.L.Rev. 801, 833–34 (1964).

35. See Ohlinger v. U.S., 135 F.Supp. 40 (D.Idaho 1955), holding that a belated motion for a jury on the second trial of a case was appropriate since a statutory change while appeal was pending authorized jury trials in actions of this kind, and since plaintiff's counsel moved for jury trial as soon as the change came to his attention.

36. See note 35, above. See also Davis v. Parkhill–Goodloe Co., 302 F.2d 489, 494 n. 5 (5th Cir.1962) (timely demand was filed, but parties later consented to trial by court).

37. Hazelrigg v. American Fidelity & Cas. Co., 241 F.2d 871, 873 (10th Cir.1957); William Goldman Theatres, Inc. v. Kirkpatrick, 154 F.2d 66, 69 (3d Cir.1946).

38. William Goldman Theatres, Inc. v. Kirkpatrick, 154 F.2d 66, 69–70 (3d Cir. 1946).

39. Hazelrigg v. American Fidelity & Cas. Co., 241 F.2d 871 (10th Cir.1957).

Although failure to make a timely demand results in a waiver of jury trial, a party may request the court to exercise its discretion under Federal Rule 39(b) to order a trial by jury on all or some of the issues.[40] This is an important and appropriate safety-valve in a system that places a high value on the jury trial right.[41] Nevertheless, a number of courts have expressed the opinion that the exercise of this discretion should not be a matter of caprice; it should be based upon adequate grounds. As stated by one district judge,

> * * * judicial indulgence ought rarely to grant a trial by jury in default of a timely request for it. Such laxity is calculated to inspire indifference to the requirements of the rules in their entirety, to countenance tardiness in procedural and trial performance, and ultimately to defeat the avowed purpose of the rules to achieve punctuality in the administration of justice. More immediately, it will inevitably create confusion in trial dockets and accomplish unanticipated and intolerable continuances of trials. The consequences are uninviting.[42]

In determining whether a late motion for jury trial should be allowed, the courts have considered several factors: whether the motion was made within a reasonable time after expiration of the period allowed by statute,[43] whether the failure to make a demand was the result of such inadvertence, mistake, or excusable neglect as should justify allowing the motion,[44] and whether permitting a jury trial would prejudice the rights of the adverse party.[45] Finally, one of the most important factors in deciding whether to exercise discretion to allow a late demand appears to be the effect it would have on the court's docket.[46]

---

40. Fed.Civ.Proc.Rule 39(b). See the discussion in 9 C. Wright & A. Miller, Civil 2d § 2334.

41. As the Supreme Court stated in Aetna Ins. Co. v. Kennedy, 301 U.S. 389, 393, 57 S.Ct. 809, 811–12, 81 L.Ed. 1177 (1937): "But, as the right of jury trial is fundamental, courts indulge every reasonable presumption against waiver."

42. Arnold v. Chicago, Burlington & Quincy R.R. Co., 7 F.R.D. 678, 680 (D.Neb. 1947).

43. See Ohlinger v. U.S., 135 F.Supp. 40 (D.Idaho 1955) (motion for jury trial was properly granted, although three months late, because counsel had discovered that a statutory change, made while an appeal of a first trial of the case was pending, permitted either party to request a jury trial); Hill v. Peres, 136 Cal.App. 132, 28 P.2d 946 (1934) (court granted jury trial when there was only one day's delay on the part of plaintiff in depositing jury fees as required by statute).

44. See Ohlinger v. U.S., 135 F.Supp. 40 (D.Idaho 1955) (three month delay was due to excusable neglect, and it was doubtful if any lawyer, under similar circumstances, would have discovered the statutory change any sooner than had plaintiff's counsel); Alfred Hofmann, Inc. v. Textile Machine Works, 27 F.Supp. 431 (E.D.Pa. 1939) (unfamiliarity with the rules for a month after their adoption, was a matter of excusable neglect in failing to demand jury trial, although the court denied jury trial for other reasons).

45. See Daly v. Scala, 39 A.2d 478 (D.C.Mun.App.1944); Aronoff v. Texas Turnpike Authority, 299 S.W.2d 342 (Tex. Civ.App.1957).

46. Beckstrom v. Coastwise Line, 13 F.R.D. 480, 483 (D.Alaska 1953). See also Wilson v. Corning Glass Works, 195 F.2d 825 (9th Cir.1952).

C.   TRIAL BY JURY

§ 11.10   Selection and Composition of the Jury

The procedures by which a jury panel is selected and its socioeconomic composition have an extremely important bearing on the utility and vitality of the constitutional right to trial by jury. The Judiciary Act of 1789 provided that jurors in federal courts were to have the same qualifications as jurors of the state in which the district court was located.[1] Congress did not impose independent federal juror qualifications until 1957.[2]

Prior to 1968, a number of federal courts employed the "key man" or "suggester" system,[3] under which persons or organizations thought to have extensive contacts in the community were requested to suggest juror candidates who met the qualifications. The suggesters were encouraged to recommend persons possessing not only the required qualifications but also additional attributes such as community esteem, "good character, approved integrity, sound judgment and fair education."[4] This system, although designed to promote the selection of competent jurors, was unlikely to produce a representative cross-section of the community.[5] Several courts had approved the use of the "key man" system,[6] but the 1966 decision by the Fifth Circuit in Rabinowitz v. United States[7] marked the turning point; the court held that the statutory qualifications were exhaustive and officials had no discretion to impose additional requirements. As one commentator observed, Rabinowitz "sounded the death knell of the key man system in the federal courts and ordered an end to the practice of jury commissioners silently raising the selection standards above those laid down in the statutes."[8]

In 1968, Congress implemented the Rabinowitz decision by revamping the statutory scheme governing the selection and qualifications of jurors in the federal courts.[9] The thrust of the amendments was to reduce the discretionary elements in the process and to introduce a degree of uniformity. The policy goals of the enactment were to guarantee juries were selected "at random from a fair cross-section of the community," to provide all citizens with the opportunity to be consid-

---

§ 11.10

1. Act of Sept. 24, 1789, § 29, 1 Stat. 88.

2. Civil Rights Act of 1957, Pub.L. 85–315, § 152, 71 Stat. 638 (1957). Although Congress enacted federal qualifications in 1948, those persons incompetent as jurors under state law were excluded from service in the federal courts of that state until the 1957 enactment. See Act of June 25, 1948, c. 121, § 1861, 62 Stat. 951.

3. Stanley, Federal Jury Selection and Service Before and After 1968, 66 F.R.D. 375, 376 (1974).

4. Form of Letter to "Suggesters" (Key–Men), attached as part of Exhibit 3 to The Jury System in the Federal Courts, 26 F.R.D. 409, 513–14 (1960).

5. See Report of the Committee on the Operation of the Jury System, 42 F.R.D. 353, 361 (1967).

6. U.S. v. Hoffa, 349 F.2d 20 (6th Cir. 1965), affirmed 385 U.S. 293, 87 S.Ct. 408, 17 L.Ed.2d 374 (1966); Dow v. Carnegie–Illinois Steel Corp., 224 F.2d 414 (3d Cir. 1955), cert. denied 350 U.S. 971.

7. 366 F.2d 34 (5th Cir.1966).

8. Note, The Congress, the Court and Jury Selection: A Critique of Titles I and II of the Civil Rights Bill of 1966, 52 Va.L.Rev. 1069, 1094–95 (1966).

9. See 28 U.S.C.A. §§ 1861–71.

ered for jury service,[10] and to prevent discrimination on the basis of "race, color, religion, sex, national origin, or economic status."[11] Two innovations were introduced into the selection process: first, the required use of lists of registered or actual voters as the source of jurors, and second, the use of objective criteria in determining juror disqualifications, exemptions, excuses, and exclusions.[12] Each district court was required to draw up a plan, consistent with these constraints, to effectuate the policy goals. Since the statutory qualifications are deemed exhaustive and random selection from voter lists is prescribed, the "key man" system effectively was abolished.[13]

The present qualifications for federal jurors require that the candidate be a United States citizen, a resident of the judicial district for one year, eighteen years of age or older, sufficiently literate to fill out a juror qualification form, fluent in the English language, mentally and physically capable of service, and free from any pending charges or past convictions of crimes punishable by imprisonment for more than one year.[14] In addition to those disqualified under this standard, the 1968 statutory scheme delineates four categories of persons who either are not permitted to serve or can be excused from service.

The first of these requires the district court plan to specify "groups of persons or occupational classes whose members shall be barred from jury service on the ground that they are exempt;" these groups must include public officials and active members of the Armed Forces and local fire and police departments.[15] The justification for these exemptions is that the indicated people perform valuable social services that are more important to the community than jury duty.

Second, "excuse groups" must be established by the district court plan, members of which can serve if they wish, but must be excused upon request.[16] The groups are to be defined in terms of the "undue hardship in traveling" to the courthouse because of distance or travel time. For example, excuse groups might be established for doctors, ministers, sole proprietors of businesses, or mothers with young children. Some commentators have suggested that the statutory creation of "excuse groups" presents significant equal protection problems.[17] But the excuse groups created by at least one district court plan have been upheld against constitutional challenge.[18]

Third, individuals who can demonstrate "undue hardship or extreme inconvenience" may be excused for a time that is discretionary

---

10. 28 U.S.C.A. § 1861.

11. 28 U.S.C.A. § 1862.

12. H.R.Rep. No. 1076, 90th Cong., 2d Sess., reprinted in 2 U.S.Code Cong. & Ad. News 1793 (1968).

13. Id. at 1794. See Davis v. U.S., 411 U.S. 233, 235 n. 2, 93 S.Ct. 1577, 1579 n. 2, 36 L.Ed.2d 216 (1973) (dictum).

14. 28 U.S.C.A. § 1865(b).

15. 28 U.S.C.A. § 1863(b)(6).

16. 28 U.S.C.A. § 1863(b)(5).

17. See Comment, Jury Selection in California, 5 Stan.L.Rev. 247, 256–57 (1953); Note, Economic Discrimination in Jury Selection, 1970 Law & Social Order 474.

18. See U.S. v. Arnett, 342 F.Supp. 1255 (D.Mass.1970).

with the court, at the expiration of which the person can be recalled for service.[19] This provision honors valid individual excuses, but, by means of the recall provision, prevents the use of pretexts to evade jury service. Grave illness in the family is an example of a sufficient excuse.

The fourth category consists of those whom the court has the power to exclude for partiality or because they are likely to be disruptive, to threaten jury secrecy, or to affect adversely the integrity of the proceedings.[20] The necessity of this type of safety valve is self-evident.

The qualifications and procedures for selecting jurors in the state court systems vary. Among the more common qualifications imposed are residency requirements, property ownership, payment of taxes, and good health.[21] The various state procedures for assembling lists of potential jurors include utilization of voting lists, property tax records, telephone directories, or personal references under the "key man" system, described earlier. Several other methods for selecting juries have been suggested, including the use of psychological tests in order to guarantee a minimum level of rationality.[22] A "Uniform Jury Selection and Service Act," based to some extent on the 1968 federal statute, has been proposed and adopted in a few states.[23]

It is most important to keep in mind that in designing their jury selection procedures the states are not constrained by the Seventh Amendment.[24] They are limited only by Fourteenth Amendment requirements. This means that no group cognizable under the Equal Protection Clause can be systematically excluded from consideration as jurors,[25] and under the Due Process Clause, litigants must be afforded procedures consistent with "fundamental fairness."[26] The federal concept of the jury as a cross-section of the community is not imposed upon the states. For example, the Supreme Court in a five-to-four decision upheld a state "blue ribbon" jury selection system by which New York courts selected for special jury service a group of individuals who were able to qualify under strict intelligence examinations.[27] Although the Supreme Court has moved gradually towards the imposition of a cross-section require-

---

19. 28 U.S.C.A. § 1866(c)(1).

20. 28 U.S.C.A. § 1866(c)(2), (5).

21. See generally A. Vanderbilt, Minimum Standards of Judicial Administration 162–71 (1949).

22. Redmount, Psychological Tests for Selecting Jurors, 5 U.Kan.L.Rev. 391 (1957); Note, Psychological Tests and Standards of Competence for Selecting Jurors, 65 Yale L.J. 531 (1956).

23. For the text and an analysis of the Act, see McKusick & Boxer, Uniform Jury Selection and Service Act, 8 Harv.J.Legis. 280 (1971). The Act is in force currently in five states: Hawaii, Idaho, Indiana, Maine, and Mississippi.

24. See § 11.7 n. 1, above.

25. States cannot systematically exclude persons from jury duty on the basis of race, for example. Smith v. Texas, 311 U.S. 128, 61 S.Ct. 164, 85 L.Ed. 84 (1940); Strauder v. West Virginia, 100 U.S. (3 Otto) 303, 25 L.Ed. 664 (1879).

26. Fay v. New York, 332 U.S. 261, 294, 67 S.Ct. 1613, 1630, 91 L.Ed. 2043 (1947). See also Witherspoon v. Illinois, 391 U.S. 510, 88 S.Ct. 1770, 20 L.Ed.2d 776 (1968).

27. Fay v. New York, 332 U.S. 261, 67 S.Ct. 1613, 91 L.Ed. 2043 (1947). Fay was a criminal proceeding, but it was decided before the Court ruled that the Sixth Amendment is applicable to the states.

ment on the states for criminal juries,[28] it is not likely that this movement will extend to civil juries.[29]

In order to select individual jurors, a series of questions are posed to each prospective juror in a process called the voir dire examination, which is designed to expose a juror's lack of qualification or bias. Various methods exist for conducting this examination; the trial judge may ask the basic questions, allowing the parties to ask supplementary questions, or the court may ask all the questions giving counsel the opportunity to request that certain inquiries be made, or the court may allow the parties' attorneys to conduct the examination, reserving the right to disallow or ask additional questions.

The voir dire procedure, particularly when left to the parties' lawyers, has both affirmative and negative aspects. On the one hand, allowing a wide scope of questioning of the prospective jurors helps guarantee the constitutional right to a fair and impartial jury. It also, however, allows clever lawyers to employ the examination to influence potential jurors, by framing inquiries in a way that amounts to a presentation of part of their case.[30] This has led some observers to suggest that the court should conduct the examination itself, after consulting with the litigants.[31] Others have suggested that the most effective screening practice would be to limit the scope of voir dire inquiry.[32]

A litigant may wish to challenge the sufficiency of the selection process itself. A procedure—called a challenge to the array—is available by which the method used in selecting prospective jurors can be attacked on the ground that constitutional or statutory standards have not been satisfied. In the federal courts, time limits within which a statutory challenge must be raised are prescribed,[33] and the objecting party must prove a "substantial failure" to comply with the provisions of the 1968 Act.[34]

Cases involving challenges to the array were common before the 1957 and 1968 statutes, which reduced judicial discretion in the juror selection process. In Ballard v. United States, the Supreme Court sustained a challenge to an array from which women had been systematically excluded.[35] In Thiel v. Southern Pacific Company,[36] the Supreme Court sustained a petitioner's challenge to a federal court jury selection prac-

---

28. See Taylor v. Louisiana, 419 U.S. 522, 530, 95 S.Ct. 692, 697–98, 42 L.Ed.2d 690 (1975). On the significance of Taylor, see Note, Taylor v. Louisiana: The Jury Cross Section Crosses the State Line, 7 Conn.L.Rev. 508 (1975).

29. See n. 27, above.

30. See, e.g., Smith v. Nickels, 390 S.W.2d 578 (Mo.App.1965). But compare Sandidge v. Salen Offshore Drilling Co., 764 F.2d 252 (5th Cir.1985) (it is improper for voir dire examination to search the result of the case in advance).

31. Note, Selection of Jurors by Voir Dire Examination and Challenge, 58 Yale L.J. 638, 643–44 (1949).

32. Note, Voir Dire—Prevention of Prejudicial Questioning, 50 Minn.L.Rev. 1088, 1098–99 (1966).

33. 28 U.S.C.A. § 1867(a)–(c).

34. 28 U.S.C.A. § 1867(d).

35. 329 U.S. 187, 67 S.Ct. 261, 91 L.Ed. 181 (1946).

36. 328 U.S. 217, 66 S.Ct. 984, 90 L.Ed. 1181 (1946).

tice under which daily wage earners systematically were struck from the jury lists. The Court held that federal court litigants are entitled to have prospective jurors selected from a cross-section of the entire community. This does not mean that a party will succeed in a challenge to the array merely because the members of the particular jury empanelled in the case fail to represent a cross-section of the entire community from which they are drawn; rather it means that the federal selection process itself may not systematically exclude a legally cognizable group or class of people from eligibility for jury service.

The litigants, based on information gathered on voir dire, also may have particular veniremen removed from the prospective jury panel by challenging them on an individual basis. This differs from the challenge to the array in that the challenge asserts that an individual, rather than the entire group, should not be allowed to sit with the jury in a certain case. Challenges to individual jurors are of two types: for cause and peremptory.

Failure to meet the statutory qualifications for jury duty, evidence of bias, and relationship to one of the litigants are all grounds for challenging a potential juror for cause. Challenges for cause are unlimited in number and may be exercised by the parties through a timely objection during the selection process, or by the court on its own motion. The important characteristic of a challenge for cause is that its validity is decided by the trial judge so that the party seeking disqualification must satisfy an objective disqualification standard. This differs from a peremptory challenge, by which a party may have a prospective juror removed without stating any reason.

In the federal courts, the number of peremptory challenges accorded a party is prescribed by statute.[37] In a civil action, each litigant is entitled to three peremptory challenges. Multiple plaintiffs or defendants may be considered a single "party" for the purpose of exercising one side's allotment of peremptories, although when there is more than one litigant, the court has discretion to grant additional challenges and to allow them to be exercised separately or jointly.

Peremptory challenges are used to disqualify jurors with occupational and attitudinal characteristics that an attorney feels are unfavorable to her client.[38] Thus, they usually are based on an assumed partiality that may not be susceptible of proof. Other commentators have suggested that a primary justification for the availability of the peremptory challenge is that it is a means of satisfying litigants that their case is being determined by an impartial group of laypeople.[39] According to this argument, allowing litigants to participate in the formation of their jury

---

37. 28 U.S.C.A. § 1870.

38. One study has shown that there is a strong correlation between certain demographic characteristics and the way in which an individual juror "feels" about a particular case. Kalven, The Jury, the Law, and the Personal Injury Damage Award, 19 Ohio St.L.J. 158, 174–75 (1958).

39. Comment, The Right of Peremptory Challenge, 24 U.Chi.L.Rev. 751, 762 (1957).

tends to reduce the feeling that the jury's composition is entirely in the hands of the judge.

Prior to the Supreme Court's 1986 decision in Batson v. Kentucky,[40] peremptory challenges could be exercised in an arbitrary and discriminatory way,[41] despite strong criticism[42] and harsh results.[43] In Batson, a criminal case, the Supreme Court held that a state denies a defendant equal protection when it puts him on trial before a jury from which members of his own race have been excluded.[44] The same equal protection principles used to determine whether there has been discrimination in selecting the jury venire thus also apply to the state's use of peremptory challenges to remove individual jurors from the petit jury.[45] In its decision, the Court noted that discriminatory jury selection undermines public confidence in the fairness of our system of justice and perpetuates racial prejudice.[46]

In Powers v. Ohio[47] the Supreme Court made clear that Batson was not limited to cases in which potential jurors of the same race as defendant were eliminated by peremptory challenge.[48] Race-based peremptory challenges violate the equal protection rights of the potential juror as well,[49] so that the race of the defendant is irrelevant in determining the constitutional challenge. The Court further determined that the defendant had standing to bring the equal protection claim on behalf of the rejected juror.[50]

These two cases were extended to civil actions in Edmonson v. Leesville Concrete Company,[51] when the Supreme Court held that a private litigant in a civil case may not use peremptory challenges to exclude jurors on the basis of their race because doing so violates the equal protection rights of the excluded jurors. Although both parties in Edmonson were private, the Court determined that the use of the peremptory challenge constituted state action and thus violated the constitution.[52] And in 1994, the Supreme Court extended its prohibition

---

40. 476 U.S. 79, 106 S.Ct. 1712, 90 L.Ed.2d 69 (1986).

41. See Swain v. Alabama, 380 U.S. 202, 85 S.Ct. 824, 13 L.Ed.2d 759 (1965) (overruled by Batson v. Kentucky).

42. People v. Wheeler, 22 Cal.3d 258, 148 Cal.Rptr. 890, 583 P.2d 748 (1978), noted 32 Stan.L.Rev. 189 (1979); Commonwealth v. Soares, 377 Mass. 461, 387 N.E.2d 499 (1979), cert. denied 444 U.S. 881. This trend has been criticized in Saltzburg & Powers, Peremptory Challenges and the Clash Between Impartiality and Group Representation, 41 Md.L.Rev. 337 (1982); Note, Rethinking Limitations on the Peremptory Challenge, 85 Colum.L.Rev. 1357 (1985).

43. See Hall v. U.S., 168 F.2d 161 (D.C.Cir.1948), cert. denied 334 U.S. 853.

44. 476 U.S. at 86, 106 S.Ct. at 1717.

45. 476 U.S. at 89, 106 S.Ct. at 1718–19.

46. 476 U.S. at 86, 106 S.Ct. at 1717.

47. 499 U.S. 400, 111 S.Ct. 1364, 113 L.Ed.2d 411 (1991).

48. 499 U.S. at 406, 111 S.Ct. at 1368.

49. 499 U.S. at 409–410, 111 S.Ct. at 1370.

50. 499 U.S. at 415, 111 S.Ct. at 1373.

51. 500 U.S. 614, 111 S.Ct. 2077, 114 L.Ed.2d 660 (1991).

52. 500 U.S. at 630, 111 S.Ct. at 2088. The Court noted the extensive use of state procedures, the significant assistance of state officers, and the substantial control of voir dire by the trial judge in making its determination. There was, however, a strong dissent by three of the justices. 500 U.S. at 631, 111 S.Ct. at 2089.

to forbid gender-based peremptory challenges.[53] Notably, the Supreme Court refused to eliminate the use of peremptory challenges altogether, stating: "Parties still may remove jurors who they feel might be less acceptable than others on the panel; gender simply may not serve as a proxy for bias."[54]

Determining just when bias is present as opposed to a decision to strike a juror because of an intuitive concern about the individual's ability to render a fair and impartial decision is an issue that has continued to bedevil the lower courts since the Batson case was decided.[55] It even has led some courts to call for the complete elimination of peremptories as inherently suspect and unnecessary to ensure a fair trial.[56] But to date the Court has been unwilling to declare that the peremptory challenge system is inherently constitutionally flawed.

Finally, Federal Rule 47(b) and a number of comparable state provisions give the trial court discretion to empanel additional jurors to serve as alternates. The purpose of this authority is to prevent a mistrial should one or more jurors in a prolonged case become unable to complete their duties or be disqualified after the trial has begun. The additional jurors must meet the same qualifications as the regular jurors, and a limited number of additional peremptory challenges is made available in connection with selecting the alternates.[57]

§ 11.11　Size of the Jury and the Requirement of Unanimity

Since the mid-Fourteenth Century, the common law trial by jury has referred to a unanimous verdict of a panel of twelve members.[1] Early Supreme Court decisions held or assumed that the Sixth Amendment's "right to a * * * trial by an impartial jury" in criminal cases and the Seventh Amendment's provision that "the right of trial by jury shall be preserved" in civil cases embodied these common law characteristics.[2] But more recent Supreme Court rulings have altered the traditional understanding regarding jury size and unanimity.

In the 1970 case of Williams v. Florida,[3] the Supreme Court held that a six-person jury in a state criminal proceeding satisfied the Sixth

---

53. J.E.B. v. Alabama ex rel. T.B., 511 U.S. 127, 114 S.Ct. 1419, 128 L.Ed.2d 89 (1994) (peremptory challenge used to strike virtually all males in a paternity action).

54. 511 U.S. at 143, 114 S.Ct. at 1429.

55. See Charlow, Tolerating Deception and Discrimination After Batson, 50 Stan. L.Rev. 9 (1997); Note, Batson's Invidious Legacy: Discriminatory Juror Exclusion and the "Intuitive" Peremptory Challenge, 78 Cornell L.Rev. 336 (1993).

56. E.g., Minetos v. City Univ. of New York, 925 F.Supp. 177 (S.D.N.Y.1996).

57. For a discussion of the selection and use of alternate jurors, see 9 C. Wright & A. Miller, Civil 2d § 2484.

§ 11.11

1. A. Scott, Fundamentals of Procedure in Actions at Law 75–79 (1922).

2. Patton v. U.S., 281 U.S. 276, 50 S.Ct. 253, 74 L.Ed. 854 (1930); Springville City v. Thomas, 166 U.S. 707, 17 S.Ct. 717, 41 L.Ed. 1172 (1897); American Publishing Co. v. Fisher, 166 U.S. 464, 17 S.Ct. 618, 41 L.Ed. 1079 (1897).

3. 399 U.S. 78, 90 S.Ct. 1893, 26 L.Ed.2d 446 (1970).

Amendment requirement of trial by jury, which has been made binding on the states through the Fourteenth Amendment.[4] In Williams, the Court concluded that nothing in the history of the Sixth Amendment suggested that twelve jurors were indispensable to the constitutional right to jury trial.

> The relevant inquiry, as we see it, must be the function that the particular feature performs and its relation to the purposes of the jury trial. Measured by this standard, the 12–man requirement cannot be regarded as an indispensable component of the Sixth Amendment.[5]

However, the Court specifically reserved the question whether the wording of the Seventh Amendment codified the common-law characteristics of the civil jury as part of the constitutional standard.[6] Doubts on this issue were resolved in Colgrove v. Battin,[7] a 1973 case in which the Supreme Court, by a vote of five to four, upheld a federal district court local rule providing for a six-person jury in civil proceedings. In Colgrove, the Court adhered to the premise of the earlier Sixth Amendment case, and held that the twelve-member panel is not a substantive aspect of the jury trial right.[8] Questions as to whether a jury composed of even less than six members is constitutionally permissible were answered in 1978 in Ballew v. Georgia,[9] in which the Supreme Court ruled that a criminal conviction returned by a five-member jury violated the Sixth Amendment guarantee. Similarly, then, a five-person civil jury should violate Seventh Amendment jury trial rights applicable to the federal courts.[10]

The Court expressed the opinion in Williams that there was little difference between the six-person jury and the twelve-person jury in terms of representing a cross-section of the community.[11] This viewpoint has been criticized and questions have been raised regarding both the estimated economy of using a smaller jury, and the assertion that the smaller panel produces a negligible difference in community representation.[12] Others have applauded the Williams decision as an important step towards alleviating the backlog of cases pending in the federal courts.[13] Not surprisingly, local district court rules under Federal Rule 83 autho-

---

4. The Sixth Amendment was "incorporated," or made applicable to the states, in Duncan v. Louisiana, 391 U.S. 145, 88 S.Ct. 1444, 20 L.Ed.2d 491 (1968).

5. 399 U.S. at 99–100, 90 S.Ct. at 1905.

6. 399 U.S. at 92 n. 30, 90 S.Ct. at 1901 n. 30.

7. 413 U.S. 149, 93 S.Ct. 2448, 37 L.Ed.2d 522 (1973).

8. 413 U.S. at 157–58, 93 S.Ct. at 2453.

9. 435 U.S. 223, 98 S.Ct. 1029, 55 L.Ed.2d 234 (1978), cert. denied 436 U.S. 962.

10. Federal Rule of Civil Procedure 48 provides for a jury of not less than six or more than twelve. The rule does allow the parties to stipulate to a verdict taken from a jury reduced in size to fewer than six members, however.

11. 399 U.S. at 102, 90 S.Ct. at 1907.

12. See Kaye, And Then There Were Twelve: Statistical Reasoning, The Supreme Court, and the Size of the Jury, 68 Calif.L.Rev. 1004 (1980); Lempert, Uncovering "Nondiscernible" Differences: Empirical Research and the Jury–Size Cases, 73 Mich. L.Rev. 643 (1975); Zeisel, ... And Then There Were None: The Diminution of the Federal Jury, 38 U.Chi.L.Rev. 710 (1970).

13. See Devitt, The Six–Man Jury in the Federal Court, 53 F.R.D. 273 (1971).

rizing six-person civil juries have become increasingly popular.[14] Indeed, a number of states have permitted the use of juries having fewer than twelve members for many years.[15]

Many state statutes or court rules also provide for a nonunanimous verdict in civil actions; typically, only nine or ten votes on a twelve-person jury are necessary to reach a decision.[16] In Apodaca v. Oregon,[17] the Supreme Court held that a statutory provision allowing the state to convict an individual with less than a unanimous verdict was constitutionally sufficient. The Court concluded that unanimity, like the size of the jury panel, did not have to be constitutionally imposed on the states by the Sixth Amendment through the Fourteenth Amendment. The Court noted that the contemporary function of the jury is to interpose the common-sense judgment of a group of laypeople between the accused and the accuser. As long as the jury is composed of a representative cross-section of the community and is free from outside influence, the Court felt that it could serve that purpose. Thus, "in terms of this function we perceive no difference between juries required to act unanimously and those permitted to convict or acquit by votes of 10 to two or 11 to one."[18]

The decision in Apodaca was a divided one. Only four members of the Court joined the plurality opinion. Justice Powell concurred, stating that although not all of the elements of the Sixth Amendment were binding on the states and a state might constitutionally provide for a less than unanimous verdict in a criminal case, a defendant in a federal court could be convicted only by a unanimous jury.[19]

Read strictly, Apodaca is a construction of the Sixth Amendment and its holding is limited to state criminal juries. Since the jury procedure in civil actions in the federal courts is governed by the Seventh Amendment, Apodaca seems inapplicable to the federal civil context. Yet, an extension of Apodaca from state criminal to federal civil jury practice on the issue of unanimity would be analogous to the Supreme Court's movement from Williams to Colgrove on the issue of jury size. Given Justice Powell's position on incorporation, unanimity still may be required in federal criminal cases.[20] If that is so, then the unanimous verdict requirement also may be viewed as part of the Seventh Amendment guarantee of federal civil jury trial.

But even if the lower federal courts may not constitutionally impose a nonunanimous verdict on litigants, Federal Rule 48 provides that the

---

14. See Fisher, The Seventh Amendment and the Common Law: No Magic in Numbers, 56 F.R.D. 507, 535 (1972).

15. E.g., Nev.Rules Civ.Proc., Rule 48; Utah Const. Art. 1, § 10.

16. See, e.g., West's Ann.Cal.Code Civ. Proc. § 618; Minn.Stat.Ann. § 546.17 (five-sixths verdict allowed after six hours of deliberation); N.J.Stat.Ann. 2A:80–2; Okl. Stat.1971 Const. Art. 2, § 19.

17. 406 U.S. 404, 92 S.Ct. 1628, 32 L.Ed.2d 184 (1972).

18. 406 U.S. at 411, 92 S.Ct. at 1633.

19. 406 U.S. at 369, 92 S.Ct. at 1637.

20. 406 U.S. at 366, 92 S.Ct. at 1635. But see The Supreme Court, 1969 Term, 84 Harv.L.Rev. 1, 168 n. 24 (1970).

parties in a civil action may stipulate to a trial by a jury of fewer than twelve, or may agree to abide by the verdict reached by a stated number of jurors.[21] Agreement to trial by fewer than twelve can prevent a mistrial in cases in which a juror becomes ill or otherwise disabled during the proceedings and no alternate juror has been impanelled.

It seems clear that use of a six-member jury and a less than unanimous verdict may have a substantial impact on the adjudicatory process in the federal courts over the long-run.[22] To be sure, these measures are designed to accommodate modern concerns for the rational allocation of limited judicial resources and perhaps are justifiable in those terms. Although the constitutionality of the six-person federal jury has been clearly established, at least in the civil context, and the constitutionality of a nonunanimous verdict may come to pass, there are serious questions whether these practices should be accommodated.

Some problems in applying a nonunanimous verdict rule have surfaced in states where it is allowed. For example, if the rule permits a verdict to be entered on the basis of the agreement of nine jurors, is it necessary that the same nine jurors agree both on liability and damages? At least four states have ruled no, recognizing that a juror who originally voted against liability, nonetheless could participate fully in the decision on damages.[23] But one might argue that the result obtained under those circumstances is a verdict with which less than nine jurors were in total agreement, departing even farther from the concept underlying the historic jury trial. A similar, but even more extreme, problem would occur if a six person jury were used in conjunction with a nonunanimous verdict. The Supreme Court already has ruled that that is violative of the Sixth Amendment,[24] at least insofar as a verdict is reached based on the agreement of less than six jurors. At some point, changes in the aspects or features of the jury to accommodate efficiency and economy may seriously erode the basic jury trial guarantee. Thus, great care must be taken in making these alterations so that the underlying rights remain inviolate.

21. In the absence of a party stipulation, Federal Rule 48 requires a unanimous verdict.

22. See an excellent discussion of this point in Zeisel, ... And Then There Were None: The Diminution of the Federal Jury, 38 U.Chi.L.Rev. 710 (1970).

23. Juarez v. Superior Ct. of Los Angeles County, 31 Cal.3d 759, 183 Cal.Rptr. 852, 647 P.2d 128 (1982); Tillman v. Thomas, 99 Idaho 569, 585 P.2d 1280 (1978); Naumburg v. Wagner, 81 N.M. 242, 465 P.2d 521 (App.1970); Ward v. Weekes, 107 N.J.Super. 351, 258 A.2d 379 (App.Div. 1969). See generally Trubitt, Patchwork Verdicts, Different–Jurors Verdicts, and American Jury Theory: Whether Verdicts Are Invalidated By Juror Disagreement on Issues, 36 Okla.L.Rev. 473 (1983).

24. Burch v. Louisiana, 441 U.S. 130, 99 S.Ct. 1623, 60 L.Ed.2d 96 (1979).

§§ 11.12–12.0 are reserved for supplementary material.

Chapter 12

VERDICTS AND JUDGMENTS

Analysis

A. DECISIONMAKING

A.   DECISIONMAKING

§ 12.1   The Verdict: Its Entry and Form

Because of its simplicity, the traditional and still most common form of verdict in jury trials is the general verdict, by which the jury finds for either plaintiff or defendant but does not disclose the grounds for the decision. But this simplicity necessarily leads to several weaknesses. One major criticism is that it is "either all wrong or all right, because it is an inseparable and inscrutable unit."[1] And this characteristic may result in problems if the verdict is appealed. For example, if a prevailing plaintiff asserts several possible theories of recovery, and the appellate court finds the evidence for one of those theories to have been admitted erroneously, a new trial on all issues will be required because there is no way of discovering which theory the jury relied on in reaching the verdict.[2] A second criticism of the general verdict is that it is virtually impossible to know whether the jury made its decision after careful consideration of the court's instructions, or whether it decided based

---

§ 12.1

1. Sunderland, Verdicts, General and Special, 29 Yale L.J. 253, 259 (1920).

2. See Mueller v. Hubbard Milling Co., 573 F.2d 1029, 1038–40 (8th Cir.1978), cert.

denied 439 U.S. 865; Morrissey v. National Maritime Union of America, 544 F.2d 19, 26–29 (2d Cir.1976).

upon emotion, popular opinion, or some other sentiment.[3]

To ameliorate these problems, the Federal Rules allow two other verdict forms.[4] Rule 49(a) authorizes a special verdict by which the court submits only a list of factual issues to the jury and requests it to make findings. The judge then applies the law to these findings to enter the appropriate judgment. Rule 49(b) authorizes a general verdict accompanied by written interrogatories by which the court instructs the jury to reach a general verdict, but also requests answers to one or more questions so that the basis for the verdict is disclosed. Similar provisions exist in the states.[5]

A major advantage of using one of these two forms is judicial efficiency.[6] If either is used instead of a general verdict in the example above, an appellate court can tell whether the jury based its decision on the erroneously admitted evidence. Depending on the nature of the issue, the court then can affirm the verdict if the error did not affect the jury's decision,[7] or if the decision were affected, it can remand for a new trial limited to the tainted issue.[8] Further, in certain cases the special verdict can obviate the need to charge the jury, saving time and eliminating a potential source of error.

Despite these advantages, many trial judges resist using these forms, particularly the special verdict.[9] A major cause of this reluctance has been the controversy surrounding their effect on the role of the jury, and the question of how much control the court should exercise over the jury. Advocates of the use of these forms emphasize that the jury's exclusive function is finding facts.[10] Further, the special verdict in particular is

---

3. For a famous discussion of the weaknesses of the general verdict by the late Judge Jerome Frank, see Skidmore v. Baltimore & O. R. Co., 167 F.2d 54 (2d Cir.1948), cert. denied 335 U.S. 816. See also § 12.5, below, on impeachment of the verdict.

4. See generally 9A C. Wright & A. Miller, Civil 2d §§ 2501–13.

The special verdict and general verdict with interrogatories may have different legal results. Diamond Shamrock Corp. v. Zinke & Trumbo, Ltd., 791 F.2d 1416 (10th Cir.1986), cert. denied 479 U.S. 1007. Thus, when there is any doubt as to the form used the party should inquire. See Reorganized Church of Jesus Christ of Latter Day Saints v. U.S. Gypsum Co., 882 F.2d 335 (8th Cir.1989).

5. E.g., West's Ann.Cal.Code Civ.Proc. §§ 624–25; Ill.—Smith–Hurd Ann. 735 ILCS 5/2–1108; La.Stat.Ann.—Code Civ. Proc. arts. 1812, 1813; N.Y.—McKinney's CPLR 4111; S.C.Rules of Civ.Proc., Rule 49.

6. See Warner–Jenkinson Co. v. Hilton Davis Chem. Co., 520 U.S. 17, 117 S.Ct. 1040, 137 L.Ed.2d 146 (1997), a patent in-fringement case resting on the application of the doctrine of equivalents to individual elements of a patent claim, in which the Court noted in a footnote that "a special verdict and/or interrogatories on each claim element could be very useful in facilitating review, uniformity, and possible postverdict judgments as a matter of law." 520 U.S. at 38 n. 8, 117 S.Ct. at 1054 n. 8.

7. E.g., Security Mut.Cas. Co. v. Affiliated FM Ins. Co., 471 F.2d 238, 244–45 (8th Cir.1972).

8. E.g., Jamison Co. v. Westvaco Corp., 526 F.2d 922, 934–36 (5th Cir.1976).

9. Brown, Federal Special Verdicts: The Doubt Eliminator, 44 F.R.D. 338, 352 (1967); Guinn, The Jury System and Special Verdicts, 2 St. Mary's L.J. 175, 178 (1970); James, Sufficiency of the Evidence and Jury–Control Devices Available Before Verdict, 47 Va.L.Rev. 218, 242–44 (1961).

10. J. Frank, Courts on Trial 141–42 (1963); Brodin, Accuracy, Efficiency, and Accountability in the Litigation Process— The Case for the Fact Verdict, 59 U.Cin.L.Rev. 15 (1990).

seen as a useful device in making the jury process more scientific.[11] Because special verdicts allow the jury to make only findings of fact and the court is not required to instruct the jurors on how the law will be applied to their findings,[12] the judge can control any tendencies the jury might have to be swayed by sympathy.[13] In the words of one commentator, the special verdict throws off the "cloak of secrecy" surrounding the jury process and "enables the public, the parties and the court to see what the jury has really done."[14]

Many distinguished scholars oppose the special verdict for exactly these reasons.[15] They argue that the jury system should not be a scientific process. Rather, the jury's greatest value is that it applies the strict and sometimes harsh principles of law with the sense of justice of the "man on the street."[16] Justices Hugo L. Black and William O. Douglas went even further, calling for the rejection of Federal Rule 49, and describing it as "but another means utilized by courts to weaken the constitutional power of juries and to vest judges with more power to decide cases according to their own judgments."[17]

Between these two extremes are those who feel the special verdict is unnecessary in simple cases,[18] and those who consider it a valuable tool

11. Nordbye, Comments on Selected Provisions of the New Minnesota Rules, 36 Minn.L.Rev. 672, 686 (1952).

12. There is considerable disagreement among courts on whether it is error to instruct the jury on the legal effect of its answers to the special verdict questions. Courts viewing such an instruction as being reversible error act on the notion that the knowledge would destroy the objectivity the device was designed to create. Brewer v. Jeep Corp., 546 F.Supp. 1147 (W.D.Ark. 1982), affirmed on other grounds 724 F.2d 653 (8th Cir.1983); McGowan v. Story, 70 Wis.2d 189, 234 N.W.2d 325 (1975). Other courts take a contrary view. Lowery v. Clouse, 348 F.2d 252 (8th Cir.1965); Seppi v. Betty, 99 Idaho 186, 579 P.2d 683 (1978). See also Wright, The Use of Special Verdicts in Federal Courts, 38 F.R.D. 199, 204–06 (1965). This is especially true when there is a danger that the jury will attempt to guess about the law. In re Aircrash in Bali, Indonesia, 871 F.2d 812, 815 (9th Cir. 1989), cert. denied 493 U.S. 917; Kaeo v. Davis, 68 Hawaii 447, 719 P.2d 387 (1986). For a discussion of this debate in connection with comparative negligence cases, see Comment, Informing the Jury of the Legal Effect of Special Verdict Answers in Comparative Negligence Actions, 1981 Duke L.J. 824. However, when the questions contain a mixture of law and fact, the court must instruct the jury as to the legal standard to apply. Landy v. Federal Aviation Administration, 635 F.2d 143, 147 (2d Cir. 1980); Kissell v. Westinghouse Elec. Corp., Elevator Div., 367 F.2d 375, 376 (1st Cir. 1966).

13. Jackson v. Ulrich Mfg. Co., 55 F.R.D. 473 (E.D.Pa.1972), affirmed 485 F.2d 680 (3d Cir.1973), cert. denied 415 U.S. 982.

14. Sunderland, Verdicts, General and Special, 29 Yale L.J. 253, 259 (1920).

15. O.W. Holmes, Collected Legal Papers 237–38 (1921); Traynor, Fact Skepticism and the Judicial Process, 106 U.Pa. L.Rev. 635, 640 (1958); Wigmore, A Program for the Trial of a Jury Trial, 12 J.Am. Jud.Soc. 166, 170 (1929).

16. Guinn, The Jury System and Special Verdicts, 2 St. Mary's L.J. 175, 181 (1970); Wigmore, A Program for the Trial of a Jury Trial, 12 J.Am.Jud.Soc. 166, 170 (1929).

17. Statement of Justices Black and Douglas issued in connection with the 1963 amendment of Rule 49, 374 U.S. 865, 867–68, 83 S.Ct. 43, 44–45 (1963).

18. The late Judge Charles E. Clark, draftsman of the Federal Rules, described Rule 49 as of "more doubtful value in a relatively simple factual situation." Morris v. Pennsylvania R. Co., 187 F.2d 837, 841 (2d Cir.1951); Nordbye, Comments on Selected Provisions of the New Minnesota Rules, 36 Minn.L.Rev. 672, 683 (1952).

in complicated, multi-issue litigation.[19] Because the general verdict with interrogatories allows the jury to retain more of its traditional role, it is less controversial and thus often is preferred by more judges over the special verdict.[20]

The choice of verdict form generally is left to the discretion of the trial judge;[21] no party has a right to a particular form of verdict.[22] Although in Wisconsin[23] and Texas,[24] the special verdict is the rule rather than the exception, in most cases whether either of these specialized forms is used depends on the particular judge's view of the debate on their usefulness and intrusiveness on the jury.[25]

When special verdicts or general verdicts with interrogatories are used, serious questions may arise concerning the procedure surrounding their use. The device is basically an adaptation of the common law special verdict,[26] which was an unworkable procedural device because it required the jury to find specifically on every material fact of the case for the party with the burden of proof, or else that party lost.[27] Modern procedural rules are designed to avoid some of the problems that arose at common law by providing that the parties waive their jury trial rights on any issue not submitted to the jury before it retires.[28] Thus, there is no necessity to define and isolate all the material issues before using this form. If the submitted questions omit a material issue of fact and no

19. Wright, The Use of Special Verdicts in Federal Court, 38 F.R.D. 199, 206 (1965). See Berkey Photo, Inc. v. Eastman Kodak Co., 603 F.2d 263, 278 (2d Cir.1979), cert. denied 444 U.S. 1093; Mueller v. Hubbard Milling Co., 573 F.2d 1029, 1038 n. 13 (8th Cir.1978), cert. denied 439 U.S. 865; Jamison Co. v. Westvaco Corp., 526 F.2d 922, 935 (5th Cir.1976); Harding v. Evans, 207 F.Supp. 852, 855 (M.D.Pa.1962).

20. Guinn, The Jury System and Special Verdicts, 2 St. Mary's L.J. 175, 179 (1970).

21. Bartak v. Bell–Galyardt & Wells, Inc., 629 F.2d 523, 531 (8th Cir.1980); Nobility Homes, Inc. v. Ballentine, 386 So.2d 727 (Ala.1980); Turney v. Anspaugh, 581 P.2d 1301 (Okl.1978). But compare West's Ann.Cal.Code Civ.Proc. § 625 (special verdict mandatory on issue of punitive damages as separate from compensatory damages). Special verdicts or general verdicts with interrogatories also have been required when comparative fault is an issue. E.g., Kan.Stat.Ann. § 60–258a(b); N.J.Stat. Ann. 2A:15–5.2; Lawrence v. Florida East Coast Ry. Co., 346 So.2d 1012, 1017 (Fla. 1977).

22. Parties also have no right to submission of particular interrogatories when either the special verdict or general verdict with interrogatories is used. Miley v. Oppenheimer & Co., 637 F.2d 318, 333–34 (5th Cir.1981); New Orleans & N.E.R.R. Co. v. Anderson, 293 F.2d 97 (5th Cir.1961). But see Norton v. Wilbur Waggoner Equip. Rental & Excavating Co., 82 Ill.App.3d 727, 38 Ill.Dec. 93, 403 N.E.2d 108 (1980) (when special interrogatory is in proper form, relating to an ultimate issue of fact, the trial court has no discretion to refuse it).

23. Wis.Stat.Ann. 805.12; Milwaukee & Suburban Transport Corp. v. Milwaukee County, 82 Wis.2d 420, 263 N.W.2d 503 (1978); Graczyk, The New Wisconsin Rules of Civil Procedure Chapters 805–807, 59 Marq.L.Rev. 671, 697 (1976).

24. Vernon's Ann.Tex. Rules Civ.Proc., Rule 277. See Survey of Special Issue Submission in Texas Since Amended Rule 277, 7 St. Mary's L.J. 345 (1975).

25. 9A C. Wright & A. Miller, Civil 2d § 2505, at 494.

26. Dobie, The Federal Rules of Civil Procedure, 25 Va.L.Rev. 261, 287 (1939). For a history of the development of special verdicts see Comment, Special Verdicts: Rule 49 of the Federal Rules of Civil Procedure, 74 Yale L.J. 483 (1965).

27. Stinson, Special Verdicts and Interrogatories, 7 Mo.L.Rev. 142 (1942).

28. Fed.Civ.Proc.Rule 49(a); Michigan Court Rule 2.514(c); N.Y.—McKinney's CPLR 4111(b); N.C.Gen.Stat. § 1A–1, Rule 49(c); Wis.Stat.Ann. 805.12(2).

timely objection is made, the court may make the findings necessary to cure the omission.[29] Findings consistent with the verdict will be implied if not expressly made.[30]

Formulating the questions or issues to be put to the jury is the most difficult part of using the special verdict. Indeed, the time required and the difficulty of formulating the questions for a special verdict, particularly in complex cases, is yet one more reason why the use of this device is not widespread.[31] For the best results, the court should present to the jury a small number[32] of simply worded,[33] unambiguous questions,[34] each limited to one issue.[35] Parties may object to the form of the questions or issues, but the objection must be timely, and may not be raised for the first time on appeal.[36]

The jury's findings on the questions or issues presented must be definite and unambiguous or the court may refuse to enter judgment on them.[37] But a failure to answer all the questions will not be harmful if those that are answered dispose of the necessary issues.[38] Furthermore, the individual findings should be consistent with each other. The court is under a duty to harmonize the answers if possible,[39] and to construe

29. Peckham v. Continental Cas. Ins. Co., 895 F.2d 830, 836 (1st Cir.1990); Hawco v. Massachusetts Bay Transportation Authority, 398 Mass. 1006, 499 N.E.2d 295, 296 (1986). But see Kinnel v. Mid–Atlantic Mausoleums, Inc., 850 F.2d 958, 965–66 (3d Cir.1988) (court is not permitted to supply finding determining a party's ultimate liability).

30. Bradway v. Gonzales, 26 F.3d 313, 317 (2d Cir.1994); Anderson v. Cryovac, Inc., 862 F.2d 910, 915–16 (1st Cir.1988); Smith v. Christley, 755 S.W.2d 525, 531 (Tex.App.1988); Regents of Univ. of Minnesota v. Medical Inc., 382 N.W.2d 201, 210 (Minn.App.1986), cert. denied 479 U.S. 910.

31. Guinn, The Jury System and Special Verdicts, 2 St. Mary's L.J. 175, 178 (1970).

32. N.C.Gen.Stat. § 1A–1, Rule 49(b), puts in statutory form the direction to the court to keep from submitting too many issues to the jury.

33. In Wyler v. Feuer, 85 Cal.App.3d 392, 405, 149 Cal.Rptr. 626 (1978), the court noted the "disadvantages of saddling a jury with lengthy and involved interrogatories, cocooned in legal terminology and garnished with words of art."

34. See Cunningham v. M–G Transport Servs., Inc., 527 F.2d 760, 762 (4th Cir.1975) (court recommended to all the district courts in its circuit that they submit questions to the jury rather than issues; it also recommended that the questions separate damages from liability).

35. See Bissett v. Ply–Gem Indus., Inc., 533 F.2d 142 (5th Cir.1976); Corceller v. Brooks, 347 So.2d 274 (La.App.1977), writ denied 350 So.2d 1223 (La.1977).

36. Bell v. Mickelsen, 710 F.2d 611 (10th Cir.1983); Fredonia Broadcasting Corp. v. RCA Corporation, 481 F.2d 781 (5th Cir.1973); W. H. Barber v. McNamara–Vivant Contracting Co., 293 N.W.2d 351 (Minn.1979). See also Patur v. Aetna Life & Cas., 90 Ill.App.3d 464, 45 Ill.Dec. 732, 413 N.E.2d 65 (1980).

37. See Iacurci v. Lummus Co., 387 U.S. 86, 87 S.Ct. 1423, 18 L.Ed.2d 581 (1967); Atlantic Tubing & Rubber Co. v. International Engraving Co., 528 F.2d 1272 (1st Cir.1976), cert. denied 429 U.S. 817; Gardner v. Kerly, 613 S.W.2d 795 (Tex.Civ. App.1981).

38. E.g., Simms v. Village of Albion, 115 F.3d 1098 (2d Cir.1997); Black v. Riker–Maxson Corp., 401 F.Supp. 693 (S.D.N.Y.1975); Barnette v. Doyle, 622 P.2d 1349, 1367–68 (Wyo.1981); Anheuser–Busch, Inc. v. Smith, 539 S.W.2d 234 (Tex. Civ.App.1976). Compare Franki Foundation Co. v. Alger–Rau & Assocs., Inc., 513 F.2d 581 (3d Cir.1975) (responses to unanswered questions were necessary).

39. Gallick v. Baltimore & Ohio R.R. Co., 372 U.S. 108, 83 S.Ct. 659, 9 L.Ed.2d 618 (1963). See also Olson v. City of Austin, 386 N.W.2d 815, 817 (Minn.App.1986); Schmit v. Stewart, 601 P.2d 256 (Alaska 1979); Rohr v. Henderson, 207 Kan. 123, 483 P.2d 1089 (1971).

them as consistent if there is a view of the case that makes them so.[40] If the answers are consistent, then the court may apply the law to those findings and enter judgment for the appropriate party.[41] If the answers are inconsistent after all attempts to harmonize them, then the court may resubmit the findings to the jury for reconsideration in hopes of curing the inconsistency.[42] Additional interrogatories also may be submitted to help cure an inconsistency.[43] However, a new trial should be ordered if the inconsistencies cannot be resolved.[44] This cluster of rules reveals the problem with special verdicts—they expose jury malfunctions that we might rather not know about.[45]

The procedure for using a general verdict with interrogatories is in some respects simpler because it usually is not as detailed as the special verdict. Nonetheless, many of the same concerns arise. The interrogatories are submitted to the jury at the same time as the general verdict form.[46] Only a small number of clearly worded interrogatories should be put to the jury, since the purpose of the device is merely to make the grounds for the decision clearer,[47] not to place a tight reign on the jury's deliberations.[48]

One problem area with this device concerns the options that exist for the judge if the jury encounters difficulty with the interrogatories. Federal Rule 49(b) directly addresses the three possible situations that may arise. First, if the answers and the verdict are harmonious, then judgment may be entered on the verdict. Second, if the answers are consistent among themselves, but one or more is inconsistent with the

---

40. The duty to view the jury's answers as consistent if possible arises out of the Seventh Amendment guarantee of a right to jury trial. Atlantic & Gulf Stevedores, Inc. v. Ellerman Lines, Ltd., 369 U.S. 355, 364, 82 S.Ct. 780, 786, 7 L.Ed.2d 798 (1962); Rohr v. Henderson, 207 Kan. 123, 483 P.2d 1089 (1971). For examples of how courts analyze what appear to be inconsistent answers, see Rose Hall, Ltd. v. Chase Manhattan Overseas Banking Corp., 566 F.Supp. 1558, 1566–70 (D.Del.1983); Van Cleve v. Betts, 16 Wn.App. 748, 559 P.2d 1006, 1013 (1977). See generally Note, Resolving Inconsistencies in Federal Special Verdicts, 53 Ford.L.Rev. 1089 (1985).

41. Robles v. Exxon Corp., 862 F.2d 1201 (5th Cir.1989), cert. denied 490 U.S. 1051.

42. Landry v. Offshore Logistics, Inc., 544 F.2d 757 (5th Cir.1977); Alston v. West, 340 F.2d 856 (7th Cir.1965).

43. Morrison v. Frito–Lay, Inc., 546 F.2d 154, 161 (5th Cir.1977).

44. Andrasko v. Chamberlain Mfg. Corp., 608 F.2d 944 (3d Cir.1979); Fugitt v. Jones, 549 F.2d 1001 (5th Cir.1977); Russell v. Pryor, 264 Ark. 45, 568 S.W.2d 918 (1978).

45. Consider Judge Learned Hand's observation that if we demanded that every jury act without bias and vote only upon the evidence heard in court, then "it is doubtful whether more than one in a hundred verdicts would stand * * *." Jorgensen v. York Ice Mach. Corp., 160 F.2d 432, 435 (2d Cir.1947), cert. denied 332 U.S. 764.

46. It is unusual for interrogatories to be requested and allowed after the charge has been read to the jury. Compare Scarborough v. Atlantic Coast Line R. Co., 190 F.2d 935 (4th Cir.1951) (allowed), with Falk v. Schuster, 171 Conn. 5, 368 A.2d 40 (1976) (not allowed).

47. Masonite Corp. v. Pacific Gas & Elec. Co., 65 Cal.App.3d 1, 11, 135 Cal.Rptr. 170, 176 (1976).

48. See the discussion in Wyler v. Feuer, 85 Cal.App.3d 392, 405–08, 149 Cal. Rptr. 626, 634–35 (1978), and the examples of the 28 overly long and involved interrogatories put to the jury in that case. See also United Air Lines, Inc. v. Wiener, 335 F.2d 379, 405 (9th Cir.1964), cert. dismissed 379 U.S. 951, vacating Nollenberger v. United Air Lines, Inc., 216 F.Supp. 734 (S.D.Cal. 1963).

general verdict, then the court may order a new trial, or it may return both to the jury for further deliberation, or it may disregard the general verdict and enter judgment in accordance with the specific answers.[49] But only when the answers and the general verdict conflict on a material issue and there is no chance for reconciliation may the specific answers prevail over the general verdict.[50]

For example, in one tort case arising out of an automobile accident the jury rendered a general verdict of $500,000 in favor of the plaintiff, but at the same time specifically found the plaintiff guilty of contributory negligence. The court entered judgment for the defendant based on the specific answer because the substantive law barred recovery if she were found contributorily negligent.[51] It was not possible to reconcile the inconsistency. In other circumstances, the court may be able to reconcile the apparent inconsistency and, as was true of the special verdict,[52] it should attempt to do so by viewing the case in the light most favorable to their consistency.[53]

The third possibility addressed by Rule 49 concerns when the answers are inconsistent with each other and one or more also is inconsistent with the verdict. When that occurs, the court may not enter judgment, it either must request further deliberation by the jury or order a new trial.[54] Under those circumstances, there is no way for the judge to surmise what the appropriate verdict should be.

In addition to the preceding options, the trial judge has discretion to withdraw certain interrogatories, even after the jury has retired, if they are unclear or ambiguous and only serve to confuse the jury. For example, in the leading case of Diniero v. United States Lines Company,[55] the trial judge submitted a general verdict form to the jury accompanied by six interrogatories. Three hours after deliberations commenced, the judge received a note from the jury asking him to interpret the meaning of one of the questions. The judge complied, but one hour later received another note saying that the jury still could not agree on that question. The judge then withdrew all of the interrogato-

---

49. Similar provisions may be found in many states. See West's Ann.Cal.Code Civ. Proc. § 625; N.Y.—McKinney's CPLR 4111(c); Marine Midland Bank v. John E. Russo Produce Co., 50 N.Y.2d 31, 427 N.Y.S.2d 961, 405 N.E.2d 205 (1980).

50. Julien J. Studley, Inc. v. Gulf Oil Corp., 407 F.2d 521 (2d Cir.1969); GNB Battery Technologies, Inc. v. Exide Corp., 876 F.Supp. 605 (D.Del.1995); Hasson v. Ford Motor Co., 19 Cal.3d 530, 138 Cal. Rptr. 705, 564 P.2d 857 (1977); Allen v. D'Ercole Constr. Co., 104 R.I. 362, 244 A.2d 864 (1968).

51. Elston v. Morgan, 440 F.2d 47 (7th Cir.1971). For another example, see Stoddard v. School Dist. No. 1, Lincoln County, Wyoming, 590 F.2d 829 (10th Cir.1979).

52. See the cases in note 39, above.

53. See Cone v. Beneficial Standard Life Ins. Co., 388 F.2d 456 (8th Cir.1968); Patur v. Aetna Life & Cas., 90 Ill.App.3d 464, 45 Ill.Dec. 732, 413 N.E.2d 65 (1980); Hasson v. Ford Motor Co., 19 Cal.3d 530, 138 Cal.Rptr. 705, 564 P.2d 857 (1977).

54. Bahamas Agricultural Indus. Ltd. v. Riley Stoker Corp., 526 F.2d 1174 (6th Cir.1975). But see Seven Provinces Ins. Co. v. Commerce & Industry Ins. Co., 65 F.R.D. 674, 689 (W.D.Mo.1975) (court said that answers were not inconsistent, but even if they were, it would not be of a sufficient magnitude to warrant a new trial).

55. 288 F.2d 595 (2d Cir.1961), cert. denied 368 U.S. 831.

ries and asked the jury merely to render a general verdict. After nearly four more hours of deliberation, the jury rendered a verdict for the plaintiff. The Second Circuit held that it was within the trial judge's discretion to withdraw "unclear and ambiguous" interrogatories for the purpose of curing obvious jury confusion. Prejudice to the defendant was absent because the jury deliberated for almost four hours after the removal of the interrogatories. The appellate court further noted that a confusing and ambiguous interrogatory cannot be considered "material" or one that is "necessary to a verdict."[56] Following the lead of Diniero, a lower federal court has held that it was within its discretion to clear up ambiguities in the jury's answers by resubmitting amended interrogatories and additional instructions to the jury.[57]

In contrast, a New York state court has ruled that it was error for the trial judge to withdraw an unanswered interrogatory after the jury had returned with the verdict.[58] The unanswered interrogatory was "material" and "necessary to the verdict" because it asked the jury to determine the plaintiff's full damages as an indispensable step in calculating the final award in a comparative negligence case. The fact that the jury obviously was confused did not warrant withdrawal of this important interrogatory after the verdict had been rendered.

As these cases suggest, great care must be taken when withdrawing interrogatories or resubmitting them to the jury. As to withdrawal, there is the concern that the jury is confused by more than an ambiguous question, and that if the verdict is allowed, it may mask jury error. With regard to resubmission, there is the concern that the court is placing undue pressure on the jurors to arrive at a decision. If they feel coerced, the resulting verdict would not be returned fairly.[59]

§ 12.2 Findings and Conclusions in Nonjury Cases

Whenever an action is tried without a jury, Federal Rule of Civil Procedure 52(a)[1] and similar state rules[2] require the trial judge to make findings of fact and conclusions of law when entering judgment. This requirement applies when the court sits with an advisory jury,[3] as well as when the judge grants or refuses an interlocutory injunction,[4] dismisses plaintiff's case on the merits at the close of plaintiff's presentation of

---

56. 288 F.2d at 599–600.

57. U.S. v. 0.78 Acres of Land, More or Less, 81 F.R.D. 618, 622 (E.D.Pa.1979), affirmed without opinion 609 F.2d 504 (3d Cir.1979).

58. Grey v. United Leasing Inc., 91 A.D.2d 932, 457 N.Y.S.2d 823 (1983).

59. See Diniero v. U.S. Lines Co., 288 F.2d 595, 598–600 (2d Cir.1961), cert. denied 368 U.S. 831, and the cases cited by the Second Circuit.

§ 12.2

1. See 9A C. Wright & A. Miller, Civil 2d §§ 2571–91.

2. Fed.Civ.Proc.Rule 52(a); Official Code Ga.Ann. § 9–11–52(a); Ky.Rules Civ. Proc., Rule 52.01.

3. Transmatic, Inc. v. Gulton Indus., Inc., 53 F.3d 1270 (Fed.Cir.1995); Reachi v. Edmond, 277 F.2d 850 (9th Cir.1960); Advisory Committee Note to the 1948 Amendment of Rule 52(a), reprinted at 5 F.R.D. 471.

4. Rosen v. Siegel, 106 F.3d 28 (2d Cir.1997); Newark Stereotypers' Union No. 18 v. Newark Morning Ledger Co., 353 F.2d 510 (3d Cir.1965).

evidence,[5] or grants a partial judgment on some of the claims in an action.[6]

The purposes of this requirement are threefold. First, it aids the appellate court by providing a better understanding of the basis of the trial court's decision.[7] Second, it clarifies precisely what is being decided, facilitating the application of res judicata and collateral estoppel principles in subsequent cases.[8] Third, it evokes care on the part of the trial judge in ascertaining the facts.[9]

Under the federal rule and the state provisions modelled after it, the requirement that the judge make special findings of fact and separate conclusions of law is mandatory,[10] and may not be waived.[11] In many states, however, the rules do not require the judge to make special findings unless a request for them is made by one of the parties.[12] Further, the findings may be made orally. Federal Rule 52(a) was amended in 1983 to make clear that the judge may make findings of fact and conclusions of law orally in open court. According to the Advisory Committee Note, the objective of the amendment was to lighten the burden on trial judges, and to reduce the number of published district court opinions that embrace written findings.[13]

The trial judge should state the factual findings separately from the conclusions of law.[14] As a general rule, findings of fact should be clear,

---

5. Lemelson v. Kellogg Co., 440 F.2d 986 (2d Cir.1971).

Findings are unnecessary, however, if the case is dismissed on a preliminary motion, such as summary judgment. Fed.Civ. Proc.Rule 52(a); Palzer v. Serv–U–Meat Co., 419 P.2d 201, 205 (Alaska 1966).

6. See Fed.Civ.Proc.Rule 52(c).

7. Snyder v. U.S., 674 F.2d 1359, 1362–63 (10th Cir.1982); Complaint of Ithaca Corp., 582 F.2d 3, 4 (5th Cir.1978); Coble v. Coble, 300 N.C. 708, 268 S.E.2d 185, 189 (1980); In re Welfare of Woods, 20 Wn.App. 515, 581 P.2d 587, 588 (1978).

8. Advisory Committee Note to 1948 Amendment of Rule 52(a), reprinted at 5 F.R.D. 433, 471, citing Nordbye, Improvements in Statement of Findings of Fact and Conclusions of Law, 1 F.R.D. 25, 26–27 (1940). See Wattleton v. International Bhd. of Boiler Makers, Iron Ship Builders, Blacksmiths, Forgers & Helpers, Local No. 1509, 686 F.2d 586, 591 (7th Cir.1982), cert. denied 459 U.S. 1208; In re Marriage of Barron, 177 Mont. 161, 580 P.2d 936, 938 (1978).

9. The Supreme Court has noted that judges "will give more careful consideration to the problem if they are required to state not only the end result of their inquiry, but the process by which they reached it." U.S. v. Merz, 376 U.S. 192, 199, 84 S.Ct. 639, 643, 11 L.Ed.2d 629 (1964). See also Rob-

erts v. Ross, 344 F.2d 747, 751–52 (3d Cir. 1965); Pruitt v. First Nat. Bank of Habersham County, 142 Ga.App. 100, 235 S.E.2d 617, 618 (1977).

10. H. Prang Trucking Co. v. Local Union No. 469, 613 F.2d 1235, 1238 (3d Cir.1980); Featherstone v. Barash, 345 F.2d 246, 249 (10th Cir.1965); Romrell v. Zions First Nat. Bank, N.A., 611 P.2d 392 (Utah 1980); Shannon v. Murphy, 49 Hawaii 661, 426 P.2d 816, 820 (1967).

11. Berguido v. Eastern Air Lines, Inc., 369 F.2d 874, 877 (3d Cir.1966), cert. denied 390 U.S. 996; Waialua Agricultural Co. v. Maneja, 178 F.2d 603 (9th Cir.1949), cert. denied 339 U.S. 920; Romrell v. Zions First Nat. Bank, N.A., 611 P.2d 392, 394–95 (Utah 1980).

12. Ariz.Rules Civ.Proc., Rule 52(a); West's Ann.Cal.Code Civ.Proc. § 632; Ohio Rules Civ.Proc., Rule 52; Or.Rules Civ. Proc., Rule 62A; Me.Rules Civ.Proc., Rule 52; Vernon's Ann.Mo.Civ.Proc.Rule 73.01(a)(2).

13. Advisory Committee Note to the 1983 Amendment of Federal Rule 52(a), reprinted in 97 F.R.D. 221 (1983).

14. Polaroid Corp. v. Markham, 151 F.2d 89, 90 (D.C.Cir.1945). This requirement is particularly important because findings of fact may be reversed on appeal

complete, and specific.[15] Findings on as many of the subsidiary facts as necessary should be included to give the appellate court an understanding of the logic used by the trial judge in reaching an ultimate conclusion on each factual issue.[16] At the very least, the findings of fact must be sufficiently clear to provide an adequate basis for the trial court's decision.[17] Thus, for example, the mere recitation of the events that took place at trial is not sufficient.[18]

Although the duty of making findings of fact and conclusions of law lies with the court, the trial judge may invite counsel to submit proposed findings and conclusions.[19] Indeed, requests for proposed findings may be particularly helpful in complex cases involving scientific or technical issues.[20] When counsel are invited to submit proposed findings and conclusions, they are obligated to assist the court,[21] and if they do not, cannot complain that the court's final findings and conclusions are incomplete.[22]

If the court asks the attorneys' aid in preparing its findings, the better practice is to request proposals from counsel for both sides, and to do so prior to the decision of the case.[23] Several courts, however, have adopted the practice of deciding a case and then asking winning counsel to prepare findings and conclusions.[24] The Third Circuit has expressly rejected this approach, stating that it "flies in the face of the spirit and

only if they are clearly erroneous. For a discussion of appellate review, see § 13.4, below.

15. Joseph A. by Wolfe v. New Mexico Dep't of Human Servs., 69 F.3d 1081 (10th Cir.1995), cert. denied 517 U.S. 1190; Lora v. Board of Educ. of City of New York, 623 F.2d 248, 251 (2d Cir.1980); American Century Mortgage Investors v. Strickland, 138 Ga.App. 657, 227 S.E.2d 460, 462–63 (1976). See also Lindsey v. Ogden, 10 Mass. App.Ct. 142, 406 N.E.2d 701, 711 (1980). For a more thorough discussion of the standard for assessing the sufficiency of the trial court's findings, see 9A C. Wright & A. Miller, Civil 2d § 2579.

16. Kelley v. Everglades Drainage Dist., 319 U.S. 415, 422, 63 S.Ct. 1141, 1145, 87 L.Ed. 1485 (1943); Duffie v. Deere & Co., 111 F.3d 70 (8th Cir.1997); Golf City, Inc. v. Wilson Sporting Goods Co., 555 F.2d 426, 432–36 (5th Cir.1977); Eagle Elec. Co. v. Raymond Constr. Co., 420 A.2d 60, 64–65 (R.I.1980).

17. Keller v. U.S., 38 F.3d 16 (1st Cir. 1994); Snyder v. U.S., 674 F.2d 1359, 1362–63 (10th Cir.1982); Coburn v. Michigan Public Serv. Comm'n, 104 Mich.App. 322, 304 N.W.2d 570 (1981); In the Matter of Lewin's Estate, 42 Colo.App. 129, 595 P.2d 1055, 1057 (1979); Fine v. Fine, 248 N.W.2d 838 (N.D.1976).

18. Fred R. Surface & Assocs., Inc. v. Worozbyt, 148 Ga.App. 639, 252 S.E.2d 67, 68 (1979).

19. U.S. v. Cornish, 348 F.2d 175, 181 n. 8 (9th Cir.1965); Featherstone v. Barash, 345 F.2d 246, 251 (10th Cir.1965); Cormier v. Carty, 381 Mass. 234, 408 N.E.2d 860, 863 (1980); Kerner v. Johnson, 99 Idaho 433, 583 P.2d 360, 376 (1978).

20. See Reese v. Elkhart Welding & Boiler Works, Inc., 447 F.2d 517, 520 (7th Cir.1971) (patent case).

21. Desch v. U.S., 186 F.2d 623 (7th Cir.1951).

22. Sonken–Galamba Corp. v. Atchison, T. & S.F. Ry. Co., 34 F.Supp. 15 (W.D.Mo.1940), affirmed 124 F.2d 952 (8th Cir.1942), cert. denied 315 U.S. 822.

23. Vicon, Inc. v. CMI Corporation, 657 F.2d 768, 772 n. 5 (5th Cir.1981); Eli Lilly & Co. v. Generix Drug Sales, Inc., 460 F.2d 1096 (5th Cir.1972); Roberts v. Ross, 344 F.2d 747, 752 (3d Cir.1965).

24. Citizens for Balanced Environment & Transp., Inc. v. Volpe, 650 F.2d 455 (2d Cir.1981); Schnell v. Allbright–Nell Co., 348 F.2d 444 (7th Cir.1965), cert. denied 383 U.S. 934; Boyer Co. v. Lignell, 567 P.2d 1112 (Utah 1977). See also Globe Drilling Co. v. Cramer, 39 Colo.App. 153, 562 P.2d

purpose * * * of Rule 52(a)."[25] The formulation of the findings and conclusions is part of the decisionmaking process. For this reason, it generally is agreed that it is ill-advised for the court to adopt the winning counsel's findings and conclusions verbatim.[26] Nonetheless, the Supreme Court has stated that the verbatim adoption of findings prepared by counsel does not require that those findings be rejected out-of-hand; they may stand if supported by the evidence.[27] However, the Court went on to comment that findings drawn with the "insight of a disinterested mind are * * * more helpful to the appellate court."[28]

As is discussed elsewhere, the standard on review is that findings of fact will not be reversed unless they are clearly erroneous.[29] In the federal courts and some states, this is true whether the evidence that was submitted was oral or documentary.[30] Of course, appellate courts are likely to review findings and conclusions prepared by a party and adopted nearly verbatim by the court more carefully than those that show evidence of the judge's own work product.[31] If the trial court fails to make sufficient findings, the appellate court either will vacate the judgment and remand for the trial judge to make the appropriate findings;[32] will remand so that the trial court may hear further evidence

762 (1977) (findings entered only after court found them to be proper).

25. Roberts v. Ross, 344 F.2d 747, 751 (3d Cir.1965). See also Callahan v. Callahan, 579 S.W.2d 385 (Ky.App.1979) (delegating to counsel should be limited to routine matters and done under close scrutiny of the trial judge).

26. Industrial Bldg. Materials, Inc. v. Interchemical Corp., 437 F.2d 1336 (9th Cir.1970); In re Las Colinas, Inc., 426 F.2d 1005 (1st Cir.1970); Compton v. Gilmore, 98 Idaho 190, 560 P.2d 861 (1977).

27. U.S. v. El Paso Natural Gas Co., 376 U.S. 651, 656, 84 S.Ct. 1044, 1047, 12 L.Ed.2d 12 (1964). See also Ramey Constr. Co. v. Apache Tribe of Mescalero Reservation, 616 F.2d 464 (10th Cir.1980); Nissho–Iwai Co. v. Star Bulk Shipping Co., 503 F.2d 596 (9th Cir.1974); Molokoa Village Development Co. v. Kauai Elec. Co., 60 Hawaii 582, 593 P.2d 375 (1979).

28. 376 U.S. at 656, 84 S.Ct. at 1047. See also Edward B. Marks Music Corp. v. Colorado Magnetics, Inc., 497 F.2d 285 (10th Cir.1974), cert. denied 419 U.S. 1120; Edward Valves, Inc. v. Cameron Iron Works, Inc., 289 F.2d 355 (5th Cir.1961), cert. denied 368 U.S. 833.

29. Fed.Civ.Proc.Rule 52(a). See § 13.4, below.

30. Federal Rule 52(a) was amended in 1985 to provide specifically that the clearly erroneous standard applies regardless of the type of evidence involved. For a discussion of the standard and its application, see Amadeo v. Zant, 486 U.S. 214, 108 S.Ct. 1771, 100 L.Ed.2d 249 (1988); Anderson v. Bessemer City, 470 U.S. 564, 105 S.Ct. 1504, 84 L.Ed.2d 518 (1985); Levine & Salans, Exceptions to the Clearly Erroneous Test After the Recent Amending of Rule 52(a) for the Review of Facts Based Upon Documentary Evidence, 10 Am.J.Trial.Advoc. 409 (1987); Note, Review of Findings Based on Documentary Evidence: Is the Proposed Amendment to Rule 52(a) the Correct Solution, 30 Vill.L.Rev. 227 (1985). Several states previously applying the de novo standard of review for documentary evidence have adopted the federal rule. E.g., Bellon v. Malnar, 808 P.2d 1089, 1092 (Utah 1991); Rapp v. Barry, 398 Mass. 1004, 496 N.E.2d 636 (1986).

31. Ramey Constr. Co. v. Apache Tribe of Mescalero Reservation, 616 F.2d 464 (10th Cir.1980); Louis Dreyfus & Cie. v. Panama Canal Co., 298 F.2d 733 (5th Cir. 1962); Cormier v. Carty, 381 Mass. 234, 408 N.E.2d 860 (1980); United Nuclear Corp. v. General Atomic Co., 96 N.M. 155, 629 P.2d 231 (1980), appeal dismissed, cert. denied 451 U.S. 901.

32. See, e.g., Touch v. Master Unit Die Prods., Inc., 43 F.3d 754 (1st Cir.1995); H. Prang Trucking Co. v. Local Union No. 469, 613 F.2d 1235 (3d Cir.1980); Golf City, Inc. v. Wilson Sporting Goods Co., 555 F.2d 426 (5th Cir.1977); Eagle Elec. Co. v. Raymond

on which to base its findings;[33] or will order a new trial.[34] If the trial court fails to make a finding on a material fact, some appellate courts assume that the judge found against the party with the burden of proof on that issue.[35] Others imply that the court made a finding on that fact consistent with its general findings.[36] Most commonly, however, the appellate court will treat the omission as reversible error and remand for further findings on that issue,[37] unless the record on appeal allows only one resolution of the issue.[38]

B. ATTACKS ON VERDICTS AND JUDGMENTS

§ 12.3 Directed Verdicts and Judgments Notwithstanding the Verdict (Judgments as a Matter of Law)

Directed verdicts and judgments notwithstanding the verdict (JNOV) are two mechanisms by which the judge controls the jury,[1] since the granting of either motion essentially takes the case out of the jurors' hands. Directed verdict motions may be made by either party at the close of their opponent's evidence.[2] For the motion to be granted the court must find that there is insufficient evidence to go to the jury or that the evidence is so compelling that only one result could follow.[3] In this way

---

Constr. Co., 420 A.2d 60 (R.I.1980); Rucker v. Dalton, 598 P.2d 1336 (Utah 1979).

33. See, e.g., Anderson v. City of Albuquerque, 690 F.2d 796 (10th Cir.1982).

34. Kruger v. Purcell, 300 F.2d 830 (3d Cir.1962) (when appellate court had only documentary evidence, and a transcript of the testimony was not available, remanding for further findings of fact would be useless, and the court therefore ordered a new trial); Keefer v. Keefer & Johnson, Inc., 361 A.2d 172 (D.C.App.1976) (because almost two years had elapsed since trial, the appellate court felt compelled to order a new trial rather than order further findings).

35. Switzer Bros., Inc. v. Locklin, 297 F.2d 39 (7th Cir.1961), cert. denied 369 U.S. 851. See Note, The Effect of an Omitted Special Finding of Fact, 33 Ind.L.J. 273 (1958).

36. Clinkenbeard v. Central Southwest Oil Corp., 526 F.2d 649 (5th Cir.1976); Burkhard v. Burkhard, 175 F.2d 593 (10th Cir.1948).

37. Rucker v. Dalton, 598 P.2d 1336 (Utah 1979); Daughtry v. Jet Aeration Co., 91 Wn.2d 704, 592 P.2d 631 (1979); Whitney v. Lea, 134 Vt. 591, 367 A.2d 683 (1976).

38. See Pullman–Standard v. Swint, 456 U.S. 273, 102 S.Ct. 1781, 72 L.Ed.2d 66 (1982); Gomez v. City of Watsonville, 863 F.2d 1407 (9th Cir.1988), cert. denied 489 U.S. 1080.

§ 12.3

1. "The vital justification for the institution of directed verdicts is found in the need to provide at least some minimal device for preserving the integrity of the legal rules given by the judges." Cooper, Directions for Directed Verdicts: A Compass for Federal Courts, 55 Minn.L.Rev. 903, 907 (1971).

For a fuller exploration of the operation of these motions in federal courts, see 9A C. Wright & A. Miller, Civil 2d §§ 2521–40.

2. See U.S. v. Vahlco Corp., 720 F.2d 885, 889 (5th Cir.1983) (directed verdict for plaintiff at close of plaintiff's evidence upheld though irregular procedure disapproved since "where there is any doubt at all as to the propriety of a directed verdict, district courts should not jump the gun but should wait until both sides have presented their evidence before ruling on motions for directed verdict"). See also Steffen, The Prima Facie Case in Non–Jury Trials, 27 U.Chi.L.Rev. 94 (1959).

3. "Hence in the end, a kind of intuitive evaluation must be made, that the verdict does not or would not shock the judicial sense of justice." Christie v. Callahan, 124 F.2d 825 (D.C.Cir.1941).

the directed verdict acts somewhat like a delayed summary judgment motion[4] in that it determines that there are no genuine issues of fact that need to be sent to the jury. Similarly, a JNOV motion may be viewed as a delayed directed verdict because it is made after the verdict is rendered and seeks a judgment contrary to the verdict on the ground that there was insufficient evidence for the jury to find as it did.[5] A 1991 amendment to the federal rule renamed the motion for a directed verdict and the motion for a judgment notwithstanding the verdict as motions for judgment as a matter of law.[6] The change in terminology underscores the common identity of the two motions, which merely are made at different times in the proceeding.

The primary use of these motions is when there is some overriding issue of law that would indicate the jury verdict is erroneous. Because the result of a successful motion for directed verdict or JNOV is to take a case away from the jury, courts exercise great care in deciding when any of these motions can and should be used so as not to intrude improperly into the jury's domain.[7]

A good example of the sensitivity to the line dividing judge and jury functions is found in federal cases involving state provisions requiring certain issues to be given to the jury. Generally when there is no evidence submitted on a question of contributory negligence, a federal judge may withdraw that issue from the jury. This is true even when the constitution of the state whose law is being applied provides that the defense of contributory negligence is a question of fact to be decided by the jury.[8] As the Supreme Court noted in Herron v. Southern Pacific Company,[9] the power to direct a verdict is part of the essential character of a federal court.

> In a trial by jury in a federal court, the judge is not a mere moderator, but is the governor of the trial for the purpose of assuring its proper conduct and of determining questions of law. This discharge of the judicial function as at common law is an essential factor in the process for which the Federal Constitution provides.[10]

---

4. See §§ 9.1–9.3, above, on summary judgment.

5. See Hauter v. Zogarts, 14 Cal.3d 104, 120 Cal.Rptr. 681, 534 P.2d 377 (1975).

6. Fed.Rule Civ.Proc. 50. Despite the difference in nomenclature, the procedure remains unchanged. Thus, throughout this chapter references to directed verdicts or JNOVs should be taken to include the now federally-named judgment as a matter of law.

7. For example, the Ninth Circuit has held that before ruling on a motion for judgment as a matter of law, the trial court must advise opposing parties of the deficiencies in their proof and give them the opportunity to present additional evidence on the dispositive facts and this duty is mandatory especially when pro se litigants are involved. Waters v. Young, 100 F.3d 1437 (9th Cir.1996).

8. Sax v. Kopelman, 96 Ariz. 394, 396 P.2d 17, 19 (1964). See also Thoe v. Chicago, M. & St. P. Ry. Co., 181 Wis. 456, 195 N.W. 407 (1923).

9. 283 U.S. 91, 51 S.Ct. 383, 75 L.Ed. 857 (1931).

10. 283 U.S. at 95, 51 S.Ct. at 384. How this characterization of the power to direct a verdict influences the question of what law governs in federal diversity actions is discussed at notes 58–62, below.

Before turning to a discussion of the standards governing directed verdict and JNOV motions, it is important to consider how the courts have reconciled the use of these devices with the right to jury trial. The major constitutional justification for these procedures is that analogous devices existed at common law. Since the Seventh Amendment to the United States Constitution and comparable provisions in state constitutions preserve the right to jury trial as it existed at common law,[11] the existence of mechanisms allowing similar judicial control at that time is seen as justifying the modern day procedures.[12] In other words, the presence of historical analogs supports the constitutionality of modern practice. But two caveats must be added.

First, the historic jury control devices—the demurrer to the evidence, nonsuit, and a motion for new trial—differ in some major respects from modern directed verdict and JNOV motions.[13] The demurrer to the evidence, like many motions at common law, required the moving party to take some risks. The movant asserted that all the evidence, viewed in the opposing party's favor, was insufficient to create an issue for the jury. If the court disagreed, it did not merely deny the motion, it entered judgment for the opponent! In that way, litigants were discouraged from using the device unless they were quite certain of succeeding, and the court's opportunities for taking the case from the jury consequently were limited.[14] The motion for nonsuit, conversely, was more gentle than the modern directed verdict in that it did not preclude the plaintiff from suing again.[15] Similarly, the new trial motion did not erode the jury's role because its grant meant that another jury would hear the case.

Despite these differences, the United States Supreme Court has ruled that the use of a directed verdict motion in the federal courts comports with the Seventh Amendment.[16] According to the Court, the important fact is that at common law there was some mechanism by which the judge could determine that the evidence was insufficient for the jury to consider.[17] Further, a directed verdict motion does not

---

11. See §§ 11.3–11.7, above, for a discussion of the right to jury trial.

12. See Smith, The Power of the Judge to Direct a Verdict: Section 457–a of the New York Civil Practice Act, 24 Colum.L.Rev. 111 (1924), tracing the various analogs to directed verdicts in England and in the states.

13. See generally J. Thayer, A Preliminary Treatise on Evidence at the Common Law 234–49 (1898); Comment, Trial Practice—Demurrer Upon Evidence as a Device for Taking a Case from the Jury, 44 Mich. L.Rev. 468 (1945).

14. See the discussion in Hopkins v. Nashville, C. & St. L. Ry., 96 Tenn. 409, 34 S.W. 1029 (1896).

15. Di Biase v. Garnsey, 104 Conn. 447, 451, 133 A. 669, 670 (1926). See Lewis

v. Bowen, 208 Ga. 671, 68 S.E.2d 900 (1952).

16. "The Amendment did not bind the federal courts to the exact procedural incidents or details of jury trial according to the common law in 1791 * * *." Galloway v. U.S., 319 U.S. 372, 390, 63 S.Ct. 1077, 1087, 87 L.Ed. 1458 (1943). For a contrary view, see Hackett, Has a Trial Judge of a United States Court the Right to Direct a Verdict?, 24 Yale L.J. 127 (1914).

17. In Galloway v. U.S., 319 U.S. 372, 391 n. 23, 63 S.Ct. 1077, 1087 n. 23, 87 L.Ed. 1458 (1943), the Supreme Court also noted that during the late eighteenth and early nineteenth centuries the nonsuit had transformed into a practice that differed from the directed verdict "only in form."

concede the opponent's right to a judgment if the standard for granting the motion is not met.[18]

The second caveat that should be noted involves the special problem regarding the constitutionality of the judgment notwithstanding the verdict. In the federal courts, the use of the JNOV confronts that clause in the Seventh Amendment stating "no fact tried by a jury, shall be otherwise re-examined in any Court of the United States, than according to the rules of the common law." Here, unlike the directed verdict, however, there do not appear to be any direct common-law analogs to validate the JNOV.[19] Nonetheless, the federal courts have upheld the constitutionality of a JNOV when it can be considered a delayed or renewed directed verdict, for which there is common-law precedent.[20] Notably, because the states are not governed by the Seventh Amendment in establishing jury trial rights in their judicial systems,[21] many allow a JNOV motion to be made without a prior directed verdict motion.[22]

In part because of the characterization of the JNOV as a delayed directed verdict, the procedure surrounding the motion is crucial. Under the Federal Rules and many state provisions, a JNOV motion can be granted only if a directed verdict motion was made prior to submission of the case to the jury,[23] so that the JNOV results from a renewed motion

---

18. See Annot., 68 A.L.R.2d 300 (1959), listing those states using a waiver approach as of that time. Indiana still holds that if both parties move for a directed verdict, the effect is to take the case from the jury. Estes v. Hancock County Bank, 259 Ind. 542, 289 N.E.2d 728 (1972). But most states have abandoned that approach. See Godell v. Johnson, 244 Or. 587, 418 P.2d 505 (1966); Smyser, Rule 50(a) Directed Verdict: Its Function and Criteria in South Dakota, 19 S.D.L.Rev. 39 (1974).

Prior to its amendment in 1991, Federal Rule 50(a) explicitly provided that if a directed verdict motion was denied, the movant could offer evidence in response to the opponent without having reserved a right to do so. That language was omitted in the 1991 revision as being unnecessary because "only the antiquities of directed verdict practice suggest that it might have been" a waiver of jury trial rights to so move. See the Advisory Committee Notes to the 1991 amendments to Rule 50, reprinted in 134 F.R.D. 679, 684.

19. At common law there was something called a motion to arrest the judgment. Although superficially this appears similar to the modern JNOV it was addressed to the sufficiency of the pleadings, not the evidence produced at trial. See Bond v. Dustin, 112 U.S. 604, 608, 5 S.Ct. 296, 298, 28 L.Ed. 835 (1884).

20. "At common law there was a well-established practice of reserving questions of law arising during trials by jury and of taking verdicts subject to the ultimate ruling on the questions reserved * * *." Baltimore & Carolina Line, Inc. v. Redman, 295 U.S. 654, 659, 55 S.Ct. 890, 892, 79 L.Ed. 1636 (1935). The Redman Court distinguished the earlier decision of Slocum v. New York Life Ins. Co., 228 U.S. 364, 33 S.Ct. 523, 57 L.Ed. 879 (1913), in which a JNOV for defendant had been overturned, even though the Court agreed that the evidence legally was insufficient to support plaintiff's claim. The Court noted that the problem in Slocum requiring reversal was that the trial court had not reserved its decision on the directed verdict, so that there was no historic support for invading the verdict. Only a new trial could be ordered.

21. See § 11.7, above.

22. E.g., West's Ann.Cal.Code Civ. Proc. § 629; Colo.Rule Civ.Proc., Rule 59(d); N.Y.—McKinney's CPLR 4404(a).

23. See, e.g., Battle v. Yancey Bros. Co., 157 Ga.App. 277, 277 S.E.2d 280 (1981).

Although the 1991 amendments to Federal Rule 50 submitted a single appellation—motion for judgment as a matter of law—for both directed verdict and JNOV motions, the use of the motion after the case has been submitted to the jury is limited to circumstances in which the party is renewing a motion made earlier, thus pre-

requesting the court to evaluate the sufficiency of the evidence. If the party fails to make a directed verdict motion, a JNOV is not available.[24] Further, a post-trial motion for judgment can be granted only on grounds advanced in the earlier motion.[25] Finally, even if a directed verdict motion was made, a JNOV motion typically cannot be entered sua sponte.[26] The rationale for this latter limitation is that the formal requirement of a motion provides the opposing party with notice so that she may request a new trial in the alternative.[27]

Despite the fact that the use of both the directed verdict and the JNOV is not deemed to violate constitutional jury trial rights, the misuse or overuse of either device obviously poses a threat to the jury's scope of operation. Thus, a significant problem is determining the proper standard to be used so that the court does not improperly intrude into the jury's sphere. The basic issue presented on either motion is the same—whether the evidence is legally sufficient to allow the jury to decide the case.[28] But what constitutes legal sufficiency?[29] The answer to that question requires an examination of the different formulations the courts have used in testing legal sufficiency, as well as consideration of how the standard relates to the burden of proof and the ability of the parties to present evidence. Courts also have developed various rules of construction that aid in making a determination of legal sufficiency.

Basically, there are two different formulations of the directed verdict standard: the scintilla test and the substantial evidence test.[30] Under the scintilla test, the judge will deny the motion and refer the case to the

serving the constitutional peg on which the Supreme Court relied in sustaining the JNOV. Fed.Rule Civ.Proc. 50(b).

24. Neely v. Martin K. Eby Constr. Co., 386 U.S. 317, 87 S.Ct. 1072, 18 L.Ed.2d 75 (1967).

As amended in 1991, Federal Rule 50(a)(2) specifically requires that the "motion shall specify the judgment sought and the law and the facts on which the moving party is entitled to the judgment." In this way courts cannot avoid the requirement by allowing something less than a formal motion to preserve a party's right to move for a judgment as a matter of law after the jury verdict is announced.

25. See Kutner Buick, Inc. v. American Motors Corp., 868 F.2d 614 (3d Cir.1989); McCarty v. Pheasant Run, Inc., 826 F.2d 1554, 1556 (7th Cir.1987).

26. Neely v. Martin K. Eby Constr. Co., 386 U.S. 317, 87 S.Ct. 1072, 18 L.Ed.2d 75 (1967); Johnson v. New York, N. H. & H. R.R. Co., 344 U.S. 48, 73 S.Ct. 125, 97 L.Ed. 77 (1952); Cone v. West Virginia Pulp & Paper Co., 330 U.S. 212, 67 S.Ct. 752, 91 L.Ed. 849 (1947). But compare First Safe Deposit Nat. Bank v. Western Union Tel. Co., 337 F.2d 743 (1st Cir.1964). For a

criticism of the Supreme Court decisions on this point, see Louis, Post–Verdict Rulings on the Sufficiency of the Evidence: Neely v. Martin K. Eby Construction Co. Revisited, 1975 Wis.L.Rev. 503.

27. Shaw v. Edward Hines Lumber Co., 249 F.2d 434 (7th Cir.1957) (court allowed to enter a delayed directed verdict when the hearing on that motion was after a verdict for plaintiff and plaintiff had an opportunity to seek a new trial).

28. See the thorough exposition of the various directed verdict standards in Cooper, Directions for Directed Verdicts: A Compass for Federal Courts, 55 Minn. L.Rev. 903 (1971).

29. See the excellent discussion of legal sufficiency in James, Sufficiency of the Evidence and Jury Control Devices Available Before Verdict, 47 Va.L.Rev. 218 (1961).

30. The Supreme Court noted the use of the different standards of proof in Galloway v. U.S., 319 U.S. 372, 395, 63 S.Ct. 1077, 1089, 87 L.Ed. 1458 (1943). For a criticism of Galloway for not providing an adequate test to substitute for the generalization of "substantial evidence," see McBaine, Trial Practice: Directed Verdicts; Federal Rule, 31 Calif.L.Rev. 454 (1943).

jury if there is any—"a scintilla of"—evidence on which the jury might possibly render a verdict for the nonmovant.[31] At the opposite end of the spectrum, under the substantial evidence test, the court will grant the motion unless there is sufficient or substantial evidence suggesting that the jury might decide for the nonmovant.[32]

The differences between these two standards reflect varying judicial attitudes regarding the importance of avoiding intrusion into the jury's sphere and the perceived need for jury control.[33] These attitudes, in turn, may be shaped, at least in part, in light of the nature of the case and the reasons for giving special respect to the jury's decisional freedom in certain areas.[34] The scintilla test tilts in favor of allowing cases to go to the jury; the substantial evidence test allows the judge much greater authority to intrude. The general trend in the courts has been toward the use of the substantial evidence test and increased court control.[35]

A brief look at one Supreme Court case rejecting the scintilla rule illustrates the difference between the two standards. In Pennsylvania Railroad Company v. Chamberlain,[36] an action was brought alleging that defendant's negligence caused the death of a brakeman. Plaintiff's theory was that the death resulted from a violent collision of a string of railroad cars causing the plaintiff to be run over. Plaintiff's case rested on the testimony of one employee, Bainbridge, who was near the place of the accident and who testified that at one point he saw the car on which the decedent was riding slowing down and other cars behind it gaining speed. Later he heard a loud noise, like a crash, but did not look immediately because loud noises were not uncommon in the railroad yard. Three other employees of the railroad who were on the other cars testified that no collision occurred. The trial court directed a verdict for the defendant and the appellate court reversed finding that there was conflicting testimony so that, under the scintilla test, a jury issue was present. The Supreme Court reversed, rejecting the scintilla rule and

31. Hanson v. Couch, 360 So.2d 942 (Ala.1978); Barber v. Stephenson, 260 Ala. 151, 69 So.2d 251 (1953).

32. E.g., Pennsylvania R. Co. v. Chamberlain, 288 U.S. 333, 53 S.Ct. 391, 77 L.Ed. 819 (1933); Combs v. Meadowcraft, Inc., 106 F.3d 1519 (11th Cir.1997), cert. denied ___ U.S. ___, 118 S.Ct. 685.

33. See the dissenting opinion of Justice Black in Galloway v. U.S., 319 U.S. 372, 396, 63 S.Ct. 1077, 1090, 87 L.Ed. 1458 (1943).

34. For example, in FELA suits the Court has found that Congress has established a clear presumption for jury trial in all but infrequent cases, thus making it harder to obtain a directed verdict. See Rogers v. Missouri Pacific R.R. Co., 352 U.S. 500, 77 S.Ct. 443, 1 L.Ed.2d 493 (1957); Wilkerson v. McCarthy, 336 U.S. 53, 69 S.Ct. 413, 93 L.Ed. 497 (1949). For a

fuller exploration of how the nature of the case may suggest the appropriate level of jury deference, see Cooper, Directions for Directed Verdicts: A Compass for Federal Courts, 55 Minn.L.Rev. 903, 921–27 (1971).

35. Pennsylvania R. Co. v. Chamberlain, 288 U.S. 333, 53 S.Ct. 391, 77 L.Ed. 819 (1933); Gunning v. Cooley, 281 U.S. 90, 50 S.Ct. 231, 74 L.Ed. 720 (1930); Boeing Co. v. Shipman, 411 F.2d 365 (5th Cir.1969) (en banc); Newing v. Cheatham, 15 Cal.3d 351, 124 Cal.Rptr. 193, 540 P.2d 33 (1975). Referring to the scintilla rule as "judicial legend," Professor James comments: "if there ever was such a notion all that remains of it today is its universal repudiation." James, Sufficiency of the Evidence and Jury Control Devices Available Before Verdict, 47 Va.L.Rev. 218, 219 (1961).

36. 288 U.S. 333, 53 S.Ct. 391, 77 L.Ed. 819 (1933).

holding that the trial judge could not allow a verdict based on facts inferred from Bainbridge's testimony when the uncontradicted testimony of unimpeached witnesses indicated that the inferred fact never occurred. There was no conflicting evidence to send to the jury because eyewitnesses denied that a collision occurred and plaintiff offered no direct rebuttal evidence.

As illustrated by Chamberlain, when evaluating whether a particular movant has met the directed verdict standard, the court may be influenced by whether the opposing party has the burden of proof as well as whether the opponent is in a position to present more evidence.[37] If the movant has the burden of proof, then the opponent's task of showing that there is substantial evidence to create an issue for the jury is much easier[38] than when the nonmoving party in meeting the substantial evidence test must show substantial evidence in compliance with his burden at trial.[39] The same would be true under the scintilla standard. Indeed, in some states, a directed verdict cannot be entered if the movant has the burden of proof unless the facts are totally uncontroverted or the parties agree to them.[40] Further, the determination whether the opposing party has sufficient evidence to prevail at trial may be influenced by whether the nonmoving party, who at the time of the directed verdict already has presented all his evidence, is able to present additional evidence.[41]

A good example of how these concerns affect the availability of a directed verdict is found in Galloway v. United States.[42] In Galloway, the plaintiff sued for insurance benefits, claiming total and permanent disability by insanity existing on May 31, 1919, when his yearly renewable term insurance lapsed for nonpayment of the premium. Evidence was introduced at trial showing that plaintiff had entered the Army in 1917, had served in France, during which time he had been hospitalized for influenza and later honorably discharged on April 29, 1919. Additional evidence showed that he had enlisted in the Navy, receiving a bad conduct discharge in July, 1920, had reenlisted in the Army, and then

37. See 9A C. Wright & A. Miller, Civil 2d § 2535. The important effect of the burden of proof on the court's willingness to grant a directed verdict is akin to that on summary judgment. See the discussion in § 9.3, above.

38. "Yet though a motion for directed verdict in favor of the proponent of an issue is cast in the same form as when made by the defending party, it requires the judge to test the body of evidence not for its insufficiency to support a finding, but rather for its overwhelming effect." Mihalchak v. American Dredging Co., 266 F.2d 875, 877 (3d Cir.1959), cert. denied 361 U.S. 901. E.g., Shaw v. Edward Hines Lumber Co., 249 F.2d 434 (7th Cir.1957).

39. See, e.g., Denman v. Spain, 242 Miss. 431, 135 So.2d 195, 197 (1961).

40. Alexander v. Tingle, 181 Md. 464, 30 A.2d 737 (1943). A few state courts also have ruled that a directed verdict cannot be entered for the person having the burden of proof even if the evidence is uncontradicted as long as it is oral. See Hoerath v. Sloan's Moving & Storage Co., 305 S.W.2d 418, 421 (Mo.1957). For a criticism and analysis of this problem, see Comment, Directing the Verdict in Favor of the Party with the Burden of Proof, 50 N.C.L.Rev. 843 (1972); Note, Directing a Verdict in Favor of the Party with the Burden of Proof, 16 Wake Forest L.Rev. 607 (1980).

41. See, e.g., Brown v. Maryland Cas. Co., 111 Vt. 30, 11 A.2d 222 (1940).

42. 319 U.S. 372, 63 S.Ct. 1077, 87 L.Ed. 1458 (1943).

deserted in May, 1922. Testimony regarding his behavior during that time was introduced. Finally, medical testimony was produced showing that he was diagnosed by the Veterans' Administration in 1930 as a "moron," in 1931 as having a psychosis, and finally in 1934, as a manic-depressive who at the time of trial was totally insane. An expert witness testified that in his judgment, based on this evidence, Galloway was born with an inherent disability and that the strain of his time in France brought on a total collapse, resulting in permanent disability. The trial court granted a directed verdict for the government and the appellate court and the Supreme Court affirmed.

As reviewed by the Supreme Court, Galloway clearly had shown his disability some time before 1930, but had failed to show that it became total and permanent prior to May, 1919. That conclusion could be reached only by drawing an inference from his failure to produce substantial evidence of his activities between 1922 and 1930, other than the fact that he was married some time during that period. Justice Rutledge, commented for the Court: "Inference is capable of bridging many gaps. But not, in these circumstances, one so wide and deep as this."[43] The Court particularly noted that plaintiff had the burden to show continuous disability and that the omission of evidence for that eight year period "was not one of oversight or inability to secure proof."[44] Thus, the evidence presented was legally insufficient to allow the jury to consider entering a verdict for the plaintiff.

When evaluating the propriety of a directed verdict or JNOV the courts also use various rules of construction that bear on whether the standard has been met. Typically, the judge must view the evidence in the light most favorable to the nonmoving party in order to determine whether there is sufficient evidence to raise a jury issue.[45] This means that the nonmovant has the benefit of all the legitimate inferences that may be drawn from the evidence.[46] The case should go to the jury even if the underlying facts are not disputed as long as conflicting inferences may be drawn from those facts.[47] Although there are some difficulties in determining whether a particular inference is legitimate and thus entitled to be drawn, no quantitative test has evolved. As noted by the Supreme Court in Lavender v. Kurn,[48]

---

43. 319 U.S. at 386, 63 S.Ct. at 1085.

44. Ibid. The Court noted, for example, that the wife did not testify although she had married the plaintiff during that period and presumably would be aware of his conduct during at least some of that time.

45. Gunning v. Cooley, 281 U.S. 90, 50 S.Ct. 231, 74 L.Ed. 720 (1930); Jones v. Associated Universities, Inc., 870 F.Supp. 1180, 1192 (E.D.N.Y.1994); Parham v. Dell Rapids Township, 80 S.D. 281, 122 N.W.2d 548 (1963).

46. Berry v. U.S., 312 U.S. 450, 61 S.Ct. 637, 85 L.Ed. 945 (1941); Gunning v. Cooley, 281 U.S. 90, 50 S.Ct. 231, 74 L.Ed.

720 (1930); Gardner v. Buerger, 82 F.3d 248 (8th Cir.1996).

47. Rogers v. Missouri Pacific R.R. Co., 352 U.S. 500, 506–07, 77 S.Ct. 443, 448–49, 1 L.Ed.2d 493 (1957); Planters Mfg. Co. v. Protection Mut. Ins. Co., 380 F.2d 869 (5th Cir.1967), cert. denied 389 U.S. 930; Lane v. Scott, 220 Va. 578, 260 S.E.2d 238 (1979), cert. denied 446 U.S. 986; Whitaker v. Borntrager, 233 Ind. 678, 122 N.E.2d 734 (1954); Dimock State Bank v. Boehnen, 46 S.D. 50, 190 N.W. 485 (1922).

48. 327 U.S. 645, 66 S.Ct. 740, 90 L.Ed. 916 (1946). Lavender does not involve a directed verdict or JNOV, but presents

Whenever facts are in dispute or the evidence is such that fair-minded men may draw different inferences, a measure of speculation and conjecture is required on the part of those whose duty it is to settle the dispute by choosing what seems to them to be the most reasonable inference. Only when there is a complete absence of probative facts to support the conclusion reached does a reversible error appear.[49]

Although all courts recognize this liberal construction principle, it is not applied uniformly. In some cases, the moving party's evidence is not considered and whether sufficient evidence is presented is determined only on the basis of the evidence introduced by the opponent.[50] This approach raises an almost impenetrable barrier to directed verdicts. Consequently, most judges consider all the evidence that has been presented at the time of the motion, resolving any credibility problems in favor of the nonmovant.[51]

The application of the directed verdict or JNOV standard has its greatest difficulty when questions of credibility are raised, because assessing the credibility of witnesses is clearly within the jury's domain.[52] Nonetheless, an assertion that credibility is at issue, resting alone, will not suffice to prevent the court from directing a verdict if all of the objective or indisputable evidence indicates that a particular piece of testimony is incredible.[53] Conversely, uncontradicted, disinterested testimony may support the entry of a directed verdict because the jury should not be allowed to disbelieve that testimony.[54] The court is not weighing the evidence under these circumstances, rather it is determining that there is not sufficient evidence to create an issue of credibility. Thus, the propriety of a directed verdict seems clear.

the question whether the appellate court can overturn a jury's verdict because the court draws different inferences from the evidence presented. See also § 11.2 at nn. 4–5, above.

49. 327 U.S. at 653, 66 S.Ct. at 744 (per Murphy, J.).

50. See Note, The Motion for a Directed Verdict in Indiana: An Evaluation of Present Standards, 32 Ind.L.J. 238 (1957).

The notion that only the opponent's evidence should be considered is supported by a statement of Justice Black in Wilkerson v. McCarthy, 336 U.S. 53, 69 S.Ct. 413, 93 L.Ed. 497 (1949). But that statement has been criticized as overly broad and may be limited to FELA cases in which the standard for obtaining a directed verdict is much higher than in other cases. See Cooper, Directions for Directed Verdicts: A Compass for Federal Courts, 55 Minn. L.Rev. 903 (1971); Currie, Thoughts on Directed Verdicts and Summary Judgments, 45 U.Chi.L.Rev. 72 (1977).

51. Simblest v. Maynard, 427 F.2d 1 (2d Cir.1970); Boeing Co. v. Shipman, 411 F.2d 365 (5th Cir.1969) (en banc).

52. See the excellent discussion of this problem in Ferdinand v. Agricultural Ins. Co., 22 N.J. 482, 126 A.2d 323 (1956). See Gunning v. Cooley, 281 U.S. 90, 50 S.Ct. 231, 74 L.Ed. 720 (1930); Cooper, Directions for Directed Verdicts: A Compass for Federal Courts, 55 Minn.L.Rev. 903 (1971); Note, The Power of the Court to Determine Witness Credibility: A Problem in Directing a Verdict for the Proponent of the Evidence, 107 U.Pa.L.Rev. 217 (1958).

53. See Pennsylvania R.R. Co. v. Chamberlain, 288 U.S. 333, 53 S.Ct. 391, 77 L.Ed. 819 (1933).

54. See Annot., Credibility of Witness Giving Uncontradicted Testimony as Matter for Court or Jury, 62 A.L.R.2d 1191 (1958). For the arguments in support of a directed verdict under these circumstances, see Cooper, Directions for Directed Verdicts: A Compass for Federal Courts, 55 Minn.L.Rev. 903, 930–40 (1971).

Less clear, however, is the question whether a directed verdict may be entered because the evidence presented is inherently incredible or because some of the evidence of physical facts suggests that other testimony is incredible and should be ignored. Some courts seem to be willing to make this assessment;[55] others refuse to do so.[56] Again this difference reflects, at least in part, the particular judge's deference to the jury.[57]

Given the somewhat different formulations of the standards for testing the legal sufficiency of the evidence, as well as varying approaches to construing the evidence, one question that must be considered is whether federal courts when sitting in diversity of citizenship are bound to apply the directed verdict standards of the state in which they are sitting.[58] It is useful to consider this question in two different contexts. The first is when the state, by statute or constitution, provides that a particular issue is solely within the purview of the jury to decide. Does this state law limit or alter the federal court's ability to direct a verdict in an appropriate case? As already indicated, the answer to this question is clear: state law "cannot alter the essential character or function of a federal court."[59]

In the second context, however, federal court authority is less clear.[60] This occurs when the state standards for granting a directed verdict differ from the federal standard. Some courts have ruled that federal law governs, viewing the power to enter a directed verdict or JNOV as a decision related to the judge-jury relationship and thus inherently federal.[61] Yet other courts find that questions relating to the sufficiency of the evidence are so bound up with the substantive rights at issue that state law must control.[62]

55. See Simblest v. Maynard, 427 F.2d 1 (2d Cir.1970); Lohmann v. Wabash R. Co., 364 Mo. 910, 269 S.W.2d 885 (1954); Potter v. Robinson, 233 Iowa 479, 9 N.W.2d 457 (1943); Nucci v. Colorado & S. Ry. Co., 63 Colo. 582, 169 P. 273 (1917). See also Gianotta v. New York, N. H. & H. R. Co., 98 Conn. 743, 120 A. 560 (1923).

56. See, e.g., Kircher v. Atchison, T. & S. F. Ry. Co., 32 Cal.2d 176, 195 P.2d 427 (1948).

57. See the dissenting opinion of Judge Scott in Nucci v. Colorado & S. Ry. Co., 63 Colo. 582, 602, 169 P. 273, 281 (1917).

58. For a discussion of the governing law in federal courts generally, see §§ 4.1–4.7, above.

59. Herron v. Southern Pac. Co., 283 U.S. 91, 94, 51 S.Ct. 383, 384, 75 L.Ed. 857 (1931).

60. The Supreme Court has declined to pass on this question. See Mercer v. Theriot, 377 U.S. 152, 84 S.Ct. 1157, 12 L.Ed.2d 206 (1964); Dick v. New York Life Ins. Co., 359 U.S. 437, 79 S.Ct. 921, 3 L.Ed.2d 935 (1959). And the lower courts are not in agreement. See notes 61–62, below.

In some cases the courts acknowledge the conflicting authority and apply both standards finding that, although different, both would be met in the particular case. E.g., Simblest v. Maynard, 427 F.2d 1 (2d Cir.1970); Seven Provinces Ins. Co. v. Commerce & Industry Ins. Co., 65 F.R.D. 674 (W.D.Mo.1975).

61. "Federal courts must be able to control the fact-finding processes by which the rights of litigants are determined * * *. Of course, we do not contend that this control will not affect state-created rights in some cases. Ultimately, however, the integrity of our fact-finding processes must outweigh considerations of uniformity." Boeing Co. v. Shipman, 411 F.2d 365, 369–70 (5th Cir.1969) (en banc). See Oldenburg v. Clark, 489 F.2d 839, 841 (10th Cir.1974).

62. Pittsburgh–Des Moines Steel Co. v. Brookhaven Manor Water Co., 532 F.2d 572 (7th Cir.1976); Thompson v. Illinois Cent. R.R. Co., 423 F.2d 1257 (6th Cir.1970).

For the most part this discussion has treated directed verdict and JNOV motions interchangeably, recognizing the latter as differing from the former mainly in their timing. This fact raises a question, which is whether there is any particular function served by the judgment notwithstanding the verdict that is not addressed by the directed verdict? The answer is yes. First, the very availability of a JNOV encourages the judge to ease back on granting the directed verdict; in most cases the verdict will be the same as the judge would have directed because the jury should agree that the evidence does not support a verdict for the opposing party. If the judge's conclusion and the jury's disposition disagree, the court still can impose the rule of law by granting of JNOV. By waiting, the judge avoids disputes about the propriety of a directed verdict, as well as appeals from its grant, and also defers to the jury. In addition, the judge may not be in as good a position to decide whether the evidence is sufficient to warrant judgment as a matter of law when a directed verdict motion is made as will be the case by the time the jury verdict is rendered.[63]

Judges also may be inclined to prefer ruling on a JNOV rather than a directed verdict because of the additional savings that will occur if that ruling is appealed and overturned.[64] In the case of an erroneous directed verdict, judgment cannot be entered for the opponent; all the appellate court can determine is that there was sufficient evidence to send the case to a jury, not who should prevail. An entire new trial will be necessary. In the case of an improperly entered JNOV, the appellate court may reverse and instruct the district court to enter judgment on the jury's verdict.[65] It is worth noting, however, that the ultimate savings in trial time on a JNOV may be offset by the fact that more appeals may be taken from JNOV rulings than from directed verdicts simply because the difference between the judge and jury on the sufficiency of the evidence is only speculative in the latter context.

The different timing of the JNOV motion, coming after the close of all the evidence, also allows the court to consider whether instead of granting a judgment contrary to the jury's verdict, a new trial should be ordered.[66] This will occur, for example, if the court determines that the evidence was not sufficient to allow the winning party under the jury's

---

63. Referring to its historical analog, the Supreme Court in Baltimore & Carolina Line, Inc. v. Redman, 295 U.S. 654, 660, 55 S.Ct. 890, 893, 79 L.Ed. 1636 (1935), said: "Fragmentary references to the origin and basis of the practice indicate that it came to be supported on the theory that it gave better opportunity for considered ruling, made new trials less frequent, and commanded such general approval that parties litigant assented to its application as a matter of course." Recognizing these advantages, Virginia procedure provides that the judge cannot enter a directed verdict. Va. Code 1950, § 8.01–378. Only a JNOV is permissible. Va.Code 1950, § 8.01–430.

64. These advantages of a JNOV have been recognized by some appellate courts. E.g., Jamesbury Corp. v. Litton Industrial Products, Inc., 839 F.2d 1544, 1550 (Fed. Cir.1988), cert. denied 488 U.S. 828; Campbell v. Oliva, 424 F.2d 1244, 1251–52 (6th Cir.1970). A directed verdict saves the time usually spent in charging the jury and in jury deliberations, however. There really is no way to know which is more efficient.

65. Dace v. ACF Industries, Inc., 722 F.2d 374, 379 n. 9 (8th Cir.1983).

66. For a discussion of the standards for granting a new trial, see §§ 12.4–12.5, below.

verdict to prevail, but that a new trial might allow that party to fill some gaps in the evidence.[67] Of course, if the court concludes that the evidence is legally insufficient even though the opposing party has produced a complete case, then a new trial would be wasted and a JNOV should be entered.

The availability of a new trial acts to undercut the potential severity of the trial judge's decision regarding the sufficiency of the evidence and further avoids any undue intrusion into the jury process because the parties may have a jury trial in the second suit.[68] Thus, it generally is held that the court may order a new trial, even if the party seeking a JNOV has not requested a new trial in the alternative.[69] Further, in the federal courts, if the judge grants a JNOV, the party against whom it is rendered then may move for a new trial instead.[70] The most common practice is for the losing party at trial to make simultaneous motions for JNOV and new trial.[71]

The last matter that must be considered is the availability and scope of appellate review of directed verdict and JNOV rulings. In a final-judgment-rule jurisdiction, such as the federal courts, the grant of either motion results in the entry of a judgment and may be appealed immediately. The denial of a JNOV also results in the court entering judgment on the jury's verdict and thus an immediate appeal may be taken. When a directed verdict is denied, however, that decision is interlocutory and appeal must wait until a judgment on the merits is reached.[72]

Appealability becomes somewhat complicated when the trial judge has considered an alternative motion for new trial with a JNOV motion.[73] Although the denial of a new trial results in a judgment that is final, the grant of such a motion typically does not.[74] Nonetheless, in order to avoid piecemeal appeals and allow the appellate court to decide whether the case should be terminated or allowed to proceed to a second trial, the federal rules and similar state provisions, generally provide that if a new trial motion is granted, but only as an alternative to the grant of a JNOV motion, then both rulings may be appealed immediate-

---

67. See Seven Provinces Ins. Co. v. Commerce & Industry Ins. Co., 65 F.R.D. 674 (W.D.Mo.1975), discussing the difference between the inquiry on a motion for a new trial and on a JNOV motion when both are made on grounds of insufficient evidence.

68. See § 12.4 at n. 27, below.

69. See, e.g., Meadows v. State Univ. of New York at Oswego, 160 F.R.D. 8 (N.D.N.Y.1995). The ground for granting a new trial must be sufficiency of the evidence, not some other error, however. Peterman v. Chicago, R. I. & Pacific R.R. Co., 493 F.2d 88 (8th Cir.1974), cert. denied 417 U.S. 947. Further, if a JNOV is not warranted, then the court cannot grant a new trial unless there has been a motion for new

trial. Jackson v. Wilson Trucking Corp., 243 F.2d 212 (D.C.Cir.1957), noted 71 Harv. L.Rev. 552 (1958).

70. Fed.Civ.Proc.Rule 50(c)(2).

71. When the court is confronted with joint motions for JNOV and new trial, both based on insufficient evidence, it must rule on both motions and cannot refuse to rule on the new trial motion on the ground that that is subsumed in the JNOV. Mays v. Pioneer Lumber Corp., 502 F.2d 106 (4th Cir.1974), cert. denied 420 U.S. 927. See Fed.Civ.Proc.Rule 50(c)(1).

72. See § 13.1, below.

73. See 9A C. Wright & A. Miller, Civil 2d § 2540.

74. See § 12.4 at n. 55, below.

ly.[75] If a new trial is granted and the JNOV motion is denied, then the case must proceed to a new trial and the denial of the JNOV cannot be reviewed until after the new trial has concluded.[76] As a practical matter this usually means that there is no appellate review of that ruling because it is difficult to show that the denial, even if erroneous, had a prejudicial effect in the second trial. Of course in jurisdictions in which the grant of a new trial is an appealable order,[77] its joinder with a JNOV motion does not pose these problems; either ruling may be appealed on its own or together.

The presence of both new trial and JNOV rulings before the appellate court also affects the appellate court's options.[78] Stated briefly, if the JNOV and new trial motions were denied, then the appeal is from the judgment entered on the jury's verdict and the court should affirm if it determines that those post-trial motions properly were denied. However, if the court decides that the original judgment is erroneous and should be reversed, it has two choices: it may reverse and order a new trial,[79] or if a new trial does not seem appropriate, it may direct the entry of a JNOV.[80]

If an appeal is taken after the trial judge granted a JNOV and made a conditional order for a new trial, the reviewing court, if it determines that the JNOV was improper, generally should remand for a new trial, in accordance with the trial judge's order.[81] The appellate court typically will be heavily influenced by the trial court's willingness to order a new trial conditionally, although it is not bound to follow the trial judge's view. Thus, if it decides that the trial judge erroneously granted the new trial, then it simply may reinstate the original judgment.[82]

Finally, if the parties moved only for a directed verdict or JNOV below and did not join a request for a new trial, the appellate court nonetheless may consider whether a new trial should be ordered if it disagrees with the trial court's denial of the JNOV. This power is particularly important because in some cases the reviewing court will determine that the evidence presented is insufficient legally to support

75. Fed.Civ.Proc.Rule 50(c)(1); West's Ann.Cal.Code Civ.Proc. § 629.

76. Montgomery Ward & Co. v. Duncan, 311 U.S. 243, 254, 61 S.Ct. 189, 196, 85 L.Ed. 147 (1940).

77. See § 12.4 at n. 58, below.

78. See Note, Post–Verdict Motions Under Rule 50: Protecting the Verdict Winner, 53 Minn.L.Rev. 358 (1968), for a thorough review of the Supreme Court's decisions on these questions.

79. The court of appeals may consider whether a new trial is warranted, but it also may exercise its discretion to remand the case to have the trial court pass on the new trial motion in light of its decision that the jury's verdict should not stand. Neely v.

Martin K. Eby Constr. Co., 386 U.S. 317, 87 S.Ct. 1072, 18 L.Ed.2d 75 (1967). See Louis, Post–Verdict Rulings on the Sufficiency of the Evidence: Neely v. Martin K. Eby Construction Co. Revisited, 1975 Wis.L.Rev. 503.

80. Neely v. Martin K. Eby Constr. Co., 386 U.S. 317, 322, 87 S.Ct. 1072, 1076, 18 L.Ed.2d 75 (1967); Montgomery Ward & Co. v. Duncan, 311 U.S. 243, 61 S.Ct. 189, 85 L.Ed. 147 (1940).

81. Federal Rule 50(c)(1) provides that "the new trial shall proceed unless the appellate court has otherwise ordered."

82. See, e.g., Berner v. British Commonwealth Pacific Airlines, Ltd., 346 F.2d 532 (2d Cir.1965), cert. denied 382 U.S. 983.

the verdict, but it will not be certain whether other evidence might exist that would allow the winning party to retain the verdict. In that event, the grant of a JNOV would be inappropriate.[83] Further, in many cases the trial judge will be in a better position to consider whether a new trial is warranted, and the appellate court merely may reverse the JNOV denial and remand the case to have the trial judge pass upon the propriety of a new trial.[84] This necessarily is a very cumbersome process and explains further why parties are encouraged to file simultaneous JNOV and new trial motions so that the appellate court will have the benefit of the trial judge's insights and can avoid piecemeal review.

§ 12.4 Motions for New Trial

All American judicial systems provide some means by which a party who is dissatisfied with the first trial in a civil case may request a new trial.[1] Although errors that occurred during the trial may be asserted on appeal,[2] they also may present the basis for obtaining a new trial in the trial court.[3] The new trial motion gives the judge the opportunity to correct any errors that occurred, avoiding appellate reversal. The trial judge, who necessarily is in a better position to know what happened than the appellate court, can assess the entire proceeding and take into account the cumulative effect of various rulings or courtroom occurrences.

Given the important corrective role of new trial motions, the discretion granted to the court is exceedingly broad.[4] The only clear limitation is one of time; most procedural rules have rigid timing restrictions in which new trial motions must be made[5]—typically 10 days after judgment has been entered. Failure to move within the period is fatal.[6] Most

83. Iacurci v. Lummus Co., 387 U.S. 86, 87 S.Ct. 1423, 18 L.Ed.2d 581 (1967).

84. Iacurci v. Lummus Co., 387 U.S. 86, 87 S.Ct. 1423, 18 L.Ed.2d 581 (1967). But compare Mays v. Pioneer Lumber Corp., 502 F.2d 106 (4th Cir.1974), cert. denied 420 U.S. 927 (when trial judge erroneously granted JNOV and refused to rule on new trial motion, appellate court reversed and ordered verdict to be reinstated).

§ 12.4

1. See generally 11 C. Wright, A. Miller & M. Kane, Civil 2d §§ 2801–21.

2. Some jurisdictions require a new trial motion to be made as a prerequisite to appeal. E.g., Vernon's Ann.Tex.Rules Civ. Proc., Rule 324.

3. In some states, all motions for post-trial relief are combined to simplify the methods for seeking relief from judgments. Thus, a single motion can seek a JNOV and a new trial, and the same procedure applies. E.g., N.Y.—McKinney's CPLR 4404; 42

Purdon's Penn.Statutes, Rule of Civil Procedure 227.1.

4. The trial judge's decision on the new trial motion will be reversed only for an abuse of discretion. See text at notes 59–62, below. Further, the question of what constitutes reversible error on appeal often is affected by the trial judge's ruling on a new trial motion. This impact is heightened in jurisdictions that require a new trial motion as a prerequisite for an appeal. See, e.g., Evans v. Wilkinson, 419 P.2d 275 (Okl. 1966); Martin v. Opdyke Agency, Inc., 156 Colo. 316, 398 P.2d 971 (1965).

5. E.g., Fed.Civ.Proc.Rule 59(b).

6. See Ehrler v. Ehrler, 126 Cal.App.3d 147, 178 Cal.Rptr. 642 (1981) (15 day period); Seale v. Seale, 339 So.2d 1028 (Ala.Civ. App.1976), cert. denied 339 So.2d 1029 (30 day period). Fed.Civ.Proc.Rule 6(b) specifically provides that the time for making a new trial motion cannot be enlarged by the court. For an interesting case, see Hulson v. Atchison, Topeka & Santa Fe Ry. Co., 289 F.2d 726 (7th Cir.1961), cert. denied 368 U.S. 835.

procedural rules also authorize the court to order a new trial sua sponte, at least within that same time period.[7] This is in keeping with the notion that this device allows the judge to correct any errors that occurred, thereby avoiding a time-consuming appeal and assuring a just and appropriate result.[8]

But the exercise of the new trial power must be used cautiously. No one would assert that the trial process is a scientific one or that a just result may be achieved only if no errors are made. To order a new trial is costly to the parties and to the judicial system.[9] Thus, the question is whether any errors have been committed that singly or taken together may have prejudiced the result.[10] Further, a series of new trial orders in jury cases in which the judge's view of the result does not comport with the jury verdicts would be inappropriate.[11] To order repeated new trials could be an intrusion on the institution of jury trial. The right to jury trial would be meaningless if verdicts could stand only if the judge would reach the same result.

A brief look at the grounds that may be asserted as the basis for new trial illustrates the breadth of the device. Under some rules, specific grounds are set out on which the new trial motion must be based.[12] For example, Minnesota Procedural Rule 59.01 lists jury misconduct, newly discovered material evidence and errors of law as reasons for ordering a new trial.[13] Other rules simply authorize the judge to grant a new trial on any ground "heretofore recognized,"[14] thereby allowing the court to consider any error that may have prejudiced the losing party. Using this authority, courts have granted new trials because of prejudicial errors[15]

7. Fed.Civ.Proc.Rule 59(d); Florida Coastal Theatres, Inc. v. Belflower, 159 Fla. 741, 32 So.2d 738 (1947).

8. One question that has arisen is whether the court can consider grounds for granting the motion that were not raised within the time period for filing the motion. In the federal courts, Federal Rule 59(d) was amended in 1966 to make clear the court's power to do so. See Kaplan, Continuing Work of the Civil Committee: 1966 Amendments of the Federal Rules of Civil Procedure (II), 81 Harv.L.Rev. 591, 598 (1968).

9. But cf. Schnapper, Judges Against Juries—Appellate View of Federal Civil Jury Verdicts, 1989 Wis.L.Rev. 237, 313 (the average civil jury trial takes less than three days, whereas the typical appeal of a civil case takes eleven months).

10. See Lewis v. Kepple, 185 F.Supp. 884 (W.D.Pa.1960), affirmed 287 F.2d 409 (3d Cir.1961).

11. See Vernon's Ann.Mo.Stat § 510.330, limiting the right to grant more than one new trial in any given case on the ground that the verdict is against the weight of the evidence.

12. E.g., West's Ann.Cal.Code Civ. Proc. § 657.

13. The trial court is limited in granting a new trial to the grounds listed in the rule. Ginsberg v. Williams, 270 Minn. 474, 135 N.W.2d 213 (1965).

14. Fed.Civ.Proc.Rule 59(a); Vernon's Ann.Mo.Stat. § 510.330.

15. Although theoretically new trial motions may be granted in judge as well as jury trials, see Fed.Civ.Proc.Rule 59(a)(2), the type of errors meriting a new trial typically arise only in jury trials. For example, even if the court erroneously receives certain evidence in a nonjury trial, the judge simply may disregard that evidence when rendering judgment, avoiding the need for a new trial. Thus, it has been suggested that few errors justify a new trial in a nonjury case. See Builders Steel Co. v. Commissioner, 179 F.2d 377 (8th Cir.1950). See also Daigle & Son, Inc. v. Stone, 387 A.2d 1115 (Me.1978). A new trial may be warranted even in a nonjury case, however, if, for example, newly discovered evidence is presented. See 11 C. Wright, A. Miller & M. Kane, Civil 2d § 2804.

in evidentiary rulings[16] or in the jury instructions;[17] for attorney[18] or juror[19] misconduct; because of newly discovered evidence;[20] or because the verdict appears against the weight of the evidence[21] or is legally excessive or inadequate in amount.[22]

New trial rulings involving the sufficiency of the evidence require some special consideration because of the overlap with motions for directed verdicts and for judgments notwithstanding the verdict, both of which also are based on the legal insufficiency of the evidence.[23] The difference is really one of degree because a new trial may be granted even though the insufficiency falls short of that required to support a directed verdict or JNOV motion.[24] The evidence may be such that reasonable people could find as the jury did, but the verdict still may be manifestly against the weight of the evidence.[25] The trial judge on a new trial motion may weigh the evidence and grant a new trial under these circumstances;[26] the judge is not allowed to weigh the evidence on a judgment notwithstanding the verdict and thus could not enter a JNOV under similar circumstances.

Although the judge's power to intrude on the jury's decision is much greater on a new trial motion, the grant of a new trial because of the insufficiency of the evidence does not violate jury trial rights. This is so in part because the impact of the decision is to send the case to a second

---

16. Florida Coastal Theatres, Inc. v. Belflower, 159 Fla. 741, 32 So.2d 738 (1947).

17. See Bateman v. Mnemonics, Inc., 79 F.3d 1532 (11th Cir.1996); Everton v. Blair, 99 Idaho 14, 576 P.2d 585 (1978); Magnani v. Trogi, 70 Ill.App.2d 216, 218 N.E.2d 21 (1966).

18. See Fineman v. Armstrong World Indus., Inc., 980 F.2d 171 (3d Cir.1992), cert. denied 507 U.S. 921; Seimon v. Southern Pacific Transportation, 67 Cal.App.3d 600, 136 Cal.Rptr. 787 (1977); Jangula v. Klocek, 284 Minn. 477, 170 N.W.2d 587 (1969).

19. See § 12.5, below.

20. See Compass Technology, Inc. v. Tseng Lab., Inc., 71 F.3d 1125 (3d Cir. 1995); Scott v. Farrar, 139 Cal.App.3d 462, 188 Cal.Rptr. 823 (1983). To obtain a new trial on this ground, the movant usually must show that he could not have reasonably discovered the evidence prior to trial. See Jones v. Jones, 250 F.2d 454 (9th Cir. 1957).

Newly discovered evidence also may be the ground for a motion for relief from judgment. See § 12.6, below.

21. See the text at nn. 23–26, below.

22. Richardson v. Communications Workers of America, AFL–CIO, 530 F.2d 126 (8th Cir.1976), cert. denied 429 U.S.

824. See Dagnello v. Long Island R.R. Co., 289 F.2d 797 (2d Cir.1961), reviewing all the authorities on this point. Substantial difficulties can arise in determining exactly what constitutes insufficiency, and judges clearly differ on this. See the majority and dissenting opinions in O'Gee v. Dobbs Houses, Inc., 570 F.2d 1084 (2d Cir.1978). In general, it is agreed that a verdict should not be set aside as excessive unless it appears so large that it must have been the result of passion or prejudice. Pistorius v. Prudential Ins. Co., 123 Cal.App.3d 541, 176 Cal.Rptr. 660 (1981); Fruit v. Schreiner, 502 P.2d 133 (Alaska 1972).

23. See § 12.3, above.

24. See § 12.3 at nn. 78–84, above, for a discussion of the standards used when joint motions for a judgment notwithstanding the verdict and for a new trial are made.

25. For a thorough review of federal court standards in assessing new trial motions based on the weight of the evidence, see 11 C. Wright, A. Miller & M. Kane, Civil 2d § 2806.

26. Bevevino v. Saydjari, 574 F.2d 676 (2d Cir.1978); Aetna Cas. & Sur. Co. v. Yeatts, 122 F.2d 350 (4th Cir.1941).

jury.[27] The party whose verdict is eliminated by a JNOV may argue that she has been denied the right to a trial by jury, but the litigant whose verdict is ousted by a motion for new trial can complain only that he gets too much jury trial, not too little. At the same time, courts recognize that the judge is not to grant a new trial lightly, simply because he disagrees with the jury.[28] Too liberal an approach to new trial could intrude improperly on the jury's decisionmaking authority.[29]

In addition to considering whether a new trial is necessary, the court may determine whether the errors that occurred may be cured by ordering only a partial new trial, thereby avoiding some of the expense of a new trial.[30] However, great care must be taken in using this device to ensure that the issues not retried are truly separable from those being resubmitted.[31] Otherwise, the second judgment will remain tainted by the errors of the first trial. Most commonly, partial new trials are used when the tainted issues relate solely to damages, so that a new trial limited to damages is appropriate.[32] By contrast, it has been held that the court should not order a partial new trial solely on liability when an erroneous instruction was given to the jury on the liability standard.[33] The jurors' decision as to the amount of damages to be awarded frequently is inextricably intertwined with their decision on liability so

27. It has been said that the authority to grant a new trial supports the right to jury trial as it protects the jury system from verdicts that are erroneous. Smith v. Times Pub. Co., 178 Pa. 481, 36 A. 296 (1897). See also Capital Traction Co. v. Hof, 174 U.S. 1, 19 S.Ct. 580, 43 L.Ed. 873 (1899).

28. Spurlin v. General Motors Corp., 528 F.2d 612 (5th Cir.1976); Faust v. General Motors Corp., 117 N.H. 679, 377 A.2d 885 (1977); Knecht v. Marzano, 65 Wn.2d 290, 396 P.2d 782 (1964).

See West's Ann.Cal.Code Civ.Proc. § 657, which provides that a new trial based on insufficiency of the evidence shall not be granted "unless after weighing the evidence the court is convinced from the entire record, including reasonable inferences therefrom, that the court or jury clearly should have reached a different verdict or decision." But see McLaughlin v. Broyles, 36 Tenn.App. 391, 397, 255 S.W.2d 1020, 1023 (1952): "The rule in this state is firmly established that the trial court shall exercise the function of a thirteenth juror upon hearing of a motion for new trial; that it is his duty to weigh the evidence and independently determine therefrom whether or not it is sufficient to sustain the verdict."

29. The difficulty in expressing a standard that the judge can apply in these cases is apparent. One suggestion is that the judge may grant a new trial if "having given full respect to the jury's findings, the judge on the entire evidence is left with the definite and firm conviction that a mistake has been committed * * *." 11 C. Wright, A. Miller & M. Kane, Civil 2d § 2806 at 75. This standard is analogous to that used by appellate courts when reviewing a trial court's findings of fact in a nonjury case. See U.S. v. U.S. Gypsum Co., 333 U.S. 364, 395, 68 S.Ct. 525, 542, 92 L.Ed. 746 (1948).

30. Partial new trials are authorized specifically in the federal rules and in many state codes. E.g., Fed.Civ.Proc.Rule 59(a); West's Ann.Cal.Code Civ.Proc. § 662; N.Y.—McKinney's CPLR 4404.

31. Gasoline Prods. Co. v. Champlin Refining Co., 283 U.S. 494, 51 S.Ct. 513, 75 L.Ed. 1188 (1931); Shu–Tao Lin v. McDonnell Douglas Corp., 742 F.2d 45 (2d Cir. 1984); Vizzini v. Ford Motor Co., 569 F.2d 754 (3d Cir.1977); Liodas v. Sahadi, 19 Cal.3d 278, 137 Cal.Rptr. 635, 562 P.2d 316 (1977).

32. E.g., Wagner v. Reading Co., 428 F.2d 289 (3d Cir.1970); Sanders v. Green, 208 F.Supp. 873 (E.D.S.C.1962).

33. Doutre v. Niec, 2 Mich.App. 88, 138 N.W.2d 501 (1965).

A stipulation by counsel that if a new trial is granted as to liability, damages need not be retried is binding and may produce partial new trials on liability alone. See Hutton v. Fisher, 359 F.2d 913 (3d Cir. 1966).

that a new jury should consider both aspects of the case. Similarly, if the judge determines that the amount awarded is legally insufficient because it is too small, a partial new trial on damages may not be appropriate. If it is possible that the verdict was the result of a compromise, then a full new trial must be ordered.[34] On the other hand, if the error appears to be the result of an incorrect instruction on what evidence might be considered in calculating damages, a partial new trial may be appropriate.[35]

When the problem or error in the first proceeding involves the size of the verdict a court can save substantial time and expense by ordering a conditional new trial.[36] Using this power, the court states that it will grant the new trial motion unless the opposing party agrees to accept a specified reduction or increase in the verdict.[37] The power to reduce damages, called remittitur, is recognized by virtually all judicial systems,[38] but the power to increase damages, additur, has not been accepted in all courts.[39] The distinction between the two, at least in the federal courts, is a result of history. Conditional new trial orders have been challenged as violative of constitutional jury trial rights because the judge effectively is supplanting the jury's decision on the amount of damages.

Remittitur clearly existed at common law and thus, insofar as the right to jury trial is tied to history,[40] it is permissible.[41] However, the Supreme Court has ruled that the use of remittitur must be coupled with the option of a new trial in order to comply with the Seventh Amendment. To impose a remittitur without that option would violate the Amendment's re-examination clause.[42] In contrast, there was no common law version of additur. Consequently, the United States Supreme Court in the early case of Dimick v. Schiedt[43] ruled, five-to-four, that the use of

34. See Southern Ry. Co. v. Madden, 235 F.2d 198 (4th Cir.1956), cert. denied 352 U.S. 953; Zerr v. Spokane City Lines, Inc., 58 Wn.2d 196, 361 P.2d 752 (1961); Kinsell v. Hawthorne, 27 Ill.App.2d 314, 169 N.E.2d 678 (1960).

35. See Wagner v. Reading Co., 428 F.2d 289 (3d Cir.1970); Rosa v. City of Chester, Pennsylvania, 278 F.2d 876 (3d Cir.1960).

36. It has been noted that conditional new trial orders are particularly appropriate in complex cases because of the savings for the parties and judicial system. U.S. v. 47.14 Acres of Land, More or Less, Situate in Polk County, Iowa, 674 F.2d 722 (8th Cir.1982). But compare Arnold v. Eastern Air Lines, Inc., 681 F.2d 186 (4th Cir.1982), cert. denied 460 U.S. 1102 (remittitur cannot be used to remedy trial judge's error in allowing pain and suffering to be included in wrongful death award).

37. Evers v. Equifax, Inc., 650 F.2d 793 (5th Cir.1981). See also Comment, Correction of Damage Verdicts by Remittitur and Additur, 44 Yale L.J. 318 (1934).

38. But see Firestone v. Crown Center Redevelopment Corp., 693 S.W.2d 99 (Mo. 1985) (remittitur abolished in Missouri).

39. For a discussion of remittitur and additur in the federal courts, see Sann, Remittitur (and Additur) in Federal Courts: An Evaluation With Suggested Alternatives, 38 Case W.Reserve L.Rev. 157 (1988).

40. See §§ 11.4–11.6, above.

41. In Dimick v. Schiedt, 293 U.S. 474, 55 S.Ct. 296, 79 L.Ed. 603 (1935), Justice Sutherland noted that the practice of remittitur was upheld by Justice Story in Blunt v. Little, 3 Fed.Cas. 760 (C.C.Mass.1822) (No. 1,578) and that although there was reason to doubt Justice Story's conclusion there, it has been accepted as law for so long that the doctrine should not be reviewed.

42. Hetzel v. Prince William County, 523 U.S. 208, 118 S.Ct. 1210, 140 L.Ed.2d 336 (1998).

43. 293 U.S. 474, 55 S.Ct. 296, 79 L.Ed. 603 (1935).

it in the federal courts violates the Seventh Amendment.[44] Although this decision has been criticized as creating a meaningless distinction between the two devices[45] and there is some reason to doubt its continued vitality under more recent Seventh Amendment decisions,[46] it remains controlling today. Nonetheless, many state courts, not bound by the Seventh Amendment, have upheld the constitutionality of additur under state constitutional jury trial provisions.[47]

A major issue when utilizing conditional new trials is determining what amount should be remitted or added.[48] There is no generally accepted formulation of the standard to be applied; different states follow different verbal standards. Among those used, three general formulations can be identified. The judge may set the amount at (1) the legally sufficient minimum the jury could have awarded;[49] (2) the maximum that would have been permitted;[50] or (3) a figure somewhere between these two extremes reflecting what the judge believes the evidence justifies.[51]

The party opposing the new trial motion who is confronted with the conditional new trial order either must accept the judge's figure or be willing to suffer the costs and uncertainties of a new trial. If the opposing party accepts the remittitur or additur, then the new trial

---

44. The Court attempted to justify the different treatment of additur and remittitur by arguing that if the verdict is legally inadequate, both parties are entitled to have a jury properly determine liability and the amount of damages. But when the verdict is excessive and the judge orders remittitur, "what remains is included in the verdict along with the unlawful excess—in that sense that it has been found by the jury—and that the remittitur has the effect of merely lopping off an excrescence." 293 U.S. at 486, 55 S.Ct. at 301.

45. See the dissenting opinion of Justice Stone in Dimick v. Schiedt, 293 U.S. 474, 488, 497, 55 S.Ct. 296, 301, 305, 79 L.Ed. 603 (1935).

46. The Dimick Court insisted that the Seventh Amendment required resort to the rules of common law as they were in 1791, not recognizing that the common law adapted itself to varying conditions. 293 U.S. at 487, 55 S.Ct. at 301. More recent Seventh Amendment cases have seemed to abandon a strictly historical approach. See, e.g., Galloway v. U.S., 319 U.S. 372, 63 S.Ct. 1077, 87 L.Ed. 1458 (1943) (on the constitutionality of directed verdict motions). See generally §§ 11.4–11.6, above, on constitutional jury trial standards.

Compare Gibeau v. Nellis, 18 F.3d 107 (2d Cir.1994), ordering the trial court to enter an award of $1 in nominal damages, when the jury had found liability but awarded no damages, because the civil

rights statute on which the claim was based compelled an award of nominal damages when a substantive constitutional violation was found.

47. See McCall v. Waer, 487 S.W.2d 308 (Tenn.1972); Jehl v. Southern Pacific Co., 66 Cal.2d 821, 59 Cal.Rptr. 276, 427 P.2d 988 (1967) (additur used in FELA suit); Bodon v. Suhrmann, 8 Utah 2d 42, 327 P.2d 826 (1958); Fisch v. Manger, 24 N.J. 66, 130 A.2d 815 (1957). Conditional new trials are codified in California in West's Ann.Cal.Code Civ.Proc. § 662.5.

48. For a thorough examination of all the questions the judge must confront in deciding whether and how to use remittitur, see Note, Remittitur Practice in the Federal Courts, 76 Colum.L.Rev. 299 (1976).

49. Wisconsin used the standard of the lowest amount that a reasonable jury could have awarded until 1960. See Powers v. Allstate Ins. Co., 10 Wis.2d 78, 102 N.W.2d 393 (1960).

50. E.g., Jenkins v. Aquatic Contractors & Engineers, 446 F.2d 520 (5th Cir. 1971).

51. See Maxey v. Freightliner Corp., 722 F.2d 1238 (5th Cir.1984), modified 727 F.2d 350 (1984) (remittitur of all punitive damages in excess of a sum equal to three times actual damages); U.S. v. 47.14 Acres of Land, More or Less, Situate in Polk County, Iowa, 674 F.2d 722 (8th Cir.1982).

motion is denied and the party who sought that ruling, if he is unhappy with the amount set by the trial court, has no alternative but to appeal, claiming that the amount set also is legally improper. Most courts have ruled that a party who accepts the remittitur or additur cannot appeal because he has acquiesced in the judgment.[52] Some courts have rejected this limitation, however,[53] and others have recognized the party's right to cross-appeal if the losing party first appeals.[54]

The preceding discussion illustrates the broad discretion given the trial judge when confronting a new trial motion. In fact, if the judge's decision is to grant a new trial, that determination is virtually unassailable. In most judicial systems, including the federal courts, an order granting a new trial is interlocutory and cannot be appealed until after a final judgment is entered at the conclusion of the second trial.[55] This delay in review necessarily decreases the likelihood of reversal. If the second trial is totally free from prejudicial error, then the appealing party is in the awkward position of seeking to overturn what appears as a fair verdict simply on the ground that the second trial was not necessary because the first trial also was free from prejudicial error.[56] Consequently, in most cases even if it were error to grant a new trial, that error will be deemed harmless or moot by the time appellate review occurs.[57]

Some systems permit the grant of a new trial to be appealed immediately;[58] additionally, if that order is joined with a ruling on a judgment notwithstanding the verdict, an immediate appeal may lie.[59] Even in these circumstances, however, reversals are infrequent.

Appellate courts will reverse a new trial ruling only for an abuse of discretion.[60] Enormous deference is given to the trial judge, at least when

52. See Donovan v. Penn Shipping Co., 429 U.S. 648, 97 S.Ct. 835, 51 L.Ed.2d 112 (1977).

A party may be able to appeal if the court has ordered remittitur unconditionally. See Staplin v. Maritime Overseas Corp., 519 F.2d 969 (2d Cir.1975).

53. U.S. v. 1160.96 Acres of Land, More or Less, in Holmes County, Mississippi, 432 F.2d 910 (5th Cir.1970). In Tennessee, the right to appeal is recognized statutorily. Tenn.Code Ann. § 20–10–101(b)(1).

54. See Jangula v. Klocek, 284 Minn. 477, 170 N.W.2d 587 (1969); Plesko v. City of Milwaukee, 19 Wis.2d 210, 120 N.W.2d 130 (1963). See generally Note, Civil Procedure—Remittitur—Remitting Parties' Right to Cross–Appeal, 49 N.C.L.Rev. 141 (1970).

55. Allied Chem. Corp. v. Daiflon, Inc., 449 U.S. 33, 101 S.Ct. 188, 66 L.Ed.2d 193 (1980) (mandamus not appropriate to obtain review of grant of new trial); Taylor v. Washington Terminal Co., 409 F.2d 145 (D.C.Cir.1969), cert. denied 396 U.S. 835;

Comment, Appellate Review in the Federal Courts of Orders Granting New Trial, 13 Stan.L.Rev. 383 (1961).

56. See, e.g., Evers v. Equifax, Inc., 650 F.2d 793 (5th Cir.1981).

57. Reversals do occur, however. See Duncan v. Duncan, 377 F.2d 49 (6th Cir. 1967), cert. denied 389 U.S. 913.

58. See Rabinowitz, Appellate Review of Trial Court Orders Granting New Trial, 8 Rut.L.Rev. 465 (1953), detailing the trend in the state courts by statute and court decision to allow immediate appeals from orders granting new trials.

59. See § 12.3 at n. 75, above.

60. Browning–Ferris Indus. of Vermont, Inc. v. Kelco Disposal, Inc., 492 U.S. 257, 279, 109 S.Ct. 2909, 2922, 106 L.Ed.2d 219 (1989); O'Gee v. Dobbs Houses, Inc., 570 F.2d 1084 (2d Cir.1978); Hill v. Cherry, 379 So.2d 590 (Ala.1980); In re Green's Estate, 25 Cal.2d 535, 154 P.2d 692 (1944). For a general discussion of the varying decisions regarding the scope of review of new

the basis for a new trial is some form of prejudicial misconduct or error of law, on the theory that the judge was present during the proceedings and thus is in the best position to evaluate the prejudicial effect of what occurred.[61] The appellate court also uses an abuse of discretion standard to review the denial of a new trial motion, although less latitude is given to the trial judge in that context. Reversals of those new trial rulings occur only when the appellate court finds that the trial judge was wrong as a matter of law as to what reasons would support the granting or denial of the motion.[62]

Strong arguments have been raised concerning the propriety of the traditional narrow review standard.[63] Some have urged utilizing more strict scrutiny, at least when the trial judge's decision is based on an evaluation of the weight of the evidence.[64] And some lower courts appeared to be moving toward this latter view.[65] The debate centers on the right to jury trial. Review of the grant of a new trial does not seem to intrude on the jury's decisionmaking authority because it focuses on the propriety of the trial judge's decision to overturn the jury. Review of the denial of a new trial, based on the ground that the evidence was legally sufficient for the jury to find as it did, does require an inquiry into the jury's role, however. And that should be attempted only under the most limited circumstances.

Whatever the merits of these arguments, the importance of utilizing only a narrow review standard when evaluating trial court decisions on motions for new trials was re-emphasized by a 1996 Supreme Court decision, Gasperini v. Center for Humanities, Inc.[66] The case involved the power of the courts to review the size of jury verdicts on grounds of excessiveness. The Court, in an opinion by Justice Ginsburg, ruled that the trial court could apply state law standards to determine what was excessive,[67] but that the appellate court when reviewing its denial of a new trial was confined to an abuse of discretion standard. Most importantly, the Court held that appellate review, limited to abuse of discre-

trial rulings, see 11 C. Wright, A. Miller & M. Kane, Civil 2d §§ 2818–19.

61. E.g., Arnold v. Eastern Air Lines, Inc., 681 F.2d 186 (4th Cir.1982), cert. denied 460 U.S. 1102.

62. See, e.g., Estate of Sheldon, 75 Cal. App.3d 364, 142 Cal.Rptr. 119 (1977).

63. Wright, The Doubtful Omniscience of Appellate Courts, 41 Minn.L.Rev. 751 (1957).

64. Carrington, The Power of District Judges and the Responsibility of Courts of Appeals, 3 Ga.L.Rev. 507, 524 (1969).

65. See Taylor v. Washington Terminal Co., 409 F.2d 145, 148 (D.C.Cir.1969), cert. denied 396 U.S. 835 ("The judge's unique opportunity to consider the evidence in the living court-room context must be respected. But against his judgment we must con-

sider that the agency to whom the Constitution allocates the fact-finding function in the first instance—the jury—has evaluated the facts differently."); Lind v. Schenley Industries, Inc., 278 F.2d 79, 90 (3d Cir. 1960), cert. denied 364 U.S. 835 (when new trial is granted because the verdict is against the weight of the evidence, the appellate court should "exercise a closer degree of scrutiny and supervision than is the case where a new trial is granted because of some undesirable or pernicious influence obtruding into the trial"). For a review of the federal cases in this area, see 11 C. Wright, A. Miller & M. Kane, Civil 2d § 2819.

66. 518 U.S. 415, 116 S.Ct. 2211, 135 L.Ed.2d 659 (1996).

67. This aspect of the decision is discussed in § 11.8, above.

tion, was consistent with the Seventh Amendment's re-examination clause "as a control necessary and proper to the fair administration of justice * * *."[68]

§ 12.5 Juror Misconduct and Impeachment of the Verdict

Various errors committed by the jury can be the basis for a challenge to the verdict either by motion for new trial or by appeal.[1] The problem must be considered on two levels. First, what constitutes juror misconduct? And, second, what evidence may be used to show misconduct?[2]

Some instances of juror misconduct are clear, as when a juror fails to answer truthfully one of the questions asked during voir dire.[3] In those circumstances, the main issue is whether the juror's response is viewed as so prejudicial that the verdict should be overturned.[4] Other forms of misconduct that occur during the deliberation process raise difficult questions concerning what the jury may consider when determining the verdict, as well as problems of whether it is proper to inquire into their deliberations at all.

The jury will have been instructed to decide the case in accordance with the law as explained by the judge in the instructions and to consider only the evidence brought forward at trial. Thus, one easily identifiable form of misconduct occurs when members of the jury engage in unauthorized conversations about the case with others,[5] or when they

---

68. 518 U.S. at 435, 116 S.Ct. at 2223.

§ 12.5

1. If the jury renders a verdict based on evidence that is insufficient as a matter of law, that result may be cured by the grant of a motion for judgment notwithstanding the verdict or for a new trial. See §§ 12.3–12.4, above. In these situations, the jurors have not malfunctioned; rather, they have been asked to decide a question that should not have been submitted to them.

2. See generally 11 C. Wright, A. Miller & M. Kane, Civil 2d § 2810.

3. See Pierce v. Altman, 147 Ga.App. 22, 248 S.E.2d 34 (1978) (juror in wrongful death suit fails to reveal that he was a defendant in a personal injury suit and he later becomes foreman); Reich v. Thompson, 346 Mo. 577, 142 S.W.2d 486 (1940) (juror in personal injury suit intentionally conceals he was a defendant in personal injury suit).

4. See Kealoha v. Tanaka, 45 Hawaii 457, 370 P.2d 468 (1962) (no prejudice when jurors drank alcoholic beverages at dinner during deliberations since no evidence that any of them were affected); Derr v. St. Louis Public Serv. Co., 399 S.W.2d 241 (Mo.App.1965) (no prejudice when juror did not intentionally conceal information that was not directly connected with case).

5. U.S. v. Harry Barfield Co., 359 F.2d 120 (5th Cir.1966) (conversation with plaintiff); Printed Terry Finishing Co. v. City of Lebanon, 247 Pa.Super. 277, 299–300, 372 A.2d 460, 469 (1977) (conversation between juror and plaintiff's counsel). Compare Adams v. Davis, 578 S.W.2d 899 (Ky.App. 1979), in which a new trial was denied although the defendant alleged that he had an unauthorized conversation with a juror. The court noted, "to allow a defendant to participate in misconduct, knowingly withhold information about it until a verdict is reached, and then complain of juror misconduct could subject every jury verdict to attack." 578 S.W.2d at 900.

Annotations dealing with unauthorized conversations regarding a case that may constitute juror misconduct include, Annot., 64 A.L.R.2d 158 (1959) (contact with outsiders generally); Annot., 62 A.L.R.2d 298 (1958) (contact with party or attorney); Annot., 52 A.L.R.2d 182 (1957) (contact with witnesses); Annot., 41 A.L.R.2d 288 (1955) (contact with judges, court officials and attendants).

consider evidence obtained outside the courtroom, such as by visiting the scene of the accident.[6] In either of these situations, a new trial may be warranted if the court determines that the information or conversations were prejudicial.[7]

A more difficult question is posed when the alleged misconduct involves information exchanged by the jurors during their deliberations. A major strength of the jury system is that it brings together a cross-section of community standards and human experiences.[8] It is expected that the jurors will bring their combined general knowledge to bear on the facts of the case.[9] At the same time, it clearly is improper for the jurors to decide the case on the basis of any personal knowledge they might have about it. Indeed, a juror with any personal knowledge of the case should have disclosed that during voir dire and, in most circumstances, the juror would be excused from serving on that case.[10]

Between these extremes, however, is the question whether it is proper for the jury to consider some specialized knowledge of one of the jurors that bears on the case.[11] The difficulty is that the parties may be unaware of that knowledge so that they would have no way to rebut it once the jury begins deliberating. It is as though the jury had before it an expert witness, not subject to cross-examination by either party.

But what constitutes specialized, as distinct from general or common, knowledge such that the losing party may claim prejudice because the jury was exposed to it?[12] Unfortunately, there is no common agreement as to where to draw the line between general experience and special knowledge.[13] For example, in some instances knowledge of the region—its physical layout and climate—appropriately is considered; in others regional information is deemed inappropriate because it seems too particularized.[14] The balance between what is appropriate and what is

---

6. Bainton v. Board of Educ. of City of New York, 57 Misc.2d 140, 292 N.Y.S.2d 229 (1968).

7. See U.S. v. Harry Barfield Co., 359 F.2d 120 (5th Cir.1966); Kohler v. Central & Southern Truck Lines, Inc., 45 Ill.App.3d 621, 4 Ill.Dec. 342, 360 N.E.2d 89 (1977).

8. See § 11.1, above, for a discussion of the role of the jury in modern society.

9. "While they cannot act in any case upon particular facts material to its disposition resting in their private knowledge, but should be governed by the evidence adduced, they may, and to act intelligently they must, judge of the weight and force of that evidence by their own general knowledge of the subject of inquiry." Head v. Hargrave, 105 U.S. (15 Otto) 45, 49, 26 L.Ed. 1028 (1881) (per Field, J.).

For a discussion of what constitutes general knowledge of which the jury may take account in rendering its verdict, compare Holt v. Pariser, 161 Pa.Super. 315, 54 A.2d

89 (1947), with Harris v. Pounds, 185 Miss. 688, 187 So. 891 (1939).

10. See § 11.10, above, on the jury selection process.

11. See Texas Employers' Ins. Ass'n v. Price, 336 S.W.2d 304, 310 (Tex.Civ.App. 1960); Texas & P. Ry. Co. v. Mix, 193 S.W.2d 542 (Tex.Civ.App.1946).

12. See the Supreme Court's statement on this question in a case involving the value of legal services, in Head v. Hargrave, 105 U.S. (15 Otto) 45, 49–50, 26 L.Ed. 1028 (1881).

13. See Harris v. Deere & Co., 263 N.W.2d 727 (Iowa 1978), in which the Iowa Supreme Court reviews all its prior decisions delimiting what type of information exchanged by the jurors was found improper and prejudicial and what was allowed.

14. See Broeder, The Impact of the Vicinage Requirement: An Empirical Look, 45 Neb.L.Rev. 99 (1966).

not is drawn so as to assure that the jury limits its inquiry to the formal evidence, buttressed only by generalized community knowledge, not specific details. The more specific the information considered, the more likely it will be deemed new evidence, inappropriately considered because it was not received in open court.

Another form of juror misconduct about which there is greater agreement involves the method of reaching the verdict itself. The classic example occurs when the jury decides on the basis of a flip of the coin or by lot.[15] More commonly, despite careful and adequate instructions by the judge, the jury errs by entering a compromise verdict or a quotient verdict. To illustrate, consider a negligence action arising out of a car collision in a unanimous verdict jurisdiction. If one or more of the jury members feels that the plaintiff has not proved liability, while other jurors feel that not only was liability shown, but damages should be $100,000, the jury may decide to break the deadlock by returning a verdict for plaintiff, but only in the amount of $25,000 for actual medical expenses. This compromise ignores the law because the failure of all the jurors to find defendant liable entitles the defendant to win the case.[16] A quotient verdict is one in which the jurors enter the jury room and, without deliberating on liability, they agree that they each will write down the amount that he or she believes the plaintiff should receive, that the amounts will then be totalled and divided by the number of jurors, and that the result will constitute their verdict.[17] What this process ignores is any discussion of liability. It may be that in reaching the end result, some jurors wrote "no damages" since they felt that liability was not proven, and yet a verdict would be rendered for the plaintiff. If evidence can be introduced to show that this has occurred, then the verdict cannot stand and a new trial is necessary.

In a small number of the situations just described,[18] jury misconduct will appear on the face of the verdict.[19] When this occurs, the judge must

---

15. West's Ann.Cal.Code Civ.Proc. § 657(2). See National Credit Corp. v. Ritchey, 252 Ark. 106, 477 S.W.2d 488 (1972).

16. See, e.g., Hatfield v. Seaboard Air Line R.R. Co., 396 F.2d 721 (5th Cir.1968). Not all compromises by jury members are subject to challenge, for the deliberation process itself is designed to allow for shifting and changing impressions or opinions. Warrender v. McMurrin, 256 Iowa 617, 128 N.W.2d 285 (1964). It is only those compromises that ignore the law that require a new trial.

17. E.g., Hukle v. Kimble, 172 Kan. 630, 243 P.2d 225 (1952). But compare Schulz v. Chadwell, 558 S.W.2d 183, 186 (Ky.App.1977) (quotient verdict allowed when there was no antecedent agreement to be bound so that "the average of the jurors' views was obtained merely as a basis for further deliberation").

18. When a special verdict or general verdict with interrogatories is used, inconsistencies in the answers may reveal jury misunderstanding of what was required. See, e.g., Fugitt v. Jones, 549 F.2d 1001 (5th Cir.1977). See generally § 12.1, above.

19. E.g., Rusidoff v. DeBolt Transfer, Inc., 251 Pa.Super. 208, 380 A.2d 451 (1977) (jury returned verdict for defendant "with reservations due to the evidence provided"); Robb v. John C. Hickey, Inc., 19 N.J.Misc. 455, 20 A.2d 707 (1941) (jury verdict finding both plaintiff and defendant guilty, comparing degrees of negligence, and recommending an award of $2,000, despite instruction that comparative negligence was immaterial).

It has been argued that a general verdict finding defendant liable, but awarding $0 damages is ambiguous or inconsistent, meriting a new trial. But not all courts have

consider whether a new trial should be ordered or whether there is some way to cure the defect, thereby avoiding the cost and delay of a new trial.[20] The judge may question the jury as to its meaning and adjust the verdict accordingly,[21] or enter a verdict that seems consistent with the jury's intent.[22] Great care is necessary in these situations to ensure that the judge in molding the verdict reflects the understanding of the jury. The error itself may reveal a basic misunderstanding by the jury tainting the verdict as a whole. Thus, although the remedy used is within the judge's discretion, it is subject to strict scrutiny on appeal; only when the jury's real purpose and intent are clear can the judge properly mold a verdict.[23]

Most often, jury misconduct is not apparent when the verdict is announced. This particularly is true when a general verdict is used and the only information given to the parties and the judge when the verdict is rendered is who is liable and for how much.[24] Under these circumstances the issue of whether the verdict may be impeached turns on the question of what evidence may be introduced to show jury misconduct[25] requiring a new trial.[26]

The historic rule was set forth by Lord Mansfield in the eighteenth century in England[27] and thus is referred to as the Mansfield Rule. That rule provides that no juror may testify as to what occurred during the jury deliberations. It is based on the belief that to allow any inquiry into what transpired during the deliberation process would threaten the entire jury system, which depends on the jurors feeling secure from investigation and free to decide the case as they see fit.[28] Therefore, juror

---

held this form of verdict defective. See Wingerter v. Maryland Cas. Co., 313 F.2d 754 (5th Cir.1963); Pitcher v. Rogers, 259 F.Supp. 412 (N.D.Miss.1966).

20. Gil de Rebollo v. Miami Heat Ltd. Partnership, 949 F.Supp. 62 (D.Puerto Rico 1996) (verdict reached either through compromise or bias requires new trial); Hanolt v. Mlakar, 421 Pa. 136, 218 A.2d 750 (1966) (unclear and inconsistent verdict that cannot be cured).

21. Sigel v. Boston & Me. R.R., 107 N.H. 8, 216 A.2d 794 (1966).

22. Gilday v. Hauchwit, 91 N.J.Super. 233, 219 A.2d 873 (App.Div.1966), reversed on other grounds 48 N.J. 557, 226 A.2d 834 (1967) (court can strike as surplusage jury's improper attempt to apportion damages among defendants); Hodgkins v. Mead, 119 N.Y. 166, 23 N.E. 559 (1890) (court enters amount when verdict for plaintiff who sought real estate commission and no issue as to amount).

23. See Kramer v. Kister, 187 Pa. 227, 40 A. 1008 (1898) (criminal action). Compare Gilday v. Hauchwit, 91 N.J.Super. 233, 219 A.2d 873 (App.Div.1966), reversed on other grounds 48 N.J. 557, 226 A.2d 834

(1967) (verdict molded), with Robb v. John C. Hickey, Inc., 19 N.J.Misc. 455, 20 A.2d 707 (1941) (improper to mold verdict).

24. See § 12.1, above.

25. For a detailed examination regarding the various rules that have been adopted concerning the use of juror affidavits to impeach the verdict, see 8 J. Wigmore, Evidence §§ 2345–56 (J. McNaughton ed.1961).

26. Most often, arguments attempting to impeach the verdict are raised on a motion for new trial. However, the availability of that motion is limited by rules to 10 days or so after judgment is entered, see § 12.4, above. Thus, if the attorney discovers the misconduct after that time has passed, then the evidence may be the basis for a motion for relief from judgment or an appeal.

27. Vaise v. Delaval, 1 Term R. 11, 99 Eng.Rep. 944 (K.B.1785).

28. "But let it once be established that verdicts solemnly made and publicly returned into court can be attacked and set aside on the testimony of those who took part in their publication and our verdicts could be, and many would be, followed by

affidavits as to what occurred during the deliberations may not be used to attack their verdict. Supporters of the Mansfield Rule point out that there is no way to ensure completely that a jury functions properly; jury deliberations are not a scientific process.[29] Additionally, the result of impeaching a verdict—a new trial—does not ensure that a more just or appropriate decision will be reached.

The price of this jury freedom is high. By preventing any inquiry into juror misconduct that depends on juror testimony, the rule effectively precludes impeachment since most often the jurors are the only persons who can explain what occurred. However, if a third party observed some conduct that was in violation of their charge, then that evidence may be used.[30] Illustratively, affidavits of third persons to the effect that the jury was seen visiting the scene of the accident may be allowed. It should be noted that a juror can testify as to misconduct during voir dire, such as perjury, because that evidence does not invade the deliberation process itself.[31] Except for these few instances, no other inquiry can be made. Although the Mansfield Rule has been soundly criticized as allowing tainted verdicts to remain undisturbed,[32] it remains controlling in a number of jurisdictions.[33]

In an attempt to ameliorate the effect of the Mansfield Rule, most jurisdictions now allow information from jurors to be introduced, but with significant restrictions.[34] Thus, it remains true today that the inquiry into the mental processes of the jurors or the effects of certain

---

an inquiry in the hope of discovering something which might invalidate the finding. Jurors would be harassed and beset by the defeated party in an effort to secure from them evidence of facts which might establish misconduct sufficient to set aside a verdict. If evidence thus secured could be thus used, the result would be to make what was intended to be a private deliberation, the constant subject of public investigation—to the destruction of all frankness and freedom of discussion and conference." McDonald v. Pless, 238 U.S. 264, 267–68, 35 S.Ct. 783, 784, 59 L.Ed. 1300 (1915) (per Lamar, J.).

29. In Jorgensen v. York Ice Machinery Corp., 160 F.2d 432, 435 (2d Cir.1947), cert. denied 332 U.S. 764, Judge Learned Hand observed that if we demanded that every juror act without bias and base his vote only upon the evidence heard in court, then "it is doubtful whether more than one in a hundred verdicts would stand such a test * * *."

30. See Christ v. Wempe, 219 Md. 627, 150 A.2d 918 (1959). But compare Central of Georgia Ry. Co. v. Holmes, 223 Ala. 188, 134 So. 875 (1931).

31. See McCoy v. Goldston, 652 F.2d 654 (6th Cir.1981). In most instances challenges based on the failure to disclose infor-

mation on voir dire are not successful, however. See the cases cited in 11 C. Wright, A. Miller & M. Kane, Civil 2d § 2810 n. 15. Some courts allow juror affidavits concerning any conduct occurring outside the jury room. See Bainton v. Board of Educ. of City of New York, 57 Misc.2d 140, 292 N.Y.S.2d 229 (1968).

32. See the dissenting opinion of Justice Peters in Sopp v. Smith, 59 Cal.2d 12, 27 Cal.Rptr. 593, 377 P.2d 649 (1963). Sopp was overruled later in People v. Hutchinson, 71 Cal.2d 342, 78 Cal.Rptr. 196, 455 P.2d 132 (1969), cert. denied 396 U.S. 994; Note, Impeachment of Jury Verdicts, 53 Marq.L.Rev. 258 (1970). See also Note, Admissibility of Evidence to Impeach Jury Verdicts, 22 U.Miami L.Rev. 729 (1968).

33. See Barsh v. Chrysler Corp., 262 S.C. 129, 203 S.E.2d 107 (1974); Eichel v. Payeur, 106 N.H. 484, 214 A.2d 116 (1965). See also Blanton v. Union Pacific R.R. Co., 289 Or. 617, 616 P.2d 477 (1980) (juror affidavit may not be used to show quotient verdict).

34. In California, a motion for new trial cannot be supported by juror testimony, only by affidavits. Linhart v. Nelson, 18 Cal.3d 641, 134 Cal.Rptr. 813, 557 P.2d 104 (1976).

matters on their mental processes is precluded totally in all systems.[35] However, juror affidavits may be used to testify as to "overt acts"[36] or independent facts involving jury members that may have been prejudicial.[37]

But what constitutes an "overt act?" The purpose of this exception is to allow in some evidence, but to protect against any inquiry into the thoughts of jurors as they deliberated. As explained by Justice Traynor, "The only improper influences that may be proved * * * are those open to sight, hearing, and other senses and thus subject to corroboration."[38] For example, in a case involving a quotient verdict, juror affidavits may be introduced to show that the jurors wrote down damage figures—the process by which the amount of the verdict was reached.[39] The permissible testimony concerns the acts of writing, adding and then dividing by twelve, not the thoughts of the jurors as to why this was appropriate or why they felt compelled to follow this approach.[40] Some courts applying this rule also allow the use of affidavits to show that extraneous information was provided by one of the jurors in the jury room.[41] The key is that no testimony can be received about the effect of that information on the minds or feelings of the jury members.

In the federal courts, Federal Evidence Rule 606(b) governs what juror testimony may be introduced to impeach a jury verdict.[42] It provides that no testimony may be used that relates to any matter or statement made during the deliberations, to the effect of anything on any juror's mind or emotions, or concerning the juror's mental process-

35. See U.S. v. Krall, 835 F.2d 711 (8th Cir.1987) (evidence that juror voted for conviction despite belief in defendant's innocence because of feared IRS retaliation deemed inadmissible); Dongieux's v. Shoaf, 271 Ark. 197, 608 S.W.2d 33 (App.1980); Kirkland v. Robbins, 385 So.2d 694 (Fla. App.1980), review denied 397 So.2d 779 (Fla.1981); Hendrickson v. Konopaski, 14 Wn.App. 390, 541 P.2d 1001 (1975).

36. People v. Hutchinson, 71 Cal.2d 342, 78 Cal.Rptr. 196, 455 P.2d 132 (1969), cert. denied 396 U.S. 994 (affidavits concerning bailiff's conduct pressuring jury to hasten decision); Wright v. Illinois & Mississippi Telegraph Co., 20 Iowa 195 (1866). Texas courts appear to be the most liberal in setting aside verdicts based on an inquiry into the deliberations. See Pope, The Mental Operation of Jurors, 40 Texas L.Rev. 849 (1962).

37. See Kilgore v. Greyhound Corp., 30 F.R.D. 385 (E.D.Tenn.1962); Kritzer v. Citron, 101 Cal.App.2d 33, 224 P.2d 808 (1950); Thomason v. Trentham, 178 Tenn. 37, 154 S.W.2d 792 (1941).

Information regarding the mental competency or physical disability of a juror may not be used to attack a verdict under Federal Evidence Rule 606(b). Government of Virgin Islands v. Nicholas, 759 F.2d 1073 (3d Cir.1985). But cf. Weaver v. Puckett, 896 F.2d 126 (5th Cir.1990), cert. denied 498 U.S. 966 (there may be an exception for "an extremely strong showing of juror incompetence") (criminal case).

38. People v. Hutchinson, 71 Cal.2d 342, 78 Cal.Rptr. 196, 201, 455 P.2d 132, 137 (1969), cert. denied 396 U.S. 994.

39. National Credit Corp. v. Ritchey, 252 Ark. 106, 477 S.W.2d 488 (1972).

40. See Johnson v. Harris, 23 Ariz. App. 103, 530 P.2d 1136 (1975) (court disallowed juror affidavit stating that one juror announced she would go along with anything the majority decided and another said that she would sign the verdict only to avoid a mistrial).

41. See Kilgore v. Greyhound Corp., 30 F.R.D. 385 (E.D.Tenn.1962); Krouse v. Graham, 19 Cal.3d 59, 137 Cal.Rptr. 863, 562 P.2d 1022 (1977); New Jersey v. Kociolek, 20 N.J. 92, 118 A.2d 812 (1955).

42. An excellent exposition of the general problems of impeachment can be found in Comment, Impeachment of Jury Verdicts, 25 U.Chi.L.Rev. 360 (1958).

es.[43] However, a juror may testify "on the question whether extraneous prejudicial information was improperly brought to the jury's attention or whether any outside influence was improperly brought to bear upon any juror."[44] Thus, the Federal Rule starts with a broad presumption against allowing testimony concerning the deliberation process unless one of the two exceptions applies.[45]

The use of the phrase "extraneous prejudicial information" rather than "overt acts" attempts to avoid the problem of defining what is an act and recognizes that a verdict is tainted when information not presented during the trial is given to the jurors and is considered by them in reaching their verdict.[46] That information may come to them by the intervention of outside parties,[47] inadvertently[48] or it may consist of one juror's revelation of specialized knowledge.[49] The court still must tackle the problem of when information is extraneous[50]—that is, whether it is part of the general knowledge that jurors ordinarily bring to bear in the deliberation process or whether it is so specialized that it effectively represents additional testimony received outside the courtroom.[51] And, even if that is so, the verdict will be overturned only if the information is

43. E.g., Robles v. Exxon Corp., 862 F.2d 1201 (5th Cir.1989), cert. denied 490 U.S. 1051 (statements by several jurors that they had misunderstood the impact of the verdict could not be used because the error implicated the jurors' mental processes).

44. The history of this provision reflects some of the serious difficulties in deciding where to draw the line concerning inquiry into juror misconduct, how that decision is influenced by varying attitudes concerning what conduct must be corrected, and when questions concerning the deliberations are least likely to threaten the sanctity of the process itself. See Mueller, Jurors' Impeachment of Verdicts and Indictments in Federal Court Under Rule 606(b), 57 Neb.L.Rev. 920, 927–35 (1978).

45. For a discussion of the application of Fed.Evid.Rule 606(b), see Mueller, Jurors' Impeachment of Verdicts and Indictments in Federal Court Under Rule 606(b), 57 Neb.L.Rev. 920 (1978); Thompson, Challenge to the Decisionmaking Process—Federal Rule of Evidence 606(b) and the Constitutional Right to a Fair Trial, 38 Sw.L.J. 1187 (1985).

46. For a discussion of the exceptions to Federal Evidence Rule 606(b) and their underlying policy considerations, see Tanner v. U.S., 483 U.S. 107, 107 S.Ct. 2739, 97 L.Ed.2d 90 (1987). The case is analyzed in Diehm, Impeachment of Jury Verdicts: Tanner v. U.S. and Beyond, 65 St. John's L.Rev. 389 (1991), and criticized in Note, The Jurisprudence of Jury Trials: The No Impeachment Rule and the Conditions for Legitimate Decisionmaking, 64 U.Colo. L.Rev. 57 (1993).

47. For a listing of the kinds of evidence that is excluded, see Mueller, Jurors' Impeachment of Verdicts and Indictments in Federal Court Under Rule 606(b), 57 Neb.L.Rev. 920, 936–43 (1978). Professor Mueller concludes his survey, saying, "clearly the counsel of the rule, however, is to be conservative in the approach to such problems and to err upon the side of exclusion rather than receipt of evidence in close cases." Id. at 943.

48. See, e.g., Farese v. U.S., 428 F.2d 178 (5th Cir.1970) (criminal case).

49. See, e.g., U.S. v. Howard, 506 F.2d 865 (5th Cir.1975) (juror affidavit to the effect that another juror had stated that defendant had been in trouble two or three times before).

50. See, e.g., Maldonado v. Missouri Pacific Ry. Co., 798 F.2d 764, 769 (5th Cir.1986), cert. denied 480 U.S. 932 (discussion of jurors regarding wealth of the railroad and whether jurors had given plaintiff benefit of the doubt is not extraneous); Shillcutt v. Gagnon, 602 F.Supp. 1280, 1282 (E.D.Wis.1985), affirmed 827 F.2d 1155 (7th Cir.1987) (racially prejudiced remark made during jury deliberations was not extraneous).

51. See Comment, Impeachment of Jury Verdicts, 25 U.Chi.L.Rev. 360, 367–68 (1958), arguing that impeachment should not be allowed on the basis of the juror's specialized knowledge. See also text at notes 9–14, above.

deemed prejudicial. A juror may testify about whether extraneous information was brought to the jurors' attention and may describe the information,[52] but prejudice will have to be inferred since Rule 606(b) precludes any testimony regarding the effect this extraneous information may have had on the members of the jury.[53]

The exception for the use of evidence showing "outside influence" makes clear the ability to receive evidence concerning attempts to bribe, coerce, or influence the jury or a jury member.[54] It does not matter whether the information imparted actually was pertinent. The threat posed by those activities to the essential fairness of the judicial system requires that the evidence be admitted and the court be given the opportunity to assure itself that the verdict was not prejudiced thereby.

As is apparent from even this brief survey of the approaches to the question of what evidence may be used to impeach the verdict, there is no common agreement as to exactly what should be permitted and what precluded. Even jurisdictions ostensibly following the same approach do not all agree concerning what constitutes an "overt act" or "extraneous prejudicial information." These differences should not be read as reflecting great foment in this area. Rather, they reveal small but continuing adjustments made to achieve an appropriate balance between assuring a fair and just verdict and protecting the jury process from destructive intrusiveness. With the increasing adoption of the Federal Evidence Rules by the states,[55] it is to be expected that its formulation will be most widely used; however, the different ways in which it will be interpreted will reflect the varying attitudes on this question. This therefore remains one area in which it is very important to review local law, for nationally uniform standards are unlikely to emerge.

§ 12.6 Motions to Alter the Judgment or for Relief From the Judgment

The entry of the judgment marks the final act in the trial court adjudication of a dispute.[1] Errors in the judgment that are the result of

---

52. Rushen v. Spain, 464 U.S. 114, 104 S.Ct. 453, 78 L.Ed.2d 267 (1983).

53. U.S. v. Calbas, 821 F.2d 887 (2d Cir.1987), cert. denied 485 U.S. 937; U.S. v. Green, 523 F.2d 229 (2d Cir.1975), cert. denied 423 U.S. 1074. But compare Whitten v. Allstate Ins. Co., 447 So.2d 655 (Ala. 1984) (jurors may testify as to whether they were influenced by extraneous matter).

54. See, e.g., Stone v. U.S., 113 F.2d 70 (6th Cir.1940) (criminal case). This exception allows evidence of any contacts by outsiders with jury members that may have been prejudicial. See note 5, above. But cf. U.S. v. Casamayor, 837 F.2d 1509, 1515 (11th Cir.1988), cert. denied 488 U.S. 1017 (juror harassment or intimidation of another juror is not competent evidence to impeach verdict) (criminal case).

55. See the listing of the state of the law in various jurisdictions on this question in 8 J. Wigmore, Evidence § 2354 (J. McNaughton ed. 1961) (1988 supplement by W. Reiser).

§ 12.6

1. The date of entry of judgment is important because typically it is from that point that the timing periods for making post-trial motions or for taking an appeal begin to run. See Fed.Civ.Proc.Rules 59 and 60, and Fed.App.Proc.Rule 4(a). The filing of post-trial motions does not extend the time for filing an appeal. Fed.App.Proc.Rule 4(a) lists the motions that do extend the time for an appeal and does not include motions under Rules 59 and 60.

clerical mistakes[2] or some omission or oversight[3] when the judgment was entered may be corrected by a motion to correct or alter the judgment. This can be done by any of the parties or by the court sua sponte.[4] Although correction may relieve a party from an erroneous judgment, it is a ministerial procedure and does not require the judgment to be formally reopened or the case to by retried. Thus, it is not very controversial. In fact, in most systems the ability to correct a judgment for clerical mistakes exists at any time;[5] the alteration of a judgment because of the omission of some element is limited to 10 days,[6] in recognition that this change may be more substantial.[7]

But the use of a motion to alter the judgment is strictly limited to clerical errors or matters of clear oversight,[8] not questions involving the right to additional recovery[9] or a reduction in an award.[10] Attempts to reopen the judgment or to alter it for some nontechnical reason or outside the time period provided must be made by a motion for a new trial[11] or by appeal.[12]

In addition to these methods, all judicial systems provide some means, typically a motion for relief from judgment, by which an aggrieved party can seek relief in the trial court. The availability of this relief is particularly important because the right to move for a new trial or to appeal also is limited to defined time periods, commonly ten and thirty days, respectively, and many errors will not be discovered in time to make use of those methods of challenge. Consequently, a motion for

2. Fed.Civ.Proc.Rule 60(a); Mich.Rules Civ.Proc. 2.612; Va.Code 1950, § 8.01–428B. See generally 11 C. Wright, A. Miller & M. Kane, Civil 2d §§ 2854–56.

3. Fed.Civ.Proc.Rule 59(e). See generally 11 C. Wright, A. Miller & M. Kane, Civil 2d § 2817.

4. American Trucking Ass'ns v. Frisco Transportation Co., 358 U.S. 133, 79 S.Ct. 170, 3 L.Ed.2d 172 (1958); Wilson v. Wilson, 88 Cal.App.2d 382, 198 P.2d 916 (1948).

5. Tillman v. Tillman, 172 F.2d 270 (D.C.Cir.1948), cert. denied 336 U.S. 954.

6. Fed.Civ.Proc.Rule 59(e). The time for making the motion cannot be extended. Fed.Civ.Proc.Rule 6(b); Scola v. Boat Frances, R., Inc., 618 F.2d 147 (1st Cir.1980).

7. For example, when a state statute requires the addition of interest from the time of injury to the verdict, the omission of interest from the judgment is a clerical error correctable under Rule 60(a). Hayden v. Scott Aviation, Inc., 684 F.2d 270 (3d Cir.1982). If the award of interest is discretionary, however, then the failure to include interest in the judgment is not a clerical error and cannot be corrected through Rule 60(a). Gray v. Dukedom Bank, 216 F.2d 108 (6th Cir.1954). It may be altered by a timely motion under Rule 59(e), however. Spur-

geon v. Delta S.S. Lines, Inc., 387 F.2d 358 (2d Cir.1967).

8. McNickle v. Bankers Life & Cas. Co., 888 F.2d 678, 682 (10th Cir.1989) (correction should require no additional proof); Employers Mut. Cas. Co. v. Key Pharmaceuticals, Inc., 886 F.Supp. 360 (S.D.N.Y. 1995) (failure to include post-judgment interest could be corrected as clerical mistake, but prejudgment interest could not be corrected because it required additional findings); Zisk v. City of Roseville, 56 Cal. App.3d 41, 127 Cal.Rptr. 896 (1976) (judgment as signed does not express actual judicial intention). Compare Dennis v. Dennis, 3 Mass.App.Ct. 361, 330 N.E.2d 490 (1975) (premature entry of decree is not clerical error).

9. See White v. New Hampshire Dep't of Employment Security, 455 U.S. 445, 102 S.Ct. 1162, 71 L.Ed.2d 325 (1982) (Rule 59(e) is not applicable to post-judgment requests for attorney fees under 42 U.S.C.A. § 1988).

10. Dow v. Baird, 389 F.2d 882 (10th Cir.1968) (attempt to eliminate punitive damages).

11. See generally §§ 12.4–12.5, above.

12. See generally Chapter 13, below.

relief from the judgment often presents the only possible means of avoiding what is claimed to be an erroneous judgment.

The question of when to allow relief from a judgment is difficult because it requires the delicate balancing of two opposing principles: the important goal of finality requiring that there be an end to litigation, and the desire to render justice in individual cases.[13] Given that courts today are overcrowded and that the person who is seeking relief already has had at least one opportunity to be heard, perhaps it is not surprising that American courts typically have given greater weight to finality in this hierarchy of values.[14]

There are essentially four different methods that may be available for seeking relief from a judgment in the trial court.[15] First, special statutes may authorize specific procedures for seeking relief from certain types of judgments.[16] Second, contemporary rules usually provide that a party may make a motion in the original trial court for relief based on certain listed grounds.[17] Third, a party may be allowed to bring an independent action challenging a judgment on grounds recognized historically in equity, or, fourth, a party may file an application to set a judgment aside for fraud, appealing to the inherent equity powers of the court.

These latter two devices represent historic methods by which law court judgments could be reopened by the equity courts on grounds not recognized at common law. With the merger of law and equity, the historic need for the independent action or special equitable relief for fraud has disappeared. Nonetheless, in some states they remain extremely important means of obtaining relief because the grounds listed in the relevant procedural rules for relief are very limited.[18] Further, these devices continue to be useful even in jurisdictions having reasonably broad motion practice when restrictions in the rules authorizing motions for relief otherwise would prevent the court from responding.

13. See generally Frankel, The Search for Truth: An Umpireal View, 123 U.Pa. L.Rev. 1031 (1975).

14. "[I]t is for the public interest and policy to make an end to litigation * * * [so that] suits may not be immortal, while men are mortal." Ocean Ins. Co. v. Fields, 18 Fed.Cas. 532, 539 (C.C.Mass.1841) (No. 10,-406).

The application of the rules of former adjudication providing for the binding effect of judgments also exemplifies the judicial preference for finality. See generally Chapter 14, below.

15. See generally 11 C. Wright, A. Miller & M. Kane, Civil 2d §§ 2857–73.

16. For a discussion of the few statutory methods of relief that currently exist, see 11 C. Wright, A. Miller & M. Kane, Civil 2d § 2869.

17. Fed.Civ.Proc.Rule 60(b). Many state rules are modelled after the federal rules and list the same grounds for relief. E.g., Mass.R.Civ.P. Rule 60(b); Minn.Rules Civ.Proc., Rule 60.02.

18. For example, in Virginia a motion for relief may be made only from a default judgment or a decree pro confesso and then only on the ground that there was a fraud upon the court, or the judgment is void or there has been an accord and satisfaction. Va.Code 1950, § 8.01–428A. Less extreme, but nonetheless limited, is California where a motion for relief is limited to a challenge that the judgment was entered through mistake, inadvertence, surprise or neglect, or is void. West's Ann.Cal.Code Civ.Proc. § 473. In these settings, the independent action or motion to set aside the judgment for fraud upon the court thus may play a very important role.

For example, an independent action may be brought in a court other than the judgment rendering court,[19] but a motion for relief from the judgment cannot.[20] Also, in many systems a motion for relief must be made within specified time periods, which is not true of the equitable devices.[21] The right to utilize an independent action is restricted only by the equitable notion of laches;[22] an application to set aside the judgment for fraud upon the court has no time limits and will not even be barred by laches.[23] Indeed, some courts have opened judgments on their own motion, invoking this equitable reserve power.[24]

But the use of an independent action or a general invocation to set aside a judgment because of fraud is limited by historic restrictions[25] and by difficulties in interpretation and definition.[26] For example, an application to set aside the judgment for fraud generally can be used only when there has been a fraud upon the court, not merely fraud between the parties.[27] The distinction between these two forms of fraud is somewhat elusive,[28] but the former generally involves showing something designed to corrupt or taint the judicial process, not merely to prevent the opposing party from prevailing.[29] Thus, simple perjury generally does not

19. Hadden v. Rumsey Prods., Inc., 196 F.2d 92 (2d Cir.1952).

If the party moves for relief first in the original judgment rendering court and, after it is denied there, brings an independent action in another court on the same grounds, res judicata may preclude the independent suit. See Locklin v. Switzer Bros., Inc., 335 F.2d 331 (7th Cir.1964), cert. denied 379 U.S. 962. But compare Caputo v. Globe Indem. Co., 41 F.R.D. 239 (E.D.Pa.1966); Verret v. DeHarpport, 49 Or.App. 801, 621 P.2d 598 (1980).

20. Taft v. Donellan Jerome, Inc., 407 F.2d 807 (7th Cir.1969).

21. Caputo v. Globe Indem. Co., 41 F.R.D. 239 (E.D.Pa.1966); Compton v. Compton, 101 Idaho 328, 612 P.2d 1175 (1980).

22. Lockwood v. Bowles, 46 F.R.D. 625 (D.D.C.1969) (laches found); Dunham v. First Nat. Bank in Sioux Falls, 86 S.D. 727, 201 N.W.2d 227 (1972) (no laches).

23. Toscano v. Commissioner of Internal Revenue, 441 F.2d 930 (9th Cir.1971).

24. Toscano v. Commissioner of Internal Revenue, 441 F.2d 930 (9th Cir.1971); Root Refining Co. v. Universal Oil Prods. Co., 169 F.2d 514, 521 (3d Cir.1948), cert. denied 335 U.S. 912.

25. Since the independent action and the motion for relief because of a fraud upon the court are appeals to the equitable powers of the court, they generally are restricted by the historic notion that they may be utilized only when there is no adequate remedy at law. If relief is possible under the ordinary procedural rules, it must be sought in that way. Taft v. Donellan Jerome, Inc., 407 F.2d 807 (7th Cir. 1969); Anderson v. Anderson, 399 N.E.2d 391 (Ind.App.1979).

26. For a statement of the requirements surrounding the use of the independent action, see National Sur. Co. v. State Bank of Humboldt, 120 Fed. 593, 599 (C.C.A.Neb.1903). See also Comment, Rule 60(b): Survey and Proposal for General Reform, 60 Calif.L.Rev. 531, 542 (1972).

When the independent action is brought in a federal court and the judgment under attack is from state court, special concerns are present. See Comment, Judgments: Fraud as a Basis for Relief in Federal Courts from Final State Court Judgments, 1964 Duke L.J. 109.

27. Travelers Indem. Co. v. Gore, 761 F.2d 1549, 1551 (11th Cir.1985); Rozier v. Ford Motor Co., 573 F.2d 1332 (5th Cir. 1978).

28. For a discussion of the difference between fraud upon the court and ordinary fraud, see Rozier v. Ford Motor Co., 573 F.2d 1332 (5th Cir.1978). See generally 11 C. Wright, A. Miller & M. Kane, Civil 2d § 2870. For a criticism of the distinction, see Note, Relief from Fraudulent Judgments in Federal Courts: Motion to Vacate or Independent Action—Opposite Sides of the Same Coin, 36 Drake L.Rev. 389 (1986).

29. The leading case exemplifying fraud upon the court is Hazel–Atlas Glass Co. v. Hartford–Empire Co., 322 U.S. 238, 64 S.Ct. 997, 88 L.Ed. 1250 (1944).

constitute fraud upon the court,[30] although attempts to bribe the judge do.[31] In any event, the circumstances qualifying as fraud upon the court are extremely limited. In a similar vein, most courts recognizing the use of an independent action restrict the challenge to judgments obtained in situations revealing extrinsic, not intrinsic, fraud.[32] As a result, the most common and preferred means of seeking relief remains a motion for relief made in the court that entered the judgment being challenged.[33]

In most judicial systems, statutes and rules provide rather specific grounds on which relief may be premised. Further, they set definite time restrictions for obtaining relief. These provisions codify well-recognized and concrete exceptions to the finality principle and represent a decision that under those circumstances the desire for truth and justice outweighs the value of immediate finality. The timing restrictions operate to protect the stability of judgments because they assure that finality merely is postponed, not avoided. The courts have discretion in applying these statutory criteria and generally have used them judiciously to remedy injustice.[34]

Federal Rule 60(b),[35] which governs relief from judgments in the federal courts, provides an excellent example of a common approach taken in deciding when and why relief is authorized. The six grounds for relief under that provision may be divided into three categories. First, there are those grounds that cannot be raised more than one year[36] after judgment has been entered.[37] A party can seek relief within this time period on the ground that judgment was entered on the basis of some mistake, inadvertence or excusable neglect,[38] or that there is newly

---

30. Petry v. General Motors Corp., 62 F.R.D. 357 (E.D.Pa.1974); Lockwood v. Bowles, 46 F.R.D. 625 (D.D.C.1969); Willis v. Willis, 93 Idaho 261, 460 P.2d 396 (1969). But see Shammas v. Shammas, 9 N.J. 321, 88 A.2d 204 (1952).

31. E.g., Root Refining Co. v. Universal Oil Prods. Co., 169 F.2d 514, 525 (3d Cir. 1948), cert. denied 335 U.S. 912.

32. Maschoff v. International Union, UAW, 23 Fed.R.Serv.2d 1204 (E.D.Mich. 1977); Rogoski v. City of Muskegon, 107 Mich.App. 730, 309 N.W.2d 718 (1981); Bennett v. Hibernia Bank, 47 Cal.2d 540, 305 P.2d 20 (1956). See generally Note, Attacking Fraudulently Obtained Judgments in the Federal Courts, 48 Iowa L.Rev. 398 (1963). The retention of the distinction between extrinsic and intrinsic fraud has been criticized. 11 C. Wright, A. Miller & M. Kane, Civil 2d § 2868.

33. See Restatement Second of Judgments § 78 (1982).

34. See generally Kane, Relief From Federal Judgments: A Morass Unrelieved By a Rule, 30 Hast.L.J. 41 (1978).

35. For a history of Federal Rule 60(b), see Moore & Rogers, Federal Relief From Civil Judgments, 55 Yale L.J. 623 (1946).

36. Some states provide an even shorter time period. See, e.g., West's Ann.Cal. Code Civ.Proc. § 473 (6 months); Utah Rules Civ.Proc., Rule 60(b) (3 months).

37. The one-year time period marks the outer limits of the period in which relief may be sought. The party also must move diligently. A motion for relief made within a year, but long after the grounds for relief should have been discovered may be denied if there is no explanation for the delay. E.g., Security Mut. Cas. Co. v. Century Cas. Co., 621 F.2d 1062 (10th Cir.1980) (115 day delay); Di Vito v. Fidelity & Deposit Co. of Maryland, 361 F.2d 936 (7th Cir.1966) (four and one-half month delay); Schildhaus v. Moe, 335 F.2d 529 (2d Cir.1964) (eight month delay).

38. Fed.Civ.Proc.Rule 60(b)(1).

For a discussion of whether Federal Rule 60(b)(1) applies to judicial errors of law, see Note, Relief from Judgment Under Rule 60(b)(1) Due to Judicial Errors of Law, 83 Mich.L.Rev. 1571 (1985).

discovered evidence,[39] or on the basis of fraud.[40] Each of these bases was a well-recognized ground for relief even before the 1938 adoption of the federal rules.[41] Each also is quite concrete and generally has been interpreted narrowly so as not to encourage sloppy practices during the first trial. A brief review of how the courts have used each of these grounds reveals their limits.

Relief is allowed on the basis of mistake, inadvertence, or neglect only when it appears to be reasonable under the circumstances[42] and is not the result of gross negligence on the part of the moving party[43] or his lawyer.[44] In practice, this means that the rule most frequently is invoked successfully in the default setting[45] or when the plaintiff's suit was dismissed for failure to prosecute[46] and judgment was entered by mistake since the party fully intended actively to litigate the dispute.[47] Outside the default setting, negligent errors of counsel are treated less sympathetically and relief frequently is denied on the ground that the negligent act was inexcusable.[48]

Federal Rule 60(b)(2), authorizing relief on grounds of newly discovered evidence, requires something more than simply the development of a new theory or newly discovered facts. A party seeking to rely on this provision must show that the evidence and the fact to which it relates

---

39. Fed.Civ.Proc.Rule 60(b)(2).

40. Fed.Civ.Proc.Rule 60(b)(3).

In some states there is no fixed time limit when seeking relief based on fraud. E.g., Del.Civ.Proc.Rule of Super.Ct. 60(b); N.Y.—McKinney's CPLR 5015(a). In California, relief sought because of intrinsic fraud is governed by the statutory 6–month time limit, but if extrinsic fraud is alleged, the time limit does not apply. Beresh v. Sovereign Life Ins. Co. of California, 92 Cal.App.3d 547, 155 Cal.Rptr. 74 (1979).

41. See, e.g., Kaw Valley Drainage Dist. v. Union Pacific R.R. Co., 163 Fed. 836 (C.C.A.Kan.1908). Relief premised on the grounds of newly discovered evidence or fraud was obtained by special writs and independent actions. See Moore & Rogers, Federal Relief from Civil Judgments, 55 Yale L.J. 623, 653–82 (1946).

42. E.g., Barber v. California Credit Council, 224 Cal.App.2d 635, 36 Cal.Rptr. 834 (1964).

43. E.g., Weinreich v. Sandhaus, 156 F.R.D. 60 (S.D.N.Y.1994).

44. The attorney's negligence generally is imputed to the client. See Link v. Wabash R.R. Co., 370 U.S. 626, 633, 82 S.Ct. 1386, 1390, 8 L.Ed.2d 734 (1962); Restatement Second of Judgments § 67, comment c (1982).

45. See Project, Relief from Default Judgments Under Rule 60(b)—A Study of Federal Case Law, 49 Ford.L.Rev. 956

(1981). E.g., Rooks v. American Brass Co., 263 F.2d 166 (6th Cir.1959). See also Mieszkowski v. Norville, 61 Ill.App.2d 289, 209 N.E.2d 358 (1965).

The New York counterpart to Rule 60(b)(1) allows relief only on the basis of "excusable default." N.Y.—McKinney's CPLR 5015(a)(1).

46. E.g., Boughner v. Secretary of HEW, 572 F.2d 976 (3d Cir.1978); Leong v. Railroad Transfer Serv., Inc., 302 F.2d 555 (7th Cir.1962).

47. See Griffin v. Kennedy, 344 F.2d 198 (D.C.Cir.1965) (erroneous stipulation of counsel in order to raise jurisdiction defense that resulted in summary judgment against client); Van Dyke v. MacMillan, 162 Cal.App.2d 594, 328 P.2d 215 (1958) (illness of counsel and misunderstanding that mail would take more than one day from Los Angeles to Yuba City).

48. See, e.g., Sparrow v. Heller, 116 F.3d 204 (7th Cir.1997); Consolidated Masonry & Fireproofing, Inc. v. Wagman Constr. Corp., 383 F.2d 249 (4th Cir.1967). For an argument that the decision to grant relief should not be tied to the negligence or nonnegligence of the moving party, but rather the focus should be on whether there was a miscarriage of justice, see Note, Negligent Litigation and Relief from Judgments: The Case for a Second Chance, 50 S.Cal.L.Rev. 1207 (1977).

were in existence at the time of the trial,[49] and that the party was unable to discover them at that time despite the exercise of due diligence in preparing the case.[50] Further, the evidence must be of such a nature that it is likely to produce a different result if the judgment is reopened and a new trial ordered.[51]

These limitations press parties to prepare fully for their first trial because equitable considerations demand that the winning party should be able to rely on the judgment, except in very exceptional circumstances. In addition, the requirement that the evidence have been in existence at the time of trial recognizes that to allow relief for evidence that was not in existence until after trial would result in the perpetual continuation of lawsuits. Thus, the subsequent development of a new medical treatment that could ameliorate plaintiff's damages[52] or later medical examinations showing that the injury is greater or more extensive than was shown at trial[53] cannot be the bases for relief. The windfall or the harm to the plaintiff as a result of changed circumstances is the result and price of the practice of awarding lump sum damages and does not alter the fact that at the time of trial the relief was appropriate.

To make a successful motion for relief because of fraud, the movant must establish the existence of the fraud by clear and convincing evidence; a mere suspicion or allegation of fraud is not sufficient.[54] Some courts have held that relief may be allowed without any necessity of showing that the result is likely to be altered in a second trial not tainted by fraud,[55] although other courts require some showing of a meritorious claim or defense.[56]

Historically, relief was granted solely for extrinsic, as opposed to intrinsic, fraud. The federal rule abandons this restriction[57] and autho-

---

49. Brown v. Pennsylvania R.R. Co., 282 F.2d 522 (3d Cir.1960), cert. denied 365 U.S. 818; Prostrollo v. University of South Dakota, 63 F.R.D. 9 (D.S.D.1974).

50. Alpern v. UtiliCorp United, Inc., 84 F.3d 1525 (8th Cir.1996); Richardson v. National Rifle Ass'n, 879 F.Supp. 1 (D.D.C. 1995); Inhabitants of Town of Kennebunkport v. Forrester, 391 A.2d 831 (Me.1978); Ashton v. Sierrita Mining & Ranching, 21 Ariz.App. 303, 518 P.2d 1020 (1974).

If the reason the party could not discover the evidence sooner was because it was fraudulently concealed by the opposing side, relief may be sought on the basis of fraud. In some instances, this will allow relief outside the timing restrictions. See text at nn. 22–24, above.

51. U.S. v. Walus, 616 F.2d 283 (7th Cir.1980); International Nikoh Corp. v. H. K. Porter Co., 374 F.2d 82 (7th Cir.1967); Cox v. Trans World Airlines, Inc., 20 F.R.D. 298 (W.D.Mo.1957).

52. Patrick v. Sedwick, 413 P.2d 169 (Alaska 1966).

53. Ryan v. U.S. Lines Co., 303 F.2d 430 (2d Cir.1962).

54. Di Vito v. Fidelity & Deposit Co. of Maryland, 361 F.2d 936 (7th Cir.1966); Brown v. Pennsylvania R.R. Co., 282 F.2d 522 (3d Cir.1960), cert. denied 365 U.S. 818.

55. Rozier v. Ford Motor Co., 573 F.2d 1332, 1339 (5th Cir.1978) ("This subsection of the Rule is aimed at judgments which were unfairly obtained, not at those which are factually incorrect.").

56. Saunders v. Saunders, 157 Cal. App.2d 67, 320 P.2d 131 (1958).

57. See generally Note, Relief from Unfairly Obtained Verdicts in Federal Court: Determination and Analysis of the Level of Fraud Required for Vacation of Judgments Under Fed.R.Civ.P. 60(b), 30 S.Car.L.Rev. 781 (1979).

rizes relief for both.[58] The difference between the two always has been elusive.[59] Stated roughly, intrinsic fraud is that which occurs in court during trial—the presentation of perjured testimony, for example—whereas extrinsic fraud involves some act of the opposing party that prevented the movant from discovering some evidence or otherwise from making some claim or defense.[60] Many states today have retained this historic distinction and permit the judgment to be opened only for extrinsic fraud.[61] This limitation is premised on the belief that the trial itself allows an opportunity to uncover intrinsic fraud, by the examination and cross-examination of the witnesses, and that the rule cannot be used to correct for trial errors.

The second category of relief motions in Federal Rule 60(b) also presents very specific grounds, but a party seeking relief under these provisions must do so only within a "reasonable time." The bases for relief are that the judgment is void,[62] or that it has been satisfied, or that the law on which the court relied has been reversed, or, if an injunctive decree is involved, that a change in circumstances makes it no longer equitable to enforce it.[63] The decision not to limit the right to raise these challenges within a set time period reflects the seriousness of the issues. In addition, in the injunction context, the time for seeking relief necessarily will depend on the circumstances of the case and will not be totally within the party's control. Indeed, motions under Rule 60(b)(4) alleging that the judgment is void often are said to have no real time limits because a void judgment cannot obtain validity through the laches of the moving party.[64] In general, under all of these provisions the moving party need show only that she acted diligently once the basis for relief became available, and that the delay in seeking relief did not cause undue hardship to the opposing party.[65]

These grounds for relief are limited strictly in their scope, however. A judgment can be challenged as void only on grounds of lack of

---

58. Peacock Records, Inc. v. Checker Records, Inc., 365 F.2d 145 (7th Cir.1966), cert. denied 385 U.S. 1003.

Although the abolition of the distinction between extrinsic and intrinsic fraud simplifies the decision whether relief is merited, there remain difficult questions of what conduct constitutes fraud. See, e.g., Buice v. T. & B. Builders, Inc., 219 Ga. 259, 132 S.E.2d 784 (1963) (failure to disclose matters that would defeat claim is not fraud justifying relief).

59. Howard v. Scott, 225 Mo. 685, 125 S.W. 1158 (1909).

60. For a discussion of the distinction, see 11 C. Wright, A. Miller & M. Kane, Civil 2d § 2861.

61. Schwartz v. Merchants Mortgage Co., 272 Md. 305, 322 A.2d 544 (1974); Smith v. Great Lakes Airlines, Inc., 242 Cal.App.2d 23, 51 Cal.Rptr. 1 (1966); Jen-

nings v. Bridgeford, 218 Tenn. 287, 403 S.W.2d 289 (1966). See also Lumbermens Mut. Cas. Co. v. Carriere, 170 N.J.Super. 437, 406 A.2d 994 (Law Div.1979).

62. Fed.Civ.Proc.Rule 60(b)(4).

63. Fed.Civ.Proc.Rule 60(b)(5).

64. Misco Leasing, Inc. v. Vaughn, 450 F.2d 257 (10th Cir.1971); Austin v. Smith, 312 F.2d 337 (D.C.Cir.1962); Jardine, Gill & Duffus, Inc. v. M/V Cassiopeia, 523 F.Supp. 1076 (D.Md.1981); Shields v. Pirkle Refrigerated Freightlines, Inc., 181 Mont. 37, 591 P.2d 1120 (1979).

65. Compare John W. Johnson, Inc. v. J. A. Jones Constr. Co., 369 F.Supp. 484 (E.D.Va.1973) (timely), with Willits v. Yellow Cab Co., 214 F.2d 612 (7th Cir.1954) (untimely).

jurisdiction[66] or for some failure of due process in the original proceeding.[67] Erroneous judgments are not void,[68] even when based on unconstitutional statutes. Further, relief will be allowed because of a change in the law only when the trial court clearly and specifically relied on some precedent that was overturned.[69] This ground for relief is not a method of bringing all judgments into conformity with one another. It is only to remedy egregious errors that become apparent within a limited time.[70] Finally, the reference to relief from injunctive decrees simply embraces the historic power of the court issuing the decree to modify it if there has been a change in circumstances.[71]

The third and final category found in Rule 60(b) for obtaining relief is on its face the broadest. It is governed only by the need to seek relief within a reasonable time[72] and covers "any other reason justifying relief from the operation of the judgment."[73] This catch-all provision preserves the courts' equitable reserve power to do justice in individual cases when it seems appropriate. And the courts have responded accordingly. For example, the most common situation in which relief has been granted under this provision is when a default judgment is involved, because the courts generally favor adjudications after an adversarial presentation.[74] Relief from a default judgment will be denied only when it is clear the defendant has no defense to the action[75] or when the defendant has delayed so long that the plaintiff would be prejudiced by being required to go to trial.[76]

Although concerns were raised that this equitable loophole effectively could destroy the restrictions imposed in the other portions of the rule[77] because it could be used to allow relief on grounds listed elsewhere, but outside the applicable time limits, or for reasons somewhat inconsis-

66. Restatement Second of Judgments §§ 65, 69 (1982).

67. Orner v. Shalala, 30 F.3d 1307 (10th Cir.1994); Aguchak v. Montgomery Ward Co., 520 P.2d 1352 (Alaska 1974).

68. Hoult v. Hoult, 57 F.3d 1 (1st Cir. 1995); In the Matter of Estate of Davis, 524 N.W.2d 125 (S.D.1994); Bowers v. Board of Appeals of Marshfield, 16 Mass.App.Ct. 29, 448 N.E.2d 1293 (1983), review denied 389 Mass. 1104, 451 N.E.2d 1167.

69. Collins v. City of Wichita, 254 F.2d 837 (10th Cir.1958), noted 44 Iowa L.Rev. 574 (1959); Berryhill v. U.S., 199 F.2d 217 (6th Cir.1952); Loucke v. U.S., 21 F.R.D. 305 (S.D.N.Y.1957).

70. See Bailey v. Ryan Stevedoring Co., 894 F.2d 157, 160 (5th Cir.1990), cert. denied 498 U.S. 829; Pierce v. Cook & Co., 518 F.2d 720 (10th Cir.1975), cert. denied 423 U.S. 1079; Hartford Ins. Co. v. Allstate Ins. Co., 68 N.J. 430, 347 A.2d 353 (1975).

71. See Agostini v. Felton, 521 U.S. 203, 117 S.Ct. 1997, 138 L.Ed.2d 391 (1997)

(fact that individual members of the Supreme Court had expressed an interest in reevaluating Court's earlier decision is not a change in circumstances meriting relief).

72. Compare King v. Mordowanec, 46 F.R.D. 474 (D.R.I.1969), with Marquette Corp. v. Priester, 234 F.Supp. 799 (E.D.S.C. 1964).

73. Fed.Civ.Proc.Rule 60(b)(6).

74. Erick Rios Bridoux v. Eastern Air Lines, Inc., 214 F.2d 207 (D.C.Cir.1954), cert. denied 348 U.S. 821.

75. See, e.g., Bell Telephone Labs., Inc. v. Hughes Aircraft Co., 73 F.R.D. 16 (D.Del. 1976).

76. Diversified Utilities Sales, Inc. v. Monte Fusco Excavating Contracting Co., 71 F.R.D. 661 (E.D.Pa.1976).

77. Note, Federal Rule 60(b): Relief from Civil Judgments, 61 Yale L.J. 76 (1952).

tent with the specific grounds delineated, this has not occurred.[78] The courts have construed this plenary power as not providing a means to escape the timing restrictions that control motions for new trial,[79] appeals,[80] or motions for relief based on mistake,[81] newly discovered evidence[82] or fraud.[83] Relief has been limited to what are deemed cases presenting "extraordinary circumstances"[84] or presenting grounds other than those listed in the rule[85] that seem to require some remedy.

Although the standard of extraordinary circumstances is somewhat vague and subject to some varying, if not conflicting, interpretations by the courts, it does suggest at least the broad contours of a test. The standard begins with a presumption that the judgment is not to be opened easily, but only when undue hardship would occur and the demands of equity and justice require it.[86]

The test was adopted by the Supreme Court in two cases. The first was Klapprott v. United States,[87] an action to set aside a four-year-old default judgment cancelling a certificate of naturalization. Petitioner claimed that he had failed to move for relief earlier because he had been jailed and was impoverished. An attempt to get the ACLU to defend him allegedly was thwarted when the FBI prevented his letter from being mailed. The Supreme Court upheld Klapprott's right to relief under Rule 60(b)(6), noting that he was entitled to a fair trial. One year later the Court was presented with another motion for relief from a four-year-old judgment cancelling a certificate of naturalization. However, in that

---

78. See Kane, Relief From Federal Judgments: A Morass Unrelieved by a Rule, 30 Hast.L.J. 41 (1978), reviewing all the decisions dealing with Rule 60(b)(6).

There are a few cases in which the courts have strained the interpretation of the rule to find that an error falling within the time restricted portion of the rule is extraordinary and thus relief is merited. See, e.g., U.S. v. Karahalias, 205 F.2d 331 (2d Cir.1953). See generally Note, Federal Rule 60(b): Relief from Civil Judgments, 61 Yale L.J. 76 (1952).

79. See Hulson v. Atchison, Topeka & Santa Fe Ry. Co., 289 F.2d 726 (7th Cir. 1961), cert. denied 368 U.S. 835.

80. Hodgson v. United Mine Workers, 473 F.2d 118 (D.C.Cir.1972).

81. Costa v. Chapkines, 316 F.2d 541 (2d Cir.1963).

82. Carr v. District of Columbia, 543 F.2d 917, 926 n. 72 (D.C.Cir.1976).

83. Petry v. General Motors Corp., 62 F.R.D. 357 (E.D.Pa.1974); Stone v. Stone, 647 P.2d 582 (Alaska 1982).

84. Webb v. Erickson, 134 Ariz. 182, 655 P.2d 6 (1982) (judgment entered against defaulting garnishee presented ex-

traordinary circumstances meriting relief); Jewell v. Division of Social Servs., 401 A.2d 88 (Del.1979) (Division's action in obtaining custody of children within 6 months of parties' stipulation that gave appellant hope of regaining custody vitiated underlying basis of settlement and provided extraordinary circumstances allowing for relief from judgment); Bowers v. Board of Appeals of Marshfield, 16 Mass.App.Ct. 29, 448 N.E.2d 1293 (1983), review denied 389 Mass. 1104, 451 N.E.2d 1167 (consent judgment involving agreement that was beyond scope of authority of government officials who acquiesced justified extraordinary relief).

85. L. M. Leathers' Sons v. Goldman, 252 F.2d 188 (6th Cir.1958) (relief from a judgment based on a settlement agreement with which the opposing party failed to comply); Armour & Co. v. Nard, 56 F.R.D. 610 (N.D.Iowa 1972) (fraud of third-party witness).

86. For an exploration of the case law applying this standard, see Kane, Relief from Federal Judgments: A Morass Unrelieved by a Rule, 30 Hast.L.J. 41, 50–62 (1978).

87. 335 U.S. 601, 69 S.Ct. 384, 93 L.Ed. 266 (1949).

case, Ackermann v. United States,[88] the petitioners had been present at their trial but had decided not to appeal when their attorney advised them of the cost, which would require the sale of their only asset—a house—and an official at their internment camp told them not to sell because it was likely that, at the end of the war, all persons in their position would be freed. The Court upheld the trial court's denial of relief, concluding "neither the circumstances of petitioner nor his excuse for not appealing is so extraordinary as to bring him within Klapprott or Rule 60(b)(6)."[89] The voluntary choice of the Ackermanns not to appeal, despite the pressures they were under, meant that extraordinary relief was not warranted.

Finally, some mention must be made about the interplay between motions for relief and appeals. If a party succeeds in obtaining relief, the judgment is opened and a new trial ordered. Hence, there can be no immediate appeal[90] in jurisdictions following the final judgment rule,[91] as the ruling is interlocutory.[92]

A serious problem is posed, however, when a party moves for relief from judgment after an appeal has been filed.[93] This has caused some difficulty because the general rule is that once appeal is taken, the trial court loses jurisdiction.[94] Yet, appeals may be pending for long periods of time and the allowance of a motion for relief in the trial court may obviate the need for appellate relief. Some older cases suggested that a party in that position should raise his grounds for relief in the appellate court, which could then remand the case to allow the district court to pass on them.[95] This approach was unnecessarily cumbersome. More recent decisions allow the motion for relief to be filed directly in the district court, and if that court indicates that it will grant relief, the appellate court then will remand.[96] If the court denies the motion, then a

---

88. 340 U.S. 193, 71 S.Ct. 209, 95 L.Ed. 207 (1950).

89. 340 U.S. at 202, 71 S.Ct. at 213. In contrasting the facts of the two cases, the Ackermann majority commented upon "the difference between no choice and choice; imprisonment and freedom of action, no trial and trial; no counsel and counsel; no chance for negligence and inexcusable negligence." Ibid.

90. Stubblefield v. Windsor Capital Group, 74 F.3d 990 (10th Cir.1996); Fisher v. Bush, 377 So.2d 968 (Ala.1979); Allen v. Cole Realty, Inc., 325 A.2d 19 (Me.1974); Hackney v. Hackney, 327 S.W.2d 570 (Ky. 1959).

91. See § 13.1, below.

92. Although historically appeals could be taken by using various extraordinary writs or special bills, see generally Moore & Rogers, Federal Relief from Civil Judgments, 55 Yale L.J. 623 (1946), the 1948 amendments to Federal Rule 60(b) specifi-

cally eliminated the availability of these devices, treating orders granting judgment relief the same as all other orders for appeals purposes. "Writs of coram nobis, coram vobis, audita querela, and bills of review and bills in the nature of a bill of review, are abolished * * *." Fed.Civ.Proc.Rule 60(b).

93. See 11 C. Wright, A. Miller & M. Kane, Civil 2d § 2873.

94. Beresh v. Sovereign Life Ins. Co. of California, 92 Cal.App.3d 547, 155 Cal.Rptr. 74 (1979).

95. Zig Zag Spring Co. v. Comfort Spring Corp., 200 F.2d 901 (3d Cir.1953); Baruch v. Beech Aircraft Corp., 172 F.2d 445 (10th Cir.1949).

96. Standard Oil Co. of California v. U.S., 429 U.S. 17, 97 S.Ct. 31, 50 L.Ed.2d 21 (1976); Puerto Rico v. SS Zoe Colocotroni, 601 F.2d 39 (1st Cir.1979); Iannarelli v. Morton, 463 F.2d 179 (3d Cir.1972); Note, Disposition of Federal Rule 60(b) Motions During Appeal, 65 Yale L.J. 708 (1956).

new appeal from the denial can be considered by the appellate court in conjunction with the appeal from the original judgment.[97]

97.   E.g., Goffman v. Gross, 59 F.3d 668 (7th Cir.1995).

§§ 12.7–13.0 are reserved for supplementary material.

Chapter 13

APPEALS

Analysis

A. APPEALABILITY

A. APPEALABILITY

§ 13.1 The Timing of Appeals—The Final Judgment Rule

In most jurisdictions today the question of when an appeal can be taken is governed by the so-called "final judgment rule."[1] As the name suggests, under this rule appeals are allowed only after all the issues involved in a particular lawsuit have been finally determined by the trial court.[2] The reliance on finality to govern the timing of appeals can be traced to early English practice when appeals from common law judgments were by writs of error that depended on obtaining a full record of the case for review.[3] Although the procedure surrounding appeals has

---

§ 13.1

1. In most jurisdictions the final judgment rule is statutory. See, e.g., 28 U.S.C.A. § 1291; West's Ann.Cal.Code Civ.Proc. § 904.1; Kansas Stat.Ann. 60–2102(4). The Supreme Court recognized the finality principle before it was made a statutory requirement for the federal courts. See McLish v. Roff, 141 U.S. 661, 12 S.Ct. 118, 35 L.Ed. 893 (1891).

2. In the federal courts, identifying whether a judgment has been entered rarely poses great difficulty because under the Federal Rules, judgments must be set forth on a separate document. Fed.Civ.Proc.Rule 58. A party need not be concerned about failing to file a timely appeal, if he waits until the separate document containing the judgment has been filed and entered. See, e.g., Cooper v. Town of East Hampton, 83 F.3d 31 (2d Cir.1996). However, the party, under certain circumstances, may file an appeal before the judgment has been separately entered; the absence of a separate judgment does not deprive the court of appellate jurisdiction. Bankers Trust Co. v. Mallis, 435 U.S. 381, 98 S.Ct. 1117, 55 L.Ed.2d 357 (1978). The main problem in determining whether an appeal is timely is whether the judgment is final.

3. See 15A C. Wright, A. Miller & E. Cooper, Jurisdiction and Related Matters 2d § 3906; Crick, The Final Judgment as a Basis for Appeal, 41 Yale L.J. 539 (1932).

changed,[4] the final judgment rule remains.

An often quoted definition of a final judgment is an order that "ends the litigation on the merits and leaves nothing for the court to do but execute the judgment."[5] The important distinction to be drawn is between an order that is final as to the particular issue at hand and one that concludes the litigation on the merits.[6] The former is interlocutory and not subject to an immediate appeal; it may be reviewed only after the entire lawsuit is concluded. Thus, interlocutory orders ultimately are reviewable,[7] but not immediately appealable. The final judgment rule determines not whether the appellate court will review a particular ruling, but when. Illustratively, the decision of the trial judge overruling counsel's challenge for cause of a particular juror is conclusive on that issue. It may be reviewed on appeal, but only after a final judgment on the merits.

It is very important to ascertain just what constitutes a final judgment because in many situations appellate courts are deemed to lack jurisdiction over other types of decisions.[8] If a final judgment is not presented, the appellate court has no recourse but to dismiss.[9] Although characterizing the rule as jurisdictional may be criticized, it is still the norm,[10] with the result that determining what orders fall within the final

---

4. There is wide variance among the appellate procedures used in different systems, and a review of the many rules that exist is beyond this volume. Care should be taken to check the relevant appellate rules in order to avoid forfeiting the right of appeal because of some technical failure.

5. Catlin v. U.S., 324 U.S. 229, 233, 65 S.Ct. 631, 633, 89 L.Ed. 911 (1945). For a review of the leading federal decisions that have attempted to give some more content to the definition of finality, see 15A C. Wright, A. Miller & E. Cooper, Jurisdiction and Related Matters 2d § 3909. Compare Altschuler v. Altschuler, 399 Ill. 559, 78 N.E.2d 225 (1948) (finality present when the only matters left for future determination were incidental to the ultimate rights already adjudicated).

6. For example, injunctive decrees are final when the court has decided all the issues and all that remains is to determine compliance with the decree. The fact that the trial court reserves jurisdiction to alter the decree should circumstances change does not make its determination interlocutory. Heath v. Kettenhofen, 236 Cal.App.2d 197, 45 Cal.Rptr. 778 (1965). See also Taylor v. Taylor, 398 So.2d 267 (Ala.1981). In contrast, a judgment specifying certain damage items, but leaving open the possibility that additional damages might be awarded in a subsequent proceeding does not end the litigation and is interlocutory. International Controls Corp. v. Vesco, 535

F.2d 742 (2d Cir.1976). See also Ball Corp. v. Loran, 42 Colo.App. 501, 596 P.2d 412 (1979) (a decree deciding liability, but deferring damages, is not final).

7. For a discussion of reviewability, see § 13.4, below.

8. Because finality is viewed as a jurisdictional requisite, the appellate court can raise the issue sua sponte and the parties consent is immaterial. Brown Shoe Co. v. U.S., 370 U.S. 294, 305, 82 S.Ct. 1502, 1513, 8 L.Ed.2d 510 (1962).

9. See Firestone Tire & Rubber Co. v. Risjord, 449 U.S. 368, 101 S.Ct. 669, 66 L.Ed.2d 571 (1981); Collins v. Miller, 252 U.S. 364, 40 S.Ct. 347, 64 L.Ed. 616 (1920); U.S. v. Girault, 52 U.S. (11 How.) 22, 13 L.Ed. 587 (1850).

10. For a practical view of finality, see Jetco Electronic Indus., Inc. v. Gardiner, 473 F.2d 1228 (5th Cir.1973), upholding appellate jurisdiction of an order dismissing one of three defendants from a case when the other claims were dismissed after the original appeal was filed. Compare Fletcher v. Gagosian, 604 F.2d 637 (9th Cir.1979), holding that plaintiff's unilateral dismissal of remaining claims did not convert a preexisting order for dismissal of count one into a final appealable order. See generally 15A C. Wright, A. Miller & E. Cooper, Jurisdiction and Related Matters 2d §§ 3914.6–3914.9.

judgment rule remains a critical threshold question on appeal. The failure to determine correctly when a final judgment is entered can result in the dismissal of an appeal, or, more drastically, in forfeiting all rights of appeal, because those rights must be exercised within strict time limits[11] once final judgment is entered.[12]

Although the application of the final judgment rule can produce some harsh results, the rationale supporting its use rests on a desire to achieve judicial economy and efficiency.[13] The assumption is that a single appeal in which all objections to the trial court's rulings are raised will be more efficient than several appeals, each requiring its own set of briefs, record, oral argument, and opinions.[14] Further, many adverse rulings never will require appellate review. A losing party on a particular motion, for example, ultimately may prevail at trial and thus will not seek an appeal at all, saving appellate court time. Additionally, by forcing the parties to wait until the trial concludes, the appellate court may be able to review the various rulings being challenged from a broadened perspective.[15] By avoiding interlocutory appeals, the trial process also may proceed more rapidly, because it will not need to be stalled while waiting for an appellate ruling on some point. Adherence to the final judgment rule also avoids the risk that immediate appeals from all trial court orders may decrease respect for the authority of the trial judge.[16] Finally, the operation of the rule prevents parties from engaging in costly delaying tactics at trial, by appealing each adverse ruling as it is entered.[17]

A few jurisdictions have not been persuaded by these arguments, however, and allow interlocutory appeals freely.[18] This is not because they do not desire judicial economy, but rather they have determined

11. Appellate rules provide a set time period, commonly 30 days, from the entry of judgment in which an appeal must be filed or the right to appeal will be lost. E.g., Fed.App.Proc.Rule 4; Ariz.App.Proc.Rule 9(a); Kansas Stat.Ann. 60–2103(a); Mass. Rules App.Proc.Rule 4(a).

12. See, e.g., Dickinson v. Petroleum Conversion Corp., 338 U.S. 507, 70 S.Ct. 322, 94 L.Ed. 299 (1950); Burgin v. Sugg, 210 Ala. 142, 97 So. 216 (1923).

13. See generally Note, Appealability in the Federal Courts, 75 Harv.L.Rev. 351 (1961).

14. Appeals can be very expensive. See Willcox, Karlen & Roemer, Justice Lost—By What Appellate Papers Cost, 33 N.Y.U.L.Rev. 934 (1958); Note, Cost of Appeal, 27 Mont.L.Rev. 49 (1965).

15. Taylor v. Board of Educ. of City School Dist. of City of New Rochelle, 288 F.2d 600 (2d Cir.1961).

16. See MDK, Inc. v. Mike's Train House, Inc., 27 F.3d 116 (4th Cir.1994),

cert. denied 513 U.S. 1000; Wright, The Doubtful Omniscience of Appellate Courts, 41 Minn.L.Rev. 751, 781 (1957) ("Every time a trial judge is reversed, every time the belief is reiterated that appellate courts are better qualified than trial judges to decide what justice requires, the confidence of litigants and the public in the trial courts will be further impaired.").

17. Waverly Mut. & Permanent Land, Loan & Bldg. Ass'n v. Buck, 64 Md. 338, 1 A. 561 (1885).

18. New York allows an appeal whenever the order involved affects a substantial right. N.Y.—McKinney's CPLR 5701. See generally Korn, Civil Jurisdiction of the New York Court of Appeals and Appellate Divisions, 16 Buffalo L.Rev. 307 (1967). Wisconsin allows nonfinal appeals by permission in order to protect petitioner from substantial or irreparable injury. Wisconsin Stat.Ann. 808.03(2)(b). See also Glover v. Baker, 76 N.H. 261, 81 A. 1081 (1911).

that allowing interlocutory appeals is more efficient.[19] This is particularly true if the issue on which an appeal is sought is one that would be determinative so that allowing an immediate appeal may avoid an unnecessary trial.[20] Allowing interlocutory review also arguably supports a better and more refined trial; by correcting the errors below as they occur, whatever judgment ultimately is reached may be less likely to be reversed, thus avoiding a wasted trial. In addition to this difference of view regarding which approach is more efficient, those systems allowing a more liberal interlocutory review focus on the task of the appellate courts to provide guidance to the lower courts concerning the interpretation of the law. Strict application of the final judgment rule effectively prevents some orders from ever receiving appellate scrutiny because, even if they are entered erroneously, the order itself will not be deemed sufficiently prejudicial to merit reversal. To avoid inconsistent lower court treatment, more constant and systematic guidance by the appellate courts over all the phases of the trial is preferred. The price for this decision is potential congestion at the appellate level.[21]

The concerns reflected by those jurisdictions preferring interlocutory appeals are not ignored in those jurisdictions following the final judgment rule. They too recognize that to adhere to finality too rigidly in some settings would create an undue hardship on the parties or actually prevent necessary trial court guidance.[22] Thus, as is discussed in the following sections, some exceptions to finality have been incorporated in specific statutes,[23] and a few well-recognized judicial doctrines[24] have developed allowing immediate appeals when they otherwise would be precluded because of a lack of finality. The difference between the two approaches to appealability consequently is not as much philosophical as

19. For arguments that the federal courts should move toward a discretionary appeal system, see Martineau, Defining Finality and Appealability by Court Rule: Right Problem, Wrong Solution, 54 U.Pitt.L.Rev. 717 (1993); Note, Replacing the Crazy Quilt of Interlocutory Appeals Jurisprudence with Discretionary Review, 44 Duke L.J. 200 (1994).

20. Under the final judgment rule, statutory and judicial exceptions provide the flexibility necessary to allow some critical interlocutory orders to be reviewed immediately. See §§ 13.2–13.3, below.

21. See Project, The Appellate Division of the Supreme Court of New York: An Empirical Study of Its Powers and Functions as an Intermediate State Court, 47 Ford.L.Rev. 929, 951 (1979). Other writers have noted the increasing problem of appellate court congestion even in the federal courts in which the final judgment rule prevails. See Wright, The Overloaded Fifth Circuit: A Crisis in Judicial Administration, 42 Texas L.Rev. 949 (1964); Note, The Second Circuit: Federal Judicial Administra-

tion in Microcosm, 63 Colum.L.Rev. 874 (1963).

22. In some states that follow the final judgment rule, the courts treat finality more flexibly than do the federal courts in order to accommodate concerns in certain cases. See, e.g., Cook v. Cook, 26 Ariz.App. 163, 547 P.2d 15 (1976); In re Marriage of Skelley, 18 Cal.3d 365, 134 Cal.Rptr. 197, 556 P.2d 297 (1976). Further, state statutory exceptions sometimes can be quite broad, effectively giving the appellate court the discretion to allow an appeal whenever necessary "in the interest of justice." N.J. Court Rules, 1969 2:2–4. Some states also exercise broader power to review through a liberal use of extraordinary writs in certain types of cases. See, e.g., Taylor v. Superior Court of Los Angeles County, 24 Cal.3d 890, 157 Cal.Rptr. 693, 598 P.2d 854 (1979) (mandamus allowed to review grant of demurrer on portion of plaintiff's complaint seeking punitive damages).

23. See § 13.3, below.

24. See § 13.2, below.

it is a difference in the method in which a particular jurisdiction has decided to balance the efficiency obtained by adherence to finality against the judicial economy and guidance promoted by allowing immediate review.

The process of determining what constitutes a final judgment is straightforward in most simple two-party, single-claim litigation.[25] In several situations, however, the finality concept has been the subject of confusion.[26] This sense of confusion is exacerbated if one compares the decisions of different jurisdictions, all claiming to follow the final judgment rule, because there is a wide variance in the way in which that rule is applied. For example, in the federal courts a trial judge's ruling rejecting a personal jurisdiction objection is interlocutory and cannot be reviewed until after a judgment on the merits is entered. However, several states, supposedly governed by the final judgment rule, have allowed immediate review of these orders[27] so as to avoid a wasted trial if jurisdiction actually is lacking.

Without doubt, the federal courts are among the most strict in adhering to the finality requirement; the federal appellate courts have been sensitive to the need to protect their dockets from numerous interlocutory appeals. Because it would be impossible to explore fully the various nuances that can be found among the states, the remaining discussion will be directed primarily to the federal approach. An understanding of the operation of the final judgment rule in that context will illustrate the application of the finality rule. But worth repeating is the warning that precedents on finality are not readily transferrable from one jurisdiction to another.

One major problem has been the application of the final judgment rule to multiple-claim, multiple-party actions.[28] If the rule is applied literally, then any appeal must wait until all the claims against all the parties have been decided.[29] This is true even though orders dismissing some claims or parties may have been entered at an early stage and several years may pass before the entire lawsuit is concluded. Recognizing that to postpone an appeal under these circumstances may result in an unnecessary delay for those parties who have received a final judgment on their claim, a special rule, Federal Rule of Civil Procedure 54(b),[30] was adopted to identify those orders in the complex litigation setting that determine finally the rights of a given party or a single claim so that an immediate appeal may be allowed. Notably, Rule 54(b) is not

25. See Note, Appealability in the Federal Courts, 75 Harv.L.Rev. 351, 354 (1961).

26. McGourkey v. Toledo & Ohio Central Ry. Co., 146 U.S. 536, 545, 13 S.Ct. 170, 172, 36 L.Ed. 1079 (1892). See Redish, The Pragmatic Approach to Appealability in the Federal Courts, 75 Colum.L.Rev. 89 (1975).

27. See, e.g., West's Ann.Cal.Code Civ. Proc. § 418.10(c) (authorizing a writ of mandate to review an order refusing to quash service).

28. See Comment, Appealability Problems in Nebraska; Advantages of Federal Rule 54(b), 53 Neb.L.Rev. 73 (1974).

29. See, e.g., Santa Clara County v. Support, Inc., 89 Cal.App.3d 687, 152 Cal. Rptr. 754 (1979).

30. See generally 10 C. Wright, A. Miller & M. Kane, Civil 3d §§ 2653–61.

an exception to the final judgment rule; rather, it is a statutory standard for applying that rule in the multiple-party, multiple-claim context.[31]

Federal Rule 54(b) provides that a trial judge in an action with multiple claims or parties may identify as appealable a particular order issued with respect to a claim or party by making an express direction for the entry of a judgment as to the claim or party involved and by certifying that there is no just reason to delay an appeal. In the absence of this trial court certification, no appeal will lie.[32] The parties need not fear losing their right of appeal by failing to file a timely notice of appeal after an interlocutory order has been entered unless a Rule 54(b) certificate has been issued. The presence of the certificate does not itself guarantee the right to an immediate appeal, however. The appellate court will review the court's order to determine whether the entry of judgment was appropriate, as well as whether there is a just reason to delay the appeal.[33]

If the basis of the Rule 54(b) order was that it was a final disposition regarding one of several claims in the case, the court of appeals will consider de novo whether in fact multiple claims are presented or whether the trial judge merely ruled on one of the alternative theories on which a single claim was based.[34] The distinction between alternative theories and separate claims is not always easy to draw. One matter that the Supreme Court has clarified is that just because the claims rest on overlapping facts or are transactionally related does not prevent a finding that separate claims are present; separate does not mean totally unrelated.[35] It has been suggested that multiple claims are presented if the theories of recovery could be separately enforced.[36] But beyond these broad guidelines, little detail can be offered.[37] The determination whether multiple parties are present is less difficult. The key is that the

31. Sears, Roebuck & Co. v. Mackey, 351 U.S. 427, 435, 76 S.Ct. 895, 899, 100 L.Ed. 1297 (1956).

32. Bader v. Atlantic Int'l, Ltd., 986 F.2d 912 (5th Cir.1993); Employees' Retirement Sys. v. Big Island Realty, Inc., 2 Hawaii App. 151, 627 P.2d 304 (1981); Geyer v. City of Logansport, 317 N.E.2d 893 (Ind. App.1974). However, a majority of the circuit courts have found that a subsequent Rule 54(b) certification will validate an appellant's otherwise premature notice of appeal as long as there is no prejudice to the nonappealing party. See, e.g., Martinez v. Arrow Truck Sales, Inc., 865 F.2d 160 (8th Cir.1988); Lewis v. B.F. Goodrich Co., 850 F.2d 641 (10th Cir.1988); Freeman v. Hittle, 747 F.2d 1299 (9th Cir.1984).

33. Schwartz v. Compagnie General Transatlantique, 405 F.2d 270 (2d Cir. 1968); Baca Land & Cattle Co. v. New Mexico Timber, Inc., 384 F.2d 701 (10th Cir. 1967); Jackson v. Burlington Northern, Inc., 201 Mont. 123, 652 P.2d 223 (1982); Marshall v. Williams, 128 Ariz. 511, 627 P.2d 242 (App.1981).

34. See Liberty Mut. Ins. Co. v. Wetzel, 424 U.S. 737, 96 S.Ct. 1202, 47 L.Ed.2d 435 (1976) (complaint resting on single legal theory applied to one set of facts but seeking several remedies presented only a single claim); U.S. v. Crow, Pope & Land Enterprises, Inc., 474 F.2d 200 (5th Cir.1973) (appeal dismissed since action involved only a single claim with different legal theories).

35. Cold Metal Process Co. v. United Engineering & Foundry Co., 351 U.S. 445, 76 S.Ct. 904, 100 L.Ed. 1311 (1956); Sears, Roebuck & Co. v. Mackey, 351 U.S. 427, 76 S.Ct. 895, 100 L.Ed. 1297 (1956).

36. Rieser v. Baltimore & Ohio R.R. Co., 224 F.2d 198 (2d Cir.1955), cert. denied 350 U.S. 1006. See General Acquisition, Inc. v. GenCorp, Inc., 23 F.3d 1022 (6th Cir. 1994).

37. See the cases collected and discussed in 10 C. Wright, A. Miller & M. Kane, Civil 3d § 2657.

judgment must conclusively determine all the claims against one of the parties. If it does not, it cannot be certified.[38]

The second part of the trial court's certification, that there is no just reason to delay appellate review, requires a careful balancing of whether an appeal could simplify the trial or whether it would result in a double review of many of the same issues after judgment is reached on the remaining claims.[39] The appellate court will review the trial court's finding on this question for an abuse of discretion.[40] Consistent with the discretionary character of this determination, there are no precise guidelines for the courts to apply,[41] other than the recognized principle that appeals using Rule 54(b) are the exception, rather than the rule, and are reserved for the "infrequent harsh case."[42]

In general, the courts may consider whether there is some reason why it would be unfair to make the parties wait until after a final judgment in the entire action is entered before obtaining review. For example, it may consider whether there will be serious economic prejudice to the judgment winner if he is forced to wait to execute on a judgment until the remaining claims are decided.[43] An early appeal also may be warranted if it would avoid further proceedings in the trial court.[44] Balanced against these concerns may be factors arguing for the avoidance of piecemeal review, such as whether the claims being appealed are closely related to those yet to be tried so that it may be necessary to review the same facts a second time when the other claims reach judgment.[45] Each case must be decided in light of the facts surrounding

---

38. Vaughn v. Regents of University of California, 504 F.Supp. 1349 (E.D.Cal. 1981); Liquilux Gas Servs. of Ponce, Inc. v. Tropical Gas Co., 48 F.R.D. 330 (D.Puerto Rico 1969).

The appellate courts are split on the question whether Rule 54(b) applies when there is a judgment in a consolidated action that does not dispose of all the claims. See the cases collected in 10 C. Wright, A. Miller & M. Kane, Civil 3d § 2656. See generally Comment, The Appealability of Partial Judgments in Consolidated Cases, 57 U.Chi. L.Rev. 169 (1990).

39. See, e.g., Panichella v. Pennsylvania R.R. Co., 252 F.2d 452 (3d Cir.1958).

40. Cold Metal Process Co. v. United Engineering & Foundry Co., 351 U.S. 445, 453, 76 S.Ct. 904, 909, 100 L.Ed. 1311 (1956); Griffin v. Bethesda Foundation, 609 P.2d 459 (Wyo.1980); Schiffman v. Hanson Excavating Co., 82 Wn.2d 681, 513 P.2d 29 (1973). See the unusual case of Continental Cas. v. Superior Court, 130 Ariz. 189, 635 P.2d 174 (1981), in which the Arizona Supreme Court ruled that the trial judge had abused his discretion in refusing to certify an appeal under Rule 54(b).

41. The Supreme Court has refused specifically to provide concrete guidelines,

commenting, "because the number of possible situations is large, we are reluctant either to fix or sanction narrow guidelines for the district courts to follow." Curtiss–Wright Corp. v. General Elec. Co., 446 U.S. 1, 10–11, 100 S.Ct. 1460, 1466, 64 L.Ed.2d 1 (1980).

42. Panichella v. Pennsylvania R.R. Co., 252 F.2d 452 (3d Cir.1958). See Comment, Appeal and Error—North Dakota Rule of Civil Procedure 54(b): Looking for the Storied "Infrequent Harsh Case," 72 N.Dak.L.Rev. 731 (1996).

43. Curtiss–Wright Corp. v. General Elec. Co., 446 U.S. 1, 100 S.Ct. 1460, 64 L.Ed.2d 1 (1980).

44. See, e.g., Continental Airlines, Inc. v. Goodyear Tire & Rubber Co., 819 F.2d 1519 (9th Cir.1987) (Rule 54(b) certification designed to produce res judicata effects in another forum); Alcan Aluminum Corp. v. Carlsberg Financial Corp., 689 F.2d 815 (9th Cir.1982) (early appeal would reduce further litigation and facilitate settlement).

45. See, e.g., ODC Communications Corp. v. Wenruth Investments, 826 F.2d 509 (7th Cir.1987); Arlinghaus v. Ritenour, 543 F.2d 461 (2d Cir.1976).

it, interpreting Rule 54(b) consistent with the policies underlying the general goal of finality that controls appellate review.

Another area in which the determination of what constitutes a final judgment has posed some difficulty is that involving trial court orders either certifying or refusing to certify a particular action for class action treatment. Several lower federal courts developed a pragmatic approach to finality in order to allow appeals from these orders.[46] An order refusing class certification was viewed as sounding the "death knell" for the lawsuit on the theory that the individual claims of class members were too small to justify continued litigation and the suit would go forward only if a class action could be maintained.[47] Conversely, when class certification was granted, the opposing parties invoked what was termed the inverse death knell doctrine, arguing that to deny immediate review and cause them to litigate the action as a class suit would be extremely burdensome and costly, particularly since, if certification were erroneous, plaintiffs would not as a practical matter be able to sue at all.[48] This latter doctrine was accepted only in the Second Circuit.[49] Although in neither situation was a formal judgment presented, allowing an immediate appeal was deemed consistent with the policies underlying the final judgment rule.

The Supreme Court rejected this attempt to expand the meaning of the final judgment rule in Coopers & Lybrand v. Livesay.[50] The case involved an application of the death knell approach, and the Court ruled that that approach was effectively a legislative attempt to alter the statutory requirement of finality to accommodate social policies underlying class actions. The Court's invitation for a legislative solution ulti-

---

46. That a pragmatic approach to finality might be appropriate has been recognized by the Supreme Court. See, e.g., Gillespie v. U.S. Steel Corp., 379 U.S. 148, 152, 85 S.Ct. 308, 311, 13 L.Ed.2d 199 (1964); Brown Shoe Co. v. U.S., 370 U.S. 294, 306, 82 S.Ct. 1502, 1513, 8 L.Ed.2d 510 (1962). And some early decisions reflect this view. See, e.g., U.S. v. Wood, 295 F.2d 772 (5th Cir.1961), cert. denied 369 U.S. 850 (immediate appeal allowed from denial of temporary restraining order on the ground that the order was a "de facto dismissal" of the suit). See also T. C. R. Realty, Inc. v. Cox, 472 Pa. 331, 372 A.2d 721 (1977). However, more recent decisions have suggested that this pragmatic approach should be construed narrowly. See, e.g., All Alaskan Seafoods, Inc. v. M/V Sea Producer, 882 F.2d 425 (9th Cir.1989). See generally 15A C. Wright, A. Miller & E. Cooper, Jurisdiction and Related Matters 2d § 3913.

47. Eisen v. Carlisle & Jacquelin, 370 F.2d 119 (2d Cir.1966), cert. denied 386 U.S. 1035.

48. See Herbst v. International Tel. & Tel. Corp., 495 F.2d 1308 (2d Cir.1974). The narrow scope of the inverse death knell was

clarified in In re Master Key Antitrust Litigation, 528 F.2d 5 (2d Cir.1975); Kohn v. Royall, Koegel & Wells, 496 F.2d 1094 (2d Cir.1974).

49. See cases cited in note 48, above. The inverse death knell doctrine was rejected in Blackie v. Barrack, 524 F.2d 891 (9th Cir.1975), cert. denied 429 U.S. 816. See also Bennett v. Behring Corp., 525 F.2d 1202 (5th Cir.1976), cert. denied 425 U.S. 975; Seiffer v. Topsy's Int'l, Inc., 520 F.2d 795 (10th Cir.1975), cert. denied 423 U.S. 1051.

50. 437 U.S. 463, 98 S.Ct. 2454, 57 L.Ed.2d 351 (1978). The Livesay decision and its ramifications are discussed in Cohen, "Not Dead But Only Sleeping": The Rejection of the Death Knell Doctrine and the Survival of Class Actions Denied Certification, 59 B.U.L.Rev. 257 (1979). The doctrine also has been rejected in Colorado. See Levine v. Empire Sav. & Loan Ass'n, 34 Colo.App. 235, 527 P.2d 910 (1974), affirmed 189 Colo. 64, 536 P.2d 1134 (1975).

mately was addressed in 1998 amendments to the federal class action rule, authorizing interlocutory appeals of class certification orders,[51] and thereby creating an exception to the finality principle.

§ 13.2 Judicial Exceptions to the Final Judgment Rule

There are two well-recognized judicial doctrines in the federal courts that allow for the immediate appeal of orders even though portions of the case remain undecided. First, and most widely used, is the collateral order doctrine,[1] which derives from the Supreme Court's decision in Cohen v. Beneficial Industrial Loan Corporation.[2] In that case, the Court upheld the right to appeal from an order refusing to direct the plaintiff in a shareholder derivative action to comply with a state statute requiring the posting of security for costs. The Court found that allowing the appeal was consistent with the underlying policies of the final judgment rule because the order itself was final on that question and would not be altered by the trial judge. Further, the failure to allow immediate review might effectively deny any right of review.

The key to invoking the Cohen doctrine is that the trial court's decision must determine a matter collateral to the rights underlying the action and one that is too important to be denied review. If these two criteria are met, then the purposes of the final judgment rule will not be undercut by allowing an appeal. The appellate court can offer guidance on important issues that otherwise might evade review without fear that the matters will result in duplicative consideration through piecemeal appeals.

The invocation of this exception necessarily depends upon finding that the order being appealed truly involves collateral matters[3] and is a final determination of those issues. A good example of the kind of refined analysis that may be required is in the class action area, since these cases frequently present a wide range of preliminary orders relating to the management of the case upon which immediate appellate review is desired because of their enormous impact. For example, the Supreme Court has ruled that a trial court order establishing notice requirements in a class action for damages and requiring the defendant to bear 90% of their cost, because there was a substantial possibility that the class would prevail on the merits, could be appealed under the collateral order doctrine.[4] The order itself was a final determination with regard to

---

51. Fed.Civ.Proc.Rule 23(f). This exception is discussed in § 13.3, below.

§ 13.2

1. The collateral order doctrine is discussed more fully in 15A C. Wright, A. Miller & E. Cooper, Jurisdiction and Related Matters 2d §§ 3911–3911.5. See also Anderson, The Collateral Order Doctrine: A New "Serbonian Bog" and Four Proposals for Reform, 46 Drake L.Rev. 539 (1998).

2. 337 U.S. 541, 69 S.Ct. 1221, 93 L.Ed. 1528 (1949).

3. See Palmer v. City of Chicago, 806 F.2d 1316 (7th Cir.1986), cert. denied 481 U.S. 1049 (an order is collateral if an appeal would not interfere with the litigation in the district court). For further discussion of what constitutes a collateral issue, see Comment, Collateral Orders and Extraordinary Writs as Exceptions to the Finality Rule, 51 Nw.U.L.Rev. 746 (1957).

4. Eisen v. Carlisle & Jacquelin, 417 U.S. 156, 94 S.Ct. 2140, 40 L.Ed.2d 732 (1974).

notice and that subject was separate from the decision on the merits. Also if the defendant were to prevail on the merits, it would be unlikely that the expenses could be recouped from the class. Consequently, the rights involved were too important to require the defendant to wait until final judgment was entered before receiving appellate review. On the other hand, court orders certifying a class action[5] or refusing to certify an action for class treatment[6] are inextricably intertwined with the merits of the case and typically are subject to revision until judgment is entered. Thus, the Court has ruled that class certification orders cannot be appealed under the collateral order doctrine.[7]

The collateral order exception is a narrow one.[8] Not all matters that are collateral and conclusively decided may fit within it. The court must be able to find that there could be no effective review of the order after a final judgment is entered.[9] This point was reaffirmed by the Supreme Court in 1981 in Firestone Tire & Rubber Company v. Risjord,[10] when it ruled that an order denying a motion to disqualify counsel could not be appealed under the Cohen exception because there was not sufficient evidence that the ruling would be effectively unreviewable after a judgment on the merits.[11] The Court noted that a view of the propriety of the court's disqualification order would be difficult to accomplish until the litigation was completed and the impact of having counsel remain could be assessed. At that time, the appellate court could determine whether allowing the continuing representation was prejudicial error. Consequently, there was no need for immediate review upon entry of the order.[12]

5. Shelter Realty Corp. v. Allied Maintenance Corp., 574 F.2d 656 (2d Cir.1978); Blackie v. Barrack, 524 F.2d 891 (9th Cir. 1975), cert. denied 429 U.S. 816.

6. In re Piper Aircraft Distribution Sys. Antitrust Litigation, 551 F.2d 213 (8th Cir.1977); Anschul v. Sitmar Cruises, Inc., 544 F.2d 1364 (7th Cir.1976), cert. denied 429 U.S. 907; Share v. Air Properties G. Inc., 538 F.2d 279 (9th Cir.1976), cert. denied 429 U.S. 923.

7. Coopers & Lybrand v. Livesay, 437 U.S. 463, 98 S.Ct. 2454, 57 L.Ed.2d 351 (1978). As a result of a 1998 amendment to the federal rules, class certification orders now may be subject to a discretionary appeal. See Fed.Civ.Proc.Rule 23(f).

8. The appellate courts generally have displayed a reluctance to read the requirements of the doctrine expansively so as to avoid the inundation of the appellate courts with appeals invoking this exception. Borden Co. v. Sylk, 410 F.2d 843, 846 (3d Cir.1969) ("To accept the appellant's view is to invite the inundation of appellate dockets with what have heretofore been regarded as nonappealable matters.") (Aldisert, J.); West v. Zurhorst, 425 F.2d 919,

921 (2d Cir.1970) ("The increase in the burden on the courts of appeals in the last decade * * * hardly suggest the desirability of an expansive reading of Cohen.") (Friendly, J.).

9. See Swint v. Chambers County Comm'n, 514 U.S. 35, 115 S.Ct. 1203, 131 L.Ed.2d 60 (1995); Puerto Rico Aqueduct & Sewer Authority v. Metcalf & Eddy, Inc., 506 U.S. 139, 113 S.Ct. 684, 121 L.Ed.2d 605 (1993); Parr v. U.S., 351 U.S. 513, 519, 76 S.Ct. 912, 916, 100 L.Ed. 1377 (1956).

10. 449 U.S. 368, 101 S.Ct. 669, 66 L.Ed.2d 571 (1981). But compare Kraus v. Davis, 6 Cal.App.3d 484, 85 Cal.Rptr. 846 (1970).

11. See generally Note, The Appealability of Orders Denying Motions for Disqualification of Counsel in the Federal Courts, 45 U.Chi.L.Rev. 450 (1978).

12. Utilizing similar reasoning, the Supreme Court also has held that an order granting a motion to disqualify counsel is not immediately appealable under the collateral order doctrine. Richardson–Merrell, Inc. v. Koller, 472 U.S. 424, 105 S.Ct. 2757, 86 L.Ed.2d 340 (1985). The question remains open whether this approach will be

The requirement that a denial of immediate review as a practical matter may preclude any review whatsoever is an important limitation on the availability of the collateral order doctrine.[13] This prerequisite has been a significant barrier to its use to obtain immediate review of discovery orders. A trial judge's order to turn over certain documents or respond to some other discovery demand, although clearly final and collateral, typically cannot be appealed under this exception to the final judgment rule.[14] A means of obtaining review does exist: the party can disobey the order, be found in contempt, and then appeal that contempt judgment.[15] Although the contempt route of appeal necessarily is a risky one,[16] as well as harsh on the appealing party, the Supreme Court generally has ruled that its availability shows that there is no need for immediate review of the discovery order as a collateral order.[17]

The second judicially developed exception to the final judgment rule involves cases in which there is some immediate harm that might occur to the appellant if review is postponed. This will occur only when the

applied to the appealability of orders denying appointment of counsel for indigent plaintiffs in civil actions. The circuit courts are split on the issue. See Note, Motions for Appointment of Counsel and the Collateral Order Doctrine, 83 Mich.L.Rev. 1547 (1985). See generally 15A C. Wright, A. Miller & E. Cooper, Jurisdiction and Related Matters 2d § 3914.21.

13. This limitation has proven dispositive in several recent Supreme Court decisions. See, e.g., Digital Equip. Corp. v. Desktop Direct, Inc., 511 U.S. 863, 114 S.Ct. 1992, 128 L.Ed.2d 842 (1994) (order vacating dismissal predicated on parties' settlement agreement cannot be appealed as a collateral order); Lauro Lines S.R.L. v. Chasser, 490 U.S. 495, 109 S.Ct. 1976, 104 L.Ed.2d 548 (1989) (denial of motion to dismiss based on contractual forum-selection clause is not immediately appealable); Stringfellow v. Concerned Neighbors in Action, 480 U.S. 370, 107 S.Ct. 1177, 94 L.Ed.2d 389 (1987) (no immediate appeal allowed from order that denied intervention as of right, but allowed permissive intervention on very restrictive grounds). See also 15A C. Wright, A. Miller & E. Cooper, Jurisdiction and Related Matters 2d § 3911.3.

14. U.S. v. Ryan, 402 U.S. 530, 91 S.Ct. 1580, 29 L.Ed.2d 85 (1971); Cobbledick v. U.S., 309 U.S. 323, 60 S.Ct. 540, 84 L.Ed. 783 (1940). But compare U.S. v. Nixon, 418 U.S. 683, 692, 94 S.Ct. 3090, 3099, 41 L.Ed.2d 1039 (1974), in which the President was allowed an immediate appeal from an order to produce certain tape recordings for examination by the federal trial judge. The President was not a party to the action

in which the recordings were sought and the Court commented that to require the President to disobey the court's order so as to obtain review would be "unseemly, and would present an unnecessary occasion for constitutional confrontation between two branches of the Government."

15. For an example of this means of obtaining review, see Hickman v. Taylor, 329 U.S. 495, 67 S.Ct. 385, 91 L.Ed. 451 (1947).

In some limited circumstances, the complaining party may be able to obtain review by mandamus. See, e.g., Schlagenhauf v. Holder, 379 U.S. 104, 85 S.Ct. 234, 13 L.Ed.2d 152 (1964). See generally § 13.3, below.

16. Appeal is allowed only from a judgment of criminal contempt. If the contempt citation is characterized as civil—intended only to coerce compliance, not punish disobedience—no appeal would be allowed because it would be interlocutory. See Fox v. Capital Co., 299 U.S. 105, 57 S.Ct. 57, 81 L.Ed. 67 (1936). See generally Andre, The Final Judgment Rule and Party Appeals of Civil Contempt Orders: Time for Change, 55 N.Y.U.L.Rev. 1041 (1980). Further, if the appellate court agrees with the trial judge, then the contempt penalty will stand.

17. See the cases cited in note 14, above. In some rare circumstances, the contempt route may not be available and an appeal may be allowed. See, e.g., Perlman v. U.S., 247 U.S. 7, 38 S.Ct. 417, 62 L.Ed. 950 (1918) (when a subpoena for documents was issued to a third party and the owner of the documents was protesting their release, an appeal was allowed since it was

trial court's determination is such that it necessarily requires some immediate act or conduct by the parties that will be irremediable should later review suggest that it was improperly ordered.[18] Thus, the exception is an extremely limited one.

The exception stems from the Supreme Court's decision in Forgay v. Conrad.[19] The trial judge in that case had found that property had been transferred by means of a fraudulent conveyance. He then ordered the property delivered to an assignee in bankruptcy and an accounting made. Although the accounting remained to be done, so that the fraud ruling was only a partial adjudication of the case, the court treated its decision as final, by directing the immediate delivery of property to the assignee. An appeal was allowed on the ground that there would have been irreparable harm to the losing party if review were delayed and he were forced to comply with the trial judge's decree since the assignee might dispose of the property before the accounting was completed.

§ 13.3   Statutory Exceptions to the Final Judgment Rule

The statutory exceptions to the final judgment rule can be placed in three categories. In the first category are very precise statutes specifying particular orders for interlocutory appeal. For example, in the federal courts, appeals specifically are allowed for interlocutory orders "granting, continuing, modifying, refusing or dissolving injunctions," or refusing to do so,[1] for orders involving the appointment or winding up of receiverships,[2] and for orders in admiralty cases that determine the rights and liabilities of the parties.[3] Other examples may be found in state statutes.[4] Illustratively, many states authorize an immediate appeal from an order vacating or sustaining an attachment[5] or from the grant of

---

unlikely the third party would risk contempt to protest their release).

18. Compare Sekaquaptewa v. MacDonald, 575 F.2d 239 (9th Cir.1978), and Penn v. Transportation Lease Hawaii, Ltd., 2 Hawaii App. 272, 630 P.2d 646 (1981), allowing an appeal, with Midway Mfg. Co. v. Omni Video Games, Inc., 668 F.2d 70 (1st Cir.1981), and Dameron v. Capitol House Assocs. Ltd. Partnership, 431 A.2d 580 (D.C.App.1981), disallowing an appeal.

19. 47 U.S. (6 How.) 201, 12 L.Ed. 404 (1848). The Forgay doctrine is examined more thoroughly in 15A C. Wright, A. Miller & E. Cooper, Jurisdiction and Related Matters 2d § 3910.

§ 13.3

1. 28 U.S.C.A. § 1292(a)(1). See 16 C. Wright, A. Miller & E. Cooper, Jurisdiction and Related Matters 2d §§ 3921–24. For examples of comparable state statutes, see Ill.S.Ct.Rule 307; Mass.Gen.Laws Ann. c. 231, § 118; Pa.Rules App.Proc., Rule 311; Va.Code 1950, § 8.01–670.

2. 28 U.S.C.A. § 1292(a)(2). See 16 C. Wright, A. Miller & E. Cooper, Jurisdiction and Related Matters 2d § 3925. For comparable state statutes, see West's Ann.Cal. Code Civ.Proc. § 904.1(g); Kan.Stat.Ann. 60–1305; Mass.Gen.Laws Ann. c. 231, § 117.

3. 28 U.S.C.A. § 1292(a)(3). See 16 C. Wright, A. Miller & E. Cooper, Jurisdiction and Related Matters 2d § 3927.

4. In some states the statutory exceptions are phrased so generally that they arguably could eradicate the final judgment rule. See, e.g., Hawaii Rev.Stat. § 641–1(b) (appeal may be allowed whenever advisable for the speedy termination of the litigation); Wisconsin Stat.Ann. 808.03(2) (appeals allowed whenever it would materially advance the termination of the litigation, protect against injury, or clarify an issue of general importance).

5. See, e.g., West's Ann.Cal.Code Civ. Proc. § 904.1(e); Fla.—West's F.S.A.Rule App.Proc.Rule 9.130(a)(3)(C)(ii); Minn. Rules Civ.App.Proc., Rule 103.03(c).

a motion for a new trial.[6]

By and large, the orders specified in these statutes represent decisions made by the legislature that certain issues require continuing appellate supervision or are so important that there would be a hardship on the parties if review were delayed.[7] Indeed, as illustrated by the federal list, the exceptions created are not actually much of a departure from finality, except in its most rigid interpretation. The injunction exception involves orders that require some immediate conduct on the parties' part so that, despite being interlocutory, the effect of the decree may be substantial on the party enjoined. The other exceptions all present orders that essentially are final on liability so that duplicative appeals are not likely.

Most of these particularized statutory exceptions are straightforward and pose few problems in interpretation. In a few instances, some difficulty arises in deciding whether a particular order falls within the class listed. In general, the courts have construed the statutory categories strictly.[8] For example, with regard to the federal exception for orders dealing with injunctions, temporary restraining orders are not considered injunctions[9] and thus do not fall within the scope of the statute.[10] Further, in actions seeking injunctive relief, only preliminary orders touching the merits of the underlying claim will be deemed to involve the injunction itself so as to qualify for an immediate appeal. It does not make a difference that as a practical matter the preliminary order may affect the scope of the ultimate injunction or may appear to deny it temporarily.[11] Despite their narrow interpretation, the availability of the statutory exceptions by and large relieves some of the burden on the appellate courts to grant extraordinary relief and ameliorates what otherwise would be the harsh effect of rigid adherence to the final judgment rule.

6. Ariz.Rev.Stat. § 12–2101F.1; West's Ann.Cal.Code Civ.Proc. § 904.1(d).

7. See Smith v. Vulcan Iron Works, 165 U.S. 518, 525, 17 S.Ct. 407, 410, 41 L.Ed. 810 (1897) (predecessor of 28 U.S.C.A. § 1292(a)(1)).

8. The Supreme Court frequently has emphasized the need to construe the statutory exceptions narrowly. E.g., Carson v. American Brands, Inc., 450 U.S. 79, 101 S.Ct. 993, 67 L.Ed.2d 59 (1981); Gardner v. Westinghouse Broadcasting Co., 437 U.S. 478, 98 S.Ct. 2451, 57 L.Ed.2d 364 (1978); Switzerland Cheese Ass'n, Inc. v. E. Horne's Market, Inc., 385 U.S. 23, 24, 87 S.Ct. 193, 194, 17 L.Ed.2d 23 (1966).

9. For a description of the difference between temporary restraining orders and preliminary injunctions, see § 15.4, below.

10. Sampson v. Murray, 415 U.S. 61, 86 n. 58, 94 S.Ct. 937, 951 n. 58, 39 L.Ed.2d

166 (1974); Grant v. U.S., 282 F.2d 165 (2d Cir.1960). A temporary restraining order that runs more than 20 days may be treated as a preliminary injunction and hence be appealable, however. National City Bank v. Battisti, 581 F.2d 565 (6th Cir.1977); Connell v. Dulien Steel Prods., Inc., 240 F.2d 414 (5th Cir.1957), noted 71 Harv.L.Rev. 550 (1958). See generally 16 C. Wright, A. Miller & E. Cooper, Jurisdiction and Related Matters 2d § 3922.

11. See, e.g., Gardner v. Westinghouse Broadcasting Co., 437 U.S. 478, 98 S.Ct. 2451, 57 L.Ed.2d 364 (1978) (denial of class certification in suit seeking injunctive relief is not appealable under Section 1292(a)(1)); Switzerland Cheese Ass'n, Inc. v. E. Horne's Market, Inc., 385 U.S. 23, 25, 87 S.Ct. 193, 195, 17 L.Ed.2d 23 (1966) (denial of summary judgment motion in an action seeking permanent injunctive relief is not appealable under Section 1292(a)(1)).

The second category of statutory exceptions is exemplified by Section 1292(b) of the United States Code,[12] added in 1958 to provide flexibility. In order to fall within its scope, the party seeking review must obtain both district judge and appellate court certification.[13] Both courts must agree that the order involves "a controlling question of law," that "there is substantial ground for difference of opinion" with regard to the issue presented, and "that an immediate appeal from the order may materially advance the ultimate termination of the litigation." This statute thus serves as a safety valve to make certain that important issues of law receive immediate review.[14]

Appeals under Section 1292(b) are subject to the discretion of the courts.[15] By requiring both the trial and appellate courts to agree that a particular order falls within the statute, each court is given the opportunity to consider both the burden of and the need for departure from the final judgment principle on the particular ruling involved. The trial court can reflect on whether the appellant truly is raising a critical and debated issue or is merely using a tactic to delay the proceedings. The appellate court, on the other hand, can assess its own appellate court workload and can make its decision as to the critical or important nature of the issues being presented free of the pressures from the litigants.[16]

A close look at the statute's language indicates that it is not designed as a broad loophole to finality and the courts have interpreted it accordingly. All three of the stated criteria must be met before review

---

12. 28 U.S.C.A. § 1292(b). See 16 C. Wright, A. Miller & E. Cooper, Jurisdiction and Related Matters 2d §§ 3929–31; Note, Interlocutory Appeals in the Federal Courts Under 28 U.S.C.A. § 1292(b), 88 Harv. L.Rev. 607 (1975).

13. Numerous opinions state that absent a trial judge's certification, there is no appellate jurisdiction. See, e.g., Memorial Hosp. Sys. v. Heckler, 769 F.2d 1043, 1044 (5th Cir.1985); Barfield v. Weinberger, 485 F.2d 696 (5th Cir.1973). But compare Gillespie v. U.S. Steel Corp., 379 U.S. 148, 154, 85 S.Ct. 308, 312, 13 L.Ed.2d 199 (1964), in which the Court upheld appellate jurisdiction despite the lack of trial and appellate certification, commenting that if the case had been certified under Section 1292(b), "the appeal unquestionably would have been proper; in light of the circumstances we believe that the Court of Appeals properly implemented the same policy Congress sought to promote in § 1292(b) by treating this obviously marginal case as final and appealable." The Gillespie case should not be read too broadly, however. The Supreme Court has refused to extend Gillespie's rationale beyond its limited facts. E.g., Coopers & Lybrand v. Livesay, 437 U.S. 463, 477 n. 30, 98 S.Ct. 2454, 2462 n. 30, 57 L.Ed.2d 351 (1978).

14. The history of the statute suggests that it was designed for protracted or complex cases. A good summary of the history can be found in Note, Interlocutory Appeals in the Federal Courts under 28 U.S.C.A. § 1292(b), 88 Harv.L.Rev. 607, 610 (1975). Although appeals under the statute clearly are not limited to "big" cases, the courts agree that they are to be granted cautiously and only in exceptional cases. E.g., Fisons Ltd. v. U.S., 458 F.2d 1241, 1248 (7th Cir. 1972), cert. denied 405 U.S. 1041; Vaughn v. Regents of University of California, 504 F.Supp. 1349, 1355 (E.D.Cal.1981). See generally Solimine, Revitalizing Interlocutory Appeals in the Federal Courts, 58 Geo. Wash.L.Rev. 1165 (1990).

15. The legislative history of the statute makes clear the discretionary character of the determinations by the trial and appellate judges. S.Rep. 2434, 85th Cong., 2d Sess., 1958, in 1958 U.S.Code Cong. & Admin.News 5255, 5257.

16. Coopers & Lybrand v. Livesay, 437 U.S. 463, 475, 98 S.Ct. 2454, 2461, 57 L.Ed.2d 351 (1978). The discretion of the appellate court has been analogized to that of the Supreme Court on certiorari petitions. See Gallimore v. Missouri Pac. R.R. Co., 635 F.2d 1165, 1168 n. 4 (5th Cir. 1981).

is appropriate[17] and, consequently, only a small class of issues or orders qualify. Further, appellate courts are very sensitive to the determinations of trial judges on these questions and, if the trial court has refused certification under the statute, courts generally have agreed that mandamus cannot be used to force the trial judge's hand.[18]

The major questions about the propriety of an appeal under Section 1292(b) typically involve the first and third criteria, because there is little difficulty in agreeing whether there is a substantial basis for different opinions on the issues involved.[19] The key in the determination of what constitutes a controlling question is not whether a reversal would be necessary if it were wrongly decided by the trial court—although that finding obviously would satisfy the statute[20]—but whether an immediate appellate reversal might save time and expense for all concerned.[21] Thus, the first and third requirements often are intertwined. Further, the last criterion under the statute—that an immediate appeal would advance materially the termination of the litigation—requires a careful balancing of whether allowing piecemeal review may delay or hinder the trial against the need for immediate appellate guidance on the issue presented by the order. The courts exercise their greatest discretion in connection with this factor and thus, perhaps not surprisingly, some conflicting determinations appear.[22] As a result, appeals have been both denied and granted on various discovery rulings,[23] as well as from orders involving class action certification.[24] But at least

17. In addition to the three requirements, and implicit in the statutory criteria, an order must be involved. The trial judge cannot simply certify an issue for an advisory appellate opinion, but must have made some ruling. Okolinsky v. Philadelphia, Bethlehem & New England R.R. Co., 282 F.2d 70 (3d Cir.1960). See Nickert v. Puget Sound Tug & Barge Co., 480 F.2d 1039, 1041 (9th Cir.1973) (pretrial ruling determining the legal consequences of one possible trial resolution of disputed issues, even though denominated a partial summary judgment, was not deemed an "order").

18. Arthur Young & Co. v. U.S. District Court, 549 F.2d 686, 698 (9th Cir. 1977), cert. denied 434 U.S. 829; Leasco Data Processing Equipment Corp. v. Maxwell, 468 F.2d 1326, 1344 (2d Cir.1972). But see Fernandez–Roque v. Smith, 671 F.2d 426, 431 (11th Cir.1982). For a discussion of mandamus generally, see text at notes 25–45, below.

19. The fact that an issue is a matter of first impression does not in itself meet the prerequisite. There must be some reason to expect that there is conflicting authority. See Castanho v. Jackson Marine, Inc., 484 F.Supp. 201, 203 (E.D.Tex.1980), appeal dismissed in part, order affirmed in part, mandamus denied 650 F.2d 546 (5th

Cir.1981); Barrett v. Burt, 250 F.Supp. 904 (S.D.Iowa 1966). See also In re Pyramid Co., 141 Vt. 294, 449 A.2d 915 (1982).

20. See Katz v. Carte Blanche Corp., 496 F.2d 747, 755 (3d Cir.1974), cert. denied 419 U.S. 885.

21. See, e.g., Garner v. Wolfinbarger, 430 F.2d 1093, 1097 (5th Cir.1970), cert. denied 401 U.S. 974; Resnick v. American Dental Ass'n, 95 F.R.D. 372, 380 (N.D.Ill. 1982).

22. Compare Atlantic City Elec. Co. v. General Elec. Co., 337 F.2d 844 (2d Cir. 1964) (application denied from order upholding objections to interrogatories directed at discovering whether plaintiffs actually sustained damages or passed them on to customers), with Commonwealth Edison Co. v. Allis–Chalmers Mfg. Co., 335 F.2d 203 (7th Cir.1964) (appeal allowed under same circumstances).

23. Compare Bourget v. Government Employees Ins. Co., 48 F.R.D. 29 (D.Conn. 1969) (appeal refused), with North Carolina Elec. Membership Corp. v. Carolina Power & Light Co., 666 F.2d 50 (4th Cir.1981) (appeal allowed).

24. Compare Katz v. Carte Blanche Corp., 496 F.2d 747 (3d Cir.1974), cert. denied 419 U.S. 885 (order certifying class

some of the different conclusions reached as to the propriety of appealing certain types of orders may reflect practical differences among the federal circuits and therefore are to be expected given the discretionary character of a Section 1292(b) appeal. Because of this phenomenon, generalizations regarding what types of orders may fall within the statute are dangerous and care must be taken to evaluate each request on the basis of its surrounding facts and the law in the relevant circuit.

The last category of statutory exceptions to finality involves applications to the appellate court for writs of mandamus or prohibition to reverse some intermediate trial court ruling.[25] The use of a so-called extraordinary writ differs from all other means of review because technically it is not an appeal, but an original proceeding in the appellate court seeking an order directing the trial judge to enter or vacate a particular order. The ability of appellate courts to review interlocutory matters by way of an extraordinary writ can be traced to England.[26]

In some states a writ of mandamus is granted relatively freely to allow review of a wide range of orders that otherwise would be denied appeal as interlocutory.[27] However, the use of extraordinary writs has been carefully limited in the federal courts.[28] Because of wide variances among jurisdictions, generalizations about the use of writs are somewhat misleading. What follows is a brief summary of how the extraordinary writ power has been applied in the federal courts.

The traditional view of federal extraordinary writ power is that it exists to aid appellate court jurisdiction by allowing the court to confine trial judges to the lawful exercise of their jurisdiction or to compel them to act if they have abdicated their jurisdictional obligations.[29] Hence it

action appealable), with In re Master Key Antitrust Litigation, 528 F.2d 5 (2d Cir. 1975) (order certifying class action held not appealable). As a result of a 1998 amendment to the class action rule, interlocutory appeals of class certification rulings now may be allowed without resort to Section 1292(b). See Fed.Civ.Proc.Rule 23(f).

25. Technically, the difference between the two writs is that mandamus orders the trial judge to do something, whereas prohibition forbids the doing of an act. Although of historical significance, the distinction between these two forms is largely meaningless today. In re Simons, 247 U.S. 231, 239, 38 S.Ct. 497, 498, 62 L.Ed. 1094 (1918). For a description of the writs at common law, see Crick, The Final Judgment Rule as a Basis of Appeal, 41 Yale L.J. 539, 554 (1932).

26. For a history of the use of extraordinary writs in England, see Jenks, The Prerogative Writs in English Law, 32 Yale L.J. 523 (1923).

27. For example, mandamus is readily available to obtain review of discovery orders in some states. See, e.g., Ex parte

Employers Nat. Ins. Co., 539 So.2d 233 (Ala.1989); Klett v. Hickey, 310 Mich. 329, 17 N.W.2d 201 (1945); Ex parte Benson, 243 Ala. 435, 10 So.2d 482 (1942). In other states, mandamus is available to review discovery orders if there is no adequate remedy by appeal, Sears, Roebuck & Co. v. Ramirez, 824 S.W.2d 558 (Tex.1992); or if there is an important question of first impression before the court, St. Vincent Medical Center v. Superior Court, 160 Cal. App.3d 1030, 206 Cal.Rptr. 840 (1984). Compare the federal view reflected in the cases cited in note 35, below.

28. The All Writs Statute, 28 U.S.C.A. § 1651, authorizes appellate review by way of extraordinary writ. For a thorough discussion of the federal authorities in this area, see 16 C. Wright, A. Miller & E. Cooper, Jurisdiction and Related Matters 2d §§ 3932–36.

29. Roche v. Evaporated Milk Ass'n, 319 U.S. 21, 63 S.Ct. 938, 87 L.Ed. 1185 (1943). See Berger, The Mandamus Power of the United States Courts of Appeals: A Complex and Confused Means of Appellate

often is said that they issue only to enforce a clear legal duty. When the issue is one committed to the discretion of the trial judge or when mere error is alleged, review cannot be achieved by way of mandamus,[30] because the writ is not deemed a general substitute for an appeal.[31] A brief look at two Supreme Court cases upholding the use of mandamus may illustrate the level or kind of abuse that may merit this extraordinary review.

The first is La Buy v. Howes Leather Company[32] in which the trial judge had used his discretion under Federal Rule 53(b) to appoint a special master to try antitrust cases. The judge justified his action on the ground that he had a congested trial calendar and, because it was expected that trial would take six weeks, it was necessary for him to turn the matter over to the master. The Supreme Court ruled that the judge had totally abdicated his judicial functions thereby depriving the parties of a trial before a judge on the basic issues in the litigation. Thus, appellate court review was imperative to order the judge to withdraw at least the liability questions from the master. In another case, the Court upheld the use of mandamus to review a discovery order requiring the defendant to submit to physical and mental examinations.[33] The order was challenged as being unconstitutional and the Court noted that the issue was a matter of first impression in the federal courts, requiring some appellate guidance. It went on to caution, however, that once it issued guidelines in its opinion, subsequent decisions applying the guidelines would not necessarily be reviewable by way of mandamus.[34]

Later opinions of the Supreme Court make clear that the two cases just described are extraordinary. Thus, the Court has disapproved the use of mandamus to review district court orders granting discovery, even though claims were raised that irreparable injury would occur unless the order were reversed immediately.[35] The writ is available only when the issue on which mandamus is sought is one that goes to the jurisdiction of the court,[36] such as an order transferring the case, the effect of which is

---

Control, 31 Buffalo L.Rev. 37, 41 (1982), for a discussion of the various "standards" suggested by the treatment of mandamus power in several Supreme Court opinions.

30. Radio Corp. of America v. Igoe, 217 F.2d 218 (7th Cir.1954), cert. denied 348 U.S. 973; Bankers Life & Cas. Co. v. Holland, 346 U.S. 379, 382, 74 S.Ct. 145, 148, 98 L.Ed. 106 (1953).

31. Roche v. Evaporated Milk Ass'n, 319 U.S. 21, 63 S.Ct. 938, 87 L.Ed. 1185 (1943).

32. 352 U.S. 249, 77 S.Ct. 309, 1 L.Ed.2d 290 (1957).

33. Schlagenhauf v. Holder, 379 U.S. 104, 85 S.Ct. 234, 13 L.Ed.2d 152 (1964).

34. 379 U.S. at 112, 85 S.Ct. at 239.

35. Kerr v. U.S. District Court, 426 U.S. 394, 96 S.Ct. 2119, 48 L.Ed.2d 725

(1976); Will v. U.S., 389 U.S. 90, 88 S.Ct. 269, 19 L.Ed.2d 305 (1967). Compare Thornburg, Interlocutory Review of Discovery Orders: An Idea Whose Time Has Come, 44 Sw.L.J. 1045 (1990) (advocating a model system of interlocutory review of discovery orders).

36. But the term jurisdiction may be interpreted broadly. See Lyons v. Westinghouse Elec. Corp., 222 F.2d 184, 186 (2d Cir.1955), cert. denied 350 U.S. 825, in which the court granted mandamus to review the trial court's order staying an antitrust case pending the determination of a related state court proceeding, commenting, "the question whether a final judgment will be an estoppel so nearly touches the jurisdiction of the district court, as to make it proper for us to entertain the petition for mandamus." Compare Radio Corp. of America v. Igoe, 217 F.2d 218 (7th Cir.

to deprive the appellate court in the circuit where the suit originally was filed of the opportunity to rule.[37] Or, more broadly, when the district judge's order is seen as a "clear" abuse of discretion[38] abdicating judicial functions or involving some issue of judicial administration that appears to have broad significance beyond the particular case.[39]

Because mandamus represents a deliberate and direct interference with the trial court during the course of trial,[40] it can be used successfully only in extreme cases. Further, as an extraordinary method of obtaining review, courts often rule that it is available only when none of the other interlocutory appeal routes can be utilized.[41] For example, the possibility that an appeal might be sought under Section 1292(b) suggests that certification should be sought under that statute before resorting to mandamus.[42] The result of this restrained exercise of mandamus authority is that a review of the cases reveals that the majority of federal opinions on mandamus present discussions of why it is not an appropriate remedy in the particular case.

But care should be taken in evaluating the fact that mandamus most often is denied. What the statistics do not reveal is that in many instances appellate courts in deciding whether they have jurisdiction to issue the writ examine the merits of the underlying dispute.[43] In this way, even though the writ ultimately is denied, they offer some guidance to the lower courts on a less formal basis, and assuredly satisfy the desire of the petitioner for appellate review of the matters involved. Although this result may appear inconsistent with the standard,[44] it avoids the necessity of the appellate court issuing what may appear a

1954), cert. denied 348 U.S. 973, refusing mandamus to review the denial of a stay.

37. E.g., In re Fireman's Fund Ins. Cos., 588 F.2d 93 (5th Cir.1979). Compare Bankers Life & Cas. Co. v. Holland, 346 U.S. 379, 384, 74 S.Ct. 145, 148, 98 L.Ed. 106 (1953) (mandamus not an appropriate remedy to vacate transfer order when transfer was to district court within the same circuit); In re Ralston Purina Co., 726 F.2d 1002 (4th Cir.1984) (mandamus not appropriate to review order refusing to sever or transfer cases).

38. Bankers Life & Cas. Co. v. Holland, 346 U.S. 379, 74 S.Ct. 145, 98 L.Ed. 106 (1953).

39. In Nixon v. Sirica, 487 F.2d 700, 707 (D.C.Cir.1973), the appellate court upheld review by mandamus of an order to the President to produce certain tape recordings for the trial judge's inspection. The court found that the issue was jurisdictional in that the question presented was whether the district judge had exceeded his authority and also was a matter of first impression on which there was great public interest in obtaining a prompt resolution. Finally, it concluded that if the only avenue

of direct appellate review was for the President to disobey the order, that was "a clearly inadequate remedy." See Note, Appealability in the Federal Courts, 75 Harv.L.Rev. 351, 377 (1961).

40. As noted the Supreme Court, "mandamus should be resorted to only in extreme cases, since it places the trial judges in the anomalous position of being litigants without counsel other than uncompensated volunteers." La Buy v. Howes Leather Co., 352 U.S. 249, 257–58, 77 S.Ct. 309, 314, 1 L.Ed.2d 290 (1957).

41. E.g., Knable v. Wilson, 570 F.2d 957, 961 (D.C.Cir.1977) (Rule 54(b)).

42. E.g., In re Missouri, 664 F.2d 178 (8th Cir.1981); Rapp v. Van Dusen, 350 F.2d 806, 813 (3d Cir.1965).

43. See, e.g., In re Halkin, 598 F.2d 176 (D.C.Cir.1979).

44. In Note, Supervisory and Advisory Mandamus Under the All Writs Act, 86 Harv.L.Rev. 595, 596 n. 7 (1973), the author argues that questions of jurisdiction should be kept separate from the standard governing whether a writ properly may issue.

rather strong remedy against the district judge and thus eases the relationship between the trial and appellate courts.[45] Issuance of mandamus itself is reserved for extraordinary situations in which a powerful rebuke is deemed necessary.

B. REVIEWABILITY

§ 13.4 The Nature and Scope of Review

The decision to take an appeal is influenced not only by considerations relating to the timing of an appeal, but also by various rules or standards involving the nature and scope of review. Not all matters that occur during the trial may be reviewed by the appellate court. Furthermore, when a matter is reviewed, the likelihood of reversal depends on the standard that is used to determine whether the trial court erred. The standards governing when review is available and when an appeal will be successful reflect determinations about the proper role of the appellate courts vis-à-vis the trial courts. Trials will not be error-free; nevertheless, appellate review will not be available to remedy all the mistakes. The concern on appeal is that the judgment that was reached was correct and was not entered on the basis of improperly submitted information or because of an erroneous view of the law as applied to the facts of the case. The appellate process is designed to review the results that were achieved below to make certain that they are not inappropriate, not to supervise the conduct of each trial to ensure that the judge adhered to all the rules of procedure and evidence that were applicable.

Thus, the scope of appellate review is limited to certain matters. First, any error that is raised on appeal must appear clearly in the trial court record[1] and the aggrieved party must have objected promptly to the allegedly erroneous ruling in the trial court.[2] This restriction encourages the parties to try to bring to the judge's attention any problems that they perceive so that they can be corrected immediately, thereby avoiding later appeals. It also allows the appellate court the benefit of a trial court ruling on the question, which may be helpful when reviewing the matter presented. Errors that are not objected to below or arguments that are not raised at trial generally cannot be raised for the first time on appeal.[3]

---

45. This justification was suggested in Berger, The Mandamus Power of the United States Courts of Appeals: A Complex and Confused Means of Appellate Control, 31 Buffalo L.Rev. 37, 86–87 (1982).

§ 13.4

1. For a criticism and discussion of the effect of the rule limiting appellate review to the trial record, see Note, Appeal and Error—New Evidence in the Appellate Court, 56 Harv.L.Rev. 1313 (1943).

2. Record Data Int'l, Inc. v. Nichols, 381 So.2d 1 (Ala.1979); Young v. Jones, 149 Ga.App. 819, 256 S.E.2d 58 (1979).

3. McGinnis v. Ingram Equipment Co., 918 F.2d 1491, 1495 (11th Cir.1990); City of Eloy v. Pinal County, 158 Ariz. 198, 761 P.2d 1102 (App.1988); Tahoe Nat. Bank v. Phillips, 4 Cal.3d 11, 92 Cal.Rptr. 704, 480 P.2d 320 (1971); Damiani v. Albert, 48 Cal.2d 15, 306 P.2d 780 (1957). A limited exception is made for errors going to the court's subject-matter jurisdiction, see § 2.2, above, or in extreme circumstances to avoid a miscarriage of justice. Easterwood

Second, winning parties may not obtain review of findings deemed erroneous if those findings are not necessary to the decree.[4] Only parties aggrieved or harmed by the judgment can appeal from it.[5] This restriction is designed to avoid needless appeals. Since, as is discussed elsewhere, unnecessary findings cannot be the basis for collateral estoppel,[6] an appeal is unnecessary because the winning party cannot be prejudiced by the trial judge's adverse ruling.

At times, particularly when multiple claims are involved, it is difficult to determine what findings are necessary. If a finding is included in the decree itself, it generally may be treated as necessary and an appeal allowed, although the appeal may be limited to reforming the decree to eliminate those findings.[7] In this way, the danger of the improper application of issue preclusion is avoided. In other instances the court must look carefully to determine whether a finding ostensibly entered only in relation to a claim that the appellant won also was essential for a claim on which the appellant lost.[8]

These two restrictions on the scope of review are not absolute. For example, if the losing party appeals, the winning party may respond by raising any issue that would sustain the judgment, even if it is not one that was clearly decided in the record below.[9] The basic standard governing whether the appellee can raise new grounds sustaining the judgment is one of fairness: Is the issue as presented on appeal in the same basic posture as it would have been had it been introduced below?

The appellate court cannot act as a trial court and receive new evidence concerning the facts.[10] However, it can address new theories or

v. CSX Transportation, Inc., 933 F.2d 1548, 1551 (11th Cir.1991), affirmed on other grounds 507 U.S. 658, 113 S.Ct. 1732, 123 L.Ed.2d 387 (1993). Martinez v. Mathews, 544 F.2d 1233 (5th Cir.1976). For an interesting perspective regarding new issues on appeal, see Martineau, Considering New Issues on Appeal: The General Rule and the Gorilla Rule, 40 Vand.L.Rev. 1023 (1987).

4. See, e.g., New York Telephone Co. v. Maltbie, 291 U.S. 645, 54 S.Ct. 443, 78 L.Ed. 1041 (1934); Burchanowski v. Lycoming County, 32 Pa.Cmwlth. 207, 378 A.2d 1025 (1977). This limitation is discussed more fully in 15A C. Wright, A. Miller & E. Cooper, Jurisdiction and Related Matters 2d § 3902.

5. Lowe v. Labor & Indus. Relations Comm'n, 594 S.W.2d 365 (Mo.App.1980); Offutt v. Montgomery County Bd. of Educ., 285 Md. 557, 404 A.2d 281 (1979); Graney Dev. Corp. v. Taksen, 66 A.D.2d 1008, 411 N.Y.S.2d 757 (1978).

6. See § 14.11, below.

7. See Electrical Fittings Corp. v. Thomas & Betts Co., 307 U.S. 241, 242, 59 S.Ct. 860, 861, 83 L.Ed. 1263 (1939) (when

district court dismissed a patent infringement suit, ruling the first claim valid, but not infringed, and the second claim invalid, petitioners could appeal "not for the purpose of passing on the merits, but to direct the reformation of the decree" to eliminate the portion of the decree adjudging the first claim valid as it was unnecessary).

8. See, e.g., Partmar Corp. v. Paramount Pictures Theatres Corp., 347 U.S. 89, 99 n. 6, 74 S.Ct. 414, 420 n. 6, 98 L.Ed. 532 (1954).

9. Schweiker v. Hogan, 457 U.S. 569, 585 n. 24, 102 S.Ct. 2597, 2607 n. 24, 73 L.Ed.2d 227 (1982); Standard Accident Ins. Co. v. Roberts, 132 F.2d 794 (8th Cir.1942); Cunningham v. Lynch–Davidson Motors, Inc., 425 So.2d 131 (Fla.App.1982), petition for review denied 436 So.2d 99.

10. For a fascinating account of the history of the treatment of new evidence on appeal in the United States, as contrasted to other countries, see Millar, New Allegations and Proof on Appeal in Anglo–American Civil Procedure, 47 Nw.U.L.Rev. 427 (1952). The rule is criticized in Note, Appeal and Error—New Evidence in the Ap-

legal arguments regarding the law applicable to the facts.[11] But new theories may be addressed only if they can be determined on the facts established at trial.[12] This conclusion is commanded in most instances because the taking of evidence would be an intrusion on jury trial rights. Although many cases do not involve jury trials, the general principle is so well entrenched that it typically is followed in all cases.[13]

The winning party at trial, as appellee, is limited to raising issues that support the judgment, unless she files a cross-appeal.[14] This requirement can become very important in the multiple party or multiple claim setting in which the appellee won on some claims, but not on others. For example, assume A sues B for car damage and B impleads C, his insurer, on an indemnity theory. If A loses, the third-party claim against C will be dismissed because the right to indemnity never arose. Thus, at the conclusion of the trial B effectively is a winning party. If A appeals and B wants to preserve his right to indemnity from C, B must file a cross-appeal against C, B cannot merely raise the issue by way of his responsive brief against A. If B fails to file a cross-appeal, the indemnity issue will be foreclosed from appellate review.[15]

In a somewhat similar vein, only those issues that are presented in the parties' briefs and the relevant portion of the trial-court record that is brought to the appellate court's attention will be reviewed.[16] The court does not independently search the record for errors below, but leaves the decision of what needs review to the litigants. To avoid surprise and to encourage well-prepared presentations, only errors presented in the papers filed on appeal will be addressed.

pellate Court, 56 Harv.L.Rev. 1313 (1943). Compare the approach taken in North Dakota where if the state Supreme Court decides that some issue not tried below is necessary to a proper disposition on appeal, it can retain jurisdiction but remand the case to the trial court for a determination of that issue. N.D.Rules App.Proc., Rule 35(b).

11. "We do not feel that we are precluded from deciding on a ground not pressed by counsel. Such a course, however, is undesirable where not necessary; it is usually better, if possible, to consider a case as it was presented to the lower court." In re Barnett, 124 F.2d 1005, 1007 (2d Cir. 1942); Ward v. Taggart, 51 Cal.2d 736, 336 P.2d 534 (1959) (court upholds judgment on theory of unjust enrichment and quasi-contract, although the case was tried on a tort theory).

12. See, e.g., Bowman v. Hall, 83 Ariz. 56, 316 P.2d 484 (1957).

13. In some states, such as California, special statutes provide that in cases in which trial by jury is not a matter of right or is waived, the appellate courts may make factual determinations contrary to or in addition to those made by the trial judge and may take additional evidence in order to do so. West's Ann.Cal.Code Civ.Proc. § 909. It has been suggested, however, that "the most significant practical characteristic of this California exception is its sparing use, especially in situations where the additional evidence aims at reversal of the judgment instead of affirmance." Louisell & Degnan, Rehearing in American Appellate Courts, 44 Cal.L.Rev. 627, 629 n. 8 (1956).

14. The most well-known statement of this rule is that of Justice Brandeis in U.S. v. American Ry. Express Co., 265 U.S. 425, 435, 44 S.Ct. 560, 564, 68 L.Ed. 1087 (1924).

15. See Whitehead v. American Sec. & Trust Co., 285 F.2d 282, 285 (D.C.Cir.1960). But compare Baker v. Texas & Pacific Ry. Co., 326 S.W.2d 639 (Tex.Civ.App.1959) (entire judgment reversed and case remanded though no formal appeal by defendant on its third-party claim because facts of both claims were intertwined).

16. National Advertising Co. v. Arizona Dep't of Transp., 126 Ariz. 542, 617 P.2d 50 (App.1980); City of Chicago v. Hutter, 16 Ill.Dec. 27, 58 Ill.App.3d 468, 374 N.E.2d 802 (1978).

Assuming that the errors properly are brought to the attention of the appellate court, the extent of the review that will be undertaken will depend on the nature of the alleged error, as well as whether the proceeding below was a jury or nonjury trial. The fullest scope of review, not surprisingly, is for errors of law; the appellate court will decide questions of law de novo.[17] For example, if one alleged error is that an erroneous jury instruction was given because the law concerning comparative negligence was misstated, the appellate court can determine independently whether the instruction accurately reflected the current state of the law in that jurisdiction. Indeed, the appellate court may conclude that the trial judge correctly applied existing law, but that existing law should be changed. Similarly, on an appeal from a summary judgment the appellate court will decide de novo whether the summary judgment standard was met.[18] The appellate court actually is in as good a position as the trial court to decide those legal questions and, indeed, ruling on questions of law is one of its functions in guiding the lower courts.

The review of fact determinations is much more restricted.[19] Since the entire trial cannot be recreated on appeal, more deference is given to the factual determinations made there.

When a judge trial is involved, procedural rules, such as Federal Rule 52(a),[20] typically provide that the judge must make findings of fact and further, that those findings are to be overturned only if they are "clearly erroneous."[21] Although it is clear that the use of a clearly erroneous standard reflects a very narrow scope of review because it establishes a presumption that the findings are correct, defining exactly what is proper under this standard has posed some problems for the appellate courts. The reason for using the clearly erroneous standard is that the trial judge is thought to have an advantage over the appellate court because of his opportunity to view the witnesses; demeanor evi-

17. See U.S. v. Mississippi Valley Generating Co., 364 U.S. 520, 526, 81 S.Ct. 294, 297, 5 L.Ed.2d 268 (1961).

In 1991, the Supreme Court resolved a conflict among the circuits by holding that the courts of appeal should review de novo district court determinations of state law. Salve Regina College v. Russell, 499 U.S. 225, 111 S.Ct. 1217, 113 L.Ed.2d 190 (1991).

18. Mayo v. Engel, 733 F.2d 807 (11th Cir.1984). See generally 10A C. Wright, A. Miller & M. Kane, Civil 3d § 2716.

19. The issue often arises on appeal after the trial judge has denied a motion for new trial on the ground that the evidence was sufficient to support the verdict. The right of the trial judge to rule on a new trial motion on the basis of the weight of the evidence is clear. See § 12.4, at n. 26, above. It also generally is agreed that the appellate courts should not substitute their judgments in this setting. See Wright, The Doubtful Omniscience of Appellate Courts, 41 Minn.L.Rev. 751 (1957). A few courts nonetheless have asserted the power to reverse when they feel the weight of the evidence does not support the verdict. Georgia–Pacific Corp. v. U.S., 264 F.2d 161 (5th Cir.1959).

20. For a more thorough discussion of appellate review under Rule 52(a), see Note, Civil Rule 52(a): Rationing and Rationalizing the Resources of Appellate Review, 63 Notre Dame L.Rev. 645 (1988). See generally 9A C. Wright & A. Miller, Civil 2d §§ 2583–91.

21. Official Code Ga.Ann. § 9–11–52(a); Ky.Rules Civ.Proc., Rule 52.01; N.D.Rules Civ.Proc., Rule 52(a).

dence is of course unavailable to the appellate court.[22] In addition, the trial judge has been able to sift through the entire case and the ultimate judgment reached may reflect this familiarity, which may provide much greater insight into the action than the limited view of specific issues or rulings that is presented on appeal.[23]

In recognition of the trial judge's special expertise, the clearly erroneous standard is said to preclude the appellate court from redetermining the weight or credibility of the evidence,[24] and from independently assessing the inferences drawn from the facts by the trial judge.[25] As expressed by the Supreme Court in an often-quoted statement,

> A finding is "clearly erroneous" when although there is evidence to support it, the reviewing court on the entire evidence is left with the definite and firm conviction that a mistake has been committed.[26]

In its most limited view, then, the clearly erroneous standard would prevent reversal unless the judge based his finding on a misunderstanding of the law[27] or it was without adequate evidentiary support.

In some earlier cases, the appellate courts advocated undertaking broader review when the trial had proceeded without live witnesses or when credibility questions were not present.[28] This approach resulted in some confusion regarding what deference should be given to those trial court findings. The issue was answered by the Supreme Court in Anderson v. City of Bessemer City.[29] In Anderson, the Court specifically rejected the view that there should be a broader scope of review if the district court's findings do not rest on credibility determinations, but are based on physical or documentary evidence or inferences from other facts.[30] Further, the Court held that when findings are based on determi-

---

22. Inwood Labs., Inc. v. Ives Labs., Inc., 456 U.S. 844, 102 S.Ct. 2182, 72 L.Ed.2d 606 (1982).

23. Wright, The Doubtful Omniscience of Appellate Courts, 41 Minn.L.Rev. 751, 782 (1957). See also Pendergrass v. New York Life Ins. Co., 181 F.2d 136, 138 (8th Cir.1950). For a contrary view, see Weiner, The Civil Nonjury Trial and the Law–Fact Distinction, 55 Calif.L.Rev. 1020, 1033 (1967).

24. Inwood Labs., Inc. v. Ives Labs., Inc., 456 U.S. 844, 102 S.Ct. 2182, 72 L.Ed.2d 606 (1982). See also Geldert v. Hawaii, 3 Hawaii App. 259, 649 P.2d 1165, 1170 (1982); Nevada v. Courtesy Motors, 95 Nev. 103, 590 P.2d 163 (1979).

25. "It is not enough that we might give the facts another construction, resolve the ambiguities differently, and find a more sinister cast to actions which the District Court apparently deemed innocent." U.S. v. National Ass'n of Real Estate Bds., 339 U.S. 485, 495, 70 S.Ct. 711, 717, 94 L.Ed. 1007 (1950); Primm v. Primm, 46 Cal.2d 690, 693, 299 P.2d 231, 233 (1956). See also Kee v. Redlin, 203 N.W.2d 423 (N.D.1972).

26. U.S. v. U.S. Gypsum Co., 333 U.S. 364, 395, 68 S.Ct. 525, 542, 92 L.Ed. 746 (1948).

27. Shull v. Dain, Kalman & Quail, Inc., 561 F.2d 152 (8th Cir.1977), cert. denied 434 U.S. 1086; Toro Mfg. Corp. v. Jacobsen Mfg. Co., 357 F.2d 901 (7th Cir. 1966). For a discussion of the review standard on issues of law, see text at notes 17–18, above.

28. See, e.g., Orvis v. Higgins, 180 F.2d 537 (2d Cir.1950), cert. denied 340 U.S. 810.

29. 470 U.S. 564, 105 S.Ct. 1504, 84 L.Ed.2d 518 (1985).

30. Additionally, Rule 52(a) was amended in 1985 to provide that findings, "whether based on oral or documentary evidence," shall not be set aside unless clearly erroneous. See generally 9A C. Wright & A. Miller, Civil 2d § 2587.

For a discussion of appellate review of factual determinations in nonjury cases, see Lea, Federal Rule of Civil Procedure 52(a): Applicability of the "Clearly Erroneous"

nations regarding the credibility of witnesses, even greater deference to the trial court is required.

Additional distinctions are sometimes drawn between questions of pure fact and mixed questions of fact and law, with the clearly erroneous standard applied only to the former. Mixed fact-law questions are subject to the same full review as are pure questions of law.[31] This distinction necessarily produces some very complicated analyses concerning when an issue is a question of pure fact.[32] At least in the federal system, the Supreme Court has made clear that the clearly erroneous review standard applies to all questions of fact, not solely to questions of ultimate fact,[33] and thus it is not necessary to inquire into fine pleading distinctions to determine the proper review standard.[34]

The types of distinctions that may be drawn is exemplified by Bose Corporation v. Consumers Union of United States, Inc.[35] The case involved a claim of product disparagement and the question presented at trial was whether a false statement in an article about the petitioner's loudspeaker systems was made with actual malice, as required under New York Times, Inc. v. Sullivan.[36] The trial judge found for the plaintiff and the appellate court reversed, ruling that it was not governed by the Rule 52(a) review standard on the question whether actual malice was present because the case raised First Amendment concerns that required an independent review of the trial judge's findings. The Supreme Court agreed.

The Court recognized that the First Amendment requires the appellate court to make an independent examination of the entire trial record

Test to Findings of Fact in All Nonjury Cases, 29 How.L.J. 639 (1986).

31. Hawkins v. Ceco Corp., 883 F.2d 977, 981 (11th Cir.1989), cert. denied 495 U.S. 935; Ashland Oil & Refining Co. v. Kenny Constr. Co., 395 F.2d 683 (6th Cir. 1968); Malarchick v. Pierce, 264 N.W.2d 478 (N.D.1978). See generally Lee, Principled Decision Making and the Proper Role of Federal Appellate Courts: The Mixed Questions Conflict, 64 S.Cal.L.Rev. 235 (1991).

32. See, e.g., Pullman–Standard v. Swint, 456 U.S. 273, 102 S.Ct. 1781, 72 L.Ed.2d 66 (1982) (question of intentional discrimination is a pure issue of fact); Reich v. Newspapers of New England, Inc., 44 F.3d 1060 (1st Cir.1995) (use of a sliding scale approach to mixed fact-law questions to determine standard of review). See generally Weiner, The Civil Nonjury Trial and the Law–Fact Distinction, 55 Calif.L.Rev. 1020 (1967).

33. See Pullman–Standard v. Swint, 456 U.S. 273, 286 n. 16, 102 S.Ct. 1781, 1788–89 n. 16, 72 L.Ed.2d 66 (1982). The Court specifically noted that insofar as the earlier decision in Baumgartner v. U.S., 322 U.S. 665, 64 S.Ct. 1240, 88 L.Ed. 1525 (1944), had seemed to suggest that ultimate fact findings could be reviewed more broadly, that case referred to findings that were a mixture of law and fact, not pure findings of fact. Ibid.

34. The distinction between law and fact can become incredibly difficult, however. In one case involving Rule 52(a), Justice Stevens, writing for the Court, commented: "At some point, the reasoning by which a fact is 'found' crosses the line between application of those ordinary principles of logic and common experience which are ordinarily entrusted to the finder of fact into the realm of a legal rule upon which the reviewing court must exercise its own independent judgment. Where the line is drawn varies according to the nature of the substantive law at issue." Bose Corp. v. Consumers Union of U.S., Inc., 466 U.S. 485, 501 n. 17, 104 S.Ct. 1949, 1960 n. 17, 80 L.Ed.2d 502 (1984).

35. 466 U.S. 485, 104 S.Ct. 1949, 80 L.Ed.2d 502 (1984).

36. 376 U.S. 254, 84 S.Ct. 710, 11 L.Ed.2d 686 (1964).

to make certain the judgment does not intrude on those rights. Further, the Court found that this conclusion was not inconsistent with the application of Rule 52(a), noting that that provision does not forbid all review, but only commands that due deference be given to the trial judge. That objective was achieved in Bose when the court of appeals deferred to the district judge on the credibility of the witnesses. Finally, the Court noted that the history of the application of the clearly erroneous review standard to judicial fact findings reveals that the presumption of deference to the judge has varied in intensity depending on the circumstances surrounding the case. The First Amendment considerations present in Bose required an independent review.[37]

When the trial is by jury rather than a judge, appellate courts give even greater deference to the findings of fact. In most instances this is because of constitutional provisions for jury trial that protect jurors' determinations of fact from full review except to the extent allowed at common law.[38] A good example of the varying scope of review for judge and jury factual findings is provided by a Sixth Circuit case, Hersch v. United States,[39] which arose out of the crash of a private airplane that killed the pilot and two passengers. Two separate actions were filed by representatives of the estates. The first was against the United States under the Federal Tort Claims Act, asserting that the negligence of an air traffic controller ultimately caused the plane to spin into the fatal crash. The second was against the manufacturer, claiming that a design defect limited the ability of the plane to recover from the spin. The actions were consolidated for trial with the judge sitting as trier of fact on the claim against the government and a jury hearing the claims against the manufacturer. After plaintiffs presented their evidence, the United States moved for an involuntary dismissal and the manufacturer moved for a directed verdict. Both motions were granted.

The appellate court affirmed, but contrasted the different standards applicable to each ruling. The trial judge could enter a directed verdict, effectively taking the case from the jury, only if there was a complete absence of proof on material issues or there were no factual issues on

---

37. The holding in Bose remains intact following the Supreme Court's decision in Anderson v. City of Bessemer City, 470 U.S. 564, 105 S.Ct. 1504, 84 L.Ed.2d 518 (1985). See, e.g., Families Achieving Independence & Respect v. Nebraska Dep't of Social Servs., 111 F.3d 1408 (8th Cir.1997); In re Capital Cities/ABC, Inc.'s Application for Access to Sealed Transcripts, 913 F.2d 89 (3d Cir.1990); Liberty Lobby, Inc. v. Rees, 852 F.2d 595 (D.C.Cir.1988), cert. denied 489 U.S. 1010. See also Note, Constitutional Fact Review: An Essential Exception to Anderson v. Bessemer, 67 Ind.L.J. 1209 (1987).

38. E.g., U.S. Const.Amend. 7 (" * * * no fact tried by a jury, shall be otherwise re-examined in any Court of the United States, than according to the rules of common law"). See generally Clark & Stone, Review of Findings of Fact, 4 U.Chi.L.Rev. 190 (1937). But compare Corcoran v. City of Chicago, 373 Ill. 567, 27 N.E.2d 451 (1940), finding authority in English history to uphold an Illinois statute authorizing appellate courts to review errors of fact in deciding whether a judgment is against the weight of the evidence. The case is criticized in Weisbrod, Limitations on Trial by Jury in Illinois, 19 Chi.–Kent L.Rev. 91 (1940). The English practice is described in Goodhart, Appeals on Questions of Fact, 71 L.Q.Rev. 402 (1955).

39. 719 F.2d 873 (6th Cir.1983).

which reasonable people might differ.[40] The trial judge could not weigh the evidence and had to view all the evidence in the light most favorable to the nonmoving party. The appellate court in reviewing a directed verdict is to be governed by the same standard and rules of construction. By contrast, the court in entering the involuntary dismissal against the government could weigh and evaluate the evidence, and the nonmoving party's evidence would not be subject to any special inferences. The appellate court on review could examine all the evidence in the record, including inferences drawn by the judge and, although it must give great deference to the findings and inferences of the trial court, it could overturn the trial court's ruling if it was clearly erroneous.

Applying these standards, the Sixth Circuit found that on the products liability claim before the jury, the relevant governing law required that the plaintiffs show there was a probability, not a possibility, that those defects were responsible for the crash. The appellate court agreed with the trial judge that the evidence produced by plaintiffs did not reveal probable cause, so the directed verdict was upheld. As to the dismissal of the nonjury claim, the appellate court reviewed the evidence presented, noting that the trial judge appeared impressed with the testimony of the air traffic controller and that the experts' testimony was conflicting so that the trial judge rejected it. This action was not clearly erroneous and thus the dismissal could stand.

Finally, it should be noted that any rulings that are within the discretion of the trial judge will be reviewed under an abuse of discretion standard.[41] As a practical matter, this means that only if an appellate court is convinced that the court below was clearly wrong will it reverse a discretionary decision. Again, this narrow scope of review reflects the desire of the appellate courts not to intrude on the trial process too readily, particularly when the trial judge may be in the best position to make the determination involved. Indeed, the decision to treat certain matters as discretionary indicates that that is the case.

40. For a discussion of directed verdict standards, see § 12.3, above.

41. See, e.g., Saunderson v. Saunderson, 379 So.2d 91 (Ala.Civ.App.1980); Keeth Gas Co. v. Jackson Creek Cattle Co., 91 N.M. 87, 570 P.2d 918 (1977); Primm v. Primm, 46 Cal.2d 690, 299 P.2d 231 (1956).

§§ 13.5–14.0 are reserved for supplementary material.

Chapter 14

FORMER ADJUDICATION

Analysis

§ 14.1　Overview and Terminology

This Chapter examines the rules and principles governing the binding effect of a judgment entered in one action on a subsequent proceeding—the doctrine of former adjudication. Since this concept necessarily is very broad, precise terminology is used to describe the principles that apply in certain contexts. Thus, before embarking on an examination of the various rules of former adjudication, it is necessary to become familiar with the nomenclature of this area of the law.

Former adjudication may be broken into two basic concepts, often called "res judicata"[1] and "estoppel by judgment." This division goes back to the beginnings of the common law. As used presently, the two terms refer to two ways that a judgment may preclude a future action. Res judicata prevents a plaintiff from suing on a claim that already has been decided; it also prevents a defendant from raising any new defense to defeat the enforcement of an earlier judgment. Estoppel by judgment precludes relitigation of any issue, regardless of whether the second action is on the same claim as the first one, if that particular issue actually was contested and decided in the first action. The differences between these two concepts are explored more fully in the next section.

Both res judicata and estoppel by judgment may be subdivided. Res judicata traditionally is divided into two closely related doctrines, "merger" and "bar." They differ only in that merger applies when a claimant has prevailed in the earlier action and bar applies when the claimant has lost. When a claimant wins a judgment, all possible grounds for the cause of action are said to be merged into that judgment and are not available for further litigation. A party who loses the first suit is said to be barred by the adverse judgment from ever raising the same cause of action again, even if he can present new grounds for recovery.[2] For example, suppose that plaintiff who was injured in an automobile accident sues alleging injury to his arm, but loses because the jury finds that he was contributorily negligent. If plaintiff files a second suit claiming head injuries from the same accident, then the earlier decision will serve to bar the second suit because it is based on the same cause of action. Suppose, however, that the plaintiff prevailed in the first action and recovered damages for his broken arm. If he files a second suit to recover damages for facial lacerations also caused by the same automobile accident, the original judgment will preclude the second action; the second claim is merged into the original claim, preventing the plaintiff from "splitting" the cause of action.[3] Claim-splitting thus is prohibited by both merger and bar.

Estoppel by judgment also may be divided into two categories: "direct estoppel" and "collateral estoppel." When an issue is estopped by a judgment on a different claim, the estoppel is collateral. An issue is precluded by direct estoppel when the prior judgment invoked as an estoppel and the present suit are both on the same cause of action.

Since subsequent suits on claims that already have been decided usually are extinguished entirely by res judicata, examples of direct estoppel are very few. Direct estoppel is used most often when the first

---

§ 14.1

1. Occasionally, courts use the term "res adjudicata." This is simply a spelling variance, synonymous in all respects with "res judicata."

2. Restatement First of Judgments §§ 47, 48 (1942).

3. "It is undoubtedly a settled principle that a party is not at liberty to split up his demands and prosecute by piecemeal, or present only a portion of the grounds upon which special relief is sought and leave the rest to be presented in a second suit if the first fails. There would be no end of litigation if such practice were permissible." Stark v. Starr, 94 U.S. (4 Otto) 477, 485, 24 L.Ed. 276 (1876). See also Cleary, Res Judicata Reexamined, 57 Yale L.J. 339, 342–44 (1948).

action results in a judgment that is not on the merits.[4] When that occurs, the determinations made on those issues actually litigated and necessarily determined in the course of handing down the judgment will be binding in all subsequent suits on the same cause of action.[5] For example, if in the course of a lawsuit the parties litigate the issue of the court's jurisdiction, and the court makes a determination on it, the doctrine of direct estoppel will preclude reconsideration of that issue in a subsequent suit brought in the same court between the same parties on the same cause of action.[6] Yet an action brought in another state would not be controlled by direct estoppel as the issue of the second court's jurisdiction would not have been litigated or decided.

Having set out these definitions, a cautionary note must be added. The terminology in this area is by no means uniform. The Restatement Second of Judgments, for example, uses "res judicata" as a general term, the equivalent of former adjudication.[7] Building on terminology suggested by Professor Vestal,[8] the Restatement suggests that res judicata then may be divided into two parts: "claim preclusion," corresponding to traditional res judicata, and "issue preclusion," the analog of estoppel by judgment. Because this new terminology has been adopted by some courts and not by others, it is necessary to look carefully at how and for what purpose the binding effect of a prior judgment is being asserted in order to determine exactly which rules need be addressed.[9] Throughout this volume the terms res judicata and claim preclusion are used inter-

---

4. See § 14.7, below, for a discussion of what constitutes a judgment on the merits.

5. An important example of a judgment that, despite being entered without a contest on the merits, is binding on suits on the same cause of action, is the default judgment. See, for example, Lockhart v. Mercer Tube & Mfg. Co., 53 F.Supp. 301 (D.Del.1943) (a default judgment against trustee in bankruptcy to test the legality of a transfer of stock was conclusive in a subsequent suit against the trustee in an action to recover said stock); Pine v. M.E. Conran Co., 51 N.Y.S.2d 34 (Sup.Ct.1944) (a default judgment in favor of the plaintiff in an action to recover payment on certain notes was conclusive on the question of the validity of the debt in a subsequent suit involving the same parties).

Some courts have stated that a default judgment finally determines issues pleaded and necessary to the judgment. The decisions, however, involve instances in which redetermination of those issues would partially or entirely nullify the effect of the default judgment. Thus, these cases can be explained as prohibitions of collateral attack on prior judgments, rather than implied determinations made conclusive in a different cause of action. See Woods v. Cannaday, 158 F.2d 184 (D.C.Cir.1946) (default judgment against the superintendent of a

club was conclusive in a subsequent action for an accounting brought against the superintendent by the club members); O'Hagan v. Kracke, 253 App.Div. 632, 3 N.Y.S.2d 401 (1938), appeal denied 278 N.Y. 741, 15 N.E.2d 682 (1938) (default judgment excluding original beneficiary from all beneficial interest under deed of trust was determinative of this issue in a subsequent suit by the original beneficiary against the trustees).

6. Restatement First of Judgments § 9, comment a (1942). In order to preserve an opportunity to attack jurisdiction collaterally, the party seeking to challenge jurisdiction must default to avoid the application of direct estoppel on the jurisdiction issue. See §§ 3.25–3.26, above, for a discussion of the binding effect of personal jurisdiction challenges, and § 2.2, above, concerning subject-matter jurisdiction challenges.

7. Restatement Second of Judgments 131 (1982).

8. See Vestal, Res Judicata/Preclusion: Expansion, 47 So.Cal.L.Rev. 357, 359 (1974).

9. See, e.g., Railway Labor Executives' Ass'n v. Guilford Transportation Indus., Inc., 989 F.2d 9 (1st Cir.1993).

changeably, as are the terms collateral estoppel and issue preclusion; unless and until the new terminology displaces the old, they are regarded as equivalents.

Before turning to an examination of the workings and scope of issue and claim preclusion, it is important to distinguish these doctrines[10] from three related, but different, concepts: stare decisis, double jeopardy, and law of the case.

Stare decisis describes the effect of previous judicial decisions on present litigation. Stare decisis principles, also referred to as the doctrine of precedent, dictate that like cases should be decided alike by courts in a single jurisdiction. To adhere to precedent is a fundamental doctrine of Anglo–American law.[11] Like former adjudication, stare decisis has the task of ensuring stability and consistency in judicial decisions, allowing people to plan their conduct. The law must appear to be rationally consistent if it is to be accepted as an impersonal arbiter of disputes.

Despite the superficial similarity to former adjudication, stare decisis may be distinguished with regard to both the persons that it binds and the issues to which it applies. Former adjudication precludes only later litigation between parties to a previous lawsuit and, in some cases, others who are in privity with the parties.[12] Stare decisis, on the other hand, applies equally to all litigants, even those having no connection with the precedent-setting lawsuit. A doctrine established by stare decisis thus outlives the litigants in the original suit. Illustratively, the requirement of complete diversity for federal subject-matter jurisdiction set out in Strawbridge v. Curtiss[13] in 1806 remains binding precedent in the federal court system, even though the litigants died long ago.

A second distinction is that stare decisis applies only to questions of law; former adjudication precludes litigation on questions both of law and fact. Former adjudication protects the judgment that is the result of rules of law applied to a specific factual situation. Title to a particular piece of land or the interpretation of a particular contract are examples of what former adjudication determines. Stare decisis, however, is unconcerned with the facts of a given case except insofar as they illustrate the legal doctrine that the case enunciates.[14] In essence, then, former adjudication establishes a judgment as final between specific litigants in a particular dispute, whereas stare decisis perpetuates the general principle by which a particular case is decided and incorporates it into the body of the law.

Stare decisis, although wider in scope than former adjudication, is far less strict in its application. A judgment between specific litigants,

---

10. When questions of res judicata and collateral estoppel are raised in an interstate context, the judgment is given effect by the Full Faith and Credit Clause of the Constitution. See § 14.15, below.

11. In re Herle's Estate, 165 Misc. 46, 300 N.Y.S. 103 (1937).

12. See §§ 14.13–14.14, below.

13. 7 U.S. (3 Cranch) 267, 2 L.Ed. 435 (1806).

14. See Brown v. Rosenbaum, 175 Misc. 295, 23 N.Y.S.2d 161 (1940), reversed on other grounds 262 App.Div. 136, 28 N.Y.S.2d 345 (1941), cert. denied 316 U.S. 689.

once final, almost never is altered. As a precedent, however, a case may be overruled directly. As noted by one court, a departure from stare decisis may be "necessary in order to vindicate plain and obvious principles of law, and to remedy a continued injustice."[15] Although subordinate courts in particular are bound by precedents proclaimed by appellate courts, courts of last resort are at liberty to revise their own precedents. In contrast, courts do not consider themselves free to interfere with their own judgments in contravention of former adjudication. The res judicata or collateral estoppel effect of a judgment will be avoided only in truly extraordinary circumstances.[16] Even when a judgment is recognized to be in error, it will not be reconsidered if it comes within the ambit of former adjudication.[17]

Double jeopardy is very similar to res judicata, and the two doctrines serve closely analogous functions. One prohibits repeated prosecution of criminal charges, the other of civil claims.[18] Both double jeopardy and former adjudication are founded on the maxim that one ought not be twice vexed by the same cause.[19] Despite these similarities, the doctrines work in different ways.

Res judicata effect is given to any valid judgment, civil or criminal, that is final and on the merits.[20] Double jeopardy depends on the concept of "jeopardy," which is unique to criminal cases. Jeopardy attaches to a criminal proceeding when the accused is in imminent danger of conviction. Once this has occurred, double jeopardy forbids the prosecution from renewing the same charges in a second proceeding no matter how the case was dealt with in the original court. Ordinarily, jeopardy is deemed to have attached when the jury is sworn, or a witness examined. Because res judicata and double jeopardy rely on different standards, one can imagine criminal cases in which one doctrine would apply but not the other. For example, if a criminal prosecution is dismissed before a jury is empanelled on a finding that the relevant statute of limitations has expired, the defendant has not yet been placed in jeopardy. Nevertheless, the defendant might avoid later prosecution for the same offense by invoking res judicata.[21]

15. McGregor v. Provident Trust Co. of Philadelphia, 119 Fla. 718, 162 So. 323 (1935).

16. See §§ 14.8, 14.12, below.

17. Independence Mortgage Trust v. White, 446 F.Supp. 120 (D.Or.1978). But compare Lytle v. Household Mfg., Inc., 494 U.S. 545, 110 S.Ct. 1331, 108 L.Ed.2d 504 (1990) (erroneous denial of jury trial outweighs judicial economy interests that otherwise would support application of preclusion).

18. The Queen v. Miles, 24 Q.B.D. 423, 431 (1890).

19. See Commonwealth v. Moon, 151 Pa.Super. 555, 30 A.2d 704 (1943).

20. See § 14.7, below.

21. This example is based on U.S. v. Oppenheimer, 242 U.S. 85, 37 S.Ct. 68, 61 L.Ed. 161 (1916). The government in that case maintained that only double jeopardy was available to prevent retrial of criminal charges. Justice Holmes wrote for the Court, "It cannot be that the safeguards of the person, so often and so mightily mentioned in solemn reverence, are less than those that protect from a liability in debt. * * * [T]he Fifth Amendment was not intended to do away with what in the civil law is a fundamental principle of justice." Id. at 87–88, 37 S.Ct. at 69.

The last doctrine to be distinguished from former adjudication is "law of the case." Law of the case refers to the principle that issues once decided in a case that recur in later stages of the same case are not to be redetermined.[22] Just as notions of collateral estoppel prevent the relitigation of the same issues in successive suits, this doctrine limits relitigation in successive stages of a single suit. For example, law of the case will apply when an issue in the case is decided by the trial court and appealed. If the appellate court reverses and rules on the law to be applied and how it affects certain issues of the case, those findings will be binding on the trial court when the action is remanded for a new trial.[23] In practice, the doctrine is not enforced with the rigor that attends the rules of res judicata and collateral estoppel. As noted by the Supreme Court, it "merely expresses the practice of courts generally to refuse to reopen what has been decided, not a limit on their power."[24]

§ 14.2 Distinguishing Between Res Judicata and Collateral Estoppel—Claim and Issue Preclusion

Although claim and issue preclusion are similar in many respects and are treated today as closely related doctrines, they have very different historical origins. Res judicata came into English law from Roman law; estoppel has its origin in Germanic law. In general, estoppel prohibits a person from contradicting what he affirmed earlier.[1] For example, estoppel in pais prevents one from denying one's own earlier assertion that another has relied upon to her detriment. Originally, estoppel by judgment also embraced the notion that a party was bound by his own admissions. In the ancient Germanic trials, the emphasis was placed on the proceedings, which were controlled largely by the litigants themselves, and not upon the judgment to which they submitted. Trials were concluded not by the findings of the court but by the litigants' own public and solemn declarations, which they could not later retract.

In contrast, res judicata stressed from its Roman beginnings the importance of the court's judgment; it was always the fact of judgment that foreclosed later actions.[2] The influence of the Roman law concepts on the English common law was pervasive, although indirect. The principle of res judicata entered England both through Norman law and through borrowings from Canon law, so that by the early 1100s the Roman law principle of res judicata was established in England.

---

22. See Vestal, Law of the Case: Single Suit Preclusion, 1967 Utah L.Rev. 1 (1967).

23. For an interesting discussion of the problems of applying law of the case when an action appears in the same appellate court for a second time, but before different judges, see Lincoln Nat. Life Ins. Co. v. Roosth, 306 F.2d 110 (5th Cir.1962), cert. denied 372 U.S. 912.

24. Messinger v. Anderson, 225 U.S. 436, 444, 32 S.Ct. 739, 740, 56 L.Ed. 1152 (1912). See also Official Code Ga.Ann. § 9–11–60(h).

§ 14.2

1. "A man's own act or acceptance stops or closes his mouth to allege or plead the truth." Caulfield v. Noonan, 229 Iowa 955, 295 N.W. 466, 471 (1940), quoting Coke, Litt. 352a.

2. "By res judicata is meant the termination of a controversy by the judgment of a court." Modestinus, Pandects, BK VII, XLII(1).

Although both principles, Roman and Germanic, appear to have coexisted in English law,[3] the principle of estoppel underwent considerable modification. Transformed, it became "estoppel by record"; an incontestable presumption of the truth of the records made by the King's Court. In its new role, it supported the preeminence of the King's courts, which were "of record," over lower courts, which did not keep formal transcripts. "Estoppel by record" thus was shorn of the characteristic that identified it as an estoppel: It no longer relied on a person's own statement for its preclusive effect. Instead, like res judicata, it was enlisted to protect the sanctity of the court's pronouncements. Still, a distinction persisted between matters precluded by the judgment of a court and matters precluded by the court's record. When the second action was no more than a repetition of the first, the existing judgment precluded the subsequent action; if the second action differed substantially from the preceding one, the parties still were forbidden to contradict directly what the court by its record had established earlier.[4]

Today, res judicata and estoppel have combined to become two arms of a single doctrine.[5] The court's records no longer are considered to be unimpeachable as the word of the King. Outside evidence may be introduced to show what was considered and what issues were decided in an earlier trial. Both estoppel and res judicata guard the finality of the court's judgment.

There are three characteristic differences between the two doctrines. Res judicata prevents relitigation of claims; collateral estoppel ends controversy over issues. Res judicata applies regardless of whether there has been an adversary contest on a particular matter; collateral estoppel operates only when an issue has been litigated fully. Res judicata precludes only subsequent suits on the same cause of action; collateral estoppel may preclude relitigation of the same issues in later suits on any cause of action.

The leading case—often described as "classic"—concerning the distinction between res judicata and collateral estoppel is Cromwell v.

---

3. In civil law countries that owe their legal systems almost exclusively to Roman law, nothing corresponding to the principle of estoppel appears. In those countries, questions decided in the course of reaching a judgment or "prejudicial questions" are not excluded from later actions between the same parties unless one of the parties specifically asks for a ruling on that issue. See Millar, The Premises of the Judgment as Res Judicata in Continental and Anglo–American Law, 39 Mich.L.Rev. 1 (1940). A request of this type amounts to a demand for a declaratory judgment in addition to the judgment in the original action. This procedure allows the parties to know beforehand precisely which issues a judgment will foreclose—an advantage not shared by the Anglo–American scheme.

4. Millar, The Historical Relation of Estoppel by Record to Res Judicata, 35 Ill. L.Rev. 41 (1940).

5. For an excellent introduction to the policy justifications underlying the doctrines of res judicata and collateral estoppel, and to the distinctions between these two, see 18 C. Wright, A. Miller & E. Cooper, Jurisdiction and Related Matters §§ 4402–03; Developments in the Law—Res Judicata, 65 Harv.L.Rev. 818, 840–50 (1952). Also useful for their historical analysis of the doctrine of collateral estoppel are Scott, Collateral Estoppel by Judgment, 56 Harv. L.Rev. 1 (1942); Polasky, Collateral Estoppel—Effects of Prior Litigation, 39 Iowa L.Rev. 217 (1954); and Rosenberg, Collateral Estoppel in New York, 44 St. John's L.Rev. 165 (1969).

County of Sac.[6] Cromwell held four bonds issued by the county in 1860 in order to build a courthouse. When some of the coupons on those bonds reached maturity, Cromwell brought suit against the county to compel payment on them. The county resisted payment, alleging that the bonds had been issued fraudulently.[7] The case reached the Supreme Court which determined (1) that because of the fraudulent inception of the bonds, they were void against the county except in the hands of a bona fide holder who had taken them for value before maturity, and (2) that Cromwell had not shown that he was a bona fide holder of the bonds in question. The first action, therefore, was decided in favor of the county.

When the bonds matured, Cromwell brought another action. The trial court held this second action to be precluded by the earlier suit, but the Supreme Court reversed. In analyzing the effect of the earlier decision on the second action, Justice Field, writing for the Court, carefully distinguished between the effects of res judicata and collateral estoppel.[8] Res judicata, which would have been an absolute bar to the subsequent action, did not apply because each bond and the interest coupons attached to it constituted a separate cause of action.[9] Cromwell's cause of action would not be rejected as a whole. Therefore, it was necessary to look to the allied doctrine of collateral estoppel in order to find what issues might be precluded by the first suit.

To determine how collateral estoppel applied, Justice Field noted that "the inquiry must always be as to the point or question actually litigated and determined in the original action, not what might have been thus litigated and determined."[10] Since the earlier action had determined that the bonds had been fraudulently issued, on that point no further litigation would be allowed. Further, Cromwell could not attempt to show that he was a bona fide holder of the coupons that had been the subject of the earlier litigation: He had failed to do that in the first suit and that cause of action was closed forever. However, he was free to show, if he could, that he was the bona fide holder for value of newly matured coupons. "The fact that a party may not have shown that he gave value for one bond or coupon is not even presumptive, much less conclusive, evidence that he may not have given value for another and different bond or coupon."[11]

Thus, collateral estoppel may have a much broader effect than res judicata in that a judgment may be applied to preclude relitigation of an issue whenever it appears in any other action. This broad scope is dangerous because an issue may resurface in unexpected contexts, presenting a risk of unhappy surprise. An issue that appeared trivial in one

---

6.   94 U.S. (4 Otto) 351, 24 L.Ed. 195 (1876).

7.   It appears that $10,000 worth of bonds had been issued by the county. The courthouse never was built and some of the bonds were used to bribe the county judge. The first action actually was brought by one Smith, but because he sued for the benefit of Cromwell, collateral estoppel applied equally to both. See § 14.13, below.

8.   94 U.S. at 352.

9.   See § 14.4, below.

10.   94 U.S. at 353.

11.   94 U.S. at 360.

action may be crucial in a later suit, and an unwary litigant may regret his earlier, lax handling of it.

Because of this potential for surprise, the application of collateral estoppel is restricted in other ways. It is narrower than res judicata in that it applies only to issues actually litigated in a previous suit. This requirement mitigates the danger of surprise, limiting preclusion to issues that have received the attention of the litigants. In addition, the issue precluded must be one that was necessary to the prior judgment, assuring that the rendering court recognized its determination to be significant and worthy of close attention. These restrictions are explored more fully later.[12] They are mentioned here merely to highlight some of the distinctions between the operation of the doctrines of claim and issue preclusion.

A. RES JUDICATA—CLAIM PRECLUSION

§ 14.3 General Principles Underlying Res Judicata

To understand res judicata, it is necessary to understand why it is desirable that once a judgment is reached on one claim, no further action on the same controversy should be allowed. Two maxims of the English common law best summarize the general policies underlying this doctrine. They are: first, that no person should be twice vexed by the same claim; and second, that it is in the interest of the state that there be an end to litigation. Thus, principles of res judicata serve both private and public interests.

The interest of the judicial system in preventing relitigation of the same dispute recognizes that judicial resources are finite and the number of cases that can be heard by the courts is limited. Every dispute that is reheard means that another will be delayed. As modern court dockets are filled to overflowing, this concern is of critical importance. Res judicata thus conserves scarce judicial resources and promotes efficiency in the interest of the public at large.

Once a final judgment has been rendered, the prevailing party also has an interest in the stability of that judgment. Parties come to the courts in order to resolve controversies; a judgment would be of little use in resolving disputes if the parties were free to ignore it and to litigate the same claims again and again. Although judicial determinations are not infallible, judicial error should be corrected through appeals procedures, not through repeated suits on the same claim. Further, to allow relitigation creates the risk of inconsistent results and presents the embarrassing problem of determining which of two conflicting decisions is to be preferred. Since there is no reason to suppose that the second or third determination of a claim necessarily is more accurate than the first, the first should be left undisturbed.

---

12. See § 14.11, below.

In some cases, the public at large also has an interest in seeing that rights and liabilities once established remain fixed. If a court quiets title to land, for example, everyone should be able to rely on the finality of that determination. Otherwise, many real estate transactions would be clouded by uncertainty. Thus, the most important purpose of res judicata is to provide repose for both the party litigants and the public.[1] As the Supreme Court has observed, "res judicata thus encourages reliance on judicial decision, bars vexatious litigation, and frees the courts to resolve other disputes."[2]

Despite the valuable policies promoted by res judicata, its application may lead to harsh consequences in some cases. A prior judgment ends litigation, not only "as to every ground of recovery that was actually presented in the action, but also as to every ground which might have been presented."[3] This characteristic, more than any other, distinguishes res judicata from its allied doctrine, collateral estoppel.[4] The preclusive breadth of the doctrine means that a judgment concludes an entire cause of action, which may encompass separate component claims.[5] A plaintiff who has been injured in an accident has claims for injuries to different parts of his body—one claim for a broken arm, another for a ruptured spleen, and so forth—but has only one cause of action for all of these injuries. Because the scope of res judicata extends beyond what actually has been litigated, it prevents the plaintiff from fragmenting his case into many separately prosecuted claims in order to harass the defendant with the expense of litigation.

In this way, res judicata serves to encourage joinder of claims, resulting in judicial economy. A danger, however, accompanies this salutary effect. Because what "might be presented" in an action is not always evident during litigation, the parties may discover after trial that claims not presented—perhaps not even contemplated—have been foreclosed by the judgment. Res judicata can preclude a plaintiff from pursuing an otherwise meritorious claim that never was litigated because of a seemingly minor procedural error or because a lawyer failed to anticipate at the time of the first action the effect that the judgment would have on future litigation.

---

§ 14.3

1. Southern Pacific R.R. Co. v. U.S., 168 U.S. 1, 18 S.Ct. 18, 27, 42 L.Ed. 355 (1897): "[The general rule of res judicata] is demanded by the very object for which civil courts have been established, which is to secure the peace and repose of society by the settlement of matters capable of judicial determination. Its enforcement is essential to the maintenance of social order; for, the aid of judicial tribunals would not be invoked for the vindication of rights of person and property, if, as between parties and their privies, conclusiveness did not attend the judgments of such tribunals in respect of all matters properly put in issue and actually determined by them." For a more recent statement of the same thought, see James v. Gerber Prods. Co., 587 F.2d 324, 327 (6th Cir.1978).

2. Brown v. Felsen, 442 U.S. 127, 131, 99 S.Ct. 2205, 2209, 60 L.Ed.2d 767 (1979).

3. Cromwell v. County of Sac, 94 U.S. (4 Otto) 351, 353, 24 L.Ed. 195 (1876).

4. See §§ 14.9–14.12, below, for a discussion of collateral estoppel.

5. See §§ 14.4–14.6, for a discussion of the scope of res judicata.

A second feature of res judicata that leads to harsh results is that it forecloses relitigation of claims regardless of whether the original decision was correct. Res judicata is rigidly formal and works mechanically. It resolutely ignores the substantive merit of the judgment it enforces. Decisions that plainly are wrong and that would be reversed on appeal, were that route available, are valid final judgments for res judicata purposes. After all, the policies of res judicata—finality of decision and protection from harassment—would be frustrated completely if a plaintiff could evade the doctrine simply by arguing that the original decision was wrong. Res judicata reflects the policy that sometimes it is more important that a judgment be stable than that it be correct.[6]

The rules of res judicata have been formulated almost entirely by courts; very few statutes or constitutional provisions provide any specific guidance.[7] In general, the common law rules that have developed fall into two categories: first, those defining the scope of a cause of action[8] and second, those pertaining to the nature of the original decision.[9] The former determine whether an earlier suit should preclude a later one by ascertaining how much is included in the cause of action decided by the first suit. The latter limitations are imposed to ensure as much as possible that the original action provided a fair and complete opportunity to litigate the claims that are to be precluded in the second lawsuit. These rules look to the form of the first proceeding and require the first judgment to be a final, not provisional, judgment; to be on the merits, not based on a preliminary or jurisdictional matter; and to be rendered by a court jurisdictionally competent to determine all parts of the plaintiff's cause of action.

Before turning to an examination of the standards for applying res judicata, it is important to keep in mind the procedure surrounding its use. Res judicata is an affirmative defense that the court ordinarily will not raise on its own initiative.[10] Therefore, it is not strictly accurate to say that res judicata prohibits relitigation of the same cause of action because the defendant in the second action may waive the defense and consent to retrying the action.

---

6. Shoup v. Bell & Howell Co., 872 F.2d 1178, 1182 (4th Cir.1989); Mitchell v. National Broadcasting Co., 553 F.2d 265, 272 (2d Cir.1977); Iselin v. Meng, 307 F.2d 455, 457 (5th Cir.1962), cert. denied 372 U.S. 909.

7. The Full Faith and Credit Clause of the Constitution, Article IV, § 1, does provide some general guidelines for interstate res judicata questions. See § 14.15, below.

8. See §§ 14.4–14.6, below.

9. See § 14.7, below.

10. Older cases emphasized the policy underlying res judicata as avoiding twice vexing the defendant, and pleading rules requiring the defendant to raise the issue or waive it were drafted at that time. See Fed.Civ.Proc.Rule 8(c). See also Cleary, Res Judicata Reexamined, 57 Yale L.J. 339, 348 (1948). As courts have become increasingly concerned with their own interests in forestalling repetitive litigation, a few have raised the question of preclusion on their own motion. See Independent School Dist. No. 283 v. S.D., 88 F.3d 556, 562 n. 5 (8th Cir.1996); Carbonell v. Louisiana Dep't of Health & Human Resources, 772 F.2d 185, 189 (5th Cir.1985); Williams v. Codd, 459 F.Supp. 804, 811 (S.D.N.Y.1978); Ocean Acc. & Guar. Corp. v. U.S. Fidelity & Guar. Co., 63 Ariz. 352, 162 P.2d 609, 614 (1945). See generally 18 C. Wright, A. Miller & E. Cooper, Jurisdiction and Related Matters § 4405.

Res judicata may be waived explicitly or implicitly. For example, a party explicitly may waive future invocation of res judicata during the original lawsuit. In this way, the parties can control the litigation's scope, deliberately removing parts of a cause of action from consideration and expressly stipulating that they are not to be considered within the scope of the judgment. A couple being divorced, for instance, may stipulate that the divorce action does not touch upon the division of property. Accordingly, a later action to enforce a property division agreement will not be precluded by the divorce decree.[11]

The defendant also may waive the defense unintentionally. By actions taken at the first trial, the defendant sometimes is found to have waived implicitly the right to assert a later res judicata defense. For example, if the plaintiff, having brought two separate suits for the same cause of action, attempts to consolidate them into one and the defendant objects successfully, the defendant may not complain thereafter that the plaintiff has split the cause of action. By preventing consolidation, the defendant implicitly waived the defense of res judicata.[12]

Waiver also may occur because of defendant's conduct in the second action. If res judicata is not raised, like other affirmative defenses it is presumed to be waived and the issue will be ignored.[13] Waiver also may occur if defendant fails to raise the defense soon enough.[14] The question of what constitutes the timely interposition of the defense depends on the circumstances of each case. The simplest case is one in which the first trial is completely finished before the second action begins. In that situation, the defendant must plead the prior judgment in the first responsive pleading.[15]

When two suits on the same cause of action are brought simultaneously, res judicata is unavailable until one of the actions reaches a final judgment. Although the defendant cannot interpose the defense until one of the two concurrent suits reaches judgment, waiver nonetheless may be implied even before either action has gone to judgment. By acquiescing to the separate suits without objecting to the other pending action, the defendant may be found to have waived any objections to the claim-splitting. Defendant may not lie in wait silently until one of the two actions is brought to judgment and then use that judgment to ambush the plaintiff and defeat the other action.[16]

---

11. Smith v. Smith, 235 Minn. 412, 51 N.W.2d 276 (1952).

12. E.g., Reeves v. Philadelphia Gas Works Co., 107 Pa.Super. 422, 164 A. 132 (1933).

13. See Marcus v. Sullivan, 926 F.2d 604 (7th Cir.1991).

14. See Annot., Waiver of, by Failing Promptly to Raise, Objection to Splitting Cause of Action, 40 A.L.R.3d 108 (1971).

15. The failure to include res judicata in the first responsive pleading is not neces-

sarily fatal because leave to amend may be granted by the court. See § 5.26, above, on the right to amend.

16. In Georgia Ry. & Power Co. v. Endsley, 167 Ga. 439, 145 S.E. 851 (1928), the plaintiff brought separate actions for personal and property damage after the defendant's streetcar collided with plaintiff's automobile. The defense of res judicata was disallowed because defendant failed to object before one of the actions had reached judgment.

Finally, the benefit of res judicata may be lost if, by fraud or other misrepresentation, the defendant actually is responsible for the claim-splitting.[17] The case of Hyyti v. Smith[18] provides a classic example. Plaintiff sued for the death of her father who was killed in an accident with the defendant. Plaintiff, who had arrived in America only recently and who spoke only Finnish, relied on the advice of the defendant's attorney and did not hire her own lawyer. The defendant's attorney did not tell her that she was entitled to sue for loss of support and punitive damages. At his advice, she brought an action only for hospital, medical, and funeral expenses. When she realized the existence of the other claims, she brought a second action, to which the defendant raised res judicata as an affirmative defense. The court overruled the defense, noting that the "plaintiff's cause of action for loss of support was omitted in the former action, but the defendant was responsible for the omission."[19]

Even innocent misrepresentation may prevent the application of res judicata. For example, in Vineseck v. Great Northern Railway Company,[20] plaintiff, a Pole who spoke very little English, was injured while working for the defendant railway. A company doctor treated him for leg and head injuries and assured him that his blurred vision was only temporary. Plaintiff sued the railway and recovered for the leg injury only, believing that the head injury was trivial. Later, the seemingly minor head injury caused the plaintiff to become permanently blind. Even though there was no proof that the railroad, through its doctor, intended to mislead the plaintiff, the court allowed the plaintiff to bring a second action for the head injury that led to his blindness. The railroad, the court held, could not object to the plaintiff's splitting of the cause of action because its doctor had helped encourage him to do so.

What is important in these cases is not the plaintiff's intentions regarding claim-splitting, but the defendant's complicity or involvement in the decision to split the claims. The defendant is estopped from protesting a result that he has brought upon himself. Equally clear is that when the plaintiff through her own carelessness has overlooked some claim that should have been brought in the first case, she cannot have a second chance. Although a few cases have held that excusable ignorance on the part of the plaintiff prevents the application of res judicata,[21] other authorities, notably the Restatement Second of Judgments,[22] insist that plaintiff's mistakes, absent fraud, concealment, or misrepresentation by the defendant, do not justify claim-splitting.[23] This

17. Restatement Second of Judgments § 26, comment j (1982). E.g., McCarty v. First of Georgia Ins. Co., 713 F.2d 609 (10th Cir.1983).

18. 67 N.D. 425, 272 N.W. 747 (1937).

19. 272 N.W. at 749.

20. 136 Minn. 96, 161 N.W. 494 (1917).

21. Zaromb v. Borucka, 166 N.J.Super. 22, 398 A.2d 1308 (App.Div.1979); Gaither

Corp. v. Skinner, 241 N.C. 532, 85 S.E.2d 909, 912 (1955); Gedney v. Gedney, 160 N.Y. 471, 55 N.E. 1 (1899). See also Developments in the Law, Res Judicata, 65 Harv. L.Rev. 818, 830–31 (1952).

22. Restatement Second of Judgments § 26, comment j (1982).

23. Cohan v. Associated Fur Farms, 261 Wis. 584, 53 N.W.2d 788 (1952). Defendant, Associated, bought contaminated feed

admittedly harsh result is supported by the systemic need for certainty and finality to litigation.

§ 14.4   The Scope of Res Judicata—What Is a Claim or Cause of Action

The basic unit of litigation to which res judicata applies is a cause of action or claim.[1] A valid and final judgment on the merits of a cause of action is treated as conclusive as to the parties' rights and accorded binding effect in all subsequent lawsuits involving the same cause of action. Merger and bar apply not only to what was litigated, but also to all aspects of the cause, as well as to all defenses, that might have been raised with respect to the cause of action adjudicated in the original lawsuit.[2] Thus, it is crucial to define the meaning of "cause of action" in order to understand the operation of the res judicata doctrine.

It was relatively easy and predictable to determine the scope of a cause of action under the writ system. Identical writs based on one event gave rise to only one cause of action; different events involving more than one writ appropriately were pursued in separate actions. Moreover, even when there was only a single transaction or occurrence, if two different writs such as detinue and trover were available, they could be sued upon separately.[3]

The merger of law and equity and the breakdown of the procedural distinctions that separated the common-law forms of action have widened the scope of the modern action as to matters that may be joined in a pleading, as well as to the relief allowed to be sought in a single action. As a result, it often is difficult to isolate units of litigation and to decide whether two claims are closely enough related to warrant preclusion by res judicata. Thus, disputes over the scope of the cause of action in an earlier suit often are critical threshold battles that determine the success or failure of a lawsuit.[4]

for its own animals from Armour and sold some to Cohan. When its animals began to die, it sued the vendor, and recovered. Cohan, whose animals died later, then sued Associated who in turn attempted to implead Armour. Armour successfully pleaded res judicata, even though at the time of the first suit Associated could not have known of the damage to Cohan's animals.

§ 14.4

1. The term "cause of action" traditionally has been used to define the limits of res judicata. This is not surprising because the concept also was used to define a litigation unit in other contexts, such as pleading, joinder, and statutes of limitations when the early procedural codes were adopted by the states. Modern procedural rules generally have substituted the notion of a "claim" for "cause of action" and,

consistent with this change, the scope of res judicata now may refer to claims. For a more thorough treatment of the scope of res judicata, see 18 C. Wright, A. Miller & E. Cooper, Jurisdiction and Related Matters §§ 4406–14.

2. Cromwell v. County of Sac, 94 U.S. (4 Otto) 351, 24 L.Ed. 195 (1876); Schuykill Fuel Corp. v. B. & C. Nieberg Realty Corp., 250 N.Y. 304, 165 N.E. 456 (1929); Reich v. Cochran, 151 N.Y. 122, 45 N.E. 367 (1896).

3. II W. Holdsworth, A History of English Law 250 (1936).

4. Even if a claim is found to be a part of a separate cause of action, the earlier judgment is not wholly irrelevant. Rather, its preclusive effect is limited to specific issues that were actually litigated and necessarily decided by the earlier suit. See §§ 14.9–14.11, below.

No precise definition of a cause of action commands universal acceptance. Moreover, "on a given set of facts there seems to be at least one rule to buttress any result, and the same tests often can sustain opposite positions."[5] To ask what might have been litigated in a former action is, in Professor Cleary's words, to "leave the workaday world and enter into a wondrous realm of words."[6]

A few things are certain: Identical complaints raise the same cause of action, and claims arising from different transactions or occurrences are distinct causes of action. But under what circumstances a single transaction or occurrence can give rise to two or more separate causes of action is not so easily agreed upon.

In general, the scope of a cause of action depends on two considerations. First, the procedural rules governing pleading, joinder of claims, jurisdictional reach, and the division of law and equity in the court in which the first action is brought, determine the extent to which it is reasonable to require litigants to advance their claims and defenses in a single lawsuit.[7] The Federal Rules, for example, provide the parties with an abundant opportunity to litigate all the claims arising from one transaction in a single lawsuit.[8] Therefore, when the Federal Rules or comparable rules are in force, it is appropriate to define the cause of action broadly to include all legal questions that may arise from the same transaction or occurrence. That approach is highly inappropriate, however, if the procedural rules neither allow free joinder of claims nor liberal amendment of pleadings, or if there is no forum in which legal and equitable claims can be combined in a single action.

The scope of a cause of action also depends on the degree to which the court is committed to promoting judicial economy. The application of res judicata fosters the policy of discouraging multifarious suits by requiring a party to "dispose of all his claims in one proceeding as expeditiously as the present law of procedure and the requirements of fairness permit."[9] When defining the scope of a particular cause of action the court often must reconcile two competing factors: the efficiency of the system as a whole and justice in the case at hand. Painstaking attention to individual cases easily could swamp the judicial machinery

---

5. Developments in the Law—Res Judicata, 65 Harv.L.Rev. 818, 825 (1952).

6. Cleary, Res Judicata Reexamined, 57 Yale L.J. 339, 343 (1948).

7. The meaning of cause of action for res judicata purposes is much broader today than it was earlier. The whole aim in pleading under the writ system was to frame a single legal issue so that the words "cause of action" had a very narrow meaning. If the theory of the second suit was unavailable under the writ used in the first suit, the plaintiff had no opportunity to litigate it and hence was not barred by res judicata. In contrast, the principle that pervades modern pleading systems, especially the

federal system, as exemplified by the free permissive joinder of claims, liberal amendment provisions, and compulsory counterclaims, is that the whole controversy between the parties may and often must be brought before the same court in the same action. Williamson v. Columbia Gas & Elec. Corp., 186 F.2d 464 (3d Cir.1950), cert. denied 341 U.S. 921. See Restatement Second of Judgments § 24, comment a (1982).

8. See Chapter 6, above, on joinder of claims and parties.

9. Schopflocher, What is a Single Cause of Action for the Purposes of the Doctrine of Res Judicata, 21 Ore.L.Rev. 319, 324 (1942).

with repetitive reviews, preventing fresh grievances from being heard. Zealous dedication to efficiency, on the other hand, has the danger of undermining the judicial system's purpose. Thus, judicial economy considerations typically favor construing the scope of the cause of action widely,[10] whereas concern for individual litigants demands adopting a narrower definition.

The tests or definitions that the courts and commentators have proposed represent two schools of thought. The transactional approach—the more contemporary of the two—is geared to maximizing efficiency consistently with individual justice. The other approach is narrower and focuses on whether the primary right or type of injury is the same in both actions. The application of these tests to a few recurrent types of situations follows.

Some courts recognize separate causes of action whenever they are satisfied that no decision in the second action would contradict the judgment in the first action.[11] This test singles out and emphasizes the importance of the stability and consistency of judgments, insisting only that once a final judgment is rendered, no later action be allowed to undermine it.

A leading case applying this test is Schuykill Fuel Corporation v. B. & C. Nieberg Realty Corporation.[12] In Schuykill, Judge (later Justice) Cardozo declared that the "decisive test" for determining whether two causes of action are the same for purposes of res judicata is "whether the substance of the rights or interests established in the first action will be destroyed or impaired by the prosecution of the second."[13] The application of this standard to the facts of Schuykill, itself, illustrates its narrowness. Judge Cardozo held that plaintiff's second action seeking reformation of a contract was not barred by an earlier action in which the plaintiff had recovered under the document as written. Although the former judgment would be conclusive as to the meaning of the contract's terms, it was not conclusive as to whether the contract should be reformed because "nothing heretofore determined nor any right secured thereby is retracted or diminished."[14] Courts applying a broader defini-

---

10. "[T]he larger the unit of litigation, the less energy will be spent per individual unit." Vestal, Res Judicata/Preclusion: Expansion, 47 So.Calif.L.Rev. 357, 359 (1974).

11. For example, in United Federation of Teachers Welfare Fund v. Kramarsky, 451 F.Supp. 333, 337 (S.D.N.Y.1978), affirmed on other grounds 650 F.2d 1310 (2d Cir.1981), the Fund sued to enjoin the Commissioner of the New York State Human Rights Division from ordering that city school personnel be provided maternity benefits. Prior to the suit several actions had been brought by the Commissioner on behalf of individual teachers against the Fund and the decisions in those suits had affirmed that maternity benefits had to be paid. The court held that the judgments in those suits did not bar the present action because the relief sought would have only prospective application and thus would not affect the earlier judgments.

12. 250 N.Y. 304, 165 N.E. 456 (1929). Although a leading New York precedent, its use is almost entirely limited to New York. A few courts in other states have used similar reasoning. See, e.g., Boucher v. Bailey, 117 N.H. 590, 375 A.2d 1160 (1977).

13. 165 N.E. at 458.

14. Ibid.

tion of cause of action have required that a plea for contract reformation be joined with the original action on the contract or be barred.[15]

The destruction-of-prior-judgment test was held to be met in Statter v. Statter,[16] in which the New York Court of Appeals held a prior judgment awarding a decree of separation to an estranged husband to be res judicata in a later action brought by the wife for the annulment of their marriage. The second action was precluded even though the validity of the marriage never actually was contested in the first suit and the wife alleged possession of new evidence showing that the husband's earlier marriage, previously unknown to her, still was valid at the time of their own. According to the court,

> a decision in the pending annulment action declaring the marriage invalid would undermine and devitalize completely the earlier separation judgment by depriving it of the very basis upon which it was rendered. The inconsistent determination would result in the alteration or dissolution of the status and concomitant rights and interests already declared to exist.[17]

As these cases illustrate, the destruction-of-prior-judgment test can result in a narrow or wide scope being given to the cause of action depending on what is considered to be within the content of a judgment. It is not clear whether what is established by a judgment and should not be disturbed includes (1) only the relief granted; or (2) the relief granted plus the judicial pronouncements concerning the litigants' rights and duties; or (3) all of these, plus the findings on disputed facts. Further, although protecting the stability and consistency of judgments is necessary to encourage optimal use of judicial resources and to avoid uncertainty in the economic affairs of the parties, this test may be criticized as merely reformulating the question, since the very problem in applying res judicata is to determine when a later action would undo a prior judgment.

Another test frequently used focuses attention on the conceptual framework of legal rights and legal wrongs that were involved in the first action. Although this test is narrower than the transactional approach, it is intended to be broad enough to prevent repetitious lawsuits based on the multiplication of grounds for the same wrong or injury.

A good example is Baltimore Steamship Company v. Phillips.[18] An eighteen-year old plaintiff had been injured seriously by the fall of a hatch cover while working on board defendant's vessel. Plaintiff first sued for negligence, alleging that the defendant had failed to provide a safe working place and that the equipment provided on the vessel had been unseaworthy. That action was dismissed on the ground that the

15. See Massari v. Einsiedler, 6 N.J. 303, 78 A.2d 572 (1951).

16. 2 N.Y.2d 668, 163 N.Y.S.2d 13, 143 N.E.2d 10 (1957). One judge dissented, believing that the public policy against bigamy was more important than res judicata.

17. 163 N.Y.S.2d at 16, 143 N.E.2d at 13.

18. 274 U.S. 316, 47 S.Ct. 600, 71 L.Ed. 1069 (1927).

plaintiff's injury had not been caused by the negligence alleged but by the negligence of other employees in the unloading operation. Although the proper course would have been to amend the plaintiff's complaint to include the additional ground for recovery, both the court and plaintiff's counsel had proceeded on the erroneous belief that the maritime law under which the suit had been brought did not allow the plaintiff to recover for the negligence of fellow crew members. When Phillips brought a new action against the Steamship Company alleging employee negligence, the district court held, and the Second Circuit affirmed, that the cause of action in the new suit was separate from the one raised in the first because distinct grounds of negligence were pleaded. The Supreme Court reversed, holding that merely alleging different grounds of negligence was not sufficient to support two separate actions when there was only "a single wrongful invasion of a single primary right of the plaintiff, namely the right of bodily safety."[19] As defined by the Court:

> A cause of action does not consist of facts, but of the unlawful violation of a right which the facts show. The number and variety of the facts alleged do not establish more than one cause of action so long as their result, whether they be considered severally or in combination, is the violation of but one right by a single legal wrong.[20]

Although this test has an intuitive appeal, its main difficulty is that there is no precise legal formula by which to determine what constitutes a single right or wrong. The traditional categories identifying legal rights are rooted in the common-law writ system. For example, under this approach, a person who is hurt in a barroom brawl may have one cause of action for the injury to his nose and another for his broken glasses, because security of the person and of property were treated as distinct legal rights.[21] This distinction can be traced to the historical fact that there were two different writs at common law, one for trespass to the person and another for trespass to chattels. Thus, using this approach to distinguish different legal rights relies on historical distinctions that do not have any modern relevance.[22]

---

19. 274 U.S. at 321, 47 S.Ct. at 602.

20. Ibid.

21. Today, the majority of jurisdictions hold personal and property damage from the same transaction to be one cause of action. See, e.g., McKibben v. Zamora, 358 So.2d 866 (Fla.App.1978). Compare International Evangelical Church of the Soldiers of the Cross of Christ v. Church of the Soldiers of the Cross of Christ of California, 54 F.3d 587 (9th Cir.1995)(right to seek damages for fraud and unjust enrichment are primary rights different from the right to enforce a trust upon assets dedicated to a particular religious doctrine).

22. Perhaps because of this anomaly, the application of the primary-rights test by modern courts in practice often is close to the transactional standard. See, e.g., Production Supply Co. v. Fry Steel Inc., 74 F.3d 76 (5th Cir.1996); Reed v. Marketing Services Int'l, Ltd., 540 F.Supp. 893 (S.D.Tex.1982); Takahashi v. Board of Educ. of Livingston Union School District, 249 Cal.Rptr. 578, 202 Cal.App.3d 1464 (1988), cert. denied 490 U.S. 1011. The transaction standard is discussed at notes 39–50, below.

Another way of distinguishing legal rights is by looking to the statutes that embody them.[23] Statutory codes often provide a convenient way of organizing legal rights into discrete units, and thus each statute may be thought of as creating a single cause of action.[24] Indeed, when arguing that two claims constitute different causes of action, it is helpful to be able to point to separate statutes as the basis of each action, although that argument alone generally is not conclusive.[25]

A good illustration of the "different-statute" approach is Harrington v. Workmen's Compensation Appeal Board.[26] Pennsylvania provided its civil servants two means for seeking compensation for employment-related injuries; they could file a claim under the Workmen's Compensation Act or under a special regulation of the Pennsylvania Civil Service Commission. Harrington, a fireman injured in an automobile accident while driving to work, first sought relief under the Civil Service regulation, but the court denied relief on the ground that his injury was not "work-related" as required by the regulation. When Harrington brought a second action for the same injury under the Workmen's Compensation Act, the court held that the new suit was not barred by res judicata because it was based on a different statute and raised a new cause of action.[27]

Another variant of the infringement-of-the-same-right-by-the-same-wrong test views a cause of action as composed of a single remedial right.[28] For example, a claim for damages at law and a claim for specific performance sometimes may be treated as separate causes of action even though both arise from the nonperformance of the same contract. Using this approach, a Pennsylvania court ruled that a contempt action against the power company for ignoring a court order to prepare plans to lower pollution levels did not bar a subsequent action for civil damages resulting from the company's delay.[29] The two suits involved distinct

23. Delicate issues of federalism can arise when both federal and state statutes are applicable to the same situation. See § 14.7, at nn. 15–28, below.

24. A similar approach may be used when constitutional and statutory claims are asserted in separate actions. E.g., Mitchell v. Board of Trustees of Pickens County School District A, 380 F.Supp. 197 (D.S.C.1973) (first action based on Equal Protection Clause of the Fourteenth Amendment; second suit based on Title VII of the 1964 Civil Rights Act).

25. See Williamson v. Columbia Gas & Elec. Corp., 186 F.2d 464, 468 (3d Cir. 1950), cert. denied 341 U.S. 921 (action under Clayton Act may preclude action under Sherman Act).

26. 15 Pa.Cmwlth. 119, 325 A.2d 337 (1974).

27. The second claim ultimately was dismissed, however, because collateral estoppel precluded the plaintiff from alleging

that his injury was work-related. Similar is Nicklos v. Firestone Tire & Rubber Co., 346 F.Supp. 185 (E.D.Pa.1972), affirmed without opinion 485 F.2d 680 (3d Cir.1973), in which the plaintiff unsuccessfully sought relief under the Workman's Compensation Act, then brought a second action asserting a common-law tort claim. The court held that the second action was on a new cause of action, but that collateral estoppel prevented the plaintiff from asserting elements essential to his claim. See §§ 14.9–14.11, below, for a discussion of collateral estoppel.

28. See McCaskill, Actions and Causes of Action, 34 Yale L.J. 614 (1925).

29. Pennsylvania Dep't of Environmental Protection v. Pennsylvania Power Co., 34 Pa.Cmwlth. 546, 384 A.2d 273 (1978), reversed on other grounds 490 Pa. 399, 416 A.2d 995 (1980).

causes of action because the "thing sued for" was different in each. Unless there are special circumstances, however, merely seeking different remedies normally will not be sufficient to support separate actions.[30]

The judicial economy objective underlying res judicata would be impaired if the factfinding effort undertaken in the original action were duplicated by a subsequent lawsuit. Thus, courts often proclaim that "to determine if the first [action] is res judicata to the second, the test to be applied is whether there is identity of facts essential to the maintenance of both cases or whether the same evidence would sustain both."[31] This definition of a cause of action[32] reflects an attempt to group the underlying facts in some functional way, a concern that stems from the nineteenth century code reforms.[33]

The application of the same-evidence test is not without difficulty and it has been used inconsistently. For example, some courts have applied the test very narrowly, requiring a complete identity of evidence for the two claims before res judicata will preclude the second suit.[34] Thus, in one case the plaintiff unsuccessfully sued the defendant estate to recover possession of real estate, alleging that he had provided consideration for the property's purchase and that the decedent had held it in trust for herself and for him. The Ohio Supreme Court held that a second action against the estate based on the allegation that plaintiff was the decedent's sole heir at law as her common-law husband raised sufficiently different evidence to constitute a distinct cause of action.[35] In a similar vein, an Illinois appellate court applied the same-evidence test to hold that an action by a former employee to recover backpay was not precluded by a prior small claims action to recover a sales commission, even though both claims arose from the same employment relation.[36] The issue of wrongful termination of employment, which was neither material nor relevant in the first action, was crucial in the second action and this evidentiary difference was sufficient to support allowing the new action to go forward.

30. See O'Brien v. City of Syracuse, 54 N.Y.2d 353, 355, 445 N.Y.S.2d 687, 688, 429 N.E.2d 1158, 1159 (1981); Golden v. Mascari, 63 Ohio App. 139, 25 N.E.2d 462 (1939). But see McCaskill, Actions and Causes of Action, 34 Yale L.J. 614 (1925), in which the author insists that rights cannot be understood apart from remedies.

31. Kahler v. Don E. Williams Co., 59 Ill.App.3d 716, 16 Ill.Dec. 927, 929, 375 N.E.2d 1034, 1036 (1978).

32. The same evidence test was incorporated in the First Restatement. See Restatement First of Judgments § 61 (1942).

33. In place of the abolished forms of action, the codes required that the complaint set out a description of the facts constituting the cause of action. See § 5.4, above. Because a cause of action for pleading purposes therefore consisted of facts and the evidence needed to support them, it is not surprising that the same definition was carried over and applied to res judicata. See Developments in the Law—Res Judicata, 65 Harv.L.Rev. 818, 826 (1952). See, e.g., Church of New Song v. Establishment of Religion on Taxpayers' Money in Federal Bureau of Prisons, 620 F.2d 648 (7th Cir. 1980), cert. denied 450 U.S. 929; Williamson v. Columbia Gas & Elec. Corp., 186 F.2d 464 (3d Cir.1950), cert. denied 341 U.S. 921; Massari v. Einsiedler, 6 N.J. 303, 78 A.2d 572 (1951).

34. See Developments in the Law—Res Judicata, 65 Harv.L.Rev. 818 (1952).

35. Norwood v. McDonald, 142 Ohio St. 299, 52 N.E.2d 67 (1943).

36. Kahler v. Don E. Williams Co., 59 Ill.App.3d 716, 16 Ill.Dec. 927, 375 N.E.2d 1034 (1978).

Not every court will deny res judicata effect to a judgment simply because there is some difference in evidentiary requirements, however. In Williams v. Jensen,[37] the Nevada Supreme Court noted that "the same cause of action exists when there is identity of the facts essential to the maintenance of the two actions." The court went on to declare, most aptly, that "the converse of this rule—namely, that when the facts are not identical, the causes of action are not the same—does not necessarily follow."[38] Thus, an action for removal of an obstruction placed on a right of way allegedly owned by the plaintiff was barred by a prior action in which the same relief had been sought, even though the obstructions whose removal was sought in the two actions had been built at different times. The court found that there was a sufficient overlap of evidentiary requirements because the basic controversy in both actions was the defendant's right to obstruct.

Just how extensive the overlap of evidentiary requirements must be before an action will preclude another cannot be answered easily. In general, the more liberally a court applies the same-evidence test, the more it will achieve judicial economy. From this perspective, in order to find that two claims are embraced by the same cause of action, it certainly should not be necessary that the evidence be absolutely identical, but merely that a substantial part of the facts to be proved under each claim be the same. Using this approach, personal injury and property damage claims arising out of a single accident would constitute a single cause of action because both would have largely overlapping evidentiary requirements, even though the damage evidence would differ. The same-evidence test thus requires supplementation by other criteria.

The last test defining the scope of res judicata is favored by the Restatement Second of Judgments, which declares that the claims extinguished by a first judgment shall include "all rights of the plaintiff to remedies against the defendant with respect to all or any part of the transaction, or series of connected transactions, out of which the action arose."[39] The test accords a broad res judicata effect and represents the modern trend toward defining claims or causes of action in terms of actual occurrences. A transaction or series of closely connected transactions is the basic unit of litigation, regardless of the variations in the legal theories, primary rights, grounds, evidence, or requested remedies.

For the purpose of applying this test, the term transaction is intended to mean "a natural grouping or common nucleus of operative facts."[40] What factual grouping constitutes a transaction is to be deter-

---

37. 81 Nev. 658, 408 P.2d 920 (1965).

38. 408 P.2d at 921.

39. Restatement Second of Judgments § 24(1) (1982). The Second Restatement also uses the word "claim" instead of the older term "cause of action." This difference in terminology, in a sense, reflects an attempt to circumvent use of older tests in the guise of newer language.

40. Restatement Second of Judgment § 24, comment b (1982). For an examination of the meaning and scope of a transaction in varying contexts, including res judicata, see Kane, Original Sin and the

mined pragmatically by considering such factors as: (1) whether the facts are closely connected in time, space, origin, or motivation; (2) whether they form a convenient litigation unit; and (3) whether treating them as a single transaction conforms with the parties' expectations and business practice.[41]

The same-transaction test for res judicata is pragmatically equivalent to a compulsory joinder rule: It requires the plaintiff to plead all transactionally related claims in one complaint under threat of precluding any subsequent action for the unasserted claims. Under a compulsory counterclaim rule,[42] the defendant must forgo all counterclaims arising out of the same transaction or occurrence that is the subject matter of the suit, unless she asserts the counterclaims in her answer. Therefore, a rule imposing a similar compulsion upon the plaintiff arguably is eminently fair in balancing the relative positions of plaintiffs and defendants. Since the Federal Rules provide for compulsory counterclaims, free joinder of claims, and liberal amendment of pleadings, the same-transaction test is especially appropriate in the federal courts and in those states that have adopted comparable rules.[43]

An illustration of the same-transaction test is provided by Fox v. Connecticut Fire Insurance Company.[44] Previously, the plaintiff had prevailed in an action compelling defendant insurance company to pay upon a fire insurance policy. The plaintiff then brought a second action against the same defendant to recover the costs of litigating the first case, plus punitive damages. The Tenth Circuit affirmed the district court's decision that the second suit involved the same cause of action as the first and that the second suit was precluded by res judicata because the damages sought in both actions grew out of the same refusal of the insurer to pay.

In another case, a federal district court ruled that a prior action in which the plaintiff unsuccessfully contended that her removal from her job was arbitrary was res judicata in a second suit based on a new allegation that the reason given for her dismissal was fraudulent.[45] The court held that the two suits involved the same cause of action because they both "deal with the same event * * * and seek the same remedy."[46] The court went on to note that "fraud is nothing more than an alternate ground for recovery that should have been asserted in plaintiff's first

Transaction in Federal Civil Procedure, 76 Texas L.Rev. 1723 (1998).

41. Ibid. For an application of the standard, see Porn v. National Grange Mut. Ins. Co., 93 F.3d 31 (1st Cir.1996).

42. Fed.Civ.Proc.Rule 13(a). See § 6.7, above.

43. Some courts explicitly have recognized the appropriateness of the expansive view of the transaction test for claim preclusion in light of the modern trend of

encouraging joinder. Manego v. Orleans Bd. of Trade, 773 F.2d 1 (1st Cir.1985), cert. denied 475 U.S. 1084; Olmstead v. Amoco Oil Co., 725 F.2d 627 (11th Cir.1984); James v. Gerber Prods. Co., 587 F.2d 324 (6th Cir.1978); Kilgoar v. Colbert County Bd. of Educ., 578 F.2d 1033 (5th Cir.1978).

44. 380 F.2d 360 (10th Cir.1967).

45. Miller v. U.S., 438 F.Supp. 514 (E.D.Pa.1977).

46. 438 F.Supp. at 522.

lawsuit."[47]

The New Jersey Supreme Court applied similar reasoning in holding that the judgment in an action for rescission of a contract was a bar against a subsequent fraud action seeking damages at law.[48] The court stated that the policy of avoiding multiplicity of litigation was important enough to uphold the defense of res judicata, even though the plaintiff had lost the prior action on the theory of ratification of the contract and thus the merits of the fraud charge had not been determined.

What underlies the transactional approach is the need to strike a balance between judicial economy and individual justice—an optimal balance between "the interests of the defendant and of the courts in bringing litigation to a close" and "the interest of the plaintiff in the vindication of a just claim."[49] Therefore, prior judgments should be given the wide binding effect permitted under the same-transaction test only if the procedural rules allow all transactionally related claims and all legal and equitable remedies to be adjudicated in one proceeding. When the same-transaction test is tailored to the rules of procedure, it can be a very effective method of determining the scope of res judicata. However, even in a jurisdiction in which the procedural rules can accommodate the demands of the transactional approach, the res judicata effect of a particular action may need to be curtailed if there are special circumstances making it clearly unjust to apply a broad standard.[50]

§ 14.5 The Scope of Res Judicata—Some Applications

Although application of the various tests that have been used to define the scope of res judicata can pose difficult problems, courts have been able to develop particular rules to deal with common cases. Consequently, one often can avoid general discussion of the precise scope of a cause of action and concentrate on limited but specific rules.

In relying on rules developed for specific cases rather than on a general conceptual scheme, doctrinal elegance is sacrificed somewhat for increased predictability and certainty of result. But whatever is lost, the resulting gain is worth the price because nowhere in the law is predictability more important than in res judicata. Indeed, it makes relatively little difference what the rules of res judicata happen to be so long as litigants and their lawyers understand them clearly enough to be able to plan litigation to avoid the pitfalls of unwanted claim preclusion. This section will describe briefly the major categorical rules that have evolved.

---

47. 438 F.Supp. at 523–24.

48. Ajamian v. Schlanger, 14 N.J. 483, 103 A.2d 9 (1954), cert. denied 348 U.S. 835. More recently, New Jersey expanded its approach by adopting the "entire controversy" doctrine, precluding any constituent component of a controversy, even if it is cognizable as a separate and independent cause of action. See Brown v. Brown, 208 N.J.Super. 372, 506 A.2d 29 (App.Div.1986).

49. Restatement Second of Judgments § 24, comment b (1982).

50. The Restatement acknowledges various exceptions to the general transactional approach. See Restatement Second of Judgments § 26 (1982). See also § 14.8, below.

In contract actions, whether two suits concern the same contract or different ones typically determines whether res judicata properly may be invoked. This rule has many advantages. A single contract is relatively easy to identify and isolate as the "single right" often referred to by courts; it is not abstract because there is usually a written document; and it generally is appropriate to use a contract as defining the cause of action because by agreeing to its terms the parties themselves have established the boundaries of their own controversy.

Unfortunately, difficult cases do surface since not all contracts fall under the simple paradigm of two parties exchanging one promise for another. A single document can contain several independent promises and thus embody a number of distinct contracts. For example, a contract to pay a certain amount for a quantity of coal appears, without more, to be a single contract. But the case may be different if the coal is to be delivered and paid for in monthly installments throughout a year. Are there then twelve separate contracts, one for each month's delivery?

To answer this question, procedure borrows from contract law the distinction between contracts that are entire and those that are several. A contract is entire if it consists of a single, indivisible promise to do some act; a contract is several if it comprises discrete promises to do different acts. The breach of a contract judged to be entire will support only one cause of action because a promise to do one thing can be broken only once. A contract that is several, on the other hand, is a compound of different promises that may be broken or performed individually and thus it may support more than one cause of action.

The early case of Pakas v. Hollingshead[1] illustrates the importance of the distinction between entire and several contracts for res judicata purposes. In Pakas, the plaintiff contracted to buy 50,000 pairs of bicycle pedals, to be delivered and paid for in separate installments. The first shipment was short by 16,892 pairs of pedals, and the buyer sued for damages. When the remaining shipments failed to arrive at all, the buyer brought a second action, but the court held the second suit to be barred by res judicata because the contract in question was entire.[2]

It remains true that an entire contract will support only one cause of action, but today an installment contract like the one in Pakas would be considered to be several.[3] A single unsatisfactory installment does not breach the entire contract unless it impairs the value of the whole; the buyer may bring an action solely for defective past installments, without affecting the contract for the future.[4] A subsequent breach would give rise to a separate cause of action.

§ 14.5

1. 184 N.Y. 211, 77 N.E. 40 (1906).

2. "There can be no doubt that the contract was entire. It could not be performed on the part of the defendant without delivery of the property stipulated in the contract and the whole of it." 184 N.Y. at 214, 77 N.E. at 41.

3. Le John Mfg. Co. v. Webb, 91 A.2d 332 (D.C.Mun.App.1952); Restatement Second of Judgments § 24, comment d (1982).

4. Uniform Commercial Code § 2–612(3).

Although a contract deemed several conceivably could support as many causes of action as the separate promises it contains, the plaintiff's ability to bring separate actions for successive breaches of the same contract is limited by what might be called, for convenience sake, "the Rule of Accumulated Breaches." Under this rule a suit for breach of a continuing contract merges all claims that arose prior to the time suit is brought.[5] Thus, if someone contracts to buy coal each month for a year, the contract generally would be considered divisible, and a suit for damages based on the fact that the first shipment failed to meet the contract's requirements would not bar a second suit if the next installment also proves inadequate. But, if the plaintiff receives three unsatisfactory shipments before suing, all three claims must be brought in one action; suing on any one alone would merge the other two claims and preclude later litigation based on them.

Negotiable instruments and other specialized contracts have developed their own special rules.[6] Separate negotiable instruments always may be sued upon separately. Because each periodic interest coupon of a bond is deemed a separate instrument, a person holding a bond may bring successive suits, one for each coupon.[7] The primary justification for permitting separate actions rests on an overriding social policy favoring free negotiability of each interest coupon.[8]

The parties to a contract may control whether a contract is to be treated as entire or several by inserting specific provisions dictating its treatment. In an installment purchase agreement, for example, a so-called acceleration clause—a provision that all payments become due automatically if the buyer defaults on any single installment—commonly is viewed as an intention to make the contract single and indivisible, since a single breach permits the creditor to recover the entire debt. If the lender sues only on a single installment, res judicata may be invoked to preclude the collection of further installments.[9] In a similar vein, claims for different types of remedies such as specific performance and damages that arise from the same breach usually are regarded as parts of a single cause of action in jurisdictions in which both may be sued upon together.[10]

Turning to the field of torts, the problem whether personal injuries and property damages resulting from a single tortious act give rise to a single cause of action or two separate causes of action is a recurring one.

---

5. Bolte v. Aits, Inc., 60 Hawaii 58, 587 P.2d 810 (1978).

6. See Cromwell v. County of Sac, 94 U.S. (4 Otto) 351, 24 L.Ed. 195 (1876). The case is discussed in § 14.2, above. It is important to realize that the Court only reached the question of collateral estoppel because the negotiable-instruments rule prevented the application of res judicata.

7. Restatement Second of Judgments § 24, comment d (1982). See also Nesbit v. Independent District of Riverside, 144 U.S. 610, 619, 12 S.Ct. 746, 748, 36 L.Ed. 562 (1892).

8. Developments in the Law—Res Judicata, 65 Harv.L.Rev. 818, 829 (1952).

9. See Jones v. Morris Plan Bank of Portsmouth, 168 Va. 284, 191 S.E. 608 (1937).

10. Sanwick v. Puget Sound Title Ins. Co., 70 Wn.2d 438, 423 P.2d 624 (1967); Gilbert v. Boak Fish Co., 86 Minn. 365, 90 N.W. 767 (1902); Restatement Second of Judgments § 25, comment i (1982).

Any litigation over a serious automobile accident may raise the question whether damage to the car and to its owner can be split into separate trials. And in every jurisdiction the question has a clear answer, although the answers differ.

Some courts follow the English precedent in Brunsden v. Humphrey[11] finding two separate causes of action. In Brunsden, a cab driver sued after collision with defendant's two-horse carriage and recovered four pounds, three shillings for damage to his cab. Plaintiff later brought a second action for injury to his legs. The court overruled the defendant's plea of res judicata, holding that personal and property damages give rise to two causes of action. Two judges concurred in the decision, one emphasizing that different evidence was needed to support claims of personal and property damages, the other stressing that the right to personal security is different from the right to the unfettered use of one's property.

Only a minority of American jurisdictions subscribe to the rule of Brunsden today, the majority find only one cause of action.[12] To most courts, a single tortious act such as in an automobile accident is a natural litigation unit that is dealt with most efficiently in one action.

In some jurisdictions in which personal and property damages arising out of a single occurrence support only one cause of action, there has developed an added rule that sometimes permits these claims to be split.[13] This secondary rule applies when part of an injured party's claim is subrogated to an insurance company. A person injured in an automobile accident, for example, may be required to assign the claim for car damages to his insurance company in order to secure reimbursement. If the insurance company sues on that claim before the victim has brought an action for physical injuries, then, applying the normal res judicata rule, the victim later may find that action precluded by the insurance company's suit.[14] In order to deal with this problem, many courts recognize a subrogation-exception to the general rule.[15] When a property-damage claim has been subrogated to an insurer, litigation or settlement of that claim does not prevent the victim from pursuing his own claim for personal injuries. This exception permits speedy settlement of property damage claims, which often are simpler and less costly than those

11.   14 Q.B. 141 (1884).

12.   Compare Parrell v. Keenan, 389 Mass. 809, 452 N.E.2d 506 (1983); Rush v. City of Maple Heights, 167 Ohio St. 221, 147 N.E.2d 599 (1958), cert. denied 358 U.S. 814; and Dearden v. Hey, 304 Mass. 659, 24 N.E.2d 644 (1939) (one cause of action), with Clancey v. McBride, 338 Ill. 35, 169 N.E. 729 (1929); and Reilly v. Sicilian Asphalt Paving Co., 170 N.Y. 40, 62 N.E. 772 (1902) (two causes of action). See generally Annot., 62 A.L.R.2d 977 (1956), listing states adhering to each position.

13.   See Travelers Indem. Co. v. Moore, 304 Ky. 456, 201 S.W.2d 7 (1947); Underwriters at Lloyd's Ins. Co. v. Vicksburg Traction Co., 106 Miss. 244, 63 So. 455 (1913).

14.   The insurance company and the insured are deemed in privity as they share identical interests and thus each is bound by any judgment entered against the other. See § 14.13, below, for a discussion of privity.

15.   Scott v. Rosenthal, 118 So.2d 555, 559 (Fla.App.1960).

for personal injury, and further promotes the important goal of trial convenience.

Although the rule that a single tort gives rise to a single cause of action appears straightforward, questions do arise concerning what constitutes a single tort. To analyze this question, a tort must be divided into two components: tortious act and injury. In general, when a single act results in several distinct injuries, a single cause of action arises. If, for example, the defendant loses control of his car and it crashes through the plaintiff's fence, runs over the plaintiff's prize flower garden, and demolishes the plaintiff's front porch, the plaintiff has suffered several separate injuries, but she has only one cause of action. She may not harass the defendant by suing initially for the ruined flowers, then for the broken fence, and yet again for the damage to the house.[16]

Conversely, when a single injury can be traced to several different wrongful acts, there is still only one cause of action.[17] This is similar to the rule that a change in legal theory will not justify bringing a new action; every ground for relief must be presented in the original lawsuit.[18] For example, suppose that a passenger alighting from B Company's streetcar slips and falls because of a defective step. Suppose further that before the passenger can get up, the conductor, without looking to be sure that all passengers have departed safely, starts the car and runs over the hapless passenger. If the passenger brings suit against B Company alleging only the negligence of the conductor, he will not be allowed to bring another suit complaining that the defective step was also the cause of his injuries.

Because only one cause of action accrues when there is either a single tortious act or one indivisible injury, anyone arguing that there are two causes of action must show both that separate acts were responsible for the alleged injuries and that the injuries themselves are distinguishable. This often involves intricate factual questions that turn on a variety of considerations unique to each case. The Restatement Second of Judgments recognizes this when it attempts to trace the boundaries of what it considers a single transaction for res judicata purposes. It notes that the determination is to be made

> pragmatically, giving weight to such considerations as whether the facts are related in time, space, origin, or motivation, whether they form a convenient trial unit, and whether their treatment as a unit conforms to the parties' expectations or business understanding or usage.[19]

---

16. See the cases cited in note 12, above. But see Missouri Pacific Ry. Co. v. Scammon, 41 Kan. 521, 21 P. 590 (1889) (train running down two animals within 165 yards of one another created separate causes of action).

17. Restatement First of Judgments § 63, comment b (1942). See also Baltimore S.S. Co. v. Phillips, 274 U.S. 316, 47 S.Ct. 600, 71 L.Ed. 1069 (1927).

18. See Stratford Place Corp. v. Capalino, 574 F.Supp. 52 (S.D.N.Y.1983), affirmed without opinion 742 F.2d 1441 (2d Cir. 1984), cert. denied 469 U.S. 824; Restatement Second of Judgments § 25, comment d (1982).

19. Restatement Second of Judgments

There is, however, another kind of tort, which is best illustrated by nuisance cases. In those situations, there are not multiple or successive acts that cause discrete injuries but a single continuous wrong that results in ongoing damage. For these chronic torts a rule analogous to that described as the "Rule of Accumulated Breaches" in contract law has developed.[20] A suit for damages caused by an ongoing nuisance is treated as conclusive of all claims up to the time suit is brought. An earlier judgment does not preclude a subsequent action for damages that accrue later, however. Consequently, a farmer whose fields adjoin a cement factory that showers them with noxious ashes may bring successive damage actions each limitations period, each suit for the period's accrued devaluation to his land.[21] In this situation, moreover, actions for damages generally do not preclude a later suit for injunctive relief, since injunctions look only to the future.[22]

There is an exception to this general principle concerning continuous torts. Either the plaintiff or the court may choose to treat the nuisance as "permanent" and award damages that are calculated to compensate for anticipated as well as past injury. In the illustration just given, a court may decide that neither of the other two options— repeated lawsuits for the same complaint or an injunction to close the factory—is acceptable economically and it may award the farmer a single lump sum to cover past and future damages.[23] A judgment awarding permanent damages precludes later suits based on the same nuisance.

Finally, some mention must be made concerning the application of res judicata when successive suits involve legal or equitable remedies. Before the merger of law and equity, an action at law generally did not preclude a later action in equity or vice-versa.[24] A claimant who lost a suit at law on a contract still might prevail in a second action in equity for reformation of the same contract.[25] On the other hand, under the "equity clean-up" doctrine, an equity court could decide any incidental legal issues that arose in the course of litigation. Thus, if equitable relief was sought first, a later action for damages was precluded because monetary relief could have been obtained in the first action.[26]

§ 24(2) (1982).

20. See text at note 5, above.

21. See Restatement Second of Judgments § 26(e) (1982).

22. A suit for an injunction may preclude a later suit for past damages, however. See text at notes 24–28, below. The asymmetry is apparent only. The crucial question is whether the injury to be redressed by the second suit already had occurred at the time of the first action.

23. The example is modelled after Boomer v. Atlantic Cement Co., 26 N.Y.2d 219, 309 N.Y.S.2d 312, 257 N.E.2d 870 (1970). The award of permanent damages effectively amounts to condemnation of the farmer's land in favor of the economically

preferred cement factory. Indeed, a limit on plaintiff's option to treat the nuisance as continuing or permanent occurs when defendant actually has eminent domain power.

24. Restatement Second of Judgments § 25, comment i(1) (1982).

25. Northern Assurance Co. v. Grand View Bldg. Ass'n, 203 U.S. 106, 27 S.Ct. 27, 51 L.Ed. 109 (1906).

26. See Falcone v. Middlesex County Medical Soc., 47 N.J. 92, 219 A.2d 505 (1966); Wischmann v. Raikes, 168 Neb. 728, 97 N.W.2d 551 (1959); Gilbert v. Boak Fish Co., 86 Minn. 365, 90 N.W. 767 (1902). See generally Annot., Decree Granting or Refusing Injunction as Res Judicata in Action for

With the unification of law and equity, it now is possible to seek both legal and equitable remedies in one action, and thus res judicata demands that all the potential remedies for a single cause of action be sought in one proceeding or be lost. Consequently, for example, after losing a suit for rescission of a contract based on a fraud theory, one cannot bring another suit for damages sustained on account of the fraud.[27] And the plaintiff who failed to prove a breach in a contract damages action no longer can bring a second suit in equity for reformation of the same contract.[28]

The one exception to the general applicability of res judicata to successive claims presenting legal and equitable remedies is suits to enjoin wrongs of a continuing nature, such as a continuing nuisance or trespass. Although it generally is true that the merger of law and equity in almost all judicial systems means that a claimant must ask for all available remedies in one action, a recovery of accrued damages for a continuing wrong still may not preclude a later request for an injunction. This exception is not based on the broader range of remedies available in equity, but on the different nature of the remedy involved. Injunctions are viewed as sterner, more direct remedies than damages because defendants are subject to contempt sanctions for noncompliance. Consequently, injunction actions for a continuing wrong are subject to further litigation concerning compliance and to the court's continuing supervision. If the plaintiff were compelled to seek an injunction along with the damage claim in order to avoid losing the former, this could force the expenditure of unnecessary judicial effort, as well as impose an unduly harsh remedy on the defendant at too early a stage; a damage award alone may encourage the defendant to abate the nuisance or cease the trespass.

An analogous problem is presented when a plaintiff sues first for declaratory relief and later seeks coercive or injunctive relief based on the same conduct of the defendant.[29] Most commonly, the injunctive claim will not be deemed merged or barred by the declaratory judgment, even when the plaintiff could have sought coercive relief in the original suit.[30] This conclusion is supported by the policy and language of the Federal Declaratory Judgments Act,[31] which permits a second action for

Damages in Relation to Matter Concerning Which Injunction Was Asked in First Suit, 26 A.L.R.2d 446 (1952).

27. Ajamian v. Schlanger, 14 N.J. 483, 103 A.2d 9 (1954), cert. denied 348 U.S. 835.

28. See Hennepin Paper Co. v. Fort Wayne Corrugated Paper Co., 153 F.2d 822 (7th Cir.1946); Restatement Second of Judgments § 25, comment i (1982). In New York the reformation action is preserved by statute. See N.Y.—McKinney's CPLR 3002(d).

29. If the plaintiff requests both a declaratory judgment and coercive or compensatory relief in the first action, then the normal rules of res judicata apply to prevent further litigation. University of New Hampshire v. April, 115 N.H. 576, 347 A.2d 446 (1975).

30. See Edward B. Marks Music Corp. v. Charles K. Harris Music Pub. Co., 255 F.2d 518 (2d Cir.1958), cert. denied 358 U.S. 831; 10B C. Wright, A. Miller & M. Kane, Civil 3d § 2771.

31. 28 U.S.C.A. § 2202. Similar language appears in the Uniform Declaratory Judgment Act § 8, adopted in many of the states.

"further relief" based on the declaratory judgment.[32] Nonetheless, a few courts erroneously have deemed the plaintiff's claim merged in the declaratory action when all the remedies could have been sought at that time.[33]

§ 14.6 The Scope of Res Judicata—The Effect of Res Judicata on Defendant's Assertions

Applying the rules of res judicata to defendant's claims poses special considerations because the defendant's role in litigation is different from that of the plaintiff.[1] The defendant may take two separate and distinct postures towards the plaintiff's action. First, the defendant's response may be no more than a defensive reaction to the plaintiff's complaint, either denying the plaintiff's allegations or introducing an affirmative defense. Second, the defendant may assert positive claims of his own, in the form of counterclaims, cross-claims, or third-party claims.

The res judicata effect of any judgment that is entered may depend on which of these two litigation postures the defendant adopts. Briefly, three general principles can be stated:

(1) Every available defense must be asserted in the first suit.

(2) Defendant need not assert any counterclaim, cross-claim, or third-party claim unless required to do so by specific statutory provision.

(3) Once asserted by the defendant, the determination of a counterclaim, cross-claim, or third-party claim will be accorded the same res judicata effect that it would have had as an original complaint.

The first principle simply recognizes that the plaintiff's entire cause of action, including all defenses that may be advanced to defeat it, should be concluded in a single lawsuit. The second rule has two parts. The rationale for the first part is protection of the defendant. The rule recognizes that litigants should be allowed to choose when and where to bring their claims and that the plaintiff should not have the advantage of compelling the defendant to bring claims prematurely. However, there is a competing objective of judicial economy that is represented in the federal compulsory counterclaim rule and similar state statutes:[2] precious judicial resources are saved if certain closely related claims can be resolved in a single proceeding.[3] Indeed, the very meaning of "compulso-

---

32. See Restatement Second of Judgments § 33, comment c (1982). But see Note, Declaratory Judgments: Federal Anticipatory Relief from State Criminal Statutes After Steffel v. Thompson, 50 Ind.L.J. 567, 579–85 (1975).

33. See Mastercraft Lamp Co. v. Mortek, 35 Ill.App.2d 366, 183 N.E.2d 12 (1962).

§ 14.6

1. See generally 18 C. Wright, A. Miller & E. Cooper, Jurisdiction and Related Matters § 4414.

2. Fed.Civ.Proc.Rule 13(a). See § 6.7, above.

3. Given the widespread adoption of compulsory counterclaim rules, the exception tends to eclipse the rule. See Buck v. Mueller, 221 Or. 271, 351 P.2d 61 (1960).

ry" is that counterclaims not asserted are precluded. Thus, the second principle acknowledges that if the jurisdiction in which the first action is brought has expressed a policy in its statutes requiring joinder of defendant's claims, then subsequent suits by the defendant on those claims will be precluded. The rationale for the third rule regarding the effect of defendant's assertions simply recognizes that a "defendant who interposes a counterclaim is, in substance, a plaintiff as far as the counterclaim is concerned."[4]

Although these rules provide a convenient framework for analyzing cases in this area, they cannot be applied in a mechanical fashion. The key distinction on which they depend—that between defense and claim for relief—is sometimes difficult to make. For example, fraud may provide a defense to a contract action and also serve as the basis for a tort claim, thus straddling the line that divides defenses from counterclaims. Consequently, a more careful inquiry into the application of these rules is necessary.

The proposition that the original judgment is conclusive of all defenses that the defendant might have asserted, as well as those that were actually put forward, is the mirror image of the res judicata rule that applies to the plaintiff. The application of this rule arises in two different contexts.

The most common situation is in an action on the judgment. If a party wins a valid judgment in one jurisdiction that remains unsatisfied because the defendant has removed itself and its assets to another state, the plaintiff can follow the defendant and bring an action to enforce the judgment in the latter state.[5] Defendant at the second proceeding is precluded from raising any defenses that could have been litigated at the previous trial.[6]

The other circumstance when the defendant may be precluded from raising defenses involves situations in which for policy reasons the plaintiff is allowed to split her cause of action. Some states, for example, provide expedited procedures for landlords to repossess their property from nonpaying tenants. These hearings are limited in scope to the right to occupy the premises; all other matters may be deferred to a later trial. But the defendant must set forth all his defenses in the first action or risk foreclosure. Thus, if a landlord sues to evict a tenant because of failure to pay rent, and the tenant fails to appear at the eviction hearing, his defenses to a later action for back rent due may be barred by res judicata.[7]

If the defendant asserts a counterclaim, that claim will be treated for res judicata purposes exactly as though it were brought as an original action. All other claims of the defendant that fall within the same cause

4. Restatement Second of Judgments § 21, comment a (1982).

5. See § 15.7, below, for a discussion of judgment enforcement.

6. Restatement Second of Judgments § 18(2) (1982).

7. Tutt v. Doby, 265 A.2d 304 (D.C.App.1970).

of action as the counterclaim will be precluded in future litigation.[8] For example, suppose that a buyer refuses to pay for the latest shipment of widgets because the last five shipments have been defective. When the seller sues for payment on that installment, the buyer counterclaims only for damages caused by defects in that latest shipment. The counterclaim will prevent the buyer from bringing a subsequent action with respect to the other four defective installments. As with plaintiff's claims, res judicata precludes not only what was litigated, but also what might have been litigated.[9]

Even when defendant does not assert a counterclaim, any potential claims may be foreclosed in a later action in one of two ways. First, as already indicated, the claim may fall within a statutory compulsory counterclaim rule, such as Federal Rule 13(a),[10] and the failure to comply with that rule will prevent a subsequent action based on that claim. But this preclusion should be viewed as the effect of an estoppel or waiver rather than res judicata because, technically, the subsequent action is prevented by a procedural court rule rather than the doctrine of former adjudication.[11] Second, some state courts require that certain counterclaims be brought even in the absence of a statutory rule, thereby effectively establishing a common-law compulsory counterclaim. Illustratively, a Georgia court barred a tenant's claim for damages based on the landlord's failure to repair the property because the tenant did not assert it as a counterclaim in a prior action by the landlord for nonpayment of rent.[12]

A permissive counterclaim—one not covered by either a statutory or common-law compulsory counterclaim rule—is not barred for failure to assert it during the plaintiff's action.[13] The defendant may choose whether to assert that claim in the first action or bring an independent action on it. This is exemplified by Mercoid v. Mid–Continent Investment Company.[14] The plaintiff sued for patent infringement. Defendant could have counterclaimed showing that the plaintiff was misusing its patents in violation of the antitrust laws, but chose not to do so. After the original suit had gone to judgment, the defendant initiated a separate action under the Clayton Act and the plaintiff raised the defense of res judicata, alleging that the claim should have been raised as a counterclaim in the first suit. The Supreme Court held that despite its close connection to the subject matter of the first suit, the defendant's claim was not covered by Federal Rule 13(a) and that nothing prevented the

---

8. See §§ 14.4–14.5, above, for a discussion of what constitutes a cause of action.

9. See 64 West Park Ave. Corp. v. Parlong Realty Corp., 77 Misc.2d 1019, 354 N.Y.S.2d 342 (1974).

10. See § 6.7, above.

11. See, e.g., Kane v. Magna Mixer Co., 71 F.3d 555 (6th Cir.1995), cert. denied 517 U.S. 1220.

12. Crow v. Mothers Beautiful Co., 115 Ga.App. 747, 156 S.E.2d 193 (1967). The court treated the tenant's claim as a form of recoupment and held that claims for recoupment are mandatory under Georgia law.

13. Joseph v. Darrar, 93 Idaho 762, 472 P.2d 328 (1970).

14. 320 U.S. 661, 64 S.Ct. 268, 88 L.Ed. 376 (1944).

defendant's assertion of that claim in a later, independent lawsuit. By analogy, because cross-claims and third-party claims are not compulsory under most procedural rules,[15] they are not precluded from a later lawsuit if not asserted in the first action.[16] The interposition of a cross-claim or third-party claim in the original suit may preclude the later litigation of additional claims between those parties, however, depending on the scope of the claims litigated.[17]

Since defenses are subject to different rules than are counterclaims for purposes of res judicata, the distinction between the two can be critical. A recurring problem is when the same facts available as a defense in the original proceeding are asserted by the defendant as the basis for affirmative recovery in a separate lawsuit. The question becomes whether a used or unused defense now may be asserted as a claim. This problem often is expressed by medieval imagery: can facts that were, or might have been, used as a "shield" in one action be made into a "sword" in a later action?

To analyze this question, one must distinguish cases in which the facts being asserted by the original defendant as the basis for affirmative recovery were raised as a defense to the first action from cases in which those facts never were introduced as a defense, although they could have been. In the first instance, some courts have held that a second use of the same facts is precluded. For example, in Mitchell v. Federal Intermediate Credit Bank,[18] a potato farmer in South Carolina found that his claim against a bank for $9,000 was forfeited because the facts upon which it was based had been the basis of his defense in a prior action. The bank had loaned the farmer $9,000, using the expected proceeds from the farmer's potato crop as security. When sold, the crop yielded $18,000. Although the bank received this money, it sued the farmer on the $9,000 note and the farmer successfully raised the bank's receipt of the $18,000 as a defense. When the farmer later attempted to recover the excess $9,000, the court held that the farmer's entire cause of action had been merged when it was asserted defensively.[19]

Similarly, if a physician sues to recover his fee and the patient defends the action by alleging that the physician was negligent and that the services rendered were worthless, the patient's later action for malpractice may be precluded.[20] Not all courts rule that the defensive use of facts precludes their later use either as a defense or as an offensive claim, however. Some jurisdictions join the Restatement Second of Judgments in maintaining that a defensive assertion of facts should not prevent a later use of the same facts by the defendant in a suit for

15. See §§ 6.8–6.9, above.

16. Hall v. Bleisch, 400 F.2d 896 (5th Cir.1968), cert. denied 393 U.S. 1083. But see Colhouer v. Union Pacific R.R. Co., 275 Or. 559, 551 P.2d 1291 (1976).

17. See §§ 14.4–14.5, above.

18. 165 S.C. 457, 164 S.E. 136 (1932). See Annot., 83 A.L.R. 642 (1933).

19. The farmer's defense of payment in the bank's action was, in effect, a set-off so the "defense" may have been viewed as at least a $9,000 claim.

20. Rose v. Treitman, 143 N.Y.S.2d 926 (Sup.Ct.1955). But see Gwynn v. Wilhelm, 226 Or. 606, 360 P.2d 312 (1961).

affirmative recovery.[21] Under this view, merely defending an action does not produce any res judicata effect as to the defendant because only the plaintiff has asserted a cause of action.

When the facts constituting both a defense and a counterclaim are not raised in the first action, there is widespread agreement that their subsequent assertion in a suit by the original defendant is not precluded. Thus if the potato farmer mentioned above had defaulted in the original suit or had not raised the $18,000 proceeds as a defense, he well might have been able to recover the full amount in a second action. Similarly, if a patient who is contemplating a lawsuit against her physician refrains from invoking the doctor's negligence in the latter's original suit for payment, a later malpractice action will not be foreclosed by res judicata.

There are extraordinary situations, however, in which courts have held that failure to interpose a defense in one action will prevent bringing an independent lawsuit later. These are cases in which the second suit is viewed as being so closely related to the first that it is hardly an independent suit at all, but is, in effect, a detached defense to the first action.[22] An early California case, Barrow v. Santa Monica Builders Supply Company,[23] is a good example. After plaintiff successfully foreclosed a mortgage, the defendant then attempted to bring a quiet title action, arguing that the plaintiff's mortgage was invalid. The court dismissed the second action, holding that it was no more than an attempt to nullify the results of the foreclosure and that if the defendant wished to show that the mortgage was invalid he had been given an opportunity to do so in the first suit.

Similar reasoning was used in another case in which the Gay Students Organization obtained declaratory and injunctive relief to prevent the University of New Hampshire administration from restricting its social activities. The University then brought its own suit, asking the court to rule that homosexuality is an illness or mental disease and accordingly to enjoin dances sponsored by the organization. The New Hampshire Court held that this claim amounted to a defense to the previous action and should have been litigated at that time.[24]

§ 14.7 Requirements for the Application of Res Judicata

In order for a judgment to be given former adjudication effect, the court must find that it meets three requirements: The judgment must be valid, final, and on the merits. Each of these requirements is explored in this section.

21. Restatement Second of Judgments § 22, comment d (1982); Schwabe v. Chantilly, Inc., 67 Wis.2d 267, 226 N.W.2d 452 (1975). See 18 C. Wright, A. Miller & E. Cooper, Jurisdiction and Related Matters § 4414.

22. E.g., Martino v. McDonald's System, Inc., 598 F.2d 1079 (7th Cir.1979), cert. denied 444 U.S. 966.

23. 9 Cal.2d 601, 71 P.2d 1108 (1937).

24. University of New Hampshire v. April, 115 N.H. 576, 347 A.2d 446, 450–51 (1975).

A challenge to a judgment's validity is a challenge to the authority of the first court to have decided the case. It does not simply suggest error in the first proceeding. Even though the earlier judgment may have been based upon an unconstitutional statute or judicial rule, it will be given full binding effect.[1] As the Supreme Court has noted: "The past cannot always be erased by a new judicial declaration."[2] Similarly, full res judicata effect will be given to judgments based on invalid judicial rules or invalid judicial procedures, so long as there was a fair opportunity to raise the issue of their validity in the first proceeding or on appeal.[3] A challenge to the validity of a judgment, then, is limited to arguments that the judgment rendering court acted beyond its subject-matter jurisdiction[4] or that it failed to secure proper personal or attachment jurisdiction.[5]

In general, a prior judgment will be given full res judicata effect even though it later appears that the judgment rendering court acted beyond its subject-matter jurisdiction if that court made a determination that it had jurisdiction. This is due, in large measure, to the principle that a court has jurisdiction to determine its jurisdiction.[6] Once a court makes a determination that it has jurisdiction, that decision is binding unless reversed on appeal. This principle was reaffirmed by the Supreme Court in Durfee v. Duke.[7] Initially, Durfee sued Duke in a Nebraska state court to quiet title to certain bottom land situated on the Missouri River, which is the boundary between Nebraska and Missouri. The Nebraska court had subject-matter jurisdiction only if the land was in Nebraska, and that depended entirely on whether a shift in the river's course had been caused by avulsion or accretion. Duke lost the action after appearing in the Nebraska court and fully litigating the issues, and the decision was affirmed by the Nebraska Supreme Court. Duke did not petition the United States Supreme Court for review.

Two months later Duke filed suit against Durfee in a Missouri state court to quiet title to the same land, arguing that it was in Missouri. After the case was removed to federal court, the Eighth Circuit ruled that res judicata did not preclude the second action because land was involved, and thus a Missouri court was free to retry the issue of the

§ 14.7

1. One notable exception is the use of the writ of habeas corpus for continued investigation into the validity of the laws that resulted in the defendant's conviction. See 17A C. Wright, A. Miller & E. Cooper, Jurisdiction and Related Matters 2d §§ 4265–67.

2. Chicot County Drainage Dist. v. Baxter State Bank, 308 U.S. 371, 374, 60 S.Ct. 317, 318, 84 L.Ed. 329 (1940).

3. See Buckeye Indus., Inc. v. Secretary of Labor, 587 F.2d 231 (5th Cir.1979).

4. See §§ 2.1–2.14, above.

5. See §§ 3.1–3.17, above. The scope of the prior judgment also may be restricted because the jurisdiction was based on at-

tachment of the defendant's property. But these limitations have their greatest implications when collateral estoppel is being used. See § 14.9, below.

6. See Underwriters Nat. Assurance Co. v. North Carolina Life & Acc. & Health Ins. Guar. Ass'n, 455 U.S. 691, 102 S.Ct. 1357, 71 L.Ed.2d 558 (1982); Dowell v. Applegate, 152 U.S. 327, 14 S.Ct. 611, 38 L.Ed. 463 (1894); Des Moines Navigation & R.R. Co. v. Iowa Homestead Co., 123 U.S. 552, 8 S.Ct. 217, 31 L.Ed. 202 (1887).

7. 375 U.S. 106, 84 S.Ct. 242, 11 L.Ed.2d 186 (1963).

Nebraska court's jurisdiction over the subject matter. The Supreme Court reversed, holding that the judgment of the Nebraska Supreme Court was res judicata as to all issues, including jurisdiction. The Court stressed that absent an overriding consideration, such as federal preemption or sovereign immunity,[8] a judgment is entitled to full faith and credit as to questions of jurisdiction when they "have been fully and fairly litigated and finally decided in the court which rendered the original judgment."[9] Even when the jurisdictional issue was not actually litigated in the prior action, some courts have reached the same result on the ground that res judicata applies not only to matters actually litigated but also to matters that might have been presented.[10]

Although the principle that a court has jurisdiction to determine its jurisdiction is well established, the Durfee Court noted that this "general rule of finality of jurisdictional determination is not without exception."[11] In particular, the Court indicated that the decision whether res judicata should apply despite a failure of jurisdiction in the judgment rendering court may depend upon balancing the underlying policies of res judicata against those supporting the particular jurisdictional limitation.[12] The factors widely recognized as relevant in this connection are: the nature of the court, that is, whether the court in the first action was a court of broad general jurisdiction only subject to a few specific limitations or a court of narrow special jurisdiction that should not be arbitrarily extended; the importance of the jurisdictional limitation that was violated; the clarity of the error; the procedures that were available in the first proceeding to obtain a ruling on that defect; collusion among the parties; and the extent of litigation in the first action.[13] Accordingly, res judicata effect will be given more readily to the judgment of a court having relatively broad general jurisdiction subject to some limitation, and not as readily to the judgment of an inferior court having very narrow special jurisdiction. Along these lines, then, state court judgments that violate exclusive federal jurisdiction are more easily vulnerable to collateral attack.[14]

A situation in which plaintiff has claims under both the state and federal antitrust laws arising from the same underlying facts presents a paradigm case raising these concerns. In this situation, the state court

---

8. See U.S. v. U.S. Fidelity & Guar. Co., 309 U.S. 506, 60 S.Ct. 653, 84 L.Ed. 894 (1940).

9. 375 U.S. at 111, 84 S.Ct. at 245. This same principle was applied in Stoll v. Gottlieb, 305 U.S. 165, 59 S.Ct. 134, 83 L.Ed. 104 (1938).

10. Lambert v. Conrad, 536 F.2d 1183, 1185 (7th Cir.1976); U.S. v. Eastport S.S. Corp., 255 F.2d 795, 803 (2d Cir.1958). See also 13A C. Wright & A. Miller & E. Cooper, Jurisdiction and Related Matters 2d § 3536.

11. 375 U.S. at 114, 84 S.Ct. at 246.

12. The Court specifically noted with approval the factors found in the Restate-

ment First of Judgments § 10 (1942). 375 U.S. at 115 n. 12, 84 S.Ct. at 247 n. 12. Most of the same factors appear in the Restatement Second of Judgments § 12 (1982).

13. For a fuller discussion, see 18 C. Wright, A. Miller & E. Cooper, Jurisdiction and Related Matters § 4428.

14. E.g., Kalb v. Feuerstein, 308 U.S. 433, 60 S.Ct. 343, 84 L.Ed. 370 (1940) (statutory policies underlying exclusive bankruptcy jurisdiction mandate federal preemption of state proceedings). Exclusive federal jurisdiction is discussed in § 2.3, above.

would not be competent to adjudicate the federal claim, because federal jurisdiction over antitrust claims is exclusive. The state antitrust claims, however, may be litigated either in a state or federal court. If the plaintiff is permitted to sue first in the state court on the state claim, and later in the federal court on the federal claim, the policies of res judicata are subverted by permitting plaintiff to split the cause of action. On the other hand, if res judicata effect is given to the state court judgment, the congressionally declared exclusivity of federal jurisdiction over the federal claim may be undermined.

The Restatement Second of Judgments[15] as well as several courts[16] have concluded that res judicata should not apply under these circumstances. This result is achieved either by holding the state and federal claims to be separate causes of action or by expressly recognizing that res judicata should not apply when both claims cannot be presented in the first court because of limitations on that court's subject-matter jurisdiction. In order to avoid duplication and promote judicial economy, the Restatement Second suggests instead that collateral estoppel may be applied to the identical issues decided in the state court action.[17]

The converse set of facts does not yield the same result, however. If the plaintiff first sues in federal court on the federal claim alone, whether she will be barred from later bringing the state claim in the state court depends on whether plaintiff can assert the state claim in federal court. Unless there is diversity of citizenship between the parties, there is no federal question basis for subject-matter jurisdiction over the state claim. Nonetheless, the federal court can exercise discretion to assert supplemental jurisdiction over that claim because it arises from the same "common nucleus of operative facts."[18] When it clearly is open to the plaintiff to advance a state law theory as well as one based on federal law in the federal action, and she fails to do so, she will be barred from maintaining a second action in state court.[19] The identification of a transactional test for defining the scope of res judicata[20] with the

---

15. Restatement Second of Judgments § 26(1)(c), comment c(1) and illustration 2 (1982).

16. See Eichman v. Fotomat Corp., 759 F.2d 1434, 1437 (9th Cir.1985); Klein v. Walston & Co., 432 F.2d 936 (2d Cir.1970); Cream Top Creamery v. Dean Milk Co., 383 F.2d 358 (6th Cir.1967); Wellington Computer Graphics, Inc. v. Modell, 315 F.Supp. 24 (S.D.N.Y.1970). See also Notes, The Effect of Prior Non–Federal Proceedings on Exclusive Federal Jurisdiction over Section 10(b) of the Securities Exchange Act of 1934, 46 N.Y.U.L.Rev. 936 (1971); 24 U.Miami L.Rev. 834 (1970); 53 Va.L.Rev. 1360 (1967); 69 Yale L.J. (1960).

17. Restatement Second of Judgments § 28, comment e, and § 86, comment d (1982). The decision whether issue preclusion is appropriate depends somewhat on the legislative intent. See § 14.12, below.

18. United Mine Workers of America v. Gibbs, 383 U.S. 715, 86 S.Ct. 1130, 16 L.Ed.2d 218 (1966). See the discussion of supplemental jurisdiction in § 2.13, above.

19. See Woods Exploration & Producing Co. v. Aluminum Co., 438 F.2d 1286, 1311–16 (5th Cir.1971), cert. denied 404 U.S. 1047; McCann v. Whitney, 25 N.Y.S.2d 354 (Sup.Ct.1941), noted 41 Colum.L.Rev. 1116 (1941); Restatement Second of Judgments § 25, comment e and illustration 11 (1982); Note, The Res Judicata Implications of Pendent Jurisdiction, 66 Cornell L.Rev. 608 (1981); Note, Judgments: Res Judicata and Pendent Jurisdiction, 28 Okla.L.Rev. 413 (1975).

20. See the discussion in § 14.4 at notes 39–50, above.

supplemental jurisdiction standard of common nucleus of operative facts[21] suggests that res judicata should be applied to preclude the assertion of any claim that would fall within the federal court's supplemental jurisdiction. Consequently, a judgment for plaintiff on a federal antitrust claim will merge the state claim as well, whether or not it actually was presented in the federal action.[22]

Some caution regarding the application of res judicata in this situation is necessary because the exercise of supplemental jurisdiction is discretionary and in some instances properly should be declined.[23] The court in the second action must assess whether the federal court would have decided to exercise its discretion in favor of asserting jurisdiction. In response to this concern, the Restatement Second of Judgments suggests: "[I]n cases of doubt, it is appropriate for the rules of res judicata to compel the plaintiff to bring forward his state theories in the federal action, in order to make it possible to resolve the entire controversy in a single lawsuit."[24]

Indeed, a few federal courts have concluded that if plaintiff sues on a state claim in a state court which is barred from entertaining a federal claim based on identical facts,[25] res judicata nevertheless applies to prevent the later assertion of the federal claim in federal court.[26] These courts have noted that as long as the plaintiff could have pursued all the claims in the federal court, then the plaintiff cannot be allowed to split those claims, burdening both the federal and state courts with their determination. The cases involved a federal antitrust plaintiff who was barred from bringing suit when he lost his state antitrust claim in the state courts.[27] In an even more far reaching decision, the Seventh Circuit, sitting en banc, barred a federal antitrust claim after a plaintiff had sued unsuccessfully for unfair competition in the state courts.[28]

21. Restatement Second of Judgments § 25, comment e, Reporter's Note 227 (1982).

22. Boccardo v. Safeway Stores, Inc., 134 Cal.App.3d 1037, 184 Cal.Rptr. 903 (1982); Belliston v. Texaco, Inc., 521 P.2d 379 (Utah 1974). Conversely, when a state action is removed to federal court on the basis of diversity of citizenship, an unasserted exclusive federal claim will be merged in the judgment. See Engelhardt v. Bell & Howell Co., 327 F.2d 30 (8th Cir. 1964).

23. See § 2.13, above.

24. Restatement Second of Judgments § 25, comment e, Reporter's Note 228 (1982).

25. See § 2.3, above, for a discussion of exclusive federal court subject-matter jurisdiction.

26. Derish v. San Mateo–Burlingame Bd. of Realtors, 724 F.2d 1347, 1350 (9th Cir.1983); Nash County Bd. of Educ. v. Biltmore Co., 640 F.2d 484, 488 (4th Cir.1981), cert. denied 454 U.S. 878. The Fourth and Ninth Circuit opinions focused heavily on the identity of issues and the fact that the plaintiff had litigated the state antitrust claim, so that the policy of judicial economy clearly dominated and the decisions rely on concerns similar to those underlying issue preclusion. See § 14.12, below.

27. See generally Note, The Res Judicata Effect of Prior State Court Judgments in Sherman Act Suits: Exalting Substance Over Form, 51 Ford.L.Rev. 1374 (1983); Comment, Exclusive Federal Jurisdiction: The Effect of State Court Findings, 8 Stan. L.Rev. 439 (1956).

28. Marrese v. American Academy of Orthopaedic Surgeons, 726 F.2d 1150 (7th Cir.1984). The Supreme Court reversed for failure below to ascertain and apply Illinois law on splitting, as required under 28 U.S.C.A. § 1738. 470 U.S. 373, 105 S.Ct. 1327, 84 L.Ed.2d 274 (1985). See § 14.15, below.

Judge Posner, writing for the majority, noted that the plaintiff could have brought a state antitrust claim in the first action and that the state and federal antitrust laws were almost identical. Plaintiff, by failing to assert the state claim in the first action, was barred from suing on it, as well as on the federal claim, in the federal courts.

These decisions reflect serious judicial concern about multiple litigation and crowded court dockets. Thus, they emphasize the policy of res judicata to foster judicial economy and ignore the more traditional emphasis on whether the first court was competent to enter a valid judgment on all the claims involved. It might be questioned whether this emphasis on economy goes too far. Nonetheless, the clear thrust is that as long as the plaintiff has a forum in which to assert all his claims, he must sue there or risk losing those claims omitted from the first proceeding in a court of limited jurisdiction.

The validity of a judgment also may be challenged on the ground that the first court lacked personal jurisdiction over the defendant. As was true with subject-matter jurisdiction, however, if the first court determines that it possesses jurisdiction, the judgment will be given res judicata effect; the defendant cannot relitigate the jurisdiction question.[29] Further, a defendant who litigates the merits of the case and does not object to personal jurisdiction generally is treated as having waived the right to raise a personal jurisdiction objection later.[30] Only a defendant who defaults in the original proceeding can raise the question of personal jurisdiction subsequently as a means of avoiding that judgment. But that approach is risky because if the second court determines that there was personal jurisdiction in the original proceeding, res judicata will apply and the defendant will be foreclosed from defending on the merits.[31]

Sometimes the first court's jurisdiction is limited, rather than totally absent, and the res judicata effect of any judgment may be restricted correspondingly.[32] For example, if the defendant cannot be reached by personal service within the state, the plaintiff must rely on the state's long-arm statute to obtain personal jurisdiction.[33] Although the plaintiff may have several theories of liability arising from the same basic facts (for example, both tort and contract theories), the state's long-arm statute may provide for asserting jurisdiction based on only one of these theories. When this occurs, plaintiff generally will not be barred from the later assertion of the other theories in a court of competent jurisdiction. Plaintiff, not being able to assert all the claims in the first suit, will not be deemed to have split the cause of action.

29. Baldwin v. Iowa State Traveling Men's Ass'n, 283 U.S. 522, 51 S.Ct. 517, 75 L.Ed. 1244 (1931). See Durfee v. Duke, 375 U.S. 106, 84 S.Ct. 242, 11 L.Ed.2d 186 (1963); In re Universal Display & Sign Co., 541 F.2d 142 (3d Cir.1976).

30. For the procedure surrounding personal jurisdiction objections, see §§ 3.25–3.27, above.

31. Hazen Research, Inc. v. Omega Minerals, Inc., 497 F.2d 151 (5th Cir.1974).

32. Restatement Second of Judgments § 26(1)(c), comment c(1) (1982).

33. See §§ 3.12–3.13, above, for a discussion of long-arm statutes.

This limitation on res judicata is particularly important when attachment jurisdiction is used in the first action.[34] A judgment in a quasi in rem action will be satisfied only to the extent of the value of the property that has been attached. Further, the judgment will be conclusive only as to the interests in the specific property or obligation under the court's control. Res judicata cannot be asserted in any subsequent action by the plaintiff to collect the remainder of the personal claim.[35]

This exception to the normal application of merger and bar principles can be criticized because it allows unnecessary relitigation of the same claim, giving the plaintiff an advantage by exposing her to no risk of losing her cause of action in an adverse judgment.[36] The better rule would be that the plaintiff is barred, or at least collaterally estopped.[37] Nonetheless, because the court lacked plenary power and the defendant was not accorded a full day in court in the first action, the parties generally are not bound by the judgment except to the extent of the specific property involved.[38]

The second requirement of res judicata is that it can be based only on a final judgment.[39] The requirement of finality asks only that nothing further remain for the judge but to order entry of judgment.[40] Finality of a judgment in this context resembles the requirement of finality for appeal,[41] although they generally are not equivalent.[42]

An interlocutory order generally never is accorded res judicata effect because by its nature it either leaves some issues for determination in

34. Attachment jurisdiction is discussed in §§ 3.8–3.9, and 3.14–3.15, above.

35. Riverview State Bank v. Dreyer, 188 Kan. 270, 362 P.2d 55 (1961); Strand v. Halverson, 220 Iowa 1276, 264 N.W. 266 (1935); Restatement Second of Judgments § 32, comment c (1982); Developments in the Law—Res Judicata, 65 Harv.L.Rev. 818, 835 (1952). But see Developments in the Law—State–Court Jurisdiction, 73 Harv. L.Rev. 909, 954–55 (1960).

36. For an argument that the limitation on the judgment establishes a fair balance of risk between the parties, see Developments in the Law—Res Judicata, 65 Harv.L.Rev. 818, 834 (1952).

37. Modern thinking does not require that estoppel be mutual. See § 14.14, below.

38. This conclusion has been reached even when the defendant has been permitted to make a limited appearance. See § 3.27, above. However, under those circumstances there is the possibility that the issues that actually are litigated will be given estoppel effect. Restatement Second of Judgments § 32 comment d (1982). See Note, Limited Appearances and Issue Preclusion: Resetting the Trap?, 66 Cornell L.Rev. 595 (1981).

39. See G & C Merriam Co. v. Saalfield, 241 U.S. 22, 36 S.Ct. 477, 60 L.Ed. 868 (1916). See also 1 Freeman, Judgments § 22 (5th ed. 1925); 1 Black, Judgments § 21 (2d ed. 1902).

40. McDaniel Nat. Bank v. Bridwell, 65 F.2d 428 (8th Cir.1933). See generally Note, Use of the Bifurcated Trial to Avoid Collateral Estoppel and the Expanding Concept of Final Judgment, 7 Sw.U.L.Rev. 161 (1975).

41. See § 13.1, above.

42. Miller Brewing Co. v. Jos. Schlitz Brewing Co., 605 F.2d 990 (7th Cir.1979), cert. denied 444 U.S. 1102; Sherman v. Jacobson, 247 F.Supp. 261 (S.D.N.Y.1965); Restatement Second of Judgments § 13, comment b (1982). But see First Alabama Bank of Montgomery, N.A. v. Parsons Steel, Inc., 825 F.2d 1475 (11th Cir.1987), cert. denied 484 U.S. 1060 (under Alabama law finality for preclusion is measured by the same test as finality for appeal).

Although finality still is observed fairly rigidly for res judicata, in recent years it has been relaxed for collateral estoppel purposes. See 18 C. Wright, A. Miller & E. Cooper, Jurisdiction and Related Matters § 4434; Restatement Second of Judgments § 13, comment g (1982).

subsequent litigation or requires the completion of certain acts or conditions before the entry of judgment.[43] Thus, a judgment determining liability will not be sufficiently final for res judicata purposes as long as damage issues are deferred for separate trial or otherwise remain unadjudicated.[44] Similarly, the grant or denial of a preliminary injunction or a temporary restraining order will not merge or bar an action for permanent injunctive relief;[45] there has been no final ruling on the underlying claim for relief. In fact, temporary relief typically is granted on less than full (sometimes ex parte) fact determinations, subject to revision. Indeed, most pretrial rulings in civil actions do not have res judicata effect because they usually are either provisional or determine only one issue.[46]

Two major problems attend the finality requirement. One is the effect of an appeal on the finality of the trial court's judgment, and the other is whether to treat declaratory judgments and injunction decrees as final for res judicata purposes.

Most courts treat a judgment as final for res judicata purposes if it conclusively disposes of the lawsuit in the rendering court, notwithstanding that an appeal has been taken or the time to appeal has not expired.[47] This is true regardless of whether an opportunity to appeal was foregone deliberately or an attempt to appeal did not succeed because of a failure to meet procedural requirements.[48] Further, just as a pending appeal or the availability of one does not defeat the finality of a judgment, neither does a motion for new trial or to vacate the judgment destroy a judgment's finality.[49]

Because an appeal does not destroy the finality of a judgment, theoretically, the judgment can be enforced even during the pendency of an appeal.[50] If a lower court's decision is vacated or reversed on appeal,

---

43. But see Note, Amalgamation of Interlocutory Orders into Final Judgments, 3 St. Mary's L.J. 207 (1971).

44. G & C Merriam Co. v. Saalfield, 241 U.S. 22, 36 S.Ct. 477, 60 L.Ed. 868 (1916). The final determination of a claim in an action involving multiple claims or parties can be given res judicata effect, however. The key is whether the court entered a final judgment on the claim decided. See Fed.Civ.Proc.Rule 54(b), discussed at § 13.1, above.

45. Hunter Douglas Inc. v. Sheet Metal Workers Int'l Ass'n, Local 159, 714 F.2d 342 (4th Cir.1983); Mesabi Iron Co. v. Reserve Mining Co., 270 F.2d 567 (8th Cir. 1959).

46. Horner v. Ferron, 362 F.2d 224 (9th Cir.1966), cert. denied 385 U.S. 958.

47. New Haven Inclusion Cases, 399 U.S. 392, 90 S.Ct. 2054, 26 L.Ed.2d 691 (1970); U.S. v. Munsingwear, Inc., 340 U.S. 36, 71 S.Ct. 104, 95 L.Ed. 36 (1950); Myers v. Bull, 599 F.2d 863 (8th Cir.1979), cert. denied 444 U.S. 901. But see Chavez v.

Morris, 566 F.Supp. 359 (D.Utah 1983). See generally Vestal, Preclusion/Res Judicata Variables: Adjudicating Bodies, 54 Geo.L.J. 857 (1966); Comment, Res Judicata— Should It Apply to a Judgment Which is Being Appealed?, 33 Rocky Mt.L.Rev. 95 (1960).

48. Hubbell v. U.S., 171 U.S. 203, 18 S.Ct. 828, 43 L.Ed. 136 (1898); Smith v. U.S., 369 F.2d 49 (8th Cir.1966), cert. denied 386 U.S. 1010; Wight v. Montana–Dakota Utilities Co., 299 F.2d 470 (9th Cir. 1962), cert. denied 371 U.S. 962.

49. See McArdle v. Schneider, 228 F.Supp. 506 (D.Mass.1964); Restatement Second of Judgments § 13, comment f (1982).

50. Deposit Bank v. Board of Councilmen of Frankfort, 191 U.S. 499, 24 S.Ct. 154, 48 L.Ed. 276 (1903); Fidelity Standard Life Ins. Co. v. First Nat. Bank & Trust Co., 510 F.2d 272 (5th Cir.1975), certiorari denied 423 U.S. 864. A stay or supersedeas order issued by the appellate court may delay enforcement, however.

however, it loses its res judicata effect because it no longer is a valid judgment.[51] Further, the preclusive effect of the original judgment is not restored by an appeal taken to the next higher appellate court.[52] When the appellate court partially affirms and partially reverses the lower court's decision, or disposes of the entire case by ruling only on some issues, res judicata generally attaches only to the matters actually decided by the appellate court.[53]

As a result of these finality rules, an anomalous situation can arise if a court holds that it is bound by a judgment in a prior suit that is subsequently reversed.[54] The Supreme Court held in Reed v. Allen[55] that the reversal of the underlying judgment does not automatically affect a later judgment based on it. However, relief from the second judgment may be authorized under the applicable procedural rules.[56]

The finality requirement also poses some difficulties when the first action involves a declaratory judgment. The Federal Declaratory Judgment Act specifically provides that a judgment under that statute has the force and effect of a final judgment or decree.[57] However, the Act also authorizes a second action for "further relief" based on the declaratory judgment.[58] Thus, res judicata is not strictly applicable because the statute specifically recognizes the right of multiple actions.[59] The preclusive effect of a declaratory judgment, therefore, is more akin to collateral estoppel, preventing relitigation of issues that actually were contested and were necessary to the judgment rendered.[60]

Traditionally, the third and final requirement for res judicata is that the judgment must be "on the merits." In general terms, a judgment is considered to be on the merits if it is a disposition based on the validity of the plaintiff's claim rather than on a technical procedural ground.[61]

51. Pope v. Shipp, 38 Ga.App. 483, 144 S.E. 345 (1928); Brooks v. Union Depot Bridge & Terminal R. Co., 215 Mo.App. 643, 258 S.W. 724 (1923); Houston Oil Co. of Texas v. McCarthy, 245 S.W. 651 (Tex. Com.App.1922).

52. Di Gaetano v. Texas Co., 300 F.2d 895 (3d Cir.1962).

53. Seguros Tepeyac, S.A. v. Jernigan, 410 F.2d 718 (5th Cir.1969), cert. denied 396 U.S. 905.

54. See, e.g., Federated Dep't Stores, Inc. v. Moitie, 452 U.S. 394, 101 S.Ct. 2424, 69 L.Ed.2d 103 (1981); Harrington v. Vandalia–Butler Bd. of Educ., 649 F.2d 434 (6th Cir.1981).

55. 286 U.S. 191, 52 S.Ct. 532, 76 L.Ed. 1054 (1932).

56. See Fed.Civ.Proc.Rule 60(b)(5). Relief from judgments is discussed in § 12.6, above. See also Butler v. Eaton, 141 U.S. 240, 11 S.Ct. 985, 35 L.Ed. 713 (1891).

57. 28 U.S.C.A. § 2201.

58. The issue of whether, despite the statute's language, modern res judicata notions compel the plaintiff to seek all possible remedies in a single action is discussed in § 14.5 at notes 29–33, above.

59. See Perez v. Ledesma, 401 U.S. 82, 91 S.Ct. 674, 27 L.Ed.2d 701 (1971); Note, Declaratory Judgments, 50 Ind.L.J. 567, 579–85 (1975); Note, The Res Judicata Effect of Declaratory Relief in the Federal Courts, 46 So.Calif.L.Rev. 803 (1973); Annot., Extent to Which Principles of Res Judicata are Applicable to Judgments in Actions for Declaratory Relief, 10 A.L.R.2d 782 (1950).

60. Kerotest Mfg. Co. v. C–O–Two Fire Equipment Co., 342 U.S. 180, 72 S.Ct. 219, 96 L.Ed. 200 (1952); Fidelity Nat. Bank & Trust Co. v. Swope, 274 U.S. 123, 47 S.Ct. 511, 71 L.Ed. 959 (1927); Jackson v. Hayakawa, 605 F.2d 1121 (9th Cir.1979), cert. denied 445 U.S. 952.

61. Saylor v. Lindsley, 391 F.2d 965, 968 (2d Cir.1968). For example, most courts

Therefore, any judgment in favor of a claimant establishing his rights and ordering relief will be on the merits for res judicata purposes. In contrast, a judgment against the claimant may or may not be on the merits because it may result either from a decision on the substantive rights involved or from a purely procedural ruling.

Unfortunately, the phrase "on the merits" has created much confusion and obscures the fact that a court decision may be given preclusive effect independent of the merits of the underlying claim.[62] Thus, a court decision such as dismissal for lack of jurisdiction is given preclusive effect on the issue of jurisdiction, even though it does not touch the merits of the plaintiff's cause of action.[63] For these reasons the Restatement Second of Judgments formulates the rules of res judicata without using the traditional phrase "on the merits."[64] Under its approach the principle of bar applies to all valid and final personal judgments, although exceptions are allowed for those cases that may be characterized as "not on the merits" under the older scheme.[65]

Many judicial decisions, rules, and statutes, however, continue to use "on the merits" to indicate what type of judgment will bar a subsequent action.[66] Moreover, the requirement that a judgment be on the merits to have full res judicata effect accords with the modern procedural notion that a claimant is entitled to a day in court and should not lose the right to a hearing on the substance of his grievance because of procedural errors. Thus, some investigation into what is considered a decision on the merits is necessary.

Judgments entered after full trial plainly are on the merits, as are summary judgments and judgments entered on a motion for a directed

---

hold that dismissals on statute of limitations grounds are not on the merits but are procedural, denying the remedy, not the rights involved, and thus they do not bar an action in another jurisdiction having a longer statute of limitations. E.g., Warner v. Buffalo Drydock Co., 67 F.2d 540 (2d Cir. 1933), cert. denied 291 U.S. 678; Taylor v. New York City Transit Authority, 309 F.Supp. 785, 790 (E.D.N.Y.1970), affirmed on other grounds 433 F.2d 665 (2d Cir. 1970); Koch v. Rodlin Enterprises, Inc., 223 Cal.App.3d 1591, 273 Cal.Rptr. 438 (1990). Compare Hamson v. Lionberger, 87 Ill. App.2d 281, 231 N.E.2d 277 (1967) (dismissal on statute of frauds grounds bars substantive right).

62. For example, in one case the plaintiff first sued to enjoin a bank from making payment on a cashier's check and that claim was defeated by the bank's defense that irreparable injury—a requirement for injunctive relief—had not been shown. The plaintiff instituted a second action seeking damages for the same conduct and the court held that the dismissal in the first

action determined only that the remedy sought there was unavailable; it was not a judgment on the merits and did not preclude a later action for damages. Foreman v. Martin, 26 Ill.App.3d 1028, 325 N.E.2d 378 (1975). Since modern procedural rules typically allow the joinder of alternative or inconsistent claims in a single proceeding, the rationale for not according res judicata effect in this situation is weak. Most courts today would find res judicata fully applicable, not relying on the remedial characterization to avoid preclusive effect. See § 14.5, at notes 24–28, above, for some examples. See generally 18 C. Wright, A. Miller & E. Cooper, Jurisdiction and Related Matters § 4435.

63. See § 14.9, below, on issue preclusion.

64. Restatement Second of Judgments § 19, comment a (1982).

65. Restatement Second of Judgments, §§ 19–20 (1982).

66. See, e.g., Fed.Civ.Proc.Rule 41, on voluntary and involuntary dismissals.

verdict or for a judgment as a matter of law.[67] The area that has posed the most difficulty in applying this requirement is voluntary dismissals or nonsuits.

Courts often specify when dismissing a case whether it is "with prejudice" or "without prejudice." Dismissal without prejudice means that the plaintiff can reassert the same cause of action by curing the defects that led to dismissal. By contrast, dismissals with prejudice are intended to bar relitigation of the same claim.[68] A question of considerable difficulty is whether and to what extent a later court can look behind the issuing court's pronouncement that the case was dismissed "with prejudice" and, by examining the grounds upon which the dismissal was based, decide for itself whether to accord the judgment res judicata effect.[69]

A common-law plaintiff could terminate the lawsuit without prejudice through the device of voluntary nonsuit any time before the verdict was rendered.[70] As discussed more fully elsewhere, most jurisdictions now limit this privilege, either by requiring it to be exercised at a much earlier stage of the proceeding or by limiting the number of times the right can be exercised without prejudice to the plaintiff's cause of action.[71] Accordingly, an attempt to obtain a second voluntary dismissal or a dismissal at a later stage in the action typically results in a determination that the dismissal is on the merits. In this way, the limitations imposed by the procedural rules are enforced.

There is a split of opinion, however, as to cases in which the plaintiff simply fails to prosecute the case after filing the complaint. In actions brought in the federal courts, Federal Rule 41(b) provides that these dismissals are treated as involuntary dismissals on the merits unless the trial court specifies otherwise.[72] But state courts differ as to whether a dismissal for failure to prosecute constitutes a judgment on the merits. Although the merits of the claim have not been adjudicated, some courts have held that the plaintiff's improper conduct justifies precluding a second suit.[73] Other state courts still adhere to the older rule that a dismissal for failure of prosecution does not result in a judgment on the

---

67. Jackson v. Hayakawa, 605 F.2d 1121 (9th Cir.1979), cert. denied 445 U.S. 952; Hubicki v. ACF Industries, Inc., 484 F.2d 519 (3d Cir.1973); Simon v. M/V Hialeah, 431 F.2d 867 (5th Cir.1970); Keys v. Sawyer, 353 F.Supp. 936 (S.D.Tex.1973), affirmed without opinion 496 F.2d 876 (5th Cir.1974); Restatement Second of Judgments § 19, comments g and h (1982).

68. For an interesting case in which defendant sought unsuccessfully to broaden the preclusive effect of a proposed dismissal with prejudice, see Ferrato v. Castro, 888 F.Supp. 33 (S.D.N.Y.1995).

69. See Weissinger v. U.S., 423 F.2d 782 (5th Cir.1968) (panel opinion), vacated 423 F.2d 795 (1970) (en banc opinion); Saylor v. Lindsley, 391 F.2d 965 (2d Cir.1968);

Ottinger v. Chronister, 13 N.C.App. 91, 185 S.E.2d 292 (1971); Overstreet v. Greenwell, 441 S.W.2d 443 (Ky.1969). See generally 9 C. Wright & A. Miller, Civil 2d § 2373.

70. See Greenlee v. Goodyear Tire & Rubber Co., 572 F.2d 273 (10th Cir.1978); Developments in the Law—Res Judicata, 65 Harv.L.Rev. 818, 837 (1952).

71. See § 9.5, above.

72. See Casto v. Arkansas–Louisiana Gas Co., 597 F.2d 1323 (10th Cir.1979).

73. E.g., Kradoska v. Kipp, 397 A.2d 562 (Me.1979). See generally Annot., Dismissal of Civil Action for Want of Prosecution as Res Judicata, 54 A.L.R.2d 473 (1957).

merits.[74] Older procedural systems discouraged the direct amendment of the pleading, so that the plaintiff was accorded greater freedom of nonprosecution as a form of altering the pleading. In contrast, modern procedural systems that are more liberal in allowing pleading amendments are properly more strict regarding plaintiff's freedom to abandon prosecution and begin again.

Involuntary dismissals also may result because of a lack of jurisdiction or venue[75] or of the failure to join an indispensable party. A dismissal on any of those grounds does not operate as an adjudication on the merits.[76] Furthermore, trial courts do not have discretion to dismiss on those grounds with prejudice.[77] The rationale for this flat prohibition is found "in the threshold character of the determination on which the judgment is based."[78] These dismissals decide only that the court is an inconvenient one or that it is without power to adjudicate the dispute; they do not reach any consideration of the merits.[79]

But what about other dismissals not specifically designated "with prejudice" by the rendering court?[80] Under Federal Rule 41(b), and comparable state provisions, "any dismissal not provided for in this rule" operates as an adjudication upon the merits unless the court specifies otherwise.[81] The difficulty with this provision is illustrated by Costello v. United States.[82] In that case, a denaturalization action brought by the government against Costello was dismissed because the government did not file with the complaint the statutorily required affidavit of good cause for initiating the action. The district court did not specify whether the dismissal was with prejudice or not. The government brought a second action against Costello on the same grounds, filing an affidavit of good cause. The Supreme Court ruled that the prior dismissal was without prejudice because it should be treated as having been based on a lack of jurisdiction. It rejected the argument that the dismissal of the first proceeding fell within the category of "dismissal[s] not provided for in [Rule 41(b)]" which would have rendered it an adjudication upon the merits. The Court based its conclusion on an analysis of the policy behind allowing some dismissals to be treated as jurisdictional and thus

---

74. McQuaid v. United Wholesale Aluminum Supply Co., 31 Md.App. 580, 358 A.2d 922 (1976).

75. Dismissals based on a lack of venue are rare, however, because transfer cures most venue problems. See § 2.17, above.

76. Restatement Second of Judgments § 20(1)(a) (1982). See also American Guar. Corp. v. U.S., 185 Ct.Cl. 502, 401 F.2d 1004 (1968) (lack of subject-matter jurisdiction); Etten v. Lovell Mfg. Co., 225 F.2d 844 (3d Cir.1955), cert. denied 350 U.S. 966 (lack of personal jurisdiction); Bauscher v. National Sur. Corp., 92 Idaho 229, 440 P.2d 349 (1968) (failure to join indispensable party).

77. See 9 C. Wright & A. Miller, Civil 2d § 2373.

78. Restatement Second of Judgments § 20, comment c (1982).

79. Direct estoppel effect will be accorded the determination on the particular venue, jurisdiction or joinder issue, however. See § 14.1, above.

80. See, e.g., McNeal v. State Farm Mut. Auto. Ins. Co., 278 So.2d 108 (La. 1973) (dismissal by Mississippi court on ground that there was no direct action statute and family immunity barred suit in Mississippi was not on the merits, so Louisiana court not bound by it).

81. See Kelley v. Mallory, 202 Or. 690, 277 P.2d 767 (1954).

82. 365 U.S. 265, 81 S.Ct. 534, 5 L.Ed.2d 551 (1961).

not preclusive of future litigation, finding that the government's failure to file the proper affidavit fell within that policy.

> The defendant is not put to the necessity of preparing a defense because the failure of the Government to file the affidavit with the complaint requires the dismissal of the proceeding. Nothing in the term "jurisdiction" requires giving it the limited meaning that the petitioner would ascribe to it.[83]

Along similar lines, dismissals of a premature suit or of an action in which plaintiff has failed to satisfy a precondition to suit typically do not bar a second action after the claim has matured or the precondition has been satisfied.[84] For example, when a suit for breach of a contract is dismissed because it has been brought before the time when the defendant is obligated to perform or because plaintiff has failed to post security for costs as provided by statute, the plaintiff can bring a second action when the defect is cured. This principle, which always was valid at common law, also operates in the federal courts, regardless of whether the trial court has specified its decision to be without prejudice as required by a literal reading of Federal Rule 41(b).[85]

Difficult questions do arise, however, as to whether a dismissal based on a demurrer or a motion to dismiss for failure to state a claim is or is not on the merits.[86] At common law, and in states not following federal practice, a dismissal entered for defendant on a demurrer generally is not considered to bar plaintiff's cause of action because plaintiff is free to correct the defects in the pleading and sue again.[87] A successful demurrer does not determine that the plaintiff has no cause of action, but only that the plaintiff has not stated one. In certain situations, however, a judgment on demurrer may be considered as going to the merits and be accorded bar effect.[88] Thus, the problem is how to determine whether a dismissal was based only upon the formal insufficiency of the pleading or upon a defect going to the merits.

83.   365 U.S. at 287, 81 S.Ct. at 546. See additionally Baris v. Sulpicio Lines, Inc., 74 F.3d 567 (5th Cir.1996) (following Costello and ruling a forum non conveniens dismissal as without preclusive effect even though entered with prejudice).

84.   Restatement Second of Judgments § 20(2) (1982). The Restatement recognizes an exception, allowing res judicata to be applied when it would be manifestly unfair to subject the defendant to a second suit. This might occur when all issues were litigated and the precondition rendering the suit premature was within plaintiff's control.

85.   See Saylor v. Lindsley, 391 F.2d 965 (2d Cir.1968), in which the dismissal of a shareholder's derivative suit for failure to post security for costs was held not to bar reassertion of the claim even though the trial court had expressly declared the dismissal "with prejudice." But see Priolo v. El San Juan Towers Hotel, 575 F.Supp. 208 (D.Puerto Rico 1983) (dismissal for failure to post nonresident bond treated as on the merits).

86.   See §§ 5.22 and 5.25, above, for a discussion of these challenges.

87.   Gould v. Evansville & C.R.R. Co., 91 U.S. (1 Otto) 526, 23 L.Ed. 416 (1875); Developments in the Law—Res Judicata, 65 Harv.L.Rev. 818, 836 (1952).

88.   Restatement First of Judgments § 50, comment c (1942). It has been suggested that the sustaining of a demurrer should not bar matters that might have been raised in the first action but were not. Developments in the Law—Res Judicata, 65 Harv.L.Rev. 818, 837 (1952). See also von Moschzisker, Res Judicata, 38 Yale L.J. 299, 319–20 (1929).

For example, the plaintiff's complaint might allege certain facts suggesting the existence of a legally cognizable claim but fail to make an allegation essential to the claim. An omission of an essential proposition generally is considered only a formal defect and will not bar later suit on a complaint containing the missing allegation.[89] On the other hand, the complaint may be defective because plaintiff is seeking relief that the law does not allow. In that event the defendant's motion to dismiss essentially is equivalent to a motion for summary judgment and, if granted, will preclude a second action.

In part because it is not always easy to articulate the distinction between dismissals based on a pleading insufficiency and dismissals on the merits, many jurisdictions today reject this distinction and simply rule that a dismissal for insufficient pleading precludes a second action.[90] The harshness of this approach is ameliorated by giving the plaintiff an opportunity to amend the complaint before final judgment is entered. Failure to use that opportunity will result in the dismissal being entered with prejudice.[91]

In the federal courts, a Federal Rule 12(b)(6) dismissal for failure to state a claim upon which relief may be granted generally will be treated as a judgment on the merits unless the court specifies that it is without prejudice.[92] Although this approach may seem unfair insofar as it requires a plaintiff to be prepared to have the whole case disposed of on a Rule 12(b)(6) motion, the courts can avoid any unfairness by granting the motion with leave to amend, and that is the prevailing practice.[93]

Two other forms of judgments have raised some questions concerning whether they should be treated as on the merits: default judgments and consent judgments. The issue arises because neither of these two judgments is the result of full litigation. Nonetheless, a default judgment is treated as an adjudication on the merits, commanding res judicata effect.[94] Full merger and bar effect are given to default judgments to prevent the defendant from stalling the plaintiff's action by defaulting

89. Gilbert v. Braniff Int'l Corp., 579 F.2d 411 (7th Cir.1978); Keidatz v. Albany, 39 Cal.2d 826, 249 P.2d 264 (1952).

90. See Restatement Second of Judgments § 19, comment d, Reporter's Note (1982); Brousseau, A Reader's Guide to the Proposed Changes in the Preclusion Provisions of the Restatement of Judgments, 11 Tulsa L.J. 305 (1976).

91. Developments in the Law—Res Judicata, 65 Harv.L.Rev. 818, 837 (1952). But compare Rost v. Kroke, 195 Minn. 219, 262 N.W. 450 (1935), in which plaintiff was given the choice between amendment and starting a new action, even though leave to amend had been granted by the trial court.

92. Ness Investment Corp. v. U.S., 219 Ct.Cl. 440, 595 F.2d 585 (1979); Mirin v. Nevada, 547 F.2d 91 (9th Cir.1976), cert. denied 432 U.S. 906.

Some courts have reached this conclusion by treating Rule 12(b)(6) dismissals under Federal Rule 41(b). Hall v. Tower Land & Investment Co., 512 F.2d 481 (5th Cir.1975). Others have so held, but have ruled that Rule 41(b) does not by itself command that result. Rinehart v. Locke, 454 F.2d 313 (7th Cir.1971). See also 9 C. Wright & A. Miller, Civil 2d § 2373.

93. See 5A C. Wright & A. Miller, Civil 2d § 1357.

94. Technical Air Prods., Inc. v. Sheridan–Gray, Inc., 103 Ariz. 450, 445 P.2d 426 (1968). See Restatement Second of Judgments § 18, comment a (1982); Annot., Doctrine of Res Judicata as Applied to Default Judgments, 77 A.L.R.2d 1410 (1961). Collateral estoppel effect may not be given to the judgment, however. See § 14.11, below.

and later challenging the judgment by a subsequent suit of his own. In the absence of claim and defense preclusion in this situation, the plaintiff would not be able to secure a binding final judgment without the defendant's cooperation.

Judgments and dismissals entered because the parties have settled their case involve additional considerations. An out-of-court settlement technically is only a contract between the parties without any adjudicatory effect. Thus, a voluntary dismissal after a settlement has been reached has no preclusive effect if the parties to the action agree that the dismissal will be without prejudice. However, to avoid the possibility of multiple actions in the event of a breach—the first on the original claim and the second for breach of the settlement contract—judgments voluntarily dismissing actions as a result of settlement agreements commonly provide that the judgment is on the merits. Nonetheless, the settlement agreement is governed by the intent of the parties and may be attacked under general contract principles for fraud or lack of consideration even when the parties have stipulated that the resulting judgment is on the merits.

In contrast to an out-of-court settlement, a consent judgment normally is given full res judicata effect in the absence of a stipulation indicating that it is not on the entire claim.[95] Because parties can waive the right to object to splitting a claim,[96] there will be a presumption of waiver when the judgment is based on an agreement that does not embody the whole claim, unless the parties stipulate otherwise.[97]

§ 14.8   Exceptions to the Application of Res Judicata

As has been discussed, applying the rules of claim preclusion, particularly to bar the litigation of matters that were omitted in an earlier proceeding, represents a decision that judicial economy concerns must predominate over the important goal of achieving individual justice. In some situations, however, additional policies would be undercut were the normal rules of res judicata to apply. Thus, a series of exceptions have evolved to accommodate what are deemed to be these more important policies.[1] When reviewing these exceptions, it is impor-

---

95. U.S. v. Southern Ute Tribe or Band of Indians, 402 U.S. 159, 91 S.Ct. 1336, 28 L.Ed.2d 695 (1971); Lawlor v. National Screen Service Corp., 349 U.S. 322, 75 S.Ct. 865, 99 L.Ed. 1122 (1955); Martino v. McDonald's Sys., Inc., 598 F.2d 1079 (7th Cir.1979), cert. denied 444 U.S. 966; Kaspar Wire Works, Inc. v. Leco Engineering & Mach., Inc., 575 F.2d 530 (5th Cir.1978); Wallace Clark & Co. v. Acheson Indus., Inc., 532 F.2d 846 (2d Cir.1976), cert. denied 425 U.S. 976.

96. See § 14.3 at notes 10–23, above.

97. See Note, "To Bind or Not to Bind": Bar and Merger Treatment of Consent Decrees in Patent Infringement Litiga-

tion, 74 Colum.L.Rev. 1233 (1974); Annot., Res Judicata as Affected by the Fact that Former Judgment Was Entered by Agreement or Consent, 2 A.L.R.2d 514, 562 (1948).

§ 14.8

1. In some situations claim preclusion may be avoided simply because the disposition of the first case did not provide a resolution of the problem. Compare Adams v. Pearson, 411 Ill. 431, 104 N.E.2d 267 (1952), with Hahl v. Sugo, 169 N.Y. 109, 62 N.E. 135 (1901).

For another example, see Mashpee Tribe v. Watt, 542 F.Supp. 797 (D.Mass.1982),

tant to note that although a number of cases may speak in terms of allowing an exception as being in the "public interest" or because it avoids "injustice," these generally are overstatements.[2] As will be seen, exceptions to res judicata most commonly and properly are invoked only in specialized situations in which a specific policy is deemed to outweigh judicial economy concerns.

To begin with, there are situations in which the normal consequences of res judicata might undermine specific objectives of legislative or constitutional provisions; when that is so, successive suits on the same claim may be permitted.[3] For example, repetitive litigation may be allowed in order to prevent an inequity that would jeopardize the carrying out of a regulatory scheme. In one well-known case, the defendant transferred 325 of her 326 shares in a bank just before its insolvency, but the transfer was not registered until later. The State Superintendent of Banks sued successfully for a shareholder's contribution due on the one remaining share. A state court subsequently decided that there was statutory liability on shares not actually transferred prior to closing, and the Superintendent then sued for a contribution on the other 325 shares. This suit ordinarily would be precluded by merger, but the Superintendent was allowed to split his claims because of the interest in uniform treatment of the bank's shareholders, which should not be compromised by a public official's mistake.[4] Another situation in which relitigation of the underlying claim is allowed is in habeas corpus proceedings, because the rights at stake are deemed so important that they outweigh the need for finality.[5]

The intention of an existing statutory scheme to allow repetitive suits also has been held to permit relitigation. For example, a landlord who brings summary proceedings to repossess property from a tenant will not be precluded from a later action for payment of the past rent due if the statutory scheme gives the landlord a choice between the expedited procedure to evict and a regular action in which all claims could be combined.[6] In a similar vein, some courts have ruled that when

affirmed 707 F.2d 23 (1st Cir.1983), cert. denied 464 U.S. 1020 (rights of American Indians are of such special concern to federal government that res judicata should not be applied as a matter of public policy).

2. Blankner v. City of Chicago, 504 F.2d 1037, 1042 (7th Cir.1974), cert. denied 421 U.S. 948. See 18 C. Wright, A. Miller & E. Cooper, Jurisdiction and Related Matters § 4415.

3. Restatement Second of Judgments § 26(d) (1982). Compare Migra v. Warren City School Dist. Bd. of Educ., 465 U.S. 75, 104 S.Ct. 892, 79 L.Ed.2d 56 (1984) (res judicata precludes omitted Section 1983 claims from state breach of contract suit) with U.S. v. American Heart Research Foundation, Inc., 996 F.2d 7 (1st Cir.1993) (successive suits under False Claims Act

allowed for injunction and then for unjust enrichment).

4. White v. Adler, 289 N.Y. 34, 43 N.E.2d 798 (1942). See also Woodbury v. Porter, 158 F.2d 194 (8th Cir.1946).

5. Sanders v. U.S., 373 U.S. 1, 8, 83 S.Ct. 1068, 1073, 10 L.Ed.2d 148 (1963): "Conventional notions of finality of litigation have no place where life or liberty is at stake and infringement of constitutional rights is alleged * * *. The inapplicability of res judicata to habeas, then, is inherent in the very role and function of the writ."

6. Tutt v. Doby, 459 F.2d 1195 (D.C.Cir.1972). See generally Restatement Second of Judgments § 26, comment d (1982). But see Jackson v. U.S. Postal Serv., 799 F.2d 1018 (5th Cir.1986).

federal and state statutes apply to the same situation,[7] an action based upon the state statute will not preclude the federal claim from being asserted in a federal court if the latter has been given exclusive subject-matter jurisdiction over causes of action under the federal statute. These opinions reflect a decision that redundancy of trial is necessary in order to effectuate the congressional intention to have certain claims, such as antitrust matters, heard exclusively in the federal courts.[8] But, as is discussed more fully elsewhere, courts more recently seem to be abandoning this exception, perhaps reflecting the conclusion that judicial economy and avoidance of duplicative litigation should predominate in this era of overcrowded courts.[9]

Although changes in law usually do not warrant the denial of claim preclusion,[10] the inflexible application of merger and bar rules may be inapposite when there is a major change in constitutional principles as applied to areas of continuing conduct that have broad public importance. Thus, a second suit on the same claim to enjoin an allegedly racially discriminatory system of state school tuition grants was allowed when in the interim the Supreme Court had struck down a similar system in a different action.[11] Similar conclusions have been reached in cases involving desegregation.[12]

B. COLLATERAL ESTOPPEL— ISSUE PRECLUSION

§ 14.9   General Principles Underlying Collateral Estoppel

As is true for res judicata,[1] the law of collateral estoppel is grounded in notions that the finality of judgments must be preserved and that judicial economy demands that cases not be retried continually.[2] When an issue has been litigated fully between the parties, spending additional time and money repeating this process would be extremely wasteful. This is particularly important in an era when the courts are overcrowded and the judicial system no longer can afford the luxury—if it ever

---

7. In some cases, it has been held that the federal and state legislation create separate causes of action because of significant differences between them, so that res judicata does not apply. See, e.g., Troxell v. Delaware, Lackawanna & W.R.R. Co., 227 U.S. 434, 33 S.Ct. 274, 57 L.Ed. 586 (1913) (state action by railroad worker's widow does not preclude FELA suit, which allows recovery for negligence of fellow employees).

8. See Cream Top Creamery v. Dean Milk Co., 383 F.2d 358 (6th Cir.1967).

9. See § 14.7 at notes 25–28, above.

10. Morris v. Adams–Millis Corp., 758 F.2d 1352 (10th Cir.1985); Gowan v. Tully, 45 N.Y.2d 32, 407 N.Y.S.2d 650, 652–53, 379 N.E.2d 177, 179–80 (1978).

11. Griffin v. State Bd. of Educ., 296 F.Supp. 1178 (E.D.Va.1969), reopening 239 F.Supp. 560 (E.D.Va.1965).

12. Christian v. Jemison, 303 F.2d 52, 55 (5th Cir.1962), cert. denied 371 U.S. 920.

§ 14.9

1. See § 14.3, above.

2. "To preclude parties from contesting matters that they have had a full and fair opportunity to litigate protects their adversaries from the expense and vexation attending multiple lawsuits, conserves judicial resources, and fosters reliance on judicial action by minimizing the possibility of inconsistent decisions." Montana v. U.S., 440 U.S. 147, 153–54, 99 S.Ct. 970, 973–74, 59 L.Ed.2d 210 (1979).

could—of allowing people to relitigate matters already decided.[3] Thus, issue preclusion operates to simplify dispute resolution[4] by considering the original court's determination on specific issues to be binding; any subsequent litigation between the parties,[5] even on different claims,[6] will be limited to only those issues being presented for the first time.[7]

Collateral estoppel operates without regard to whether the first determination of a particular issue was correct. The court does not concern itself with the rightness of the findings.[8] Its only inquiry is whether a particular issue is one that clearly was decided in a prior proceeding and whether the issue was necessary to the determination of that proceeding.[9]

Because collateral estoppel focuses on the avoidance of relitigating issues, rather than precluding entire claims for relief or causes of action, it is used in a number of contexts in which res judicata is not available.[10] For example, interlocutory orders that include findings on specific issues may be given collateral estoppel effect,[11] even when their lack of finality prohibits their use for res judicata purposes.[12]

In a leading case, Lummus Company v. Commonwealth Oil Refining Company,[13] on an appeal in his first action the plaintiff had obtained an interlocutory order for arbitration of his contract disputes, but the federal district court in New York in a second action ordered a stay of arbitration pending trial. The Second Circuit overruled, holding that the decision in the first action, albeit reached in an interlocutory proceeding, was final for collateral estoppel purposes on the issue of arbitrability.

---

3. In fact, although certain exceptions have been recognized to the normal applicability of collateral estoppel to respect statutory policies that seem to require a redetermination of a particular issue, recent cases appear to be leaning toward allowing the use of collateral estoppel, finding that the need of judicial economy outweighs statutory concerns. For a discussion of this problem, see § 14.12, below.

4. It has been suggested that the potential of conclusiveness on litigated issues may encourage more extensive litigation in the first action and thus actually may not reduce the burden on courts. Polasky, Collateral Estoppel—Effects of Prior Litigation, 39 Iowa L.Rev. 217, 220 (1954). Further, one author has asserted that the lack of clarity of existing collateral estoppel rules creates increased lawyering and court costs. Richardson, Taking Issue with Issue Preclusion: Reinventing Collateral Estoppel, 65 Miss.L.J. 41 (1995).

5. In some instances collateral estoppel may be used by persons who were not parties to the first action. See § 14.14, below.

6. Repetitive litigation between the same parties on the same claim will be precluded by res judicata and collateral estoppel, see § 14.3, above.

7. Scott, Collateral Estoppel by Judgment, 56 Harv.L.Rev. 1, 3 (1942).

8. For a discussion of the various interests served by issue preclusion, as well as its dangers, see 18 C. Wright, A. Miller, & E. Cooper, Jurisdiction and Related Matters § 4416.

9. The requirements for collateral estoppel are discussed in § 14.11, below.

10. The doctrines of collateral estoppel and res judicata are complimentary; the decision as to the definition of a claim for res judicata purposes often is influenced by the breadth of the rule of issue preclusion. Restatement Second of Judgments, Introductory Note 249 (1982).

11. Restatement Second of Judgments § 13, comment g (1982). For an interesting discussion of the possibility of using collateral estoppel in the bifurcated trial setting, see Note, Res Judicata, and the Bifurcated Trial, 16 U.C.L.A.L.Rev. 203 (1968).

12. See § 14.7 at notes 39–60, above.

13. 297 F.2d 80 (2d Cir.1961), cert. denied 368 U.S. 986.

Writing for the majority, Judge Friendly said: " 'Finality' in the context here relevant may mean little more than that the litigation of a particular issue has reached such a stage that a court sees no really good reason for permitting it to be litigated again."[14]

In a similar vein, a preliminary injunction may have collateral estoppel effect if it is based on a determination that constitutes an insuperable obstacle to success on the merits. This was the situation in Miller Brewing Company v. Jos. Schlitz Brewing Company.[15] In the first suit on an appeal from a preliminary injunction order, the court held as a matter of law that the brand name "Lite" could not have trademark protection. This determination was held to be final and conclusive in a second action. On the other hand, court findings that are inherently provisional do not have preclusive effect even for purposes of collateral estoppel. Thus, for example, when a ruling on a motion to suppress a confession on the ground that it was involuntary was only provisional under state law, because the issue of voluntariness ultimately had to be left to the jury in the criminal trial, that ruling was held not binding on a civil jury in an action for damages alleging mistreatment by the police officer.[16] Whether an order is final for purposes of collateral estoppel, then, will depend on factors such as "the nature of the decision (i.e., that it was not avowedly tentative), the adequacy of the hearing, and the opportunity for review."[17] As long as the determination was definitive, it may be treated as final for purposes of issue preclusion.

Collateral estoppel effect also may be given to judgments entered by courts of limited jurisdiction, when those jurisdictional limits ordinarily would prevent the use of res judicata.[18] For example, if a court obtains attachment jurisdiction[19] over a nonresident defendant by bringing within its power some property belonging to him, and the defendant makes a limited appearance[20] to defend the property, any issues that necessarily are determined in that first proceeding may be given preclusive effect in later actions seeking to obtain further relief.[21] The judgment itself will not have merger or bar effect. It has been suggested that it is improper to permit such a judgment to have even collateral estoppel effect because that is inconsistent with the notion of a limited appearance and may be unfair.[22] However, as long as the defendant fully litigated the issues in the first action,[23] judicial economy compels that the determination of

14. 297 F.2d at 89.

15. 605 F.2d 990 (7th Cir.1979), cert. denied 444 U.S. 1102.

16. Spencer v. Town of Westerly, 430 F.Supp. 636 (D.R.I.1977).

17. Lummus Co. v. Commonwealth Oil Refining Co., 297 F.2d 80, 89 (2d Cir.1961), cert. denied 368 U.S. 986.

18. See § 14.7 at notes 32–38, above.

19. See §§ 3.14–3.16, above, for a discussion of attachment jurisdiction.

20. See § 3.27, above.

21. Restatement Second of Judgments § 32(3) (1982). See also Harnischfeger Sales Corp. v. Sternberg Dredging Co., 189 Miss. 73, 191 So. 94 (1939); 189 Miss. 73, 195 So. 322 (1940).

22. For an exploration of the arguments for and against the issue preclusive effect of limited appearances, see 18 C. Wright, A. Miller & E. Cooper, Jurisdiction and Related Matters § 4431.

23. When attachment jurisdiction could be premised solely on the presence of the defendant's insurance company in the forum, it was held that the allowance of

those issues be given complete binding effect.[24]

Collateral estoppel effect also may be accorded to judgments entered in actions brought in a court of limited subject-matter jurisdiction, even though the issues involved would be beyond the court's jurisdiction in most circumstances.[25] The decision whether to uphold issue preclusion in these cases depends on a number of factors.[26] First, the court must consider whether it would be inconsistent with the policies behind the subject-matter jurisdiction limits to allow issues decided in the first court to be treated as conclusive in a later court of more general jurisdiction.[27] Second, the court must consider whether the limited authority of the original trial court suggests some reason why it would be unwise to rely on the determination it reached.[28] The courts have not been uniform in evaluating this last question, and decisions can be found both upholding and overruling issue preclusion in similar settings.[29] These differences simply reflect the fact that to allow collateral estoppel depends on a variety of factors[30] involving the nature of the litigation and the underlying justification for the limitations imposed by the legislature on the court's authority to handle certain disputes.[31]

collateral estoppel would be inconsistent with due process. Minichiello v. Rosenberg, 410 F.2d 106, 112 (2d Cir.1968), cert. denied 396 U.S. 844. This method of obtaining jurisdiction no longer is available, however. Rush v. Savchuk, 444 U.S. 320, 100 S.Ct. 571, 62 L.Ed.2d 516 (1980).

24. Restatement Second of Judgments § 32, comment d (1982).

25. This issue arises when a court incidentally determines a matter that it would not have had jurisdiction to rule on directly. Thus, in a state court breach of contract suit, for example, the defendant may defend on the ground that the contract is illegal as it violates the antitrust laws. In order to resolve the contract issues, the court may rule on the federal antitrust defense, even though federal antitrust matters are within the exclusive jurisdiction of the federal courts.

26. See generally 18 C. Wright, A. Miller & E. Cooper, Jurisdiction and Related Matters § 4428.

27. Although most courts agree that res judicata should not be applied when exclusive subject-matter jurisdiction has been given to the second court, see § 14.7 at notes 14–17, above, the question whether the overlapping issues should be given collateral estoppel effect is less clear and depends on the particular facts and policies involved. See, for example, Brown v. Felsen, 442 U.S. 127, 99 S.Ct. 2205, 60 L.Ed.2d 767

(1979), holding that a prior state court judgment in a suit for collection would not be given res judicata effect in a later bankruptcy court proceeding. The Court specifically noted that collateral estoppel might be used, however. 442 U.S. at 139 n. 10, 99 S.Ct. at 2213 n. 10. This issue is discussed more fully in § 14.12, below.

28. Professor Vestal has argued that "inferior courts with *very limited jurisdiction* should not be able to preclude further litigation of a point." But that "a court limited, for example, to suits involving 10,-000 dollars or less, should * * *." Vestal, Preclusion/Res Judicata Variables: Adjudicating Bodies, 54 Geo.L.J. 857, 868 (1966).

29. See Brownell v. Union & New Haven Trust Co., 143 Conn. 662, 124 A.2d 901 (1956) (refusing); Niles v. Niles, 35 Del.Ch. 106, 111 A.2d 697 (1955) (upholding).

30. Compare Vella v. Hudgins, 20 Cal.3d 251, 142 Cal.Rptr. 414, 572 P.2d 28 (1977), with Wood v. Herson, 39 Cal.App.3d 737, 114 Cal.Rptr. 365 (1974).

31. The Restatement Second takes the position that "preclusive effect should turn in each case on an analysis of the comparative quality and extensiveness of the procedures followed in the two courts, of their relative competence to deal with the particular issue, and of the legislative purpose in allocating jurisdiction between them." Restatement Second of Judgments § 23(3), Reporter's Note 287 (1982). Special prob-

Finally, the procedure for raising the defense of collateral estoppel is the same as for res judicata. Collateral estoppel is an affirmative defense[32] that must be pleaded or it will be waived.[33] It may be raised in a responsive pleading, but more commonly it is included in a motion for summary judgment or partial summary judgment.[34] The key is that the defense must be raised early in the litigation so that, if it is upheld, judicial economy will be fostered by eliminating that issue from the dispute.

Despite the fact that the operation of collateral estoppel benefits both parties and courts by avoiding needless relitigation, courts generally do not raise the matter sua sponte.[35] In most instances the judge would not know of the prior litigation unless one of the parties refers to it, so perhaps this is not a very important limitation. In those few cases in which the court is aware of a prior judgment, however, placing the sole responsibility for introducing the defense on the parties seems somewhat anomalous. Thus, in times in which judicial economy concerns are dominant, it is not surprising that some courts are raising issue preclusion on their own motion.[36]

§ 14.10   The Scope of Collateral Estoppel—Defining an Issue

Just as res judicata requires that the cause of action to be precluded be identical to the one already litigated, collateral estoppel demands identity of issues.[1] Consequently, for collateral estoppel, the problem of defining the scope of a single issue takes a place analogous to determining the scope of a cause of action for res judicata.[2] Unlike "cause of action," however, the term "issue" is not encrusted with historical associations. Whether issues in two actions are the same typically depends upon straightforward considerations such as factual identity, legal standards, and the burden of proof imposed on the parties in each

---

lems arise when the litigation is in both state and federal courts. See § 14.15, below.

32. Fed.Civ.Proc.Rule 8(c); Barker v. Norman, 651 F.2d 1107, 1130 (5th Cir. 1981); Dellums v. Powell, 566 F.2d 167, 177 n. 13 (D.C.Cir.1977), cert. denied 438 U.S. 916; LaSalle Nat. Bank v. County of Du-Page, 77 Ill.App.3d 562, 32 Ill.Dec. 935, 938 n. 1, 396 N.E.2d 48, 51 n. 1 (1979).

33. The liberal amendment provisions of most judicial systems are used to preserve the defense beyond the initial pleading stages, however. See § 5.26, above, on amendments.

34. Summary judgment is more common because it allows presentation of evidence of the prior judgment which usually is necessary in order to establish that the collateral estoppel standard is met. See Crutsinger v. Hess, 408 F.Supp. 548

(D.Kan.1976). See generally 10B C. Wright, A. Miller & M. Kane, Civil 3d § 2735.

35. "[T]he fact that a party can waive the application of collateral estoppel suggests that the needs of judicial administration are, at best, of subsidiary value; * * *." Technograph Printed Circuits, Ltd. v. U.S., 372 F.2d 969, 977 (Ct.Cl.1967).

36. E.g., LaRocca v. Gold, 662 F.2d 144 (2d Cir.1981); Jones v. Beasley, 476 F.Supp. 116, 117 (M.D.Ga.1979); Sherwood v. Brown, 209 Neb. 68, 306 N.W.2d 171 (1981).

§ 14.10

1. See 18 C. Wright, A. Miller & E. Cooper. Jurisdiction and Related Matters § 4417.

2. See §§ 14.4–14.5, above.

lawsuit.[3]

The requirement that issues be identical is construed strictly. As the Supreme Court noted in Commissioner of Internal Revenue v. Sunnen,[4] the doctrine "must be confined to situations where the matter raised in the second suit is identical in all respects with that decided in the first proceeding and where the controlling facts and applicable legal rules remain unchanged."[5] Thus, the Court articulated a narrow standard for the application of collateral estoppel: "If the relevant facts in the two cases are separable, even though they be similar or identical, collateral estoppel does not govern the legal issues which recur in the second case."[6]

The application of this standard to the facts of Sunnen resulted in the denial of collateral estoppel effect. In 1928 Sunnen assigned to his wife the right, title, and interest to a patent that he held. In a 1935 suit before the Board of Tax Appeals it was determined that money paid to the wife under that contract was not to be considered part of Sunnen's taxable income. Sunnen then assigned other patents to his wife in documents similar in all important respects to the 1928 contract. When a suit was brought concerning the taxability of income under these later contracts, the Court held that the prior Tax Board determination did not affect the second action. "For income tax purposes, what is decided as to one contract is not conclusive as to any other contract which is not then in issue, however similar or identical it may be."[7]

The passage of time between two sets of very similar events, each giving rise to a separate lawsuit, often will prevent collateral estoppel from being applied because the underlying facts of each set will not be identical. For example, in one case plaintiff claimed that proceeds from the sale of certain breeding cattle between 1951 to 1953 should be taxed as capital gains, not as ordinary income. The Tax Court disallowed that claim. In a later action, the plaintiff claimed capital gains treatment for breeding cattle sold between 1957 and 1960. No collateral estoppel effect was given to the prior judgment because that judgment concerned different cattle.[8] The issue decided in the first action was not the plaintiff's procedures for selling cattle, but the procedures for selling those cattle at that time. In a similar vein, a determination that a farm held by a religious society was ineligible for a state tax exemption in one

---

3. Although the identification of issues is not itself problematic, significant difficulties arise in determining what issues were actually and necessarily decided in the first action. See § 14.11, below. Further, court decisions exploring the propriety of using collateral estoppel often intertwine questions of whether the parties in the first action could foresee that a particular issue litigated there would become critical in later suits with determinations of what should be the proper scope of a particular issue. See Restatement Second of Judg-

ments § 27, comment c (1982). For purposes of this volume, these questions are kept separate.

4. 333 U.S. 591, 68 S.Ct. 715, 92 L.Ed. 898 (1948).

5. 333 U.S. at 599–600, 68 S.Ct. at 720.

6. 333 U.S. at 601, 68 S.Ct. at 721.

7. 333 U.S. at 602, 68 S.Ct. at 721.

8. Moore v. U.S., 246 F.Supp. 19 (N.D.Miss.1965).

year was held not to be preclusive in the following year.[9] The court noted: "The issues are not the same. The issue as to each year depends upon what took place that year."[10]

The assessment of the similarity of issues necessary to decide whether collateral estoppel should preclude relitigation of a particular issue varies with the facts of each case.[11] The court will balance the significance of the change in circumstances against the burden of repeated litigation. The differences shown must be significant ones; the passage of time alone will not always be significant. As explained by Professor Wigmore, "That a soap bubble was in existence half an hour ago affords no inference at all that it is in existence now; that Mt. Everest was in existence ten years ago is strong evidence that it exists yet."[12] Thus, a judgment that determined the existence of an enduring condition raises a presumption that the condition will continue to exist, and collateral estoppel may be applied. The presumption shifts the burden of initiative on to the opposing party to show a change of circumstances such that the issues are not identical.[13]

Illustratively, if one action set aside a contract between the parties because the defendant was mentally incompetent when the contract was made, the plaintiff, trying to enforce a different contract made with the defendant the following day, would be obliged to prove the defendant's miraculous recovery. Otherwise, collateral estoppel would apply to the issue of the defendant's lack of contractual capacity. Other determinations that have raised similar presumptions that issues are identical include findings of permanent disability,[14] the character of a neighborhood[15] and the relative value of a tenant's lease for the purposes of rent-control.[16]

Collateral estoppel also may depend on the way that an issue is framed or worded.[17] Illustratively, in one case, a negligently built drain

9. People ex rel. Watchtower Bible & Tract Soc., Inc. v. Haring, 286 App.Div. 676, 146 N.Y.S.2d 151 (1955).

10. 146 N.Y.S.2d at 156.

11. A stricter or narrower standard for finding identical issues often is used for issues of law, see text at notes 37–52, below, and in tax cases. See Pelham Hall Co. v. Hassett, 147 F.2d 63, 67 (1st Cir.1945) ("To minimize the recurring hardship to the taxpayer or prejudice to the revenue (as the case may be), with respect to the taxes for all succeeding tax years, neither the taxpayer nor the government should be precluded from raising a relevant point of law unless it appears beyond doubt that the precise point was actually contested and decided (not merely assumed) in the prior litigation."). For criticism of this view, see Restatement Second of Judgments § 27, Reporter's Note 265 (1982).

12. 2 Wigmore on Evidence § 437, at 513 (Chadbourne Rev.1979).

13. Napper v. Anderson, Henley, Shields, Bradford & Pritchard, 500 F.2d 634, 637 (5th Cir.1974), cert. denied 423 U.S. 837.

14. Anderson v. U.S., 126 F.2d 169 (3d Cir.1942). Compare Rose v. U.S., 513 F.2d 1251, 1257 n. 5 (8th Cir.1975) ("the competency of an accused cannot be rendered an immutable historical fact, for the mental condition of an accused may change drastically in a matter of months").

15. St. Lo Constr. Co. v. Koenigsberger, 174 F.2d 25 (D.C.Cir.1949), cert. denied 338 U.S. 821.

16. Application of Fifth Madison Corp., 3 A.D.2d 430, 161 N.Y.S.2d 326 (1957), affirmed 4 N.Y.2d 932, 175 N.Y.S.2d 173, 151 N.E.2d 357 (1958).

17. A factual issue decided in one action for one purpose may not be the same when it is used for another purpose. E.g., Local 32B–32J Service Employees Int'l Un-

caused periodic flooding of the plaintiff's land. The plaintiff sued once for damages and prevailed. When another flood caused further damage, plaintiff brought a second action[18] and the town tried to invoke the doctrine of municipal immunity. The court held the town to be estopped by the previous action. Although a different flood was involved in the second suit, it was caused by the same drain. "Every essential element bearing upon the liability of the town is the same in all this litigation."[19] The issue was defined as "whether the town is liable for floods caused by this drain"; not "whether the town is liable for damage caused by this flood."

Differences in the burden of proof in the first and second actions may result in the denial of collateral estoppel with respect to an issue that on its face appears identical in both suits.[20] If the party against whom collateral estoppel is being asserted bears a less onerous burden of proof in the second trial, then a different outcome is possible and the issues should not be treated as identical.[21] The best example of this occurs when common issues are present in civil and criminal actions.[22] Stated generally, issues clearly decided against the defendant in a criminal action may be asserted as collateral estoppel in a later civil action,[23] but issues decided first in a civil proceeding normally will not preclude relitigation in a later criminal proceeding.[24] The distinction arises because the standard of proof in criminal cases—beyond a reasonable doubt—is greater than that in civil cases—a preponderance of the evidence. Thus, a finding in a criminal case that the defendant drove recklessly by exceeding the speed limit will preclude the defendant from denying that fact in a later action for damages allegedly caused by the

ion, AFL–CIO v. NLRB, 982 F.2d 845 (2d Cir.1993) (holding that new employer was a "successor" to the duty to arbitrate in the labor contract was not preclusive on the question whether it was a "successor" with respect to other legal obligations in the contract); First Charter Land Corp. v. Fitzgerald, 643 F.2d 1011 (4th Cir.1981) (determination that a particular person was not an agent of defendant for long-arm jurisdiction purposes did not preclude a determination that he was an agent for other purposes involved with the same transaction).

18. When a single negligent act causes repeated damage, the plaintiff may elect to bring successive actions for each trespass because each is considered to be a separate cause of action. See § 14.5 at n. 21, above.

19. Wishnewsky v. Town of Saugus, 325 Mass. 191, 89 N.E.2d 783, 786 (1950).

20. See, e.g., In re C.M.H., 413 So.2d 418, 8 Family L.Rep. 1110 (Fla.App.1982); Gelardi v. Gelardi, 205 Misc. 348, 127 N.Y.S.2d 802 (1953).

21. This may occur when an issue is common to a defense as well as a claim, or when the same conduct results in both civil

and criminal actions. Restatement Second of Judgments § 28(4) (1982).

22. Restatement Second of Judgments § 85 (1982); Vestal & Coughenour, Preclusion—Res Judicata Variables, Criminal Prosecutions, 19 Vand.L.Rev. 683 (1966).

23. Roshak v. Leathers, 277 Or. 207, 560 P.2d 275 (1977); Levy v. Association of the Bar of the City of New York, 37 N.Y.2d 279, 372 N.Y.S.2d 41, 333 N.E.2d 350 (1975); Teitelbaum Furs, Inc. v. Dominion Ins. Co., 58 Cal.2d 601, 25 Cal.Rptr. 559, 375 P.2d 439 (1962), cert. denied 372 U.S. 966; 18 C. Wright, A. Miller & E. Cooper, Jurisdiction and Related Matters § 4474.

24. U.S. v. Casale Car Leasing, Inc., 385 F.2d 707 (2d Cir.1967). See also West Virginia v. Miller, 194 W.Va. 3, 459 S.E.2d 114 (1995).

In some cases when the government sues civilly and then criminally, the burden of proof is the same and collateral estoppel may be asserted if all the requirements for doing so otherwise are met. See Yates v. U.S., 354 U.S. 298, 335, 77 S.Ct. 1064, 1085, 1 L.Ed.2d 1356 (1957).

reckless driving. A finding of reckless driving in a civil case by a preponderance of the evidence does not ensure that defendant would be found reckless beyond a reasonable doubt, however. The potential of a different outcome requires the issues to be litigated. Similarly, if the defendant first is acquitted in a criminal trial, collateral estoppel cannot be used in a later civil action because the prosecution's failure to prove certain conduct beyond a reasonable doubt does not establish that the conduct could not be proven under a lesser standard.[25]

In addition to limiting collateral estoppel to identical issues, courts sometimes have distinguished between "ultimate" and "mediate" facts when determining whether issues decided in one suit will be viewed as preclusive in a later one.[26] The most influential explanation of this distinction is found in Judge Learned Hand's opinion in The Evergreens v. Nunan.[27] Imagine a lawsuit as a logical structure resembling a pyramid. At its base are the facts introduced into evidence. From these facts are drawn conclusions which, when combined with other deductions or evidence, lead eventually to "ultimate facts" that establish a legal right, duty, or status. The ultimate facts are the summit of the structure; all that supports them are "mediate data." The Evergreens case held that only matters constituting ultimate facts in the second action are subject to being precluded by collateral estoppel.

The controversy in The Evergreens turned on the value for tax purposes of cemetery lots appropriated by the City of New York. The lots were of two kinds, improved and unimproved. An earlier proceeding had determined the value of the improved lots and that determination was accepted in the later action without dispute. The earlier proceeding also had fixed the cost of upgrading the unimproved lots to improved status. The plaintiff maintained that these two findings taken together should determine the value of the unimproved lots: The uncontested value of the improved lots minus the cost of improving them should be taken as the value of the unimproved lots.

The Second Circuit rejected this argument, relying on the distinction between ultimate and mediate facts. Judge Hand first noted that authorities differed concerning whether mediate facts or only ultimate facts in the first suit are decided conclusively by the judgment.[28] The question presented, however, was whether a determination, either mediate or ultimate in the first suit, could establish a mediate fact in the

---

25. U.S. v. One Assortment of 89 Firearms, 465 U.S. 354, 104 S.Ct. 1099, 79 L.Ed.2d 361 (1984); One Lot Emerald Cut Stones v. U.S., 409 U.S. 232, 93 S.Ct. 489, 34 L.Ed.2d 438 (1972); Younge v. State Bd. of Registration for Healing Arts, 451 S.W.2d 346 (Mo.1969), cert. denied 397 U.S. 922.

26. E.g., Yates v. U.S., 354 U.S. 298, 338, 77 S.Ct. 1064, 1087, 1 L.Ed.2d 1356 (1957); Abeles v. Wurdack, 285 S.W.2d 544 (Mo.1955).

27. 141 F.2d 927 (2d Cir.1944), cert. denied 323 U.S. 720.

28. The question whether collateral estoppel effect ought to be given to mediate facts in the first action involves concerns whether mediate facts were necessary to the first determination, such that it is likely the parties fully litigated them. See § 14.11, below.

second suit. On this question, authority was silent; Judge Hand decided that collateral estoppel could not be used.

This determination rested on the notion that the conclusion that would result if estoppel were to apply might be both unintended and unjust. The deductions that may be drawn from a given fact are unpredictable. Restricting the use of collateral estoppel to ultimate issues in the second suit attempts to ensure that the consequences of issues decided by the first judgment are plainly visible when that judgment is entered.

> What jural relevance facts may acquire in the future it is often impossible even remotely to anticipate. Were the law to be recast, it would therefore be a pertinent inquiry whether the conclusiveness * * * might not properly be limited to future controversies which could be thought reasonably in prospect when the first suit was tried. That is, of course, not the law as it stands * * *.[29]

The "law as it stands" has changed since The Evergreens decision. Now many jurisdictions acknowledge the policies outlined in the opinion, but not necessarily the technical separation of mediate from ultimate facts. The Restatement First of Judgments distinguished these two kinds of facts,[30] but the Restatement Second abolishes the distinction.[31] The formalism of the mediate/ultimate facts approach was difficult to apply and unhelpful in practice because facts are not clearly mediate or ultimate.[32] Decisions on how to apply these labels often depended on the policy considerations suggested by Judge Hand—whether the situation in which estoppel is to be applied was foreseeable at the time of the first suit,[33] and whether the issue was necessary to that judgment.[34] The Second Restatement, therefore, abandons the terminology of mediate and ultimate facts and appeals directly to foreseeability.[35] Identical issues will not be given preclusive effect if "it was not sufficiently foreseeable at the time of the initial action that the issue would arise in the context of a subsequent action."[36]

Finally, it should be noted that sometimes it is stated broadly that collateral estoppel applies only to issues of fact, not to issues of law.[37]

29. 141 F.2d at 929.

30. Restatement First of Judgments § 68, comment p (1948).

31. Restatement Second of Judgments § 27, comment j (1982).

32. The Evergreens rule has been strongly criticized by commentators. See Heckman, Collateral Estoppel as the Answer to Multiple Litigation Problems in Federal Tax Laws: Another View of Sunnen and The Evergreens, 19 Case W.Res.L.Rev. 230 (1968); Rosenberg, Collateral Estoppel in New York, 44 St. John's L.Rev. 165, 182 (1969).

33. See Laughlin v. U.S., 344 F.2d 187, 191 (D.C.Cir.1965); Hyman v. Regenstein,

258 F.2d 502, 510–11 (5th Cir.1958), cert. denied 359 U.S. 913.

34. The requirement that matters precluded were "necessarily litigated" is discussed in § 14.11, below.

35. For a fuller discussion see 18 C. Wright, A. Miller & E. Cooper, Jurisdiction and Related Matters § 4424.

36. Restatement Second of Judgments § 28(5)(b) (1982). See also Synanon Church v. U.S., 820 F.2d 421 (D.C.Cir.1987).

37. The Supreme Court has noted the importance of not giving preclusive effect to pure legal issues in constitutional adjudication. "Unreflective invocation of collateral estoppel against parties with an ongoing

This limitation rests on the premise that issues of law by nature are general,[38] whereas the scope of collateral estoppel is restricted to very specific findings. Although this simple generalization is helpful to remember, it must be qualified. First, issues of law and fact are not easily identified. The line between issues of fact and issues of law is hard to draw because courts do not concern themselves either with fact or law issues in isolation but with the application of the one to the other. Moreover, collateral estoppel can preclude clear issues of law in some limited circumstances. Thus, the premise that issues of law require different treatment presents some of the most difficult problems in delineating the scope of collateral estoppel.[39]

The danger in allowing collateral estoppel to apply freely to issues of law is that the doctrine might cause inequities among litigants[40] when the law has changed and estoppel is asserted for findings based on the earlier law. Discarded rules of law would apply between particular parties whenever an issue recurs between them that was the subject of a previous lawsuit. For example, if a taxpayer obtained a judgment that a certain transaction is tax exempt, collateral estoppel arguably would preclude the Internal Revenue Service from relitigating the same legal issues with the same taxpayer if the transaction were to be repeated during the next taxable year. To allow collateral estoppel to work in that way would give that taxpayer an unfair advantage if, in accordance with a subsequent reinterpretation of the law, other taxpayers are taxed for similar transactions. This possibility was discussed by the Supreme Court in Commissioner v. Sunnen.

> Such consequences, however, are neither necessitated nor justified by the principle of collateral estoppel. The principle is designed to prevent repetitious lawsuits over matters which have once been decided and which have remained substantially static, factually and legally. It is not meant to create vested rights in decisions that have become obsolete or erroneous with time, thereby causing inequities among taxpayers.[41]

A leading case for the proposition that collateral estoppel is inapplicable to issues of law is United States v. Moser.[42] Moser was a captain in the United States Navy. Upon retirement in 1904, Moser sued for and received enhanced retirement benefits under a statute providing that officers who had served in the Civil War should receive retirement

---

interest in constitutional issues could freeze doctrine in areas of the law where responsiveness to changing patterns of conduct or social mores is critical." Montana v. U.S., 440 U.S. 147, 163, 99 S.Ct. 970, 978, 59 L.Ed.2d 210 (1979).

38. Some certainty is provided for pure issues of law by virtue of stare decisis. See § 14.1, above.

39. See generally 18 C. Wright, A. Miller & E. Cooper, Jurisdiction and Related Matters § 4425; Buckley, Issue Preclusion & Issues of Law: A Doctrinal Framework Based on Rules of Recognition, Jurisdiction & Legal History, 24 Hous.L.Rev. 875 (1987); Hazard, Preclusion as to Issues of Law: The Legal System's Interest, 70 Iowa L.Rev. 81 (1984).

40. Scott, Collateral Estoppel by Judgment, 56 Harv.L.Rev. 1, 7 (1942).

41. 333 U.S. 591, 599, 68 S.Ct. 715, 720, 92 L.Ed. 898 (1948).

42. 266 U.S. 236, 45 S.Ct. 66, 69 L.Ed. 262 (1924).

benefits for the next highest rank. During that war he had been a midshipman at the Naval Academy. Subsequently, another decision held that service at the Naval Academy did not qualify for retirement benefits, citing a statute that had been overlooked in the first Moser trial. That decision notwithstanding, Moser, relying on his original judgment, prevailed in three later suits for additional retirement benefits withheld by the Navy. The third action was appealed to the Supreme Court. The government contended that collateral estoppel could not preclude relitigation of an issue of law that had been decided wrongly in the first trial. The Court agreed that collateral estoppel does not apply to pure issues of law, but held that this case involved "a fact, question or right distinctly adjudged in the original action" which "cannot be disputed in a subsequent action, even though the determination was reached upon an erroneous view or by an erroneous application of the law."[43] Thus, collateral estoppel may preclude "mixed issues of law and fact." The problem becomes identifying what constitutes a mixed law/fact issue.

The Restatement First of Judgments sought the same general result as arrived at in Moser by suggesting that determination of an issue of law is not conclusive in a later lawsuit unless both suits concern the same subject matter or transaction.[44] The idea was to restrict collateral estoppel to particular rulings about particular events. If the same legal issue arises between the same parties fortuitously in two unrelated proceedings, no estoppel is created. If by sheer coincidence two motorists collide with one another while driving on separate occasions—different days and places—legal issues such as the standard for negligence decided in one trial may not be imposed by collateral estoppel on the other. Either party would be free to relitigate all legal issues as if that party had collided with any other driver on the road; a party would not be estopped because of the bizarre misfortune of having had an accident with someone with whom he had collided before.

Some litigants are so situated that they come into conflict repeatedly over the same legal issues. The most notable examples of this are actions between the Internal Revenue Service and taxpayers.[45] A taxpayer who conducts the same type of business continuously through several taxable years may face the Service in litigation on the same legal issues annually. If an issue of law decided in one year has no collateral estoppel effect on the next year's transactions, then much wasteful and repetitive litigation may ensue.

Recognizing this, the Restatement Second of Judgments has provided that preclusive effect may be given to issues of law unless the two actions present claims that are "substantially unrelated" or "a new determination (of the issue) is warranted in order to take account of an

---

43. 266 U.S. at 242, 45 S.Ct. at 67.

44. Restatement First of Judgments § 70 (1942).

45. For old but still valuable discussions of collateral estoppel principles in the tax area, see Griswold, Res Judicata in Federal Tax Cases, 46 Yale L.J. 1320 (1937); Sellin, The Sunnen Case—A Logical Terminus to the "Issue" of Res Judicata in Tax Cases, 4 Tax L.Rev. 363 (1949).

intervening change in the applicable legal context or otherwise to avoid inequitable administration of the laws."[46] This clause is meant to cover situations such as arose in the Sunnen case.[47] As already described,[48] the taxpayer there made several contracts to transfer income from various patents to his wife. Prior determinations concerning the taxability of earlier contracts could not be invoked as collateral estoppel for later, similar contracts. A somewhat different question was presented, however, by successive payments made under a single contract. A 1935 judgment had held that installments paid from 1928–1934 under a particular contract were not taxable to Sunnen. Should collateral estoppel exempt later installments paid under the same contract from taxation?

The situation appears closely analogous to Moser's retirement benefits. The Moser Court held that the earlier decision had been on a mixed issue of law and fact so that collateral estoppel should apply. The Sunnen Court held that collateral estoppel effect should be denied, noting in particular that, since the earlier suit, several important cases had been decided on the issue of taxability of transferred assets. Had the original case been presented after these cases, it probably would have been decided differently. The change in the "legal climate" necessitated a new trial of the facts.[49] Otherwise, the Court reasoned, some taxpayers—namely those who had obtained judgments before the shift in legal doctrine—would be favored, and others correspondingly harmed.

Similarly, in Young Men's Christian Association of St. Louis v. Sestric,[50] three prior court opinions had affirmed that the St. Louis Y.M.C.A. building was liable for taxes because it was not a charitable institution. Although the facts concerning the Y.M.C.A. operation had not changed materially, later decisions by the state supreme court ruled that similar operations run by the Salvation Army and Goodwill were tax exempt. When the Y.M.C.A. tried a fourth time to gain tax exempt status, the state supreme court held that collateral estoppel could not be invoked to preclude this fourth attempt.

> To hold this case res judicata would result in applying forever one rule of law between two parties (Y.M.C.A. and the City of St. Louis) and another rule of law among all other parties in similar or the same factual situations. The injustice of any such application of res judicata or collateral estoppel is at once apparent.[51]

---

46. Restatement Second of Judgments § 28(2) (1982). For an example of how this standard is applied, see Burlington N. R.R. Co. v. Hyundai Merchant Marine Co., 63 F.3d 1227 (3d Cir.1995).

47. Commissioner v. Sunnen, 333 U.S. 591, 68 S.Ct. 715, 92 L.Ed. 898 (1948).

48. See text at notes 4–7, above.

49. In some instances the change in the law will be clear, as when a statute on which the first judgment is based has been amended or a new statute is enacted. See, e.g., Grosz v. City of Miami Beach, Florida, 82 F.3d 1005 (11th Cir.1996); Continental Oil Co. v. Jones, 176 F.2d 519 (10th Cir. 1949). In other cases, such as Sunnen, the law changes more slowly or sometimes, more subtly by judicial decisions, and there may be some disputes concerning whether there actually has been a change in the law. See, e.g., North Georgia Elec. Membership Corp. v. City of Calhoun, Georgia, 989 F.2d 429 (11th Cir.1993).

50. 362 Mo. 551, 242 S.W.2d 497 (1951).

51. 242 S.W.2d at 507.

The concern that the vagueness of issues of law makes them unreliable for preclusion purposes is accommodated by taking into account changes in the underlying facts or in the legal climate. In making this determination, a court should consider the clarity of any particular change in the law or facts, the need for equality between litigants at any particular point in time, and the goals of finality and certainty promoted by the application of collateral estoppel. Although balancing these concerns in particular cases may not be easy, it is certain to be more meaningful than engaging in semantic arguments concerning what constitutes an issue of law as opposed to a mixed issue of law and fact. Thus, perhaps not surprisingly, most modern courts seem to have rejected the law/fact distinction as an automatic barrier to collateral estoppel.[52]

Although abandoning the rule that issues of pure law should not be given preclusive effect has much to commend it, one Supreme Court decision suggests that when this is done other problems may arise. The case, United States v. Stauffer Chemical Company,[53] involved attempts by the Environmental Protection Agency (EPA) to inspect plants for purposes of enforcing national air quality standards. The EPA had attempted to use private contracting firms to carry out inspections of Stauffer plants in Tennessee and Wyoming, and Stauffer had refused entry on the ground that the Clean Air Act provided for inspections only by "authorized representatives," not by private contractors. The Tenth Circuit upheld Stauffer's interpretation, and when the case from Tennessee reached the Sixth Circuit, it gave issue preclusive effect to the Tenth Circuit determination. The Supreme Court affirmed, noting that the cases arose from "virtually identical facts" and that the application of estoppel would foster judicial economy and protect Stauffer from burdensome litigation. Thus, the preclusive effect of a pure issue of law was recognized.

The decision creates a serious problem, however, in that Stauffer also maintained plants in California, where the Ninth Circuit had ruled in a different case with different parties that private contractors could be used. Did the Supreme Court's ruling mean that the EPA could not sue Stauffer in the Ninth Circuit to force compliance? If so, then unequal treatment would be accorded businesses in the Ninth Circuit depending on whether they had achieved a favorable ruling in some other circuit. Justice Rehnquist, who wrote for the Court, refused to answer the question, commenting that that issue was not before the justices.[54] In a concurring opinion, Justice White suggested that Stauffer could not use the Tenth Circuit ruling as collateral estoppel in the Ninth Circuit, distinguishing the present case on the ground that the Sixth Circuit had not ruled on the question so that the application of collateral estoppel

---

52. See U.S. v. Stauffer Chem. Co., 464 U.S. 165, 104 S.Ct. 575, 78 L.Ed.2d 388 (1984); U.S. v. Mendoza, 464 U.S. 154, 104 S.Ct. 568, 78 L.Ed.2d 379 (1984). These cases and their implications for suits against the government are explored in Levin & Leeson, Issue Preclusion Against the United States Government, 70 Iowa L.Rev. 113 (1984).

53. 464 U.S. 165, 104 S.Ct. 575, 78 L.Ed.2d 388 (1984).

54. 464 U.S. at 174, 104 S.Ct. at 580.

there did not create an intra-circuit conflict. The need to promote even-handed application of the law within each circuit may require that collateral estoppel effect not be given to a particular judgment.[55]

Whether Justice White's solution to the problem posed by intercircuit conflicts will be adopted remains unclear. The important thing to note is that there exist difficulties and conflicting policies that must be addressed when collateral estoppel is asserted to preclude litigation on issues of pure law.[56]

§ 14.11 Requirements for the Application of Collateral Estoppel

The requirements for collateral estoppel are easier to state than to apply.[1] As already noted, the court first must find that the issues on which collateral estoppel is being asserted are identical in both actions.[2] In addition, the person asserting estoppel must show that the issue to be precluded actually was litigated and decided in the prior action and that it was necessary to the court's judgment.[3]

Because collateral estoppel may be used in cases involving different claims and, in some instances, even different parties[4] than the original proceeding, it has the potential to trap unwary litigants who might have litigated the first suit differently had they realized the far reaching effects the determination might have. These requirements thus serve to assure that only those issues that were fully and fairly decided will be binding in subsequent litigation.

In many instances, an inquiry into whether a particular issue actually was litigated in a prior action will pose few problems because the pleadings and the judgment will make it clear whether the issue was fully tried. Similarly, it generally is agreed that default judgments,[5] admissions made during discovery[6] or stipulations made prior to trial[7]

---

55. 464 U.S. at 178, 104 S.Ct. at 581, 582.

56. For some other policy issues that have arisen, see § 14.12, below.

§ 14.11

1. See 18 C. Wright, A. Miller & E. Cooper, Jurisdiction and Related Matters §§ 4419–21.

2. See § 14.10, above.

3. Restatement Second of Judgments § 28 (1982).

4. See § 14.14, below.

5. The early rule was that default judgments preclude litigation of every issue that would have to be resolved to support the judgment after a full trial, and some courts still adhere to that rule. See Kapp v. Naturelle, Inc., 611 F.2d 703 (8th Cir.1979); Reich v. Cochran, 151 N.Y. 122, 45 N.E. 367 (1896). However, that rule has been soundly criticized. See Rosenberg, Collateral Estoppel in New York, 44 St. John's L.Rev.

165, 173 (1969); Note, Collateral Estoppel in Default Judgments: The Case for Abolition, 70 Colum.L.Rev. 522 (1970). And the weight of authority now supports the conclusion that default judgments generally should not be given any issue preclusive effect. See Matter of McMillan, 579 F.2d 289 (3d Cir.1978); Baron v. Bryant, 556 F.Supp. 531 (D.Hawai'i 1983); Gwynn v. Wilhelm, 226 Or. 606, 360 P.2d 312 (1961). When a party has appeared and litigated a matter, a default judgment entered as a penalty for discovery violations may support collateral estoppel effect on the litigated issue, however. See In re Ansari, 113 F.3d 17 (4th Cir.1997), cert. denied ___ U.S. ___, 118 S.Ct. 298.

6. Any admission by a party pursuant to a request for admission under Fed.Civ. Proc. Rule 36 "is for the purpose of the

7. See note 7 on page 690.

should not be a basis for according issues collateral estoppel treatment because in none of these situations were the issues actually tried, that is, subject to an adversary presentation and consequent judgment. By requiring that the issues be litigated, not stipulated or conceded, the courts foster the ability of parties to agree on certain issues before trial without concern that an agreement not to contest a particular issue will have an adverse impact in ways not foreseen at that time. For these reasons, consent judgments[8] or judgments entered as a result of a settlement[9] typically cannot be used as the basis for issue preclusion.[10] Conversely, summary judgments[11] or judgments entered on a directed verdict motion[12] may be given collateral estoppel effect. Although the litigation terminated before a full trial was completed, the judgment was not a product of the parties' consent and is a final decision on the merits.

The requirement of actual adjudication causes particular problems when a review of the pleadings or pretrial orders and the resulting judgment fails to reveal whether certain issues framed at an early stage in the proceedings actually were litigated at trial and thus are embraced in the judgment.[13] This problem can become particularly acute in complex or multiple claim cases when the pleadings, although meeting the notice standards of the pleading rules,[14] do not provide sufficient detail to expose adequately all the issues that might have been raised, and the judgment sheds no additional light on the question.[15] The problem is not

pending action only and is not an admission for any other purpose nor may it be used against the party in any other proceeding." Fed.Civ.Proc. Rule 36(b).

7. Sekaquaptewa v. MacDonald, 575 F.2d 239 (9th Cir.1978); Environmental Defense Fund, Inc. v. Alexander, 467 F.Supp. 885, 903 (N.D.Miss.1979), affirmed on other grounds 614 F.2d 474 (5th Cir.1980), rehearing denied 616 F.2d 568, cert. denied 449 U.S. 919; Seay v. International Ass'n of Machinists, 360 F.Supp. 123 (C.D.Cal.1973).

8. U.S. v. International Bldg. Co., 345 U.S. 502, 73 S.Ct. 807, 97 L.Ed. 1182 (1953); Lipsky v. Commonwealth United Corp., 551 F.2d 887 (2d Cir.1976); U.S. v. California Portland Cement Co., 413 F.2d 161 (9th Cir.1969). See Shapiro, Should a Guilty Plea Have Preclusive Effect?, 70 Iowa L.Rev. 27 (1984).

9. Standard Oil Co. of Kentucky v. Illinois Cent. R.R. Co., 421 F.2d 201 (5th Cir. 1969); McLellan v. Atchison Ins. Agency, Inc., 81 Haw. 62, 912 P.2d 559 (Ct.App. 1996).

10. Collateral estoppel effect may be given to consent judgments or stipulated issues if it is clear that the parties intended their agreement to have that effect. Green v. Ancora–Citronelle Corp., 577 F.2d 1380 (9th Cir.1978). See James, Consent Judg-

ments as Collateral Estoppel, 108 U.Pa. L.Rev. 173 (1959).

11. Exhibitors Poster Exchange, Inc. v. National Screen Serv. Corp., 421 F.2d 1313, 1319 (5th Cir.1970), cert. denied 400 U.S. 991; Eidelberg v. Zellermayer, 5 A.D.2d 658, 174 N.Y.S.2d 300 (1958), affirmed 6 N.Y.2d 815, 188 N.Y.S.2d 204, 159 N.E.2d 691 (1959).

12. Simon v. M/V Hialeah, 431 F.2d 867 (5th Cir.1970).

13. For an example of the kind of detailed inquiry that may be required, see Henderson v. Snider Bros., Inc., 409 A.2d 1083 (D.C.App.1979) (Maryland decree effecting sale and foreclosure of property owned by plaintiffs had no collateral estoppel effect on plaintiffs' later claim that they were induced fraudulently to purchase the property when plaintiffs pleaded fraud only as an offset to any judgment entered in the Maryland suit, no evidence concerning fraud was presented in that suit, and the Maryland court took no explicit position on the fraud issue).

14. See §§ 5.7–5.9, above, on pleading standards.

15. Judgments entered as a result of a general verdict reveal only whether liability was found and, if so, for how much. It is only when special verdicts are used or when

one of a failure of proof; an issue may be fully litigated even though the ultimate decision is that the party with the burden of proof failed to adduce sufficient evidence to establish that issue at trial.[16] Rather, the question that arises is whether an issue suggested in the pleadings actually was in contest during trial or, even if it were litigated at the trial, whether the judgment that was entered necessarily embraced that issue.

Assume Alpha and Beta are involved in an auto collision. A sues B, claiming that B was negligent, causing a series of injuries for which A seeks damages. B defends by asserting that A was contributorily negligent, which would completely bar recovery under the governing law. If a general verdict is rendered for B, it may have resulted because the jury found A to be negligent, or B to be free from negligence, or both. However, in the absence of a reliable way of determining which of the grounds actually was decided, the judgment cannot be given collateral estoppel effect.

The party asserting collateral estoppel bears the burden of showing what issues actually were decided.[17] In some instances the party may satisfy this burden simply by showing that, given the judgment rendered and the issues raised in the pleadings, the logical inference is that a particular issue must have been litigated and decided in order for the particular result to be reached.[18] Thus, in the hypothetical above, if A had prevailed, that judgment would be reached only if B were found negligent and A free from negligence; both issues were necessarily and actually decided and may be given collateral estoppel effect.

If inferences cannot be drawn because the presence of multiple claims or alternative defenses prevents any inference about which claims or issues support the judgment, evidence extrinsic to the formal record may have to be used.[19] Although the use of extrinsic evidence is well-recognized,[20] some suggestion has been made that only evidence that supports the judgment, not that which undermines it, may be considered.[21] It also is stated that only evidence of "open and tangible" facts may be received, no evidence may be used of subjective matters such as

findings of fact are utilized in judge trials that the judgment may include the information necessary to decide questions of issue preclusion. See §§ 12.1–12.2, above, for a discussion of findings and verdicts.

16. Continental Can Co. v. Marshall, 603 F.2d 590 (7th Cir.1979); U.S. v. Silliman, 167 F.2d 607 (3d Cir.1948), cert. denied 335 U.S. 825; Patterson v. Saunders, 194 Va. 607, 74 S.E.2d 204 (1953), cert. denied 345 U.S. 998.

17. Spilman v. Harley, 656 F.2d 224 (6th Cir.1981); Gulf Tampa Drydock Co. v. Germanischer Lloyd, 634 F.2d 874 (5th Cir. 1981); Illinois Cent. Gulf R.R. Co. v. Parks, 181 Ind.App. 141, 390 N.E.2d 1078 (1979).

18. Grubb v. Public Utilities Comm'n, 281 U.S. 470, 477, 50 S.Ct. 374, 377, 74 L.Ed. 972 (1930); Wishnewsky v. Town of Saugus, 325 Mass. 191, 89 N.E.2d 783 (1950).

19. Russell v. Place, 94 U.S. (4 Otto) 606, 608, 24 L.Ed. 214 (1876).

20. Miles v. Caldwell, 69 U.S. (2 Wall.) 35, 43, 17 L.Ed. 755 (1864); Home Owners Federal Savs. & Loan Ass'n v. Northwestern Fire & Marine Ins. Co., 354 Mass. 448, 238 N.E.2d 55 (1968).

21. Washington, A. & G. Steam Packet Co. v. Sickles, 72 U.S. (5 Wall.) 580, 592, 18 L.Ed. 550 (1866); Slater v. Skirving, 51 Neb. 108, 70 N.W. 493 (1897).

testimony of the judge as to what was intended by the judgment.[22] In any event, if the party asserting collateral estoppel fails to introduce sufficient extrinsic evidence, and an ambiguity remains, issue preclusion will be denied.[23]

Even if it is clear that an issue has been fully litigated, it may not be given collateral estoppel effect unless the court can find that the determination of that issue in the prior lawsuit was necessary or essential to the judgment.[24] Incidental issues or those that merely provide evidence relevant to the determination of the major matters in the dispute,[25] although actually litigated, have no collateral estoppel effect.[26]

There are several important reasons for this limitation. Notions of fairness require that only those issues that have been fully litigated and considered by the parties should be excluded from future actions. Nonessential issues, even though discussed at trial, ought not to be given binding effect because they may have received only passing attention by either or both of the parties, or, for that matter, the judge. On the other hand, issues that were necessary for the judgment presumably will have been given the complete attention of the parties, as well as the court or fact-finder.[27] Finally, findings not necessary to a lawsuit's result seldom are reviewable by an appellate court, especially when they are decided in

22. "[N]o testimony should be received except of open and tangible facts—matters which are susceptible of evidence on both sides. A judgment is a solemn record. Parties have a right to rely upon it. It should not lightly be disturbed, and ought never to be overthrown or limited by the oral testimony of a judge or juror of what he had in mind at the time of the decision." Fayerweather v. Ritch, 195 U.S. 276, 307, 25 S.Ct. 58, 67–68, 49 L.Ed. 193 (1904).

The protection of the sanctity of the jury deliberation process also supports the refusal to allow juror testimony explaining what was included in the verdict. Ohio–Sealy Mattress Mfg. Co. v. Kaplan, 90 F.R.D. 11 (N.D.Ill.1980), affirmed in part, reversed in part on other grounds 745 F.2d 441 (7th Cir.1984), cert. denied 471 U.S. 1125. See generally § 12.5, above.

23. Glass v. U.S. Rubber Co., 382 F.2d 378 (10th Cir.1967); Stout v. Pearson, 180 Cal.App.2d 211, 4 Cal.Rptr. 313 (1960). But see Kelley v. Curtiss, 16 N.J. 265, 108 A.2d 431 (1954) (jury verdict for defendant in negligence suit held to include findings that defendant was free from negligence and plaintiff was contributorily negligent).

24. Block v. Bourbon County Commissioners, 99 U.S. (9 Otto) 686, 693, 25 L.Ed. 491 (1878); Fletcher v. Atex, Inc., 68 F.3d 1451 (2d Cir.1995); Synanon Church v. U.S., 820 F.2d 421 (D.C.Cir.1987).

25. The distinction between mediate and ultimate facts for issue preclusion purposes rests on the same concerns as does the requirement that the issues precluded be essential: is it reasonable to assume that the parties in the first action foresaw the possibility that an adverse determination on some issue could be used in a different lawsuit to their detriment. See the discussion in § 14.10 at notes 26–36, above. Some courts discuss whether an issue is essential in terms of whether it relates to an ultimate fact. E.g., Hinchey v. Sellers, 7 N.Y.2d 287, 197 N.Y.S.2d 129, 165 N.E.2d 156 (1959). It has been argued most persuasively, however, that courts would be better served if they abandoned the attempt to distinguish between mediate and ultimate facts and instead focussed on whether "the fact in question was a necessary step in arriving at the final judgment, provided that at the time it was foreseeable that the fact might be of importance in future litigation." Developments in the Law—Res Judicata, 65 Harv.L.Rev. 818, 843 (1952). See also Restatement Second of Judgments § 27, comment j (1982).

26. See, e.g., Association of Bituminous Contractors, Inc. v. Andrus, 581 F.2d 853 (D.C.Cir.1978); Wilson v. Wilson, 186 Mont. 290, 607 P.2d 539 (1980); Thal v. Krawitz, 365 Pa. 110, 73 A.2d 376 (1950).

27. The Evergreens v. Nunan, 141 F.2d 927, 929 (2d Cir.1944), cert. denied 323 U.S. 720.

favor of the prevailing party.[28] Although availability of appellate review is not an absolute prerequisite for applying collateral estoppel, the absence of review of nonessential findings lends further weight to those arguments against their collateral estoppel effect.

Consider, again, the car collision involving Alpha and Beta. Assume that the court explicitly finds both drivers negligent and gives judgment for B, as required by the law of contributory negligence. If B now sues A for her injuries, A cannot successfully urge collateral estoppel on the issue of B's negligence. Once the first court decided that A was negligent it was obliged to give judgment for the defendant and the further determination that B also was at fault was not necessary or essential.[29] B, as the winning party in that first suit, had no incentive or ability to appeal that adverse determination. A's chance to avoid relitigation and a possible conflicting result depends on whether claim preclusion may be invoked on the ground that B omitted her personal injury claim in the first action and cannot raise it now.[30]

On the other hand, alternative grounds for a particular judgment may be given full preclusive effect.[31] The courts will not attempt to discern which ground was the necessary one when either would support the judgment. In this situation, it is presumed that the court fully considered all the issues raised and the losing party had a full incentive to obtain appellate review.[32] Consequently, there is not the same concern about whether there was a full opportunity and incentive to litigate all the adverse findings.[33]

§ 14.12 Exceptions to the Application of Collateral Estoppel

Even when an issue has been fully litigated in a lawsuit, and its determination was necessary to the outcome of the trial, there still are a

---

28. See Bell v. Dillard Dep't Stores, Inc., 85 F.3d 1451 (10th Cir.1996) (party had no opportunity to appeal pretrial probable cause finding after ultimate dismissal of the charges at trial); Rios v. Davis, 373 S.W.2d 386, 387–88 (Tex.Civ.App.1963) ("Since the judgment was in favor of Rios he had no right or opportunity to complain of or to appeal from the finding that he was guilty of such negligence even if such finding had been without any support whatever in the evidence. The right of appeal is from a judgment and not from a finding.").

29. Rios v. Davis, 373 S.W.2d 386 (Tex. Civ.App.1963); Cambria v. Jeffery, 307 Mass. 49, 29 N.E.2d 555 (1940).

30. See § 14.6, above.

31. Winters v. Lavine, 574 F.2d 46 (2d Cir.1978); Malloy v. Trombley, 50 N.Y.2d 46, 427 N.Y.S.2d 969, 405 N.E.2d 213 (1980); Patterson v. Saunders, 194 Va. 607,

74 S.E.2d 204 (1953), cert. denied 345 U.S. 998. But see C.B. Marchant Co. v. Eastern Foods, Inc., 756 F.2d 317, 319 (4th Cir. 1985); Halpern v. Schwartz, 426 F.2d 102 (2d Cir.1970).

32. This will not always be true. A losing party who is convinced that one of the grounds on which the decision is based is correct so that there is no chance of reversal will have no incentive to file an appeal as to the other ground, even though it was tainted with error.

33. The Restatement Second takes the position that alternative determinations by a court of first instance ought not to be given collateral estoppel effect. Restatement Second of Judgments § 27, comment i (1982). If an appeal is taken and the appellate court affirms the judgment on both alternative grounds, then issue preclusion will apply. Restatement Second of Judgments § 27, comment o (1982).

few instances in which collateral estoppel will not be applied.[1] Stated generally, exceptions to the normal application of collateral estoppel will be made when other substantive policies are deemed to outweigh the policies of judicial economy and avoidance of inconsistent results that are fostered by issue preclusion. The number of substantive policies deemed significant enough to override collateral estoppel necessarily is limited and depends upon the facts and circumstances of each case. Further, the growing awareness that the courts are overcrowded has served to heighten the emphasis on judicial economy, making the courts less receptive to arguments that other policies require relitigation of issues that appear to have been fully determined. A brief exploration of a few of the cases involving the question when exceptions are appropriate best illustrates their scope and limits.

One of the most notable examples of a substantive policy exception to collateral estoppel involves antitrust litigation and is traceable to Judge Learned Hand's 1955 decision in Lyons v. Westinghouse Electric Corporation.[2] The case raised the question whether a state court determination that a contract was not illegal under federal antitrust laws would be binding in a later federal antitrust action brought by the former defendant in the state court proceeding. Judge Hand recognized that ordinarily antitrust matters are within the exclusive jurisdiction of the federal courts, but that the antitrust issue was properly before the state court because it was necessary for that court to determine the contract's legality to render its decision. However, the question whether that determination should be given collateral estoppel effect depended upon whether the grant of exclusive jurisdiction suggested that only federal courts should make the ultimate determination of whether those laws were violated for purposes of imposing liability.[3] Judge Hand concluded that the exclusive federal court jurisdiction over antitrust matters was designed to promote the uniform administration of the antitrust laws and that that could be accomplished only "by an untrammeled jurisdiction of the federal courts."[4] Thus, the decision to assert exclusive federal jurisdiction was linked to a congressional desire for uniform statutory interpretation that arguably could be satisfied only by allowing relitigation of any antitrust issue decided by a state court.[5]

This exception is less broad than it first seems. Judge Hand retained for the federal courts the exclusive authority to determine the ultimate question whether the antitrust laws had been violated. He suggested, however, that findings on the underlying facts concerning the parties'

---

§ 14.12

1. The question whether issue preclusion applies when there has been a change in the law is discussed in § 14.10 at notes 46–52, above.

2. 222 F.2d 184 (2d Cir.1955), cert. denied 350 U.S. 825.

3. The case also raised the issue whether if the jurisdiction of the state court is limited, rulings on matters normally beyond its authority should not be binding in

subsequent cases. 222 F.2d at 188–89. This issue is discussed at notes 21–28, below.

4. 222 F.2d at 189.

5. The policies and arguments surrounding the use of collateral estoppel in actions within the exclusive jurisdiction of the federal courts are explored more fully in 18 C. Wright, A. Miller & E. Cooper, Jurisdiction and Related Matters § 4470.

business arrangements could be given collateral estoppel effect.[6] For example, if the state court ruled on the existence of a contract between the parties and what that contract required, including what the geographic scope of the agreement was, those findings, he intimated, would not have to be relitigated in a subsequent antitrust action in which the defendant was charged with monopolizing the market. Similar conclusions have been reached in other contexts in which the federal courts have exclusive jurisdiction; issue preclusion has been allowed with respect to state court decisions on the underlying facts in patent,[7] securities,[8] and bankruptcy actions.[9]

Many courts[10] have declined to follow Lyons and thus have rejected any notion that exclusive federal jurisdiction, alone, poses a barrier to the use of collateral estoppel. The impact of that conclusion is most important because several states have adopted state antitrust and securities laws that virtually are identical with the federal schemes. Conse-

6. Judge Hand reached this conclusion by interpreting the Supreme Court's decision on a similar issue in the patent field, Becher v. Contoure Labs., Inc., 279 U.S. 388, 49 S.Ct. 356, 73 L.Ed. 752 (1929). Reviewing that decision, he concluded that it "looks as though the distinction were between the finding of one of the constituent facts that together make up a claim and the entire congeries of such facts, taken as a unit; an estoppel is good as to the first but not as to the second." 222 F.2d at 188. This distinction is tied to the one then recognized between mediate and ultimate facts, with collateral estoppel effect given only to the latter. For a discussion of that distinction, see § 14.10 at notes 26–36, above.

7. Becher v. Contoure Labs., Inc., 279 U.S. 388, 49 S.Ct. 356, 73 L.Ed. 752 (1929) (plaintiff in patent infringement suit estopped by state court determination that defendant was the true inventor and plaintiff had obtained the patent surreptitiously); Vanderveer v. Erie Malleable Iron Co., 238 F.2d 510 (3d Cir.1956), cert. denied 353 U.S. 937 (collateral estoppel applied to state court determination that licensee's product was not within scope of patent). See generally Cooper, State Law of Patent Exploitation, 56 Minn.L.Rev. 313, 322 (1972). Compare In re Convertible Rowing Exerciser Patent Litigation, 814 F.Supp. 1197 (D.Del. 1993) (collateral estoppel effect given to fact finding of International Trade Commission regarding patent validity).

8. Calvert Fire Ins. Co. v. American Mut. Reinsurance Co., 600 F.2d 1228, 1236 n. 18 (7th Cir.1979); Connelly v. Balkwill, 174 F.Supp. 49 (N.D.Ohio 1959), affirmed per curiam 279 F.2d 685 (6th Cir.1960). See generally Note, The Res Judicata and Collateral Estoppel Effect of Prior State Suits on Actions Under SEC Rule 10b–5, 69 Yale L.J. 606 (1960).

9. The use of collateral estoppel in bankruptcy is well-recognized. See Heiser v. Woodruff, 327 U.S. 726, 66 S.Ct. 853, 90 L.Ed. 970 (1946). However, the 1970 amendments to Section 17 of the Bankruptcy Act place the issue of dischargeability within the exclusive jurisdiction of the federal bankruptcy courts so that state court or other federal court findings regarding dischargeability should not be binding. On the other hand, determinations that a particular transaction was fraudulent may be given preclusive effect. The question left to the bankruptcy court is whether the fraud found by the prior court should result in making the debt nondischargeable. See In re Houtman, 568 F.2d 651 (9th Cir.1978) (state court judgment based on fraud establishes a prima facie case that it represents a nondischargeable debt). See also Brown v. Felsen, 442 U.S. 127, 139 n. 10, 99 S.Ct. 2205, 2213 n. 10, 60 L.Ed.2d 767 (1979). For a discussion of the issue, see Donald & Cooper, Collateral Estoppel in Section 523(c) Dischargeability Proceedings: When Is a Default Judgment Actually Litigated, 12 Bank.Dev.J. 321 (1996).

10. See, e.g., Azalea Drive–In Theatre, Inc. v. Hanft, 540 F.2d 713 (4th Cir.1976), cert. denied 430 U.S. 941; In re TransOcean Tender Offer Secs. Litigation, 427 F.Supp. 1211, 1221 (N.D.Ill.1977) (Securities Exchange Act litigation). One law review comment after Lyons suggests that many courts refused to follow its result. See Note, Collateral Estoppel of State Court Judgment in Federal Antitrust Suits, 51 Calif.L.Rev. 955, 964 (1963).

quently, if an action is brought first in the state courts under the applicable state law, most of the issues ruled upon will be identical to those necessary for federal liability.[11] As a practical matter, applying collateral estoppel to those underlying facts will preclude the possibility of a different result in the federal courts.[12] Indeed, more recent decisions in the Courts of Appeals have suggested that whatever the perceived need for uniform interpretation of the federal laws at the time of Judge Hand's opinion, that no longer is the case and the need for judicial economy outweighs the desire for exclusivity.[13]

In the past, strong arguments also were raised for an exception to collateral estoppel in actions involving federally protected civil rights.[14] It was argued that, although the federal courts were not given exclusive jurisdiction to determine actions brought under the various civil rights statutes, there was reason to believe that Congress created a federal remedy because the state courts were not able to protect adequately the rights of the persons involved. Thus, the guarantee of a federal forum in which to litigate fully questions concerning the enforcement of federal law was necessary, and the enforcement scheme could be impaired substantially if collateral estoppel effect were given to state court determinations in subsequent federal civil rights litigation.

The Supreme Court has put these contentions to rest. In Allen v. McCurry,[15] it ruled that collateral estoppel could be used in a Section 1983[16] suit raising Fourth Amendment search and seizure issues that were determined against the federal plaintiff in a state criminal trial. The Court found nothing in the statute's legislative history that suggested that Congress intended to create an exception to the normal preclusion rules.[17] As long as fair procedures were used in the state trial courts,

---

11. There have been some suggestions that res judicata should prevent any federal litigation, although the traditional rule has been that because the plaintiff was not permitted to join the federal claims in the state action, res judicata would not be applied. See § 14.7 at notes 14-17, above.

12. Some courts have noted the identity between the federal and state schemes finding that the state and federal claims comprise one cause of action and thus that the federal suit is barred by res judicata. See, e.g., Derish v. San Mateo–Burlingame Bd. of Realtors, 724 F.2d 1347 (9th Cir. 1983); Nash County Bd. of Educ. v. Biltmore Co., 640 F.2d 484 (4th Cir.1981), cert. denied 454 U.S. 878. Because these cases all arose after full litigation in the state court, they involve the question whether the same issues should be relitigated, not whether omitted facts or theories may be raised in the federal courts. Thus, although they speak in terms of res judicata, they express preferences for avoiding duplicative litigation and inconsistent results, the policies underlying collateral estoppel.

13. See Marrese v. American Academy of Orthopaedic Surgeons, 726 F.2d 1150 (7th Cir.1984), reversed on other grounds 470 U.S. 373, 105 S.Ct. 1327, 84 L.Ed.2d 274 (1985) (res judicata opinion). For a somewhat different approach to reconciling exclusive jurisdiction and the policies underlying collateral estoppel, see Note, The Collateral Estoppel Effect of Prior State Court Findings in Cases Within Exclusive Federal Jurisdiction, 91 Harv.L.Rev. 1281 (1978).

14. See 18 C. Wright, A. Miller & E. Cooper, Jurisdiction and Related Matters § 4471; Vestal, State Court Judgment as Preclusive in Section 1983 Litigation in a Federal Court, 27 Okla.L.Rev. 185 (1974).

15. 449 U.S. 90, 101 S.Ct. 411, 66 L.Ed.2d 308 (1980).

16. 42 U.S.C.A. § 1983.

17. "The actual basis of the Court of Appeals' holding appears to be a generally framed principle that every person asserting a federal right is entitled to one unencumbered opportunity to litigate that right

there was no justification for allowing relitigation of the federal issues. Further, in Kremer v. Chemical Construction Corporation,[18] the Court similarly concluded that nothing in the legislative history of Title VII prevented a federal court from giving collateral estoppel effect to a state court decision upholding a state administrative agency's rejection of an employment discrimination claim.[19]

The key question in these cases was whether there was some legislative purpose or policy underlying the particular remedial scheme that suggested that interpretations of that law should be solely within the competence of the federal courts.[20] That such a policy may exist must be considered when determining whether issues decided in a state court may be precluded in later litigation in a federal court. However, as the preceding discussion illustrates, the Supreme Court has yet to identify any federal statute as embracing an implied exclusivity principle that would prevent the normal operation of collateral estoppel.

Having said this, it is necessary to return briefly to Judge Hand's opinion in Lyons v. Westinghouse Electric Corporation, in which he made a second argument that collateral estoppel may be disallowed because the jurisdiction of the tribunal that rendered the first judgment was limited.[21] As discussed earlier, the fact that the judgment rendering court was one of limited jurisdiction does not necessarily prevent giving full collateral estoppel effect to its judgments.[22] If the limitations on the court reflect some significant differences between the quality and extensiveness of the procedures available in that court,[23] however, so that a party receiving an adverse determination there rightly might claim that there was not a full opportunity to litigate,[24] then collateral estoppel may

in a federal district court, regardless of the legal posture in which the federal claim arises. But the authority for this principle is difficult to discern. It cannot be in the Constitution, which makes no such guarantee, but leaves the scope of jurisdiction of the federal district courts to the wisdom of Congress. And no such authority is to be found in § 1983 itself." 449 U.S. at 103, 101 S.Ct. at 419.

18. 456 U.S. 461, 102 S.Ct. 1883, 72 L.Ed.2d 262 (1982).

19. The Court's holding in Kremer has been buttressed by its more recent ruling that state courts enjoy concurrent jurisdiction over Title VII claims. Yellow Freight System, Inc. v. Donnelly, 494 U.S. 820, 110 S.Ct. 1566, 108 L.Ed.2d 834 (1990).

20. The possibility of a legislative policy exception is recognized in Restatement Second of Judgments § 28, comments d and e (1982).

21. See 18 C. Wright, A. Miller & E. Cooper, Jurisdiction and Related Matters § 4423; Vestal, Preclusion/Res Judicata Variables: Adjudicating Bodies, 54 Geo.L.J. 857 (1966).

22. See § 14.9 at notes 25–31, above.

23. One of the difficult areas in which this exception arises is when the prior determination was made by an administrative agency rather than a court. In some instances administrative determinations partake of an adjudicatory model and full collateral estoppel effect is appropriate. See People v. Sims, 32 Cal.3d 468, 186 Cal.Rptr. 77, 651 P.2d 321 (1982); Dawson, Why a Decision by the NLRB Under 8(b)(4) Should Be Determinative on the Issue of Liability in a Subsequent Section 303 Damage Suit, 27 Okla.L.Rev. 660 (1974). In others, this is not the case. See generally Mogel, Res Judicata and Collateral Estoppel in Administrative Proceedings, 30 Baylor L.Rev. 463 (1978).

24. The Supreme Court has recognized on several occasions that a denial of a full opportunity to litigate because of varying procedures may serve to prevent the assertion of collateral estoppel. Kremer v. Chemical Constr. Corp., 456 U.S. 461, 481, 102 S.Ct. 1883, 1897, 72 L.Ed.2d 262 (1982); Montana v. U.S., 440 U.S. 147, 164, 99 S.Ct. 970, 979, 59 L.Ed.2d 210 (1979); Parklane

be denied.[25] For example, estoppel effect typically is not given to judgments of small claims courts or justice courts that are designed to provide an expedited and inexpensive process.[26] Exactly what other differences in procedure may require the denial of issue preclusion must be decided on a case by case basis,[27] although the Supreme Court has ruled that the availability of a jury trial in the second action is not the type of difference that will prevent collateral estoppel from being utilized.[28]

The final exception to collateral estoppel that should be noted arises in litigation in which the government is a party. The government is not in the same position as most private litigants because it is likely to be involved in nationwide litigation involving identical legal issues. If an adverse result in the first completed suit were to receive full collateral estoppel effect in all future and pending cases, the government would have to appeal each trial determination to the Supreme Court in order to ensure a full review of its interpretation of the law and avoid the freezing effect of a lower court decision on a matter of public importance. Recognizing this problem, the Supreme Court has ruled that nonparties cannot use collateral estoppel offensively[29] to preclude the relitigation of issues decided against the government in other cases.[30] The Court concluded that the avoidance of collateral estoppel

> will better allow thorough development of legal doctrine by allowing litigation in multiple forums. Indeed, a contrary result might disserve the economy interest in whose name estoppel is advanced by

Hosiery Co. v. Shore, 439 U.S. 322, 333, 99 S.Ct. 645, 652, 58 L.Ed.2d 552 (1979).

25. Desotelle v. Continental Cas. Co., 136 Wis.2d 13, 400 N.W.2d 524 (App.1986), review denied 136 Wis.2d 563, 407 N.W.2d 560; Vella v. Hudgins, 20 Cal.3d 251, 142 Cal.Rptr. 414, 572 P.2d 28 (1977); Niles v. Niles, 35 Del.Ch. 106, 111 A.2d 697 (1955). "[P]reclusive effect should turn in each case on an analysis of the comparative quality and extensiveness of the procedures followed in the two courts, of their relative competence to deal with the particular issue, and of the legislative purpose in allocating jurisdiction between them." Restatement Second of Judgments § 28, Reporter's Note 287 (1982).

26. In several states the fact that judgments in various state tribunals are not to be given any collateral estoppel effect is specifically found in statutes. See Note, Article 2226a: Its Effect on Res Judicata and Collateral Estoppel, 17 Baylor L.Rev. 221 (1965).

27. When the issue of whether fair procedures were used in a state court determination arises in later federal court litigation, statutory full faith and credit obligations limit the federal court's inquiry to whether the state proceedings "satisfy the

minimum procedural requirements of the Fourteenth Amendment's Due Process Clause * * *." Kremer v. Chemical Constr. Corp., 456 U.S. 461, 481, 102 S.Ct. 1883, 1897, 72 L.Ed.2d 262 (1982). For a discussion of the special considerations arising when full faith and credit is involved, see § 14.15, below.

28. "[T]he presence or absence of a jury as fact-finder is basically neutral, quite unlike, for example, the necessity of defending the first lawsuit in an inconvenient forum." Parklane Hosiery Co. v. Shore, 439 U.S. 322, 334 n. 19, 99 S.Ct. 645, 652 n. 19, 58 L.Ed.2d 552 (1979). But cf. Lytle v. Household Mfg., Inc., 494 U.S. 545, 110 S.Ct. 1331, 108 L.Ed.2d 504 (1990) (the wrongful denial of a jury trial in the first action prevents the application of collateral estoppel to the district court's ruling that Title VII provides the exclusive remedy when plaintiff filed claims under both Title VII and 42 U.S.C.A. § 1981).

29. The use of collateral estoppel by nonparties is discussed in § 14.14, below.

30. U.S. v. Mendoza, 464 U.S. 154, 104 S.Ct. 568, 78 L.Ed.2d 379 (1984).

requiring the government to abandon virtually any exercise of discretion in seeking to review judgments unfavorable to it.[31]

But this exception is limited strictly to situations in which collateral estoppel is being asserted by someone who was not a party to the prior government litigation. In a companion case, the Supreme Court rejected arguments that collateral estoppel never should apply in government litigation because it would freeze the development of the law on matters of public importance.[32] When the same party is involved and the facts are virtually identical, judicial economy concerns predominate.[33]

C.   WHO CAN BE BOUND

§ 14.13   General Principles Governing Who Is Bound

The decision as to who will be bound by a judgment rests on a very straightforward rule:[1] Only persons who were parties[2] or who are in privity with persons who were parties in the first action may be bound.[3] Our notions of due process require this result because individuals who are tied to a judgment in a suit in which they had no opportunity to be heard rightly could claim that there had been a denial of due process.[4] Indeed, in order to ensure that each person has a full opportunity to be heard on issues in which he has an interest, it also is held that issue preclusion may be asserted only against someone who was an adverse party in the prior action.[5] Coparties in the first suit are not prevented

---

31. 464 U.S. at 163, 104 S.Ct. at 574.

32. U.S. v. Stauffer Chem. Co., 464 U.S. 165, 104 S.Ct. 575, 78 L.Ed.2d 388 (1984).

33. See Levin & Leeson, Issue Preclusion Against the United States Government, 70 Iowa L.Rev. 113 (1984). For a discussion of the problems presented when collateral estoppel is limited to parties, see § 14.10 at notes 53–56, above.

§ 14.13

1. See generally 18 C. Wright, A. Miller & E. Cooper, Jurisdiction and Related Matters §§ 4448–62.

2. Nominal parties typically are not bound by res judicata or collateral estoppel. See Restatement Second of Judgments § 37 (1982), for a discussion of who is a nominal party. Only those who actively participate in the first action are precluded in subsequent lawsuits. See U.S. v. 111.2 Acres of Land, 293 F.Supp. 1042 (E.D.Wash.1968), affirmed 435 F.2d 561 (9th Cir.1970); In re Morgan Guar. Trust Co., 28 N.Y.2d 155, 320 N.Y.S.2d 905, 269 N.E.2d 571 (1971), cert. denied 404 U.S. 826. Further refinements may be drawn when a person litigates in two capacities. The fact that a person was a named party in both lawsuits

will not necessarily result in preclusion. The question becomes whether the individual clearly litigated in one capacity and now is appearing in a different capacity, presenting interests that were not previously represented. See Restatement Second of Judgments § 36 (1982). See, e.g., Freeman v. Lester Coggins Trucking Co., 771 F.2d 860 (5th Cir.1985); Brown v. Osier, 628 A.2d 125 (Me.1993); Smith v. Bishop, 26 Ill.2d 434, 187 N.E.2d 217 (1962).

3. This section deals only with the question of who may be bound by a judgment. The question of who may take advantage of a favorable judgment is discussed in § 14.14, below.

4. Richards v. Jefferson County, Alabama, 517 U.S. 793, 116 S.Ct. 1761, 135 L.Ed.2d 76 (1996); Blonder–Tongue Labs., Inc. v. University of Illinois Foundation, 402 U.S. 313, 329, 91 S.Ct. 1434, 1443, 28 L.Ed.2d 788 (1971); Zenith Radio Corp. v. Hazeltine Research, Inc., 395 U.S. 100, 89 S.Ct. 1562, 23 L.Ed.2d 129 (1969).

5. Potomac Design, Inc. v. Eurocal Trading, Inc., 839 F.Supp. 364 (D.Md.1993); Nickert v. Puget Sound Tug & Barge Co., 335 F.Supp. 1162 (W.D.Wash.1971); Marcum v. Mississippi Valley Gas Co., 672 So.2d 730 (Miss.1996); Freightliner Corp. v.

from litigating the same issues between themselves in a second lawsuit if they remained in a nonadversarial position toward one another throughout the first action.[6] By requiring that an adversarial relationship be found between parties before issue preclusion may be used, the courts ensure that the parties specifically and knowingly litigated the issues in controversy. The one historically recognized exception to the rule involves judgments in class actions.[7] In that context, any judgment that is entered will be given full res judicata and collateral estoppel effect, binding all absent class members. Due process concerns are satisfied by finding that the members were represented adequately and properly notified in the first suit.[8]

The scope of judgments have been expanded to bind nonparties typically by a determination that a nonparty is in privity with a party. Persons in a privity relationship are deemed to have interests so closely intertwined that a decision involving one necessarily should control the other. It is expected that the person who was the named party adequately represented the interests of the other when litigating the first action because it was in that party's own selfish interest to do so.

The difficulty comes in defining what constitutes privity for preclusion purposes. A showing of similar interests is not enough to bind a nonparty.[9] But what is? It has been suggested that privity is merely a conclusory label applied by the courts when they determine that there is a sufficient identity of interest between a party and nonparty to allow a judgment to bind both.[10] Thus, rather than focussing on who is in privity, a more profitable analysis of when nonparties may be bound

Rockwell–Standard Corp., 2 Cal.App.3d 115, 82 Cal.Rptr. 439 (1969).

Some courts appear to have abandoned the adversity requirement, focussing solely on whether the party against whom estoppel is asserted had a full and fair opportunity to litigate the issues in the first action. See Scooper Dooper, Inc. v. Kraftco Corp., 494 F.2d 840 (3d Cir.1974).

6. The traditional view was that coparties may adopt an adversarial position toward one another solely by the assertion of claims between them. See Hellenic Lines, Ltd. v. The Exmouth, 253 F.2d 473 (2d Cir.1958), cert. denied 356 U.S. 967. More recently, some courts have not required that claims be asserted between the parties to establish adversity, but have looked to the litigation postures that were adopted, allowing, for example, the codefendants' attempts to shift blame on each other to satisfy the need for adversity. See Nevada v. U.S., 463 U.S. 110, 103 S.Ct. 2906, 77 L.Ed.2d 509 (1983); McLellan v. Columbus I–70 West Auto–Truckstop, Inc., 525 F.Supp. 1233 (N.D.Ill.1981). The adversity requirement is explored more fully in 18 C. Wright, A. Miller & E. Cooper, Jurisdiction and Related Matters § 4450.

7. Hansberry v. Lee, 311 U.S. 32, 61 S.Ct. 115, 85 L.Ed. 22 (1940).

8. For a discussion of the binding effect of class action judgments, see § 16.8, below.

9. Collins v. E.I. DuPont de Nemours & Co., 34 F.3d 172 (3d Cir.1994); Hardy v. Johns–Manville Sales Corp., 681 F.2d 334 (5th Cir.1982). Thus, for example, family members generally are treated as not being in privity even though they may have similar interests in the outcome of particular actions. E.g., Commonwealth v. Johnson, 7 Va.App. 614, 376 S.E.2d 787 (1989); Land v. Sellers, 150 Ga.App. 83, 256 S.E.2d 629 (1979). See generally 18 C. Wright, A. Miller & E. Cooper, Jurisdiction and Related Matters § 4459.

10. "Privity states no reason for including or excluding one from the estoppel of a judgment. It is merely a word used to say that the relationships between the one who is a party on the record and another is close enough to include that other within the res judicata." Bruszewski v. U.S., 181 F.2d 419, 423 (3d Cir.1950) (Goodrich, J., concurring), cert. denied 340 U.S. 865. See, e.g., Safeco Ins. Co. of America v. Yon, 118 Idaho 367, 796 P.2d 1040 (App.1990).

requires an inquiry into whether the facts and circumstances in the first action raise the presumption that the nonparty's interest was fully and adequately presented.[11] Some courts seem receptive to this analysis.[12] Regardless of the merits of this approach, a brief review of the common privity relationships that have been recognized is useful to at least outline the principle's scope.[13]

The historic and most common situation in which privity is found is when a person acquires an interest in the subject matter of the suit after it was filed or decided.[14] Successors in interest, whether they obtain their interests by virtue of an assignment, by inheritance, or by law are bound along with their predecessors by res judicata and collateral estoppel.[15] This is necessary in order to preserve the finality of judgments; otherwise a person confronted with an adverse decision might subject the winning party to the prospect of continual litigation simply by transferring his interest in the subject matter of the suit to another who could begin the suit anew.[16]

A second well-defined privity relationship arises when legally appointed representative parties, such as trustees and executors, are involved; those individuals are deemed in privity with those whom they represent.[17] Since parties litigating in a representative capacity have no interests of their own, but either sue or are sued on behalf of the beneficiaries, any judgment that is entered will bind not only them, but the individuals whom they serve.[18]

11. For an insightful examination of what standards should govern the binding of nonparties to judgments, see Note, Collateral Estoppel of Nonparties, 87 Harv. L.Rev. 1485 (1974).

12. In particular, a focus on the adequacy of the first proceeding and the expectation that a different result is unlikely to be achieved in the second action has appeared in some cases, suggesting a theory of virtual representation that allows the judgment to bind an absent nonparty. See, e.g., Tyus v. Schoemehl, 93 F.3d 449 (8th Cir. 1996), cert. denied ___ U.S. ___, 117 S.Ct. 1427; Shaw v. Hahn, 56 F.3d 1128 (9th Cir.1995), cert. denied 516 U.S. 964; Benson & Ford, Inc. v. Wanda Petroleum Co., 833 F.2d 1172 (5th Cir.1987). For a discussion of this line of cases, see 18 C. Wright, A. Miller & E. Cooper, Jurisdiction and Related Matters § 4457.

13. See Developments in the Law: Res Judicata, 65 Harv.L.Rev. 820, 855–61 (1952).

14. "What is privity? As used when dealing with the estoppel of a judgment, privity denotes mutual or successive relationship to the same right of property." Bigelow v. Old Dominion Copper Mining & Smelting Co., 225 U.S. 111, 128–29, 32

S.Ct. 641, 643, 56 L.Ed. 1009 (1912) (joint tortfeasors are not in privity).

15. See 18 C. Wright, A. Miller & E. Cooper, Jurisdiction and Related Matters § 4462.

16. The notion that successive owners are bound by any judgments affecting the property at issue also is expressed as a principle of property law. Justice Pitney described the basis for this rule as "the estoppel runs with the property, that the grantor can transfer no better right or title than he himself has, and that the granter take cum onere." Postal Telegraph Cable Co. v. City of Newport, 247 U.S. 464, 38 S.Ct. 566, 62 L.Ed. 1215 (1918).

17. The class of persons who may be deemed as litigating in a representative capacity has been expanded in modern times to include persons or agencies invested by law to represent a person's interest, as well as those specifically designated by the represented party to do so. See Restatement Second of Judgments § 41 (1982).

18. Sea–Land Serv., Inc. v. Gaudet, 414 U.S. 573, 593–94, 94 S.Ct. 806, 819, 39 L.Ed.2d 9 (1974); Chicago, R.I. & P. Ry. Co. v. Schendel, 270 U.S. 611, 46 S.Ct. 420, 70 L.Ed. 757 (1926).

Privity also has been universally recognized when it is determined that the newly named party in the second suit actually controlled[19] or participated in litigating the first action. Although the nonparty will not be bound by res judicata because different claims are involved,[20] identical issues that were necessarily and actually litigated will be precluded.[21] Having received one opportunity to defend or prosecute those issues, the nonparty may not be allowed another.[22] Under this principle, for example, liability insurers who actually control litigation on behalf of their insureds are bound, even though they were not named parties.[23]

Finally, privity has been recognized in a wide range of commercial relationships. The application of res judicata or collateral estoppel principles in these situations is difficult to classify because the decision whether privity is found and a judgment deemed to be binding depends heavily on the substantive law that regulates the relationship. Thus, it is necessary to review carefully the underlying law in order to determine whether preclusion can be asserted against a nonparty who falls into one of these relationships.[24]

Although it is beyond the scope of this volume to explore all the various distinctions that have been drawn as to when persons are or are not in privity, two examples may suffice to illustrate the complicated nature of the rules that have evolved. The first involves insurance litigation. When an insurance company pays the insured's property damages, it is subrogated to that claim, and thus can bring an action against a tortfeasor who caused the damage. Suppose, however, that the insured already has sued and obtained a judgment against that tortfeasor for personal injuries arising out of the same accident, and that the jurisdiction in which suit was filed follows the majority rule that all damages from a single occurrence constitute but one claim. In that event

19. For further elaboration on who may be deemed a "controlling" party, see Restatement Second of Judgments § 39 (1982).

20. Montana v. U.S., 440 U.S. 147, 154, 99 S.Ct. 970, 974, 59 L.Ed.2d 210 (1979); Vanguard Recording Soc., Inc. v. Fantasy Records, Inc., 24 Cal.App.3d 410, 100 Cal.Rptr. 826 (1972).

21. Montana v. U.S., 440 U.S. 147, 99 S.Ct. 970, 59 L.Ed.2d 210 (1979); Patterson v. Saunders, 194 Va. 607, 74 S.E.2d 204 (1953), cert. denied 345 U.S. 998. Although a controlling nonparty will be bound by the judgment, it will not be allowed to take advantage of a favorable judgment by asserting issue preclusion offensively against the prior party. Restatement Second of Judgments § 84 (1982).

22. There has been a suggestion in some cases and commentary that preclusion may extend to certain nonparties who failed to intervene in a pending action. Provident Tradesmens Bank & Trust Co. v. Patterson, 390 U.S. 102, 114, 88 S.Ct. 733, 740, 19 L.Ed.2d 936 (1968); Note, Preclusion of Absent Disputants to Compel Intervention, 79 Colum.L.Rev. 1551 (1979); Comment, Nonparties and Preclusion by Judgment: The Privity Rule Reconsidered, 56 Cal.L.Rev. 1098, 1122 (1968). The Supreme Court resolved the question in Martin v. Wilks, 490 U.S. 755, 109 S.Ct. 2180, 104 L.Ed.2d 835 (1989), holding that a party seeking a judgment binding another cannot obligate that person to intervene, but must formally join the person.

23. See, e.g., Charter Oak Fire Ins. Co. v. Sumitomo Marine & Fire Ins. Co., 750 F.2d 267 (3d Cir.1984); Inland Seas Boat Co. v. Buckeye Union Ins. Co., 534 F.2d 85 (6th Cir.1976).

24. See 18 C. Wright, A. Miller & E. Cooper, Jurisdiction and Related Matters § 4460.

the insurer's subrogation action will be precluded.[25] As the real party in interest in the first suit, the insured had the ability to combine the personal injury and property damage claims and should have done so.[26] The insurance company stands in the shoes of its insured. Since the latter would be barred, so is the former. This result is not unduly harsh because the insurer can, before paying for the property damage, take steps to ensure that its subrogation rights will be protected. On the other hand, if the insurer had sued first, the insured would not have been precluded from bringing a later personal injury action.[27] This conclusion has been reached on the theory that two causes of action exist or, more appropriately, by finding that it would not be fair to hold the insured in privity because the insured had no control over the insurance company's litigation and no way to safeguard the right to sue on the personal injury claim.

The second important context in which complex and sometimes seemingly inconsistent[28] rules of privity have been developed involves derivative liability growing out of such relationships as employer and employee, principal and agent, guarantor and debtor, etc. An injured party may sue to collect damages from the individual who caused the harm or the person who is derivatively liable. The question is when, if at all, the plaintiff can sue each of them in successive actions.[29]

Suppose, for example, a plaintiff brings a negligence action against E, an employee of F, for injuries arising out of an auto collision. A jury finds for E. Plaintiff cannot now sue F to collect for those injuries. It would be highly unjust to hold F liable for the negligence of E after E already has been exonerated in a prior suit.[30] Moreover, it would be wasteful of the court's time and energy to allow relitigation of the same issues. Should the result be the same if plaintiff first had sued F, the employer, and lost, and then filed a second action against E, the employee? There would not be the same manifest injustice because E would be called to defend only his own conduct, but there would be a waste of resources. Therefore, the second action should be precluded. It is important to note, however, that this would be the result only if the first suit against F was decided on the merits of E's conduct. Thus, if F won not because E was not negligent but solely because E was not acting within the scope of his employment for F at the time of the accident, then plaintiff's second action against E should be allowed to go forward.

25. Hayward v. State Farm Mut. Auto. Ins. Co., 212 Minn. 500, 4 N.W.2d 316 (1942).

26. Real party in interest concepts are discussed in § 6.3, above.

27. Reardon v. Allen, 88 N.J.Super. 560, 213 A.2d 26 (Law Div.1965). This exception to the normal operation of res judicata is discussed in § 14.5 at notes 13–15, above.

28. E.g., "[A]lthough a master has privity with his servant, a servant is not in privity with the master." Land v. Sellers, 150 Ga.App. 83, 256 S.E.2d 629, 630 (1979).

29. See U.S. v. Gurley, 43 F.3d 1188 (8th Cir.1994), cert. denied 516 U.S. 817 (employer-employee liability); Good Health Dairy Prods. Corp. v. Emery, 275 N.Y. 14, 9 N.E.2d 758 (1937) (derivative liability); City of Anderson v. Fleming, 160 Ind. 597, 67 N.E. 443 (1903) (subrogee-subrogor).

30. New Orleans & N.E.R. Co. v. Jopes, 142 U.S. 18, 12 S.Ct. 109, 35 L.Ed. 919 (1891).

Similar rules apply to questions of damage. If plaintiff prevails either against E or F, the amount of damages will be held binding; plaintiff cannot bring a second suit to obtain a higher award.[31]

§ 14.14   The Doctrine of Mutuality

Although requirements of due process govern the determination of who may be bound by a judgment, the question whether a nonparty may take advantage of a prior decree raises other concerns. Nonetheless, history and tradition have induced courts to treat these two matters as the same: Only parties and their privies may be bound or may take advantage of a judgment.[1]

Whether a nonparty may be benefitted by a decree arises only in the context of collateral estoppel. When new parties are involved, the courts generally have ruled that the two actions do not constitute a single cause of action or claim and thus are not barred by res judicata.[2] However, identical issues can be presented in separate actions involving different parties and it may be clearly established that those issues were actually and necessarily litigated and determined in the first proceeding, thereby meeting the basic requirements for issue preclusion.[3] What prevents the use of collateral estoppel is the doctrine of mutuality.

As the term suggests, mutuality is premised on the notion that all litigants should be treated equally,[4] that no person should benefit from a judgment when he stood to lose nothing by it. Since someone who was a party to the first proceeding could not assert any judgment that was entered against a nonparty because that person had no opportunity to present evidence or argument at the first trial, the nonparty likewise should not be able to use the judgment against the party.[5] Thus, mutuality operates in favor of prior parties because it affords them the opportunity to litigate a second time in the hope that a different determination will be reached.[6] At the same time, it sacrifices judicial

---

31. Land v. Sellers, 150 Ga.App. 83, 256 S.E.2d 629 (1979).

§ 14.14

1. The mutuality rule may be explained historically by the fact that originally it evolved from a practice that limited estoppel to the parties on record. See Miller, The Historical Relation of Estoppel by Record to Res Judicata, 35 Ill.L.Rev. 41 (1940).

2. See Lawlor v. National Screen Serv. Corp., 349 U.S. 322, 75 S.Ct. 865, 99 L.Ed. 1122 (1955). See also the discussion of what constitutes a cause of action in § 14.4, above.

In certain exceptional circumstances, nonparties have been allowed to rely on res judicata. See, e.g., Nevada v. U.S., 463 U.S. 110, 143–44, 103 S.Ct. 2906, 2925, 77 L.Ed.2d 509 (1983). However, mutuality typically is an essential element of res judi-

cata. Beard v. O'Neal, 728 F.2d 894 (7th Cir.1984), cert. denied 469 U.S. 825.

3. See §§ 14.10–14.11, above.

4. See Bigelow v. Old Dominion Copper Mining & Smelting Co., 225 U.S. 111, 32 S.Ct. 641, 56 L.Ed. 1009 (1912); Ralph Wolff & Sons v. New Zealand Ins. Co., 248 Ky. 304, 58 S.W.2d 623 (1933).

5. For an argument supporting the retention of mutuality except in certain limited areas involving derivative or secondary liability, see Moore & Currier, Mutuality and Conclusiveness of Judgments, 35 Tul. L.Rev. 301 (1961).

6. One author has argued, using probability theory, that mutuality also allocates trial risks consistent with the burden of persuasion and thus that its abandonment "strikes at the heart of the trial process." Note, A Probabilistic Analysis of the Doc-

economy and raises the possibility of inconsistent results, all in an attempt to treat litigants equally.[7]

Although mutuality still limits the application of collateral estoppel in a number of jurisdictions,[8] adherence to the doctrine has been steadily eroding. The case that began this trend is Bernhard v. Bank of America National Trust and Savings Association,[9] in which Justice Roger Traynor ruled that there existed no supportable reasons justifying mutuality. He noted that many courts implicitly had recognized this by allowing the expansion of the notion of who was in privity in order to permit a broader binding effect.[10] Thus, he concluded that the only pertinent questions in deciding whether to apply issue preclusion should be (1) whether identical issues are involved; (2) whether there is a final judgment on the merits; and (3) whether the person against whom estoppel was asserted was a party or in privity with a party to the prior law suit.[11]

Following Justice Traynor's lead, many jurisdictions have abandoned mutuality.[12] They have noted that a person should not be able to continue to try an issue, particularly when there is no reason to suspect that the result will be different. As long as the issue or issues are identical in both suits and a full opportunity was present in the first action to litigate those issues, a nonparty may assert collateral estoppel against someone who was the losing party there.

But this move away from mutuality has been in stages and jurisdictions vary as to when they will allow nonparties to assert issue preclusion against a party to earlier litigation.[13] Many courts have made this decision depend on the litigation posture of the parties in the first and second action.

The most common situation in which mutuality has been abandoned is when the party against whom estoppel is asserted was in an offensive posture in the first suit (a plaintiff) and when the person who is

trine of Mutuality of Collateral Estoppel, 76 Mich.L.Rev. 612, 619 (1978).

7. See Semmel, Collateral Estoppel, Mutuality and Joinder of Parties, 68 Colum.L.Rev. 1457 (1968).

8. E.g., Goodson v. McDonough Power Equipment, Inc., 2 Ohio St.3d 193, 443 N.E.2d 978 (1983); Newport Div. Tenneco Chemicals, Inc. v. Thompson, 330 So.2d 826 (Fla.App.1976); Keith v. Schiefen–Stockham Ins. Agency, Inc., 209 Kan. 537, 498 P.2d 265 (1972); Howell v. Vito's Trucking & Excavating Co., 386 Mich. 37, 191 N.W.2d 313 (1971).

9. 19 Cal.2d 807, 122 P.2d 892 (1942).

10. See § 14.13, above.

11. 122 P.2d at 895.

12. See generally Taylor, Kentucky Courts and Non–Mutual Collateral Estoppel, 24 N.Ky.L.Rev. 297 (1997); Note, Col-

lateral Estoppel: The Changing Role of the Rule of Mutuality, 41 Mo.L.Rev. 521 (1976).

Several of the cases involving mutuality since Bernhard are collected and discussed in the Appendix to Currie, Civil Procedure: The Tempest Brews, 53 Calif.L.Rev. 25, 38 (1965).

13. The trend is toward steady abandonment of the mutuality requirement, but the process is not invariable. Compare Crowall v. Heritage Mut. Ins. Co., 118 Wis.2d 120, 346 N.W.2d 327 (App.1984) (conviction of misdemeanor drunk driving held preclusive on issue of who was driving in later civil action), with Trucking Employees of North Jersey Welfare Fund, Inc. v. Romano, 450 So.2d 843 (Fla.1984) (prior felony conviction not preclusive in later civil proceeding).

asserting estoppel is doing so defensively in the second action.[14] This was the situation in the Bernhard case itself.[15] In this context there is little disposition to allow a losing claimant to continue litigating the same issues simply by switching adversaries in the hope that a different result will occur.

There also was an early suggestion that collateral estoppel never should be available to a nonparty who is asserting it against someone who was a defendant in the first action.[16] This limitation reflected a presumption that defendants always are at a disadvantage because they do not choose the time or place of suit. Under this rationale, to avoid any possibility that this inherent disadvantage might have prevented a full defense, a defendant should be bound only in subsequent actions between the same parties. However, most courts now have rejected this limitation as unnecessarily broad.[17]

A number of courts have drawn a line when the person asserting collateral estoppel is doing so offensively, for purposes of establishing a claim for relief.[18] Thus, some courts have ruled that mutuality should control, at least when the party against whom estoppel is being asserted was a defendant in the prior litigation.[19] Other courts have gone further and have refused to allow nonparties to benefit from issue preclusion whenever they are asserting the judgment offensively.[20]

14. E.g., Fisher v. Jones, 311 Ark. 450, 844 S.W.2d 954 (1993), noted 47 Ark.L.Rev. 701 (1994); Sanderson v. Balfour, 109 N.H. 213, 247 A.2d 185 (1968). See Crutsinger v. Hess, 408 F.Supp. 548 (D.Kan.1976), deciding that the Kansas Supreme Court would abandon mutuality when collateral estoppel was asserted defensively against a prior plaintiff, even though offensive use of collateral estoppel by a nonparty had been rejected in Adamson v. Hill, 202 Kan. 482, 449 P.2d 536 (1969).

15. In Bernhard, a beneficiary of an estate sued the administrator claiming that he improperly had transferred money of the decedent to his own account. The administrator won, defending on the ground that the transferred money was a gift. After his discharge, the former plaintiff was appointed executrix and she then sued the bank claiming that it had improperly allowed the prior administrator to remove the deposit. The bank defended on the ground that the withdrawal of funds was proper because it was a gift, as it had been found to be in the first action. Collateral estoppel was upheld.

16. This limitation was suggested by Professor Brainerd Currie in Mutuality of Collateral Estoppel: Limits of the Bernhard Doctrine, 9 Stan.L.Rev. 281 (1957). He later retracted this view, arguing that the death of mutuality "should rest on particularized inquiry rather than on rules of thumb."

Currie, Civil Procedure: The Tempest Brews, 53 Calif.L.Rev. 25, 31 (1965).

17. Zdanok v. Glidden Co., 327 F.2d 944 (2d Cir.1964), cert. denied 377 U.S. 934; Bahler v. Fletcher, 257 Or. 1, 474 P.2d 329, 337 (1970); Teitelbaum Furs, Inc. v. Dominion Ins. Co., 58 Cal.2d 601, 25 Cal. Rptr. 559, 375 P.2d 439 (1962), cert. denied 372 U.S. 966.

18. For a thorough discussion of the distinction between offensive and defensive use of collateral estoppel by nonparties, see Note, The Impacts of Defensive and Offensive Assertion of Collateral Estoppel by a Nonparty, 35 Geo.Wash.L.Rev. 1010 (1967).

The Restatement Second of Judgments § 29 Reporter's Note 299 (1982) states that the current trend is not to distinguish between offensive and defensive uses of collateral estoppel, except to require a stronger showing that the prior opportunity to litigate was adequate when preclusion is asserted offensively.

19. Reardon v. Allen, 88 N.J.Super. 560, 213 A.2d 26 (Law Div.1965); First Nat. Bank of Cincinnati v. Berkshire Life Ins. Co., 176 Ohio St. 395, 199 N.E.2d 863 (1964); Nevarov v. Caldwell, 161 Cal.App.2d 762, 327 P.2d 111 (1958).

20. Spettigue v. Mahoney, 8 Ariz.App. 281, 445 P.2d 557 (1968); Albernaz v. City of Fall River, 346 Mass. 336, 191 N.E.2d

The rationale for not allowing a nonparty to assert collateral estoppel offensively is twofold. First, there is the concern that abandoning mutuality under those circumstances would encourage people to adopt a wait-and-see attitude after one suit was filed. If that suit were completed successfully, they could take advantage of the judgment by collateral estoppel, but if the suit were unsuccessful, they could claim a due process right to litigate the issues anew. This result somehow seems unfair to the defendant. A second concern first raised by Professor Brainerd Currie was the possibility of inconsistent and anomalous judgments in a situation in which multiple suits are filed arising out of a single event, such as an air collision or bus accident.[21] If the first several judgments were for the defendant, due process would allow other injured passengers to continue to litigate the question of defendant's negligence. However, if mutuality were abandoned totally and a later case resulted in a plaintiff's judgment, subsequent claimants all could rely on that determination, even though it was likely that that verdict was an aberration. To avoid that possibility, it is argued that collateral estoppel effect must be denied.[22]

Not all jurisdictions simply draw lines defining when they are willing to abandon mutuality. Some, like New York,[23] have adopted a fluid test. In each case in which a nonparty attempts to benefit by asserting collateral estoppel, the court must determine whether a full and fair opportunity was present in the first action to explore the issues on which an estoppel is asserted so that it would be unlikely that a different determination would be reached in a second trial.[24] Under this approach, the presumption is to allow issue preclusion because the burden is on the party opposing its use to demonstrate why the first opportunity was unfair and what will be different in a second adjudication.[25]

In 1979, the Supreme Court provided guidelines for the federal courts evaluating assertions of collateral estoppel by nonparties. Several years earlier the Court had endorsed the abandonment of mutuality in

771 (1963). See also Flanagan, Offensive Collateral Estoppel: Inefficiency and Foolish Consistency, 1982 Ariz.St.L.J. 45.

21. Currie, Mutuality of Collateral Estoppel: Limits of the Bernhard Doctrine, 9 Stan.L.Rev. 281, 289 (1957).

22. State Farm Fire & Cas. Co. v. Century Home Components, Inc., 275 Or. 97, 550 P.2d 1185 (1976).

Obviously, a rule of thumb is not the only way to handle the possibility that the first judgment rests on an erroneous verdict. See Taylor v. Hawkinson, 47 Cal.2d 893, 306 P.2d 797 (1957) (collateral estoppel effect denied when the judgment might have resulted from a compromise verdict).

23. The New York cases on mutuality of estoppel are discussed extensively in 5 J.

Weinstein, A. Miller & H. Korn, New York Civil Practice ¶ ¶ 5011.32–.42.

24. See Waitkus v. Pomeroy, 31 Colo. App. 396, 506 P.2d 392 (1972), reversed on other grounds 183 Colo. 344, 517 P.2d 396 (1973); B. R. DeWitt, Inc. v. Hall, 19 N.Y.2d 141, 278 N.Y.S.2d 596, 225 N.E.2d 195 (1967); Israel v. Wood Dolson Co., 1 N.Y.2d 116, 151 N.Y.S.2d 1, 134 N.E.2d 97 (1956).

25. State Farm Fire & Cas. Co. v. Century Home Components, Inc., 275 Or. 97, 550 P.2d 1185 (1976); Schwartz v. Public Administrator of Bronx County, 24 N.Y.2d 65, 298 N.Y.S.2d 955, 246 N.E.2d 725 (1969). But see Waitkus v. Pomeroy, 31 Colo.App. 396, 506 P.2d 392 (1972), reversed on other grounds 183 Colo. 344, 517 P.2d 396 (1973).

the defensive setting in Blonder–Tongue Laboratories, Inc. v. University of Illinois Foundation[26] when it ruled that a patentee could be precluded from relitigating the validity of a patent that had been declared invalid in prior litigation against other alleged infringers. This conclusion was necessitated as a matter of sound policy. As described by Justice White, in his opinion for the Court, "In any lawsuit where a defendant, because of the mutuality principle, is forced to present a complete defense on the merits to a claim which the plaintiff has fully litigated and lost in a prior action, there is an arguable misallocation of resources."[27] Not long afterward, in Parklane Hosiery Company v. Shore,[28] the Court confronted the question whether a nonparty could assert collateral estoppel offensively against someone who was a defendant in the prior action— the most troublesome situation for the lower courts. In an opinion by Justice Stewart, the Court upheld the use of collateral estoppel, but issued a caveat, as follows: "The general rule should be that in cases where a plaintiff could easily have joined in the earlier action or where * * * the application of offensive estoppel would be unfair to defendant, a trial judge should not allow the use of offensive estoppel."[29] Thus, the Court endorsed the complete abandonment of mutuality in the federal courts. It substituted a discretionary standard by which the trial judge is to assess whether allowing a nonparty to assert issue preclusion in a particular case raises any of the concerns or problems that have encouraged some courts and commentators to reject its use.

Four factors are specifically mentioned. First, could the nonparty have joined the prior litigation?[30] If so, then estoppel may not be proper, for its availability then would encourage a wait-and-see attitude on the part of claimants and that ultimately could increase the total amount of litigation.[31] Second, was the subsequent litigation foreseeable at the time of the first suit so that the defendant had every incentive to defend that action vigorously?[32] Third, is the judgment being relied upon consistent with prior judgments against this defendant so that there need be no

---

26. 402 U.S. 313, 91 S.Ct. 1434, 28 L.Ed.2d 788 (1971).

27. 402 U.S. at 329, 91 S.Ct. at 1443. The misallocation of resources occurred because "the defendant's time and money are diverted from alternative uses—productive or otherwise—to relitigation of a decided issue." Further, to allow plaintiff to relitigate "as long as the supply of unrelated defendants holds out reflects either the aura of the gaming table or 'a lack of discipline and of disinterestedness on the part of the lower courts, hardly a worthy or wise basis for fashioning rules of procedure.' "Ibid.

28. 439 U.S. 322, 99 S.Ct. 645, 58 L.Ed.2d 552 (1979).

29. 439 U.S. at 331, 99 S.Ct. at 651–52.

30. This question was answered easily in Parklane since the first proceeding was

an SEC action in which private parties could not join.

31. As noted by the Court, "potential plaintiffs will have everything to gain and nothing to lose by not intervening in the first action." 439 U.S. at 330, 99 S.Ct. at 651.

32. On the issue of foreseeability, compare Zdanok v. Glidden Co., 327 F.2d 944 (2d Cir.1964), cert. denied 377 U.S. 934, with Berner v. British Commonwealth Pac. Airlines, Ltd., 346 F.2d 532 (2d Cir.1965), cert. denied 382 U.S. 983.

For an example of how this factor is applied in successive employment discrimination suits, see Meredith v. Beech Aircraft Corp., 18 F.3d 890 (10th Cir.1994).

fear of the multiple-claimant phenomenon?[33] Fourth, are there any procedural opportunities available to the defendant in the second action that did not exist in the first, so that a different result might ensue if the issues are retried? The Court offered some guidance as to this last factor. It first specifically rejected the argument raised in Parklane that the availability of a jury trial in the second action was just such a procedural opportunity, declaring that "the presence or absence of a jury as fact-finder is basically neutral * * *."[34] Justice Stewart described the kind of circumstances that might suggest that it would be inappropriate to employ issue preclusion as those arising when the defendant is forced to defend in an inconvenient forum and is unable to engage in full discovery or to call witnesses.[35] An analysis of these four questions should fully appraise the trial judge whether or not the defendant had a full and fair opportunity to defend the first action so that the use of collateral estoppel seems appropriate.

What is notable about the Parklane criteria is their direct response to the concerns raised. As mentioned earlier, many state courts have abandoned mutuality, but when confronted with the problems that have been raised, they either have limited their move away from mutuality to only certain settings or have used a general standard, requiring some assessment of whether the first proceeding was fair. Parklane provides specific guidelines for how to assess that fairness question.[36]

The success of the Parklane standard necessarily will be determined by its ease of application.[37] A brief look at the criteria reveals that some ambiguities remain.[38] For example, with regard to the first factor—easy joinder—although it often may be simple to determine that a particular litigant was adopting a wait-and-see attitude, as when the party original-

---

33. Notably (as in Parklane itself) in most cases involving multiple claimants, collateral estoppel may be asserted after the first determination so that there are no inconsistent judgments as of that time and this factor will not come into play. Although a question might be raised concerning whether we can determine if the first judgment itself is an aberration, that concern is answered by an analysis of the other factors, which require a finding that there has been a full and fair opportunity to defend in the first suit.

34. 439 U.S. at 332 n. 19, 99 S.Ct. at 652 n. 19. For a discussion of jury trial and collateral estoppel, see Shapiro & Coquillette, The Fetish of Jury Trial in Civil Cases: A Comment on Rachal v. Hill, 85 Harv.L.Rev. 442 (1971); Note, Mutuality of Estoppel and the Seventh Amendment: The Effect of Parklane Hosiery, 66 Cornell L.Q. 1002 (1979).

35. 439 U.S. at 331 n. 15, 99 S.Ct. at 651 n. 15.

36. The Restatement Second of Judgments § 29 (1982) adopts the Parklane cri-

teria for purposes of determining whether issue preclusion may be used in suits with strangers to the first proceeding.

37. For some discussion of the implications of Parklane, see Callen & Kadue, To Bury Mutuality, Not to Praise It: An Analysis of Collateral Estoppel After Parklane Hosiery Co. v. Shore, 31 Hast.L.J. 755 (1980); Statman, The Defensive Use of Collateral Estoppel in Multidistrict Litigation After Parklane, 83 Dick.L.Rev. 469 (1979). For an interesting analysis of one area in which the use of offensive nonmutual collateral estoppel has not been successful, see Green, The Inability of Offensive Collateral Estoppel to Fulfill Its Promise: An Examination of Estoppel in Asbestos Litigation, 70 Iowa L.Rev. 141 (1984).

38. The easiest factor to apply is the third because when inconsistent determinations occur they should be readily apparent. See, e.g., Standefer v. U.S., 447 U.S. 10, 23 n. 17, 100 S.Ct. 1999, 2007 n. 17, 64 L.Ed.2d 689 (1980); Hardy v. Johns–Manville Sales Corp., 681 F.2d 334 (5th Cir. 1982).

ly was joined in the first suit but obtained a severance, in others the reasons for not joining will not be clear. Further, in most instances the courts have not adopted a principle of compulsory intervention. They have allowed individuals to control their own disputes, giving them tactical decisionmaking authority. Thus, a party who did not participate in any way in a prior proceeding for sound tactical reasons, but who was not simply sitting on the sidelines hoping to capitalize on a favorable result, should not be denied the benefits of collateral estoppel.[39] Consequently, only a careful factual inquiry into the nonparty's decision not to join the first suit will reveal whether this concern merits a denial of preclusion.[40]

Under Parklane the court must evaluate on a case-by-case basis whether it is necessary to allow what appears to be duplicative litigation to ensure the reliability and fairness of a judgment; no precise rules can or should be formulated. This approach has much to recommend it because it allows the courts to maintain the advantages of collateral estoppel while protecting the parties' interests. However, the Parklane standard is applicable only to the federal courts.[41] State courts are not obligated to follow the Supreme Court's lead.[42] Consequently, it is necessary to search carefully the law of the judgment-rendering court to determine whether it has abandoned mutuality and, if so, to what extent, because variations in treatment remain.

D. INTERSYSTEM PROBLEMS OF FORMER ADJUDICATION

§ 14.15 Principles Governing Judgment Recognition Across System Lines

As has been seen throughout this Chapter, when a party seeks to rely on a judgment entered in a previous action, judicially developed rules of claim and issue preclusion will determine whether and to what degree that judgment will be binding. When the first action is heard in one judicial system and the second action in another, the decision to accord respect for the judgment in the first suit is controlled by principles of full faith and credit.[1] Full faith and credit thus may be seen as

---

39. See, e.g., Starker v. U.S., 602 F.2d 1341 (9th Cir.1979) (tactical considerations suffice to explain nonjoinder). See generally Note, Offensive Assertion of Collateral Estoppel by Persons Opting Out of a Class Action, 31 Hast.L.J. 1189 (1980).

40. Collins v. Seaboard Coastline R.R. Co., 681 F.2d 1333 (11th Cir.1982) (inquiry required as to why wife had not joined her loss of consortium claim to husband's personal injury claim against railroad).

41. For a thorough treatment of the mutuality doctrine in the federal courts, see 18 C. Wright, A. Miller & E. Cooper, Jurisdiction and Related Matters §§ 4463–65.

42. See Davidson v. Lonoke Production Credit Ass'n, 695 F.2d 1115 (8th Cir.1982), which contains an interesting analysis of the Arkansas precedents on mutuality and collateral estoppel, concluding why it is likely that the Arkansas Supreme Court would follow the lead of Parklane Hosiery.

§ 14.15

1. Full faith and credit principles are explored in several excellent articles. See Carrington, Collateral Estoppel and Foreign Judgments, 24 Ohio St.L.J. 381 (1963); Casad, Intersystem Issue Preclusion and the Restatement (Second) of Judgments, 66

assuring intersystem former adjudication.[2]

Article IV, Section 1 of the United States Constitution provides that each state must accord the judgments of sister states full faith and credit. This principle is found and expanded upon in Section 1738 of the United States Code,[3] in which it is stated that courts of one state must give the judgments of courts in another state the same faith and credit that they would be given in the judgment-rendering state. Further, federal courts must treat the judgments of state courts with the same respect that those judgments would receive in the state in which they were rendered. Although neither the statute nor the Constitution mentions what obligations exist for state courts confronting federal court judgments, it is well recognized that the same compulsion controls and thus state courts must treat federal judgments as those judgments would be treated by the federal courts themselves.[4] The presence of this compulsion is very important, for without it each judicial system would be free to ignore the judgments coming from other court systems. Consequently, full faith and credit serves as "a nationally unifying force."[5]

When arguments are raised that an exception should be made to avoid giving the normal binding effect to a prior judgment rendered by a court in a different court system, the question is not simply whether as a policy matter the court in its discretion should decide to ignore the judgment, but whether there is some policy that would override constitutional and statutory full faith and credit obligations. Necessarily, exceptions are few in number. When one state is enforcing the judgment of another state only some other constitutional imperative can outweigh the Article IV obligation. For example, when there was no personal jurisdiction in the first court so that a failure of due process is established, an exception to full faith and credit will be recognized.[6] However,

---

Cornell L.Q. 510 (1981); Degnan, Federalized Res Judicata, 85 Yale L.J. 741 (1976); Lilly, The Symmetry of Preclusion, 54 Ohio St.L.J. 289 (1993); Scoles, Interstate Preclusion by Prior Litigation, 74 Nw.U.L.Rev. 742, 748 (1979).

Although full faith and credit principles govern all preclusion issues in intersystem cases, they do not control the "time, manner, and mechanisms for enforcing judgments." Baker v. General Motors Corp., 522 U.S. 222, 118 S.Ct. 657, 665, 139 L.Ed.2d 580 (1998). For a discussion of how judgments are enforced, see §§ 15.7–15.8, below.

2. When the binding effect of another nation's judgment is involved, comity principles control. The effect to be given foreign country judgments is outside the scope of this volume. For extended treatment of this question, see E. Scoles & P. Hay, Conflict of Laws §§ 24.3–24.7 and 24.33–24.45 (2d ed.1992).

3. 28 U.S.C.A. § 1738.

4. Stoll v. Gottlieb, 305 U.S. 165, 59 S.Ct. 134, 83 L.Ed. 104 (1938); Crescent City Live–Stock Co. v. Butchers' Union Slaughter–House Co., 120 U.S. 141, 7 S.Ct. 472, 30 L.Ed. 614 (1887); Embry v. Palmer, 107 U.S. (17 Otto) 3, 2 S.Ct. 25, 27 L.Ed. 346 (1882); Loveridge v. Fred Meyer, Inc., 72 Wn.App. 720, 864 P.2d 417 (1993).

5. Magnolia Petroleum Co. v. Hunt, 320 U.S. 430, 439, 64 S.Ct. 208, 214, 88 L.Ed. 149 (1943).

6. Pennoyer v. Neff, 95 U.S. (5 Otto) 714, 24 L.Ed. 565 (1877); Restatement Second of Judgments § 81 (1982). Even an attack on a judgment for lack of jurisdiction will be limited, however, to situations in which that issue was not litigated in the first suit. See the discussion in § 14.7 at notes 29–38, above.

when the issue arises between the state and federal systems, the question that must be answered is different. Since the full faith and credit obligation in that setting is statutory only, Congress could decide to abandon or alter the requirement because of some other legislative objective,[7] and the court must consider whether it has done so.[8] As was discussed earlier, although there have been various situations in which arguments have been raised that some substantive statutory policy requires res judicata or collateral estoppel not be applied, to date there are few instances in which that argument has been upheld.[9] Full faith and credit principles have controlled.

The main area in intersystem preclusion cases in which there has been some difficulty is in determining what law should be consulted when deciding whether res judicata or collateral estoppel has been asserted appropriately.[10] The question of governing law is a very important one because, as much of the earlier discussion in this Chapter has illustrated, courts in different jurisdictions often disagree concerning the scope of these two doctrines. Illustratively, the law in the judgment-rendering court may provide that personal injury and property damage arising out of a single occurrence constitute one cause of action or that collateral estoppel may be asserted only by persons who were parties to the litigation that produced the judgment. But the law in the court in which the judgment is being asserted may be that two causes of action are presented by claims for personal injury and property damage or that jurisdiction may have abandoned mutuality, allowing nonparties to assert collateral estoppel against prior parties. Deciding what law controls will determine whether the particular judgment will preclude further litigation.

In all of these circumstances, the language of Section 1738 must be applied literally. Thus, it is necessary to look to the judgment-rendering court's law to determine all binding effect questions.[11] This is true when a state court judgment is asserted later in a federal tribunal,[12] as well as

7. Restatement Second of Judgments § 86, comment d (1982).

8. See Migra v. Warren City School Dist. Bd. of Educ., 465 U.S. 75, 104 S.Ct. 892, 79 L.Ed.2d 56 (1984) (42 U.S.C.A. § 1983 is not an exception; res judicata precludes litigation of federal claim omitted from state action); Kremer v. Chemical Constr. Corp., 456 U.S. 461, 102 S.Ct. 1883, 72 L.Ed.2d 262 (1982) (Title VII is not an exception; collateral estoppel precludes employment discrimination claim); Allen v. McCurry, 449 U.S. 90, 101 S.Ct. 411, 66 L.Ed.2d 308 (1980) (collateral estoppel effect must be given to state judgment, precluding federal action under 42 U.S.C.A. § 1983).

9. See §§ 14.8 and 14.12, above. For an example of a statutory policy deemed to override Section 1738, see U.S. Fidelity &

Guar. Co. v. Hendry Corp., 391 F.2d 13 (5th Cir.1968), cert. denied 393 U.S. 978.

10. For useful discussions of this question, see Degnan, Federalized Res Judicata, 85 Yale L.J. 741 (1976); Vestal, Res Judicata/Preclusion by Judgment: The Law Applied in the Federal Courts, 66 Mich.L.Rev. 1723 (1968).

11. For a more detailed examination of the problems of the law governing res judicata in the federal system, see 18 C. Wright, A. Miller & E. Cooper, Jurisdiction and Related Matters §§ 4466–73.

12. See Growe v. Emison, 507 U.S. 25, 113 S.Ct. 1075, 122 L.Ed.2d 388 (1993); Marrese v. American Academy of Orthopaedic Surgeons, 470 U.S. 373, 105 S.Ct. 1327, 84 L.Ed.2d 274 (1985); Oklahoma Packing Co. v. Oklahoma Gas & Elec. Co., 309 U.S. 4, 8, 60 S.Ct. 215, 217, 84 L.Ed.

when a federal court judgment subsequently is asserted in a state court action.[13] Even in cases in which the court that rendered the judgment erroneously failed to give preclusive effect to an earlier judgment, the court in which the judgment is being asserted as preclusive is bound to honor it.[14]

The source of governing law has produced special problems when a judgment is entered by a federal court in one state and questions of preclusion arise in a federal court in another state. Full faith and credit no longer controls because the question of judgment recognition pertains only to one judicial system—federal.[15] Thus, federal law should control. As argued persuasively by Professor Degnan,[16] even if the first action was a federal diversity case, the scope of the judgment should be controlled by federal law, not by a reference to the state law where the federal court was sitting.[17] Although there is some conflicting authority, at least in this last situation,[18] the Restatement Second of Judgments[19] also has agreed that the decision regarding the preclusive effect of federal judgments is controlled by federal law rather than by principles derived from the Supreme Court's decision in Erie Railroad Company v. Tompkins.[20]

537 (1940); Aquatherm Indus., Inc. v. Florida Power & Light Co., 84 F.3d 1388 (11th Cir.1996).

The deference required by federal courts to state court judgments is underscored in Matsushita Elec. Industrial Co. v. Epstein, 516 U.S. 367, 116 S.Ct. 873, 134 L.Ed.2d 6 (1996), in which the Court held that a Delaware state court class action settlement judgment was entitled to full faith and credit in a California federal class suit even though the released claims were within exclusive federal court jurisdiction. The decision is criticized in Kahan & Silberman, Matsushita and Beyond: The Role of State Courts in Class Actions Involving Exclusive Federal Claims, 1996 Sup.Ct.Rev. 219, and Casenote, 110 Harv.L.Rev. 297 (1996).

13. See the cases cited in note 4, above.

14. Parsons Steel, Inc. v. First Alabama Bank, 474 U.S. 518, 106 S.Ct. 768, 88 L.Ed.2d 877 (1986) (failure of second judgment to give full faith and credit to first judgment is preclusive on that issue and only may be corrected on appeal in the courts of the second state).

15. Baldwin v. Iowa State Traveling Men's Ass'n, 283 U.S. 522, 51 S.Ct. 517, 75 L.Ed. 1244 (1931).

16. Degnan, Federalized Res Judicata, 85 Yale L.J. 741 (1976).

17. J.Z.G. Resources, Inc. v. Shelby Ins. Co., 84 F.3d 211 (6th Cir.1996); Havoco of America, Ltd. v. Freeman, Atkins & Coleman, Ltd., 58 F.3d 303 (7th Cir.1995); Adkins v. Allstate Ins. Co., 729 F.2d 974 (4th Cir.1984); Hardy v. Johns–Manville Sales Corp., 681 F.2d 334 (5th Cir.1982); Aerojet–General Corp. v. Askew, 511 F.2d 710 (5th Cir.1975), cert. denied 423 U.S. 908.

18. E.g., Follette v. Wal–Mart Stores, Inc., 41 F.3d 1234 (8th Cir.1994), cert. denied 516 U.S. 814; McCarty v. First of Georgia Ins. Co., 713 F.2d 609 (10th Cir. 1983); Provident Tradesmens Bank & Trust Co. v. Lumbermens Mut. Cas. Co., 411 F.2d 88 (3d Cir.1969).

19. Restatement Second of Judgments § 87 (1982).

20. 304 U.S. 64, 58 S.Ct. 817, 82 L.Ed. 1188 (1938). The Erie doctrine is discussed in §§ 4.1–4.7, above.

§§ 14.16–15.0 are reserved for supplementary material.

Chapter 15

SECURING AND ENFORCING JUDGMENTS

Analysis

---

§ 15.1 Overview

Because a defendant may dispose of his property in such a way as to put it beyond the court's reach, or because he may engage in acts that might render the plaintiff's requested relief ineffectual, states have provided that, under specified circumstances, a plaintiff may invoke certain protective measures—typically called provisional remedies—pending a final resolution of the controversy on the merits.[1] By using one of these remedies, the plaintiff may ensure that should she prevail on the merits, there will be assets available from which to collect any damages that are awarded[2] or, in the case of injunctive relief, that the status quo will not be disturbed while the litigation is pending.[3]

The first question that must be asked when utilizing any provisional remedy is whether the statutory procedure meets due process standards, which require notice and an opportunity to be heard before a party may

---

§ 15.1

1. In this area of the law, the federal rules, which so dominate other procedural devices, generally have deferred to the states, so that state law must be consulted to determine the exact scope and availability of most provisional remedies, even when

in federal court. One exception is preliminary injunctions. See § 15.4, below.

2. See §§ 15.2–15.3, and §§ 15.5–15.6, below.

3. See § 15.4, below.

be deprived of his property, even temporarily. The Supreme Court's articulation of due process criteria to evaluate prejudgment remedies was discussed in an earlier Chapter.[4] Suffice it to say at this point that the development of those standards, the exact boundaries of which still remain unclear, has had considerable impact on the procedural requirements for provisional remedies. Once the Supreme Court had spoken, states quickly amended their statutes to bring them within permissible constitutional limits, and all this change has created some confusion. This Chapter explores the mechanics and scope of prejudgment remedies as they generally are applied today.

At the opposite end of the litigation spectrum are devices for enforcing judgments. When a losing defendant is unwilling to give the plaintiff the remedy to which the court has declared her entitled, state statutes provide a series of procedures for discovering the judgment debtor's assets and for collecting them.[5] When injunctive relief is involved, whether preliminarily or as a final decree, the court has the power to enforce compliance by holding those who disregard its decree in contempt of court.[6] Although a full exploration of the intricacies of the state procedures for enforcing judgments and the courts' contempt power is outside the scope of this volume, a brief discussion of how each operates and to what they pertain is included.

A. PROVISIONAL REMEDIES

§ 15.2 Attachment

Attachment is a procedure by which the court, at the instance of the plaintiff, directs an officer of the court—in most jurisdictions, a sheriff—to seize or, in the case of nonmovable property, to assert dominion and control over the defendant's assets.[1] Attachment may be used either to obtain jurisdiction over the defendant when the defendant is not otherwise amenable to service of process[2] or to prevent the defendant from disposing of or otherwise impairing the value of property that might be used to satisfy the judgment in an action.[3]

Most states have limited by statute the availability of this provisional remedy to certain prescribed situations.[4] For example, New York will permit attachment only when (1) the defendant is a foreign corporation

---

4. See § 3.21, above.

5. See § 15.7, below. Here, too, state law dominates. See note 1, above.

6. See § 15.8, below.

§ 15.2

1. The description of the provisional remedy of attachment in this section also pertains to other specialized attachment devices such as garnishment, which is the attachment of intangibles, and sequestration, which has equitable origins but now exists in statutory form in some states.

2. See § 3.16, above.

3. Mindlin v. Gehrlein's Marina, Inc., 58 Misc.2d 153, 295 N.Y.S.2d 172 (1968); Elliott v. Great Atl. & Pac. Tea Co., 11 Misc.2d 133, 171 N.Y.S.2d 217 (1957), affirmed 11 Misc.2d 136, 179 N.Y.S.2d 127 (1958).

4. For a summary of procedures and methods of obtaining a prejudgment attachment in ten European countries, see How to Gain Prejudgment Attachment, Int'l Fin. L.Rev. 29 (Oct. 1983).

neither located within the state nor qualified to do business within the state; (2) the defendant is a resident of the state but cannot be served with process despite diligent efforts to do so; (3) the defendant, with the intent to defraud creditors, has assigned, secreted, disposed of, encumbered or removed property from the state or is about to do any of those acts; (4) the action is brought by the victim or the representative of the victim of a crime; or (5) the cause of action is based on a judgment entitled to full faith and credit or to recognition by the state.[5] California even more narrowly restricts the use of attachment to cases involving commercial transactions.[6]

Perhaps reflecting the courts' hesitance about depriving a litigant of property rights prior to a determination on the merits, the statutory criteria for obtaining an attachment typically are construed strictly against the person seeking it.[7] Further, an application for an attachment is addressed to the court's discretion and the court may refuse to grant it even though the statutory criteria are met.[8] This may occur, for example, when allowing the attachment would be oppressive or would cause irremediable harm to the defendant.[9]

The procedures to be followed for obtaining an order of attachment (normally referred to as a "writ" or "warrant") in a particular jurisdiction must be scrutinized carefully to determine whether they comport with the constitutional due process requirements that a defendant be given fair notice and an opportunity to be heard in the action.[10] To obtain a warrant of attachment, state statutes usually require the petitioning litigant to submit an affidavit and any other papers demonstrating that he has a cause of action and that one or more of the statutory grounds for attachment exists.[11] The filing of a complaint is not necessary for the issuance of the writ in some states.[12] If, however, it

---

5. N.Y.—McKinney's CPLR 6201. See generally 7A J. Weinstein, H. Korn & A. Miller, New York Civil Practice ¶ ¶ 6201.01–6201.17.

6. West's Ann.Cal.Code Civ.Proc. § 483.010.

7. Yorkwood Savs. & Loan Ass'n v. Thomas, 379 So.2d 798 (La.App.1980); Englebrecht v. Development Corp. for Evergreen Valley, 361 A.2d 908 (Me.1976); Landewit v. Spadea, 32 Misc.2d 995, 224 N.Y.S.2d 782 (1962).

8. Elliott v. Great Atl. & Pac. Tea Co., 11 Misc.2d 133, 171 N.Y.S.2d 217 (1957), affirmed 11 Misc.2d 136, 179 N.Y.S.2d 127 (1958).

9. Waterman–Bic Pen Corp. v. L.E. Waterman Pen Co., 19 Misc.2d 421, 190 N.Y.S.2d 48 (1959), reversed on other grounds 8 A.D.2d 378, 187 N.Y.S.2d 872 (1959).

10. See § 3.21, above.

11. E.g., West's Ann.Cal.Code Civ. Proc. § 484.020; N.Y.—McKinney's CPLR

6212(a). See Connolly v. Sharpe, 49 N.C.App. 152, 270 S.E.2d 564 (1980).

Since the attachment will be effective only to the extent of the amount claimed in the action plus interest and expenses, some states also require that the plaintiff state the amount of damages demanded from the defendant. See Buxbaum v. Assicurazioni Generali, 175 Misc. 785, 25 N.Y.S.2d 357 (1941). Others require only that the plaintiff state the amount to be secured by the attachment. See West's Ann.Cal.Code Civ. Proc. § 484.020(b).

12. Great Lakes Carbon Corp. v. Fontana, 54 A.D.2d 548, 387 N.Y.S.2d 115 (1976); Beltran Assocs., Inc. v. Steamaster Automatic Boiler Co., 92 N.Y.S.2d 691 (1949); N.Mex.Stat.Ann.1978, § 42–9–4. See also Ala.Code 1975, § 6–6–140 (complaint must be filed within 15 days after suing out the attachment).

Indeed, because the writ is issued primarily on the basis of affidavits, if a complaint is filed, any defects in it may be

clearly appears from the papers presented that the plaintiff's cause of action ultimately will fail, the court may refuse to issue a writ of attachment.[13]

Most commonly, before a writ of attachment will issue, the person seeking it must deposit an undertaking with the court for the purpose of compensating the defendant for any damages sustained should the attachment later be proven wrongful.[14] When an attachment has been vacated because of some significant irregularity or impropriety, such as a lack of jurisdiction, a suit may be brought in the nature of a trespass against the party who obtained the attachment;[15] however, when there has been mere error, the defendant's only redress is upon the plaintiff's undertaking, which is the source and measure of the latter's liability.[16]

A writ of attachment usually is directed to the sheriff in the county in which any property of the defendant, real or personal, tangible or intangible, is located. The sheriff is ordered to levy against that property or against any debts owed to the defendant.[17] The sole restriction on the type of property that may be attached is that it must be such as could be subjected to execution for the satisfaction of a judgment.[18] For example, a contingent debt may not be attached in some jurisdictions because until the contingency has occurred there is nothing that may be used to satisfy the judgment.[19] The premise of this limitation is obvious: since the purpose of attachment is to provide security for any judgment entered for the plaintiff, it is necessary to secure only property that may be used to enforce the judgment.

Ordinarily, a defendant whose property has been attached is given an opportunity to repossess the attached items. Upon giving notice to the sheriff and the plaintiff, paying the sheriff's fees and expenses, and depositing an undertaking equal to the value of the property attached, or a statutorily required higher sum, the defendant may move for a discharge of the attachment.[20] Further, some states expressly have

---

ignored. See United Steel Warehouse Corp. v. Del–Penn Steel Co., 212 N.Y.S.2d 157 (1961); Brown v. Chaminade Velours, Inc., 176 Misc. 238, 26 N.Y.S.2d 1009 (1941), affirmed 261 App.Div. 1071, 26 N.Y.S.2d 1012 (1941).

13. Bernstein v. Van Heyghen Freres Societe Anonyme, 163 F.2d 246 (2d Cir. 1947), cert. denied 332 U.S. 772; American Reserve Ins. Co. v. China Ins. Co., 297 N.Y. 322, 79 N.E.2d 425 (1948). See also Good v. Paine Furniture Co., 35 Conn.Sup. 24, 391 A.2d 741 (1978).

14. West's Fla.Stat.Ann. § 76.12; N.Mex.Stat.Ann.1978, §§ 42–9–4, 42–9–7.

15. See Pourney v. Seabaugh, 604 S.W.2d 646 (Mo.App.1980); Audit Servs. Inc. v. Haugen, 181 Mont. 9, 591 P.2d 1105 (1979).

16. Subin v. U.S. Fidelity & Guar. Co., 12 A.D.2d 49, 208 N.Y.S.2d 278 (1960).

17. Although the levy by the sheriff typically results in the sheriff taking custody of the property, if that is not practicable, adequate notice that the property is within the court's control will suffice. The key is whether the sheriff's acts sufficiently place the property outside the control of the defendant so that the court can find that the attachment was accomplished. See National Am. Corp. v. Federal Republic of Nigeria, 448 F.Supp. 622 (S.D.N.Y.1978), affirmed on other grounds 597 F.2d 314 (2d Cir. 1979); State ex rel. Mather v. Carnes, 551 S.W.2d 272 (Mo.App.1977).

18. See § 15.7, below, on execution.

19. See, e.g., Javorek v. Superior Ct., 17 Cal.3d 629, 131 Cal.Rptr. 768, 552 P.2d 728 (1976).

20. Official Code Ga.Ann. § 18–3–33; Minn.Stat.Ann. § 570.131.

provided that moving to discharge an attachment does not constitute a general appearance[21] so that defendant retains the right to object to the court's personal jurisdiction over him.[22]

§ 15.3   Civil Arrest

Historically, the procedural remedy of civil arrest—the capias ad respondendum—was a device for obtaining jurisdiction over the defendant by which the defendant would be taken into custody and physically restrained until bail was posted or judgment was rendered. The abuses that often accompanied this practice led numerous state legislatures either to prohibit or to restrict the availability of civil arrest.[1] Further, even in those jurisdictions that retained civil arrest, modern courts do not look upon this provisional remedy with favor because of its drastic—indeed, quasi-penal—character.[2]

For example, prior to 1979 when the device was abolished in New York, the courts there ruled that the remedy would not be granted unless there was clear proof that the defendant fell within the provisions of the statute and that its use was necessary to protect the interests of the plaintiff.[3] Moreover, if complete protection could be afforded the plaintiff by some other provisional remedy—attachment, most typically—civil arrest was not ordered.[4] New York courts also exercised their discretion to find that certain persons were immune from the device.[5] For example, public officials were not subject to civil arrest because the public interest would suffer if persons entrusted with the performance of public duties are unavailable to perform them.[6] Similarly, in most states, a nonresident who comes into the state voluntarily to be a witness or who is a party in a civil action has been deemed immune from civil arrest while attending court and while en route to or from the courthouse, provided that only a reasonable time is spent in making these journeys.[7]

To obtain an order of civil arrest, the plaintiff must file with the court, along with a complaint, an affidavit showing that one or more of the statutory grounds for the remedy have been satisfied. Sometimes, statutes require that the affidavit detail facts from which the amount of the bail that should be required of the defendant may be computed.[8]

---

21. N.Y.—McKinney's CPLR 6222.

22. See § 3.26, above, for a discussion of the procedure for making a challenge to jurisdiction.

§ 15.3

1. E.g., N.J.S.A. 2A:15–41, 15–42; S.C.Code 1976, § 15–17–20.

2. North Cent. Investment Co. v. Vander Vorste, 81 S.D. 340, 135 N.W.2d 23 (1965).

3. Todd–Buick, Inc. v. Smith, 118 Misc. 102, 192 N.Y.S. 459 (1922), affirmed 202 App.Div. 774, 194 N.Y.S. 985 (1922).

4. Ibid.

5. Rosenblatt v. Rosenblatt, 110 Misc. 525, 180 N.Y.S. 463 (1920); Kutner v. Hodnett, 59 Misc. 21, 109 N.Y.S. 1068 (1908).

6. Family Finance Corp. v. Starke, 36 N.Y.S.2d 858 (1942).

7. Turner v. McGee, 217 Ga. 769, 125 S.E.2d 36 (1962).

8. See Allison v. Ventura County, 68 Cal.App.3d 689, 137 Cal.Rptr. 542 (1977) (a party may sue for false imprisonment when arrested pursuant to a defective warrant not specifying the amount of bail or the cause or reason for plaintiff's arrest).

Moreover, the court may require the plaintiff to deposit an undertaking with the court for the purpose of covering any damages that might be suffered by the defendant should the arrest prove wrongful.

If an order of arrest is granted, the attorney for the plaintiff typically delivers it to the sheriff. The order will direct the sheriff to arrest the defendant forthwith and bring him into court for a hearing. It also ordinarily will state the amount of bail that will be required to secure the defendant's release from custody. The defendant must be provided a hearing within a statutorily designated period of time or he will be released.[9]

A defendant may secure release from custody by posting the bail specified by the court and promising to make himself available to court process. The posted bail will be used as security for any judgment that the plaintiff may recover in case the defendant later refuses to honor the judgment.

§ 15.4   Preliminary Injunctions

Preliminary injunctions[1] and temporary restraining orders are court orders entered prior to trial for the purpose of protecting the rights of the plaintiff from irreparable injury during the pendency of the action. The orders can be molded to fit the exigencies of each case and thus provide an extremely flexible remedy. For example, they may require the continuation of a course of action, the observance of certain standards of conduct, or that certain acts not be performed. Although affirmative acts may be required of the defendant, the hallmark of the preliminary injunction and the temporary restraining order is that they are intended primarily to preserve the status quo.[2]

A plaintiff may obtain a preliminary injunction by demonstrating to the court that the defendant is acting in a manner that will irreparably injure the plaintiff or that will render a final judgment on the merits ineffectual.[3] This showing is to be made at a hearing that will be held after the defendant has been given notice of the application for preliminary relief.[4] A plaintiff who can show that immediate and irreparable

9. Cf. Thurston v. Leno, 124 Vt. 298, 204 A.2d 106 (1964) (defendant arrested on civil process must be given opportunity to apply to reduce attachment or post security and time of hearing must be set by judge before the defendant can be committed to jail).

§ 15.4

1. Preliminary injunctions also sometimes are referred to as interlocutory or temporary injunctions.

2. Benson Hotel Corp. v. Woods, 168 F.2d 694, 696 (8th Cir.1948); Hoppman v. Riverview Equities Corp., 16 A.D.2d 631, 226 N.Y.S.2d 805 (1962); Board of Higher Educ. of City of New York v. Marcus, 63 Misc.2d 268, 311 N.Y.S.2d 579 (1970).

3. N.Y.—McKinney's CPLR 6301. See generally Bell v. Gitlitz, 38 A.D.2d 656, 327 N.Y.S.2d 437 (1971); Graham v. Board of Supervisors, Erie County, 49 Misc.2d 459, 267 N.Y.S.2d 383 (1966), modified on other grounds 25 A.D.2d 250, 269 N.Y.S.2d 477 (1966), appeal dismissed 17 N.Y.2d 866, 271 N.Y.S.2d 295, 218 N.E.2d 332 (1966). For an excellent discussion of the application of the irreparable injury requirement in preliminary relief cases, see D. Laycock, The Death of the Irreparable Injury Rule 110–132 (1991).

4. For a description of the procedure for obtaining a preliminary injunction in the federal courts, see 11A C. Wright, A. Miller & M. Kane, Civil 2d § 2949.

harm is likely to take place prior to that hearing may obtain a temporary restraining order.[5] Because the temporary restraining order is an emergency device used to protect the plaintiff's rights before the plaintiff and defendant can be brought together for the preliminary injunction hearing, it is by practical necessity granted ex parte. The fact that notice may not be given to all the parties before the court must decide whether to issue a temporary restraining order raises a serious possibility of unfairness to the absentee. Thus, the rulemakers in some jurisdictions have imposed conditions upon the granting of temporary restraining orders[6] and the procedure governing their issuance will be applied scrupulously. Further, a temporary restraining order remains in effect only until the hearing on the motion for the preliminary injunction can be held.[7]

The decision to grant or deny a motion for a preliminary injunction or temporary restraining order lies in the discretion of the court.[8] However, this discretion cannot be exercised unless the plaintiff has made a prima facie showing that he has a cause of action against the defendant.[9] Because even a temporary injunction may do substantial injury to the defendant and because it is granted prior to a determination of the dispute's merits, courts will exercise their discretion to award preliminary relief only when a clear case of entitlement has been demonstrated by the plaintiff.[10] If the facts are in dispute, the court normally will refuse to grant the injunction.[11]

Courts also will use extreme caution if the preliminary injunction requested by the plaintiff would be substantially the same as the remedy that might be awarded at the end of the trial,[12] and the remedy will not

5. See, e.g., U.S. v. Washington Post Co., 446 F.2d 1322 (D.C.Cir.1971). See generally 11A C. Wright, A. Miller & M. Kane, Civil 2d § 2951, discussing the grounds for obtaining a temporary restraining order.

6. See Fed.Civ.Proc.Rule 65(b); 11A C. Wright, A. Miller & M. Kane, Civil 2d § 2952.

7. Most rules authorizing temporary restraining orders provide that they will remain in effect only for a limited period of time, typically ten days, unless the court extends the time "for good cause shown" or the other party consents to an extension. E.g., Official Code Ga.Ann. § 9–11–65(b) (order expires as court fixes, not to exceed 30 days); Vernon's Ann.Mo.Civ.Proc.Rule 92.02(b) (order expires by its terms, not to exceed 10 days). In practice this means that the order remains in effect until the preliminary injunction hearing.

8. R & J Bottling Co. v. Rosenthal, 40 A.D.2d 911, 337 N.Y.S.2d 783 (1972); McHugo v. Kozak, 18 Misc.2d 53, 188 N.Y.S.2d 253 (1958).

9. Crowther v. Seaborg, 415 F.2d 437 (10th Cir.1969); Weisner v. 791 Park Ave. Corp., 7 A.D.2d 75, 180 N.Y.S.2d 734

(1958), reversed on other grounds 6 N.Y.2d 426, 190 N.Y.S.2d 70, 160 N.E.2d 720 (1959). Courts use a variety of formulations to suggest that the applicant for preliminary relief must show some likelihood of success on the merits. See 11A C. Wright, A. Miller & M. Kane, Civil 2d § 2948.3 nn. 2–3.

10. Dymo Indus., Inc. v. Tapeprinter, Inc., 326 F.2d 141, 143 (9th Cir.1964); Valentine v. Indianapolis–Marion County Bldg. Authority, 355 F.Supp. 1240 (S.D.Ind.1973); Russian Church of Our Lady of Kazan v. Dunkel, 34 A.D.2d 799, 311 N.Y.S.2d 533 (1970).

11. See Miller v. American Tel. & Tel. Corp., 344 F.Supp. 344 (E.D.Pa.1972); Tuvim v. 10 E. 30 Corp., 75 Misc.2d 612, 345 N.Y.S.2d 258 (1971), modified on other grounds 38 A.D.2d 895, 329 N.Y.S.2d 275 (1972), affirmed 32 N.Y.2d 541, 347 N.Y.S.2d 13, 300 N.E.2d 397 (1973); Jaymar's Inc. v. Schwartz, 37 Misc.2d 314, 235 N.Y.S.2d 449 (1962).

12. Bailey v. Romney, 359 F.Supp. 596 (D.D.C.1972); Acorn Employment Serv., Inc. v. Moss, 261 App.Div. 178, 24 N.Y.S.2d

be awarded unless there is a clear showing of necessity.[13] That is, the applicant must show that he is likely to suffer irreparable harm before a decision on the merits can be reached.[14] In considering whether necessity exists, the court ordinarily will balance the relative inconveniences to the parties.[15] If granting the injunction would do more damage to the defendant than denying it would do to the plaintiff, the request should be refused.[16] In analyzing this relative-injury calculus in a particular case, the court may consider injury to the public welfare as well as to the parties.[17]

Preliminary injunctions and temporary restraining orders are equitable remedies; hence, the maxim that an equitable remedy will not be given when the plaintiff has adequate redress at law is applicable.[18] For example, in one early case persons who had speculatively purchased tickets to a baseball game and who were reselling them at a substantial profit when it appeared that the game would be a sellout, sought a preliminary injunction to restrain the baseball club from refusing admission to the purchasers of their tickets. The court refused to grant the preliminary injunction on the ground that the speculators could maintain an action for the price of any tickets that the baseball club wrongfully refused to honor and therefore had an adequate remedy at law.[19]

Although preliminary injunctions and temporary restraining orders are granted prior to a full adjudication on the merits, they have all the force of a permanent injunction during their periods of effectiveness. Thus, these orders bind the defendant, the defendant's servants and agents, and those acting in conjunction with or for the benefit of the defendant, just as would a permanent decree.[20] And, the failure to obey

669 (1941), appeal denied 261 App.Div. 897, 26 N.Y.S.2d 315 (1941).

13. Russian Church of Our Lady of Kazan v. Dunkel, 34 A.D.2d 799, 311 N.Y.S.2d 533 (1970); McKesson & Robbins Inc. v. New York State Bd. of Pharmacy, 226 N.Y.S.2d 271 (1962).

14. Compare Omega Importing Corp. v. Petri–Kine Camera Co., 451 F.2d 1190 (2d Cir.1971) (irreparable harm found when high probability of confusion between products in trademark infringement case and harm not fully compensable in damages), with Cheese Shop Int'l, Inc. v. Wirth, 304 F.Supp. 861 (N.D.Ga.1969) (irreparable injury not found by threat of breach of covenant not to compete).

15. Board of Trustees of Community College District No. 508 v. Bakalis, 64 Ill. App.3d 967, 21 Ill.Dec. 732, 382 N.E.2d 26 (1978); Mantle Men & Namath Girls, Inc. v. LCR Temporaries, Inc., 39 A.D.2d 681, 331 N.Y.S.2d 987 (1972); Gilbert v. Burnside, 6 A.D.2d 834, 175 N.Y.S.2d 989 (1958).

16. Herwald v. Schweiker, 658 F.2d 359 (5th Cir.1981); Gilbert v. Burnside, 6

A.D.2d 834, 175 N.Y.S.2d 989 (1958); Chapman v. Hapeman, 8 Misc.2d 19, 167 N.Y.S.2d 342 (1957).

17. See Yakus v. U.S., 321 U.S. 414, 440, 64 S.Ct. 660, 675, 88 L.Ed. 834 (1944); DePina v. Educational Testing Serv., 31 A.D.2d 744, 297 N.Y.S.2d 472 (1969); International Ry. Co. v. Barone, 246 App.Div. 450, 284 N.Y.S. 122 (1935).

18. See A. L. K. Corporation v. Columbia Pictures Indus., Inc., 440 F.2d 761 (3d Cir.1971); People v. Teague, 83 Ill.App.3d 990, 39 Ill.Dec. 463, 404 N.E.2d 1054 (1980); Mantle Men & Namath Girls, Inc. v. LCR Temporaries, Inc., 39 A.D.2d 681, 331 N.Y.S.2d 987 (1972). See generally 11A C. Wright, A. Miller & M. Kane, Civil 2d § 2944, for a discussion of what constitutes an adequate legal remedy.

19. Levine v. Brooklyn Nat. League Baseball Club, 179 Misc. 22, 36 N.Y.S.2d 474 (1942).

20. For a discussion of who is bound by an injunction, see 11A C. Wright, A. Miller & M. Kane, Civil 2d § 2956.

the injunction may be punishable by contempt.[21]

§ 15.5   Temporary Receivers

The appointment of a temporary receiver is a procedure by which a plaintiff, or in some states any person having an interest in property that is the subject of a lawsuit, requests that the court appoint a competent person to manage some or all of the defendant's property until the resolution of the underlying controversy.[1] Typically, statutes permit the appointment of a temporary receiver when there is a substantial danger that property will be removed from the state, lost, materially injured or destroyed.[2] In practice, however, it is the actual or potential insolvency of the defendant that prompts a party to request that the defendant's property be turned over to a receiver.

The decision to appoint a receiver during the pendency of an action rests in the discretion of the court.[3] Because it represents an interference with the defendant's peaceful enjoyment of his property, a receiver normally will not be appointed unless there is clear and convincing proof of necessity,[4] such as a showing of a likelihood of irreparable harm to the property.[5]

The receiver is an officer of the court who has been appointed for a specific purpose. He is at all times subject to the court's control and possesses only those powers conferred by the order of appointment. The receiver should show complete impartiality as to all those claiming an interest in the property in custody.[6] The receiver's role as an officer of the court makes it unlawful for him to delegate his powers or responsibilities to others.[7] He stands in a fiduciary relationship to those who claim an interest in the property, and is held to the same standard of care as is a trustee in the management of a trust.[8]

To qualify as a receiver, an individual must be a person of unimpeachable reputation. Someone who is about to become a receiver has an affirmative duty to inform the court of any matter that concerns his

---

21. See § 15.8, below.

§ 15.5

1. The appointment of a receiver is ancillary to other remedies and cannot be the sole relief sought by an action. Petitpren v. Taylor School District, 104 Mich.App. 283, 304 N.W.2d 553 (1981); Nigro v. First Nat. Bank of Boston, 7 Mass.App.Ct. 903, 387 N.E.2d 1196 (1979); Northampton Nat. Bank of Easton v. Piscanio, 475 Pa. 57, 379 A.2d 870 (1977).

2. Fed.Civ.Proc.Rule 66; West's Ann. Cal.Code Civ.Proc. § 564; N.Y.—McKinney's CPLR 6401. See generally 12 C. Wright, A. Miller & R. Marcus, Civil 2d §§ 2981–86.

3. Theatres of America, Inc. v. State, 577 S.W.2d 542 (Tex.Civ.App.1979); Lieb-

man & Co. v. Institutional Investors Trust, 406 A.2d 37 (Del.1979).

4. See Commodity Futures Trading Comm'n v. Comvest Trading Corp., 481 F.Supp. 438 (D.Mass.1979); Northampton Nat. Bank of Easton v. Piscanio, 475 Pa. 57, 379 A.2d 870 (1977); Saull v. Seplowe, 218 N.Y.S.2d 777 (1961).

5. S.Z.B. Corporation v. Ruth, 14 A.D.2d 678, 219 N.Y.S.2d 889 (1961).

6. Continental Ins. Co. v. Equitable Trust Co., 229 App.Div. 657, 243 N.Y.S. 200 (1930), affirming 137 Misc. 28, 244 N.Y.S. 377 (1930).

7. In re Stoll–Meyer Woodcrafters, Inc., 84 N.Y.S.2d 757 (1948).

8. Slack v. McAtee, 175 Misc. 393, 23 N.Y.S.2d 785 (1940).

reputation or integrity, and a failure or omission to do so is considered a fraud upon the court.[9] In addition, state statutes ordinarily require that the receiver take an oath to discharge faithfully and fairly the trust conferred upon him[10] and a receiver normally will be required to file an undertaking in an amount fixed by the court. The undertaking is the maximum limit of the receiver's liability if, when acting within the scope of his authority, an occurrence arises for which liability is sought to be imposed. If the receiver acts outside the scope of his authority, individual liability may be imposed for the full amount of any proven damages.[11]

§ 15.6　Notice of Pendency

A notice of pendency, also referred to as lis pendens, is a mechanism by which a plaintiff in litigation concerning property may guarantee that nothing will occur during the course of the lawsuit that will create a defect in the defendant's title to the property at issue. Filing a notice of pendency gives constructive notice that the title to the property is the subject of pending litigation.[1] The notice is not an injunction and it does not restrain the conveyance of land; however, any grantee will take the property subject to the interests that the plaintiff may establish as a result of a determination of the litigation in her favor.[2] The notice of pendency thus may be viewed as a benefit to potential encumbrancers and vendees because in order to determine whether property is the subject of pending litigation, all one need do is look through the property records for a notice of pendency.[3]

A lis pendens typically may be filed in any action in which the judgment demanded would affect the title to, or the possession, use, or enjoyment of real property, except in a summary proceeding brought to recover the possession of real property.[4] A few states also authorize its use in actions affecting personal property.[5] To determine whether the action is for a judgment that would affect the title to or enjoyment of property, the court will look to the face of the complaint.[6] If it appears

9. Cohen v. Hechtman, 187 Misc. 994, 66 N.Y.S.2d 305 (1946).

10. E.g., N.Y.—McKinney's CPLR 6403. See generally 7A J. Weinstein, H. Korn & A. Miller, New York Civil Practice ¶¶ 6403.01–6403.06.

11. See Becknell v. McConnell, 142 Ga. App. 567, 236 S.E.2d 546 (1977); State Through State Bd. of Equalization v. Stewart, 272 Cal.App.2d 345, 77 Cal.Rptr. 418 (1969); Birch–Field v. Davenport Shore Club, Inc., 223 App.Div. 767, 227 N.Y.S. 624 (1928).

§ 15.6

1. See Albertson v. Raboff, 46 Cal.2d 375, 295 P.2d 405 (1956).

2. Bagnall v. Suburbia Land Co., 579 P.2d 914 (Utah 1978); Fiddlers Green Ass'n v. Construction Corp. of Long Island, Inc., 20 Misc.2d 473, 190 N.Y.S.2d 17 (1959),

reversed on other grounds 12 A.D.2d 501, 207 N.Y.S.2d 81 (1960).

3. E & E Hauling, Inc. v. DuPage County, 33 Ill.Dec. 536, 77 Ill.App.3d 1017, 396 N.E.2d 1260 (1979).

4. E.g., N.Y.—McKinney's CPLR 6501. See Hammersley v. District Court In & For Routt County, 199 Colo. 442, 610 P.2d 94 (1980) (proceeding to enforce adherence to criteria with respect to construction of improvements). See generally 7A J. Weinstein, H. Korn & A. Miller, New York Civil Practice ¶¶ 6501.01–6501.15

5. E.g., West's Fla.Stat.Ann. § 48.23; Ohio Rev.Code § 2703.26.

6. See Boca Raton Land Dev., Inc. v. Sparling, 397 So.2d 1053 (Fla.App.1981); Siegel v. Silverstone, 250 App.Div. 784, 294 N.Y.S. 385 (1937); Starkie v. Nib Constr. Corp., 235 App.Div. 699, 255 N.Y.S. 401 (1932).

that the action is based on grounds unrelated to the property, even though the property may be mentioned or described in the complaint, lis pendens is not proper.[7] The action itself must involve or be directed at the title to or enjoyment of the property in some way; the mere possibility that ownership will be affected by proceedings for the satisfaction of the judgment is not sufficient. Thus, a notice of pendency may not properly be filed in anticipation of an action for money damages,[8] an action based on a personal obligation,[9] or an action to recover the reasonable value of the plaintiff's services in real estate negotiations.[10]

Like all prejudgment remedies, the lis pendens procedure must comport with due process requirements, which mandate some form of notice or hearing before defendant's property can be affected.[11] Typically, a notice of pendency must be filed with the clerk of the county in which the property is situated, along with a copy of the complaint.[12] The notice itself states the names of the parties to the action, the object of the action, and a description of the property affected. The county clerk is required to record the notice of pendency and index it in connection with the affected property. Under some statutes, the notice also may be required to be mailed to all adverse parties and owners of record in order to be effective.[13] The current requirements applicable in each state should be consulted carefully because many states have changed their procedures in recent years in an effort to comply with the Supreme Court's due process pronouncements.[14]

B. ENFORCEMENT OF JUDGMENTS

§ 15.7 Executions and Levies

For those litigants who seek damages from their opponents, a favorable judgment on the merits may prove to be only the first skirmish in what turns out to be a very long, hard-fought battle to collect the award. The entry of a judgment against a defendant ordinarily is merely declaratory of the fact and amount of liability. Many defendants are reluctant to pay judgments entered against them, and it is the judgment creditor's responsibility to commence collection proceedings.

State statutes provide a number of devices by which a judgment winner may collect an award.[1] The classic one, typically called execution,

---

7. Zanfardino v. Newberg, 145 N.Y.S.2d 15 (1955).

8. Bramall v. Wales, 29 Wn.App. 390, 628 P.2d 511 (1981); Oster v. Bishop, 20 Misc.2d 446, 186 N.Y.S.2d 737 (1959).

9. Zanfardino v. Newberg, 145 N.Y.S.2d 15 (1955).

10. Ryan v. La Rosa, 22 Misc.2d 125, 202 N.Y.S.2d 802 (1960).

11. See Kukanskis v. Griffith, 180 Conn. 501, 430 A.2d 21 (1980).

12. See Dunn v. Stack, 394 So.2d 1076 (Fla.App.1981).

13. E.g., West's Ann.Cal.Code Civ. Proc. § 405.22.

14. See § 3.21, above.

§ 15.7

1. The law in this area is mostly state created. The federal courts use whatever statutory procedures are available in the states in which they are sitting. See Fed. Civ.Proc.Rule 69(a).

assumes varying forms depending upon the nature of the property of the judgment debtor that will be used to satisfy the judgment. In general, however, executions are papers issued from the clerk of the court[2] or, in some jurisdictions, from the attorney for the judgment creditor,[3] authorizing the sheriff to seize or to assert dominion over the property of a judgment debtor.[4]

The availability of execution to enforce a judgment is limited to certain types of property. First, execution typically may be used only on property that the debtor may transfer voluntarily or assign. For example, many jurisdictions provide that contingent remainders are not subject to either lien or levy, representing as they do a mere expectancy.[5] Further, an execution will reach only property in which the judgment debtor has a property interest at the time the execution is served.[6] Consequently, although the execution will reach money not yet due under an existing contract, it will not reach funds paid to the judgment debtor pursuant to a contract made after the service of the execution.[7] This doctrine was carried to its logical limits in one New York case in which an execution against an overdrawn bank account was held invalid.[8] The bank was not required to pay out money at the time of the execution; nor did the execution create a lien on the account. Money deposited thereafter would not have to be paid to the judgment creditor.

Finally, special problems are presented when the creditor attempts to execute on property that is not solely owned by the judgment debtor, or when the judgment debtor was sued in a representative capacity, and execution is sought against his personal property. For example, in jurisdictions that permit a partnership to be sued in its own name, a judgment may be entered against all the partners even though less than all have been served with process. But an execution to collect that judgment will reach only the property of the partnership and not the partners' personal property unless they have been served in their individual capacities with process.[9] Furthermore, in some states an execution against property held in a tenancy by the entirety will be ineffective during the term of the entirety.[10] It is necessary to check state law carefully to ascertain exactly what and whose property may be subject to execution.

2. Neb.Rev.St. § 25–1501.

3. N.Y.—McKinney's CPLR 5230(b).

4. For a discussion of what happens when execution must take place in a jurisdiction other than the one rendering the original judgment, see text at notes 39–43, below.

5. See Halbach, Creditors' Rights Against Contingent Remainders, 43 Minn. L.Rev. 217 (1958).

6. Kazanjian v. Jamaica Sav. Bank, 105 Misc.2d 228, 432 N.Y.S.2d 62 (1980) (certificate of deposit is present debt).

7. In re Lindenwald Bottling Corp., 23 N.Y.S.2d 768 (1940).

8. Douglas v. Fassoulis, 17 Misc.2d 911, 186 N.Y.S.2d 537 (1959).

9. Detrio v. U.S., 264 F.2d 658 (5th Cir.1959); Martinoff v. Triboro Roofing Co., 228 N.Y.S.2d 139 (1962). Compare First Nat. Bank of Southglenn v. Energy Fuels Corp., 200 Colo. 540, 618 P.2d 1115 (1980) (execution on real property held in joint tenancy acts only on interest of judgment debtor).

10. Bostian v. Jones, 244 S.W.2d 1 (Mo.1951).

In addition to the above limitations, state statutes also typically provide for the exemption of certain kinds of property from execution. A common provision is one exempting various types of personal property in order to make certain that the judgment debtor and his family are able to maintain a household and some modest, minimal standard of living.[11] Because of the overriding need to protect the health and safety of the public, the property of a municipality also has been deemed exempt from execution.[12]

In most states, if the judgment creditor waits too long before instituting enforcement proceedings, the judgment will expire.[13] In some cases, however, it may be impossible to commence collection proceedings until after the expiration date has passed, as, for example, when the judgment debtor has left the jurisdiction. The absence of the debtor may be ameliorated by state tolling statutes.[14] Alternatively, some states permit the judgment creditor to apply for a writ of scire facias,[15] which, if granted, revives the original judgment for a period of time at the expiration of which an application for another writ of scire facias may be made. By repeating this procedure, a judgment may be kept alive until the debtor and his property are found.

A writ of execution is a powerful device because it gives the judgment creditor a direct means of enforcement against the property of the judgment debtor.[16] When the execution is delivered to the sheriff, it operates as a lien against the personal property of the judgment debtor that is subject to execution.[17] The execution authorizes the sheriff to seize or levy upon any property belonging to the judgment debtor.[18]

---

11. See, e.g., N.Y.—McKinney's CPLR 5205(a). New York enforcement practice is discussed at length in Volume 6 of J. Weinstein, H. Korn & A. Miller, New York Civil Practice. See the discussion of the Alaska exemption statutes in Gutterman v. First Nat. Bank of Anchorage, 597 P.2d 969 (Alaska 1979). See generally Vukowich, Debtors' Exemption Rights, 62 Geo.L.J. 779 (1974).

12. Union Reddi–Mix Co. v. Specialty Concrete Contractor, 476 S.W.2d 160 (Mo. App.1972); Burgess v. Kansas City, 259 S.W.2d 702 (Mo.App.1953). Compare Fed. Civ.Proc.Rule 69(b) (execution against revenue officers and officers of Congress limited).

13. E.g., West's Ann.Cal.Code Civ. Proc. § 337.5 (10 years); So.Dak.Codified Laws 15–18–1 (20 years).

14. E.g., Vernon's Tex.Code Ann. Civ. Prac.Rem.Code § 16.063; West's Rev.Code Wash.Ann. 4.16.180.

15. See Nowels v. Bergstedt, 120 Ariz. 112, 584 P.2d 576 (App.1978); Driscoll v. Konze, 322 S.W.2d 824 (Mo.1959), cert. denied 360 U.S. 931; Kennedy v. Boden, 241 Mo.App. 86, 231 S.W.2d 862 (1950).

16. Rosenthal v. Graves, 168 Misc. 845, 6 N.Y.S.2d 766 (1938).

In some instances this direct means of enforcement may not be feasible, as when the property is held by the judgment debtor at his home and the sheriff thus is prevented from entering and seizing it. In these cases, some states provide an alternative remedy: the creditor can apply to the court for an order of payment directing that property be turned over in compliance with it. E.g., N.Y.—McKinney's CPLR 5225. Failure to comply with the court's order may result in contempt.

17. Art–Camera–Pix, Inc. v. Cinecom Corp., 64 Misc.2d 764, 315 N.Y.S.2d 991 (1970); Meyerhardt v. Heinzelman, 71 N.Y.S.2d 692 (1947), affirmed 272 App.Div. 800, 71 N.Y.S.2d 925 (1947).

18. If jurisdiction in the underlying lawsuit was based on the attachment of property, only the property that was attached for jurisdiction purposes is subject to execution. Benadon v. Antonio, 10 A.D.2d 40, 197 N.Y.S.2d 1 (1960), modified on other grounds 10 A.D.2d 929, 205 N.Y.S.2d 800 (1960).

Usually the sheriff has a limited amount of time within which to levy pursuant to the execution. In New York, for example, the sheriff must return the execution, whether satisfied or not, to the proper clerk or support collection unit within sixty days from the date on which it was delivered to him.[19] The sheriff's return must set forth the steps that were taken pursuant to the execution.

It should be noted that it is not necessary for the sheriff or his agent physically to seize the property in order for a levy to be effective. All that is required is that the sheriff assert dominion over it.[20] For example, in one case[21] an execution was delivered to the deputy sheriff who then went to the site of an old school house that had been purchased recently by the judgment debtor. The deputy informed the debtor that the property was being levied upon and that no part of the building or its contents should be carried from the premises. Subsequently, the judgment debtor tore down the building and carried it away. The court held that the deputy's verbal notice was sufficient to constitute a valid levy and that the judgment debtor's willful disregard of the levy was punishable as contempt.

When a judgment calls for the delivery of certain specified property, as when a court order of specific performance is involved, the execution will describe the property to be awarded, direct the sheriff to seize the property from the judgment debtor, and order it delivered to the person named in the execution.[22] If the specific property cannot be found within the sheriff's jurisdiction, and if the judgment is for the delivery of a chattel or its value, the sheriff may be authorized to levy upon any property within the jurisdiction, just as if the execution were in satisfaction of a money judgment.

If the judgment for which execution is sought is an award of money damages, the sheriff usually will sell the property rather than deliver it to the judgment creditor. Most statutes provide that the sale must be by public auction.[23] Since the objective is to secure a fair price for the property, in some states the sheriff may postpone the sale, if he believes there is an insufficient number of bidders. In addition, the sheriff usually is required to sell for cash only.[24] The proceeds of the sale, after deducting the sheriff's fees and other costs of the auction, are applied toward the satisfaction of the judgment. If, after satisfying the judgment, some proceeds remain, they will be turned over to the judgment debtor.

Procedural defects in the sale or in the notice may render the auction void, and if the judgment creditors are aware of the defects and

19. N.Y.—McKinney's CPLR 5230(c).

20. Alcor, Inc. v. Balanoff, 45 A.D.2d 795, 357 N.Y.S.2d 160 (1974).

21. Burton v. Jurgensen, 138 Misc. 69, 244 N.Y.S. 320 (1930).

22. N.Y.—McKinney's CPLR 5102.

23. The sheriff typically is required to give some form of public notice for a prescribed period of time prior to the date of the sale. E.g., N.J.Stat.Ann. 2A:17–33, 17–34, 17–35; N.Y.—McKinney's CPLR 5233.

24. Flagship State Bank of Jacksonville v. Carantzas, 352 So.2d 1259 (Fla.App. 1977), cert. denied 361 So.2d 830 (Fla.); Watson & Pittinger v. Hoboken Planing Mills Co., 156 App.Div. 8, 140 N.Y.S. 822 (1913).

permit the sale to continue, they may be liable for conversion. Illustratively, in one case the sheriff levied against the personal property of the judgment debtor at his farm home. At the execution sale, the judgment debtor's wife protested on the ground that she had a half interest in the property being sold and that the notice was given only on the day of the sale instead of six days prior thereto, as the statute required. The court held that in light of the judgment creditor's knowledge of these defects, his acquiescence in the continuation of the sale and receipt of the proceeds constituted conversion.[25]

A levy of execution is not limited to property in the possession of the judgment debtor; it may be directed against property held by a third person. When this occurs, the proceeding usually is called a garnishee execution. It has been held that because an execution is not an order of the court, a failure by the garnishee to surrender the property to the sheriff may not be punishable as contempt.[26] However, noncompliance with a restraining notice—an instrument issued by the clerk or support collection unit prohibiting the garnishee from transferring a judgment debtor's property—may result in the garnishee being liable to the creditor for the value of the property.[27]

A judgment creditor also may cause an execution to be issued against the income of the judgment debtor. If the income execution is served upon the judgment debtor and the latter fails to pay the installments specified in the execution, some states provide that the sheriff may serve an endorsed copy of the execution on the person obligated to pay income to the judgment debtor. The garnishee—usually the judgment debtor's employer—then must withhold a specified percentage or dollar amount of the debtor's wages as if the execution had been served upon him originally.[28] A garnishee who fails to withhold income pursuant to the execution may become liable for the amount not withheld.[29]

Rather than using an income execution—or wage garnishment as it is commonly called—a judgment creditor may elect to request the court to issue an order requiring the defendant to satisfy the judgment in installment payments.[30] There is some confusion as to whether a judgment creditor first must attempt an ordinary garnishment proceeding before requesting this remedy. Some cases[31] hold that the court will not permit a direct action against the judgment debtor ordering him to pay installments when there is a reasonable chance of collecting the judg-

---

25. White v. Page, 275 App.Div. 871, 88 N.Y.S.2d 373 (1949), reargument denied 275 App.Div. 972, 91 N.Y.S.2d 515 (1949).

26. Smith v. Top Notch Bakers, Inc., 206 Misc. 265, 134 N.Y.S.2d 744 (1954), affirmed 286 App.Div. 1016, 144 N.Y.S.2d 536 (1955), appeal denied 1 A.D.2d 785, 149 N.Y.S.2d 226 (1956).

27. N.Y.—McKinney's CPLR 5222.

28. Neb.Rev.St. § 25–1558; N.Y.—McKinney's CPLR 5231.

29. Flaherty Assocs., Inc. v. Fairway Motor Sales, Inc., 23 N.Y.S.2d 34 (1940).

30. N.Y.—McKinney's CPLR 5226.

31. Industrial Bank of Commerce v. Kelly, 28 Misc.2d 889, 215 N.Y.S.2d 644 (1961); Adirondack Furniture Corp. v. Crannell, 167 Misc. 599, 5 N.Y.S.2d 840 (1938); Metropolitan Life Ins. Co. v. Zaroff, 157 Misc. 796, 284 N.Y.S. 665 (1935).

ment through other devices; but other cases[32] assert that the choice of procedures is left entirely to the judgment creditor. The latter view seems preferable when the applicable statutes do not expressly require the unsuccessful resort to an income execution as a prerequisite to the granting of an order for installment payments. It is clear that the judgment creditor may use only one of the two procedures. She cannot simultaneously receive payments under an income execution and an order for installment payments.[33]

Regardless of which form of income execution is used, the judgment debtor should be given an opportunity to demonstrate his reasonable needs and those of his family. The exact amount to be deducted from the judgment debtor's wages is discretionary with the court.[34] Indeed, it has been held that even the judgment debtor's stipulation to pay a specified amount is not controlling, especially if the debtor's circumstances change after signing the stipulation.[35] However, some state legislatures have limited the courts' discretion by declaring that no more than a certain percentage or a fixed dollar amount may be deducted from a wage earner's income,[36] and Congress has enacted a statute providing that no court—state or federal—may authorize a deduction from a judgment debtor's wages that will leave his remaining income less than 75% of his take-home pay or 30 times the minimum hourly wage, whichever is greater.[37]

In some states, proceedings against real property for the satisfaction of judgments are governed by different rules from those that apply to personal property or income. For example, a lien against personal property typically is established when the execution is delivered to the sheriff, but a lien against real property is established when the judgment is docketed with the clerk of the county in which the real property is situated.[38] It is most important that the appropriate procedure be used because an error in docketing that has misled a bona fide purchaser will give that purchaser rights in the property superior to those of the judgment creditor.

All the preceding discussion about judgment execution assumes that property is available within the jurisdiction of the court that rendered the underlying judgment. When the judgment creditor is forced to seek property outside the jurisdiction of the judgment court, then traditionally the creditor must bring an action on the judgment in the court where property is found because a court cannot issue an order of execution

32.   Olson v. Olson, 275 App.Div. 60, 87 N.Y.S.2d 709 (1949); Yamamoto v. Costello, 73 Misc.2d 592, 342 N.Y.S.2d 33 (1973); Goodman v. Owen, 28 Misc.2d 1045, 214 N.Y.S.2d 963 (1961).

33.   McDonnell v. McDonnell, 281 N.Y. 480, 24 N.E.2d 134 (1939).

34.   Wood v. Paolino, 116 R.I. 106, 352 A.2d 397 (1976); Uni–Serv Corp. v. Linker, 62 Misc.2d 861, 311 N.Y.S.2d 726 (1970); Amato v. Amato, 45 N.Y.S.2d 371 (1943).

35.   Wells v. Hollister, 265 App.Div. 603, 40 N.Y.S.2d 166 (1943).

36.   Colo.Rev.Stat.Ann.   § 13–54–104; Tenn.Code Ann. § 26–2–106; Utah Rules Civ.Proc., Rule 64D(d).

37.   15 U.S.C.A. § 1673.

38.   Asher v. U.S., 436 F.Supp. 22 (N.D.Ill.1976), affirmed 570 F.2d 682 (7th Cir.1978); N.Y.—McKinney's CPLR 5203.

outside its own territorial limits.[39] Although the Full Faith and Credit Clause of the United States Constitution[40] assures that in most instances the court in which execution is sought will not look behind the judgment and reopen the case on the merits, the requirement of filing a new action and effectuating service is costly and certainly more complex than ordinary execution. To ameliorate this, a special federal statute exists providing for the registration of judgments between federal courts.[41] Several states also have adopted the Uniform Enforcement of Foreign Money Judgments Act,[42] which allows similar simplified procedures when execution is sought between state courts.[43] In the absence of these special statutory procedures, however, attempts to execute a judgment across state lines require the filing of a formal action on the judgment to obtain a new judgment in the second state on which execution can issue.

Additional problems in execution are presented when property levied upon by the sheriff is claimed by persons other than the judgment debtor. When this occurs, the individual claiming an interest in property in the custody of the sheriff may institute a proceeding to obtain a judicial determination of who has the superior interest.[44] If issues of fact are in dispute, a separate trial will be ordered. As long as the value or the utility of the property will not be impaired, custody of the property will remain with the sheriff during the course of these proceedings.

A more common difficulty in execution is the problem of locating the judgment debtor's assets. It must be remembered that the typical civil judgment declares liability and its amount, but does not order the losing party to pay money or indeed to do anything. Hence a recalcitrant judgment debtor, through concealment of assets or fraudulent conveyance, can frustrate enforcement of the judgment.

Equity courts responded to this perceived inadequacy of execution process by creating two remedies that now have been applied in all jurisdictions by statute or court decision. The first of these is exemplified by the Uniform Fraudulent Conveyance Act, which nullifies transactions by which a judgment debtor renders himself insolvent through the transfer of his property for less than its value. That Act has been widely adopted.[45] The second remedy to prevent abuse usually is referred to as

---

39. National Equipment Rental, Ltd. v. Coolidge Bank & Trust Co., 348 So.2d 1236 (Fla.App.1977). See generally Pennoyer v. Neff, 95 U.S. (5 Otto) 714, 24 L.Ed. 565 (1878).

40. U.S.C.A. Const. Art. IV, § 1. Full faith and credit is discussed in § 14.15, above.

41. 28 U.S.C.A. § 1963.

42. 13 Uniform Laws Ann. 152.

43. E.g., N.Y.—McKinney's CPLR 5401 to 5408.

44. E.g., N.Y.—McKinney's CPLR 5239.

When this remedy is available, it should be pursued by the claimant rather than attempting to induce the judgment debtor to resist the levy. Should the latter course be taken, the property may be sold anyway and the judgment debtor may be held in contempt of court. See Burton v. Jurgensen, 138 Misc. 69, 244 N.Y.S. 320 (1930).

45. Uniform Fraudulent Conveyance Act, 7A Uniform Laws Ann. 427. Twenty-five states, plus the Virgin Islands, have adopted the act to date and others achieve the same result by court decision. The widespread recognition of the practice is reflected in Fed.Civ.Proc.Rule 18(b).

supplementary proceedings. Upon a showing that the sheriff is unable to locate property of the debtor subject to execution, the debtor can be subjected to examination under oath to disclose the location of assets and to trace property that has disappeared or been transferred.[46]

These devices remain creatures of equity. Thus they are outside the ambit of jury trial, and they continue to lend to the judgment the coercive power of contempt sanctions. False swearing or noncompliance with a subpoena issued to respond to post-judgment discovery consequently may be punishable as contempt.[47]

§ 15.8 Contempt

As noted in earlier sections of this Chapter, a party's noncompliance with a direct court order may be punished by declaring the miscreant to be in contempt of court.[1] Historically, contempt was the normal procedure for enforcing decrees issued by the equity courts. Unlike the garnishment of the judgment debtor's wages or the levying of an execution against his property, a citation for contempt operates against the person of the contemnor, rather than his property.

There are two distinct types of contempt—civil and criminal. The distinction between the two depends upon the objective to be achieved by the contempt citation.[2] If its purpose is remedial and it is intended to coerce the contemnor into performing an act required by the court's decree or refraining from conduct proscribed by the court, the contempt should be characterized as civil.[3] If the purpose is to vindicate the authority of the court and punish disobedience of its order, the contempt is criminal in nature.[4] Contempt sanctions may be a fine or imprisonment, or both, but the form in which these sanctions may be administered differs depending on the type of contempt involved. Although a fine or incarceration inevitably will have some punitive and deterrent effect, in the civil contempt context, because the fine typically is paid to the

46. E.g., Fed.Civ.Proc.Rule 69. See U.S. v. Earl Phillips Coal Co., 66 F.R.D. 101 (E.D.Tenn.1975); 12 C. Wright, A. Miller & R. Marcus, Civil 2d § 3014.

47. In re Fellerman, 149 Fed. 244 (S.D.N.Y.1907). But cf. Fromme v. Gray, 148 N.Y. 695, 43 N.E. 215 (1896) (only refusing to testify, not false swearing, is punishable as contempt).

§ 15.8

1. Contempt may be sought in response to a violation of preliminary court orders, such as those that arise in discovery, from the failure to comply with a final injunction decree, or from the disobedience of a court order to turn over property subject to execution. It is the latter two types that are of interest in the present context, although many of the principles discussed apply to all forms of contempt.

2. Shillitani v. U.S., 384 U.S. 364, 86 S.Ct. 1531, 16 L.Ed.2d 622 (1966); Penfield Co. of California v. SEC, 330 U.S. 585, 67 S.Ct. 918, 91 L.Ed. 1117 (1947); Ex parte Grossman, 267 U.S. 87, 45 S.Ct. 332, 69 L.Ed. 527 (1925); Gompers v. Buck's Stove & Range Co., 221 U.S. 418, 31 S.Ct. 492, 55 L.Ed. 797 (1911).

3. Shillitani v. U.S., 384 U.S. 364, 86 S.Ct. 1531, 16 L.Ed.2d 622 (1966); Nye v. U.S., 313 U.S. 33, 61 S.Ct. 810, 85 L.Ed. 1172 (1941); McCrone v. U.S., 307 U.S. 61, 59 S.Ct. 685, 83 L.Ed. 1108 (1939); Latrobe Steel Co. v. United Steelworkers of America, AFL–CIO, 545 F.2d 1336 (3d Cir.1976).

4. U.S. v. United Mine Workers of America, 330 U.S. 258, 67 S.Ct. 677, 91 L.Ed. 884 (1947); In re Osborne, 344 F.2d 611 (9th Cir.1965).

injured party it must be primarily compensatory in nature.[5] The amount must be reasonably calibrated to compensate the beneficiary of the court's order who has been injured by reason of the contemnor's non-compliance. As in the case of fines, incarceration may have either a coercive or punitive purpose. In the civil contempt context, it must be designed to coerce the contemnor into compliance with the court's order.[6]

The case of In re Lazarus[7] provides an excellent illustration of the difference between incarceration for civil contempt and imprisonment for criminal contempt. The contemnor had refused to answer questions before a grand jury pursuant to a court order. The judge ordered him to be held until he agreed to answer the questions. The fact that imprisonment was conditioned upon his continued refusal to answer indicates that the contempt was civil in nature. The incarceration was not penal because the contemnor had the keys to the jail house door. Had the contemnor been ordered to be held for a fixed period of time with no opportunity to end the incarceration, the contempt would have been criminal and the procedural safeguards employed in criminal contempt proceedings would have been available.[8]

Except for its brevity and summary character, a civil contempt proceeding is litigated as is any other civil action and is governed by the jurisdiction's general rules of civil procedure. Typically, the proceeding is treated as an extension of the original action. If the civil contemnor was not an actual party in the underlying action, he must be validly served with process to bring him within the jurisdiction of the court. If the civil contemnor was a party to the underlying lawsuit, no new process is required because he already is within the court's jurisdiction, although notice is necessary.[9]

Civil contempt proceedings are brought at the instance of private individuals—not the government. Usually the complainant's papers must contain a statement of the grounds on which the court's subject-matter jurisdiction is based. Because a purely civil contempt proceeding is for the benefit of a private party, the contempt proceeding may be terminated at any time by the complainant.[10] However, there may be a difference in the burden of proof between a civil contempt proceeding and an ordinary action at law. A finding of liability in an ordinary civil action is based on a preponderance of the evidence; in some jurisdictions, before an individual may be held in civil contempt, the proof may have to be clear and convincing.[11]

5. In re D. I. Operating Co., 240 F.Supp. 672 (D.Nev.1965).

6. Shillitani v. U.S., 384 U.S. 364, 86 S.Ct. 1531, 16 L.Ed.2d 622 (1966); Skinner v. White, 505 F.2d 685 (5th Cir.1974).

7. 276 F.Supp. 450 (C.D.Cal.1967).

8. See the discussion at notes 16–24, below.

9. James v. Powell, 32 A.D.2d 517, 298 N.Y.S.2d 840 (1969).

10. Flight Engineers Int'l Ass'n v. Eastern Air Lines, Inc., 301 F.2d 756 (5th Cir.1962).

11. Stringfellow v. Haines, 309 F.2d 910 (2d Cir.1962); Telling v. Bellows–Claude Neon Co., 77 F.2d 584 (6th Cir. 1935), cert. denied 296 U.S. 594; Louisiana

A finding of civil contempt is interlocutory in character, and thus, in a final-judgment-rule jurisdiction, such as the federal courts, appeal must await a final judgment in the underlying suit.[12] If, however, the civil contemnor is not a party to the original suit,[13] or if the contempt is criminal as well as civil[14] in nature, the contempt judgment is final, and an immediate appeal is available.

As indicated earlier in this section, the primary purpose of criminal contempt is to enforce respect for the authority of the court and to punish disregard of it. Since criminal contempt is punitive in character, there must be an element of intent, just as is required for a criminal conviction. Accordingly, willfulness is an essential element of criminal contempt.[15]

Inasmuch as the distinction between civil and criminal contempt depends upon the purpose to be served by the sanction and not upon the nature of the underlying action, a criminal contempt proceeding may be ancillary to either a criminal or a civil case.[16] Moreover, the same conduct may constitute both civil and criminal contempt, and unless the alleged contemnor is told, a party may not be able to determine whether she is being charged criminally or civilly. Therefore, the notice of the contempt proceeding should inform the alleged contemnor of the nature of the proceeding.[17] This conclusion was reached by the United States Supreme Court in Gompers v. Buck's Stove & Range Company,[18] in which the Court said, "He is not only entitled to be informed of the nature of the charge against him, but to know that it is a charge, and not a suit."[19] When a contempt proceeding is both criminal and civil, it will be treated procedurally as if it were entirely criminal in order to protect the accused.[20]

Educ. Ass'n v. Richland Parish School Bd., 421 F.Supp. 973 (W.D.La.1976), affirmed without opinion 585 F.2d 518 (5th Cir. 1978); Coca–Cola Co. v. Feulner, 7 F.Supp. 364 (S.D.Tex.1934).

Some courts have designated all contempt proceedings quasi-criminal and thus subject to the criminal burden of proof standard of "beyond a reasonable doubt." Ross v. Superior Court of Sacramento County, 19 Cal.3d 899, 141 Cal.Rptr. 133, 569 P.2d 727 (1977); Paasch v. Brown, 199 Neb. 683, 260 N.W.2d 612 (1977).

12. McCrone v. U.S., 307 U.S. 61, 59 S.Ct. 685, 83 L.Ed. 1108 (1939); Fox v. Capital Co., 299 U.S. 105, 57 S.Ct. 57, 81 L.Ed. 67 (1936). For a discussion of the final-judgment rule, see Chapter 13, above.

13. Bessette v. W. B. Conkey Co., 194 U.S. 324, 24 S.Ct. 665, 48 L.Ed. 997 (1904).

14. Penfield Co. of California v. SEC, 330 U.S. 585, 67 S.Ct. 918, 91 L.Ed. 1117 (1947); Union Tool Co. v. Wilson, 259 U.S. 107, 42 S.Ct. 427, 66 L.Ed. 848 (1922).

15. U.S. v. United Mine Workers of America, 330 U.S. 258, 67 S.Ct. 677, 91

L.Ed. 884 (1947); Chapman v. Pacific Tel. & Tel. Co., 613 F.2d 193 (9th Cir.1979); In re Joyce, 506 F.2d 373 (5th Cir.1975); Shook v. Shook, 242 Ga. 55, 247 S.E.2d 855 (1978). But see U.S. v. Schlicksup Drug Co., 206 F.Supp. 801 (S.D.Ill.1962).

16. Walker v. City of Birmingham, 388 U.S. 307, 87 S.Ct. 1824, 18 L.Ed.2d 1210 (1967); U.S. v. United Mine Workers of America, 330 U.S. 258, 67 S.Ct. 677, 91 L.Ed. 884 (1947).

17. The notice of the proceeding need not contain the word "criminal" if the contemptuous conduct is described fully and the contemnor is not confused as to the nature of the proceeding. See FTC v. Gladstone, 450 F.2d 913 (5th Cir.1971).

18. 221 U.S. 418, 31 S.Ct. 492, 55 L.Ed. 797 (1911).

19. 221 U.S. at 446, 31 S.Ct. at 500.

20. Penfield Co. of California v. SEC, 330 U.S. 585, 67 S.Ct. 918, 91 L.Ed. 1117 (1947); Nye v. U.S., 313 U.S. 33, 61 S.Ct. 810, 85 L.Ed. 1172 (1941).

Unlike civil contempt, a criminal contempt proceeding is a completely separate action.[21] It is instituted and controlled entirely by the court or a prosecuting agency. Since the government is proceeding against an individual for committing a public wrong, the litigation will be conducted in much the same way as would a criminal case.[22] The penal character of criminal contempt proceedings dictates that the various due process rights and constitutional procedural safeguards available in ordinary criminal proceedings also apply.[23] The Supreme Court has held, for example, that there is a constitutional right to a jury trial in criminal contempt proceedings, except for petty offenses.[24] Moreover, jurisdiction and venue must be established anew for a criminal contempt proceeding. Because a court should be able to punish a person for disregarding the authority of the court wherever the contempt takes place, venue usually poses no problem.

Finally, the scope of review in contempt proceedings must be considered. Many judicial systems, including the federal courts, have provided that the validity of the underlying court order ordinarily may not be challenged in a criminal contempt proceeding. This is true even for persons who have been convicted of contempt for violating orders that were either unconstitutional or issued by a court lacking jurisdiction to make the order.[25] This seemingly harsh rule is justified in terms of the importance of obeying court orders and not resorting to self-help to challenge them, as well as the notion that a court has the power to preserve the status quo while determining whether to assert jurisdiction.[26] The court is said to have jurisdiction to determine jurisdiction.

In some contexts, however, the refusal to question the validity of the underlying order is limited to orders that are designed to preserve the status quo. Thus, persons faced with orders calling for affirmative acts have been permitted to challenge the validity of the underlying order in criminal contempt proceedings.[27] In addition, a criminal contemnor may

---

21. The procedure may vary depending on whether direct or indirect criminal contempt is involved. For example, Federal Rule of Criminal Procedure 42(a) states that direct contempts are punishable summarily if the judge certifies that he or she saw or heard the actual contemptuous behavior—that it was committed within the presence of the court. This summary power allows the judge to terminate conduct disruptive of the orderly conduct of the trial without having to set a separate time for hearing the contempt charge. See Sacher v. U.S., 343 U.S. 1, 72 S.Ct. 451, 96 L.Ed. 717 (1952); In re Osborne, 344 F.2d 611 (9th Cir.1965); Skolnick v. Indiana, 180 Ind.App. 253, 388 N.E.2d 1156 (1979), cert. denied 445 U.S. 906. Because contempt that occurs as a result of failing to obey an injunction or an order to turn over property most commonly involves conduct outside the courtroom, these summary powers are not available.

22. See generally 3 C. Wright, Criminal 2d §§ 707–15.

23. See In re Oliver, 333 U.S. 257, 68 S.Ct. 499, 92 L.Ed. 682 (1948); Armentrout v. Dondanville, 24 Ill.Dec. 688, 67 Ill.App.3d 1021, 385 N.E.2d 829 (1979).

24. Bloom v. Illinois, 391 U.S. 194, 88 S.Ct. 1477, 20 L.Ed.2d 522 (1968); In the Matter of Evans, 411 A.2d 984 (D.C.App. 1980).

25. Walker v. City of Birmingham, 388 U.S. 307, 87 S.Ct. 1824, 18 L.Ed.2d 1210 (1967); U.S. v. United Mine Workers of America, 330 U.S. 258, 67 S.Ct. 677, 91 L.Ed. 884 (1947).

26. See generally 13A C. Wright, A. Miller & E. Cooper, Jurisdiction and Related Matters 2d § 3537.

27. Maness v. Meyers, 419 U.S. 449, 95 S.Ct. 584, 42 L.Ed.2d 574 (1975); U.S. v. Thompson, 319 F.2d 665 (2d Cir.1963); In re Stern, 235 F.Supp. 680 (S.D.N.Y.1964).

be able to challenge the validity of the underlying order if he attempted to have the order vacated before violating it, but was unable to do so.[28] This distinction was emphasized by the Supreme Court in Walker v. City of Birmingham.[29] In that case, the Court refused to examine the constitutional validity of an underlying state court decree, which sought to prevent a public demonstration concerning racial equality, because the contemnors had not attempted to vacate the order before violating it. The Court did say, however: "This case would arise in quite a different constitutional posture if the petitioners, before disobeying the injunction, had challenged it in the Alabama courts, and had been met with delay or frustration on their constitutional claims."[30] Along similar lines, the Supreme Court ruled in United States v. Ryan[31] that because an order denying a motion to quash a grand jury subpoena duces tecum is not appealable, a person might refuse to comply with it and then challenge its validity in the event that contempt proceedings are brought.

Further, although the Supreme Court has upheld the right of a system to limit the scope of review on criminal contempt, several state courts have not done so. Rather, they have allowed contemnors to challenge underlying decrees on grounds of jurisdiction,[32] invalidity,[33] and constitutionality.[34] Thus, it is necessary to consult local law to determine what scope of review is permissible.

The ability to challenge the underlying decree in a contempt proceeding is more frequently available when the contempt is civil. Some courts permit an examination of the order itself in civil contempt proceedings on the theory that since the sanction is designed to provide the beneficiary with the fruits of the court order, it should not be imposed if the underlying decree is invalid because the original plaintiff is not entitled to have the order enforced.[35]

28. In re Green, 369 U.S. 689, 82 S.Ct. 1114, 8 L.Ed.2d 198 (1962).

29. 388 U.S. 307, 87 S.Ct. 1824, 18 L.Ed.2d 1210 (1967).

30. 388 U.S. at 318, 87 S.Ct. at 1831.

31. 402 U.S. 530, 91 S.Ct. 1580, 29 L.Ed.2d 85 (1971).

32. Armentrout v. Dondanville, 24 Ill. Dec. 688, 67 Ill.App.3d 1021, 385 N.E.2d 829 (1979); Mellor v. Cook, 597 P.2d 882 (Utah 1979).

33. State ex rel. Girard v. Percich, 557 S.W.2d 25 (Mo.App.1977).

34. In re Berry, 68 Cal.2d 137, 65 Cal. Rptr. 273, 436 P.2d 273 (1968); Board of Medical Examiners v. Terminal–Hudson Electronics, Inc., 73 Cal.App.3d 376, 140 Cal.Rptr. 757 (1977).

35. U.S. v. United Mine Workers of America, 330 U.S. 258, 294–95, 67 S.Ct. 677, 696, 91 L.Ed. 884 (1947); ITT Community Dev. Corp. v. Barton, 569 F.2d 1351 (5th Cir.1978); Latrobe Steel Co. v. United Steelworkers of America, AFL–CIO, 545 F.2d 1336 (3d Cir.1976). But compare City of Lebanon v. Townsend, 120 N.H. 836, 424 A.2d 201 (1980) (collateral attack not allowed when party never raised challenge on direct appeal).

§§ 15.9–16.0 are reserved for supplementary material.

Chapter 16

SPECIALIZED PROCEEDINGS: CLASS ACTIONS, DERIVATIVE SUITS, AND INTERPLEADER

Analysis

A.   CLASS ACTIONS

1.   in General

§ 16.1   Purpose and History

The class action permits a lawsuit to be brought by or against large numbers of individuals or organizations whose interests are sufficiently

736

related so that it is more efficient to adjudicate their rights or liabilities in a single action than in a series of individual proceedings.[1] In modern times the class action has become an extremely popular, albeit controversial, procedure. In the federal courts, it has been used extensively in antitrust, securities, and environmental cases, in suits charging race and sex discrimination, in actions regarding governmental benefits, and, in the 1990s, with increasing frequency in products liability and toxic tort cases.

This increase in class action activity often is attributed to the revision of Federal Rule 23 in 1966.[2] However, the trend probably reflects doctrinal changes in the fields of substantive law mentioned above, increased social action litigation, and the attractiveness of using the class action device when there is a prospect of receiving court-awarded or statutorily provided attorney's fees.[3] Whatever the cause or causes, the class action has imposed additional burdens on the judicial system and certain classes of litigants, leading some to challenge it as a "Frankenstein monster."[4] On the other hand, the procedure may represent the only viable method for people with small claims to vindicate their rights or for important social issues to be litigated. The controversy between proponents and opponents of the class action has escalated in recent years with the filing of numerous nationwide or multistate products liability and consumer fraud class actions that have challenged the traditional procedures and rules surrounding class litigation. The suits raise important issues regarding the rights of individuals to control their own claims, the power of the courts to shape the class device to provide binding adjudications over massive controversies, and the role of the lawyers in conducting and settling these actions.[5] Many proposals

§ 16.1

1. See generally Developments in the Law—Class Actions, 89 Harv.L.Rev. 1318 (1976).

An alternative to class actions is found in procedures authorizing the transfer and consolidation of individual lawsuits for aggregated or coordinated treatment in a single court. However, that alternative currently has several limitations. First, transfer is restricted within a single judicial system and thus consolidation between state courts and across state lines is impossible. Second, in the federal courts transfer for consolidation is limited to pretrial purposes. 28 U.S.C.A. § 1407. Third, parties must have claims sufficiently large to merit filing them individually so that, unlike class actions, it does not provide a remedy for small claimants. Proposals to increase the utility of transfer and consolidation procedures were adopted by the American Law Institute in 1993. See ALI, Complex Litigation: Statutory Recommendations and Analysis (1994).

2. See, e.g., American Bar Association, Report of Pound Conference Follow Up

Task Force 30, reprinted in 74 F.R.D. 159, 194 (1976).

3. Miller, Of Frankenstein Monsters and Shining Knights: Myth, Reality and the "Class Action Problem," 92 Harv.L.Rev. 664 (1979).

4. The term was used first by Chief Judge Lumbard in his dissenting opinion in Eisen v. Carlisle & Jacquelin, 391 F.2d 555, 572 (2d Cir.1968), to describe that case. Other judges and authors have since used it to refer to class actions generally.

5. For some articles discussing many of these issues, see Coffee, Class Wars: The Dilemma of the Mass Tort Class Action, 95 Colum.L.Rev. 1343 (1995); Green , Advancing Individual Rights Through Group Justice, 30 U.C. Davis L.Rev. 791 (1997); Marcus, They Can't Do That, Can They? Tort Reform Via Rule 23, 80 Cornell L.Rev. 858 (1995); Shapiro, Class Actions: The Class as Party and Client, 73 Notre Dame L.Rev. 913 (1998).

have been made for changes that would stabilize the situation and resolve some of the policy issues that underlie the debate,[6] but to date no major changes have been adopted.[7]

The precursor of the modern class action was a procedure known as the bill of peace.[8] It was developed by the English court of chancery so that a number of individuals with small claims who were united in interest were not prevented from enforcing their equitable rights; nor were a comparable group of wrongdoers given what was tantamount to immunity from suit. A bill of peace was permitted if the plaintiff could show that, because of the large size of the group, joinder would be impossible or impracticable, that all persons possessed a joint interest in the issue to be litigated, and that the named parties would adequately represent the interests of the absentees.[9] If these prerequisites were met, the action could proceed on a representational basis and the final decree would bind all class members whether or not they were actual parties to the litigation.

Because the class action had its origins in the English chancery courts, it was cognizable only in equity and this limitation found its way into early American practice.[10] However, when the state codes brought about the fusion of law and equity in the nineteenth century, class actions became available in actions at law as well.[11]

Prior to the merger of law and equity in the federal courts in 1938, the availability of a class action was controlled by the Federal Equity Rules. It never became clear under the Federal Equity Rules whether absent class members were bound by the court's decree or whether the

---

6. Some proposals have been statutory, See, e.g., Mullenix, Class Resolution of the Mass Tort Case: A Proposed Federal Procedure Act, 64 Texas L.Rev. 1039 (1986); Rowe, Beyond the Class Action Rule: An Inventory of Statutory Possibilities to Improve the Federal Class Action, 71 N.Y.U. L.Rev. 186 (1996). Others have focussed on amending Rule 23. See, e.g., Cooper, Rule 23: Challenges to the Rulemaking Process, 71 N.Y.U. L.Rev. 13 (1996).

7. In 1996, the Advisory Committee on the Civil Rules offered several proposed amendments to Rule 23, which were circulated for comment. In October 1997, the Committee decided to drop most of the proposals, leaving the matter open for future consideration and forwarding to the Supreme Court only an amendment to authorize the interlocutory appeal of some class certification decisions. That provision is discussed in § 13.3, above.

8. Z. Chafee, Some Problems in Equity 200–01 (1950); Walsh, Equity § 118, at 553–60 (1930); Yeazell, From Group Litigation to Class Action: Part I: The Industrialization of Group Litigation, 27 U.C.L.A.L.Rev. 514 (1980); Developments

in the Law—Multiparty Litigation in the Federal Courts, 71 Harv.L.Rev. 874 (1958).

9. Adair v. New River Co., 11 Ves.Jr. 429, 443–45, 32 Eng.Rep. 1153, 1158–59 (Ct.Ch.1805) (dictum).

10. For a description of how nineteenth century American cases incorporated the English bill of peace mechanism, see Yeazell, From Group Litigation to Class Action: Part II: Interest, Class, and Representation, 27 U.C.L.A.L.Rev. 1067 (1980).

11. Stearns Coal & Lumber Co. v. Van Winkle, 221 Fed. 590 (C.C.A.Ky.1915), cert. denied 241 U.S. 670; Colt v. Hicks, 97 Ind. App. 177, 179 N.E. 335 (1932).

Most codes allowed class suits upon a showing that a large number of individuals held a common or general interest or that the class was so numerous it would be impracticable to join everyone in a single action. See, e.g., West's Ann.Cal.Code Civ. Proc. § 382; R.I. Sup.Ct.Rules Civ.Proc., Rule 23. Other codes required a showing of both commonality of an interest among a group of persons and the impracticability of their joinder. See, e.g., Conn.Gen.Stat. § 5519 (1930); Fla.Stat.Ann. § 63.14 (1931).

procedure simply functioned as a permissive joinder device.[12] Some of the confusion, at least for a time, was reduced by the Supreme Court's decision in Supreme Tribe of Ben–Hur v. Cauble,[13] in which all the members of a beneficial organization were bound by a decree affecting the control and disposition of that institution's funds. The Court stated: "If the decree is to be effective and conflicting judgments are to be avoided, all the class must be concluded by the decree."[14] Despite this language, doubts remained respecting the effect that a decree in a federal class suit would be given.[15]

The promulgation of Federal Rule of Civil Procedure 23 in 1938 represented an attempt to expand the usefulness of the class action device in the federal system, and it was made available in actions at law as well as suits in equity. Rule 23 divided class actions into three categories that were described in terms of the jural relationships among the class members. The so-called "true" class action was available when the rights were "joint" or "common," or "secondary" in the sense that the owner of the primary right of action refused to enforce it. A "hybrid" class suit was permitted when the rights among class members were "several" and the object of the action was the adjudication of claims affecting specific property involved in the action. The so-called "spurious" class action also required that the jural relationships among the class members be "several"; however, a "spurious" class action could go forward when there was a common question of law or fact affecting the "several" rights and when common relief was sought.[16]

Unquestionably, the most controversial of these three categories was the "spurious" class suit, which was little more than a liberal joinder device because only the named parties were bound by the court's decree.[17] The principal confusion stemmed from the requirement that "common" relief be sought. Some courts asserted that when litigants possessed individual rights to damages, a class suit was not maintainable; the more accepted view, however, was that it was sufficient if the same kind of relief was sought by or against the class members.[18]

12. Equity Rule 48—in force from 1842 to 1912—had as its concluding sentence: " * * * in such cases the decree shall be without prejudice to the rights and claims of the absent parties." Despite this language the Supreme Court in at least one case bound all parties whether they had been brought before the court or not. Smith v. Swormstedt, 57 U.S. (16 How.) 288, 14 L.Ed. 942 (1853).

13. 255 U.S. 356, 41 S.Ct. 338, 65 L.Ed. 673 (1921).

14. 255 U.S. at 367, 41 S.Ct. at 342.

15. For a more extensive discussion of the historical development of the class action prior to 1938, see 7A C. Wright, A. Miller & M. Kane, Civil 2d § 1751.

16. For a complete description of the practice under original Rule 23, see 7A C.

Wright, A. Miller & M. Kane, Civil 2d § 1752.

17. "Spurious" class suits were popular in litigation involving the Fair Labor Standards Act, e.g., Pentland v. Dravo Corp., 152 F.2d 851 (3d Cir.1945) (employer's suit); mass torts, e.g., Kainz v. Anheuser–Busch, Inc., 194 F.2d 737 (7th Cir. 1952), cert. denied 344 U.S. 820; and antitrust matters, e.g., Kainz v. Anheuser–Busch, Inc., 194 F.2d 737 (7th Cir.1952), cert. denied 344 U.S. 820.

18. The common relief requirement was satisfied either when all the class members sought damages or all sought equitable relief, as opposed to the situation in which some class members were seeking damages and others presented claims for injunctive

A major difficulty with original Federal Rule 23 was the nebulous, conceptual character of the jural relationships that supposedly defined the boundaries separating the three class action categories.[19] A second problem grew out of the fact that once the requisite jural relationships were found to exist, the class suit was maintainable without any showing that common questions were significant or predominated over individual issues. This deficiency permitted the maintenance of class actions that were overburdened by substantial individual issues, so that there was no assurance that judicial economy would be achieved. To exacerbate the problem, the text of the class action rule did not provide any guidance to the district judge as to how to handle individual issues and, if literally construed, did not seem to permit the court to segregate them for separate individual determinations.

Dissatisfaction with this arbitrary and conceptualistic tripartite division of class actions led the Advisory Committee on Civil Rules to revise Federal Rule 23, and its work product became effective in 1966. The present Federal Rule reflects an attempt to determine whether a class action is proper in functional terms.[20] Moreover, the rule gives the court substantial guidance as to the measures at its disposal in handling a class action.[21] A number of states that have revised their class action rules since 1966 have embraced the approach embodied in current Federal Rule 23, with certain exceptions,[22] so that an understanding of the federal practice has significant application.

2.   Prerequisites

§ 16.2   Federal Class Action Prerequisites

Determining the propriety of giving federal class action treatment to a case typically is a two stage process. First, it must be determined whether several procedural prerequisites have been satisfied.[1] Second, it must be ascertained whether the particular class action falls within the

relief. Oppenheimer v. F. J. Young & Co., 144 F.2d 387 (2d Cir.1944).

19. This confusion is illustrated in the various opinions that grew out of Deckert v. Independence Shares Corp., 27 F.Supp. 763 (E.D.Pa.1939), reversed 108 F.2d 51 (3d Cir.1939), affirmed 311 U.S. 282, 61 S.Ct. 229, 85 L.Ed. 189 (1940), on remand 39 F.Supp. 592 (E.D.Pa.1941), affirmed 123 F.2d 979 (3d Cir.1941). The plaintiffs claimed that their suit on behalf of defrauded creditors was "hybrid." The defendant asserted that it was "spurious." The district court stated merely that it was a class bill. In reversing, the circuit court of appeals characterized the suit as "spurious." When the case came to the Supreme Court, the suit was held to be maintainable, but the Court did not characterize it. Upon remand, the district judge classified the suit as "hybrid," and finally, when the case was

appealed to the circuit court of appeals for the second time, the court declared that names were not important.

20. Although current Rule 23 also divides class actions into three types, that is where the similarity to its predecessor ends and any attempts to perpetuate the former practice or the labels "true," "hybrid," and "spurious" would be inappropriate. The current federal provision is discussed at § 16.2, below.

21. See § 16.5, below.

22. See § 16.3, below.

§ 16.2

1. See Fed.Civ.Proc.Rule 23(a). The Rule 23(a) requirements are examined in detail in 7A C. Wright, A. Miller & M. Kane, Civil 2d §§ 1759–71.

definition of one of the permissible types of class suits set out in the rule.[2] Although a thorough review of all of the problems and questions that have arisen at both of these stages is beyond the scope of this volume, a brief look at each stage follows.

Before a class action of any type may proceed in the federal courts, all of the following questions must be answered in the affirmative. (1) Is there an identifiable class? (2) Are those purporting to represent that class members of it? (3) Is the class so large that joinder is impracticable? (4) Are there questions of law or fact common to all the class members? (5) Are the claims or defenses of the representatives of the class typical of those of other class members? (6) Will the representatives adequately represent and protect the interests of the absent class members? Ordinarily, the judge has broad discretion in determining whether these requirements have been met.[3] If any of the prerequisites is not satisfied—and the party seeking class action treatment has the burden of showing that they are—the case cannot proceed on a class basis.[4]

In the past, some federal courts also required the representatives, when a plaintiff class was involved, to demonstrate that there was a significant possibility that they would succeed on the merits, or that their claims were not frivolous, before the suit was permitted to proceed as a class action.[5] The obvious rationale behind this requirement was to ensure that a substantial claim existed before the extremely expensive and time-consuming class action machinery was activated. The practice was dubious. Requiring a preliminary showing of a substantial claim is an inappropriate threshold burden to place on class plaintiffs and well might prove to be cumbersome and more costly of resources than simply proceeding in the usual fashion. Fortunately, the Supreme Court's decision in Eisen v. Carlisle & Jacquelin[6] eliminated the practice.

It is axiomatic that before a class action should be permitted to proceed as such, an identifiable class must exist.[7] This does not mean that every member of the represented group must be identified, or even

---

2. See Fed.Civ.Proc.Rule 23(b). The Rule 23(b) categories are examined in detail in 7A C. Wright, A. Miller & M. Kane, Civil 2d §§ 1772–80; 7B C. Wright, A. Miller & M. Kane, Civil 2d §§ 1781–84.

3. Coley v. Clinton, 635 F.2d 1364 (8th Cir.1980); Gold Strike Stamp Co. v. Christensen, 436 F.2d 791 (10th Cir.1970).

4. Williams v. Weinberger, 360 F.Supp. 1349 (N.D.Ga.1973); Southern v. Board of Trustees for Dallas Independent School District, 318 F.Supp. 355 (N.D.Tex.1970), affirmed per curiam 461 F.2d 1267 (5th Cir. 1972). The failure of the action as pleaded to meet all the requirements does not necessitate dismissal, however, if the class can be redefined or the representation altered to meet the prerequisites. Geraghty v. U.S. Parole Comm'n, 719 F.2d 1199 (3d Cir. 1983), cert. denied 465 U.S. 1103; DeBre-

maecker v. Short, 433 F.2d 733 (5th Cir. 1970); Shivelhood v. Davis, 336 F.Supp. 1111 (D.Vt.1971).

5. Milberg v. Western Pacific R.R. Co., 51 F.R.D. 280 (S.D.N.Y.1970); Dolgow v. Anderson, 43 F.R.D. 472 (E.D.N.Y.1968), grant of summary judgment reversed 438 F.2d 825 (2d Cir.1970).

6. 417 U.S. 156, 94 S.Ct. 2140, 40 L.Ed.2d 732 (1974).

7. In re A.H. Robins Co., 880 F.2d 709 (4th Cir.1989), cert. denied 493 U.S. 959; United Bhd. of Carpenters & Joiners of America, Local 899 v. Phoenix Assocs., Inc., 152 F.R.D. 518 (D.W.Va.1994). For a thorough discussion of the identifiability of a class, see 7A C. Wright, A. Miller & M. Kane, Civil 2d § 1760.

be identifiable, at the outset of the litigation.[8] Rather, the general contours of the class should be delineated sufficiently so that it would be feasible for the court to ascertain whether particular individuals are or are not members of it.[9] Indeed, this type of determination may have to be made in order to send notice of the action to the class members or to distribute any recovery that may be secured. Serious ambiguity as to the dimension or nature of the class also can create problems of determining who is bound by any judgment that is entered in the action.

The second requirement that the representatives be members of the class is premised on the notion that if they have a personal stake in the outcome of the litigation, the representatives are likely to undertake a full prosecution or defense.[10] Class membership offers some assurance that the representative will adequately protect the interests of the absent class members.[11] It also can be thought of as in the nature of a standing requirement. But not every representative need be a member of the class; it may be sufficient if one of them is a class member.[12]

The third prerequisite for bringing a class suit is that the class must be so large that joinder of all its members would be impracticable.[13] This requirement—sometimes inelegantly called numerosity—demands no more than extreme difficulty or inconvenience of joinder; a showing of impossibility is not necessary.[14] The requirement reflects a desire to avoid class actions that will not achieve judicial economy. If a controver-

8. Carpenter v. Davis, 424 F.2d 257 (5th Cir.1970); Ashe v. Board of Elections in City of New York, 124 F.R.D. 45 (E.D.N.Y.1989).

9. Compare Hilao v. Estate of Marcos, 103 F.3d 767 (9th Cir.1996) (class of Philippine citizens who were or whose decedents were tortured, summarily executed, or "disappeared" while in custody during a 14–year period was sufficiently definite), with Newton v. Southern Wood Piedmont Co., 163 F.R.D. 625 (S.D.Ga.1995) (class definition including people who had been exposed to chemicals from a wood treatment plant and had experienced keratosis deemed too vague).

10. Initially there was some problem in applying this requirement to cases in which an unincorporated association, such as a labor union, seeks to represent its members in a class suit because the association technically is not a class member if it is not seeking any remedies for itself. See, e.g., Air Line Stewards & Stewardesses Ass'n, Local 550 v. American Airlines, Inc., 490 F.2d 636 (7th Cir.1973), cert. denied 416 U.S. 993. Courts allowed the suit to be brought if the organization had specific authority from its members to sue on their behalf or if the organization was created for the purpose of protecting the very interests that were the subject of the lawsuit. See Norwalk CORE

v. Norwalk Redevelopment Agency, 395 F.2d 920 (2d Cir.1968). Today most of the problems in suits brought by or against unincorporated associations are dealt with in the federal courts under Federal Rule 23.2. That provision is discussed in 7C C. Wright, A. Miller & M. Kane, Civil 2d § 1861.

11. A finding that the representative is not a class member frequently is phrased as a lack of adequate representation. See, e.g., Alexander v. Yale University, 631 F.2d 178 (2d Cir.1980); Phillips v. Brock, 652 F.Supp. 1372 (D.Md.1987), vacated on other grounds 854 F.2d 673 (4th Cir.1988).

12. Hunter v. Atchison, T. & S.F. Ry. Co., 188 F.2d 294 (7th Cir.1951), cert. denied 342 U.S. 819. But compare the decision in La Mar v. H & B Novelty & Loan Co., 489 F.2d 461 (9th Cir.1973), a suit under the Truth in Lending Act against a number of pawnbrokers, in which the court held that the plaintiff could represent only those people who had been injured by the same pawnbroker, in effect requiring the formation of separate classes against each pawnbroker.

13. Fed.Civ.Proc.Rule 23(a)(1).

14. Robidoux v. Celani, 987 F.2d 931 (2d Cir.1993); Roman v. Korson, 152 F.R.D. 101 (W.D.Mich.1993).

sy can be resolved reasonably, effectively, and efficiently through individual suits or other joinder procedures, there is no reason to mobilize the often costly class machinery. But when joinder is impracticable and it seems likely that the judicial system will be burdened with a substantial number of individual suits, handling the controversy as a class action may represent a significant economy.

Factors other than mere numbers play an important role in determining the feasibility of joinder. Some of them are: (1) the nature and complexity of the action,[15] (2) the size of individual claims,[16] and (3) the geographic distribution of the members of the class.[17] In addition, turnover in class membership may be an appropriate consideration inasmuch as it would be intolerable to require a litigant to join a number of people who are similarly situated but whose identity is constantly changing—for example, as a result of births, deaths, or rapid changes in employment.

The fourth prerequisite to the maintenance of a class action is that common questions of law or fact must exist, thus tying the class members together.[18] All questions of law or fact need not be common or classwide,[19] however. For example, the requirement has been satisfied when a pattern of discriminatory conduct was alleged, despite the fact that the conduct might have affected various class members in different ways.[20] On the other hand, if an isolated incident is alleged that does not implicate any common policy or practice, the requirement is not satisfied.[21]

The fifth prerequisite for a class action is that the claims or defenses of the representatives must be typical of the claims or defenses of all the class members—the "typicality" requirement.[22] It is not entirely clear what the rulemakers intended to achieve with this requirement.[23] Typicality often is tested in terms of a lack of antagonism among the claims and defenses of the representatives and those of the class members.[24]

---

15. E.g., Patrykus v. Gomilla, 121 F.R.D. 357 (N.D.Ill.1988); Armstead v. Pingree, 629 F.Supp. 273 (M.D.Fla.1986).

16. E.g., Dirks v. Clayton Brokerage Co. of St. Louis, Inc., 105 F.R.D. 125 (D.Minn.1985); Leist v. Shawano County, 91 F.R.D. 64 (E.D.Wis.1981).

17. E.g., Garcia v. Gloor, 618 F.2d 264 (5th Cir.1980), cert. denied 449 U.S. 1113; Markham v. White, 171 F.R.D. 217 (N.D.Ill. 1997); Gentry v. C & D Oil Co., 102 F.R.D. 490 (W.D.Ark.1984).

18. Fed.Civ.Proc.Rule 23(a)(2).

19. Forbush v. J.C. Penney, 994 F.2d 1101 (5th Cir.1993); Cox v. American Cast Iron Pipe Co., 784 F.2d 1546 (11th Cir. 1986), cert. denied 479 U.S. 883.

20. E.g., Jordan v. County of Los Angeles, 669 F.2d 1311 (9th Cir.1982); Christman v. American Cyanamid Co., 92 F.R.D. 441 (D.W.Va.1981); Molthan v. Temple University of Commonwealth Sys. of Higher Educ., 83 F.R.D. 368 (E.D.Pa.1979). For an extensive collection of the varying factual patterns in which common questions of law or fact have been found to exist, see 7A C. Wright, A. Miller & M. Kane, Civil 2d § 1763.

21. E.g., Stewart v. Winter, 87 F.R.D. 760 (N.D.Miss.1980), affirmed 669 F.2d 328 (5th Cir.1982).

22. Fed.Civ.Proc.Rule 23(a)(3).

23. A more detailed discussion of the typicality requirement may be found in 7A C. Wright, A. Miller & M. Kane, Civil 2d § 1764.

24. E.g., Inmates of the Attica Correctional Facility v. Rockefeller, 453 F.2d 12 (2d Cir.1971); Tenants Associated for a Better Spaulding (TABS) v. U.S. Dep't of Housing & Urban Dev. (HUD), 97 F.R.D. 726 (N.D.Ill.1983).

This formulation, however, is practically indistinguishable from the requirement, discussed later, that the representatives adequately protect the interests of absent class members. But perhaps the overlap between the typicality and adequacy of representation requirements is intentional.[25] As described by Professor Degnan, "[T]he adversary system is confident that it works well only when the litigant who does his best for himself also inescapably benefits his fellow class members."[26] Thus, courts have ruled that the representative's claim need not be identical to those of the absent class members,[27] and typicality usually will be found if the claims or defenses of the representative and the class stem from the same events or rest on the same legal theory.[28] Only when the representative's claim is markedly different from that of the other class members will typicality be lacking.[29]

The final prerequisite for the maintenance of a class suit is that the named representatives fairly and adequately protect the interests of the absent class members.[30] This requirement has a due process dimension to it. Because considerations of efficiency and judicial economy have led to a relaxation in the class action context of the ordinary guarantee of a right to be present in the courtroom when one's rights or liabilities are adjudicated, courts are especially careful to ensure that the absent members have a suitable surrogate.[31] Unless great care is taken to

25. See Rosado v. Wyman, 322 F.Supp. 1173, 1193 (E.D.N.Y.1970), affirmed on other grounds 437 F.2d 619 (2d Cir.1970), affirmed without opinion 402 U.S. 991, 91 S.Ct. 2169, 29 L.Ed.2d 157 (1971). See also Gonzales v. Cassidy, 474 F.2d 67 (5th Cir. 1973).

26. Degnan, Foreword: Adequacy of Representation in Class Actions, 60 Calif.L.Rev. 705, 716 (1972).

27. Markham v. White, 171 F.R.D. 217 (N.D.Ill.1997); Jones v. Blinziner, 536 F.Supp. 1181 (N.D.Ind.1982). But compare Insley v. Joyce, 330 F.Supp. 1228 (N.D.Ill. 1971) (class action denied because interests not coextensive).

28. E.g., Baby Neal for & by Kanter v. Casey, 43 F.3d 48 (3d Cir.1994) (action to force city human services department to comply with statutes and constitution regarding provision of child care services); Haley v. Medtronic, Inc., 169 F.R.D. 643 (C.D.Cal.1996) (products liability action against manufacturer of allegedly defective pacemaker leads); Holland v. Steele, 92 F.R.D. 58 (N.D.Ga.1981) (class action challenging defendant's policy of denying access to counsel at jail to all prisoners under his supervision); In re Screws Antitrust Litigation, 91 F.R.D. 52 (D.Mass.1981) (Clayton Act suit).

29. E.g., Kalodner v. Michaels Stores, Inc., 172 F.R.D. 200 (N.D.Tex.1997) (typi-cality lacking when representative in securities fraud action was a "professional plaintiff" subject to unique defenses).

The Supreme Court has ruled that an employee denied a promotion on allegedly discriminatory grounds could not bring a class action challenging the entire spectrum of the employer's practices. Typicality was lacking without a showing that discrimination manifested itself in the same general fashion in other areas, such as hiring. General Telephone Co. of the Southwest v. Falcon, 457 U.S. 147, 102 S.Ct. 2364, 72 L.Ed.2d 740 (1982). For a discussion of the impact of the Falcon decision on the lower courts' application of Rule 23, see 7A C. Wright, A. Miller & M. Kane, Civil 2d § 1771.

30. Fed.Civ.Proc.Rule 23(a)(4).

31. The court need not dismiss the action if it finds the existing representation inadequate. It may divide the class into subclasses, each with its own representative, In re Mut. Savs. Bank Secs. Litigation, 166 F.R.D. 377 (E.D.Mich.1996); it may narrow or redefine the class to avoid any conflicting interests, Gibb v. Delta Drilling Co., 104 F.R.D. 59 (N.D.Tex.1984); or it may appoint additional representatives, Brewer v. Swinson, 837 F.2d 802 (8th Cir. 1988), or additional counsel, Cullen v. New York State Civil Service Comm'n, 566 F.2d 846 (2d Cir.1977).

ensure adequacy of representation, an absent class member can avoid being bound by the judgment by attacking it as being constitutionally flawed. If that occurs, then the efficiencies and economies sought by permitting the class action in the first instance will be nullified.[32]

The representative need not have explicit authority from the class members to act on their behalf.[33] Further, adequacy of representation is demonstrated not so much by the number of representatives as by their quality, and that of their counsel.[34] The quality of the representation depends on both the named representatives and the competence of the selected counsel.[35] The latter entails consideration of numerous elements,[36] including the lawyer's experience, especially with regard to the particular field of litigation involved in the specific suit,[37] and the quality of the papers submitted to the court.[38] The stature of the named parties, their motivation for bringing the litigation, and their interest in its result also may be considered.[39] Because the maintenance of a class action often is extremely protracted and may involve a substantial outlay of funds for expenses, the representatives' ability not only to persevere

---

32. See Gonzales v. Cassidy, 474 F.2d 67 (5th Cir.1973).

33. Mason v. Garris, 360 F.Supp. 420 (N.D.Ga.1973), judgment amended 364 F.Supp. 452 (1973). If the representative does have specific authority, the adequacy of the representative is more or less assumed. Anderson v. City of Albany, 321 F.2d 649 (5th Cir.1963).

34. Korn v. Franchard Corp., 456 F.2d 1206 (2d Cir.1972); Twyman v. Rockville Housing Authority, 99 F.R.D. 314 (D.Md. 1983).

35. To ensure objectivity, several courts have ruled that a person cannot serve both as class counsel and class representative. See Wagner v. Taylor, 836 F.2d 578 (D.C.Cir.1987); Zylstra v. Safeway Stores, Inc., 578 F.2d 102 (5th Cir.1978); Brick v. CPC International, Inc., 547 F.2d 185 (2d Cir.1976).

Because of perceived abuses in securities fraud class actions and concerns that those suits were essentially attorney, rather than client, controlled, Congress enacted special legislation in 1995 that requires the court to identify and designate a lead plaintiff deemed to be the best representative of the class, not simply an adequate representative. The statute also includes special requirements for designating lead counsel. Pub.L. 104–67, Dec. 22, 1995, 109 Stat. 737–765. The details of the additional statutory requirements are discussed in 7B C. Wright, A. Miller & M. Kane, Civil 2d § 1806.

36. Serious concerns have been raised regarding ethical problems facing class counsel, and courts and commentators have been focusing on methods and means of overseeing the attorney's conduct to avoid conflicts of interest. See generally Garth, Conflict and Dissent in Class Actions: A Suggested Perspective, 77 Nw.U.L.Rev. 492 (1982); Rhode, Class Conflicts in Class Actions, 34 Stan.L.Rev. 1183 (1982); Note, Conflicts of Interest in Class Representation Vis-à-Vis Class Representative and Class Counsel, 33 Wayne L.Rev. 141 (1986). For a discussion of the factors courts consider in assessing the quality of class counsel, see 7A C. Wright, A. Miller & M. Kane, Civil 2d § 1769.1.

37. See, e.g., Lynch v. Rank, 604 F.Supp. 30 (N.D.Cal.1984), order affirmed 747 F.2d 528 (9th Cir.1984). Perhaps not surprisingly, pro se class actions have been found lacking in adequacy of representation. Oxendine v. Williams, 509 F.2d 1405 (4th Cir.1975).

38. See, e.g., Williams v. Balcor Pension Investors, 150 F.R.D. 109 (N.D.Ill. 1993); Aguinaga v. John Morrell & Co., 602 F.Supp. 1270 (D.Kan.1985).

39. Epstein v. Weiss, 50 F.R.D. 387, 392 (E.D.La.1970). The actual party should be able to exercise independent judgment. Thus, some courts have ruled that there should not be any significant family or financial relationship between the representative and counsel. See In re Goldchip Funding Co., 61 F.R.D. 592 (M.D.Pa.1974). For an argument that focusing on the individual characteristics of the named plaintiffs is inappropriate, see Burns, Decorative Figureheads: Eliminating Class Representatives in Class Actions, 42 Hast.L.J. 165 (1990).

but to prosecute the action vigorously are very pertinent. Although the size of the representatives' individual claims is not determinative,[40] the court may consider whether the representatives have sufficient financial means to be able to absorb the costs necessary for the litigation.[41]

The most critical factor to be scrutinized when determining adequacy of representation is whether conflicting or antagonistic interests exist between the representatives and other members of the class. However, only a conflict or antagonism that goes to the heart of the controversy will be fatal.[42]

The leading case on this point is Hansberry v. Lee,[43] in which members of a class seeking to set aside a racially restrictive covenant were held by the Illinois Supreme Court to be bound by a prior class suit brought by an owner of one of the lots subject to the covenant to enjoin the violation of the covenant by other owners who allegedly were subject to it. The covenant itself stated that it would not be effective unless signed by ninety percent of the owners. That fact was stipulated by both plaintiffs and defendants in the first suit, although, in fact, less than seventy percent had signed. The United States Supreme Court held that those seeking to challenge the racially restrictive covenant were not bound by the prior judgment because their interests had not been adequately represented by class representatives whose objectives had been to establish the validity of the covenant, rather than to strike it down.

The lesson is a clear one. To ensure that there is neither conflict nor collusion, as in Hansberry, there must be careful judicial scrutiny of the representative's relationship with both the other class members and those opposing the class. The basic objective is for the court to be certain that the representative will prosecute the action with forthrightness and vigor.[44] Thus, one troublesome aspect of the adequacy requirement is

---

40. See, e.g., Eisen v. Carlisle & Jacquelin, 391 F.2d 555 (2d Cir.1968) (representative's claim was for $70); In re South Central States Bakery Prods. Antitrust Litigation, 86 F.R.D. 407 (M.D.La.1980). In contrast, in 1995 Congress enacted special legislation governing securities fraud class actions providing, as part of the new requirements for those suits, that a lead plaintiff be designated and that there is a presumption that the individual with the largest financial stake is the designated party. 15 U.S.C.A. § 77z–1(a)(3)(B)(iii); 15 U.S.C.A. § 78u–4(a)(3)(B)(iii).

41. Compare McGowan v. Faulkner Concrete Pipe Co., 659 F.2d 554 (5th Cir. 1981) (plaintiff's failure to pursue discovery for two years, and inability to pay $421 for documents copied for them by defendant, justified denying class certification), with George v. Beneficial Finance Co. of Dallas, 81 F.R.D. 4 (N.D.Tex.1977) (legal foundation where plaintiffs' attorneys were employed had sufficient resources to finance action).

Recognition that it is legitimate to consider the representative's financial adequacy has produced some disputes concerning the right to discover the representative's assets and the financial arrangements with counsel. See 7A C. Wright, A. Miller & M. Kane, Civil 2d § 1767.

42. Berman v. Narragansett Racing Ass'n, 414 F.2d 311 (1st Cir.1969), cert. denied 396 U.S. 1037; Redmond v. Commerce Trust Co., 144 F.2d 140 (8th Cir. 1944), cert. denied 323 U.S. 776. What constitutes antagonism sufficient to defeat class certification is explored in more detail in 7A C. Wright, A. Miller & M. Kane, Civil 2d § 1768.

43. 311 U.S. 32, 61 S.Ct. 115, 85 L.Ed. 22 (1940).

44. The mere presence of an ulterior motive does not necessarily constitute a

determining in defendant class actions whether a reluctant representative possesses, by the fact of reluctance alone, an interest so antagonistic to the members of the class that the suit should not go forward on a representative basis.[45]

If the class action prerequisites just discussed are satisfied, the court then must proceed to the next stage of the inquiry: whether the action falls into one of the categories of cases permitted under Rule 23(b). The first category set out in Rule 23(b)(1) permits a class action (a) when the prosecution of separate actions might result in inconsistent or varying adjudications that would establish incompatible standards of conduct for the party opposing the class, or (b) when individual litigation might result in judgments that would be dispositive of the interests of other members of the class who are not parties to those individual actions.[46] It is not necessary to satisfy both of these standards and nothing turns on which of the tests is met. In fact, in many suits requesting mandatory or prohibitory relief, both elements usually are present. Loosely conceived, this category might be thought of as the "anti-prejudice" class action.[47] It permits class action treatment if individual actions would result in prejudice to the party opposing the class or to members of the class itself.

Pragmatic considerations dictate whether prejudice will be found. The opposing party can be threatened by individual adjudications only if there is a real possibility that separate actions will be brought,[48] and if that individual or entity is required by law or practical necessity to act in the same manner respecting each class member. In that event, differing results in separate cases might force the defending party to violate its legal duty to some of the class members.[49] Prejudice is not found when the risk merely is that the opposing party will have to pay damages to some claimants and not others, as might occur if individual actions are brought following a mass accident.[50]

conflict of interest. First Am. Corp. v. Foster, 51 F.R.D. 248 (N.D.Ga.1970).

45. Research Corp. v. Pfister Associated Growers, Inc., 301 F.Supp. 497 (N.D.Ill. 1969). For a more extended treatment of the question of the reluctant representative, see 7A C. Wright, A. Miller & M. Kane, Civil 2d § 1770.

46. See generally 7A C. Wright, A. Miller & M. Kane, Civil 2d §§ 1772–74.

47. The similarity between the criteria for a class action under Rule 23(b)(1) and the standards for determining when a party is needed for a just adjudication under Federal Rule 19 should be noted. The latter are discussed in § 6.5, above.

48. If the class members' individual claims are extremely small, there is little danger of multiple litigation. See Eisen v. Carlisle & Jacquelin, 391 F.2d 555 (2d Cir. 1968).

49. Larionoff v. U.S., 533 F.2d 1167 (D.C.Cir.1976), affirmed 431 U.S. 864, 97 S.Ct. 2150, 53 L.Ed.2d 48 (1977) (naval enlisted men suing to recover variable reenlistment bonuses); Kjeldahl v. Block, 579 F.Supp. 1130 (D.D.C.1983) (action challenging Secretary of Agriculture's refusal to implement loan program created by statute); Collins v. Bolton, 287 F.Supp. 393 (N.D.Ill. 1968) (a statutory assessment).

50. Attempts have been made in nationwide products liability litigation to obtain class certification under Rule 23(b)(1) on the theory that the class action presented the only way to ensure all members some recovery because if suits proceeded individually they would rapidly overwhelm defendant's assets. In general, courts have used a very high threshold and have refused certification on the ground that insufficient evidence existed to demonstrate the defendant's likely insolvency. See, e.g., In re

Similarly, the absent class members need not show that they would be bound legally by the separate adjudications under notions of claim or issue preclusion in order to demonstrate prejudice.[51] The effect of the individual litigation should be something more than the impact of stare decisis, however.[52] For example, Rule 23(b)(1) may be invoked when individual class members are seeking to recover out of a limited common fund. If portions of the fund are distributed in individual suits on a first-come, first-served basis, the fund may be completely exhausted before some class members have had an opportunity to litigate their claims[53] and individual litigation thus may threaten the class members' rights as a practical matter.

The second type of class action,[54] found in Federal Rule 23(b)(2), is permitted when (1) the party opposing the class has acted or refused to act on grounds generally applicable to the class as a whole, and (2) the class representatives are seeking final injunctive relief or corresponding declaratory relief.[55] It is this category of Rule 23 that is used most often for civil rights suits and in other constitutional litigation,[56] although any action seeking to alter defendant's conduct also may qualify.[57] The requirements for Rule 23(b)(2) will be met if the class opponent either has acted in a consistent manner towards the class members so that it amounts to a pattern of activity,[58] or the party has imposed a regulatory scheme that affects all members of the class.[59] It is not necessary that

School Asbestos Litigation, 789 F.2d 996 (3d Cir.1986); In re Northern District of Cal. Dalkon Shield IUD Prods. Liability Litigation, 693 F.2d 847 (9th Cir.1982), cert. denied 459 U.S. 1171. But see In re "Agent Orange" Prod. Liability Litigation, 100 F.R.D. 718 (E.D.N.Y.1983), mandamus denied sub nom. In re Diamond Shamrock Chemicals Co., 725 F.2d 858 (2d Cir.1984), cert. denied 465 U.S. 1067. Of course, when defendant has become insolvent, then the use of Rule 23(b)(1) has been upheld. E.g., In re Joint E. & S. District Asbestos Litigation, 982 F.2d 721 (2d Cir.1992).

51. La Mar v. H & B Novelty & Loan Co., 489 F.2d 461 (9th Cir.1973); Rodriguez v. Barcelo, 358 F.Supp. 43 (D.Puerto Rico 1973).

52. Larionoff v. U.S., 533 F.2d 1167 (D.C.Cir.1976), affirmed on the merits 431 U.S. 864, 97 S.Ct. 2150, 53 L.Ed.2d 48 (1977); LaMar v. H & B Novelty & Loan Co., 489 F.2d 461 (9th Cir.1973).

53. See, e.g., In re Drexel Burnham Lambert Group, Inc., 960 F.2d 285 (2d Cir. 1992); In re Greenman Secs. Litigation, 94 F.R.D. 273 (S.D.Fla.1982). See also note 50, above.

54. For a more detailed discussion of this category, see 7A C. Wright, A. Miller & M. Kane, Civil 2d §§ 1775–76.

55. The rule appears to authorize only actions by a class seeking to enjoin conduct

and most courts have ruled that actions to enjoin a class from pursuing or failing to pursue some conduct are outside its scope. E.g., Thompson v. Board of Educ. of Romeo Community Schools, 709 F.2d 1200 (6th Cir.1983); Paxman v. Campbell, 612 F.2d 848 (4th Cir.1980), cert. denied 449 U.S. 1129; Stewart v. Winter, 87 F.R.D. 760 (N.D.Miss.1980), affirmed on other grounds 669 F.2d 328 (5th Cir.1982).

56. E.g., Riley v. Nevada Supreme Court, 763 F.Supp. 446 (D.Nev.1991) (action challenging Nevada procedural rules in death penalty cases); Singleton v. Drew, 485 F.Supp. 1020 (E.D.Wis.1980) (action to require due process for rejected public housing applicants).

57. E.g., Califano v. Yamasaki, 442 U.S. 682, 99 S.Ct. 2545, 61 L.Ed.2d 176 (1979) (social security act suit); Environmental Defense Fund, Inc. v. Corps of Engineers of U.S. Army, 348 F.Supp. 916 (N.D.Miss.1972), affirmed on other grounds 492 F.2d 1123 (5th Cir.1974) (environmental suit); Van Gemert v. Boeing Co., 259 F.Supp. 125 (S.D.N.Y.1966) (suit to require conversion of debentures into common stock).

58. See, e.g., Ashmus v. Calderon, 935 F.Supp. 1048 (N.D.Cal.1996).

59. See, e.g., Sorenson v. Concannon, 893 F.Supp. 1469 (D.Or.1994).

every class member be affected directly by the actions of the opposing party or feel aggrieved by them,[60] as might be true in a case attacking an institutional dress code. Further, the relief sought must be final in character; requests solely for preliminary injunctions or temporary restraining orders will not suffice. However, the mere fact that the complaint requests an award of damages in addition to injunctive or declaratory relief does not defeat certification under Rule 23(b)(2),[61] as long as the damages sought are viewed as incidental.

The most controversial of the three types of class actions is the "common question" or "damage" class action authorized in Federal Rule 23(b)(3).[62] The three elements necessary for its maintenance are: (1) common questions of law or fact must predominate over questions that only affect individual class members, (2) the class action procedure must be superior to other means of adjudicating the controversy, and (3) the best notice practicable must be given to the class members of the institution of the action and of their right to exclude themselves from the class.[63]

The requirements for a common question class action reflect an attempt to accommodate two somewhat opposing policies. On the one hand, judicial economy and litigation efficiency point towards the combining of legally and factually similar actions into one suit to avoid duplication and inconsistent adjudications. Indeed, class action treatment may enable persons with claims too small to justify individual litigation to vindicate their rights through collective action.[64] On the other hand, traditional notions of due process and procedural fairness may be put in jeopardy when an individual has no control over litigation affecting him and is forced to share an attorney with hundreds or even thousands of others.[65]

The requirement that common questions of law or fact predominate over questions affecting only individual class members attempts to achieve a balance between these opposing policies.[66] Even when it appears that the individual issues may consume more time than the common questions, the class suit still may be permitted if it appears that

60. See, e.g., Johnson v. American Credit Co. of Georgia, 581 F.2d 526 (5th Cir.1978); Hess v. Hughes, 500 F.Supp. 1054 (D.Md.1980).

61. Eubanks v. Billington, 110 F.3d 87 (D.C.Cir.1997); Probe v. State Teachers' Retirement Sys., 780 F.2d 776 (9th Cir.1986), cert. denied 476 U.S. 1170.

62. For a more detailed discussion of the Rule 23(b)(3) requirements, see 7A C. Wright, A. Miller & M. Kane, Civil 2d §§ 1777–80; 7B C. Wright, A. Miller & M. Kane, Civil 2d §§ 1781–84.

63. This third requirement is not stated as a formal requirement in Rule 23(b)(3) but is made mandatory by Rule 23(c)(2) to all actions under that subdivision. Since

numerous cases have been dismissed because of an inability or an unwillingness to give the class members notice of the action, notice should be treated as a co-equal requirement for the maintenance of a common question class action.

64. Comment, Rule 23: Categories of Subsection (b), in The Class Action—A Symposium, 10 B.C.Ind. & Com.L.Rev. 539, 555 (1969).

65. Frankel, Some Preliminary Observations Concerning Civil Rule 23, 43 F.R.D. 39, 43 (1967).

66. Compare   Fed.Civ.Proc.Rule 23(a)(2), which only requires that common questions exist, not predominate. See the discussion at notes 18–21, above.

doing so will be substantially more efficient than leaving the parties to individual adjudications in separate suits.[67] Thus, courts frequently approach the predominance question by inquiring whether there is a significant common nucleus of factual and legal issues,[68] but it is not necessary that this common nucleus include all issues that would be dispositive of the case.[69] In cases involving securities fraud and antitrust violations,[70] for example, predominance may be found if the defendant's challenged activities stem from a single, class-wide course of conduct, so that the issue of statutory liability is common to the class, even though there may be separate individual issues such as damages, and in securities cases, reliance.[71] On the other hand, products liability actions often fail to meet this requisite because the individual character of the issues of causation and damages predominates over any common questions.[72]

Indeed, this point was underscored by the Supreme Court's 1997 decision in Amchem Products, Inc. v. Windsor,[73] which involved the certification for settlement purposes of a proposed nationwide class of future asbestos claimants.[74] The Court held that the common issue concerning the health consequences of asbestos exposure was outweighed by the individual questions posed concerning class members with varying levels of exposure, from different products, over different time periods, as well as those who had suffered varying injuries or no injuries at all. The fact that differing state laws applied to the claimants further exacerbated the problem.[75]

In addition to finding that common questions predominate, the court in a Rule 23(b)(3) action must consider whether there are any other methods for resolving the controversy that would be more advantageous than a class action. Other adjudicatory procedures include, most obviously, remitting the dispute for individual adjudication, joinder of

---

67. Compare Minnesota v. U.S. Steel Corp., 44 F.R.D. 559, 569 (D.Minn.1968) (class action allowed), with Bonner v. Texas City Independent School Dist. of Texas City, Texas, 305 F.Supp. 600, 617 (S.D.Tex. 1969) (class action not allowed).

68. Esplin v. Hirschi, 402 F.2d 94, 99 (10th Cir.1968), cert. denied 394 U.S. 928; Kristiansen v. John Mullins & Sons, Inc., 59 F.R.D. 99 (E.D.N.Y.1973); Illinois v. Harper & Row Publishers, Inc., 301 F.Supp. 484, 488 n. 7 (N.D.Ill.1969).

69. Lockwood Motors, Inc. v. General Motors Corp., 162 F.R.D. 569 (D.Minn. 1995); Kleiner v. First Nat. Bank of Atlanta, 97 F.R.D. 683 (N.D.Ga.1983).

70. For a fuller discussion, see 7B C. Wright, A. Miller & M. Kane, Civil 2d § 1781.

71. E.g., Kirkpatrick v. J.C. Bradford & Co., 827 F.2d 718 (11th Cir.1987) (common course of misrepresentation by affirmative acts and omissions in securities ac-

tion); Stephenson v. Bell Atlantic Corp., 177 F.R.D. 279 (D.N.J.1997) (same showing of anticompetitive conduct and monopolistic pricing required in antitrust action).

72. See, e.g., Raye v. Medtronic Corp., 696 F.Supp. 1273 (D.Minn.1988); Caruso v. Celsius Insulation Resources, Inc., 101 F.R.D. 530 (M.D.Pa.1984); Payton v. Abbott Labs., 100 F.R.D. 336 (D.Mass.1983).

73. 521 U.S. 591, 117 S.Ct. 2231, 138 L.Ed.2d 689 (1997).

74. The implications of the decision on settlement classes are discussed in § 16.7, below.

75. Other courts also have ruled that mass tort suits, which derive from multiple state laws, fail to satisfy the predominance requirement in part because of the multiple laws that must be applied. See, e.g., Castano v. American Tobacco Co., 84 F.3d 734 (5th Cir.1996); In the Matter of Rhone–Poulenc Rorer Inc., 51 F.3d 1293 (7th Cir. 1995), cert. denied 516 U.S. 867.

the absent class members through interpleader[76] or intervention,[77] consolidation of separate cases for common adjudication, transfer to a single court for consolidated and coordinated pretrial activities,[78] remitting the matter to an administrative body,[79] and treating one or more of the claims as a test case.[80] If a comparison of the alternative adjudicatory techniques reveals that the benefits of a class action warrant the expenditure of the judicial energy necessary to manage it and to run the risks of mass litigation, the class suit should proceed.

To aid the court in making this assessment, the Federal Rule contains a nonexhaustive list of factors to be considered.[81] These are intended to focus the judge's attention on the objectives of the common question class suit and to ensure that an action is maintained on that basis only when it is the most efficient means of proceeding. Thus, the judge is invited to inquire whether individual class members have an interest in controlling the prosecution or defense of individual suits involving their rights.[82] A strong desire for individual control may reflect dissatisfaction with the representation or may lead a significant number of class members to opt-out of the action,[83] undermining the utility of proceeding on a class basis. Similarly, the judge will consider whether other actions concerning the controversy already are pending.[84] Unless those suits can be enjoined or stayed, or if they will provide an effective adjudication of the dispute, the class action simply will be an additional burden on the judicial system.[85] Moreover, if individual actions are pending, that itself provides evidence that some class members have an interest in controlling the course of litigation involving their rights.

The third factor that the court may consider is the desirability of having the controversy resolved in one action. This factor entails an evaluation of whether permitting a class suit to proceed will minimize the potential for duplication of effort and the possibility of inconsistent results.[86] It also requires some assessment of whether the forum selected for the class action represents an appropriate place to resolve the controversy. The propriety of the forum may depend on the citizenship

76. See §§ 16.10–16.13, below.

77. See § 6.10, above.

78. This procedure is permitted under 28 U.S.C.A. § 1407; it is an alternative only in the federal system, and is limited to transfer for pretrial only.

79. Schaffner v. Chemical Bank, 339 F.Supp. 329, 337 (S.D.N.Y.1972). See, e.g., Pattillo v. Schlesinger, 625 F.2d 262 (9th Cir.1980).

80. See, e.g., Yeager's Fuel, Inc. v. Pennsylvania Power & Light Co., 162 F.R.D. 482 (E.D.Pa.1995); Perez v. Government of Virgin Islands, 109 F.R.D. 384 (D.Vi.1986).

81. See Fed.Civ.Proc.Rule 23(b)(3)(A–D).

82. See, e.g., Commander Properties Corp. v. Beech Aircraft Corp., 164 F.R.D. 529 (D.Kan.1995).

83. The right to opt out is provided in Fed.Civ.Proc.Rule 23(c)(2).

84. See Kamm v. California City Dev. Co., 509 F.2d 205 (9th Cir.1975) (state action pending).

85. A federal court cannot enjoin ongoing state actions. 28 U.S.C.A. § 2283. Federal Rule 23 has been held not to be an exception to the anti-suit injunction statute. In re Federal Skywalk Cases, 680 F.2d 1175 (8th Cir.1982); In re Corrugated Container Antitrust Litigation (Three J. Farms, Inc.), 659 F.2d 1332 (5th Cir.1981), cert. denied 456 U.S. 936.

86. Carpenter v. Hall, 311 F.Supp. 1099, 1112 (S.D.Tex.1970).

of the interested parties, the availability of witnesses and evidence, and the condition of the court's calendar, among other things.[87]

The fourth factor, which often is given the most intensive scrutiny of all, requires the court to appraise the management difficulties likely to arise if the action is maintained as a class suit.[88] This requires a consideration of, among other elements, the size of the class, the onerousness of the notice requirement, the potential number of intervenors, and the presence of special individual issues. The difficulties likely to arise are weighed against the benefits to be derived from representative adjudication.[89]

The final prerequisite for a common question class action is that the best notice practicable of the action and the right to opt out be given to identifiable class members. In the federal courts, notice is required to be given to each class member whose identity is ascertainable with reasonable effort.[90] The problems of giving notice are discussed in a later section.[91] Suffice it to note at this point that the costs of complying with these notice requirements in large class suits can be so prohibitive as to preclude the action from being brought.

A class suit may meet the requirements for two or all three of the class action categories just discussed. Difficulties will arise only when the action qualifies under both the "common question" and one of the other class action categories.[92] In that event, many courts have ruled that because of the special notice requirement and opt-out privilege that pertain to the common question suit, it is more expeditious not to characterize the action as falling within that category.[93] Although it can be argued that the availability of the special procedural safeguards that attend the "common question" class action should not turn on expediency, the closer relationship of the class members and claims that meet the criteria of Rule 23(b)(1) or (b)(2)[94] justifies their certification without those added safeguards.

§ 16.3   State Class Action Prerequisites

Although the precise requirements for bringing a class action vary from state to state, the types of statutes that exist can be grouped

---

87. See Hobbs v. Northeast Airlines, Inc., 50 F.R.D. 76 (E.D.Pa.1970).

88. For an interesting, albeit restrictive, application of manageability, see In re Hotel Telephone Charges, 500 F.2d 86 (9th Cir.1974).

89. Chevalier v. Baird Savs. Ass'n, 72 F.R.D. 140 (E.D.Pa.1976); In re Memorex Sec. Cases, 61 F.R.D. 88, 103 (N.D.Cal. 1973); Brennan v. Midwestern United Life Ins. Co., 259 F.Supp. 673 (N.D.Ind.1966).

90. Eisen v. Carlisle & Jacquelin, 417 U.S. 156, 94 S.Ct. 2140, 40 L.Ed.2d 732 (1974).

91. See § 16.6, below.

92. It is unnecessary to choose between categorizing an action as a (b)(1) or a (b)(2) suit because the notice provisions and binding effect are identical for both types of actions.

93. DeBoer v. Mellon Mortgage Co., 64 F.3d 1171 (8th Cir.1995), cert. denied 517 U.S. 1156; Tober v. Charnita, Inc., 58 F.R.D. 74 (M.D.Pa.1973); Walker v. City of Houston, 341 F.Supp. 1124 (S.D.Tex.1971).

94. The requirements for Rule 23(b)(1) and 23(b)(2) actions are discussed at notes 46–61, above.

roughly into four categories.[1] The two most common forms are modelled after federal practice. Thus, some states adopted as their class action rules the 1938 version of Federal Rule 23, classifying class actions as "true," "hybrid," and "spurious" depending on the type of interests presented by the class.[2] More commonly, however, states have enacted the 1966 version of Federal Rule 23.[3] In those states in particular, federal court interpretations of the various requirements are most influential, if not absolutely binding.

The third type of state class action statute is exemplified by Section 382 of the California Code of Civil Procedure, which simply provides that "when the question is one of a common or general interest, of many persons, or when the parties are numerous, and it is impracticable to bring them all before the court, one or more may sue or defend for the benefit of all."[4] The most striking difference between the California provision and those in states that follow the federal text is that California courts are not required to determine whether the particular suit falls within a prescribed class action category. A brief look at how the California statute has been applied reveals a few additional insights.

The first thing to note is that the statute appears to present only two requirements: that there be a community of interest among the members and that joinder be impracticable. In addition, and implicit in these requirements, however, California courts insist on a showing that there is an identifiable class.[5] As is true in the federal courts,[6] this does not mean that the representatives must be able to identify each class member at the outset.[7]

The major hurdle in satisfying the statute is the showing that there is a community of interest sufficient to merit class action treatment. Departing from those states that interpreted this requirement as necessitating some bond of privity between the class members,[8] the California

---

§ 16.3

1. An excellent discussion of state class action practice up to 1971 can be found in Homburger, State Class Actions and the Federal Rule, 71 Colum.L.Rev. 609 (1971).

2. E.g., Mich.Gen.Ct.Rule 1963, 208. See also Official Code Ga.Ann. § 9–11–23 (only "true" and "hybrid" suits authorized). The statute is examined in Casurella & Bevis, Class Action Law in Georgia: Emerging Trends in Litigation, Certification, and Settlement, 49 Mercer L.Rev. 39 (1997). West Virginia, which amended its class action rule in 1978, has an unusual provision combining the 1938 requirements referring to joint and several interests with the additional authorization of class relief if the action would fall into what is Federal Rule 23(b)(1). See W.Va.Rules Civ.Proc., Rule 23(a).

3. E.g., Ala.Rules Civ.Proc., Rule 23; Alaska Rules Civ.Proc., Rule 23; Fla.— West's F.S.A.Rules Civ.Proc.Rule 1.220;

Idaho Rules Civ.Proc., Rule 23(a); 12 Okl. St.Ann. § 2023.

4. The California provision is essentially that of the Field Code, adopted first in New York in 1849. New York has since abandoned this approach. See the discussion at note 19, below. However, some states still retain similar provisions. E.g., Neb.Rev.St. § 25–319; Wis.Stat.Ann. 803.08.

5. Lazar v. Hertz Corp., 143 Cal. App.3d 128, 191 Cal.Rptr. 849 (1983); Hebbard v. Colgrove, 28 Cal.App.3d 1017, 105 Cal.Rptr. 172 (1972).

6. See § 16.2 at nn. 7–9, above.

7. Daar v. Yellow Cab Co., 67 Cal.2d 695, 63 Cal.Rptr. 724, 433 P.2d 732 (1967).

8. See Hall v. Coburn Corp. of America, 26 N.Y.2d 396, 311 N.Y.S.2d 281, 259 N.E.2d 720 (1970); Society Milion Athena, Inc. v. National Bank of Greece, 281 N.Y.

Supreme Court has ruled that it is satisfied if there is an ascertainable class and a common definable interest in the questions of law or fact affecting the class members.[9] The standard is a balancing one—the court weighs the economies to be gained by allowing the action to proceed against the concerns of adequacy of representation and cohesiveness of interests on the part of the class members.[10] It is interesting to note that in evaluating these factors California courts have looked for assistance to the federal class action requirements and their interpretation in federal courts.[11] Thus, California judges have attempted to ascertain that there are common questions of law or fact,[12] that the interests of the representatives are typical of those of other class members, and that the representatives will adequately protect the interests of the absentees,[13] in order to find that a community of interest is present. Judicial economy is assured by considering whether the common questions raised by the class predominate over any questions to be adjudicated on an individual basis.[14] Nonetheless, it is important to bear in mind that federal law, though influential, is not binding,[15] allowing the California courts more discretion in shaping class action requirements in light of changing times.

The last type of class action statute that should be identified is found in those states that have newly revised their statutes in light of the federal experience. Like Federal Rule 23, these statutes generally attempt to take a pragmatic approach. They include not only prerequisites, but also provisions concerning notice, fees, types of remedies, and other management concerns.[16] In order to simplify class certification, these provisions typically have eliminated the need to find that the class

282, 22 N.E.2d 374 (1939). The New York statute was completely revised in 1975. See text at note 19, below.

9. Daar v. Yellow Cab Co., 67 Cal.2d 695, 63 Cal.Rptr. 724, 433 P.2d 732 (1967).

10. Compare Vasquez v. Superior Court, 4 Cal.3d 800, 94 Cal.Rptr. 796, 484 P.2d 964 (1971) (consumer class action for fraud upheld), with Caro v. Procter & Gamble Co., 18 Cal.App.4th 644, 22 Cal.Rptr.2d 419 (1993) (class action charging fraud and deceit in orange juice labeling and advertising not allowed).

11. In addition to decisions looking to federal law for guidance, some superior courts have adopted local rules patterned in large measure on Federal Rule 23. See, e.g., Los Angeles County Superior Court Class Action Manual, Rules 401–470. Further, the California Consumers Legal Remedies Act has within it provisions for consumer class actions including requirements identical to those in Rule 23(a). West's Ann.Cal.Civ. Code § 1781.

12. Gerhard v. Stephens, 68 Cal.2d 864, 69 Cal.Rptr. 612, 442 P.2d 692 (1968); Slakey Bros. Sacramento, Inc. v. Parker,

265 Cal.App.2d 204, 71 Cal.Rptr. 269 (1968).

13. San Jose v. Superior Court of Santa Clara County, 12 Cal.3d 447, 115 Cal. Rptr. 797, 525 P.2d 701 (1974).

14. Weaver v. Pasadena Tournament of Roses Ass'n, 32 Cal.2d 833, 198 P.2d 514 (1948); Silva v. Block, 49 Cal.App.4th 345, 56 Cal.Rptr.2d 613 (1996); Kennedy v. Baxter Healthcare Corp., 43 Cal.App.4th 799, 50 Cal.Rptr.2d 736 (1996); Lazar v. Hertz Corp., 143 Cal.App.3d 128, 191 Cal.Rptr. 849 (1983).

15. Most notably, the California courts have not followed the federal lead, which requires individual notice in common question damage class actions, see § 16.6 at nn. 20-21, below. California also permits fluid recoveries, see § 16.5 at nn. 25–29, below.

16. See, e.g., N.Y.—McKinney's CPLR 901–909. The most extensive attempt to provide statutory guidance is found in the Uniform Class Action Rule, currently adopted in North Dakota. See N.D.Rules Civ.Proc., Rule 23(f)–(r).

action falls into a particular category,[17] as is necessary under Federal Rule 23(b).[18] New York, for example, simply requires for all class actions that common questions of law or fact predominate and that class relief be superior to other available adjudicatory techniques.[19]

§ 16.4   Personal and Subject–Matter Jurisdiction Requirements

Special problems and questions have arisen in the class action context concerning how courts should treat absent class members for purposes of satisfying personal[1] and subject-matter[2] jurisdiction requirements.

With regard to personal jurisdiction, early federal decisions ruled that when a defendant class action was involved, all the unnamed class members could be bound to any judgment entered in the action as long as the court properly obtained in personam jurisdiction over the representative parties.[3] Questions concerning the need to obtain personal jurisdiction over absent plaintiff class members never were raised. However, over time, courts[4] and commentators[5] began to look carefully at whether traditional personal jurisdiction requirements must be met for all absent class members, whether a plaintiff or defendant class is involved.[6] This question has become particularly important as the Supreme Court restrictions on the availability of federal class relief have forced more litigants into the state courts,[7] so that those courts now are

---

17. See, e.g., Mass.Rules Civ.Proc., Rule 23; R.I.Sup.Ct.Rules Civ.Proc., Rule 23. New Mexico's class action rule has provisions like current Federal Rule 23, except that it eliminated the (b)(3) category. Rule 1–023 N.M.R.A. 1998. In contrast, the Uniform Class Action Rule, adopted in North Dakota, although it eliminates the class action categories, substitutes a list of thirteen factors to be considered in deciding whether class treatment will present a fair and efficient adjudication of the controversy. N.D.Rules Civ.Proc., Rule 23(c).

18. See § 16.2, above.

19. N.Y.—McKinney's CPLR 901a.

§ 16.4

1. See generally Chapter 3, above.

2. See generally Chapter 2, above.

3. Canuel v. Oskoian, 23 F.R.D. 307 (D.R.I.1959), affirmed on other grounds 269 F.2d 311 (1st Cir.1959); Griffin v. Illinois Cent. R.R. Co., 88 F.Supp. 552 (N.D.Ill. 1949); Salvant v. Louisville & N.R. Co., 83 F.Supp. 391 (W.D.Ky.1949).

4. In re Northern District of California "Dalkon Shield" IUD Prods. Liability Litigation, 526 F.Supp. 887 (N.D.Cal.1981), class certification reversed on other grounds 693 F.2d 847 (9th Cir.1982), cert.

denied 459 U.S. 1171; Schlosser v. Allis–Chalmers Corp., 86 Wis.2d 226, 271 N.W.2d 879 (1978); Shutts v. Phillips Petroleum Co., 222 Kan. 527, 567 P.2d 1292 (1977), cert. denied 434 U.S. 1068.

5. See Note, Multistate Plaintiff Class Actions: Jurisdiction and Certification, 92 Harv.L.Rev. 718 (1979); Comment, Toward a Policy–Based Theory of State Court Jurisdiction Over Class Actions, 56 Texas L.Rev. 1033 (1978).

6. An interesting approach to this problem is taken by the Uniform Class Action Statute, adopted in North Dakota. The statute suggests that personal jurisdiction over the absent members should be asserted only if jurisdiction could be asserted in an action against the person, or if the state where the member resides, by class action rule or law, has made its residents subject to the jurisdiction of North Dakota. In other words, jurisdiction may be premised on reciprocity. See N.D.Rules Civ.Proc.Rule 23(f).

7. In particular, the Supreme Court's decisions prohibiting aggregation to meet the amount in controversy requirements, see the discussion at notes 18–27, below, and requiring the plaintiff to bear the cost of individual notice in damage actions, see

being confronted with multistate controversies that do not fall easily within the traditional framework for asserting personal jurisdiction. The state courts that addressed the problem did not agree on the solution.[8]

The Supreme Court finally resolved the issue in Phillips Petroleum Company v. Shutts,[9] holding that it was not necessary to satisfy the minimum contacts standard normally applied to out-of-state defendants in order to obtain a judgment binding out-of-state, absent plaintiff class members. The Court found that class action plaintiffs are in a very different posture from defendants because the burdens placed on them are not the same as those imposed on a defendant. It noted specifically that "the plaintiffs in this suit were not haled anywhere to defend themselves upon pain of a default judgment," and that "[u]nlike a defendant in a civil suit, a class-action plaintiff is not required to fend for himself."[10] Finally the Court noted that other procedural protections provided to the absent class members, including notice and the opportunity to opt out,[11] satisfied due process concerns so that the absent plaintiffs did not need as much protection from state court jurisdiction as do defendants.[12]

Shutts involved only the question whether it was necessary for state courts to satisfy personal jurisdiction requirements with regard to absent plaintiff class members in order to enter binding judgments. In a footnote, the Court specifically limited its decision to plaintiff class actions, refusing to state how it would deal with the issue were absent defendant class members involved.[13] Also unanswered is whether the same due process restraints exist for federal class actions that exist for state class suits. Of course, insofar as Shutts permits the state courts to rely on procedural requirements other than personal jurisdiction to satisfy due process concerns, it is clear that the federal courts also would not be required to apply the minimum contacts standard to obtain a judgment binding absent class plaintiffs if they use similar protections.[14]

§ 16.6 at notes 9–14, below, have had this effect.

8. Miner v. Gillette Co., 87 Ill.2d 7, 56 Ill.Dec. 886, 428 N.E.2d 478 (1981), cert. dismissed 459 U.S. 86 (1982); Schlosser v. Allis–Chalmers Corp., 86 Wis.2d 226, 271 N.W.2d 879 (1978).

9. 472 U.S. 797, 105 S.Ct. 2965, 86 L.Ed.2d 628 (1985). The Shutts case is examined extensively in Miller & Crump, Jurisdiction and Choice of Law in Multistate Class Actions After Phillips Petroleum Co. v. Shutts, 96 Yale L.J. 1 (1986).

10. 472 U.S. at 809, 105 S.Ct. at 2973.

11. For a discussion of the requirements necessary to obtain a binding class action judgment, see § 16.8, below.

12. For an interesting case, which distinguished Shutts on the ground that the

absent parties, who were from Arizona, were afforded fewer procedural protections than the absent plaintiffs in Shutts when the opposing party sought an injunction from a Pennsylvania district court to prevent the absent parties' Arizona suit, see In re Real Estate Title & Settlement Servs. Antitrust Litigation, 869 F.2d 760 (3d Cir. 1989), cert. denied 493 U.S. 821.

13. 472 U.S. at 811 n. 3, 105 S.Ct. at 2974 n. 3.

14. Some courts have ruled that the absent members impliedly consent to jurisdiction either by failing to opt out or by contesting inclusion in the class. See, e.g., White v. National Football League, 41 F.3d 402 (8th Cir.1994), cert. denied 515 U.S. 1137; In re Prudential Ins. Co. of America Sales Practices Litigation, 962 F.Supp. 450 (D.N.J.1997).

However, it remains questionable whether they may use lesser or other procedures and, nonetheless, comport with due process.[15]

Two questions have arisen concerning federal subject-matter jurisdiction over class actions under Federal Rule 23. First, whose citizenship should control when determining whether diversity of citizenship exists? Second, may the claims of individual class members be aggregated to meet the amount in controversy requirement?

As to the first, it is well settled that only the citizenship of the named representatives is considered in determining whether federal diversity jurisdiction may be invoked.[16] In view of the complete diversity requirement,[17] taking account of the citizenship of all class members would seriously impair the availability of class actions.

Turning to the second query, according to decisions by the United States Supreme Court, each class member must have a claim that satisfies the amount in controversy requirement,[18] except when the class members are seeking to enforce a single title or a right in which they assert a common and undivided interest.[19] Unfortunately, this standard preserves much of the conceptualism of pre–1966 class action practice. At that time aggregation was permitted in "true" class actions when the members' rights were joint or common. Aggregation was not permitted in the "spurious" or "hybrid" class suits since the class members' rights were "several" in nature.[20] It had been hoped that these arbitrary and conceptualistic distinctions would be eliminated by the new rule.

The no aggregation rule has a particularly inhibiting effect in federal class actions brought by persons who have small claims even though the totality of the alleged harm caused by the defendant is substantial. The result is illustrated by the Supreme Court's decision in Zahn v. International Paper Company,[21] in which four named represen-

---

15. For a fuller discussion, see 7B C. Wright, A. Miller & M. Kane, Civil 2d § 1789.

16. Supreme Tribe of Ben–Hur v. Cauble, 255 U.S. 356, 41 S.Ct. 338, 65 L.Ed. 673 (1921).

17. The complete diversity rule is discussed in § 2.5, above.

18. Note, however, that the amount in controversy requirement is not satisfied only if a claim appears to a "legal certainty" to be less than the jurisdictional amount. See St. Paul Mercury Indem. Co. v. Red Cab Co., 303 U.S. 283, 289, 58 S.Ct. 586, 82 L.Ed. 845 (1938). Thus, in In re School Asbestos Litigation, 921 F.2d 1310 (3d Cir.1990), cert. denied 499 U.S. 976, the court of appeals upheld the district court's decision to defer the amount in controversy issue until trial when the plaintiffs conceded that a small number of school districts would not be able to show the requisite amount of damages, rather than to try

to determine which districts those were at the outset of the litigation.

19. Zahn v. International Paper Co., 414 U.S. 291, 94 S.Ct. 505, 38 L.Ed.2d 511 (1973); Snyder v. Harris, 394 U.S. 332, 89 S.Ct. 1053, 22 L.Ed.2d 319 (1969).

20. See § 16.1, above.

21. 414 U.S. 291, 94 S.Ct. 505, 38 L.Ed.2d 511 (1973). The Zahn case is discussed more thoroughly in 14A C. Wright, A. Miller & E. Cooper, Jurisdiction and Related Matters 2d § 3705; Riddell & Davis, Ancillary Jurisdiction and the Jurisdictional Amount Requirement, 50 Notre Dame Law. 346 (1974); Thies, Zahn v. International Paper Co. The Non–Aggregation Rule in Jurisdictional Amount Cases, 35 La.L.Rev. 89 (1974); Note, Unnamed Plaintiffs in Federal Class Actions: Zahn v. International Paper Co. Further Restricts the Availability of the Class Suit, 35 Ohio St. L.J. 190 (1974).

tatives—each having a claim in excess of the jurisdictional amount—sued on behalf of themselves and several hundred other similarly situated lake-front owners who allegedly had been injured by the defendant's pollution. Because the rights asserted by each of the represented lake-front owners did not involve more than the $10,000 then required to satisfy the diversity statute[22] and their claims were deemed several instead of common or joint, the federal court was said to be without subject-matter jurisdiction.[23]

The no aggregation rule has little effect in Federal Rule 23(b)(2) class actions for injunctive relief, at least when suit is brought to rectify racial discrimination, because these actions have no amount in controversy requirement.[24] The same is true, with rare exceptions, of any actions arising under a federal law since they do not require an amount in controversy.[25] In addition, diversity suits under Federal Rule 23(b)(1) typically will be unaffected by Zahn because the rights of class members in these actions ordinarily are deemed joint or common.[26] The greatest impact of the no aggregation rule, therefore, is in the common question class action for damages, when jurisdiction is based on diversity, and when the individual claims are not large—in consumer and environmental litigation, for example. The application of the no aggregation rule means that these actions must be filed in state courts, which may or may not be able to handle them as class actions.[27]

The enactment in 1990 of the supplemental jurisdiction statute[28] has raised some question whether it impliedly overruled Zahn so that class actions now may be brought as long as one of the representatives possesses a claim satisfying the jurisdictional amount requirements, with the smaller claims of the other class members being deemed supplemental.[29] The courts are divided on the issue because the legislative history surrounding the statute suggests that there was no intention to alter class action practice, but the failure to include class actions as one of the statute's explicit exceptions means that the plain meaning of the statute suggests otherwise.[30]

---

22. The diversity statute currently requires that the amount in controversy be more than $75,000. 28 U.S.C.A. § 1332(a).

23. There have been numerous cases trying to distinguish claims that can be aggregated from those that cannot. Compare Gallagher v. Continental Ins. Co., 502 F.2d 827 (10th Cir.1974) (aggregation permitted), with Burns v. Massachusetts Mut. Life Ins. Co., 820 F.2d 246 (8th Cir.1987) (aggregation not permitted).

24. 28 U.S.C.A. § 1343.

25. The amount in controversy requirement in federal question cases is discussed in § 2.8, above.

26. E.g., Eliasen v. Green Bay & W.R.R. Co., 93 F.R.D. 408 (E.D.Wis.1982), affirmed without opinion 705 F.2d 461 (7th Cir.1983), cert. denied 464 U.S. 874; Cass Clay, Inc. v. Northwestern Public Serv. Co.,

63 F.R.D. 34 (D.S.D.1974). Federal Rule 23(b)(1) is not co-extensive with the former "true" class action classification, however, and aggregation will be permitted only if the rights of the class members are found to be "joint" or "common."

27. See generally § 16.3, above.

28. 28 U.S.C.A. § 1367. The statute is discussed in §§ 2.13–2.14, above.

29. Compare Snider v. Stimson Lumber Co., 914 F.Supp. 388 (E.D.Cal.1996) (Zahn authoritative), with In re Prudential Ins. Co. of America Sales Practices Litigation, 962 F.Supp. 450 (D.N.J.1997) (Zahn overruled).

30. See Arthur & Freer, Grasping At Burnt Straws: The Disaster of the Supplemental Jurisdiction Statute, 40 Emory L.J. 963, 981 (1991); Rowe, Burbank & Mengler,

3.   Special Procedures and Problems

§ 16.5   Procedures in Class Actions

Because class actions embrace the rights of so many persons[1] and often present highly complex issues to resolve, the courts must use special procedures to manage or control the litigation so as to assure fair representation of all the interests involved.[2] In particular, as discussed in the following two sections, special rules concerning notice to absent members[3] and settlements[4] have been developed. This section discusses some of the other procedural issues that have arisen and explores the range of management devices that may be used by the trial judge, from the certification process to the distribution of damages.

The first problem facing the court is the certification process itself. As soon as practicable after a suit has been commenced as a class action, the court will determine whether the litigation should proceed in that format.[5] Although either the plaintiff or the defendant may seek this determination,[6] the court need not wait for a motion. Indeed, the judge is obligated to determine whether the suit can be maintained as a class action even if neither party initiates the inquiry.[7] Since there is no occasion for notifying the nonparty class members until after the court has determined that the action is a proper class suit, certification should

Compounding or Creating Confusion About Supplemental Jurisdiction? A Reply to Professor Freer, 40 Emory L.J. 943, 960 (1991).

§ 16.5

1. See § 16.8, below, on the binding effect of class action judgments.

2. Certain problems common to all litigation have received special consideration in class actions. For example, there was some question about the right to jury trial in a class suit because the class device originally was a creature of equity, where no jury trial was available. See Industrial Waxes, Inc. v. International Rys. of Cent. America, 193 F.Supp. 783, 786 n. 8 (S.D.N.Y. 1961). However, the Supreme Court's decision in Ross v. Bernhard, 396 U.S. 531, 90 S.Ct. 733, 24 L.Ed.2d 729 (1970), upholding the right to a jury trial in a shareholder derivative suit, has clarified that a jury trial now will be readily available if the nature of the underlying issues in the action so requires. Only the question whether a proper class action is brought remains equitable, to be tried by the judge. The right to jury trial is discussed in Chapter 11, above. When a jury is required, problems of how to conduct the trial on the class issues while still preserving individual jury rights have surfaced in several cases. See, e.g., In re Fibreboard Corp., 893 F.2d 706 (5th Cir.1990); In re Estate of Marcos Human Rights Litigation,

910 F.Supp. 1460 (D.Haw.1995), affirmed 103 F.3d 767 (9th Cir.1996).

Another example of a common problem that has surfaced in class actions is the right to immediate appellate review of many of the court's preliminary class action orders, see Chapter 13, above.

3. See § 16.6, below.

4. See § 16.7, below.

5. In New York, a motion for certification must be made within sixty days after answers have been filed. N.Y.—McKinney's CPLR 902. A more detailed discussion of the certification process in the federal courts may be found in 7B C. Wright, A. Miller & M. Kane, Civil 2d § 1785.

6. Cook County College Teachers Union, Local 1600, Am. Federation of Teachers, AFL–CIO v. Byrd, 456 F.2d 882 (7th Cir.1972), cert. denied 409 U.S. 848.

7. Gore v. Turner, 563 F.2d 159 (5th Cir.1977).

Theoretically the judge has the authority to certify a class action even if neither party requests it. However, this course is fraught with problems because it may result in unwilling class representatives and counsel. See, e.g., In re Northern District of Cal. Dalkon Shield IUD Prods. Liability Litigation, 693 F.2d 847 (9th Cir.1982), cert. denied 459 U.S. 1171.

occur at very early stages in the litigation so that class members can be given a meaningful opportunity to opt out, to make an appearance in the action, or to object to the representation.

The facts and circumstances of each case will control the timing of the decision as to the certification of the class action. In any event, a favorable decision as to the maintainability of the action as a class suit is not final; future events may cause the court to reverse its determination and order that the class allegations be stricken from the pleadings.[8]

Some considerations that may bear on when it is practicable to make the determination include the existence of related pending suits[9] and the possibility that discovery may be necessary before a determination can be made.[10] In the federal courts, the certification decision may not depend upon a preliminary inquiry into the merits,[11] however. In a few instances, certification has been delayed until after the decision on the merits,[12] although great care must be taken to ensure that this result is fair to all concerned.[13]

The court has wide discretion in determining whether a suit is maintainable as a class action. Factors other than those specifically mentioned in the applicable rule or statute often will be considered.[14] For example, several courts confronted by potential class actions for injunctive relief have considered whether class relief is necessary or whether, if the case were to proceed on an individual basis, any injunction that was entered necessarily would benefit all affected by the challenged practice or policy.[15]

The trial judge also has considerable flexibility in fashioning the order to be issued upon certification. For example, the court may determine that the action should be maintained as a class suit only with regard to particular issues or as to certain parties[16] or it may divide the

---

8. E.g., Forehand v. Florida State Hosp. at Chattahoochee, 89 F.3d 1562 (11th Cir.1996); Hervey v. City of Little Rock, 787 F.2d 1223 (8th Cir.1986).

9. Berland v. Mack, 48 F.R.D. 121, 126 (S.D.N.Y.1969) (determination postponed for two years because of pending SEC claim).

10. See, e.g, Chateau de Ville Productions, Inc. v. Tams–Witmark Music Library, Inc., 586 F.2d 962 (2d Cir.1978); Connett v. Justus Enterprises of Kansas, Inc., 125 F.R.D. 166 (D.Kan.1988).

11. Eisen v. Carlisle & Jacquelin, 417 U.S. 156, 94 S.Ct. 2140, 40 L.Ed.2d 732 (1974).

12. Alexander v. Aero Lodge No. 735, Int'l Ass'n of Machinists & Aerospace Workers, AFL–CIO, 565 F.2d 1364 (6th Cir. 1977), cert. denied 436 U.S. 946; McLaughlin v. Wohlgemuth, 535 F.2d 251 (3d Cir. 1976). But see Peritz v. Liberty Loan Corp., 523 F.2d 349 (7th Cir.1975).

13. See Watson v. Secretary of HEW, 562 F.2d 386 (6th Cir.1977); Nance v. Union Carbide Corp., Consumer Products Div., 540 F.2d 718 (4th Cir.1976), cert. denied 431 U.S. 953.

14. In re A.H. Robins Co., 880 F.2d 709, 740 (4th Cir.1989), cert. denied 493 U.S. 959; Bermudez v. U.S. Department of Agriculture, 490 F.2d 718 (D.C.Cir.1973), cert. denied 414 U.S. 1104; Carter v. Butz, 479 F.2d 1084 (3d Cir.1973), cert. denied 414 U.S. 1103.

15. E.g., Kansas Health Care Ass'n v. Kansas Dep't of Social & Rehabilitation Servs., 31 F.3d 1536 (10th Cir.1994); Donovan v. University of Texas at El Paso, 643 F.2d 1201 (5th Cir.1981). But see Fujishima v. Board of Educ., 460 F.2d 1355 (7th Cir. 1972). See generally 7B C. Wright, A. Miller & M. Kane, Civil 2d § 1785.2.

16. See Fed.Civ.Proc.Rule 23(c)(4)(A). E.g., Jenkins v. Raymark Indus., Inc., 782 F.2d 468 (5th Cir.1986); Stong v. Bucyrus–

class into subclasses[17] each with its own representative and counsel.[18] The ability to fashion subclasses is a particularly useful tool for managing very complex class actions.[19] In this way, the advantages and economies of a single adjudication of issues that are common to the entire class can be secured even though other issues in the case may have to be adjudicated separately with respect to each class member.[20]

The certification process is just the beginning of the management problems inherent in a class action. The complexity of many class actions and the danger of violating the due process rights of absent class members have led to a general understanding that the trial judge must be prepared to exercise considerable authority to control and manage numerous aspects of these cases. Accordingly, Federal Rule 23(d) contains a nonexhaustive list of the types of orders that a court may issue during a class action. In addition, the Manual for Complex Litigation, Third, issued by the Judicial Conference of the United States, contains an elaborate discussion of numerous procedures that judges may employ to manage class actions effectively.

The specifics of the Federal Rule are worth examining in order to appreciate the broad authority given to the judge. First, in order to promote the logical and efficient processing of the case, the trial judge may issue orders to determine the course of proceedings and prescribe measures to prevent undue repetition or confusion in the presentation of evidence or argument.[21] Second, in order to protect the interests of the class members and to promote the fair conduct of the litigation, the judge may order that notice be given to class members of any step in the

---

Erie Co., 481 F.Supp. 760 (E.D.Wis.1979); McCoy v. Salem Mortgage Co., 74 F.R.D. 8 (E.D.Mich.1976).

The decision to create subclasses based on particular issues must be done in such a way as to avoid intruding on or overlooking individual issues not susceptible to a common adjudication or jury trial. Compare Castano v. American Tobacco Co., 84 F.3d 734 (5th Cir.1996), and In the Matter of Rhone–Poulenc Rorer, Inc., 51 F.3d 1293 (7th Cir.1995), cert. denied 516 U.S. 867 (reversing subclassing), with In re Telectronics Pacing Sys., Inc., 172 F.R.D. 271 (S.D.Ohio 1997) (upholding subclassing).

17. See Fed.Civ.Proc.Rule 23(c)(4)(B). E.g., Margaret S. v. Edwards, 488 F.Supp. 181 (E.D.La.1980); Vuyanich v. Republic Nat. Bank of Dallas, 82 F.R.D. 420 (N.D.Tex.1979). But compare In re Tetracycline Cases, 107 F.R.D. 719 (W.D.Mo.1985) (class certification denied because issues most susceptible to class treatment would require creation of numerous subclasses that the jury might have difficulty keeping separate).

18. When subclasses are formed, the court must make a determination that each

subclass meets the prerequisites for certification.

19. E.g., In re Baldwin–United Corp., 770 F.2d 328 (2d Cir.1985) (class certification approved for imminent settlements of cases consolidated under federal multidistrict procedures).

The court's authority to divide the action into subclasses or to order only a partial class action continues throughout the litigation. See In re NASDAQ Market–Makers Antitrust Litigation, 172 F.R.D. 119 (S.D.N.Y.1997); Johnson v. ITT–Thompson Indus., Inc., 323 F.Supp. 1258 (N.D.Miss. 1971); Sol S. Turnoff Drug Distributors, Inc. v. N. V. Nederlandsche Combinatie Voor Chemische Industrie, 51 F.R.D. 227, 233 (E.D.Pa.1970).

20. For a more detailed discussion of the court's power to order a partial class action or to establish subclasses, see 7B C. Wright, A. Miller & M. Kane, Civil 2d § 1790.

21. Fed.Civ.Proc.Rule 23(d)(1). For an analysis of the flexible and imaginative procedures that may be implemented in managing a class action, see 7B C. Wright, A. Miller & M. Kane, Civil 2d § 1792.

action, or of the proposed extent of the judgment, or of the opportunity of class members to signify their satisfaction or dissatisfaction with the quality of the representation, or to intervene for any purpose or to come into the action in some other fashion.[22] Third, the trial judge is empowered to impose conditions upon the class representative or intervenors,[23] and fourth, the court may order that all allegations as to the representative character of the suit be stricken from the pleadings and that the suit proceed as an individual action.[24]

In addition to the kinds of orders specifically authorized in Federal Rule 23(d), judges have been called upon to fashion special orders regarding damages. For example, courts have faced significant difficulties in deciding how to administer a class damage remedy in an efficient and inexpensive fashion without significantly impairing the sums recovered. Additional remedial problems have been presented in various consumer class actions in which, although liability is easily established, it is not clear that the members of the public ever could be identified in an economical way to distribute the damages. The device that has been used to combat these problems was developed originally in the California state courts and is called "fluid recovery" or "cy pres recovery."[25] Under this approach, the court may assess a lump sum damage award against the defendants based on their own records of illegal profits or overcharges.[26] Then, the defendants may be ordered to reduce prices for some period in the future until that amount has been expended. In this way the same general class of the public who was harmed—for example, all taxicab users or potato chip eaters—receives the benefit of the award, even though the identical persons harmed may not be compensated.[27]

22. Fed.Civ.Proc.Rule 23(d)(2). See 7B C. Wright, A. Miller & M. Kane, Civil 2d § 1793.

Because a class suit may have a substantial impact on persons who have not actually been before the court, the possibility that class members will seek to intervene to protect their rights is much greater than in the ordinary two party lawsuit. Indeed, some have argued that a nonparty class member has an automatic right to intervene in a common question class action. Cohn, The New Federal Rules of Civil Procedure, 54 Geo.L.J. 1204 (1966); Comment, The Litigant and the Absentee in Federal Multiparty Practice, 116 U.Pa.L.Rev. 531 (1968). However, it now generally is agreed that an absent class member may intervene only after satisfying the ordinary requirements for intervention. See Kaplan, Continuing Work of the Civil Committee: 1966 Amendments of the Federal Rules of Civil Procedure (I), 81 Harv.L.Rev. 356, 392 n. 137 (1967). Intervention is discussed in § 6.10, above.

23. Fed.Civ.Proc.Rule 23(d)(3). For a compilation of situations in which conditions have been imposed upon class representatives and intervenors, see 7B C. Wright, A. Miller & M. Kane, Civil 2d § 1794.

24. Fed.Civ.Proc.Rule 23(d)(4).

25. See State v. Levi Strauss & Co., 41 Cal.3d 460, 224 Cal.Rptr. 605, 715 P.2d 564 (1986); Daar v. Yellow Cab Co., 67 Cal.2d 695, 63 Cal.Rptr. 724, 433 P.2d 732 (1967). See generally McCall, Sturdevant, Kaplan & Hillebrand, Greater Representation for California Consumers—Fluid Recovery, Consumer Trust Funds, and Representative Actions, 46 Hast.L.J. 797 (1995); Comment, Damage Distribution in Class Actions: The Cy Pres Remedy, 39 U.Chi.L.Rev. 448 (1972).

26. The nature of the damages sought must be calculable in a lump sum or by review of the defendant's records. Otherwise the damage calculation itself may be unmanageable. See Devidian v. Automotive Service Dealers Ass'n, 35 Cal.App.3d 978, 111 Cal.Rptr. 228 (1973).

27. Although the fluid recovery concept recognizes that the persons receiving the benefits of the award need not necessar-

This method of altering the traditional method of computing and assessing damages has come under strong attack and has been rejected by several federal courts as being outside the authority conveyed to them by the Federal Rule.[28] The Supreme Court has not yet ruled on its validity, and it remains a viable judicial management device in the state courts.[29]

The management aspects of many modern class actions represent what probably is their most controversial characteristic. Many judges feel that they should not be required to engage in extensive administrative duties in connection with these suits.[30] But if the judges fail to participate in the shaping of these large and complex cases, the inevitable effect will be that they will become amorphous and unstructured, remain on the court's docket indefinitely, and ultimately consume more time and energy than would be expended if they were under the firm direction of the judge. Many lawyers also are apprehensive about judicial management of their cases because it is inconsistent with the traditional model for litigation in which the attorneys control the direction and development of lawsuits and judges act as impartial arbiters.[31] There is no question that if the class action is to have utility in large scale cases, the judge must work in collaboration with counsel to expedite the processing of the litigation. Moreover, new techniques and support staffing—perhaps wider use of magistrates or masters—must be employed.

§ 16.6 Notice

Like other requirements for maintaining a class action, the rules relating to the obligation to notify absent class members of the pending litigation reflect an attempt to secure the efficiency of the class action without sacrificing the important right of individual class members to have their day in court or to monitor the conduct of the case. Adequate notice helps to secure the binding effect of any judgment that is entered,[1] so that multiple actions will be avoided. Thus, a vital question is what

ily be those who were injured, it cannot be used if there is no way to define a current user class that has the same interests and characteristics as the injured class. See Blue Chip Stamps v. Superior Court of Los Angeles County, 18 Cal.3d 381, 134 Cal.Rptr. 393, 556 P.2d 755 (1976).

28. The federal courts rejecting the notion of a fluid recovery generally have addressed the issue at the class certification stage, finding that the device could not be used to overcome management problems that made certification improper. See, e.g., Eisen v. Carlisle & Jacquelin, 479 F.2d 1005 (2d Cir.1973), affirmed on other grounds 417 U.S. 156, 94 S.Ct. 2140, 40 L.Ed.2d 732 (1974); In re Coordinated Pretrial Proceedings in Antibiotic Antitrust Actions, 410 F.Supp. 706 (D.Minn.1975). However, the Ninth and Eleventh Circuits have approved the use of a fluid recovery to distribute

unclaimed funds after the class had prevailed at trial. See Six (6) Mexican Workers v. Arizona Citrus Growers, 904 F.2d 1301 (9th Cir.1990); Nelson v. Greater Gadsden Housing Authority, 802 F.2d 405 (11th Cir. 1986). And it also has been used to distribute unclaimed settlement funds. See, e.g., In re Wells Fargo Secs. Litigation, 991 F.Supp. 1193 (N.D.Cal.1998).

29. Some state class action rules even contain specific authorization for a fluid recovery. E.g., N.D.Rules Civ.Proc., Rule 23(*o*)(3).

30. See, for example, the comments of Judge Sneed in La Mar v. H & B Novelty & Loan Co., 489 F.2d 461 (9th Cir.1973).

31. See § 1.1, above.

§ 16.6

1. See § 16.8, below.

constitutes adequate notice to absent class members. The answer requires a dual inquiry: first, into notice provisions required by statutes or rules, and second, into constitutional due process standards governing adequate notice.[2]

The most common notice provisions are found in Federal Rule 23 and its state counterparts.[3] The provisions for giving notice to absent class members are set forth in subdivisions (c)(2) and (d)(2) of the Federal Rule. If the court permits a class action to be maintained under Rule 23(b)(3)—namely, a class action for damages involving questions of law or fact common to the class members—the court must direct to the class members "the best notice practicable under the circumstances, including individual notice to all members who can be identified through reasonable effort."[4] Federal Rule 23(d)(2) is the discretionary notice provision. It authorizes the court to order notice to be given "for the protection of the members of the class or otherwise for the fair conduct of the action * * *." The manner and scope of the notice are left to the court's discretion, subject, of course, to due process restraints.

Turning first to the mandatory notice provision, what constitutes the "best notice practicable" must be determined on a case-by-case basis.[5] The requirements of Rule 23 do not contemplate compliance with the formalities of service of process.[6] If the class is very large, notice by ordinary mail may suffice, and notice by publication may be employed for those class members who cannot be identified through reasonable effort; the basic requirement is that the method chosen must be reasonably calculated to reach the absent class member.[7] The standard of "reasonable effort" in identifying class members is also somewhat indefinite. However, if any existing document identifying class members is available, such as a list of stockholders, owners, taxpayers, or others, individual notice must be given to all class members named in that document.[8]

The requirement of individual notice to identifiable class members may place so severe a financial burden on the representative of a plaintiff class that the suit cannot be maintained as a class action. This requirement thus greatly undercuts the potential effectiveness of the class action as a device to vindicate congressional policies such as the private enforcement of antitrust, securities, environmental and consum-

2. For a discussion of notice requirements in civil actions generally, see §§ 3.19–3.21, above.

3. E.g., Ariz.Rules Civ.Proc., Rule 23.

4. See generally 7B C. Wright, A. Miller & M. Kane, Civil 2d § 1786.

5. West Virginia v. Chas. Pfizer & Co., 440 F.2d 1079 (2d Cir.1971), cert. denied 404 U.S. 871; In re Four Seasons Secs. Laws Litigation, 63 F.R.D. 422 (W.D.Okl. 1974), opinion supplemented 64 F.R.D. 325 (1974), affirmed 525 F.2d 500 (10th Cir. 1975).

6. Advisory Committee Note to the 1966 Amendments to Rule 23, reprinted in 39 F.R.D. 98, 107 (1966).

7. See Mullane v. Central Hanover Bank & Trust Co., 339 U.S. 306, 70 S.Ct. 652, 94 L.Ed. 865 (1950). Mullane is discussed in § 3.19, above.

8. See, e.g., Mader v. Armel, 402 F.2d 158 (6th Cir.1968), cert. denied 394 U.S. 930; Bunch v. Barnett, 62 F.R.D. 615 (D.S.D.1974); Korn v. Franchard Corp., 50 F.R.D. 57 (S.D.N.Y.1970), appeal dismissed 443 F.2d 1301 (2d Cir.1971).

er protection laws when the class is large, but the individual claims are small. Nevertheless, Rule 23's individual notice requirement has been construed literally by the Supreme Court.

In Eisen v. Carlisle & Jacquelin,[9] the Second Circuit held, and the Supreme Court agreed, that Federal Rule 23(c)(2) requires that individual notice be sent to all identifiable class members. In that case the plaintiff class numbered some 6,000,000, of whom over 2,000,000 could be "easily identified" through the analysis of computer tapes,[10] and the cost of individual notice was estimated at $225,000.[11] Notice by publication plus individual notice to a portion of the class was held inadequate, and the cost of sending notice was not allowed to be shifted to the defendant despite the trial court's determination of the likely success of the plaintiff class on the merits.[12]

The practical impact of Eisen was extended in Oppenheimer Fund, Inc. v. Sanders, in which the Supreme Court held that the burden of identifying class members could not be shifted to the class opponent under the guise of a discovery request, because the information would not be relevant to the subject matter of the action.[13] Ordering the defendant to bear the cost of identification was an abuse of discretion: "Courts must not stray too far from the principle underlying Eisen * * * that the representative plaintiff should bear all costs relating to the sending of notice because it is he who seeks to maintain the suit as a class action."[14]

9. 479 F.2d 1005 (2d Cir.1973), petition for rehearing en banc denied 479 F.2d 1020 (2d Cir.1973), affirmed 417 U.S. 156, 94 S.Ct. 2140, 40 L.Ed.2d 732 (1974). See also Bennet, Eisen v. Carlisle & Jacquelin: Supreme Court Calls for Revamping of Class Action Strategy, 1974 Wis.L.Rev. 801; Dam, Class Action Notice: Who Needs It?, 1974 Sup.Ct.Rev. 97.

10. 479 F.2d at 1008.

11. 417 U.S. at 167, 94 S.Ct. at 2147. The Supreme Court noted, "There is nothing in Rule 23 to suggest that the notice requirements can be tailored to fit the pocket-books of particular plaintiffs." 417 U.S. at 176, 94 S.Ct. at 2152.

12. 417 U.S. at 177, 94 S.Ct. at 2152. The Supreme Court expressly disapproved the trial judge's attempt to make some assessment of plaintiff's probable success on the merits in order to determine whether to shift some of the notice costs to defendants, finding no authorization in Rule 23 for such a preliminary merits determination.

13. 437 U.S. 340, 351–52, 98 S.Ct. 2380, 2390, 57 L.Ed.2d 253 (1978). But compare Hoffmann–La Roche Inc. v. Sperling, 493 U.S. 165, 110 S.Ct. 482, 107 L.Ed.2d 480 (1989), in which the Court upheld the district court's grant of discovery of the names and addresses of all simi-

larly situated employees in an action under the Age Discrimination in Employment Act.

The appropriate scope of discovery requests is governed by Fed.Civ.Proc.Rule 26(b)(1) and is discussed in § 7.2, above.

14. 437 U.S. at 359, 98 S.Ct. at 2392 (per Powell, J.). The Court did note that when the defendant can identify class members more efficiently or less expensively than the representative plaintiff, the court may order defendant to do so under Federal Rule 23(d). However, defendant cannot be required to pay for identification unless the cost is insubstantial.

For an interesting case that shifted the burden of giving notice onto defendant, see Mountain States Tel. & Tel. Co. v. District Court, 778 P.2d 667 (Colo.1989), cert. denied 493 U.S. 983, in which the state supreme court upheld an order requiring defendant telephone company to enclose the notices required by Rule 23(c)(2) in its billing mailings to nearly 1.5 million customers, because this method would reduce substantially the cost of giving notice. The court observed that Mountain Bell could notify class members at no significant additional expense to itself by merely enclosing the class notices in billing envelopes routinely sent to its customers. Id. at 673.

It is important to note that the Eisen Court grounded its opinion on its interpretation of Rule 23, rather than on the Constitution.[15] The drafters of the rule[16] thought that its notice standards were dictated by the due process notions embodied in the Supreme Court's decision in Mullane v. Central Hanover Bank & Trust Company.[17] Under the Eisen Court's interpretation, however, the notice standards of Rule 23(c)(2) appear more stringent than due process requires: In Eisen, financial considerations were found to be irrelevant,[18] but in Mullane the cost of notice was a factor in deciding what form of notice was required by due process.[19] Thus, perhaps it is not surprising that many states have not felt themselves bound by Eisen and either have interpreted their provisions more liberally, not necessitating individual notice in all common question suits,[20] or have adopted notice provisions that clearly give the court discretion to determine whether individual notice should be required.[21]

Federal Rule 23 only mandates notice to be given in damage actions brought under subdivision (b)(3). As a matter of rule or statutory law, class actions involving joint interests or for injunctive or declaratory relief maintained under Rule 23(b)(1) and Rule 23(b)(2), respectively, fall within the discretionary notice provisions of Rule 23(d)(2).[22] This discrepant treatment reflects the different nature of the classes described in subdivision (b).[23] In actions maintained under the first two categories, the class generally will be more cohesive than will be true under Rule 23(b)(3). Often each member of a (b)(1) or (b)(2) class would be affected by a judgment obtained in an individual action instituted by another member of the class. Moreover, in those classes, there are fewer special defenses or issues relating to individual class members. Therefore, it is more likely that the named representatives, by presenting their own claims, will protect the interests of the absent members, and the courts need be less concerned about making certain that each member of the class is given notice and an opportunity to be present.[24] In addition, members of classes in (b)(1) and (b)(2) actions may not exclude them-

---

15. "[Q]uite apart from what due process may require, the command of Rule 23 is clearly to the contrary." 417 U.S. at 177, 94 S.Ct. at 2152.

16. See Advisory Committee Note to the 1966 Amendments to Rule 23, reprinted in 39 F.R.D. 98, 107 (1966). But see Comment, Adequate Representation, Notice and the New Class Action Rule: Effectuating Remedies Provided by the Securities Laws, 116 U.Pa.L.Rev. 889 (1968).

17. 339 U.S. 306, 70 S.Ct. 652, 94 L.Ed. 865 (1950). Mullane is discussed in § 3.19, above.

18. 417 U.S. at 176, 94 S.Ct. at 2152.

19. 339 U.S. at 313–20, 70 S.Ct. at 657–60.

20. Cartt v. Superior Court, 50 Cal. App.3d 960, 124 Cal.Rptr. 376 (1975).

21. E.g., Mass.Rules Civ.Proc., Rule 23(d); N.Y.—McKinney's CPLR 904. But compare N.D.Rules Civ.Proc., Rule 23(g)(4), requiring individual notice to any class member who has a damage claim for more than $100, and who can be identified by reasonable diligence.

22. In a few states some form of notice is mandatory in all class actions. See Fla.—West's F.S.A. Rules Civ.Proc.Rule 1.220(d)(1); N.D.Rules Civ.Proc., Rule 23(g)(1).

23. See § 16.2 at nn. 46–94, above.

24. See, e.g., the Court's reasoning in Mullane v. Central Hanover Bank & Trust Co., 339 U.S. 306, 70 S.Ct. 652, 94 L.Ed. 865 (1950).

selves from the action[25] so there is no need to make certain they understand their right to opt out. Of course, should it appear necessary, the court has discretionary power to order that notice be given in those actions "for the protection of the members of the class or otherwise for the fair conduct of the action."[26]

In suits under Rule 23(b)(3), class members typically are associated with one another only by the fact that their claims assert common issues of law or fact. Usually no pre-existing or ongoing legal relationships exist among them, and individual members may have different remedial objectives. This lack of cohesiveness engenders increased concern about whether the interests of absent class members are identical with those of the class representative.[27] Further, because a judgment in a Rule 23(b)(3) action binds only those class members who do not expressly request exclusion from the action, notice apprises members of their right to be excluded and thus not be bound by any judgment that is entered. Alternatively, notice permits them to decide whether to enter an appearance with their own counsel if they believe that that would enable them to protect their rights better.[28]

However significant these distinctions may be, the question whether some form of notice should be mandatory in all class actions has not been resolved uniformly by the courts. Although some courts have

25. In a footnote to the majority opinion in Phillips Petroleum Co. v. Shutts, 472 U.S. 797, 105 S.Ct. 2965, 86 L.Ed.2d 628 (1985), the Supreme Court limited its holding that due process requires that an absent plaintiff be provided with the opportunity to opt out of the class to "those class actions which seek to bind known plaintiffs concerning claims wholly or predominantly for money judgments." Id. at 811 n. 3, 105 S.Ct. at 2974 n. 3. The Court "intimate[d] no view concerning other types of class actions, such as those seeking equitable relief." Id.

Since then, several courts have explicitly held that there is no constitutional right to opt out from the class in an action seeking predominantly equitable relief, even as to aspects of the case that seek money damages. See, e.g., Colt Indus. Shareholder Litigation v. Colt Indus., Inc., 77 N.Y.2d 185, 565 N.Y.S.2d 755, 566 N.E.2d 1160 (Ct.App. 1991); Nottingham Partners v. Dana, 564 A.2d 1089 (Del.1989).

26. Fed.Civ.Proc.Rule 23(d)(2). See Berman v. Narragansett Racing Ass'n, 48 F.R.D. 333, 338 (D.R.I.1969).

27. Some courts have suggested that because of the nature of the common question class action, it well might violate the due process rights of the absent class members to bind them to a class judgment without notice. Appleton Elec. Co. v. Advance–United Expressways, 494 F.2d 126 (7th Cir. 1974); Lynch v. Sperry Rand Corp., 62 F.R.D. 78, 85 n. 8 (S.D.N.Y.1973). See also the discussion in § 16.8, below.

28. Federal Rule 23(c)(2) specifically provides that the notice must apprise the class member: (1) that he may opt out of the class if he requests to be excluded before a specified date; (2) that the judgment will bind all class members who do not request exclusion; and (3) that any member who does not request exclusion may enter an appearance through counsel.

Some courts also have included forms in notices requiring the recipient to file a proof of claim. E.g., Kyriazi v. Western Elec. Co., 647 F.2d 388 (3d Cir.1981). This practice seems inconsistent with both the philosophy and the specific language of the rule, however, which states that the recipient will be considered part of the class if he does not affirmatively opt out. To insist the form be filed in response to the notice, appears to oblige the member to opt-in to the action. See Korn v. Franchard Corp., 50 F.R.D. 57 (S.D.N.Y.1970), appeal dismissed 443 F.2d 1301 (2d Cir.1971). Of course, after liability has been determined, a proof of claim form can be required in order to permit individual members to partake of the award.

decided that no notice is required,[29] others have ruled that notice is mandatory,[30] indeed may be required as a matter of due process.[31] Given this confusion, the better or safer practice is to provide for some notice to assure the adequate protection of the interests of the unnamed class members.

In any event, the manner and form of notice in actions other than those based solely on common questions remain within the court's discretion. Individual notice need be given only if it seems necessary under the facts of the case and its cost is not so great as to prevent plaintiff from going forward. Thus, although the method of giving notice may vary from case to case, publication plus actual notice to a random sample of class members commonly is deemed adequate.[32] In some instances even notice by television or radio may be held appropriate.[33] The key is to develop a notice scheme that is most likely to reach and inform[34] the vast majority of class members.

§ 16.7 Dismissal and Compromise

To provide additional protection for absent class members, most class action provisions specifically require court approval of any compro-

29. Johnson v. General Motors Corp., 598 F.2d 432 (5th Cir.1979); Elliott v. Weinberger, 564 F.2d 1219 (9th Cir.1977), affirmed in part, reversed in part on other grounds sub nom. Califano v. Yamasaki, 442 U.S. 682, 99 S.Ct. 2545, 61 L.Ed.2d 176 (1979); W.P. v. Poritz, 931 F.Supp. 1187 (D.N.J.1996); McKay County Election Comm'rs for Pulaski County, Arkansas, 158 F.R.D. 620 (D.Ark.1994).

Compare the approach taken in New York, in which notice need not be given in actions for injunctive or declaratory relief unless the court feels it necessary to protect the interests of the class members and finds that the cost will not be prohibitive. N.Y.—McKinney's CPLR 904(a).

30. Eisen v. Carlisle & Jacquelin, 391 F.2d 555 (2d Cir.1968); Hoston v. U.S. Gypsum Co., 67 F.R.D. 650 (D.La.1975); Alexander v. Avco Corp., 380 F.Supp. 1282 (M.D.Tenn.1974).

31. Eisen v. Carlisle & Jacquelin, 391 F.2d 555, 564 (2d Cir.1968); Lopez v. Wyman, 329 F.Supp. 483 (W.D.N.Y.1971), affirmed without opinion 404 U.S. 1055, 92 S.Ct. 736, 30 L.Ed.2d 743 (1972). Whether notice is required to enter a binding class action judgment is discussed more fully in § 16.8, below.

32. See, e.g., In re Agent Orange Prods. Liability Litigation, 818 F.2d 145, 168–69 (2d Cir.1987), cert. denied 484 U.S. 1004; Montelongo v. Meese, 803 F.2d 1341 (5th Cir.1986); In re Cherry's Petition to

Intervene, 164 F.R.D. 630 (E.D.Mich.1996). Under some state class action rules, the court is given complete discretion in determining the method of notice and is directed to weigh factors such as the cost, resources of the parties, and stake of individual members when deciding what scheme to authorize. See, e.g., West's Ann.Cal.Civ.Code § 1781(d) (California Consumers Legal Remedies Act); N.Y.—McKinney's CPLR 904(c).

33. See N.D.Rules Civ.Proc., Rule 23(g)(5).

34. Serious problems arise concerning how to draft notices that are likely to inform the recipients of their rights. It generally is agreed that at the least, any notice must contain a description of the dispute, the nature of the action, the issues being litigated, and the address to which any reply should be directed. See, e.g., Kyriazi v. Western Elec. Co., 647 F.2d 388 (3d Cir. 1981). In addition, if the members have a right to opt out, they must be given sufficient information to be able to determine whether to exercise that right or take some other procedural step. See, e.g., Abulaban v. R. W. Pressprich & Co., 51 F.R.D. 496 (S.D.N.Y.1971) (notice contained information that there was a counterclaim against the class). But practical problems of conveying this information to a lay recipient sometimes seem insurmountable. See generally Miller, Problems of Giving Notice in Class Actions, 58 F.R.D. 313 (1973).

mise or dismissal of the class claims arranged by the parties.[1] This is designed to prevent an unjust or unfair settlement resulting either from the class representatives becoming faint-hearted or having been bought off by the class' opponent.[2] Provisions for judicial involvement in the settlement arena are unique in American law because they are inconsistent with the general principle that litigants are free to settle, terminate, or discontinue a lawsuit as they see fit.

Ordinarily, the judge does not participate in the settlement negotiations. Only after a proposed agreement has been reached does the court appraise the fairness of its terms[3] and indicate whether it is in the best interest of those who will be affected by it.[4] In scrutinizing the settlement, the judge is limited to either approving or disapproving the entire proposal.[5] Among the factors that have been thought relevant in assessing fairness are the following: (1) the extent to which class members object to the settlement,[6] (2) the likelihood of the class ultimately succeeding in the litigation, (3) the complexity of the factual and legal issues in the case, (4) the amount of the settlement compared to the amount that might be recovered, (5) the costs that would be incurred if the action went forward, (6) the plan for distributing the settlement and the extent to which it is likely to succeed, and (7) whether proper procedures have been provided for notifying absent class members.[7]

Notice of a proposed compromise must be given class members to afford them an opportunity to intervene and object or to aid the court in identifying members who will be willing to continue the suit as a class action should the original representatives drop out of the litigation.[8] If

---

§ 16.7

1. Fed.Civ.Proc.Rule 23(e); Ariz.Rules Civ.Proc., Rule 23(e); Mass.Rules Civ.Proc., Rule 23(c); N.Y.—McKinney's CPLR 908.

2. See generally, Note, Abuse in Plaintiff Class Action Settlements: The Need for a Guardian During Pretrial Settlement Negotiations, 84 Mich.L.Rev. 308 (1985).

To effectuate the inquiry in fairness, objectors to a settlement have been allowed to discover matters relating to the conduct of the settlement negotiations. See In re General Motors Corp. Engine Interchange Litigation, 594 F.2d 1106, 1123 (7th Cir. 1979), cert. denied 444 U.S. 870.

3. Zerkle v. Cleveland–Cliffs Iron Co., 52 F.R.D. 151, 159 (S.D.N.Y.1971); Matthies v. Seymour Mfg. Co., 23 F.R.D. 64, 77 (D.Conn.1958), reversed on other grounds 270 F.2d 365 (2d Cir.1959).

4. Young v. Katz, 447 F.2d 431 (5th Cir.1971); Wainwright v. Kraftco Corp., 53 F.R.D. 78 (N.D.Ga.1971).

5. Evans v. Jeff D., 475 U.S. 717, 106 S.Ct. 1531, 89 L.Ed.2d 747 (1986).

6. The presence of objectors may aid the court in evaluating the fairness of the settlement as it will result in an adversary presentation of the various elements involved. See In re Corrugated Container Antitrust Litigation, 643 F.2d 195 (5th Cir. 1981). However, although it is clear that the fact that some class members object does not alone suggest that the proposed settlement is improper, see, e.g., In re Chicken Antitrust Litigation Am. Poultry, 669 F.2d 228 (5th Cir.1982); In re Southern Ohio Correctional Facility, 173 F.R.D. 205 (S.D.Ohio 1997), what weight the court should give to their interests remains unclear. This problem of divergent views as to what is in the best interests of the class is particularly acute in class actions seeking institutional reform. See generally Rhode, Class Conflict in Class Actions, 34 Stan. L.Rev. 1183 (1982).

7. A fuller discussion of the factors the court will scrutinize in evaluating the fairness of a particular proposal is found in 7B C. Wright, A. Miller & M. Kane, Civil 2d § 1797.1.

8. The contents of the notice and the methods of distributing it are generally within the discretion of the judge, but are to be determined so as to effectuate inform-

notice has been given, a class member who neglects to protect his rights during the settlement process by voicing objections or by other means[9] will be barred from attacking the agreement on appeal[10] or collaterally.[11]

Because of the expense of notifying absent class members of a proposed settlement and the difficulties encountered as a result of the need to obtain judicial approval, many attorneys seek to avoid these requirements by attempting to settle the action prior to its certification as a class suit. Most courts, however, treat the action as a class action during the precertification period for purposes of the applicability of the requirement of judicial approval.[12]

A serious problem is posed, however, by these precertification settlements because they require the court to evaluate the fairness of a settlement in the absence of a finding as to the scope of the class and its membership. Further questions are raised concerning whether the normal requirements for certification should be relaxed when considered in the context of a settlement class. The potential for collusion between the attorneys also exists so that the court may not receive the benefit of a full adversarial presentation on the class certification issues.

Because of these concerns, the lower courts were not agreed as to whether or how to handle the certification of settlement classes. The Supreme Court addressed the question in its 1997 decision in Amchem Products, Inc. v. Windsor.[13] It ruled that settlement classes could be certified under Rule 23, but that courts should be particularly careful when reviewing whether the action satisfied the rule's requirements to ensure that the absentees' rights have been adequately protected.[14] One

---

ing the members in the best fashion possible what is at stake. In securities fraud class suits, however, Congress in 1995 enacted some special requirements that need to be followed. 15 U.S.C.A. § 77z–1(a)(7); 15 U.S.C.A. § 78u–4(a)(7).

9. Class settlements may provide that members may opt-out and pursue their own individual claims. See, e.g., Holmes v. Continental Can Co., 706 F.2d 1144 (11th Cir. 1983). Compare Officers for Justice v. Civil Service Comm'n of City & County of San Francisco, 688 F.2d 615 (9th Cir.1982), cert. denied 459 U.S. 1217 (not an abuse of discretion to approve settlement with no opt-out procedure), and Nottingham Partners v. Dana, 564 A.2d 1089 (Del.1989) (there is no constitutional right to opt out of a (b)(2) settlement even when some money damages are involved).

10. Shults v. Champion Int'l Corp., 35 F.3d 1056 (6th Cir.1994); Marshall v. Holiday Magic, Inc., 550 F.2d 1173 (9th Cir. 1977).

11. In re Antibiotic Antitrust Actions, 333 F.Supp. 296 (S.D.N.Y.1971), affirmed per curiam sub nom. Connors v. Chas. Pfiz-

er & Co., 450 F.2d 1119 (2d Cir.1971), cert. denied 408 U.S. 930.

12. E.g., Baker v. America's Mortgage Servicing, Inc., 58 F.3d 321 (7th Cir.1995); Diaz v. Trust Territory of Pacific Islands, 876 F.2d 1401 (9th Cir.1989); Shelton v. Pargo, Inc., 582 F.2d 1298, 1308 n. 31 (4th Cir.1978). The opposing party may negotiate settlements with individual class members without judicial approval, however, even if the ultimate result of those settlements is to reduce the number of claimants so that class certification no longer is viable. See In re General Motors Corp. Engine Interchange Litigation, 594 F.2d 1106 (7th Cir.1979), cert. denied 444 U.S. 870; Weight Watchers of Philadelphia, Inc. v. Weight Watchers Int'l, Inc., 455 F.2d 770 (2d Cir. 1972).

13. 521 U.S. 591, 117 S.Ct. 2231, 138 L.Ed.2d 689 (1997).

14. In the Amchem case itself, the Court found that certification had been improper because of serious concerns involving adequacy of representation and notice, given the broad class definition involved. Amchem presented the additional problem

area was identified, however, in which the application of Rule 23 to settlement classes might differ from that in the trial setting and thus may affect the court's analysis of whether certification is permissible. That arises in the assessment of superiority under Rule 23(b)(3), which ordinarily requires the court to consider any possible management problems if the case were to proceed as a class suit. Management concerns necessarily are not pertinent if the case is to be settled so that no trial is envisioned and thus they do not pose a potential barrier to finding that the superiority requirement is met for a settlement class.

§ 16.8   Binding Effect of a Class Action Judgment

If all the requirements and prerequisites for a class action have been satisfied, the resulting decree will be binding on all class members whether they actually participated in the case or not.[1] This is an exception to the general rule that persons who have not had their own day in court cannot be bound by any judgment.[2] It reflects a recognition that an overburdened judicial system must be able to avoid the delay and expense of multiple litigation. The conditions under which a class action may go forward therefore represent a compromise by which some aspect of an individual's normal right to control civil litigation affecting him is sacrificed to the demands of judicial efficiency.[3]

But the effects of a class action judgment often are not as apparent as the preceding paragraph suggests. Because a court cannot predetermine the res judicata effect of its own judgment,[4] class action provisions typically provide only that the court's decree should define and describe the members of the class in order to aid in any future determination of the judgment's binding effect.[5] Further ambiguity is generated by the fact that even though specifically named in the decree, an absent class member will not be bound if the absentee can demonstrate either that

---

of whether the settlement of future asbestos claims can be achieved through a class judgment. That issue continues to plague the courts and a Fifth Circuit decision, which attempted to distinguish itself from Amchem, but which involves similar issues, is pending review in the Supreme Court. See Flanagan v. Ahearn, 134 F.3d 668 (5th Cir.1998), cert. granted sub nom. Ortiz v. Fibreboard Corp., ___ U.S. ___, 118 S.Ct. 2339.

§ 16.8

1. Cooper v. Federal Reserve Bank of Richmond, 467 U.S. 867, 104 S.Ct. 2794, 81 L.Ed.2d 718 (1984); Hansberry v. Lee, 311 U.S. 32, 61 S.Ct. 115, 85 L.Ed. 22 (1940); Supreme Tribe of Ben–Hur v. Cauble, 255 U.S. 356, 41 S.Ct. 338, 65 L.Ed. 673 (1921). See generally 7B C. Wright, A. Miller & M. Kane, Civil 2d § 1789.

2. See Chapter 14, above.

3. Several courts even have held that absent class members cannot appeal a decision with which the named representatives are satisfied. See, e.g., Walker v. City of Mesquite, 858 F.2d 1071 (5th Cir.1988); Guthrie v. Evans, 815 F.2d 626 (11th Cir. 1987).

4. Gonzales v. Cassidy, 474 F.2d 67 (5th Cir.1973); Battle v. Liberty Nat. Life Ins. Co., 770 F.Supp. 1499 (N.D.Ala.1991), affirmed per curiam 974 F.2d 1279 (11th Cir.1992), cert. denied 509 U.S. 906.

5. E.g., Fed.Civ.Proc.Rule 23(c)(3). The Rules Enabling Act provides that no rule may enlarge, abridge, or modify any substantive right. 28 U.S.C.A. § 2072. Thus, if the Federal Rule were construed to permit the court to predetermine the binding effect of its judgment, it might violate the Act because questions involving the scope of judgments ordinarily are considered to be substantive in nature.

the representation was inadequate[6] or that the notice[7] given was insufficient; in either event the member's due process rights may be violated.[8]

In its 1985 decision in Phillips Petroleum Company v. Shutts,[9] the Supreme Court enumerated four conditions that must be met in a Rule 23(b)(3) damage class action[10] for absent plaintiff class members who are outside the jurisdiction of the court[11] to be bound by the judgment, consistent with due process concerns. First, the absentee must receive notice plus an opportunity to be heard. Second, the notice must meet the standards of Mullane v. Central Hanover Bank & Trust Company.[12] Third, the absent class member must be provided an opportunity to opt out of the action, and lastly, the named plaintiff must adequately represent the class. Although the Court's statement of these prerequisites was quite straightforward, questions exist concerning the scope of its ruling and whether it is necessary that all four conditions be satisfied in all cases.[13] For example, if the class is composed only of instate

---

6. Compare Grigsby v. North Mississippi Medical Center, Inc., 586 F.2d 457 (5th Cir.1978), and Gonzales v. Cassidy, 474 F.2d 67 (5th Cir.1973) (representation inadequate), with Dosier v. Miami Valley Broadcasting Corp., 656 F.2d 1295 (9th Cir.1981), and Fowler v. Birmingham News Co., 608 F.2d 1055 (5th Cir.1979) (representation adequate). Adequacy of representation is discussed in more detail in § 16.2, at notes 30–45, above.

In one case, the Ninth Circuit held that federal plaintiffs could collaterally attack on grounds of inadequate representation a state class action judgment that was entered as part of a global settlement, even though the state court had found the representation adequate. Epstein v. MCA, Inc., 126 F.3d 1235 (9th Cir.1997). The decision is criticized in Kahan & Silberman, The Inadequate Search for "Adequacy" in Class Actions: A Critique of Epstein v. MCA, Inc., 73 N.Y.U. L.Rev. 765 (1998).

7. See Anderson v. John Morrell & Co., 830 F.2d 872 (8th Cir.1987); Penson v. Terminal Transport Co., 634 F.2d 989 (5th Cir.1981); Pearson v. Easy Living, Inc., 534 F.Supp. 884 (S.D.Ohio 1981).

8. Some courts have suggested that notice may cure any failure in representation. In re Four Seasons Secs. Laws Litigation, 493 F.2d 1288 (10th Cir.1974). Conversely, the failure to receive notice may be ignored if the class member was adequately represented. Johnson v. American Airlines, Inc., 157 Cal.App.3d 427, 203 Cal.Rptr. 638 (1984). This problem is discussed in Note, Collateral Attack on the Binding Effect of Class Action Judgments, 87 Harv.L.Rev. 589 (1974); Comment, The Importance of Being Adequate: Due Process Requirements

in Class Actions Under Federal Rule 23, 123 U.Pa.L.Rev. 1217 (1975).

9. 472 U.S. 797, 105 S.Ct. 2965, 86 L.Ed.2d 628 (1985).

10. The Shutts case was a Kansas state class action brought under rules parallel to Federal Rule 23(b)(3). The Court specifically limited its decision to damage actions and did not express an opinion on whether the same requirements would be necessary in suits for injunctive relief or those filed under Rule 23(b)(1). 472 U.S. at 811 n. 3, 105 S.Ct. at 2974 n. 3. Several lower courts thus have limited Shutts to actions filed under Rule 23(b)(3) and have held class judgments to be binding even though no right to opt out was available. See, e.g., In re Joint E. & S. District Asbestos Litigation, 78 F.3d 764 (2d Cir.1996); Brown v. Ticor Title Ins. Co., 982 F.2d 386 (9th Cir.1992), cert. dismissed 511 U.S. 117; White v. National Football League, 822 F.Supp. 1389 (D.Minn.1993), affirmed 41 F.3d 402 (8th Cir.1994). But the issue of whether there is a constitutional right to opt out and thereby avoid the binding effect of a class judgment remains a troubling one for the courts. See, e.g., Colt Indus. Shareholder Litigation v. Colt Indus., Inc., 77 N.Y.2d 185, 565 N.Y.S.2d 755, 566 N.E.2d 1160 (1991).

11. For a discussion of the Shutts case as it related to personal jurisdiction requirements in class actions, see § 16.4, above.

12. 339 U.S. 306, 70 S.Ct. 652, 94 L.Ed. 865 (1950).

13. The issue of whether a right to opt out must be provided to satisfy due process, regardless of other protections, has been before the Supreme Court twice since

plaintiffs so that there are no personal jurisdiction limits, due process considerations might be satisfied by adequate representation and a notice scheme comporting with Mullane even if a particular class member never actually received notice. These and other interpretation questions remain,[14] so that ambiguity as to when and whether an absent class member successfully may escape the binding effect of a class judgment still exists.

As an additional wrinkle, some courts have concluded that if an absent class member is not bound by an adverse decision when his interests were inadequately represented, the party opposing the class also should be able to avoid the decree by demonstrating that members of the class were denied due process, even though the court reached a favorable result for the class.[15] But this approach smacks of the now discredited notion of mutuality of estoppel,[16] which having been rejected in most jurisdictions as neither fair nor logical, should not be embraced in the class action setting. There is no policy reason justifying the need to treat all the parties identically regarding whether they are benefitted or burdened by a judgment. Encouraging attacks by persons who are on opposite sides in a class suit will result in a multiplicity of actions—the very evil that the procedure was designed to avoid. Of course attention must be paid to procedural fairness to the nonclass party. This can be accomplished by reviewing the first proceeding to make sure that the parties to the class action completely litigated the issues and that there is no reason to believe that the class opponent was misled into preparing a defense only with respect to those class members who were present in the action.

Another unsettled question is whether persons who have opted out of a common question class action later can claim the benefits of a result favorable to the class.[17] Although this problem raises many of the same concerns as the general mutuality of estoppel notion, two additional factors in the opt-out setting appear to justify something in the nature of quasi-mutuality treatment. First, if class members who opt out are permitted to claim the benefits of a favorable decree, there would be no reason not to opt out. Widespread opting out would impair the utility of

---

Shutts, but in both cases the Court ultimately dismissed certiorari as improvidently granted, with opinions noting the importance of the issue. See Adams v. Robertson, 520 U.S. 83, 117 S.Ct. 1028, 137 L.Ed.2d 203 (1997); Ticor Title Ins. Co. v. Brown, 511 U.S. 117, 114 S.Ct. 1359, 128 L.Ed.2d 33 (1994).

14. For a more detailed examination of Shutts, see 7B C. Wright, A. Miller & M. Kane, Civil 2d § 1789.

15. McCarthy v. Director of Selective Serv. Sys., 322 F.Supp. 1032 (E.D.Wis. 1970), affirmed on other grounds 460 F.2d 1089 (7th Cir.1972); Pasquier v. Tarr, 318 F.Supp. 1350 (E.D.La.1970), affirmed 444 F.2d 116 (5th Cir.1971).

16. Mutuality of estoppel is discussed in § 14.14, above.

17. Compare Saunders v. Naval Air Rework Facility, 608 F.2d 1308 (9th Cir. 1979) (collateral estoppel allowed), with Premier Elec. Constr. Co. v. National Elec. Contractors Ass'n, 814 F.2d 358 (7th Cir. 1987) (no collateral estoppel). See generally George, Sweet Use of Adversity: Parklane Hosiery and the Collateral Class Action, 32 Stan.L.Rev. 655 (1980); Note, Offensive Assertion of Collateral Estoppel by Persons Opting Out of a Class Action, 31 Hast.L.J. 1189 (1980).

the class action device; occasionally it might reduce the class so drastically that the joinder of the remaining members no longer would be impracticable and the class action would fail because of not satisfying one of its essential prerequisites. Second, as an historic matter, the pre–1966 version of Federal Rule 23, as well as comparable state class action provisions, were construed to permit so-called "one-way intervention," allowing absent class members to wait until a favorable result had been achieved before intervening; an unfavorable judgment would be ignored. The 1966 revision was designed to end that practice.[18]

B. SHAREHOLDER DERIVATIVE SUITS

§ 16.9 Shareholder Derivative Suits

A shareholder derivative suit is an action maintained for the benefit of a corporation by a shareholder when the people ordinarily entrusted with the responsibility for vindicating the corporation's rights—typically the management—have refused to do so. Because it is a representative action, many of the policy questions concerning judicial economy and the binding of absentees to the judgment that are raised in class actions also are pertinent in the derivative suit context.[1] Further, as is true for class actions, special prerequisites exist to ensure that a proper derivative suit is brought and that the shareholder-plaintiff is an appropriate person to bring the action on behalf of the corporation.[2] Additionally, most derivative suit provisions require court approval before settlement is permitted, and notice of any proposed compromise or dismissal usually must be given to the shareholders in a manner directed by the court.[3] A brief look at some of the special derivative action prerequisites and rules follows.

A derivative suit plaintiff is seeking to redress a claim that technically belongs to the corporation, and consequently must allege that the harm is peculiar to the corporation and ordinarily would be only indirectly detrimental to the interests of the shareholders.[4] Often the test for determining whether a suit is derivative is to ask whether the harm was an invasion of the shareholder's rights as opposed to an injury to the corporation; only the latter qualifies for derivative treatment.[5] For example, if the challenged conduct damaged the corporation but only reduced the market value of the shareholder's stock, the claim belongs to the corporation and a derivative suit may be brought.[6] On the other

---

18. See Kaplan, Continuing Work of the Civil Committee: 1966 Amendments of the Federal Rules of Civil Procedure (I), 81 Harv.L.Rev. 356, 391 n. 136 (1967).

§ 16.9

1. See §§ 16.1 and 16.8, above.

2. A complete discussion of the requirements for bringing a shareholder derivative suit may be found in 7C C. Wright, A. Miller & M. Kane, Civil 2d §§ 1821–41.

3. See 7C C. Wright, A. Miller & M. Kane, Civil 2d § 1839. A discussion of class action settlements is found in § 16.7, above.

4. Reifsnyder v. Pittsburgh Outdoor Advertising Co., 405 Pa. 142, 173 A.2d 319 (1961).

5. An action that seeks to redress the shareholder's own rights might be brought as a class action.

6. Lewis v. Chiles, 719 F.2d 1044 (9th Cir.1983); Smith v. Bramwell, 146 Or. 611, 31 P.2d 647 (1934).

hand, an action seeking to compel the corporation to declare a dividend is an attempt to vindicate only the shareholders' rights, not the corporation's, and is not a proper derivative suit.[7]

In order to ensure that a derivative suit is necessary because the persons in authority have failed to vindicate the corporation's rights, Federal Rule 23.1 and most state derivative suit provisions require that the plaintiff allege that a demand has been made upon the board of directors to bring the action.[8] Further, applying what is termed the business judgment rule, most courts have ruled that if the board refuses to accede to a demand to sue on the basis of an honest business judgment, then a derivative action cannot be maintained.[9] The demand requirement thus promotes intracorporate settlement of the dispute without litigation. On the other hand, the demand requirement may be dispensed with if the plaintiff can demonstrate that it would be futile.[10] Futility may be shown by allegations such as that a majority of the board is controlled by directors who are the alleged wrongdoers.[11]

Some state rules also require a demand upon the shareholders.[12] The rationale behind this requirement is that the shareholders may decide to replace the board with directors who will bring suit, or that the shareholders will decide to ratify the board's refusal to sue, thereby avoiding suit entirely.[13] Hence, some states will not require a demand on the stockholders when non-ratifiable misconduct by the board has been alleged or when the shareholders are so widely scattered that the demand requirement would force the litigant to engage in a debilitating proxy fight prior to bringing a derivative suit.[14] Yet, other jurisdictions— apparently in the hope of avoiding "strike suits"[15]—require that the demand be made even when the complaint alleges fraud,[16] which typically cannot be ratified.

A third requirement imposed by Federal Rule 23.1 and comparable state provisions is that the plaintiff must own the stock at the time of the alleged wrong, or the securities must have devolved upon the

---

7. Doherty v. Mutual Warehouse Co., 245 F.2d 609 (5th Cir.1957).

8. See 7C C. Wright, A. Miller & M. Kane, Civil 2d § 1831.

9. Evangelist v. Fidelity Management & Research Co., 554 F.Supp. 87 (D.Mass. 1982); Rosengarten v. International Tel. & Tel. Corp., 466 F.Supp. 817 (S.D.N.Y.1979).

10. Nussbacher v. Continental Illinois Nat. Bank & Trust Co. of Chicago, 518 F.2d 873 (7th Cir.1975); Brooks v. Brooks Pontiac, Inc., 143 Mont. 256, 389 P.2d 185 (1964); Bartlett v. New York, N. H. & H. R. Co., 221 Mass. 530, 109 N.E. 452 (1915).

11. See, e.g., Lewis v. Curtis, 671 F.2d 779 (3d Cir.1982), cert. denied 459 U.S. 880; Ono v. Itoyama, 884 F.Supp. 892 (D.N.J.1995).

12. Federal Rule 23.1 does not include a shareholder demand requirement. Rather, it defers to state law by requiring the plaintiff to plead the facts surrounding efforts to obtain shareholder approval, "if necessary."

13. Halprin v. Babbitt, 303 F.2d 138 (1st Cir.1962).

14. Mayer v. Adams, 37 Del.Ch. 298, 141 A.2d 458 (1958); Levitt v. Johnson, 334 F.2d 815 (1st Cir.1964), cert. denied 379 U.S. 961.

15. A "strike suit" is an action brought by a person who has no bona fide claim. The theory is to harass the corporation by burdensome pretrial procedures into a remunerative out-of-court settlement.

16. Claman v. Robertson, 164 Ohio St. 61, 128 N.E.2d 429 (1955).

plaintiff by operation of law.[17] Even if the plaintiff is alleging a series of wrongful transactions, a derivative suit can be brought only on the basis of events transpiring while plaintiff owned the stock.[18] The purpose of this requirement is to prevent the purchasing of lawsuits.[19] In the federal courts the requirement also prevents the collusive invocation of diversity jurisdiction.[20]

In some states, a fourth requirement obliges plaintiffs to demonstrate that they own either a specified dollar amount or percentage of the corporation's stock.[21] In addition, it may be necessary for derivative suit plaintiffs to post a bond to cover the opponent's expenses.[22] The policy behind these requirements again is to discourage "strike suits." A requirement that the plaintiff shareholder have substantial holdings in the defendant corporation or be willing to post a large sum arguably discourages faint-hearted plaintiffs and frivolous claims.[23]

Because the plaintiff in a derivative suit seeks to vindicate the rights of a corporation, the outcome of the action may have a substantial impact on other shareholders. Should the plaintiff lose, the corporate right will be foreclosed forever and the shareholders thus also will lose.[24] Of course, the converse is true: The shareholders will be benefitted, albeit indirectly, if plaintiff succeeds in vindicating the corporation's interests. For this reason, a derivative action plaintiff also must demonstrate that she will fairly and adequately represent the interests of other shareholders, a requirement analogous to the adequacy of representation prerequisite in the class action context.[25]

---

17. See 7C C. Wright, A. Miller & M. Kane, Civil 2d § 1828. Since only shareholders may bring a derivative action, the plaintiff also must be a shareholder at the time suit is filed. Lewis v. Knutson, 699 F.2d 230 (5th Cir.1983); Kauffman v. Dreyfus Fund, Inc., 434 F.2d 727 (3d Cir.1970), cert. denied 401 U.S. 974. See 7C C. Wright, A. Miller & M. Kane, Civil 2d § 1826.

18. See McDonough v. American Int'l Corp., 905 F.Supp. 1016 (M.D.Fla.1995); Brambles USA, Inc., v. Blocker, 731 F.Supp. 643 (D.Del.1990). This restriction has posed serious problems for the courts in defining what constitutes a single transaction when a series of events are involved. Compare Herald Co. v. Seawell, 472 F.2d 1081 (10th Cir.1972) (notion of continuing wrong antedating plaintiff's purchase of stock rejected), with Bateson v. Magna Oil Corp., 414 F.2d 128 (5th Cir.1969), cert. denied 397 U.S. 911 (continuing wrong theory used).

19. Cohen v. Beneficial Indus. Loan Corp., 337 U.S. 541, 556, 69 S.Ct. 1221, 1230, 93 L.Ed. 1528 (1949); Home Fire Ins. Co. v. Barber, 67 Neb. 644, 93 N.W. 1024 (1903).

20. Hawes v. City of Oakland, 104 U.S. (14 Otto) 450, 26 L.Ed. 827 (1881).

21. N.Y.—McKinney's Bus.Corp.Law § 627.

22. West's Ann.Cal.Corp.Code § 800 (c); N.Y.—McKinney's Bus.Corp.Law § 627. Federal Rule 23.1 is silent regarding bond requirements. However, some federal statutes give the court authority to order a bond to be posted. See, e.g., Fed.Secs.Act of 1933, § 11(e), 15 U.S.C.A. § 77k(e) and Fed.Secs.Exchange Act of 1934, § 9(e), 15 U.S.C.A. § 78i(e). See also the discussion at note 41, below.

23. It has been argued that if the concern is to discourage weak plaintiffs and frivolous claims, a ban on out-of-court settlements would be a better remedy than a bond requirement. Hornstein, New Aspects of Stockholders' Derivative Suits, 47 Colum.L.Rev. 1 (1947). Judicial approval is required in most jurisdictions for the settlement of derivative suits.

24. See 7C C. Wright, A. Miller & M. Kane, Civil 2d § 1840, for a discussion of the effect of a judgment in a shareholder derivative action.

25. See the discussion of the adequacy of representation prerequisite in § 16.2 at notes 30–45, above.

The other procedural rules applicable to derivative suits are the same as in civil suits generally, although some special problems or questions have arisen.[26] For example, because the corporation ultimately is the beneficiary of the litigation it must be made a party. Because its board of directors has refused to bring the action, it initially will be named as a defendant. However, since the company's ultimate interest is more closely related to those of the shareholders, arguably it should be realigned as a party plaintiff. The problem is that realignment in a federal diversity case almost always will destroy the court's subject-matter jurisdiction because the state citizenship of the corporation usually will be the same as at least some members of its board of directors, who are named as individual defendants in the action. In light of this difficulty and because, realistically, the corporation may be controlled by people who are more concerned about their own interests than that of the corporation, it is settled that if corporate management is antagonistic to the plaintiffs, and may have acted in a manner injurious to their rights, the corporation should not be realigned, regardless of its ultimate interest.[27]

The amount in controversy requirement for diversity jurisdiction has received a similar, practical interpretation. Because it is the corporation that is the ultimate beneficiary of the suit, the satisfaction of the jurisdictional amount requirement is determined by reference to the potential recovery by the corporation.[28] Moreover, individual shareholders may intervene in the action regardless of the size of their claims or their citizenship.[29]

In the federal courts, a special venue provision permits a derivative suit to be brought in any jurisdiction in which the corporation might have sued.[30] The statute's language seems clear, yet complicated factual settings have given some courts difficulty in construing it.[31]

An example of the utility of the special venue provision is as follows. Plaintiffs, residents and citizens of State A, bring a derivative suit

26. Two problems that are discussed elsewhere in this volume involve pleading and jury trial. Although typically pleadings do not have to be verified, derivative suits are an exception to this practice. See § 5.11, above. Although derivative suits had their beginnings in equity where there was no jury trial, a jury trial now can be demanded in a derivative suit when the underlying claim is one that would have been cognizable at law if the corporation had sued on it. Ross v. Bernhard, 396 U.S. 531, 90 S.Ct. 733, 24 L.Ed.2d 729 (1970). See § 11.5, above.

27. Koster v. (American) Lumbermens Mut. Cas. Co., 330 U.S. 518, 67 S.Ct. 828, 91 L.Ed. 1067 (1947); Doctor v. Harrington, 196 U.S. 579, 25 S.Ct. 355, 49 L.Ed. 606 (1905); 7C C. Wright, A. Miller & M. Kane, Civil 2d § 1822.

28. Koster v. (American) Lumbermens Mut. Cas. Co., 330 U.S. 518, 67 S.Ct. 828, 91 L.Ed. 1067 (1947); Bernstein v. Levenson, 437 F.2d 756 (4th Cir.1971); 7C C. Wright, A. Miller & M. Kane, Civil 2d § 1823.

29. Weinstock v. Kallet, 11 F.R.D. 270 (S.D.N.Y.1951).

30. 28 U.S.C.A. § 1401.

31. Another federal statute pertaining to derivative suits permits serving process on the corporation outside the state in which the action is brought. 28 U.S.C.A. § 1695. This provision has been construed as applying only to actions in which the special venue statute has been utilized. King v. Wall & Beaver Street Corp., 145 F.2d 377 (D.C.Cir.1944); Greenberg v. Giannini, 140 F.2d 550 (2d Cir.1944).

naming the corporation, which is incorporated and is doing business in State B, and several individual defendants, who are residents and citizens of States B, X, Y, and Z. Prior to 1991 when it was amended, the general venue provision would permit suit to be brought either in the state in which the claim arose or in the state in which all the plaintiffs or all the defendants reside. If the claim did not arise in State B, suit could be brought only in State A, which might be an inconvenient forum.[32] The language of the special statute permits venue in State B because that is where the corporation could have sued, basing venue on its own residence as plaintiff.[33] Notably, the corporation could not have sued the individual defendants in a federal court because some of them had the same citizenship as the corporation. Nonetheless, in determining where the corporation could have sued the individual defendants, the court will consider only venue limitations. The fact that diversity of citizenship would have been lacking will be disregarded.

Finally, it must be noted that although most corporate law is state made, most derivative suits are brought in the federal courts. This has produced special congeries of governing law questions in the federal courts, since the court often is exercising diversity jurisdiction.[34] In some instances Federal Rule 23.1 is explicit about certain prerequisites and, in that event, the federal requirements control, regardless of any contrary state ones. This is true, for example, regarding the applicability of the contemporaneous ownership rule even when the state in which the court sits does not have a comparable requirement.[35] On the other hand, when the Federal Rule explicitly defers to state law, as is true regarding the requirement of a demand on the shareholders, then state law applies.[36] More frequently, the Federal Rule is silent and some special state provision exists, raising the question whether the federal court should follow the state rule because it represents an attempt to regulate corporations, not merely the procedure in state courts.[37]

Necessarily the determination of this last question requires a close examination of the type of rule involved and the activity to which it is directed, as well as whether or what federal interest exists in ignoring state law on the question. For example, although some federal courts have permitted equitable owners of stock at the time of the wrong to bring derivative suits regardless of state law,[38] the prevailing view is that state law should govern in defining stockholder status because the question of who is a stockholder appears to be more than a mere rule of

---

32. For an exploration of venue requirements under the amended statute, see § 2.15, above.

33. Van Gelder v. Taylor, 621 F.Supp. 613 (N.D.Ill.1985); Dowd v. Front Range Mines, Inc., 242 F.Supp. 591 (D.Colo.1965). See also 7C C. Wright, A. Miller & M. Kane, Civil 2d § 1825.

34. When the underlying claims are based on federal law and the court is exercising federal question jurisdiction, state law may be disregarded. See, e.g., Levitt v.

Johnson, 334 F.2d 815 (1st Cir.1964), cert. denied 379 U.S. 961.

35. See 7C C. Wright, A. Miller & M. Kane, Civil 2d § 1829.

36. See note 12, above.

37. The standard for ascertaining governing law in federal diversity actions generally is discussed in §§ 4.3–4.4, above.

38. HFG Company v. Pioneer Pub. Co., 162 F.2d 536 (7th Cir.1947).

procedure.[39] A similar conclusion has been reached with regard to the demand on directors. The Supreme Court has ruled that Rule 23.1 sets forth only a pleading requirement, and that whether a demand must be made, as well as what constitutes an adequate demand or an excuse for failing to make one, is intimately bound up with decisions regarding how to regulate corporations so that state law controls those issues in diversity suits.[40] Finally, the Supreme Court has ruled that federal courts should apply state security-for-expenses statutes, requiring the posting of a bond before allowing the action to proceed.[41] The Court found the statute to be a substantive regulation because it imposed the defendant's costs on the plaintiff if he lost, thereby creating a liability that otherwise did not exist, and because the posting of a bond had a significant impact on plaintiff's right to maintain the underlying action.

C. INTERPLEADER

§ 16.10 Purpose and History

Interpleader is an equitable procedure by which a person holding property (commonly called a stakeholder) who is or who may be subject to inconsistent claims on that property (the stake) can bring together all the claimants in a single action. Interpleader is thus a form of joinder designed to protect the stakeholder.[1] Without it, the stakeholder might be compelled to guess, perhaps incorrectly, which claimant is entitled to the stake, the penalty being multiple litigation with the possibility of inconsistent verdicts resulting in multiple liability. Even a stakeholder who has guessed correctly risks the vexation and expense of becoming embroiled in several lawsuits with each of the claimants. Thus, in addition to its function of protecting the stakeholder, interpleader conserves judicial resources by condensing several disputes into one. Interpleader also avoids a "race to judgment" by claimants seeking a disproportionate share of a limited fund. Finally, because the stake or a sum equivalent in value most commonly will be deposited with the court, much of the delay and expense often attending the enforcement of a money judgment are eliminated.[2]

The origins of interpleader may be traced to the law side of the English courts, but it has been predominantly a creature of equity.[3] Until the twentieth century, its usefulness was limited by restrictions

---

39. Gallup v. Caldwell, 120 F.2d 90 (3d Cir.1941); Rosenfeld v. Schwitzer Corp., 251 F.Supp. 758 (S.D.N.Y.1966). See 7C C. Wright, A. Miller & M. Kane, Civil 2d § 1829.

40. Kamen v. Kemper Financial Servs., Inc., 500 U.S. 90, 111 S.Ct. 1711, 114 L.Ed.2d 152 (1991).

41. Cohen v. Beneficial Industrial Loan Corp., 337 U.S. 541, 69 S.Ct. 1221, 93 L.Ed. 1528 (1949). See 7C C. Wright, A. Miller & M. Kane, Civil 2d § 1835.

§ 16.10

1. Sanders v. Armour Fertilizer Works, 292 U.S. 190, 54 S.Ct. 677, 78 L.Ed. 1206 (1934).

2. State Farm Fire & Cas. Co. v. Tashire, 386 U.S. 523, 533, 87 S.Ct. 1199, 1205, 18 L.Ed.2d 270 (1967).

3. Rogers, Historical Origins of Interpleader, 51 Yale L.J. 924 (1942).

and requirements that may be divided into two categories: those generated by the principles of equity jurisprudence and those generated by considerations of jurisdiction and venue. There were four equity requirements for a "strict" bill of interpleader: (1) the same thing, debt, or duty had to be claimed by all the parties against whom interpleader was demanded; (2) all of the claimants' adverse titles or rights had to be dependent upon or be derived from a common source; (3) the plaintiff-stakeholder could not claim any interest in the subject matter of the interpleader (the stake); and (4) the person seeking the remedy must have incurred no independent liability to any of the claimants—the stakeholder had to stand perfectly indifferent among them.[4] Although adherence to these restrictions severely curtailed the use of interpleader, equity courts were willing to relax them when the proceeding was a "bill in the nature of interpleader." In such a case, the plaintiff-stakeholder did not have to be disinterested, but could cite "some special ground for equitable relief beyond the assertion of multiple claims against him."[5]

The problems of jurisdiction and venue and their limitations on the usefulness of interpleader is illustrated by the case of New York Life Insurance Company v. Dunlevy,[6] decided by the United States Supreme Court in 1916. In Dunlevy, the Court held that an interpleader action was an in personam proceeding so that the attachment of the debt—the proceeds of a life insurance policy—was not sufficient as a basis for in rem jurisdiction over nonresident claimants. In personam jurisdiction was required over all the claimants and the stakeholder. Thus, unless all the claimants consented to jurisdiction, the court could not guarantee full protection of the stakeholder. In Dunlevy, itself, because the interpleader court did not obtain in personam jurisdiction over one of the claimants, the judgment that was entered in that action was not entitled to full faith and credit and the insurance company was compelled to pay twice on the same policy.

The implications for cases arising in interstate commerce were clear: unless all the claimants resided in the forum state or consented to suit there, interpleader was not available. Because at the time of Dunlevy the power of federal district courts to obtain personal jurisdiction ordinarily was coterminous with the borders of the state in which they sat, claimants residing outside the forum state could not be bound by any interpleader judgment entered therein, unless they consented to appear. Because state courts had the same difficulty,[7] stakeholders seeking interpleader could not be assured full protection from having to satisfy

---

4. The most often quoted statement of these requirements may be found in J.N. Pomeroy, Equity Jurisprudence § 1322, at 906 (5th ed. Symons 1941). In Hazard & Moskovitz, An Historical and Critical Analysis of Interpleader, 52 Calif.L.Rev. 706, 708 (1964), the authors have criticized Pomeroy's statement as "the product of uncritical reading and uncritical thinking."

5. C. Wright, Law of Federal Courts § 74, at 532 (5th ed.1994).

6. 241 U.S. 518, 36 S.Ct. 613, 60 L.Ed. 1140 (1916).

7. The expansion of long-arm jurisdiction by the states is a more recent development. See §§ 3.12–3.13, above. However, the territorial restrictions on state jurisdiction still exist for interpleader. See § 16.12, below.

the same liability more than once. (Moreover, thanks to the requirement of complete diversity between the stakeholder on the one hand and all claimants on the other,[8] if the stakeholder was from the same state as one of the claimants, the federal court could not hear the action due to the lack of diversity).

All but the last of the restrictions at equity have been eliminated in modern federal practice and in most states; in addition, as is discussed more fully later, Congress has relaxed considerably jurisdiction and venue requirements in actions of interpleader and in the nature of interpleader.[9] The effort to reform interpleader was triggered by widespread dissatisfaction with the Dunlevy decision and its implications. Led by Professor Zachariah Chafee, who was its most prolific and eloquent spokesman,[10] it culminated in the Federal Interpleader Act of 1936,[11] of which Chafee was chief draftsman, and in Rule 22 of the Federal Rules of Civil Procedure. After some controversy about whether statutory interpleader was intended to be the only authorized type,[12] the prevailing view is that statutory and rule interpleader co-exist and are complementary.[13]

Both the statute and the rule expressly abolish the first two historic requirements for interpleader. The third requirement, that the stakeholder be disinterested, was expressly abolished by the rule. Although the interpleader statute is silent regarding this prerequisite, it generally is recognized that the requirement no longer applies, as it is inconsistent with the liberal approach taken by the statute.[14]

The fourth requirement, that the stakeholder may not have any independent liability to any of the claimants, has proved most resistant to change. The restriction itself appears to be based on the concern that the stakeholder would tend to favor the claimant to whom he had some independent ground of liability. Although Professor Chafee seemed to believe that the fourth restriction was abolished by implication in the rule and the statute,[15] and although English practice has rejected it,[16]

---

8. See § 16.12, below.

9. Ibid.

10. Professor Chafee penned several articles over twenty years that constitute a classic discussion of interpleader: Chafee, Modernizing Interpleader, 30 Yale L.J. 814 (1921); Chafee, Interstate Interpleader, 33 Yale L.J. 685 (1924); Chafee, Interpleader in the United States Courts, 41 Yale L.J. 1134 (1932), 42 Yale L.J. 41 (1932); Chafee, The Federal Interpleader Act of 1936: I & II, 45 Yale L.J. 963, 1161 (1936); Chafee, Federal Interpleader Since the Act of 1936, 49 Yale L.J. 377 (1940); Chafee, Broadening the Second Stage of Interpleader, 56 Harv. L.Rev. 541, 929 (1943).

11. 49 Stat. 1096 (1936); Judicial Code § 24(26), 28 U.S.C.A. § 41(26). The interpleader statute now is codified in 28 U.S.C.A. §§ 1355, 1397, and 2361.

12. Compare Eagle, Star & British Dominions v. Tadlock, 14 F.Supp. 933, 940 (S.D.Cal.1936), with Security Trust & Savs. Bank v. Walsh, 91 F.2d 481 (9th Cir.1937), overruling the holding in the Eagle case that statutory interpleader did away with the older equitable version.

13. 7 C. Wright, A. Miller & M. Kane, Civil 2d § 1701.

14. See Pan Am. Fire & Cas. Co. v. Revere, 188 F.Supp. 474, 479 (E.D.La. 1960); 7 C. Wright, A. Miller & M. Kane, Civil 2d § 1701.

15. The no independent liability requirement was viewed as a specific application of the restriction that the claims have a common origin. Thus, the abolition of that requirement impliedly also affected the former. See Chafee, Federal Interpleader Since

---

16. See note 16 on page 782.

some American courts still have insisted on preserving this restriction.[17] Thus, for example, if an allegation is made that an insurance company stakeholder may be independently liable to its insured because of bad faith in processing the claim, the courts will try the facts as to the alleged existence of the bad faith claim; if the claim is not upheld, interpleader is ordered, but if the claim is valid, that is sufficient ground to deny the application for interpleader.

The flexibility and adaptability of modern procedural systems suggest that there are other ways to settle the problem of possible bias due to the stakeholder's independent liability. Thus, it has been argued that because the independent liability restriction has only its antiquity to support it, it should not be retained as a bar to interpleader.[18] Perhaps, not surprisingly, therefore, American courts increasingly have accepted this view and ignored the requirement.[19]

§ 16.11   Modern Interpleader: Practice and Procedure

Despite the existence of two different forms of interpleader in federal courts,[1] and variants among the states,[2] interpleader procedure does have some basic principles and characteristics in common. To begin with, there are two stages of any interpleader proceeding. In the first, the stakeholder's application for an order to interplead is reviewed by the court. If there is no obstacle to granting the order, the proceeding then moves to the second stage for a consideration of the merits, during which the claimants fight it out among themselves. If the stakeholder has no interest in the final outcome of the dispute, it withdraws at the end of the first stage, having committed the stake to the custody of the court. If the stakeholder does have an interest—for example, an insurance company that wants to contest payment to any of the claimants because the premiums had not been paid and the policy consequently lapsed—it remains in the action and participates in the second stage as another claimant.

the Act of 1936, 49 Yale L.J. 377, 412 (1940). See also Note, The Independent Liability Rule as a Bar to Interpleader in the Federal Courts, 65 Yale L.J. 715, 719 (1956).

16. Ex parte Mersey Docks & Harbour Bd., 1 Q.B. 546 (1899).

17. Nevada Eighty–Eight, Inc. v. Title Ins. Co. of Minnesota, 753 F.Supp. 1516 (D.Nev.1990); Poland v. Atlantis Credit Corp., 179 F.Supp. 863 (S.D.N.Y.1960); American–Hawaiian S.S. Co. (Del.) v. Bowring & Co., 150 F.Supp. 449 (S.D.N.Y.1957). See also McKeithen v. S.S. Frosta, 430 F.Supp. 899, 901 (E.D.La.1977).

18. C. Wright, Law of Federal Courts § 74, at 533 (5th ed.1994); 7 C. Wright, A. Miller & M. Kane, Civil 2d § 1706.

19. Libby, McNeill, & Libby v. City Nat. Bank, 592 F.2d 504 (9th Cir.1978); Dakota Livestock Co. v. Keim, 552 F.2d 1302 (8th Cir.1977); Knoll v. Socony Mobil Oil Co., 369 F.2d 425, 428–29 (10th Cir. 1966), cert. denied 386 U.S. 977; Stuyvesant Ins. Co. v. Dean Constr. Co., 254 F.Supp. 102, 109 (S.D.N.Y.1966), affirmed per curiam sub nom. Stuyvesant Ins. Co. v. Kelly, 382 F.2d 991 (2d Cir.1967).

§ 16.11

1. The major differences between rule and statutory interpleader are the jurisdictional and venue requirements applicable to both. See § 16.12, below.

2. See, e.g., West's Ann.Cal.Code Civ. Proc. § 386; N.Y.—McKinney's CPLR 216.

Unlike historic interpleader, it is not necessary for the stakeholder to be confronting actual claims that already have been asserted. The remedy now is available even though one or more (or even all) of the claimants have not brought suit against the stakeholder or even made a formal demand for the stake. The emphasis in the first stage is on deciding whether the remedy should be granted, not on evaluating the merits of the claims the stakeholder is confronting or may confront. Thus, the claims, whether in contract or tort, need not be liquidated or reduced to judgment for purposes of deciding the initial question whether interpleader should be granted.[3]

Although it may not be necessary for some or all of the claims to have been asserted at the time interpleader is requested, the stakeholder must be able to show that the claimants are "adverse" to each other. Adversity is expressly required by the interpleader statute.[4] It would be necessary even in the absence of explicit statutory language, however, because if the claimants' interests in the stake are not adverse, there is no need to protect either the stakeholder or the claimants.[5] Even though it is the usual practice to defer examination of the merits of the claims until after interpleader has been granted, courts will dismiss an application for interpleader when it is clear that the stakeholder is not threatened by multiple liability or litigation. Consequently, if the stakeholder presents two alleged claimants and one of them has dropped her claim,[6] or if the claims are not asserted against the same fund,[7] or if the stakeholder may be legally liable to both claimants,[8] then interpleader ordinarily will be denied.

When, however, the claims are not technically adverse but in the aggregate they exceed the limited fund held by the stakeholder, interpleader becomes available.[9] Consider, for example, an insurance company that has issued an automobile policy with a limitation of $10,000 per accident. If its insured is involved in a serious accident with a bus, the company may file an interpleader action requesting the court to decide how to allocate the $10,000 among the many bus passengers alleging injuries. Even though a decision that one claimant's claim is meritorious does not implicate the legal validity of any other person's claim, as a practical matter, in the absence of interpleader, the satisfaction of the

3. 7 C. Wright, A. Miller & M. Kane, Civil 2d § 1704.

4. 28 U.S.C.A. § 1335(a)(1).

5. Indianapolis Colts v. Mayor & City Council of Baltimore, 741 F.2d 954 (7th Cir.1984), cert. denied 470 U.S. 1052; 7 C. Wright, A. Miller & M. Kane, Civil 2d § 1705.

6. Bierman v. Marcus, 246 F.2d 200 (3d Cir.1957), cert. denied 356 U.S. 933 (1958); John Hancock Mut. Life Ins. Co. v. Beardslee, 216 F.2d 457 (7th Cir.1954), cert. denied 348 U.S. 964.

7. See, e.g., Wausau Ins. Cos. v. Gifford, 954 F.2d 1098 (5th Cir.1992); Interfirst Bank Dallas, N.A. v. Purolator Courier Corp., 608 F.Supp. 351 (N.D.Tex.1985).

8. See, e.g., Bradley v. Kochenash, 44 F.3d 166 (2d Cir.1995); General Elec. Credit Corp. v. Grubbs, 447 F.2d 286 (5th Cir. 1971), reversed on other grounds 405 U.S. 699, 92 S.Ct. 1344, 31 L.Ed.2d 612 (1972).

9. State Farm Fire & Cas. Co. v. Tashire, 386 U.S. 523, 87 S.Ct. 1199, 18 L.Ed.2d 270 (1967). See also Cory v. White, 457 U.S. 85, 102 S.Ct. 2325, 72 L.Ed.2d 694 (1982).

first claim to reach judgment could result in the depletion of the fund so that the remaining claimants would have no recourse.

Traditionally, the stakeholder either has been required to place the money or property under the control of the court or to post a bond sufficient to ensure compliance with any future order disposing of the stake. In the federal courts, this requirement is preserved in the interpleader statute itself[10] and is treated as a jurisdictional prerequisite to invoking statutory interpleader. Federal Rule 22 does not include a deposit requirement, however.[11] Of course, the district courts have the equitable power to receive a deposit, even though the rule does not require one.[12]

The amount of the deposit required generally is equal to the largest claim against the stake.[13] The fact that the stakeholder claims an interest in the stake does not permit any deductions in the deposit to offset its claim.[14] Conversely, complying with the deposit requirement does not constitute a waiver of that interest;[15] the second stage of the proceedings will determine the merits of the stakeholder's claim. Once the merits of the claims have been determined, the stake and any interest that has accrued on it[16] will be distributed to the prevailing claimants.

The remedy of interpleader is not limited to an original action by a plaintiff stakeholder. It also is available to any defendant exposed to a threat of multiple liability.[17] Thus, a defendant-stakeholder may obtain interpleader by way of cross-claim or counterclaim.[18] Courts also have

---

10. 28 U.S.C.A. § 2361. Although the courts strictly enforce the deposit requirement, they generally will accord the stakeholder a second opportunity to comply before dismissing the action for noncompliance. See, e.g., Prudential Ins. Co. of America v. Bennett, 299 F.Supp. 451 (S.D.Ga.1969); American Smelting & Refining Co. v. Naviera Andes Peruana, S.A., 182 F.Supp. 897 (S.D.N.Y.1959).

11. The different bond requirements for federal rule and statutory interpleader have had the unfortunate effect of creating some disputes about which form of interpleader is involved when the stakeholder wishes to avoid depositing the stake. 7 C. Wright, A. Miller & M. Kane, Civil 2d § 1716.

12. Corrigan Dispatch Co. v. Casa Guzman, S.A., 569 F.2d 300 (5th Cir.1978); Bank of China v. Wells Fargo Bank & Union Trust Co., 209 F.2d 467, 473 (9th Cir. 1953).

13. In re Sinking of M/V Ukola, 806 F.2d 1 (1st Cir.1986); National Union Fire Ins. Co. v. Ambassador Group, Inc., 691 F.Supp. 618 (E.D.N.Y.1988).

14. See Metal Transport Corp. v. Pacific Venture S.S. Corp., 288 F.2d 363 (2d Cir.1961).

15. Moseley v. Sunshine Biscuits, Inc., 110 F.Supp. 157 (W.D.Mo.1952); John Hancock Mut. Life Ins. Co. v. Yarrow, 95 F.Supp. 185 (E.D.Pa.1951); Johnston v. All State Roofing & Paving Co., 557 P.2d 770, 773 n. 13 (Alaska 1976).

16. See Webb's Fabulous Pharmacies, Inc. v. Beckwith, 449 U.S. 155, 101 S.Ct. 446, 66 L.Ed.2d 358 (1980), in which the Supreme Court struck down a state statute declaring all interest earned on any interpleader deposits to be income of the office of the county clerk as violative of the Fifth Amendment. The Court did leave open the possibility that a fee for services rendered in maintaining the deposit could be charged. 449 U.S. at 164, 101 S.Ct. at 452.

17. See, e.g., West's Ann.Cal.Code Civ. Proc. § 386(b).

18. Grubbs v. General Elec. Credit Corp., 405 U.S. 699, 705 n. 2, 92 S.Ct. 1344, 1349 n. 2, 31 L.Ed.2d 612 (1972). Federal Rule 22(1) specifically provides: "A defendant exposed to similar liability may obtain such interpleader by way of cross-claim or counterclaim." Although the federal interpleader statute contains no similar language, courts have held that stakeholders

held that a stakeholder may intervene in an existing action between the claimants,[19] or may interpose an interpleader claim as a third-party claim.[20] The purpose of making interpleader available to defendant-stakeholders is to allow them to avoid the cumbersome procedure of instituting a separate interpleader action and then moving to consolidate the two actions to bring about the same result. Of course, a defendant only may employ interpleader when he would be exposed to multiple liability upon the same obligation that underlies the original action; he may not counterclaim or cross-claim for interpleader in the absence of a nexus with a party already in the case.[21]

Finally, although questions of governing law in the federal courts are covered in more depth elsewhere,[22] it should be noted that insofar as different procedural requirements exist between available state and federal interpleader statutes, a federal court will be governed by federal law.[23] Even though the federal court is sitting in a state preserving the older equity restrictions for interpleader, and the application of those restrictions to the facts of the case before it would prevent the forum state's courts from granting interpleader, the federal court can allow interpleader, either under the rule or the statute. However, during the second stage of interpleader when the claimants' rights to the stake are litigated, state law will govern the determination of those substantive legal issues,[24] except in those rare instances in which the claims themselves rest on some federal right.

The distinction between the various stages of the interpleader proceeding also is important when evaluating the availability of jury trial in these actions. The long history of interpleader as an equitable remedy originally led most to conclude that trial by jury was inappropriate in interpleader actions.[25] However, the Supreme Court's holding in Beacon Theatres, Inc. v. Westover[26] that the right to trial by jury in a merged system cannot be determined simply by labeling the action "legal" or "equitable," requires the court to determine whether jury trial is appro-

---

may utilize statutory interpleader by way of counterclaim. See, e.g., Humble Oil & Refining Co. v. Copeland, 398 F.2d 364 (4th Cir.1968); New York Life Ins. Co. v. Welch, 297 F.2d 787 (D.C.Cir.1961); Walmac Co. v. Isaacs, 220 F.2d 108 (1st Cir.1955).

19. Mallonee v. Fahey, 117 F.Supp. 259 (S.D.Cal.1953).

20. Home Ins. Co. of New York v. Kirkevold, 160 F.2d 938 (9th Cir.1947).

21. Grubbs v. General Elec. Credit Corp., 405 U.S. 699, 705 n. 2, 92 S.Ct. 1344, 1349 n. 2, 31 L.Ed.2d 612 (1972).

22. See Chapter 4, above.

23. 7 C. Wright, A. Miller & M. Kane, Civil 2d § 1713. See generally Hanna v. Plumer, 380 U.S. 460, 85 S.Ct. 1136, 14 L.Ed.2d 8 (1965).

24. See Great Falls Transfer & Storage Co. v. Pan Am. Petroleum Corp., 353 F.2d 348 (10th Cir.1965); Kerrigan's Estate v.

Joseph E. Seagram & Sons, Inc., 199 F.2d 694 (3d Cir.1952); Metropolitan Life Ins. Co. v. McCall, 509 F.Supp. 439 (W.D.Pa. 1981).

Additionally, the Supreme Court has ruled that even in a statutory interpleader action, the federal court must look to the forum state's choice of law rules to determine which state's law will govern the rights of the claimants. Griffin v. McCoach, 313 U.S. 498, 61 S.Ct. 1023, 85 L.Ed. 1481 (1941). Griffin is discussed in § 4.5, above.

25. This conception was reinforced by Chief Justice Taft's dictum in Liberty Oil Co. v. Condon Nat. Bank, 260 U.S. 235, 241, 43 S.Ct. 118, 120, 67 L.Ed. 232 (1922).

26. 359 U.S. 500, 79 S.Ct. 948, 3 L.Ed.2d 988 (1959).

priate for each of the issues in the action.[27] Of the three fundamental issues raised by interpleader proceedings, the first—whether to permit interpleader—always must be a question for the court as it is a purely equitable issue.[28] The second question—which claimant is entitled to the fund—on the other hand, is the sort of question that could, in the absence of the interpleader proceeding, be brought before a court as a "legal" action and thus might be tried to a jury. If so, it would be unreasonable to deny the claimants jury trial in an interpleader proceeding when they would have it in a noninterpleader proceeding.[29] As for the nature and extent of the stakeholder's liability to the claimants, both historical and systemic arguments suggest that these issues, as well, should be submitted to jury trial, unless jury trial would be unavailable in a noninterpleader proceeding involving those same matters.[30]

§ 16.12 Jurisdiction and Venue

When all the claimants reside in a single state, state court interpleader is readily available. However, if the parties prefer to be in a federal forum or if the claimants are more widely dispersed, then significant problems are presented in determining where suit may be brought because of limitations concerning personal and subject-matter jurisdiction and venue. Further, in the federal courts, the major differences between rule and statutory interpleader are the particular jurisdiction and venue rules applicable to each type of interpleader. An understanding of these differences thus is necessary in order to be able to assess the availability of interpleader in a particular forum.

As discussed earlier, the United States Supreme Court in New York Life Insurance Company v. Dunlevy[1] made clear that it is necessary to obtain in personam jurisdiction over each of the nonresident claimants in order to enter a binding judgment involving their rights. As a practical matter this restriction has limited the use of state court interpleader to actions in which only resident claimants are involved. This is so for two reasons. First, most states do not have long-arm statutes that can be interpreted to reach the claimants because the typical long-arm statute addresses persons or entities doing business or committing torts, or accomplishing some other act in the forum that the state has determined brings the defendant within its courts' power.[2] Further, even in those states with statutory authorization for jurisdiction,[3] it is necessary to satisfy the due

27. See the discussion in §§ 11.5–11.6, above.

28. Savannah Bank & Trust Co. v. Block, 175 F.Supp. 798, 801 (S.D.Ga.1959); American–Hawaiian S.S. Co. (Del.) v. Bowring & Co., 150 F.Supp. 449 (S.D.N.Y.1957).

29. 7 C. Wright, A. Miller & M. Kane, Civil 2d § 1718.

30. Ross v. Bernhard, 396 U.S. 531, 90 S.Ct. 733, 24 L.Ed.2d 729 (1970); Pan Am. Fire & Cas. Co. v. Revere, 188 F.Supp. 474, 483 (E.D.La.1960); Savannah Bank & Trust Co. v. Block, 175 F.Supp. 798, 801 (S.D.Ga.

1959); John Hancock Mut. Life Ins. Co. v. Yarrow, 95 F.Supp. 185, 188 (E.D.Pa.1951).

§ 16.12

1. 241 U.S. 518, 36 S.Ct. 613, 60 L.Ed. 1140 (1916). See § 16.10, above.

2. See §§ 3.12–3.13, above, for a discussion of various types of long-arm statutes.

3. E.g., West's Ann.Cal.Code Civ.Proc. § 410.10 (allowing long-arm jurisdiction whenever the Constitution permits).

process requirements of minimum contacts and fair play and substantial justice before the assertion of jurisdiction will be upheld.[4] Since in most interpleader actions the claimants essentially are passive, that standard cannot be met.[5] Thus, unless the nonresident claimants willingly consent to state court interpleader jurisdiction,[6] state courts typically are not viable fora.

Federal rule interpleader actions are limited by similar personal jurisdiction restraints. Service of process for rule interpleader cases is governed completely by Federal Rule 4.[7] That provision authorizes the federal district court to serve process, and thereby obtain personal jurisdiction, within the borders of the state where the court is sitting or pursuant to state law.[8] This means that the federal court may make use of any applicable state long-arm statute, but, as just discussed, this does not provide any significant opportunity to reach nonresident claimants.[9]

By contrast, Congress has provided for nationwide service of process on all claimants in actions under the federal interpleader statute.[10] Thus, in statutory interpleader actions, only those claimants who cannot be found[11] or who reside outside of the United States[12] are beyond the reach of the statute.[13] Further, the assertion of jurisdiction under the statute need not be tested against the minimum contacts standard, for it represents an assertion of federal, not state, court jurisdiction, mandated by Congress and thus controlled only by Fifth Amendment Due Process restraints.[14] Since the reason for the federal enactment was a recognition of the need to protect the stakeholder from multiple liability,[15] and the

---

4. See §§ 3.10–3.11, above, for a discussion of the current constitutional requirements for asserting state court jurisdiction.

5. An ingenious method of satisfying the standard was employed in Atkinson v. Superior Court, 49 Cal.2d 338, 316 P.2d 960 (1957), cert. denied 357 U.S. 569 (per Traynor, J.), although the case is somewhat limited by its peculiar facts.

6. The New York interpleader statute attempts to encourage consent by providing that notice be given to all nonresident claimants by mailing copies of the summons and complaint. The court then stays the interpleader action for one year, unless a claimant intervenes (thereby consenting to jurisdiction) or begins an action elsewhere. N.Y.—McKinney's CPLR 216. If a claimant fails to come into the New York action or file suit elsewhere, his claim is barred from suit in New York, as well as in any state having a borrowing statute.

7. See 7 C. Wright, A. Miller & M. Kane, Civil 2d § 1711.

8. Fed.Civ.Proc.Rule 4(k)(1)(A).

9. A very limited opportunity may be provided if interpleader is defensive and the

stakeholder is interpleading by way of a counterclaim or cross-claim. Additional claimants, if deemed to be necessary under Rule 19, may be joined under Rule 13(h) and Rule 4 then authorizes service within 100 miles of where suit was filed, even across state borders. See Fed.Civ.Proc.Rule 4(k)(1)(B).

10. 28 U.S.C.A. § 2361.

11. U.S. v. Swan's Estate, 441 F.2d 1082 (5th Cir.1971); Metropolitan Life Ins. Co. v. Dumpson, 194 F.Supp. 9 (S.D.N.Y. 1961).

12. Cordner v. Metropolitan Life Ins. Co., 234 F.Supp. 765, 767 n. 2 (S.D.N.Y. 1964).

13. The assertion of jurisdiction over claimants residing in foreign countries may be accomplished by utilizing Federal Rule 4(f), governing service in foreign countries. See generally 4A C. Wright & A. Miller, Civil 2d §§ 1133–36.

14. For a discussion of governing law on personal jurisdiction questions, see § 3.18, above.

15. In cases involving questions concerning the jurisdiction of a state court to determine title to abandoned tangible per-

state courts could not provide that protection because of Dunlevy, the assertion of jurisdiction under those circumstances clearly would survive constitutional scrutiny.

Although the ability to obtain personal jurisdiction over nonresident claimants suggests that if the stakeholder wishes to bring the action in the federal courts statutory interpleader usually will be preferred to rule interpleader, important differences exist between these two forms of federal interpleader relating to subject-matter jurisdiction and venue that may bear on that choice. To begin with, in statutory interpleader, subject-matter jurisdiction is determined on the basis of diversity of citizenship between the claimants.[16] In Treinies v. Sunshine Mining Company,[17] the Supreme Court pointed out that the actual controversy in an interpleader action is between the claimants; the citizenship of the stakeholder is irrelevant. In 1967, the Court went even further, holding in State Farm Fire & Casualty Company v. Tashire[18] that all that was required was "minimal diversity"—only one claimant must be a citizen of a state different from that of the other claimants.

Since Tashire, the lower federal courts have ruled that minimal diversity is satisfied in cases in which all the claimants are citizens of the same state but there is an interested stakeholder who is a citizen of a different state; the theory behind this extension apparently is that the stakeholder who has an interest in the disposition of the case ultimately becomes a claimant, creating minimal diversity.[19] Utilizing a minimal diversity standard broadens the availability of interpleader and thus is consistent with the main purpose behind the creation of statutory interpleader. The availability of statutory interpleader is enhanced further by the amount-in-controversy requirement; the minimum amount necessary to maintain an action under the statute is $500.[20]

The subject-matter jurisdiction requirements for rule interpleader, on the other hand, are the same as those governing any other civil action in the federal courts. There must be either a federal question[21] or there must be complete diversity between the stakeholder and all the other

sonal property through the state's power to escheat, the Supreme Court has stated that notions of due process prohibit forcing the holder of property within a state from relinquishing the property unless it is protected against the possibility of subsequent liability on a claim against the same property. Western Union Tel. Co. v. Pennsylvania, 368 U.S. 71, 82 S.Ct. 199, 7 L.Ed.2d 139 (1961). Although the Supreme Court has not extended the rationale underlying the escheat cases to private litigation, the importance of the threat of multiple liability as a factor to be considered in evaluating the propriety of asserting jurisdiction is clear. See Harris v. Balk, 198 U.S. 215, 25 S.Ct. 625, 49 L.Ed. 1023 (1905); Atkinson v. Superior Court, 49 Cal.2d 338, 316 P.2d 960 (1957), cert. denied 357 U.S. 569.

16. 28 U.S.C.A. § 1335.

17. 308 U.S. 66, 60 S.Ct. 44, 84 L.Ed. 85 (1939). On the same subject, see Pan Am. Fire & Cas. Co. v. Revere, 188 F.Supp. 474 (E.D.La.1960).

18. 386 U.S. 523, 87 S.Ct. 1199, 18 L.Ed.2d 270 (1967).

19. Mt. Hawley Ins. Co. v. Federal Savs. & Loan Ins. Corp., 695 F.Supp. 469 (C.D.Cal.1987). See also 7 C. Wright, A. Miller & M. Kane, Civil 2d § 1710.

20. 28 U.S.C.A. § 1335.

21. See, e.g., Commercial Union Ins. Co. v. U.S., 999 F.2d 581 (D.C.Cir.1993); St. Louis Union Trust Co. v. Stone, 570 F.2d 833, 835 (8th Cir.1978); Bank of China v. Wells Fargo Bank & Union Trust Co., 209 F.2d 467 (9th Cir.1953).

claimants.[22] If jurisdiction is premised on diversity, the amount in controversy also must exceed $75,000.[23]

Note that both for statutory and rule interpleader cases, the value of the stake determines whether the amount requirement is satisfied.[24] It will not be sufficient to aggregate the claims against the stake to reach the minimum requirement since the total possible recovery is necessarily limited by the stake, which is the basis of the requested relief.

Federal question jurisdiction in interpleader is very limited because it is most unusual for the rights to a particular fund or stake to find their source in federal law. Consequently, if the stakeholder is a citizen of the same state as any one of the claimants or if the amount involved is not greater than $75,000, then rule interpleader is not available and statutory interpleader must be invoked. The one exception to this limitation on the availability of rule interpleader occurs when interpleader is asserted by way of a compulsory counterclaim or by way of a cross-claim. In that situation, the interpleader claim may come within the supplemental jurisdiction of the court and the complete diversity and amount requirements may be ignored.[25]

Differences in the venue rules applicable to statutory and rule interpleader also affect the availability of each of these devices.[26] The provision governing venue for statutory interpleader cases allows the action to be brought in a judicial district where one or more of the claimants reside.[27] Because venue is premised on residence rather than citizenship, if one of the claimants is a corporation, a statutory interpleader action may be filed in any district where the corporation is incorporated or licensed to do business or is doing business, even though it may not be deemed a citizen there for diversity purposes.[28] Remembering that a stakeholder utilizing statutory interpleader may use nationwide service of process, this broad and liberal venue provision allows stakeholders a wide range of forum choices.[29]

22. See, e.g., Angst v. Royal Maccabees Life Ins. Co., 77 F.3d 701 (3d Cir.1996); Aetna Life & Cas. Co. v. Spain, 556 F.2d 747 (5th Cir.1977); First Nat. Bank & Trust Co. of Oklahoma City, Oklahoma v. McKeel, 387 F.2d 741 (10th Cir.1967).

23. 28 U.S.C.A. § 1332.

24. See 6247 Atlas Corp. v. Marine Ins. Co., 155 F.R.D. 454 (S.D.N.Y.1994).

25. See, e.g., Guy v. Citizens Fidelity Bank & Trust Co., 429 F.2d 828 (6th Cir. 1970); Ciechanowicz v. Bowery Savings Bank, 19 F.R.D. 367 (S.D.N.Y.1956). Supplemental jurisdiction is discussed in § 2.14, above.

26. As is true with civil actions generally, even if venue is proper, an interpleader action may be transferred to any other district where it might have been brought. 28 U.S.C.A. § 1404(a); Preston Corp. v. Raese, 335 F.2d 827 (4th Cir.1964); Fidelity & Cas.

Co. of New York v. Levic, 222 F.Supp. 131 (W.D.Pa.1963). See generally § 2.17, above.

27. 28 U.S.C.A. § 1397.

28. Gannon v. American Airlines, Inc., 251 F.2d 476 (10th Cir.1957); Moseley v. Sunshine Biscuits, Inc., 110 F.Supp. 157 (W.D.Mo.1952).

29. The breadth of venue in statutory interpleader actions may be extended even further if the 1988 amendments to the general venue statute, 28 U.S.C.A. § 1391(c), defining corporate residence as "any judicial district in which it is subject to personal jurisdiction at the time the action is commenced" are deemed applicable, because effectively nationwide venue would be authorized. The propriety of that extension has been questioned. See Welkowitz, Some Thoughts on Corporate Venue and Other Foibles, 10 Whittier L.Rev. 721 (1989).

In contrast to statutory interpleader, venue in cases brought under Federal Rule 22 is governed by the general venue statute applicable to other federal civil actions. If based on federal question jurisdiction, venue is proper in the district where any defendant-claimant resides, if all defendants reside in the same state, or where a substantial part of the events or omissions giving rise to the claim arose.[30] Since the concept of where the claim arose is a rather meaningless one in the interpleader context, the result is that venue will be proper only if all the claimants reside in the same district—a not too common occurrence. Venue in diversity actions confronts similar limitations.[31]

§ 16.13   Federal Injunctions Against Other Judicial Proceedings

Since the adoption of the first interpleader act in 1926,[1] Congress has authorized the federal courts to issue injunctions restraining other proceedings relating to the subject matter of the interpleader.[2] The purpose of this federal injunctive power is to preserve the effectiveness of the interpleader remedy. Allowing a federal court to enjoin other proceedings involving the same matters prevents multiple litigation and reduces the possibility of inconsistent determinations or the inequitable distribution of the fund.[3]

This statutory grant of injunctive power does not apply to interpleader actions under Rule 22 because the language of the statute makes it clear that it is applicable only to statutory interpleader cases. Further, a court may utilize this authority only when a deposit has been made or a bond provided by the stakeholder as required by the statute.[4] After the injunction is issued, the court then may proceed to hear the case and, if appropriate, discharge the plaintiff-stakeholder from further liability;[5] it also may make the injunction permanent.[6]

Although there is no explicit statutory authorization for federal courts in rule interpleader cases to enjoin state court proceedings, it has been suggested that a federal court may have that power under Section 2283 of Title 28.[7] Under that statute, a federal court may issue an order

---

30. 28 U.S.C.A. § 1391(b).

31. 28 U.S.C.A. § 1391(a).

In cases in which a defendant seeks interpleader, the plaintiff claimant effectively has waived venue objections by bringing the initial action, although venue still must be established for any additional claimants. See 7 C. Wright, A. Miller & M. Kane, Civil 2d § 1712.

§ 16.13

1. 44 Stat. 416 (1926).

2. The current statutory provision embodying this authority is 28 U.S.C.A. § 2361. It authorizes the court to restrain all claimants from instituting any actions in state or federal court affecting the property, instrument, or obligation involved in the interpleader suit.

3. 7 C. Wright, A. Miller & M. Kane, Civil 2d § 1717.

4. Austin v. Texas–Ohio Gas. Co., 218 F.2d 739 (5th Cir.1955). See § 16.11, above, for a discussion of the deposit or bond requirements.

5. Baron Bros. Co. v. Stewart, 182 F.Supp. 893 (S.D.N.Y.1960).

6. See, e.g., Francis I. du Pont & Co. v. Sheen, 324 F.2d 3 (3d Cir.1963); Melton v. White, 848 F.Supp. 1513 (D.Okl.1994).

7. 7 C. Wright, A. Miller & M. Kane, Civil 2d § 1717.

to stay proceedings in a state court "where necessary in aid of its jurisdiction, or to protect or effectuate its judgments." Insofar as state court actions may be deemed to interfere with the federal court's power to control the distribution of the stake, an injunction against them appears to fall within this authority.[8] Also, a federal court may bar the parties in an interpleader action before it from pursuing another federal court action or prevent the parties in the interpleader suit from instituting a state court action,[9] for neither of these orders violates the prohibition against federal injunctions of ongoing state actions.

It must be pointed out, however, that even if the court has authority to issue an injunction, it may refuse to do so. Federal courts always have been reluctant to issue injunctions against state court proceedings because of federalism concerns. Thus, the power to issue an injunction is used cautiously.[10] For example, the court may refuse an injunction if there is no real threat of litigation relating to the subject matter of the interpleader action.[11] Further, the scope of any injunction that is issued will be narrowed to prohibit only those suits that pose a threat to the stakeholder; all related actions will not necessarily be enjoined.[12] This point was underscored by the Supreme Court in State Farm Fire and Casualty Company v. Tashire.[13] The Court ruled that the trial court had abused its discretion when interpleader was sought by an insurance company against persons with unliquidated tort claims against the insured and the trial court enjoined all claimants from proceeding in any other fora to have their claims against the insured established. The injunction was proper only insofar as it prohibited the claimants from asserting their rights to the insurance proceeds in any forum other than the interpleader action. As the Court noted, "There is nothing in the statutory scheme * * * which requires that the tail be allowed to wag the dog in this fashion."[14]

Even though the normal procedure for seeking injunctive relief governs applications for injunctions under the interpleader statute, there is some question whether the federal rules' provisions governing notice and hearing requirements for injunctions are applicable to injunctions in interpleader cases.[15] Although adhering to strict notice and hearing requirements in a nationwide interpleader proceeding might not be possible with sufficient speed to give effect to the court's order, they

---

8. See, e.g., General Ry. Signal Co. v. Corcoran, 921 F.2d 700 (7th Cir.1991); Truck–A–Tune, Inc. v. Re, 856 F.Supp. 77 (D.Conn.1993), affirmed on other grounds 23 F.3d 60 (2d Cir.1994).

9. Pan Am. Fire & Cas. Co. v. Revere, 188 F.Supp. 474, 483 n. 46 (E.D.La.1960).

10. See Comment, Deference to State Courts in Federal Interpleader Actions, 47 U.Chi.L.Rev. 824 (1980).

11. Walmac Co. v. Isaacs, 220 F.2d 108 (1st Cir.1955) (dictum).

12. See, e.g., Emcasco Ins. Co. v. Davis, 753 F.Supp. 1458 (D.Ark.1990); Empire

Fire & Marine Ins. Co. v. Crisler, 405 F.Supp. 990 (S.D.Miss.1976).

13. 386 U.S. 523, 87 S.Ct. 1199, 18 L.Ed.2d 270 (1967).

14. 386 U.S. at 535, 87 S.Ct. at 1206.

15. Holcomb v. Aetna Life Ins. Co., 228 F.2d 75, 82 (10th Cir.1955), cert. denied 350 U.S. 986. The court relied on the language in Rule 65(e) that the rules do not modify any statutes including "the provisions of Title 28, U.S.C., sec. 2361, relating to preliminary injunctions in actions of interpleader * * *."

should not be discarded when there is reason to believe that they are necessary to protect the interests of one or more claimants and to reach a sound conclusion as to whether interpleader is appropriate.[16]

16. Prudential Ins. Co. v. Shawver, 208 F.Supp. 464 (W.D.Mo.1962); 7 C. Wright, A. Miller & M. Kane, Civil 2d § 1717.

APPENDIX

RESEARCHING THE LAW OF CIVIL PROCEDURE ON WESTLAW®

Analysis

Section 1. Introduction

Civil Procedure, Third Edition, provides a strong base for analyzing even the most complex problem involving the law of civil procedure. Whether your research requires examination of rules, statutes, case law, expert commentary or other materials, West books and Westlaw are excellent sources of information.

To keep you abreast of current developments, Westlaw provides frequently updated databases. With Westlaw, you have unparalleled legal research resources at your fingertips.

Additional Resources

If you have not previously used Westlaw or have questions not covered in this appendix, see the *Westlaw Reference Manual* or call the West Group Reference Attorneys at 1–800–REF–ATTY (1–800–733–2889). The West Group Reference Attorneys are trained, licensed attorneys, available 24 hours a day to assist you with your Westlaw search questions.

Section 2.   Westlaw Databases

Each database on Westlaw is assigned an abbreviation called an *identifier*, which you use to access the database. You can find identifiers for all databases in the online Westlaw Directory and in the printed *Westlaw Database Directory*. When you need to know more detailed information about a database, use Scope. Scope contains coverage information, lists of related databases and valuable search tips. To access Scope, click the **Scope** button while in the database.

The following chart lists Westlaw databases that contain information pertaining to civil procedure. For a complete list of civil procedure databases, see the online Westlaw Directory or the printed *Westlaw Database Directory*. Because new information is continually being added to Westlaw, you should also check the Welcome to Westlaw window and the Westlaw Directory for new database information.

Selected Westlaw Databases

Database	Identifier	Coverage
Federal Rules, Orders and Statutes		
Federal Rules	US–RULES	Current data
Federal Orders	US–ORDERS	Current data
Federal Rules of Practice & Procedure Advisory Committee Minutes	US–RULESCOMM	Varies by committee
United States Code Annotated®	USCA	Current data
United States Public Laws	US–PL	Current data
Congressional Bills	CONG–BILLTXT	Current Congress
Federal and State Case Law Combined		
Federal & State Case Law	ALLCASES	Begins with 1945
Federal & State Case Law— Before 1945	ALLCASES–OLD	1789–1944
Federal Case Law		
Federal Case Law	ALLFEDS	Begins with 1945
Federal Case Law—Before 1945	ALLFEDS–OLD	1789–1944
U.S. Supreme Court Cases	SCT	Begins with 1945
U.S. Supreme Court Cases— Before 1945	SCT–OLD	1790–1944
U.S. Courts of Appeals Cases	CTA	Begins with 1945
U.S. Courts of Appeals Cases— Before 1945	CTA–OLD	1891–1944
U.S. District Courts Cases	DCT	Begins with 1945

Database	Identifier	Coverage
U.S. District Courts Cases—Before 1945	DCT–OLD	1789–1944

State Rules, Orders and Statutes

Database	Identifier	Coverage
Individual State Court Rules	XX–RULES (where XX is a state's two-letter postal abbreviation)	Varies by state
State Court Rules	RULES–ALL	Varies by state
Individual State Court Orders	XX–ORDERS (where XX is a state's two-letter postal abbreviation)	Varies by state
State Court Orders	ORDERS–ALL	Varies by state
Individual State Statutes–Annotated	XX–ST–ANN (where XX is a state's two-letter postal abbreviation)	Varies by state
State Statutes–Annotated	ST–ANN–ALL	Varies by state

State Case Law

Database	Identifier	Coverage
State Case Law	ALLSTATES	Begins with 1945
State Case Law Before 1945	ALLSTATES–OLD	1821–1944
Individual State Cases	XX–CS (where XX is a state's two-letter postal abbreviation)	Varies by state

Texts, Periodicals and Research Tools

Database	Identifier	Coverage
Texts & Periodicals–All Law Reviews, Texts & Bar Journals	TP–ALL	Varies by publication
Federal Rules Decisions (Articles from the West Reporter)	FEDRDTP	Begins with 1986 (vol. 108)
Litigation–Law Reviews, Texts & Bar Journals	LTG–TP	Varies by publication
PLI Litigation and Administrative Practice–Litigation Course Handbook Series	PLI–LIT	Begins with June 1984
Restatement of the Law—Conflict of Laws	REST–CONF	Current data
Restatement of the Law—Judgments	REST–JUDG	Current data
California Procedure	WITPROC	Volumes 1–8: Third Edition Volumes 9–10: Fourth Edition
The Rutter Group™—California Practice Guides: Multibase	TRG–CA	Current editions
The Rutter Group—California Practice Guide: Alternative Dispute Resolution	TRG–CAADR	1997 edition
The Rutter Group—California Practice Guide: Civil Appeals and Writs	TRG–CACIVAPP	1998 edition
The Rutter Group—California Practice Guide: Civil Procedure Before Trial	TRG–CACIVP	1998 edition
The Rutter Group—California Practice Guide: Civil Trials and Evidence	TRG–CACIVEV	1997 edition
The Rutter Group—California Practice Guide: Enforcing Judgments and Debts	TRG–CADEBT	1998 edition
The Rutter Group—California Practice Guide: Federal Civil Procedure Before Trial	TRG–CAFEDCIVP	1998 edition
The Rutter Group—California Practice Guide: Ninth Circuit Civil Appellate Practice	TRG–CA9CIR	1998 edition

Database	Identifier	Coverage
The Rutter Group—Texas Practice Guide: Multibase	TRG–TX	Current editions
The Rutter Group–Texas Practice Guide: Federal Civil Procedure Before Trial, 5th Circuit Edition	TRG–TXFCIVP	1998 edition
The Rutter Group—Texas Practice Guide: Texas Civil Evidence	TRG–TXEV	1997 edition
The Rutter Group—Texas Practice Guide: Discovery	TRG–TXDIS	1997 edition
West's® McKinney's® Forms—Civil Practice Law and Rules Index	NYFORMSIDX–CPLR	Current through July 1997
News and Current Events		
All News	ALLNEWS	Varies by source
Westlaw Topical Highlights— Litigation	WTH–LTG	Current data
West Legal Directory™		
West Legal Directory—Courts	WLD–COURT	Current data
West Legal Directory—Judges	WLD–JUDGE	Current data
West Legal Directory–Litigation	WLD–LIT	Current data

Section 3. Retrieving a Document with a Citation: Find and Jump

3.1 Find

Find is a Westlaw service that allows you to retrieve a document by entering its citation. Find allows you to retrieve documents from anywhere in Westlaw without accessing or changing databases. Find is available for many documents, including rules (state and federal), the *United States Code Annotated*, state statutes, case law (state and federal), administrative materials, texts and periodicals.

To use Find, simply access the Find service and type the citation. The following list provides some examples:

To Find This Document	Access Find and Type
International Shoe Co. v. State of Washington, 66 S. Ct. 154 (1945)	**66 sct 154**
United States v. Offshore Marine, 179 F.R.D. 156	**179 frd 156**
Schaeffer v. Moody, 705 S.W.2d 318 (1986)	**705 sw2d 318**
Federal Rules of Civil Procedure, Rule 11	**frcp rule 11**
28 U.S.C.A. § 1367	**28 usca 1367**
California Code of Civil Procedure § 86	**ca civ pro 86**

For a complete list of publications that can be retrieved with Find and their abbreviations, consult the Find Publications List. Click the **Pubs List** button after accessing Find.

3.2 Jump

Use Jump markers (> or f) to move from one location to another on Westlaw. For example, use Jump markers to go directly from the statute, case or law review article you are viewing to a cited statute, case or article; from a headnote to the corresponding text in the opinion; or from an entry in a statutes index database to the full text of the statute.

Section 4. Searching with Natural Language: WIN—Westlaw is Natural

Overview: With WIN, you can retrieve documents by simply describing your issue in plain English. If you are a relatively new Westlaw user, Natural Language searching can make it easier for you to retrieve cases that are on point. If you are an experienced Westlaw user, Natural Language gives you a valuable alternative search method.

When you enter a Natural Language description, Westlaw automatically identifies legal phrases, removes common words and generates variations of terms in your description. Westlaw then searches for the concepts in your description. Concepts may include significant terms, phrases, legal citations or topic and key numbers. Westlaw retrieves the 20 documents that most closely match your description, beginning with the document most likely to match.

4.1 Natural Language Search

Access a database, such as Federal Case Law (ALLFEDS). If the Terms and Connectors Query Editor is displayed, click the **Search Type** button and choose **Natural Language**. At the Natural Language Description Editor, type a Natural Language description such as the following:

what are the requirements for the application of collateral estoppel

4.2 Next Command

Westlaw displays the 20 documents that most closely match your description, beginning with the document most likely to match. If you want to view additional documents, click your right mouse button and choose **Next 10 Documents** from the pop-up menu, or choose **Next 10 Documents** from the Browse menu.

4.3 Natural Language Browse Commands

Best Mode: To display the best portion (the portion that most closely matches your description) of each document in your search result, click your right mouse button and choose **Next Best** from the pop-up menu or click **Best** f.

Standard Browsing Commands: You can also browse your Natural Language search result using standard Westlaw browsing commands, such as citations list, Locate, page mode and term mode. When you browse your Natural Language search result in term mode, the five portions of each document that are most likely to match your description are displayed.

Section 5.   Searching with Terms and Connectors

Overview: With Terms and Connectors searching, you enter a query, which consists of key terms from your issue and connectors specifying the relationship between these terms.

Terms and Connectors searching is useful when you want to retrieve a document for which you know specific details, such as the title or the fact situation. Terms and Connectors searching is also useful when you want to retrieve documents relating to a specific issue. If the Natural Language Description Editor is displayed when you access a database, click the **Search Type** button and choose **Term Search**.

5.1   Terms

Plurals and Possessives: Plurals are automatically retrieved when you enter the singular form of a term. This is true for both regular and irregular plurals (e.g., **child** retrieves *children*). If you enter the plural form of a term, you will not retrieve the singular form.

If you enter the nonpossessive form of a term, Westlaw automatically retrieves the possessive form as well. However, if you enter the possessive form, only the possessive form is retrieved.

Automatic Equivalencies: Some terms have alternative forms or equivalencies; for example, *5* and *five* are equivalent terms. Westlaw automatically retrieves equivalent terms. The *Westlaw Reference Manual* contains a list of equivalent terms.

Compound Words, Abbreviations and Acronyms: When a compound word is one of your search terms, use a hyphen to retrieve all forms of the word. For example, the term **cross-claim** retrieves *cross-claim*, *cross claim* and *crossclaim*.

When using an abbreviation or acronym as a search term, place a period after each of the letters to retrieve any of its forms. For example, the term **f.r.c.p.** retrieves *frcp*, *f.r.c.p.*, *f r c p* and *f. r. c. p.* Note: The abbreviation does *not* retrieve *federal rules of civil procedure* or *Fed. Rules Civ.Proc.*, so remember to add alternative terms to your query such as **"federal rules of civil procedure"** or **"fed.rules civ.proc."**

The Root Expander and the Universal Character: When you use the Terms and Connectors search method, placing the root expander (!) at the end of a root term generates all other terms with that root. For example, adding the ! to the root *discover* in the query

discover!   /5   scope

instructs Westlaw to retrieve such terms as *discover, discovered, discoverable* and *discovery*.

The universal character (*) stands for one character and can be inserted in the middle or at the end of a term. For example, the term

withdr*w

will retrieve *withdraw* and *withdrew*. Adding two asterisks to the root *jur*

jur**

instructs Westlaw to retrieve all forms of the root with up to two additional characters. Terms such as *jury* or *juror* are retrieved by this query. However, terms with more than two letters following the root, such as *jurisdiction,* are not retrieved. Plurals are always retrieved, even if more than two letters follow the root.

Phrase Searching: To search for an exact phrase, place it within quotation marks. For example, to search for references to *supplemental jurisdiction,* type **"supplemental jurisdiction"**. When you are using the Terms and Connectors search method, you should use phrase searching only if you are certain that the terms in the phrase will not appear in any other order.

5.2 Alternative Terms

After selecting the terms for your query, consider which alternative terms are necessary. For example, if you are searching for the term *supplemental,* you might also want to search for the terms *ancillary* and *pendent.* You should consider both synonyms and antonyms as alternative terms. You can also use the Westlaw thesaurus to add alternative terms to your query.

5.3 Connectors

After selecting terms and alternative terms for your query, use connectors to specify the relationship that should exist between search terms in your retrieved documents. The connectors are described below:

Use:	To retrieve documents with:	Example:
& (and)	both terms	**diversity & counter-claim**
or (space)	either term or both terms	**abstention abstain*****
/p	search terms in the same paragraph	**discovery /p "order for protection"**
/s	search terms in the same sentence	**interplead** /s statut*****
+s	the first search term preceding the second within the same sentence	**burden +s prov*** proof**
/n	search terms within "n" terms of each other (where "n" is a number)	**summary /3 judgment**
+n	the first search term preceding the second by "n" terms (where "n" is a number)	**pennoyer +3 neff**
" "	search terms appearing in the same order as in the quotation marks	**"res judicata"**

Use:	To exclude documents with:	Example:
% (but not)	search terms following the % symbol	**attorney lawyer /5** **client /s privileg! %** **sy,di(work-product)**

5.4   Field Restrictions

Overview: Documents in each Westlaw database consist of several segments, or fields. One field may contain the citation, another the title, another the synopsis and so forth. Not all databases contain the same fields. Also depending on the database, fields with the same name may contain different types of information.

To view a list of fields for a specific database and their contents, see Scope for that database. Note that in some databases not every field is available for every document.

To retrieve only those documents containing your search terms in a specific field, restrict your search to that field. To restrict your search to a specific field, type the field name or abbreviation followed by your search terms enclosed in parentheses. For example, to retrieve a case in the Supreme Court Cases database (SCT) entitled *Burger King Corporation v. Rudzewicz,* search for your terms in the title field (ti):

ti("burger king" & rudzewicz)

The fields discussed below are available in Westlaw databases you might use for researching civil procedure issues.

Digest and Synopsis Fields: The digest (di) and synopsis (sy) fields, added to case law databases by West's attorney-editors, summarize the main points of a case. The synopsis field contains a brief description of a case. The digest field contains the topic and headnote fields and includes the complete hierarchy of concepts used by West's editors to classify the headnotes to specific West digest topics and key numbers. Restricting your search to the synopsis and digest fields limits your result to cases in which your terms are related to a major issue in the case.

Consider restricting your search to one or both of these fields if

- you are searching for common terms or terms with more than one meaning, and you need to narrow your search; or

- you cannot narrow your search by using a smaller database.

For example, to retrieve U.S. courts of appeals cases that discuss the principal place of business of unincorporated entities in relation to federal court jurisdiction, access the U.S. Courts of Appeals Cases database (CTA) and type the following query:

sy,di(principal /s business /p unincorporated /p jurisdiction)

Headnote Field: The headnote field (he) is part of the digest field, but does not contain topic numbers, hierarchical classification information or key numbers. The headnote field contains a one-sentence summary for each point of law in a case and any supporting citations given by the author of the opinion. A headnote field restriction is useful when you are searching for specific statutory sections or rule numbers. For example, to retrieve headnotes from federal cases that cite 28 U.S.C.A. § 1441, access the Federal Case Law database (ALLFEDS) and type the following query:

he(28 +5 1441)

Topic Field: The topic field (to) is also part of the digest field. It contains hierarchical classification information, including the West digest topic names and numbers and the key numbers. You should restrict search terms to the topic field in a case law database if

- a digest field search retrieves too many documents; or
- you want to retrieve cases with digest paragraphs classified under more than one topic.

For example, the topic Interpleader has the topic number 222. To retrieve U.S. courts of appeals cases that discuss attorney fees in interpleader matters, access the U.S. Courts of Appeals Cases database (CTA) and type a query like the following:

to(222) /p attorney /3 fee

To retrieve cases classified under more than one topic and key number, search for your terms in the topic field. For example, to search for cases discussing remittitur, which may be classified to Courts (106), Federal Civil Procedure (170a), Federal Courts (170b) or Pretrial Procedure (307a), among other topics, type a query like the following:

to(remittitur)

For a complete list of West digest topics and their corresponding topic numbers, access the Key Number Service: click the **Key Number Service** button or choose **Key Number Service** from the Services menu.

> *Note:* Slip opinions, cases not reported by West and cases from topical services do not contain the digest, headnote and topic fields.

Prelim and Caption Fields: When searching in a database containing statutes, rules or regulations, restrict your search to the prelim (pr) and caption (ca) fields to retrieve documents in which your terms are important enough to appear in a section name or heading. For example, to retrieve federal statutes relating to interpleader actions, access the United States Code Annotated database (USCA) and type the following:

pr,ca(interpleader)

5.5 Date Restrictions

You can use Westlaw to retrieve documents *decided* or *issued* before, after or on a specified date, as well as within a range of dates. The following sample queries contain date restrictions:

da(1999) & amend! /5 complaint pleading

da(aft 1995) & amend! /5 complaint pleading

da(9/26/1998) & amend! /5 complaint pleading

You can also search for documents *added to a database* on or after a specified date, as well as within a range of dates. The following sample queries contain added-date restrictions:

ad(aft 1996) & amend! /5 complaint pleading

ad(aft 2–1–1998 & bef 2–17–1998) & amend! /5 complaint pleading

Section 6. Searching with Topic and Key Numbers

To retrieve cases that address a specific point of law, use topic and key numbers as your search terms. If you have an on-point case, run a search using the topic and key number from the relevant headnote in an appropriate database to find other cases containing headnotes classified to that topic and key number. For example, to search for state cases containing headnotes classified under topic 267 (Motions) and key number 33 (Quashing or dismissal), access the State Case Law database (ALLSTATES) and enter the following query:

267k33

For a complete list of West digest topic and key numbers, access the Key Number Service: click the **Key Number Service** button or choose **Key Number Service** from the Services menu.

> *Note:* Slip opinions, cases not reported by West and cases from topical services do not contain West topic and key numbers.

Section 7. Verifying Your Research with Citator Services

Overview: A citator service is a tool that helps you ensure that your cases are good law; helps you retrieve cases, legislation or articles that cite a case, rule or statute; and helps you verify that the spelling and format of your citations are correct.

7.1 KeyCite

KeyCite is the citation research service from West Group that integrates all case law on Westlaw. KeyCite helps you trace the history of a case, retrieve a list of all cases and selected secondary sources that cite a case, and track legal issues decided in a case.

KeyCite provides both direct and negative indirect history for any case within the scope of its coverage. The History of the Case window displays a case's direct appellate history and its negative indirect history, which consists of cases outside the direct appellate line that may have a negative impact on its precedential value. The history also includes related references, which are opinions involving the same parties and facts but resolving different issues.

In addition to case history, the Citations to the Case window in KeyCite lists all cases on Westlaw and secondary sources, such as law review articles and ALR® annotations, that cite the decision. These citing references are added to KeyCite as soon as they are added to

Westlaw. All citing cases on Westlaw are included in KeyCite—even unpublished opinions.

For citation verification, the KeyCite result provides the case title; parallel citations, including many looseleaf citations; the court of decision; the docket number; and the filing date.

7.2 Westlaw As a Citator

For citations not covered by the citator services, including persuasive secondary authority such as restatements and treatises, use Westlaw as a citator to retrieve cases that cite your authority.

Using Westlaw as a citator, you can search for documents citing a specific statute, rule, regulation, agency decision or other authority. For example, to retrieve federal cases citing 28 U.S.C.A. § 1334, access the Federal Case Law database (ALLFEDS) and type a query like the following:

28 +5 1334

Section 8.   Researching with Westlaw—Examples

8.1 Retrieving Law Review Articles

Recent law review articles are often a good place to begin researching a legal issue because law review articles serve 1) as an excellent introduction to a new topic or review for a stale one, providing terminology to help you formulate a query; 2) as a finding tool for pertinent primary authority, such as rules, statutes and cases; and 3) in some instances, as persuasive secondary authority.

Suppose you need to gain more background information on supplemental jurisdiction.

Solution

- To retrieve recent law review articles relevant to your issue, access the Litigation–Law Reviews, Texts & Bar Journals database (LTG–TP). Using the Natural Language search method, enter a description like the following:

supplemental jurisdiction

- If you have a citation to an article in a specific publication, use Find to retrieve it. For more information on Find, see Section 3.1 of this appendix. For example, to retrieve the article found at 49 Baylor L. Rev. 1069, access Find and type

49 baylor l rev 1069

- If you know the title of an article but not which journal it appeared in, access the Litigation–Law Reviews, Texts & Bar Journals database (LTG–TP) and search for key terms from the title in the title field. For example, to retrieve the article "Pandora's Box or Treasure Chest?: Circuit Courts Face 28 U.S.C. § 1367's Effect on Multi–Plaintiff Diversity Actions," type the following Terms and Connectors query:

ti(pandora & treasure)

8.2   Retrieving Rules or Statutes

Suppose you need to retrieve Iowa rules or statutes dealing with vacating a judgment.

Solution

- Access the Iowa Statutes–Annotated database (IA–ST–ANN). Search for your terms in the prelim and caption fields using the Terms and Connectors search method:

pr,ca(vacat! & judgment)

- When you know the citation for a specific rule or statute, use Find to retrieve it. For example, to retrieve Iowa Code Ann. § 624A.3, access Find and type

ia st 624a.3

- To look at surrounding statutory sections, use the Table of Contents service. Select a Jump marker in the prelim or caption field. You can also use Documents in Sequence to retrieve the section following § 624A.3, even if that following section was not retrieved with your search or Find request. Click the **Docs in Seq** button.

- When you retrieve a statute on Westlaw, it will contain an Update message if legislation amending or repealing it is available online. To display this legislation, select the Jump marker in the Update message.

> Because slip copy versions of laws are added to Westlaw before they contain full editorial enhancements, they are not retrieved with Update. To retrieve slip copy versions of laws, access the United States Public Laws database (US-PL) or a state's legislative service database (XX-LEGIS, where XX is the state's two-letter postal abbreviation). Then type **ci(slip)** and descriptive terms, e.g., **ci(slip) & vacat! /p judgment.** Slip copy documents are replaced by the editorially enhanced versions within a few working days. Update also does not retrieve legislation that enacts a new statute or covers a topic that will not be incorporated into the statutes. To retrieve this legislation, access US-PL or a legislative service database and enter a query containing terms that describe the new legislation.

8.3   Retrieving Case Law

Suppose you need to retrieve Iowa case law in which the Iowa courts discuss vacating a default judgment.

Solution

- Access the Iowa Cases database (IA–CS). Type a Natural Language description such as the following:

vacating a default judgment

- When you know the citation for a specific case, use Find to retrieve it. (For more information on Find, see Section 3.1 of this appendix.) For example, to retrieve *Hastings v. Espinosa*, 340 N.W.2d 603 (Ia. Ct. App. 1983), access Find and type

340 nw2d 603

- If you find a topic and key number that is on point, run a search using that topic and key number to retrieve additional cases discussing that point of law. For example, to retrieve cases containing headnotes classified under topic 228 (Judgment) and key number 143(3) (Mistake, surprise, or excusable neglect in general), type the following query:

228k143(3)

- To retrieve cases written by a particular judge, add a judge field (ju) restriction to your query. For example, to retrieve cases written by Justice Harris that contain headnotes classified under topic 228 (Judgment), type the following query:

ju(harris) & to(228)

8.4   Using KeyCite

Suppose one of the cases you retrieve in your case law research is *Suss v. Schammel*, 375 N.W.2d 252 (Ia. 1985). You want to determine whether this case is good law and to find other cases that have cited this case.

Solution

- Use KeyCite to retrieve direct history and negative indirect history for *Suss v. Schammel*. While viewing the case, click the **KeyCite** button.

- Use KeyCite to display citing references for *Suss*. From the History of the Case, click the **Citations to the Case** button.

8.5   Following Recent Developments

As the litigation specialist in your firm, you are expected to keep up with and summarize recent legal developments in this area of the law. How can you do this efficiently?

Solution

One of the easiest ways to stay abreast of recent developments in the area of civil procedure and litigation is by accessing the Westlaw Topical Highlights–Litigation database (WTH–LTG). The WTH–LTG database contains summaries of recent legal developments, including court decisions, legislation and changes in the area of litigation. Some summaries also contain suggested queries that combine the proven power of West's topic and key numbers and West's case headnotes to retrieve additional pertinent cases.

- When you access WTH–LTG you will automatically retrieve a list of documents added to the database in the last two weeks.

- To read a summary of a document, double-click its entry in the list.

- To view the full text of a document, access Find while viewing its summary.

- To search this database, choose **New Search** from the Search menu. At the Terms and Connectors Query Editor, type your query. For example, to retrieve references discussing federal removal jurisdiction, type a query like the following:

  remov! /s jurisdiction

Table of Cases

K

M

U

Table of Statutes And Rules

UNITED STATES CODE ANNOTATED
15 U.S.C.A.—Commerce and Trade

Sec.	This Work Sec.	Note
5	3.18	3
15	2.2	22
15	2.15	3
22	3.18	3
25	3.18	3
26	2.2	23
77k(e)	16.9	22
77v	2.3	8
77vvv(b)	2.3	8
77z–1(a)(3)(B)(iii)	16.2	40
77z–1(a)(7)	16.7	8
78aa	2.3	8
78i(e)	16.9	22
78u–4(a)(3)(B)(iii)	16.2	40
78u–4(a)(7)	16.7	8
79y	2.3	8
80a–43	2.3	8
80b–14	2.3	8
1673	15.7	37

18 U.S.C.A.—Crimes and Criminal Procedure

Sec.	This Work Sec.	Note
3231	2.2	23
3500	7.4	11

28 U.S.C.A.—Judiciary and Judicial Procedure

Sec.	This Work Sec.	Note
24(26)	16.10	11
41(26)	16.10	11
80	2.7	7
131	1.2	6
639—653	7.1	6
1251(a)(1)	4.7	17
1252—1258	1.2	12
1291	13.1	1
1292(a)(1)	13.3	1
1292(a)(1)	13.3	7
1292(a)(1)	13.3	11
1292(a)(2)	13.3	2
1292(a)(3)	13.3	3
1292(b)	13.3	
1292(b)	13.3	12
1292(b)	13.3	13
1330	2.6	34
1330	11.6	29
1330(a)	11.6	30
1331	2.3	
1331	2.3	6
1331	2.4	1
1331	2.8	8
1331	2.8	37
1331	2.12	36
1331(a)	4.7	7
1332	2.6	

UNITED STATES CODE ANNOTATED
28 U.S.C.A.—Judiciary and Judicial Procedure

Sec.	This Work Sec.	Note
1332	2.10	
1332	16.12	22
1332(a)	2.6	
1332(a)	2.6	38
1332(a)	2.8	4
1332(a)	5.14	14
1332(a)	16.4	22
1332(a)(1)	2.6	
1332(a)(1)	2.6	1
1332(a)(2)	2.6	
1332(a)(2)	2.6	15
1332(a)(2)	11.6	29
1332(a)(4)	11.6	29
1332(b)	2.8	17
1332(c)	2.6	
1332(c)	2.6	45
1332(c)	2.6	48
1332(c)	2.6	63
1332(c)	2.7	
1332(c)(2)	2.6	33
1332(d)	2.6	12
1333	2.3	
1333	2.10	
1334	2.2	23
1334	2.3	10
1335	2.6	6
1335	2.7	9
1335	16.12	20
1335	16.15	16
1335(a)(1)	16.11	4
1337	2.3	37
1338	2.3	11
1338(a)	2.2	23
1343	2.3	9
1343	16.4	24
1345	2.10	
1346	2.8	10
1346(a)(1)	11.3	13
1346(a)(2)	2.10	11
1351	2.2	23
1355	16.10	11
1359	2.7	
1367	2.12	21
1367	2.13	
1367	2.13	10
1367	2.14	
1367	3.18	
1367	16.4	28
1367(a)	2.13	
1367(a)	2.13	10
1367(a)	2.14	
1367(b)	2.13	
1367(b)	6.9	38
1367(b)	6.10	57
1367(c)	2.13	
1391	2.15	
1391(a)	16.12	31
1391(a)(2)	2.15	
1391(b)	16.12	30

UNITED STATES CODE ANNOTATED

31 U.S.C.A.—Money and Finance

Sec.	This Work Sec.	Note
3727	6.3	9
3729	6.3	19

42 U.S.C.A.—The Public Health and Welfare

Sec.	This Work Sec.	Note
1981	14.12	28
1983	4.7	28
1983	14.8	3
1983	14.12	16
1983	14.15	8
1988	12.6	9

45 U.S.C.A.—Railroads

Sec.	This Work Sec.	Note
51 et seq.	11.3	11
56	2.15	3
56	4.8	7

46 U.S.C.A.—Shipping

Sec.	This Work Sec.	Note
183—189	2.10	19
688	2.3	37
688	2.11	3
688	2.15	3
688	11.6	1

49 U.S.C.A.—Transportation

Sec.	This Work Sec.	Note
20(11)	3.18	6

STATUTES AT LARGE

Year	This Work Sec.	Note
1789, Sept. 24, c. 20, 1 Stat. 73	2.2	8
1789, Sept. 24, c. 20, 1 Stat. 92	4.1	1
1789, Sept. 24, c. 20, § 11, 1 Stat. 73	2.5	2
	2.7	7
	2.8	1
1789, Sept. 24, c. 20, § 11, 1 Stat. 78	2.5	2
	2.8	1
1789, Sept. 24, c. 20, § 11, 1 Stat. 79	2.7	7
1789, Sept. 24, c. 20, § 12, 1 Stat. 73	2.11	2
1789, Sept. 24, c. 20, § 29, 1 Stat. 88	11.10	1

STATUTES AT LARGE

Year	This Work Sec.	Note
1792, May 8, c. 36, § 2, 1 Stat. 275	4.3	4
1792, May 8, c. 36, § 2, 1 Stat. 276	4.3	4
1801, Feb. 13, § 11, 2 Stat. 89	2.3	2
1801, Feb. 13, § 11, 2 Stat. 92	2.3	2
1802, Mar. 8, § 1, 2 Stat. 132	2.3	3
1866, July 27, c. 287, 14 Stat. 306	2.11	37
1872, June 1, c. 255, 17 Stat. 197	5.1	11
1872, June 1, c. 255, § 5, 17 Stat. 197	4.4	1
1875, Mar. 3, c. 135, 18 Stat. 470	2.3	4
	2.11	38
1875, Mar. 3, c. 135, § 1, 18 Stat. 470	2.5	3
1875, Mar. 3, c. 137, § 5, 18 Stat. 470	2.7	7
1875, Mar. 3, c. 137, § 5, 18 Stat. 472	2.7	7
1887, Mar. 3, c. 373, 24 Stat. 552	2.8	2
1908, Mar. 22, P.L. 60–100, 35 Stat. 65	11.3	11
1911, Mar. 3, P.L. 61–475, 36 Stat. 1091	2.8	2
1926, May 8, P.L. 69–203, 44 Stat. 416	16.13	1
1934, June 19, c. 651, 48 Stat. 1064	4.2	1
	4.4	4
1936, Jan. 20, P.L. 74–422, 49 Stat. 1096	16.10	11
1940, April 20, c. 117, 54 Stat. 143	2.6	12
1948, June 25, c. 121, § 1861, 62 Stat. 951	11.10	2
1948, June 25, c. 646, 62 Stat. 935	2.15	18
1949, May 24, c. 139, § 81, 63 Stat. 101	2.17	2
1957, Aug. 7, P.L. 85–315, § 152, 71 Stat. 638	11.10	2
1958, July 25, P.L. 85–554, 72 Stat. 415	2.8	3
1958, July 25, P.L. 85–554, § 2, 72 Stat. 415	2.6	45
1963, Dec. 23, P.L. 88–235, 77 Stat. 473	2.15	10

ILLINOIS SUPREME COURT RULES

Rule	This Work Sec.	Note
201(i)	7.8	3
202	7.17	11
212(b)	7.17	11
215(a)	7.12	3
216(c)	7.10	23
307	13.3	1

INDIANA ACTS

Year	This Work Sec.	Note
1927, Ch. 227	3.5	6

INDIANA RULES OF TRIAL PROCEDURE

Rule	This Work Sec.	Note
8(B)	5.19	4
11(A)	5.11	2
12(C)	5.22	7
15(B)	5.26	17
16	8.1	8
24	6.10	10
26(B)	7.2	2
26(B)	7.2	3
26(D)	7.8	24
26(E)(1)	7.13	3
26(E)(2)	7.13	4
33(E)	7.9	14
34(A)	7.11	3
34(B)	7.11	5
35(B)(2)	7.12	19
37(A)(1)	7.16	19
41(E)	9.5	20
45(B)	7.11	23
45(F)	7.8	30

IOWA CODE ANNOTATED

Sec.	This Work Sec.	Note
42, § 617.3	3.13	3

IOWA RULES OF CIVIL PROCEDURE

Rule	This Work Sec.	Note
22	6.6	17
31	6.6	17
33	6.8	2
72	5.19	10
75	6.10	10
76	6.10	10
122(c)	7.5	27
125(a)(2)(B)	7.6	12

IOWA RULES OF CIVIL PROCEDURE

Rule	This Work Sec.	Note
126(c)	7.9	14
127	7.10	1
129	7.11	3
133(b)	7.12	19
140(c)(2)	7.8	31
147(b)	7.8	24
149(b)	7.8	6
153	7.8	1
181	10.1	3
191	10.1	25
215	9.5	11

KANSAS STATUTES ANNOTATED

Sec.	This Work Sec.	Note
17–7303	3.13	53
60–212(b)(1)—(b)(5)	5.24	8
60–212(b)(7)	5.24	8
60–217(a)	6.3	11
60–226(b)	7.2	2
60–226(b)	7.2	3
60–226(b)(3)	7.5	37
60–226(b)(4)(A)(ii)	7.6	13
60–226(e)	7.13	1
60–230(b)	7.8	18
60–230(g)(2)	7.8	31
60–234(a)	7.11	3
60–236	7.9	7
60–236	7.10	1
60–237(a)(1)	7.16	19
60–237(d)	7.16	2
60–241(b)	9.5	22
60–258a(b)	12.1	21
60–409	5.22	20
60–1305	13.3	2
60–2102(4)	13.1	1
60–2103(a)	13.1	11
60–3703	5.16	41

KANSAS UNITED STATES DISTRICT COURT LOCAL RULES

Rule	This Work Sec.	Note
16	8.2	2

KENTUCKY RULES OF CIVIL PROCEDURE

Rule	This Work Sec.	Note
26.05(b)	7.13	4
26.05(c)	7.13	5
43.02	10.1	25
45.01	7.8	29
45.01	7.11	25
51(2)	10.1	54
52.01	12.2	2
52.01	13.4	21

MICHIGAN COURT RULES

Rule	This Work Sec.	Note
2.116	9.1	7
2.116	9.3	1
2.116(I)(2)	9.2	6
2.302(B)(4)(a)(i)	7.6	11
2.302(B)(4)(a)(ii)	7.6	12
2.310	7.11	6
2.310(c)	7.8	29
2.310(c)	7.11	25
2.312	7.10	1
2.313	7.13	10
2.514(c)	12.1	28
2.612	12.6	2

MICHIGAN GENERAL COURT RULES

Rule	This Work Sec.	Note
203.1	6.6	18
208	16.3	2

LOCAL RULES OF PRAC. & PROC. OF U.S. DIST. COURT FOR WESTERN DIST. OF MICHIGAN

Rule	This Work Sec.	Note
5	8.2	2

MINNESOTA STATUTES ANNOTATED

Sec.	This Work Sec.	Note
546.17	11.11	16
570.131	15.2	20

MINNESOTA RULES OF CIVIL PROCEDURE

Rule	This Work Sec.	Note
9.01	6.3	48
14.01	6.9	20
26.02(b)	7.2	18
26.02(d)(2)	7.6	23
26.05(c)	7.13	5
30.01	7.8	19
30.02(f)	7.8	16
31	7.8	37
33.01(a)	7.9	19
34.01	7.11	6
34.02	7.11	5
35	7.12	3
35.01	7.12	5
36.01	7.10	2
37	7.14	6
37.04	7.16	12
45.01	7.11	23
45.02	7.11	23
59.01	12.4	
60.02	12.6	17

MINNESOTA RULES OF CIVIL PROCEDURE

Rule	This Work Sec.	Note
103.03(c)	13.3	5

MISSISSIPPI CODE ANNOTATED

Sec.	This Work Sec.	Note
13–3–57	3.12	7
13–3–57	3.13	17

VERNON'S ANNOTATED MISSOURI STATUTES

Sec.	This Work Sec.	Note
510.130(1)	9.5	11
510.130(2)	9.5	11
510.140	9.5	22
510.330	12.4	11
510.330	12.4	14

MISSOURI RULES OF CIVIL PROCEDURE

Rule	This Work Sec.	Note
52.11	6.9	8
52.12(a)	6.10	13
55.06	6.6	14
55.07—55.09	5.17	1
55.09	5.18	1
55.10	5.17	5
55.13	6.3	48
55.27	5.17	2
55.32(a)	6.7	15
55.32(b)	6.7	15
56.01(b)(2)	7.2	18
56.01(b)(4)	7.5	6
56.01(b)(4)(a)	7.6	11
56.01(b)(4)(b)	7.6	12
57.03(a)	7.8	19
57.03(b)(4)	7.8	16
57.04	7.8	37
58.01(b)	7.11	6
58.01(b)	7.11	11
60.01	7.12	3
60.01(a)	7.12	5
61.01	7.14	6
62.01	8.1	4
73.01(a)(2)	12.2	12
92.02(b)	15.4	7

MISSOURI SUPREME COURT RULES

Rule	This Work Sec.	Note
56.01(e)	7.13	7

MONTANA CODE ANNOTATED

Sec.	This Work Sec.	Note
28–2–708	2.17	8

MONTANA RULES OF CIVIL PROCEDURE

Rule	This Work Sec.	Note
26(b)(2)	7.2	18
26(b)(4)(B)	7.6	24
31	7.8	39
32(a)(3)	7.17	10
34(b)	7.11	6
35(a)	7.12	6
36(a)	7.10	2
37(b)(2)(E)	7.16	25
42(a)	5.28	17

NEBRASKA REVISED STATUTES

Sec.	This Work Sec.	Note
25–319	16.3	4
25–832	5.13	12
25–833	5.6	2
25–852	5.26	15
25–1107	10.1	25
25–1107	10.1	54
25–1335	9.3	38
25–1501	15.7	2
25–1558	15.2	28

NEVADA RULES OF CIVIL PROCEDURE

Rule	This Work Sec.	Note
48	11.11	15

NEW HAMPSHIRE SUPREME COURT RULES

Rule	This Work Sec.	Note
36	7.9	7

NEW JERSEY STATUTES ANNOTATED

Sec.	This Work Sec.	Note
2A:15–5.2	12.1	21
2A:15–41	15.3	1
2A:15–42	15.3	1
2A:17–33	15.7	23
2A:17–34	15.7	23
2A:17–35	15.7	23
2A:80–2	11.11	16

NEW JERSEY COURT RULES

Rule	This Work Sec.	Note
1:4–8	5.11	8

NEW JERSEY COURT RULES

Rule	This Work Sec.	Note
2:2–4	13.1	22
4:5–1	5.21	16
4:5–8(b)	5.16	8
4:6–4	5.23	6
4:9–3	5.27	1
4:9–3	5.27	22
4:10–2(d)(3)	7.6	24
4:14–9	7.8	5
4:15–1	7.8	39
4:16–1(c)	7.17	10
4:17–7	7.13	7
4:25	8.1	8
4:25–1(a)	8.2	1
4:36–2	10.1	3

NEW MEXICO STATUTES ANNOTATED

Sec.	This Work Sec.	Note
42–9–4	15.2	12
42–9–4	15.2	14
42–9–7	15.2	14

NEW MEXICO RULES OF CIVIL PROCEDURE

Rule	This Work Sec.	Note
1–010(B)	5.13	4
1–011	5.11	6
1–016	8.3	2
1–031(a)	7.8	40

NEW YORK, MCKINNEY'S CONSTITUTION

Art.	This Work Sec.	Note
I, § 2	11.7	7
I, § 2	11.7	10
VII, § 2	11.7	6
XLI	11.7	5

NEW YORK, MCKINNEY'S BUSINESS CORPORATION LAW

Sec.	This Work Sec.	Note
627	16.9	21
627	16.9	22
1301(b)	3.13	53

NEW YORK CIVIL PRACTICE ACT

Sec.	This Work Sec.	Note
424	11.7	29

NEW YORK, MCKINNEY'S CIVIL PRACTICE LAW AND RULES

Sec.	This Work Sec.	Note
6212(a)	15.2	11
6222	15.2	21
6301	15.4	3
6401	15.5	2
6403	15.5	10
6501	15.6	4

NEW YORK CODE OF CIVIL PROCEDURE

Sec.	This Work Sec.	Note
974	11.7	28

NEW YORK LAWS

Year	This Work Sec.	Note
1847, c. 59, § 8	5.1	4
1848, c. 379	5.1	13
1848, c. 379	6.1	2
1848, c. 379, § 133	5.11	42
1849, c. 438, § 157	5.11	43
1851, c. 479, § 1	5.4	1

NEW YORK, MCKINNEY'S GENERAL ASSOCIATIONS LAW

Sec.	This Work Sec.	Note
13	6.3	32

NEW YORK RULES OF COURT

Rule	This Work Sec.	Note
699.14	6.2	21

RULES OF THE UNITED STATES DISTRICT COURT FOR THE NORTHERN DISTRICT OF NEW YORK

Rule	This Work Sec.	Note
12	10.1	2
16	10.1	2

NORTH CAROLINA GENERAL STATUTES

Sec.	This Work Sec.	Note
1–69.1	6.3	32
1–75.2(1)	3.13	2
1A–1	5.22	4
1A–1	5.28	8
1A–1	8.3	1
1A–1	12.1	28
1A–1	12.1	32

NORTH CAROLINA GENERAL STATUTES

Sec.	This Work Sec.	Note
55–145 (repealed)	3.13	23

NORTH CAROLINA RULES OF CIVIL PROCEDURE

Rule	This Work Sec.	Note
8(a)(1)	5.15	1
8(b)	5.19	4
12	5.22	4
15(c)	5.27	22
15(d)	5.28	8
34(b)	7.11	11
45(c)	7.8	29
45(c)	7.11	25
49(b)	12.1	32
49(c)	12.1	28

LOCAL RULES OF PRAC. & PROC. OF U.S. DIST. CT. FOR EASTERN DIST. OF N. CAROLINA

Rule	This Work Sec.	Note
25.02	8.2	7

NORTH DAKOTA RULES OF APPELLATE PROCEDURE

Rule	This Work Sec.	Note
35(b)	13.4	10

NORTH DAKOTA RULES OF CIVIL PROCEDURE

Rule	This Work Sec.	Note
23(c)	16.3	17
23(f)	16.4	6
23(f)—(r)	16.3	16
23(g)(1)	16.6	22
23(g)(4)	16.6	21
23(g)(5)	16.6	33
23(o)(3)	16.5	29
35	7.12	3
52(a)	13.4	21
56(c)	9.2	6

OHIO REVISED CODE

Sec.	This Work Sec.	Note
2703.26	15.6	5

OHIO RULES OF CIVIL PROCEDURE

Rule	This Work Sec.	Note
10(b)	5.13	4

OHIO RULES OF CIVIL PROCEDURE

Rule	This Work Sec.	Note
15(b)	5.26	16
16	8.1	8
26(B)(3)	7.5	11
26(B)(4)(c)	7.6	27
30(B)(5)	7.8	17
31(A)	7.8	40
32(A)(3)(b)	7.17	12
34	7.11	2
34(D)(3)	7.3	6
35(A)	7.12	6
36(A)	7.10	3
37(A)(2)	7.16	16
37(A)(3)	7.16	16
37(B)(2)	7.16	26
52	12.2	12
55(A)	9.4	7
56(C)	9.2	5
56(E)	9.2	20

OKLAHOMA CONSTITUTION

Art.	This Work Sec.	Note
2, § 19	11.11	16

OKLAHOMA STATUTES ANNOTATED

Tit.	This Work Sec.	Note
12, § 1441	5.4	9
12, § 1701.01 et seq. (repealed)	3.11	22
12, § 2009	5.16	4
12, § 2009	5.16	5
12, § 2012	5.17	2
12, § 2012	5.23	10
12, § 2015C	5.27	24
12, § 2023	16.3	3

OREGON RULES OF CIVIL PROCEDURE

Rule	This Work Sec.	Note
15	5.17	6
17B	5.11	3
21A	6.3	23
22A	6.6	17
24A	6.6	17
36B(2)	7.2	20
62A	12.2	12

PENNSYLVANIA STATUTES

Tit.	This Work Sec.	Note
2, § 1401	3.5	31
42, § 8301(b)	6.3	6
42, § 8301(d)	6.3	7

PENNSYLVANIA CONSOLIDATED STATUTES ANNOTATED

Tit.	This Work Sec.	Note
15, § 4122(a)	3.13	53

PENNSYLVANIA RULES OF APPELLATE PROCEDURE

Rule	This Work Sec.	Note
311	13.3	1

PENNSYLVANIA RULES OF CIVIL PROCEDURE

Rule	This Work Sec.	Note
214	10.1	7
214	10.1	11
1024	5.11	46
1035.5(b)	9.1	7
2252	6.9	8
2327	6.10	1
2328	6.10	1

RHODE ISLAND GENERAL LAWS

Sec.	This Work Sec.	Note
9–5–33	3.12	9

RHODE ISLAND SUPERIOR COURT RULES OF CIVIL PROCEDURE

Rule	This Work Sec.	Note
12(b)	5.22	18
12(c)	5.22	18
23	16.1	11
23	16.3	17

RHODE ISLAND RULES OF CIVIL PROCEDURE

Rule	This Work Sec.	Note
13(a)	6.7	15
26(b)(2)	7.2	20

SOUTH CAROLINA CODE

Sec.	This Work Sec.	Note
15–17–20	15.3	1

SOUTH CAROLINA RULES OF CIVIL PROCEDURE

Rule	This Work Sec.	Note
49	12.1	5

SOUTH CAROLINA RULES OF CIVIL PROCEDURE

	This Work	
Rule	Sec.	Note
55(b)(1)	9.4	25

SOUTH DAKOTA CODIFIED LAWS

	This Work	
Sec.	Sec.	Note
15–6–15(a)	5.26	10
15–18–1	15.7	13

TENNESSEE CODE ANNOTATED

	This Work	
Sec.	Sec.	Note
20–2–214(a)(3)	3.13	48
20–10–101(b)(1)	12.4	53
26–2–106	15.7	36

TENNESSEE RULES OF CIVIL PROCEDURE

	This Work	
Rule	Sec.	Note
7.01	5.24	2
15.01	5.24	2
15.02	5.24	2
15.04	5.24	2
36.01	7.10	3

V.T.C.A., CIVIL PRACTICE AND REMEDIES CODE

	This Work	
Sec.	Sec.	Note
16.063	15.7	14
17.042(1)	3.12	7
17.042(1)	3.13	17
17.042(2)	3.13	13

TEXAS RULES OF CIVIL PROCEDURE

	This Work	
Rule	Sec.	Note
40	6.4	5
45	5.11	2
48	5.12	9
57	5.11	2
58	5.13	9
120a	3.26	14
166(c)	7.8	3
166–A	9.3	1
215(5)	7.13	10
265	10.1	25
277	12.1	24
324	12.4	2

LOCAL RULES OF UNITED STATES DISTRICT COURT FOR THE WESTERN DISTRICT OF TEXAS

	This Work	
Rule	Sec.	Note
300.6	8.2	7

UTAH CONSTITUTION

	This Work	
Art.	Sec.	Note
1, § 10	11.11	15

UTAH RULES OF CIVIL PROCEDURE

	This Work	
Rule	Sec.	Note
12(f)	5.5	23
12(f)	5.24	5
26(b)(3)	7.5	11
26(b)(4)(A)(ii)	7.6	13
26(b)(4)(C)(ii)	7.6	27
30(b)(2)	7.8	20
30(b)(6)	7.8	17
32(a)(3)(B)	7.17	12
33	7.9	1
35(a)	7.12	6
36(a)	7.10	4
37(a)(2)	7.16	16
37(a)(3)	7.16	16
37(b)(2)	7.16	26
56	5.22	17
60(b)	12.6	36
64D(d)	15.7	36

VERMONT RULES OF CIVIL PROCEDURE

	This Work	
Rule	Sec.	Note
7(c)	5.22	2

VIRGINIA CODE

	This Work	
Sec.	Sec.	Note
8.01–378	12.3	63
8.01–428A	12.6	18
8.01–428B	12.6	2
8.01–430	12.3	63
8.01–670	13.3	1

RULES OF THE SUPREME COURT OF VIRGINIA

	This Work	
Rule	Sec.	Note
3:10(b)	6.9	1
4:1(b)(3)	7.5	23
4:1(b)(4)(C)	7.6	30
4:5(b)(2)	7.8	20
4:8	7.9	1
4:10(a)	7.12	6
4:11(a)	7.10	4
4:12(a)(2)	7.16	16
4:12(a)(3)	7.16	16
4:12(b)(2)	7.16	26

WEST'S REVISED CODE OF WASHINGTON ANNOTATED

	This Work	
Sec.	Sec.	Note
4.16.180	15.7	14

WASHINGTON SUPERIOR COURT CIVIL RULES

Rule	This Work Sec.	Note
10(b)	5.13	4
26(b)(3)	7.5	23
26(b)(4)(C)	7.6	30
26(c)	7.11	7
30(b)(2)	7.8	20
33(a)	7.9	3
34(b)	7.11	5
34(b)	7.11	7
37(a)	7.11	7
37(a)(2)	7.16	16
37(a)(3)	7.16	16
37(b)(2)	7.16	26

WEST VIRGINIA RULES OF CIVIL PROCEDURE

Rule	This Work Sec.	Note
23(a)	16.3	2
26(b)(4)(A)(ii)	7.6	13

WISCONSIN STATUTES ANNOTATED

Sec.	This Work Sec.	Note
802.01(1)	5.21	9
802.03(7)	5.9	7
802.06	3.26	16
802.08(6)	9.2	6
803.05(2)	6.9	1
803.08	16.3	4
803.09	6.10	13
804.01(5)(1)	7.13	3
804.01(5)(2)	7.13	4
804.07(i)(c)(2)	7.17	11
805.12	12.1	23
805.12(2)	12.1	28
806.02(1)	9.4	25
808.03(2)	13.3	4
808.03(2)(b)	13.1	18

WYOMING CONSTITUTION

Art.	This Work Sec.	Note
1, § 9	11.1	2

WYOMING RULES OF CIVIL PROCEDURE

Rule	This Work Sec.	Note
12(d)	5.20	15
15(a)	5.24	4
35	7.12	3

FEDERAL RULES OF APPELLATE PROCEDURE

Rule	This Work Sec.	Note
4	13.1	11

FEDERAL RULES OF APPELLATE PROCEDURE

Rule	This Work Sec.	Note
4(a)	12.6	1
38	4.4	37

FEDERAL RULES OF CIVIL PROCEDURE

Rule	This Work Sec.	Note
1	1.1	3
1	11.4	9
2	11.4	9
3	2.5	31
3	4.4	
3	4.4	27
3	4.4	37
4	3.18	
4	4.3	
4	5.27	20
4	16.12	
4	16.12	9
4(a)	3.22	18
4(c)(1)	3.22	4
4(c)(2)	3.22	7
4(c)(2)(C)(i)	16.12	8
4(d)	3.20	
4(d)(1)	3.20	28
4(d)(1)	4.3	
4(d)(2)	3.20	27
4(d)(2)(B)	3.20	25
4(d)(2)(G)	3.20	25
4(d)(3)	3.18	
4(d)(7) (former)	3.18	20
4(e)	3.18	
4(e)	3.18	5
4(e)	4.4	
4(e)(1)	3.18	
4(e)(1)	3.18	20
4(e)(2)	3.18	
4(e)(2)	3.18	8
4(e)(2)	3.20	
4(f)	3.18	
4(f)	16.12	13
4(h)	3.20	20
4(i)(2)	3.18	
4(j)	5.27	
4(j)	5.27	20
4(k)	3.18	
4(k)	3.18	4
4(k)	3.27	
4(k)(1)	3.18	
4(k)(1)(A)	3.18	5
4(k)(1)(B)	3.18	
4(k)(1)(B)	16.12	9
4(k)(2)	3.18	
4(l)	3.21	
4(m)	3.22	8
4(m)	5.27	20
4(n)	3.27	
4(n)(2)	3.16	13
6(b)	5.17	7
6(b)	12.4	6

Index

References are to Pages